ENCYCLOPEDIA OF
American
Urban History

ENCYCLOPEDIA OF

American Urban History

1

David Goldfield
University of North Carolina, Charlotte

A SAGE Reference Publication

SAGE Publications
Thousand Oaks ▪ London ▪ New Delhi

For information:

 SAGE Publications, Inc.
2455 Teller Road
Thousand Oaks, California 91320
E-mail: order@sagepub.com

SAGE Publications Ltd.
1 Oliver's Yard
55 City Road
London EC1Y 1SP
United Kingdom

SAGE Publications India Pvt. Ltd.
B-42, Panchsheel Enclave
Post Box 4109
New Delhi 110 017 India

Printed in the United States of America.

Library of Congress Cataloging-in-Publication Data

Encyclopedia of American urban history/editor, David R. Goldfield.
    p. cm.
(A Sage reference publication)
Includes bibliographical references and index.
ISBN 0-7619-2884-7 or 978-0-7619-2884-3 (cloth) (2 vols.)

    1. Metropolitan areas—United States—History—Encyclopedias. 2. Cities and towns—United States—Growth—History—Encyclopedias. 3. Urbanization—United States—History—Encyclopedias. I. Goldfield, David R., 1944–
HT123.E49 2007
307.76′40973—dc22   2006025882

This book is printed on acid-free paper.

06   07   08   09   10   10   9   8   7   6   5   4   3   2   1

Publisher:	Rolf Janke
Developmental Editor:	Paul Reis
Reference Systems Coordinator:	Leticia Gutierrez
Project Editor:	Astrid Virding
Copy Editors:	Barbara Ray, Jamie Robinson, Pam Suwinsky, Jackie Tasch, and April Wells-Hayes
Typesetter:	C&M Digitals (P) Ltd.
Proofreader:	Scott Oney
Indexer:	Kathy Paparchontis
Cover Designer:	Candice Harman

Contents

Editorial Board

List of Entries

Reader's Guide

The Reader's Guide provides a way to locate related entries in the encyclopedia. For example, if you look under Finances and Commerce, you will find a list of the main entries on that topic, including Trade and Commerce and Urban Housing. Similarly, if you are interested in busing, you will find the entry under the heading Transportation, where you will also notice reference to other related entries, including Commuting, Congestion, and Rapid Transit. The Reader's Guide also provides an overview of all the entries in the encyclopedia. Simply look through the listing of headings, such as Finances and Commerce or Transportation, and pick one of particular interest to you, then choose the entries you might want to read. Some entries may be listed in more than one category.

Biographies

Abbott, Edith
Abrams, Charles
Ackerman, Frederick L.
Addams, Jane
Anderson, Sherwood
Armour, Philip Danforth
Armstrong, Louis
Barry, Marion S., Jr.
Bartholomew, Harland
Bauer, Catherine
Bellows, George
Benton, Thomas Hart
Bogart, Humphrey
Brice, Fanny
Burgess, Ernest W.
Burnham, Daniel H.
Byrne, Jane M.
Capone, Al
Chaplin, Charlie
Cooley, Charles Horton
Coughlin, John Joseph
Crump, Edward H.
Curley, James Michael
Daley, Richard J.
Dinkins, David N.
Du Bois, W. E. B.

Fitzgerald, F. Scott
Ford, Henry
Frazier, E. Franklin
Gilman, Charlotte Perkins
Gladden, Washington
Hague, Frank
Hatcher, Richard
Hearst, William Randolph
Hopper, Edward
Horne, Frank S.
Howard, Ebenezer
Howe, Frederic C.
Howells, William Dean
Hoyt, Homer
Jackson, Maynard
Jacobs, Jane
Jenney, William Le Baron
Joplin, Scott
Kahn, Louis I.
Kelley, Florence
Kenna, Michael "Hinky Dink"
Kerouac, Jack
Koch, Edward Irving
La Guardia, Fiorello
Lawrence, David L.
Levitt, William
Lindsay, John V.
Logue, Edward

Doctrines, Actions, Movements, and Religions

Education and Schools

About the Editor

David R. Goldfield is the Robert Lee Bailey Professor of History at the University of North Carolina, Charlotte. A native of Memphis, he grew up in Brooklyn, New York, and attended the University of Maryland. He is the author or editor of 13 books dealing with the history of the American South, including two works, *Cotton Fields and Skyscrapers: Southern City and Region* (1982) and *Black, White, and Southern: Race Relations and Southern Culture* (1991), that were nominated for the Pulitzer Prize in history; both of these also received the Mayflower Award for Non-fiction. *Still Fighting the Civil War: The American South and Southern History* appeared in 2002 and received the Jules and Frances Landry Prize and was named by *Choice* as an Outstanding Non-fiction Book. His most recent book is *Southern Histories: Public, Personal, and Sacred,* published by the University of Georgia Press in 2003. He is currently working on a reinterpretation of the Civil War, *Rebirth of a Nation: America During the Civil War Era,* for Holt Publishing. The Organization of American Historians named him Distinguished Lecturer in 2001. Goldfield is the editor of the *Journal of Urban History* and a coauthor of *The American Journey: A History of the United States* (2005).

He serves as an expert witness in voting rights and death penalty cases, as a consultant on the urban South to museums and public television and radio, and with the U.S. State Department as an Academic Specialist, leading workshops on American history and culture in foreign countries. He also is on the Advisory Board of the Lincoln Prize. Among his leisure-time activities are reading Southern novels, listening to Gustav Mahler and Buddy Holly, and coaching girls' fast-pitch softball.

Contributors

Carl Abbott
Portland State University

Elaine S. Abelson
New School University

Marsha E. Ackermann
Eastern Michigan University

Thomas Adam
University of Texas, Arlington

Julie Adkins
Southern Methodist University

Jeffrey S. Adler
University of Florida

John H. Akers
Tempe Historical Museum

Mary Anne Albanza Akers
University of Georgia

Thomas G. Alexander
Brigham Young University

Nedda C. Allbray
Brooklyn, New York

Nicholas Anastasakos
Brown University

Jerry Anthony
University of Iowa

Jo Ann E. Argersinger
Southern Illinois University, Carbondale

Elif S. Armbruster
Arlington, Massachusetts

Robert Armstrong
Lehigh University

Özgür Avci
University of Wisconsin, Madison

Eric Avila
University of California, Los Angeles

Jeremiah B. C. Axelrod
Occidental College

Robin F. Bachin
University of Miami

David A. Badillo
Bronx Institute, Lehman College

Allison Baker
Santa Monica College

Davarian L. Baldwin
Somerville, Massachusetts

Peter C. Baldwin
University of Connecticut

Carlos J. L. Balsas
Arizona State University

Dalit Baranoff
University of Maryland

Robert G. Barrows
Indiana University at Indianapolis

Hugh Bartling
DePaul University

John F. Bauman
Southport, Maine

Ronald H. Bayor
Georgia Tech University

Thomas Beal
State University of New York, Oneonta

Robert A. Beauregard
New School University

Janet R. Daly Bednarek
University of Dayton

Margaret Bendroth
American Congressional Association

F. Kaid Benfield
Natural Resources Defense Council

Larry Bennett
DePaul University

Roger Biles
Northern Illinois University

Michael J. Birkner
Gettysburg College

Alan A. Block
Pennsylvania State University

Jack S. Blocker Jr.
University of Western Ontario

Barbara Blumberg
Teaneck, New Jersey

Douglas K. Bohnenblust
Cheyenne, Wyoming

Christopher Bonastia
Queens College

Michael Ian Borer
Furman University

Joseph Boskin
Boston University

Nisha D. Botchwey
University of Virginia

Jamie M. Bradley
University of Maryland, Baltimore County

Martha Bradley
University of Utah

Amy Bridges
University of California, San Diego

Michael K. Brown
University of California

Cecelia Bucki
Fairfield University, Connecticut

John D. Buenker
University of Wisconsin, Parkside

Kristopher Burrell
New York, NY

Thomas J. Campanella
University of North Carolina, Chapel Hill

Walter F. Carroll
Bridgewater State College

Sundiata Keita Cha-Jua
University of Illinois, Urbana–Champaign

Brigitte Charaus
Marquette University

Howard P. Chudacoff
Brown University

William Clayson
Community College of Southern Nevada

Bell Clement
George Washington University

Alfredo Manuel Coelho
UMR Moïsa, Montpellier, France

David R. Colburn
University of Florida, Gainesville

James J. Connolly
Ball State University

Bernard Dov Cooperman
University of Maryland

Christopher Coutts
University of Michigan

Aaron Cowen
Cincinnati, Ohio

Margaret Crawford
Harvard University

Lawrence Culver
Utah State University

John T. Cumbler
University of Louisville

Susan Curtis
Purdue University

Donald L. Deardorff II
Cedarville University

Julie A. Dercle
California State University, Northridge

Tracey Deutsch
University of Minnesota

Richardson Dilworth
Drexel University

Darren Dochuk
Purdue University

James F. Donnelly
Miami Design Preservation League

Jack Dougherty
Trinity College

Gregory J. Downey
University of Wisconsin, Madison

Gina Marie Dreistadt
George Mason University

Louise Nelson Dyble
University of California, Berkeley

Stephanie Dyer
Sonoma State University

Michael H. Ebner
Lake Forest College

David J. Edelman
University of Cincinnati

Paul S. Edwards
University of Nottingham

Sarah Elkind
San Diego State University

Philip J. Ethington
University of Southern California

Andrew Feffer
Union College

Marjorie N. Feld
Babson College

Gail Fenske
Roger Williams University

Gary Fields
University of California, San Diego

Donovan Finn
University of Illinois, Urbana–Champaign

Maureen A. Flanagan
Michigan State University

Richard Flanagan
College of Staten Island, City University of New York

Steven Flusty
Toronto, Ontario, Canada

Laura Milsk Fowler
Southern Illinois University, Edwardsville

David M. P. Freund
Princeton University

John W. Frick
University of Virginia

Monroe Friedman
Eastern Michigan University

Catherine C. Galley
Texas Tech University

Wendy Gamber
Indiana University

Margaret Garb
Washington University

Todd K. Gardner
U.S. Census Bureau

Mark I. Gelfand
Boston College

Gene C. Gerard
Tarrant County College

Michelle A. Gilbert
Shaker Heights, Ohio

Howard Gillette Jr.
Rutgers University

Todd Gish
University of Southern California

Joseph Goddard
University of Copenhagen

Christian Gonzales
University of California, San Diego

Joanne L. Goodwin
University of Nevada, Las Vegas

William Gorham
The Urban Institute

Kevin Fox Gotham
Tulane University

Chiori Goto
University of California, San Diego

Kevin Grace
University of Cincinnati

Amy S. Greenberg
Pennsylvania State University

Catherine Devon Griffis
Rosalind Franklin University of Medicine and Science

Max Grinnell
University of Wisconsin, Madison

J. Philip Gruen
Washington State University

Owen D. Gutfreund
Barnard College

Marta Gutman
City College of New York

Dale Allen Gyure
Lawrence Technological University

Devon Hansen
Boston University

Richard Harris
McMaster University

Maureen Hays-Mitchell
Colgate University

Leslie Heaphy
Kent State University

Kenneth J. Heineman
Ohio University, Lancaster

A. Scott Henderson
Furman University

James Higgins
Lehigh University

Patricia Evridge Hill
San Jose State University

Arnold R. Hirsch
University of New Orleans

Bernard Hirschhorn
New York, New York

Amy Hodgin
University of North Carolina, Charlotte

Lisa M. Hoffman
University of Washington, Tacoma

Peter C. Holloran
Worcester State College

Michael W. Homel
Eastern Michigan University

Clifton Hood
Hobart and William Smith Colleges

Mervyn Horgan
York University

Darci L. Houser
Cleveland State University

Amy L. Howard
Center for Civic Engagement

Ella Howard
Boston University

D. Bradford Hunt
Roosevelt University

Laura Huntoon
University of Arizona

Andrew Hurley
University of Missouri, St. Louis

Ray Hutchinson
University of Wisconsin, Green Bay

Sharon Irish
University of Illinois, Urbana–Champaign

William Issel
San Francisco State University

Seema D. Iyer
University of Pennsylvania

Thomas J. Jablonsky
Marquette University

Kenneth T. Jackson
Columbia University

Kent James
Washington, Pennsylvania

Volker Janssen
University of California, San Diego

Edward J. Jepson Jr.
University of Tennessee

Jason Jindrich
University of Minnesota

David A. Johnson
University of Tennessee

David C. Johnson
Fordham University Lincoln Center

David R. Johnson
University of Texas, San Antonio

Janice E. Jones
Alverno College

Richard Junger
Western Michigan University

Seth Kamil
Big Onion Walking Tours, New York

Ronald Dale Karr
University of Massachusetts, Lowell

Nicholas Katers
University of Wisconsin, Milwaukee

William Dennis Keating
Cleveland State University

Barbara M. Kelly
Hofstra University

Tim Kelly
San Francisco Landmarks Board

Robert V. Kemper
Southern Methodist University

Judith Kenny
University of Wisconsin, Milwaukee

Thomas Kessner
CUNY Graduate Center

Margaret J. King
*The Center for Cultural Studies &
Analysis, Philadelphia*

Christopher Klemek
American Academy of Arts & Sciences

Matthew Klingle
Bowdoin College

Andrea Tuttle Kornbluh
University of Cincinnati

Dejan Kralj
Loyola University Chicago

Carl E. Kramer
Kramer Associates, Jeffersonville, Indiana

Kevin M. Kruse
Princeton University

Ben Kuhlman
University of Wisconsin, Milwaukee

Nancy Kwak
Columbia University

Michael Kwartler
Environmental Simulation Center

Peter Kwong
*Hunter College, City University of
New York*

Louis M. Kyriakoudes
University of Southern Mississippi

Tim Lacy
Loyola University Chicago

James B. Lane
Indiana University Northwest

Jason S. Lantzer
Indiana University

Kristin Larsen
University of Florida

Matthew D. Lassiter
University of Michigan

Ute Lehrer
Brock University

Daniel J. Lerner
Binghamton University

Elaine Lewinnek
California State University, Fullerton

Robert Lewis
University of Toronto

Ariane Mary Liazos
Harvard University

Teresa Lingafelter
University of California, Los Angeles

Kyle M. Livie
Petaluma, California

Jared Lobdell
Millersville University

Carrie Logan
University of Georgia

Roger W. Lotchin
University of North Carolina, Chapel Hill

Mary Ting Yi Lui
Yale University

Catherine Maddison
University of Cambridge

Patrick Mallory
Loyola University Chicago

Paul B. Manchester
*United States Department of Housing
and Urban Development*

Seth R. Marcus
*United States Department of Housing
and Urban Development*

James Marten
Marquette University

Robert W. Matson
University of Pittsburgh, Johnstown

Glenna Matthews
*Institute of Urban and Regional
Development, Berkeley, California*

Paul Mattingly
New York University

Alan Mayne
University of Melbourne

Bernadette McCauley
*Hunter College, City University of
New York*

Dennis McClendon
Chicago CartoGraphics

Lorraine McConaghy
Museum of History and Industry

Gerald W. McFarland
University of Massachusetts

Stephen J. McGovern
Haverford College

Eileen McGurty
Johns Hopkins University

Andrew Meyers
Ethical Culture Fieldston School

Christopher Miller
Marquette University

La Shonda Mims
Charlotte, North Carolina

Gregory Mixon
University of North Carolina, Charlotte

Raymond A. Mohl
University of Alabama, Birmingham

Kate Mollan
University of Wisconsin, Milwaukee

Christian Montès
University Lyon, France

Ian Morley
Ming Chuan University

Eric J. Morser
University of New Mexico

Roberta M. Moudry
Cornell University

Edward K. Muller
University of Pittsburgh

Douglas Muzzio
Baruch College, City University of New York

Patrick Naick
University of Iowa

Douglas Nelson
Mill Valley, California

Barbara Stabin Nesmith
New York, New York

Caryn E. Neumann
Ohio State University

Scott A. Newman
Loyola University Chicago

Becky Nicolaides
University of California, San Diego

Micheline Nilsen
Ernestine M. Raclin School of the Arts

Thomas J. Noel
University of Colorado, Denver

Timothy J. O'Brien
University of Houston

Thomas H. O'Connor
Boston College

Robert S. Ogilvie
University of California, Berkeley

Kathy Ogren
University of Redlands

Janet C. Olson
Northwestern University

Itohan Osayimwese
Ypsilanti, Michigan

Dominic A. Pacyga
Columbia College

Howard Padwa
University of California, Los Angeles

Brian D. Page
Ohio State University

Mark Peel
Monash University

Thomas R. Pegram
Loyola College

David N. Pellow
University of California, San Diego

Emily Pettis
Madison, Wisconsin

Susan A. Phillips
Pitzer College

Wendy Plotkin
Arizona State University

Carrie M. Poteat
University of North Carolina, Charlotte

Madelon Powers
University of New Orleans

David Kenneth Pye
University of California, San Diego

Nancy Quam-Wickham
California State University, Long Beach

James Ralph
Middlebury College

CindyAnn M. Rampersad
Pennsylvania State University

James K. Reap
University of Georgia

Gordon Reavley
The Nottingham Trent University

Teresa M. Reinders
University of Wisconsin, Parkside

Stella Ress
Loyola University Chicago

Mary Stovall Richards
Brigham Young University

Amy G. Richter
Clark University

Joseph A. Rodriguez
University of Wisconsin, Milwaukee

Mark H. Rose
Florida Atlantic University

Nicholas G. Rosenthal
University of California, Los Angeles

Reuben Skye Rose-Redwood
Pennsylvania State University

Matthew W. Roth
University of Southern California

A. K. Sandoval-Strausz
University of New Mexico

Eric Sandweiss
Indiana University

Pierre-Yves Saunier
Lyon, France

David Schuyler
Franklin & Marshall College

David G. Schwartz
University of Nevada, Las Vegas

Cord Scott
Loyola University Chicago

Robert O. Self
Brown University

Amanda I. Seligman
University of Wisconsin, Milwaukee

Harriet F. Senie
City College of New York

Allen J. Share
University of Louisville

Martin Shefter
Cornell University

Samuel C. Shepherd Jr.
Centenary College of Louisiana

Abraham J. Shragge
University of California, San Diego

Lindsay Silver
Brandeis University

Roger D. Simon
Lehigh University

Christina Slattery
Madison, Wisconsin

Robert A. Slayton
Chapman University

David Charles Sloane
University of Southern California

Wendy Slone
Cleveland, Ohio

Carl Smith
Northwestern University

Christa Smith
Clemson University

Kennedy Lawson Smith
The Community Land Use and Economics Group

Michael O. Smith
Wayne State University

Joseph Michael Sommers
University of Kansas

J. Mark Souther
Cleveland State University

Daphne G. Spain
University of Virginia

Judith Spraul-Schmidt
University of Cincinnati

Amy Squitieri
Madison, Wisconsin

Sumeeta Srinivasan
Harvard University

Jason Stacy
Loyola University Chicago

Marc Stein
York University

Chris Stonestreet
University of North Carolina, Charlotte

David Stradling
University of Cincinnati

Doreen Swetkis
Cleveland State University

Julie Sze
University of California, Davis

Joel A. Tarr
Carnegie Mellon University

Jon C. Teaford
Purdue University

Dianne T. Thompson
United States Department of Housing and Urban Development

Claudette L. Tolson
Loyola University Chicago

Judith Ann Trolander
University of Minnesota, Duluth

Joe W. Trotter
Carnegie Mellon University

Barbara Truesdell
Indiana University

Kazuyo Tsuchiya
University of California, San Diego

Bas van Heur
Utrecht University

Philip R. VanderMeer
Arizona State University

Thomas J. Vicino
University of Maryland

Avis C. Vidal
Wayne State University

Domenic Vitiello
University of Pennsylvania

Matthew L. Wagner
University of Wisconsin, Milwaukee

Stacy Warren
Eastern Washington University

Kimberley Green Weathers
University of Houston

Andrew Wiese
San Diego State University

Geoffrey S. Wiggins
University of New Orleans

Mark Wild
California State University, Los Angeles

Dan Levinson Wilk
Duke University

Mary Lethert Wingerd
St. Cloud State University

Dale Winling
University of Michigan

Dan Wishnoff
John Jay College of Criminal Justice

David B. Wolcott
Miami University

David A. Wolff
Black Hills State College

Michael Wolford
University of North Carolina, Charlotte

Gwendolyn Wright
Columbia University

James Wunsch
New York, New York

Carl Zimring
Oberlin College

Introduction

We are an urban nation and have been so, officially at least, since the early 20th century. But long before then, our cities played crucial roles in the economic and political development of the nation, as magnets for immigrants and as centers of culture and innovation. They still do. Yet, the discipline that we call "urban history" is really a phenomenon of post–World War II scholarship. And it was not until the 1970s that a body of research emerged to justify a journal—the *Journal of Urban History*—as a showcase for that scholarship. Now, after a generation of pathbreaking scholarship that has reoriented and enlightened our perception of the American city, an interdisciplinary group of scholars offers both a summary and a prospectus of the field in this *Encyclopedia of American Urban History*.

Ours is an interdisciplinary field. Architects, planners, sociologists, environmentalists, political scientists, and economists, among others, are better informed in their work if they are aware of the urban process in historical context. The interdisciplinary nature of the field is reflected both in the variety of entries and in the diversity of contributors. Although historians predominate, the Editors and Advisory Board of these volumes have invited individuals inside and outside the academy and social scientists from a number of disciplines.

It is fair to ask, then, if in fact, like our contemporary cities, the field has become the intellectual version of sprawl. Is it possible to make sense out of what seems to be a Jackson Pollock scholarly canvas? Not any more than in most other social science fields, the Editors believe; the difficulty of synthesizing burgeoning research is a common scholarly lament. It is, in fact, a reflection of dynamic scholarship: Urban historical research is so rapidly expanding into new areas of inquiry and offering new perspectives and innovations in methodology and sources that a synthesis would at once be heroic and quickly out of date. The value of this encyclopedia is that it affords an opportunity to take stock, to see where we are in the field and where we might be going. Perhaps some scholar will find these entries useful in fashioning that long-awaited synthesis, but this is not the primary purpose of the volumes. Rather, the Editors and Advisory Board hope to expose the leading scholarship by both prominent and up-and-coming academics and practitioners as not only a state-of-the-art summary of American urban history but as a valuable reference work to guide future researchers.

Our distinguished Editorial Advisory Board has thought long and hard on these issues, and one member, Kenneth T. Jackson, has thought longer and harder than the rest of us, having directed the highly regarded *Encyclopedia of New York City* (1995). The complexity of the field reflects the complexity of the city, complicating the selection of entries. But the eclectic nature of the field and the entity we study has also allowed for wide latitude. Tim Gilfoyle, Associate Editor of the *Journal of Urban History,* and an Advisory Board member, has noted that cities are complex phenomena, requiring urbanists to break them down into constituent parts in their attempts to make sense of them. Cities, Gilfoyle avers, defy easy generalization and definition. Urban history thus remains a topic absent any totalizing theory or universal paradigm. For nearly 30 years, urban history has flourished in interdisciplinary chaos, with many of the works written by individuals who do not define themselves as "urbanists" or "urban historians." Urban history benefits from the absence of a canon. While that means the field lacks a certain glue to hold it together, the multiple methodologies and subjects encompassed by "urban history" make for a more invigorating field, albeit a more difficult one to teach or promote. The influence of nonhistorians and nonurbanists in the field of urban history presents an ongoing and historic tradition.

Much of this urban historical research has focused on the past 150 years of American urban history, and this is the emphasis of the encyclopedia. This is the time period when the American city came into its own, when the United States transformed from being a nation of shopkeepers and farmers to an urban industrial, and then postindustrial, society. This transformation was sudden (in historical terms) and dramatic. Henry Adams's comment that "in the essential of life . . . the boy of 1854 stood nearer the year one than to the year 1900" underscores the metamorphosis. The scale of cities, the types of people living in them, the diversity of activities within and on the periphery, and the technology that drove these changes are the subjects of these volumes.

Carl Abbott, who is a contributor to these volumes and teaches in a city planning program, recalled that pioneering urban historian Richard Wade used to tell his students that urban history was not an independent subspecialty but an essential way to explore the development of the United States as a whole, and that scholars should think of themselves as U.S. historians first, urban historians second. The scholarship bears him out, especially recent work. The study of cities and groups within cities is thriving under the banner of many other "histories," such as environmental, educational, ethnic, racial, immigration, gender, social, and regional. There is interesting work on historical aspects of urban development in sociology, political science, geography, urban planning, and other closely related disciplines. The journals surveyed and books read by urban historians are wide-ranging and interdisciplinary, as are these volumes.

Most members of the Advisory Board are identified with multiple subareas and do not identify themselves exclusively as urban historians. Thus, Raymond A. Mohl is identified with ethnicity and infrastructure, Joe Trotter with labor and African American history, Lizabeth Cohen with labor and social history, Becky Nicolaides with American studies and gender, Maureen Flanagan with gender, and Tim Gilfoyle with sexuality and popular culture, but all happen to focus their research on cities. Ken Jackson's most cited work, *Crabgrass Frontier,* is about suburbs. What binds these individuals together as urban historians is their interest in the interaction between the urban process—how and why cities grow—and the specific subjects on which they focus. As with most of our contributors, they view the city as a dynamic entity shaping and being shaped by an array of peoples and events. It is this interactive quality that the contributions to these volumes bring to the field of urban history.

As Carl Abbott has noted, new ideas, more often than not, come out of dissonance and conflict rather than consensus. Permeable disciplinary boundaries tend to be highly productive of new ideas and insights. A long tradition in social theory argues that people on the edges and frontier zones of social groups, those whose status and standing are uncertain and contested, are the most active agents of social change. In the realm of scholarship, new ideas also come from the margins. The interaction between urban and environmental history offers an example. It is a productive area of inquiry because urban historians are being drawn to environmental questions and because environmental historians are finding it useful to ask "urban history" questions that lead them toward the examination of social and ethnic groups, neighborhood dynamics, and local political power and institutions.

To study the history of cities, Abbott concludes, is essentially to study the creation and character of the modern, and perhaps postmodern, world. To make things manageable, urban historians have often focused on specific topics that repay concentrated analysis by many scholars. Topics such as intercity competition and rivalry, the origin of public services, and social and economic mobility were hot in the 1960s and 1970s, but are less so now. They have been replaced by equally interesting topics such as women's urban experiences and institutions, cities as arenas for sexual choices, the complex character of suburbanization, and the symbolic meanings of the built environment. Because pursuit of these topics may take groups of researchers into different scholarly realms, the field can look fragmented—or it can look vital.

Selecting entries for such a broad field was our most challenging task. Members of the Advisory Board, chosen not only for their expertise in a particular subfield but also because of their comprehensive knowledge of the field in general, submitted entries in four categories, ranging from most significant (requiring at least 2,500 words) to important (entries of 500 words). Their suggestions totaled more than 1,000 entries. Eliminating duplicate and overlapping suggestions, the Editors of these volumes developed a list of more than 500 entries and then set about pairing the entries with contributors, again taking the suggestions of the Advisory Board members. Deciding which entries belonged in which categories was a daunting task as well and was accomplished after several months of consultations between the Editor and Assistant Editor and the Advisory Board members. The Editors and Board members have also defined *urban* broadly, including suburban environments, and even something new and, literally, far out, called *penurbia*. The approach was both referential and reverential: to produce a work that would function as a research tool and as a commemoration of scholarship.

The entries reflect not only an expansive view of "urban" but also the nature of American urbanization itself. American cities were not created by administrative fiat or royal command, but usually by economic forces and geographical imperatives. Their development was likewise not carefully controlled; it was driven by the desire for land and by the hunger of the huge markets that arose in that quest. Land speculation was a major factor behind the location and development of cities, the creation of urban wealth, the development of new transportation technologies, and the provision of city services (the value of land rose dramatically with the extension of water and sewer lines, paved streets, and police and fire protection). American cities are, perhaps to a greater extent than cities anywhere else in the world, the products of exuberant capitalism. The entries reflect the Editors' view of cities as engines of development and of the great diversity of peoples attracted by the opportunities that development presented.

The entries also indicate the shifting nature of the field. During the 1950s and 1960s, urban biographies—historical analyses of major cities—dominated the subject. With the rise of the "new urban history" of the 1960s and 1970s, more quantitative approaches gained favor, particularly those related to social and geographic mobility. Also at this time, historians made connections with geographers, sociologists, and architects to extend a multidisciplinary analysis to urban development that emphasized the evolution and allocation of urban space and structure. By the 1980s, urban historical research followed general historiographical trends using race, class, and gender as analytical categories, though with a continued awareness of how space and power interacted with those categories. At the same time, interest in suburban research grew, a reflection of the fact that the 1970 census indicated that more Americans lived in suburbs than in central cities.

In fact, urban historians have seemed to follow contemporary research trends. This should not imply we are "presentists." But it is true that we believe that urban historical research definitely has contemporary policy implications. Many of the entries bear out that parallel. Public health, the environment, infrastructure, law enforcement, and the new immigration are prominent policy issues in the contemporary metropolis. In turn, they are also important topics for urban historical research. Such subjects also indicate how comfortable urban historians are researching and writing in an interdisciplinary milieu. It is really not a choice, it is a necessity, and the contributions to these volumes reflect that.

The entries also say a great deal about the contributions to the encyclopedia: that urban historical research is carried out in a variety of settings. While most of the authors are connected with colleges and universities, a significant number of writers represented here work for nonprofits, governments, and corporations. These settings have a significant stake in the urban process, and understanding that process is essential to their well-being. So, while the Editors and Advisory Board present this encyclopedia as history, these volumes are also reflections of the present day and of the future. In other words, if you live in a metropolitan area, regardless of what your professional interests might be, these volumes will help you to understand the place where you live and work, how it came to be that way, and what, perhaps, might make it better. Urban scholars and practitioners deal with the urban process, the constantly changing nature of the city and of the people who compose it. For urban historians and our numerous fellow travelers in the social sciences and sciences, the Editors and Board members have fashioned this as a fundamental reference work to ground and inspire future research in our field. It is a measure of what we have accomplished to this point, and what we may do in the future.

David Goldfield
Editor

Kathryn B. Wells
Assistant Editor

ABBOTT, EDITH

Edith Abbott (1876-1957) was born in Grand Island, Nebraska. She was one of the first women in America to earn a doctoral degree. In 1924, she became the dean of the School of Social Service Administration at the University of Chicago, a position she held for 18 years. As such, she had a profound influence on the emerging field of social work.

Abbott came from a family that had an intense interest in social activism. Her mother participated in the abolitionist and women's rights movements. Abbott's sister, Grace, served as the chief of the Children's Bureau within the U.S. Department of Labor from 1921 to 1934. Abbott graduated from a girls' boarding school in Omaha in 1893.

Although Abbott wanted to attend college, her parents could not afford it at the time. Consequently, Abbott returned to Grand Island and taught high school for 2 years. She eventually attended the University of Nebraska, graduating in 1901. She went on to attend the University of Chicago, earning a Ph.D. in economics in 1905. The following year she continued her studies in England, attending both the University College of London and the London School of Economics and Political Science. It was at the London School that she was exposed to new methods of combating poverty.

After returning to America, she joined her sister Grace in 1908 in Chicago to volunteer at Hull-House, the first settlement house founded in the country.

Settlement houses were community centers in poor neighborhoods that were staffed and managed by college-educated women. While working at Hull-House Abbott promoted improvements in housing for the poor, as well as new laws to protect immigrants, working women, and children.

She became an assistant to Sophonisba Breckinridge, the director of social research at the Chicago School of Civics and Philanthropy. In this capacity, she contributed to many studies of juvenile delinquents.

In 1920, Abbott helped move the School of Civics and Philanthropy to the University of Chicago, where it became the School of Social Service Administration. It was the first graduate school of social work at an American university. Abbott taught in the school for 33 years, and she served as dean from 1924 to 1942.

Abbott had a significant effect on the new profession of social work. She firmly believed that universities should oversee education for social work and should be conducted at the graduate school level. In addition, she was convinced that a sound education in social work must include fieldwork, where students could gain actual experience. Abbott not only created the curriculum for social work education but also wrote all of the early literature necessary to teach social work students, amounting to over 100 books and studies.

After retiring from the University of Chicago in 1953, she returned to her family's home in Nebraska. She died in 1957.

—Gene C. Gerard

Further Readings and References

Costin, L. (1983). *Two sisters for social justice: A biography of Grace and Edith Abbott.* Urbana, IL: University of Illinois Press.

Ladd-Taylor, M. (1997). *Gender and the politics of welfare reform: Mothers' pension in Chicago, 1911–1929.* Chicago: University of Chicago Press.

ABRAMS, CHARLES

Charles Abrams (1902-1970) was a scholar, lawyer, and administrator whose views helped shape government policies and popular conceptions concerning cities, urban growth, and public housing in mid-20th-century America.

Born in Tsarist-controlled Poland, Abrams and his family immigrated to the United States in 1904, eventually settling in the Williamsburg neighborhood of Brooklyn, New York. Abrams quickly developed an appreciation for the diverse communities that urban environments foster. He received his law degree from Brooklyn Law School in 1922, and within a few years, he had amassed significant wealth from his work as a real estate lawyer and speculator. He married Ruth Davidson, an aspiring artist, in 1928.

New York City Mayor Fiorello La Guardia, aware of Abrams's expertise in real estate, urged him to assist in drafting the New York Municipal Housing Authorities Law. Enacted in 1933, this legislation became a model for subsequent federal and state housing laws. Later, as the New York City Housing Authority's first general counsel (1934–1937), Abrams successfully established the legality of eminent domain proceedings for slum clearance and construction of public housing.

In addition to his support of public housing, Abrams was also an avid crusader for open-housing laws. In 1955, Governor Averell Harriman appointed Abrams to run the New York State Commission Against Discrimination (SCAD). As head of SCAD, Abrams drafted legislation to include FHA (Federal Housing Administration) and VA (Veterans Administration) financed housing under the New York State Law Against Discrimination. Soon after leaving SCAD in 1959, Abrams accepted the presidency of the National Committee Against Discrimination in Housing (1961–1965). Under Abrams's leadership, that organization led a successful fight for an Executive Order barring discrimination in federally subsidized housing.

Abrams was one of the founders of the discipline of urban studies, the systematic study of cities and their inhabitants. As a visiting professor at numerous institutions, including the New School for Social Research, the University of Pennsylvania, MIT, and Columbia University, he inspired students to embrace his analytical, but humane approach to examining the urban landscape. He also disseminated his ideas in seven books (the most often cited remains his classic 1955 survey of housing discrimination, *Forbidden Neighbors*), dozens of articles, and hundreds of newspaper stories. Written for general audiences, these publications avoided technical terms and jargon, making Abrams one of the era's best-known public intellectuals.

Abrams's career extended beyond the United States. He undertook several overseas missions for the United Nations, helping to establish housing authorities and planning schools in developing countries. He summarized these trips in his influential 1964 book, *Man's Struggle for Shelter in an Urbanizing World.*

Throughout his life, Abrams criticized the misuse of urban space. It was therefore fitting—if also contrary to his Jewish heritage—that Abrams requested that his body be cremated, a request that his family honored.

—*A. Scott Henderson*

See also Housing Segregation; La Guardia, Fiorello; Public Housing; Restrictive Deed Covenants

Further Readings and References

Abrams, C. (1964). *Oral history interview.* Columbia University Oral History Collection, New York.

Henderson, A. S. (2000). *Housing and the democratic ideal: The life and thought of Charles Abrams.* New York: Columbia University Press.

Taper, B. (1967, February 4). A lover of cities, I. *The New Yorker.*

Taper, B. (1967, February 11). A lover of cities, II. *The New Yorker.*

ACKERMAN, FREDERICK L.

An architect and housing reformer, Frederick Lee Ackerman (1878–1950) supported proactive engagement of the federal government to supply quality housing for the working class and to oversee national planning, integrating transportation, housing, commercial uses, and open space responsive to community needs. He participated in the federal government's earliest housing program, collaborated with architects Clarence S. Stein and Henry Wright on their celebrated projects Sunnyside (1924) and Radburn (1928), and worked for the New York City Housing Authority. While he favored traditional architecture and lower income housing, one of his most acclaimed designs was a modernist, luxury apartment building in New York City.

Following a trip to Great Britain in 1917 at the behest of Charles Whitaker, editor of the *Journal of the American Institute of Architects,* to survey that country's government housing program, Ackerman became town planner for the United States Shipping Board's Emergency Fleet Corporation, overseeing the design of new communities for war workers. Ackerman advocated large-scale development efficiently realized through combining individual lots and locating the structures, typically low-scale garden apartments, on the perimeter with common open space in the interior, a layout employed at Sunnyside and the early public housing projects of the 1930s. He shared the community-building ideas of Stein and Wright, advocating deconcentration of the congested metropolis into autonomous, interconnected new towns of limited population with communal land ownership and joined these architects in forming the Regional Planning Association of America (RPAA).

Considered by social critic and fellow RPAA member Lewis Mumford among the most radical thinkers of that group, Ackerman based his proposals for restructuring the capitalist system of land ownership and development to better accommodate the working class on the ideas of social economist Thorstein Veblen and land reformer Henry George. The technical expert or *technocrat* had the expertise to formulate new strategies of land development informed and coordinated by centralized government to ensure that any increase in property values due to population growth or public improvements accrued to the people rather than to a few land speculators. Ackerman believed that the architect, armed with a combination of planning tools, cost analysis, design skills, and a holistic, regionalist perspective, occupied a central role in this process.

Following the establishment of the federal public housing program, Ackerman headed the technical staff of the New York City Housing Authority (1934–1939). He designed a variety of projects from faculty housing at his alma mater Cornell University to New York City's first public housing project to the commercial Plaza Building at Radburn. His circa 1938 luxury apartment building in New York City at East 83rd Street is renowned for its modern exterior featuring glass block that expressed the technological advances inside—the first apartment building in the city with central air.

—*Kristin Larsen*

See also Garden Cities; Mumford, Lewis; Regional Planning Association of America; Stein, Clarence S.; Wright, Henry

Further Readings and References

Lang, M. (2001). Town planning and radicalism in the Progressive Era: The legacy of F. L. Ackerman. *Planning Perspectives, 16,* 143–167.

ADDAMS, JANE

Jane Addams (1860-1935) intended to live a life of purpose. A social activist and reform-minded woman of the late 19th century, she initiated the settlement movement in the United States when Hull-House opened in 1889. Addams was born to a middle-class family in Cedarville, Illinois in 1860, and thus the world offered her a life of idleness befitting a woman of her status. Jane Addams, however, wanted to accomplish more with her life. While on a Grand Tour of Europe in 1887, she made a visit to Toynbee Hall. Named for its founder, Arnold Toynbee, an Oxford-educated gentleman, the settlement house, located in the deplorable Whitechapel district of London, sought to bring education and social uplift to the poor.

Jane Addams modeled Hull-House after Toynbee Hall. Located on Halsted Street, in a working-class district of Chicago, Hull-House sought to remedy the disparity that existed between the classes in many industrial cities. With the rise of industrialization in Northern cities, the United States experienced an influx of European immigration. These immigrants represented the working-class residents who made their homes in ramshackle tenement houses amid filth and disease. To remedy such conditions of early urbanization, Hull-House's philosophy rejected religious tenets for scientific theory. Victorian-era reformers, such as Addams, dismissed the biblical foundations of the inherent depravity of the individual and instead proposed that their environment influenced humans' condition. The women of Hull-House provided various intellectual and cultural programs as a means to foster self-improvement among those in Chicago's new immigrant populations.

Jane Addams faded into obscurity in the early 20th century with the start of the First World War. As a pacifist and Women's Peace Party chairperson, she vigorously protested the morality of the war. Her unpopular political views made her a target of the Red Scare of approximately 1918 to 1920. Nevertheless, she was awarded the Nobel Peace Prize in 1931 for her work. With the government's proactive stance to its citizenry, most notably in the New Deal, the nature of charity changed. The state took up the burden of the nation's poor, and Jane Addams died after years of illness on May 31, 1935.

—Carrie M. Poteat

Further Readings and References

Addams, J. (1910). *Twenty years at Hull-House with autobiographical notes.* New York: MacMillan.

Diliberto, G. (1999). *A useful woman: The early life of Jane Addams.* New York: Scribner.

ADDICTION

Though the connection between narcotics and deviance is often taken for granted, the arrival of these substances on the sociocultural margins is a relatively recent phenomenon. Until the turn of the 20th century, the use of drugs that are now illicit was socially acceptable and actually quite common. Morphine became a painkiller of choice thanks to the increased availability of the hypodermic syringe after the Civil War, while opiates were used widely in popular cures for gastrointestinal illness and hangovers and were even used in sleeping agents for infants. Cocaine was a main ingredient in hay fever medicines and popular tonics and beverages (including Coca-Cola), while cannabis was an ingredient in ordinary pharmaceutical preparations. Yet as use of these substances became prevalent in the late 19th century, doctors began to notice that many of their patients, especially

those who used morphine, developed both a tolerance to and a physical dependence on these drugs—in short, they became addicted. Increasingly aware of the potential dangers of addiction, doctors became reluctant to prescribe narcotics, and the 1906 Pure Food and Drug Act led pharmaceutical manufacturers to decrease the narcotic levels in their products.

As the medical use of narcotics declined, the demographic of the typical user shifted dramatically: The once common type of addict—a middle-aged, middle- or upper-class female who became addicted because of a doctor's careless prescription habits—became increasingly rare as medical professionals and consumers became more careful with narcotics. In place of the well-to-do victims of medically induced addiction emerged a new kind of addict—a person who began using narcotics recreationally and was likely to be a working-class and nonwhite young male. Consequently, stereotypes linking heroin with inner city immigrants and radicals, opium with Chinese laborers in the West, marijuana with Mexicans, and cocaine with Southern blacks worked to create powerful discursive links between drug use and foreignness, social disorder, and decay. This shift in popular perceptions of both drug use and drug users helped lay the ideological and political groundwork for the stringent legal controls over these substances that would emerge in the 1910s and 1920s.

While some states had passed laws against morphine and cocaine in the late 19th century, the federal government became involved in narcotics control by prohibiting the importation of smoking opium into the United States, and the 1914 Harrison Act required anyone who imported, sold, or prescribed opiates or coca leaves to register with the federal government and pay a special tax. The Harrison Act was buffered by a series of Supreme Court decisions, highlighted by *Webb et al. v. United States* (1919), which established that doctors could not prescribe controlled substances to addicts so addicts could maintain their drug-taking habits. Shortly thereafter, narcotic clinics, which had opened in about a dozen major cities to help addicts gradually reduce their drug intake, were shut down. Thus by the mid-1920s, addicts were left with little choice but to either enter treatment or turn to what had become a growing black market in the narcotics trade.

In the 1920s, law enforcement became the major weapon in the struggle against addiction, operating under the assumption that stiff penalties and severe enforcement measures were the best way to ensure public compliance with the federal drug control regime. By 1928, almost one third of the inmates in federal prisons were incarcerated for violating narcotics laws, more than the total of the next two categories of lawbreakers (violators of liquor prohibition and car thieves) combined. To alleviate the strain on the prison system in the 1930s, the federal government created separate facilities for drug addicts, which came to be known as "narcotic farms." The two farms—one in Lexington, Kentucky, the other in Fort Worth, Texas—were ostensibly treatment facilities designed to give addicts a retreat from the rigors of modern life in the city, which were held to have been a key factor in causing addiction. However, the farms ultimately proved to be more like prisons or labor camps than treatment facilities, as medical practitioners played a relatively minor role in what came to be a rather harsh program of rehabilitation that was imposed on addicts.

The number of drug users in the United States dropped with America's entry into the Second World War, as the state of national emergency allowed the government to tighten its controls over both the international traffic and domestic distribution of drugs. By the late 1940s, Congress no longer felt it necessary to increase the narcotics-control budget, even though new hotspots for smugglers and dealers emerged in the Puerto Rican and black ghettos of Northern cities.

In the early 1950s, the popular press seized upon what it perceived to be skyrocketing levels of drug use in American cities, especially among teenagers. Seven major cities—New York, Baltimore, Philadelphia, Detroit, Chicago, New Orleans, and Washington, D.C.—were seen as the centers of the narcotic problem, while affluent suburbs and rural areas were considered generally free from narcotic abuse. Thus, beginning in the 1950s, American drug policy was constructed with two main goals: to check and contain the spread of drug abuse where narcotics were prevalent and to keep it out of areas where abuse was not widespread. Stiff penalties were meted out to drug dealers, with long prison sentences and mandatory minimums for certain offenses, while the legal arsenal aimed against organized drug trafficking expanded dramatically.

By the mid-1960s, however, narcotics use had become increasingly popular outside of the disadvantaged urban population. But unlike in the late 19th century, the prevalence of drug use among the more affluent did not make it more socially acceptable. Co-opted into the antiwar movement and hippie culture that was embraced by many middle- and upper-class youths, drugs maintained their links with countercultural and disruptive behavior, especially with the proliferation of psychedelic substances like LSD. Yet despite their continued association with deviance and disorder, the late 1960s and 1970s saw a major shift in the direction of American drug policy. With the spread of addiction among the better off, funding and support for treatment and prevention programs increased under the Nixon administration, and they have continued growing through the present day. But notwithstanding the development of a more demographically, geographically, and socially heterogeneous addict population, many Americans continue to associate the ravages of addiction with the degradation of urban ghettos and crime, as they have for over a century.

—Howard Padwa

Further Readings and References

Belenko, S. R. (Ed.). (2000). *Drugs and drug policy in America: A documentary history.* Westport, CT: Greenwood Press.

Courtwright, D. T. (1982). *Dark paradise: Opiate addiction in America before 1940.* Cambridge, MA: Harvard University Press.

Morgan, H. W. (Ed.). (1974). *Yesterday's addicts: American society and drug abuse, 1865–1920.* Norman, OK: University of Oklahoma Press.

Musto, D. F. (1987). *The American disease: Origins of narcotic control.* New York: Oxford University Press.

AFRICAN AMERICAN BUSINESS DISTRICTS

Throughout American history, a community's Main Street business district has served as a cultural reflection of free enterprise and a focal point for its social, political, religious, and economic fabric. For African Americans in the 1880s to early 1960s, a parallel form took shape through the development of African American business districts within the segregated South, and later throughout the country as African Americans migrated North seeking labor opportunities.

Many have characterized the development of African American business districts in the past as a "golden age" for African American business, while others have contended the racial oppression brought upon by segregation and federal policies constrained opportunities for additional business growth. In the end, the dollars invested in African American business districts produced a great deal of self-pride, self-determination, and self-sufficiency for African Americans. From Harlem to Beale Street, the cultural, social, and economic value endemic to historic African American business districts is now being rediscovered and mined through dedicated preservation and redevelopment efforts.

After the Civil War, skills that were once bound by the institution of slavery were commercialized in a free society. Southern states responded to the growth of African American enterprise by creating Jim Crow or segregation laws, which restricted where businesses owned by African Americans could be located, stifling and precluding African Americans' participation in the country's economic growth. Thus in Southern cities, free African Americans who owned successful enterprises on Main Street before the Civil War were forced, along with newly freed African Americans, to operate only in African American communities. As a result numerous African American business districts formed, including Miami's Overtown District, Atlanta's Sweet Auburn Street, and the "Black Wall Streets" of Greenwood in Tulsa, Oklahoma, and Hayti in Durham, North Carolina.

With the discovery of oil, Tulsa in 1920 was a thriving, enormously wealthy town. However, Tulsa was a tale of two cities isolated from one another. Like most Southern communities, African Americans could neither live among whites nor patronize their businesses. African Americans developed their own separate business communities. In Tulsa, the Greenwood district was so vibrant and successful that during a visit, Booker T. Washington bestowed on it the moniker "Negro Wall Street."

By 1921, the Greenwood business district contained two theaters, three drug stores, four hotels, and community institutions such as a hospital, schools, and two newspapers. In addition there were more than 150 two- and three-story brick commercial buildings that housed apparel and food stores, cafes, nightclubs, and a number of professional services including doctors, lawyers, and dentists.

Unfortunately, it was this success that often led to increased racial tension and retribution in the South. The alleged assault of a white woman by an African American man in Greenwood triggered unprecedented civil unrest. The worst riot in American history, the Tulsa Race Riot of 1921 destroyed people, property, and African American commerce. Hundreds of people died or were injured. Property damage ran into the millions of dollars. The Greenwood district burned to the ground. Prior to the massacre, which wiped out an estimated 1,500 homes and businesses owned by African Americans, Tulsa boasted an unprecedented 10 African American millionaires and more than 600 African American residents with assets of $5,000 to $500,000.

Much of the Greenwood business district was patterned after the development of the Hayti district in Durham, North Carolina. African Americans began settling on the southwest edge of Durham shortly after the Civil War. Originally viewed as a labor pool for Durham's tobacco warehouses, Hayti soon prospered with African American entrepreneurship, leading to the founding of several large institutions, including the North Carolina Mutual Insurance Company and North Carolina Central University, a historically black college and university founded by James Shepard, a registered pharmacist and business owner.

Starting in 1910 and lasting until 1970, there was a demographic shift involving the "Great Migration" of Southern African Americans seeking higher wages and political rights in the North. This created another wave of prosperous, but still segregated, African American business districts.

Chicago's Bronzeville district characterized the Northern African American business community. While not segregated by law, Bronzeville was a city within a city, offering a commercial alternative to the indifference that characterized Chicago at the time. The dramatic rise in Bronzeville's economic and social base led many to refer to the district as "African American Metropolis."

Milwaukee's Walnut Street was the Cream City's version of the great African American business districts that once thrived in the nation's largest cities. Jazz and blues clubs owned or managed by African Americans had been part of Milwaukee's scene since the late 1920s. "Black and Tan" clubs such as the Metropole and the Club Congo made an impression on mainstream Milwaukee with a diverse mixture of white and African American patrons.

African American business districts began to show signs of weakness beginning in the 1940s and 1950s. As African Americans began to gain additional freedoms, many chose to shop in other areas of the city, where better capitalized white merchants offered greater selection of goods and lower prices. Further economic pressure resulted from federal policies such as the Urban Renewal Act and Interstate Highway Act, which began to dismantle the surrounding African American neighborhoods with projects designed to remove urban blight and pave the way for America's suburban growth.

While discrimination, increasing competition, and physical removal may have dismantled many districts, their legacy continues to be celebrated through the vibrant blues and jazz music heritage grounded in the heart of historic African American business districts. Hayti in Durham, North Carolina, had a homegrown music scene in the Piedmont Blues, nurtured by native sons like Blind Boy Fuller and Bull City Red.

The bustling nightclubs of Overtown's hotels, referred to as Miami's "Black Broadway," hosted national celebrities such as Cab Calloway, Lena Horne, Count Basie, and Nat King Cole. The Fillmore District in San Francisco became the "Harlem West" beginning in the 1940s, as jazz musicians such as Duke Ellington and Count Basie performed at the famed Fillmore Theater on a regular basis.

Elmore James, Sonny Boy Williamson, Little Milton, and James Waller, musical powerhouses, spun vinyl recordings and furthered their recording careers on Trumpet Records, the little label founded in the early 1950s on once-thriving Farish Street, the historic African American business district of Jackson, Mississippi. What caused it to spring to life along Farish Street is an unlikely tale. A white woman named Lillian McMurry and her husband purchased a hardware store on Farish Street, then a location on the boundary between the city's white and African American business and entertainment districts. While renovating the building, she discovered a stack of unsold records, including Wynonie Harris's recording of "All She Wants to Do Is Rock." Curious, McMurry played it on the store's record player and became so inspired that she decided to record more music like it. Thus was born Trumpet Records. The life of the studio along Farish Street was brief, but it stands at the forefront of what would later become rock and roll.

—*Matthew L. Wagner*

Further Readings and References

Butler, J. S. (1991). *Entrepreneurship and self-help among black Americans: A reconsideration of race and economics.* Albany, NY: State University of New York Press.

Goings, K. W., & Mohl, R. A. (Eds.). (1996). *The new African American urban history.* Thousand Oaks, CA: Sage.

Johnson, H. B. (1998). *Black Wall Street: From riot to renaissance in Tulsa's historic Greenwood district.* Austin, TX: Eakin Press.

Ryan, M. W. (2004). *Trumpet Records: Diamonds on Farish Street.* Jackson, MS: University Press of Mississippi.

Vann, A. D., & Washington Jones, B. (1999). *Durham's Hayti.* Mount Pleasant, SC: Arcadia.

AFRICAN AMERICAN MAYORS

The passage of the Voting Rights Act of 1965 ended nearly a century of legalized segregation and hastened the integration of African Americans into the political mainstream. Within 2 years of the act's adoption, African American mayors were elected in two of the nation's major cities, signaling a new chapter in the black experience and in urban politics. The elections of Richard Hatcher in Gary and Carl Stokes in Cleveland—alongside the assassination of the Reverend Martin Luther King Jr. in 1968—placed in stark contrast what Bayard Rustin described as the transition of black activism from the streets to the halls of government.

Since 1968, African American mayors have governed nearly every large city as well as many mid-size ones. One hundred and fourteen were elected mayors in citywide campaigns in 72 cities (with over 50,000 people), with the largest number serving in cities with a mayor-council form of government and a strong and independent mayoral system of government.

The first mayoral campaigns of African Americans took place in the midst of racial unrest and rioting in several major cities and reflected efforts by black leaders to test the public's commitment to the Voting Rights law. The fact that such campaigns occurred first in the North resulted from certain political realities. Blacks in this region had the suffrage and were not dependent on lawyers from the Department of Justice to help them register. They had also gained valuable political experience in the urban political machines, which proved essential in mounting campaigns, raising funds, mobilizing support, and ultimately governing large, complex cities.

An analysis of the 114 African American mayors who were elected from 1968 to 2005 reveals that they shared a variety of characteristics. Most represented the educational elite of the country, having obtained law degrees, master's degrees, and doctorates. All of these mayors also had extensive political experience at the federal, state, and local levels. Such backgrounds and credentials proved crucial in gaining support of white voters as well as in securing black votes. The support of many older blacks, who had been accustomed to voting for whites, was often conditional on having a well-educated, experienced black candidate.

Another inescapable feature of these mayors was their maleness. Only 15 women, among them Sharon Sayles Belton of Minneapolis and Carrie Saxon Perry of Hartford, have been elected mayors of large American cities since 1980. The dominance of male candidates is analogous to the prominence of black men in the leading civil rights organizations, in local politics, and in the business community. Gender relations in black America have often mirrored the gendered construction of white society.

Whether in the campaign of Harvey Gantt in Charlotte or David Dinkins in New York, economic issues have dominated the campaign platforms of African American mayors. In virtually every campaign, they called for programs to enhance economic development, recruit new businesses, and develop enterprise zones. Combating crime stood a strong second, and education ranked third, with many candidates for mayor proposing funding increases for public schools. Urban renewal stood fourth and housing fifth. These issues resonated almost equally with urban white and black voters throughout the period from 1968 to 2004, although blacks more consistently supported new housing and greater economic opportunity, while whites favored schools and business recruitment.

The deteriorating economic conditions in many Northeastern and Midwestern cities, and the general level of national economic uncertainty from 1973 to 1992, caused many mayors to call for programs to spur economic growth. The populations and economies of most Rustbelt cities fell below their 1930 levels, and major corporations led the exodus.

However, African American mayors also have governed some of the most prosperous cities in the nation—from Norman Rice in Seattle to Wellington Webb in Denver, Thomas Bradley in Los Angeles, Clarence Lightner in Raleigh, and Ron Kirk in Dallas. These cities flourished under their leadership, and African American mayors pursued programs to spur further economic development alongside education, so that opportunities were made available to all residents. The election process in these cities revealed that campaign platforms of African American mayoral candidates were quite diverse and encompassing.

In most campaigns from 1967 to 1976, race defined the voting results. Victorious African American candidates typically captured 90 percent of the black vote and between 10 and 20 percent of the white vote. The racial split between voters was profound, and in many cases whites, who were lifelong Democrats, chose to vote for the white candidate, even when he was a Republican. Nevertheless, even in these campaigns, black candidates would not have won without support from white voters.

In the older, large metropolises of the Northeast, the Midwest, and the South, African American mayoral candidates sought to mobilize as much support among black constituents as possible. The rhetoric of campaigns in black neighborhoods was rooted initially in the Civil Rights Movement and in an emerging black consciousness.

Black churches served as the organizational base for all African American mayoral campaigns, but candidates also called on a variety of black organizations, including fraternities, sororities, civil rights groups, newspapers, radio stations, and unions to sponsor meetings with the candidates and to help increase registration and turn out the vote. This strategy was crucial in the early period because African Americans lacked connections with white civic organizations and the media that they needed to draw upon to publicize their candidacies. The political strategies of black candidates in these older cities often paralleled those of an earlier generation of Irish American politicians who appealed to the church, the pub, and the neighborhood to mobilize Irish voters.

A second key to victory for black candidates in the older cities of the Northeast and Midwest involved capturing at a minimum 10 percent of the white vote.

The election of an African American mayor occurred generally after an election or series of elections in which a black-white coalition helped elect a white candidate and in which the white mayor eased the transition to African American mayoral leadership by appointing African Americans to leadership positions in city government. The prominence of blacks in local leadership positions and the cooperation between white and black managers eased white fears about the ability of blacks to govern and about a black takeover.

Whether seeking white votes in the older, mayor-council communities or in the newer, mayor-commissioner cities, black candidates looked principally to middle- and upper-class whites. Thomas Pettegrew observed that white supporters of black candidates in Cleveland, Gary, Los Angeles, and Newark were disproportionately upper status and college educated. Despite some claims that these black candidates were able to construct a biracial coalition across class lines, the coalition almost exclusively included black candidates, white elites, and liberal members of the white middle class.

In the newer, mayor-commissioner cities in the Sunbelt and in the West, black candidates also began by securing their base in the black community and then reached out to white civic and business groups and liberal organizations. Because black candidates for mayor were initially quite novel, they commanded a great deal of attention. The free publicity cut two ways: It gave these candidates free advertising and thus an early boost, but it also generated hostility among some whites. The skill with which these candidates used this political advantage and the receptivity of whites to a black candidate ultimately determined the electoral outcome.

Paradoxically, despite sharp racial divisions in voting, race seldom became a blatant issue, even though it was often part of the strategy employed by both white and black candidates. The absence of overt appeals did not mean, however, that race was absent from these campaigns. The percentage of white and black voters casting ballots for someone of their own race, especially in the older cities, made clear that race was a very important factor.

As black challengers emerged as serious opponents, white candidates resorted to what political scientist Asher Avian described as a racial agenda, including crime, drugs, homelessness, and urban violence, and most black candidates found it necessary to take strong stands on these issues or face losing white support.

While white candidates manipulated race to their political advantage, black candidates were not averse to employing their own racial strategies. Stokes's case was typical, when he reassured a white Cleveland audience that his victory would not signal a black "takeover. " But Stokes and others appealed directly to black residents to vote for one of their own.

As a result of the achievements of African American mayors, most whites have come to recognize that black representation is a legitimate part of the democratic process. African American mayors have often breathed new life into communities in economic and social turmoil, offering hope and opportunity to groups of citizens who had not been privy to such possibilities previously. They did this, for the most part, with remarkably traditional campaign platforms. At the same time, their campaigns also offered inclusion and political opportunity to people who had been previously ignored and oppressed, and their leadership gave these cities a political future, even under extraordinarily difficult social and economic circumstances.

—David R. Colburn

See also Civil Rights; Politics in Cities

Further Readings and References

Bernard, R. (1990). *Snowbelt cities: Metropolitan politics in the Northeast and Midwest since World War II.* Bloomington, IN: Indiana University Press.

Keech, W. (1968). *The impact of negro voting: The role of the vote in the quest for equality.* Chicago: Rand McNally.

Kleppner, P. (1985). *Chicago divided: The making of a African American mayor.* DeKalb, IL: Northern Illinois University Press.

Thernstrom, S., & Thernstrom, A. (1997). *American in black and white.* New York: Simon & Schuster.

AFRICAN AMERICANS IN CITIES

The black urban population had its origins in the European colonization of North America and the enslavement of African people. With the onset of the Great Migration of the 20th century, the black population moved from a predominantly rural Southern setting into the urban North, West, and South. During the late 20th century, black migration turned southward again, but this movement swelled Southern cities and suburbs rather than Southern agriculture. Nonetheless, at different points in time, black urbanization reflected the African American search for freedom, jobs, and social justice as well as the evolution of new patterns of race, class, and ethnic relations in American society.

As early as 1565, some 100 Africans (including a few women) had entered what is now the United States with Spanish explorers and helped to establish St. Augustine, Florida, the first permanent non-Indian settlement in North America. Nearly 200 years later, enslaved Africans also played a role in the French settlement of Louisiana and the growth of New Orleans (under French control until the early 19th century). Beginning during the early 17th century, in British America, the marketing demands of Southern staple crops—tobacco, rice, indigo, sugar, and later grain—stimulated the early growth of the black population in cities like Charleston (Charles Town until 1783), Savannah, Baltimore, and Norfolk. By the onset of the American Revolution, blacks made up nearly 50 percent of the total population in New Orleans and Charleston. At the same time, the extensive commercial activities of Northeastern seaports pushed the number of African Americans to over 1,500 in Boston, 1,400 in Philadelphia, and over 2,000 in New York.

In the colonial North and South, the wealthiest white urbanites belonged to the slaveholding class. A few small shopkeepers and artisans also owned a handful of slaves, but pre-Revolutionary War black urban life unfolded in close conjunction with the experiences of other unfree workers. In addition to blacks, before the Revolution, white indentured servants, Native Americans, and low-wage white laborers also faced mistreatment at the hands of colonial elites. Such mistreatment of poor and working-class people stimulated substantial cooperation across the color line. Throughout the mid-18th century, colonial newspapers reported recurring acts of resistance among black and white seamen in the port cities of the North and South, including New York, Boston, and Norfolk, Virginia.

The American Revolution changed the socioeconomic and political context of African American life. It not only intensified the growth of black urban communities during the late 18th and early 19th centuries, but it also sharpened the color line between blacks and whites. Initially, however, the promise of the Revolution found its greatest expression in the rise of the free black population. Most of the 5,000 blacks who had served in the Continental Army soon gained their freedom, and through natural increase, fugitives, and immigration, among other sources, the free black population increased from negligible numbers at the onset of the American Revolution to 60,000 in 1790 and to 234,000 in 1820. While legal restrictions on manumission limited its growth thereafter, the free black population nonetheless increased to nearly 500,000 by 1860. Over 33 percent of free blacks in the South and virtually all of those in the North lived in cities, compared to only 5 percent of slaves, and little more than 15 percent of Southern and Northern whites.

Antebellum free blacks became the most highly urbanized component of the United States population, but their lives were closely intertwined with those of enslaved blacks. Although slaves gradually declined as a percentage of the urban population in most cities, their absolute numbers increased in New Orleans, Charleston, Louisville, Richmond, and Mobile. By 1860, Charleston (with 13,900 blacks) and New Orleans (with 13,400 blacks) had the first and second highest number of enslaved urban blacks. With nearly 28,000 blacks, Baltimore had the largest concentration of blacks of any Southern city, most of which were free people of color before the Civil War. Because urban bondspeople gained opportunities to arrange contracts with employers, compete with white workers, and move from one industrial site to another, some contemporary observers suggested that slavery simply could not survive in the dynamic and competitive social environment of cities.

Although free people of color made up only a tiny fraction of the total black population, they had a disproportionately large impact on antebellum African American culture, communities, and politics. In both the North and South, free people of color could legally marry, own property, and establish their own institutions. As America moved toward the enfranchisement of working-class and poor white men during the early 19th century, however, free black men and women faced economic exploitation, disfranchisement, segregation, and the intensification of the colonization movement. Formed in 1817, the American Colonization Society aimed to transport free people of color to Africa and secure the United States as a republic of slaves and free whites.

Free blacks lived and labored on the precarious borders of antebellum slave society, but they were by no means quiescent. They built their own institutions, strengthened ties with enslaved Africans and sympathetic white allies, and pushed for the abolition of slavery and the acquisition of full citizenship for all blacks. As early as the 1790s, blacks had launched the African Methodist Episcopal Church in Philadelphia, followed closely by the African Methodist Episcopal Zion Church in New York, and the Baptist Church in both cities. Antebellum black churches played a key role in the abolitionist movement and the development of the Underground Railroad. In the years after the Civil War, several generations of free blacks would build upon this antebellum legacy and continue to fight for full citizenship rights and economic democracy in American society.

In the wake of the Civil War and emancipation, the black urban population increased from an estimated 5 to 7 percent in 1860 to over 25 percent in 1910. Former bondsmen and women repeatedly equated life in cities with freedom. Yet, despite the freed people's optimistic turn toward cities after the Civil War, contemporary whites viewed black urbanization with alarm in the urban North and South, and they took steps to suppress the movement. Partly designed to curb black urbanization, destructive race riots broke out in New Orleans and Memphis in 1866; Philadelphia in 1871; Danville, Virginia in 1883; Wilmington, North Carolina in 1898; New York in 1900; Atlanta in 1906; and Springfield, Illinois in 1904 and 1908. White mobs entered black communities, destroyed property, and beat, killed, and injured scores of people, forcing many to flee for their lives.

The increasing incidence of mob violence—coupled with the intensification of institutional segregation, disfranchisement, and exploitative conditions in Southern agriculture—set the stage for the onset of the Great Migration. Under the impact of World War I (particularly the labor shortages precipitated by the cessation of massive European immigration), an estimated 700,000 to 1 million blacks left the South between 1917 and 1920. Another 800,000 to 1 million left during the 1920s. In the Northeast, New York City's black population trebled from 100,000 to over 300,000. In the Midwest, Detroit's black population increased by 611 percent during the war years and by nearly 200 percent during the 1920s, rising from less than 6,000 to over 120,000. In the urban far West, the black population increased most dramatically in Los Angeles, growing from 7,600 in 1910 to nearly 40,000 in 1930.

The Great Migration fueled the emergence of a new black industrial working class. Southern black sharecroppers, farm laborers, sawmill hands, dockworkers, and railroad hands all moved into new positions in the urban economy—in meatpacking, auto, steel, and other mass production industries. In Cleveland, Pittsburgh, Detroit, and Milwaukee, the percentage of black men employed in industrial jobs increased from an estimated 10 to 20 percent of the black labor force in 1910 to about 60 to 70 percent in 1920 and 1930. Black women also entered industrial jobs, although their gains were far less than those of black men. In Chicago, the percentage of black women in manufacturing trades increased from less than 1,000 in 1910 to over 3,000 in 1920. Industrial jobs made up 15 percent of the black female labor force, compared to less than 7 percent in 1910. Although less intensely than the urban North, Western cities such as Seattle, Los Angeles, and those in the San Francisco Bay area also gradually recruited black workers for industrial jobs.

Based upon better social conditions, higher wages, and the franchise, the first wave of African American migrants viewed the Great Migration to Northern cities in biblical terms as going to "The Promised Land," the "Flight out of Egypt," and "Going into Canaan." But such favorable commentary on life in the urban North did not blind African Americans to patterns of inequality in Northern cities. Alongside the growth of the black urban proletariat, residential segregation increased in all major cities. Between 1910 and 1930, the index of dissimilarity (a statistical device for measuring the extent of residential segregation) rose from 66.8 to 85.2 percent in Chicago, 60.6 to 85.0 percent in Cleveland, 64.1 to 77.9 percent in Boston, and 46.0 to 63.0 percent in Philadelphia. As early as 1909, a Seattle realtor took an African American home buyer to court (but lost) for moving into a previously all-white neighborhood and presumably driving property values down. When the legal tactics of white property owners and their associations failed, whites often resorted to violence and intimidation. Aimed at restricting African American competition in the job and housing market, among other objectives, racial violence erupted in Chicago, East St. Louis, Washington, D.C., Tulsa, Charleston, Knoxville, and Philadelphia during the era of the Great Migration. Race riots not only reinforced residential segregation in Northern cities but also highlighted the growing nationalization of the "race question" in American society.

In order to counteract the impact of class and racial discrimination on their lives, African Americans developed cross-class alliances and fought inequality in the housing, institutional, and political life of the city. Following the Civil War, black churches, fraternal orders, and social clubs had proliferated at the local and regional levels. During the late 19th and early 20th centuries, African Americans turned increasingly toward the formation of national bodies such as the National Baptist Convention (1895–1896), the National Medical Association (1895), and the National Association of Colored Women (1896). The National Association of Colored Women mobilized and supported a variety of social welfare activities: homes for the aged, young women, and children, relief funds for the unemployed, and legal aid to combat injustice before the law. Supplementing the activities of black churches and women's clubs were a variety of mutual aid societies and fraternal orders, including the Masons, Odd Fellows, and Independent Order of St. Luke, among others. Black consciousness and racial solidarity across class and status lines intensified with the rise of the "New Negro" during World War I and the 1920s. The ideas and aspirations of the New Negro gained expression in the Harlem Renaissance, the Brotherhood of Sleeping Car Porters, and the Universal Negro Improvement Association (the Garvey Movement).

The alliance between black workers and black urban elites was hardly unproblematic. As the new black middle class expanded during the 1920s, for example, it slowly moved into better housing vacated by whites, leaving the poorest blacks concentrated in certain sections of the black community. Moreover, the rise of organizations like the Universal Negro Improvement Association created substantial conflicts between black workers and established middle-class leadership. While race-conscious black business and professional people endorsed aspects of Marcus Garvey's ideas, they feared his mass appeal and often complained that his message attracted the "ignorant class" of newcomers from the South.

At the same time, although both interracial and intraracial conflicts reflected the growing segregation of blacks in the urban environment, African Americans cultivated and retained a core of white allies. Black-white alliances emerged before World War I—particularly with the formation of the National Urban League in 1911 and the National Association for the Advancement of Colored People (NAACP) in 1909—and expanded during and after the war. Under the impact of the Great Depression and World War II,

interracial and intraracial unity gained even greater expression with the rise of the Congress of Industrial Organizations, New Deal social welfare programs, and the March on Washington Movement (MOWM). In 1941, Franklin D. Roosevelt issued Executive Order 8802, calling for the establishment of the Fair Employment Practices Committee (FEPC) to eliminate racial barriers in defense industries. The FEPC and MOWM not only represented major victories against racial exclusion and exploitation, but also stimulated the emergence of the modern Civil Rights and Black Power Movements during the post–World War II years.

In the postwar years, the technological revolution in Southern agriculture, the expansion of the welfare state, and the militant Civil Rights and Black Power Movements all helped to complete the long-run transformation of blacks from a predominantly rural to a predominantly urban people. Distributed almost equally between regions, the African American population increased from 13 million in 1940 to over 22 million in 1970 and to 35 million in 2000. The proportion of blacks living in cities rose to over 80 percent, 10 percent higher than in the country at large. Black migration and urban community development had run its familiar 20th century course. Beginning as the most rural of Americans, blacks had become the most urbanized.

During the late 20th century and into the 21st century, African American urban life entered a painful transition from the old industrial to the emerging postindustrial economy. As mass-production industries increasingly gave way to the new computer-driven service economy, African Americans experienced large and disproportionate levels of unemployment, out-of-wedlock births, drug addiction, and violent forms of interracial and intraracial conflict. Unlike in previous periods in the nation's history, African American urban life also unfolded within the context of large-scale immigration from Latin America and Asia rather than from Europe. By 2000, the United States Census reported that the Latino/a American population had exceeded the African American population in size. Numerically, blacks are no longer the nation's principal minority group.

The new configuration of color and culture complicates the traditional black-white divide and reshapes the color line and racial conflict in American society. Growing numbers of Southern-born blacks and their children responded to these changes by returning home during the 1980s and 1990s. After declining for more than a century, the proportion of African Americans living in the South increased. Moreover, by the turn of the 21st century, the volume of black migration to suburbs had surpassed the Great Migration to industrial America. While the full results of these changes are yet to be determined, they demonstrate that blacks and the nation have entered another era of profound urban transformation.

—Joe W. Trotter

Further Readings and References

Grossman, J. R. (1989). *Land of hope: Chicago, black Southerners, and the Great Migration.* Chicago: University of Chicago Press.

Harris, L. M. (2003). *In the shadow of slavery: African Americans in New York City, 1626–1863.* Chicago: University of Chicago Press.

Hirsch, A. R. (1983). *Making the second ghetto: Race and housing in Chicago 1940–1960.* Chicago: University of Chicago Press.

Hunter, T. W. (1997). *To joy my freedom: Southern black women's lives and labors after the Civil War.* Cambridge, MA: Harvard University Press.

Lewis, E. (1991). *In their own interests: Race, class, and power in 20th century Norfolk.* Berkeley, CA: University of California Press.

Phillips, K. L. (1999). *Alabama North: African-American migrants, community, and working-class activism in Cleveland, 1915–45.* Urbana, IL: University of Illinois Press.

Sugrue, T. J. (1996). *The origins of the urban crisis: Race and inequality in postwar Detroit.* Princeton, NJ: Princeton University Press.

Taylor, Q. (1998). *In search of the racial frontier: African Americans in the American West.* New York: Norton.

Trotter, J. W. (Ed.). (1991). *The Great Migration in historical perspective: New dimensions of race, class, and gender.* Bloomington, IN: Indiana University Press.

Trotter, J. W., Lewis, E., & Hunter, T. W. (Ed.). (2004). *The African American urban experience: Perspectives from the colonial period to the present.* New York: Palgrave Macmillan.

African Americans in Suburbs and African American Towns

At first glance, African American towns and African American suburbs appear to be the products of oppositional ideologies. Black town formation was an element of a nationalist African American ideology and practice. Conversely, black suburbanization is usually understood as a consequence of the Civil Rights Movement (1955–1968), specifically the passage of the 1964 Civil Rights and the 1968 Fair Housing Acts. Yet, as sociologist Bruce D. Haynes reminded us in 2001 in *Red Lines, Black Spaces,* African American suburbanization actually began during the first Great Migration of 1910 to 1929. In the popular imagination, black suburbanization is also seen as a result of urban decline and as a reflection of the class aspirations and racial ambiguities of the African American middle class. It is considered an expression of an *integrationist* perspective. Although black towns and African American suburbanization *may* represent different approaches to African Americans' search for a better a life, both reflect their quest for personal security and the right to determine their own destinies. This relationship is complex, revealing apparent oppositions, yet striking similarities.

This essay explores the origins and development and the scope and significance of black towns and African American suburbanization. It places their construction over time in sociohistorical context and situates them within the ideological matrix of the black intellectual tradition. Finally, it articulates an underlying unity that belies the apparent ideological differences between black town formation and African American suburbanization.

Black Towns in Sociohistorical Context

Black town construction is the most concrete example of African American nationalism. Much of African American civil society reflects a *proto-nationalist* ethos. That is, a sense that African Americans are a distinct people whose fate is interconnected, a pragmatic allegiance to an autonomous associational life, and a commitment to collective survival and advancement. Black town formation, however, differs from African Americans' maintenance of independent social, political, and cultural institutions. Historically, the building of black towns represented something more; these towns were a more explicit nationalist project, a manifestation of African Americans' aspiration for self-governance. Like *emigrationism,* the inspiration for black town development was rooted in African Americans' desire for freedom, self-development, and self-determination. But while emigration has received more scholarly attention, the significance of the 10,000 or so African Americans who emigrated from the United States pales in comparison to that of the hundreds of thousands of blacks who took up residence in black towns. And although a constant undercurrent in black politics, the dream of an independent African American nation-state has never stimulated a mass movement among African Americans. Among the nationalist projects, only black town creation has stimulated mass migration.

Most black towns were built during what historian Wilson Jeremiah Moses referred to as Black Nationalism's "golden age"—1850 to 1925. The story of black town formation is rightly dominated by the drama of the struggle to gain political control of the Kansas-Oklahoma territory. Yet, African Americans' yearning for autonomy was not confined to the Midwest region, and their desire for self-governance transcended the historical moment historian Rayford Logan called the "nadir"—1877 to 1917. Black town construction has occurred mainly during four historical moments: (1) slavery, particularly between 1819 and 1860; (2) emancipation and Reconstruction, from 1865 to 1876; (3) the nadir, from 1877 to 1915; and (4) the Great Migration, from 1910 to 1929.

The political lineage of black towns can be traced to fugitive and quasi-free blacks' creation of maroon societies, organized black communities and freedom villages. In the United States, maroon societies operated on the periphery of slavery, in the swamps, and in areas controlled by Native Americans or foreign governments. In 1738, 100 black maroons from Carolina who had aligned with the emerging Seminole Nation were granted control of Gracia Real de Santa Teresa de Mose or Fort Mose by Manuel de Montiano, the Spanish governor. Located in northeastern Florida, near St. Augustine, Fort Mose is considered the first "sanctioned" free black settlement in North America. At Fort Mose, self-liberated Africans built a farming community that also served as a front line of defense against British and eventually United States invasion. In 1863, the populations of Mose and St. Augustine were evacuated to Cuba after the British gained control of the territory. Fort Mose is one of a few well-documented African American maroon societies.

Emerging a little later, *organized black communities* (OBCs) were mainly created in Canada and in the Old Northwest Territory, in states that today comprise the upper Midwest. According to William and Mary

Pease, about a score of these communities were organized between 1800 and 1860. Unlike maroon societies, organized black communities derived from collaborations between white philanthropists and African Americans. OBCs sought to demonstrate that blacks could be productive operating their own communities. Some were attempts by white reformers to find an equivalent but domestic alternative to the repatriation proposed by the American Colonization Society (ACS; 1816 to 1964). A few were created through the process of manumission. For example, in 1819, Edward Coles, a former secretary to President James Madison and future governor of Illinois, manumitted 17 of his slaves and moved them to Illinois. There he distributed farmland among the now quasi-free families who established a small farming community in Pinbush Parrish near Edwardsville, in Madison County, thus founding the first organized black community.

Others sought to establish a refuge outside the U.S. and to avoid the stigma associated with the ACS. One such community was Elgin located in North Buxton, Ontario, Canada (1849). Elgin was established by the Reverend William King (1812–1895), who took the 15 slaves he had inherited after his father-in-law's death from Louisiana to Canada, where he freed them. Abraham Doras Shadd and his daughter, Mary Anne Shadd Cary (1823–1893), helped transform the Elgin Settlement into a beacon of liberty. Another venture, the Dawn Settlement, established by Josiah Henson (1789–1877) in 1836 near Dresden in Ontario, Canada, was a genuine product of African American agency. In *Uncle Tom's Cabin,* Harriet Beecher Stowe loosely based her character Uncle Tom on Henson. However, contrary to the docile character Beecher created and to popular perception, Henson was a courageous freedom fighter. At its peak, 500 fugitives and their families lived and worked in Dawn's farms, mills, and brickyard. However, at the center of the Dawn Settlement was the British-American Institute, a general education, manual arts and teacher training school. The school closed in 1868 after nearly 20 years of financial problems. Eventually, most residents left, either returning to the U.S. or moving to other Canadian communities.

Organized black communities were accomplishments—they provided blacks with a haven, a chance to live as free men and women, and opportunities to own their own land and to educate themselves and their children. Ultimately, they demonstrated blacks' capacity for self-sufficiency. In the end, these experiments failed, largely because blacks did not gain control of the decision-making apparatuses. Despite their mixed legacy, OBCs left black town builders a heritage to build on.

Freedom villages are the most direct link to black towns. Like the OBCs, freedom villages were generally small farming communities located in the Old Northwest Territory, though some, like Lawnside, New Jersey (1840) were built in the Northeast. But unlike the OBCs, freedom villages were generally the result of African American agency—the self-activity of blacks in their own interest. In 1836, Thomas and Jemima Woodson established one of the first freedom villages at Berlin Crossroads in Milton Township in Jackson County, Ohio. Some scholars consider their oldest child, Lewis, the "father of Black Nationalism," rather than Dr. Martin Robinson Delany (1812–1885), whom he taught. Reverend Lewis Woodson's Black Nationalist ideas were developed from his experiences in the Berlin Crossroads community. Lyles Station, Indiana, Menifee, Arkansas, and Brooklyn, Illinois were other freedom villages.

The Woodson family also had a connection to the first incorporated black town, Brooklyn, Illinois. Sarah, Thomas and Jemima's daughter, would eventually marry Winston Early, a carpenter and African Methodist Episcopal minister who built the community's first institution, Brooklyn, A.M.E., in 1832. According to oral tradition, Brooklyn originated in the late 1820s. Around 1829, "Mother" Priscilla Baltimore led a band of 11 fugitive and quasi-free families across the Mississippi River into the wilderness in St. Clair County, Illinois, where they established a separate settlement. In 1837, five white male abolitionists platted the land and named it Brooklyn, transforming it into a community with a seven-eighths majority black population. In July of 1873, Brooklyn was incorporated as a village, and 13 years later, in 1886, blacks led by John Evans seized control of both the village and school boards. Black acquisition of all the apparatuses of government activated a process of white flight that transformed Brooklyn into a 99 percent black community.

Popularly known as Lovejoy, in honor of martyred abolitionist Elijah Lovejoy, Brooklyn was initially an anomaly among black towns. Brooklyn was created in the heart of an expanding urban-industrial complex in the St. Louis Metro-east region, whereas most black towns were rural farming villages in the South or West, such as Princeville, North Carolina (which was

called Freedom Hill when it was founded in 1865 and Princeville when it was incorporated in 1885); Kendelton, Texas (1867); Nicodemus, Kansas (1877); Mound Bayou, Mississippi (1887); and Boley, Oklahoma (1904). Brooklyn foreshadowed the working-class commuter black towns, like Robbins, Illinois (1917) and Lincoln Heights, Ohio (1920s) that would develop on the rim of industrial cities in the wake of the Great Migration. And although these suburban industrial commuter towns represent the dominant form of contemporary black towns, they are not the image that dominates popular conceptions.

The popular image of black towns is derived from the communities created by two social movements, the *Exodus of 1879* and what sociologist and "father of black town studies" Mozell C. Hill called the "Great Black March West" from 1890 to 1910. In the *Exodus of 1879,* Benjamin "Pap" Singleton and the Tennessee Emigration Society and Henry Adams and the Colonization Councils organized between 25,000 and 60,000 Blacks from Alabama, Louisiana, Mississippi, North Carolina, Tennessee, and Texas to migrate to the Oklahoma and Kansas territories. The Exodus was a response to labor exploitation and the rampant racial violence unleashed by white terrorists after President Rutherford B. Hayes withdrew the federal troops from the South. Adams, a former slave from Shreveport, Louisiana articulated the nationalist attitude undergirding the *Exoduster* movement. In a letter to the U.S. Attorney General in 1878, Adams wrote that he trusted God to give black people their own territory to work instead of being worked to death or simply killed by slaveholders. The violence was not curtailed and the *Exodusters* sought their territory in the form of self-governing black towns.

The "Great Black March West" built on the Exodusters' pioneering migration to the Kansas and Oklahoma territories. Stimulated by another resurgence in racial oppression during the 1890s, upwards of 60,000 black Southerners fled westward. Led by Edward P. McCabe and the First Colored Real Estate Homestead and Emigration Association, African Americans built over 60 black towns in the Kansas and Oklahoma territories between 1890 and 1910. Building on themes expressed earlier by Adams, McCabe wrote a letter to the *New York Times* detailing his dream that blacks would soon own their homes and govern themselves. Here, perhaps, more clearly than any other proponent, McCabe communicated the nationalist premise behind the black town movement.

McCabe's dream was unrealized. Whites became the majority population in Kansas and Oklahoma. They enacted state constitutions that enshrined segregation, thus killing the Black Nationalist dream of a state governed by African Americans. Yet, the Great March was not a failure. Although the black migrants did not gain political control of a territory, they did succeed in building countless black towns, including Nicodemus, Kansas, Boley, Oklahoma, Allensworth, California (1909) and an estimated 60 to 100 other all-black towns in the region. Moreover, black town formation would continue be a feature of African American life across the United States; today there are approximately 300 black towns in the United States.

Black Suburbs in Sociohistorical Context

Overshadowed by the dramatic urbanization of African Americans during the 20th century, African American suburbanization has only recently become a significant topic of scholarship. Black suburbanization has paralleled the urbanization of blacks throughout the 20th century. Black suburbs are a product of the same forces that created the urban ghetto—mass black migration from the South, employment discrimination, racial steering, and housing discrimination. Two core concepts relevant to this discussion are worth distinguishing: black suburbanization and black suburbs. *Black suburbanization* refers to African Americans' residing near but outside the corporate boundary of a central city, while *black suburbs* refers to majority black communities on the periphery of a city. Although this distinction is important analytically, because racism tended to restrict most black suburbanites to majority black suburbs, in life the two experiences usually were intertwined.

The new scholarship has identified three historical periods during which African Americans moved to suburbs in the 20th century: (1) the first Great Migration to World War II, from 1910 to 1940; (2) the second Great Migration, from the 1940s to the late 1960s; and (3) from 1970 to the mid-1990s. I suggest that there is a fourth period that began during the mid-1990s. During each period, (a) black suburbs were diverse, running the gamut from older previously rural underdeveloped black towns (Brooklyn, Illinois), to working-class commuter communities (Robbins, Illinois), to affluent jurisdictions that mirrored the socioeconomic attributes of middle-class white suburbs (Fairmount Heights, Maryland), and (b) the number and percentage of blacks residing in the suburbs grew, with the most dramatic increase occurring in the third period. This period was also marked by the greatest shift in the class structure of black suburbanites, from working class (defined occupationally as blue-collar workers) to middle class (defined occupationally as white-collar workers).

Scholars have generally used two definitions to characterize *suburbia*. One definition is based on geographic-spatial considerations. The other relies on socioeconomic criteria. The first definition describes all communities just beyond a city's corporate boundaries as *suburban*. The second includes only communities with high percentages of homeownership, middle-class occupations, and low numbers of racial minorities. The second definition gained preeminence because it characterized the racially and class homogeneous communities created by post–World War II suburbanization. The nation's rapid suburbanization between 1940 and 1970 has often been referred to as "white flight" because simultaneously as 4 million African American migrants poured into the cities whites departed, decreasing the share of the white community residing in cities from 55 to 30 percent. Put another way, during these years the share of the white community residing outside of the cities increased from 45 to 70 percent.

Until recently, scholars of suburbia have been guided by the 1950s definition. Black suburbs generally contradicted the image of a homogeneous white middle-class community, thus they fell beneath scholars' radar. Reliance on the 1950s socioeconomic definition led scholars such as geographer Harold Rose to argue that black communities like Robbins, Illinois were not suburbs. According to Rose, these communities did not conform to the dominant suburban concept of middle-class Euro-American communities. During the early 1960s, using the socioeconomic criteria, Rose compared the factors of poverty, homeownership, and percentage of substandard housing in black "suburban" communities to the same factors in inner city ghettos and in neighboring predominately white suburbs. Not surprisingly, he discovered that black suburban communities resembled ghettos more than they did suburbs. Historian Andrew Wiese challenged Rose 40 years later. Wiese noted that contemporary urbanists using U.S. Census data to map changing demographic trends were recovering the heterogeneity of suburbs that had been rendered invisible by the 1950s suburban concept.

Much of the new research is re-creating residential patterns before 1940 and recovering the history of African American suburbanization. African American suburbanization began during the Great Migration, and it is generally believed racial discrimination kept the number and percentage of blacks living in suburbs very small. Wiese's research questions this assumption. According to him, Southern black migrants moved to the suburbs between 1910 and 1940, encompassing about 15 percent (about 285,000 people) of black population growth in the North and West during that time. Weise also noted that by 1940, close to 500,000 African Americans lived in suburbs outside the South, representing nearly 20 percent of the African Americans in metropolitan areas of these regions.

The new research leaves us with an apparent contradiction. Though a much larger percentage of blacks resided in suburban communities than previous scholarship reported, the percentages have remained quite small. For instance, African Americans composed only 4.8 percent of the suburbanization population in 1970.

The major impetuses to African American suburbanization came from two factors, the unprecedented economic growth in the United States between 1950 and the mid-1970s and the socioeconomic and cultural changes generated by the Black Freedom movement, in its Civil Rights and Black Power phases, from 1955 to 1975. Stimulated by economic transformation (transition from an industrial to an informational political economy) and the opportunities opened by the Black Freedom movement, the size of the black middle class rapidly expanded. For instance, the percentage of black women in clerical jobs more than doubled from 10 to 22 percent between 1960 and 1970 and the percentage of black males in the rapidly growing technical-managerial sector grew from 1.8 to 7 percent, while the percentage of black proprietors and managers grew from 1.3 to 3 percent. The transformation and growth of the black middle class from 1955 to 1975 is directly responsible for the rise in the percentage of blacks residing in suburbs, which had increased to 6.1 percent by 1980 and to 8.5 percent by 1990. And by 1998, the percentage of African Americans living in suburban communities increased to 31 percent. Economic restructuring and the Civil Rights and Black Power Movements not only accelerated the suburbanization of blacks, they also created a different type of black suburbanite. The suburbanization of blacks since the Civil Rights and Black Power Movements has largely been a middle-class migration.

The black middle class, however, is a highly diverse group. They continue to endure racial discrimination in social goods, particularly in wealth, occupation, and housing. Yet, as Haynes points out in the case of Runyon Heights residents, these middle-class homeowners have found it in their material interest to keep physical and social distance between themselves and the bulk of blacks. The intersection of race, class, and place is often cross-cutting. Thus, the Runyon Heights Improvement Association overcame strained relations with whites in the neighboring community of Homefield to oppose a proposed low-income housing development. This class-based unity across racial lines is rare because African Americans moving into predominately white suburbs still often face hostility. According to Haynes, much of middle-class white suburbia remains opposed to black neighbors, regardless of class. A history of racial exclusion; continuing hostility, economic resources, and racial steering; and a desire to maintain familial and sociocultural ties to black civil society largely explain why black suburbs are often proximate to working-class and poor black communities. For instance, according to Valerie Johnson in 2002 in *Black Power in the Suburbs,* one reason Prince Georges County was attractive to middle-class blacks was its proximity to largely African American Washington, D.C. This situation underscores the organic relationship between the black middle class and working-class and poor blacks.

The combination of racial hostility and the second white flight, as well as blacks' reluctance to play the role of desegregation pioneer and their desire for institutional linkages to black civil society, has led black suburbanization to continue to be largely a process of the creation of black suburbs. The middle-class suburbanization that characterized African American suburbanization after the Civil Rights and Black Power Movements is being supplemented by the suburbanization of working-class and poor African Americans in the wake of the destruction of public housing. The escalating dislocation of the former public housing tenants constitutes a new period in the suburbanization of blacks.

Historically, the social processes that led blacks to create black towns and those that produced African American suburbs have been quite similar, despite apparent ideological differences. Once we rid ourselves of the fixation on the Western black towns created during the nadir, the link between black towns and black suburbs becomes readily visible. Not only were they created by similar social processes, but they were initially populated mainly by working-class Southern migrants who sought to create a haven from the worst aspects off racial oppression. Using the geographic-spatial definition of a suburbia, places such as Brooklyn, Illinois; Robbins, Illinois; Kinloch, Missouri; and the communities established on the periphery of urban areas during the Great Migration occupied both categories. African American suburbanization may have been motivated in part by a commitment to integration, but the form it has taken, majority black suburbs, partly reflects a proto-nationalist social consciousness as well.

—*Sundiata Keita Cha-Jua*

See also Housing Segregation; Race Riots; Racial Zoning

Further Readings and References

Cha-Jua, S. K. (2000). *America's first black town, Brooklyn, Illinois, 1830–1915.* Urbana, IL: University of Illinois Press.

Deagan, K., & MacMahon, D. (1995). *Ft. Mose, Colonial America's black fortress of freedom.* Gainesville, FL: University of Florida Press.

Hamilton, K. M. (1991). *Black towns and profit: Promotion and development in the Transapplachian West, 1877–1915.* Urbana, IL: University of Illinois Press.

Haynes, B. D. (2001). *Red lines, black spaces: The politics of race and space in a black middle class suburb.* New Haven, CT: Yale University Press.

Johnson, V. C. (2002). *Black Power in the suburbs: The myth or reality of African American suburban political incorporation.* Albany, NY: State University of New York Press.

Landers, J. (1991). Gracia Real de Santa Teresa de Mose: A free black town in Spanish colonial Florida. *St. Augustine Historical Society, 28,* 81–112.

Mobley, J. A. (1986). On the shadow of white society: Princeville, a black town in North Carolina, 1865–1915. *North Carolina Historical Review, 63*(3), 340–384.

Painter, N. I. (1992). *Exodusters: Black migration to Kansas after Reconstruction.* New York: Norton.

Pease, W., & Pease, M. (1963). *Black Utopia: Negro communal experiments in America.* Madison, WI: Wisconsin State Historical Society.

Rose, H. (1976). The All-Negro town: Its evolution and function. *Geographic Review,* pp. 352–367.

Wiese, A. (1999). Black housing, white finance: African American housing and home ownership in Evanston, Illinois, before 1940. *Journal of Social History, 33.*

Wiese, A. (2004). *Places of their own: African American suburbanization in the twentieth century.* Chicago: University of Chicago Press.

AIR CONDITIONING

The advent early in the 20th century of mechanical air-conditioning systems designed to simultaneously control indoor heat and humidity helped to reshape urban America. As its use spread, starting in the nation's largest, wealthiest, and most important cities, the rhythms of city life changed as buildings and work schedules responded to the promise and problems of a new kind of indoor control. After World War II, air conditioning would play a central role in the ascendancy of Sun Belt metropolitan areas.

Worries about summer heat and humidity predated the arrival of systems designed to fix them. As cities like New York, Chicago, and St. Louis grew in population, industrial might, and building density in the late 19th century, thermal comfort and temperature control became life-or-death concerns. While dozens, mainly children, died daily of heat stroke in congested slums, wealthy urbanites fled city summers for cooler mountain and shore locations. In major cities, theaters, department stores, and museums catering to the middle and upper classes would close for much of the summer.

The success of refrigerated cold storage facilities in several cities by the late 1880s provoked engineers and others to consider how to bring similar coolness to spaces inhabited by humans. One pioneer was heating and ventilating engineer Alfred R. Wolff, who in 1889 equipped New York's Carnegie Hall with air ducts that could hold ice for summer cooling and in 1902 designed a cooling system for the New York Stock Exchange's new trading room.

That same year, Willis Haviland Carrier, an engineer employed by Buffalo Forge, designed what is generally considered the world's first modern air-conditioning system for Brooklyn's Sackett-Wilhelms Lithographing & Publishing Company. On humid summer days, inks would smudge the colorful covers of *Judge,* a national political humor magazine. Carrier's system of cold-water pipes, sprays, and circulators attempted to keep relative humidity at 55 percent and the summertime indoor temperature at 80 degrees.

Despite these projects, it would be some 15 years before cooling technology would become a significant presence in U.S. cities. At first, heat and humidity control systems were marketed not for human comfort but to enable consistent and efficient industrial processes. Only when air conditioning went to the movies did it begin to become a fixture of urban life. In 1917, Chicago entrepreneurs Barney Balaban and Sam Katz opened the Central Park Theater, the world's first movie house to use mechanical cooling rather than fans blowing over blocks of ice. By the 1920s, "picture palaces," accommodating 2,000 or more moviegoers at a time, occupied prime urban real estate in the Northeast and Midwest. In 1925, Willis Carrier's company outfitted the Rivoli in Times Square with bypasses meant to gently infuse cool air instead of blasting icy breezes at foot level. During the Depression, smaller theaters, especially in the South and West, began installing more compact and efficient cooling units as moviegoing for both entertainment and heat relief purposes soared, marking the beginning of the summer "blockbuster" season.

Soon, other city institutions were feeling the heat. In 1925, the 21-story J. L. Hudson's on Detroit's Woodward Avenue became the nation's first air-conditioned department store. For many years, only its Bargain Basement was cooled, attracting low-class and middle-class Detroiters unable to leave the city during hot summer months. Macy's in New York's Herald Square, Filene's and Jordan Marsh of Boston, and Chicago's Marshall Field soon followed J. L. Hudson's and installed air conditioning. The spread of cooling in the economically lagging South was slower. Rich's of Atlanta did not air condition any part of its "great white store" until 1937, 20 years after it opened.

Before World War II, no American city was more air conditioned than Washington, D.C. Attempts to cool official Washington, defined by British diplomats as a "tropical" posting, began in 1881 when President James A. Garfield, felled by an assassin's bullet, lay dying in the White House. Navy engineers used a blower, boxes of ice, and tin pipes, later replaced with canvas ducts to reduce noise, in an attempt to alleviate Garfield's discomfort.

In 1928, after extensive hearings designed to forestall political charges of self-indulgent extravagance, air conditioning was installed in the chambers of the U.S. Senate and House of Representatives. By 1929, offices and workspaces at the White House were likewise outfitted with air conditioning. The new Supreme Court, completed in 1935, was air conditioned from the start. Although President Franklin D. Roosevelt personally detested mechanical cooling and refused to use it, he saw the technology as a way to assure maximum bureaucratic efficiency during the

long (and especially hot) years of the Depression. By 1942, the District of Columbia's electric utility recorded a summer usage peak, years before these would begin to appear in other U.S. cities.

Air conditioning came more slowly to the multi-story urban office building, even as these huge structures began to dominate downtowns across America in the 1920s and 1930s. Issues of architectural custom, cost, and technical complications meant that even New York's Chrysler, Woolworth, and Empire State Building skyscrapers had windows that could be opened for light and air instead of mechanical cooling. Not until 1928 was San Antonio's 21-story Milam Building constructed with a year-round modern air-conditioning system.

The first fully air-conditioned U.S. residence was built in Minneapolis in 1914. Not until after World War II, however, did residential cooling really become feasible, with cities participating to some extent in the boom that swept the new postwar suburbs. Initially, politicians and promoters in such cities as Miami, New Orleans, and Phoenix claimed that their communities had little need for air conditioning, or were adequately served by low-tech solutions, like Southwestern desert coolers, but before long, newly arrived residents would massively air condition Sun Belt cities and suburbs.

Urban air conditioning created new ways of interacting with neighbors. In a 1954 essay, sociologist William H. Whyte Jr. showed how window-mounted cooling units multiplied in Philadelphia neighborhoods via word-of-mouth and status competition among middle-class row house owners. As cities have become more air conditioned, thousands of units expelling hot air have intensified normal urban heat island effects.

Recent U.S. Census figures show that air conditioning is now available in 83 percent of U.S. households, with commercial installations almost certainly higher. Yet heat wave occurrences since the ascendancy of mechanical cooling revealed the limitations on urban comfort and control. In 1980, a month-long heat wave gripped the central southern U.S., killing 1,265 people. In St. Louis, where 112 died, wards in its 75-year-old City Hospital, serving mainly poor, elderly, and African American patients, recorded 95-degree nighttime temperatures. A 6-day Chicago heat wave in 1995 was blamed for some 700 deaths. The high cost of operating air conditioning has proved to be one factor in these disturbing results.

After more than 100 years, air conditioning has not eliminated problems of heat and humidity, but it has made urban living, work, shopping, and entertainment generally more comfortable and consistent in all seasons. By leveling natural climatic benefits and disadvantages, air conditioning has also reshaped the political and economic map of the United States. As naturally warmer cities of the South and West continue to attract newcomers and jobs, the losers are mainly those Northeastern and Midwestern metropolises that pioneered the use of air conditioning in its earliest days.

—Marsha E. Ackermann

Further Readings and References

Ackermann, M. E. (2002). *Cool comfort: America's romance with air-conditioning.* Washington, DC: Smithsonian Press.

Cooper, G. (1998). *Air-conditioning America: Engineers and the controlled environment, 1900–1960.* Baltimore, MD: Johns Hopkins University Press.

Whyte, W. H., Jr. (1954, November). The web word of mouth. *Fortune,* p. 140.

AIR POLLUTION

Urban life in America has included several factors that have compromised the quality of the air residents breathe. Among these factors are industrial processes, transportation, heat, and the reliance upon fossil fuels to provide the energy for commercial and residential activity. This dynamic was in place in the colonial period; Thomas Jefferson lamented the development of industry in America, concerned that it would bring the smoke and corruption of European urbanization (where complaints of smoke produced by coal date back to the 1400s) to the pristine landscape. By the time Jefferson had ascended to the presidency, this transition had already begun in the colonies, with smoke and odors from New England lumber mills befouling local air.

Jefferson's concerns anticipated the toll of industry, and as American cities developed large steel, textile, and transportation industries over the 19th century, the use of coal to fuel production belched large and constant clouds of smoke and sulphur dioxide over urban skies. Smoke and ash became particularly acute problems in the second half of the

19th century. Factors contributing to urban smoke included industrial smokestacks, the incineration of municipal waste, widespread use of railroads for commerce and transit, and domestic heating and cooking. Most of these activities involved the burning of coal as the primary source of fuel, and soft grades of coal produced highly visible plumes of black smoke and fly ash. The concentration of smoke in Northern cities grew especially severe during winter months when thousands of stoves burned coal to warm homes; on some days, cities such as Pittsburgh and Saint Louis would have black skies at noon.

Public health advocates worried about the effects of smoke on children, the infirm, and workers. By the end of the 19th century, women's associations such as civic associations and smoke abatement leagues emerged to critique the problem of smoke. Between 1890 and 1940, these associations teamed with civic engineers to compel several cities using soft coal for heating and industry to pass smoke control regulations. Several measures passed with limited success. Municipalities began using the Ringelmann Chart to measure coal smoke in the early 1900s. The technique, developed by Maximillian Ringelmann of France in the late 1800s, measured the darkness of smoke with four different black grids on a white background, which was placed a distance away from smokestacks for a set time. Smoke control efforts in Chicago and other cities quickly adopted the technique, defining air pollution as visible smoke in need of control. Engineering developments joined with public pressure to keep smoke control a priority in local politics. The Smoke Abatement League of Saint Louis erected billboards in 1939 claiming smoke cost each resident of the city $19 per year because of cleaning and health costs.

Coal-washing municipal ordinances (pioneered in Saint Louis in 1940 and adopted by dozens of cities by the end of 1941) and a gradual transition in urban domestic heating fuel supplies away from coal in favor of natural and manufactured gas and oil mitigated the smoke problem between 1940 and 1950, though industrial uses, power plants, and railroads continued to put visible smoke into urban skies. The days of black skies at noon were over.

By 1950, however, use of oil in transportation contributed to a different air pollution problem in the nation's metropolitan areas. The automobile replaced the train as a source of transportation both for urban residents and for the growing numbers of Americans who chose to move to the suburbs and commute in to the city centers. Access from the suburbs via the automobile sped flight from the smoky cities to the fresh air of the suburbs (a contrast remarked upon by suburban developers in advertisements between the wars). Ironically, the daily use of the automobile to commute between suburb and city helped contribute to the most pressing issue in urban air pollution after World War II.

Smog, a combination of smoke and fog containing several gases, produced yellowy clouds of dirty air. In Los Angeles, smog was sufficiently prevalent in the 1940s to become an integral element in noir fiction. As the United States became a more suburban nation between 1945 and 1980, smog became a problem in most metropolitan areas.

Industrial emissions continued to pollute the air. Occasionally the results were sudden and tragic. In Donora, an industrial town south of Pittsburgh, air pollution inversion (cool air trapped by warm air above it keeps pollution from dispersing) trapped sulfur dioxide, carbon monoxide, and metal dust emitted from local plants and coal furnaces in October 1948. The resulting smog killed 20 people and sickened over 7,000 residents.

The Donora tragedy and resulting public concern spurred a sustained period of attempts to control air pollution from industrial and consumer sources in the second half of the 20th century. Similar to the smoke abatement groups of the early 20th century, postwar air pollution organizations, including the Group Against Smog and Pollution (GASP) founded in Pittsburgh in 1969, demanded local and national political action to combat the growing threat to human health. Public concern produced a sustained period of attempts to control air pollution in the second half of the 20th century at the local, state, and national levels.

National regulation of air quality was a post–World War II development. Congress passed the Air Pollution Control Act of 1955, which identified air pollution as a national problem and allocated $5 million annually for 5 years for research by the Public Health Service for additional research on the sources and consequences of air pollution. In 1963, Congress passed the Clean Air Act, allocating $95 million over 3 years for states and municipalities to set emissions standards for stationary sources of pollution, including power plants and steel mills. Amendments to the Clean Air Act passed in 1965, 1966, 1967, and 1969. In 1967, Congress passed the Air Quality Control Act, setting timetables for states to establish air quality standards.

Three years later Congress passed the Clean Air Act of 1970, establishing more stringent national air quality standards. The Clean Air Act of 1970 allowed citizens the right to take legal action against anyone or any organization, including the government, who is in violation of the emissions standards. Among the significant consequences of the new legislation in the 1970s involved changes to the nation's automobiles, including a ban on leaded gasoline and requirements for catalytic converters in automobiles to reduce hydrocarbons, carbon monoxide, and nitrogen oxide emissions.

Although the Reagan Administration stymied further amendments to the Clean Air Act, 1990 brought new revisions to require cities to enact specific air pollution control measures, raised automobile emissions standards, and set a definite timetable. Research into atmospheric pollution since the earlier amendments indicated that urban air pollution's consequences included smog, the accumulation of ground-level ozone, airborne carcinogens such as benzene, linking sulfur dioxide to the production of acid rain and the use of chlorofluorocarbons (CFCs) in industry and consumer products contributed to global ozone depletion. The 1990 Clean Air Act attempted to reduce the levels of these pollutants to stem the local, regional, and global effects of air pollution.

These attempts have had limited success. Air pollution relating to fossil fuels is now linked to the increased diagnosis of several respiratory illnesses, including asthma, among urban residents. Today, the largest source of pollution in most urban areas remains the use of motor vehicles, and although national curbs on industrial emissions are half a century old, enforcement in the early 21st century is not systematic in many cities. The fast-growing sprawling metropolitan regions in the South and West feature some of the most concentrated smog problems. In the more densely settled Northeast, concern over transboundary air pollution increased at the end of the 20th century, as New Yorkers voiced concern over coal smoke from power plants in Ohio and Pennsylvania.

At the beginning of the 21st century, research and public concern over air pollution produced an evolving understanding that air pollution did not simply comprise visible smoke and particulate matter, affecting the local environment, but included both visible and invisible pollutants which contributed to human health problems in the local environment, as well as a series of detrimental effects on the local, regional, and global scale. Though these perceptions had produced a series of local, state, national, and even (if we consider the Kyoto Protocol of 1997 that the United States did not join) global political efforts to curb air pollution, continued use of fossil fuels by drivers, industries, and consumers meant that air pollution remained a critical issue in urban American life.

—Carl Zimring

Further Readings and References

Davis, D. L. (2002). *When smoke ran like water: Tales of environmental deception and the battle against pollution.* New York: Basic Books.

Melosi, M. V. (2000). *The sanitary city: Urban infrastructure in America from colonial times to the present.* Baltimore, MD: Johns Hopkins University Press.

Stradling, D. (1999). *Smokestacks and Progressives: Environmentalists, engineers, and air quality in America, 1881–1951.* Baltimore, MD: Johns Hopkins University Press.

Tarr, J. A. (1996). *The search for the ultimate sink: Urban pollution in historical perspective.* Akron, OH: University of Akron Press.

Tarr, J. A., & Zimring, C. (1997). The struggle for smoke control in St Louis: Achievement and emulation. In A. Hurley (Ed.), *Common fields: The environmental history of Saint Louis* (pp. 190–220). Saint Louis, MO: Missouri Historical Society.

AIRPORTS

The airports serving the airline passengers of the early 21st century are the product of more than 80 years of experimentation and development. For much of the first half of the 20th century, airports were in many ways peripheral to the lives of Americans. Air travel was an elite experience and most major airports were located at some distance from the center of population. Today, however, the emergence of air travel as a mass phenomenon and urban sprawl have worked to increase the contact and connections between Americans and their local airports. Over the course of the first century of staffed, powered, heavier-than-air flight, airports emerged as vital parts of the national transportation infrastructure.

The history of commercial airports in the United States can be divided into two broad periods. The first period stretched from the end of World War I through the end of World War II. During these decades many of the basic patterns of United States airport development emerged as airports evolved from relatively simple facilities, often privately owned, serving the Post Office and the military, to more complex, expensive, publicly owned facilities serving a growing traveling public and receiving federal aid, in part due to their continued role in national defense. Driving much of the activity during this early time period were civic boosterism, aviation enthusiasm, and, as suggested, military needs. The second period covers the decades from the end of World War II to the present, although the events of September 11, 2001 may prove an important watershed as well. This postwar period witnessed the emergence of a number of issues and developments. First, and most important, complaints about aircraft noise made campaigns to expand airports, not to mention build new ones, extremely contested affairs. Second, the volatility of the airline industry made airport planning extremely difficult. Finally, new technologies—from jet airliners to ground control radars—made airports even more complex and expensive than many early airport boosters could ever have imagined.

The first "customers" for airports in the United States were the Post Office and the military. Both began approaching local civic leaders on the subject of building such facilities immediately following World War I. Though even at that date many expressed the idea that airports ought to be publicly owned, a variety of local circumstances, not the least of which was a lack of necessary enabling legislation, often led private interests to take the lead in the earliest airport construction initiatives. Over time, however, a number of factors came together to favor public over private ownership of those airports serving the traveling public. As aircraft technologies advanced, many improvements required certain changes at the airports. For example, the early technologies allowing for day-and-night, all-weather flying depended upon extensive airport lighting and hard-surfaced runways. Growing complexity brought higher expenses. At this early stage airports struggled to break even, let alone make a profit. Therefore, it became apparent to many that public ownership and financing would be the only way to guarantee that airports witnessed the needed improvements. Finally, the Works Projects Administration, a major source of federal funding for airport construction in the 1930s, required that any airport receiving federal aid had to be publicly owned.

Though in the years before World War II, especially, airport profits proved illusive, civic boosterism, aviation enthusiasm, and national defense provided sufficient incentives to promote airport construction projects. As early as the 1920s and certainly by the 1930s, airports emerged as a "must have" on the list of local boosters. Modern up-to-date cities needed modern up-to-date airports. These decades also witnessed a great deal of enthusiasm for the potential of aviation, particularly following Charles Lindbergh's flight from New York to Paris in 1927. In the wake of that event, states across the nation passed airport enabling legislation and cities pressed forward with airport plans. And though airports played host to military units since 1918, in the late 1930s the role of airports in national defense went far in justifying the first direct federal aid—not based on work relief—for airport construction and improvement.

To a great extent the aviation landscape of the United States was in place by the end of World War II. With few exceptions, all the sites for the nation's major airports had already been identified as serving aviation purposes. These sites included existing airports and military airfields in the process of or soon to be converted to civilian uses, an example being Chicago's O'Hare Airport. A number of factors contributed to the dearth of new major airport construction following World War II, the most important being the public's reaction to increasing aircraft noise. Noise complaints dated back at least to the 1930s. However, as cities grew outward, bringing residential developments closer to previously isolated airports, aircraft noise complaints began to mount, especially after the introduction of the first jet airliners in the late 1950s. By the late 1960s, aircraft noise had been defined as a form of pollution and airport construction subject to environmental impact assessments addressing the noise issue.

The imprecision of airline travel forecasts further complicated efforts to plan and build airports to meet demand. Travel by airline generally increased after World War II, especially in the 1960s and again after the deregulation of airlines in the late 1970s. Predicting overall growth was not the problem. Rather, predicting exactly where the growth would occur—especially which airports would see the most growth—proved more difficult. Atlanta, Georgia, for example, undertook a major expansion of its airport in the early 1960s only to find it inadequate to meet actual demands. Such uncertainty—resulting in either underbuilt or overbuilt airports—made local airport operators cautious, often demanding multiple studies before authorizing construction. The time between the initial proposal to expand or build an airport and the completion of construction increasingly stretched to years, even decades.

As symbolized by the new airport in Denver, further adding to the complexity surrounding airport expansion or construction was increasing costs. The necessity to mitigate noise problems as well as the complexity of the planning process added costs of their own. In Denver, for example, in an effort to address the noise issue the city located its new airport on a remote 53-square-mile site. Throughout the postwar period, many new technologies also added to the cost of airports, including the wider, thicker, longer runways needed by the larger, faster aircraft, new navigational aids, more extensive lighting systems, ground-tracking radars, and people movers. Further, desires to meet the demands of the traveling public inspired the construction of larger, more amenities-laden airport terminals. In the end, Denver's new airport cost over $5 billion to build.

To a great extent airports remain works in progress, continually facing new challenges. This was evident following the terrorist attacks of September 11, 2001. In the wake of that event, airports became "ground zero" in the scramble to reassure Americans on the safety of the air transportation system. Airports became the location where Americans were most likely to encounter some of the most visible symbols of the new federal homeland security measures—the agents of the Transportation Security Administration. With facilities designed for a different security environment, many airport managers had to act quickly to reconfigure terminals to accommodate the new measures. In addition, the future of airline passenger travel remains difficult to predict. Some envision a decentralization of airline travel with a shift from the current hub-and-spoke system focused on a few major airports to a system built on point-to-point travel that utilizes many of the nation's smaller airports and involves creation of a fleet of smaller aircraft. On the other hand, Airbus is planning to introduce a 550-passenger civilian airliner, the A380, the size and capacity of which will restrict its use to only the largest airports. Regardless, airports will continue to evolve as air travel evolves.

—*Janet R. Daly Bednarek*

Further Readings and References

Bednarek, J. R. D. (2001). *America's airports: Airfield development, 1918–1947.* College Station, TX: Texas A&M University Press.

Braden, B., & Hagan, P. (1989). *A dream takes flight: Hartsfield Atlanta International Airport and aviation in Atlanta.* Atlanta, GA: Atlanta Historical Society; Athens, GA: University of Georgia Press.

Dempsey, P. S., Goetz, A. R., & Szyliowicz, J. S. (1996). *Denver International Airport: Lessons learned.* New York: McGraw-Hill.

Albuquerque, New Mexico

Located 60 miles southwest of the state capitol of Santa Fe, surrounded by the mountains and plateaus which form the Rio Grande River Valley, Albuquerque is the largest city in the state of New Mexico. It is the center of the state's business, manufacturing, and medical industries. The city reflects a mix of Native American and European influences via its culture and envelopment within the enormous expanses of desert landscape.

Albuquerque was one of the first villages colonized by the Spanish in North America. In 1706, Governor Francisco Cuervo y Valdes named a villa along the Rio Grande River after the Duke of Alburquerque (the first "r" was later dropped), Viceroy of New Spain, possibly as a gesture of goodwill since he did not have the preapproval of the king or viceroy. Over a century later, the governance of Albuquerque would change hands between Spain, Mexico, and the United States within a 25-year span.

Claimed by the United States by the turn of the 20th century, Albuquerque was quickly becoming an urban center in the West and surpassed Santa Fe as a commercial and population hub. The arrival of the Atchison, Topeka and Santa Fe (AT&SF) railroad in the 1880s allowed the incorporated City of Albuquerque to exploit the economic potential of its surrounding forest and mining resources. The Booster's Association trumpeted the city's "healing capacities" to lure emigrants from the Eastern states, and real estate salesmen promised fertile soils and high yields to Eastern buyers looking for farmlands. Agriculture, however, failed to provide the economic strength the boosters had envisioned. It was the continued growth of railroading and manufacturing that would attract settlers from around the country and Mexico.

As the population increased, so did the need for housing and buildings to support Albuquerque's new inhabitants. The Spanish and Mexican architecture that had dominated Albuquerque was considered humble and out of date for a burgeoning American city. Since most of the land developers were from the East Coast, new structures were predominantly Victorian. The regimented Victorian-style buildings constructed along the rail line were a radical departure from the requirements of the early Albuquerque, which was a central plaza surrounded by municipal buildings and churches that gave way to small farm plots.

The rapid emigration near the turn of the century began to crowd what was to be called the "New Town" area where the affluent resided. As suburban developments were added, the space between New Town and Old Town was gradually filled in to accommodate the influx of emigrants to Albuquerque searching for cheaper land, commercial opportunities, and healthier living. Although the automobile would be one of the facilitators in the rise of suburban growth, the street railcar enabled the initial movement to the outskirts. When automobiles eventually replaced streetcars as the primary means of transport, gas stations and motels began to appear amid the commercial activity lining Railroad Avenue. Renamed Central Avenue in 1912, it remained the main east-west thoroughfare in the city. Central Avenue became part of the popular highway Route 66 until the 1960s when Interstate 40 was completed and diverted much of the traffic from Route 66 and downtown Albuquerque.

After World War I, Albuquerque fell into an economic recession due to the plummeting of agricultural and livestock prices. Businesses in the city faltered, and Albuquerque's growth slowed. In 1924, local businessmen formed the Civic Council in an effort to formulate a plan to revitalize Albuquerque. Ultimately it would be their promotion of Albuquerque's "healthy climate" that would once again attract people to the city and help Albuquerque rebound from its postwar recession. This rebound included a continued population growth, the alteration of Albuquerque's skyline with the nine-story First National Bank, and the construction of one of the first airfields in the West.

A recovering Albuquerque did not suffer the same economic devastation that enveloped the country in the stock market crash of 1929. The city's small businesses and shops reliant on Route 66 tourist traffic were affected when traffic dropped to half of its pre-crash volume. In 1935, local businessmen once again gathered to formulate means to invigorate

Albuquerque's faltering but not yet stagnant economy. The result was a "Golden Jubilee" celebration to mark Albuquerque's 50th anniversary as an incorporated city. A keynote address from Governor Clyde Tingley and a telegram from Franklin Roosevelt congratulating the city's anniversary contributed to the success of the celebration, and from 1935 through the rest of the decade, Albuquerque's economy began to revive.

Once America entered World War II, Albuquerque quickly became a popular location for military training and military testing. The vast open spaces, relatively sparse surrounding population, and climate facilitated the building of military airstrips. Military leaders realized the importance of Albuquerque's isolated location in the desert, and weapons testing locations near Albuquerque attracted chemists and atomic scientists from all over the country. Los Alamos laboratories, near Santa Fe, employed some of the best scientists in the United States, and Albuquerque remained the center through which atomic research materials and other weaponry passed. In July of 1945, the first atomic bomb was detonated at the Trinity Site, and Albuquerque's future as an epicenter of military weapons systems development and nuclear research was secured.

During the World War II era, new military installations were built in and around Albuquerque, and urban growth boomed into the 1950s when the Cold War accelerated the weapons development and testing industry. The steadily increasing population created unprecedented suburban growth. The face of Albuquerque began to resemble a modern city, and little heed was paid toward preserving the city's unique architecture or open space. In 1975, in the midst of being designated by the FBI as having the highest crime rate of any city in the country, Albuquerque developed the first plan that directly addressed the sprawling suburbs, the loss of historic landmarks, increased pollution, and the importance of preserving the buildings and southwestern architecture. By 1989, Albuquerque had the fifth largest holding of urban open space in the nation, and Old Town became one of the city's biggest tourist attractions because of its mud streets, adobe buildings, and distinct "old Western town" feel. This is remarkable considering that by the 1980s less than 20 percent of the city's residents could claim Albuquerque as their birthplace, and half of Albuquerque's population had been residents for less than 5 years.

Present-day Albuquerque remains a culturally diverse city due to a large scientific community originating from all over the country and world and its mingling of current and historical Native American, Spanish, and Mexican influence. Many of the historic landmarks still stand in the midst of a very modern city of high-tech industry due to an active effort to preserve that which makes Albuquerque unique: its architecture, plazas, and diverse heritage.

—*Christopher Coutts*

Further Readings and References

Price, V. B. (1992). *A city at the end of the world.* Albuquerque, NM: University of New Mexico Press.

Simmons, M. (1982). *Albuquerque.* Albuquerque, NM: University of New Mexico Press.

ALLEY HOUSING

Passageways for services within city blocks were once a necessary feature of the well-designed city; alleys neatly separated pedestrian traffic from the noisome activities of waste removal and the stabling of horses. The covert and distasteful functions of alleys have ensured that they have remained a persistently underserviced and ugly feature of many American cities. Despite the obvious inconveniences of living in an alley, rear lot housing has been a feature of the American city since colonial times, but it was during the late 19th century period of rapid urbanization and attendant housing shortages that alley housing became common. Because of the low quality and cost of most of the housing, alleys of that era often became associated with particular low-status residents in ways that reflected regional differences, the best documented examples being enclaves of Jews in New York, Chinese along the West Coast, and blacks throughout the South.

Never regarded highly, the reputation of alley housing went into a steep decline following the publication of Jacob Riis's *How the Other Half Lives* (1890), which explicitly linked the depravity of the residents of the Lower East Side of Manhattan to their appalling living conditions. The opening chapter identifies the rear-house tenement as the archetype of the Hell's Kitchen slum, abandoned by the city and shunned by anyone with the means to live elsewhere, representing a baseline of misery and squalor. As repellant as the scenes of degradation in the main avenues of the Bowery were, Riis argued that alleys were the actual epicenters of antisocial behavior because they were sanctuary for those who could not meet even the incredibly low standards of the Bowery. This effective embodiment of late-Victorian preoccupations with hygiene, environment, sex, and race in the alley residents of the Bowery ensured that alley slums would remain a primary subject of social reform for decades.

Following Riis's example, representations of residence alleys throughout the Progressive Era emphasized their alien nature as places where the rules of American society were suspended and normal standards of behavior were perverted. Inspired by Riis's example, urban hygiene programs began emphasizing tenement demolition and dispersal of alley residents, programs that accelerated through the 1920s aided by a vibrant urban economy and a widespread building boom that eased housing shortages. Following upon two decades of high-profile efforts, the Great Depression all but ended progress in slum clearance as demand for low-cost housing increased and funds for demolition vanished. The Depression also marked a significant change in the makeup of alley communities, transferring the racialized spatial patterns of the South to the industrial cities of the North and changing the meaning of slum clearance in those cities entirely.

The association of blacks with alley housing in the American South long predates emancipation, going back to when domestic slaves were commonly housed in outbuildings along alleys and freed Africans were deterred from living on main streets. After emancipation this pattern of living "behind the front house" persisted in Southern cities, and alleys became the thoroughfares of segregated cities that were all but invisible to whites. The degree of separation in a single block could be impressive; John Borchert calculated in 1980 that in the first decade of the 20th century, some blocks of Washington, D.C., were 97 percent white occupancy in the front houses and 93 percent black occupancy in the rear housing and alleys contained 78 percent of all black residences throughout the city.

Where blacks concentrated in alleys, in the North or South, their presence complicated clearance programs with concerns that they would be displaced into white neighborhoods. A watershed moment was reached when in 1934 Congress reinvigorated Washington, D.C.'s alley clearance program by combining it with subsidized public housing, a solution that cleared tenements but accelerated the concentration of black residents into specific neighborhoods. This strategy spread across the United States in the following decades, aided by federal funding. Urban renewal programs of the 1950s and 1960s particularly targeted black-occupied rear tenements by eliminating alleys altogether through "super-block" and parking lot developments and replacing low-rise buildings with tower-block public housing that quickly replaced the tenement house as the icon of the inner city ghetto. Despite their high visibility, post–World War II slum clearance programs were much less effective than the automobile in ending widespread alley residence. Cars encouraged lower population densities that undercut the demand for alley housing and encouraged "white flight" to suburbs, creating a surplus of inner city housing. Automobiles also increased the value of alleys for garages and off-street truck delivery, displacing other uses. Simultaneously, as conditions in the remaining residences gradually improved through minimum housing standards, the stigma attached to alley housing decreased.

In the 1970s the precursors of the New Urbanism movement reassessed alley housing and declared them ripe for redevelopment, as noted by Grady Clay in 1978. The successes of coach house gentrification in the alleys of Georgetown in Washington, D.C., and Greenwich Village in New York City have sparked a widespread gentrification of alley housing in recent decades, including new and exclusive "court" and "mews" developments as well as a return of affordable rental units in the form of "granny flats." Alleys, which were once a liability, no longer bear many of the unpleasant associations of the past—they are valued for their insularity and have become a key part of the American city.

—*Jason Jindrich*

Further Readings and References

Beasley, E. (1996). *The alleys and back buildings of Galveston.* Houston, TX: Rice University Press.

Clay, G. (1978). *Alleys: A hidden resource.* Louisville, KY: Grady Clay.

Ling, H. (2002). "Hop alley": Myth and reality of the St. Louis Chinatown, 1860s–1930s. *Journal of Urban History, 28*(2), 184–220.

Riis, J. A. (1890). *How the other half lives: Studies among the tenements of New York.* New York: Scribner.

AMERICAN STATE CAPITALS

A state capital is at once a capitol (both words are pronounced identically), a municipality, and a symbol of the state. This refers to Americans' relationship to their cities as well as to the links between capital cities and other cities in their states.

In the American federal system, urban primacy and politics follow a different logic. State capitals are highly heterogeneous and form a parallel urban network, disconnected from the classical American urban network, largely based on economic dynamics and linkages. The population of state capitals ranged from 8,035 (in Montpelier) to 5,819,000 (in Boston) in 2000, and capitals' share of the state's population ranged from 7 percent (Frankfort, Annapolis, and Jefferson City) to 113 percent (in Providence, Rhode Island, where the metropolitan area exceeds the limits of the state).

Capitals are singular in the American urban fabric, from physical and social points of view. It could be contended that capitals are the "most American" of the nation's cities because, owing to their diversity, they are symbols of the United States of America.

Their platting stages and translates the polity in the physical pattern of the capital city. Carefully planned under public initiative and investment, they mostly depart from the supposed uniformity of American cities through the erection of monuments on symbolic locations, the most impressive of which are the capitols. Once symbols of the reality of statehood, they have become symbols of permanence, linking the states with their history. Capitals host and stage the most important public spaces and places in their states, capitol grounds being the most visible ones. However, unanimity was never reached, since these "public" places were mainly built by white men for the white Anglo-Saxon Protestant majority, thus excluding numerous minorities, including Native Americans, African Americans, and women.

The absence of unanimity was very visible during the processes of capital choice, and the aftermath of these selection processes continues even today. Indeed, a common factor in the history of American state capitals is their instability: American states (including during the colonial and territorial periods in some cases) had an average of 3.8 successive capitals. No clear geographical pattern emerges from the capital migrations that all but eight states have experienced.

To find an explanatory model, several factors have to be intertwined. Most of the current state capitals were selected during the 19th century, 35 of them before 1861, an era of pioneer and idealized territorial vision. Their story thus connects them with the Jeffersonian ideal—a democracy based upon small but educated farmers. The search for centrality in the location of capitals was indeed not merely a geographical wish. It was linked to the representation regime and expressed the principle of equality in geographical terms. But today, only 13 capitals (26 percent) are geographically central in their states. The ideals of Puritanism and the small town were mostly a marginal rhetoric during the selection process. Distrust of the "big" cities was rarely present, Baton Rouge being the most explicit case. Better suited were the booster and the gateway models. Capitals fully participated in the construction of urban America (one fourth were built from scratch) in a framework of intense competition between communities: becoming a capital brought the hope that the town would survive and thrive. The naming of the capital was often considered in this perspective, as it was for Augusta, Olympia, and Lincoln, but some cities changed their names after being selected as capitals, such as Pumpkinville, which became Phoenix. Very often, the choice of a capital illustrated the balance of powers inside a state. Capitals' locations shifted as political factions grabbed control and railway companies fought over new territories, as in South Dakota. The selection process was firmly in the hands of white men and linked to eastern capital. Locating the capital was indeed not a way to translate the democratic wish of the citizens, because *they, the people*, seldom chose directly. Most of the time, Congress, governors, or the state legislature made the choice—with the helping hand of lobbyists and town boosters and sometimes despite legislative requirements that called for popular referenda on the matter. The overall process might be abbreviated under the "BBC theme": Boosterism, Bribery, and Compromise.

The process of selecting a capital location thus shed all the divisive factors in a state as, at the very same time, it brought everyone to think about unity: one capital to represent and manage a single political unit, the state. Although choosing a capital was not the unique factor that consolidated state consciousness, it did help. Not necessarily at once, but in the long term, almost all citizens were to accept the fact that the capital, however difficult had been the selection process, was to last.

Once chosen, capitals had to survive the initial limited boom that followed their designation. The fate of former capitals proves that although hosting the capitol did not often induce large growth processes, being the seat of government did qualify cities accorded such a status for a better fate than cities that lost the privilege. But not a grand fate: The records of capital cities before the second half of the 20th century do not seem very brilliant, with some exceptions, such as Boston, Atlanta, and Indianapolis. In a fast-growing nation, only half the capitals belonged at one moment to the 100 most populated American cities during the 1790 to 1950 period. Of these capitals, 19 out of 25 faded. Thirty-six capitals (three quarters) proved unable to broaden their economic base far beyond state government during that period. Not that their elites were willing to be secluded from economics. On the contrary, those with power in capital cities dreamt of the cities becoming economic metropolises. The capitals' developmental delay is often charged to a corrupt government on one side and a relatively unenlightened citizenry on the other. Such a combination did not help to attract as many prospective investors as it had been hoped by the city fathers. A second cause to the capitals' economic delay was the frequent dichotomy between political and economic territories. Capitals ruled over areas that had not often been drawn according to economic logic. A third cause—partly resulting from the former two—was the fact that railroads often bypassed capitals, kicking them astray from the urban growth channels of industrialization, and vice versa.

The "purgatory years" of state capitals lasted into the 1950s. The capitals' aggiornamento has since seen them modeling their evolution on mainstream America. The state capitals escaped remaining public *company towns* primarily because of the changes in government since the 1940s. As federal and state budgets expanded and most states opened to more political honesty, capitals expanded more quickly demographically and economically than did other cities. As a result, governmental centers grew in importance in the new division of labor that was emerging. The latest economic trends are indeed based on the traditional assets of capitals: white-collar dwellers and urban amenities. A high quality of life—in a successful economic environment—attracts most Americans to areas. Juneau, Olympia, Helena, Santa Fe, and Annapolis fully gain from the booming leisure economy by treasuring their modest and pleasurable size and atmosphere. But capitals that are also academic

centers fare better (see Austin and Raleigh) than other capitals at exploiting the new niches, while state universities have often been offered to cities that had lost the capital fight.

If manufacturing dominates at the regional level, state capitals do not have the best cards to play, because of the population manufacturing tends to attract. If agriculture dominates, capitals, if centrally located, can easily play the role of supply and trade centers. When the economic base is diversified, the case is more complex. This diversity is a trademark of most capitals and enables them to profit from a stable and growing economic base through public employment (around one half of the total workforce for the smallest capitals and one quarter for the medium-sized ones). Being diversified in a mono-industrial state enables the capital to react better to economic downturns (like Columbus and Cheyenne did).

However, the recent growth of American capitals has not fundamentally modified the national urban hierarchy. Some capitals certainly became metropolises (Atlanta, Salt Lake City, and Austin), but, while 26 percent of the state capital municipalities had more than 250,000 inhabitants in 2000 and 30 percent were millionaire metropolitan areas, 24 percent still had less than 50,000 inhabitants. Under a certain threshold, it is impossible to turn a "village-capital" into a "new economy" boomtown.

The current modification of the image of capitals testifies to the modernization of the way politics are conducted as well as of their economies. This means that state capitals are more than simply symbolic towns; they are clear bases of the American identity.

—*Christian Montès*

See also Company Towns

Further Readings and References

Bromley, R. (1990). *Doing business in a capital city: Report of the Capital Cities Project.* Albany, NY: University at Albany Foundation and Norstar Bank of Upstate New York.

Goodsell, C. T. (2001). *The American statehouse: Interpreting democracy's temples.* Lawrence: University Press of Kansas.

Moussalli, S. D. (1997). Choosing capitals in antebellum Southern frontier constitutions. *Southwestern Historical Quarterly, 101,* 58–75.

Zagarri, R. (1988). Representation and the removal of state capitals, 1776–1812. *Journal of American History, 74,* 1239–1256.

AMERICANIZATION MOVEMENT

The Americanization movement refers to a disparate set of programs and institutions designed to incorporate immigrants, and in some cases native-born Americans, into the broad parameters of middle-class American culture. The premise of these programs—that qualified reformers could both improve material conditions and foster a unified national identity—represented a key element of Progressive Era thought and undergirded the idea of the United States as a "melting pot." The popularity of Americanization crested in the early 20th century, but during the late 1910s, World War I and fears of political radicalism prompted a shift in programs from cultural uplift to a more conservative nationalism. A decade later the movement withered under a widespread pessimism about the ability or willingness of immigrants to assimilate into mainstream society.

Americanization's intellectual origins lay in the settlement house movement that emerged in response to the late 19th century influx of immigrants, especially from eastern and southern Europe, and the proliferation of crowded immigrant ghettos. A concept imported from Great Britain, the settlement provided welfare services and educational programs to nearby residents, and it often became active in attempts to rid neighborhoods of pollution, substandard housing, vice, and crime. Church-led settlements added evangelism to their efforts. By the early 20th century, many religious and secular settlements had begun to encapsulate their goals under the rubric of *Americanization*. The term reflected a sense that cultural, spiritual, and economic uplift could foment a cohesive, virtuous national identity. Most reformers advocated naturalization for those eligible (federal law during this period prevented Asian immigrants from naturalizing) and encouraged immigrants to become active in the political life of the country. But they placed an equal emphasis on everyday practices, from English language skills to housekeeping to cooking styles (reformers believed "American" food to be healthier than that of other ethnicities). Many of these efforts focused on the domestic duties of immigrant women, under the logic that mothers would transmit the values they learned to their children. Thus Americanization, especially before World War I, involved much more than citizenship and patriotism. Many reformers believed that those native-born African Americans and Anglos who fell short of middle-class living standards were equally suitable targets for their programs.

At its high point the Americanization movement extended its influence well beyond reformers' circles. President Theodore Roosevelt championed Americanization as a way to unify a country increasingly characterized by cultural diversity. Henry Ford required his immigrant workers to attend English language and citizenship classes. In some cases government agencies explicitly adopted Americanization principles. California's Commission on Immigration and Housing, for example, invoked the movement's philosophy in promoting public education, housing reform, and immigrant welfare policies. Indeed, some of government's first forays into regulating the private lives of American residents occurred under the auspices of Americanization.

The onset of World War I and the subsequent entry of the United States into the conflict inspired a second wave of Americanization efforts, albeit of a different sort than their predecessors. These new programs focused more on nationalism and the suppression of labor organizations, and they reflected a growing suspicion of the loyalties of recent arrivals. The high-profile National Americanization Committee, which exchanged its progressive ideals for a nationalist focus during the war, illustrated this ideological shift. By the end of the 1910s, those programs emphasizing cultural pluralism or shop floor mobilization found their financial support dwindling, sometimes under allegations of disloyalty.

The Americanization movement faded during the 1920s amid mounting reservations about the assimilability and loyalty of immigrants. These concerns led to the passage in 1921 and 1924 of strict federal quotas that curbed immigration from eastern and southern Europe, thereby reducing the number of clients for settlements and related programs. Though western cities continued to receive newcomers from Mexico, reformers became more cynical about the ability of Mexicans to assimilate. Toward the end of the decade, for instance, California's Commission of Immigration and Housing began to call for restrictions on immigration from Mexico. Although some social workers continued to use the term *Americanization* during and after the 1930s, the economic upheavals of the Great Depression created new social problems that made Americanization seem less critical.

Scholars remain divided over the impact of the Americanization movement. Some emphasize the important material benefits these programs provided and credit the movement for encouraging cultural unification. Others contend that Americanization demeaned, either implicitly or explicitly, immigrant cultures and did little to counter ethnic or racial inequality. The difficulty of assessment arises in part from the diversity of organizations that embraced the concept of Americanization. Jane Addams's Hull-House in Chicago, for instance, adopted a pluralist view of American culture and encouraged immigrants to maintain at least some aspects of their ethnic heritage. At the other end of the spectrum, the Better America Federation, formed by California business leaders at the end of World War I, cast its programs almost exclusively in nationalist terms and attacked more liberal versions of Americanization.

Overall, the Americanization movement provided tangible benefits to thousands of newcomers, many of whom did adopt middle-class customs and patriotism. European immigrants, the focus of most programs, proved the most amenable to this outreach effort. Nevertheless, many other immigrants, particularly those of color, ignored or rejected the lure of Americanization in whole or in part. Accounts by social reformers and missionaries from the period frequently contrast the relative willingness of immigrants to avail themselves of welfare programs with their reluctance to embrace U.S. citizenship and/or Christianity. The limits of Americanization remain apparent at least in part in the persistence of ethnic communities and practices into the beginning of the 21st century.

—Mark Wild

See also Addams, Jane; Settlement House Movement

Further Readings and References

Higham, J. (2002). *Strangers in the land: Patterns of American nativism, 1860–1925.* New Brunswick, NJ: Rutgers University Press.

Lissak, R. S. (1989). *Pluralism and Progressives: Hull-House and the new immigrants.* Chicago: University of Chicago Press.

Sanchez, G. (1990). Go after the women: Americanization and the Mexican immigrant woman, 1915–29. In E. C. DuBois & V. Ruiz (Eds.), *Unequal sisters: A multi-cultural reader in U.S. women's history.* New York: Routledge.

AMUSEMENT PARKS

Descendants of the medieval trade fairs and European pleasure gardens of the late 17th and 18th centuries, amusement parks have evolved from providing adult entertainment to being one of American families' favorite recreational places as leisure time and disposable personal income increased.

Originally picnic grounds including a few primitive rides, the first American amusement parks developed at the end of the 19th century under the influence of the trolley companies, which wanted to stimulate weekend ridership to generate additional revenues and maximize the flat monthly rate charged by the electric light and power companies, and Chicago's Columbian Exposition of 1893, which introduced the key elements of modern amusement parks. The World's Fair unveiled the exotic enticements of the Midway Plaisance and the first Ferris wheel, which provided visitors with a spectacular view of the city from 264 feet above the ground. The White City offered also the safe experience of an enclosed and temporary ideal world artificially produced by architects, engineers, and planners. The following year, Captain Paul Boynton launched Chutes Park in Chicago, the first enclosed amusement park charging an admission fee; and in 1895, he opened Sea Lion Park at Coney Island, Brooklyn, New York, which inspired many amusement parks in the United States, such as Sea World in California and Florida.

Coney Island, once called the Empire of the Nickel, started its metamorphosis from a traditional seaside resort into the world's most popular playground with the completion of Andrew Culver's Prospect Park and the Coney Island Trailway in 1875. From the 1890s until the mid-1950s, it epitomized the American amusement park tradition. Steeplechase Park (1897–1964), Luna Park (1903–1947), and Dreamland (1904–1911) attracted millions of working-class New Yorkers who wanted to escape their responsibilities and mundane urban daily life to enjoy the intense thrills provided by the scary roller coasters and the wonderful atmosphere of fantasy, sensuality, and chaos created by the gaudy architectural structures, impressive lighting, and disorienting attractions.

By 1920, more than 1,800 amusement parks, usually located at the end of a trolley line, operated in the United States. Nevertheless, this golden age subsided quickly and a dramatic decline started in the 1920s as Americans enjoyed the new mobility provided by automobiles. Unable to provide adequate parking facilities and affected by Prohibition, some years of bad summer weather, the acquisition of parks by private individuals, the Stock Market Crash of 1929, and the Great Depression, numerous urban amusement parks closed. By 1939, only 245 parks remained and the downward sloping trend continued during World War II.

The postwar baby boom and the creation of "kiddielands" allowed amusement parks to experience some brief revival, but the dramatic cultural transformations of the 1950s (such as the suburbanization of the middle class, the intensification of racial tensions, and inner city decay) made them increasingly obsolete, unable to compete with shopping malls, the television, and more sophisticated entertainments. The traditional parks irreversibly deteriorated, but a new concept soon emerged. It was Walt Disney's $17 million brilliant and iconic dream.

On July 17, 1955, Walt Disney's Magic Kingdom, more commonly referred to as Disneyland, opened in Anaheim, California. The first modern U.S. theme park was born and radically affected the future development of the amusement park industry. Despite the early skepticism generated by the absence of traditional attractions, it became an instant success. Disneyland featured five separate fantasy worlds—Main Street, U.S.A., Fantasyland, Adventureland, Frontierland, and Tomorrowland—and included themes borrowed from Disney's popular motion pictures. In 1956, Disneyland attracted nearly four million tourists who delighted in discovering different times and spaces with maximum thrill and illusion of danger while simultaneously experiencing a spotless and idyllic universe without sex, violence, or social problems. The 50-millionth visitor entered the turnstiles in 1965 and the park has maintained its exceptional popularity ever since, becoming a pilgrimage destination for middle-class families. Contrary to the traditional amusement park, which attracted undesirable guests such as prostitutes, rakes, smugglers, and thieves, and the development of criminal activities as their popularity grew, Disneyland is the prototypical theme park, planned and engineered down to the tiniest detail to ensure perfect safety, control, and predictability.

Disneyland's triumph was not easily replicable, but in 1961, Six Flags over Texas opened and became the first successful regional theme park, followed in 1967 by Six Flags over Georgia. During the late 1960s and 1970s, large corporations such as Anheuser-Busch, Harcourt Brace Jovanovich, Marriott Corporation, MCA, Inc., and Taft Broadcasting invested in theme parks well connected to the interstate highway system and would dominate the industry. In 1971, Walt Disney World, the world's largest tourist attraction, opened on 27,500 acres in Lake Buena Vista, Florida. Costing $250 million, it was the most expensive theme park of that time, a comprehensive vacationland with theme attractions, hotels, resorts, and numerous recreational facilities. Less than 10 years later, in 1982, the $900 million futuristic EPCOT Center was added. In the 1980s, facing the threat of domestic market saturation, the industry successfully exported the amusement park concept throughout the world. Meanwhile, the growing interest for historic preservation allowed some old amusement parks to regain some of their appeal. In 1987, Kennywood, in Pittsburgh, Pennsylvania, and Playland, in Rye, New York, became the first operating amusement parks to be listed on the National Register of Historic Places.

Despite their popularity, theme parks have been controversial and severely condemned by the intellectual community. Most criticisms focus on the inauthentic and fictitious character of the utopian visions offered; the controlled, passive, and sanitized experience they provide; the insidious promotion of an unchallenged belief in consumerism and technologies to answer political and social problems; and their spatial and social segregation. On the other hand, theme park visitors are certainly not so gullible as to believe in the reality of the experience they purchase, which allow them to become again for a few hours worry-free children filled with wonder and fascination.

—*Catherine C. Galley*

See also Theme Parks

Further Readings and References

Adams, J. A. (1991). *The amusement park industry: A history of technology and thrills.* Boston: Twayne.

Mangels, W. F. (1952). *The outdoor amusement industry from earliest times to present.* New York: Vantage Press.

Samuelson, D., & Yegoiants, W. (2001). *The American amusement park.* Osceola, WI: Motorbooks International.

ANDERSON, SHERWOOD

Sherwood Anderson (1876–1941) was an American author best known for his collection of stories, *Winesburg, Ohio* (1919). Anderson saw himself in the literary tradition of Whitman, Twain, and Dreiser, in that he sought to capture the essence of American life unadulterated by artistic pretense. Anderson portrayed Winesburg as a microcosm of modern America wherein he explored the dilemmas of modernity: the disappearance of the pastoral, the erosion of local traditions, and the advent of a monolithic popular culture and consumerism.

Anderson was born in Camden, Ohio, to Erwin and Emma Anderson. The family was forced to move frequently because of his father's fluctuating business prospects and eventually settled in Clyde, Ohio, in 1884. As a young adult, Anderson lived in Chicago and worked as an unskilled laborer until enlisting in the U.S. Army at the outbreak of the Spanish-American War. After the war, Anderson secured a job as a copywriter in Chicago and married Cornelia Lane. While in Chicago, Anderson became friends with many of the writers who would later influence his work: Floyd Dell, Theodore Dreiser, Ben Hecht, and Carl Sandburg.

In 1906, Anderson relocated to Cleveland to work as a manager at a mail-order house. In November of 1912, however, Anderson left his office midday, disappeared, and was found 4 days later in Cleveland, having suffered a mental breakdown. Anderson would later refer to this episode as his break with the materialistic existence he had thus far led and the beginning of his career as an artist and social critic of modern America.

In 1914, Anderson began to publish his work in the leftist journal *The Masses*. These early writings included stories that formed the nucleus of what became *Winesburg, Ohio*. Also during this formative period, Anderson published *Poor White* (1920), *The Triumph of the Egg* (1921), *Many Marriages* (1923), *Horses and Men* (1923), and *Dark Laughter* (1925).

Winesburg, Ohio is Anderson's best-known work and contains many of the themes important to his later writings. The book itself is a collection of 23 stories about a small Ohio town. Though written over a 4-year period (1915–1919), and often published individually as short stories, Anderson considered the work a cohesive whole as stated in his *Memoirs:*

"I felt that, taken together, they made something like a novel, a complete story." In this work, the narrator often uses a mock sentimentality toward Winesburg to express a reaction against the disintegration of community in the face of materialism and the lack of individual identity that resulted from this disintegration. Similar themes can also be found in the works of later modernists such as Hemingway, Fitzgerald, and Eliot.

While on a visit to Panama with his fourth wife, Eleanor Copenhaver, Anderson died of peritonitis brought on by swallowing a toothpick.

—*Jason Stacy*

Further Readings and References

Anderson, D. (Ed.). (1981). *Critical essays on Sherwood Anderson.* Boston: G. K. Hall.

Papinchak, R. (1992). *Sherwood Anderson: A study of the short fiction.* New York: Twayne.

Townsend, K. (1988). *Sherwood Anderson.* Boston: Houghton Mifflin.

ANNEXATION

Annexation of land is the principal means by which the territorial jurisdictions of local governments in the United States are expanded. Since land is a state subject, the statutes of at least 44 of 50 U.S. states identify conditions and procedures for annexation, as noted in 1993 by David Rusk. Almost all states in the Midwest and South have such laws while very few in the Northeast do.

Annexation can result in advantages and disadvantages for those whose property is annexed as well as for the annexing municipality. For owners of annexed land, possible benefits include better or cheaper access to municipal services and higher property prices (especially if the property is undeveloped and can be developed at higher densities or intensities after annexation). The disadvantages they may face include higher property taxes and a real or perceived dilution of political control. For cities, annexation helps in efforts toward orderly development in fringe areas, allowing for expansion of the local tax base, and developing the potential for economies of scale in the provision of municipal services from the larger population served. However, the greater need for capital expenses to build infrastructure in newly annexed areas can be a significant drain on municipal budgets, as noted by Eric Damien Kelly in 1993.

The process of annexation can be initiated by a property owner wanting to be annexed to a city or by a city wanting to annex land outside its jurisdiction. Voluntary annexation is when both parties, that is, the property owners and the municipality, are supportive of the action. By and large, this is the only type of annexation allowed in Northeastern states. When cities choose to annex extraterritorial land without the consent of landowners, which cities sometimes do, it is termed *involuntary annexation.* Since municipal approval is required for annexations in all but five states, as Kelly wrote, annexation is rarely involuntary for a municipality.

Requirements for annexations when specified in state statutes typically include conditions of contiguity, appropriate authority (or authorities), application procedures, guidelines for determination of annexation fees, hearing and review processes, and timelines for decisions. Several states require approval by a third party: in the case of 5 states, a judicial review, whereas in 10 states, approval by a quasijudicial body, as noted by Kelly. Eleven states require approval by the county government. About 19 states require annexation proposals to be approved by a majority of owners of the area being annexed, while a smaller number of states require approval from a majority of the voters within the annexing city, as noted by Rusk. Washington has a triple majority requirement requiring approval of annexation proposals by majorities of the annexing city, as well as of land parcels and land valuations involved; on the other hand, Idaho, Nebraska and North Carolina allow unilateral annexation by the municipality, as noted by Thomas D. Galloway and John D. Landis in 1986. About three fifths of the states require annexation proposals to be debated in public hearings. Since 1971, concerned about municipalities using annexation powers to add primarily white areas to cities and thereby diluting the political strength of other racial and ethnic groups, many states have required municipalities to have their annexation proposals cleared by the U.S. Department of Justice, as noted by Rusk.

By way of example, some of the statutory regulations pertaining to annexation in the Midwestern state of Iowa are as follows.

- Criteria for annexation: The land in question must adjoin current city limits for a minimum of 50 feet and if annexed, must not create an island of unannexed land surrounded by the city.

- Types of annexations: Iowa statues differentiate between voluntary and involuntary annexations; in voluntary annexations up to 20 percent of the total land area may be annexed without the owner's consent.

- Process for involuntary annexation: A petition for involuntary annexation of surrounding land may be filed by a city council with the state land development board, with a copy served upon governing bodies of all affected jurisdictions. This petition must include various types of demographic and socioeconomic information as well as a description of existing municipal services in the land to be annexed and plans for extension of municipal services by the annexing city. The petitioner is required to publish notice of the proposed annexation, hold a public hearing about the proposal, and disseminate the minutes of that public meeting to all concerned governing bodies.

In growing urban areas, cities within the region may engage in competing efforts and acrimonious debates to annex adjacent lands. Often smaller cities, with lower tax rates and significant growth prospects, win such battles, leaving older, larger cities with less potential for increasing their taxable land base. Annexation processes are also influenced by the degree of state support for incorporation of new municipalities. Kelly wrote that states such as Oregon and Illinois allow for easier incorporation that may thwart annexation efforts, while Rusk noted that states such as New Mexico, which requires a 5-mile distance between an existing municipality and a newly incorporated one, may encourage annexation.

In the recent past there have been more and more public and political debates about the phenomenon of urban sprawl, and annexation powers of municipalities can affect sprawl. Some urban scholars contend that if municipal annexation powers are very broad, then annexation wars in urban areas with multiple local governments can promote sprawl. Other scholars disagree by noting that broad annexation powers can be used to prevent fragmentation of urban governance, an oft-cited limitation to potential benefits from many quality-of-life enhancing programs.

—Jerry Anthony

Further Readings and References

Galloway, T. D., & Landis, J. D. (1986). How cities expand: Does state law make a difference? *Growth and Change, 17,* 25–45.

Kelly, E. D. (1993). *Managing community growth.* Westport, CT: Praeger Press.

Porter, D. (1997). *Managing growth in America's communities.* Washington, DC: Island Press.

Rusk, D. (1993). *Cities without suburbs.* Baltimore, MD: Johns Hopkins University Press.

APARTMENT BUILDINGS

Apartment building is a general term used to describe a variety of multifamily dwelling types. Ranging from small to large, modest to luxurious, apartment buildings contain suites of rooms which include all the basic functions necessary for domestic life. As American urban populations grew dramatically in the 19th century, demand for housing skyrocketed. Lack of widespread, affordable transit meant that more and more people were concentrated in a limited area. This drove land costs up, and made single-family housing less and less financially feasible. All different kinds of apartment buildings were designed and built to accommodate the surge in population in the available urban space.

Aside from the physical differences between the apartment building and its counterpart, the single-family dwelling, residential tenure has played another, significant role in differentiating between the two in American society. While either may be owned or rented, it is generally true that apartment dwellers rent and house occupants own or purchase. A long-standing cultural and public policy bias favoring ownership over tenancy has combined with a similarly constructed predisposition for freestanding houses over multistory apartments. The result is that, despite the popularity and sometimes luxurious conditions of apartment living, this residential choice has long suffered second-class status in the United States.

Though apartment buildings began to appear in growing European cities during the 1500s, they date from much earlier. Multistory *insulae* were common in Rome during antiquity, as that city and others grew much faster in population than in area. After centuries of urban depopulation, places such as Paris and Berlin gradually became characterized by concentrations of large and elaborate apartment structures, home to elite and middle-class urbanites—although less distinguished buildings occupied by laborers were quite common. In Europe, a civic culture evolved wherein the need for residential density combined with the prestige of living near the center city to make urban apartment buildings perfectly respectable shelter for all social classes. This contrasted sharply with the distinctly subordinate position for downtown apartment living in the United States.

Apartments came to North American cities later, for a number of reasons. Dispersed settlement patterns kept most urban land relatively affordable until later in the 19th century, when an increasing convergence of social and economic forces significantly altered the housing market. Immigration, migration, and industrialization were nothing new, yet by the 1800s these factors interacted at a higher order of magnitude, dramatically driving up many cities' populations. Still, affordable, transit-enabling, large-scale decentralization was not yet viable. All of this resulted in a constantly expanding demand for shelter within the same amount of space. Smaller houses on smaller lots offered one solution for increasing density, but this was nowhere near sufficient in the largest cities.

New York City—Manhattan—showed these urban symptoms in highest relief, since its boundaries were fixed on all sides by water. Poor immigrants and American laborers packed into the first multiple dwellings, tenements, beginning in the 1830s. By the 1850s it was apparent that middle-income households would not be able to afford a row house or detached residence for much longer. And, while multifamily housing already existed for the poor, this idea of sharing a structure with other households offended "proper" sensibilities about family domesticity. The skyrocketing costs of land and housing trumped the social question, however. Apartment buildings were built and filled at an astonishing pace. As other U.S. cities grew and the Yankee experiment with so-called French flats proved economically feasible (if culturally suspect), apartment buildings began appearing in many places, like Chicago, Boston, and Washington, D.C.

The first apartment building in the United States is often considered to be Stuyvesant House in New York City, completed in 1870. Recent scholarship has indicated, however, that experimentation by builders, architects and realtors with the multiple-unit dwelling designed for middle-class occupancy began at least a decade earlier. This innovation came as a direct result of the notorious reputation of the proliferating tenement, an earlier multifamily structure infamous for crowding, poor construction, and inadequate sanitation. The apartment building was, in essence, a superior version of the tenement house. Both were multifamily housing, but apartment developers typically built their properties more substantially and provided them with more space, additional amenities, and better locations.

Not all apartment buildings are the same. Architecturally, they can be anything from a small, two-story building to a massive high-rise block with hundreds of units. The term *apartment building* is commonly used for anything larger than a duplex (two-unit structure) or triplex (three units). The all-inclusive *apartment* label obscures some important distinctions between larger and smaller multiple dwellings, however. Not only does each have different physical and economic characteristics; each varies in relative "acceptability" when compared to single-family housing in mainstream United States culture. Big apartment buildings have long been considered nuisances by neighboring home-owners; yet smaller structures of a few units—sometimes actually designed to resemble a large house—have often escaped this disapproval.

Though multifamily housing began in dense urban settings, as the 20th century progressed "garden-style" apartments (set on large landscaped lots) began to appear in both urban and suburban settings. Such development became popular as demand for affordable rental housing grew. Garden apartments were particularly favored by emerging municipal housing authorities as the model for new public housing projects starting in the 1930s.

Despite a cultural emphasis on ownership of detached dwellings and a concomitant suspicion of rented and "shared" housing, apartments became very popular. Some in America even saw promise for social betterment in this unusual housing form. Some utopians, such as Edward Bellamy, envisioned a positive future for American cities of multifamily housing set in parks. One segment of late-19th-century feminists regarded the newly popular multiple-dwelling structures—especially those with common kitchens, dining rooms, and play areas—as the best hope for the liberation of women from the burdens of housework and child care.

—*Todd Gish*

See also Tenement

Further Readings and References

Baar, K. (1992). The national movement to halt the spread of multifamily housing, 1890–1926. *Journal of the American Planning Association, 58,* 39–48.

Cromley, E. (1990). *Alone together: A history of New York's early apartments.* Ithaca, NY: Cornell University Press.

Doucet, M., & Weaver, J. (1991). The North American apartment building as a matter of business and an expression of culture: A survey and case study, 1900s–1980s. In *Housing the North American city* (pp. 388–419). Montreal: McGill-Queen's University Press.

Hancock, J. (1980). The apartment house in urban America. In Anthony D. King (Ed.), *Buildings and society: Essays on the social development of the built environment* (pp. 151–189). London: Routledge & Kegan Paul.

Hayden, D. (1981). *The grand domestic revolution.* Cambridge, MA: MIT Press.

Wright, G. (1981). The advantages of apartment life. In *Building the dream: A social history of housing in America* (pp. 135–151). Cambridge, MA: MIT Press.

ARCHITECTURE

American urban architecture is vast and complex, yet particular building types or architectural theories can be read in parallel with larger shifts in American society. What follows is a broad outline of American urban architecture, mixing a selection of notable buildings with ordinary ones. Together, they compose the architecture of the American city.

Early America

The earliest American city (and, subsequently, the earliest urban architecture) may have been the Mississippian Native American site of Cahokia and its mounds, an approximately 6-square-mile site located near the confluence of the Mississippi, Missouri, and Illinois Rivers in present-day East St. Louis, Illinois. Thriving between 900 and 1200, records indicate that as many as 30,000 people may have lived in and around this site by the late 1100s—a figure which, if true, makes Cahokia the largest North American settlement until the rise of Philadelphia in the late 18th century. As many as 120 mounds (raised pyramidal earthworks) along with six large plazas marked the site. Most significant was the broad, 100-foot, earth-built terraced "Monk's Mound," a platform for royal, ritual, or administrative functions. Yet it remains unclear whether Cahokia was a permanent urban settlement with a complex social structure or, perhaps like Poverty Point in Louisiana's West Carroll Parish (circa 1000 BCE), an occasional ceremonial or pilgrimage site.

Beginning around 900 in the arid setting of Chaco Canyon, New Mexico, the Ancestral Pueblos, or *Anasazi,* also began erecting a number of large masonry complexes. The largest of these, the D-shaped Pueblo Bonito, featured as many as 800 rooms, 30 of which resemble circular, subterranean ritual spaces knows as *kivas.* Because of ancient roads stretching some 65 miles to other ancestral pueblo sites, Pueblo Bonito has been variously interpreted as a royal residence, an ancient apartment building, or the urban center of an extensive ancient economic or political network. Whether the Chacoan settlements, as well as the cliff dwellings of Mesa Verde in nearby southwestern Colorado (1100–1300), constitute examples of early American urban architecture also remains unclear.

More is known about the architecture of early British colonial towns in New England and Virginia, of which settlers intended some of the buildings as part of a communal, if not urban, environment. Despite its almost complete restoration, Williamsburg, Virginia, is noted for a handful of impressive administrative buildings based upon English Baroque precedents. Together with the main building for the College of William and Mary (1695–1702), the Capitol Building (1701–1705), and the Governor's Palace (1706–1720) were a series of less permanent residences, shops, pharmacies, and taverns lining muddy streets. In such buildings and spaces, much of the everyday work of the colony took place.

Eighteenth-century colonial cities remained small, however. The largest were the principal seaports: Philadelphia, Boston, New York, Newport, and Charleston. In 1765, Philadelphia was the biggest, boasting 20,000 people, with its State House (Independence Hall) (1732–1753) and Christ Church (1727–1754) among its most prominent buildings. Their towers, or steeples, featured an eclectic array of ornament that suggested colonial builders' awareness of British church architecture. This is understandable, for colonial builders had access to British architectural pattern books such as James Gibbs's *Book of Architecture* (1728). Pattern book templates for church design directly influenced Boston's Christ Church (Old North) (1723) and its Old South Meetinghouse

(1729–1730), as well as Charleston's St. Michael's Church (1752–1761).

An Architecture of Democracy

Following the Revolution, Thomas Jefferson (an architect as well as a politician) turned to the architecture of ancient Rome as an appropriate model for a new nation because of its suggestions of civic virtue. While Jefferson's buildings were mostly rural, by the 1810s his adoption of antiquity spurred a national revival of classically inspired buildings. While Jefferson favored Rome (as in his 1785 to 1792 design for the state capitol in Richmond, Virginia), architects and builders also considered ancient Greek architecture an architectural precedent for a democratic nation. Private buildings with an important civic presence, such as William Strickland's Second Bank of the United States in Philadelphia (1818–1824), Alexander Parris's main building at Quincy Market in Boston (1825), and J. C. Bucklin and Russell Warren's Providence Arcade (1827–1829), borrowed from the Greek tradition. Public buildings were also erected as part of this "Greek Revival," including the Ohio State Capitol in Columbus (1839–1861) and the Fairmount Water Works in Philadelphia (1812–1815).

Yet the Greek Revival did not dominate the national urban scene, even in Washington, D.C. Thomas U. Walter's redesign of the U.S. Capitol Building, with its cast-iron dome, drew upon the European Renaissance (1851–1865); Robert Mills's Washington Monument, after a slow start, rose in the manner of an Egyptian obelisk (1848–1884); and James Renwick's Smithsonian Institution Building (1847–1855) brought a version of the Romanesque to the national mall. In the early 19th century, however, Washington, D.C., principally remained an administrative center with monumental buildings; it lacked the urban infill, or the substantial population, constitutive of a city.

Industry and Expansion

Industrialization, however, attracted tens of thousands of immigrants to other early-19th-century cities along the eastern seaboard. New urban building types, including hotels, tenements, railway stations, warehouses, and factories emerged in the wake of industrialization and immigration. The mass production of iron and glass also expanded architectural possibilities.

Following the 1825 opening of the Erie Canal, immigrants to New York City crowded into Manhattan's Lower East and West sides to take advantage of work opportunities. By the 1850s, many had moved into "railroad tenements," thin, subdivided blocks of two-room apartments that lacked plumbing and proper ventilation but nonetheless provided an upgrade from previous living conditions. An 1879 tenement house law required developers to build on smaller lots and provide better ventilation, resulting in the popular dumbbell plan soon adopted for thousands of tenements. By 1900, tenements housed more than three quarters of the city's 20 million people, but they were overcrowded and unsanitary despite some improvements. Architecturally, however, they put on a memorable urban face: cornices topped their brick facades, and window surrounds included decorative arches with voussoirs and keystones.

In general, 19th-century American cities struggled to mediate between their rapid industrialization and their physical appearance. Mass-produced row houses in cities such as Baltimore and Philadelphia usually featured some level of architectural detail, and even the cast-iron fronts of dry goods warehouses, department stores, and shops in cities nationwide were built to suggest they were traditional building types made of stone. The cast-iron façade of John P. Gaynor's E. P. Haughwout Store in New York (1857) resembled that of a Renaissance palazzo; similarly, the façade of the Zion's Co-operative Mercantile Institution in Salt Lake City (1876) was cast into Corinthian pilasters and decorative brackets. Such exterior treatment countered the industrial character of the materials and served to temper the commercial activity located within. In New Orleans, lacy decorative ironwork ascribed to no particular style, but nonetheless appeared on the façades of numerous downtown buildings and single-family homes.

As urban development stretched westward in the early 19th century, builders, architects, and urban elites counteracted the otherwise haphazard and shoddily-built appearance of these "frontier" or "instant" cities with imposing stone or brick buildings designed in traditional styles. Yet such architecture masked other circumstances—and a less-refined built environment. Tucked behind the financial districts of Western American cities were areas of neglect or ill repute. In San Francisco, blatant discrimination relegated Chinese immigrants to a 9-square-block area just northwest of downtown, composed of speculative buildings erected in the early years of settlement in the 1850s. San Francisco's Chinatown gradually established its own distinctive architectural character, but ethnic neighborhoods in 19th-century American cities were rarely afforded the dignified treatment of the business district.

Commerce and Civility

The introduction of steel into the late-19th-century architectural lexicon permitted the world's first skyscrapers. Coupled with elevators and fireproofing techniques, many skeletal steel frames rose in the wake of Chicago's 1871 fire, none grander than that provided for Burnham and Root's Masonic Temple (1892), which at 22 stories and 302 feet was once the world's tallest building. Architects who designed skyscrapers responded to developers' wishes to maximize office space within tight downtown lots, but they did so with respect to potential clients or consumers who preferred luxury and tradition to technological innovation. Thus, it was not uncommon to discover skyscrapers with ornate, atrium-style lobbies and decorative façades. Louis Sullivan's Schlesinger & Mayer Store (1899–1904), which is now Carson Pirie Scott owned by Sak's Incorporated, featured elaborate iron ornamentation at street level, intended to capture the attention of passersby; early skyscrapers in New York, meanwhile, commonly featured spires resembling those found on medieval churches or guild halls.

Given this ideological climate, it is not surprising that the Richardsonian Romanesque, derived from the work of architect Henry Hobson Richardson, found an appropriate home in the late-19th-century American city. Buildings erected in this style, with their heavy rusticated stone walls, bold massing, and large arches, conveyed an air of solidity and permanence popular with civic structures. These buildings included Pittsburgh's Allegheny County Courthouse and Jail (1884–1888), begun by Richardson and completed by his successor firm, Shepley, Rutan and Coolidge, as well as a series of buildings erected in Seattle's Pioneer Square in the 1890s that signaled that city's resurgence after a disastrous 1889 fire.

On the edges of American downtowns, balloon-frame construction, machine-made lumber, and mass-produced nails contributed to rapid residential construction. With the development of the electric streetcar, developers bought land along or near rail lines and erected thousands of residential dwellings, many of which featured identical floor plans but exterior detail that recalled medieval traditions. With milling machinery and plentiful wood, such detail was not expensive. In San Francisco, the ubiquitous "Victorians" were predominantly of this sort; erected en masse by the 1870s to house a working- and middle-class urban population, but doing so with an architectural panache that belied their assembly-line production.

Representative of the long-standing effort to combat the industrial and commercial city was the 1893 World's Columbian Exposition in Chicago. Daniel Burnham orchestrated the grand, Baroque plan and hired architects trained at the classically oriented École des Beaux-Arts in Paris to design the fair's principal buildings, including George B. Post, Richard Morris Hunt, and the firm of McKim, Mead and White. Most of the building façades were produced in white plaster, but their classical details, shared massing, and generally consistent roofline suggested a civilized, orderly city that contrasted sharply with the haphazard skyline of the 19th-century commercial and industrial metropolis. Although no American cities were completely reorganized along these lines, the fair inspired the City Beautiful Movement and helped legitimize revival styles for urban architecture until well into the 20th century—an attempt to put a civilized face on the metropolis. Among the more notable examples were Burnham's own classical Union Station in Washington, D.C. (1903–1907) and Cass Gilbert's Woolworth Building in New York City (1911–1913)—a Gothic skyscraper popularly dubbed the "Cathedral of Commerce."

Optimism and Decline

Revival styles continued to dominate the urban scene for important buildings beyond the First World War. But zoning ordinances passed in cities such as New York (1916) and Chicago (1923) to reduce skyscraper bulk and bring more light and air into downtowns required developers to step back their buildings above a certain height. The jagged profile of a number of skyscrapers was the result, and a few cities adopted this profile even when there was no need. Some buildings were particularly flamboyant: William Van Alen's Chrysler Building in New York (1928–1930) featured a frieze of stylized hubcaps, tires, and gargoyles resembling hood ornaments. Given the growth of advertising and marketing, such "Art Deco"

imagery seemed appropriate for the optimistic 1920s. Meanwhile, the new cinemas, such as Meyer and Holler's Grauman's Chinese Theater in Los Angeles (1923), frequently drew from non-Western precedents to suggest the exotic—an allusion to the fantasy and escape shown on the screens inside.

American cities continued to be places of residence in the interwar years, as well as places of work. Although most of the middle and upper classes had moved to the suburbs, thousands of apartments and residential hotels existed in the shadow of the high-rise office towers. Some apartment buildings, especially in New York and Chicago, were lavishly apportioned and housed the fairly well off. Yet there were also many unadorned, single-room occupancy hotels housing temporary or full-time, working-class residents and retirees. As late as 1930, as many as 18 residents shared a single toilet per floor in these hotels.

Conditions were especially difficult for American cities during the Great Depression, and privately funded construction virtually came to a halt. With some exceptions, such as the collection of small Art Deco hotels and apartments lining Miami Beach, most urban developments in the 1930s were federally sponsored public buildings that emerged from New Deal legislation, such as courthouses, city halls, post offices, and mints. To suggest confidence and resiliency, these buildings, such as those in Washington, D.C.'s Federal Triangle, were designed in a stripped-down classical mode. The New Deal also created the Public Works Administration, which provided funds for public housing. Borrowing from European housing of the 1910s and 1920s, American developments were characterized by low-rise blocks with flat roofs organized around courtyards. Although a few exceptions were sensitive to their urban contexts and outfitted with a range of communal services, such as Oskar Stonorov and Albert Kastner's Carl Mackley Houses in Philadelphia (1932–1934), many were poorly maintained, designed with minimal detail, and set back from the street.

Modernist Visions

Mass housing, built in conjunction with shipbuilding and airplane manufacturing, composed urban architecture during World War II. Western cities and regions received the bulk of this construction, especially in Los Angeles, the San Francisco Bay Area,

Portland, and Seattle. In Vanport, Oregon, and Hanford, Washington, assembly-line construction created "instant" cities of minimally apportioned single-family residences for workers and their families.

In the postwar years, publicly funded high-rise housing projects, built on cleared land near the city center, dominated the image of American urban housing. Erected primarily for poor residents in eastern and midwestern cities, these projects, like their 1930s forebears, were set back from the street and featured little ornament. Yet they were significantly taller, and many lacked play areas and sufficient green space. The much-maligned collection of Pruitt-Igoe Houses in St. Louis (1950–1964) were 11 stories each; the towers that composed the Robert Taylor Homes in Chicago (1960–1962) were 16 stories.

Housing projects were debatably part of an urban strategy to remove older housing stock—and the urban poor—from the city center. Also rising were concrete, glass, and steel office buildings, civic centers, hotels, theaters, plazas, and stadiums that, together, provided a new image for the postwar American city. New skyscrapers followed the lead of German émigré Ludwig Mies van der Rohe, whose 860–880 Lake Shore Drive Apartments in Chicago (1949–1951) offered a prototype for the modernist, "international style" high-rise: minimally detailed, raised steel boxes with flat roofs and glass curtain walls, set back from the street in their own plazas. The largely undifferentiated and seemingly nonhierarchical façades of Mies van der Rohe's buildings, despite his exquisite materials and fine proportions, gave them a rational, utilitarian look that suggested progress and appealed to private developers. They turned to architects such as Skidmore, Owings, and Merrill (SOM) to design corporate headquarters in the Mies van der Rohe manner, even if their budgets did not permit a similar level of detail. Nonetheless, the principles of setting a sculptural concrete, steel, or glass tower away from the city persisted. Along with the ribbons of freeways cutting into, around, and through cities, modernist skyscrapers ushered in a clean, organized, and pragmatic architectural vision for the postwar American city.

The Future Past

According to urban critic Jane Jacobs, this vision was also dull and, even worse, destructive. In her influential book *The Death and Life of Great American Cities* (1960), Jacobs castigated postwar urban American planning for "sacking" American cities, obliterating the traditional street, and ruining public life. She favored, instead, the everyday urban environment of sidewalks, walk-up apartments, parks, stores, and bars which she discovered in New York's Greenwich Village and Boston's North End.

Although the destruction of older buildings and neighborhoods for modernist high rises and expressways dominated the American urban landscape in the 1960s and 1970s, there were moments of preservation and adaptive reuse that signaled a renewed attention to the historic fabric and the walking city that loosely subscribed to Jacobs's ideals. Victor Gruen's pedestrian malls appeared in downtown Kalamazoo, Michigan (1959) and Fresno, California (1964), while Wurster, Bernardi, and Emmons transformed old chocolate factory buildings into the Ghirardelli Square shopping center in San Francisco (1962–1967). Developer James Rouse hired Benjamin Thompson and Associates to remake Boston's Quincy Market into the Faneuil Hall Marketplace (1971–1976), a pedestrian-oriented "festival marketplace" featuring shops, restaurants, and plazas that attracted tourists and suburbanites back to the urban heart.

In the late 1970s and 1980s, a number of architects turned their attention away from modernist aesthetics. Michael Graves's Portland Public Services Building (1978–1982) in Portland, built on a tight budget, featured a pastel-colored façade with a giant keystone, pilasters, decorative garlands, and an enormous sculpture—defying the modernist desire to strip façades to their minimum. Charles Moore's Piazza d'Italia (1978–1989), a sculptural ensemble designed for New Orleans' Italian-American community, offered another version of "postmodern" urban architecture. Hard up against the modernist high-rises of Canal Street, Moore combined stainless steel and neon with intentionally ironic references to architectural classicism. Philip Johnson and John Burgee, meanwhile, designed a glass skyscraper in the form of a Gothic tower for the Pittsburgh Plate Glass Company in Pittsburgh (1982).

Cities of Culture

Yet many of these postmodern gestures were little more than façade changes, and not all late 20th-century architects turned back to the past in any event. Helmut Jahn was one of many architects noted for exposing the structural attributes of his buildings, as demonstrated most explicitly in his James R. Thompson Center (1980–1985) and United Airlines Terminal in Chicago (1985–1989)—both decidedly modernist gestures. Even the idea of the traditional downtown came in for question, as corporate high- and low-rises, housing, and shopping appeared regularly on the far-flung edges of American cities, often well beyond the postwar suburbs. These "Edge Cities"—such as Tyson's Corner, Virginia; Plano, Texas; and Irvine, California—rarely featured signature works by noted architects, but their reflective glass office buildings and lack of pedestrian activity continued the modern urban and architectural legacy. To help counter the progressive flight of residents from American cities, developers renovated decayed houses or converted warehouses into lofts. This frequently spurred downtown gentrification, making early 21st-century cities the residential provinces of the wealthy.

The turn of the millennium has also witnessed urban development turning increasingly toward entertainment and "culture" rather than commerce—a reversal of the late-19th-century trend. Buildings regularly making a splash in the headlines are museums, concert halls, or libraries designed by superstar architects or architectural firms. While American architects, such as Frank Gehry, Richard Meier, and I. M. Pei, have gained some of these commissions, international architects garner the lion's share in an increasingly competitive global architectural climate. Medium-sized cities such as Cincinnati, Milwaukee, and Fort Worth have looked to privately funded buildings by the likes of Zaha Hadid, Santiago Calatrava, or Tadao Ando to resuscitate their flagging local economies, while larger cities, such as Seattle, with its public library by Dutch architect Rem Koolhaas (2004), and San Francisco, with its de Young Museum by the Swiss architects Jacques Herzog and Pierre de Meuron (2005), banked upon high-profile buildings to transform their architectural reputations. The desire for highly iconic architecture in American cities has not diminished, despite the coordinated attacks that destroyed New York's World Trade Center on September 11, 2001, and increased attention to surveillance and security in new urban developments.

Examples of "sustainable" or "green" architecture have also made their way into American cities, in part because urban governments have offered incentives for buildings that meet environmental criteria for energy efficiency. Croxton Collaborative provided a model with their renovation of an 1890s building in New York City for the National Audubon Society (1989–1992). Stripped-down modernist housing projects are also no longer considered a panacea for low-income urban residents. Many have been demolished in favor of colorful, mixed-use, low-rise developments with gables, bays, pitched roofs, and courtyards intended to foster a sense of urban community. Michael Pyatok has produced a number of these in Oakland and Seattle.

—*J. Philip Gruen*

See also Balloon-Frame Construction; Burnham, Daniel H.; Chicago School of Architecture; Chrysler Building; City Beautiful Movement; Elevators; Ethnic Neighborhoods; Financial Districts; Gentrification; Greenwich Village; Historic Preservation; Housing Act of 1949; Jacobs, Jane; Movie Theaters and Urban Space; Museums; Pedestrian Malls; Philadelphia, Pennsylvania; Plazas; Postmodernism; Pruitt-Igoe Housing Project; Rouse, James W.; Skyscrapers; Streetcar Suburbs; Sullivan, Louis Henri; World Fairs and Expositions; Woolworth Building

Further Readings and References

Dickens, C. (1966). *American notes and pictures from Italy.* London: Oxford University Press. (Original work published 1842)

Ford, L. R. (1994). *Cities and buildings: skyscrapers, skid rows, and suburbs.* Baltimore: Johns Hopkins University Press.

Gelernter, M. (2001). *A history of American architecture: Buildings in their cultural and technological context.* Hanover, NH: University Press of New England.

Ghirardo, D. (1996). *Architecture after modernism.* London: Thames & Hudson.

Girouard, M. (1985). *Cities and people: A social and architectural history.* New Haven, CT: Yale University Press.

Gowans, A. (1964). *Images of American living: Four centuries of architecture and furniture as cultural expression.* Philadelphia: J. B. Lippincott.

Handlin, D. P. (2004). *American architecture* (2nd ed.). London: Thames & Hudson.

Jacobs, J. (1960). *The death and life of great American cities.* New York: Random House.

Roth, L. M. (2001). *American architecture: A history.* Boulder, CO: Westview Press.

Upton, D. (1998). *Architecture in the United States.* Oxford, UK: Oxford University Press.

ARMOUR, PHILIP DANFORTH

In the history of Chicago's manufacturing might, one of the key sources of employment for Chicago, as well as a key part of its growth, was the meatpacking industry of the Stockyards district (from 39th to 47th streets, Ashland to Halsted). Of the major employers in the Stockyards area, the two largest were the Swift company, run by Gustavus Swift, and the Armour company, run by Philip Danforth Armour (1832–1901).

Born into a farming family near Oneida, New York, in 1832, Armour sought riches early on. At the age of 17, he left for the California Gold Rush. After spending time in California, where he earned a small fortune ($8,000, by some accounts), he moved to Cincinnati, then Milwaukee, where he worked in the meatpacking industry. Finally, he moved to Chicago and set up operation where he could be closer to the railheads and therefore the animals from the Great Plains.

Armour believed that all of the animal should be used in production. He was innovative in the use of the disassembly line, where dozens of workers, usually lesser skilled immigrants, would cut apart a pig or cow with an efficiency that would make the Stockyards a tourist attraction in Chicago. A crew of up to 200 men was able to process an animal from a living beast to processed meat in less than 10 minutes. Armour believed that all parts of the animal should be used, and his fortune was made on the by-products that would be thrown away by smaller butchers: hair for brushes, bones for glue, hides for leather, and so on. Armour was proud of his work. In fact the motto of the company was quite simple, yet bold in scope: "We Feed the World."

To achieve the profits necessary to operate, Armour invested in new ideas such as reefer (refrigerated) cars on trains, ice-cutting stations (to furbish the reefer cars), and butcher shops on the East Coast in cities like New York and Boston. Whenever local butchers posed any sort of resistance to Armour, he simply undercut them, and then hired the butchers to sell Armour meats.

He had connections to the greatness that defined Chicago in the Gilded Age. His offices were in the Home Insurance Building (the first skyscraper), and his patronage of education resulted in the Armour Institute, now known as the Illinois Institute of Technology. He had his detractors, however. His use of pacers to speed up production often resulted in injuries on the job. He also had no compunctions in firing anyone who encouraged unionization of the workers. In the late 1800s, his offices were rocked by scandal, when it was revealed that the company mixed in tainted meat to make a profit. Regardless of how employees felt about him, his stature was large in Chicago. When he died in January of 1901, the papers noted that a driving force of Chicago had passed. If Armour had lived through the muckraking attacks several years later, his reputation may have been tarnished. But as it was, his name was synonymous with the opulence of Chicago.

—*Cord Scott*

Further Readings and References

Miller, D. (1996). *City of the century.* New York: Touchstone.
Spinney, R. (2000). *City of big shoulders.* DeKalb: Northern Illinois University Press.

ARMSTRONG, LOUIS

Louis Daniel Armstrong (1900–1971) was born in the Storyville District of New Orleans on August 4, 1900. Armstrong, who first began playing the cornet as a boy, was a musical sensation by the time he was 22 years old. Armstrong's mastery of the cornet and jazz improvisation brought him professional and artistic acclaim over the course of his career. He toured the world for over five decades, bringing joy to a countless number of people. Both his talent and longevity helped make him one of the most influential jazz musicians of the 20th century.

Armstrong grew up hustling for money on the streets of New Orleans. His mother was a part-time prostitute and his father abandoned the family shortly after Armstrong was born. As a result, Armstrong spent most of his childhood helping his mother earn extra money. Arrested for firing a friend's gun into the air on New Year's Eve, Armstrong spent several months in the Colored Waifs Home in 1913. It was there that Armstrong received his first formal music lessons. He learned to play the cornet over the course of his stay and became an active member in the home's brass band.

Armstrong began hanging around local music clubs following his release in 1914. His favorite act was Joe "King" Oliver, a local musician who played with the Kid Ory Band. Oliver immediately took a liking to the young Armstrong, even offering to buy him his first cornet. It was not long before Armstrong was getting paid to sit in with Oliver and his band.

Oliver and Armstrong moved their act to Chicago in 1922, when they joined forces in Oliver's Creole Jazz Band. The group's brand of New Orleans jazz took the town by storm. By the mid-1920s, Armstrong was a star in his own right and ready to strike out on his own. He left Oliver to form his own band, called Louis Armstrong and the Hot Five, in 1925. Although they never toured, Armstrong and the Hot Five (later the Hot Seven) recorded several albums that went on to become jazz classics. It was during this period that Armstrong recorded the famous "St. Louis Blues" featuring Bessie Smith.

In 1929, Armstrong organized a touring band and set off on a tour that lasted almost 6 years. The band played for audiences all over the United States and Europe, including the King of England in 1932. However, big orchestras began to lose their popularity following World War II, forcing Armstrong to reevaluate his act. Despite his unique frontline formation of a single horn player, Armstrong and his manager, Joe Glaser, still felt the act needed to be updated. They hired a whole new group of musicians in 1947 and named them the Louis Armstrong All-Stars. The smaller band toured endlessly throughout the next two decades. They played all over the United States, Africa, Asia, South America, and Europe.

Armstrong's popularity reached its peak in the 1960s. He was known as America's Goodwill Ambassador and scored several number one hits, including "What a Wonderful World" and "Hello, Dolly." Armstrong continued to record throughout the last few years of his life. He died in his sleep on July 6, 1971.

—*Catherine Devon Griffis*

Further Readings and References

Armstrong, L. (1999). *Louis Armstrong in his own words.* Oxford, UK: Oxford University Press.

Bergreen, L. (1997). *Louis Armstrong: An extravagant life.* New York: Broadway Books.

ART AND PUBLIC SPACE

Art in public space is not the same as public art; the latter implies a large, general audience suggesting an ideal genre for a democracy. Yet, since the formation of the United States, issues surrounding the appropriate form and placement of art in public space, as well as its funding, have made the concept of public art all but an oxymoron, an object of controversy more often than consensus or celebration. Nevertheless, the implicit intension of all art placed in public space is that it is, in some often undefined way, for a public (as opposed to private) audience.

Today public art may take any form: abstract sculpture or figurative mural, city park, street furniture or lighting, and even community-based events with a sociopolitical focus organized by artists. However, the most familiar form of art in urban space remains memorial sculpture, and for centuries it was the only kind. Historically, commemorative monuments celebrated heroic men, deeds (usually of war), or virtues. Although George Washington was an undisputed national figure worthy of commemoration, finding a suitable memorial for him proved problematic in the extreme. Horatio Greenough, commissioned by Congress to create a portrait of our first president for the Capitol Rotunda, produced a 12-foot-high seated figure in classical Greek robe that became an instant object of controversy and graffiti. As a result, his *George Washington* (1832–1841) was removed to a more neutral and less visible outdoor location on the Capitol grounds and subsequently to even safer turf, the entrance hall of the Smithsonian Museum of History and Technology. The Washington Monument, a 555-foot obelisk on the Mall in the nation's capital, remains the structure most associated with the first president, yet it does not bear his image. The product of a lengthy and fraught process, it was designed by Robert Mills and completed in 1885, over a century after Congress voted to honor the first president with a monument.

Commemorating war was no less problematic. Building memorials raises issues regarding a particular war specifically and war in general. Traditional forms of war memorials such as victory arches or columns didn't reflect these problems. Debates began after World War I and became widespread after World War II as to whether it might not be better to build useful memorials, such as libraries or swimming pools, rather than structures whose only purpose was commemorative. The hope was that this might shift the focus from a controversial subject or structure to a general public benefit. From a public space perspective, this pitted social amenity against memorial object.

During the postwar period, at a time when the art world increasingly championed modern styles of art favoring abstraction, there was a concern that something could not be both modern and a monument; if it was not exclusively about art issues, it could not be art. There were only a few artists whose figurative memorials were accepted as art, notably George Segal with *In Memory of May 4, 1970, Kent State: Abraham and Isaac* (1978, now on the Princeton University campus), *Gay Liberation* (1980, in Sheridan Square Park, New York City), *The Steelmakers* (1980, in Youngstown, Ohio), and *The Holocaust* (1982, in San Francisco). The situation of artists of memorials not receiving art world approbation did not change until Maya Lin's Vietnam Veterans Memorial (1981) was installed on the Washington Mall between the Washington Monument and Lincoln Memorial. The wall takes the form of minimal sculpture, two 250-foot-long walls tapering to ground level at each end and rising in the middle to a height of 10 feet at the center where they meet. Made of black granite with a highly polished surface, listing the names of all the war dead or missing according to the day they died or disappeared, with its back embedded in the earth, it suggests a large national tombstone or house of death. Its audience moves along the memorial in a specific choreographed way, first into the space of death and then out again. The Vietnam Veterans Memorial, once the object of a huge controversy that resulted in the addition of a compromise figurative sculpture, *Three Fighting Men* (1984) by Frederick Hart, opposite its reflective wall, is today the most visited memorial in the nation's capital. Lin's use of the visual vocabulary of minimal sculpture (influenced by Richard Serra, who was teaching at Yale where she was an architecture student) and her listing of the names became a model for subsequent memorial sculpture. By providing both a mobile and tactile experience for the viewer, Lin's sculpture and many of its offshoots in effect created their own distinct and dedicated urban space.

Art in urban space that was not commemorative in nature was, for a time, sponsored by the federal government in response to the Great Depression of the 1930s. Art commissioned for federal buildings fell under the jurisdiction of the Treasury Department's Section of Painting and Sculpture (later the Section of Fine Arts). This agency, a precursor of the later Art-in-Architecture program of the General Services Administration (GSA), used 1 percent of construction costs for art. Much of the commissioned art was directly attached to public buildings in the form of murals or relief sculpture. Stylistically it expressed the streamlined mode typical of the 1930s design in architecture and industry. Concurrently, but under private patronage, Rockefeller Center (1931–1940) in the center of Manhattan, which is often cited as a paradigm of enlightened urban design, included an extensive public art program. Although the artworks as a whole have not been much admired, John D. Rockefeller Jr. set a precedent for urban design and art inclusion that was followed, with varying degrees of success, by his sons: John D. Rockefeller III at Lincoln Center in New York City; David Rockefeller at the Chase Manhattan Bank headquarters, also in New York City; and Nelson Rockefeller at the Empire State Plaza in Albany, New York.

Since the late 1960s, artworks, in ever increasing numbers and for various reasons, have been commissioned for public spaces. In terms of public policy, this publicly funded art was an extension of the liberal social-welfare programs of the Kennedy and Johnson administrations. The Great Society Task Force was created in 1964, the Department of Housing and Urban Development was created in 1965, and a year later the Model Cities Act was passed. By the decade's end, the National Endowment for the Arts inaugurated its Art in Public Places program with the installation of Alexander Calder's *La Grande Vitesse* (1969) in Grand Rapids, Michigan. Here Calder's sculpture became the focal point for much more than an empty urban space. Initially it prompted a controversy focused on the decision to replace the intended fountain with art, the American artist's choice to live and work in France and his abstract style. Ultimately, however, the sculpture became a civic symbol, the logo on official stationery and city vehicles, including garbage trucks. Eventually its site was renamed Calder Plaza.

Two years earlier the Chicago Picasso, also the object of much debate, eventually became a civic emblem as well. The commission, sponsored entirely by private funds, was spearheaded by William Hartmann of Skidmore Owings & Merrill (SOM), one of the architectural firms involved in building the Chicago Civic Center. Significantly, the civic center was one of the first modern buildings to include open public space in its design. In an attempt to respond to the style and nature of the building as well as to improve the quality of downtown life, the architects were motivated by European precedent. Mayor Richard Daley's support of the work by "the best artist in the world" (Pablo Picasso) insured a grudging acceptance. At the mayor's death, a local cartoonist depicted the sculpture shedding a tear. Although the work is an abstract conflation of Picasso's wife at the time, Jacqueline, and his pet Afghan hound, Kaboul, decidedly private references that have nothing to do with Chicago, it is a highly visible landmark in a significant urban space.

Similarly, abstract art in public places may also be used as corporate emblems. George Rickey's kinetic *Triple L Excentric Gyratory Gyratory II* (1986) consists of three L-shaped aluminum elements that move in the wind. When it was placed in front of Coca-Cola headquarters in Atlanta, Georgia, corporate executives renamed it *Leadership*. A brochure advertising the corporate art collection links the sculpture to qualities that distinguish the company's products and style of leadership: never static, always evolving.

As the public art revival of the late sixties expanded, artists and commissioners alike began thinking that art should have a significant connection to its local site. Site specific public art denotes work that is created for a particular space. It may be linked to that space through formal means, for example, shape or color or by embodying references to the history or nature of the site. By contrast, the works by Calder, Picasso, and Rickey discussed above relate to their urban sites only in a very general aesthetic way. In many instances the artists had never even visited the cities, let alone the specific places, where their art would be located. The development of site specific public art was an acknowledgment that placing art in an urban space was not enough. To justify the placement of art in the public domain, it was now felt, the work had to be linked to it in a meaningful way. However, site specificity didn't always translate clearly into the visual vocabulary of contemporary art. Thus, to an audience unfamiliar with such art, the nature of its site specificity often remained as obscure as the work itself.

As public art evolved during the 1970s and 1980s, concern over its relationship with its site was expressed in various ways. One way was to provide an urban counterpoint by introducing references to the unbuilt landscape using natural materials, primarily stone (like Noguchi's *Landscape of Time,* 1975, and Michael Heizer's *Adjacent, Against, Upon,* 1977, both in Seattle). Another was to introduce elements of water through contemporary fountains (such as Noguchi's *Horace E. Dodge and Son Memorial Fountain,* 1978, in Hart Plaza, Detroit, Michigan; Claes Oldenburg and Coosje van Bruggen's *Dropped Bowl With Scattered Slices and Peels,* 1990, in downtown Miami). Nancy Holt created urban sculptures that referenced natural phenomena like the summer and winter solstice (for example, *Annual Ring,* 1980–1981, in Saginaw, Michigan). Other artists created minilandscapes for urban sites (such as Elyn Zimmerman, *Marabar,* 1984, the National Geographic Building in Washington, D.C.). Another approach was to provide art that directly or indirectly addressed environmental issues. Patricia Johanson's *Fair Park Lagoon* (1981–1986, in Dallas), in the form of local flora, actually functions as land reclamation sculpture, controlling problems of erosion at the site, while Athena Tacha's *Green Acres* (1986, Department of Environmental Protection in Trenton, New Jersey) contains sandblasted photographic images that call attention to current environmental problems. Landscape elements appear accessible and engaging to all. Seen in the larger context of city planning, they have a vital function by introducing some of the proven restorative effects of nature. Many of these projects function equally as urban amenities and art. The expansion of public sculpture from single to site specific object to entire site was accompanied by an expansion of the definition of sculpture itself, which allowed for the inclusion of use. The notion of use in relationship to art challenged well-established definitions of art in Western European culture where art, that is to say high art, traditionally was not functional. In an urban context, however, use made sense. By the end of the 1980s the boundary between high and low art blurred, especially in the context of a growing focus on public art as an element of urban design rather than an adjunct to architecture. Thus George Sugarman included seating in his public art commissions (*Baltimore Federal,* 1975–1977; *A Garden of Sculpture,* 1989). Scott Burton created hybrid categories of sculpture/furniture (*Viewpoint,* 1981–1983, NOAA Western Regional Center in Seattle; *Untitled,* 1985–1986, Equitable Life in New York City). Siah Armajani created sculpture/architecture (*Irene Hixon Whitney Bridge,* 1985, in Minneapolis), and R. M. Fischer created a number of gates (*MacArthur Park Gateway,* 1985, in

Los Angeles; *Rector Gate,* 1985–1989, in Battery Park in New York), as did Lauren Ewing (*Endless Gate,* 1985, Seattle Center), while Donna Dennis focused on fences that depicted something of the history of the site (*Dreaming of Far Away Places: The Ships Come to Washington Market,* 1988, P.S. 234 in New York). A number of artists also created light sculptures, which added yet another urban amenity. Rockne Kreb's *Miami Line* (1984–1985), a 154-foot-long anodized steel and neon sculpture, creates a nocturnal rainbow along the local metrorail system, while Stephen Antonakos's *Neons for Exchange Place* (1990, Path Station, Jersey City, New Jersey) offers a constantly changing visual experience over the entire length of an escalator.

Beyond creating elements for the built environment such as street furniture or lighting that function as urban amenities as well as art, some artists created entire sites using the visual vocabulary of architecture. Ned Smyth created *Reverent Grove* (1978, Federal Courthouse, Charlotte Amalie, St. Thomas, U.S. Virgin Islands) as well as *Upper Room* (1987, Battery Park, New York), Andera Blum created *Ranier* (1984–1986, State Mental Health Facility in Buckly, Washington), and Kit-Yin Snyder created *Margaret Mitchell Square* (1986, Atlanta, Georgia). And one of the pioneers of public art in many categories, Isamu Noguchi, created playgrounds, notably *Playscapes* (1976, Atlanta, Georgia). Arguably, these artists assumed something of the function of both architect and urban designer.

With each new development in public art, focus turned more and more to perceived public needs in the urban environment. From art, to site specific art, to the evocation of landscape, and finally street furniture and the design of entire urban plazas, artists and their patrons sought to address perceived physical deficiencies in the urbanscape. In recent years, the focus has turned increasingly toward perceived social problems. Thus, in a period when postcolonial theory and social inequities dominated art world concerns, public art evolved to create public discourse rather than objects or sites in the public realm.

Over time, the NEA's Art in Public Places program, which was founded in 1967, reflected these developments. By 1974 it encouraged art that was "appropriate to its immediate site." Four years later it called for artists "to approach creatively the wide range of possibilities for art in public situations." This was followed the next year with a requirement for accompanying "methods to insure an informed common response to the project." By 1983, projects had to include planned activities "to educate and prepare the community" and "plans for community involvement, preparation, and dialogue." At the start of the 1990s the agency responsible for funding much of the art in contemporary urban spaces encouraged "educational activities which invite community involvement."

A series of exhibitions curated by Mary Jane Jacob illustrate the general evolution toward redefining the public element in public art. For *Places With a Past,* organized for the 1991 Spoleto Festival in Charleston, South Carolina, she selected well-established public artists to interpret sites that revealed the city's "forgotten history" rather than its well-known tourist sites. Two years later, in *Culture in Action,* curated for Sculpture Chicago, she involved artists directly with a variety of community groups rather than with a site. This resulted in temporary events such as a parade organized by Daniel Martinez and Vinzula Kara intended to foster civic pride and a video show created by teens working with Inigo Manglano-Ovalle and Robert Peters, installed in a neighborhood vacant lot. Both briefly redefined their urban environment in terms of community ownership. The video project was subsequently adopted by a local youth organization as a regular program. Another project, a hydroponic garden intended to grow organically pure products for an AIDS hospice (created by the artists' collaborative Haha) was also adopted by a community group and maintained for a number of years. In 1996 Jacob redefined public art and thereby its surrounding public space by further emphasizing its public dimension. *Conversations at the Castle: Changing Audiences and Contemporary Art,* created for the Olympics in Atlanta, consisted primarily of conversations that brought members of the public together with artists, critics, and curators. Instead of art in a public space, public art was now defined as civic dialogue. By implication, its attendant public space thus became a forum.

Today, at the start of the 21st century, all types of public art continue to be commissioned and installed in our urban spaces. From the art object that may serve as a memorial or simply as a photo op (or a climbing opportunity for the younger public audience) to urban amenities in the form of seating, lighting, or an entire urban plaza to temporary sociopolitical intervention—our relationship to our urban spaces is redefined.

—Harriet F. Senie

Further Readings and References

Bogart, M. H. (1989). *Public sculpture and the civic ideal in New York City 1890–1930.* Chicago: University of Chicago Press.

Costonis, J. J. (1989). *Icons and aliens: Law, aesthetics, and environmental change.* Urbana, IL: University of Illinois Press.

Doss, E. (1995). *Spirit poles and flying pigs: Public art and cultural democracy in American communities.* Washington, DC: Smithsonian Institution Press.

Finkelpearl, T. (2000). *Dialogues in public art.* Cambridge, MA: MIT Press.

Jacob, M. J., Brenson, M., & Olson, E. M. (1995). *Culture in action.* Seattle, WA: Bay Press.

Kramer, J. (1994). *Whose art is it?* Durham, NC: Duke University Press.

Mitchell, W. J. T. (Ed.). (1992). *Art and the public sphere.* Chicago: University of Chicago Press.

Senie, H. F. (1992). *Contemporary public sculpture: Tradition, transformation, and controversy.* New York: Oxford University Press.

Senie, H. F. (2002). *The tilted arc controversy: Dangerous precedent?* St. Paul: MN: University of Minnesota Press.

Senie, H. F., & Webster, S. (Eds.). (1998). *Critical issues in public art: Content, context, and controversy.* Washington, DC: Smithsonian Institution Press.

ASHCAN SCHOOL

The term *Ashcan School,* first used retrospectively by Holger Cahill and Alfred Barr in 1934, was loosely applied to American urban realist painters. Specifically, it referred to those members of The Eight, a group who after 1900 began painting ordinary aspects of city life. The group coalesced in Philadelphia around 1891 when Robert Henri attracted artist-reporters and newspaper illustrators around him. Henri, John Sloan, William J. Glackens, Everett Shinn, George Luks, Ernest Lawson, Maurice Prendergast, Arthur B. Davies, and later, George Bellows, were the informal core of painters who reacted against prevailing restrictive traditions and academic exhibition procedures.

Following consolidation of the five boroughs into New York in 1898, the city's transformation from a 19th-century manufacturing center and seaport into a 20th-century commercial metropolis occurred alongside population growth from immigration and migration, a subway infrastructure that promoted the movement of people and goods, and the consequent shifting of commercial and residential boundaries. The resulting sprawl led to increasing illegibility; the city evolved into a totality that was nevertheless composed of neighborhoods, subdivided into enclaves segregated along class and ethnic lines. Ashcan painters believed that the city was made more knowable by discerning the totality in each fragment and the group emphasized the street over the panorama, the local over the universal, domesticating the city by representing localities where life was distinguished by intimate knowledge of immediate surroundings. Painters selected just enough from the web of overlapping edges to suggest what they took to be the city.

The beginnings of industrialization and urbanization were ignored by the majority of painters, but modernization after 1900 inspired and affected American Impressionists and the Ashcan School. Mass immigration led to social, class, and ethnic tensions, and economic depression and industrial unrest contributed to a desire among cultural producers to promote and maintain a sense of a unified, harmoniously ordered world. Documentary photographic realism is almost entirely absent from painting until the emergence of the Ashcan School and even then, most painters, with the possible exception of Sloan, celebrated the vitality of the lower classes rather than criticizing their living conditions.

While pursuing themes similar to those of the Impressionists, Ashcan painters chose not to celebrate architectural transformation but to portray the city from the street up, and despite stylistic divergence, they shared a preference for a worm's-eye perspective. They presented the city as a mosaic of little worlds and communities, using a dark, subdued palette, resulting from Henri's trip to Europe, where he was influenced by Francisco José de Goya, Diego Velazquez, Franz Hals, and Édouard Manet. Ashcan paintings are fluid and spontaneous, very different from the polish of the work done in American academies at the time. Rapid handling of thickly applied paint left individual brushstrokes, but despite its apparent spontaneity, most Ashcan art is a carefully composed synthesis by a less than objective interpreter who, through careful, selective omission, arrived at a distanced and detached viewpoint.

Just as representations of the "ideal" city were believed to help assimilate immigrants, architects and planners claimed that public works as symbols of civic unity would enhance the city and Americanize a fragmented population. Despite its planned grid, the reality of New York's disordered chaos inspired Ashcan artists. The idea of New York as a City Beautiful was stimulated by pictures; magazines were illustrated with drawings while plans show open vistas and city functions separated and partitioned. Although considered more realistic, photographers were still selective, and they depicted the city as chaotic and illegible.

Photographs and, by extension, rapidly executed illustrations and paintings would most accurately depict, and so make legible, the single element and the whole. Ashcan painters became materialist historians, selecting fragments that could reveal the worlds residing in the smallest details. New York had by then become the center for nationally distributed illustrated magazines and, although photographs began to replace illustrations, the latter were still widely used. Images were important in the evolution of commercial culture, appearing as illustrations in the popular press and on the increasingly evident billboards and posters. Ashcan work shared similar thematic concerns with more commercial sources but, in American painting at least, there were few precedents for their urban subjects, and Ashcan painters were as prone to euphemism, selective omission, and optimism as most contemporary artists.

Public parks were originally conceived as part of plans for improvement through contact with nature. By 1900, Central Park, which was originally intended as a retreat, was crowded with the activities that Ashcan painters pictured as thoroughly integrated with the urban fabric. Glackens's *May Day, Central Park* (1905) emphasizes the crowd and belies the conformity of City Beautiful imagery. By distancing the spectator, Glackens makes unpredictability enjoyable. Depictions of Lower East Side streets show markets and sidewalk stands as social spaces, passages between distinct neighborhoods. Despite planners' rhetoric about the public good, attempts to force stands into special districts were part of an effort to divide the city into identifiable zones, symptomatic of constant attempts to replace randomness with planned districts. However, as with the Ashcan artists' preference for romanticizing street life, the reality of markets often challenged the representation. Hester Street merchants served the needs of the Lower East Side, which was by this time one of the world's most densely settled areas. In *Hester Street* (1905), Luks reduced the stands from an estimated 2,500 to a single example demonstrating

the strategies of editing and euphemism that he, among others, employed to domesticate the subject. Despite the crowds, the painting contains none of the chaos of contemporary photographs.

The defining characteristic and strength of Ashcan art is the painters' intimate knowledge of the "walking locales" and neighborhoods that defined the city. Many "true" versions of New York were possible, and thus a widely divergent iconography and partiality are evident in Ashcan art. The painters captured the diversity and heterogeneity of formative New York when verticality replaced horizontality.

Although the painters' subject matter was radical, stylistically, their art was conservative and therefore unequal to modern New York. Yet through them the city acquired a distinctive iconography well before images commonly associated with early modernists such as Marin, Stella, and Weber. Despite the conservatism, sentimentality, and literal nature of Ashcan paintings, they established all the important elements of an urban iconography, representing a vital transition between the 19th and 20th centuries. The impact of the Armory Show in 1913 and the outbreak of World War I signaled the decline of realism and the emergence of modernism. Their legacy can be seen in Reginald Marsh's overripe Coney Island women, which are clearly derived from Sloan, as are Hopper's detached spectators, staring out of city windows.

—*Gordon Reavley*

See also Marsh, Reginald

Further Readings and References

Perlman, B. P. (1988). *Painters of the Ashcan School: The immortal eight.* New York: Dover.
Zurier, R., Snyder, R., & Mecklenburg, V. (1996). *Metropolitan lives: Ashcan artists and their New York.* New York: Norton.

ASIAN AMERICANS IN THE SUBURBS

After World War II, the anti-Chinese sentiment in the United States eased and American-born second-generation Chinese Americans were able to find jobs in the American labor market beyond restaurant, laundry, and other ethnicity-bound service trades. At the same time, Chinese Americans were able to move out of Chinatowns into racially tolerant urban neighborhoods. Some even ventured into the few suburbs that were willing to accommodate them. There, they were soon followed by Chinese professionals who immigrated to the United States after World War II from Mainland China, Taiwan, and Hong Kong. Many Chinese scientists, doctors, and engineers came to the United States as graduate students and stayed on as refugees after the communist takeover of the Chinese mainland in 1949, whereas others gained their legal residence status by taking advantage of the professional preference quota set by the 1965 immigration law. They were individuals of privileged background in China, and once in the United States, they shunned Chinese urban enclaves. They preferred the safe environment and open space of the suburbs, and particularly the good suburban public schools for their children. As a result, while working-class non-English-speaking Chinese immigrants continue to congregate in urban centers to this day, a high percentage of others, especially the highly trained professionals, live in the suburbs (41 percent of all Chinese, compared to 33.7 percent of white Americans, as revealed in the 1993 census).

The Chinese people who choose to live in the suburbs have similar priorities and therefore end up flocking to the same areas, setting into motion a resegregation process of sorts. To begin with, 70 percent of all Chinese people in the U.S. are concentrated in five states. California and the Greater New York City metropolitan region claim three fifths of all Chinese in the nation. Furthermore, the Chinese people continue to favor three cities and their surrounding suburbs—San Francisco, Los Angeles, and New York—all of which were the oldest Chinese settlements in the country. Today, the suburban sprawl of Santa Clara County outside San Francisco and San Gabriel Valley outside Los Angeles claim larger numbers of Chinese than the urban core of those cities. In the New York metropolitan region, Chinese people have spread to Connecticut, Long Island, and Westchester County, while the number of those who reside in the city's three main suburban counties in New Jersey doubled during the 1990s.

The surge in suburbanization of Chinese America went hand in hand with the influx of Chinese immigrant professionals. The first wave came to alleviate America's shortage of trained scientists in competition with the Soviet Union during the Cold War. The second occurred in the 1970s, in response to America's economic restructuring from manufacturing to high-tech industries. The latest was brought to address America's move to the cyberinformation age. Chinese professionals have also been recruited to assist in corporate trans-Pacific expansion by acting as subcontractors and facilitators for American firms setting up operations in Asia. Their entry to the United States has been helped by aggressive measures adopted by the Congress, which tripled annual quotas set for immigrant professionals and broadened the definition of desired professionals to include those with entrepreneurial skills and those willing to invest in the U.S. economy.

The latest group of Chinese immigrants gravitates toward the most desirable suburbs and has practically formed a class of its own. Having come from the upper crust of cosmopolitan cities like Taipei and Hong Kong in their prime, members of this group are self-confident and want to enjoy creature comforts that they were accustomed to at home. Ethnic Chinese businesses understand their needs and have moved to the suburbs to offer, first, food and grocery stores, then bilingual services of all types. The result is a visibly Chinese commercial district in many of these suburbs. As it replicates many features of an urban Chinatown, this ethnic suburban enclave phenomenon has been called *ethnoburb,* denoting an area in which one ethnic group, although not its absolute majority, is present in a concentrated enough fashion to appear as a recognizable ethnic residential and business cluster.

One of the first Chinese ethnoburbs in the U.S. was Monterey Park in the San Gabriel Valley on the outskirts of Los Angeles. Immigrants from Taiwan arrived there in the 1970s with money to buy homes. Before long, the area's main thoroughfares were peppered with Chinese-owned restaurants, bookstores, banks, and beauty salons. The existence of a visibly Chinese commercial district attracted more Chinese immigrants to move in. Soon their presence spread to the surrounding San Gabriel Valley. As the economy of new ethnoburbs expanded, the increased need for ethnic Chinese services created job opportunities for working-class Chinese who were until then living in the economically stagnant L.A. Chinatown. Following their new jobs, the working-class Chinese also began to migrate to the suburbs, adding a multiclass dimension to the Chinese ethnoburbs. In 1983, about half of the Chinese-owned businesses in the Greater

Los Angeles area were located in Chinatown, and one third in the San Gabriel Valley. By 1992 merely 6 percent remained in Chinatown, while 55 percent were in the valley, with 12 percent in Monterey Park. Several other Chinese ethnoburbs have emerged around Silicon Valley south of San Francisco to act as both homes and workplaces of Chinese high-tech scientists and entrepreneurs. The demographic change has brought Chinese-language signs, opulent homes, and giant Asian shopping malls selling Chinese produce to almost exclusively Chinese customers.

In some cases the existence of a suburban Chinese community is indicated only by an "oriental" supermall. In Rockville, Maryland, for instance, an otherwise invisible community came to light when Chinese residents of the Washington, D.C., area forsook the traffic congestion surrounding old Chinatown located near the capitol for more leisurely shopping at Wintergreen Plaza on Rockville Pike. There are several major Chinese supermall chains around the country, including Hong Kong Foods, Asian Food Markets, and 99 Ranch, which has 21 stores in California alone. These malls are almost identical to Wal-Marts, but the majority of their merchandise is imported from China, Hong Kong, and Taiwan to suit Chinese tastes. There are over 60 supermalls of this type in Southern California, and roughly 140 more around the country.

Residents of the diffuse Chinese suburbia stay connected with the help of locally based Chinese language papers. The papers carry advertising for every conceivable type of business and service—all offered by Chinese professionals to Chinese-speaking residents of the neighboring suburban areas—those in accounting, medicine, law, construction, music education, and restaurants, of course. These papers serve as focal points for Chinese speakers in the geographic areas they cover, making the otherwise disconnected Chinese immigrants feel that they belong to a community.

The main Chinese "institution" in suburbia is Chinese-language schools for American-born second-generation Chinese. There are some 800 of them around the country. A number of the schools have expanded to serve as local Chinese culture centers staging art exhibitions and performances. Some have evolved into community centers to host professional seminars and fundraising events for Asian American politicians.

As the number of Chinese Americans in suburbia increased and as their stake in their new communities became more apparent, they began to realize that they had to organize politically. Quite often, this realization was forced upon them by the people they were displacing. In Monterey Park, for instance, older white residents greeted the increased Chinese presence and the proliferation of Chinese malls and condominiums with complaints that the Chinese were "taking over their community." They used their established political power to pass "slow-growth" legislations to curb further influx of immigrant businesses and residents. They even resorted to xenophobic appeals. The all-white city board passed a resolution declaring English the official language and presided over battles over whether to allow Chinese lettering on the storefronts of Chinese-owned businesses or Chinese-language books in the library. Confronted with this kind of attack, Chinese suburban professionals have demonstrated that they are both willing and able to fight back through active involvement in mainstream electoral politics. A number of them have run for elected posts. They have successfully solicited campaign funds from Chinese communities across the country, formed coalitions with liberal white and other racial minorities, and devised programs that can win them support beyond ethnic Chinese voters.

The results achieved by the wealthy, resourceful, and well-connected new immigrant Chinese professionals and entrepreneurs in the political arena, compared to the progress made through earlier efforts by American-born Chinese civil rights activists, have been striking. Today, the majority of Monterey Park's city council are ethnic Chinese. Elsewhere in Southern California, three Chinese immigrants won city council seats in 2003, in Cerritos, San Gabriel, and Claremont. In Cupertino, the Silicon Valley home of Apple Computers headquarters as well as of many affluent Chinese high-tech professionals (23.8 percent of the city population is of Chinese descent), 9 out of the 28 elected officials are Chinese Americans. The emerging prominence of ethnic Chinese in suburban public life signals a new trend in the suburbanization of America. Having picked the suburbs where they want to live, raise their children, and do business through the support of their ethnic networks, new immigrant professionals want to continue to speak their mother tongue and keep close ties to their countries of origin. They are also more than willing to participate in local politics to defend their choices.

—Peter Kwong

Further Readings and References

Chan, W. K. K. (2002). Chinese American business networks and trans-pacific economic relations since the 1970s. In P. H. Koehn & Y. Xiao-huang (Eds.), *The expanding roles of Chinese Americans in U.S.–China Relations* (pp. 145–161). Armonk, NY: M. E. Sharpe.

Fong, T. (1994). *The first suburban Chinatown: The remaking of Monterey Park, California.* Philadelphia: Temple University Press.

Horton, J. (1995). *The politics of diversity: Immigration, resistance, and change in Monterey Park, California.* Philadelphia: Temple University Press.

Koo, G. (2002, August 3). *Chinese American contribution to Silicon Valley.* Speech given at the 20th Anniversary Banquet of the Chinese American Forum, St. Louis, MO.

Li, W. (1998). Anatomy of a new ethnic settlement: The Chinese ethnoburb in Los Angeles. *Urban Studies, 35*(2), 470–501.

Tseng, Y.-F. (2000). The mobility of entrepreneurs and capital: Taiwanese capital-linked migration. *International Migration, 38*(2), 143–166.

Wong, B. (1998). *Ethnicity and entrepreneurship: The new Chinese immigrants in the San Francisco Bay Area.* Boston: Allyn & Bacon.

Atlanta, Georgia

Atlanta, Georgia, the gate city of the South, began in 1842 as a railroad center called Terminus, was then renamed Marthasville in 1843, and was finally given its present name in 1847. From the beginning, industry, commerce, and transportation defined the city. It was the commercial center of the Confederacy during the Civil War, part of the "New South," and by the late 20th century the commercial core and airline hub of the southern Sunbelt.

Largely destroyed during the Civil War, Atlanta took as its symbol the legendary Phoenix as it emerged out of devastation to become the leading city of the "New South." The spirit of entrepreneurship and the prominent role played by its commercial elite forged a city with a determination to continue its dramatic economic development and population growth. By 1870, the city's population had more than doubled (to 21,789) over its 1860 figure. Aiding Atlanta's progress was its designation as state capital in 1868, the repairing and extension of the rail lines, and its marketing and processing facilities, especially in regard to cotton.

Other than commerce, the major aspect of Atlanta's success has been image. The city's business elite was protective of Atlanta's progressive reputation in regard to welcoming Northern capital, emphasizing growth, and claiming better race relations than elsewhere in the South. Boosterism has been the city's hallmark into the present day. The International Cotton Exposition (1881), in which Henry Grady, of the *Atlanta Constitution*, was an important voice for the New South, indicated the central place of the city in southern industrial and commercial growth, and the Cotton States and International Exposition (1895) in which Booker T. Washington offered his "Atlanta Compromise" speech calling for social separation of the races but unity in economic progress forged Atlanta's identification with business growth and racial harmony.

The business aspect was correct, but racial togetherness was never a realistic description of Atlanta's history. Most notable was the 1906 race riot—a brutal 4-day attack on the black community that resulted in numerous casualties. The result of the riot was to further separate the races as African Americans began congregating on the west side and in the Fourth Ward, especially along Auburn Avenue. "Sweet Auburn," as it came to be called, became the business center and home to many of the black middle class, most notably the family of Martin Luther King Jr. Another infamous event that brought Atlanta unwelcome national attention was the trial and 1915 lynching of Leo Frank, a Jewish American, in close-by Marietta, which led to both the creation of the Anti-Defamation League of B'nai B'rith and the reemergence of the Ku Klux Klan, with its initial meeting on nearby Stone Mountain and its national offices in Atlanta.

Atlanta during the early 20th century evidenced serious racial and ethnic bigotry and violence. However, its entrepreneurial spirit was to eventually cross most barriers to growth. A major fire in 1917 that destroyed a good part of the east side (73 square blocks) barely slowed the city's development and boosterism as it marched onward with the Chamber of Commerce's "Forward Atlanta" campaign of the 1920s. The effort to market Atlanta, as well as to govern it, was the work of a relatively small number of interconnected white families who had school, marriage, economic, and background ties. This elite, which included the heads of various companies—Coca Cola, Haverty's Furniture, Rich's Department Store, and others—guided the city with their vision of what represented good, efficient, beneficial leadership. Many firms relocated to Atlanta, drawn by the campaign ads' claims of good weather, a ready-to-work and cheap labor force, and effective transportation connections. The 1930s Depression temporarily dampened the 1920s economic boom but brought some benefits as well. The New Deal gave Atlanta the nation's first federal public housing projects, but the new housing maintained the segregated housing patterns already evident in the city. Techwood Homes, designated as a white-only project, opened in 1936; its black counterpart, University Homes, opened in 1937. Replacing slum housing, these projects became the prototype for other cities. The 1920s economic growth restarted during World War II. War industries such as the Bell Bomber plant (the precursor to Lockheed) in Marietta brought larger numbers of workers to the city and metropolitan areas as did army bases and military supply depots.

As much as the war grew Atlanta's economy, the city further benefitted from postwar changes related to transportation and commerce—the 1950s interstate highway system and urban renewal, as well as the continued development of the airport, particularly as the hub for Delta Airlines, gave the city a national rather than just a regional importance. The population by 1950 was 331,300 (with 36.6 percent African American). The late 1940s and 1950s represented the beginning of a new stage for the city in size, politics, race relations, and national attention.

Atlanta's major annexation in 1952 with its "Plan of Improvement" increased the city's area from 37 to 118 square miles. This augmentation was partly due to racial issues as whites began their flight to the suburbs and blacks, now a voting force of considerable strength, pushed for new sections to live in that could be politically approved (that is, not near white neighborhoods). Politics had changed considerably as of 1946, due to the Primus King decision (*Chapman v. King*) in which federal courts ended Georgia's white-only Democratic Primary. A primary win guaranteed election in the general contest. Once blacks were able to vote in the primary, registration boomed and African American votes carried some weight. Working within the Atlanta Negro Voters League, which united black Democrats and Republicans, the African American community was able to bring pressure on Atlanta's last white mayors (William Hartsfield, Ivan Allen Jr., and Sam Massel) and secure various necessities—hiring of black police officers and firefighters, more attention to black neighborhoods,

and a quickened desegregation pace. It was during the Hartsfield administration that the mayor coined the phrase "A city too busy to hate." That perfect imagery of an active, entrepreneurial city so interested in business success that it had no time for bigotry became Atlanta's theme.

The coalition of the white business-commercial upper middle class and upper class with the black community led by clergy, teachers, and business leaders served both sides suitably at first, especially in keeping segregationists such as Lester Maddox out of city hall. However, it was not sufficient as Atlanta, and the nation, moved into the years of civil rights protests. Atlanta had always been a city of black activism and intellectual fervor, largely due to the black colleges (Morehouse, Morris Brown, Clark, Spelman, Atlanta University, and the Interdenominational Theological Center) located in the city and a financially successful black elite (particularly Alonzo Herndon and Jesse Hill of Atlanta Life Insurance Company). Also a number of black leaders have resided in Atlanta and affected the city's racial situation: for example, W. E. B. Du Bois, John Lewis, Julian Bond, Andrew Young, and Martin Luther King Jr.). It was not surprising then that the city became the nerve center of the Civil Rights Movement. The Southern Christian Leadership Conference (SCLC), the Student Non-violent Coordinating Committee (SNCC), and the Southern Regional Council were all based in Atlanta, as the Commission on Interracial Cooperation had been earlier.

Compared to cities such as Birmingham and Selma, Atlanta was a safe haven, but nonetheless it had extensive problems with racism in schools, medical care, city services, housing, and employment. The 1973 election of Atlanta's first black mayor, Maynard Jackson, led to the correction of some of these issues. Most important were his innovative affirmative action and minority business enterprise programs. Firms doing business with the city had to agree to minority hiring goals, and the mayor greatly increased the percentage of city contracts going to minority firms. This effort substantially increased the number of black-owned businesses and led to the significant growth of the black middle class.

However, Atlanta continued to develop with more emphasis on image and commerce than solutions to social and economic problems. Most notable was the city's experience after securing the 1996 Summer Olympics. The focus of Olympic planning was economic development and downtown revitalization.

A new baseball stadium for the Atlanta Braves was built in an area in dire need of new housing, and a park (Centennial Olympic Park) was developed in the downtown area replacing a dilapidated commercial section, using corporate contributions that were needed for neighborhood redevelopment. The business community benefitted through downtown improvement, an increase in the tourist trade, and an international stage to showcase the city's success.

Atlanta is a city of contradictions—gleaming skyscrapers overlooking slum areas. It is a city that contains a substantial black middle class and is considered a black Mecca, but which has a persistent black low-income group that has benefitted little from black political empowerment. Suburban growth and sprawl has led to upper-income black housing and some black movement out of the city, while gentrification has started to bring whites back into Atlanta. It is also a city of increasing Hispanic and Asian immigration, which is changing its historical biracial identification.

What has not changed over the years is that Atlanta is still a city on the make where commerce and image still rule.

—Ronald H. Bayor

See also African Americans in Cities; Jackson, Maynard; Sunbelt and Snowbelt Cities

Further Readings and References

Bayor, R. H. (1996). *Race and the shaping of twentieth-century Atlanta.* Chapel Hill, NC: University of North Carolina Press.

Keating, L. (2001). *Atlanta: Race, class, and urban expansion.* Philadelphia: Temple University Press.

Kuhn, C., Joye, H., & West, E. B. (1990). *Living Atlanta: An oral history of the city, 1914–1948.* Athens, GA: University of Georgia Press.

Russell, J. M. (1988). *Atlanta 1847–1890: City building in the old South and the new.* Baton Rouge, LA: Louisiana State University Press.

Stone, C. N. (1989). *Regime politics: Governing Atlanta, 1946–1988.* Lawrence, KS: University Press of Kansas.

AUSTIN, TEXAS

In 1839, a site-selection commission for the new Republic of Texas chose a settlement then known as Waterloo to serve as the nation's capital. The committee purchased 7,735 acres of land located on the Colorado River and hired Edwin Waller to plan and construct the new city. Waller laid out the city on a grid of 14 square blocks dominated by "Capitol Square."

By the time the Texas Congress convened in November of 1839, temporary buildings served as government headquarters. The body incorporated Austin on December 27, and in January of 1840, Waller became its first mayor. The first 856 inhabitants included diplomatic representatives from France, England, and the United States, as well as 145 slaves.

In 1842, Mexican troops captured the nearby city of San Antonio and reopened debate over the safest location for the Texas capital. Former General and President Sam Houston wanted the capital to be in Houston, closer to the Gulf Coast and further from Mexico. In response to the Mexican threat, he ordered the Texas archives moved to Houston for safekeeping. Austinites refused to move the archives, but President Houston moved the capital anyway. The dispute became known as the Archive War when Houston sent an armed contingent to seize the General Land Office in Austin. Without its political base, Austin's growth stalled, until a constitutional convention in 1845 voted to bring the capital back. The United States annexed Texas in February of 1846, and in 1850, voters made Austin the permanent state capital. The new capitol building at the top of Congress Avenue opened in 1853, followed by the governor's mansion in 1856. By 1860, the population numbered 3,546, including 1,019 slaves and congregations of Presbyterians (who built the first church in 1839), Methodists, Catholics, Baptists, and Episcopalians.

Austinites voted against secession, but once the Civil War commenced at least 12 local volunteer companies joined the Confederacy. Union occupation at the end of the conflict brought immense numbers of emancipated slaves to Austin, increasing the city's black population by over 50 percent. By 1870, over a third of Austin's population was African American.

Postwar growth continued with a railroad connection on the Houston and Texas Central Railway. As the westernmost terminus for the railroad, Austin became a trading center for western Texas. In 5 years, with the addition of numerous residents from Europe and Mexico, the city's population doubled to 10,363 people. Austin took on a modern character with gas street lamps, a streetcar line, and an elevated bridge across the Colorado River. As the railroad industry spread to nearby towns, however, the city's economic boom ended.

Austin turned to politics and education to distinguish itself. In 1872, the city survived challenges to its seat as state capital and constructed a new capitol building, the "seventh largest building in the world." The 1880s brought numerous educational institutions to the city, beginning with a public school system. In 1881, it became the home of the new University of Texas (UT) despite objections from parents that going to school so close to politicians would corrupt their children. The Tillotson Collegiate and Normal Institute provided education to the African American community.

City leaders approved construction of the 60-foot-high Austin Dam on the Colorado River to generate electricity and attract manufacturing. The initial project was completed in 1893, but the dam did not live up to expectations. Not only did Austin not become a manufacturing center, but the water and electric systems experienced frequent outages and the dam collapsed 7 years later. Seven more government-funded dams followed by 1938. This activity marked the entrance of future president Lyndon Baines Johnson into government work.

The oil boom essentially bypassed Austin, and the city fell from the fourth largest in the state to the tenth largest in 1920. By 1905, the municipality had only one paved street, no public parks, and a severely limited sewer system. In 1909, A. P. Wooldridge became mayor and spent a decade improving the city. Most notably, Wooldridge acquired Barton Springs, the spring-fed pool that came to symbolize Austin's landscape. The reformist mayor retired in 1919, but Progressivism continued to dominate city planning, particularly urban beautification. Austinites adopted the council-manager system of city government in 1926 and initiated a $4.25 million bond issue to provide for infrastructure, a city hospital, and an airport.

Austin fared well during the Great Depression, experiencing significant population growth and benefitting greatly from New Deal programs thanks to the election of Lyndon Baines Johnson to Congress in 1937. In 1942, the Del Valle Army Air Base (later the Bergstrom Air Force Base) brought the benefits of military investment to the city as well.

Following World War II, Austin continued to build on its strengths as a political and educational center. In 1956, UT became the first major university in the South to allow black enrollment. Segregation receded with the Civil Rights Act of 1964, and by the 1970s, both African Americans and Hispanics were represented in city government. Also in the 1970s, Austin began to earn its reputation as a center for high technology. Prompted by research programs at UT, IBM moved to Austin in 1967. Texas Instruments established its headquarters there in 1969, and Motorola followed in 1974. Such corporate growth continued into the 1980s when Michael Dell, a UT dropout, founded Dell Computers.

Rapid growth in the 1970s spurred revolt from Austin environmentalists. Over 150 groups sprang up around the city, angered by heavy population growth and accompanying traffic congestion and determined to preserve Austin's natural resources. These organizations won significant victories in a series of environmental ordinances in the 1970s and 1980s.

At the dawn of the 21st century, Austin boasted high rankings on national surveys of the best places to live in the United States. UT enjoyed equal prominence for many academic programs, and the city remained a destination for high-technology innovation. Austin was also characterized as the self-proclaimed music capital of the country and hosted numerous musical festivals throughout the year, including the notable South by Southwest Festival.

—Kimberley Green Weathers

Further Readings and References

Humphrey, D. C. (1997). *Austin: A history of the capital city.* Austin, TX: Texas State Historical Association.

Humphrey, D. C. (2005, July). Austin, TX. In *Handbook of Texas online.* Retrieved June 14, 2006, from http://www.tsha.utexas.edu/handbook/online/articles/AA/hda3.html

Orum, A. M. (1987). *Power, money, and the people: The making of modern Austin.* Austin, TX: Texas Monthly Press.

BACK OF THE YARDS

Back of the Yards in Chicago is one of the most famous urban neighborhoods, in large part because it was home to the Union Stockyards. Originally a rural district, the section was part of the Township of Lake, so named because of the marshy countryside, only a few feet higher than Lake Michigan. In 1865, when locals decided to incorporate as a separate village, there were fewer than 700 residents.

A number of developments, both industrial and technological, transformed this area. Chicagoans had been engaged in the wholesale buying and selling of cattle since at least the 1840s; by the time of the Civil War, the city's entrepreneurs were beginning to challenge the dominant meat market in the country, Cincinnati, with yards all over the Windy City.

In 1865, a group of investors led by John Sherman decided to build a unified stockyards with adjoining industrial park. In their search for an appropriate site, they settled on a 320-acre site in the Town of Lake. Over a thousand workers toiled on the project, and on December 25, 1865, the Union Stockyards opened for business.

While a number of businesses took root quickly— Armour arrived in 1867, Swift in 1875—the real burst of expansion followed the introduction of the refrigerated railroad car, first patented in 1868 but made workable by a system Gustavus Swift invented in 1879. For the first time, it now became economically efficient to slaughter cattle in one large complex, then ship dressed meat to markets across the country.

Other crucial developments that built Chicago's meatpacking industry included the introduction of assembly-line methods long before Henry Ford used these to build cars; in this case, it was actually a disassembly process, but the work was eventually broken down into small, repetitive movements. In addition, packers learned to make use of all possible by-products, prompting the cliché, "They used everything but the squeal."

At its height, the Yards included a vast enterprise of 500 acres, with 13,000 pens and 300 miles of railroad tracks. In 1919, the myriad companies processed 14,903,487 animals.

As a result of these developments, the surrounding community grew enormously. In 1920, the peak year, local population reached 75,920. The original residents were mostly Irish and German, but by the turn of the 20th century the neighborhood had become predominantly Eastern European. In 1920, 43 percent of the population was foreign born; of these, 45 percent were Polish, 16 percent either Bohemian or Slovak, 12 percent Russian, and 7 percent Lithuanian.

Most of the increase, of course, was due to the plants and the jobs they offered; a 1919 federal study showed that total employment in Chicago's meat industry was 45,696 workers, and that one Swift & Company plant in the Yards had over 11,000 workers. A 1923 survey indicated that 54 percent of all local heads of household worked in meatpacking.

By then, work in these plants had changed from skilled butchering to routine factory work, and the Union Stockyards came to symbolize the horrors of the industrial age. Wages were low; a 1900 study found that annual income averaged only $347.36, while a 1910 survey discovered that fewer than half the workers made over $600 a year. In addition, the Yards had become a very dangerous place to work; half of Armour's workforce became ill or injured each year. Some of the jobs were just plain dirty, such as squeegeeing blood down drains and squeezing kidneys to get the urine out.

As a result, workers and their families used several mechanisms to make life better. Efforts to unionize began early, particularly among the skilled butchers, but the first real effort at mass organizing came with the Amalgamated Meat Cutters and Butcher Workmen in the 1890s. While they were effective in organizing local workers, they could not overcome the packers' power and lost important strikes in 1904 and 1921. The former episode also led to Upton Sinclair becoming interested in the neighborhood, prompting him to do local research and write his classic muckraking novel, *The Jungle*.

Thus, a great deal of local efforts centered on building a viable community instead. The most important institution was the church, and local residents were overwhelmingly Roman Catholic. Edifices dotted the area, each filled to the brim during the numerous masses each Sunday. These places provided not just solace and religious celebration, but a variety of efforts to foster community, including social services, financial assistance, and serving as a local center for activities.

The one problem associated with the churches, however, was that they divided the community. Despite their common religion, local houses of worship defined themselves in ethnic terms; residents referred to the "Irish church" or the "Slovak church." Thus, they perpetuated the antagonisms brought over from Europe and divided residents.

In 1939, a visiting social worker, Saul Alinsky, teamed up with a local parks director, Joseph Meegan, to found one of the oldest community organizations in America, the Back of the Yards Neighborhood Council (BYNC). The two men built on the existing social structure, granting equal membership to 76 organizations, ranging from athletic teams to Holy Name Societies. The BYNC thus permitted a variety of particularities, but it established one venue where, once a month, everyone could come together for the common good. Its motto read, "We The People Will Work Out Our Own Destiny."

The council's first efforts centered on two issues: labor activism and child welfare. Granting assistance to the new CIO unions in the Yards—first the Packinghouse Workers Organizing Committee and then the United Packinghouse Workers of America—in 1946 council leaders, including priests, joined the union's picket lines and urged the entire community to support what became a successful strike action. The Council also established one of the nation's first school lunch programs using federal funds, and set up programs to deal with juvenile delinquency.

In the 1950s and 1960s, the neighborhood faced devastation from urban blight and an aging housing stock, and the council concentrated on this issue. It launched a variety of programs, and its home improvement drive begun in 1953 resulted in 9,000 out of 11,000 homes being upgraded within 10 years.

By the late 1960s, the Yards had gone, and the neighborhood was undergoing a demographic change that would continue for decades. By 2000, the area was 50 percent Hispanic, 35 percent black, and 13 percent white.

Slowly, the Back of the Yards Neighborhood Council shifted to deal with these conditions, and by the 1980s was focusing on economic development. The council had won designation for the Yards as Empowerment and Enterprise Zones, as well as gaining status for the area as a Tax Increment District. It maintained a Small Business Development Center in its office, as well as a Business Technology Center. As a result of these and other initiatives, the old stockyards site—now the Stockyards Industrial Park—became home to 110 companies that employ 15,000 workers.

—*Robert A. Slayton*

Further Readings and References

Barrett, J. (1987). *Work and community in the jungle.* Urbana, IL: University of Illinois Press.

Jablonsky, T. (1993). *Pride in the jungle.* Baltimore, MD: Johns Hopkins University Press.

Pacyga, D. (1991). *Polish immigrants and industrial Chicago.* Columbus, OH: Ohio State University Press.

Slayton, R. (1986). *Back of the Yards.* Chicago: University of Chicago Press.

Wade, L. (1987). *Chicago's pride.* Urbana, IL: University of Illinois Press.

BALLOON-FRAME CONSTRUCTION

Balloon-frame construction represented a monumental breakthrough in the manufacture of shelters. Prior to this new construction method, house building was a time-consuming process. Specialized workers were needed to fit the pieces, called a mortise-and-tenon joint frame, together, and the houses were solidly built. The way builders constructed these wooden portions of the house was to take the posts, cut down one end so that it had a protruding tongue (called a tenon) and fit it into a hole (called a mortise) in the adjoining beam. In this manner, houses were constructed without metal fasteners. While sturdy, these houses required a vast amount of lumber to form the walls and roofs, not to mention several skilled workers who had to hand fabricate the dowels to secure the wood together. Balloon-frame construction changed all of this in several important aspects.

The origin of the style has been contested: Some believe it was created by George Washington Snow, and others believe it was the work of Augustine Taylor. The first documented year of its use was 1833 in Chicago, with Taylor's construction of St. Mary's Church, located near the current intersection of Wabash and Madison streets. Chicago was a perfect city in which to try the new style for several reasons. First, the city was arranged on a grid, which suited the style. Second, easy sales of plots created a need for structures that could be assembled quickly and with minimal cost to the developer. Balloon-frame construction called for a series of uniformly cut 2-inch by 4-inch pine boards, assembled into a frame 16 inches apart, with clapboards nailed to the frame. The frame without the clapboards looked as if it would blow away like a balloon at the first strong wind, hence the name. The method used mass-produced nails to hold the studs and clapboard together. With these nails, the building was constructed much faster (no need for mortise and tenon) and with unskilled labor. Because of Chicago's growing immigrant population, construction was an easy job to acquire, as few communication skills were needed. Third was the location of Chicago itself. As more and more contactors shifted to this new method of construction, companies needed more lumber. Since Chicago was located on major waterways, near the forests of Michigan, Wisconsin, and Minnesota, and was also a rail hub, lumber was a large commodity traded in the region. Chicago not only was built with this lumber, but it also became a key shipping point to the West and South for the major lumber companies.

Balloon-frame construction had its shortcomings, however. Since it was used as quickly as possible, the lumber was sometimes of poor quality, and would warp, sending the building out of alignment. Another problem was the fear of fire due to the lumber and the tar paper construction of the roof. The buildings were put up far too close to each other in many cities, and this led to potential fire hazards. Chicago's 1871 conflagration was in part due to the lack of safety concerns about lumber storage, as well as buildings in extremely close proximity to one another. Another fire danger inherent in the balloon frame was the fact that the earliest designs had space between the frame studs, and this allowed a fire below to be channeled to the roof, like a chimney. After a few incidents, this flaw was discovered, and lateral or diagonal cross braces were installed. These cross members not only eliminated the flue problem but also gave further support to the frame. After the "Great Fire," Chicago set standards on distances between houses, and also banned the use of wood-framed structures in the downtown district.

Despite its problems, the balloon-frame construction method did influence the wider architectural community. If one looks closely at the construction plans of William Le Baron Jenney's first "skyscraper" (the Home Insurance Building, erected in 1885), the skeletal frame is directly reminiscent of the balloon-frame construction—except for its being made with heavier materials. Other features of the balloon-frame construction that directly influenced home building were the ease of construction and the effectiveness of shipping. The Sears and Roebuck Catalog Company of Chicago boasted that by 1900 they were selling some 12,000 prefabricated balloon-frame houses through their mail-order business. The kits consisted of all the materials to fabricate a house, complete with plans, and rail delivery to the closest station. Many houses on the Great Plains are from the Sears catalogue and were originally built with wood shaped in and shipped from Chicago.

Many Europeans complained that the new form of construction looked shoddy, especially in comparison to the solid European homes. They also noted that European houses would last hundreds of years. For Americans, with limited money and an immediate need for housing (not to mention weakened ties to the "old country"), the balloon frame was what fit the need. Theoretically, the wood could also be salvaged for other building projects if the need warranted it. In the ever-changing cityscapes of the late 1800s, this feature also proved valuable.

After catastrophes in the major cities, as well as in the smaller towns, balloon-frame construction represented a visible sign of life and the return to some sense of normalcy. Pictures taken soon after the Chicago fire and the San Francisco earthquake, for example, show frames of buildings going up in quick succession. In fact, one of the most notable pictures from the aftermath of the Chicago fire was of a balloon-frame building hastily erected by D. W. Kerfoot, with a sign that noted: "All gone but wife, children, and energy." Writers from the 1860s noted that if not for the use of balloon-frame construction, Chicago and San Francisco would not have grown as quickly as they did.

Still used today in various forms, the balloon-frame method of construction has proven itself to be cheap, economical, and in other ways directly related not only to the industrial revolution but to the rise of the city as well. Balloon-frame construction is yet another example of mass production of goods, unlike the work the artisans of the guilds created out of wood. While more workers obtained jobs in construction, pay was less than it had been for the woodworkers of the past. As more people immigrated to urban centers, the need for cheap, affordable housing increased substantially. As the population spread out across the country and moved into places with no natural building supplies, such as timber, the balloon-frame house proved itself to be of prime importance, as well as a source of income and control for those who controlled the railroads and the lumberyards.

—Cord Scott

Further Readings and References

Cronon, W. (1992). *Nature's metropolis.* New York: Norton.

Mayer, H., & Wade, R. (1969). *Chicago: Growth of a metropolis.* Chicago: University of Chicago Press.

Miller, D. (1996). *City of the century.* New York: Simon & Schuster.

Spinney, R. (2000). *City of big shoulders.* DeKalb, IL: Northern Illinois University Press.

Upton, D. (1998). *Architecture in the United States.* New York: Oxford University Press.

BALTIMORE, MARYLAND

One of the nation's major cities, Baltimore grew fitfully from its founding in 1729. Situated near a deep harbor, it had an emerging trade economy tied to tobacco and linked to milling and iron operations; an ambitious merchant class; a network of roads; and an influx of entrepreneurial German immigrants. The American Revolution prompted real growth in Baltimore when merchants responded to wartime demands and the elimination of mercantile restrictions by establishing new trade routes, manufacturing enterprises, and city markets. Population increased, the city was incorporated in 1796, and a new generation of leaders emerged. Baltimoreans began to refer to their community as a city—not merely a town.

Cycles of growth and stagnation and periods of division and calm characterized Baltimore in the 19th century. The War of 1812 brought prosperity, and Baltimoreans celebrated victory at Fort McHenry—where Francis Scott Key penned the "Star Spangled Banner." But in 1819, the economy sank into recession, mirroring the national slump and aggravating religious, ethnic, and racial tensions in the city.

Transportation developments, including the nation's first railroad, the Baltimore & Ohio (B&O), and the city's famed clipper ships, increased commercial prosperity. Migration and immigration expanded Baltimore's population from over 35,000 in 1820 to more than 210,000 in 1860, a third of whom were Germans, Irish, or African Americans. To house the growing population, construction soared, including the creation of Canton, one of the nation's earliest planned residential and industrial communities. But municipal services lagged behind and sanitation, fresh water, and protection from fires, floods, and disease remained inadequate. Public-private partnerships were formed to deliver city services—a model that continued through the 20th century and beyond.

Racial and ethnic animosities made the pre–Civil War era in Baltimore both volatile and dangerous. Political reforms extended the vote to all tax-paying white males and created a public school system—for white children only. But Irish Americans were attacked at the polls by nativist Know-Nothings; in 1856, 15 people were killed in election-day violence. Baltimore, the nation's largest center of free blacks, became known as "Mobtown" for its marauding white gangs, corruption, and fraud—even Edgar Allan Poe experienced "cooping," when he was rounded up by thugs and forced to vote as directed.

The Civil War further divided the city. Secessionist sentiments ran high and residents attacked Union soldiers who marched through Baltimore. Federal troops jailed the mayor and occupied the city throughout the war. The war's political legacy lasted through much of the 20th century: the Democratic party, wedded to states' rights and racism, took over the city's machinery with rare challenges.

The pattern of boom and bust hindered sustained growth and swelled the population of the poor. Hard times exacerbated the conflict between labor and management, as revealed by the Great Strike of 1877 against the B&O Railroad, in which federal troops fired on workers and their families, leaving 10 dead and others wounded.

By 1900, Baltimore ranked third nationally in trade but was changing from a commercial into an industrial city. Population growth, economic specialization, and residential segregation combined to redraw the spatial configuration of the city, dividing fashionable neighborhoods from the city's distinctive row homes for immigrant and native workers, crowding African Americans into the worst housing in the city, and creating a thriving garment industry of "skyscraping factories" alongside a retail shopping district showcasing emporiums of consumer elegance. City boosters pointed to the foundries, canneries, copper and iron processing plants, fertilizer producers, and machine shops as signs of economic growth and to the museums, parks, and the Johns Hopkins University and hospital as proof of cultural advancement. But they also lamented the limits of Baltimore's progress and pressed for a more robust industrial expansion. Only after the Great Fire of 1904 did the city establish an adequate water system, but sewage remained a problem.

Known as a "blue-collar town," Baltimore was home to poor whites and blacks from rural areas who provided cheap labor, discouraging large numbers of newer immigrants from settling in Baltimore. However, the garment and canning industries did attract Italians, Jews, Poles, Bohemians, and Lithuanians, creating ethnic enclaves and sweatshops. Progressive Era reforms attempted to eliminate child labor and "sweating," but working-class neighborhoods were ravaged by tuberculosis and typhoid. Progressive leaders revived city planning and, with the Olmsted Brothers, attempted to slow suburbanization through a new park system linked by parkways and planned elegant neighborhoods for the wealthiest citizens. But much of the city's population remained economically marginal, and sporadic efforts of reformers did little to strengthen what one observer has called a "weak tradition of civic action."

Between 1917 and 1945, Baltimore experienced significant economic and political growth. World War I attracted rural migrants and produced competition for jobs and houses marked by racism, segregation, and an active Klan. Wartime production led to an overexpansion of the garment industry, and the postwar recession and 1930s Depression signaled its ultimate demise. The death of key political leaders resulted in Democratic factionalism that stifled reform. United primarily by a commitment to states' rights, the Democratic Party leadership remained generally hostile to the New Deal, but rank-and-file white and black voters overwhelmingly endorsed Franklin Roosevelt and the New Deal and demanded jobs, relief, and public housing.

World War II created a short-lived boom that could not reverse the effects of the Depression and the city's declining position as a port and an industrial center. Postwar Baltimore witnessed the disappearance of trolleys, which were replaced by autos that brought congestion to city streets; the acceleration of suburbanization, which left vacant and decaying areas; the shift of industries to surrounding counties; and periodic efforts at "slum clearance" and urban renewal. What had always been two cities, divided by color, saw the departure of white residents, especially after the riots in 1968. Population declined, the tax base shrunk, schools deteriorated, and jobs disappeared—an all-too-familiar pattern in American cities. Between the 1960s and 1980s, Baltimore lost a fifth of its population and nearly half its manufacturing jobs. By 1987, African Americans, representing 60 percent of the city's population, had become politically organized and elected a black mayor. Yet 45 percent of the city's population over 16 did not have jobs.

Still, Baltimore has enjoyed some success in urban renewal. Strong mayoral and business leadership succeeded in revitalizing the downtown. In particular, the quirky but powerful William Donald Schaefer, who was elected in 1971 and served four terms, was a white mayor in a city with a black majority who was instrumental in attracting business support and pitching Baltimore as a special place to live and to visit. Turning to tourism and marketing, Schaefer and city leaders transformed the city's Inner Harbor into a major attraction. Assisted by the local media, Schaefer so successfully marketed himself and the city that he was named best mayor in America in 1984 by *Esquire* magazine and the Inner Harbor was featured in *Time* magazine. Even the *London Sunday Times* trumpeted the Inner Harbor in 1987 as one of "America's top tourist draws," adding that in Baltimore, "urban unemployment is falling fast." But the redevelopment of the downtown has not mitigated the city's social and economic problems, halted the loss of jobs (between 1970 and 2000, there was a decrease of over 10 percent in the number of jobs), or contributed substantially to the tax base. As one observer noted, there was much "rot beneath the glitter." Recent city boosters have attempted to reposition the downtown as a source of both tourism and job development with the "Digital Harbor"—the "next hub for high-tech and internet business." But whether tourism and the harbor can overcome the city's divided past to bring jobs and adequate housing to its poor remains to be seen.

—*Jo Ann E. Argersinger*

Further Readings and References

Argersinger, J. E. (1988). *Toward a New Deal in Baltimore: People and government in the Great Depression.* Chapel Hill, NC: University of North Carolina Press.

Argersinger, J. E. (1999). *Making the amalgamated: Gender, ethnicity, and class in the Baltimore clothing industry, 1899–1939.* Baltimore, MD: Johns Hopkins University Press.

Durr, K. D. (2003). *Behind the backlash: White working-class politics in Baltimore, 1940–1980.* Chapel Hill, NC: University of North Carolina Press.

Fee, E., Shopes, L., & Zeidman, L. (Eds.). (1991). *The Baltimore book: New views of local history.* Philadelphia: Temple University Press.

Greene, S. E. (1980). *Baltimore: An illustrated history.* Woodland Hills, CA: Windsor.

Olson, S. H. (1980). *Baltimore: The building of an American city.* Baltimore, MD: Johns Hopkins University Press.

BANKS AND BANKING

Over the past decades, the banking industry has experienced a major worldwide restructuring. This movement has reshaped regional economies and urban spaces across the United States. Banks today offer a wider range of products and services than in the past, and deliver them faster and more efficiently. However, the bank's central purpose remains what it has always been, putting the community's surplus resources (deposits and investments) to work by lending the resources to citizens and companies.

If there were one industry with the stigma of being old and stodgy, it would have to be banking; however, the global trend of deregulation has created new business possibilities in banking. Deregulation, coupled with technological developments such as online banking and ATMs, is giving the banking industry an opportunity to shed its lackluster image.

Banks have begun to use asset-building plans to stimulate asset-based development in areas of the United States such as low-income and minority urban spaces. These plans have focused on creating more real estate development and removing urban "blight" (real estate based asset building). Banks' efforts have also encouraged community-based financial and business enterprises.

There are two main types of banks in the United States: regional (and thrift) banks and major (mega) banks. The first type includes smaller financial institutions that primarily focus on one geographical area. In the U.S., there are six such geographical areas: the Northeast, Southeast, Central or Midwest, Northwest, Southwest, and Far West. Providing depository and lending services is the regional banks' primary line of business. The second type of bank includes banks that operate local or regional branches but whose main line of business is in financial centers; an example is New York City, where banks get involved with international transactions, underwriting, and so on.

The United States government is very involved in the banking industry, as it sets restrictions on borrowing limits and the amount of deposits that banks must hold in their vault. Also, the Federal Reserve Bank has a major influence on the bank's profitability, as it sets the interest rates which influence the credit market (loans).

A Short History of U.S. Banks and Banking

The history of the United States banking system has been largely influenced by the decisions of the American government. Initially, the banking industry was operated and regulated by the specific state where it resided and the banks required special authorization from the specific state government to open and operate.

The history of banking in the United States did not begin with the Federal Reserve Bank. Originally, an additional layer of oversight was provided by the Bank of the United States, a central bank that received its charter in 1791 from the United States Congress. When the congressional charter expired in 1811, the Second Bank of the United States was created in 1816 and operated until 1832. However, this Second Bank met with considerable controversy. Those with agrarian interests were opposed to the bank because they feared it would benefit commercial and industrial interests over their own. In those days, city bankers tended to be extremely cautious about to whom they lent money and for how long, as they wanted to make sure they had enough cash available to meet unexpected demands from depositors. The typical banker of the time generally made short-term loans. Typically, manufacturers and shopkeepers would use their own funds to pay their suppliers and workers until they could sell the goods to customers. After selling their goods they would pay off the bank loan.

A National Banking System: 1832 to 1864

Because of the unpredictability of weather and market conditions, loan losses tended to be higher in less settled parts of the country. When the Second Bank of the United States went out of business in 1832, state governments took over the job of supervising banks. In the absence of a national banking system, state banks increased in number and influence. Private banks sprang up, each with its own policies and currency. State government supervision often proved inadequate. In those days banks made loans by issuing their own currency. It was sometimes difficult or impossible to detect which notes were sound and which were not. By 1860, more than 10,000 different bank notes circulated throughout the country. Commerce suffered as a result. Counterfeiting was epidemic. Hundreds of banks failed. Throughout the country, there was an insistent demand for a uniform national currency acceptable anywhere without risk.

The Independent Treasury System, a network of federal offices that handled United States government money, could not manage the banking system adequately. In response, Congress passed the National Currency Act in 1863 and the National Banking Act in 1864. These laws were enacted to stabilize the banking system. A new system of national banks and a new government agency was established. The economy's money supply was once again left in the hands of state banks. The National Banking Act put a reserve system in place, with small banks able to borrow reserves from city banks, which could in turn borrow from central reserve city banks. However, this structure was not flexible. Sudden economic downturns could cause a chain reaction, with few banks able to borrow from city banks that could in turn borrow from central reserve city banks.

A National Currency: 1865 to 1914

The banks were required to purchase United States government securities. Most paper currency circulated between the Civil War and World War I consisted of National Bank Notes. On the rare occasion that a national bank failed, the government sold the securities held on deposit and reimbursed the note holders. National bank notes were the mainstay of the nation's money supply until Federal Reserve notes appeared in 1914. The Federal Reserve Act of 1913 created the Federal Reserve System to stabilize the banking system and a formal decentralized Central Bank.

Banks in Crisis: 1929 to 1933

The Great Depression, which began with the stock market crash in October 1929, extended worldwide until about 1939. It was a disaster for the banking system. Many banks had invested in the stock market and failed when the demand for money outweighed the amount of currency they possessed. Also, many businesses failed and could not pay back their bank loans. On March 6, 1933, newly elected president Franklin D. Roosevelt proclaimed the closure of all banks in the United States in order to save the remaining assets of banks (a bank holiday was declared).

In June 1933, Congress created federal deposit insurance and required the separation of commercial banking from investment banking activities in the Glass-Steagall Act. Accounts were insured up to $2,500 per depositor. These reforms were aimed at improving the regulation of bank activities and competition.

A New Competitive Era in Banking: The 1960s

Banking in the early 1960s largely remained the same as it had been in the 1930s during its reshaping: banking markets were segmented by geography and product line; banking loan and deposit customers had virtually no alternatives to banks; maximum demand and time deposit rate maxima were set under Regulation Q; and demand deposits were protected by deposit insurance. However, a robust home mortgage market had arisen, with half of all mortgages issued by either the Federal Housing Administration (FHA) or Veterans Administration (VA) programs.

By the mid-1960s, banks were beginning to emerge from a long era of competitive lethargy. The impetus came from money-center banks, which were losing high-balance customers to broker-dealers. The money-center banks created a number of liability-side innovations to retain these customers. Prior to 1960, only very few American commercial banks had any foreign operations. During the 1970s and 1980s, the largest United States commercial banks expanded abroad.

Banks faced competitive pressure as a result of the high inflation environment of the late 1960s and 1970s. High inflation reduced the attractiveness of deposits in bank accounts whose interest rates were subject to the 1933 Act (Regulation Q). This provision limited competition within banking and thereby strengthened the banks. High inflation encouraged the alternative of intermediaries such as money-market mutual funds.

A Revolution in Banking: The 1970s to Today

Domestic commercial banks entered the international market during the 1960s and the 1970s. American bank globalization peaked in the late 1970s, and with very small exceptions, commercial banking in the United States has returned to being a resolutely domestic business, in contrast to both investment banking and industry in general in this country. In the mid-1970s, banks of all sizes faced a customer loss problem when intermediaries such as the newly created money-market mutual funds paid more through liquid short-term savings than Regulation Q permitted.

Furthermore, during the last quarter century, banking has undergone a revolution. Technology has transformed the way Americans obtain financial services. Telephone banking, debit and credit cards, and automatic teller machines are commonplace, and electronic money and banking are evolving.

Patterns of financial exclusion coincided with the emergence of many cities. In the second half of the 1970s, many organizations attempted to fight urban housing abandonment by focusing on the problem of access to banking credit. Banks sometimes would neither nurture the potential loan demand of the new (minority) residents of the inner city areas they served nor the demand of existing (mostly white) residents. The term *redlining* was coined to denote banks' refusal to make loans—especially home loans—in inner city areas. The destabilization of contiguous inhabited neighborhoods has been attributed to redlining, and redlining has become a national issue.

Redlined areas contain traditionally underserved communities—minority and low-income populations. Consequently, multiracial alliances for "reinvestment" by banks have emerged. Further, some steps were taken to give access to credit to members of those communities with two crucial pieces of federal legislation: the Home Mortgage Disclosure Act of 1975 and the Federal Community Reinvestment Act of 1977. The Federal Community Reinvestment Act was designed to eliminate all redlining practices. However, this legislation created incentives for predatory lending and Wall Street became a major player by investing in these sub-prime loans.

Since the beginning of the 1980s, the bank merger has led to a dramatic reshaping of the banking industry. However, as noted by Mark Mizruchi and Gerald Davis in 2004, there was a substantial attenuation of the trend toward branch globalization. In the early 1980s, new entrants in the banking industry encountered markets undergoing a rapid change.

The Financial Services Modernization Act of 1999 removed many of the post-Depression laws that promoted an increasing separation between banking, insurance, and securities. As a result, commercial banks and savings institutions began to lend funds. The other institutions not regulated by the Federal government (mortgage banking affiliates, insurance companies, etc.) took the biggest share of this market. The influence of the Community Reinvestment Act declined.

The Costs and Benefits of Bank Mergers

The ongoing consolidation of the banking industry creates the scales of efficiency necessary to offer such services. Concentration is more pronounced among larger banks. In recent years, the 100 largest banks have increased their share of domestic bank assets. United States regulations now permit interstate banking and nationwide branching. Competitive pressures have motivated mergers, technological advances, diversification of product offerings, market globalization, and increased efficiency.

Urban markets have disproportionately more mergers than rural markets, and mergers with targets in urban areas account for the largest share of acquired deposits and offices. Urban markets are also more likely than rural markets to be the location of a merger in which the acquirer had an office previously.

The mega-mergers that have occurred since the 1990s have provided upsides and downsides for bank stakeholders. A stronger job market and low interest rates have advanced mortgage lending—the lifeblood of community development. According to the Federal Reserve Bank, lending to low-income, community development, and minority borrowers has risen at a faster rate than lending to all borrowers. Bank consolidation in metropolitan areas has not adversely or disproportionately affected mortgage lending to minority and lower income customers. In general, increased lending by independent mortgage companies and others has offset reductions in lending by merged banks.

The consolidation trends in banking in the same local market have increased local banking market concentration, which in some cases can weaken competition. Antitrust enforcement carried out, in part, by the Federal Reserve Bank has helped limit an increase in concentration in local markets due to mergers.

Employees and Community Groups

Employment in the financial services industry in the United States, including banks, brokerage firms, and insurance companies, has in general increased (it even outpaced overall private sector job growth between 1980 and 1997, when it climbed 38.4 percent). Nevertheless, individual bank mergers have led to significant job losses. For example, BankAmerica cut 18,000 jobs as a result of its merger with NationsBank.

Community groups have gained concessions from banks to increase lending, keeping branches open or providing development funds. For example, following the 1998 merger between BankAmerica and NationsBank, the merger bank agreed to reach low- to moderate-income and minority home credit lending customers at a level similar to the general penetration rate.

Transformation of Urban Spaces by U.S. Banks

Deregulation is reinforcing the development process by encouraging the installation of the most sophisticated systems in urban centers that already are the hubs for leading financial and business services.

In many aspects, urban decay is not as severe a problem in other countries as it is in the United States. Community investing addressed the financial needs of low-income and underserved communities. Firstar Banks was one of the first banks in the United States to form a community development corporation—they went into depressed neighborhoods and spent millions of combined dollars to revitalize the neighborhoods.

Banks are among the Community Financial Development Institutions (CDFIs) that provide many investment opportunities, diverging from where investment capital is applied and to what degree of risk is involved. These organizations put community investment capital to work and share in common investment, placing the funds directly in the hands of those that need the most—people who do not have access to capital through conventional channels.

Community Development Banks and credit unions are the only CDFIs that are regulated and insured. Instead of placing their depositors' money wherever they can get the greatest financial return, these banks and credit unions dedicate their funds to local disadvantaged communities and promote community revitalization programs. There are a handful of community development banks in the United States, led by the South Shore Bank, which over two decades years ago revitalized a failed bank to directly serve Chicago's beleaguered inner city.

Another consequence of the concentration and growth of banks in downtown areas is the emergence of new land-use patterns, such as the development of central business districts on high-value land with the highest concentration of traffic and activities. The specialization of these functions accompanies urban growth. During the 20th century, the growing volume of persons and goods and services like banking built urban land use patterns that have since become obsolete.

Downtown areas have the highest concentration of banks. The concentration of banks in turn encourages a concentration of service activities associated with banks and their staffs. However, some of the "poorest" locations exist around the corner or across the street from some of these "central business districts." For many years, urban land patterns were influenced by market decisions created by real estate operators. This phenomenon had many controversial consequences, such as real estate speculation, concentration, and social exclusion. It was only in the late decades of the 20th century that public regulations started to have a strong influence on these patterns by establishing public policies about land use and urban planning.

Does technological innovation in banking restrict the ability of the poor and the elderly to access services? While new technological innovations have reinforced the role of the office building in some areas of the financial sector, they have led to a dispersion of routine and retail financial services. Nowhere is this more apparent than in the consolidation of local banks into interstate banking companies and the replacement of the local branch offices with the spread of electronic communications (automated teller machines, or ATMs, 24-hour banking). The spread of electronic communications has expanded into local communities through supermarkets, drugstores, and gas stations. Another new field is online brokering, which is growing much faster than online banking.

Retail banks, once built in order to reassure depositors that their savings were safe and secure, are no longer defined by real estate but by electronic networks. This has led many communities to protest the loss of the locally owned and managed bank. Low-income households and people lacking resources (technology and money) to purchase these innovations may be excluded from or have limited access to those services.

Of even more importance, some banks now operate solely in electronic space rather than in physical space. Internet banks such as Security First Network Bank, Atlanta Internet Bank, and ComuBank offer 24-hour service on their Web sites. This new way of banking presupposes access to and literacy in communications technology, which is still lacking in many communities.

The unique position of the financial industry in urban redevelopment is another important issue to be considered. The importance of the Community Reinvestment Act and other forms of federal and state regulations of the banking industry may play a role in this redevelopment process, in that cities without strong financial anchor firms may not be candidates for this type of revitalization.

Recently many banks have established in-house "community development corporations" for the specific purpose of promoting redevelopment lending. Although the nomenclature is slightly confusing, community development banking is a vital component in allowing private capital to invest in the redevelopment effort. Redevelopment has become more reliant on private than public capital, with banks encouraged through the Community Reinvestment Act to actively participate.

Ethnically Owned Banks' Role in Community Development

Given the rapid increase of immigrant populations and ethnic communities in the United States, ethnically owned banks have an increasing role in community development. The discriminatory and exclusionary practices of mainstream banks and other financial institutions play a significant role in impoverishing urban, low-income areas. Banks owned by Korean Americans, African Americans, and Chinese Americans, to name a few, address this problem. Some banks simply grow organically, while others are instrumental in helping the community (for example, those in Los Angeles County such as Chinatown and the San Gabriel Valley ethnoburb). Community partnerships are a very important means of reaching each specific community. In addition, the economic conditions of some low-income neighborhoods have allowed for the creation of ethnically owned banks to eliminate discriminatory lending practices, that is, when bankers pass up the credit requests of those in poorer neighborhoods because of racial and ethnic bias.

The American Bankers Association has begun to address this problem by promoting best practices in lending to immigrants, equal opportunity staffing, and promoting close ties to the community through a number of channels and underwriting standards (for example, nontraditional criteria for making loans). These are among the practices of ethnically owned banks in the United States.

Conclusion

A new community gap is emerging in many neighborhoods, and many grassroots coalitions are forcing banks to eliminate redlining of urban neighborhoods and predatory lending. On the other hand, there is little understanding of how banks have been successful in turning around the process of urban decay and degeneration. The successful urban redevelopment is most likely to come from development coalitions and partnerships (stakeholders) established among local governments, shareholders, for-profit developers, banks, and community development corporations. Finally, the emerging patterns of banks in urban spaces have lead to a growing momentum at the local level for progressive urban growth policies.

—*Alfredo Manuel Coelho*

Further Readings and References

Dimsky, G. A., Li, W., & Zhou, Y. (1998). *Ethnobanks and ethnoburbs in Los Angeles County: Framework and initial empirical findings.* Unpublished manuscript, Department of Economics, University of California, Riverside.

Dymski, G. A., & Mohanty, L. (1999). Credit and banking structure: Asian and African American experience in Los Angeles. *American Economic Review, 89*(2), 362–366.

Dymski, G. A., & Veitch, J. (1996). Financial transformation and metropolis: Booms, busts, and banking in Los Angeles. *Environment and Planning, 28*(7), 1233–1260.

Mizruchi, M. S., & Davis, G. F. (2004). The globalization of American banking, 1962–1981. In F. Dobbin (Ed.), *The sociology of the economy.* New York: Russell Sage Foundation.

Pollard, J. S. (1996). Banking at the margins: A geography of financial exclusion in Los Angeles. *Environment and Planning, 28,* 1209–1232.

Santos, J. A. C. (1998). Banking and commerce: How does the United States compare to other countries? *Economic Review, Federal Reserve Bank of Cleveland, 34*(4), 14–26.

Schuler, K. (2001). Note issue by banks: A step toward free banking in the United States? *Cato Journal, 20*(3), 453–465.

Schwartz, A. (1998). Bank lending to minority and low-income households and neighborhoods: Do community reinvestment agreements make a difference? *Journal of Urban Affairs, 20*(3), 269–301.

BAR CULTURE

From colonial times to today, the barroom has provided a convenient entrée into city life. Here a person familiar with drinking traditions and barroom etiquette might swiftly form a circle of acquaintances with whom to relax, play games, enjoy music, and swap stories. Cultivating such barroom contacts might also prove useful in gaining information about the city itself: where to eat and stay, what jobs are available, and who's who in the neighborhood and at city hall. As both a social club and a connection to urban society at large, the barroom has long served an important dual purpose in the lives of city dwellers.

The duality so noticeable in bar culture is in fact present in most aspects of urban life, as sociologist Ferdinand Tonnies pointed out in the late 19th century and historians Thomas Bender, Gary Nash, and others have expanded upon in recent decades. People cultivate relationships characteristic of the community (*gemeinschaft*) and the society or marketplace (*gesellschaft*). Relationships based on communal needs grow spontaneously and organically out of a fundamental desire for companionship; those based on marketplace needs are deliberately constructed alliances built on mutual self-interest. It is this pronounced duality that makes urban bars urban. Though similar in appearance and basic amenities to small-town and rural bars, urban establishments offer both a greater variety of communal pastimes and a far more sophisticated network of marketplace connections.

The evolution of the dual nature of urban bar culture can be traced to colonial drinking establishments, then commonly called *taverns* or *inns.* In the early 1600s, just as English settlers were first building taverns in their fledgling New World towns, taverngoers on both sides of the Atlantic began using the verb *to club* to mean to combine into a drinking group, with each member contributing equally toward the cost of the beverages (usually ale or rum punch). This clubbing arrangement simplified the evening's finances and defined the drinking circle with the collection of dues.

Groups who routinely clubbed for drinks soon themselves became known as *clubs,* as did the drinking establishments that hosted them. Such tavern clubs constituted an elementary form of voluntary association, with their defined memberships, regular meetings, dues collections, and shared social goals. By the late 18th century, the club idea became so popular that people began applying the term *club* to any group, tavern based or not, that collected dues toward a mutually agreeable end.

Among drinkers, meanwhile, the custom of clubbing continued, whether participants chipped in all their dues at once or took turns paying for rounds, known as "treating." In this manner, countless drinking clubs have taken shape in bars over the centuries, most of them short-lived and devoted strictly to social ends. Some, however, have evolved into more elaborate and lasting endeavors. In the late 19th century, the urban barroom, with its clubbing tradition, became the principal host and facilitator of all manner of voluntary associations, particularly among workers. These groups included ethnic lodges, trade union chapters, political parties, mutual aid associations, singing societies, and amateur sports teams. All compensated the bartender for meeting space by clubbing for drinks, a strategy that smoothly combined the commercial with the communal.

In the 20th century, many of these groups moved away to more sober and permanent headquarters, especially when Prohibition closed down legitimate bars from 1920 to 1933. To the present day, however, recreational groups such as darts leagues, poker clubs, and the smaller Mardi Gras krewes of New Orleans still hold meetings and recruit members in neighborhood bars. In addition, individuals continue to use their favorite haunts as information centers, check-cashing facilities, and message services.

The communal pastimes in city bars chiefly involve drink, food, storytelling, music, and games. Treating, the most spontaneous form of clubbing for drinks, remains central to barroom socializing. On the surface, this custom may seem deceptively simple. One person offers to buy a drink for another, who reciprocates with a second round. Yet drinking is an activity laden with cultural meaning. To drink *with* another is to affirm fellowship and mutual esteem. Drink itself symbolizes well-being and good fortune. This is revealed in medicinal remedies like the hot toddy (brandy or rum with honey and lemon) for colds, as well as in toasts such as "To your health" and "Here's to success." Breaches of treating etiquette are met with contempt, as when the recipient dares to order a fancier drink, fails to reciprocate, or worst of all, refuses a treat. Before 1920, when bars were largely a male preserve, such dishonorable conduct sometimes provoked altercations. Most treating episodes, however, are amicable and equitable exchanges, reinforcing the barroom's communal creed.

Changes in drinking preferences over the centuries reflect the influence of immigration and technological advances. Rum, ale, and hard cider were the colonial favorites, but the arrival of skilled Scottish and Irish distillers after 1790 and expert German brewers after 1840 eventually made whisky and lager beer the American drinks of choice. Wine did not become a barroom standard until the late 20th century. Cocktails, which combine hard liquor like bourbon with mixers like soda, were available throughout the 19th century. But most bargoers dismissed them as "sissy drinks," fit only for effete elites, until the low-quality liquor of the Prohibition era gave mixed drinks a new appeal. Female customers, more numerous in the post-Prohibition era, also boosted the cocktail's popularity. Modern bars offer a dazzling array of bottles to choose from. Yet in the typical establishment, the customer who orders a grasshopper (featuring green crème de menthe) will still get a roll of the eyes from the regulars, who tend to favor beer, wine, and the simpler cocktails.

The consumption of food as a communal activity has long been a part of bar culture. In the colonial and antebellum eras, many taverns offered a cheap midday meal called an "ordinary." By the late 19th century, more foods from faraway suppliers became available to the typical urban bar, by then known by the more fanciful name of "saloon." With the backing of major breweries, which increasingly gained control of urban bars from 1880 to 1920, saloonkeepers began to feature the "free lunch," a buffet open to anyone who bought a 5-cent beer. Some larger saloons provided a veritable feast, augmented with ethnic and regional touches. To the outrage of temperance advocates, these noontime bonanzas attracted hoards of both female and male workers. After Prohibition, when reform legislation mandated a greater separation of the brewery and bar businesses, the free lunch came to an end. Instead, many bars now simply sell low-cost meals and snacks, though some provide free hors d'oeuvres (usually liberally salted) at happy hour.

Urban bars have always been lively centers of conversation and storytelling. Political discussions filled the tavern air during the colonial and Revolutionary War eras, with debates over British policies gradually turning to talk of rebellion. In the 19th century, politicians met with their supporters in antebellum grogshops and postbellum saloons, eventually building political machines that would dominate the urban landscape. Though post-Prohibition politicians no longer routinely plot their campaigns in bar back rooms, the bargoers themselves continue to pick apart public policies and devour the latest political scandals.

Much bar talk concerns neighborhood and personal matters. Regulars confide problems to their bar mates and bartenders, brag of their accomplishments, and vie to tell the best stories. Among the most striking changes to verbal bar lore has been the decline of lengthy recitation pieces. In the late 19th century, amusing multi-versed narratives like "The Shooting of Dan McGrew" and "Casey at the Bat" were barroom staples. In the 20th and 21st centuries, however, the most favored category has been the joke, whether told to comrades as a fix-phrased piece or told on them as a free-form anecdote. Jokes, according to folklorists, are a subcategory of the folktale genre, characterized not only by wit, but by brevity. Perhaps here lies the key to their popularity. As cities have mushroomed and the pace of urban life has increased, people now prefer their stories "quick and dirty," so to speak. In modern bars, a call for jokes will usually produce a lively round of story swapping.

Singing of the spontaneous and homegrown sort was common among bargoers from the colonial era to the early 20th century. Folksongs were the colonial favorites, joined in the late 19th century by labor anthems, immigrant airs, and the sentimental melodies of Tin Pan Alley's professional songsmiths. Bars have traditionally offered occasional live performances as well, from colonial fiddlers to 19th-century German bands to present-day blues guitarists. Once radio, recorded music, and jukeboxes became widely available after Prohibition, however, bargoers' vocalizing rapidly fell to a sing-along hum. Yet though self-produced music has waned, drinkers still exercise considerable choice in their barroom music. A survey of any jukebox's most-played tunes will provide a revealing portrait of the regular customers' class, ethnicity, age, and worldview. The music may not be live, but the communal spirit it evokes lives on.

A wide variety of games also promote barroom camaraderie. Regulars have played dominoes, chess, and backgammon since colonial times. Particularly popular in saloons of the late 19th century were contests amenable to small-stakes gambling, including games of chance like dice, roulette, and lotteries, as well as games of skill like pool, darts, and cards. In modern bars, drinkers have enthusiastically embraced technological advances, such as video poker machines and televised sporting events. Yet many bars still use poster board to devise their own homemade betting pools, in which participants wager on squares representing possible scoring outcomes.

Games, according to scholars of the genre, create a kind of separate reality with clear rules and results, unlike the ambiguities of ordinary life. As a consequence, game participants derive a sense of order, justice, and reward from playing games, in addition to amusement and emotional release. Such factors help explain the enduring appeal of games in taverns as well as their role in bolstering the communal aspects of bar culture.

Most institutions generate a characteristic culture: One hears of "prison culture," "theater culture," "Pentagon culture," and the like. But few examples are as colorful and complicated as bar culture, due in large part to the centrality of drink in bar life. Drinking is a fun but risky business. Where there is adventure and risk, there tends also to be a sizable body of customs, beliefs, superstitions, proverbs, jokes, and other lore that people use to bring order to a volatile setting. So it is with bars, particularly those in big cities where customers must contend daily with the demands of the marketplace on the one hand and the need for community on the other. Bar culture in urban America has evolved over 4 centuries to meet these dual needs, providing both practical assistance and communal pleasure to customers coping with the pressures of urban living.

—*Madelon Powers*

Further Readings and References

Duis, P. R. (1983). *The saloon: Public drinking in Chicago and Boston, 1880–1920.* Urbana, IL: University of Illinois Press.

Powers, M. (1998). *Faces along the bar: Lore and order in the workingman's saloon, 1870–1920.* Chicago: University of Chicago Press.

Rorabaugh, W. J. (1979). *The alcoholic Republic: An American tradition.* New York: Oxford University Press.

Rosenzweig, R. (1983). *Eight hours for what we will: Workers and leisure in an industrial city, 1870–1920.* New York: Cambridge University Press.

Rotskoff, L. (2002). *Love on the rocks: Men, women, and alcohol in post-World War II America.* Chapel Hill, NC: University of North Carolina Press.

Salinger, S. V. (2002). *Taverns and drinking in early America.* Baltimore, MD: Johns Hopkins University Press.

Sinclair, A. (1962). *Era of excess: A social history of the Prohibition movement.* New York: Harper & Row.

BARRY, MARION S., JR.

Four-time mayor of Washington, D.C., Marion Barry is a charismatic and controversial figure in American city politics. Barry brought energy and initiative to the fledging Washington, D.C., home rule government, but his mayoralty was stained by allegations of corruption. His 1990 conviction on misdemeanor charges of crack-cocaine possession forced him out of office and made the District of Columbia and its African American–led government an object of national derision.

Barry was born in 1936 in Itta Bena, Mississippi, a tiny delta community. His father died when Barry was a young child, and his mother moved the family to Memphis, Tennessee in 1940. His mother remarried, and Barry grew up in a working-class household which included his two sisters, two half sisters, and three stepsisters. He attended LeMoyne College in Memphis, and went on to do graduate work in chemistry at Fisk University in Nashville, at the University of Kansas, and at the University of Tennessee.

Barry's entry into politics came in 1960 when, while still a graduate student at Fisk, he became a part of the Nashville lunch counter sit-ins. In that same year, he was elected the first chairman of the Student Non-violent Coordinating Committee (SNCC). In 1964 he abandoned his graduate studies to become a full-time civil rights activist and SNCC fundraiser, assigned first to New York City and then, in 1965, to Washington, D.C.

Once in Washington, Barry quickly established himself on the local political scene, organizing bus boycotts to protest fare increases and initiating the "Free D.C." movement, which worked to gain home rule for the city. In 1967, Barry established a job training program, Pride, Inc., which was generously supported by federal Department of Labor grants. The program was ultimately damaged by corruption scandals, however. In 1971, Barry won a seat on Washington's first elected school board. In 1973 the city was granted partial home rule, and Barry won election as an at-large member of the D.C. Council in 1974 and again in 1976.

In 1978, Barry won the mayoralty with strong support from white liberals and an effusive *Washington Post* endorsement. He was credited in his first term both with opening up Washington government to the city's underrepresented African American community and with bringing order to the city's chaotic finances. He was reelected in 1982, and again in 1986, but by that time his political base had eroded due both to the city's downward financial spiral and to allegations of his drug use and sexual misconduct. In January 1990, Barry was videotaped smoking crack-cocaine by an FBI sting operation. After serving a 6-month prison term on a misdemeanor conviction, Barry returned to Washington, winning election to the D.C. Council in 1992 and regaining the mayoralty in 1994.

Barry's fourth mayoral term was marred by congressional imposition of a federal control board that sought to salvage the nation's capital from its precarious financial situation by placing the majority of city agencies into receivership. Barry declined to run for a fifth term, and he was succeeded in office by the city's CFO, Anthony Williams. Barry aborted a 2002 Council race after a confrontation with police who alleged they had found traces of crack and marijuana in Barry's car. In 2004, Barry won election to a 4-year Council term.

—*Bell Clement*

Further Readings and References

Agronsky, J. I. Z. (1991). *Marion Barry: The politics of race.* Latham, NY: British American Publishing.

Barras, J. R. (1998). *The last of the black emperors: The hollow comeback of Marion Barry in the new age of black leaders.* Baltimore, MD: Bancroft Press.

Jaffe, H. S., & Sherwood, T. (1994). *Dream city: Race, power, and the decline of Washington, D.C.* New York: Simon & Schuster.

BARTHOLOMEW, HARLAND

Born in 1889, Harland Bartholomew spent his early years on the East Coast. His tertiary education was limited to 2 years at Rutgers University, where he studied civil engineering. He then accepted a job with the city of Newark as a planning consultant, and subsequently became one of the earliest full-time municipal planners in the United States. Bartholomew retired in 1961 and died in 1989.

Bartholomew pursued a tripartite career: as director of planning for Newark, St. Louis, and Washington, D.C.; in private practice as the founder of Harland Bartholomew Associates; and as an instructor at the University of Illinois. Urban planning was an emerging discipline in the 1910s, and Bartholomew was able to influence the field in discernible ways. His primary concern was planning a scientific enterprise. Accordingly, he expanded upon the concept of the "comprehensive plan." The comprehensive plan combined zoning and land use, major streets, transit, transportation, recreation, and civic art into a single entity. It considered past trends and made long-term projections.

Unlike many of his contemporaries, Bartholomew recognized the interrelatedness of social, economic, and physical criteria in urban development. His firm developed more than 500 comprehensive plans for American cities between 1919 and 1984. Two innovations facilitated this feat. Recognizing the disadvantages of the dominant "hit and run" consulting system, Bartholomew established longer term associations between planners and communities. A planner was assigned to a community for 2 to 4 years, during which he worked with a planning commission to develop a comprehensive plan. To encourage continuous activity, this "field man" was encouraged to remain with the community after the contract period as director of planning. Thus, Bartholomew was partly responsble for the acceptance of planning as a legitimate concern of local governments, as well as the dispersion of planners across the country. In addition, he was one of the first to organize an interdisciplinary practice that included architects, landscape architects, and civil engineers. The immediate availability of necessary expertise streamlined the planning process. Also important in Bartholomew's oeuvre are his contributions to the development of urban renewal as a national and local concern and the initiation of a comprehensive interstate highway system. Bartholomew saw himself as an advocate for his profession and for urban constituencies. He was prominent in professional organizations, including the American Institute of Certified Planners, the Society of Landscape Architects, and the Society of Civil Engineers.

Yet, many of the charges leveled against the discipline also apply to Bartholomew's work. Cities like Battle Creek, Michigan, for which Bartholomew's firm developed a comprehensive plan, are still attempting to overcome their traumatic experiences of urban renewal, slum clearance, and highway expansion. Former residents of declared "slum areas" still contend that their neighborhoods were not slums. As minorities, residents were excluded from decision-making processes. Fifty years later, resentment still thrives because of the limited provisions made for housing and the lack of attention paid to the effects of displacement. Despite their best intentions, Bartholomew and his colleagues were not able to develop the level of foresight necessary to preclude the urban crisis.

—*Itohan Osayimwese*

Further Readings and References

Harland Bartholomew and Associates. (1949). *Comprehensive city plan, Battle Creek, Michigan. Prepared for City Planning Commission and City Commissioners.* St. Louis, MO: Harland Bartholomew Collection, University Archives, Washington University Libraries.

Johnston, N. J. (1994). Harland Bartholomew: Precedent for the profession. In D. A. Krueckeberg (Ed.), *The American planner: Biographies and recollections* (pp. 217–240). New Brunswick, NJ: Center for Urban Policy Research.

Lovelace, E. (1993). *Harland Bartholomew: His contributions to American urban planning.* Urbana, IL: University of Illinois Press.

BASEBALL AND BALLPARKS

Despite the myth of Abner Doubleday's invention of baseball in the small upstate New York town of Cooperstown, the sport actually had urban origins. Derived from the English game of rounders, "the New York game" started in the 1840s as a gentlemanly recreation for a group of white-collar professionals. One participant, Alexander Cartwright, first recorded the official rules of the game in 1845, when the original club started competing with others from New York and Brooklyn. Variations of the sport were played in different parts of the Northeast, but Cartwright's version grew into the national pastime.

At first, the game spread slowly, to New Jersey when one of the New York clubs moved, and to California when Cartwright joined the Gold Rush in 1849. It spread faster, though, in the 1850s, after New York newspaper reporter Henry Chadwick started reporting box scores as well as team and individual statistics. Within a few years, clubs formed in every major city in the Northeast, with three or four apiece in bigger cities like New York and Brooklyn. As interclub and crosstown rivalries developed, the clubs formed the National Association of Base Ball Players, to resolve disputes and standardize rules.

The Civil War era saw the expansion and professionalization of baseball. The war itself spread the game, as knowledgeable soldiers taught their uninitiated compatriots. Meanwhile, back home in Brooklyn in 1862, an entrepreneur built the first fenced-in field for baseball and charged admission to spectators. (It was this park that originated the practice of playing "The Star Spangled Banner" at the beginning of games, half a century before it was adopted as the national anthem.) Soon, promoters and club organizers began paying some of the better players, and by the end of the decade the Cincinnati Red Stockings fielded a fully professional team, thereby starting baseball's gradual transition from recreation to big business. At first, gate charges were only 5 or 10 cents.

By 1867, there were more than 30 major clubs in the old association, but the group's limited mandate and amateur emphasis were deemed obsolete. The association was replaced, in 1871, by the National Association of Professional Baseball Players, which devised a schedule for its member club, making it the first real baseball league. As gate fees escalated, reaching 50 cents for big games, clubs started building ballparks with bigger grandstands, and there was also an increased need for a stronger league structure. In 1876, the new association was replaced by the National League of Professional Baseball Clubs, a more profit-oriented group that was created in New York by a small coterie of club owners. This is the same National League that still functions today.

The National League, with its profit-driven model focused on maximizing gate fees, decided to limit its franchises to eight teams in the biggest cities, leaving smaller cities to amateur teams and to "minor" leagues. Competing leagues formed, granting franchises to owners in smaller cities, but these leagues and most of their franchises failed. Sometimes the remnants of these failures merged into the National League, or individual franchises were absorbed. The only lasting challenger was the American League, which was recognized as a major league by formal agreement in 1901. Baseball's fastest growth, in both the major and minor leagues, was at this time, from the 1880s until World War I. This growth was aided by the increasing coverage of the sport by newspapers nationwide. During the 1880s, Chicago newspapers in particular introduced a more colorful and opinionated style of reportage, which supplemented the date-based methods that had been pioneered in New York earlier. This proved a winning combination, and many newspapers made baseball coverage the anchor of their new "sports pages."

As the professional sport grew in cities nationwide, so too did the recreational version—not just among kids, but also through adult amateur leagues. By this time, baseball's base had changed. While the sport was still an urban phenomenon, the young professional gentlemen who started it had given way to working-class men. On the other hand, fans came from all sectors of society, and ballparks became multiclass and multiethnic melting pots. Immigrants and reformers alike embraced the sport, the former as a symbol of prideful Americanization, the latter because of the wholesome combination of discipline, exercise, rules, teamwork, and sportsmanship. However, African Americans were banned from the major leagues in 1898, prompting the creation of so-called "Negro Leagues." Reintegration, which started in 1947, most visibly with Jackie Robinson and the Brooklyn Dodgers, was slow. Despite the availability of outstanding players competing in the Negro Leagues, some teams did not sign their first black players for many years.

Baseball's growing popularity created opportunities for businessmen willing to invest in bigger ballparks. In the 1880s, the crude fenced-in fields with simple wooden bleachers were eclipsed by much larger and more ambitious structures designed to hold thousands of paying fans. Sometimes, transit operators participated in the development of these new ballparks to boost ridership and jumpstart real estate development along new routes, like Lakefront Park in Chicago (1883). Wooden fences and grandstands soon gave way to more elaborate steel and masonry ballparks, typically designed with traditional-looking

architectural street façades that blended into the surrounding streetscape. The state of the art was advanced again in 1909, when Shibe Park was built in Philadelphia, the first of a wave of new concrete and steel parks with seats for 20,000 to 25,000 fans. Team owners built more than a dozen such edifices during this era, some of which were used throughout the 20th century and into the 21st and became fixtures in the urban cultural and physical fabric of their cities, most notably Comiskey Park (1910) and Wrigley Field in Chicago (1914), Tiger Stadium in Detroit (1912), and Fenway Park in Boston (1912).

After World War I, the New York Yankees emerged as the dominant major league franchise. Great players (like Babe Ruth, purchased from Boston in 1920) and their success helped to attracted record numbers of paying fans, which financed the construction of Yankee Stadium in 1923—a gigantic new modern ballpark with three decks and seating capacity of 67,224, much higher than that in any other venue. The new park, the first to be called a stadium, was itself an attraction. The grandeur of the stadium and the dominating success of the team brought in even more fans and generated more gate revenues, some of which the owners used to retain top players and buy others from poorer teams, perpetuating the successful cycle. Attendance was also helped by the modification of the city's blue laws in 1919 to permit baseball games on Sundays, which were easier for working-class fans to attend than the weekday afternoon games that had traditionally made up most of the schedule. In comparison to Yankee Stadium, other major ballparks were small, obsolete, and in some cases in need of expansion, even those built recently and at great expense. Ebbets Field (1913), home of the Brooklyn Dodgers, originally had a seating capacity of 18,000, but it was expanded to provide seating for 31,497 fans. The Polo Grounds, owned by the New York Giants and home field for the Yankees up until 1920, was built in 1911 with a seating capacity of 38,000. And Comiskey Park, the home of the Chicago White Sox, seated 32,000.

The growth of the sport between the wars was also advanced by technology. For example, live broadcasts on radio and later television, after 1939, fostered a broader fan base, and eventually provided a substantial new source of revenue for major league franchises. Also, electric lighting facilitated the introduction of regular night games, starting with a 1939 game at Comiskey Park, where there had been experiments with artificially lit night games as early as 1910.

There was remarkable franchise stability in the major leagues for the first half of the 20th century, with no teams moving from 1903 until 1952. When the Boston Braves moved to Milwaukee in 1953, and then two of the New York teams moved to California in 1957, it was a harbinger of changes to the sport. The economic and civic dimensions of baseball soon eclipsed all other aspects of the sport.

Ebbets Field, home of the Brooklyn Dodgers, was typical of many of the older urban ballparks—small, obsolete, and hemmed in by urban development on a cramped 4.5 acre site. Easy access from the streets and by mass transit, formerly an essential quality for ballparks, now went hand-in-hand with inadequate parking and poor access by automobile. Also, many of the older urban ballparks were in neighborhoods that had been destabilized by the rapid middle-class migration to the suburbs. Franchise owners like Dodgers' owner Walter O'Malley sought newer arenas that were more accessible to automobiles—arenas with ample space for access roads and parking. He moved the Dodgers to Los Angeles in 1957, and the New York Giants moved to San Francisco immediately afterward—in both cases lured not only by population growth in western cities unserved by the major leagues but also by the opportunity to build profitable new stadiums on expansive plots of land. However, the movement of the Dodgers also revealed that baseball teams had become, for many Americans, an embodiment of civic pride and identity. This marked the beginning of a new era, not only for baseball, but also for ballparks and their host cities, as older cities struggled to retain their franchises and newer cities fought to acquire their own, to establish their status as "major league cities."

In this new era, almost all new stadiums were supported by public subsidy through varying combinations of public financing, low-cost or free land, or outright public ownership. Eventually, by the beginning of the 21st century, these government subsidies amounted to hundreds of millions of dollars for some teams. All the new stadiums were near major new superhighways, placed in the suburbs or—especially later—in abandoned downtown neighborhoods in the hopes of stimulating downtown revitalization. This latter objective was mostly unsuccessful until the 1990s, when some new stadiums were reconnected to the urban fabric by mass transit access and designed to reproduce the pedestrian-scale experience of older ballparks. The first of these was Baltimore's retro-styled Camden Yards, which was built in 1992. In the meantime, the innovation of covered stadiums, starting with the $545 million Houston Astrodome in 1965, eased the league's expansion into hotter southern cities. Most of the ballparks built after 1960 were considerably smaller than the standard set by Yankee Stadium, typically with a seating capacity of 40,000 to 45,000. Attendance at baseball games has declined, while television's importance to the sport has grown. Symbolic of these changes, when Yankee Stadium was renovated in 1971, its capacity was reduced to 57,545 seats.

—Owen D. Gutfreund

Further Readings and References

Benson, M. (1989). *Ballparks of North America.* Jefferson, NC: McFarland.

Gershman, M. (1993). *Diamonds: The evolution of the ballpark, from Elysian Fields to Camden Yards.* Boston: Houghton Mifflin.

Reiss, S. (1989). *City games: The evolution of American urban society and the rise of sports.* Urbana, IL: University of Illinois Press.

Seymour, H. (2005). *Baseball.* New York: Oxford University Press.

BASKETBALL

A Canadian named James Naismith invented the sport of basketball in 1891 at a Springfield, Massachusetts, YMCA. The game quickly spread to other YMCA facilities and expanded throughout the northeastern United States within a year. By the first decade of the 20th century, basketball had swept across many parts of the country both as an amateur sport in high schools, colleges and universities, and recreational leagues and as a continuously growing professional game. The game grew to encompass cities throughout the United States during the 20th century and became one of the most sought-after athletic diversions for both participation and spectatorship. From the outset, the game of basketball was linked to the American city. Basketball's successful early development and the success of today's game can be linked to the relationship the sport had and has with urban centers. The professional sports teams of American cities, including basketball teams, are the hallmarks of urban boosterism and help emphasize the importance of the city.

Naismith created the game of basketball to enable the Springfield YMCA to provide a safe and convenient form of exercise during the Massachusetts winter months. The earliest YMCA teams quickly adopted a match play style in which "Y" teams would play one another. Throughout the 1890s, these recreational and amateur games were staged in places like Trenton, Brooklyn, Buffalo, and Springfield. Within a decade the sport had been adopted by colleges and universities and had attracted professional players. Ironically, by the end of the 19th century, the YMCA facilities that had originally encouraged basketball debated the value and violence of the sport.

The game of basketball was quickly embraced by colleges and universities: During the first decade of the 20th century, several prestigious universities in the East formed the Ivy League and universities in the Midwest formed the Big Ten athletic conference. During this same decade, the National Collegiate Athletic Association took over as the governing body of basketball. In the first half of the 20th century, colleges and universities led the development of the game. Throughout these decades basketball remained on the periphery of American sports, but it began to achieve prominence by the 1930s. Madison Square Garden in New York City exhibited basketball contests between universities. These contests developed into the current National Invitation Tournament and the National Collegiate Athletic Association Tournament that still determine collegiate basketball champions. Both tournaments are held annually in large American cities and continue to be the most important part of the season for both participants and fans of collegiate basketball. The opportunity to hold these tournaments is a boon to cities, as the tournaments provide both economic possibilities and national prominence.

Professional basketball has played a larger role in the American city than that played by the amateur game, especially since the Second World War. From the very early years of basketball in the 19th century, athletes were paid for their participation. The first professional basketball team originated in Trenton, New Jersey, in 1896 and soon was followed by a number of marginal professional organizations. Although certainly professional, these early basketball teams remained on the sidelines of American sports throughout the first half of the 20th century. The Original Celtics were the first dominating professional team. Originating in Manhattan, this team stormed through the 1920s and became the paragon of American basketball. Their dominance waned as the decade closed, but the Original Celtics helped to usher in the age of popular professional basketball. Early professional basketball organizations, like the Original Celtics, suffered due to the poor performance of the first leagues. The constant financial collapse of the first professional leagues caused many more successful teams to rely on barnstorming to make ends meet.

Many leagues came and went over the first 30 years of professional basketball. During the 1930s, collegiate basketball dominated the sport and the attention of the fans, so when a new league, the National Basketball League (NBL), was formed in 1937 in the Midwest, it attempted to model the college game and recruit college stars for professional basketball. Cities involved in the 12-year existence of the NBL included Chicago, Akron, Detroit, Fort Wayne, Cleveland, Minneapolis, Indianapolis, and Sheboygan, among others. Throughout the 1940s, the NBL experienced setbacks and competition from other basketball organizations, even though the league had emerged as the most powerful league in professional basketball's short history. During the Second World War the growth of the fledgling league came to a halt, and by the end of the decade the Basketball Association of America appeared and put pressure on the NBL to disband, which the league finally did.

The Basketball Association of America (BAA) was born in 1946. During the first 2 years the league existed, its main center of competition was the East Coast. By the 1949 season, several teams from the NBL had joined the BAA and created what became a true national major league for basketball. By 1950 the BAA included the most dominating teams from both the East Coast and the Midwest and officially changed its name to the National Basketball Association (NBA). From 1950 to the present the NBA has dominated the professional ranks of basketball throughout the United States. The number of teams and locations has continually changed over the years; at present there are 30 teams stretching from Los Angeles to Boston and from Toronto to San Antonio.

African American teams began to emerge as highly competitive with the powerful Renaissance Big Five of Harlem during the 1930s. White teams needed to barnstorm to supplement the income of league play, whereas early African American teams constantly traveled after being barred from the league play of white teams. In addition to the Renaissance squad, the most popular and long-standing African American barnstorming team emerged during this era as well. The team began in the late 1920s in the city of

Chicago, and after several years they took the name Harlem Globetrotters in order to appear worldly to the Midwestern fans. Over the decades, the Globetrotters traveled to more countries than any other basketball team and became the unofficial ambassadors of the game. By 1950, after years of inclusion in the college game, African American players were admitted into professional basketball by the newly formed National Basketball Association.

—*Patrick Mallory*

Further Readings and References

Hollander, Z., & Sachare, A. (Eds.). (1989). *The official NBA basketball encyclopedia.* New York: Villard Books.

Peterson, R. W. (1990). *From cages to jumpshots: Pro basketball's early years.* New York: Oxford University Press.

Riess, S. (1989). *City games: The evolution of American urban society and the rise of sports.* Urbana, IL: University of Illinois Press.

BAUER, CATHERINE

Neither licensed architect nor credentialed planner, Catherine Bauer (1905–1964) had by the 1950s emerged as one of America's most influential voices in housing policy and urban planning. As the foremost advocate in the 1930s for "modern housing," she played a dominant role in shaping the nation's first permanent public housing program. Throughout her long career as America's premier "houser," Bauer stood for a "balanced" program of housing and regional development.

Born May 11, 1905 in Elizabeth, New Jersey, of middle-class parents, Catherine Lucy Stone Bauer graduated in 1927 from Vassar College. A postgraduate tour of Europe introduced Bauer to the ideas of Le Corbusier and modern "mass-produced," "machine-age" housing. Back in America, living an "avant-garde" life in Greenwich Village and doing publicity for Harcourt Brace publishers, Bauer met Lewis Mumford. The philosopher-urbanist became not only her lover but her entrée to the Regional Planning Association of America (RPAA) and its vision of "balanced" regional growth and nonspeculative housing in planned neighborhoods.

Bearing letters of introduction from Mumford, Bauer in 1930 traveled to Europe where she met such modernist architects and planners as Walter Gropius, Mies Van der Rohe, and Ernst May. Gropius's streamlined *bau haus* complex Romerstadt outside Frankfurt am Main especially impressed her. With Mumford she visited Europe again in 1932, and 2 years later she published *Modern Housing* (1934). The book established her as a housing expert. In *Modern Housing* she argued that affordable, well-planned, nonspeculative housing, like that at Romerstadt, derived from the active political involvement of the workers themselves. She extolled Europe's experiment with government-aided shelter, much of which featured the streamlined Bauhaus architecture of the period. By contrast, American housing had popped up chaotically and did not provide sufficiently for the needs of the workers. Bauer believed that the United States, like Europe, needed to make housing a right and a public utility and that the impetus for reform needed to come from the workers themselves. Mass evictions and mortgage foreclosures during the early years of the Great Depression vindicated Bauer's fears about the inadequacy of American housing.

The Great Depression convinced Bauer that America was ripe for modern, government-aided housing. In 1933 Franklin D. Roosevelt's New Deal created the Public Works Administration (PWA), whose Housing Division promised to rehouse America's ill housed in affordable, limited-dividend, *bau haus*-type complexes, such as the Oscar Stonorov-designed Carl Mackley Homes built by the PWA for Philadelphia textile workers. The latter sparked the founding in 1933 of the Labor Housing Conference (LHC), which lobbied for a national housing program; Bauer served as its executive secretary.

Bauer and the LHC opposed linking housing and slum clearance and centralizing the administration of government housing in Washington, which were policies favored by the PWA's Harold Ickes. Instead, Bauer and the American Federation of Labor-backed LHC espoused the limited-dividend, worker-managed Mackley model. The public housing program spawned by the 1937 Wagner-Steagall bill fell far short of Bauer's vision of modern housing as the crucible for working-class communalism. Nevertheless, in 1939 she directed the United States Housing Authority's Research and Information Division.

On the eve of World War II, Bauer accepted a teaching post at the University of California–Berkeley. There she met and married architect William (Bill) Wurster. Bauer lived in San Francisco and worked for the California Housing Authority in addition to teaching at Berkeley. In 1943 she followed Wurster back east to Harvard, where she joined Dean William Hudnut, Marcel Bruere, and Walter Gropius on the faculty of the Harvard School of Design. Increasingly, Bauer's interest broadened from housing to regional planning and to the concern for housing as a vital element in modern community building.

From 1946 to 1949, Bauer pushed for enactment of the Wagner-Ellender-Taft law, hoping it would reinvigorate the moribund prewar public housing program. However, she found the 1949 W-E-T law a mongrelized "redevelopment" bill, a ploy for "saving the central cities." In 1950 she returned with Wurster to California and to Berkeley, where she resumed her active role as a faculty member and then dean of the Architecture School and as an internationally renowned expert on housing and regional planning. In the mid-1950s, she decried the high-rise "supertenements" erected to shelter the human chaff of urban renewal. In 1957, having become a disillusioned houser, she wrote about the "dreary deadlock of public housing." Bauer was always in love with the outdoors, and she died in 1964 after accidentally falling while hiking in the Berkeley Hills.

—John F. Bauman

See also Housing Act of 1949; Mumford, Lewis; Regional Planning Association of America

Further Readings and References

Bauer, C. (1934). *Modern housing.* New York: Houghton Mifflin.

Bauer, C. (1957). The dreary deadlock of public housing. *Architectural Forum, 106*(5), 140–142.

Bauman, J. F. (2002). *Catherine Bauer: The struggle for modern housing in America, 1930–1960.* In R. Biles (Ed.), *The human tradition in urban America.* Wilmington, DE: Scholarly Resources Books.

Oberlander, P. H., & Newbrun, E. (1999). *Houser: The life and work of Catherine Bauer.* Vancouver: University of British Columbia Press.

Radford, G. (1996). *Modern housing for America: Policy struggles in the New Deal era.* Chicago: University of Chicago Press.

BELLOWS, GEORGE

George Wesley Bellows (1882–1925), a painter and printmaker of urban scenes, was born in Columbus, Ohio, on August 12, 1882, the only child of builder George Bellows and Anna Smith Bellows. Bellows entered Ohio State University in 1901 and left without completing his degree in 1904 to study illustration at the New York School of Art. He worked under Robert Henri, founder of the Ashcan School, which specialized in gritty paintings of urban life. Fascinated by the teeming life around him, Bellows gradually abandoned mannered drawings in favor of realistic depictions of street life. By 1906, he had opened his own studio.

Bellows, known for the remarkable diversity as well as the realism of his work, made an unusually rapid rise to the top of the art world. *Cross-Eyed Boy* (1906), a study of a New York street urchin, first attracted the public to Bellows's art. *Forty-two Kids* (1907), his first sale, showed a group of naked boys frolicking along the dirty waterfront of the East River in the manner that children had once gathered along swimming holes. With *North River* (1908), a portrayal of an urban landscape, Bellows had the honor of seeing his work purchased by the Pennsylvania Academy of the Fine Arts for its permanent collection. *Stag at Sharkey's* (1907), the most popular of Bellows's six boxing paintings, spotlighted brutal fighters and the pleasure of bloodthirsty spectators. It is the best known of his works today. *Cliff Dwellers* (1913) depicted wash day among the working class on New York's Lower East Side. *A Day in June* (1913) showed a fashionable throng in Central Park. The portrait *Little Girl in White* (1907) won the National Academy of Design's first Hallgarten Prize in 1913. Elected to the National Academy in 1909, Bellows became a full member in 1913.

Bellows, never particularly strong as a colorist, limited his palette to a range that verged on monochromatic. Toward the end of his short life, he began using more color. His first painting method combined thoughtful premeditation with spontaneous self-expression. By 1913, Bellows displayed a growing interest in laws of design and in carefully composing his canvases in accordance with them. His compositions were built along a geometrical framework.

Though best known for his oil paintings, Bellows provided illustrations for mass-circulation magazines, including *Collier's, Everybody's, Harper's Weekly,* and *Century.* In 1913, after embracing socialism, he contributed free illustrations to the radical magazine *The Masses.* In 1916, Bellows began making lithographs, and his work contributed to the revival of interest in lithography in the United States.

Bellows married Emma Story in 1910. A devoted family man, Bellows featured his wife and two daughters in many of his paintings and drawings, and the oil painting *Emma and Her Children* (1923) is considered among his best works. Bellows succumbed to a ruptured appendix on January 8, 1925.

—Caryn E. Neumann

See also Ashcan School

Further Readings and References

Boswell, P., Jr. (1942). *George Bellows.* New York: Crown.

Eggers, G. W. (1931). *George Bellows.* New York: Whitney Museum of American Art.

Oates, J. C. (1995). *George Bellows: American artist.* Hopewell, NJ: Ecco Press.

Benjamin Franklin Parkway

The Benjamin Franklin Parkway in Philadelphia, Pennsylvania, ranks among the most notable of early-20th-century City Beautiful projects. The parkway cuts a wide diagonal across the city's street grid, creating a vast open space for public events. Construction began in 1909 and the roadway opened in 1918.

Although several proposals to link the downtown to Fairmount Park surfaced in the late 19th century, it was the combination of national interest in city planning and local pressure to build an art museum that led, in 1907, to a detailed parkway plan aligning with an art museum on the hilltop site of the reservoir. It would be a grand urban parkway, with major cultural institutions clustered at its base and other buildings lining the route. The proposed roadway would be four lanes between City Hall and Logan Square, and then widen to the museum.

In 1916, taking advantage of a new state law giving cities the authority to control land development adjacent to parkland, the city gave control of the entire parkway to the Fairmount Park Commission, which established both height and land use regulations along the route. In 1917, the commission hired Jacques Gréber, a French landscape architect and planner, to reexamine the design. Gréber altered the earlier plans in a fundamental way. Instead of an urban boulevard, the parkway became an extension of Fairmount Park itself. The line of buildings along the route disappeared. Gréber proposed only a few public buildings in their place. Logan Square shrank to a Circle, stranded in a swirl of traffic.

The Philadelphia Museum of Art opened in 1928, but most of the proposed civic structures never materialized. West of Logan Circle only the Rodin Museum (1928) and the city's juvenile detention center (1952) were built. The cluster of civic buildings occurred on the blocks surrounding Logan Circle where the Free Library (1927), the Franklin Institute (1934), and the Municipal Court (1941) joined the Cathedral Church of Saints Peter and Paul (1864) and the Academy of Natural Science (1873). Commercial buildings and a hotel lined the blocks east of Logan Circle. In the 1960s, the block closest to City Hall was closed off and rebuilt as a plaza, popularly known as LOVE Park, after the sculpture there by Robert Indiana. In 2004, the city proposed construction of a new museum for the Barnes Collection on the site of the juvenile detention center.

In its early decades, the Benjamin Franklin Parkway served mostly as an attractive automobile route from the park drives to Center City. With 10 lanes of traffic and few buildings, it has never attracted many pedestrians. Only much later in the 20th century did it become the city's principal venue for ethnic festivals, July fourth celebrations, and parades.

—Roger D. Simon

See also City Beautiful Movement; Philadelphia, Pennsylvania

Further Readings and References

Brownlee, D. B. (1989). *Building the city beautiful: The Benjamin Franklin Parkway and the Philadelphia Museum of Art.* Philadelphia: Philadelphia Museum of Art.

Benton, Thomas Hart

The portrait of Thomas Hart Benton (1889-1975) painted by others is of a hardworking, hard-drinking, opinionated, and controversial artist. Benton was a member of the Regionalist school, an American artistic movement that promoted realistic scenes of everyday American life. Benton and fellow Regionalists Grant Wood and John Steuart Curry were successful in briefly moving the focus of the American art world from New York to the Midwest.

Benton was born in Neosho, Missouri into a political family. His uncle and namesake was one of the first two U.S. Senators of the state, and his father was an attorney and career politician. Much to his father's chagrin, Benton had no desire to become a lawyer or a politician. He had encouragement from his mother to pursue his artistic inclinations, and obtained his first professional artist position at the age of 17 as a newspaper cartoonist. After a 3-month stint at military school, Benton attended the Chicago Institute of Art. Benton left the Institute for Paris, eventually landing in New York in 1912. The New York art world became a great disappointment for Benton. He perceived a disconnect between the world of art and everyday experiences of common Americans. Benton believed art should be representative, with the subject as the focal point. He wanted to paint reality, not representation through abstract forms or color. Benton's technique for obtaining this reality was to create three-dimensional clay models of his human subjects before painting these figures in two-dimensional form on the canvas.

In his 1937 autobiography, *An Artist in America,* Benton chronicled in words and sketched his experiences as he traveled throughout different regions of the country. Benton wanted to capture what he loved about America before it disappeared. Although Benton viewed the skyscraper as evidence that Americans were regaining artistic awareness, he blamed urban dwellers for pursuing *progress* as the quintessential American value.

Following Japan's attack on Pearl Harbor, Benton painted 10 huge propaganda pieces titled *The Year of Peril.* As Regionalism's popularity waned after the war, Benton tried to find a new place in the American art world. Viewing the rapid postwar urbanization as stripping Americans of their unique characteristics, Benton turned his attention to landscape painting.

Benton is best known for his public murals hanging in Missouri, in the Missouri State Capital Building in Jefferson City and the Harry S. Truman Library in Independence, and in Tennessee, in the Country Music Hall of Fame and Museum in Nashville. Virtually every mural unveiling created a flurry of controversy, and criticism came from all corners. Art critics claimed his work was too cartoonish; social realists criticized his murals because he did not blame capitalism for America's hardships; Midwestern political elites criticized them as tawdry.

Benton chronicled the activities of everyday American people, which he captured in his murals, paintings, and drawings. In essence, Thomas Hart

Benton was a recorder of 20th-century American history. He died in his studio in January 1975.

—Doreen Swetkis

Further Readings and References

Benton, T. H. (1983). *An artist in America* (4th rev. ed.). Columbia, MO: University of Missouri Press.
Burns, K. (Writer/Director). (1988). *Ken Burns' America collection: Thomas Hart Benton* [Motion picture]. Boston: Florentine Films in association with WGBH-TV.
Yeo, W., & Cook, H. K. (1977). *Maverick with a paintbrush: Thomas Hart Benton.* New York: Doubleday.

BLACK PANTHER PARTY

Founded by Oakland, California, residents Huey Newton and Bobby Seale in 1966, the Black Panther Party was one of the most influential radical African American organizations of the late 1960s and early 1970s. The Panthers emerged out of and gave voice to a generation of urban black residents for whom poverty, racial segregation, police brutality, and neighborhood decline constituted their daily environment. By the early 1970s, the Oakland-based Panthers had inspired the formation of dozens of chapters in cities across the country, from Los Angeles to Seattle, Chicago to New Haven. The Panthers spoke out against the class and racial segregation that underlay postwar metropolitan growth and deindustrialization, and they organized their communities to seek remedies. They did so in a political language of anticolonialism and radical black nationalism inspired by Malcolm X, Karl Marx, Vladimir Lenin, and Mao Zedong. Their Ten Point Program, entitled "What We Want, What We Believe," was a seminal document of the late Civil Rights Movement.

Originally known as the Black Panther Party for Self Defense, the Panthers first gained national attention in 1967 when they marched into the California state capitol building in Sacramento bearing rifles and wearing leather jackets and black berets. They had come to testify in defense of California's existing weapons laws, which allowed registered guns to be carried openly, but their larger message was clear. Black people living in the nation's central cities would no longer tolerate indiscriminate police brutality and harassment—they would fight back. The Panthers encouraged black people to defend their communities and to resist the intimidation tactics used by all-white (or nearly all-white) urban police forces. They did so with more than guns. Panther volunteers patrolled the streets of Oakland with California statute books in hand, prepared to inform black citizens of their rights when stopped by police. Within 2 years of their founding, the Panthers had become symbols of black pride and political militancy.

In the early 1970s, the Panthers expanded the scope of their efforts in urban African American communities. They founded free breakfast programs for children, modeled after Head Start. They established Liberation Schools that taught black history. They held free sickle-cell anemia testing (sickle-cell anemia is more common in black than in white populations) and free grocery giveaways for the poor, and they instituted free ambulance service and a host of other basic social services aimed at improving the lives of impoverished urban residents. Collectively, these were known as "Survival Programs." Many of these programs were founded by and most were operated by women, who held few leadership positions in the Party but whose volunteer labor, organizing skills, and community outreach formed an essential component of the daily operations of the Panthers. In addition to the Survival Programs, the Panthers published the *Black Panther*, a radical political newspaper that frequently denounced the police, the war in Vietnam, and the politically powerful "white establishment." The paper was also an early forum for the emerging Black Arts Movement, best represented by the artist Emory Douglas, whose drawings, posters, and brilliant montages frequently adorned the cover. In all of their endeavors, particularly in Oakland, the Panthers combined a radical, class-based analysis of urban economy with black pride and an ultimately optimistic vision of the rebirth of American cities as a kind of physical, spiritual, and political homeland for African Americans.

This vision reached its fullest expression between 1973 and 1975, when Bobby Seale ran for mayor of Oakland and Elaine Brown twice ran for city council under the banner of the Black Panther Party. Calling for a "People's Economy" in Oakland, Seale and Brown orchestrated the first grassroots electoral campaign the city had seen since the 1940s. Sponsoring a massive voter registration and get-out-the-vote drive, the Panthers performed like an old-time urban political party, although one with a radical platform: community control of the Port of Oakland; a major affirmative action program in local hiring; and a new municipal revenue plan designed to redistribute the tax burden from neighborhood residents to downtown property owners. With African Americans a near majority of Oakland's population by 1973, the Panther candidates had widespread support. They were defeated nonetheless: Seale forced a run-off with the Republican mayor, John Reading, in 1973, but lost overwhelmingly in the general election; Brown came close in both 1973 and 1975 but lost by narrow margins each time. Brown continued to play an active role in Oakland politics, however, and worked to elect Lionel Wilson Oakland's first African American and reform mayor in 1977.

The Black Panther Party left an important legacy in urban African American communities by drawing attention to the price of deindustrialization and the resegregation of the nation after World War II. But the Party was not without flaws, and it has remained extraordinarily controversial. Newton, Seale, and Eldridge Cleaver, among other Panthers, frequently called for armed resistance and revolution. Their open display of weapons, their street bravado, their connection to activities of questionable legality, and their revolutionary speeches provoked an aggressive, often violent response from both local and federal authorities. The Oakland Police Department engaged the Panthers in a 3-year campaign of intimidation, harassment, and violence that many likened to a guerilla war. Nationwide, by the early 1970s, dozens of Panthers had been shot by police, dozens more were in prison, and several police officers had been killed. In addition, the counterintelligence program (COINTELPRO) of the Federal Bureau of Investigation (FBI) worked to infiltrate, destabilize, and discredit the Panthers, often through violent means of their own. Many Panther leaders found themselves caught in a cycle of violence and recrimination for which they were partly responsible (as were local and federal authorities), but which had grown beyond their control. Many among the Party's rank and file, however, escaped this turbulence and continued their community outreach, political work, and operation of the Survival Programs into the 1980s.

—*Robert O. Self*

Further Readings and References

Jones, C. (Ed.). (1998). *The Black Panther Party reconsidered.* Baltimore: Black Classic Press.

Self, R. (2003). *American Babylon: Race and the struggle for postwar Oakland.* Princeton, NJ: Princeton University Press.

Williams, Y. (2000). *Black politics/white power, civil rights, black power, and the Black Panthers in New Haven.* Naugatuck, CT: Brandywine Press.

BLACK POWER

Black Power is a term generally used to describe the struggle for civil rights for black people that took place between 1965 and the early 1970s. This period saw rising militancy, greater attention to politics, and a deeper commitment to the internal economic development of black communities under the overall umbrella of civil rights struggle. *Black Power* also refers to ideas, institutions, and cultural expressions that emphasize political and economic power for African American communities within the United States. In the urban context, Black Power was the central organizing concept for a range of movements in major American cities in the 1960s and 1970s that sought to bring historically marginalized black communities into full power sharing within the political and economic institutions that dominate big-city life. Black Power advocates took up a range of activities: running for mayor, school board, and city council; encouraging small businesses, homeownership, and entrepreneurial endeavors; advocating for black history in the schools and black studies programs in the universities; seeking redress for police brutality; fighting poverty; and in some cases advocating for a revolutionary remaking of the nation's political and economic system.

Black Power as a phrase entered the American lexicon in 1966, when Stokely Carmichael and Willie Ricks of the Student Non-violent Coordinating Committee (SNCC) used the term during a rally in Mississippi. Carmichael deployed the phrase to emphasize that the legislative and legal victories of the Civil Rights Movement would be rendered meaningless as long as black people had no real power in the United States. *Black Power* thus became the signifier of a shift in the tone and tactics of the long postwar black liberation movement: from an emphasis on legislation and moral suasion to an emphasis on building African American political and economic capacity and on full resistance to white violence, intimidation, and repression. In major cities, black Americans had long held these latter goals, but Black Power nonetheless proved a potent and generative concept around which a diverse array of movements and individuals mobilized. Black Power stands as one of the most important urban reform movements of the 20th century, on a par with those of the Progressive and New Deal eras.

Black Power was (and remains) an extraordinarily broad term. In the 1960s and 1970s, it meant everything from revolution to electing school board members to wearing a dashiki and celebrating the cultural power of African traditions. Its flexibility was part of its attractiveness. Within its broad outlines, however, three distinct tendencies could be observed. First, Black Power advocates in American cities sought to develop and expand the electoral power of African American communities. By the early 1970s, many large cities had black majorities, including Detroit, Newark, and Atlanta. Other cities, like New Orleans, Baltimore, Oakland, and Camden, had black near-majorities. In still others, including the largest cities in the nation (New York, Chicago, and Los Angeles), black communities formed a critical bloc of between one quarter and one third of the voting population. Postwar white out-migration and African American in-migration had transformed urban demographics in the space of a generation, an epochal remaking of the nation's urban populations. In this historic context, Black Power acquired concrete meaning: Black communities could determine who controlled city government.

Black Power politics was not of a single piece. Many Black Power advocates—the Revolutionary Action Movement in Detroit, for instance, and the Black Panther Party in Oakland—believed that racism and imperialist capitalism went hand in hand, and that black political power absent a radical transformation of the nation would not alter the exploitive economic system. Liberal and moderate Black Power advocates eschewed such revolutionary thinking and instead likened the objectives of Black Power to the historic demands of other American ethnic groups (the Germans, Irish, and Italians, for instance) that had sought urban political power in earlier eras as leverage in the rough-and-tumble struggle for group progress. Still others insisted that African American political power was the only thing that would put an end to police brutality, concentrated black poverty, and continued discrimination in education and employment. The nation's large cities elected an unprecedented number of black mayors and city council members between 1964 and the early 1980s. Most of them were liberal Democrats who carefully steered clear of radical affiliations but nonetheless drew on the grassroots influence of more militant groups.

Second, Black Power advocates sought a range of remedies for African Americans' historic economic marginalization. They called for a dramatic expansion of the War on Poverty in the mid-1960s to assist the most destitute urban residents. They called for a program of economic assistance to stimulate small businesses and other entrepreneurial activity in black communities. They fought for affirmative action in hiring and fair housing and lending in the home mortgage market. In sum, they called for an enormous range of reforms, from the radical left to the liberal center, designed to develop economic capacity, wealth, and capital accumulation in African American communities.

Third, Black Power represented an enormous variety of efforts to cultivate black pride and to develop the cultural resources of African Americans. Most important, this included teaching black history in urban school districts and establishing black studies programs and departments in major colleges and universities. Long denied access to their own history and subjected to demeaning racial stereotypes in both northern and southern schools, African Americans, Black Power advocates argued, deserved full and truthful representation in the American educational system. The Black Power period also saw the rise of the Black Arts Movement, a flowering of poetry, visual and graphic art, and theater in which artists combined protest politics with black cultural traditions and themes into unique forms of expression. Politically varied and culturally rich, Black Power continues to influence urban politics, culture, and economic development.

—*Robert O. Self*

Further Readings and References

Colburn, D., & Adler, J. (2001). *African American mayors: Race, politics, and the American city.* Urbana: University of Illinois Press.

Self, R. (2003). *American Babylon: Race and the struggle for postwar Oakland.* Princeton, NJ: Princeton University Press.

Singh, N. (2004). *Black is a country: Race and the unfinished struggle for democracy.* Cambridge, MA: Harvard University Press.

Van Deburg, W. (1992). *New day in Babylon: The Black Power movement and American culture, 1965–1975.* Chicago: University of Chicago Press.

Woodard, K. (1999). *A nation within a nation: Amiri Baraka (LeRoi Jones) and Black Power politics.* Chapel Hill: University of North Carolina Press.

BLACKOUTS

Urban areas are no longer uniquely vulnerable to interruptions of artificial light, as electrical grids now encompass both densely and sparsely settled territories. Yet lighting systems and their problems originated in cities. Even today, power failures continue to pose special challenges for urban areas, which are dependent on electricity for rapid transit and elevator service. In cities, too, blackouts tend to provoke greater concern about social disorder than they do in the suburbs or countryside.

The term *blackout,* drawn from stage lighting directions, became commonly applied to cities during World War II, when citizens were asked to cover their lights during air raid drills. But large-scale interruptions of electrical service date back to the 1880s, and American cities experienced failures of artificial illumination during the gaslight era as well.

Gaslight was introduced in most major American cities between 1820 and 1860. Illuminating gas at this time was manufactured by heating resin or coal in ovens called retorts. Supplies of gas were stored at the gasworks, in large pressurized tanks called *gasometers,* usually allowing service to continue even during hours when consumption outpaced production. Gas lighting could nevertheless be interrupted if gas production stopped for an extended time, or if the storage or distribution system was damaged.

Gas manufacturers preferred to build their plants along waterfronts in order to gain easy access to coal shipments and unlimited water, but this location left them vulnerable to floods that could seriously damage the equipment or at least extinguish the fires in the retorts. Fires and explosions at the gasworks also caused interruptions of gas service, as did strikes among the workers.

Newspaper articles and cartoons from the period indicate a range of reactions to failures of light. One of the common observations, still made today, was that a blackout temporarily erased technological progress and forced people to rely on their own ingenuity. Some people were said to enjoy the blackout, as a break from everyday life, with heavy drinking and erotic activity. Another response was to blame the blackout on the utility company's incompetence. Many people also expressed fears about social upheaval. In response to an 1873 gasworks strike, *Harper's Weekly* warned that if New York suffered a prolonged blackout, lawlessness and destruction would surely follow. This concern, evidently inspired by the belief that light prevents crime, continued into the electric era even in the absence of any significant blackout riot. When a generating plant explosion shut down Minneapolis's electricity in 1911, for instance, the entire police force was kept ready to fight an anticipated crime wave.

The introduction of electric lighting in the late 1870s and 1880s created a competing illumination system that temporarily mitigated the inconvenience caused by a blackout; if one system was disrupted, the other continued to function. Such was the case, for instance, when Baltimore's electric service was disrupted by a strike in 1900.

Electric supply systems had different vulnerabilities from gas systems. But power companies installed multiple generating stations, providing some insurance from technological failure as well as a flexible response to changing power demands through the day. Two other vulnerabilities presented problems that were more persistent. First, the consequences of any interruption of electricity became increasingly painful as electricity was applied to streetcars, elevators, and manufacturing equipment in the 1890s. Second, unlike gas systems, the electricity in most cities was transmitted by above-ground networks that could be damaged by severe weather.

New York, for instance, suffered its first major failure of electrical power during the blizzard of March 1888, when heavy snow and wind knocked down poles and wires throughout the metropolitan region. Electric streetlights and theater marquees stayed dark that night. As gas was still used for interior lighting in homes and most businesses, the power failure was less disruptive to daily life than the difficulty of traveling through snowy streets.

The consequences of power failures grew more severe in the 20th century with the growth of residential electric lighting, and with the heavy use of electric machinery in homes, businesses, and public spaces. For instance, the expanding use of electric refrigerators and traffic signals after about 1925 meant blackouts caused food spoilage and traffic jams. In the latter half of the 20th century and into the 21st, an urban blackout meant a radical disruption of daily life. People had to vacate workplaces rendered unusable by the failure of machinery, computers, elevators, and ventilation systems. Travel home was snarled by the disruption of traffic lights, subways, and commuter trains. Home life was made unpleasant by the loss of every appliance from the television to the kitchen stove.

The scale of power failures also expanded in the 20th century, until blackouts became regional rather than purely local events. Utility companies around 1900 began drawing power from distant hydroelectric dams, and soon from regional coal-fired generating plants as well. Some of these generating facilities served more than one city, as well as rural areas along the transmission lines. After 1935, electric service spread far beyond its previous domain of cities, suburbs, and interurban electric rail lines. The rural electrification efforts of the 1930s made increasing numbers of farms and remote villages subject to the same power disruptions that plagued cities. A continental grid soon linked electric companies throughout most of the United States and Canada.

On November 9, 1965, an equipment failure on a transmission line in Ontario set off a series of overloads on other lines, ultimately shutting off power to 30 million people in the northeastern United States and Ontario. Despite fears about the possibility of urban disorder, New Yorkers were law-abiding and often festive during the 13-hour blackout; power was restored more quickly in Boston and other cities. A blackout of this scale had been considered by the power industry to be impossible, but it was followed by another large-scale blackout in the Mid-Atlantic region in June 1967.

The New York City blackout on July 13 and 14 in 1977, which was caused by lightning hitting transmission lines north of the city, was a comparatively localized event but became infamous for its accompanying riots. Finally, events matched the fears of disorder that had historically accompanied blackouts, as looters broke into some 2,000 stores and arsonists set hundreds of fires.

Two huge blackouts shut off power to millions of people in western states in the summer of 1996, but the largest blackout in American history was the one that began on the afternoon of August 14, 2003. Originating at a generating plant near Cleveland, the power failure quickly spread throughout much of the Midwest, Northeast, and Ontario. New Yorkers, in particular, initially feared that blackout was the result of a terrorist attack like the one that had hit the city 2 years earlier. The event passed without major incident, and city residents suffered or enjoyed the experience much as they had in nearly every other blackout.

—Peter C. Baldwin

See also Infrastructure and Urban Technical Networks; Rioting; Street Lighting

Further Readings and References

Baldwin, P. C. (2004). In the heart of darkness: Blackouts and the social geography of lighting in the gaslight era. *Journal of Urban History, 30*(5), 749–768.

Federal Power Commission. (1967). *Prevention of power failures: Vol. 1. Report of the commission.* Washington, DC: Government Printing Office.

Nye, D. E. (1990). *Electrifying America: Social meanings of a new technology.* Cambridge, MA: MIT Press.

BLOCKBUSTING

Blockbusting is certain real estate dealers' practice of using racial scare tactics to persuade whites to sell their homes, buying them themselves, and then reselling the properties to African Americans. Blockbusting accounted for much of the racial succession and segregation in private housing in American cities during the 20th century. In the decades after World War II, the speed and scale of blockbusting made it seem that white urbanites were participating in massive "white flight." Blockbusters, the real estate speculators who engineered the transfers, exploited both property sellers and buyers. White sellers frequently sold their property at a loss, while black buyers paid blockbusting intermediaries substantially more than the previous owners had sold for. Despite the inflated resale prices, the financial losses whites suffered from blockbusting fed the perception that blacks lowered property values.

The word *blockbusting* came into popular use in the late 1950s, when African Americans resumed the interwar Great Migration and sought housing in increasingly crowded urban centers. During the blitz of London in World War II, the word *blockbuster* described aerial bombs that destroyed whole blocks; white Americans' sense that the arrival of blacks doomed a community was reflected by their adoption of the wartime metaphor. The term *panic peddling,* which emphasizes the psychological state of the property owner rather than the geography of the sale, was used synonymously.

Real estate speculators in Harlem who realized that black urbanites desperately needed housing pioneered the practice that later became known as blockbusting. Even before African Americans crowded into cities like New York and Chicago in the tens of thousands in the 1910s, real estate dealers understood that they could profit from whites' distaste for African American neighbors. After moving one or two black families into a block, they could persuade white homeowners to sell their properties at reduced prices and introduce more African American residents. The existence of separate housing markets for whites and blacks enabled the creation of expensive, crowded ghetto neighborhoods from which African Americans were eager to escape.

In the years after World War II, blockbusting became one of the primary methods by which African Americans purchased homes in Northern cities. Blockbusters worked by reinforcing whites' racist beliefs about the damage created by the presence of African Americans in the neighborhood. The first step in busting a block was advising incumbents that blacks' arrival was imminent. Blockbusters directly solicited property owners by mail and telephone, while also arranging for African Americans to promenade on targeted blocks and call white homeowners in the middle of the night. They told potential sellers that the first homeowner on a block to sell could receive a "market rate" price, but that subsequent sellers would be grateful to sell at any price. Once a blockbuster made a purchase on a block and enabled a black family to move in, remaining white residents sold out rapidly, for ever-decreasing prices. The less blockbusters paid for these homes, the greater their profits when they resold them to African Americans. Blockbusters also retained some properties and rented them to blacks who could not afford to purchase a home. Because federal policy discouraged banks from issuing mortgages in black neighborhoods until the late 1960s, African American buyers financed their properties with large cash down payments and unorthodox lending methods such as contract sales (in which late or missed payments could result in the prompt repossession of the property by the blockbuster, because buyers did not gain title to the property until they paid off the entire loan).

African Americans who gained access to housing in this way had mixed feelings about blockbusters. On the one hand, paying exorbitant prices to rent deteriorated and overcrowded slum properties made the prospect of owning one's own home appealing. Black home buyers who calculated that access to private housing was a vital improvement credited the real estate agents as community builders. On the other hand, African Americans knew they were paying higher prices than whites for the same properties. Those who resented this differential understood blockbusters as exploiters. For their part, whites often felt shame at selling under such circumstances and contributing to the breakdown of their communities. Whites used a range of vicious epithets to describe blockbusters and sought to stop them.

In the first half of the 20th century, many white property owners signed restrictive covenants with their neighbors, agreeing not to permit blacks, Asians, or Jews to purchase or occupy their homes, except as servants. After World War II, neighborhood activists tried to ban the posting of "for sale" signs, which they believed encouraged panic. They also petitioned municipal and state authorities to revoke the sales licenses of blockbusting real estate dealers. Neighborhood organizations attempted to repurchase homes that panicked whites sold to blockbusters. Anti-blockbusting activists asked city governments to outlaw the practices associated with blockbusting, such as threatening racial change; this tactic failed because of the constitutional protection of free speech. Neighborhood groups also returned blockbusters' harassment by picketing their offices and homes. In Chicago, rules against blockbusting were incorporated into the city's fair housing law, but they were enforced only erratically. The federal Fair Housing Act of 1968 outlawed blockbusting, as well as racial discrimination in sales, but likewise enjoyed only imperfect enforcement. By the beginning of the 21st century, neighborhood groups had become less concerned about blockbusting and worried instead about its less racist, but still exploitative, cousin property flipping.

—*Amanda I. Seligman*

See also African Americans in Cities; Fair Housing Act of 1968; Federal Housing Administration; Restrictive Deed Covenants

Further Readings and References

Meyer, S. G. (2002). *As long as they don't move next door: Segregation and racial conflict in American neighborhoods.* Lanham, MD: Rowman & Littlefield.

Orser, W. E. (1994). *Blockbusting in Baltimore: The Edmondson Village story.* Lexington: University Press of Kentucky.

Seligman, A. I. (2001). Apologies to Dracula, Frankenstein, Werewolf: White homeowners and blockbusters in postwar Chicago. *Journal of the Illinois State Historical Society, 94,* 70–95.

Blues Music

Blues is a vernacular musical form that grew out of the African American experience in the early 20th century. It generally consists of a 12-bar song structure and features the tonic-subdominant-dominant (I-IV-V) chord cadence and the prominent use of the flatted seventh note, also known as the *blue note* or *dominant seventh.* While there is evidence that the dominant seventh is related to West African musical forms, the blues has also been accommodated within European harmonic theory, in which it corresponds with the mixolydian scale. The blues provided the basis for much of the American music that followed: rock and roll, soul, and much of gospel and jazz are all variations of the blues.

Guitar-based instrumentation, the frequent use of call-and-response, and the narrative themes of loss and longing place the blues squarely within African American life in the South during the Jim Crow era. Much of the popular tradition surrounding the origins of the blues emphasizes an atavistic connection with the experience of slavery and its aftermath, but recent scholarship has determined that the blues was a syncretic form that incorporated ideas from ragtime, vaudeville, and other popular music that was widely available on radio, records, and sheet music by the 1920s. Its hybrid origins help to explain the protean quality of the blues, its ability to adapt and develop in a variety of musical and cultural contexts. Robert Johnson, who is often cited, incorrectly, as the inventor of the blues, sang stories of sex, violence, and damnation as these were understood within the religion of the Mississippi Delta region, but in songs such as "Red Hot," he also assimilated the tempo of jug-band music and the vocal range of bluegrass. In "Sweet Home Chicago," Johnson expressed a vision of the city as a hopeful alternative to the sharecropping and racial violence of African American life in the South.

Because blues was originally shaped in part by urban institutions such as radio, it did not evolve smoothly from acoustic, rural, and primordial to electrified, citified, and sophisticated. It nonetheless played a distinctive role in African American urban experience during the post–World War II period. Blues provided much of the soundtrack of working-class black life around the shipyards of Oakland, the stockyards of Chicago, and the auto plants of Detroit. Its song structure and instrumentation shaped the transition from big bands to small combos. The business of music, particularly blues, also represented a crucial economic strategy for urban African Americans. During the 1930s and 1940s and beyond, many African Americans worked as musicians and music teachers in Los Angeles and other cities. Even more important, blues provided the basis for black-owned businesses in the form of nightclubs, record stores, and radio.

Musical production remained firmly in the hands of white company owners until the 1960s, even while black producers had principal responsibility for selecting the artists and making the records. Such figures as Willie Dixon in Chicago, Don Robey in Houston, and Dave Clark in Memphis served as talent scouts, arrangers, engineers, and often salesmen too. In the 1940s and 1950s, along with their counterparts in other cities, they constructed regionally distinctive bodies of work around the talents of more famous artists, including McKinley Morganfield (better known as Muddy Waters) in Chicago, Bobby "Blue" Bland in Houston, and Aaron "T-Bone" Walker in Los Angeles. These were the people who carried the blues into the period when it would be "rediscovered" by white audiences in Europe and America interested in the origins of rock and roll.

B. B. King, who grew up in the Mississippi Delta and recently marked his 80th birthday, is probably the most recognized blues artist of the 21st century. His nightclub chain, along with the similarly themed House of Blues, has established a nominal presence for the blues in the shopping malls, theme parks, gambling casinos, and other venues of contemporary mass-market entertainment. The protean qualities of blues have hardly diminished, and it still inspires creative interpretation, mostly out of the sight of modern mass culture. Venerable figures such as Mickey Champion, once a protégé of T-Bone Walker, can be heard on Saturday night in Los Angeles; Bobby Rush remains a popular figure in the nightclubs serving black audiences across the southern tier of the United States; and the blues continues to evolve in the hands of younger professionals such as Zac Harmon, Ray Bailey, and Arthur Adams. The blues still offers an engaging musical format for the artistic expression of passion and pain.

—*Matthew W. Roth*

Further Readings and References

Nelson, G. (1988). *The death of rhythm and blues.* New York: Pantheon.
Wald, E. (2004). *Escaping the delta: Robert Johnson and the invention of the blues.* New York: HarperCollins.

BOGART, HUMPHREY

Humphrey DeForest Bogart (1899–1957) was born in New York, and his on-screen persona reflected the world-weary sardonic spirit of the city. Humphrey DeForest Bogart, or Bogie, as he was known, had an elite background. He was born on December 25, 1899, the son of Manhattan physician Belmont DeForest Bogart and prominent magazine illustrator Maud Humphrey Bogart. After being expelled from Phillips Academy in Andover, Massachusetts, he served in the United States Navy in World War I, and in 1921 he became a Broadway stage actor. By 1930, he had become a Fox Studio contract actor and appeared in John Ford's *Up the River* (1930), Raoul Walsh's *Women of All Nations* (1931), and Mervyn Le Roy's *Big City Blues* (1932). After playing the ruthless killer Duke Mantee in Robert Sherwood's drama *The Petrified Forest* on Broadway, he reprised the role in the 1936 Warner Brothers movie version of the play.

Thereafter, the gentlemanly Bogart played a series of big-city hoodlums in movies such as Raoul Walsh's *The Roaring Twenties* (1939), in which he played opposite cinema tough guy James Cagney. Bogart embodied the caustic and cynical hero adhering to his own strict code in many roles at Warner Brothers studio, including his roles in *The Great O'Malley* (1937), *San Quentin* (1937), *Kid Galahad* (1937), *Angels With Dirty Faces* (1939), and *They Drive by Night* (1940).

Bogart may be remembered best as the streetwise San Francisco private eye Sam Spade in John Huston's *The Maltese Falcon* (1941). His weather-beaten face, withering snarl, and trademark lisp, from an injury to his lip in the Navy, added to his unconventional screen image. Comedians often exaggerated these traits, making Bogie one of the most impersonated movie stars. In *Casablanca* (1942), Bogie's acting reached a new level when he played a bitter romantic from New York City whose anti-Nazi heroism awakens a sleeping isolationist America to the threatening war. This role as Rick Blaine made Bogart an international movie star who dominated the golden years of Hollywood with his stoical persona and reputation as a consummate actor.

In 1941, Bogart met Howard Hawks and Lauren Bacall, and together the three of them made two masterpieces, *To Have and Have Not* (1944) and *The Big Sleep* (1946). In 1945, Bogart married Bacall. With John Huston, Bacall and Bogart starred in *Key Largo* (1948). Bogie played a war veteran confronted by Chicago gangsters during a Florida hurricane. He tackled more complex roles as paranoid, suspicious antiheroes in John Huston's *The Treasure of Sierra Madre* (1948) and Edward Dmytryk's *The Caine Mutiny* (1954). He won an Oscar for his leading role in John Huston's offbeat *The African Queen* (1951). Already ill with cancer, Bogie turned to comedy with mixed results in Huston's *Beat the Devil* (1954) and Billy Wilder's *Sabrina* (1954) and *We're No Angels* (1955). In his last feature film, *The Harder They Fall* (1956), Bogart played a hardboiled press agent with a tender heart, a role he filled effortlessly and often.

Known to the FBI since the 1930s for his liberal political views, Bogart, along with Bacall, protested the anti-Communist witch hunts of the House Un-American Activities Committee in 1947, but unlike many Hollywood figures, his career was unaffected. Bogart's tempestuous life off screen, his three marriages, and his disputes with studio executives were zealously concealed from the media. After appearing in more than 70 movies, Bogart died in Los Angeles on January 14, 1957, the most popular American actor of the century. Harvard University students soon thereafter created the Bogie cult at the Brattle Theater in Cambridge, Massachusetts, a small art house theater where devoted fans and film buffs could go each winter to see *Casablanca* and many other Bogart movies. Bogart's blunt, manly, and witty manner appealed to the coffeehouse existentialists and counterculture youths. In the 1960s, Bogie's habit of dangling a Chesterfield cigarette from his lips spawned the marijuana smokers' phrase "Don't bogart that joint." Bogart, one of Hollywood's legendary figures and a popular culture icon today, received first place on the American Film Institute's list of the greatest screen actors.

—*Peter C. Holloran*

See also Hollywood; Motion Pictures and Cities and Suburbs

Further Readings and References

McCarty, C. (1965). *Bogey: The films of Humphrey Bogart.* New York: Citadel Press.

Meyers, J. (1997). *Bogart: A life in Hollywood.* Boston: Houghton Mifflin.

Sperber, A. M., & Lax, E. (1997). *Bogart.* New York: William Morrow.

BOHEMIANISM

Bohemianism has been an important feature of urban life for the last 150 years. In the 19th century, chroniclers described the bohemian's fate as tied to the city, the site of novel experience and nonconventional life. Twenty-first-century urban boosters, concerned about the fate of the city, claim bohemianism as savior of the economic life of the city.

As popularized by writer Henri Murger in the 1840s, bohemianism was the way of life for Parisian artists, writers, and musicians who were newly severed from the old system of art patronage and thrown into the market. In Murger's stories, new urban amenities such as furnished rooms, apartments, hotels, pawnshops, and restaurants, as well as a commercial market for art, facilitated the ability of individuals to live unconventional lives, but urban conditions did not create bohemians. In these years, urban bohemians also appeared in venues such as Thackeray's *Vanity Fair,* with its bohemian heroine Becky Sharp. In the 1850s, a group of New York writers, artists, and musicians meeting at Pffaf's restaurant declared themselves bohemians. To them this meant cosmopolitan, sympathetic to the fine arts, unbound by convention, and open-minded. Like their Parisian counterparts, the mid-19th-century American bohemians used urban institutions (such as restaurants) as public amenities and as frameworks for unconventional lives. Mid-19th-century self-defined bohemians, whether in Paris or New York, typically led sexual lives unconstrained by marriage.

In the 1890s, American cities across the nation took up the Bohemian banner and gave it a new meaning. George DuMaurier's bestselling novel *Trilby* (1894), which describes the bohemian life of Parisian artists, became a popular play and reintroduced bohemianism to Americans. Giacomo Puccini's 1896 opera, *La Boheme,* retold, again, Murger's stories and played in Los Angeles and New York. Cities such as Buffalo, Boston, Oakland, Fort Worth, and Cincinnati created new publications with titles like *The Bohemian,* the *New Bohemian,* and the *Amateur Bohemian.* The bohemians behind these magazines often saw themselves as promoters of art and culture, but they had little in common with their more unconventional ancestors. The Fort Worth publication, for example, had a section for temperance and Bible stories, and the Cincinnati magazine promoted service, uplift, and efficiency. But in the 1890s, to be bohemian was to be up-to-date, and in many cities restaurant owners advertised their bohemian atmospheres.

It was, however, Greenwich Village that in the years from 1890 to 1920 became the quintessential bohemian neighborhood. Rather than a collection of individual bohemians, the Village fostered networks of people promoting the development of new art, new literature, new politics, and new gender relations. In the Village, a pluralistic mixing of classes, ethnic groups, and the sexes helped to produce a new American culture and a new enthusiasm for the potential of urban life. The bohemian mix of radical politics, culture, and modernity helped make New York City the leading American city. But bohemia also could be found in small scale cosmopolitan centers like Taos, New Mexico; Woodstock, New York; Carmel, California; and Davenport, Iowa. In Greenwich Village, it was not simply urban amenities that helped to sustain the bohemian quarter—it was the diverse cultural experiences made possible by the metropolis which bohemians in the Village promoted as the modern way of life.

Pioneering urban sociologists W. I. Thomas and F. Znaniecki shared this view, creating a typology of social personalities that included the bohemian, which they described as a type shaped by a desire for new experience and a high degree of adaptability to new conditions. Potentially antisocial because of their alienation from established society, bohemians—along with their opposites, the philistines, and the creative individuals occupying the middle ground—formed new urban personalities. Other sociologists noted that, unlike other urban groups of the 1930s, bohemia itself was heterogeneous and cosmopolitan.

By the 1920s, the reputation of Greenwich Village as a bohemian center had been made, even as the radical nature of the prewar era faded, challenged by both political repression and changing taste. Tourists, encouraged by restaurants, theaters, and magazines as well as the newspapers, arrived in the Village by sightseeing buses and taxis; but many of the previous generation of radical bohemians had departed. Rents were too high for aspiring writers and the communal connections of the earlier age, and literary and political movements declined.

The post–World War II urban crisis prompted urban boosters to identify people who liked city life; thus bohemians and their neighborhoods proved helpful in promoting a positive attitude toward cities. In the 1950s, beatniks, described by some contemporaries as

descendants of bohemians, took root in urban neighborhoods like Greenwich Village; Telegraph Hill and North Beach, in San Francisco; and Venice Beach in California. They promoted poetry, jazz, and Zen Buddhism, as well as a rejection of the "square world." The hippies of the 1960s built countercultural urban communes in such places as Haight-Ashbury in San Francisco and the East Village in New York, promoting a critique of the materialism and militarism of contemporary society and laying the groundwork for future urban gentrification.

At the dawn of the 21st century, contemporary observers thought the position of bohemians had moved again, from margin to mainstream. Journalist David Brooks characterized the "bobos," a hybrid between the bohemians and the bourgeoisie, as the new elite. Members of this educated class, residents of expensive suburbs, not crumbling inner cities, were characterized not by their critiques of society but by their consumption patterns. In a similar manner, economist Richard Florida developed and popularized a theory of economic growth which suggested that places with high concentrations of gay and bohemian populations would have higher rates of innovation and economic growth. Calculating a number which he termed "The Bohemian Index," he claimed to measure the number of artistically creative people in a given locale. Florida, who also measures the "Gay Index" of cities, suggests that for the 21st century, cities with high concentrations of gays and bohemians also score highly as "family-friendly" locales.

Richard Florida's bohemians are apolitical, but they share a lust for experience that can most easily be satisfied in urban settings. They dislike the term *bohemian,* which seems to imply alienation, and prefer to be called "the creative class." Now, rather than being marginal, as they were in the 19th century, bohemians appear to be central to successful urban life.

—*Andrea Tuttle Kornbluh*

Further Readings and References

Brooks, D. (2000). *Bobos in paradise: The new upper class and how they got there.* New York: Simon & Schuster.

Florida, R. (2002). *The rise of the creative class and how it's transforming work, leisure, community and everyday life.* New York: Basic Books.

Murger, H. (2004). *The bohemians of the Latin quarter.* Philadelphia: University of Pennsylvania Press.

Stansell, C. (2001). *American moderns: Bohemian New York and the creation of a new century.* New York: Owl Books.

Thomas, W. I., & Znaiecki, F. (1927). *The Polish peasant in Europe and America.* New York: Knopf.

Boom Towns

Boom towns can be either new or existing communities that experience unprecedented and explosive growth because of mineral wealth that is discovered in the area or a major construction project (or sometimes because they are in a location that allows them to draw the trade of an area). In most cases, when the physical feasibility and economic payoff of the mineral extraction have been exhausted or when the construction project has been completed, the boom town is abandoned and becomes a ghost town, whereas in other cases, the communities actually survive the bust that follows the boom and become viable communities that are not based on whatever originally drew people to them.

With boom towns, while the boom is occurring, there tends to be the opportunity for wealth in the mines or well-paying jobs on the construction project. This makes it difficult to find labor for other work. It also causes inflation, in which wages and the prices for goods and services all rise above what can be earned in other areas.

Even though many boom towns are in new areas, the people who are settling them still have all of their existing problems. The 19th-century boom towns faced problems similar to those of their 20th- and 21st-century counterparts, such as prostitution, gambling, alcohol, and drug use and abuse. There were also problems that can be found in other urban settings, like the need for clean and reliable water sources, the removal of waste products, managing livestock as well as pets, effective self-government, and law enforcement.

During the 19th century in the American West there were many boom towns, the best known of which are those associated with mining and railroads.

Mining Boom Towns

Some of the first mining boom towns in the United States were actually at the southern end of the Appalachian mountain range in northern Georgia. Two towns were founded because of a gold rush in the 1830s in this region: Auraria and Dahlonega.

A very good example of explosive growth because of the discovery of gold is seen in California. The discovery of gold on January 24, 1848, by John Sutter on the American River launched the most famous American Gold Rush. When the gold was discovered, there were approximately 7,300 people of either European or Hispanic decent living in California. By the end of 1849, this population had exploded to more then 60,000, the population that the United States required a territory to have when applying for statehood. In 1850, California entered the Union as a free state.

In 1859, with gold and silver deposits discovered in the border area of Nevada and California as well as in the mountains of Colorado, there were new rushes. The camps and boom towns that would form near mines tended to be of a temporary nature, but two cities near the mining regions of California and Colorado, San Francisco and Denver, exploded with population growth and became the dominant cities of their respective regions.

Railroad Towns

The transcontinental railroad, which included the Union Pacific and Central Pacific railroads, was a major construction project that started in Omaha, Nebraska. The railroad was viewed as a method of getting goods that were arriving in the ports of California to the markets of the eastern United States; it was also viewed as a way of settling the western United States. In addition, the railroad opened up large tracts of land for settlement across Nebraska, Wyoming, Utah, and Nevada. Part of the financing for the railroads came from the government, which specified that for each mile of track a company laid, it was to receive 20 square miles of federal land. The land was allotted in alternating sections for 20 miles on either side of the right-of-way.

There was a great need for towns to supply water and fuel for the steam locomotives. As the technology improved, the Union Pacific stopped needing support in so many locations, and without the support of the railroads, some of the towns disappeared. In Wyoming, many of the towns that had once thrived—like Sherman, Bear River City, Ramsey, Percy, and Dana—disappeared, while others—like Cheyenne, Laramie, Hanna, Rawlins, and Evanston—survived and became the major population centers for the state of Wyoming up through World War I.

Oil Towns

As the 19th century closed and the 20th began, a new mineral resource was the driving force for new boom towns—oil. The oil and gas production industry was responsible for much of the development in Texas and Oklahoma and for the growth of small towns into small cities.

World War II

During World War II, two wartime boom cities sprang up around the Manhattan Project. The first and best known was Los Alamos, New Mexico. It was an existing community when the U.S. Army came in 1942 to set up research facilities. The area still houses military weapons and other research facilities.

The other boom town and research facility was where the uranium production for the atomic bomb took place—Oak Ridge, Tennessee. The construction of the plant and the city began in 1942. At the peak in 1942, there were 47,000 construction workers at the site. By 1945, there were 75,000 people living in Oak Ridge.

Energy Boom Towns

The energy boom towns that appeared in the Rocky Mountains were a response to the energy crises of the 1970s. Not only were oil and gas found in Colorado, Utah, Idaho, New Mexico, Arizona, Wyoming, and Montana, but there were also rich coal fields and oil shale found in some of these states. In the western portion of Colorado, there are large coal reserves, and throughout western Colorado, southwestern Wyoming, and eastern Utah there are large deposits of oil shale. In the mid- to late 1970s and early 1980s, it looked like the oil shale industry would be the replacement for the traditional gas and oil industries. In western Colorado, small towns like Parachute, Meeker, Silt, and Rangely all experienced great prosperity. There were large expenditures for new schools, roads, sewers, and water treatment plants. Yet, for all the money that the oil companies were pouring into research and development of oil shale, none of them could make it profitable. This led the companies to slowly withdraw and shut down their operations, leaving the small towns that had seen such promise to collapse, following the trend of so many boom towns before,

because they were unable to absorb the suddenly jobless workforce and had no method for dealing with an increased tax burden.

—*Douglas K. Bohnenblust*

Further Readings and References

Gulliford, A. (1989). *Boomtown blues: Colorado oil shale, 1885–1985*. Niwot: University Press of Colorado.

Head, S., & Etheridge, E. W. (1986). *The neighborhood mint: Dahlonega in the age of Jackson*. Macon, GA: Mercer University Press.

Klein, M. (1987). *Union Pacific: Vol. 1. Birth of a railroad, 1862–1893*. New York: Doubleday.

Malamud, G. W. (1984). *Boomtown communities*. Environmental Design Series, Vol. 5. New York: Van Nostrand Reinhold.

BOOSTERISM

Boosterism, or the practice of urban self-promotion, has been part of the American scene for two centuries. Boosterism has been both a tool and an ideology of urban rivalry. Boosters write for nonresidents, trying to persuade outsiders to settle and invest in their particular cities. They also write for a local audience, in arguing that the same expanding economy that directly benefits local real estate and business indirectly helps everyone in the community. In so doing, they may try to divert attention from internal conflicts, mobilize residents around the common cause of growth, and generate enthusiasm for public investment in public facilities and transportation improvements.

There is direct continuity between the often-florid rhetoric of 19th-century newspaper editors and the slick brochures produced by the economic development arms of 21st-century city governments. In the early 19th century, boosters were usually individual journalists, land speculators, or commercial entrepreneurs. By the second half of the 20th century, they were increasingly professionals within public and private economic development organizations. *Pure* boosterism can be defined as the publication and dissemination of positive comments and evaluations of a city's economic position and prospects. *Applied* boosterism shades imperceptibly into targeted business recruitment, an activity that benefits from a community's positive reputation but which also involves specific inducements and subsidies (whether free land for early railroads or tax abatements for modern manufacturing concerns).

Boosterism in the 19th century was especially prevalent on the urban frontiers of the Midwest and Far West. When English-speaking settlers reached these frontiers, they faced the necessity and opportunity to construct an urban system from scratch. As a result, nearly any river junction, lakeshore harbor, or road crossing *might* be the seed for an important city. The early annals of nearly every state are filled with fierce battles between rival settlements, fought in part as battles of words between rival editors and publicists. Was Toledo to be the major city on the lower Maumee River, or would the prize go to any of half a dozen rival townsites? Which of the rival townsites, separated only by a sluggish river, promised to become the core of Milwaukee? Would Seattle, Tacoma, Everett, or Bellingham emerge as the principle railroad terminus and port on Puget Sound?

Visitors from the East Coast and Europe remarked on the eagerness of Americans to expound on the virtues of their new communities and on the optimism and grandiloquence of their language. James Fennimore Cooper satirized the tendency through the character of land speculator Aristabulus Bragg in *Home as Found* (1835). In *Martin Chuzzlewit* (1844), Charles Dickens sharply observed boosterism by telling the story of Eden, a town far grander in word than in fact. Traveler John White, on a junket sponsored by the Union Pacific Railroad, found that Cheyenne, Wyoming, in 1867 did not quite live up to its billing and commented accordingly in *Sketches From America* in 1870.

Frontier boosters made energetic use of the local and national press. One of the primary functions of frontier newspapers was to talk up the advantages of their town and point out the disadvantages of rivals. Sometimes a newspaper began boosting a new town before anyone actually lived there. Editor William Byers first labored on behalf of Omaha, but packed up his printing press in 1859 and followed the Pike's Peak gold rushers to Denver, where his *Rocky Mountain News* helped to make that city the preeminent city of Colorado. Boosters also found a new outlet with the emergence of national business periodicals before the Civil War, especially *Hunt's Merchants Magazine* and *DeBow's Review.* Intended audiences for antebellum boosters included potential settlers, investors, and railroad builders.

Boosters on the urban frontier often spoke the language of geographic determinism, and they were often unabashed in adopting the premises of manifest destiny and of European cultural or racial superiority that were common in the 19th century. A mere glance at the map, said the typical booster, made it obvious why Chicago (or Terre Haute or Tacoma) was fated for greatness. Several writers, notably Jesup W. Scott and William Gilpin, developed elaborate statistical and geographical theories that claimed to pinpoint the location of the next great world city. In Scott's case that site was on the Great Lakes; in Gilpin's it was at Kansas City and later at Denver. Promoters of individual cities offered their own explanations of their community's obvious natural advantages, as Logan U. Reavis did in *St. Louis: The Future Great City of the World* (1870). The San Diego Chamber of Commerce, in the same decade, lauded its city's harbor and location. Even towns with little distinguishing geography made the most of what they had: Fresno, "the Raisin City," would surely prosper because it was smack dab between Los Angeles and San Francisco.

In towns that survived their first decades to achieve a second and third generation of growth, boosters added the task of inventorying and recording past and present accomplishments as proofs of future success. The goal was to demonstrate that prosperity and refinement went hand in hand, and young cities worked hard to show that they were safe, sober communities with "eastern" amenities. Boosters such as Cincinnati's Charles Cist produced city histories and statistical compendia that offered the hard data of progress and enlisted the past to prove future success. They published sketches of early growth; lists of schools, newspapers, and charitable societies; and tables showing manufacturing output, wheat shipments, street paving, taxes, births, real estate prices, and other quantifiable indicators.

During the late 19th and early 20th centuries, boosterism became more specialized and organized. Boosters began to offer arguments that focused on a city's advantages for specific economic functions— Atlanta as a wholesaling center for the South; Colorado Springs and San Diego as health resorts; Phoenix as the "Valley of the Sun" for long winter vacations (the name coined by an advertising agency in the 1930s). Cities also relied on organizations rather than individuals to sing their praises. The number of local chambers of commerce in the United States grew from 10 in 1858 to several hundred by 1900. In the late 19th century, Milwaukee had an Association for the Advancement of Milwaukee, Indianapolis had a Manufacturers and Real Estate

Exchange and a Board of Trade, and Los Angeles had the All-Year Club of Southern California.

At the turn of the 20th century, cities also resorted to indirect public relations. They built industrial and commercial exhibition halls as standing trade shows. They purchased advertisements in national magazines, a technique especially favored by Southern cities. They competed for national conventions and staged expositions, special events, and festivals such as Pasadena's Tournament of Roses. Imitating the undeniably successful World's Columbian Exposition in Chicago in 1893, cities from Norfolk (1907) to San Diego (1915) and Buffalo (1901) to Seattle (1909) mounted their own world's fairs. All these activities were designed to enrich cities directly by attracting big-spending visitors and indirectly by "putting the city on the map."

Although boosterism is often treated as an urban phenomenon, many of the promotional impulses and techniques of boosterism have been employed to sell entire states and regions. In the 19th century, railroads and state immigration offices published reams of pamphlets to talk up the advantages of settling in their western service territories. More recently, state departments of economic development have taken on the challenges of securing new investment in a competitive global economy—an activity sometimes characterized as "smokestack chasing."

In the last decades of the 20th century and on into the 21st century, American cities continued to pursue special events (the Olympic games held in Los Angeles in 1984, Atlanta in 1996, and Salt Lake City in 2000, for example). They scrambled for recognition and reputation as "major league cities" by subsidizing professional sports teams with tax-financed stadiums and arenas. Their economic development departments also practiced the modern version of booster writing with glossy brochures that proclaimed their advantages as places to do business. The comparative statistics, bright pictures, and carefully oriented maps of such promotional literature are identical in concept to those of the booster publications of the 1850s. The numbers may be more accurate, the pictures are now in full color, the targeted audience is likely to be manufacturing firms rather than land speculators and railroad moguls, and the language references industrial clusters and the costs of doing business rather than geography, but the underlying message and purpose are essentially the same.

—*Carl Abbott*

Further Readings and References

Abbott, C. (1981). *Boosters and businessmen: Economic thought and urban growth in the antebellum Middle West.* Westport, CT: Greenwood Press.

Burbank, M. J., Andranovich, G. D., & Heying, C. H. (2001). *Olympic dreams: The impact of mega-events on local politics.* Boulder, CO: Lynn Reinner.

Emmons, D. (1971). *Garden in the grasslands: Boomer literature of the Central Great Plains.* Lincoln, NE: University of Nebraska Press.

Glaab, C. (1962). *Kansas City and the railroads.* Madison, WI: State Historical Society of Wisconsin.

Hamer, D. (1990). *New towns in the new world: Images and perceptions of the nineteenth-century urban frontier.* New York: Columbia University Press.

Logan, J., & Molotch, H. (1987). *Urban fortunes: The political economy of place.* Berkeley, CA: University of California Press.

Wrobel, D. (2003). *Promised lands: Promotion, memory, and the creation of the American West.* Lawrence, KS: University Press of Kansas.

BOSSES AND MACHINES

The political boss and the citywide machine are among the most indelible popular images of American urban politics. Envisioned either as a cheerful figure distributing turkeys or buckets of coal in working-class neighborhoods while lining his pockets with honest graft or as a faceless, quiet presence awarding jobs, influencing officials, and managing elections, the boss was reputed to be at the center of a disciplined political organization that built urban infrastructure, dominated government, and provided social services during the explosive period of urban growth between the Civil War and the Great Depression.

Urban political machines developed out of the social and political circumstances of mid-19th-century America. The convergence of popular democracy, strong party identification and organization, sustained immigration, ethnic division, and rapid urban spatial and population expansion created sturdy political associations and loyal constituencies, along with demands for effective mechanisms of control in growing cities. City governments often lacked the centralized authority to respond to these needs. County and state controls over city budgets, parks, utilities, and even police weakened mayors and divided government responsibility. Exemplified by the Tammany Hall organization of William Marcy Tweed in

New York City, political machines bypassed the inadequate formal structure of governance and directly distributed resources, provided jobs, and carried out public works. This informal governance operated on an illicit flow of money and the exchange of votes for services. The corruption of machines (and their connection to working-class, ethnic communities) prompted middle-class reformers in the late 19th century and the Progressive Era to enact urban home rule, centralized mayoral powers, executive budgets, and expert administration of municipal services to undercut the power of political organizations and party bosses. During the 1930s, the expansion of federal government supports created another potential rival to bosses and machines. Yet some urban machines prospered well into the 20th century. Richard J. Daley's Chicago machine, which combined political and governmental control to an unprecedented degree, developed in the 1950s, long after the urban age that supposedly fostered boss rule. Even so, recent historical interpretations have revised the long-standing image of the boss and the urban machine. Many urban historians question the centrality of the boss and machines to urban governance. Some even deny the widespread existence of citywide political machines allied with immigrant, working-class voters.

The most influential impressions of bosses and urban political machines came from the observations of Lord James Bryce and the example of the Tammany Hall machine in New York City. In *The American Commonwealth* (1888), Bryce, an English analyst of American politics, portrayed the urban boss as a uniquely powerful, unelected, secretive, and disreputable figure whose dominance of urban public life condemned American cities to poor governance. Tammany Hall furnished an example of thorough organization and an array of colorful leaders that came to define machine politics and boss rule in both positive and negative ways. Tammany Hall was a faction in the New York City Democratic Party. It was associated with the New York Irish, at a time when Irish and German immigrants were the largest elements in an immigrant stream that by 1870 made up 44 percent of the city's population. In the late 1860s, Tweed became the first figure to dominate New York City politics through the organization. Tweed controlled appointments and policy to an unusual extent by means of combined office holding in state, county, and city government as well as his chairmanship of the Tammany party organization. Although a native-born Protestant, Tweed recognized the rising

influence of immigrants and included Irish and Germans in patronage and policy matters. Yet Tweed was also corrupt and ostentatious, a combination that led him to prison and the image of the boss into infamy. Later Tammany leaders Richard Croker (1886–1901) and Charles Francis Murphy (1903–1924), the latter the personification of the quiet, unobtrusive machine leader, perfected the organizational and electoral mechanism of Tammany. A vertical network of committees linked the boss through the party hierarchy down to block captains and voters. One high-level figure in this chain, George Washington Plunkitt, became the public face of machine politics through a series of published interviews with journalist William Riordan begun in 1897 and appearing in book form in 1905. Plunkitt's genial observations on professional politics and public service softened the criminal image of political bosses left by Tweed and furthered by Croker's reputation for violent acts and corruption. Plunkitt, in contrast to these bosses, emphasized constituent service and community involvement to the exclusion of most national political issues. Even though Plunkitt had served in the New York State Assembly and Senate, his political horizon was limited to his city, his district, and the Tammany Democratic organization. Plunkitt brightly admitted to graft, but only in terms of using his knowledge of city politics to make profitable business deals. Reformers expressed outrage, but Plunkitt's "plain talks on practical politics" helped cement the image of political machines as essential distributors of social services in an age of immature governance.

Between the 1880s and 1920s, other political leaders and organizations in large and small cities approached the level of centralization and control exercised by the Tammany machine. Urban growth, disorder, and fragmented city services gave George B. Cox the opportunity to construct a powerful Republican machine in Cincinnati in the 1890s. Baltimore's Isaac Freeman Rasin, Christopher Buckley of San Francisco, and Hugh McLaughlin in Brooklyn presided over centralized Democratic organizations. In Kansas City, Tom Pendergast amassed power between 1918 and 1924, then bossed the most tightly organized urban machine of its time between 1925 and 1939, at which point he followed Tweed's path into prison. Yet the dominant boss at the apex of a citywide machine was more of a rarity than the Tammany model suggested. The political structure of late 19th century cities was ward-based rather than centralized. That system gave rise to factions and strong neighborhood leaders rather than a top-down party arrangement. Chicago and Boston did not have citywide machines at the turn of the 20th century, but they contained locally powerful figures such as John Powers and Michael "Hinky Dink" Kenna in Chicago and Martin Lomasney in Boston. Most city machines were alliances between such "ward bosses" and were more decentralized and fragile than the language of bosses and machines indicates. Tweed's organization itself was a "ring" of conspirators rather than the fully developed machine later run by Murphy. Cox and Pendergast were ward-based politicians who were unusually successful at defeating and then dominating their factional rivals. Moreover, most bosses were political leaders rather than policymakers. Many departments in city government operated relatively independent of machine control.

The nexus of immigrant support, corruption, and reform in relation to city machines was also complex. Urban machines served the needs of immigrant, ethnic, and working-class constituents, but not to the exclusion of other groups. Political organizations depended on close cooperation with urban business and commercial interests, often through public building programs and franchise awards. Pendergast wooed elite support through such measures. He also grew wealthy off paving contracts and subsidized vice. The corrupt links between machines, business, and public works prompted reformers to press for urban home rule and increased mayoral authority and more formal government control over city services. These measures inadvertently enabled machine rule to take root in some cities. Boss rule in Philadelphia was promoted by the state Republican machine and a reform city charter passed by the Pennsylvania legislature in 1885. The charter allowed party officials to reduce the autonomy of ward politicians and centralize power. A similar charter reform enacted in Boston in 1909 had the same effect. The adoption of the city manager system in Kansas City in 1925 became a key element in the most dominant period of the Pendergast machine, since the boss named and controlled the manager. Reforms intended to bypass political machines thus sometimes made machines more efficient. Rather than undercutting machine rule everywhere, federal money from New Deal programs in cities like Kansas City and Pittsburgh was absorbed into the local organization's distribution of jobs and resources.

The enhanced power of mayors in 20th-century cities introduced another innovation to machine rule—the consolidation of party and government power in the office of the mayor. In 1914, James Michael Curley joined the traditional ethnic constituency of urban machines with the Progressive Era expansion of executive authority to dominate politics and governance in Boston through four mayoral terms. Unlike the invisible government of the late 19th century machine, Curley became the visible symbol of Irish aspirations and power in Boston. The new machine, combining political and governmental control, reached its culmination in Chicago under Richard J. Daley. Daley first achieved prominence as Democratic leader of Cook County and then was elected mayor in 1955, serving in both roles until his death in 1976. Daley had political clout, access to patronage, and, as mayor, could deliver dependable city services to all Chicagoans. But as political loyalties diminished and city governments turned from issues of growth to those of management and declining population, the organizational system that Daley had perfected faded away.

—*Thomas R. Pegram*

Further Readings and References

Allswang, J. M. (1977). *Bosses, machines, and urban voters.* Baltimore, MD: Johns Hopkins University Press.

McCaffery, P. (1993). *When bosses ruled Philadelphia: The emergence of the Republican machine, 1867–1933.* University Park, PA: Pennsylvania State University Press.

Merriam, C. E. (1929). *Chicago: A more intimate view of urban politics.* New York: Macmillan.

Riordon, W. L. (1994). *Plunkitt of Tammany Hall* (T. J. McDonald, Ed.). Boston: Bedford Books/St. Martin's Press.

Stave, B. M., Allswang, J. M., McDonald, T. J., & Teaford, J. C. (1988). A reassessment of the urban political boss: An exchange of views. *The History Teacher, 21,* 293–312.

Teaford, J. C. (1984). *The unheralded triumph: City government in America, 1870–1900.* Baltimore, MD: Johns Hopkins University Press.

BOSTON, MASSACHUSETTS

Boston was founded in 1630 by English Puritans who established the Massachusetts Bay Colony on the Shawmut Peninsula. Under Governor John Winthrop, the Puritans created their own form of worship based on John Calvin's doctrine of predestation. As members of the "elect," the Puritans created a theocratic government restricted to members of the Congregational church. With few natural resources, Bostonians turned to the sea, and they were soon involved in fishing, shipbuilding, and international commerce.

In 1660, King Charles passed Navigation Acts to curtail American commerce, but Bostonians ignored the regulations until the king revoked the charter and made Massachusetts a royal colony. When William and Mary came to the throne in 1688, they gave Massachusetts a new charter, but they had the governor appointed by the Crown. The religious requirement was removed, so that most English Protestants could participate in the political affairs of the colony.

Crown and Colony

With a new charter, an enlarged electorate, and an expanding economy, by the start of the 18th century Boston was a bustling seaport town. The new royal governor and his officials built fine houses in the center of town and established an active social life. A number of local Bostonians also established themselves as gentlemen of influence, and their commercial enterprises brought prosperity to the town.

As long as Great Britain was at war with France, Boston was able to continue its independent ways. Once Britain had defeated France in 1763, however, the British took steps to bring the colonies under control. Local patriots like James Otis and Samuel Adams protested strongly against British attempts to tax Americans without going through their colonial legislatures. In 1770, tensions in Boston became so great that British soldiers fired upon a mob of civilians in what became known as the Boston Massacre. Three years later, the passage of the Tea Act led a group of patriots to throw boxes of tea into the harbor in what was called the Boston Tea Party. Britain responded to this indignity with a series of Coercive Acts that closed the port of Boston and established martial law. Boston became an occupied town, with a diminished population and an unproductive economy, until March 1776, when General George Washington fortified Dorchester Heights and forced the British soldiers and loyalist civilians to evacuate the town. Boston then took the opportunity to rebuild itself.

From Town to City

With independence and a new federal Constitution, the town's economy revived. Yankee ships resumed commerce with old markets and discovered new markets in South America and the Far East. The population of the town grew steadily from 25,000 in 1800 to 30,000 in 1810, while new building projects created a new State House as well as a residential area around Beacon Hill. Although a second war with Britain in 1812 seriously endangered the future of shipping, Boston merchants successfully invested their capital in textile manufacturing.

After transforming Boston from a town into a city in 1822, a group of wealthy and public-spirited men took steps to raise the intellectual level of the citizens and make Boston the "Athens of America." The literary accomplishments of Ralph Waldo Emerson, Henry David Thoreau, and Henry Wadsworth Longfellow led Oliver Wendell Holmes to call Boston "the hub of the solar system." Josiah Quincy, the second mayor, greatly improved and upgraded the old town, while his associates organized temperance movements, engaged in prison reform, and built hospitals and asylums. Horace Mann created a public school system; Samuel Gridley Howe worked with the blind; Dorothea Dix established facilities for the mentally ill.

There were other reformers who wanted more substantial changes. A number of Bostonians organized a movement for universal peace, while women like Elizabeth Cady Stanton, Lucretia Mott, and the Grimke sisters agitated for equal legal, political, and civil rights. And with the publication of *The Liberator* on January 1, 1831, William Lloyd Garrison started the Abolition movement that labeled slavery as a moral evil and called for total and immediate emancipation. Growing demands throughout the North that slavery should be either abolished outright, or prevented from spreading any further, provoked an angry response from the slaveholding South. The election of Abraham Lincoln in November 1860 led to the formation of the Confederate States of America, and in April 1861, the bombardment of Fort Sumter, a federal fort in Charleston Harbor, produced the opening shots in the Civil War.

Volunteer regiments from Massachusetts were among the first to respond to Lincoln's call for troops, and the Bay State continued to provide men for the Union forces throughout the war. In 1861, Governor John Andrew authorized the formation of two units of Irish-American troops; and in 1863, after Lincoln's Emancipation Proclamation went into effect, he also authorized the formation of two African American regiments. With the surrender in 1865 of General Robert E. Lee to General Ulysses S. Grant at Appomattox, Virginia, the Civil War finally ended.

Changing Cultures

After the Civil War, Boston expanded considerably in size through the annexation of neighboring communities and the filling in of waters along the bay to create a large residential area called the Back Bay. A steady growth in both local numbers and foreign immigrants increased the population from 140,000 in 1865 to over 340,000 in 1875.

During the first part of the 19th century, most immigrants to Boston came from Northern and Western Europe—English, French, Germans, and especially Irish after the great potato famine brought death and starvation to their land. By the late 19th century, a second wave of immigrants came from southern and eastern Europe—Italians, Greeks, and Austrians, Jews, Poles, and Russians. Many native Bostonians feared Irish Catholics, Jews, and other strangers would have adverse effects upon their traditional Protestant culture, and they tried to hold the line against their rise and advancement.

As the earliest and largest of the immigrant groups, the Irish moved into Boston politics, took over control as ward bosses at the local level, and by the 20th century had gradually increased their power at City Hall. Elected mayor of Boston for the first time in 1914, James Michael Curley used personality and patronage to solidify the ethnic vote. While Yankee Republican Protestants still controlled the city's financial institutions, Irish Democratic Catholics dominated the political system. With neither side willing to cooperate with the other, by the 1940s Boston had become a badly divided city, with dire consequences to its public finances and physical infrastructure.

A New Boston

The defeat of Curley in 1949 by John B. Hynes, a moderate collaborationist, brought together both financiers and politicians to work for the benefit of the city. Hynes's vision of urban renewal was carried into effect by his successor, John F. Collins, whose urban planner, Edward Logue, helped create the modern designs of the New Boston. This gave Kevin H. White, who had an unprecedented four terms in office as mayor, from 1967 to 1983, the opportunity to hail Boston during the bicentennial years as a livable city.

During the 1950s the number of African Americans in Boston increased substantially, and by the 1960s Boston's African Americans were demanding better housing, jobs, and education. Failure of the all-white Boston School Committee to respond to calls for school desegregation led black leaders to bring suit in federal court. Judge W. Arthur Garrity declared the Boston public schools guilty of a systematic program of segregation, and he ordered a program of busing to correct the situation. Many of the city's ethnic neighborhoods reacted violently against court-ordered busing and, starting in September 1974, they took to the streets to prevent its implementation. Motorcycles and special police were needed to protect students on the yellow buses on their way to school.

By the time that Raymond L. Flynn was elected mayor of Boston in 1983, the worst of the busing crisis had run its course, but the city had to deal with more complex demographic changes. During the 1960s and 1970s, a new wave of immigration had brought newcomers to Boston from different parts of the world. At first Latino/as came from Puerto Rico, Cuba, and Haiti; then others arrived from countries like Colombia, El Salvador, and Nicaragua. And at the same time, large numbers of Asian people came from Vietnam and Laos, as well as from China, Japan, and India. When Thomas M. Menino became mayor in 1993, the city's population had become more than 50 percent nonwhite—with school figures indicating an even wider gap in the near future.

During this same period of demographic change, Boston also became a multicultural metropolis specializing in high-tech industry and high-end services. An economy once based on fishing, commerce, factories, and textile mills now owes its prosperity to universities, medical establishments, microelectronics firms, and complex financial services. The completion of the so-called Big Dig, the largest civil-engineering project in U.S. history, promises to unify some of the oldest and most historic parts of downtown Boston.

—*Thomas H. O'Connor*

Further Readings and References

Beatty, J. (1992). *The rascal king: The life and times of James Michael Curley, 1874–1958.* Reading, MA: Addison-Wesley.

Brooks, V. W. (1936). *The flowering of New England.* New York: Modern Library.

Handlin, O. (1941). *Boston's immigrants, 1790–1865.* Cambridge, MA: Harvard University Press.

Lukas, J. A. (1985). *Common ground: A turbulent decade in the lives of three American families.* New York: Knopf.

O'Connor, T. H. (1997). *Civil War Boston: Home front and battlefield.* Boston: Northeastern.

Rutman, D. (1965). *Winthrop's Boston: Portrait of a Puritan town.* Chapel Hill: University of North Carolina.

Bowery, The

Initially an Algonquin footpath running along a north-south ridge in Manhattan, the Bowery ultimately became one of the most important commercial thoroughfares in New York City and an internationally recognized urban legend. In 1637, Dutch colonial governor Wilhelm Keift used the *bouwerij,* meaning a farm with some cleared land, as a formal lane connecting the emerging New Amsterdam with the rural settlements to the north. By the 1650s it was a well-traveled road, and in 1673 it became the first route for overland post delivery. During the colonial period Bouwerie Lane was also known as the Boston Post Road, the primary overland route connecting New York to Boston.

With the arrival of the English, Bouwerie Lane was Anglicized to the modern Bowery. Throughout the 18th century, the Bowery was home to many prominent New Yorkers and numerous significant estates. New York City, and the Bowery, saw a rapid social and economic transformation between the decades of 1790 and the 1840s. In the early period, the DeLancey estate leased land along the southern Bowery and the adjacent Collect Pond to 46 artisans and butchers. The economic and residential transformation of this period gradually took place along the Bowery. During the antebellum era, the Bowery, beginning at its southern end, commenced a slow evolution from being the home of bourgeois citizenry to a place of commerce and industry. The Bowery had become a place where prominent citizens lived alongside prostitutes, groggeries, and manufacturing sites.

Conflict along the Bowery was both economic and racial. The nativist Bowery Boys, emerging in the 1830s, became one of the perennial symbols of the Bowery. These native-born artisans and workers, threatened by the Irish and free blacks of neighboring Five Points, often took to the street and violently exerted their rights as Americans. Such conflict was often centered on the theaters of the Bowery. Conflict erupted often, culminating with the 1849 Astor Place Theater Riot when mobs of nativists protested the presence of an Irish actor onstage. Within 6 weeks of the riot, the remaining bourgeois Bowery residents petitioned the City of New York to rename the street and thus salvage its tarnished reputation. City leaders renamed the Upper Bowery, from Astor Place to Union Square, and so as not to risk another incident, it was called Fourth Avenue rather than named to honor a prominent American.

Throughout the 1850s, the Bowery became an increasingly working-class commercial district. Saloons, inexpensive boarding houses, tattoo parlors, auctioneers, and melodramatic theaters flourished. The Bowery has often been described as a center of working-class and artisan culture during the antebellum era. While this description may be an accurate generalization, the street also was increasingly becoming a gathering point for the homeless and impoverished of New York City.

Following the Civil War, veterans and countless displaced persons attempted to find a home in New York City. During a 6-month period in 1853, the Municipal Lodging Houses of Manhattan sheltered 24,893 people. Following the Civil War, during the late 1860s, they housed an average of 86,214 per year, as noted by Kenneth Scherzer in 1992. As the numbers of New York City's homeless rose after the Civil War, the Bowery increasingly became a concentrated place of the disaffiliated.

In 1873 the Reverend John Dooley opened the first cheap Bowery hotel. The Bowery Mission opened its doors in 1879, followed by many institutions, all attempting to gather in the overflow of homeless from the burgeoning Municipal Lodging Houses and the cellars of local police precincts. During the 1880s the All Night Mission, the Salvation Army dormitory, the St. Barnabas House for Women, and the Brace Memorial Newsboys' House and, by the early 20th century, the Hadley Mission could all be found along the Bowery, as noted by Kenneth Jackson in 1987.

In 1884, 27 percent of all arrests in New York City took place along the Bowery. In the same year, some 82 saloons or drinking establishments were located along the mile between Chatham Square and Cooper Union, making an average of 6 establishments per block. By the year 1890, there were an estimated 9,000 homeless people along the Bowery between City Hall and Cooper Union. This number increased almost 200 percent within 20 years, to 25,000 by 1907. By that date, the Bowery had become an almost exclusively male enclave, as noted by Howard Bahr in 1973.

It was in the late 19th century that homelessness became institutionalized and segregated in American cities. Toward the last quarter of the century, skid row areas, with sections inhabited mainly by homeless men, were established in each of our major cities. The New York City police reported in 1890 that over the previous decade the department had provided lodgings in jails and lockups to 150,000 persons annually (making it the largest lodging supplier in the city), as noted by Peter Rossi in 1989. The Bowery was New York City's Skid Row.

The City of New York began to turn its back on the Bowery in the late 19th century, allowing it to further decline. This is best illustrated by the turmoil over the Bowery Elevated Train. The Bowery El opened on August 26, 1878, with a single track in each direction built over the sidewalks. The tracks were built so that while the buildings were shaded, the street was lit. These tracks were destroyed in 1911, and 4 years later rebuilt as four tracks across the entire street. This action, done at a time when many of Manhattan's elevated tracks were being moved below ground, condemned the Bowery to economic underdevelopment and a drastic lowering of real estate values. It is quite possible that those involved in the decision had come to the conclusion that it was acceptable to cover the Bowery and allow the infamous street to be darkened not only by reputation, but by steel as well.

The homeless played a crucial role on the Bowery. This street was considered the dumping ground for New York City's human refuse in the late 19th and early 20th centuries. By the year 1890 there were an estimated 9,000 homeless people living on the Bowery, and that number increased 200 percent, to 25,000, by 1907. While the number continued to grow, but as poverty and homelessness increasingly became a national issue, the Bowery as the locale played a less significant role. The numbers of homeless along the Bowery during the Great Depression are almost uncountable. But following World War II the homeless population began to significantly decline. One study claimed that in 1949, only 13,975 homeless were on the Bowery, and that number dropped sharply to 7,611 by 1964, as noted in *The Bowery Project* in 1965.

The 20th century brought benign neglect along the Bowery that prevented significant structural changes to most of the buildings. Until the late 1990s the Bowery held an extraordinary array of 19th-century urban architecture. With the coming of the 21st century gentrification began to take its toll.

Numerous buildings have been torn down and replaced with modern anonymous residential structures. Saloons have been replaced by fashionable nightclubs and there appears to be a wholesale commercial transformation. However, there remain nearly a half-dozen cheap "flophouse" hotels, numerous charitable missions, and, although numbering in the hundreds and not thousands, the homeless.

—*Seth Kamil*

See also Five Points; New York, New York

Further Readings and References

Bahr, H. (1973). *Skid Row: An introduction to disaffiliation.* New York: Oxford University Press.

Bureau of Applied Social Research. (1965). *The Bowery project.* New York: Columbia University Press.

Jackson, K. (1987). The Bowery: From residential street to Skid Row. In R. Beard (Ed.), *On being homeless: Historical perspectives.* New York: Museum of the City of New York.

Rossi, P. H. (1989). *Down and out in America: The origins of homelessness.* Chicago: University of Chicago Press.

Scherzer, K. (1992). *The unbounded community: Neighborhood life and social structure in New York City, 1830–1875.* Durham, NC: Duke University Press.

BRICE, FANNY

Fanny Brice (1891–1951) is best known for her successful career as an entertainer and comedienne, her starring role in Ziegfeld's "Follies" for over two decades, and her work in radio and film throughout the early 20th century.

The third child and second daughter of Rose Stern, a Hungarian immigrant, and Charlie Borach, a French bartender, Fania Borach, as she was named at birth, grew up in a nonreligious Jewish middle-class household in Newark, Brooklyn, and Manhattan. She began her life of performance as a young girl, singing and dancing on top of the bar at her father's saloon, while he, her first big supporter, tossed her coins. When she was 15, Brice, who adopted the name of family friends for the stage, began performing on "Amateur Night" at Keeney's Theater in Brooklyn, the leading vaudeville theater of the era. Her first impromptu performance there was met with a standing ovation, and her career as a singer and entertainer was launched.

In 1909, when she was 17, Brice received her first contract to perform in a touring burlesque show called "The College Girls." In 1910, she left "The College Girls" to join Florenz "Flo" Ziegfeld's 3-year-old "Follies," a new genre of musical theater combining burlesque and comedy. She soon became the audience's favorite performer and was a perennial of the Follies until its demise in 1931. Brice attained real stardom in the 1921 edition of the Follies, in which she introduced a French torch song, "My Man," which became her trademark. Other songs identified with her were "Second Hand Rose," "I Should Worry," and "Rose of Washington Square."

In 1919, Brice married her long-time boyfriend Julius "Nick" Arnstein, a charming con man who became one of the most wanted fugitives in the United States in the 1920s; they had two children together. After Brice divorced Arnstein in 1927, she married the songwriter Billy Rose in 1929, divorcing him in 1938.

Owing to her success with Ziegfeld's Follies, in the 1930s, Brice began to appear in Broadway shows and motion pictures with such major performers as W.C. Fields, Eddie Cantor, and Will Rogers; she starred in *My Man* (1928) and *Be Yourself!* (1930). In *Crazy Quilt* (1931), she introduced the character of Baby Snooks, a mischievous brat she had first played in vaudeville in 1912. Baby Snooks later became a Follies favorite, and Brice played the character on radio from 1936 until her death in 1951.

Following her divorce from Billy Rose, Brice moved to California, where she lived for the rest of her life. She continued to work in radio and film, appearing in *The Great Ziegfeld* (1936) and *Everybody Sing* (1938). Her life was the subject of the film *Rose of Washington Square* (1939) and of *Funny Girl,* a Broadway musical (1964) and a motion picture (1968).

—*Elif S. Armbruster*

See also Burlesque

Further Readings and References

Goldman, H. G. (1992). *Fanny Brice: The original funny girl.* New York: Oxford University Press.

Grossman, B. (1991). *The life and times of Fanny Brice.* Bloomington, IN: Indiana University Press.

Katkov, N. (1953). *The fabulous Fanny: The story of Fanny Brice.* New York: Alfred A. Knopf.

BROADACRE CITY

Broadacre City is the plan for an ideal community that was designed by architect Frank Lloyd Wright. In direct contrast to fellow architect Le Corbusier's highly urban "Contemporary City for Three Million Inhabitants," Broadacre City represented Wright's posturban, agrarian vision of the United States. The name Broadacre City was derived from Wright's notion that each citizen should own at least an acre of land. Wright had been working on the project, originally called "Usonia" after his name for its citizens, for quite some time when the 1929 stock market crash convinced him that the country was in need of drastic change. Wright's first public introduction of Broadacre City was during the Kahn Lectures at Princeton University in 1930, and he offered a detailed exposition of his plan in *The Disappearing City,* first published in 1932.

In *The Disappearing City,* and a later revision published in 1958 as *The Living City,* Wright contrasted what he saw as the inhuman, congested conditions of modern urban life to his own low-density city form. To Wright, modern cities were plagued with traffic jams, petty crime, and slums, and their architecture had lost all sense of human proportion, while contemporary uses of industrial technology alienated human beings and made them servants to machines. Rather than abandon technology, however, Wright proposed that it be put to better uses. Technological advances like automobiles and personal aircraft allowed people to traverse great distances quickly, telephones reduced the need for personal contact, and improvements in lighting, heating, and refrigeration methods made it possible for people to spread out across the land. These advancements enabled the decentralization of the city over a vast area, and the creation of Broadacre City, a city in the country. Rather than live in cramped urban quarters, families would own between 1 and 5 acres of land, and the farming and light industry that they undertook on their land would be the center of social and economic life. In Wright's view, this radical decentralization of the city would lead to the dissolution of "mobocracy," a resurgence of individuality, and a revival of Jeffersonian-style democracy based on individualism. Individual ownership of physical and intellectual property would eliminate the systems of "rent" of labor, property, and ideas that caused people to live vicarious lives and lose the ability to see themselves as productive individuals. Wright felt that when every citizen owned, lived on, and worked on his or her own land, the modern fragmentation between things like urban and rural life, physical and mental labor, and work and leisure would be eliminated.

True to his desire to see a resurgence of individualist democracy, Wright envisioned a nation with a very limited government. He did see the need for a uniform system of money or some form of social credit, but he saw no need for a large national government. Instead, the primary locus of government would be the county, and the most powerful official in Broadacre City would be the county architect. Trained in the principles of organic architecture, the county architect's primary responsibility would be road design, a central component in Wright's vision. This radical decentralization extended to education as well. Elementary schools would have no more than 40 students, classes would have no more than 10 students, and the curriculum would include cooking, gardening, and drawing. Large universities, too, would be eliminated and replaced by small institutes, fellowships, and style centers like Wright's own Taliesin.

Although Wright's plan was for a highly decentralized and family-based community life, he also acknowledged that people needed to come together for social and economic reasons. To this end, he created roadside markets for cooperative exchange as well as community centers, or "automobile objectives," automobile-accessed destinations built in places of natural beauty that included golf courses, racetracks, zoos, aquariums, planetariums, sports clubs and arenas, art galleries, museums, and botanical gardens. In addition to the roadside market and automobile objective, Wright designed centers of religious worship; his nonsectarian cathedrals for universal religious worship and fellowship consisted of multiple chapels around a large communal worship space devoid of any particular denominational symbolism.

While Broadacre City was intended to be primarily agrarian, Wright also planned small factories with living quarters on the top floor, apartment buildings, and houses with laboratory space. However, because most families would be small-scale farmers, Wright concentrated on his prototypical "Usonian" houses. The Broadacre City landowner would assemble a home from mass-produced components designed with enough flexibility to allow customization. Perhaps better known than Broadacre City itself, many Wright-designed Usonian houses were actually constructed throughout the United States. These modest dwellings feature open floor plans, great rooms, and one or more carports. Their horizontal lines and use of native materials allow them to blend with their environment and give them an aesthetically pleasing yet unassuming character, while natural heating, cooling, and lighting make them environmentally friendly.

Although Wright's vision was radical and comprehensive, he offered no specific plan for its implementation. Rather, Broadacre City was a prediction of the gradual disappearance of urban centers and a proposal for what the country could look like in the absence of such centers. In the winter of 1934 to 1935, Wright's students at Taliesin created a scale model of a sample 4-square-mile section of a hypothetical Broadacre City, which Wright insisted was merely a suggestion of what Broadacre City could look like, not an actual design to be copied. In 1940, a Detroit group interested in resettling auto workers on the land asked Wright to design a community of homesteads for 15 families. Wright designed the community, but the group never followed through with their plan. Because Broadacre City was never built, Wright's vision remains theoretical. Still, Broadacre City should not be dismissed. Not only does Broadacre City bring together many of Wright's ideas about architecture and society; it is also notable for its predictive quality as suburban sprawl and edge cities displace urban centers as the focus of social and economic life in the United States.

—*Gina Marie Dreistadt*

See also Wright, Frank Lloyd

Further Readings and References

DeLong, D. G. (Ed.). (1998). *Frank Lloyd Wright and the living city.* Milan: Skira Editore S.P.A.

Fishman, R. (1977). *Urban utopias in the twentieth century: Ebenezer Howard, Frank Lloyd Wright, and Le Corbusier.* New York: Basic Books.

Rosenbaum, A. (1993). *Usonia: Frank Lloyd Wright's design for America.* Washington, DC: Preservation Press.

Wright, F. L. (1958). *The living city.* New York: Horizon Press.

BROOKLYN, NEW YORK

Today, Brooklyn, an 81-square-mile area at the western end of Long Island, is the most populous of New York City's five boroughs. Among other things, it is known for the Brooklyn Bridge, its vibrant ethnic neighborhoods, Coney Island, the West Indian Carnival celebration, and the Brooklyn Dodgers—-the baseball ghosts that still haunt it after almost 50 years.

The first European settlers of Brooklyn were the Dutch, who claimed the area as part of their New Netherlands territories early in the 17th century. They established five Dutch farming communities and one English one: Flatlands (1636), Brooklyn (1646), Flatbush or Midwood (1652), New Utrecht (1657), and Bushwick (1660), as well as the English town Gravesend (1645), founded by Lady Deborah Moody, who with her followers had fled New England seeking religious freedom. Although all of the towns were stable and prospered, of the six, Flatbush, which was centrally located and served as the administrative, economic, and religious hub until the 1830s, and Brooklyn, located on the great harbor opposite lower Manhattan, were the most important.

On August 27, 1776, the Battle of Long Island, the first and biggest engagement of the American Revolution, took place in the towns of Flatbush and Brooklyn. The battle was won decisively by the British, who routed the American troops. The American Revolution almost ended with that battle. However, on August 29, fog and night made fighting another day possible when the remaining troops, with George Washington aboard the last boat, were able to escape across the East River to Manhattan.

After the British left in 1783, the towns, which had been devastated by the occupation, began to rebuild themselves. With the exception of Brooklyn, the towns remained sparsely populated farming communities until the late 19th century. Because the land in those towns stayed in the same families for generations, the combination of strong social and kinship ties and lack of economic necessity made it possible for them to withstand pressures to urbanize. The town of Brooklyn, because of its location on the East River, grew rapidly.

Brooklyn's transformation to an urban manufacturing and industrial center began with the development of its waterfront. In 1801, the federal government opened the Brooklyn Navy Yard on the East River. Shipbuilding in the Navy yard reached its peak during World War II, when more than 70,000 men and women worked around the clock 7 days a week in support of the war effort. In 1966 the government closed the yard and turned it over to New York City, which has developed it into an industrial park. The closure of the yard coincided with the decline of Brooklyn's manufacturing base and waterfront activities and the beginning of its shift to a service economy. Today, Brooklyn's once working waterfront is being turned into a large urban park.

Throughout the 19th century and well into the 20th century, the Brooklyn waterfront was an industrial powerhouse. In 1814, regular commuter steam ferry service began on the East River, making the commute between the town of Brooklyn and Manhattan easier and safer. The convenience allowed more people to move to Brooklyn, which was considered a healthier environment for families than crowded Manhattan. Many of the landholders, particularly on Brooklyn Heights, began to subdivide their holdings for housing, creating the first suburb.

In 1825, the opening of the Erie Canal, with the town of Brooklyn as its southern terminus, added to the already thriving industrial port. In 1834 the town of Brooklyn became the City of Brooklyn. By 1839 there was a city plan that mapped its streets along a grid. Work on its new City (now Borough) Hall was completed in 1849. With its annexation of the towns of Williamsburg and Bushwick in 1855, Brooklyn became the third largest city in the United States. Factories, port facilities, and warehouses stretched for miles along the shore of the East River from South Brooklyn to Greenpoint and Newtown Creek on the north. They produced a wide variety of products that were shipped across the country and around the world. With the influx of new immigrants from the 1840s onward, the City of Brooklyn was a microcosm of the world.

Even before its city charter, Brooklyn, unlike the other towns in Kings County, began to build cultural institutions. In 1823 the Brooklyn Apprentice Library, the forerunner of the Brooklyn Museum, was founded. In 1861 the Brooklyn Academy of Music (BAM) opened on Montague Street. When it was destroyed by fire in 1908, it was rebuilt at its present location on Lafayette Avenue in Fort Greene. Newly refurbished, BAM is the cornerstone of the new Fort Greene Arts District. In 1863 the Long Island Historical Society, now the Brooklyn Historical Society, was founded. The year 1897 marked the beginning of the Brooklyn Public Library system and the opening of Steeplechase amusement center in Coney Island. Major league baseball began at Ebbetts Field, home of the Brooklyn Dodgers, in 1913. In 1947 Jackie Robinson joined the team as the first African American major league player, a historic moment for baseball and civil rights.

The two most important construction projects were Prospect Park, which was completed in 1874, and the Brooklyn Bridge, which opened in 1883. Prospect Park, designed by Frederick Law Olmsted and Calvert Vaux, broke land barriers between the towns. Flatbush Avenue, a narrow road that predated European settlement, became a major roadway linking Brooklyn and the towns to its south. In addition to the 526-acre park, Olmsted and Vaux designed two grand avenues, Eastern Parkway, which connected east and west, and Ocean Parkway, which connected the park to the beaches at Brighton and Coney Island. In 1878 the Brooklyn-Flatbush-Coney Island Railroad, the predecessor to the subway system's Q line, began operating between the Park and Coney Island. The new subway lines and trolley cars which began to crisscross the area in the 1890s brought an end to farming and massive residential housing development. The Brooklyn Bridge made travel between Manhattan and Brooklyn easy and efficient. At the beginning of the 20th century, two other East River bridges were built, the Williamsburg Bridge in 1903 and the Manhattan Bridge in 1909.

In 1894 the City of Brooklyn annexed the towns of Flatbush, Gravesend, and New Utrecht. It became coterminus with Kings County in 1896 with the annexation of Flatlands. In 1898 it was consolidated into the city of Greater New York and became one of its five boroughs.

During the first half of the 20th century, Brooklyn's growing population of immigrants and their first- and second-generation children created expanding vibrant ethnic neighborhoods. However, at the end of World War II, federal housing policies encouraged people to look to the suburbs for new housing. By the 1960s Brooklyn was in decline. That decline started to be reversed in the late 1960s and early 1970s as ethnically diverse young families began to move to old neighborhoods and renovate the row houses, generically known as "brownstones." The movement was supported by the 1965 New York City Landmarks Preservation law. Although Brooklyn Heights had held its own during the decline, the neighborhoods surrounding it had not. Suddenly those neighborhoods were in demand, and for the last 40 years Brooklyn has undergone a major revival most visible in places like Park Slope and Fort Greene and in the turn-of-the-20th-century enclaves of Victorian Flatbush.

—*Nedda C. Allbray*

See also New York, New York

Further Readings and References

Allbray, N. C. (2004). *Flatbush, the heart of Brooklyn.* New York: Arcadia.

Lancaster, C. (1979). *Old Brooklyn Heights: New York's first suburb.* New York: Dover.

Snyder-Grenier, E. M. (1996). *Brooklyn: An illustrated history.* Philadelphia: Temple University Press.

Stiles, H. R. (1867). *A history of the city of Brooklyn.* New York: Author.

Willensky, E. (1986). *When Brooklyn was the world: 1920–1957.* New York: Harmony.

BROOKLYN BRIDGE

The Brooklyn Bridge captures the complexities of late-19th-century architecture in a single sweep. At that time, eclecticism, industrialization, technology, and urbanization drove the production of new building types maximizing the use of new materials produced through manufacturing. Embodying the dichotomy between engineering and architecture, the Brooklyn Bridge is at once beautiful and sweeping and immensely powerful, a workhorse facilitating transportation across the river and into the city. Social issues drove the construction of the bridge— traffic that accompanied the expanding urban population base required a more efficient way for rail, pedestrian, and vehicular travel to proceed simultaneously on the same bridge. Indeed, there are multiple methods of movement across the bridge: two lanes on the edge of the road for carriages, inside lanes for streetcars, and an elevated path for pedestrians that made possible a luxurious and safe walk to enjoy the view. John Augustus Roebling began the bridge in 1869 and was later joined by his son, Washington August Roebling, in 1883.

The building of the Brooklyn Bridge was accomplished through the maximization of the forces of both compression in the massive piers and suspension in the huge steel cables that hang from the piers and hold the roadbed in the air. It is a suspension bridge composed with a form endowed with great visual comprehensibility and beauty of form and line. Although the massive piers are in some ways simple and even plain, they reveal an eclectic mix of historical revival styles. Described best as Egypto-Gothic-Roman, the weight, the taper, and the modulation of the surface represent influences from each architectural tradition and project a significant impression of strength and weight while at the same time doing what they were intended to do. The simple Gothic lancet arches present the principal openings for the roadbed to pass through, and the cables function in two ways, both according to structural logic. The buttresses attached to the sides of the Roman arches are another reference to Gothic architecture. The roadbed itself soars in a single gesture, gliding and curving with the river from one side to the other, expressing neither compression nor tension, but moving because of both. The result is a dramatic interaction among forces, materials, forms, and visual lines—all created in heroic dimensions and scale.

Roebling was recognized for his double system of steel suspension cables, which demonstrate new engineering knowledge and the use of newest materials. To support the enormous weight of the bridge, two different systems of cables were used. The first were vertical cables moving in parabolic curves from the tops of the piers. The second were cables that moved directly from the top of one pier to the next. Roebling is also known for the innovative method of spinning high tensile steel cables as well as radiating stays, which created aerodynamic stability for the bridge suspended high above the river. The tensile strength of the spidery steel cables pulls them into stretched curves, raylike lines in the sky, and plumb lines reflective of harps. Significant bracing was required from the deck to resist wind and vibration.

When it was dedicated in 1883, the Brooklyn Bridge was described as both America's Arch of Triumph and New York's Brandenburg Gate. It represented an important and metaphoric point of welcome and announcement of this American city of industry, finance, and immigration.

—*Martha Bradley*

See also New York, New York

Further Readings and References

McCullough, D. (1972). *The great bridge.* New York: Simon & Schuster.

Trachtenberg, A. (1979). *Brooklyn Bridge: Fact and symbol.* Chicago: University of Chicago Press.

BUILDING INDUSTRY

The building industry is responsible for the construction of dwellings. Including builders, subcontractors, tradesmen, and retail building suppliers, it is a major employer in every city. It makes economic growth possible by housing workers and their families, and frames much of the urban landscape. Organized on a local basis, its members are closely connected with other real estate interests, including agents, lawyers, architects, engineers, land developers, and mortgage lenders. These companies are local boosters and influence municipal politics.

The activities of the building industry should interest economic, business, urban, social, and labor historians. In fact, scholars have neglected it. Information about builders is scattered and has commonly been ignored. From the 1920s to the 1970s, many criticized the industry as "backward" because it failed to conform to the ideal of mass production exemplified by auto assembly. *Fortune* magazine declared that house building was the industry capitalism forgot. Recent scholarship has shown that this is not so. Technological change has been steady and cumulatively substantial in the building industry; building materials have long been mass produced; using subcontractors and just-in-time deliveries from suppliers, on-site assembly can be highly efficient; moreover, the immobility of housing and the cyclical character of housing demand (which varies seasonally and over the business cycle) put a premium on flexibility. Views of the building industry are more positive today than they have been in decades.

The Blurred Boundaries of the Industry

There have always been builders, but the "building industry" was a project of the 1930s. Through a new agency, the Federal Housing Administration (FHA), the United States government worked to make this disparate sector into an object of economic management. It met with limited success, and the industry's boundaries remain blurred.

At different times and in varying degrees, house builders have overlapped with other types of construction companies, land subdividers, suppliers, subcontractors, and tradespeople. This was especially true in those cities (on the East Coast) where or at those times (1880s, 1920s, 1960s) when many multistory dwellings were built. In most North American urban areas, family homes, commonly detached, have been the predominant house type. The building technology for these homes is simpler than it is for other structures, and most house builders have confined themselves to this field. Those responsible for multifamily dwellings, however, have also built factories and offices, switching their focus according to business conditions.

Great fluidity has marked the connections between house builders, land subdividers, and building suppliers. In the 1800s, land subdividers, with exceptions such as Chicago's Samuel Gross, rarely erected houses. Vertical integration became more common in the 20th century. Large builders such as the Levitt brothers acquired land to support their building activities; landowners tightened control of development indirectly, by imposing building regulations, and directly by building. This blurring of lines between subdivider and builder was signaled by use of a new term—*developer*. Other companies bridged building and supply. In the United States, lumber has been the chief building material and lumber dealers the main source of supplies and short-term credit. Local dealers have sometimes found it profitable to enter the building business themselves, especially during booms, retreating to their core business during recessions. In the late 1960s, for example, one third of lumber dealers also built homes; almost half undertook subcontracting; and two fifths manufactured roof trusses, an innovation of the early postwar era that replaced labor-intensive rafter-and-joist roofing systems.

National companies that have produced homes in factories have challenged the identity of the building industry. Early in the 20th century, mail-order companies such as Aladdin, Van Tyne, and Sears, Roebuck produced kit homes that could be erected by amateurs as well as by contractors. In the 1940s, the federal government subsidized experiments with wholesale prefabrication that proved unsuccessful. Since the 1960s, the makers of mobile homes (now also known as manufactured housing) have consistently won at least a

quarter of the market for new homes, mostly in the Sun Belt. They have enlarged the building industry, but most homes are still assembled locally and on-site.

The Organization of Site Production

Most builders have assembled dwellings on-site, and site builders operate locally. Until World War II, it was exceptional for a builder to operate outside the urban area in which he was based. (Most builders have been male.) This local focus shaped, and was influenced by, locally variable building regulations. The postwar period saw the intermittent growth of companies that operate regionally, but the general picture has not changed greatly. According to a 1949 survey, in 21 out of 24 major urban centers across the United States, at least 98 percent of builders operated only locally. Even in the 1990s in Southern Ontario, local builders erected more than four fifths of all dwellings.

Site builders have oriented themselves to the market in one of two ways. Residential contractors have erected homes for specific clients, sometimes in collaboration with architects. They have been most common in smaller communities and in the affluent suburbs of larger metropolitan centers. In contrast, speculative builders have erected homes for an anonymous market. They have catered to the large group of middle-income buyers and have been especially, and increasingly, common in the larger metropolitan centers where demand is large and relatively predictable. In the early 1920s, some speculative builders began to erect "model homes" as a promotional tool. Since then, and especially in recent years, many have offered customized versions of such models, requiring down payments on each dwelling before construction begins. This hybrid method has reduced the builder's risk while offering choice to mass-market buyers. Beyond the bounds of the professional building industry, a third category of builders exists—those who have built homes for themselves. They have been more common around smaller urban centers, especially in unincorporated fringe areas that have limited regulations and services. Amateurs last played a substantial role in home building in the decade after 1945 when, for a time, they accounted for more than a quarter of housing starts.

All types of builders, including amateurs, have employed subcontractors to complete specific tasks. For some decades, observers deplored this practice as a sign of the industry's disorganization. In fact, the rise of subcontracting in the late 18th and early 19th centuries signaled the emergence of capitalism in housing provision. Subcontracting allows producers to respond quickly to changes in the level and character of demand, both prominent features of house building. Its growth has supported specialization. Distinctions have long existed between carpenters, masons, and plasterers; other tradespeople, such as plumbers and electricians, were added later, and all have subdivided. Paperhangers set themselves apart from painters, for example, and in larger metropolitan areas many focus more narrowly on just vinyl, fabrics, or metals.

The efficient specialization of subcontractors has enabled small builders to remain competitive and to play a large role in the industry. The 1949 survey showed that more than 96 percent of builders erected fewer than 25 dwellings; collectively, they were responsible for almost half of all housing starts. Their market share has since fallen but is still significant. This fact is associated with the high rate of churning: every year about a third of all builders leave or enter the business. This is easy because companies require so little capital. In a classic study, Sherman Maisel found that in San Francisco in the early 1950s the average builder owned $2,700 of equipment, the equivalent of a pickup truck and a tool bag. Most entrants into the business were once subcontractors or tradespeople. Occupational mobility in this industry has assisted generations of skilled and unskilled immigrants, while churning has influenced labor relations by blurring the lines between employer and employee.

The Effects on the Landscape

Each type of builder has left a distinctive mark on the urban landscape. In unregulated areas, amateurs have produced an anarchic landscape of modest, one-story frame houses with varied street setbacks. The custom builder has not always produced unique, imposing, architecturally designed homes. Many have used stock plans to erect dwellings similar to those being built by their counterparts in other subdivisions in other cities. Because these have been one-off productions, though, their accumulation has created variety, especially where particular blocks or areas have taken a decade or more to develop. Much of the charm of smaller towns and older, slow-growing suburbs stems from this manner of development. In contrast, landscapes produced by speculative builders have been more uniform. Where builders were small, as in late-19th-century Boston, the enduring impression is one

of many minor variations on a common theme. Where large, as in some early postwar suburbs, uniformity is striking. Builders sometimes have softened this visual monotony by offering variations on a few basic designs, by reversing frontages, or by presenting a choice of cladding. Later adaptations made by owners also added variety.

The landscapes of different builders have become more and more segregated. Increasingly, unplanned areas have been avoided by professional, and especially speculative, builders. By imposing building and subdivision controls, more subdividers have sought to create exclusive enclaves in which most homes are custom built and architecturally designed. Especially since 1945, mass builder-developers have created their own subdivisions. The urban landscape offers many clues to the way that builders have operated.

—Richard Harris

See also Building Regulations and Building Codes; Land Developers and Development; Zoning

Further Readings and References

Harris, R., & Buzzelli, M. (2005). House building in the Machine Age, 1920s–1970s: Realities and perceptions of modernisation in North America and Australia. *Business History, 47,* 2.

Maisel, S. (1953). *Housebuilding in transition.* Berkeley: University of California Press.

Powell, C. G. (1996). *The British building industry since 1800: An economic history.* London: E & FN Spon.

Rilling, D. (2001). *Making houses, crafting capitalism: Builders in Philadelphia, 1790–1850.* Philadelphia: University of Pennsylvania Press.

Schweitzer, R., & Davis, M.W.R. (1990). *America's favorite homes.* Detroit, MI: Wayne State University Press.

Wallis, A. (1991). *Wheel estate: The rise and decline of mobile homes.* New York: Oxford University Press.

Warner, S. B. (1962). *Streetcar suburbs: The process of growth in Boston, 1870–1900.* Cambridge, MA: Harvard University Press.

Building Regulations and Building Codes

Today, building regulations govern the construction and renovation of buildings, while building codes offer models. (Housing codes control maintenance.)

Both regulations and codes have evolved steadily, initially in response to fires, later to promote health and safety, and recently to reduce energy usage. Their form and enforcement have been controversial. Collectively, they have shaped the built environment and the building industry.

Character and Merits

Early regulations took the form of specification codes that mandated or prohibited the use of particular materials, for example, by requiring that wall framing use 2-inch by 4-inch lumber on 16-inch centers. Specification codes are easily enforced, even by unqualified personnel. Because they inhibit technological change, they have generally been replaced by performance codes that emphasize capacities, not materials: for example, a flat roof system may be required to be able to carry a specified snow and dead load. Structural regulations are supplemented by electrical and mechanical requirements pertaining to plumbing, elevators, gas fitting, and boilers.

Proponents of regulations portray them as instruments of the public good. Early critics pointed out that they embodied labor practices and social interests that may resist change. For example, in the mid-1960s most municipalities prohibited the use of pre-assembled plumbing or electrical systems; a decade later a third of municipalities still prohibited ABS (plastic) pipe, a material invented in 1948 and approved by the Federal Housing Administration in 1960. The use of performance codes has been justified as scientific. Arguably, however, it entails a shift in responsibility and power from builders and tradespeople to engineers, architects, and manufacturers. Regulations have also been criticized as a restraint of trade and limitation of choice. As their elaboration raised construction costs, especially of small homes, some have argued that regulations should vary, offering consumers tradeoffs between housing costs and safety, or the option of undertaking staged improvements of dwellings and related services.

History

In many countries, building regulations were first introduced to reduce the risk of fire. In North America, early initiatives prohibited the use of thatch for roofing and of wood for chimneys. Because fire spreads easily, risk varies with the density of the settlement. In the second half of the 19th century, major conflagrations such as Chicago's Great Fire of 1871 provoked cities to prohibit wood-frame construction in central areas by defining "fire limits." Cities were less healthy than rural areas, and by 1900 overcrowding and poor sanitation had pushed the mortality rate in cities higher than it was in rural areas. Concerns about public health and fire hazards were expressed, notably in New York, where bylaws created "model" multistory tenements with air shafts. Everywhere, cities began to regulate room sizes, ventilation, and sanitary facilities.

At first, each municipality devised its own regulations, seeking local advice from qualified persons, including engineers, builders, and tradespeople associated with the building industry. Regulations solidified practices that served the interests of these groups. The complexity of regulations, and special interests, discouraged revisions to accommodate use of new materials and techniques. Especially from the 1920s, regulations were attacked for raising the costs of construction. Attempts at standardization were made in order to facilitate revision and to enable builders and manufacturers to produce for wider markets. In the 1940s, manufacturers of prefabricated housing found it impossible to satisfy even a majority of local regulations. Partly for that reason most, notably Lustron, foundered.

In other countries, national governments led the drive for standardization of regulations. In England and Wales, for example, national legislation in 1877 affected framed house construction everywhere. Later, in Canada, a National Building Code was first published in 1941 and was widely adopted. In the United States, the earliest and most effective attempts to promote standardization were made by private agencies. Because of common concerns, in 1866 insurers established a National Board of Fire Underwriters, which in 1905 published the first "model code" that municipalities could adopt or adapt. Three other agencies have since produced widely used models. By the 1980s, one or another had been used by three quarters of the local governments that had building regulations.

The greatest opportunities for standardization lie in house building. Offices, factories, and stores are erected as custom projects for particular clients. They are each either unique or one of a small group. Housing is produced in larger quantities and, because shelter is a necessity, there is widespread concern that regulation should not raise housing costs. In 1922, a new Building Code Committee of the Department of Commerce published a model code for small homes that was used by

350 municipalities before the committee's activities were curtailed in 1934. During World War II, federal regulations facilitated the use of prefabricated units in defense communities. Subsequently, the four private agencies have continued to promote standardization, in part through publication of a simplified joint code for small homes.

After 1973, rising energy costs sparked interest in conservation. The National Conference of States helped develop a Model Energy Conservation Code that covered appliances, insulation, and air conditioning. By 1980, 44 states had enacted energy codes, and their use was encouraged by federal legislation in 1987 and 1992. In 1988 the provisions of the Fair Housing Act were extended to include the disabled. The Department of Housing and Urban Development (HUD) has produced guidelines to promoted the physical accessibility of multifamily dwellings and encouraged states and local governments to conform. In theory, codes now help to save energy and promote accessibility, health, and safety, while enabling efficient production by facilitating the adoption of new materials and methods.

Geography

The diversity of building regulations reached its apogee in the early 1900s. By then, major cities had enacted regulations, but the use of model codes was limited and the situation in suburbs was very varied. After 1900 the pace of municipal annexation slowed and most new development occurred beyond city limits. Affluent suburbs enacted strict regulations as a method of social exclusion. Industrial suburbs cautiously regulated construction, not wishing to inhibit house building for local workers. Extensive, unincorporated fringe areas were unregulated. The metropolitan geography of regulation was highly variable.

Efforts at standardization have reduced but not eliminated diversity. In 1967, the National Commission on Urban Problems found that a small majority of local governments still had no building regulations. This included 31 percent of the municipalities in standard metropolitan statistical areas (SMSAs). Even those with regulations based on one of the national codes did not necessarily agree: Most had introduced their own amendments, and many failed to keep up-to-date. The commission's survey showed that 8 out of 14 important building practices that were approved by all four of the national codes were prohibited by more than a quarter of municipalities. Building regulation is

a police power usually delegated to municipalities by the states. One means of regulation standardization has been the creation of statewide codes, often modeled on one of the four national codes. Municipalities may be encouraged or required to conform; in some states, those without regulations may be automatically covered by the state's code. Even so, diversity has persisted. In the mid-1970s, many states still did not have their own building code. Those with codes enforced them variously through departments of buildings, housing, health, public works, insurance, planning, or the fire marshal. Some but not all were mandatory; some, concerned with safety, specified minimum standards; others, concerned with social exclusion, set maxima; some set both; some allowed local amendments. The regional geography of regulation had no logic. New Jersey had comprehensive structural and mechanical codes with maximum and minimum standards. Next door, Pennsylvania lacked any statewide codes, except for codes for elevators.

For decades the mobile home industry was self-regulating. To encourage it, while enhancing public safety, since 1976 HUD has enforced national performance standards. When these were revised in 1981, "manufactured housing" replaced "mobile home."

Administration and Impact

The impact of regulations depends on administration. The amount spent on enforcement has been far less than the value of the investments at stake, and enforcement has commonly been inadequate. As late as the 1960s fewer than one quarter of the local governments with building regulations had a full-time inspector. Incentives for bribery and corruption have been strong. In New York City in the 1970s, almost all employees of the buildings department knew of, or participated in, corrupt acts. In recent years, bribery has expedited the approval process rather than securing approval for illegal structures. Some flexibility in the enforcement of regulations is necessary since circumstances vary. It is desirable when regulations were ill-conceived or become outdated, and in times of need. After the Chicago fire, new regulations that prohibited frame construction were not at first enforced. After 1945, inspectors bent rules to allow veterans to build in stages.

Building regulations have accomplished their purposes, at a price. In the early 1900s fires were more common in North America than in Europe, partly because of the prevalence of frame construction and wood shingles. In the 1910s, Toronto had three times as many fire alarms as Glasgow, Scotland, a city of comparable size. Regulations reduced fire risk. From 1900 to 1910, fire losses across the U.S. were 63 cents for every $100 of insured property. By 1940 the figure had almost halved. Greater declines in infant mortality over the same period were partly due to better construction and sanitation. The price, especially in the mid-20th century, was a lower rate of technical change in the building industry, the discouragement of mass production, and rising minimum costs. Until the late 1950s, the diversity of municipal regulation made it possible to build modestly and in stages in some fringe areas. Since then, wider adoption of national codes has limited this option.

—Richard Harris

See also Building Industry; Federal Housing Administration; Zoning

Further Readings and References

Cooke, P. W., & Eisenhard, R. M. (1977). *A preliminary examination of building regulations adopted by the states and major cities.* Washington, DC: National Bureau of Standards.

Gaskell, S. M. (1983). *Building control: National legislation and the introduction of local bye-laws in Victorian England.* London: Bedford Square Press.

Harris, R. (1991). The impact of building controls on residential development in Toronto, 1900–1940. *Planning Perspectives, 6,* 269–296.

National Commission on Urban Problems. (1968). *Building the American city.* Washington, DC: Government Printing Office.

Rosen, C. M. (1986). *The limits of power: Great fires and the process of city growth in America.* New York: Cambridge University Press.

Seidel, S. (1978). *Housing costs and government regulations.* New Brunswick, NJ: Center for Urban Policy Research.

Slaton, A., & Abbate, J. (2001). The hidden lives of standards: Technical prescriptions and the transformation of work in America. In M. T. Allen & G. Hecht (Eds.), *Technologies of power* (pp. 95–143). Cambridge, MA: MIT Press.

Vitale, E. (1979). *Building regulations: A self-help guide for the owner-builder.* New York: Scribners.

BUNGALOW

One of the most common forms of residential architecture in the world, the *bungalow* is perhaps the most influential home style in United States history. Its basic structure is simple: a low, gabled house, with one or one and a half stories, and a roof extended at the front to cover a porch. Such houses have been most commonly constructed of wood, with shingle roofs and a brick or cobblestone chimney, though stucco variants also appear. This simplicity of structural form, however, conceals great complexity of cultural meaning.

The bungalow originated in 17th-century India with the *banggolo,* a typical Bengalese peasant hut. It was adapted by the British, who found it an acceptable residence for the warm Indian climate, offering ventilation and overhanging rooflines that offered protection from the elements. The British constructed similar structures in other tropical regions of their empire, from Africa to Australia. Over time, however, the bungalow transitioned from Raj to resort, emerging as a form of inexpensive housing ideal for beachfront resort towns and vacation homes. It was in this incarnation, as a house offering leisure and a return to the "simple life," that the bungalow proved most appealing to Americans.

In the United States this housing form served as the apotheosis of a new, middle-class suburban ideal—a home separated from other residences, intended for a single family, with its own plot of land for lawn and garden. Rarely has architecture so embodied the aspirations of a class and an era. The bungalow, however, did not begin as housing for the masses. The Arts and Crafts Movement, originating in Britain and popularized by William Morris (1834–1896), argued for a return to the "simple life," with houses built for living rather than show, and filled with handmade furniture and crafts. "Simple," however, did not equal inexpensive, as all the labor required to produce all those handmade furniture pieces and architectural elements did not come cheap.

The American proponent of a more democratic Arts and Crafts residential architecture was Gustav Stickley (1848–1942). Stickley's magazine, *The Craftsman,* which began publication in 1901, contained innumerable illustrations of furniture, houses, and house plans, all intended to offer a simple, refined mode of living, where furniture and home merged into a *gesamtkunstwerk,* the "total work of art." Similar motives drove Frank Lloyd Wright to develop his Prairie House style in the same era, and his innovative designs owe something to the bungalow. Unlike Morris, and unlike Wright in most of his house designs, Stickley made his designs affordable, even incorporating machine manufacturing methods. He would later be driven into bankruptcy by "counterfeiters" creating inexpensive Craftsman furniture. Stickley nevertheless played a central role in the popularization of the bungalow in the United States.

Though a national architectural phenomenon, the bungalow achieved its greatest popularity in California, particularly in Los Angeles and other Southern California communities, such as the "Bungalow Heaven" neighborhood of Pasadena. Yet timber-frame and shingle houses were not the most logical housing type for a city built in a semiarid region with limited timber. The remarkable popularity of the bungalow in Southern California can be attributed to multiple factors. The region experienced a series of real estate booms from the 1880s through the 1920s, and the bungalow was a popular housing form during much of this era. Bungalows were inexpensive to build, and therefore appealing to home builders and home buyers alike. The balmy climate of the region also made the bungalow advantageous.

The fact that new housing tracts, cities, and the region as a whole were promoted by a massive promotional effort certainly helped as well. In boosterist rhetoric and imagery Los Angeles and the rest of Southern California were presented as an Arcadian ideal, a pastoral escape from the urban, industrial East. The bungalow, with its connotations of leisure and openness to the outdoors, was the perfect residential architecture for this Anglo-American imagined region. Indeed, the garden was an integral element of the bungalow ideal, and residents exploited the floral possibilities of the Southern California climate with exotic flowers and trees. The backyard became another social and leisure space for the house, relegating the living room to a retreat in inclement weather.

The greatest architects in the bungalow style were brothers Charles Greene (1868–1957) and Henry Greene (1870–1954). Their houses, "ultimate bungalows" built for the affluent, hardly qualified as bungalows at all. Yet such structures employed the bungalow style and philosophy, albeit on a magnified and magnificent scale. Horizontal rooflines followed the landscape, and rooms extended outward into exquisite gardens. Every element, from doorknobs to light fixtures, was carefully detailed and lovingly crafted. The woodwork, from doors and windows to elegantly complex structural elements supporting roofs and sleeping porches, was perhaps the single most striking element of such houses. Like many Arts and Crafts proponents, the Greenes exhibited a fascination with Japanese art and design, and some

Japanese elements can be seen in their houses. Such Asian influences also seemed suitable for houses built on America's Pacific coast.

Surviving Greene and Greene homes, such as Pasadena's Gamble House, are monuments to the bungalow movement at its most extravagant. By the 1920s, however, Spanish Revival and other styles had supplanted bungalow residences in Southern California. In reality, many of those later styles, perhaps most notably the ubiquitous "ranch" house of midcentury America, were descendants of the bungalow, even though they were often mass-produced. This freestanding suburban home, constructed horizontally like the bungalow and linked to a domestic ideal that merged family, leisure, and the outdoors, was an heir to the same cultural desires and imperatives.

—*Lawrence Culver*

Further Readings and References

Bosley, E. R. (2003). *Greene and Greene.* New York: Phaidon.

Cathers, D. (2003). *Gustav Stickley.* New York: Phaidon.

King, A. D. (1995). *The bungalow: The production of a global culture* (2nd ed.). New York: Oxford University Press.

BURGESS, ERNEST W.

Ernest Watson Burgess was born on May 16, 1886, in Tilbury, Ontario, Canada. Burgess attended Kingfisher College in Oklahoma, receiving a bachelor of arts degree in 1908. Burgess then went to the University of Chicago for graduate studies in sociology and received his Ph.D. in 1913. He taught at several midwestern schools before returning to the University of Chicago as an assistant professor in sociology in 1916. His career spanned many different phases of sociology at the University of Chicago—from the early years within a department that included anthropologists to later years where there were specialized centers for social phenomena. Ernest Watson Burgess died on December 27, 1966.

In the 1920s, Robert E. Park (1864–1944) and Ernest W. Burgess founded a program of urban research at the University of Chicago. They trained a group of students in the 1920s and early 1930s called the first "Chicago School" of sociology. Park and Burgess and their students developed a theory of "urban ecology." This theory suggested that urban environments were like natural environments and were governed by many of the same forces as the Darwinian theory of evolution. Competition, they suggested, was one of the most important of these forces. The competition for scarce resources divided urban space into zones where people shared similar social characteristics. Competition for land and infrastructure ultimately, according to this theory, differentiated urban space into zones, and more desirable areas had higher land values. Park and Burgess called *succession,* a term borrowed from plant ecology, the process by which people moved out of the city as their incomes rose. Their theory of land use in the city, known as *concentric zone theory*, predicted that cities would take the form of five concentric rings, with dilapidated areas concentrated near the city center and relatively prosperous areas located near the urban periphery. Park and Burgess and their students used the concentric zone theory to explain the existence of social problems, including unemployment and crime in certain locations within Chicago. Their research used mapping to reveal the spatial distribution of social problems in order to contrast different locations. Burgess and his students collected data for the city of Chicago to make maps. They obtained information from city agencies and made more extensive use of census data than any other social scientists of that time, as noted by Martin Bulmer in 1984.

After World War II, these urban models were deemed overly simplistic and superficial. In particular, critics suggested that their theory neglected issues of class, race, and ethnicity. However, the concentric rings model is still useful in introducing the complexities of urban land use change. In *Ecology of Fear* (1998), Mike Davis used the concentric rings model to describe Los Angeles. Another legacy of Burgess and the Chicago School is improvements in the methodological toolkits that are used by social scientists. Burgess wrote in 1929 that prediction is the goal of social sciences, just as it is for the physical sciences. Empirical data were a basis for all of his projects. However, he balanced statistical tools like factor analysis with case study methods. Finally, one of the most important legacies of urban ecology studies was the use of spatial data to create maps in emerging disciplines such as sociology, criminology, planning, and public policy.

—*Sumeeta Srinivasan*

See also Chicago, Illinois

Further Readings and References

Bulmer, M. (1984). *The Chicago School of Sociology: Institutionalization, diversity, and the rise of sociological research.* Chicago: University of Chicago Press.

Burgess, E., & Bogue, D. J. (Eds.). (1967). *Urban sociology.* Chicago: University of Chicago Press.

Davis, M. (1998). *Ecology of fear: Los Angeles and the imagination of disaster.* New York: Henry Holt.

Park, R., Burgess, E. W., & McKenzie, R. D. (1925). *The City.* Chicago: University of Chicago Press.

BURLESQUE

American burlesque was little more than a strip show that featured a scantily clad female gyrating in stylized motion. Yet, to mid-19th-century audiences, burlesque was a rich source of music and comedy designed to elicit audience laughter and a transgressive, lowbrow entertainment intended to subvert highbrow art.

In the 16th century, *burle* were extended "sight gags" in Commmedia dell'Arte, the Italian street theater that was popular with the lower classes; while during the 19th century in both England and America, burlesques—short comic plays that lampooned more serious works from *Hamlet* to *The Pirates of Penzance* and artists from Shakespeare to Jenny Lind—were employed as afterpieces to featured entertainments. Over the course of the 19th century, however, the display of female flesh, characteristic of the so-called girlie show, increased in importance while comic elements diminished.

In the United States, the antecedents of the girlie show were many and varied. During the 1840s, living statuary—women in revealing tights posing as classical statuary—gained respectability and was tolerated by the authorities as long as the models did not move; while during the same decade, women's bodies were on nightly display in disreputable urban concert saloons. In 1861, Adah Issacs Menken brought the perception of female nudity to the mainstream theater and gained notoriety as the "Naked Lady" when she appeared in "fleshlings" (flesh-colored tights) in *Mazeppa,* the stage version of Byron's poem. Five years later, seeming nudity on a grander scale was displayed by the chorines in *The Black Crook,* a theater piece created by joining a melodramatic potboiler to the scenery, costumes, and chorus of a Parisian dance troupe that had been stranded in New York when the theater in which they were scheduled to appear burned to the ground. Regarded by theater historians as the prototype of the American musical, *The Black Crook* can lay equal claim to being the forerunner of the American burlesque show of the 20th century.

Also during the the 1860s, British burlesque entrepreneurs were likewise relying more upon the display of shapely, underdressed women to attract audiences. At a time when proper Victorian ladies went to great lengths to mask their bodies beneath layers of clothing, women appearing on stage in flesh-colored tights were clearly subversive and a challenge to public taste. In 1868, England exported its idea of the girlie show to America in the person of Lydia Thompson and her "British Blonds," women in tights playing men in shows like *Ixion,* thereby creating the opportunity for exposing women's bodies and setting the stage for a generation of underdressed women playing sexual aggressors. Thompson and her Blonds punctuated their onstage personae as transgressive females by such offstage behavior as smoking in public.

While both *The Black Crook* and Thompson and her troupe were somewhat foreign to American audiences, spectators to M. B. Leavitt's burlesques were treated to what was arguably the first American-born girlie show that adopted the form of the minstrel show in the 1870s and achieved immediate popularity and success. Billed as *Mme Rentz's Female Minstrels,* Leavitt's shows incorporated many of the elements of earlier girlie shows—classic statuary; women dressed as men to reveal seemingly bare "flesh"—into the familiar minstrel show format. With increased display of flesh and story lines that were minimal, if they existed at all, female minstrels rendered the transforming burlesque show truly American, moved burlesque one step closer to the "skin show" of the 20th century, reduced the role of comedy in burlesque even further, and made it the target of editorials and sermons that condemned burlesque as indecent and immoral.

By the 1880s, male managers had ostensibly appropriated the form, virtually replacing feminine wit with the display of as much of the female body as local laws would allow. The final element in burlesque's transition into striptease was introduced in 1893 when at the Chicago World's Fair a dancer named Little Egypt performed for the first time the "hootchie-cooch"—an erotic, teasing, bawdy dance that is what most consider to be modern burlesque, as noted by Robert Toll in 1976. With ever-increasing competition from other entertainment forms—for example, musical comedies like *Yankee Doodle Dandy* (1898), which starred a "leggy" Edna Wallace Hopper; vaudeville with performers like Eva Tanguay, who sang songs with provocative titles like *I Want Someone to Go Wild With Me* and whose theme song was *I Don't Care;* and reviews like *The Ziegfeld Follies*—burlesque, in desperation, was virtually forced to respond to the challenges and to offer audiences increased female sexuality.

Thereafter, all that remained was for burlesque promoters like the Minsky brothers to take the striptease out of the back rooms and put it on the main stages. By 1905, burlesque had become big business as theater owners formed vaudeville-style circuits of theaters that they called "wheels" because performers and companies played these theaters in regular rotations.

The early years of the 20th century were also the era of the star in burlesque. Arguably, the first star of the striptease was Millie De Leon, "The Girl in Blue," who emerged during the second decade of the 20th century and who ended her striptease by throwing blue garters with her picture attached to them to her male fans. De Leon's on-stage energy, lack of inhibitions, and increasingly frenzied cooch dance prompted an even further emphasis upon the display of the seminude female body; comedy, although bawdier than ever and still on the bill of the burlesque show, was no longer a key attraction. By the 1930s, with the appearances of strippers like Georgia Sothern, Sally Rand, Ann Corio, and the legendary Gypsy Rose Lee, the modern striptease, with increasingly more flesh being shown, had realized its final form and was in full bloom.

However, even as burlesque reached its acme, the end was near. In the 1920s, burlesque wheels began to disappear to the extent that, once again, individual theater owners were forced to survive without the support of the booking circuits. At roughly the same time, local authorities began to focus their attention on the "sleazy," degenerate shows in their cities, and raids upon burlesque halls increased, with the most public raids conducted at the direction of New York's Mayor Fiorello La Guardia. When the police raided and closed Minsky's legendary burlesque hall in New York, the end of one of the most famous burlesque houses represented the impending end of burlesque, just as the closing of the Palace Theater symbolized the demise of vaudeville.

Now long gone and largely forgotten, burlesque's legacy lived on for years in the person of the performers who trained there—stars like Jackie Gleason,

Fanny Brice, Bert Lahr, W.C. Fields, Red Skelton, Phil Silvers, Bob Hope, and Mae West—all, ironically, comics in an art form that had de-emphasized comedy.

—*John W. Frick*

Further Readings and References

Allen, R. C. (1991). *Horrible prettiness: Burlesque and American culture.* Chapel Hill, NC: University of North Carolina Press.

Kendrick, J. (1996/2004). *History of burlesque, part 2.* Retrieved from http://www.musicals101.com/burlesque2.htm

Shteir, R. (2004). *Striptease: The untold history of the girlie show.* New York: Oxford University Press.

Toll, R. (1976). *On with the show: The first century of show business in America.* New York: Oxford University Press.

Zeidman, I. (1967). *The American burlesque show.* New York: Hawthorn Books.

Burnham, Daniel H.

Architect Daniel H. Burnham (1846–1912) was born in Hudson, New York. After unsuccessful attempts to study at Yale and Harvard, Burnham served an apprenticeship under the noted designer William LeBaron Jenney (1832–1907) in Chicago. After learning his trade under the tutelage of LeBaron Jenney, Burnham gained employment in the early 1870s at the Chicago-based office of Carter, Drake and Wright, where he met John Wellborn Root (1850–1891). With Root, Burnham designed many edifices, including one of America's earliest skyscrapers, the Masonic Temple Building in Chicago, and in so doing helped establish the partners in the famous Chicago School of Design.

With Root's premature death, Burnham was left with the task of continuing alone, including planning the World's Columbian Exposition (1893) in Chicago, a huge celebration of the 400th anniversary of Columbus's arrival on the North American continent. Furthermore, following Root's death Burnham opened himself up to less pragmatic and more classically formed design styles. Greece and Rome became his new models, and Burnham became integral in America's Classical Revival. Through his work at the World's Columbian Exposition, Burnham demonstrated to the American public the virtues of a large-scale, orderly and clean, planned environment—the

event thus being the first major example of comprehensive planning in the United States. With grandly designed buildings, broad boulevards, and monumental vistas, Burnham helped to propagate notions of rational Beaux Arts planning and publicize neoclassical architectural forms in the United States. Visitors to the exposition could not help but be impressed by the event's environment, and consequently many public and private clients of American architects sought something similar.

Due to his applauded successes, Burnham played a central role within the City Beautiful Movement which from the 1890s sought to create modern beauty in the American urban environment through the use of classically styled buildings and formal civic center schemes. The movement marked an important stage in the development of landscape architecture, municipal improvement, and civic design in modern American history and, as noted previously, the 1893 Columbian Exposition had a major impact not only on the City Beautiful Movement but also on the American public, as did Burnham's subsequent Plan for Chicago (1909), with Edward H. Bennett—the first modern attempt in America to plan and control the growth of a large metropolis. As the leading planning authority of early-20th-century America, Burnham also became involved in significant projects in cities such as Washington, D.C., Cleveland, and San Francisco. The large scale typified Burnham's work, and he somewhat infamously remarked, "Make no little plans, as they have no magic to stir men's blood." Consequently, his planning schemes were often huge and his buildings high. At the time of his death, Burnham was of such professional standing that he had the largest architectural office in the world. His significance within American architectural and planning history remains to this day.

—*Ian Morley*

See also Chicago, Illinois; City Beautiful Movement; World Fairs and Expositions

Further Readings and References

Burnham, D. H. (1993). *The plan of Chicago.* New York: Princeton Architectural Press.

Emerson, W. (1893). The World's Fair buildings, Chicago. *Journal of the Royal Institute of British Architects, 1,* 65–74.

Schaffer, K. (2003). *Daniel H. Burnham: Visionary architect and planner.* New York: Rizzoli.

BUSING

In 1970, U.S. President Richard Nixon declared court-ordered busing to be a violation of the doctrine of neighborhood schools and a futile effort at achieving a multiracial society. Two years later, Alabama governor George Wallace lambasted busing as, among other epithets, "asinine" and "mean." As the antibusing backlash spread across the nation, the Leadership Conference on Civil Rights warned that the United States faced a stark choice between living up to the promise of equal educational opportunity in the 1954 *Brown* decision or retreating to the 1968 Kerner Commission's forecast of separate and unequal black and white societies.

Battles over court-ordered busing to overcome residential segregation—a school desegregation technique often labeled "mandatory busing," "forced busing," or "busing for racial balance"—exploded across metropolitan America in the late 1960s and throughout the 1970s. But the origins of the busing conflict can be traced to the immediate aftermath of the *Brown v. Board of Education* decision, when urban school districts in the South began to adopt Northern-style desegregation plans that revolved around the allegedly race-neutral assignment of students to "neighborhood schools." According to the pervasive regional distinction, enshrined in constitutional law and popular discourse, educational patterns in the South resulted from segregation in law (*de jure*), while schooling and housing patterns outside the South represented segregation in fact but not enforced by law (*de facto*). During the first half of the 1960s, the NAACP filed hundreds of desegregation lawsuits against Southern school districts and simultaneously initiated dozens of legal and administrative challenges to de facto segregation in the cities and suburbs of the North and West. The federal courts rejected almost all of the initial NAACP lawsuits against de facto segregation outside the South on the grounds that school districts were not responsible for racial imbalances that resulted from the housing market. The U.S. Congress endorsed this constitutional interpretation in the Civil Rights Act of 1964, which specifically excluded from the scope of federal desegregation policy the transportation of students outside of their neighborhoods for the purpose of racial integration.

In a 1968 case involving a rural county in Virginia, the U.S. Supreme Court charged localities that had operated legally segregated school systems with taking all necessary steps to eliminate racial discrimination. The NAACP responded with a comprehensive assault on the constitutional distinction between de jure and de facto segregation in metropolitan school districts, including exposure of the government policies that had produced and reinforced residential segregation in all parts of the nation, not just in the Jim Crow South. The spatial development of the postwar metropolitan landscape depended upon generous subsidies for suburban sprawl and efficient implementation of housing segregation, including discriminatory home mortgage financing by federal agencies, urban renewal and highway construction programs that concentrated minorities in inner city ghettos, and exclusionary municipal zoning policies that sorted neighborhoods by race and class. In 1969, the NAACP's effort to link discriminatory housing policies to school desegregation litigation achieved its first major breakthrough in a case involving Charlotte, North Carolina, a consolidated district that included the surrounding suburbs of Mecklenburg County. In a landmark decision, District Judge James B. McMillan ordered the comprehensive integration of the countywide school system, including two-way busing that exchanged white students from the outlying suburbs and black students from the inner city.

As the national test case for a comprehensive busing plan to overcome residential segregation, *Swann v. Charlotte-Mecklenburg* set off a firestorm that fueled the grassroots revolt of the Silent Majority and rippled upward into national politics. White leaders in Charlotte appealed the decision to the Supreme Court based on the argument that the district already had complied fully with *Brown v. Board of Education* through its race-neutral neighborhood schools formula, meaning that any remaining racial segregation resulted from de facto housing patterns that were identical to those in the metropolitan North. Tens of thousands of white suburban families joined forces in the Concerned Parents Association, which adopted a color-blind platform that denounced "forced busing" as reverse racism and depicted residential segregation as the outcome of upward mobility in the free market rather than the unconstitutional product of racially discriminatory public policies. Mobilizing under the banner of the Silent Majority, the suburban activists in the Concerned Parents Association also pressured the Nixon administration to intervene in the Charlotte litigation. Richard Nixon promptly released a major antibusing statement that sharply distinguished between the unconstitutional de jure segregation of the Jim Crow era and the constitutionally permissible de facto segregation found in Charlotte and other metropolitan regions across the country. But in the spring of 1971, in a closely watched civil rights showdown, the Supreme Court upheld the two-way busing decree in Charlotte-Mecklenburg. The inclusion of the middle-class suburbs in Charlotte's integration formula mitigated "white flight" and ultimately produced one of the most successfully integrated urban school districts in the nation.

Following the victory in *Swann,* the NAACP launched a major drive to overcome residential segregation and transcend the urban-suburban divide by securing school integration remedies on a metropolitan scale in the major cities of the South and the North. Notwithstanding the emerging political consensus that busing caused the destruction of urban school systems, the highest levels of racial integration and the lowest levels of white flight occurred in the largest city-suburban consolidated school districts of the South—including Charlotte and other county-wide systems such as Raleigh, Nashville, Tampa, and Jacksonville. Court-ordered busing plans in these Southern metropolises encompassed the middle-class suburbs through comprehensive formulas that placed the bulk of the transportation burden on black students and avoided the "tipping point" by maintaining white majorities in most individual facilities. Based on the recognition that busing would prove unworkable in majority-black urban districts, the NAACP also pursued metropolitan integration remedies through the consolidation of city and suburban school systems. The civil rights group met with defeat in a 1973 case involving Richmond, Virginia, where the appellate courts overturned a district judge's order that would have merged the majority-black city school system with two overwhelmingly white suburban counties. And in Atlanta, legal efforts to enact a metropolitan integration plan dissolved after local civil rights activists who were skeptical of busing struck a bargain with white business leaders that delivered administrative control of the public school system to the African American community and confined the desegregation remedy to the city district alone.

Outside the South, busing also emerged as a volatile political issue during the early 1970s, as civil rights litigants challenged claims of de facto segregation in cities from San Francisco and Los Angeles to Boston and New York. Public opinion polls revealed overwhelming opposition among white parents in all parts of the country to the policy of busing for racial integration (as well as significant uncertainty among many black parents), and many political leaders in both parties criticized the federal courts for exceeding their constitutional authority. In 1971, racial extremists bombed 10 buses in the industrial town of Pontiac, Michigan, and a group of working-class white mothers organized boycotts of the public schools. Nearby in Detroit, District Judge Stephen J. Roth ruled that formal government policies and suburban practices of deliberate racial exclusion were responsible for the residential segregation of the metropolis, and he devised a remedy that would have required the consolidation of 54 independent districts in a three-county region and the two-way busing of almost 800,000 students to maintain a white majority in every school. Riding a powerful wave of antibusing backlash, George Wallace won the 1972 Democratic presidential primary in Michigan, along with victories in Maryland and three Southern states. President Nixon responded by proposing an extraconstitutional moratorium on court-ordered busing and endorsing an antibusing amendment to the U.S. Constitution. During his successful reelection campaign against liberal Democrat George McGovern, Nixon denounced busing as an injustice to black and white citizens from all regions of the country and defended the right to attend neighborhood schools as a centerpiece of his outreach to the Silent Majority.

Although federal district courts began to order busing in cities outside the South in the late 1960s, the first major case involving a non-Southern urban school system did not reach the Supreme Court until 1973. In the *Keyes* litigation, a divided Supreme Court applied a standard of "segregative intent" to require busing inside the city limits of Denver, Colorado as a remedy for the racial gerrymandering of attendance zones and other deliberate forms of de jure segregation. One year later, as grassroots antibusing movements mobilized in almost every affected city and suburb across the United States, the justices heard the appeal of the Detroit consolidation case. In 1974, *Milliken v. Bradley,* the most pivotal school desegregation decision since *Brown,* overturned the NAACP's quest for metropolitan integration through the merger of city and suburban school districts by a 5-to-4 majority. Chief Justice Warren Burger's opinion dismissed the factual findings in the trial court that government policies from the federal to the municipal levels had caused the residential segregation, and therefore the school segregation, that dominated the metropolitan region. The dissenting justices accused the majority of exempting the white suburbs from the scope of *Brown* and sentencing minority students to hypersegregated urban schools that did not even live up to the standard of "separate but equal." Justice Thurgood Marshall directly accused the *Milliken* majority of allowing the political backlash against busing to thwart the constitutional mandate of equal protection under the law, and he echoed the Kerner Commission in warning that the Supreme Court was now complicit in the division of the American metropolis into separate cities and suburbs, racially divided and inherently unequal.

The *Milliken* decision accelerated the expansion of court-ordered busing in the North and West but essentially redrew the de jure/de facto distinction at the city-suburban boundary. In Detroit, as in many other large cities, the exclusion of the suburbs confined integration remedies to urban neighborhoods that were already undergoing racial transition long before the arrival of busing. In the major urban centers of the Rust Belt, this meant that integration formulas imposed busing burdens primarily on the working-class areas of cities where large numbers of white families then departed for the suburbs or private schools. In the mid-1970s, the white violence that accompanied a city-only busing plan in Boston became etched in national consciousness as the essence of busing itself, a searing reminder of how civil rights organizations and liberal policymakers destroyed urban public schools by pushing too fast and too far. A broader perspective on the metropolitan dynamics of the busing battles that polarized the nation reveals a more complicated story. In cities such as Boston, the exemption of the affluent suburbs from the requirements of desegregation transformed the busing saga into a class war between struggling urban neighborhoods as much as a racial showdown between whites and blacks. In metropolitan regions such as Detroit, the suburban escape from consolidation accelerated white flight from the city to the places that enjoyed immunity from the reach of the busing decree. And across the nation, cities that operated under neighborhood schools plans experienced comparable degrees of white out-migration (and later middle-class black departures) to cities that fell under court-ordered busing mandates.

Charlotte-Mecklenburg and the other consolidated countywide school districts in the South demonstrated that metropolitan integration remedies, while certainly capable of galvanizing political backlash, were nevertheless more workable and less disruptive than city-only busing plans. In Raleigh, North Carolina, where the city's business leadership voluntarily consolidated the urban school system with suburban Wake County in 1976, the percentage of white students actually increased during the next two decades despite the existence of a metropolitan desegregation plan. In a few smaller metropolitan areas, most notably Louisville, Kentucky and Wilmington, Delaware, civil rights plaintiffs managed to meet the *Milliken* decision's rigorous standard of proof of explicit suburban responsibility for urban housing segregation. Federal courts ordered city-suburban consolidation and comprehensive school integration in both of these regions, and white flight from the public schools proved to be minimal compared to other cities with limited or even nonexistent busing remedies. In another approach that became popular in the 1980s, federal courts in cases involving St. Louis and Kansas City turned to magnet schools and parental choice programs after finding these urban school systems guilty of unconstitutional racial segregation. In St. Louis, the district court order required the state government to spend substantial funds to improve the majority-black city school system and especially the enhanced magnet facilities designed to achieve voluntary integration by attracting white students from the suburbs. The St. Louis plan also permitted about 14,000 black students to transfer to suburban public schools during the 1980s.

In the 1980 presidential election, Ronald Reagan campaigned on a "color-blind" platform that condemned "forced busing" as a failed liberal experiment and promised to allow American students of all races to attend their neighborhood schools. The Reagan administration subsequently intervened in a hotly debated resegregation case involving Norfolk, Virginia, where the school board was attempting to dismantle busing as a strategy to attract more white families to live in the city. In the 1986 *Riddick* decision, the Fourth Circuit Court of Appeals allowed the adoption of a neighborhood schools assignment plan on the grounds that Norfolk had dismantled all vestiges of de jure segregation. The NAACP argued that the existence of all-black neighborhood schools reflected a historical legacy of deliberate residential segregation that continued to shape the relationship between race and space in Norfolk, but the Supreme Court declined to hear the appeal. During the next two decades, federal courts approved the switch from busing to voluntary magnet schools plans in a number of urban districts, and a return to largely segregated neighborhood schools in other systems. As desegregation case law evolved toward a stricter "color-blind" standard, resegregation trends appeared most clearly in the South, the region that had achieved the most racially integrated public schools in the nation during the 1970s under the direct supervision of the federal courts. In 1999, three decades after Charlotte-Mecklenburg became the national testing ground for busing to overcome housing segregation, the desegregation stories of the metropolis and the nation came full circle after a reverse discrimination lawsuit filed by white suburban parents resulted in a federal court order prohibiting the school district from employing the category of race in student assignments.

—*Matthew D. Lassiter*

See also Civil Rights; National Association for the Advancement of Colored People; Nixon Administration: Urban Policy; Reagan Administration: Urban Policy

Further Readings and References

Douglas, D. M. (Ed.). (1994). *School busing: Constitutional and political developments* (2 vols.). New York: Garland.

Edsall, T. B., & Edsall, M. D. (1991). *Chain reaction: The impact of race, rights, and taxes on American politics.* New York: Norton.

Formisano, R. P. (1991). *Boston against busing: Race, class, and ethnicity in the 1960s and 1970s.* Chapel Hill, NC: University of North Carolina Press.

Hochschild, J. L. (1984). *The New American dilemma: Liberal democracy and school desegregation.* New Haven, CT: Yale University Press.

Lassiter, M. D. (2006). *The silent majority: Suburban politics in the sunbelt South.* Princeton, NJ: Princeton University Press.

Orfield, G. (1978). *Must we bus? Segregated schools and national policy.* Washington, DC: Brookings Institution.

Orfield, G., & Eaton, S. E. (1996). *Dismantling desegregation: The quiet reversal of Brown v. Board of Education.* New York: The New Press.

Wilkinson, J. H., III. (1979). *From Brown to Bakke: Thirty years of school desegregation.* Knoxville, TN: University of Tennessee Press.

BYRNE, JANE M.

Jane Byrne (1934-) often is viewed as someone who relied on gimmicks and publicity stunts to make a mark on the city of Chicago. Her legacy is far more than what is commonly known of her, however. A lifelong Chicagoan, she was born to Edward and Margaret Burke on Chicago's far northwest side on March 24, 1934. She married William Byrne, a Marine aviator, who was killed not long after the birth of their only child.

Her first position in Chicago politics was when she was appointed to the position of Consumer Sales Commissioner under the powerhouse of the Chicago political machine led by Richard J. Daley in 1968. Her appointment was initially seen by many as patronage for her work on Daley's previous campaigns, as well as a response to complaints that Daley did little to cater to women and minorities within his administration. Because of her upper-class upbringing, she often did not have to endure the glad-handing that many other mayors had to go through. This circumvention of the system allowed her to think differently, but some saw it as an unorthodox way of thinking that set a bad precedent for the future.

Her chance at the mayorship of Chicago occurred when Daley's successor, Michael Bilandic, failed to get the streets cleaned following one of Chicago's infamous snowstorms. By the time of the March 1979 Democratic Primary (effectively the election of the mayor, since the last Republican mayor was William "Big Bill" Thompson in 1929), Byrne ran as a mayor who would not let the basic needs of Chicago citizens go unheeded. She won that election and became mayor of Chicago in 1979, the first woman ever elected to the post, as well as one of the few women to hold sway in any major American city.

Byrne was beset by several major crises during her tenure. Several city employee groups (city transportation workers, teachers, and firefighters) went on strike in the first 2 years of her administration, often giving Chicago the reputation of the city that doesn't work. Her most famous publicity stunt centered around the plight of Chicago's minorities who lived in the city's housing projects, in particular the infamous, crime-ridden Cabrini-Green project: She stayed in one of the apartments overnight, albeit in an apartment that was considered by the residents to be better than most.

Her legacy was one of division. By 1983, when her term was up, she was challenged by Richard M. Daley (the former mayor's son and heir apparent), as well as a former U.S. representative from Chicago, Harold Washington. Because little serious attention was paid to Washington, Daley and Byrne campaigned for many of the same votes, and in the end, Washington won the Democratic nomination. Byrne's term was seen by some as a blip on the political radar of Chicago. For others, however, her tenure was a small yet positive step for women in the United States.

—Cord Scott

Further Readings and References

Byrne, J. (2004). *My Chicago.* Evanston, IL: Northwestern University Press.

Chicago Tribune. *Chicago days: 150 defining monuments in Chicago's history.* Cantigny, IL: First Division Foundation.

Green, P., & Holli, M. (Eds.). (1995). *The mayors: The Chicago political tradition.* Carbondale, IL: Southern Illinois University Press.

CABRINI-GREEN

Cabrini-Green is a complex of ill-fated public housing projects on Chicago's near-north side comprising the Frances Cabrini Homes (completed in 1942), Cabrini Extension (1958), and the William Green Homes (1962). At its peak, the complex included 3,600 low-income apartments, mostly in high-rise buildings. Begun with the best of intentions, Cabrini-Green spiraled downward in the 1960s under the weight of concentrated poverty, social isolation, and mismanagement. In its early years, the low-rise, racially integrated Cabrini Homes showed promise, but the addition of large-scale high-rises created an oppressive aesthetic that stifled community. The project's proximity to the city's most affluent neighborhood, however, made its problems a magnet for media attention and its location increasingly valuable. Beginning in the mid-1990s, the Chicago Housing Authority (CHA) began to tear down, redevelop, and reconfigure the Cabrini community in ways both dramatic and controversial.

Cabrini-Green cleared a slum once known as "Little Sicily," populated largely by Italian Americans and a growing African American minority. The site lay only a mile west of the city's Gold Coast neighborhood, a juxtaposition described in 1929 by Harvey Warren Zorbaugh in his book *The Gold Coast and the Slum*. The area had been targeted for clearance by reformers and the federal Public Works Administration's Housing Division in 1934, but the resistance of numerous owner-occupants convinced federal officials that the cost of assembling land in the area would be too high. In 1939, the CHA, under the leadership of progressive Elizabeth Wood, returned to the area and chose a smaller site to clear as part of its broader agenda of slum clearance.

The resulting 586-unit, low-rise Mother Frances Cabrini Homes row houses opened in 1942 amid controversy surrounding the project's tenant selection practices. Local Italian American leaders wanted the project to enforce residential segregation and exclude African Americans; Wood and CHA leaders followed existing federal guidelines and chose not to disrupt pre-existing racial patterns on the site. Before clearance, 20 percent of the site's residents had been African American, so the CHA reserved the same percentage for the new project. As a result, Italian Americans shunned the new apartments, and vacancies existed until war workers were given priority. Despite this rocky start, Cabrini recovered and served as a model of carefully managed racial integration through the late 1940s and early 1950s, with an active sense of community fostered by Wood and local settlement houses.

In 1949 the CHA proposed a vast expansion of Cabrini by clearing neighboring slums to the north and east. Wood wanted to protect the CHA's original investment and argued that larger projects offered greater economies of scale. Furthermore, Wood and other city planners believed that large swaths of the city needed redevelopment; clearing the rest of Little Sicily would begin this process. Importantly, the decision to expand Cabrini was not driven by the city's racist aldermen; Wood wanted the site, and it met with approval from city progressives. Like the original Cabrini, however, clearance removed a racially integrated, if not well-housed, low-income community with a surprisingly high number of owner-occupants.

Wood's plans for Cabrini Extension called for a series of midrise elevator buildings in a park-like setting. Truman Administration housing officials, however, demanded cost savings that required reducing the number of buildings while increasing the height of those remaining, thereby reducing per-unit costs. When completed in 1958 at a cost of $26 million, Cabrini Extension included 1,921 units designed by A. Epstein and Sons in a series of seven-, ten-, and nineteen-story buildings faced in red brick. In 1955 an additional parcel to the north was selected (again, to protect Cabrini and clear slums) for the William Green Homes. This third project, designed by Pace Associates, consisted of 1,099 units laid out in eight monolithic 16-story buildings fabricated largely from concrete. Residents quickly took to calling Cabrini-Extension "the reds," the William Green Homes "the whites," and the original Cabrini Homes "the row houses."

The tenant population at Cabrini Homes experienced racial transition before completion of the Extension. After Wood's ouster in 1954 over her principled insistence on integrating the CHA's remaining all-white projects, the CHA abandoned managed integration and adopted a first-come, first-served policy. High demand from African Americans coupled with low demand and high turnover among whites meant Cabrini Homes went from 29 percent black in 1950 to 82 percent black in 1958. By 1963, the completed project was 90 percent African American. At that time tenants were still largely working-class, two-parent families. But by 1974, only 15 percent of families reported income from nongovernment sources. A myriad of problems, including high densities of youth, chronic breakdowns of elevators, and rising crime, contributed to the exodus of employed tenants. Inadequate resources compounded the deepening crisis. Maintenance budgets were derived from rents, but rents were set as a function of income. Increasingly poor tenants could pay little toward maintenance, and additional federal subsidies after 1970 could not stem the downward spiral.

Several high-profile incidents created an image of Cabrini-Green as an alien landscape in the minds of Chicagoans. The shooting of two police officers by a sniper in 1970 shocked the city and added to Cabrini-Green's reputation as an exceedingly dangerous place. Over the next decade, the CHA poured millions into security initiatives, but to little effect. In 1981, then-Mayor Jane Byrne moved in to a fourth-floor Cabrini Extension apartment for three weeks, but her short stay sent mixed messages about conditions in public housing. By the mid-1980s, gang and drug violence had further cemented the image of a project out of control. Finally, in 1992, a sniper shot and killed seven-year-old Dontrell Davis while Davis's mother walked him to school, a murder that led to another round of urban angst over public housing.

While Cabrini-Green remained mired in social isolation and crime, its physical location made it highly desirable to city real estate interests. During the 1980s and 1990s, gentrification edged toward the complex on all sides. The CHA sought to capitalize on this trend by leveraging its land to raise redevelopment funds and by using the Department of Housing and Urban Development's (HUD) Hope VI program to transform Cabrini-Green into a viable mixed-income community. Plans, however, called for demolishing 1,300 units while providing only 325 replacement units. In response, activists, including Chicago's Coalition to Protect Public Housing, called the plan a "land grab" and "urban cleansing." Despite lawsuits and numerous design iterations, by 2004 most of the high-rises had been torn down (although the row houses remain) and major pieces of a new Cabrini had been built, including new luxury townhomes, a shopping center, two new schools, a new police station, and a revitalized park. Cabrini's remaining public housing residents are still wary, however, of a CHA that has made promises in the past but failed to keep them. The future success of a transformed Cabrini remains an open question.

—D. Bradford Hunt

See also New Urbanism; Public Housing; Robert Taylor Homes

Further Readings and References

Bowly, D. (1978). *The poorhouse: Subsidized housing in Chicago, 1895–1976.* Carbondale, IL: Southern Illinois University Press.

Guglielmo, T. A. (2003). *White on arrival: Italians, race, color, and power in Chicago, 1890–1945.* New York: Oxford University Press.

Marciniak, E. (1986). *Reclaiming the inner city: Chicago's near north revitalization confronts Cabrini-Green.* Washington, DC: National Center for Urban Ethnic Affairs.

Whitaker, D. T. (2000). *Cabrini-Green: In words and pictures.* Chicago: W3 Chicago.

Zorbaugh, H. W. (1929). *The Gold Coast and the slum.* Chicago: University of Chicago Press.

CANALS

A canal is a waterway used for the shipping of goods and for transportation between two points. A canal can be built where there is no existing waterway, or it can be a river modified to handle such traffic. Canals also are used to move water to irrigate farmland.

The earliest canals were canalized rivers, and their design included methods for bypassing obstacles such as rapids or waterfalls. The first canal in the United States was on the Connecticut River at South Hadley, Massachusetts; it was built in 1793 and designed to detour rapids on the river.

Canals tend to be level or have a slight incline. For canals to be effective over great distances and through different elevations, a canal lock is required. A canal lock is an enclosure in the canal that has gates on each end. As a boat enters the canal lock, the gate is closed behind it, and water is let in to the lock to allow the boat to rise to the next level of the canal, or water is let out so it is lowered to the next level. The second gate is then opened, and the boat continues on its journey.

Canals have proven to be useful tools in opening up frontiers as well as in helping business interests, not only at the canal ends, but also in the communities along the route. Shipping products on canals was not limited to transporting goods from one end to the other; there was also traffic among towns and cities along the canals. For the most part, canals were used to ship manufactured goods from seaport cities to the hinterland, while agricultural products, timber, stone, and coal were shipped from the hinterland to the large seaport cities.

During the colonial period of American history, factories and mills were located near waterfalls, which powered these industries. Because locks were built to guide boats around these obstacles, factory and mill owners built docks for easy loading of products onto the boats. Thus, their products could be shipped to other towns along the canal or to the port cities. Between 1815 and 1860, a total of 4,254 miles of canal were completed in the United States.

Erie Canal

The first major canal built in the United States was the Erie Canal. Construction began in 1817, and the canal opened for traffic between New York City and Buffalo, New York, in 1825. The Erie Canal was built between Buffalo and a point on the Hudson River just south of Albany. It took advantage of the Hudson River, the only natural breach in the Appalachian Mountain Range, which starts in Maine and runs south to Georgia. Goods shipped from New York City would sail north along the Hudson River to the Erie Canal just south of Albany, New York, where the boats would then head west across northern New York to Buffalo, which is on Lake Erie.

Soon after completion, it became evident that in addition to being a commercial success, the Erie Canal also aided development. Not only did New York City and Buffalo experience growth; so did many smaller cities and towns. The success of the Erie Canal and the benefits that it brought to the entire state of New York were studied by other states that wanted their cities to do just as well.

Pennsylvania Mainline

In Philadelphia, a group of businessmen sought to emulate the Erie Canal's success in their own state. They created the Pennsylvania Mainline in December of 1824, with the idea that they needed to find a way to quickly build their canal line to compete with the Erie Canal. The Pennsylvania Mainline had the physical barrier of the Allegheny Mountains (part of the Appalachian Range), which rise up to heights of 3,000 feet above sea level. The final route was a combination of canals and railroads, including a tunnel under the summit of the Alleghenies. In 1834, the Pennsylvania Mainline was completed.

The Pennsylvania Mainline left Philadelphia and followed the Philadelphia-Columbia Railroad to Columbia, a length of 82 miles. In Columbia, shipments were transferred to the Eastern Division of the Mainline Canal, and they stayed on the canal boats until reaching Hollidaysburg, a length of 172 miles. At Hollidaysburg, goods were transferred to the Allegheny Portage Railroad, which ran to Johnstown, a distance of 32 miles. At Johnstown, the goods were transferred again to canal boats on the Western Division of the Mainline and taken to Pittsburgh, a distance of 105 miles. From Pittsburgh, goods could be shipped north by river and canal to Erie, Pennsylvania, which is on the shore of Lake Erie, or into Ohio. The Erie Canal was 363 miles long and had a summit of 650 feet above sea level, while the Pennsylvania Mainline was 395 miles long and had a summit of 2,322 feet above sea level.

The Pennsylvania Mainline remained the primary form of transportation across Pennsylvania until a railroad was completed between Philadelphia and Pittsburgh in 1852. In 1857, the Pennsylvania Mainline was sold to the Pennsylvania Railroad.

Chesapeake and Ohio

Another canal, the Chesapeake and Ohio, started in Washington, D.C., and reached Cumberland, Maryland, 182 miles to the north and west. The original goal for this canal was to reach Ohio. The Potomac Company was created in 1785 to make improvements to the Potomac River. The primary use of this canal was to carry coal and building materials from West Virginia, southern Pennsylvania, and western Maryland to Washington, D.C.

In 1889, the Baltimore and Ohio Railroad gained control of the canal, and it was abandoned in 1938.

Ohio Canals

The state of Ohio saw a great deal of canal development, with Lake Erie as the destination to the north and the Ohio River, which flowed to the Mississippi River, on the south. There was the Ohio and Pennsylvania Canal between New Castle, Pennsylvania, and Akron, Ohio, as well as the Sandy and Beaver Canal from Beaver, Pennsylvania, to Bolivar, Ohio. The Ohio and Erie Canal was one of the longest; it stretched from Cleveland on Lake Erie to Portsmouth on the Ohio River. This canal passed through cities including Akron, Bolivar, Roscoe, and Carroll and went just south of Columbus.

Another major canal in Ohio was the Miami and Ohio, which started out in Toledo and followed the Maumee River south to the Miami River to Cincinnati on the Ohio River.

Other Major Canals

Wabash and Erie started in Toledo, Ohio, entered Indiana, crossed Indiana following the Wabash River to the White River, and followed that to Evansville, Indiana.

In Illinois there was the Chicago–La Salle Canal, which flowed from Chicago to La Salle, Illinois. From there it was possible to go down the Illinois River to the Mississippi and on to New Orleans.

Virginia had the James River and Kanawha Canal, which left Richmond, Virginia, and followed the James River to Buchanan, Virginia, in the Appalachian Mountains.

—*Douglas K. Bohnenblust*

See also Erie Canal

Further Readings and References

Carter, G. (Ed.). (1961). *Canals and American economic development*. New York: Columbia University Press.
Hahn, T. F. (1984). *Chesapeake and Ohio Canal*. Metuchen, NJ: Scarecrow Press.
Scheiber, H. N. (1969). *Ohio Canal era: A case study of government and the economy, 1820–1861*. Athens: The Ohio University Press.

Capone, Al

Alphonse Capone (1899–1947) was one of the most notorious Italian American gangsters during the Prohibition era. After moving to New York City from his birthplace of Naples, Italy, Capone quickly became involved in gang activities in Brooklyn during his early teenage years. From his petty childhood crimes of vandalism, theft, and fighting, he soon moved up into the famous Five Points gang and earned power and prestige with the group for his ability to strong-arm opponents. Capone was involved in many altercations over turf, money, power, and women, including an incident with fellow gangster Frank Gallucio in which Capone's face was slashed three times with a knife, giving him the nickname "Scarface" for the rest of his life.

In 1920, Capone moved to Chicago as right-hand man to John Torrio, an infamous gangster. Torrio eventually relinquished his power to Capone after an assassination attempt, and Capone quickly worked to become king of the corrupt city of Chicago during the 1920s. He owned speakeasies, brothels, and gambling houses and distributed alcohol across the city. He was taking in up to $60 million a year, but he also paid up to $30 million a year in protection from corrupt government leaders and police officials.

Capone is most famous for the St. Valentine's Day Massacre on February 14, 1929, in which members of the rival gang of George "Bugs" Moran were gunned down by Capone's henchmen dressed as police officers. This event solidified Capone's status and power in Chicago.

Capone's public image was vastly different from his true personality. He was quiet, professionally dressed, and generous with his money, which he often gave to charity. He was able to maintain this contradiction because the authorities were never able to find any evidence of his illegal activities. Most of the crimes he committed were out of the jurisdiction of the federal government, and all of the local police and government officials had been bribed to keep quiet about his actions. Eventually, Capone was brought up on charges in 1931 and found guilty of the lesser crime of tax evasion by Eliot Ness and the so-called "Untouchables" of the federal government. He was sentenced to 11 years in prison and $80,000 in fines and court costs and served his time first in Atlanta and then Alcatraz. He was released in 1939 and suffered from mental and physical illness due to syphilis. He retired to his home in Palm Island, Florida, and remained there until he died of a stroke in 1947 at the age of 48.

—Michael Wolford

See also Chicago, Illinois; Crime and Criminals

Further Readings and References

Bergreen, L. (1994). *Capone: The man and the era.* New York: Simon and Schuster.
Burdick Harmon, M. (2001). Badfella, the life and crimes of Al Capone. *Biography, 5,* 100–106.
Guthrie, M. (1995). Capone, Al. *Collier's Encyclopedia.*

CARTER ADMINISTRATION: URBAN POLICY

For the nation's cities, the one-term presidency (1977–1981) of Jimmy Carter marked the first concerted effort by the executive branch to develop a comprehensive and coordinated urban policy. After more than 40 years of enacting narrowly focused and often contradictory programs designed to meet specific problems of municipal authorities and city residents, the federal government would now attempt to bring coherence to its urban-related activities. Characteristic of the Carter administration, this endeavor generated more promises than results, more confusion than clarity.

The search for a national urban strategy reflected larger trends at work in the Carter presidency. An engineer by training, Carter valued order, direction, and economy in the conduct of government; as governor of Georgia his principal achievement had been administrative reorganization. Transforming the way the federal government operated meant not only realigning agencies, but also more clearly defining objectives and the means by which they were to be achieved. The focus was to be on policy, not programs, and the Carter White House launched highly publicized inquiries to rethink completely what the federal government did in regard to energy, welfare, and the cities. Welfare reform blew up in the administration's face, while the energy proposals enjoyed some legislative success; urban policy fell somewhere in between.

A thorough reexamination of urban issues also served the president's personal predilections and political needs. Unlike his immediate Democratic predecessors in the White House, Carter did not believe that increased federal spending was a necessarily productive response to the plight of the nation's urban areas. Furthermore, having made a virtue during his presidential campaign of his lack of Washington credentials, Carter wanted to remain aloof from the interest-group politics that dominated the nation's capital; by subjecting urban programs to intensive scrutiny, he could claim the higher ground in the inevitable bargaining with Congress. Yet if Carter was seeking over the long term to restructure American politics, he also realized that in the short run he had to satisfy the expectations of two of the mainstays of the Democratic Party (big-city mayors and urban blacks) for at least the prospect of much greater federal largesse. By putting the White House imprimatur on the urban policy review, Carter met that need.

Although the municipal chief executives and racial minorities continued to press their demands as if the urban crisis of the 1960s still claimed the nation's attention, the facts were quite different. New York and some other cities might be in severe financial distress, but layoffs of city workers and reductions in services did not elicit widespread sympathy for the affected communities. Similarly, the relative quiet of the inner city ghettos (broken frighteningly but only briefly in New York during an electrical power outage in summer 1977) fed the popular impression that the peculiar circumstances that had set these neighborhoods aflame in the previous decade no longer applied. With urban problems off the front pages, the basic trends (e.g., loss of industrial jobs, middle-class population movement to the suburbs, in-migration of lower income groups, racial tension) persisted in undermining the economic and social vitality of cities without generating a commensurate sense of urgency for action. Compared with the energy and welfare policy-making processes, the urban policy review would have to overcome general public indifference to the subject.

A year elapsed between the president's appointment of the Urban and Regional Policy Group (URPG) and Carter's unveiling in late March 1978 of "The New Partnership to Conserve America's Communities." Originally expected to be ready for the president's scrutiny by the fall of 1977, the report was so delayed that Carter was placed in the embarrassing position of having nothing substantive to say about urban issues in his January 1978 State of the Union message. The discomfiture did not end there: Important changes in the president's endorsement of specific proposals were being made in the final minutes before Carter's appearance before a large audience of invited guests at the White House in March. What had begun as a deliberate process of analysis had degenerated into a frantic effort to appease various interest groups and to construct a façade of consistency.

Unlike the bold initiatives of Lyndon B. Johnson's Great Society, which had emerged from panels of non-governmental experts meeting in secret, Carter's "New Partnership" was the product of an interagency task force, composed of representatives from six federal executive departments (Housing and Urban Development; Health, Education, and Welfare; Commerce; Labor; Transportation; and Treasury), which began by operating behind closed doors but ended up publicly seeking input from interested parties. Only close supervision by top members of the White House staff enabled URPG to complete its assignment, albeit much later than originally anticipated.

URPG's difficulties revealed not only the perennial turf battles among competing Washington bureaucracies, but the fundamental dilemmas besetting any attempt to respond to the nation's urban problems: the vast diversity in the nature of urban conditions, making any cookie-cutter solution impossible; the political dangers of concentrating federal assistance in the most "distressed communities" as opposed to spreading federal funds across as many localities as might be interested in such aid; and the wisdom of basing policies on the preservation of existing urban places (no matter how distressed) or investing resources in people and encouraging them to relocate to more promising locations. After considerable discussion, URPG recommended, and Carter accepted, a policy that recognized differences in urban situations and tried to make an asset of them by emphasizing local solutions, that highlighted the problems of particularly troubled communities while not ruling out support for those not yet desperate, and that unequivocally, as the very title of the president's policy statement proclaimed, endorsed a "place-based" strategy of federal assistance.

The New Partnership was heavy on process and light on funding. Falling far short of the "Marshall Plan for the Cities" that the mayors and civil rights groups had demanded, the proposal envisioned only small increases in the estimated $30 billion that the federal government channeled annually into urban areas. The emphasis was on more efficient coordination of existing programs; greater cooperation with state and municipal governments, as well as with neighborhood organizations; and making cities more attractive to business investment, while also discouraging suburban sprawl. Although some of these goals would require legislative action, the bulk of the policy recommendations were to be carried out by executive order. Besides directing federal agencies to put their offices in central cities and to make their purchases from companies operating in depressed urban areas, the White House established an Interagency Coordinating Council to facilitate implementation of the new policies and required all agencies to develop internal management procedures to identify whether their programs had an adverse impact on sound urban development.

Useful as these executive orders were to fulfilling Carter's managerial objectives, they had no measurable effect on urban areas and lacked the political appeal that could mobilize the president's electoral constituency. The single element of the New Partnership that held the potential for galvanizing this support was the proposal for creating an Urban Development Bank ("Urbank"), which would guarantee billions of dollars in loans to entrepreneurs expanding or locating their businesses in urban areas of high unemployment. But Carter had avoided deciding what in March 1978 was the most sensitive issue concerning the bank: whether to lodge control with the Department of Housing and Urban Development (which was attuned to city interests) or with the Department of Commerce (which had an excellent track record in dealing with business). The decision to provide for tripartite administration—HUD, Commerce, and Treasury—excited no one, and the narrow window of opportunity for congressional action on the idea closed as national economic conditions deteriorated and foreign policy concerns intensified. The four years of the Carter administration ended without a single significant legislative initiative in the area of urban policy.

Urban issues had not figured prominently in the 1976 election campaign when Carter narrowly defeated the Republican incumbent, Gerald Ford. Nor did the problems of cities assume any importance in the presidential contest four years later, as Carter lost badly to Ronald Reagan. The two candidates were virtually indistinguishable on urban questions: the president had little to point to beyond his urban policy review, and his challenger did not question the review's emphasis on better coordination, more power to states and localities, and additional incentives for business. The shift from Carter to Reagan would mean reduced attention to urban matters, but the difference was less a matter of kind than of degree.

Ironically, the sharpest cut to Carter's urban policy was inflicted not by his successor, but by an advisory panel the president had appointed to prepare a "national agenda for the eighties." Its report, released just days before the end of Carter's term, rejected the basic premise of "The New Partnership to Conserve America's Communities" by urging that the federal government's resources be directed at people rather than places. The panel claimed that seeking to revive distressed cities was both wasteful and hopeless, and that programs such as a guaranteed minimum income and national health insurance presented better approaches to urban problems. Carter repudiated the group's recommendations, but it demonstrated to the bitter end his administration's inability to forge a consensus on urban issues.

—*Mark I. Gelfand*

Further Readings and References

Kaplan, M. (1990). National urban policy: Where are we now? where are we going? In M. Kaplan & F. James (Eds.), *The future of national urban policy* (pp. 171–184). Durham, NC: Duke University Press.
Scruggs-Leftwich, Y. (1995). *Consensus and compromise: An analysis of the national urban policy development process (Carter Administration)*. Unpublished doctoral dissertation, University of Pennsylvania.
Sugrue, T. J. (1998). Carter urban policy crisis. In G. M. Fink & H. D. Graham (Eds.), *The Carter presidency: Policy choices in the post–New Deal era* (pp. 137–157). Lawrence, KS: University Press of Kansas.

CATHOLICISM

In the three great waves of immigration to American cities—1840 to 1860, 1890 to 1914, and 1980 to 2000—the majority of Roman Catholics seeking new lives claimed rural, agricultural backgrounds. Most Catholic immigrants did not become urban dwellers and factory workers until they settled in America. Disorder often accompanied this transition. Complicating matters was the fact that while America's Revolutionary War generation founded the new nation upon an inclusive ideal of liberty, rather than along exclusive sectarian lines, many native-born Protestants responded poorly to Catholic immigrants. To make matters worse, each of the successive waves of immigration, disorder, and nativist backlash caught the urban Catholic Church unprepared.

Origins of American Catholicism

Great Britain's Calvert (Lord Baltimore) family envisioned Maryland as a 17th-century haven for persecuted Roman Catholics. When it became apparent that an explicitly Catholic colony was not politically possible, the Calverts pledged religious toleration for all. By the eve of the Revolution, Maryland, and what became its chief city, Baltimore, served as a center of American Catholicism.

In 1789 Baltimore became the first Roman Catholic diocese in the United States. Although Catholics, even in colonial Maryland, had experienced some discrimination, they participated in the drafting of the Declaration of Independence and the U.S. Constitution. Then again, Catholics accounted for just 1 percent of the U.S. population in 1790, and that may have lessened Protestant fears of religious subversion.

Urban Catholicism and the First Immigrant Wave

Protestant toleration of Catholics declined in the early 19th century as millions of Irish and German immigrants poured into the United States. Eighty percent of Irish Catholic immigrants settled in cities—chiefly the ports where they had disembarked. By the 1850s, more than half the residents of Boston were foreign-born, while 60 percent of New York City's 500,000 residents claimed foreign—most frequently, Irish Catholic—origins.

In the 1850s, New York City's Irish Catholics, although representing 30 percent of the population, accounted for 60 percent of the poor and 50 percent of the criminals. Irish Catholics led New York in child abandonment and filled the ranks of criminal gangs.

Nativists argued that Catholics had brought crime and poverty to America's hitherto pristine cities. A few Catholic leaders, notably New York Archbishop John Hughes (1797–1864), recognized that their Church had to deal with the urban immigrant crisis. Archbishop Hughes exhorted Catholic immigrants to embrace the Church and reject gang membership. He hoped that parochial schools would strengthen urban Catholic morality.

Urban Catholics fully engaged the secular political process. Many historians regard New York's Tammany Hall as the first urban political machine. Established in 1787 as a social club, Tammany evolved into a powerful arm of the Democratic Party in New York. Although Tammany's initial Democratic leaders were Protestant, they quickly saw the political potential in organizing Irish Catholic immigrants into a voting bloc. Tammany forever became associated in the public mind with corrupt big-city Catholic politicians.

The Challenges of the Second Immigrant Wave

By 1890 the American Catholic Church had achieved some reduction in urban crime among its members, built a religious and educational infrastructure, and rejoiced when a select few attained political power as mayors of Boston (Hugh O'Brien, 1882) and New York (William Grace, 1880). Whatever satisfaction church leaders could take in these achievements, however, was short-lived. A new and much larger Catholic (and Jewish) immigrant wave was beginning to flow over American cities.

Between 1890 and 1924, 20 million immigrants, mainly Catholics and Orthodox Jews from southern and eastern Europe, settled in America. Most went to port cities and the growing industrial centers of the Midwest. By 1920 Chicago claimed 500,000 Polish Catholics, New York had 391,000 Italians, and Pittsburgh boasted the largest number of Croatians and Slovakians outside Europe. The Diocese of Pittsburgh struggled to keep pace with its swelling population, erecting a new church every month for the first 20 years of the 20th century.

Nativists in 1887 had founded the first national anti-immigrant lobby, the American Protective Association (APA). The APA's 2.5 million members, who were concentrated mainly in rural America, vowed neither to hire nor to vote for Catholics and Jews. In general, however, the political will to restrict immigration was not in place before World War I. Most industrialists supported unrestricted immigration, liking inexpensive workers who did not vote or join unions.

That calculus changed with the U.S. entrance into World War I. Finding its European source of labor cut off, many industrialists recruited African American workers from the South. When hundreds of thousands of southern and eastern European Catholics and Jews went on strike in 1919, industrialists joined nativists in the embrace of immigration restriction. National-origins quotas—put in place in 1921 and tightened further in 1924—discriminated against immigrants from southern and eastern Europe.

On the positive side for urban Catholic America, restriction forced immigrants and their children to assimilate. Furthermore, restriction stabilized ethnic neighborhoods whose transient populations had flowed back and forth across the Atlantic. By the 1930s, assimilation and community stabilization made it possible for the children of immigrants to mobilize politically and to organize labor unions.

A New Deal for Urban Catholics

The Great Depression (1929 to 1940) hit urban America hard. While the national unemployment rate stood at 25 percent in 1932, it soared to 40 percent or higher in idled industrial centers such as Pittsburgh and Toledo. United by economic hardship, a culturally improbable coalition of Southern white and Northern black Protestants and urban Catholics and Jews forged a Democratic electoral majority behind President Franklin D. Roosevelt (1933 to 1945).

In retrospect, the 1930s were the heyday of both urban America and urban Catholicism. Overall voter turnout between 1920 and 1936 rose 40 percent, with most of this increase concentrated in Northern and West Coast cities. Decisive voter margins in urban counties such as Allegheny (Pittsburgh), Cook (Chicago), Cuyahoga (Cleveland), and Wayne (Detroit) led to key state wins and victory in the Electoral

College. By 1944, one fourth of the national Democratic vote came from Catholics who lived mainly in cities.

Urban Catholics in the 1930s also formed the membership base and, often as not, the leadership of the industrial union movement. Affiliates of the Congress of Industrial Organizations (CIO, 1935–1955) appeared in most Northern and Western cities with significant Catholic and Jewish populations. Three of the five ranking leaders of the CIO in the 1930s—Philip Murray, James Carey, and John Brophy—were Irish Catholic Pittsburghers.

Reformers in the American Catholic Church, inspired by the prolabor encyclicals of Leo XIII, *The Condition of Labor* (in 1891), and of Pius XI, *Reconstructing the Social Order* (in 1931), championed the CIO. This support was vital to the CIO in Buffalo, Chicago, Cleveland, Detroit, Milwaukee, and San Francisco, where Catholics were often suspicious of outsiders, particularly if they were of a different religious faith. "Labor priests" and bishops provided the religious language necessary to build a noncommunist union movement among urban Catholics.

The Decline of Urban Catholicism

World War II set into motion forces that radically changed urban America and Catholicism. War-spurred Southern black migration into Northern and West Coast cities continued unabated, with an additional five million arriving between 1946 and 1960. Many working-class Catholics associated growing post–World War II urban crime rates with Southern black migration and on occasion violently resisted the racial integration of their neighborhoods.

Thanks in part to the 1944 Servicemen's Readjustment Act (a.k.a. the GI Bill of Rights), low-cost loans made it possible for more working-class city dwellers to move to the suburbs. The typical home-owner in the Chicago suburb of Rolling Meadows, for instance, was a working-class Catholic war veteran. With the decline in religious discrimination and the opening of economic and educational opportunities, American Catholics gained acceptance. The election of the first Catholic president in 1960, however, also marked the devolution of a unified New Deal voting bloc into a welter of Republicans, Independents, and Democrats divided along the lines of class, educational attainment, and religious devotion.

By the 1980s, the decline of manufacturing and the rise of a postindustrial economy completed the

depopulation of many cities as middle-class African Americans followed Catholics and Jews to the suburbs. Many bishops believed that they had little choice but to close urban parishes and parochial schools.

Ironically, the process of Catholic institutional disengagement from urban America neared completion just as a new third wave of poor Catholic immigrants—largely from Mexico and Latin America—came to the cities. While some inner city Catholic parishes have been revitalized by this most recent immigration, Pentecostal churches have moved in to assist, educate, and convert such people. In the meantime, yet another anti-immigrant political backlash appeared in the offing.

—*Kenneth J. Heineman*

See also Chicago, Illinois; Ethnic Neighborhoods; Great Depression and Cities; Philadelphia, Pennsylvania; Pittsburgh, Pennsylvania; Religion in Cities and Suburbs; Tammany Hall

Further Readings and References

Anbinder, T. (2001). *Five Points: The 19th-century New York City neighborhood that invented tap dance, stole elections, and became the world's most notorious slum.* New York: The Free Press.

Durr, K. (2003). *Behind the backlash: White working-class politics in Baltimore, 1940–1980.* Chapel Hill. NC: University of North Carolina Press.

Erie, S. P. (1988). Rainbow's end: Irish-Americans and the dilemmas of urban machine politics, 1840–1985. Berkeley, CA: University of California Press.

Heineman, K. J. (1999). *A Catholic New Deal: Religion and reform in Depression Pittsburgh.* University Park, PA: Pennsylvania State University Press.

Higham, J. (1988). *Strangers in the land: Patterns of American nativism, 1860–1925.* New Brunswick, N.J.: Rutgers University Press.

Morris, C. R. (1997). *American Catholic: The saints and sinners who built America's most powerful church.* New York: Random House.

CELEBRATION, FLORIDA

Celebration, Florida, is a planned community located in Osceola County, Florida. Developed in the early 1990s, it is significant for being one of the most publicized examples of "new urbanist" planning in the United States and for being a residential housing development undertaken by the Walt Disney Company—a large, multinational corporation known primarily for its movies, television shows, and tourist theme parks. Residents first settled in Celebration in 1994, and the community is expected to grow to a population of 12,000 residents.

From the late 1960s when Disney started acquiring property in central Florida, a residential community figured into their plans. A 1967 film narrated by the company's founder, Walt Disney, and shown following his death described a prototype community that would showcase the latest in technological innovation. The film was shown as part of the company's successful effort to convince the state of Florida to grant them the municipal powers of planning, zoning regulation, and the levying of bonds.

When the "experimental prototype community of tomorrow" (EPCOT) was finally opened in 1979, it was not a residential community at all, but rather a second theme park to complement Walt Disney World. By the late 1980s and with Osceola County threatening to rezone some of the company's undeveloped land from agriculture to a higher tax usage, Disney CEO Michael Eisner sought to develop parts of the company's underutilized land holdings and revived the idea of a planned community that integrated residential and commercial development.

Disney board member and architect Robert A. M. Stern was hired to develop the Celebration master plan, in which he and his colleague Jacqueline Robertson followed the tenets of the emerging planning framework of New Urbanism. As such, the town was developed with a traditional, mixed-use downtown that has multifamily apartment and condominium dwellings abutting restaurants, shops, and services. Single-family residential housing was situated nearby, providing pedestrian access to the development's amenities. Lot sizes for private homes were smaller than similar developments in the region, but parks and public spaces were developed both in the commercial district and throughout the various neighborhoods to act as community gathering places. In a departure from new urbanist influences, Stern situated a large regional hospital and two office towers on the outskirts of the development.

While the architecture of the community's housing stock employed a variety of traditional influences (Colonial, Spanish Mission, Cape Cod, Victorian), Disney hired many well-known modern and postmodern architects to design buildings in the commercial districts, including Philip Johnson, Michael Graves, Cesar Pelli, and Aldo Rossi.

Because of the involvement of Disney and the major size of the project, Celebration received significant national attention. Critics immediately seized upon connections among the rather traditional look of the town's architecture, the new urbanist penchant for building pedestrian-friendly communities that resemble small-town Americana, and Disney's long experience of representing nostalgic versions of United States history in its entertainment business. They denounced Celebration as being sentimental, artificial, and overly subject to corporate control.

While critics of the development were numerous and vocal, their exhortations did not negatively influence sales in the development, as it attracted an initial interest that outpaced supply. Unusual for a suburban planned community, numerous residents moved to Celebration primarily because of their enthusiasm for Disney. Expressing admiration for the company as a well-run organization, they had similar hopes for a well-run community.

Politically, the community exhibited contradictory tendencies, and the tensions between residential enthusiasm and the company's interest in realizing success in its investment often resulted in publicized clashes. While Disney marketed Celebration as a community embodying the values and feel of a "small town," it lacked the one institutional structure that most often acts as the mediator of a community's values: local government. Legally, Celebration was an unincorporated part of the larger Osceola County and governed locally through a Community Development District (CDD). CDDs are quasi-municipalities authorized by the state of Florida and created by developers to fund and maintain large common-interest developments. Under the Celebration CDD's terms of incorporation, the developer effectively controlled basic elements of the development relating to appearance and the maintenance of common areas until a critical mass of residents settled in the development. As Disney sought to change or expand its development plans, residents lacked official mechanisms of influence, leading them to often "expose" the company's plans to local and national press outlets seeking controversial stories involving Disney, the region's largest corporation.

Some of the more controversial subjects that emerged for residents were the effectiveness of the school's curriculum and the company's desire to expand the community beyond the original plan accepted by Osceola County. In each case, vocal groups of residents were notable for being sophisticated in their organizational acumen by opposing Disney in arenas outside the CDD, most notably in the Osceola County Board of Education and the Osceola County Commission.

Resident organizing also has been complemented by the fast emergence of strong voluntary institutions of civil society that frequently articulate concerns of various constituencies. These include the bimonthly newspaper, *The Celebration Independent*; a local Rotary Club; and other groups organized around common interests.

Celebration's perceived success has influenced scores of other new urbanist developments that mimic Celebration's architecture and marketing strategies, making New Urbanism one of the most popular approaches to planning large-scale communities in the late 1990s and the early part of the 21st century.

—Hugh Bartling

See also New Urbanism

Further Readings and References

Bartling, H. E. (2002). Disney's Celebration, the promise of new urbanism, and the portents of homogeneity. *The Florida Historical Quarterly, 81*(1), 44–67.

Foglesong, R. E. (2001). *Married to the mouse: Walt Disney World and Orlando.* New Haven, CT: Yale.

Frantz, D., & Collins, C. (1999). *Celebration U.S.A.: Living in Disney's brave new town.* New York: Henry Holt.

Ross, A. (1999). *The Celebration chronicles: Life, liberty, and the pursuit of property value in Disney's new town.* New York: Ballantine.

CENTRAL PARK

Central Park, in New York City, is the first great urban public park constructed in the United States. Extending from 59th to 110th streets and from Fifth to Eighth avenues, the park occupies 843 acres, 153 city blocks, and 9,792 standard 25-by-100-foot Manhattan building lots. The park's design was determined by a public competition, won by Frederick Law Olmsted, Sr., and Calvert Vaux in 1858. Olmsted was appointed architect-in-chief and superintendent, and Vaux was named consulting architect while directing the construction of the park.

Central Park is completely a humanly created landscape. Images of the park prior to construction reveal a treeless, scarred landscape. A small African American community, Seneca Village, extended from 82nd to 88th streets on the park's west side, while clusters of dwellings occupied by German or Irish immigrants stood elsewhere on the site. More than 1,600 residents were displaced when the city acquired the land, removed or demolished 300 houses as well as a number of factories, slaughterhouses, and other nuisance uses, and commenced construction of the park in 1857.

Olmsted and Vaux's challenge in designing the park was to transform an unattractive site into a place of seemingly natural beauty. Olmsted later calculated that between 1857 and 1870 workers handled 4,825,000 cubic yards of stone and earth during construction, which, if placed in the standard one-horse carts then in use, would have extended from New York to San Francisco and back again five times. So much stone and earth was moved during construction that Olmsted estimated that it was equivalent to changing the grade of the park by four feet. As many as 3,800 men were employed during the peak of construction: In addition to the dramatic reshaping of the landscape, workers dug the ponds and planted acres of grass as well as some 270,000 trees and shrubs, creating, in every sense of the word, the park. Olmsted and Vaux's "Greensward" plan gave the park its most distinctive landscape features—broad meadows, water courses and ponds, rocky outcrops, and heavily forested hillsides—as well as the complete separation of traffic within the park and the sunken transverse roads that carry city traffic across the park. Vaux and his collaborators designed more than 20 bridges and underpasses to separate pedestrian paths from bridle paths and carriage drives, as well as several buildings and dozens of structures to meet the needs of visitors to the park.

Construction of Central Park took place within the tumultuous political culture of New York City in the middle decades of the 19th century. As the city's Democratic Party grew in power, the state legislature, dominated by upstate Republicans, enacted a new charter in 1857 that severely limited the city's ability to govern itself. That charter, a patently undemocratic document, replaced the Municipal Police, whose members were appointed by the mayor, with a

Metropolitan Police force controlled by five state-appointed commissioners. The new charter created several other state-appointed commissions, including one to regulate the harbor and, fearing that park construction would become a source of patronage to city Democrats, another to build Central Park. The Board of Commissioners of the Central Park was dominated by Republicans and exercised stewardship over construction and use until 1870, when a new city charter (often called the "Tweed charter," after Tammany Hall political boss William Marcy "Boss" Tweed) replaced it with a Department of Public Parks, whose members were appointed by the mayor.

As superintendent of construction, Olmsted had to organize a disciplined workforce. New York's working class in the 1850s was experiencing pressure from industrialization, which increased work discipline, and from record high levels of immigration, which produced a surplus of labor that depressed job opportunities and wages. Workers were fractious and attempted to protect their interests through rallies and strikes. Olmsted and the park commission determined to hire laborers as public employees and to regulate their work closely, which conflicted with the expectations of many of the city's workers. Olmsted organized the workers into teams of 30 to 40 men, each with a foreman who was responsible for taking roll, directing the work, and preparing a daily report on the work accomplished. Eight general foremen supervised the foremen to ensure that all laborers were complying with park policies and Olmsted's expectations of efficient work. Between 1857 and 1870 Olmsted estimated that the park commission spent $8,900,000 constructing Central Park.

Managing Central Park—educating the public in the proper use of the park, overseeing maintenance and ongoing improvements, and ensuring the public's safety—was, Olmsted recognized, equally important as design and superintendence of construction. Prior to construction of the park, a number of newspapers expressed what Olmsted called false, craven conservatism. This was the belief that democracy was a decivilizing process that would establish the lowest common denominator in American political, social, and intellectual life. Any recreational or cultural institution open to the public would effectively be defined by the behavior of the rudest, least reputable members of society, with the result that the middle and upper classes would not frequent such places.

Olmsted realized that maintaining order and ensuring the public's safety in the park was essential to its

success. In February 1858, he assumed responsibility for training and administering a force of keepers to maintain order in the park. Olmsted envisioned that the principal responsibility of the keepers would be to educate the public in the proper use of the park. He shaped the keepers into a highly effective force, and their impact on the park was obvious: One writer told of encountering in the park one of the city's most notorious saloonkeepers, who had come there one Sunday to visit former customers who found the park a more attractive place than his bar. The fears of social conservatives notwithstanding, Central Park was a safe, well-ordered landscape.

The keepers were essential to Olmsted's vision of the park as a democratic, social space. He saw it as the one place in a city stratified by class, race, and ethnicity that welcomed all residents. In 1859, when describing his vision for the park, he insisted that it would be the primary or sole source of recreation for residents of all classes. In 1870, when urging citizens of Boston to establish a large park in their city, Olmsted observed that Central Park and Prospect Park, in Brooklyn, were the only places in their respective cities where there was equality, without competition or jealousy. His was a vision of the park as a civic space that included, indeed welcomed, all residents of the city.

Central Park was a creative response to New York City's dramatic growth in the middle decades of the 19th century, a remarkable act of stewardship that set aside 843 acres for public recreation. Olmsted and Vaux designed the park's curvilinear paths and naturalistic landscape to stand in striking contrast to the straight lines and sharp angles of the expanding city. Through boundary plantings, transverse roads, and the complete separation of traffic throughout the park, Olmsted and Vaux minimized the degree to which the city would intrude upon the landscape. But the park was, and remains, an urban institution: It was conceived not as a withdrawal from or repudiation of the complexities of the city but as part of what Olmsted later characterized as the complex physical fabric and the general economy of the city.

Central Park has experienced shifting fortunes in its 150 years. During the Tweed "ring," park administrators, in Olmsted's estimation, compromised the original design and failed to ensure proper maintenance and public safety. Cuts in funding for maintenance have occurred whenever the city faced straitened financial conditions. Robert Moses rehabilitated the park in the 1930s but also widened roads to accommodate the automobile and added playgrounds and facilities for active recreation that brought the noise, energy, and competition of the city into the park. The park again suffered deferred maintenance during the fiscal crisis of the 1970s but was renovated and restored in the closing decades of the 20th century.

Central Park inspired the creation of similar large parks in other American cities in the second half of the 19th century. Recognition of its importance in the history of landscape architecture and city planning came in 1965, when Central and Prospect parks were the first landscapes entered in the National Register of Historic Places. For more than 150 years, the park has been an incalculable resource for residents of New York City.

—*David Schuyler*

See also New York, New York; Olmsted, Frederick Law, Sr.

Further Readings and References

Beveridge, C. E., & Hoffman, C. F. (Eds.). (1997). *The papers of Frederick Law Olmsted. Supplementary Series: Vol. 1. Writings on public parks, parkways, and park systems.* Baltimore: Johns Hopkins University Press.

Beveridge, C. E., & Schuyler, D. (Eds.). (1983). *The papers of Frederick Law Olmsted: Vol. 3. Creating Central Park, 1857–1861.* Baltimore: Johns Hopkins University Press.

Board of Commissioners of the Central Park. (1863). *Sixth Annual Report.* New York: Author.

Miller, S. C. (2003). *Central Park: An American masterpiece.* New York: Harry N. Abrams, Inc. in association with the Central Park Conservancy.

Reed, H. H., & Duckworth, S. (1967). *Central Park: A history and a guide.* New York: Clarkson N. Potter.

Rosenzweig, R., & Blackmar, E. (1992). *The park and the people: A history of Central Park.* Ithaca, NY: Cornell University Press.

CENTRAL PLACE THEORY

Under the broad aegis of economic geography, central place theory attempts to offer some explanation as to why economic goods and services are offered only in some locations and not homogeneously distributed across space. The basic essence of the theory suggests that a spatial economy emerges from the trade-off between the economies of scale that sellers face while producing goods and the transportation costs that consumers must absorb when purchasing goods, as noted by Masahisa Fujita, Paul Krugman, and Anthony J. Venables in 1999.

As an introduction to the basic concepts within the theory, imagine a hypothetical, topologically neutral plain uniformly inhabited by wheat farmers. One of the farmers decides to produce beer and sell the product to other farmers. The neighboring farmers decide that traveling to buy the beer is more cost-effective than producing it themselves. But, for the neighbors of the neighbors, the time away from the farm and the cost of traveling some distance, x, outweigh the cost of producing their own beer. So, beer is produced in a "central place," as some farmers choose to enter the beer-producing market and serve other farmers who do not; furthermore, there is a spatial uniqueness as to who chooses which option, depending primarily on the price of beer.

The origins of central place theory (and location theory more generally) come from a long tradition of German intellectual thought. Its roots began in the 1850s, but because of the language barrier, location theory did not enter the American discourse until Walter Isard began his writings a century later. Johann von Thünen is considered the father of the field with his book, *The Isolated State*, in which he articulated a model analyzing rent differentials (what has become known as bid-rent analysis) that accounted for the different types of agricultural land uses around a monocentric city (von Thünen's work was revisited in the 1960s by William Alonso, Edwin Mills, and R. Muth, who replaced farmers with commuters and the central city with the central business district). This body of work essentially became known as the New Urban Economics.

Refinements to central place theory itself came from Walter Christaller's book, *Central Places in Southern Germany* (published in German in 1933), in which he presented evidence that the "laws" governing the number, sizes, and distribution of towns in space emerge into a hierarchical urban landscape. To begin his analysis, Christaller defined an inner and outer range of an economic good. The *inner range* consisted of the minimum radius from a location that if the entire population within the ring purchased the good, the costs of production would equal the revenues. The *outer range* of any good or service was the farthest distance from the central place that buyers would be willing to travel. If the outer and inner ranges were not equal, the difference between the two rings would represent the potential profit for the good. The relative sizes of each range would determine the number and rank of central places within a region. For example, if the population was equally distributed around a central place and the inner range was very low compared to the outer range, the central good would be offered at another central place located nearby. The potential profit of the good (measured by the difference between the two ranges) would induce people in nearby central places to provide the good. If the two ranges were roughly equal, the central good could only be offered profitably at precisely that central place. Of course, if the inner range exceeded the outer range, the good would yield negative profits and not be offered at all.

This interaction between inner and outer ranges for all economic goods formed the basis for ranking central places into a hierarchy. Goods with very low inner ranges, meaning profitable even with fewer purchases, would be offered in many places; places that offered *only* such "low-ranged" goods would rank lower than places that additionally offered "high-ranged" goods. Christaller went on to describe (and calculate) the locational patterns of hierarchically ordered central places. Recall the original formulation of the problem, that is, how central places emerge from a landscape of uniformly distributed farmers. To satisfy the condition that the settlement pattern is uniform, the farmers must be distributed within a hexagonal lattice. (A square pattern does not satisfy the condition of uniform distribution; the distance along the diagonal is longer than the sides.) Central places of increasingly higher order would *also* be uniformly distributed and, hence, follow a hexagonal (albeit of larger area) pattern as well.

Christaller recognized that the range of a good was not independent of the distribution and size of the central places themselves. In order to incorporate the effects of history and physical geography, he developed spatial organizing principles that were governed by the market, transportation infrastructure, or political jurisdictions. If cities are formed primarily because of the economic range of goods, the development of central places occurs according to what Christaller called the *marketing* principle. When transportation modes were not dense radially from the center, central places developed in a more linear fashion according to the *transportation* principle. Rail lines and roadways would be laid primarily to connect the highest ranked central places and would incidentally pass through towns of lower rank located along the way. Although rail transportation was in its heyday in the 1930s, Christaller foretold that, in contrast, transportation via truck or automobile would lead to the decentralization of a region as the advantages of residing close to the center or transportation economies of scale diminished. Finally, he articulated an *administrative* principle that would generate distinct or separable districts centering on a "capital."

Christaller's theory was later refined by August Lösch in his book, *The Economics of Location*, published in German in 1940. Based on the same initial assumptions of a uniformly distributed population, Lösch articulated the effect of distance on the demand for a good, that is, the spatial demand curve. Going back to the beer example, the price that a farmer chose for the beer would determine the quantity sold as well as the distance over which buyers chose to travel to obtain it. As is well established in classic economic theory, as the price of any good increases, the quantity demanded decreases. Lösch observed that for any particular price, the quantity demanded would *also decrease by distance*. Therefore, the price that the farmer chooses to set for the beer determines what Christaller termed the outer range of the good. Across the entire plain, the "market area" for all beer producers will be precisely the distance (and therefore price) at which the costs of production equal revenues.

The writings of Christaller and Lösch (particularly after being translated into English in 1966 and 1954, respectively) and central place theory in general have spawned a variety of research strains on the spatial organization of economic activity, including the geometrical and mathematical structure of the system, identification of central place hierarchies through statistical analysis, and applicability to economic development and regional planning.

—*Seema D. Iyer*

See also Economy of Cities

Further Readings and References

Christaller, W. (1933). *Central places in southern Germany*. English translation, Prentice-Hall, Inc. 1966.

Fujita, M., Krugman, P., & Venables, A. J. (1999). *The spatial economy: Cities, regions and international trade*. Cambridge, MA: MIT Press.

Isard, W. (1956). *Location and space-economy*. Cambridge, MA: MIT Press.

King, L. (1984). *Central place theory*. Thousand Oaks, CA: Sage.

Century of Progress

From May to November of 1933 and 1934, the city of Chicago commemorated its centennial by hosting the World's Fair, also known as the "Century of Progress." Built around the theme of scientific progress, the fair showcased the accomplishments of human endeavor in the areas of science, industry, and culture to millions of visitors. Amid the misery of the Great Depression, the Century of Progress—and Chicago itself—provided relief from hard times, showcased a celebration of past achievements, and offered a hopeful outlook for the country's future.

Origins of the Fair

Planning began in 1926; the fair's board of directors, who were members of Chicago's business and political elite, first convened in 1927. Oil and banking tycoon Rufus Dawes was the fair's chairperson. Retired army officer and engineer Lenox Lohr was the general manager. In the early planning stages, the fair was known simply as "Chicago's Second World's Fair," a reference to the famous World's Columbian Exposition that Chicago hosted in 1893. In 1929, the board settled on science as its theme. It then renamed the fair "A Century of Progress." Fair organizers commissioned the National Research Council, a group that coordinated scientific research in industry and universities, to develop a plan for what scientific topics ought to be exhibited.

Financing the Fair

Most of the fundraising for the fair coincided with the onset of the Great Depression. Despite that challenge, the board raised more than $630,000 by selling "memberships" in a booster organization called the Chicago's World's Fair Legion. The board also offered a $10 million bond issue, of which slightly more than half was paid. Contracts to concessionaires raised another $3 million. Numerous exhibitors, including the federal government, spent millions to construct their own pavilions and exhibit halls.

Location and Architecture

The fair's site was a narrow, three-mile-long span of lakeshore south of Chicago's downtown area, stretching southward from 12th Street to 39th Street. The tract covered 427 city acres composed of solid earth, landfill, and lagoons. Supervision of the design and construction fell to Daniel Burnham Jr., son of the famed architect by the same name who built the World's Columbian Exposition in 1893 and authored the famous *Plan for Chicago* in 1909. The layout of the fair was similar to the Columbian Exposition, but the younger Burnham's design reflected the architectural trends of his day. He rejected the neoclassicism of 1893 in favor of modern, Bauhaus-inspired design. Board members intended the buildings to reflect the theme of scientific progress. This directive, and the financial difficulties caused by the Great Depression, led the architects to construct inexpensive buildings with few windows. They enhanced the largely plain structures with innovative uses of light and color. The most famous and perhaps most controversial of the buildings was the Travel and Transport Building, whose dome was suspended by an array of cables and towers.

Key Exhibits

Visitors to the fair enjoyed a mixture of educational exhibits and entertainment. In the planning stages, the board determined that the fair itself would operate the "pure science" exhibits and leave the applied science exhibits to private industry. The Hall of Science featured exhibits on geology, physics, biology, chemistry, and other core sciences. Elaborate exhibits operated by some of the country's largest corporations—General Motors, Sears Roebuck, and Standard Oil, for example—demonstrated the application of scientific knowledge in the production of consumer goods. For the 1934 season, the Ford Motor Company spent $5 million to construct a huge pavilion and adjacent band shell that spanned 11 acres. The federal government exhibited at the fair, too, spending $1.75 million to construct the U.S. Government Building. Other popular exhibits included replicas of the 18th-century cabin inhabited by Jean Baptiste Point DuSable, thought to be the city's first non-Indian resident, and Fort Dearborn, the first American outpost in what later became the city of Chicago. Just a few blocks north of the fairgrounds, several Chicago landmarks, old and new—the Art Institute (founded in 1879), Field Museum of Natural History (1893), Shedd Aquarium (1929), and Adler Planetarium (1930)—contributed exhibition space and other resources.

The entertainment section of the fair was called the Midway. There visitors toured replicas of European cities and villages, enjoyed films projected on giant screens, and explored a host of other entertainments. The most remembered of these is surely Sally Rand, the "Fan Lady." Her burlesque alternately thrilled and outraged visitors and earned her two arrests. The entertainment program also spawned related sports events organized by the fair's Sports Committee. Soldier Field hosted five collegiate football games during the two fair seasons. The first All-Star game in major-league baseball history, organized by *Chicago Tribune* sports editor Arch Ward, was held at nearby Comiskey Park on July 6, 1933.

Racial Controversy

African American civic leaders disagreed on whether to support the fair. The *Chicago Defender*, an influential black newspaper, initially urged African Americans to support the fair. Others demurred, pointing out that fair organizers employed few blacks during construction. After the fair opened, several revelations further cooled black support. The fair employed very few African Americans, and most of those worked in the toilet concession. In addition, some concessionaires flatly refused to serve black patrons. There were other racial problems, such as with the popular Sky Ride, a cable-car ride traversing the fairgrounds several hundred feet in the air. It was suspended by twin towers named "Amos" and "Andy," a reference to a popular but racially insensitive radio show. Furthermore, plans for a concession showcasing the educational, industrial, and cultural progress of African Americans never came to fruition. Instead, visitors toured "Darkest Africa," an exhibit that presented pygmies, cannibals, hot-coal walkers, and fire-eaters. Many black Chicagoans found this exhibit degrading, and they voiced their concerns publicly. To mollify African Americans, fair organizers set aside August 12, 1933, as "Negro Day," which featured events designed to celebrate African American life and culture. Before the opening of the 1934 season, the Illinois State Legislature pressured fair organizers and concessionaires not to discriminate against African Americans. The legislature also provided a mechanism for blacks to formally lodge their complaints with the authorities.

End of the Fair

Despite such controversies, the Century of Progress was very successful. More than 48 million visitors toured its grounds. Although it was a nonprofit venture, the fair netted $160,000. Chicago's South Park District, the Field Museum, Shedd Aquarium, Adler Planetarium, and other groups divided this surplus.

—Daniel J. Lerner

Further Readings and References

Findling, J. E. (1994). *Chicago's great world's fairs.* Manchester, UK: Manchester University Press.

Holt, B. (1986). *An American dilemma on display: Black participation at the Chicago Century of Progress Exposition, 1933–1934.* Report for the Chicago Urban League Research and Planning Department.

Meier, A., & Rudwick, E. (1966). Negro protest at the Chicago World's Fair, 1933–1934. *Journal of Illinois State Historical Society, 59,* 161–167.

Rydell, R. (1993). *World of fairs: The century of progress expositions.* Chicago: University of Chicago Press.

Rydell, R., Findling, J. E., & Pelle, K. (Eds.). (2000). *Fair America: World's fairs in the United States.* Washington, DC: Smithsonian Institution Press.

Chain Stores

Chain stores are groups of retail businesses that share the same name and logo, sell the same array of branded goods, and are owned by or managed according to the guidelines of the same firm. Chain stores have come to dominate the suburban retailing landscape and to epitomize American consumer culture.

The first chain stores opened in the latter half of the 19th century. The Great Atlantic & Pacific Tea Company (A&P) opened its first grocery store in 1859, and F. W. Woolworth, the entrepreneur behind "five-and-dimes," opened his first variety store in 1879 in Utica, New York.

Fueled by a stock-market boom, rising profits, and new commercial districts in urban neighborhoods, chain-store firms grew enormously in the 1910s and 1920s. This was true both in terms of sales and in terms of number of stores owned. By 1929, chain stores accounted for 22 percent of total U.S. retail sales, and they were an expected presence in the commercial districts of urban neighborhoods. Growth was most dramatic in the fields of grocery retailing and in variety stores. But other kinds of chains also proved successful. These included tobacco stores (United Cigar Stores), drug stores (Liggett), candy stores, and restaurants such as J. R. Thompson and Howard Johnson's.

Chain stores promised low prices and standardized (and therefore trustworthy) goods. Advertisements of chain groceries and restaurants prominently featured sale items. The emphasis on low price was both a marketing strategy and the result of chains' ability to rely on economies of scale. That is, they purchased or processed standardized goods in large quantities to lower the cost of each item. To further lower costs, chains often also operated their own warehouse and distribution systems, thus eliminating the cost of outside wholesalers.

Some stores also promised "self-service"—that is, that customers could choose goods themselves from store shelves without a clerk's assistance. This was especially compelling because tensions often surrounded the more personal, but potentially discriminatory or invasive, service by clerks. Promises of autonomy and independence were targeted especially to white, middle-class, female customers but also had special appeal to white working-class and African American customers, who appreciated the possibilities for equal treatment and access to name-brand goods. Not all firms enforced this policy, and some products (for instance, meat and produce) continued to be held behind counters. Nonetheless, chains regularly marketed themselves as places where all customers would be treated equally and with discretion. Thus, social dynamics as well as low price help to explain the success of chain stores.

Chain stores did not, however, experience trouble-free growth. High rents and costs of store locations and the fixed costs of operating such large businesses worried many firms. Because of these and other concerns, some types of chain stores disappeared or became only small players in retailing. This was true of tobacco and many candy stores. Also, independent druggists and grocers urged Congress and state legislatures to protect independently owned firms by taxing or otherwise impeding chains. Although anti-chain legislation was passed at both the state and federal level, no political movement proved effective in stopping the growth of chains or, more important, in providing significant help to smaller, independently owned stores.

Indeed, the promises of chain stores were so compelling that many smaller, independent stores attempted to adapt chain strategies. Forming agreements to purchase some items collectively and often sharing similar logos, advertising, and store design, these "voluntary chains" or "retailer-cooperatives" deepened the visual and cultural impact of chains. Independent grocers, for instance, formed the Independent Grocers Alliance, while hardware dealers organized True Value chains. In the postwar period, independent proprietors working with large firms made another important innovation. Franchises, or stores owned by individuals but operated under the name and strict supervision of a national chain firm, reinforced the standardization of the American mass market.

By the 1960s, chain stores had come to epitomize American mass consumption, particularly in new suburban commercial areas. Previously independent department stores opened branches in suburban commercial districts, malls, and shopping centers. These selling spaces came to feature national clothing, department store, and variety chains.

Chains' importance was reinforced by the dramatic increases in consumer purchases that marked the post–World War II period. Chains served as crucial sources of consumer goods at the very moment when consumer purchasing assumed new economic and cultural significance in Americans' lives. Food, clothing, and housewares were bought via large, centrally managed chain stores. In this way, chains responded to and shaped middle-class Americans' increasing reliance on mass-produced, standardized goods.

In recent years, enormous "big-box" stores like Best Buy and Home Depot have spread the chain-store model to sales of appliances, electronics, building supplies, and tools. Larger variety stores like Target and Wal-Mart have forced smaller, older chains located in cities to move or to close. Although anti-chain sentiments continue, and many national firms have opened smaller chains that target particular racial or ethnic groups or socioeconomic classes, the growth of chain stores has continued to define retailing and to define many Americans' shopping.

—*Tracey Deutsch*

See also Supermarkets

Further Readings and References

Cohen, L. (1990). *Making a new deal: Industrial workers in Chicago, 1919–1939*. Cambridge and New York: Cambridge University Press.

Deutsch, T. (2001). Untangling alliances: Social tensions at neighborhood grocery stores and the rise of chains. In W. Belasco & P. Scranton (Eds.), *Food nations: Selling taste in consumer societies*. New York: Routledge.

Strasser, S. (1989). *Satisfaction guaranteed: The making of the American mass market*. New York: Pantheon.

Tedlow, R. (1990). *New and improved: The story of mass marketing in America*. New York: Basic Books.

CHAPLIN, CHARLIE

Charles Spencer Chaplin (1889–1977) was born on April 16, 1889, in London, England, to music-hall entertainers. He debuted on stage at age five but spent most of his early years as a street urchin, receiving little formal schooling, joining a band of roving performers, and working odd jobs to stay alive. Despite his Dickensian childhood, Charlie Chaplin became the most successful, in terms of longevity, and universally well-loved genius in motion-picture history. Through combined talents as actor, writer, director, and producer, he poked fun at the human condition while questioning the moral underpinnings of the Industrial Age.

Chaplin first came to the United States in 1910, in a touring vaudeville troupe. In late 1913, he signed with Mack Sennett at Keystone Studio and moved to Hollywood, making a staggering 35 one-reelers in his first year alone. In his second film, *Kid Auto Races at Venice* (1914), he introduced the screen persona that would star in Chaplin's first directorial masterpiece, *The Tramp* (1915). His happy-go-lucky vagabond with the toothbrush-sized moustache, baggy pants, floppy shoes, derby hat, and cane became the ultimate underdog, waddling through reels of encounters with unforgiving environments and showcasing Chaplin's gifts for improvisation, pantomime, acrobatic timing, and ballet-dancer agility. His alter ego became a universal icon vigorously promoted through merchandising, other media, and amateur look-alike contests. As a result, the fees Chaplin could demand skyrocketed. By 1919, after short-lived stints at a string of studios, he joined actors Douglas Fairbanks and Mary Pickford and director D. W. Griffith to form their own independent film company, United Artists.

Through Chaplin's obsessive artistic control and his novel blend of slapstick and pathos, his Little Tramp brought laughter to the masses, especially needed after World War I and during the dark years of the Depression. The lighthearted tales of woe were also a vehicle for Chaplin's biting social commentary. His reoccurring themes of destitution, desolation, and concern for the downtrodden—most likely based on his upbringing—found their way into his most famous silent features, including *The Kid* (1921), his first as producer for United Artists, and *The Gold Rush* (1925), his highest grossing silent picture. *City Lights* (1931) and *Modern Times* (1936), his two final Little Tramp features, remained uncharacteristically silent in an era of talkies. In *The Great Dictator* (1940), Chaplin spoke on-screen for the first time, playing dual roles as a Tramp-like Jewish barber and a thinly disguised Adolf Hitler, closing his film with an emotional plea against Nazi aggression and to end pre-World War II U.S. isolationism. He would make two other notable works, *Monsieur Verdoux* (1947) and *Limelight* (1952). However, as a critic of America's class-based disparities and other injustices, Chaplin had become the target of an ongoing FBI witch hunt, culminating in pro-Communist accusations by the House Un-American Activities Committee, which proved false. In 1952, weary of living in a celebrity-induced fishbowl, having endured nearly 40 years of sex scandals, disastrous marriages, income-tax woes, and political investigations played out in the press, Chaplin left the United States in disgust. He vowed never to return and did not until Hollywood honored him in 1972 with a special Oscar. On Christmas Day in 1977, 2 years after England's Elizabeth II conferred Chaplin with knighthood, he died in his sleep at his home in Switzerland.

—*Julie A. Dercle*

Further Readings and References

Chaplin, C. (1978). *My autobiography*. New York: Simon & Schuster.

Vance, J. (2003). *Chaplin: Genius of the cinema*. New York: Harry N. Abrams.

CHARITY ORGANIZATION SOCIETY

The Charity Organization Society (COS) movement of the late 19th century aimed to coordinate more effectively the delivery of relief to "deserving" members of the urban poor. There had been earlier attempts—notably in New York (1819) and Boston

(1828)—to ensure cooperation among the dozens of charities that assisted people affected by destitution and disaster. In the 1870s, the COS, which began in Britain and spread through the United States, Europe, and Australia, undertook a more determined crusade for "organized" and "scientific" charity. The underlying beliefs and principles that informed charity organization remained a significant element in how urban Americans thought about poverty and welfare into the 1920s and beyond.

One of America's first COS societies was formed by Episcopal clergyman S. Humphreys Gurteen in Buffalo, New York in 1877. It was typical: begun by Protestant clergymen and well-off citizens, it aimed to coordinate local charities, which had become, they argued, too specialized and too isolated from each other. It did not want to dispense material relief, but guidance, with trained investigators judging the merits of each case and volunteer "friendly visitors" then steering the poor—by advice and by example—toward moral improvement. The outcome was idealized in a common COS slogan: "not alms, but a friend."

Other societies appeared in Northeastern and Midwestern cities from Boston to Chicago, sometimes taking the name Associated Charities or United Charities. Where and when societies emerged and indeed survived depended in part on the strong personalities of their founders, such as New York City's Josephine Shaw Lowell. Yet the initiators of each local body shared a relatively consistent point of view, which identified poverty's origins in individual and not structural flaws. They emphasized drink, dissolution, and idleness rather than the low wages, unemployment, and ill health highlighted by an alternative tradition of progressive and radical reform. They stressed middle-class virtues such as self-control, thrift, and sobriety because they believed that such traits—rather than inheritance, privilege, or good fortune—explained their own social advantages. They disliked some of the consequences of class inequality, especially a growing gulf between rich and poor, but held fast to the conviction that this was best addressed by improving the behavior rather than the economic circumstances of the poor. To them, relief without moral reformation was at best naïve and at worst an active encouragement of "pauperism" (their term for what would become known as "welfare dependence").

In many ways, the leaders of charity organization offered a 19th-century diagnosis of poverty while initiating some key elements of a 20th-century approach to its treatment. One of those was the principle of coordination. The solution to "indiscriminate benevolence" was careful oversight of all forms of relief, which would ensure that only the "truly needy" received assistance. This relied on rigorous record keeping, often through a central index or similar register, which listed each applicant's dealings with every local charity and every form of public assistance. In some cities, the society certified the eligibility of applicants for free medical or dental treatment or advised government agencies dealing with unemployment relief on the worthiness of individual applicants. They set up woodyards, sewing rooms, and domestic-service agencies, confident that only the deserving poor would be willing to perform manual labor in return for assistance.

Organization proved difficult to achieve and sustain, however. Existing charities and services developed by the Catholic Church or the Salvation Army were hostile to the Protestant COS. In part because they depended on a sizable body of benevolent visitors, few societies emerged outside the larger cities. Charity organization also ignored strong traditions of mutual self-help among workers and immigrants and failed to comprehend that poor people used specific services for specific needs and preferred practical help to ineffectual "guidance." The COS also more or less deliberately ignored what late-19th-century Americans called "the Negro problem"; poverty among African Americans was considered a separate issue best left to their own organizations.

The COS's most enduring legacy for the 20th century was perhaps its emphasis on investigation and making judgements about whether individuals were or were not deserving. Applicants were asked to share the stories of their lives, often in intimate detail, as the willingness to give information readily was one sign that someone deserved assistance. COS visitors, often women, would then visit applicants in their homes, not so much to befriend them as to identify and diagnose their problems before offering and sometimes enforcing solutions. Applicants' reputations were checked by asking neighbors and local shopkeepers, and visitors would canvas the opinions of priests, schoolteachers, nurses, and policemen. Visiting looked more and more like detective work.

With investigation came an increasing reliance on paid workers, or "agents," and an emphasis on skills and training. Friendly visiting gave way to rigorous social investigation and "casework." The transition is perhaps best exemplified by Mary Richmond, who worked for COS in Baltimore, Philadelphia, and

New York before becoming one of the nation's leading welfare theorists and educators. Richmond's first book was *Friendly Visiting Among the Poor* (1899). Her most influential, published in 1917, was *Social Diagnosis*; it described systematic casework and became one of the most important texts for American social work.

The charity-organization movement suffered a series of setbacks in the 1890s. The local bodies often failed to achieve their aims, and that decade's savage depression starkly revealed the limits of an individualistic approach to poverty. The COS's emphasis on separating the "deserving" from the "undeserving" poor made it unpopular with other reformers, such as Jane Addams, and its reputation for "cold charity" gave it few admirers among the poor themselves. Some local societies withered, but others maintained an influence over welfare in their cities by adapting COS ideas to changing circumstances and developing new programs in areas such as work relief. As such, they lost some of their original distinctive purpose and became more like other welfare providers. Some turned themselves into different sorts of organizations and chose new names—Family Welfare Association was common—to match a changed direction. In the first 30 years of the 20th century, as the social welfare mainstream developed a greater focus on social reform, public responsibility, and structural poverty, any local society that did not change became marginalized. By the time of the New Deal in the 1930s, old-style "charity organization" seemed a language and a belief of the past.

Yet charity organization remains an important part of America's urban history, for at least two reasons. First, as they sallied forth into the alleys and tenements of America's burgeoning cities, the investigators and agents of the COS produced tens of thousands of case records, which constitute a rich and still relatively untapped body of sources for urban social and cultural history. As historians such as Michael Katz and Emily Abel have shown, they provide one of our most significant windows into ideas about poverty, welfare, gender, class, character, and social order.

Second, beliefs about the need to "improve" poor people and to undertake searching investigations of their eligibility proved very resilient indeed. So did the conviction that many of those who receive welfare, whether from public funds or private benevolence, do not really deserve it, while even those who do are at constant risk of "welfare dependence." The COS may be gone, but the anxieties that spawned it seem as strong as ever in urban America.

—*Mark Peel*

See also Poverty and Welfare in Cities; Social Services and Charity

Further Readings and References

Abel, E. K. (1997). Medicine and morality: The health care program of the New York Charity Organization Society. *Social Service Review*, 634–651.

Katz, M. (1986). *In the shadow of the poorhouse: A social history of welfare in America*. New York: Basic.

Kusmer, K. L. (1973). The functions of organized charity in the Progressive Era: Chicago as a case study. *Journal of American History, 60,* 657–678.

Waugh, J. (2001). "Give this man work!" Josephine Shaw Lowell, the Charity Organization Society of the City of New York, and the depression of 1893. *Social Science History, 25,* 217–246.

CHARLOTTE, NORTH CAROLINA

Charlotte, North Carolina, a sprawling metropolis of freeways, suburbs, and strip malls, is often seen as the quintessential "New South" city, given its long-term domination by business interests, intense boosterism, and progressive image.

Founded in 1768 in the Carolina Piedmont as the seat of Mecklenburg County, Charlotte's growth was first spurred by the nearby discovery of gold in 1799. When the California Gold Rush of 1849 threatened to end this prosperity, local businesspeople funded the development of a railroad linking Charlotte to Columbia and Charleston, which opened in 1852. This was a crucial development, as it allowed goods to be transported to market without navigating the difficult Piedmont geography and turned Charlotte into a local center of commercial and mercantile activity. For the first time, it began to overtake North Carolina port cities such as Wilmington for pre-eminence in the state. By the end of the 19th century, Charlotte was the principal trading center in the Carolinas.

Rather than interrupting Charlotte's growth, the Civil War facilitated it, as the city became a center for war production, including a Confederate naval yard. Despite this military presence, Charlotte escaped attack, which meant that after the war its goods were in high demand in damaged areas of the South. This strong economic position made Charlotte a natural adherent to the New South creed of industrial progress, and the already high cotton yields from surrounding farmlands made the construction of cotton mills a logical development. Twelve mills had been built by 1900, yet Charlotte never relied solely on cotton, maintaining a diverse economic base, particularly in terms of distribution and finance interests. This diversity later allowed Charlotte to weather the decline of the textile industry and enter the post–World War II information-based economy with relative ease.

African Americans have always been a significant presence in Charlotte: in 1880 they numbered nearly half of its people (44%), although this has steadily declined, dropping to 33% by 2000. As in other Southern cities, both the actions of African Americans and the responses of city leaders have been crucial in shaping Charlotte's development. Such was the case in the 1890s, when populism, with its anti-elite, reformist message, found a ready audience among the mill workers, small farmers, and African Americans of Mecklenburg County, already disgruntled by the dominance of local merchants and wealthy farmers. As occurred across the South, populism was beaten back by appeals to white supremacy and discriminatory laws. However, the state laws that restricted African American voting also limited that of poorer whites, rendering the city's electorate primarily middle-class. This allowed the pre-eminence of business figures in political life to go largely unopposed and the disproportionate power of the city's southeast, the richest and whitest section, to remain unchecked. This dominance was reinforced by an at-large electoral system, instituted in the 1930s, that favored candidates wealthy enough to campaign citywide.

This business leadership was, however, more progressive than in many Southern cities, and in the postwar years, especially under Stanford Brookshire (mayor from 1961 to 1969), Charlotte eagerly took advantage of federal programs. It was one of the first Southern cities to undertake large-scale urban renewal and among the first nationwide to be named a Model City. This also meant that, when African Americans again attacked racial inequality in the 1960s, business leaders were at the forefront of Charlotte's response. Recognizing the damage done to the reputation of cities that had resisted integration, such as Little Rock, they agreed to a program of desegregation, largely avoiding mass protests. Consequently, Charlotte was hailed as a rare example of a Southern city that had

solved its racial problems, making it a popular choice for companies relocating to the South, even though economic inequalities and residential segregation remained.

This view of Charlotte as "the city that made it work" was seriously challenged in 1971 by a landmark Supreme Court case, *Swann v. Charlotte-Mecklenburg Board of Education*, originating from a suit brought by African American parents fighting Charlotte's continued school segregation. *Swann*, which allowed busing as a means of achieving racial balance in schools, threatened to precipitate conflict, as similar orders to bus had done in cities such as Boston. However, anger over the issue was largely refocused on Charlotte leaders because of their attempts to exempt southeastern schools from busing: this, along with the formulation of a more equitable plan by an interracial citizens' group, is credited with easing racial tensions. The resulting successful busing operation further enhanced Charlotte's image, facilitating its continuing growth. However, in 1999, busing was ended following a suit brought by white parents, and Charlotte's schools have since begun to resegregate.

The busing crisis proved costly for Charlotte's leadership in unexpected ways, as the African American and working-class white coalition behind the citizens' plan forced a city referendum in 1977 that instituted district representation. For the first time, women, African Americans, and people from outside the southeast were fully represented on the City Council. The extent of this shift was illustrated in 1983, when African American architect Harvey Gantt was elected mayor by an electorate that was four-fifths white.

Despite this changed political structure, Charlotte has maintained its prodevelopment stance, especially as African American leaders have mostly chosen to cooperate with business. This continued commitment to growth is shown by ambitious projects such as the redevelopment of the downtown area in the 1970s, the construction of a football stadium in 1996, and the commencement of a light-rail system in 2005. Charlotte has maintained its regional hegemony, while its status as America's third largest banking center illustrates its growing national importance.

The 2000 census reported that the Charlotte region included almost 1.5 million people, representing a 29 percent increase from 1990. The Queen City, although only the 34th largest metropolitan area in America, ranked 19th in terms of numeric population change in the 1990s. Its popularity as a destination for migrants from both within and outside the United States (such as its growing Asian and Hispanic communities) indicates its continuing vitality as it enters the 21st century.

—*Catherine Maddison*

See also Busing; Desegregation of Education; Model Cities; Urban Renewal and Revitalization

Further Readings and References

Douglas, D. M. (1995). *Reading, writing and race: The desegregation of the Charlotte schools.* Chapel Hill, NC: University of North Carolina Press.

Gaillard, F. (1988). *The dream long deferred.* Chapel Hill, NC: University of North Carolina Press.

Greenwood, J. T. (1994). *Bittersweet legacy: The black and white "better classes" in Charlotte, 1850–1910.* Chapel Hill, NC: University of North Carolina Press.

Hanchett, T. W. (1998). *Sorting out the New South city: Race, class and urban development in Charlotte, 1875–1975.* Chapel Hill, NC: University of North Carolina Press.

Smith, S. S. (2004). *Boom for whom? Education, desegregation and development in Charlotte.* Albany, NY: State University of New York Press.

CHICAGO FIRE

The Great Chicago Fire of October 8–9, 1871, is the best recalled of the citywide conflagrations of the 19th- and early-20th-century United States. It devastated the greatest city of the American West, left its mark in popular culture, and helped to bring about far-reaching changes in fire codes, construction, and insurance pricing. Despite the magnitude of the destruction, Chicago quickly rebuilt and continued its rapid growth.

Fire was the great scourge of American cities of the period. Haphazard construction of closely spaced buildings entirely or partly of wood; the use of coal, kerosene, and gas fuels; inadequate water supplies; and limited firefighting capabilities produced highly combustible environments. Other cities that suffered great blazes include New York (1835), Charleston (1837), St. Louis (1849), Portland, Maine (1866), Boston (1872), Baltimore (1904), and San Francisco (earthquake and fire, 1906).

In the three decades before the Great Fire, Chicago had grown from a small outpost into a major

metropolis. The city had 298,977 residents in the Census of 1870, making it the fifth-largest American city. With its 10 railroads and its thriving industries, including lumber, meatpacking, and manufacturing, Chicago was a major commercial center.

Chicago in 1871 was primarily a wooden city. Most homes were built of wood and stood closely together. The majority of sidewalks were also wood, with many streets paved in wood as well. Even some of the grander marble and stone structures in the wealthier sections of town were in fact wood structures with facades.

The weeks before the fire were extremely dry. In the first week of October, the fire department fought 20 fires, including one the night of Saturday, October 7, that consumed 20 acres of lumberyards and coal yards. The Great Fire began as a small blaze the next evening in the city's Western Division, where homes were crowded around factories.

The most enduring tale of the fire is the story of Mrs. O'Leary's cow, which supposedly started the fire in a barn by kicking over a lantern. The wife of a laborer and mother of five children, Catherine O'Leary ran a neighborhood milk business out of her barn. While the fire probably started in the barn or its vicinity, some historians have suggested that Mrs. O'Leary, as an Irish-Catholic immigrant, may have served as a convenient scapegoat. The press typically depicted her either as a comical figure or as a drunk and a welfare cheat. For years after the fire, Mrs. O'Leary refused to speak with journalists, which failed to deter many from simply concocting stories about her. Other identities have been suggested for the culprit, including an O'Leary neighbor, boys smoking in the barn, and even a meteor.

Whatever its cause, the blaze quickly swept out of the Western Division toward the city center, pushed by a southwest wind. As the wind gained force, the fire became unstoppable, skipping from structure to structure, moving in different directions. The fire engulfed lumberyards, rail yards, and grain elevators before crossing the Chicago River. It spread from house to house through the city's South Division, until it reached a gasworks, which exploded. As it spread to the north and east, the fire consumed some of the city's finer homes and business structures.

Exhausted from the previous night's blaze, firefighters waged a futile struggle against the flames that jumped from block to block. The storehouse for extra fire hoses was soon destroyed, followed later by the water pumping station. Around 1:30 a.m., the fire reached the courthouse. The tower collapsed, silencing the bell that for hours had been ringing out warning. The fire progressed to the lake and west along the river, consuming bridges, shipping vessels, warehouses full of goods, stacks of lumber and coal along the river, and frame structure after frame structure. By Monday morning, little in the city's north side was left to burn.

Next, the fire moved south, destroying some of the city's most valuable real estate, including the post office, the *Chicago Tribune* building, and numerous grand hotels and churches. It then moved east, to the palatial residences along the lake. As the fire approached the business section, goods were removed from warehouses and stores and piled along the lakeshore. By Monday night, even these stacks of goods had ignited. On Tuesday morning, a merciful rain extinguished the flames.

The Chicago of October 10, 1871, was a smoldering ruin. Nearly 3½ square miles, more than 2,000 acres, were ash and rubble. The fire had burned almost 18,000 buildings. The business structures destroyed included most of Chicago's banks and insurance offices and all of the city's newspapers. Two hundred and fifty people had lost their lives.

During the terror of the conflagration, about 100,000 Chicagoans, a third of the population, fled their homes, carrying what they could. Driven from one point to another by the flames, the refugees finally gathered in Lincoln Park and on the open prairie along Lake Michigan. Despite the devastation of the city's center, some areas remained untouched. There, many found shelter with relatives, friends, and strangers.

Members of the commercial elite feared that Chicago's disaster would attract criminals and looters. Lacking confidence in the local authorities, a number of wealthy businessmen secured the mayor's acquiescence and convinced U.S. Army Lieutenant General Philip Sheridan, then stationed in Chicago, to restore order. Sheridan's force, consisting of regular troops, militia units, police, and volunteers, imposed *de facto* martial law in Chicago for 2 weeks after the fire.

Relief efforts had begun even before the flames were fully extinguished. City officials appointed a group of elected officials and private citizens to administer and distribute the money, food, and supplies arriving from around the country and the world, whose value would eventually total around $5 million.

In the hands of the Chicago Relief and Aid Society, the relief effort soon became a means for restoring the class hierarchy that had existed before the fire. The committee sought to distinguish worthy fire victims, meaning previously independent middle-class residents, from less worthy immigrant and working-class victims. Many of the prefabricated "shelter houses" provided by the relief society went to those who had previously owned their own homes. Similarly, the distribution of relief funds tended to favor those who had prospered before the fire, in a concerted attempt to restore them to independence. Meanwhile, the able-bodied working poor were expected to find employment. Those who required housing were put up in simple barracks.

Not everyone required charitable assistance. Many property owners carried insurance. The adjusters who arrived within days of the fire to review claims (from temporary offices) found that the fire had consumed $200 million worth of property, close to one-third of the value of all the property in the city. Well over half of the property lost had carried some amount of insurance, with just over $100 million of the property in the burnt district covered (not considering the uncovered value of partly insured property). Policyholders could rebuild their homes and businesses, assuming their insurance companies could pay the claims. Unfortunately, many could not. The fire bankrupted 68 insurance companies. As a result, only 40 percent of the insured property value lost in the fire was recovered.

For some, the fire provided an opportunity to rebuild Chicago as a grander, safer city, its widened avenues lined with fire-resistant brick and stone structures. But homeowners of modest means, who could not afford to rebuild in expensive materials, opposed proposals to ban wooden construction. Similarly, manufacturers protested laws aimed at removing fire-hazardous industries from the city center. Only in 1875, after insurers threatened to stop covering property in the city, were stricter building codes enacted and the fire department reformed. Within a few years, Chicago was rebuilt on a larger scale. The new downtown that arose was twice the size of the old, with many taller buildings. Whereas in the old Chicago, commercial and residential areas had been intermixed, the two became increasingly separated, with new residential areas, separated by class, built away from the city center.

Chicago's most valuable infrastructure, the rail lines linking it with East and West, had survived the fire, even as rail stations and depots burned. Stockyards and other heavy industry were located outside of the burnt district as well. Thus the city's industries were able to recover quickly. Despite the economic downturn following the Panic of 1873, the city continued to grow. The Census of 1880 recorded Chicago's population as 503,185.

In combination with the Boston fire of 1872, the Chicago fire provided the impetus to reshape fire insurance and prevention in the United States. After the fires, surviving insurance firms organized under the aegis of the National Board of Fire Underwriters in an attempt to halt the intense price competition of previous years, which had left many firms underfunded when the citywide fires occurred. By the early 1880s, a new system of local insurance cartels finally succeeded in stabilizing prices. Improved fire codes and safer construction techniques began to appear nationally around the same time.

The Chicago fire was a national event, figuring into the popular culture of the time. Hundreds of news stories, illustrations, eyewitness accounts, sermons, novels, poems, and songs appeared in the years following the fire. Few Americans of the period could escape the tale of Chicago's destruction or its phoenix-like rebirth. To this day, Americans are more likely to recall the Chicago fire than any of the other great fires of the past.

—Dalit Baranoff

See also Chicago, Illinois

Further Readings and References

Baranoff, D. (2003). *Shaped by risk: The American fire insurance industry, 1870–1920*. Doctoral dissertation, The Johns Hopkins University Press.
Bureau of the Census. (1870/1880). *United States Census, 1870, 1880*. Washington, DC: Government Printing Office.
The Chicago fire. (1874). *Insurance year book*, 242–251.
The Great Fire: A comprehensive account of the conflagration. (1871). In *The Chicago fire and the fire insurance companies*. New York: J. H. and C. M. Goodsell.

CHICAGO SCHOOL OF ARCHITECTURE

Chicago's rapid growth, from its founding as an outpost on the banks of Lake Michigan through the 1920s, has been a chief source of invention,

innovation, and inspiration to many architects. The construction methods have been often admired, emulated, and copied. Perhaps the most influential style of construction was the technique of design known as the Chicago school (or style) of architecture. This particular style centered on the skyscraper but spread further into the development of housing as well.

The Chicago school is, at its core, centered on the skyscraper. The first building commonly accepted as a modern skyscraper was the Home Insurance Building on LaSalle Street, erected in 1885 and designed by architect William Le Baron Jenney. While Jenney's style of design was considered by some to be ornamentally a mix of European and American styles, the core concept was based on the principles established by wooden balloon-frame construction. As its skeleton, steel frames were used to construct the wall and floor frames and were covered by glass and masonry exteriors, which gave support to the outer frame as well as light to the interior. In addition, steel girders were driven into the ground dozens of feet to give additional support to the metal frame. One French architect, who visited Chicago during the Columbian Exposition, marveled that unlike most American architecture, which seemed entirely utilitarian in nature, the skyscraper took on a certain elegance of its own. Often the buildings appeared as though they were boxes stacked on one another. As many would not see the upper levels, minimal design embellishment was used above the third floor, and it consisted mostly of cornice or window-frame work. On the main floor, however, the designs were ornate.

Chicago owed its great design boom to tragedy. The Great Fire of 1871 obliterated all of the downtown area. While the fire caused substantial property damage and was a tragedy in suffering, others, steeped in the "can do" attitude of Chicago's boosters, saw opportunity. Architects flocked to Chicago in the 1870s as a tabula rasa presented itself. The city had a chance to rebuild itself with the latest in design techniques and materials. The new boom in construction also was fueled by the natural boundaries of the downtown Chicago area. It is hemmed in to the north and west by the Chicago River, to the south by the terminals of several rail lines, and to the east by Lake Michigan. Given the relatively small area of land and the prime value of the real estate, there was only one effective way to continue building: up. Hence, the need for better technological advances in building, better materials (such as Bessemer processed steel), and more audacious designs that could both incorporate the needs of a major city and give it a stylistic flair.

While Jenney started the concept of the Chicago school, it was the designs of Dankmar Adler and Louis Sullivan that truly set the standard for many of the Chicago school buildings. Sullivan, whose axiom "form follows function" was a defining part of the Chicago school, was responsible for the Auditorium Building, which embraced the new style of embellishment when needed yet was simple when form dictated. This design method allowed costs to be limited, while ornate features could be seen by those on the ground. Sullivan's later design work was exemplified by the Carson Pirie Scott department-store building, located in the heart of Chicago's Loop area. The Carson store featured large windows that not only allowed light into the building but also allowed people to look into the interior, creating an enticement to enter. Above the windows was wrought-iron cornice work that gave a distinct look to the building yet was relatively lighter and less expensive than the usual masonry.

Another major architect in the Chicago school was Daniel Burnham. He and his partner John Wellborn Root were another of the premiere architectural teams in Chicago. Their offices at the Rookery Building on LaSalle Street still exemplify the new style of office construction, with embellishments located where they would be most noticed by passersby. The terra-cotta outer skin used on many of the buildings designed by Burnham, Sullivan, and the other Chicago school architects was an improvement, as it was self-cleaning and had a natural sheen that made the building shine in certain lights. With the addition of Chicago-style windows (three panes, with the two outer ones opening to allow ventilation into the building), these buildings impressed those who were used to the low buildings of the Plains or the massive stone buildings of the East.

The new form of construction was quickly emulated in other major cities around the United States. Major metropolises such as New York, Philadelphia, Boston, and Cleveland quickly adopted the skyscraper as a means of construction. Soon it was also a race to see who could have the highest buildings. Here, New York succeeded with its towers, best exemplified by the Empire State Building. But it was not without the inspiration of the Chicago school.

Many examples of both the simplicity and the majesty of these buildings remain in the Loop area of Chicago today. Simply go to the Rookery Building on LaSalle Street and join the architectural tours that walk the downtown area. One also can see these magnificent buildings on one's own, such as the Manadnock Building, the Fair Building, the original Marshall Field's building, or many of the buildings along Michigan Avenue. Sadly, the one building that started it all, the Home Insurance Building, was torn down in 1930 to make room for the new Chicago Board of Trade, which later moved to the end of LaSalle Street. For most of the other famous buildings, historic preservation and national register status have been granted so that the style can be preserved.

In addition to this new building style downtown, the prairie style of construction, led by Frank Lloyd Wright (who served under Louis Sullivan at one time), came into existence in Chicago's immediate suburb of Oak Park. While the two styles were similar in form, they focused on different aspects of building. The prairie style was predominantly concerned with low buildings or houses. The Chicago style worked with the professional buildings of high-rises.

The Chicago school not only accomplished a new style of building; it also gave rise to some of the most influential architectural firms of the day: Holabird and Roche, Root and Burnham, and Sullivan and Adler. These men all had an influence on the buildings in downtown Chicago and at one time had connections to Jenney. As the city hosted the 1893 World's Columbian Exposition, the new architecture continued in the fair buildings themselves, with several architects lending a hand to the designs. While the fair's buildings were temporary, they exhibited the style and passion of the day. As people flocked to the "White City" to see the sights of the fair, many also took a trip downtown to see the buildings that reached to the sky. They marveled at the elevators, the immense structures that housed thousands of people, and the canyons of steel and masonry. As one looks at the interior of the Rookery, for instance, he or she cannot help but be amazed by the style that still is timeless in the early 21st century.

For the Chicago school, the first signs of the waning of the old guard occurred in two general stages. First, by the early 1900s Daniel Burnham shifted his focus from architecture to city planning, which culminated in the 1909 plan for Chicago. It focused on grand boulevards, many parks, and central streets, not necessarily on skyscrapers. The second sign was the death of several of the original architects. Jenney died in 1907, Burnham in 1912, and Sullivan in 1924. Most architectural historians marked the end of the Chicago school in 1922, when the Tribune Building was erected and brought forth a neoclassical style, while other buildings were designed in the new art deco style. Yet the Chicago style did not end entirely. By the 1930s, Ludwig Mies van der Rohe had emigrated to Chicago, where he altered the Chicago style to fit his needs. His famous axiom "less is more" was a defining feature of his style—and was in many ways reminiscent of the original Chicago style.

—*Cord Scott*

Further Readings and References

Bach, I. (Ed.). (1980). *Chicago's famous buildings*. Chicago: University of Chicago Press.

Blaser, W. (1993). *Chicago architecture: Holabird and Root 1880–1992*. Basel, Switzerland: Birkhauser Verlag.

Condit, C. (1964). *The Chicago school of architecture*. Chicago: University of Chicago Press.

Kogan, H., & Kogan, R. (1976). *Yesterday's Chicago*. Miami, FL: E. A. Seeman.

Meyer, H., & Wade, R. (1969). *Chicago: Growth of a metropolis*. Chicago: University of Chicago Press.

Miller, D. (1996). *City of the century*. New York: Simon & Schuster.

CHICAGO, ILLINOIS

Chicago, Illinois, owes its existence to its location on both the Chicago River and the Great Lakes. From its "discovery," in 1673, by the French explorers Father Jacques Marquette, a Jesuit missionary, and Louis Jolliet, Chicago developed as a bridge between the natural resources of the North American continent and the vast Atlantic market. Originally, the fur trade encouraged the integration of the Chicago region with the expanding European economy.

Involvement with Europe meant involvement in its politics and wars, especially the French and Indian War, in 1756. After 1763, France lost its North American holdings. Twenty years later, political control of the region passed to the newly created United States. Jean Baptiste Pointe DuSable, the son of a French fur trader and a black Haitian, came to Chicago in 1781 as the first permanent resident after being imprisoned for anti-British activities. His cabin, near the mouth of the Chicago River, provided a focus for the local fur trade.

It took the military campaigns of General "Mad" Anthony Wayne to bring effective American rule. In 1791, Wayne's victories ended in the Treaty of Greenville, which granted federal control to the mouth of the Chicago River. The U.S. Army began construction of Fort Dearborn in 1803. By that time, DuSable had sold his cabin to Jean La Lime, who in turn sold it to John Kinzie. Fort Dearborn provided an American military presence in the West and a focal point for trade. The War of 1812 brought about the fort's destruction by Native Americans. The second Fort Dearborn (1816) marked the permanent establishment of American control in the area. A lively society of fur traders evolved alongside the military post. At the same time, Chicago became a focal point for Yankee migration west from New England and upstate New York.

Chartered as a town in 1833, Chicago became four years later a city of roughly 5,000 inhabitants. The Blackhawk War and an aggressive federal policy forced Indian removal by 1837. The Erie Canal (1825) significantly changed and improved Chicago's ties to the East. Merchants gathered and distributed grain, lumber, livestock, and other natural resources while dispensing manufactured products across the American economy.

In 1836, Chicagoans began building their own canal, the Illinois-Michigan Canal, which allowed the city to compete with St. Louis for the Western trade. The depression-plagued canal finally opened in 1848. In 1847, the McCormick Reaper Works opened in Chicago and helped to usher in both the industrial and agricultural revolutions in the Midwest. By 1848, the city housed roughly 20,000 inhabitants and looked forward to continued growth.

That same year Chicago entrepreneurs embraced yet another transportation technology, the railroad. The Galena-Chicago Union Railroad was the first railroad in Chicago. By 1854, Chicago emerged as an important railroad hub. The trade routes that developed as a result of the canals were reinforced and expanded with railroad connections between Eastern cities and Chicago. In turn, Chicago's railroads pushed west and crossed the Mississippi. The city's population and industrial base increased dramatically between 1850 and 1900. The emergence of the meatpacking and steel industries brought about yet another economic phase, the production of goods for national and international distribution.

Chicago grew haphazardly. Balloon-frame buildings accounted for much of the residential construction. Sidewalks, plank roads, and many city streets were wooden. In 1869, the city created a professional fire department replacing various volunteer fire brigades. Still the threat of fire hung over the city. On the night of October 8, 1871, a fire broke out in the barn of the O'Leary family house on the West Side of the city, resulting in the tragic Chicago Fire. Twenty-one hundred acres and more than 17,000 buildings were destroyed in the conflagration. But the fire did not destroy Chicago's economic base. The disaster actually provided an opportunity for the young city. In the aftermath, Chicago modernized laws, stimulated a building boom, and attracted many new residents.

Chicago grew to the status of a world-class city when it held the World's Columbian Exposition in 1893. Its population reached more than one million in 1890, making it the second largest city in the United States, a rank it held until the 1990 census. To a degree, this rapid population growth resulted from Chicago's annexation of most of its immediate suburbs in 1889.

Chicago attracted waves of both American migration and international immigration. Northern and Western Europeans dominated early immigration. Native Protestants, primarily from New England, controlled its economic, cultural, and political life. Shortly the Yankee elite lost demographic, and therefore political, dominance. Many moved to the original railroad suburbs just outside the city. Newer groups, largely Eastern and Southern Europeans, came to Chicago. In 1910, the foreign-born and their children made up nearly 80 percent of the city's population.

The outbreak of World War I cut off immigration as wartime production increased, resulting in a new migration. From 1915 to 1920, Chicago's African American population doubled in population. African Americans tended to settle on Chicago's South Side, where a large ghetto emerged as a result of segregation. In July 1919, a race riot broke out that shook the city and resulted in 38 deaths (23 blacks and 15 whites) and more than 500 injuries.

Chicago's political machine developed late in the history of urban machines. Mayor William H. Thompson's election in 1915 marked an attempt to create a citywide Republican machine. Thompson included the growing African American community in his coalition. The Thompson years also marked the creation of a citywide organized-crime machine headed by Al Capone and often allied with the local Republican Party. In 1931, the Democratic Party challenged Thompson under the leadership of Czech-born Anton Cermak, the only immigrant mayor in the city's history. Cermak created a powerful machine based on the city's important white ethnic neighborhoods.

Blacks joined the Democratic machine in the late 1930s. Cermak's victory marked the end of a vital Republican Party in the city. No Republican has gained the mayoralty since Thompson's defeat in 1931.

Following Cermak's assassination, in 1933, the Democrats placed Edward J. Kelly as mayor (1933–1947). After the two-term administration of Martin H. Kennelly (1947–1955), Richard J. Daley became Chicago's most powerful politician, winning six mayoral elections before his death on December 20, 1976. He must be credited with Chicago's development, after 20 years of depression and war, as a still-vital city at the center of an expanding metropolitan area. Nevertheless, the post-1945 era witnessed the erosion of much of the city's traditional manufacturing base. Chicago entered the postindustrial era.

After 1940, Chicago saw the continued growth of the city's African American population. Chicago's white population began to move to the suburbs. In 1940, Chicago contained 73 percent of the population of northeastern Illinois. By 2000, despite renewed population growth thanks largely to Hispanic immigration, that figure slipped to below 35 percent of the metropolitan area. Whites made up less than one-third of Chicago's population. African Americans, and a quickly growing Hispanic population, provided more than two-thirds of the city's residents.

These demographic developments, in motion since 1950, when the city hit its peak population of 3,620,962, influenced the Democratic Party, as blacks played an increasingly important role. After Daley died, his machine split apart along racial and ethnic lines. Daley's immediate successor, Michael J. Bilandic, kept the machine united for a short period of time, but in 1979 he lost the mayor's office to Jane Byrne, the first female mayor of Chicago. Byrne made an alliance with regular Democrats and seemed invincible, but she lost to Harold Washington in a three-way race for mayor in 1983. Washington served as the city's first African American mayor, winning a second term in 1987. His first administration was bogged down in a fight for power with white ethnic aldermen. Washington died in office on November 25, 1987. A struggle for power occurred immediately, resulting in the brief mayoralty of another African American mayor, Eugene Sawyer (1987–1989). After a special election in 1989, Richard M. Daley, the son of the man who had forged the most powerful machine in the city's history, came to power.

By 2000, Hispanic and Asian immigrants brought change to the city. Gentrification and new investment along the lakefront and in some outlying neighborhoods transformed Chicago. The city still maintained a large industrial base, but the service economy saw the greatest growth. New sports complexes were built. The downtown or "Loop" remained vital, but it also changed as investors converted much of the area's structures to apartments. Educational institutions moved into or expanded in the business district. As Chicago entered the 21st century, it maintained itself as a vital center for northern Illinois, but it was no longer the population, economic, and political powerhouse that it had once been. Much of the region's power had shifted to the suburbs, as the metropolis spread across portions of Illinois, Indiana, Wisconsin, and Michigan.

—Dominic A. Pacyga

See also Bosses and Machines; Byrne, Jane M.; Capone, Al; Chicago Fire; Chicago School of Architecture; Daley, Richard J.; Thompson, William Hale "Big Bill"; Washington, Harold; World Fairs and Expositions

Further Readings and References

Biles, R. (1995). *Richard J. Daley: Politics, race, and the governing of Chicago*. DeKalb, IL: Northern Illinois University Press.

Bluestone, D. (1991). *Constructing Chicago*. New Haven and London: Yale University Press.

Cronon, W. (1991). *Nature's metropolis: Chicago and the Great West*. New York: W.W. Norton & Company.

Green, P. M., & Holli, M. G. (Eds.). (1987). *The mayors: The Chicago political tradition*. Carbondale and Edwardsville, IL: Southern Illinois University Press.

Mayer, H. M., & Wade, R.C. (1969). *Chicago: Growth of a metropolis*. Chicago: University of Chicago Press.

Pacyga, D. A., & Skerrett, E. (1986). *Chicago: City of neighborhoods*. Chicago: Loyola University Press.

CHILD LABOR

Child labor has a long, complex, and controversial history in the United States. Its roots begin in the traditions and practices of the Old World. Children have always worked, whether in their masters' fields, in the homes of their parents, or in the shops of local artisans. In colonial America and before, children's work was not considered child labor. It was a child's duty to help his or her parents and family in any and all

possible ways. Usually this took the form of manual labor, such as lending a helping hand around the house or on the family farm. Parents instilled the very young with the Protestant work ethic with which they had grown up. Work was considered good for a child. It provided him or her with experience, valuable knowledge and skills, a respect for hard work, and a desire to earn the fruits of one's labor. In essence, children learned to earn their keep and the values in doing so.

As the country moved from rural, agrarian farms to industrialized, urban communities, child work was increasingly divided by gender. The separation of the public and private sphere laid the groundwork for the kinds of work that female and male children were expected to perform. In the early 19th century, for example, middle-class daughters worked inside the home, watching younger siblings, cleaning the house, or cooking meals. In some instances, girls were hired out to mend, wash laundry, and make clothes piecemeal, all activities easily accomplished within the confines of the home. On the other hand, a young boy adapted to the world outside of the home and to the physical challenges it demanded of him, often apprenticed to a nearby artisan or to the nearest relative who could provide for him. Charged with providing services much like a common servant, as well as making time for study of a particular trade or craft, these children worked twice as hard for their room and board.

European children of more modest means were brought to the colonies under indentured servitude, in which they pledged seven years of service in exchange for passage to the American colonies. Frequently, these children had a hard journey across the Atlantic Ocean, in cramped, disease-ridden ships, only to come to a country where the promise of opportunity disappeared under the often cruel tutelage of the rich who bought their passage tickets. Similarly, African children and their African American counterparts slaved away day after day without pay or sympathy.

Prior to the 19th century, however, the abuse of child work, which eventually led to its label as child labor, was not systematically documented or readily noticeable. The personal experience of one or two children was not alarming enough to alert the nation. With rapid industrialization, however, the notion of child labor appeared. As dangerous factories opened up, businessmen looked to the young, knowing that they could exploit their labor by paying them less than the average adult male. With more and more children leaving the house to work arduous hours in the factories, social concern arose. Reformers were concerned not only about the children's diminishing quality of life, but also about the kind of prospects these youth heralded. As children were seen as the key to the future, the broken bodies and uneducated minds of these youngsters, results of long hours in backbreaking labor, represented a bleak fate indeed.

Equally spurred by working conditions of the very young and the seemingly dim future these children foreshadowed, progressive reformers such as Jane Addams and Florence Kelley truly began to take notice and commit themselves to action in the late 19th century. As a result of public outcry in 1904, the National Child Labor Committee (NCLC) was organized. The NCLC, along with various other state organizations, developed the methodology used for years to come that documented and transcribed the often tragic lives of child laborers through photographs, investigations, pamphlets, and lobbying. The NCLC began the campaign for state legislation with a ringing victory, as many states enacted child-labor laws without federal involvement. Realizing that many states were resistant to child-labor laws, reformers recognized the need for federal legislation. In 1916, federal legislation passed, only to be revoked by the United States Supreme Court, which declared the legislation unconstitutional in the *Hammer v. Dagenhart* case of 1918. Undeterred by this setback, another piece of legislation was adopted that same year. Once more, however, the Supreme Court overruled the legislation, this time in the *Bailey v. Drexel Furniture Company* case in 1922.

Now fully aware of the power, capabilities, and techniques of the detractors of such federal legislation on child labor, reformers tried to fight back with a Constitutional amendment. Adopted by Congress in 1924, a child-labor amendment went to the states for ratification. By 1925, only four states, Arkansas, Arizona, California, and Wisconsin, had signed the amendment. It was never ratified.

As much as progressive reformers and sympathizers fought for child-labor regulation, lasting reform was not created until the Great Depression of the 1930s. Once the Depression hit, millions of strong, able-bodied American men were out of work. This tragedy provided the single most effective catalyst in pushing children out of the workforce and into the classroom. Every state had adopted a compulsory school-attendance law by 1933, requiring children 14 years old and younger to attend school regularly. These state laws, coupled with the legislation of such acts as the Public Contracts Act (1936) and the Beet Sugar Act (1937), increasingly edged children out of the workforce. They provided a minimum age of employment, prohibited children from certain hazardous or dangerous jobs, and set standards on the number of days and/or hours children could work. Yet this type of legislation was too exclusive, by not providing federal regulation for children in all parts of the country employed in a variety of occupations. This was soon remedied with the Fair Labor Standards Act (FLSA) of 1938. This federal mandate fixed the minimum age requirement across the nation at 16 years old during school hours.

Since then, child labor has increasingly declined, and only relatively recently has it resumed its position as child work. The abolition of child labor, however, has never been fully achieved; it has merely been transformed. Today, children are once again encouraged to work outside the home. Many students of all ages work a part-time job at the local mall, gas station, or restaurant. Youth continue to be exploited by their employers, as many of them work for minimum wage to earn "spending cash" of their own. Children also are working and are often employed inside the home as well, earning wages or "allowance" money in exchange for completing household tasks. These kinds of child labor are viewed as beneficial to both children and the American society they will one day inherit and transform.

Furthermore, although many American children now spend their mornings behind a desk in school and their evenings working comfortable and relatively light labor in sales, for example, their immigrant counterparts are found in the fields with their parents. Involved with exhausting agricultural labor and usually paid well below the minimum wage, these children and their conditions are habitually ignored by federal legislators and the public alike. Finally, although many American children are no longer employed in dangerous factories performing menial and tedious tasks, U.S. companies continue to relocate outside of the country, where children can still work freely in such conditions and at pitiful wages.

—*Stella Ress*

See also Addams, Jane; Children in Cities and Suburbs; Kelley, Florence; Progressivism; Youth Culture

Further Readings and References

Clark, C. (1996, August). Child labor and sweatshops. *CQ Researcher,* 723–730.

Levine, M. J. (2003). *Children for hire: The perils of child labor in the United States.* Westport, CT: Praeger.

Sanderson, A. R. (1974). Child-labor legislation and the labor force participation of children. *Journal of Economic History, 34*(1), 297–299.

Taylor, R. (1973). *Sweatshops in the sun: Child labor on the farm.* Boston: Beacon Press.

Zelizer, V. A. (1985). *Pricing the priceless child: The changing social value of children.* New York: Basic Books.

CHILDREN IN CITIES AND SUBURBS

Cities and suburbs have provided dramatically different realities for American children and conflicting images of American childhoods. Almost since the first suburbs were formed, the differences in the popular images of urban and suburban childhoods were stark. A Boston social worker named Philip Davis stated the case against city childhoods in 1915, when he wrote that the city life and childhood are not compatible.

Some of our most striking images of children and of cities are the photographs taken by Jacob Riis (1849–1914), the reformer and photographer who exposed the difficult lives of urban children in *How the Other Half Lives* (New York: Charles Scribner's Sons, 1890). From child pieceworkers toiling in tenement apartments to "street arabs" sleeping in alleyways, and from litter-strewn "playgrounds" to young street traders peddling their wares, Riis chronicled in sensationalistic detail the grim lives of city children. Suburban childhoods, on the other hand, have appeared in the wholesome television comedies of the 1950s and 1960s and, slightly differently, in the 1980s and 1990s movies of the director John Hughes. These popular media images present suburbs as affluent, child-centered, and homogeneous places populated by slightly naughty but generally good-hearted children and youth.

Of course, the differences in the experiences of urban and suburban children and youth transcend the ways they are presented in popular culture and encompass ethnicity, class, education opportunities, and physical surroundings, among other factors. These differences widened during the last quarter of the 19th century.

The population growth of Gilded Age and early-20th-century cities was fueled to a great extent by the millions of immigrants flowing into the United States between the Civil War and the 1920s. In most cities during this time, children younger than age 18 composed between 30 and 40 percent of the population. These youngsters filled public schools and took up diverse street trades. Educators designed school curricula to inculcate "American" values and to downplay students' "foreignness."

Alarmed by the crowded living conditions, severe health problems, and unsafe streets, reformers often targeted the working class, mostly immigrant children living in American cities. In the 1850s, Charles Loring Brace's famous "orphan trains" and other child placement services began transporting tens of thousands of children out of eastern cities and into western towns and farms. The settlement-house movement of the 1890s and beyond created kindergartens and nurseries for children, while other Progressive Era reformers established juvenile courts, playgrounds, and milk and nutrition programs. They also attempted to regulate child labor, including the thousands of "newsies" and other street traders clogging urban streets.

Throughout the rest of the 20th century, Americans often perceived the urban environment as one of the main problems facing children. This was apparent in the periodic panics over juvenile delinquency and other disruptions by children and youth. American urban youth had formed gangs since the mid-19th century; gangs became a way for working-class and ethnic youth to form social groups and communities. Fond memories of fights between white ethnic gangs in the early 20th century became a staple of urban immigrant autobiographies; more serious issues like drug dealing and deadly violence characterized discussions of inner city gangs—particularly among African American and Hispanic youth—during the second half of the 20th century. Solutions for these peculiarly urban problems were sought in the formation of countless and wide-ranging programs and organizations: Boys and Girls Clubs, Catholic Youth Organization sports leagues, and 1960s government initiatives such as Head Start and Job Corps.

Progressive Era reformers had often blamed urban conditions for the health and developmental problems facing children. During the New Deal, the federal government recognized the commonly held belief that cities were unhealthy places for children. Designed as an antidote to the crowded, polluted, vaguely degrading environment of the city, the "Greenbelt Cities" led to the establishment of only three communities (in Maryland, Ohio, and Wisconsin). But they became prototypes for the suburbs that would develop after the Second World War. Families lived in single-family or two-family houses built alongside wandering residential streets with pedestrian access to parks, shops, and recreation centers.

Parents seeking to escape the real and perceived problems of inner cities began moving to the suburbs early in the 20th century. Of course, the "baby boom" inspired the striking growth of suburbs after the Second World War. Between 1946 and 1964, 75 million babies were born, and the average birthrate was 3.6 children per woman—twice the rate in the 1930s. Parents desiring to create child-centered spaces for their growing families embraced the economical and relatively spacious ranch and Cape Cod homes, with their "family" rooms and big yards. They took advantage of government loan programs that favored new housing construction in suburbs and relegated housing projects for low-income families to inner cities. With shops, schools, and playgrounds located within walking distance—or, increasingly, a short drive—of every home, the suburbs became synonymous with white, middle-class, family-centered values. Nuclear families predominated, and communities revolved around schools and churches.

By late in the 20th century, urban and suburban governments were battling over resources for schools in the form of debates over property taxes and school voucher programs and revisiting in often contentious ways metropolitan school integration programs. Extracurricular activities in urban schools were funded at lower levels than in suburban school districts. Although suburban school systems were hardly immune from the budget crunch, urban districts suffered the most from a declining tax base, rising health care costs, and the pressures of meeting state and federal mandates. Social welfare programs that affected urban residents, especially children, suffered disproportionately from severe cuts in federal and state funding.

The middle-class ideal—if not always the reality—of child-centered families survives in the suburbs. Yet suburban youth look to the cities for their culture. Indeed, youth culture developed first in urban areas, as institutions and organizations developed to meet the needs and desires of children and youth. Perhaps the most important was the creation of high schools. Although they first appeared before the Civil War, it was not until the late 19th and early 20th centuries that most urban areas had high schools, where urban adolescents could participate in numerous extracurricular activities, clubs, and sports. This officially sanctioned form of youth culture paralleled the growth of a popular culture intended solely for young Americans. From the nickelodeons at the turn of the 20th century to the swing music of the 1930s and 1940s through the rap music of the late 20th century, the music, fashions, and other elements of youth culture have radiated out from the nation's cities.

The demographics of urban and suburban childhoods still differ dramatically. In terms of race, the 2000 census discovered that a majority of the nation's major cities were now "majority-minority," with less than half of their populations non-Hispanic whites. A study of the 2000 census funded by the Annie E. Casey Foundation found that the percentage of children living in "severely distressed neighborhoods" (high poverty rates, high percentages of female-headed households, high drop-out rates, and high unemployment rates among adult males) had grown by nearly 20 percent. The vast majority of children living in severely distressed neighborhoods lived in metropolitan areas and were black or Hispanic. For instance, 28.1 percent of black children live in such areas, compared to 1.4 percent of white children. Another study measuring the long-term effects on young children of poverty, family structure, and the educational attainment of parents showed that children living in central cities were two times more likely to be poor and unemployed as adults than suburban children. By 1996, nearly 20 percent of urban children were "at risk" of growing up in poverty and without jobs.

These troubling statistics overshadow the vitality of institutions and neighborhoods that provide good educations and safe havens for a still sizable number of urban children. The reality of life for urban children lies somewhere between David Nasaw's celebration of the immigrant children who made the streets their play and workplaces early in the 20th century, and the recent, well-known account of life in Chicago's housing projects whose title bitterly declared, *There Are No Children Here*.

—James Marten

See also Community in the Cities; Community in the Suburbs; Desegregation of Education; Education in Cities; Families in Cities and Suburbs; Juvenile Delinquency and the Juvenile Justice System; Playgrounds; Public Education; Youth Culture

Further Readings and References

Davis, P. (1915). *Street land: Its little people and big problems.* Boston: Small, Maynard, and Company.

Graff, H. J. (1995). *Conflicting paths: Growing up in America.* Cambridge, MA: Harvard University Press.

Illick, J. E. (2002). *American childhoods.* Philadelphia: University of Pennsylvania Press.

Kotlowitz, A. (1991). *There are no children here: The story of two boys growing up in the other America.* New York: Doubleday.

Mintz, S. (2004). *Huck's raft: A history of American childhood.* Cambridge, MA: Harvard University Press.

Nasaw, D. (1986). *Children of the city: At work and at play.* New York: Oxford University Press.

O'Hare, W., & Mather, M. (2003). *The growing number of kids in severely distressed neighborhoods: Evidence from the 2000 census.* Washington, DC: Annie E. Casey Foundation and the Population Reference Bureau.

Sawhill, I., & Chadwick, L. (1999). *Children in cities: Uncertain futures.* Washington, DC: Brookings Institution.

CHILDS, RICHARD SPENCER

Richard Spencer Childs (1882–1978) was born in Manchester, Connecticut. His father, William Hamlin Childs, became a wealthy businessman from his Bon Ami Company. When Richard was 10 years old, his father moved the family to Brooklyn, then a city. Childs attended the Polytechnic Preparatory School from 1897 to 1900; he earned a B.A. degree from Yale University in 1904. He joined the City Club of New York and the National Municipal League in 1908 and the Citizens Union of the City of New York in 1909. Childs married Grace Pauline Hatch, of Chicago, in 1912 and took up residence in Manhattan. That same year they both were delegates to the Syracuse convention of the National Progressive Party in the State of New York. Childs was president of the City Club of New York from 1926 to 1938, president of the National Municipal League from 1927 to 1931, and chairman of the Citizens Union from 1941 to 1950. He began his business career in advertising and later held several corporate positions. In 1947 he retired from the American Cyanamid Company to work full-time without salary on his reform agenda at the National Municipal League in Manhattan, a project that lasted 30 years.

Childs's exposure to the machinations of politicians in the state and local governments began in the November election of 1903 in Brooklyn, when he was confronted with a long ballot. He recognized the first four candidates by name but not the other 15. Childs became a political reformer; he understood that while politicians blamed voter apathy for imperiling the democratic process, it was the structure of government that needed to be changed. To end oligarchic rule required simplification of the ballot, he asserted. That meant, he explained, that only the most visible offices—about five of conspicuous importance—would attract public scrutiny. Childs's 1908 essay, "The Doctrine of the Short Ballot," a pamphlet that won the praise of scholars including college presidents, was published in *Outlook* on July 17, 1909. That year Childs organized the National Short Ballot Organization, with himself as secretary and Woodrow Wilson, then president of Princeton University, as its president. The short-ballot movement spread across the nation. By 1921, with the Progressive Era coming to a close, the National Short Ballot Organization was absorbed into the National Municipal League.

Childs invented the council-manager plan of municipal government when he attached to the commission plan the concept of a city manager. In 1912, Sumter, South Carolina, became the first council-manager city. The single, small, nonpartisan council was the government, with council members preferably elected at large rather than in wards. The council appointed a city manager, usually selected from out of town, who served at its pleasure. As chief administrator, the city manager appointed and supervised department heads. Moreover, Childs anticipated the rise of a city-manager profession. The council, including its chairman—a "mayor" without veto power—voted on policy issues. Such a structure made the council solely responsible for city governance. Today the council-manager plan is the most widely used form of government in American municipalities with populations of more than 10,000.

Other democratic reforms for which Childs battled included the integration of state administration, single-house legislatures, appointive judges, proportional representation, reapportionment of gerrymandered state legislatures, replacement of elective lay county coroners with appointive professional medical examiners, and presidential primary reform.

—*Bernard Hirschhorn*

See also New York, New York; Progressivism

Further Readings and References

Childs, R. S. (1911). *Short-ballot principles.* Boston and New York: Houghton Mifflin.

Childs, R. S. (1952). *Civic victories, The story of an unfinished revolution.* New York: Harper & Brothers.

Childs, R. S. (1965). *The first 50 years of the council-manager plan of municipal government.* New York: National Municipal League.

Hirschhorn, B. (1997). *Democracy reformed: Richard Spencer Childs and his fight for better government.* Westport, CT: Greenwood Press.

CHRYSLER BUILDING

The Chrysler Building, designed by architect Walter Van Alen, is located at 405 Lexington Avenue in New York City. Completed in 1930, the 77-story skyscraper is among the city's most admired and recognizable architectural landmarks. It is a soaring monument to both the automobile, quintessential symbol of the Industrial Age, and the American dream of the hardworking laborer rising to dominate the urban skyline.

The Chrysler Building is considered one of the greatest expressions in the United States of the modernist style popularly known as art deco. Van Alen, who trained in Paris, designed the building originally for William H. Reynolds, a New York state senator-turned-developer most famous for Dreamland Park at Coney Island. In an era of economic decline, Reynolds had leased a site for a speculative 56-story office building at the corner of 42nd and 43rd streets on the east and more affordable side of Manhattan. Financially unable to finish the project, however, he sold it to Walter P. Chrysler, the automobile magnate.

Kansas-born Chrysler, the son of a railroad worker, had apprenticed as a mechanic and climbed his way up the auto industry. In 1928, he founded the giant Detroit-based corporation that still bears his name. To herald his success, Chrysler commissioned Van Alen to complete the building as his New York City headquarters. Competition among developers to build the world's tallest building was running high, and Chrysler was not to be outdone. His building went up at the rate of four floors per week, and no workers were killed during construction. To beat out the rivals, Van Alen modified the design and erected in secret the 185-foot apex. Delivered in sections through the center of the building to the 65th floor, it was assembled inside, then hoisted into place in less than 2 hours. The glittering Chrysler Building stood 1,046 feet tall. It had surpassed both Gustave Eiffel's tower in Paris and H. Craig Severence's Bank of Manhattan tower at 40 Wall Street. For a brief moment in history, it was the world's tallest human-made structure and building, only to be eclipsed several months later by the 1,244-foot Empire State Building.

Nonetheless, Chrysler's building is Van Alen's greatest work, a streamlined cathedral he called his "fire tower," a collision of Jazz Age sensibility with traditional building elements. The sunburst design of the crowning, intricate "vertex" contains seven radiating floors that overlap like fish scales, pierced with triangular windows along the four intersecting facades that reach up to the spire. The entire pinnacle is clad in shiny Nirosta stainless steel, the first use in a building exterior in the U.S. of the new chromium nickel alloy from Germany. Although the rest of the brick building below seemed lackluster and conventional in comparison, the architect employed a lexicon of automotive references as ornamentation, from bands of abstracted cars to stylized hubcaps and eagle-like gargoyles resembling Chrysler hood ornaments. Inside, the Chrysler Building was a city within a city, a self-contained and controlled environment accessed swiftly via 32 state-of-the-art Otis elevators, ascending from a triangular lobby covered over with Edward Turnbull's ceiling mural, entitled "Energy, Result, Workmanship, and Transportation." In 1995, after years of weathering, the Chrysler Building was extensively restored to its original Machine Age glory.

—Julie A. Dercle

Further Readings and References

Dupre, J. (1996). *Skyscrapers.* New York: Black Dog and Leventhal.

Shivers, N. (1999). *Chrysler Building.* Princeton, NJ: Princeton Architectural Press.

CINCINNATI, OHIO

Cincinnati, Ohio, was the most important city west of the Appalachian Mountains in the first half of the 1800s. Cincinnati's phenomenal 19th-century growth reflected both the rapid settlement of the Ohio Valley and the importance of river travel in the nation's interior. By 1850, the still-young city's success had become emblematic of the rise of the American West. Although Cincinnati grew for another 100 years, a new economic geography—created by railroad infrastructure—favored other places. The city's 20th-century economic and demographic trajectory, featuring slowing growth followed by gradual decline, mirrored that of many other Midwestern cities.

The River City

Settled in 1788 as part of the post-Revolution speculation in Ohio lands, the fledgling village first bore the name Losantiville. Conflicts with Native Americans stunted its growth, but in 1789 Losantiville became the home of Fort Washington, which garrisoned the federal troops that would sweep most natives from Ohio by the mid-1790s. The fort provided protection for Losantiville, and eventually it led to the city's new name, put forward by General Arthur St. Clair, who disapproved of the initial name's awkwardness. St. Clair took the new name from the Society of the Cincinnati, an organization of former Continental Army officers, of which he was a member.

Cincinnati was one of dozens of Ohio River settlements that boosters hoped would become a commercial center. However, Cincinnati had several advantages over would-be competitors. Its high, flat basin kept it mostly dry during floods, and, more important, its proximity to several small rivers, including the Licking, Little Miami, and Great Miami, gave it easy access to good farmland. During the first two decades of the 1800s, the region filled with farmers, and the young city benefitted from agricultural trade, especially in grain and pork. In the late 1820s, Ohio joined the national canal-building craze, and by the 1830s the Miami Canal connected Cincinnati with Dayton and other growing cities to the north. The canal extended Cincinnati's commercial reach and encouraged its industrial development. Cincinnati also benefitted from another transportation innovation, the steamboat, which allowed commerce to travel upstream as well as down, greatly facilitating trade along the Ohio and Mississippi rivers. Cincinnati benefitted doubly, since it became a shipbuilding center.

By 1840, Cincinnati had become the Queen City of the West, famed for its phenomenal growth and seemingly endless potential. By 1850, Cincinnati's population had surged to 115,000, having more than doubled in each of the previous five decades, and it had grown to be the nation's sixth largest city.

Industrial Diversification

Until the Civil War cut off Cincinnati from its natural trading partners to the south, the city grew right along with inland river trade. With its strong economy, the city attracted European immigrants, especially Germans, and became a significant destination for African Americans fleeing the South, despite overt racism in Cincinnati. With so much of its economic activity focused on the riverfront and along the canal, Cincinnati's diverse population lived in an extremely compact city, one of the nation's most densely settled places. The "walking city," in which most of the population moved from home to work and shopping all on foot, featured a remarkable mixing of race and class, but some separation developed. While not truly segregated, African Americans clustered in two low-rent areas, one along the public landing in a neighborhood called "Little Africa" and the other near a polluted stream in a neighborhood known as "Bucktown." More famously, Germans flooded into the expanding neighborhood north of the canal that took its name from the immigrant population—Over-the-Rhine. (The canal served as the Rhine.) Germans arrived in such large numbers through midcentury that they exerted great influence over the city's culture, especially through the development of a lively saloon culture and a large brewing industry, but also through the creation of several musical institutions.

Although lager beer helped define the city, the most important product moving through Cincinnati's public landing was pork. Farmers and drovers led hogs into the city, where butchers and meatpackers turned them into dozens of salable products. Much of the meat, cured in barrels, traveled downriver to feed slaves in the cotton South. By 1830 Cincinnati had become America's largest pork-packing center and had already earned the nickname "Porkopolis." At the industry's peak, around 1850, more than a thousand Cincinnati workers packed more than 500,000 hogs a year. Although the packing industry created considerable water pollution and foul odors, other by-products proved beneficial to the city, including the large quantities of waste fat. Sold to soap and candle companies, pork fat became the major ingredient in the city's other great industry. Although dozens of local firms manufactured fat-based products, one, Procter & Gamble, founded in 1837, became the city's largest homegrown company, spurred by the invention of a floating soap—Ivory—in 1879.

Meatpacking was critical to Cincinnati, but even in the 1850s the city's economy was very diversified. Furniture and carriage manufacturers employed thousands until the end of the century. The machine tool industry remained important to the local economy even longer. Still, as the national economy shifted toward rail transportation and the production of steel in the second half of the 1800s, Cincinnati lost its competitive advantage over places like Chicago, Cleveland, and Pittsburgh. Although Cincinnati never manufactured much steel, in the early 20th century it became home to some automobile production. However, the Cincinnati area did not gain a major new industry until 1940, when the federal government built a massive aircraft-engine plant in suburban Evendale. By 1942, Wright Aeronautical employed 30,000 workers at the plant, making it the region's largest employer. After the war, General Electric purchased the plant, expanded it, and began manufacturing jet engines.

Suburban Sprawl and Urban Decline

Cincinnati's population peaked around 1950 at more than 500,000, but during the next 50 years the city lost one third of its population. While the metropolitan region continued its modest growth, the city could not keep pace with its own suburbs, especially as white, middle-class families sought refuge outside Cincinnati. At the same time, Cincinnati engaged in a series of large-scale projects designed to "modernize" the city. The city's 1948 Master Plan envisioned two major highways that would improve commuter access to downtown and simultaneously demolish wide swaths of troubled neighborhoods, including the predominantly African American West End. Although the highway building would await federal funding through the 1956 Interstate Highway Act, Cincinnati got a head start on urban renewal in the West End, using federal dollars to replace dilapidated tenements with new public housing beginning in the 1930s. In the process, however, the city created many fewer housing units than it destroyed, giving further impetus to the depopulation of the city's core.

Modernization through depopulation continued through the 1960s, as the city demolished the entire neighborhood that ran between Third Street and the river. The new riverfront, completed in 1970, featured a wide, trenched highway, a new baseball stadium, surface parking for commuters, and almost no housing. At the same time, the redevelopment of Fountain Square, at the city's heart, demolished old landmarks like the Albee Theater, replacing them with modern glass towers. The modern city would cater to auto commuters, who needed ample parking and modern offices, at the expense of previous center-city residents. In the decade following these modernization efforts, the city lost 67,000 residents.

Following national trends, more and more Cincinnatians traded their aging homes for new construction outside the city. In addition to finding that their money went further at initial purchase, these new suburbanites also saved on property taxes. Although the suburbs had these and other attractions, the city's problems undoubtedly contributed more to "white flight." Skyrocketing crime in the 1960s and two race riots, in 1967 and 1968, convinced many to leave. The desegregation of city schools, accomplished by busing children away from neighborhood schools, provided more incentive for whites to flee to suburban districts, most of which remained overwhelmingly white—and unaffected by laws requiring integration.

Despite this depopulation, Cincinnati did not experience the economic shocks that rolled through "Rust Belt" cities such as Cleveland and Detroit, since the Queen City was not dependent on steel, automobiles, or other faltering industries. Still, the city's economy slowly weakened. By the 1970s, retail had followed wealthy residents into the suburbs, and eventually so too did other types of employers, including those in high-paying white-collar sectors.

By the turn of the 21st century, Cincinnati was a polarized metropolis, afflicted by race and class segregation. Residents still expressed pride in the city's history, and Cincinnatians regularly referred to the era when the Queen City earned national prominence and international attention. Most Cincinnatians reflected fondly on the city's German heritage, its role as Porkopolis, great Reds baseball teams, and the building of its many venerable cultural institutions. Still, the city itself continued to lose population and, to some degree, faith in itself. New urbanist trends have reached Cincinnati, though, with young professionals and empty nesters stimulating renewal in some neighborhoods, giving hope that the long decline may soon be over.

—David Stradling

Further Readings and References

Aaron, D. (1992). *Cincinnati: Queen City of the West, 1819–1838*. Columbus, OH: Ohio State University Press.

Glazer, W. S. (1999). *Cincinnati in 1840: The social and functional organization of an urban community during the pre–Civil War period*. Columbus, OH: Ohio State University Press.

Miller, Z. L. (1968). *Boss Cox's Cincinnati: Urban politics in the Progressive Era*. Chicago: University of Chicago Press.

Miller, Z. L., & Tucker, B. (1998). *Changing plans for America's inner cities: Cincinnati's Over-the-Rhine and twentieth-century urbanism*. Columbus, OH: Ohio State University Press.

Ross, S. J. (1985). *Workers on the edge: Work, leisure, and politics in industrializing Cincinnati, 1788–1890*. New York: Columbia University Press.

Shapiro, H. D., & Sarna, J. D. (Eds.). (1992). *Ethnic diversity and civic identity: Patterns of conflict and cohesion in Cincinnati since 1820*. Urbana, IL: University of Illinois.

Stradling, D. (2003). *Cincinnati: From river city to highway metropolis*. Charleston, SC: Arcadia Press.

Taylor, H. L. (Ed.). (1993). *Race and the city: Work, community, and protest in Cincinnati, 1820–1970*. Urbana, IL: University of Illinois Press.

CITY BEAUTIFUL MOVEMENT

By the end of the 19th century, the functional and aesthetic failings of the large-sized industrial city had been recognized not only in Britain but in the United States and Germany as well. In the United States at this time, a group of designers sought to address this situation by instilling beauty in the urban environment through architectural principles such as proportion, symmetry, and scale in the design of large-sized, classically styled buildings and within the establishment of Beaux-Arts–inspired planning schemes for civic centers, expositions, or university campuses. Such was the significance of the "City Beautiful Movement" on American public architecture and city design that American practice seemingly from the 1890s to about 1920 can be described as being a settled policy with established designs and methods. This evolutionary route, and its methods, affected the development of landscape architecture, municipal improvement, and civic design in modern America and was so successful that it influenced architecture and urban design in Britain, particularly in London, Liverpool, and Cardiff, the capital city of Wales.

To comprehend fully what the City Beautiful Movement was about and what its objectives were, it is necessary to examine the urban context in late-19th-century America. By the 1880s, American cities were characterized by a number of elements, most of which were negative in nature. These included government corruption, poverty, social unrest, crime, poor housing, overcrowding, and seemingly uncontrolled urban growth. Jacob Riis, Theodore Dreiser, Stephen Crane, and Frank Norris all ably described the situation of the urban poor, and given the contemporary fluctuations of the nation's economic system, many social reformers in America were gravely concerned about the threat that urbanization posed as a catalyst for stimulating social discord. Thus armed with moral and civic codes of virtue, the City Beautiful Movement may be most simply defined as being a progressive reform movement created by a range of American designers. Importantly, these professionals distinguished themselves by employing classical design and planning forms to bring beauty, aesthetic order, and grandeur to urban environments as a means to offset the perception of moral deficiency and impact of poverty within urban America. Significantly, too, these individuals, such as Daniel Burnham (1846–1912), Frederick Law Olmsted Jr. (1870–1922), John Russell Pope (1874–1937), and Charles McKim (1847–1909), believed that reestablishing beauty in urban America would have a number of major social impacts. These included, for example, bringing wealthy citizens back into the cities to live and work, putting settlements in America on a cultural level similar to or equal to places in Europe, and removing many social ills in United States society.

A turning point in the history of the City Beautiful Movement was the World's Columbian Exposition, held in Chicago in 1893. Described as a triumph of Beaux-Arts classicism by renowned architectural historian Nikolaus Pevsner, the event unveiled to America a lively interest in monumental architecture and the apparent virtues of comprehensive planning. The exhibition explicitly displayed the benefits of creating large-scale architectural schemes, placed in symmetrical arrangements governed by prominent axial lines that could, ideally, be tied to the existing urban form and layout of the urban settlement. The physical form of the World's Fair by Burnham superimposed on the mind a vision of freshness and unity between the buildings within the scheme, set against the backdrop of difficulties within existing towns and cities. With its white buildings, decorated in similar fashion to each other and of a similar design style, the World's Fair, placed in the context of urban sprawl, unrest, and blight, must have appeared to some individuals as somewhat utopian.

Despite its ephemeral existence, the World's Fair provided immediate inspiration for civic beautification and generated a newfound sense of social confidence in the American architect. Its success assured that its design and planning principles, based on the grouping of buildings, not only consolidated existing aesthetic and planning knowledge but could be applied to real, as opposed to temporary, spatial forms. In short, the success of the World's Fair and subsequent expositions like those at Buffalo, St. Louis, and San Francisco demonstrated the following qualities in urban planning: the architectural advantages of an ordered arrangement of buildings, the fact that buildings gain visually from being grouped, the value of focal points and vistas, the significance of unity by color, the effect of scale, and the need for stylistic homogeneity. However, it was not until 1901 that the first explicit attempt was made to use the design ideas applied at the World's Fair in Chicago for the intent of urban amelioration. This endeavor was by Daniel Burnham in the McMillan Plan (1901–1902) of Washington, D.C., which along with later plans for Chicago and San Francisco highlighted the importance of the monumental perspective, large scales, and proportions in contemporary American city planning, as well as those qualities highlighted previously in exposition designing. In Washington, D.C., City Beautiful classicism was employed to establish a monumental center that would invoke European and classical forms in order to legitimize the power of the growing national government, and America as a nation, upon the international arena. It was intended to provide a focus for civic and national pride, which would in turn somehow ameliorate the city's and nation's economic and social problems.

The grouping of semipublic or public buildings formed one of the major elements within the City Beautiful Movement and was often of a scale larger than that evident in contemporary European civic design. By promoting concepts such as unity, proportion, symmetry, and harmony through similarities in height, bulk, color, material, and treatment of the main elevations, grand civic ensembles could be produced that highlighted not only design composition but the relation between the structure and its surroundings.

Such schemes also provided opportunities for the creation of grand vistas. The City Beautiful Movement judged the concept of urban beauty as being more than just surface decoration. It was suggested that no single building could achieve such visual effect, although some architects quickly realized that modifying a building's design through its facade elements so that it would be in accord with its setting—as was done with McKim, Mead, and White's Public Library building at Boston (1888–1895), one of the most influential buildings upon the revival of classical design in America—also permitted the creation of corresponding effects. Such design activity in many respects epitomized American civic design at the turn of the 20th century, which encouraged individual artistic ingenuity in achieving larger, somewhat idealized design notions. Thus, within a well-organized settlement, individual expression was to be subordinate to the civic expression of the city as a whole, and such a view was confirmed by City Beautiful practice in the 1890s and early 1900s.

For many advocates of the City Beautiful approach, architecture and large-scale planning were not merely used to elevate the visual standards of modern American cities but, in addition, provided a means to elevate the sense of citizenship, as large-scale architectural design of a particular manner apparently offered a symbolic language that gave benign assistance, it was believed, to the betterment of society. The idiom used within modern civic centers was usually the Beaux-Arts classical style, which brought about design order and perhaps also harmony and dignity—a style that was perceived to induce social order and respectability. Furthermore, this style was highly flexible in terms of both design details and the size and function of the structure to which it could be applied, an important matter because of the emergence of new building types such as railway stations and office buildings in American towns and cities.

As highlighted previously, the City Beautiful Movement proved successful both in terms of what it represented to the American public at a time when cities were perceived to be riddled with problems and also in terms of what it contributed to the evolution of American architecture and city planning (both in theory and in practice). The City Beautiful Movement is often wrongly characterized as being a group of professionals interested solely in monumentalism, arguably characterized by the work of Daniel Burnham in Chicago at the 1893 exposition or in his 1909 plan for the city (never undertaken), and in the plan for Washington, D.C., but as Wilson (1994) has shown, this is not the case. Small and large-scale designs fell under the movement's umbrella. While classical architecture was the public face of the City Beautiful Movement, the movement must be viewed in a broader perspective. Understanding the social condition of America is vital to understanding the City Beautiful philosophy and practice, and its legacies still remain, such are their strengths. By way of example, Washington, D.C., with its Mall is still a place of national pride, the movement's adoption of classicism helped bring to a conclusion America's search at the end of the 19th century for an effective and socially expressive building style, and the group helped to establish practical skills in America's planning profession.

—Ian Morley

Further Readings and References

Boyer, P. S. (1978). *Urban masses and moral order in America, 1820–1920.* Cambridge, MA: Harvard University Press.

Hegemann, W., & Peets, E. (1922). *The American vitruvius.* New York: Architectural Book Publishing Co.

Lang, J. (1994). *Urban design: The American experience.* New York: Van Nostrand.

Mumford, L. (1961). *The city in history.* New York: Harcourt.

Sutcliffe, A. (1981). *Towards the planned city.* Oxford: Basil Blackwell.

Wilson, W. H. (1994). *The City Beautiful Movement.* Baltimore: Johns Hopkins University Press.

CITY EFFICIENT MOVEMENT

The City Efficient Movement was the product of a marriage between two of the most significant phenomena of the Progressive Era: the municipal reform movement and what has been dubbed the "efficiency craze."

Periodic efforts at municipal reform dating from the early 1870s concentrated on infusing city government with "honesty" and "economy" by replacing "bad" men with "good" and by reducing municipal expenditures, workforces, and "unnecessary" services. A growing number of reformers began to propose more systematic solutions to the burgeoning urban crisis, such as nonpartisan elections, a stronger executive, or the separation of administration from politics. The first comprehensive analysis appeared in 1888 in

The American Commonwealth by Lord James Bryce, in which he contended that municipal government was the one conspicuous failure of the American experiment. Bryce blamed that deplorable state of affairs on four root causes: (1) unfaithful office holders who squandered resources and raised taxes to disastrous levels, (2) partisan politicians who enriched themselves, pandered to immigrant voters, and drove conscientious citizens from the political arena, (3) the increasing intrusion of state legislatures into municipal affairs, and (4) structural defects in city government. Bryce's book brought the growing urban malaise to the center of national attention and provided the blueprint for what historians have dubbed "structural reform." Always implicit in structural reform was the transference of political power from the "masses" to the "classes" and the use of the modern business corporation as an organizational model.

Municipal reform gained irresistible momentum because the severe economic depression of 1893–1897 wrought particular devastation upon the nation's cities. Economic disaster gave rise to a significant cohort of "social reformers" who responded by attempting to lower costs for such vital public services as gas, light, heat, and transportation, redistributing the tax burden onto those most able to bear it, providing public-works projects for the unemployed, and "humanizing" the urban environment by building parks, playgrounds, and public baths. Their numbers were dwarfed, however, by the growing legions of middle- and upper-class reformers who founded citizens' associations and taxpayers' leagues dedicated to "retrenchment" by eliminating "waste," cutting costs, and lowering taxes. Their movement was institutionalized with the formation of the National Municipal League (NML) at its First National Conference for Good City Government in 1894. Within the next few years, the NML proliferated into branches in hundreds of cities, established a national network of municipal correspondents, and held several national conferences to analyze the nature and causes of the urban malaise.

In its early stages, the efficiency movement existed in a parallel universe of mechanical engineers. The concept of mechanical efficiency developed out of the application of the laws of thermodynamics to the technology of the steam engine. As engineers strove to upgrade their status from that of trade or craft to profession, they proclaimed scientific efficiency to be the touchstone of their expertise. As machines became ever larger and more powerful, engineers and their industrial employers sought ways to augment their speed, precision, and productivity with a minimum expenditure of energy, time, money, and materials. So bountiful and beneficial were the fruits of enhanced mechanical efficiency that Americans envisioned the machine as a metaphor for society. Efficiency soon became a virtual synonym for progress.

As the literature of efficiency proliferated, three important variations on the central theme emerged: personal efficiency, commercial efficiency, and social efficiency (the achievement of social harmony under the guidance of "experts" and "professionals"). All four meanings of efficiency—mechanical, personal, commercial, and social—were amalgamated in the program of "scientific management" developed by Frederick W. Taylor and his disciples. For Taylor, the factory was a metaphorical machine in which all tasks were precisely arranged and performed under the constant supervision of experts, so that everyone could realize the maximum benefit appropriate to their function and status. "Efficiency experts" used time-motion studies, microcosmic cost accounting, detailed job analyses, and motion pictures to maximize productivity and efficiency, and they developed pay scales based on differing piece rates. All tasks that involved thought or judgment were the exclusive prerogative of top management. Those scientific-management advocates especially devoted to "social efficiency" convinced some more sophisticated employers to experiment with "welfare work" or "industrial sociology," by providing "qualified" employees with recreational and entertainment facilities, educational programs, insurance and pension plans, savings and loan operations, affordable housing, incentive pay, company unions, and health, safety, and sanitation measures.

It did not take long for municipal structural reformers and industrial efficiency experts to discover common ground. Indeed, many individuals were already prominent in both movements. While the former craved "scientific" justification for their political revolution, the latter sought to convert as many individuals and institutions as possible to the "gospel of efficiency." To a large extent, the tenets of efficiency had permeated the program of municipal reformers from the outset: nonpartisanship, executive hegemony and the separation of administration from politics. By the turn of the century, "efficiency" had been joined with "honesty" and "economy" as the tripartite slogan of structural reformers. Within a remarkably short period of time, efficiency became first, the ideal means to achieve honesty and economy and finally, the *raison d'être* of municipal government itself. Taylor himself

made the connection explicit in an article entitled "Government Efficiency," while former president Grover Cleveland addressed a Dartmouth College conference on "The Application of Scientific Management to the Activities of State and Municipal Government." Future president Woodrow Wilson wrote an article in the *Atlantic Monthly* on "Democracy and Efficiency," while such progressive thinkers as Herbert Croly, Walter Lippmann, and Louis Brandeis increasingly celebrated efficiency as a key to reform. By 1912, few structural reformers disputed the claim that the "government best administered is best."

The triumph of the City Efficient Movement manifested itself primarily in three ways. The first was the proliferation of bureaus of municipal research that transformed inchoate expressions of indignation into the systematic, standardized, and objectifiable channels of scientific management. First and foremost was the New York Bureau of Municipal Research (NYBMR), founded in 1906. The bureau and its various emulators persuaded hundreds of cities to adopt detailed budgeting, more accurate accounting and auditing systems, time and motion studies, inventory controls, and devices for measuring and improving the efficiency and productivity of individual municipal employees. The NYBMR aimed to create "efficient citizens" as well as "efficient officials," although it regarded the former primarily as informed taxpayers who would make intelligent choices among the spending and taxing options proffered by the latter. During the short-lived "efficiency administration" of New York mayor John Purroy Mitchel, the bureau had unrestricted access to city hall. Mitchel's Philadelphia counterpart, Rudolph Blankenburg, went directly to Taylor for advice and appointed the latter's colleague, Morris L. Cooke, as director of public works. Municipal research bureaus played a major role in the city-planning movement that emerged after 1900.

The second result of the efficiency craze was three new types of municipal government based on the corporate model: the strong mayor-council system, the commission form, and council-city manager arrangement. In the strong mayor-council form, the mayor, as chief executive, wields comprehensive administrative and policy-making authority, including the power to draft a budget, set a legislative agenda, veto ordinances, and hire and fire city employees. The commission plan unifies authority in a small body of commissioners comparable to a corporate board of directors combining policy-making and day-to-day administration. In the council-manager system, the council makes policy, passes ordinances, votes appropriations, and exercises overall supervisory authority, while the mayor presides at meetings and acts as ceremonial head. The council hires (and fires) a professional manager to supervise day-to-day operations, draft a preliminary budget, research and make recommendations about topics of interest, meet with citizens, and act as chief executive officer.

The third manifestation of the City Efficient Movement was the attempted adoption of scientific-management tools and techniques to reshape the behavior of municipal employees and to function as agents of social control in the workplace. Charging that the average efficiency level of city workers in big cities did not exceed 50 percent and that one tenth of city payrolls was squandered by padded payrolls, inferior service, and wasted energy, in 1912 the NYBMR recommended the use of close supervision, comparison of time reports, cost data, and efficiency reports as remedies. Both New York and Chicago conducted secret time studies of city employees, but such efforts generally faced stiff opposition from trade unions and civil libertarians.

So irresistible was the efficiency craze that even social reformers incorporated it into their programs. In their view, honest, efficient, and economical government could fund schools, parks, playgrounds, health clinics, natatoriums, and public works for the unemployed. The NYBMR saw government as an efficient welfare state, while the Milwaukee Bureau of Efficiency and Economy's promised motto pledged to deliver services to the poor and working classes with the utmost efficiency.

Although the term City Efficient was seldom heard after World War I, most of the movement's assumptions, values, methods, and institutions continue to permeate municipal government today. The quest for efficiency and economy continues to be challenged by demands for greater citizen access and responsiveness to the increasing service needs of urban dwellers.

—John D. Buenker

Further Readings and References

Fox, K. (1977). *Better city government: Innovations in American urban politics.* Philadelphia: Temple University Press.

Haber, S. (1964). *Efficiency and uplift: Scientific management in the Progressive Era, 1890–1920.* Chicago: University of Chicago Press.

Holli, M. G. (1974). Urban reform in the Progressive Era. In L. L. Gould (Ed.), *The Progressive Era* (pp. 133–152). Syracuse, NY: Syracuse University Press.

Rice, B. R. (1977). *Progressive cities: The commission government movement in America, 1901–1920.* Austin, TX: University of Texas Press.

Schiesl, M. J. (1977). *The politics of efficiency: Municipal administration and reform in America, 1880–1920.* Berkeley, CA: University of California Press.

CITY IN LITERATURE

Two opposing visions frame discussions of the city in American literature, and both were voiced well before the United States became an urban nation. In the sermon "A Model of Christian Charity," in 1630, John Winthrop reminded his fellow Puritans as they reached the New World that their exalted purpose was to establish a holy community. Thomas Jefferson spoke less abstractly when he expressed the hope in *Notes on the State of Virginia* (1781–1782) that the new country would forever remain a nation of farmers.

Winthrop and Jefferson argued from the same premise: that the American experiment has a special relationship with God and history. Winthrop imagined this relationship, metaphorically at least, as a harmonious urban society, while Jefferson denied that such a society could exist. He believed that urbanization was a betrayal of all that was best about America's character, which depended on its remaining an agrarian republic. Much classic American literature shares Jefferson's suspicion of urban society. Thoreau retreated to Walden Pond convinced that his fellow citizens in towns, let alone cities, pursued lives of quiet desperation. New York is the embodiment of the commercial culture in which Melville's passively defiant Bartleby the scrivener refuses to participate. The authorities declare Bartleby a vagrant and cast him into the aptly named Tombs, the prison that is emblematic of Manhattan as a whole.

Huckleberry Finn, refusing to be degraded by civilization, decided to set out for the unsettled territory, where James Fenimore Cooper's Natty Bumppo headed decades earlier at the end of *The Pioneers* (1823). Although Midwesterner Nick Carraway, narrator of *The Great Gatsby* (1925), marveled at New York as a place where anything could happen, he concluded that the city was also steeped in falseness and corruption. He finally returned to the hinterland beyond Chicago, where he could melt reassuringly into the authenticity and honesty of snow. In *I'll Take My Stand* (1930), a dozen of the nation's most accomplished Southern writers attacked industrialization and urbanization as being antithetical to the profoundest needs of the human spirit, including religion and art.

But most American authors have accepted urbanization, for better or worse, as a settled fact. Despite the difficulties and doubts she encounters in her passage from small-town Wisconsin to Chicago and then on to New York in Theodore Dreiser's *Sister Carrie* (1900), Carrie Meeber never seriously considered returning home. Her career was typical of countless other individual American journeys and the transformation of the nation from rural to urban. It also resembles the personal stories of so many writers, including Dreiser, whose decision to move to a cosmopolitan city was a necessary step in their artistic growth. While New York is by far the dominant example, other American cities also proved to be, to borrow a metaphor from *Sister Carrie*, magnets attracting would-be writers seeking contact with other creative people, as well as access to publishers and audiences. Some urban institutions, such as the City Lights bookstore, founded in San Francisco in 1953, have provided all three.

Urbanization also has been one of the driving forces behind significant developments in literary aesthetics. Precisely because urban life is the leading edge of the transformation of public and personal experience in the United States, the city has demanded translation into words if literature is to be relevant to its times. The emergence of literary realism is coincident with the rapid rise of cities in the second half of the 19th century, as the industrial-capitalist urban world came to define "reality." While varieties of realism were succeeded by modernism and postmodernism, the city, as the center of modernity and postmodernity, has remained the most compelling literary setting.

Regardless of the particular genre or aesthetic, the most distinctive urban literature captures an experiential sense of encountering the overwhelming and contradictory details and impressions of city life while offering an interpretation of what this complex place means. From the tension between the appeal and the resistance of the city to the literary imagination, several significant conventions have emerged. Those most identifiably American explore the implications of urban life for this country's core values of democracy, individualism, and mobility.

America's greatest celebrant of urban democracy is arguably its most original and influential literary voice. In "Crossing Brooklyn Ferry" (1856), Walt Whitman pondered the throngs who rode the ferry between Manhattan and Brooklyn, leading him to meditate on the mysteries of personal and collective identity. To Whitman and his many literary heirs, the sheer numbers of people in cities that repelled Jefferson are the source of its essential strength. At the end of the poem, Whitman declares that all the people who make up the urban population and, for that matter, all the natural and man-made elements of the cityscape that he surveys from the deck of the ferry are infused with the transcendent spirit of perfection dwelling in the creation, including the urban creation.

Perhaps the most popular theme in American urban literature is the one, as noted, that is most personally familiar to many writers—the city as site of individual fulfillment. The story of a young man or woman (like Sister Carrie, or opera singer Thea Kronborg in Willa Cather's 1915 *The Song of the Lark*) from the provinces who comes to the city to find personal realization cuts across the literatures of many countries. Its American permutation emphasizes the extent to which the nation in general, and the city in particular, is a place of limitless opportunity. The archetype is the *Autobiography* of Benjamin Franklin. In its iconic scene, Franklin described his bedraggled arrival in Philadelphia at the age of 17, with no assets but his training as a printer, his intellectual gifts, his self-discipline, and his ambition. He fled Boston and his apprenticeship to his brother, who represents the restrictions of family and past that do not obtain in a fluid American urban world where a man can and must succeed on his own. This narrative recurs in manifold variations, especially in popular literature, the best-known examples of which are the so-called rags-to-riches novels written by Horatio Alger in the late 19th century.

The literary conceptions of the city as a locus of democracy and individualism conjoin in works that emphasize urban mobility. The mobility pertains not only to the shifting social and economic status of characters like the hero of Alger's *Ragged Dick* (1867) but also to the social and economic nexus in which they move. Benjamin Franklin changed malleable Philadelphia as he fashioned himself, doing well by doing good. The challenge of capturing the incessant motion and energy that characterize city life has consistently fascinated writers. Whitman set "Crossing Brooklyn Ferry" on a ferry of swarming commuters traversing a river that rises and falls with the tide. In William Dean Howells's *A Hazard of New Fortunes* (1890), magazine editor Basil March most fully comprehended New York's dynamism as he surveyed the cityscape from a speeding elevated train. In *Manhattan Transfer* (1925), John Dos Passos located the principle of modern American urban motion in that omnipresent architectural feature, the revolving door.

The most insightful works are those that convey the ironies and ambiguities inherent in city life, dramatizing how democracy and individualism coexist with exclusion, alienation, chaos, confusion, and anomie; how mobility can lead downward as readily as upward; and how urban energy can turn destructive. Irony and ambiguity complicate even the earliest examples of American city literature, such as *Arthur Mervyn* (1799), Charles Brockden Brown's novel of Philadelphia under the siege of yellow fever. In "My Kinsman, Major Molineux" (1831), Nathaniel Hawthorne depicted the experience of coming from the country into the city as baffling, while Edgar Allan Poe's "The Man of the Crowd" (1830) was a sketch of desperate isolation among the urban multitude. The subtitle of Melville's major New York novel, *Pierre: or, the Ambiguities* (1852), revealed its major thematic concern. The ensemble of leading characters in *A Hazard of New Fortunes* is made up of people who are drawn to New York in search of fulfillment, but while some of them find it in some form, it is never quite what they anticipated, and the careers of others lead to disappointment and even death. Basil March's initially exhilarating impressions of the urban panorama from the elevated train never gather into a coherent, imaginative purchase on city life. He, like all the other characters, received an unexpected but inevitable education in urban contingency.

Similarly, the "best" New York society fatally preys on heroine Lily Bart, the most admirable person among them, in Edith Wharton's *The House of Mirth* (1905) as cold-heartedly, if less graphically, as the stockyards, the epicenter of modern industrial Chicago in Upton Sinclair's *The Jungle* (1906), dissected the immigrant workers along with the livestock that passed through its gates. Fallen from his comfortable position as the sociable manager of a swell saloon in Chicago and on a heartbreakingly gradual descent toward lonely suicide in a cheap New York hotel, Dreiser's Hurstwood in *Sister Carrie* came to

understand the urban world as a walled city defined by whom it kept out. The point of noir crime fiction from Poe and George Lippard to Raymond Chandler, Dashiell Hammett, and James Ellroy was that the city is a place of imperfectly hidden perversity and evil that easily crack its brittle veneer of civilization and civility.

Some of the most textured variations on American urban literary conventions have been written by people understood by others and themselves as outsiders. Just as the city has been the port of entry and the most common place of settlement for the waves of immigrants who to such a great extent define American urban life, the writings of foreign-born Americans and their descendants have powerfully contributed to urban literature. The laureate of the city as melting pot was the Jewish poet Emma Lazarus, whose "The New Colossus" (1883) welcomed the huddled masses, a statement engraved in the pedestal supporting the Statue of Liberty. But Jewish American writers from Abraham Cahan and Henry Roth to Saul Bellow and Philip Roth have chronicled the contradictions and anxieties of city life for those suspended between the clannishness and prejudice on one hand and, on the other, ethnic pride and the existential price of assimilation. The salience of ethnic urban literature lies not only in its revelations of subcultures but in the perceptions it offers on the mainstream by outsiders on the inside. Maxine Hong Kingston's exploration of New York from the point of view of a Chinese laundryman in *China Men* (1980) and Sandra Cisneros's handing the narrative voice of *The House on Mango Street* (1989) to a Mexican American girl in Chicago make the deceptively familiar cityscape strange and enable readers to see it as if for the first time.

In this respect, African American writers have made a special contribution to American urban literature. In *The Autobiography of Malcolm X* (1965), Malcolm Little's recollection of his entrance into Boston as a rube from Mason, Michigan, and of a career that leads from crime to a jailhouse conversion to Islam to his split from the Black Muslim leadership offers a vivid counterpoint to the affirmative urban narratives of Franklin and Alger. The "fulfillment" of Bigger Thomas's Great Migration journey from Mississippi to Chicago in Richard Wright's *Native Son* (1940) is his execution for an unpremeditated murder that the circumstances of his life as a young black man in the American city virtually destined him to commit. Gwendolyn Brooks brilliantly employed the diction of jive in the poem "We Real Cool" (1960) to express from the inside out the suicidal nihilism induced by the dead-end prospects of the youthful members of black street gangs.

Lorraine Hansberry's *A Raisin in the Sun* (1959) was one in a long list of examples of the way in which female writers have provided consistently penetrating insights into domestic relations in the city, although her point is how intensely the black family is under siege, even from such supposedly benign sources as white "family values," which threaten to turn violent if black families like the Youngers try to escape their "place" in the segregated city. Like Bigger Thomas, the only job Walter Younger can find is as a chauffeur for a white family, when he so desperately wants to direct his own life rather than take others where they order him to go. His sister Beneatha, who wishes to become a doctor, seriously considers whether her best option is to abandon Chicago, the only place she has ever known, for a "return" to Africa. Hansberry takes her title from a poem by Langston Hughes, a main figure in the Harlem Renaissance, that compares the thwarted dreams of African Americans to a ripe fruit condemned to dry up, rot away, or, as in the case of Bigger Thomas, explode.

After a series of tragicomic attempts at meaningful engagement with the world, the narrator of Ralph Ellison's *Invisible Man* (1952) embraces on the literal level the symbolic status of the Biggers, Walters, and Beneathas and disappears. His retreat to a warm and brightly lit basement "hole" reflects the fact that to the white world, he and other African Americans do not exist. His withdrawal is a more radical version of the strategy of characters in novels in which blacks erase their identity and "pass" as white, such as James Weldon Johnson's *The Autobiography of an Ex-Colored Man* (1912) and Nella Larsen's *Passing* (1929). Both Wright and Ellison took things another step, however, in arguing that the black American urban experience is perhaps more representative than the white one. Beyond its very real racial particulars, Wright explained, the story of Bigger was that of the human condition under urban industrial capitalism, trapped in a world that makes people anxious and fearful, and they in turn become violent. Ellison's more philosophical and sardonic universalization of urban invisibility is, if anything, more chilling and haunting for the reader.

—*Carl Smith*

See also Fitzgerald, F. Scott; Sinclair, Upton

Further Readings and References

Bremer, S. H. (1992). *Urban intersections: Meetings of life and literature in United States cities.* Urbana, IL: University of Illinois Press.

Lehan, R. (1998). *The city in literature: An intellectual and cultural history.* Berkeley, CA: University of California Press.

Machor, J. L. (1987). *Pastoral cities: Urban ideals and the symbolic landscape of America.* Madison, WI: University of Wisconsin Press.

Rotella, C. (1998). *October cities: The redevelopment of urban literature.* Berkeley, CA: University of California Press.

Williams, R. (1973). *The country and the city.* New York: Oxford University Press.

CITY PLANNING

City planning attempts to reduce uncertainty in urban change processes and to provide knowledge to public and private decision making. In their growth processes, human communities are in constant mutation. The results can be orderly progress or chaotic decline. City planning helps communities cope with change in ways that can improve their livability and quality of life. Cities are by nature complex entities, and a planner's main task is to help make informed decisions, thereby creating healthy and safe living conditions, efficient transport, adequate public facilities and aesthetic surroundings and broadening employment, housing, shopping, and educational and recreational opportunities.

Even though city-planning activities tend to react to socioeconomic forces already in motion, city planning's ultimate goal is to assist the achievement of desirable futures. In addition to working on different types of plans (master, strategic, site, etc.), city planners are responsible for collecting and analyzing data, ensuring and setting standards, creating and proposing programs, analyzing development proposals, enabling discussions, mediating conflicts, and achieving consensus and/or compromises, among many other activities, as noted by Barry Cullingworth and Roger Caves in 2003.

City planning is known by different names in other countries, such as "town planning" in the United Kingdom and "urbanisme" in France. Planning happens within a legal framework of plans, ordinances, regulations, laws, policies, and guidelines. These legal frameworks also differ from country to country. Planning involves multiple areas of urban intervention, such as land use, housing, transportation, and economic development. Planning activities also happen at a variety of different scales: site, neighborhood, city, regional, national, and global.

Even though planning emerged from other disciplines, such as architecture, engineering, and economics, it requires more than a narrow specialist view. Planning is highly interdisciplinary, and while planners do not replace other professionals, they are able to speak diverse technical languages and integrate knowledge in ways that no other professionals do. Planners study multiple subjects in school (e.g., demographics, infrastructure, law, public finance, and ecology). Because of their unique background, they are able to bring added value to the way cities develop. Planners support the emergence of more equitable, efficient, and sustainable cities.

Planners in the United States are represented by two main professional organizations: the American Planning Association (APA) and the American Institute of Certified Planners (AICP). The APA is a nonprofit public-interest and research organization representing more than 30,000 practicing planners, officials, and citizens involved with planning matters. More than half of APA's members work for state and local government agencies. APA resulted from the consolidation of the American Institute of Planners, founded in 1917, and the American Society of Planning Officials, established in 1934. The AICP is APA's professional institute, certifying planners who have met specific educational and work criteria and passed a certification exam. Planners are bound by the APA and AICP codes of conduct and professional practice.

Deliberate planning activities are many centuries old. They include the arrangement of housing in regular patterns, the location of civic and religious structures along main roads, and the creation of squares and open spaces in central areas of cities. The Greek and Roman civilizations gave particular attention to planning. In the Greek era, streets were arranged in a grid pattern, and urban development was implemented according to defense principles. Romans made full use of symmetry in their planning of cities and military camps, as well. During the medieval age, European cities and towns were planned around castles and monasteries with informal street patterns. The Renaissance period revived city planning along Greco-Roman classical orientations. In the U.S., these orientations can be seen in Pierre Charles L'Enfant's 1791 plan for Washington, D.C. The plan included wide streets, parks, malls, open spaces, and public buildings (e.g., the Capitol and the White House) in a grand design.

Even though there was city planning of Spanish influence in North America before the United States existed, modern city planning is usually traced to the hygienist and City Beautiful movements at the beginning of the 20th century. The Industrial Revolution brought progress to society, but with it also came pollution, ugliness, grimness, traffic congestion, and loss of open space. Cities grew rapidly because of population migration and an increase in job opportunities. But the majority of the urban population lived in overcrowded conditions, without proper water and sewer systems. City planning emerged to provide sanitary conditions and to regulate density in tenement housing. Early planning activities included the development of utility systems, the creation of open spaces, and the assurance of sunlight and ventilation in cities.

The provision of open spaces was a priority in many cities in the second half of the 19th century. Today, the Emerald Necklace in Boston, Central Park in Manhattan, and the lakefront park in Chicago are good testimonies of these urban and landscape planning practices. These parks characterize the beginning of a new phase in the history of city planning: the City Beautiful Movement. The 1893 World's Columbian Exposition in Chicago, organized to celebrate the 400th anniversary of the discovery of America, sparked an interest in municipal aesthetics, including public art, civic improvements, architectural ornamentations, and landscape design. The Columbian Exposition was designed by Daniel Burnham and Frederick Law Olmsted. These two architects portrayed Chicago as a "White City" in opposition to the industrial and overcrowded image that characterized Chicago at that time. As a result of the great success of this exposition, Burnham was commissioned to develop a plan for the entire city of Chicago. Published in 1909, this plan was considered very innovative because of its regional perspective and integration of transportation, parks, streets, and public buildings.

The year 1909 also saw the First National Conference on City Planning, held in Washington, D.C., and the first major use of land-use zoning to direct future development in Los Angeles. Zoning regulations were developed to separate incompatible land uses and to preserve real estate values. Public control over privately owned land, as well as the creation of advisory city-planning commissions, brought an increase in city-planning activity. Starting with New York City's historic zoning ordinance of 1916, zoning had been adopted by more than 750 communities by the end of the 1920s, as noted by Peter Hall in 2002. The number of municipal planning commissions also increased dramatically during the 1920s. In 1928, the United States Department of Commerce released a Standard City Planning Act, which was basically a procedural template to help cities guide their planning efforts. The 1920s showed the need to address planning problems at a regional scale. For instance, awareness of suburbanization and the rapid growth of the automobile led the Russell Sage Foundation to fund the Regional Survey of New York and Its Environs, a major study by the Regional Planning Association of America (RPAA) for the New York City region.

During the Great Depression of the 1930s, the national government made full use of its planning powers. President Franklin Roosevelt established the New Deal program and the Public Works Administration to implement a series of capital improvements. The Tennessee Valley Authority was created to plan and develop the Tennessee River Valley. The federal government also provided funding for the creation of entire planning departments. The federal government helped provide low-cost housing, not only as a way to improve housing for the poor, but also to promote construction and boost the economy. In addition, the Federal Housing Administration (FHA) mortgage insurance and VA loans also became important in city building.

The period after World War II saw a radical change in planning intervention. Postwar planning activities relied on private initiatives. Suddenly, suburban housing subdivisions and their transportation needs dominated the planning scene. In 1949, the Housing Act authorized federal funding for urban renewal. The main goal was to replace slums with new developments in inner city areas. The National Defense Highway Act of 1956 initiated the interstate highway system, allowing people to move out of consolidated urban areas and into the new countryside subdivisions. The Housing Act of 1959 made matching funds available for the preparation of comprehensive plans at the metropolitan, regional, and state levels.

The main influence on planning activities in the 1960s and 1970s came from changing federal policies, primarily in the areas of community development and environmental planning. In 1963, the Community Renewal Plan efforts of many cities were redirected toward assisting lower-income groups to improve their economic opportunities. The creation in 1965 of the U.S. Department of Housing and Urban Development (HUD) was a major recognition of the need to plan and develop urban areas. Initially, HUD provided rent aid payments to those below the poverty line and loans with very low interest rates to low- and moderate-income families. In 1966, President Johnson created the Model Cities program, a more bottom-up program in which residents in designated Model City districts identified and proposed their own means of solving problems in their districts. Environmental planning rose in prominence at the end of the 1960s because of increasing damage to the natural environment. This led to the approval of the National Environmental Protection Act (NEPA) in 1969, which created the Environmental Protection Agency (EPA). The two energy crises in the 1970s also brought increased attention to the field of energy planning, as noted by John Levy in 2002.

The history of city planning in the early 1970s was marked by the Nixon administration's New Federalism programs. Many federal urban development programs were terminated and replaced by a system of community development based on decentralized programs and federal revenue sharing. The most important piece of legislation of the New Federalism package was the Community Development Block Grant (CDBG), which was approved by Congress in 1974. Local governments had discretion in the use of these funds, but instead of using them to benefit minorities and lower income groups, local councils used them mainly in capital projects. The Housing and Community Development Act of 1977 created the Urban Development Action Grant (UDAG) to aid cities experiencing economic and physical distress. This program required a commitment by private investors and the assurance that grant funds would be augmented. The competitive nature of the UDAG program distinguished it from previous urban renewal efforts; however, according to Laurence Gerckens in 1988, by the end of the 1970s, there were almost no federal funds earmarked for planning activities.

Ronald Reagan's victory in 1980 was based on the promise that the free market would solve economic and social problems without government intervention. Between 1981 and 1983, the Reagan administration eliminated 62 urban grant programs and combined several others into block grants, whose purpose would be determined locally. But the most distinct feature of the 1980s was what Hall called planning-as-real-estate-development in 2002. The models were Baltimore's Inner Harbor, Boston's Quincy Market and waterfront, and San Diego's Horton Plaza, among other smaller ones. These projects were mega-developments of a large site through a public-private partnership, which involved major public investments. Enterprise Zones were also implemented in the early 1980s. This was a concept adopted from England that provided various types of incentives to investors in depressed, industrial inner city areas. Almost a decade later, a similar type of concept, the Empowerment Zone, was implemented by the Clinton administration.

The 1990s continued to see the growth of the suburbs, most intensively around Sunbelt cities, with Atlanta, Georgia, and Phoenix, Arizona, being paradigmatic examples of what today is called urban sprawl. However, central cities also have received increased planning attention with an intensification of center-city real estate developments. Providence, Chicago, and Philadelphia are examples of this trend. Center-city living gained popularity, especially among the baby-boomer generation. Downtown revitalizations and brownfield redevelopments have gained notoriety in many Rustbelt cities, as have the creation of business-improvement districts and new urbanism developments elsewhere. New urbanism is probably one of the major planning and architecture influences of the 1990s. A movement started by Andres Duany and Elisabeth Plater-Zyberk in the 1980s, new urbanism advocates the use of traditional neighborhood design to build walkable, mixed-use neighborhoods and towns that constitute an alternative to low-density, single-use, and automobile-dependent development patterns.

In the 21st century, one can argue that the three most important contemporary planning issues are the sustainability and smart-growth movements, terrorism, and the return of a public-health dilemma. Sustainability and smart growth involve a set of attempts to control suburban growth and decrease excessive automobile dependence with all their negative consequences, such as environmental pollution, depletion of natural resources, direct and indirect costs associated with traffic congestion, and accidents, among other factors. The 9/11 terrorist attack in New York City showed the need to add an additional layer of protection to the way we build cities. City planners are now asked to ensure the safety of communities and to establish policies regarding the security of infrastructure. Finally, modern city-planning activity emerged at the beginning of the 20th century as a response to a public health crisis in overcrowded inner city areas. Almost 100 years later, the planning

profession is being required to provide better built environments, mainly in the suburbs, that can foster active living, such as walking and bicycling, and indirectly help reduce the obesity epidemic. These are not easy challenges and should not be looked upon lightly. However, once again the city-planning profession will have a chance to demonstrate the added value it brings to the proper functioning of safe, efficient, and sustainable cities.

—*Carlos J. L. Balsas*

Further Readings and References

Birch, E. (1980). Advancing the art and science of planning, planners and their organizations. *Journal of the American Planning Association, 46*(1), 22–49.

Bohl, C. (2003). To what extent and in what ways should governmental bodies regulate urban planning? *Journal of Markets and Morality, 6*(1), 213–226.

Campbell, S., & Fainstein, S. (Eds.). (2003). *Readings in planning theory* (2nd ed.). Malden, MA: Blackwell Publishing.

Cullingworth, J., & Caves, R. (2003). *Planning in the USA: Policies, issues and processes* (2nd ed.). New York: Routledge.

Dalton, L., Hoch, C., & So, F. (Eds.). (2000). *The practice of local government planning* (3rd ed.).Washington, DC: ICMA.

Duany, A., Plater-Zyberk, E., & Speck, J. (2000). *Suburban nation*. New York: North Point Press.

Gerckens, L. (1988). Historical development of American city planning. In F. So & J. Getzels (Eds.), *The practice of local government planning* (2nd ed., pp. 20–59). Washington, DC: ICMA.

Hall, P. (2002). *Cities of tomorrow: An intellectual history of urban planning and design in the twentieth century* (3rd ed.). Oxford, MA: Blackwell Publishing.

Levy, J. (2002). *Contemporary urban planning* (6th ed.). Englewood Cliffs, NJ: Prentice Hall.

Sutcliffe, A. (1981). *The history of urban and regional planning: An annotated bibliography*. New York: Facts on File.

CIVIL RIGHTS

Urban places have been a decisive battleground for civil rights. The status of African Americans has been the critical issue in this contest. In the 1950s and 1960s, cities were the sites of major victories in the cause of full, inclusive citizenship, but the broader story of civil rights—freedom from discrimination in everyday social, economic, and political pursuits—in urban America is very complex.

An attachment to individual rights runs deep in urban America. Philadelphia, Boston, New York, and other large seaports, although all featuring slavery, numbered among the most open and least deferential places in colonial British North America. Their inhabitants rushed to protect cherished liberties against British authority in the 1760s and 1770s. Later, as democratic impulses swept across the new nation in the first decades of the 19th century, the country's growing and proliferating cities were hotbeds of market capitalism and political mobilization. Defenders of a more traditional, hierarchical society were in retreat. White men emerged as the principal beneficiaries of the rising egalitarian theme, while blacks remained confined to the bottom of American society.

Before the Civil War, urban slaves in the South enjoyed greater autonomy than plantation slaves, but they were nonetheless property. Confronting a staggering array of civil disabilities, free blacks in Southern cities were more denizens than citizens. Even though slavery had largely faded by 1830, blacks in Northern cities faced civil, political, and economic constraints as well. As the historian C. Vann Woodward noted, Jim Crow practices thrived first in Northern cities, not in the American South.

Northern blacks, possessing more resources to fight for their rights than their Southern counterparts, pressed for equal access. They staged rallies, took legal action, and engaged in direct-action protests. The edifice of racial segregation did not readily collapse, although black activism did lead to some successes. In 1856, for instance, the Massachusetts state legislature outlawed school segregation after blacks had protested the placement of black students in a single school in Boston.

The Civil War and the subsequent Reconstruction effort transformed the status of black Americans and the concept of civil rights. With emancipation, freed people flowed into Southern towns and cities. Southern urban blacks sought to become full participants in shaping the destiny of a new South. They were aided in this quest by federal legislation: first, the Civil Rights Act of 1866, which enumerated specific rights all citizens possessed; then, the 14th Amendment, in 1868, which invigorated the concept of national citizenship; next, the 15th Amendment, in 1870, which secured the franchise for all adult men regardless of their race; and finally, the Civil Rights Act of 1875, which banned racial discrimination in public accommodations (although not in public schools).

The full promise of Reconstruction never reached urban black Southerners, however. No Southern city had more fluid race relations in the South in the decade after the Civil War than New Orleans. Blacks and whites mixed, for instance, on streetcars, and blacks served on the city council. Yet despite state and federal civil rights laws, blacks in this city were regularly discriminated against in soda shops, hotels, and theaters. The railroad companies were especially reluctant to drop Jim Crow practices. Most whites, moreover, denounced calls for "social equality." Black and white children attended separate schools in New Orleans. And with the end of Reconstruction by the late 1870s, the prospects for black advancement diminished in New Orleans as they did across the South.

The articulation of national civil rights improved the status of blacks in Northern cities. Reconstruction opened more doors for blacks, for example, in Cleveland, a city known for its inclusive race relations even before the Civil War. By 1870, blacks could readily vote in Cleveland, and they had more legal weapons to combat discrimination than ever before. The effects of Reconstruction were even more pronounced in a more racist Ohio city, Cincinnati. There the white population had supported state laws that dramatically limited the pre–Civil War rights of blacks.

After the war, race relations in Cincinnati were never as harmonious as in Cleveland, but blacks now could vote, serve on juries in cases involving whites, and use public transportation without facing segregation. And even after the U.S. Supreme Court dramatically scaled back the scope of federal civil rights protection in 1883, Ohio, like many other Northern states, passed a state civil rights law. This law was, in many ways, more honored in the breach than in practice, but it offered a tool by which Ohio's blacks and their white allies could fight for their civil rights.

The deterioration of the status of blacks in the urban South accelerated in the last decade of the 19th century. A potent campaign for white supremacy erupted to stifle incipient coalitions between blacks and ordinary whites and to formally designate a subordinate place for blacks. The white-supremacist project most affected Southern towns and cities, places where people mingled because of the flow of urban life. From 1890 to 1910, Southern states and municipalities legally separated blacks from whites in virtually every public space and institution. The federal government stood on the sidelines as legal segregation limited the rights of black Southerners. The Supreme Court's decision in *Plessy v. Ferguson* in 1896 essentially gave constitutional sanction to the installation of a Jim Crow regime.

The disfranchisement of blacks was also an important part of the white-supremacist campaign, and the dwindling number of eligible black voters ensured that blacks were unable to turn to electoral politics to resist the oppressive trend. In a number of Southern communities, blacks did mobilize to protect their rights, but these protests, defensive by nature, tended to be short-lived and largely ineffective.

There were limits to the campaign to isolate Southern blacks. Calls for their removal from the country never gained substantial support among Southern whites. And the U.S. Supreme Court in 1917 refused to sanction residential segregation laws that would have formally instituted apartheid.

The impulse to demarcate white privilege affected other groups as well. In Southwestern cities, Mexican Americans were often excluded from public places and restricted to their own schools. Asian Americans, especially in Western cities, endured segregation in public accommodations, housing, and even public schools.

The hardening race relations in the South propelled hundreds of thousands of black Southerners to seek out opportunities in the urban North. The black population in New York, Chicago, Detroit, Cleveland, and many other industrial centers soared between 1915 and 1930. Blacks paid a price because of their growing numbers as race riots erupted in East St. Louis (1917), Chicago (1919), and elsewhere. Moreover, the outlines of modern urban ghettoes were fashioned during the era of the Great Migration as whites sought through collective violence and restrictive covenants to restrict blacks to designated areas. Nevertheless, Northern blacks did not face a public ideology of racial domination. Although they were often excluded from hotels, restaurants, and places of amusement and relegated to the lowest paying jobs, they were able to ride streetcars and subways without restriction, and, most important, they could vote.

It was in response to the race riot in Springfield, Illinois in 1908 that the following year the most important civil rights organization, the National Association for the Advancement of Colored People (NAACP), was founded. By developing branches across the country and locating an activist headquarters in New York City, the NAACP became the pre-eminent voice for equal citizenship for the next 50 years.

By 1930, the Jim Crow policies had become so engrained in Southern life that whites now viewed them as natural and enduring. Southern blacks chafed at the disabilities and indignities they faced, but they rarely mounted collective frontal assaults. There were, however, signs of change. The participation of a growing number of blacks in the industrial unionism movement of the late 1930s and 1940s not only brought blacks and whites together to fight for benefits in the workplace but also led to critiques of Jim Crow practices in Southern cities like Memphis and Winston-Salem, North Carolina.

In 1942 black and white activists in Chicago deployed a new tactic, Gandhian nonviolent direct action, which would later lead to great civil rights victories. These activists staged sit-ins against local eateries and recreational sites that refused to serve blacks. They formed the Congress of Racial Equality, which soon had affiliates sprinkled throughout the Midwest and Northeast that challenged local Jim Crow practices. The work of these activists was enhanced because of a growing discomfort among Northern whites with overt racism. The United States during World War II had defined itself against the racial supremacy of the Nazis, and this definition, in the wake of the deadly Detroit race riot of 1943, spurred Northern cities to found human-relations commissions to address problems of intergroup tensions. In many Northern cities, these commissions were the first municipal governmental effort to advance the ideal of racial equality. By the early 1960s, blatant discrimination in public accommodations across the North and West against blacks and other minorities had become rare.

The U.S. Supreme Court's decision against "separate but equal" facilities in the *Brown v. Board of Education* decision of 1954 forced Southern cities with extensive segregated public school systems to face squarely the growing national opposition to Jim Crow practices. In general, white civic leaders offered modest rhetorical concessions that forestalled major integration. In Little Rock, Arkansas in 1957, the federal government intervened to insure the desegregation of the city's high school. Despite this show of force, it was not until a decade later that Southern cities, responding to new federal pressure, began to integrate their public schools in earnest.

Although the widespread use of direct action against Jim Crow policies erupted later in Southern cities than elsewhere in the country, nowhere did it have greater consequences than in the South. The first sustained boycott against segregated seating on public buses took place in Baton Rouge, Louisiana in 1953.

Two years later, black residents in Montgomery, Alabama staged a 381-day boycott that led to a Supreme Court decision outlawing segregated seating in public transportation. Blacks organized to combat segregation in Birmingham, Alabama; Tallahassee, Florida; New Orleans; and other Southern cities. In 1957 the organizing committees of these protests became the core of a new civil rights organization, the Southern Christian Leadership Conference (SCLC), with Martin Luther King Jr. of Montgomery as its president.

The next round of civil rights activism in the South again was centered in Southern cities. The decision of four black college students to seek service at the Woolworth's lunch counter in downtown Greensboro, North Carolina in February 1960 sparked a wave of similar sit-ins in cities across the South. A group of determined black citizens and students in Nashville, Tennessee, for example, put enough pressure on local political and business leaders to ease Jim Crow practices in downtown businesses. By early 1963, because of civil rights activism, many other Southern cities, especially outside of the deep South, had followed suit.

From 1963 to 1965, the Southern Christian Leadership Conference targeted three Southern cities for major campaigns to highlight the immorality of Jim Crow policies for the entire nation. In each city, the SCLC worked closely with local activists. The campaigns in Birmingham and St. Augustine, Florida helped build support for the sweeping Civil Rights Act of 1964, which dismantled the legal underpinning for segregation in public accommodations. The campaign in Selma, Alabama in 1965 spurred the passage of the Voting Rights Act of 1965. This act, in turn, opened the doors to greater political participation by blacks in Southern politics that further undercut the Jim Crow regime that had reigned for 70 years. The election of blacks as mayors of Atlanta, Georgia in 1973 and then Birmingham, Alabama in 1979 dramatized how fully the Voting Rights Act altered Southern politics.

The Southern struggle sparked supportive demonstrations in Northern cities and helped to spur attacks against Northern segregation and discrimination. The second wave of the Great Migration, which began in the early 1940s in response to war-time labor needs and continued into the 1960s, greatly enlarged the black population in major cities like New York City, Chicago, Philadelphia, Detroit, and Cleveland as well as midsize cities ranging from Peoria, Illinois to Richmond, California. Most of the newcomers to major cities found themselves trapped in expanding ghettoes, which were largely a product of white hostility, discriminatory real estate practices, and local, state, and federal policies.

By the early 1960s, inner city blacks were mobilizing against the consequences of ghettoization. In 1963 and 1964, they staged major school boycotts to protest racial isolation and inferior education in New York City, Chicago, and Boston. In Chicago, a coalition of civil rights groups formed the Coordinating Council of Community Organizations (CCCO), which sought to ensure first-class citizenship for all residents. Similar broad-based coalitions emerged in other Northern cities as well.

The concentrated poverty, lack of opportunity, and regular mistreatment at the hands of police made the ghettoes of the 1960s swirling cauldrons of racial animosity. In 1964, blacks in Harlem, Philadelphia, and Rochester, New York took to the streets in anger. The next year, the lid blew off of the Watts ghetto in Los Angeles. Two years later Newark, New Jersey, and Detroit erupted in two of the most deadly episodes of urban disorder of the 20th century.

Following the Watts riot, Martin Luther King and the SCLC joined forces with the CCCO to launch the Chicago Freedom Movement, an ambitious effort to use nonviolence to improve the conditions of urban blacks. In the end, the Chicago Freedom Movement targeted the metropolitan region's dual housing market and staged dramatic open-housing marches into white neighborhoods across the city and into the suburbs. While the open-housing campaign did not transform life for black Chicagoans, it did compel leading Chicagoans to fight against housing discrimination and set the table for the passage of a national fair-housing law in 1968.

By the late 1960s, then, an array of anti-discrimination measures protected the civil rights of urban blacks and other racial and ethnic minorities. In recent years, cities have been the sites of campaigns to extend civil rights protections to cover sexual orientation, gender, and physical impairment. And yet, even despite agitation for affirmative-action programs in urban America to advance economic opportunities in the late 1960s and 1970s, many urban blacks and Hispanics today, confined to the worst neighborhoods and confronting limited prospects in an economy shedding good-paying, semiskilled jobs, question the extent of the civil rights advances of the past generation.

—James Ralph

Further Readings and References

Horton, J. O., & Horton, L. (1997). *In hope of liberty: Culture, community, and protest among Northern free blacks, 1700–1860*. New York: Oxford University Press.

Morris, A. (1984). *The origins of the Civil Rights Movement: Black communities organizing for change*. New York: Free Press.

Rabinowitz, H. (1978). *Race relations in the urban South, 1865–1890*. New York: Oxford University Press.

Theoharis, J., & Woodard, K. (Eds.). (2003). *Freedom north: Black freedom struggles outside the South, 1940–1980*. New York: Palgrave.

CLINTON ADMINISTRATION: URBAN POLICY

William Jefferson "Bill" Clinton served as the 42nd president of the United States from 1993 to 2001. Born and raised in Arkansas—which is primarily rural and one of the poorest states in the nation—he was consistently concerned about the well-being of poor and middle-class families and deeply committed to racial equality, but he lacked a strong urban orientation. Even though race riots in Los Angeles in 1992 drew national attention to inner city distress, urban policy played no role in either of his presidential campaigns, and with the exception of the Empowerment Zone and Enterprise Communities Program, he did little to formulate policy specifically for cities. Nevertheless, urban residents generally benefitted from the Clinton presidency more than they had from prior Republican administrations or even from the presidency of Jimmy Carter, who articulated the first national urban policy. Several factors account for this outcome.

First, Bill Clinton presided over the longest economic expansion in the country's history. The federal budget deficit had mushroomed under President Ronald Reagan. Balancing the budget was an important campaign issue for candidate Clinton and a high priority for President Clinton. His 1993 budget cut federal spending and increased taxes (mainly for the wealthy), stimulating the economy; the policies of the Federal Reserve Board supported Clinton's efforts. Tax hikes contributed to the loss of Democratic control of both houses of Congress in the 1994 elections, but deficits began to decline, and by the end of Clinton's presidency the federal budget was in the black for the first time in 30 years.

The resulting sustained economic growth was good for cities and the low-income people disproportionately concentrated in them. Older central cities, especially those in the Northeast and Midwest with a traditionally industrial base, tend to be hit hardest and first by recessions; conversely, when the economy grows, they recover late. Over a sustained period, the combination of low inflation, low interest rates, and falling unemployment helped to stimulate investment, reduce unemployment, and enabled many low- and moderate-income households—especially African Americans and Latinos—to become first-time homeowners.

Second, a number of explicit policies pressed by the Clinton administration bolstered these effects. The president's 1993 budget package substantially expanded the Earned Income Tax Credit (EITC), which had been on the books but modest in impact since 1975. This credit, which reduces the taxes of low-income workers, was popular not only with traditional advocates for the poor but also with New Democrats like Clinton and conservative Republicans because it linked public assistance to work; in short, it "makes work pay." By the end of Clinton's second term, the EITC was considered by some observers the nation's most effective anti-poverty program, responsible for raising 4.8 million people out of poverty annually. The same legislation made permanent the Low Income Housing Tax Credit (LIHTC), which offers tax benefits to developers of housing in exchange for commitments to maintain rents at affordable levels for 15 years. It had been in existence since 1986 on an annually renewable basis; making it permanent reduced uncertainty for developers and thus greatly increased its value and use.

Also enacted in 1993 was the Empowerment Zone and Enterprise Communities (EZ/EC) Program, the administration's response to increasingly concentrated urban and rural poverty. It built on an idea long popular with Republicans but supplemented tax breaks targeted to firms in distressed communities with grants that localities could use to support a wide variety of community revitalization activities. Designed by an interagency task force chaired by Vice President Al Gore, the program was administered by the Department of Housing and Urban Development (HUD) but dispensed Social Security Block Grants (also called Title XX funds) that are normally administered by the Department of Health and Human Services (HHS). Program guidelines emphasized the importance of resident participation in the development of local strategic plans and of using federal dollars to leverage investments from other sources; both weighed heavily in the selection process. Funds were appropriated to support 100 zones in the first round of designations in 1994, of which 72 were urban. The six initially designated urban EZs each received $100 million of Title XX funds over 10 years; Enterprise Communities received $3 million over five years. A second round of designations in 1997 bestowed tax benefits and the use of tax-exempt bonds on 15 more urban areas, but Title XX funds were no longer available.

On a smaller scale, Clinton sought and won approval in 1994 to provide federal support for community development financial institutions (CDFIs). Inspired when he was governor of Arkansas by the work of a community development bank in Arkadelphia, Clinton hoped to create an expanding network of financial institutions with an explicit community development mission—institutions that would make capital flow to disinvested communities where mainstream banks had long been reluctant to do business. A substantial majority of these CDFIs either serve urban areas or include cities in their service areas (e.g., statewide funds).

Republican takeover of the Congress in 1994 forced the Clinton administration into a more defensive posture. President Clinton wrangled frequently with powerful House Speaker Newt Gingrich and his conservative supporters and sought to prevent adoption of what he considered the most objectionable elements of the conservative-proposed Contract With America. Clinton's own agenda could be advanced only through compromise and bridge-building across partisan lines—and this definitely limited what he could accomplish legislatively. Initiatives he succeeded in advancing, to the benefit of city residents, included the expansion of Head Start and Early Head Start, which support preschool programs for low-income children; an increase in the minimum wage; creation of the New Markets Tax Credit, which rewards investors who channel capital into qualified distressed neighborhoods through community development organizations; and the establishment of Americorps.

HUD came under immediate attack by Congress, which made consistent attempts to slash its funding or even eliminate the agency altogether. With housing a low national priority and leaner government the order of the day, the administration moved to reorganize HUD and make it more efficient. Despite these efforts, the department lost about one fourth of its funding in fiscal year 1995 and incurred additional significant cuts in 1996, forcing major reductions in the agency's programs and workforce.

Finally, the Clinton administration used its regulatory powers to benefit disadvantaged communities. For example, the Federal Deposit Insurance Corporation (FDIC) developed new regulations under the Community Reinvestment Act (CRA), the law that prohibits redlining by banks. For the first time, bank CRA ratings became based on bank performance: actual lending, investing, and providing basic banking services. Similarly, the administration pressed Fannie Mae and Freddie Mac (private, government-sponsored secondary mortgage market institutions) to develop marketing strategies and financial products that would facilitate home purchase by low- and moderate-income families and by African Americans and Latinos, in particular.

—*Avis C. Vidal*

Further Readings and References

Burns, J. W., & Taylor, A. J. (2001). A new Democrat? The economic performance of the Clinton presidency. *The Independent Review, 3,* 387–408.

Dumas, E. C. (2005). *Bill Clinton*. Microsoft Encarta Online Encyclopedia.

Interim Assessment of the Empowerment Zones and Enterprise Communities (EZ/EC) Program: A Progress Report. (2001).

COAL TOWNS

Most often, coal towns have been identified by their close proximity to coal mines, but in reality, coal towns were much more complex. The earliest examples appeared in the 1840s, as the Industrial Revolution sparked a demand for coal, and during the next century, coal operators created thousands of towns across the country. They were frequently established in rural settings, dictated by the location of the coal seam, but the ultimate location, growth, and demise of a coal town also depended on the intent of the mine owner. Beginning essentially as frontier camps, coal towns changed over the years, with company towns becoming popular in the late 1880s, followed by model towns in the 1910s, ultimately yielding to independent communities by the 1950s.

Many of the earliest coal camps had limited company influence. When developers acquired a coal seam, they also acquired the surface rights. They wanted to own the land so that nothing would interfere with the mine's growth. Upon this land, however, close to the mine's mouth, a small town would spring up. Most early coal operators gave little thought to developing a town, leaving that task to workers. They were more interested in selling coal. The operators, however, did see the value of company stores, and these became a standard feature in coal towns, often serving as the physical, social, and economic center of the town.

With little company direction, the first towns often took on a haphazard appearance, with a variety of accommodations, from tents and shacks to clapboard houses, springing up wherever the landscape allowed. The population of these early coal towns varied from 100 to possibly as many as 1,000, with men dominating the gender mix. Transient miners often came to new locations, and these men were generally single. Boardinghouses then became a fixture in the early camps. This pattern of frontier camps, where the coal company controlled the ground and ran a store but allowed independent influences, spread from East to West as coal mining spread.

As the coal industry matured by the 1880s, many companies decided to develop full company towns and take firmer control of their communities. Here, the operators built not only stores, but also houses. They eliminated any competing businesses and allowed only employees and their families to live in their towns. Mine superintendents ran these communities, from collecting rent to providing law and order. This second generation of coal towns also took on a more ordered appearance. If the town sat in a valley, a neat row of houses generally ran down the valley. If it sat on flat terrain, the houses were placed in a regular grid pattern, with dirt streets defining the blocks. The houses in each camp looked alike, but they often varied from camp to camp, from four-room bungalows to shotgun houses. So many coal companies developed full company towns that coal mining and company towns became synonymous.

Coal companies established full company towns for three reasons. First, they saw company housing as a way to attract new workers, especially immigrant families. Indeed, the number of men and women in these communities became nearly equal. Second, operators saw company housing as a means to bring more order to the workforce. A miner could be evicted on short notice from a company-owned house,

discouraging labor disturbances. And third, companies saw potential profit in renting houses.

Other types of coal towns, however, existed in this company-town era. Some of the earlier frontier camps had evolved into towns fully independent of company control. They still may have had a company store, but a variety of merchants and people not directly associated with the coal company lived in these towns. As well, some business entrepreneurs developed a second type of independent coal town by building a small community just off coal-company property, next to an established company town. In these auxiliary towns, merchants opened stores to compete with the neighboring company store. They just needed to convince the miners and their families to walk off company property to do their shopping.

In the second decade of the 20th century, coal companies began remodeling older towns and building new "model" communities. Motivated by the new ethos of corporate responsibility and by a desire to improve labor relations, companies built larger homes, recreation centers, schools, and improved water and sewage systems. The companies also tried to develop positive community relations by sponsoring baseball teams, bands, and garden contests.

Just as the model coal towns became the norm, however, coal towns began to disappear in the 1920s. Automobiles allowed mining families to live where they wished, and oil began displacing coal as a fuel, causing mines and towns to close. Companies either abandoned their towns or sold the houses and property to those who wished to remain. This turned former coal towns into independent or self-sufficient locations, but while coal mining no longer occurred, many were still known as coal towns.

Since the Arab Oil Embargo of 1973, coal has again become an important energy source. With the reopening of coalfields, mining families returned to old coal towns. But with modern mining techniques requiring a smaller workforce, few towns depend solely on mining families for their existence, and when a mine is opened in a rural setting, coal companies seldom establish new towns. Generally, they expect the mining families to live where they choose; they no longer wish to be in the town business. But for more than 150 years, towns either dependent on the coal industry or under the control of a coal company have been an important part of America's landscape.

—*David A. Wolff*

Further Readings and References

Mulrooney, M. M. (1989). *A legacy of coal: The coal company towns of southwestern Pennsylvania.* Washington, DC: National Park Service.

Shifflet, C. A. (1991). *Coal towns: Life, work, and culture in company towns of southern Appalachia, 1880–1960.* Knoxville, TN: University of Tennessee Press.

Wolff, D. A. (2003). *Industrializing the Rockies: Growth, competition, and turmoil in the coalfields of Colorado and Wyoming, 1868–1914.* Boulder, CO: University Press of Colorado.

COLLEGE TOWNS

The communities that are home to America's institutions of higher education have long been complicated places of cultured tradition, social and intellectual vitality, fiercely territorial local politics, and actors alternately partnering and at odds with their colleges. Their importance in urban history became particularly notable in the period after World War II but goes back to the colonial era. *College towns* are best identified not by their size, but by whether the local college or university is prominent or even dominant in the city's culture, economy, and politics. Thus, cities such as Boston and Chicago, although home to many colleges and universities, are not generally considered college towns. However, many relatively small towns such as Brockport, New York and Arcata, California—homes to the State University of New York–Brockport and Humboldt State University, respectively—are thought of as college towns. More typical examples include Ann Arbor, Michigan, home to the University of Michigan, and Norman, Oklahoma, home to the University of Oklahoma.

The nation's first college, Harvard, was a seminary situated in Cambridge, Massachusetts, geographically removed from the influences of Boston in a tightly knit community. While the college was located at the edge of the New England town, the college fathers played a role in Cambridge religious life. Harvard's colonial contemporary, the College of William and Mary, was founded in Williamsburg, Virginia just before it became the capital of the Commonwealth. That college's founders and campus architect initially emulated the quadrangles of Oxford and Cambridge in order to keep students separated from the rest of the community. Such strategies are indicative of the tensions felt between town and gown even in the colonial period. The enduring popularity of the quadrangle plan and the influences of planners like Frederick Law Olmsted are testament to this equivocal relationship between town and gown. That frequent ambiguity and sometimes outright hostility between educational enterprises and their communities has continued in varied forms to this day.

Breaking from the cloistered traditions of English universities, American colleges opened up to their communities in the 19th century, and the college town as we know it was born. Increased enrollment surpassed the housing capacity of many colleges and universities by the latter stages of the 19th century, and students began to room in their host cities. Several universities, led by Harvard and Michigan, turned away from on-campus housing in this period and embraced the German tradition of the urban research university. Reform in student housing and college curricula promoting more liberal, modern coursework offered opportunity for greater student participation in community life and freedom from the constraints of faculty supervision. Literary clubs, intercollegiate athletics, and fraternities were all expressions of this new autonomy and became institutions in the culture of college towns. Intercollegiate athletics, in particular, have become important features of cities with colleges and an economic boon to communities with large universities.

The 20th century saw an explosion in higher education, particularly after the 1944 Serviceman's Readjustment Act (GI Bill) subsidized the education of millions of veterans and the baby boom swelled college enrollments in the 1960s. Despite robust and federally aided building programs at colleges, students increasingly chose to live off campus in rental housing. This pressure on the housing market and student migration into residential neighborhoods frequently led to restrictive zoning and punitive measures in an attempt to contain student behaviors in "student ghettos." These areas of high student concentration have increasingly become battlegrounds as student violence erupts in the streets and community interests mount political campaigns against student excess and encroachment, even as businesses court student patronage.

Since the early days of American higher education, cities have sought and subsidized the establishment of colleges within their boundaries in order to marshal their economic and intellectual resources. These efforts have become increasingly important in sustaining the lives of college towns, as cities have faced industrial decline and have reinvented themselves as centers of culture and technological innovation. College towns frequently boast musical venues, museums, libraries, and other cultural centers rivaling those of much larger cities because of the ongoing creative collaborations between communities and campuses. Cities such as College Station, Texas (Texas A&M) and Madison, Wisconsin (University of Wisconsin–Madison) also feature research parks that promote science and engineering partnerships between university researchers and private business enterprises. This type of collaboration has frequently yielded economic development and redeemed the early investments of city boosters in education.

The intellectual and social nexus between college faculty and local society has helped shape the broader politics of college towns. Up until the beginning of the 20th century, colleges were renowned as conservative institutions in both their curriculum and their social thought. The predominance of neoclassical and Gothic architecture on early college campuses mirrors the enduring strength of the intellectual tradition shaping those colleges. However, during the late 19th and 20th centuries, college towns and especially college campuses became loci of intellectual independence and political progressivism. Early on, several colleges emerged to provide women with quality liberal arts education, and as many colleges later took steps toward coeducation, college towns frequently became places more accepting of women's rights. Since the 1960s, college towns have been notorious for displays of liberal politics. The upheaval of the Civil Rights Movement, the women's liberation movement, and anti-Vietnam sentiment frequently resulted in violence in cities such as Oxford, Mississippi (University of Mississippi) and Berkeley, California (University of California, Berkeley). The shift of politics in academia since that era has been markedly to the left, and graduates, faculty, and students now help shape the progressive political life of college towns by participating in city government and championing political causes.

College towns—regardless of their size and location—have, since the postwar era, become places of great ethnic, social, and intellectual diversity. Frequently drawing students, faculty, and entrepreneurs from around the country and around the world, college towns offer a mix of culture, education, and economics that, despite the transience of much of their populations, has become an enduring feature of the urban social landscape.

—Dale Winling

Further Readings and References

Leslie, W. B. (1992). *Gentlemen and scholars: College and community in the "Age of the University," 1865–1917.* University Park, PA: Penn State University Press.

Rudolph, F. (1962). *The American college and university: A history.* New York: Knopf.

Smith, R. (1988). *Sports and freedom: The rise of big time college athletics.* New York: Oxford University Press.

Turner, P. (1984). *Campus: An American planning tradition.* Cambridge, MA: MIT Press.

COLUMBIA, MARYLAND

One of the first planned suburban cities in the United States, Columbia, Maryland can be distinguished as the flagship suburb of the New Town Movement. The product of land developer and community builder James Rouse, Columbia was touted as the solution to sustainable suburban growth and the urban problem of central cities. Rouse, regarded as an urban forward thinker of his time, envisioned a utopian suburban community like no other. The Rouse Company was formed to advocate the New Town Movement of the 1960s. The movement shepherded an era of new suburban living, fostering racially and economically integrated neighborhoods, a pristine landscape, and profit-driven development. Rouse believed in stimulating the private market to produce public goods. Proponents of Columbia argued for the creation of a new town that was driven by the market to spur further growth and development while maintaining the social ideals of President Lyndon Johnson's Great Society. When the city's first residents arrived in 1967, they garnered a reputation as urban pioneers. Columbia became known as the "next America," a place where the next wave of suburban residents would be able to live, work, and play in one sustainable environment. The city became the Rouse Company's prized experiment, a social laboratory that served as an alternative mode of living to the cookie-cutter Levittown suburbs of the day.

Columbia is nestled in Howard County, Maryland, located 15 miles southwest of downtown Baltimore and 20 miles north of the U.S. Capitol in Washington, D.C., which served as an ideal locale for Rouse's vision of a new town. The community draws its name from U.S. Route 29, originally called Columbia Pike after the District of Columbia. The route transects Columbia, linking Washington with Baltimore. The city is an unincorporated suburb that both of the region's central cities claim. Situated in the highly urbanized Baltimore-Washington corridor, Columbia is home to an estimated 96,000 people today—just short of its planned optimal size of 100,000. In 1970, the city's population stood at 8,701. Most of the growth occurred during the 1970s, when the population increased six-fold to 52,518. Growth slowed in subsequent decades, adding approximately 20,000 residents in the 1980s and 18,000 residents in the 1990s.

The demographic composition of Columbia reflects Rouse's ideals. Evidence from Census 2000 reveals that Columbia is one of the most diverse suburbs in an otherwise highly segregated metropolitan area. The city is 64 percent white, 21 percent black, 10 percent Asian, and 4 percent Hispanic; 13 percent of the population is foreign-born.

Rouse's community values of justice, equity, and quality of life are reflected in the planning and design of Columbia. The city's master and strategic planning processes emphasize the importance of community integration, diversity, and respect for land and nature through new town zoning. This is a method for achieving openness and integration through multipurpose zoning of houses. No single housing type prevails in Columbia, lending to the notion that one's economic class should not define a community. Thus, the neighborhoods of the city's villages all contain an array of townhouses, single-family houses, garden apartments, and low-income housing. Rouse insisted that the city reserve 10 percent of its housing stock for low-income families.

The city's village structure was designed to foster community and social interaction among residents. Columbia is composed of nine villages: Dorsey's Search, Harper's Choice, Hickory Ridge, Kings Contrivance, Long Reach, Oakland Mills, Owen Brown, River Hill, and Wilde Lake. A distinct nomenclature for streets was chosen. Street names in the villages honor the words of American literature and poetry. Community mailboxes were installed to encourage interaction among neighbors. Each village contains about five residential neighborhoods. They each feature elementary schools that are within walking distance, community parks, and neighborhood centers. Learning in elementary schools features classrooms without walls and common open spaces called "pods," designed to strengthen group learning and friendships among children. The villages each maintain a village center, which is the focal point for grocery shopping, recreation, church, and secondary education. Five "interfaith centers" integrate Catholic, Protestant, and Jewish religions in one common place of worship.

The Town Center brings together the nine villages by anchoring the business and retail communities. The Mall in Columbia functions as a retail hub of 190 stores and five department stores amid many restaurants. Densely built midrise corporate office buildings surround the mall. In the center of Columbia is Lake Kittamaqundi, a local Indian word meaning "meeting place." The official symbol of Columbia is the "People Tree," which is a large tree sculpture with arms as branches. It stands tall next to the lake and represents the city's founding principle of unity.

A green environment aids the quality of life in this new town. Columbia's urban landscape covers 27 square miles, spanning approximately 14,000 acres. Rouse envisioned a pristine environment where humans and nature peacefully coexist. One third of the land is permanently preserved for open and green space, parks, and recreation. Eighty-three miles of pathways and green trails connect the nine villages and allow residents to walk, jog, and bike. Three lakes and 19 ponds are scattered among the city's villages. In the Town Center, a 40-acre wooded park, named Symphony Woods, houses Merriweather Post Pavilion, an outdoor amphitheatre that holds 15,000 people.

The local governance of Columbia is unique. The suburb is self-governed through a private association. The Columbia Association is a nonprofit community-service organization whose 10-member board of directors is directly elected by residents of each of the nine villages (and the Town Center). The association manages all public spaces and activities in Columbia. The provision of public services is provided by the Howard County Government.

Nearly four decades have passed since the inception of Columbia. Since the 1990s, its pattern of development reflects the growth of an edge city. Columbians are increasingly dependent on automobiles and a large network of highways. Also, the region's housing boom has dramatically raised the cost of housing in

Columbia. The average housing unit sold for more than $300,000 in 2004. The restructuring of the Department of Housing and Urban Development's Section 8 voucher program has decreased the number of affordable housing units in the city.

In November 2004, the Rouse Company was sold to General Growth Properties of Chicago for $12.6 billion, ending the 65-year reign of Rouse's development practices and philosophies.

—*Thomas J. Vicino*

See also Rouse, James W.; Social Geography of Cities and Suburbs; Suburbanization

Further Readings and References

Bloom, N. D. (2001). *Suburban alchemy: 1960s new towns and the transformation of the American dream.* Columbus: Ohio State University Press.

Bloom, N. D. (2004). *Merchant of illusion: James Rouse, America's salesman of the businessman's utopia.* Columbus: Ohio State University Press.

Columbia Association. (2003). *Strategic plan, strategic initiatives.* Columbia, MD.

Levinson, D. M. (2003). The next America revisited. *Journal of Planning, Education and Research, 22*(4), 328–344.

Olsen, J. (2003). *Better places, better lives: A biography of James Rouse.* Washington, DC: Urban Land Institute.

COLUMBUS, OHIO

Columbus, the capital of the Buckeye State, is Ohio's largest city and the 15th-largest municipality in the country. It was founded in 1812 by the General Assembly of the state as its third capital (Chillicothe was the first), but, as noted by Charles C. Cole in 2001, it has remained one of the least chronicled of the country's major metropolitan areas. This is remarkable since Columbus is the large and dynamic capital of one of the country's most important industrial states. It is readily accessible, and the presence of major east-west and north-south interstate highways and the I-270 beltway around the city have spurred the development of an expanding warehouse and distribution industry. Moreover, the geography of its location has changed through time because of technological changes, first in transportation and more recently in communications. One consequence of the communication revolution has been the reorganization of the urban economy into a dynamic service economy with international dimensions, not simply one dependent on Ohio and the Midwest.

In recent years, the city government's annexation policy has led to the growth and expansion of the city, and this has made Columbus a more powerful political force within the state at the expense of Cleveland and Cincinnati. This policy has its roots in the outward movement to the lower density suburban areas of the region by manufacturing; commercial business, especially retail trade; and the residential population following World War II. In the 1950s, Columbus was less than 50 square miles in land area and still had room to grow in all directions. It had a relatively few small suburbs. Much of the county (Franklin) was made up of unincorporated agricultural lands in several townships.

During the administration of Mayor Maynard D. "Jack" Sensenbrenner in the 1950s, however, Columbus embarked on an ambitious program of territorial annexation. At the heart of the program was the issue of how to capture for the city some of the growth in industry, business, and residential population that was taking place, especially in the unincorporated areas beyond the city's political jurisdiction. Sensenbrenner sought through the annexation process to avoid many of the problems confronting America's cities, such as the loss of urban residents, businesses, industries, and their tax bases as a result of frozen political boundaries that were the reflection of the existing annexation law. The experiences of Cleveland and Cincinnati, cities that in the 1950s were already hemmed in by smaller political units and had no opportunities for expansion, were familiar to the mayor, encouraging the aggressive annexation movement in Columbus.

As a result, the annexation policy not only served to expand the area base of political Columbus (now more than 200 square miles) but resulted in a dynamic city, no longer dominated by a single large urban core but one with a series of nuclei, each providing most of the services and functions of the core at accessible points on and within the regional transportation system. It was in many ways a visionary policy that has reaped tremendous benefits for the city.

Moreover, as Henry Hunker noted in 2000, of the 25 largest cities in the country in 1990, only 7 increased their populations in the next decade at a higher rate than Columbus, and all of those were Sun Belt cities. This is in contrast to all other major cities in the state (i.e., Cleveland, Akron, Toledo, Dayton, and Cincinnati), which lost population during the same period and continue to do so. In addition, the ethnic mix of the city is changing as it is nationally with migration from Latin America and Asia, although not as fast as elsewhere. In 1990, the white population of the city was nearly 75 percent, while the black population composed about 22.6 percent. African Americans have lived in the city since its founding and have long played an important role in the community. Black Entertainment Television has ranked it the best city in America for African American families in a national study of homeownership, income, employment, education, and crime. Columbus has, however, become a more cosmopolitan community in the 1990s, and it has evolved a culture that embraces a wide range of the arts, from a symphony orchestra, ballet, art museums, and science center to a more diversified sports culture, both amateur and professional. It has also become a major center for the "Information Age" and for the activities associated with it.

With its creation as a state capital, the city's economy has always revolved around this function. It wasn't until World War II that a new focus—manufacturing—really developed. Even in the 1960s, when more than 35 percent of the labor force in most of Ohio's large industrial centers was engaged in manufacturing—and this figure rose to more than 50 percent in some of the smaller industrial towns—it was just under 30 percent for the Columbus region. By 2000, this had declined to only 11 percent, as noted by Hunker. Thus, while the loss of manufacturing during this period devastated the economies of many of Ohio's cities, in Columbus, while the loss was pronounced, it was buffered by the continuing growth of employment in the service sector of the city's increasingly diversified economy. By 2000, the five largest employers were the state of Ohio; the federal government; The Ohio State University, which has developed into the nation's second largest research university; Honda; and Bank One Corporation. Moreover, Honda was the only manufacturing firm in the top 10 employers, and there is only one other, Lucent Technologies, in the top 25. Few other state capitals in the United States have grown to the size of Columbus or have evolved its complex and stable economy, and in March 2002, *Smart Money* named Columbus the nation's second hottest job market, while *Employment Review* placed it in the top 10 list of places to live and work.

Columbus is now the home to five Fortune 500 company headquarters and one Fortune 1000 company headquarters; numerous Fortune 500 companies also have operations in the region. In addition, Columbus has become a launching pad for corporations and inventions known worldwide. Among the flagship enterprises born in the city are The Limited, Wendy's International, Nationwide, Bank One, Worthington Industries, Longaberger Baskets, Cardinal Health, Intimate Brands, and the Scotts Company. Part of this success is due to the educational and research endowment of the area. Home to 17 colleges and universities, including The Ohio State University, the flagship of the Ohio State system, and 102,000 college students (one of the largest college populations in the country), Columbus also boasts several internationally known research institutions in addition to Ohio State. These include Battelle, the OCLC Online Computer Library Center, and the Chemical Abstracts Service.

—*David J. Edelman*

Further Readings and References

Cole, C. C. (2001). *A fragile capital: Identity and the early years of Columbus, Ohio.* Columbus, OH: Ohio State University Press.

Columbus Chamber of Commerce Web site. http://www.columbus.org, accessed on December 3, 2004.

Hunker, H. L. (2000) *Columbus, Ohio: A personal geography.* Columbus, OH: Ohio University Press.

COMMERCIAL STRIP

The commercial strip is a linear grouping of commercial properties along a major road or highway. It is made up of a wide range of property types geared toward the automobile traveler and area resident. In addition to commercial space, integral components include the commercial sign and parking lot. The sign is designed to draw the attention of the passing motorist, and the parking lot serves the automobile consumer, to whom the strip caters. Strips are typically removed from the downtown of small and large cities. Many towns have a commercial strip located on either end of Main Street, outside the central business area.

Although early commercial strips developed along trolley lines and roads that radiated outward from the central city, the automobile and postwar suburban movement had the largest impact on strip development. As the American public became more mobile and moved to newly developed suburban areas, commercial centers continued to expand along established highways. This commercial expansion resulted in clusters of businesses arranged in a linear fashion along roads, commonly referred to as commercial strips. In many areas, the strip quickly replaced the downtown as a shopping destination. Shoppers appreciated avoiding the traffic congestion of the central city and enjoyed the off-street parking provided by strip businesses.

The strip contained a variety of business types and appealed to several groups of people. It included motels, hotels, gas stations, diners, and fast-food restaurants geared toward the traveling motorist. Businesses geared to the suburban resident included supermarkets, florists, dry cleaners, clothing stores, and a wide variety of retail establishments. It became possible to purchase anything you needed without making a trip into the central city. Because the strip catered to the automobile owner, it also included a concentration of automobile-related businesses. It was common for the strip to include service stations, new and used automobile dealerships, automobile parts stores, and salvage yards. This variety of business types created a varied commercial landscape.

The placement and architecture of commercial buildings evolved to become more visible to the automobile traveler. Everything was designed to be perceptible to the motorist traveling at a speed of 30 miles per hour. This resulted in larger signs with bold, simple language. Signs were typically located at the street, separated from the building by a parking lot, and used simple English words that provided succinct information on the goods and services available. For example, *eat*, *food*, *gas*, *motel*, and *free TV* were common terms along the roadside. New buildings were constructed at the rear of the lot and parallel to the street to increase both parking and storefront display space. Buildings took the form of the popular and eye-catching art deco and streamline moderne styles, which used smooth wall surfaces, horizontal emphases, and geometric motifs.

As the commercial strip developed, the strip mall became a popular addition. The strip mall consisted of a large building with several storefronts that housed various retail and service stores with a large private parking area. The building was typically one-story with large storefront windows for displaying products. Storefronts were often sheltered by a canopy or located within an arcade, so that shoppers were protected from the elements. The L-plan and rectangular form were the most popular, as they maximized the lot

space, provided adequate parking, and allowed window displays to be seen by the passing motorist. The U-plan with central courtyard parking was the least popular because the motorist passing at a moderate speed was not able to see the window displays and signage clearly.

Strip malls were often anchored by a supermarket, pharmacy, or department store and also included many of the businesses already located on the strip, including dry cleaners, florists, and salons. It became common for the shopper to visit multiple stores within a mall during the same trip, making the proximity to other retail establishments in the strip mall advantageous.

The franchise was a common addition to the commercial strip. The franchise, or chain store, was easily identified by a distinctive architectural design that was used regionally or nationally. Distinguishing features typically included logos, trademark colors, architectural motifs, and signage, which often featured distinctive images. Fast-food restaurants and gas stations used roof forms, such as the mansard, to be easily identified by the traveling motorist. These stores were constructed as both freestanding units on a commercial strip and components within larger strip malls.

The commercial strip and associated strip mall began to decline in popularity with the rise of the indoor suburban shopping mall, chain store, and big-box discount retailer, which offered a wide variety of goods at lower prices than locally owned stores. The strip began to lose popularity for the same reason of improved access that had originally attracted shoppers from downtown areas. Expanding urban areas had resulted in increased traffic congestion that made strip businesses more difficult to access. In addition, suburbanites wanted to shop close to home in the expanding suburban area, not in areas that had once been but were no longer located on the edge of town. Outdated commercial strip buildings were replaced with malls and national chain stores housed in more appealing buildings. Those that survived were remodeled to reflect a more modern appearance, or they evolved to serve new functions. Religious groups began using the large, open commercial space for church services, and local governments use the spaces for branch offices that appeal to suburban residents.

The commercial strip is making a comeback and is reappearing at the outer edges of cities. Its modern form is different from that of its predecessor, in that it is removed from the highway and has its own street network, rather than being located along an established road. The contemporary version is larger than the original strip and encircled by large parking lots. Perhaps the largest difference is that rather than serving as a convenient stopping place along a travel route, the modern strip mall has become a shopping destination.

Wilshire Boulevard in Los Angeles, known as the "Miracle Mile," was one of the most famous early examples of the commercial strip. During the 1920s, developer A. W. Ross transformed an unpaved farm road to a commercial area that rivaled downtown Los Angeles, hence the name Miracle Mile. It was developed to attract and serve automobile traffic rather than pedestrians. Ross required that merchants provide private parking lots and that building facades be designed to be best viewed through windshields. The success of Wilshire Boulevard contributed to Los Angeles's reputation as a city dominated by the automobile. Other communities quickly began to establish similar strips and referred to them as their own miracle mile.

—Emily Pettis
—Amy Squitieri

See also Chain Stores; Downtown

Further Readings and References

Davis, T. (1997). The Miracle Mile revisited: Recycling, renovation, and simulation along the commercial strip. In A. Adams & S. McMurry (Eds.), *Exploring everyday landscapes, perspectives in vernacular architecture, VII* (pp. 93–114). Knoxville: University of Tennessee Press.

Liebs, C. H. (1985). *Main Street to Miracle Mile*. Baltimore: Johns Hopkins University Press.

MacDonald, K. (1985). The commercial strip: From Main Street to Television Road. *Landscape, 28*, 2, 12–18.

Miracle Mile, Los Angeles, California. Answers.com Accessed at http://www.answers.com/topic/miracle-mile-los-angeles-california

COMMUNITY DEVELOPMENT BLOCK GRANTS

The Community Development Block Grant (CDBG) program, administered by the U.S. Department of Housing and Urban Development (HUD), provides annual grants on a formula basis to state and local governments to improve housing conditions, increase the stock of affordable housing, encourage economic development, and expand community services in high-poverty neighborhoods.

The CDBG program, initiated in 1974, is one of the oldest programs administered by HUD. For federal fiscal year 2005, the annual expenditure for the CDBG program was about $4.5 billion. HUD distributes CDBG funds to cities, counties, and states based on a formula designed to provide larger grants to municipalities with relatively greater needs.

Grantees can use CDBG funds for a variety of activities, including housing rehabilitation, construction of new housing, economic development, infrastructure (such as streetlights, parks, and water/sewer lines), preservation of historic properties, and construction, renovation, and operation of community centers.

HUD requires that CDBG applicants hold public meetings so citizens and community groups can identify their needs and propose projects to be funded. Applicants then submit this information as part of their Consolidated Plan to HUD. The Consolidated Plan must also contain maps, tables, and demographic data showing which low- and moderate-income census tracts are targeted for projects.

History of the CDBG Program

Since the early 1900s, the federal government has used various methods to address urban poverty. Many urban researchers agree that early efforts were uncoordinated and underfunded and relied on a "top-down" approach that did not solicit input from the communities they served. As a result, these efforts were not very effective in reducing poverty. One of the largest of such programs, Urban Renewal, was criticized for displacing residents, tearing down viable neighborhoods, ignoring the social needs of the community, and shifting poverty from one area to another. In many communities, opposition to eminent domain and the so-called "federal bulldozer" added further controversy to Urban Renewal and other early federal efforts.

Urban Renewal, combined with other push factors such as blockbusting and redlining, encouraged millions of middle-class families to relocate to the suburbs during the 1940s and 1950s. In addition, pull factors, including construction of the interstate highway system, availability of long-term amortized home loans, implementation of the mortgage interest tax deduction, increased popularization of the automobile, availability of cheap, mass-produced housing, and the dream of owning a house in a quiet, clean, safe, suburban environment, further encouraged suburbanization. As a result, many urban neighborhoods suffered devastating population and economic losses.

Starting in 1966, the newly formed cabinet-level agency HUD tried a new approach to curing urban ills: specific geographic targeting of funds for community improvement. This approach, called Model Cities, targeted large grants to specific neighborhoods in a few cities to eradicate slum conditions, construct affordable housing, and incorporate a wide range of social services. For the first time, HUD used census and other demographic data to identify areas with the largest needs. Although considered a novel approach with much potential, Model Cities attracted criticism because Congress distributed funds based on their political preference, arguably spreading the money too thin to do any good.

President Gerald Ford was looking for a new way to attack poverty in America's urban neighborhoods, and he found it in 1974 with the CDBG program. Instead of politicians or planners in Washington determining how and where money would be spent, the new CDBG program would be a "bottom-up" approach. Communities would document their own needs, and funds would be distributed based on a formula. HUD hoped the more equitable approach offered by the CDBG program would prevent politics from influencing funding decisions and lead to significant reductions in urban poverty rates.

The CDBG Formula

Initial studies by HUD's Office of Policy Development and Research showed that using a formula did result in a more equitable distribution of funds. However, these studies recommended adjusting the formula to assist cities with different types of problems. The Congress agreed, and when they reauthorized the CDBG program in 1978, they instituted a dual formula based on these recommendations.

HUD calculates both formulas for all grantees and awards the larger amount, minus a pro-rata reduction depending on congressional appropriation. Formula A, based 50 percent on poverty, 25 percent on population, and 25 percent on overcrowding, tends to benefit rapidly growing cities with high poverty that lack affordable housing. Formula B is based 50 percent on pre-1940 housing, 30 percent on poverty, and 20 percent on growth lag and usually benefits communities that have lost population and have a large stock of old and deteriorating housing.

In addition to instituting the dual formula, the 1978 reauthorization required that some program funds also be given to rural areas. This change

required HUD to distribute no more than 70 percent of CDBG funds to what are known as entitlements (cities and counties meeting a minimum population threshold) and earmark 30 percent for states to fund projects in rural, nonentitlement communities with significant needs.

Other recent legislative changes have added several small provisions within CDBG targeted to specific needs. The Disaster Recovery Assistance provision gives flexible grants to communities to help low- and moderate-income areas recover from presidentially declared disasters. In 1996, Congress enacted this provision by appropriating $4.2 billion in CDBG Disaster Recovery funds for the state of Louisiana to rebuild infrastructure and housing after Hurricane Katrina. Other CDBG provisions include the Section 108 loan guarantee, which offers a source of financing for large-scale rehabilitation and economic development projects, and the Section 107 provision, which provides technical assistance awards to CDBG grantees and certain minority-serving colleges and universities. In addition, the Insular Area provision is a special set-aside to help U.S. territories meet their community development needs.

Evaluating the CDBG Program

Implementation of the CDBG program represented a significant change in the way the federal government attacked urban problems. Some urban researchers argue that by involving the community in a "bottom-up" approach and by using a formula-based allocation, the CDBG program was more successful in ameliorating poverty than were previous programs. Other researchers have concluded that the CDBG program did benefit many inner city neighborhoods and succeeded in meeting some of its objectives.

However, some researchers have criticized the CDBG program for having a conflicting purpose: Grantees must target funds to low-income areas but also may use their funds for almost any urgent community need. Other scholars have suggested that increased funding and improved targeting would make CDBG a more effective program. Recently, some politicians have called for consolidating the CDBG program with other federal initiatives or eliminating it altogether.

—*Seth R. Marcus*

See also Johnson Administration: Urban Policy; Model Cities; Suburbanization; Urban Renewal and Revitalization

Further Readings and References

Bratt, R. G., & Keating, W. D. (1993). Federal housing policies and HUD: Past problems and future prospects for a beleaguered bureaucracy. *Urban Affairs Quarterly, 29,* 3–27.

Bunce, H., & Glickman, N. (1980). The spatial dimensions of the Community Development Block Grant Program: Targeting and urban impacts. In N. Glickman (Ed.), *The urban impacts of federal policies* (pp. 515–541). Baltimore: Johns Hopkins Press.

Dommel, P. R., & Rich, M. J. (1987). The rich get richer: The attenuation of targeting effects of the Community Development Block Grant Program. *Urban Affairs Quarterly, 22,* 552–579.

HUD (1978). *Third annual Community Development Block Grant report.* Washington, DC: United States Department of Housing and Urban Development.

Marcus, S. R. (1999). *Assessing the impact of community development block grants on inner-city neighborhoods.* Unpublished master's thesis, University of South Carolina.

Pascal, A. H., & Williams, B. (1980). *Appraising HUD strategies for economic and community development: An analysis of the CDBG, Section 312, and UDAG programs.* Santa Monica, CA: RAND.

COMMUNITY IN THE CITIES

Although the definition of community is subject to interpretation, both academic discourse and popular culture generally use the term to connote a shared connection or a sense of belonging, based on personal and family values, including cultural, religious, or political beliefs, to the national society and culture. Given this notion of community, it is no surprise that locating and historicizing communities in American cities, which can be places of great social interaction, diversity, and exchange, is a complex task. Over the decades, many scholars, including historians, sociologists, and political scientists, have endeavored to make sense of the meaning, extents, limits, and overall experience of community and community life in the American metropolis.

In the late 19th century, Ferdinand Tonnies, a German sociologist, examined the change in community from a traditional village-like society connected by bonds of kinship, friends, and neighbors to the impersonal, modern, and urban world where social roles are dispersed among various people. He labeled this process of community decline as the transition from *Gemeinschaft*, or society characterized by strong mutual bonds of sentiment and family, to *Gesellschaft*, or society distinguished by more distant relationships and best represented by modern cities. Tonnies's theoretical framework, which culminated in a 1938 article in *The American Journal of Sociology* by Louis Wirth, dominated the historical scholarship on community life for years. But in the mid-20th century, scholars began to challenge Tonnies's dichotomy by unearthing stories of community ties in urban centers, particularly among African Americans and other minority groups. In recent decades, new scholarship and discussions about the significance of urban communities have continued to complicate the Gemeinschaft to Gesellschaft binary as well as its authority. Still, the debate between proponents of the community decline theory and those who argue for the endurance of community ties remains central to any discussion of the role of American cities in the modern world.

The impact and longevity of Tonnies's theory can be in large part explained by the change in community life over the centuries. The contrast between the colonial village communities in the pre-industrial 17th century and the diverse, urban neighborhoods of modern America raises questions about the evolving form and function of communities. In the 17th century, Europeans who migrated to the New World established tight, local villages, each with distinct cultural values and communal life. Centered on institutions such as the church and school, these small villages were contained social units and constituted the center for economic, political, social, and religious lives for their residents, often a homogenous group within an increasingly heterogeneous continental culture.

The era of the American Revolution forever changed colonial life by bringing together different local communities into towns that collectively formed the United States. Although the local communities formed by European migrants remained bound by kinship ties during the course of the 19th century, new market forces as well as the acceleration of westward expansion, geographic mobility, and interpersonal correspondence changed the American landscape and thus the configuration of communities. At the end of the Civil War, social and political life in America was still oriented around a local community or a small town. But in the postbellum period, as urban centers increased in size and population, traditional conceptions of idyllic community life would give way to new brands of communities in diversified city spaces.

In the late 19th century, mass industrialization, immigration, and urbanization were blamed for undermining old forms of community and neighborliness. Local towns were quite literally carried into the metropolis by technological innovations such as the railroads, and people moved from their contained villages to cities in search of economic and social opportunities that the rising urban centers might offer. But the demographic change gave rise to new communities in the cities: rather than living in communities isolated by the geographic boundaries of town or village, urban dwellers established communities in city residential spaces. Thus, while the decades of the late 19th to early 20th century arguably saw the decline of what historian Robert Wiebe described as *island communities*, or disconnected, local communities, it also saw the rise of urban communities that, although still bearing an ostensibly homogenous composition, had frequent interactions with several other groups in their daily lives.

Of the many people moving to the cities during this period, major groups included immigrants and African Americans. During the last third of the 19th century, nearly 12 million people immigrated to the United States, and the majority settled in urban centers. Just as European migrants in the 17th century formed village-like networks, so too did these 19th-century ethnic groups, including Italians, Germans, Canadians, Jews, and other Eastern Europeans. Although the neighborhoods they formed tended to be structured according to race, class, ethnicity, and gender, municipalities were often heterogeneous, with, for example, Irish blocks adjacent to Italian areas, or Jewish neighborhoods near African American ones.

While living conditions in tenement apartments, where many of these new immigrants lived, were considerably poor, the very tight quarters also put people in close proximity to each other, and this nurtured a sense of community. Historical accounts of immigrants during the period have uncovered evidence of city dwellers preserving strong personal, family, and communal ties despite the difficulties of immigration and tenement living. Similarly, historians have revealed how laborers, artisans, and factory workers held on to institutions of mutual support, shared culture, and local cooperation amidst the chaos of industry and urbanization.

The 20th century also saw a massive influx of African Americans from the rural South into urban centers, particularly in the North. Once in cities, African Americans, challenged by widespread racial discrimination, found ways to establish cohesive communities. This was due in part to patterns of racial segregation, which severely restricted the geographical size and location of African American residential neighborhoods. Although families might move, and indeed, residential turnover was high, if they stayed in the same city they were ultimately bound to remain close to family and friends. The shared sentiment among neighbors was also a result of necessity as much as it was physical proximity: because of the inadequacy of living conditions in individual apartments, African American urban dwellers were forced to share facilities.

During the 1930s, these communities became more militant, uniting residents against established authorities. For example, scholars have shown that during the Great Depression, some African American women came together to withhold money from rent-raising landlords or to block the eviction of a neighboring family. African Americans also organized celebrations such as rent parties in Northern ghettoes, which brought neighbors together in a show of community and collective survival. These examples highlight the importance of urban communities during the first half of the 20th century and demonstrate the potential of community in the cities to bring people together to demand social justice.

The role of urban communities during the first half of the 20th century is particularly significant given the post–World War II rise of the suburb, which effectively remapped the American metropolis as well as community life. By luring people, initially white and middle class, away from the crowding urban centers, suburbanization caused greater segregation by race and class. As the city lost its wealthier residents and thus its businesses and tax base, city living conditions and facilities deteriorated. In the 1950s and into the 1960s, federal and state governments initiated urban renewal programs, or the redevelopment of slums and ghettoes, to revitalize urban neighborhoods. Because urban renewal threatened to raze specific urban communities, many of which were composed of minorities, the initiatives often met great controversy and drew resistance from residents in targeted areas. In their collective resistance of urban renewal initiatives, city residents demonstrated various forms of attachment to their community: to the place, the people, or a combination of both. In the latter part of the 20th century, government officials continued to initiate polices aimed at restoring communities, but they often had qualified success.

Contemporary communities in cities can take various forms, including diverse neighborhoods that share common resources and institutions or an urban gay community. While community life in the city continues to evolve and should not be idealized, evidence suggests that modern cities should not be represented only as vehicles of community decline. Rather, community in cities is a vital unit of study in both American history and life.

—*Lindsay Silver*

See also Community in the Suburbs; Wirth, Louis

Further Readings and References

Bender, T. (1978). *Community and social change in America.* New Brunswick, NJ: Rutgers University Press.

Borchert, J. (1982). *Alley life in Washington: Family, community, religion & folklife in the city, 1850–1970.* Urbana, IL: University of Illinois Press.

Issenberg, A. (2004). *Downtown America: A history of the place and the people who made it.* Chicago: The University of Chicago Press.

Nash, G. (1998). The social evolution of preindustrial American cities, 1700–1820. In R. Mohl (Ed.), *The making of urban America* (pp. 15–36). Wilmington, DE: Scholarly Resources.

Putnam, R. (2000). *Bowling alone: The collapse and revival of American community.* New York: Simon & Schuster.

Wirth, L. (1938). Urbanism as a way of life. *The American Journal of Sociology, 44,* 1–24.

COMMUNITY IN THE SUBURBS

It has been a long haul from John Adams to *Desperate Housewives*. Life distanced from city noise, crowds, grime, and crime has long appealed to affluent Americans. Planned suburban communities for the elite date to the mid-19th century, and movement into pleasing "borderlands" became increasingly commonplace early in the 20th. But suburbia in the guise that dominates popular imagination is a 20th-century phenomenon, connected to the mass migration from American cities in the wake of the Second World War.

Most suburbs in the early 20th century were indistinguishable in location, demographics, and mores from the small towns (what Thomas Jefferson called "little republics") that dotted the American landscape. But the explosive growth of suburbia in the wake of World War II heralded a new kind of American community. Older towns, particularly those immediately surrounding each major city, grew first and fastest. Meanwhile, innumerable new developments, from Lakewood, California, to Levittown, New York, rose in response to the postwar housing shortage. Popular writers and scholars began taking the temperature of life on the outskirts of the nation's overcrowded cities, although there was no consensus on what to make of it.

Community in the new suburbs (as well as fast-growing older ones) was founded on the notion of a haven for family life. Returning GIs wanted to start life fresh, in traditional homes on individual lots large enough to offer elbow room and verdant vistas. Aided by government policies, including 3 percent veterans' mortgages that encouraged homeownership, and spurred by developers advertising the affordability of the suburban dream, the newly returned GIs rushed to sign on. The United States was morphing into a suburban nation.

The new suburban communities wrought nothing less than a social revolution. The cover of *Time* magazine on July 3, 1950, featuring Levittown's chief promoter, William Levitt, captured the significance of what Levitt and Sons had wrought: They were selling a new way of life.

That new way of life was one of networking and vibrant community institutions. At the heart of the networking was the neighborhood. Neighbors replaced family and friends left behind in the city and provided essential counsel on "fitting in." Informal conversations over coffee and cards or over the fence while doing yard work, and in posher suburbs, during the cocktail party, were staples of suburban community. Post–World War II suburban communities, moreover, witnessed an outpouring of activism. Church groups, youth sports leagues, civil-defense drills, civic organizations like the PTA, and service clubs brought people together regularly in common cause. Political and social justice–oriented activism tended to be less important to suburbanites, although participation in civic rituals like voting remained strong until the 1970s.

Because suburban life more commonly entailed coffee klatches, Tupperware parties, swim outings, and Little League baseball games than the pursuit of high culture, city-based observers were quick to criticize suburbs as dull and conformist. Suburbia's critics failed to notice that working- and middle-class Americans living in cities more frequently spent their free time talking with one another on neighborhood stoops or at baseball stadiums than at museums and symphony halls. And contrary to the depiction in popular media of a stultified "split-level trap" environment, residents of post–World War II suburbs experienced a higher degree of social capital than have Americans in the years since the Nixon presidency.

Suburban communities before the mid-1960s were socially amorphous but racially restrictive. Among whites, ethnicity mattered little. People looked for— and welcomed—"compatible" neighbors, but there were few expectations from new neighbors beyond friendliness and keeping up one's property. Blue-collar workers found a niche in suburban America, folding comfortably into the rubric of modest middle class. By contrast, African Americans were discouraged from buying homes in suburbia or steered by realtors to enclaves where minorities were already established. For example, in Bergen County, New Jersey, of 71 incorporated communities, African Americans counted for more than a tiny fraction of the population in only three towns—Hackensack, Teaneck, and Englewood.

As racial exclusion dissipated in the wake of the civil rights laws of the 1960s, a new suburban phenomenon became more notable: economic segregation. Community builders designed rings of suburbs based on housing prices, thereby reinforcing homogeneity in terms of wealth if not ethnic or social background. Perhaps most remarked upon has been the emergence of the "McMansion," whether sited on a Toll Brothers grid, located on a five-acre lot in what had recently been farmland in the exurbs, or nestled on a small inner suburban lot (say, in Evanston, Illinois, or Bethesda, Maryland) after tearing down the original, and much smaller, home.

Contemporary suburban communities are more than ever automobile-centered places. Major department stores began relocating to new suburban malls in the 1950s and, in the late 20th century, to the exurbs beyond the inner suburbs. The fast-rising cost of housing in older suburbs has led families to buy homes and build lives ever farther from the metropolitan core. Inevitably this has had consequences for suburban community.

Because commuting can occupy upward of 4 hours a day, not only does membership in social organizations and coaching in children's sports leagues

become less feasible; more parents are not seeing their children (for whom the move to exurbia was made) awake during the week. One new suburbanite, Lou Friscella, moved with his family from Staten Island in New York City to Pennsylvania's Lehigh Valley in 2002. Friscella leaves for his job as a computer network engineer in Manhattan each morning at 6:15 a.m. and returns home after his three children are in bed. But neither Friscella nor his wife, Stephanie, expressed discontent with their decision to relocate. They came to the suburbs for open space and good schools, not for a 1950s version of suburban community.

Equally noteworthy is the rise of new suburban subdivisions in the South and West, in places like Douglas County, Colorado (located between Denver and Colorado Springs); Henderson County, Nevada, just outside Las Vegas; Loudon County, Virginia; Gwinnett County, Georgia; Scottsdale, Arizona; and Union County, North Carolina. These places and others like them are growing rapidly. They highlight the new dynamic of suburban community, which is placing paramount emphasis on the home as haven and showcase, personal comforts, and individual freedom.

These new suburban communities are more dependent on automobiles than traditional suburbs ever were. Cutting through the landscapes of these communities are broad commercial thoroughfares—often accommodating six lanes of traffic—with two-tier big-box malls on either side. Common spaces, where casual contacts resulting from pedestrian traffic and face-to-face interaction through organizations are the glue of a community, have yielded to a more individualistic, auto-dominated subculture.

Yet there is no single trend-line in contemporary suburbia. For two decades, an alternative, *New Urbanist* concept for reenvisioning suburbia has gained increasing attention among planners and developers. The premise of this New Urbanism is that given a choice, home buyers will prefer living in a mixed-use, pedestrian-friendly environment where family members can walk to schools, shopping, church, doctors, and recreational facilities. Seaside, Florida, was designed with this vision in mind. More successful as a concept than as a community, it nonetheless has served as a model for such successful planned suburbs as Kentlands in Gaithersburg, Maryland, and Celebration, Florida, among others.

If new suburban communities have outpaced the popularity of new urbanist designs, it is also fair to say that frequent job relocation and lack of time rather than the lack of will has attenuated community or redefined suburban community life. In the universe of urban sprawl, community is engaged in two primary ways: first, through stay-at-home parents who embrace community projects and local volunteer work (often with the aid of the Internet), and second, in virtual communities. In subdivisions where people do not mow their own lawns or have time for coffee klatches with neighbors, listserves and Internet chat rooms provide a measure of interaction and intimacy. Residents post pictures of their children and information about themselves on Web sites; many individuals engage in conversations on topics ranging from child rearing to politics, some of which doubtless mature into personal connections, face-to-face. How viable such community can or will be compared to traditional recreational, church, and service-based activity remains unclear. A community in which breadwinners are spending so much time on the road that they cannot join the PTA or coach a sports team is a community with pieces missing.

Americans seeking the good life in suburbia have consistently valued freedom as a primary priority. But satisfied suburbanites have always cited "community" as a major reason for their sense of well-being. Even the desperate housewives of Wisteria Lane have forged a meaningful community. It's a marked distance from John Adams chortling over the size of his manure pile in Braintree, Massachusetts, in 1800, but at least the neighbors are talking.

—*Michael J. Birkner*

See also Family in Cities and Suburbs

Further Readings and References

Baxandall, R., & Ewen, E. (2000). *Picture windows: How the suburbs happened.* New York: Basic Books.

Duany, A., Plater-Zyberk, E., & Speck, J. (2000). *Suburban nation: The rise of sprawl and the decline of the American dream.* New York: North Point Press.

Fishman, R. (1987). *Bourgeois utopias: The rise and fall of suburbia.* New York: Basic Books.

Gans, H. (1967). *The Levittowners: Ways of life and politics in a new suburban community.* New York: Pantheon.

Lindstrom, M. J., & Bartling, H. (Eds.). (2003). *Suburban sprawl: Culture, theory and politics.* New York: Rowman and Littlefield.

Putnam, R. D. (2000). *Bowling alone: The collapse and revival of American community.* New York: Simon & Schuster.

COMMUTING

In the urban context, commuting is characterized by the use of a transportation mode to go back and forth from work to home every day (as between a suburb and a city). The phenomenon of commuting is closely linked with the growth of suburbs in the United States. The word *suburb* refers to an unincorporated area outside of a central city. The growth of suburbs or suburbanization was initially facilitated by the development of zoning laws that allocated business or commercial land use at the center of the city and residential land use along the periphery. In the older cities of the United States, suburbs developed along streetcar lines that could shuttle workers into and out of city centers, where the jobs were located. The development of transportation modes such as streetcars and, later, automobiles and highways allowed middle-class workers to commute to the city from the suburbs.

It is true that suburbanization after World War II was unprecedented in its scale and its use of the personal vehicle as a mode of transportation. However, the postwar period was not the first major suburban movement in the United States. Very early on, railroads built stations in rural villages on the outskirts of large cities. In New York City, commuter travel by rail began as early as 1832. The railroad along Long Island Sound reached New Haven by 1882. Population growth along the railroad tracks was rapid, and by 1898 the ridership on the passenger lines to the north of the city was more than 100,000 daily commuters. Growth in ridership in railroads happened in other cities as well. By 1900, railroad commuting was well established in Philadelphia, Boston, and Chicago. Compared to other forms of public transportation, steam-based railroad travel was expensive, unlike the horsecar or the electric streetcar.

Sam Bass Warner's *Streetcar Suburbs* in 1978 looked back at the process of suburbanization in Boston between 1870 and 1900. He suggested that suburban growth was made possible by the streetcar. Warner argued that 19th-century suburbanization was spurred on by socioeconomic considerations. The middle class had lived with the lower classes in downtown Boston for centuries. According to Warner, the middle class had three major reasons for fleeing the city by the 1850s. The first reason was the growing immigrant population in Boston, especially of Irish Catholics, which led to representational conflicts with the Protestant majority. The second reason was that these immigrants tended to work in heavy industries that were also usually located in central Boston. The third reason was the rural ideal that was influenced by the urban parks designed by Frederick Law Olmsted. The middle class moved away from the city toward this rural ideal. By 1900, the center of every American city had become an area of office and commercial uses. Close to them were the industrial land uses, and within walking distance were the poor, the unskilled workers, and the recent immigrants. Beyond the walking city were the streetcar suburbs. The relatively wealthy railroad commuters lived in houses that represented the American rural ideal.

Simultaneously, the private automobile became the primary form of transportation in the United States. Led by Henry Ford and his assembly line, American automobile registrations climbed from one million in 1913 to 10 million in 1923. By 1927, when the American total had risen to 26 million, there was one motor vehicle for every five people in the country. This was aided by American federal policy like the Interstate Highway Act of 1956, and by 1991 the United States had the world's best highway system. The mass production of automobiles reinforced by federally aided highway construction meant that by 1970, the real price of both cars and fuel had dropped since the first cars were available to Americans in the early 20th century. Even in 2000, the cost of driving a car was cheaper in the United States than in other advanced nations. Peter Mueller in *Contemporary Suburban America* noted that by opening up the unbuilt areas lying between suburban rail axes, the car allowed real estate developers to build away from the streetcar corridors to the more profitable interstices. The developers were also aided by the creation of the Federal Housing Authority (FHA) to guarantee housing loans. By the 1940s, the suburbs were characterized by a diffuse settlement fabric that was dependent on near total automobility, according to Mueller. After World War II, the federal government approved billions of dollars of mortgage insurance for the FHA. Encouraged by zoning laws and the FHA mortgage insurers that wanted neighborhoods to be good investments, many subdivisions did not allow minority homeowners to buy homes. Suburbs were therefore characterized by racial and socioeconomic homogeneity.

Three period labels can characterize the geographic history of employment within an older American city like Boston, according to Sam Bass Warner in 1999. The first is that of the domination of the sea and rivers, the years from about 1600 to about 1870. The second era was the time of the domination of the railroad and the newly paved streets, roads, and state and U.S. highways, a period spanning from 1870 to 1960. The third era was the time of the limited-access freeways and the new interstate highway network, 1960 to the present. Since 1960, Warner notes, warehouses, factories, office buildings, stores, and malls sprinkle themselves along the rings and spokes of the highway network and take up open land wherever a road offers a convenient connection. Employees in the city now commute all over the metropolitan region, and their employers differ greatly from their predecessors—the factories. This transformation since 1960, Warner suggested, was happening all over North America. In 1991, Joel Garreau called these clusters of jobs along highways *edge cities* because they are usually built on the edge of town, on land that a few decades ago was agricultural or residential in terms of land use.

Richard Harris and Robert Lewis cautioned in 2001 that the geography of employment does not conform to a simple model, and neither do the spatial patterns of residence. They noted that even before World War II, residential suburbs were not affluent. By 1940, they reported, many low-income families lived in the suburbs and not necessarily in the shadow of the mills. By the 1930s, Harris and Lewis suggested, automobiles allowed some workers to scatter into the rural-urban fringe, and this was most common around small- and medium-sized industrial centers such as Eugene, Oregon; Flint, Michigan; Rochester, New York; and Norwich, Connecticut. By 1950, suburbanization was encouraged by but by no means dependent on the decentralization of manufacturing. Harris and Lewis also observe that these trends were true even where women also commuted to work, and more jobs for women were created in fringe areas. By the 1950s, in many suburban areas, women in the labor market had a range of choices. Alan Pisarski noted in 1996 that continued dispersal toward the fringes of American metropolitan areas seems a given for both jobs and population. He suggested that prospects for a reformation in land preferences toward higher densities are limited but have several avenues of potential development. The first is that as the population ages, there may be greater interest in higher density clusters, where walking is convenient. Developers, he noted, have responded to these special-interest groups and to the need sensed for new family-oriented communities with greater walking and access opportunities and greater control of vehicles.

Pisarki observed that the future of local nonwork commuting belongs to the car (and to walking in pedestrian malls). The development of shopping malls has been a response to that need for nonwork commuting. The growth of female employees in the workplace has also introduced new patterns in work-based commuting. The need to combine several activities besides work on a trip, or "trip chaining," and the need for work-scheduling flexibility is now integral to work commutes. Flexible commutes allow for variation in arrivals and departures, as well as in the length of workdays. Pisarski also suggested that firms' willingness to be flexible will increase in the future as some skills become even scarcer and firms compete for the best, and that firms will tend to relocate where skilled employees, their scarcest resource, are located. This may, according to Pisarski, tend to push firm locations to where people want to be: higher income neighborhoods. This will probably result in more reverse commuting from the city center to the outer suburbs, or regionally, to and from the outer edges of the metropolitan area or the edge cities. At a national level, he suggests, those areas that are pleasant and attractive to live in, such as the "Sunbelt" states in the South and the West, could become more attractive to urban residents.

—*Sumeeta Srinivasan*

Further Readings and References

Garreau, J. (1991). *Edge city: Life on the new frontier.* New York: Anchor Books.

Harris, R., & Lewis, R. (2001). The geography of North American cities and suburbs, 1900–1950: A new synthesis. *Journal of Urban History, 27,* 262–292.

Mueller, P. (1981). *Contemporary suburban America.* Englewood Cliffs, NJ: Prentice Hall.

Pisarski, A. E. (1996). *Commuting in America II.* Lansdowne, VA: Eno Foundation for Transportation, Inc.

Warner, S. B., Jr. (1978). *Streetcar suburbs.* Cambridge, MA: Harvard University Press.

Warner, S. B., Jr. (1999). Today's Boston: A history. *The Massachusetts Historical Review.* Retrieved June 2005 from www.historycooperative.org/journals/mhr/1/warner.html

COMPANY TOWNS

It is deceptively easy to define a company town as a human settlement built by a single business enterprise in a landscape conveniently located near a mine, forest, or other industry. The company town supports a single company and its employees and typically includes homes, community buildings, and a town store designed to benefit the town's residents, who are themselves the company's workers. A simple formula enough, but an infinite variety of towns resulted during the 19th and early 20th centuries. Each company town was an expression of a particular set of company needs, a particular environment, and a unique population of workers.

The descriptor *company town* was first used in the late 19th century to describe the mining camps and accompanying smelters located in the Appalachian and Monongahela Valley region. But quickly, the term took hold as a perfect way of describing a particular approach to mobilizing and attracting workers, in some cases to exploiting and manipulating the interests of employees in an environmental way or physical setting. Related in ways to capitalism and the market economy, company towns flourished where industry drove the extraction of raw materials and the production of mass goods for sale in national markets.

Company towns arose in part out of necessity. For instance, mining companies prospecting in isolated regions of mountainous areas were forced to build housing to lure miners to the site. Because the land itself held the same promise of riches beyond surface view, the company retained ownership of the land and instead housed workers as part of their compensation. Company towns were dependent in every way on resource sites, whether for the material that was extracted or for water that would power the company mill, or to provide resources to sustain the resident population and the company itself. Once a company had a critical number of workers in such settlements, out of necessity they developed other systems to serve their needs. These included other architecture such as community centers or schools, stores, or places for medical care. Beyond the more typical regulations of working in the company industry were community regulations or rules and ordinances that governed the ways the workers related to each other in the context of the company town.

Local cultures emerged from the unique combination of ethnic immigrant workers or those from particular social classes who tended to migrate toward such work settings. The hierarchies relative to positions in the company or work-related tasks created equivalent hierarchies in the community beyond the work setting. Mining towns were critical to the expansion of the mining and eventually lumbering industries of the United States and participated in the movement into the western frontier and settlement of the West.

Besides basic housing and recreational facilities, the company town typically operated, again as part of the business, a store and sometimes a hotel or hospital. Regardless of the variety in the formula, everything in the company town was subordinate to the company itself. Workers purchased goods based on credit or through a scrip system. Leading in some cases to widespread exploitation and oppression, in others the company operated such enterprises in ways designed to support workers.

Although it was not necessarily part of the initial formula, the best company towns seem to demonstrate significant paternalism, in which company owners or managers worked to create not only appropriate or adequate work environments but opportunities for enrichment and education. An acknowledgment of the impact of the physical environment on one's morals or values embedded in the ideas of environmental determinism stimulated interest in experiments in social engineering and landscape planning. The work of social reformers such as Ebenezer Howard influenced these experiments and fueled a paternalism that assumed that taking the urban poor out of the city and giving them the "opportunity" to work in an enlightened company town would give them a better life.

While it is true that some company towns arose spontaneously or haphazardly, others were carefully planned. Obviously, in mountainous regions where lumber towns or mining towns were laid out and developed, geography dictated the end result. In planned communities, the town typically revolved around a focal point or town center where the store, the school, or community hall were located. Houses or residential sections of town were arranged around this central point, which identified or represented the collective of the company itself.

Frequently, in such towns, the architecture exhibited a sameness. When you come upon a company town in the American landscape, you know that you have arrived someplace different. The company and the total orientation toward company interests form this difference. These towns were typically small and compact, with total populations rarely exceeding a few thousand.

Perhaps the most famous company town was Pullman, Illinois, built first in 1880 by George Pullman for railway workers. Seizing public attention in 1894, the Pullman Strike of the American Railway Union, led by Eugene V. Debs, brought the plight of the car builders who lived at Pullman into national focus. The national depression of 1893 resulted in significant layoffs and reduced work schedules at Pullman, but requirements for rents or payments for purchases at the company store did not stop. Workers were pressed into an impossible situation and organized in a strike to demand a response. One result was that the town was annexed by Chicago and dissolved its special corporate nature. Earlier, Pullman had been applauded as better than most industrial company towns for its generous expenditures reserved for gas and lighting, water, and garbage and sewage removal, equivalent to even the most luxurious suburbs of Chicago. The park at the town center complete with streetlights, park benches, and grassy parkways eventually became a scene of crime, vandalism, and urban decay. Its original innovative vision was nothing more than a memory floating in the wind.

In total, company towns and the housing and lifestyle they provided employees formed a powerful bond between workers and company owners. Based on a significant and powerful investment in real estate, architecture, and systems, in some cases the company town was the embodiment of belief and theory, and in others an opportunity to maximize profits and exploit workers powerless to defend themselves against the dark side of American capitalism, an urban experiment in the landscape of industrialization.

—*Martha Bradley*

See also Howard, Ebenezer; Pullman, Illinois

Further Readings and References

Allen, J. B. (1966). *The company town in the American West.* Norman, OK: University of Oklahoma Press.

Garner, J. S. (1992). *The company town: Architecture and society in the early Industrial Age.* New York: Oxford University Press.

CONCENTRIC ZONE MODEL

The concentric zone model is a highly influential representation of urban form and residential segregation. Formulated by the Chicago sociologist Ernest Burgess in a 1925 paper, the model is both a description and an explanation of the changing social geography of the modern American city. The concentric zone model was probably the first systematic overview of the internal structure of the modern industrial metropolis. Despite deep flaws, the model remains one of the most enduring academic expressions of the form of the American city.

Burgess made two major claims. First, he argued that the metropolitan area (which he called the city) was laid out in a series of zones that rippled out from the central core to the edge of the built-up environs. At the center was the "Loop," or central business district (CBD), the home of the city's main financial, civic, retail, and entertainment functions. This was surrounded in succession by a "zone of transition," occupied by an assortment of immigrants, migratory workers, and bohemians as well as warehouses and light manufacture; a "zone of workingmen's homes," where second-generation immigrants and blue-collar workers lived in close proximity to work; a "residential zone," where the middle class resided in well-to-do apartments and residential districts; and a "commuters' zone," the district of suburban areas and satellite cities outside the city proper.

Second, Burgess claimed that these social and geographical zones could be explained through the theory of social ecology. Deploying ideas taken from plant and human biology, he argued that the internal structure of the modern city formed out of the residential shifting and sorting of people by ethnicity, race, and occupation. Rooted in a particular version of social Darwinism, Burgess argued that urban-ecological change resulted from competitive succession, a process involving the expansion of one zone by the invasion of the occupants of the next zone. These ecological patterns were reinforced by the metabolic processes of social organization and disorganization, the antagonistic yet complementary processes of concentration and decentralization, and the social division of labor. Together, these processes formed a dynamic model of shifting and sorting by natural area and by zone and established the basis for differentiated economic and cultural groupings by space. They established the basis for residential segregation, the defining geographic feature of the modern city.

Burgess's views on the social ecology of the city were framed at the University of Chicago and in Chicago itself. Burgess learned his trade and developed his ideas in what was America's leading sociology department between 1915 and 1940. He was plugged into an exciting and vibrant environment at the university. The department was the home of several leading sociologists, such as Robert Park, who collaborated with Burgess to develop new theories and research questions. Department faculty and graduate students worked collaboratively, forming strong ties with the university's other social scientists such as George Herbert Mead and with Chicago social reformers and politicians such as Jane Addams. The result was that Burgess was able to blend theory, empirical research, and a concern with pressing social issues to create a particular style of sociological inquiry and a distinctive research agenda.

At the same time, Chicago itself was a laboratory where Burgess formulated and tested his ideas about urban society. A rapidly expanding urban place, Chicago grew from a small town on the eve of the Civil War to the second largest city in the United States by 1890. With a population of more than three million by 1930, the city contained a diverse population, a gigantic and dynamic industrial economy, and a tremendously segregated and unequal society. It was in this milieu that Burgess, as both an academic and a social reformer, sought to map and change the city.

Paradoxically, the zonal model's power lay in the very aspects that made it problematic as a model of sociographical patterning and as a theoretical construct. In the first place, it has endured as a model of urban reality despite the fact that it was empirically selective. Missing from the Chicago case, for example, were affluent downtown districts (the Gold Coast), factory districts that cut through zones (along the two branches of the Chicago River) and developed as nodes on the urban fringe (South Chicago, Pullman, Cicero, and Gary), and the socially mixed country towns (Blue Island) and satellite cities (Joliet, Aurora, and Elgin). Despite these empirical weaknesses, the model captured a sufficient number of significant sociogeographical elements—the CBD, ghetto, Little Sicily, and middle-class bungalow section, to name just a few—to convince many that it was a realistic mapping of the modern metropolis. The very divisions that were everyday for people were there on the map. Even though the model was criticized from the beginning, successive generations of scholars reread the text and the maps and found the model relevant for their understanding of the social groupings within the metropolis. Regardless of the actual empirical precision of the model, its simplicity rang true for succeeding bodies of social scientists. It made sense.

Second, the concentric zone model made a powerful argument about the relationship of urban space to social class, social mobility, and assimilation. Burgess linked social characteristics (class, race, and ethnicity) to geographical elements (zones and natural areas) along a social gradient leading out from the CBD. The composition of the metropolis changed as one moved out from the Loop. The lower classes, unassimilated immigrants, artists, and the young and the restless, lived in the slums, badlands, submerged regions, immigrant colonies, and underworlds of the zone of transition. The respectable, settled, and second-generation immigrant lived in the adjacent zone. As Burgess wrote in 1925, this zone of workingmen's homes was the first spatial step up the social ladder for those who had escaped the deteriorating districts of the zone of transition and who wanted access to the standards of living promised by the American way of life. The next two zones, the residential and com-muters', were the home of restricted neighborhoods and bungalows where the assimilated well-to-do American resided. Burgess was quite clear about the relationship among physical distance, social distance, and urban form. In the concentric model, assimilation, social class, and social mobility were geographically embodied in the very fabric of the city.

Third, despite its determinism, the social ecological vision of city form that Burgess constructed was rooted in a strong and dynamic body of ideas. Even though the theoretical underpinnings of human ecology have undergone significant change during the past 100 years, it has remained a vital element of the social sciences. In his elaboration of the concentric model, Burgess deployed midrange theories that have managed to maintain a place in the explanation of urban change. Despite their faults, concepts such as filtering (the passing down of housing to the working class by the middle class as they move farther out from the core) continue to play a part in the elabora-tion of neighborhood change and residential segrega-tion. Burgess's ideas also were deeply rooted in the writings of an impressive body of scholars, such as Charles Horton Cooley, Max Weber, William Thomas, Émile Durkheim, and, most important, Georg Simmel, whose ideas about social change continue to hold sway over social scientists. Finally, the linking of the social division of labor and social disorganization, organization and differentiation with processes of suc-cession, concentration, and decentralization form the basis for a flawed yet dynamic theory that appeals to scholars from a variety of disciplinary backgrounds.

Despite all of the model's problems, both as a map and as an explanatory framework for understanding urban change, it remains an important, influential, and foundational text for social scientists interested in the modern metropolis. Ideas about boundaries separating different economic and social groups and the internal dynamics of neighborhoods continue to play a central role in the understanding of the city, in both its historic and its contemporary forms. The social-geographic gradient, with the poor and immigrants trapped in the central city and the wealthy living in the suburbs, continues to be a well-accepted descriptor of the American city, especially before the supposed mass suburbanization of white, blue-collar workers after World War II. The simplistic and determinist ecologi-cal theory used by Burgess and his colleagues at the University of Chicago sociology department has been modified and used by a variety of scholars working on the historical, geographical, and sociological charac-ter of the modern metropolis.

—Robert Lewis

Further Readings and References

Alihan, M. (1938). *Social ecology: A critical analysis.* New York: Columbia University Press.

Bulmer, M. (1984). *The Chicago school of sociology: Institutionalization, diversity and the rise of sociological research.* Chicago: University of Chicago Press.

Burgess, E. (1925). The growth of the city: An introduction to a research project. In R. Park, E. Burgess, & R. McKenzie (Eds.), *The city* (pp. 47–62). Chicago: University of Chicago Press.

Burgess, E. (1928). Residential segregation in American cities. *Annals of the American Academy of Political and Social Science, 140,* 105–115.

Harris, R., & Lewis, R. (1998). Constructing a fault(y) zone: Misrepresentations of American cities and suburbs, 1900–1950. *Annals of the Association of American Geographers, 88,* 622–639.

CONEY ISLAND

Located in New York City, Coney Island is a four-mile-long and one-half-mile-wide peninsula occupy-ing the southern end of the borough of Brooklyn, nine miles from Manhattan. The neighborhoods of Brighton Beach and Manhattan Beach are on the east-ern end of the island, with the neighborhoods of Coney Island proper and Sea Gate on the island's western end. Synonymous with its amusement areas and beach, the neighborhood of Coney Island was a very popular resort town from the middle of the 19th century to the era immediately following World War II. The three original large amusement parks of Coney Island—Steeplechase (1897), Luna Park (1903), and Dreamland (1904)—are icons of early-20th-century popular culture, luring millions of New Yorkers away from their relatively mundane existence with the promise of thrills at the end of the subway line. Indeed, the importance of Coney Island to the development of 20th-century urban America cannot be underestimated, since it was there that the first true amusement parks were built.

During the early 19th century, Coney Island was a sleepy resort area that attracted wealthier New Yorkers eager to remove themselves from the busy, crowded streets of Manhattan to the relatively peaceful enclave of the seashore. Prior to the Civil War, vacationers on weekend getaways arrived by steamboat from Manhattan and stayed at the Coney Island House, a centrally located hotel. However, it was also during this period that Norton's Point, on the western end, became a magnet for, as written by J. F. Kasson, a host of con men and other such hustlers who preyed on the unsuspecting outside the surveillance of New York law-enforcement officials. After the Civil War, the island changed dramatically as developers and speculators invested heavily in Coney real estate, establishing Brighton Beach and Manhattan Beach as respectable alternatives to the old Coney Island proper. Developers even renamed the original Coney section of the island as West Brighton to attract an upscale clientele, although this renaming did not last very long.

One of the most important hotel landmarks, The Elephant, built in 1882, brought many visitors to the area, and the term "seeing the elephant" became a euphemism for the pleasures that visiting the island brought to visitors, as noted by Kasson. It was behind The Elephant Hotel that Paul Boyton opened the world's first outdoor amusement park, Sea Lion Park, in 1895. While modest by future Coney standards, Boyton pioneered the idea of enclosing the amusement area and charging an admission at the gate, a feature that continues to distinguish the amusement park from midway, carnival, and boardwalk rides.

The transformation of Coney Island from seaside resort to amusement destination during the late 19th century was a result of the seaside area becoming accessible by the Coney Island and Brooklyn Railroad, which reached the island in the 1870s along with a variety of steamboat and ferryboat lines. While the Brooklyn Bridge had connected Brooklyn and Manhattan in 1883, it was the introduction of the nickel fare on the trolley in 1895 that brought the masses from Manhattan and other points to the island. Finally, the subway extended to Coney Island in 1920, although New Yorkers had been making day excursions for decades by that time.

While new forms of mass transportation certainly encouraged more visitors to Coney Island, the trolley companies wanted a fuller return on their investments, and for this, they turned to the new amusement parks. Indeed, if city people had a reason to ride the rails seven days a week, the trolley companies would increase their profits (Nasaw, 1993, p. 80). The first grand amusement park, Steeplechase Park, built by George C. Tilyou and opened in 1897, featured the slogan "Steeplechase—Funny Place" and had a large, maniacally smiling face as its symbol, one that became synonymous with Coney Island for millions of Americans. Tilyou realized that people came to his amusement park to be relieved of their everyday concerns and to forget their roles in the everyday world of work and home.

It was, however, the creation of Luna Park in 1903 by Frederic Thompson and Skip Dundy, two former partners of Tilyou, that transformed the amusement park into what David Nasaw noted as an artificial resort base teeming with excess. Built on the grounds of the former Sea Lion Park, Luna was transformed at night into a fairyland illuminated by 250,000 electric bulbs, enchanting visitors with its exotic and ornate architecture.

Finally, there was the creation of Dreamland in 1904, located directly across from Luna Park on Surf Avenue, by a group of politicians led by William H. Reynolds. Dreamland outdid Luna in every aspect, from its million lights to more disaster spectacles, such as "Fighting the Flames," a live-action fire complete with real firefighters, all for the delight of the spectator. This would prove to be an unfortunate harbinger of things to come, as Dreamland, the grandest of the three large parks, burned to the ground in 1911, never to be rebuilt. Steeplechase Park also burned in 1907, as did Luna Park in the 1940s. Steeplechase was rebuilt in 1908 and remained open until 1964, the last vestige of Coney's glory days.

In the post–World War II era, Coney Island went through a period of decline, as New York City Parks Commissioner Robert Moses discouraged the expansion of amusement parks. Instead, Moses and others in city government built low- and moderate-income housing projects on ground once occupied by the grand parks. During New York City's fiscal crisis of the 1970s, the area seemed destined to be in a permanent state of decline.

Currently, however, Coney Island has rebounded as a resort area, with renewed interest from the city, historic preservationists, and the public, who are returning to the concessions and rides. Its attractions include AstroLand, featuring the Cyclone, a 1927 roller coaster; Nathan's Hot Dogs; a large boardwalk with concessions; freak shows; the annual Mermaid Parade held in June; the Wonder Wheel, a 1920 Ferris wheel; and the Cyclones, a minor-league baseball team in the New York Mets system.

—*Robert Armstrong*

Further Readings and References

Kasson, J. F. (1978). *Amusing the million: Coney Island at the turn of the century.* New York: Hill and Wang.

Nasaw, D. (1993). *Going out: The rise and fall of public amusements.* New York: Basic Books.

Peiss, K. (1986). *Cheap amusements: Working women and leisure in turn-of-the-century New York.* Philadelphia: Temple University Press.

CONGESTION

Congestion, directly related to density and commerce, is inherent to cities. For most of American history, slow-moving traffic on city streets, whether composed of pedestrians, horse-driven vehicles, streetcars, buses, private automobiles, or some combination thereof, has been seen as a major urban problem. Not only is traffic congestion frustrating to travelers and commuters, it can slow or inhibit commerce, limit development, and contribute to pollution. Ports, waterways, and airports also have faced frequent congestion, which often has been met with immense public investments in infrastructure and innovations in government. However, congestion always has positive connotations as well, indicative of a healthy urban economy and the hallmark of vibrant business districts. In recent decades, many planners and policymakers have focused on the positive side of congestion, even cultivating it as a means of influencing public-transportation choices.

Congestion arose in the United States along with the first cities. Urban streets, freely used as marketplaces, playgrounds, political forums, and parade routes, would seem crowded, chaotic, and dangerous to modern observers. Pedestrians confronted equestrians and teamsters on dirty and crowded urban streets, and fatalities were not unusual; early subway projects in Boston and New York enjoyed the overwhelming support of a frustrated public. American cities generally confronted congestion by expanding infrastructure, granting generous franchises and subsidies to private companies willing to invest in bridges, roads, and streetcars, which ultimately allowed for growth, development, and more traffic. Progressive Era support for public enterprise led to direct action by cities; San Francisco established the first municipal railway in the country in 1900.

Intercity traffic congestion also generated public responses; heavy use on the Erie Canal inspired a plethora of public canal-building projects in the 1830s. Regulating, coordinating, and maximizing traffic in American seaports were major concerns that led to the creation of powerful port boards and commissions in the 19th century and the influential Port Authority of New York and New Jersey in 1921. Today, many of the governmental entities that operate airports, public bus and rapid transit systems, and bridges and toll roads are modeled after this agency.

The rapid adoption of the automobile in the early 20th century caused an unprecedented crisis of congestion on city streets, which was very costly to modify. Motorists could and did take advantage of every space available to get through dense neighborhoods, endangering pedestrians, spooking horses, blocking and cutting off streetcars on fixed tracks, and parking haphazardly.

By the 1920s, it was common for pedestrians to move faster than automobiles in American downtowns during rush hour. As the problem grew, motorists themselves took action to relieve congestion, reduce accidents and confrontations, and prevent gridlock. Standardized systems of traffic laws and signals had been adopted nationwide by the 1930s, designed by professional traffic engineers and promoted by private auto clubs and motorists' associations.

Cities also responded by transforming city streets to accommodate the automobile at the expense of mass transportation. Streetcars were increasingly unreliable, uncomfortable, unpopular, and unprofitable. Automobiles were seen as the harbinger of progress, and boosters boasted of high per-capita automobile registrations as a measure of status and prosperity. Around the country, rails were removed, streets were widened, and parking facilities constructed at considerable public expense. Sidewalks became more common, and street activities were conscribed and segregated.

During the middle decades of the 20th century, planners and developers sought to ease traffic pressure by decentralizing population; widespread automobile ownership made large, low-density suburbs possible. Suburban life would be healthier and more convenient, they argued, removed from the crowds and filth of inner cities. However, congestion did not subside; rather, it changed and expanded. In Eastern cities such as Boston, the design of narrow, winding streets built primarily for pedestrians were frequently blamed for traffic congestion. The experience of many Western cities that were custom-built for the private automobile demonstrates that congestion is not necessarily an engineering or infrastructure problem. Wide streets and ample parking did nothing to alleviate the ubiquitous post–World War II traffic dilemma: peak-hour congestion. In the 1950s and 1960s, road and freeway building boomed with ample state and federal funding, based on the expectations of high-speed travel through and between cities. However, suburban developers followed the paths of highway engineers, and right on their heels came more cars, more congestion, air pollution, and public frustration.

The continued reality of urban and suburban congestion propelled several important movements in the late 20th century. Awareness of the environmental and aesthetic consequences of suburbanization, as well as unpleasant daily commutes, helped make environmentalism and the open-space movement powerful political forces in the 1970s. Starting in San Francisco in 1959, popular protest against the endless cycle of infrastructure and traffic resulted in freeway revolts across the country. Large-scale mass-transportation projects enjoyed enormous political support, as light rail took the place of previous streetcar systems. Traffic congestion also sparked movement of population and capital investment from suburbs back into inner cities starting in the 1980s, increasing property values and reversing economic decline. Interest in limiting traffic supported a new generation of planners interested in promoting density, mixed-use development, and mass transportation. By the end of the 20th century, slow-moving traffic and limited parking were seen more often as a boon to urban neighborhoods than a problem.

—*Louise Nelson Dyble*

Further Readings and References

Barrett, P. (1983). *The automobile and urban transit: The formation of public policy in Chicago, 1900–1930.* Philadelphia: Temple University Press.

Bottles, S. L. (1987). *Los Angeles and the automobile: The making of the modern city.* Berkeley, CA: University of California Press.

Fogleson, R. M. (2001). *Downtown: Its rise and fall, 1880–1950.* New Haven, CT: Yale University Press.

Foster, M. S. (1981). *From streetcar to superhighway: American city planners and urban transportation, 1900–1940.* Philadelphia: Temple University Press.

McShane, C. (1999). The origins and globalization of traffic control signals. *Journal of Urban History, 25,* 379–404.

Ryan, M. P. (1997). *Civic wars: Democracy and public life in the American city during the 19th century.* Berkeley, CA: University of California Press.

Taylor, G. R. (1951). *The transportation revolution, 1815–1860.* New York: Rinehart.

Weinstein, A. (2002). *The congestion evil: Perceptions of traffic congestion in Boston in the 1890s and 1920s.* Doctoral dissertation, University of California, Berkeley.

CONSERVATISM

In the earlier days of the American Republic—and largely until the present day—the cities played the more radical or liberal part, with the countryside the more conservative. Certainly during the push westward in the 19th century, towns and the laws they produced (or that produced them) were a conservative influence against the frontier and farmer or prairie radicalism—or at the very least represented a society rooted in law against the rootlessness of the frontier. (See, for example, some of the early mining laws and town codes in early mining towns, edited by Nolie S. Mumey.) Societies, as J. G. A. Pocock wrote, exist in time and conserve images of themselves as continuously so existing. An essential feature of society is tradition, meaning the handing on of formed ways of acting—tradition being immemorial, prescriptive, and presumptive. What stands outside tradition is charismatic, whether postulating timeless existence or sacred origin (which includes creative origin). All classical (as opposed to romantic) social systems are of this traditionalist sort. Note that cities in the first push westward were formed on classical models—Cincinnati is an example, with (even) a classical name.

Because societies necessarily—in order to be societies—conserve images of themselves as existing (and acting in a certain way) *nemo meminisse contradicente*, there is conservatism in the very idea of a society. Societies conserve tradition and are thus conservative, even if the tradition they conserve is not a conservative tradition. In fact, already existing cities, or parts of cities, may preserve a radical tradition, as against the conservative tradition of the countryside. But new classically planned cities—and perhaps especially new towns, and most especially in the American 19th-century West and Midwest—may be considered as playing a conservative part for the creation of order. The political descendants of the town founders in those areas in that century were the backbone of the Republican Old Right up to the 1920s. In parts of Kansas, for example, the farmers (many of them Populists) were often more radical than the townsmen (many of them Republicans).

In the 1920s and 1930s came the new (and anti-Communist) conservatism of the Southern Agrarians, whose name explains itself. The first Agrarian manifesto was essentially, as one might expect, Agrarian—the second was anti-Communist. But the word *conservatism* was not the key here. The use of the words *conservative* and *conservatism* to represent a certain "individualist" (and anti-Communist, anti-liberal) line of thought connected with the name of William F. Buckley Jr. comes in part from the influence of Russell Kirk and his study *The Conservative Mind* (1953)—even, indeed, before it was published. The archetypical publication for the American (U.S.) Conservative Movement for the years from 1955 to the present has been Buckley's *National Review*, published from 150 East 35th Street in Manhattan, with its biweekly editorial luncheons at a restaurant at Lexington Avenue and 34th Street. For much of that time Buckley maintained a home on the East Side of Manhattan.

But with the exception of his sister Priscilla—the managing editor, with reporting experience in Paris—and Suzanne LaFollette, who grew up in Washington, D.C., where her father was a congressman (not from Wisconsin!), it is noteworthy that most of the editors were self-exiled to the countryside, sometimes to isolation in the countryside. Frank S. Meyer (1909–1972), former Communist organizer in London and Chicago, lived on a mountaintop (Ohayo Mountain) in Woodstock, New York. James Burnham (1905–1987), a former Trotskyite in New York, was off in the wilds of Connecticut. Russell Kirk fled the "city" (!) of Lansing, Michigan, to be the Sage of Mecosta, Michigan. Whittaker Chambers lived in the remotest parts of

Maryland. The Europeans such as Willi Schlamm and Erik von Kuehnelt-Leddihn had not fled the cities, but then European cities were not linked to modernity (or even radicalism), as U.S. cities were. If one founds a magazine dedicated to standing athwart the course of history and shouting "Stop!"—then one is unlikely to be promoting cities or urban life or values.

One other complicating factor here lies in the support of anti-Communism by Boston and other city Irish. Quite probably, if *National Review* had not been located in New York, and if the Buckley family had not been (Roman) Catholic Irish, the American conservative movement during the past 50 years would have been even more agrarian and less urban than it has been. Towns and even smaller cities in the West and Midwest have remained relatively conservative (as Sinclair Lewis protested in *Babbitt* and elsewhere), but the cities, even those classically founded (such as Cincinnati), have become less so. It remains to be seen whether the separation between conservatism and the urban environment can be narrowed. There is an interesting 40-year-old document on the separation in William F. Buckley Jr.'s *The Unmaking of a Mayor* (1965), but in general the only parts of American 20th-century conservatism with an urban tinge are libertarianism on the one hand and neoconservatism on the other, both with city origins or at least breeding grounds.

One other strand in American conservatism might be noted here—what is sometimes called business conservatism. The American Enterprise Institute (AEI), founded in Washington, D.C., in 1943, was originally conservative and business-oriented. It is now the American Enterprise Institute for Public Policy Research, with its "business" and almost "Chamber of Commerce" origins pretty much forgotten. But even though it still has business connections—officers and fellows have included Paul O'Neill and Richard Cheney—and although it is located in northwest Washington, and although business growth is historically connected with urban growth, the AEI is only minimally concerned with urban issues. Even the conservative Manhattan Institute (in Manhattan, as one would expect, founded with Rite-Aid money) is not especially an institute for studying the problems of Manhattan or cities in general, and it reflects no connection between business and conurbation.

—*Jared Lobdell*

See also Cincinnati, Ohio

Further Readings and References

Buckley, W. F., Jr. (1955). *Up from liberalism*. New York: McDowell, Obolensky.

Buckley, W. F., Jr. (1961). *Odyssey of a friend: Letters of Whittaker Chambers to William F. Buckley Jr., 1954–1961*. Chicago: Regnery.

Burnham, J. (1967). *The war we are in*. New Rochelle, NY: Arlington House.

Kirk, R. (1953). *The conservative mind*. Chicago: Regnery.

Meyer, F. S. (1967). *The conservative mainstream*. New Rochelle, NY: Arlington House.

Pocock, J. G. A. (1989). *Politics, language, and time*. New York: Athaneum.

Wade, R. (1953). *The urban frontier*. Chicago: University of Chicago Press.

CONSOLIDATION

In recent years, as state and federal funding for municipal governments has declined and calls for greater efficiency in government services have increased, the prospect of municipal "city-county" consolidation has grown more attractive. *Consolidation* is the restructuring of municipal governance by eliminating the structural boundaries between city and regional (county-level) government. The argument for consolidation is simple: A large metropolitan area can function more efficiently if control of social services, planning, and public safety are centralized in a single government rather than having the urban core and the county governments providing duplicate services and arguing over jurisdiction over the same areas of governance. Unlike annexation, in which one body absorbs another under its control, city-county consolidation theoretically fuses two separate governments in a single, new body. Most efforts at consolidation have targeted rapidly growing, midsize communities in the West, South, or Sunbelt regions of the United States that have experienced an accelerated development of urban or suburban communities.

Although most efforts at city-county consolidation occurred in the United States after the urban/suburban expansion following World War II, the notion of consolidation itself is rooted in late-19th-century progressivism and attempts to reform the inefficiency (and corruption) of city governments. Progressive reformers saw the benefit of city-county consolidation as laying in the expansion of public power to regulate the actions of government and check for corruption in crowded urban settlements. Even with such a glowing ideal, the actual practical application of city-county consolidation was an extremely unusual phenomenon until the second half of the 20th century, and even then, it was governed by a complicated and often unsuccessful political and legal process. In recent history, most attempts at consolidation have originated as acts of city and county government via local referenda rather than from state legislative action. Given the more volatile nature of the referendum, less than 25 percent of measures seeking approval since 1945 have been approved and survived legal challenges. The most successful consolidations often incorporate some level of autonomy for outlying, unincorporated areas or isolated, small communities that would be disproportionately burdened by the loss of independent county government.

Since the explosion of suburban development beginning in the 1940s, city-county consolidation has increasingly appeared as an attractive way to aid beleaguered urban centers with increased revenue and popular power brought by suburban regions. Yet, while the consolidation of city and county governments appears appealing structurally and financially in most cases, strong opposition has appeared in most consolidation efforts. Urban denizens, particularly in politically underrepresented minority groups, fear the prospect of losing control over issues of local governance and the political sway won over several decades of successful lobbying efforts. The influence levied over such issues as restructuring urban renewal programs or the distribution (and form) of social service programs would be lost, they argue, to a larger and less invested governing body.

More so than their urban counterparts, suburban communities have demonstrated great reluctance to shoulder the often unwieldy costs of urban social services and infrastructure like police forces, sewer systems, and education. Fittingly, suburban activists have increasingly (and generally, successfully) fought consolidation on the grounds of the loss of local control since the late 1960s, which in turn has sponsored politicians representing these constituencies to oppose any state-level attempt at either consolidation legislation or measures that would help urban governments to achieve the same goal. The distaste for the potential of increased taxes to support areas that are often far from proximate to their own homes or reflective of their own needs generally disposes suburbanites against consolidation, further compounded by the fear that city residents will gain control of zoning and development throughout the county. Such control, often cited by opponents of consolidation as a source of sprawl and poor development, would in the eyes of these activists diminish the quality of life for citizens in suburban and rural communities and given them little voice (relative to the large number of city dwellers) in matters of local interest.

Indeed, efforts at consolidation have also sparked opposition in more recent history because of the dilution in power held by smaller suburban or rural communities in the most outlying areas of a particular county or regional bloc. Such communities, historically autonomous and often built with an identity in direct opposition to that of the metropol, see consolidation as a meddling force that would not only rob community members of local jurisdiction in terms of development, but also strip away the identity of a region in favor of the new, larger whole. Separate county-level governments often allot local jurisdiction, particularly over issues of planning, to smaller incorporated areas while prioritizing services for unincorporated areas, as larger communities are assumed to have the resources to institute such services for themselves. Ironically, community leaders involved in such opposition often cite the less advantageous position such communities would occupy in terms of spurring commercial or residential development, which is of course the process these communities cite as being accelerated by the loss of local autonomy.

Movements toward city-county consolidation increased during the last two decades of the 20th century, responding not only to increased metropolitan sprawl, but also to the fiscal pressures created by the demand for social services in large urban areas. Yet, even as successful examples of regional consolidation have appeared across the globe, especially in Japan and Australia, American efforts still face considerable obstacles toward achieving the goals first envisioned by progressives at the end of the 19th century. Certainly, debates over consolidation demonstrate the complex nature of urban, suburban, and rural governance in an increasingly developed and divided American landscape.

—*Kyle M. Livie*

See also Annexation

Further Readings and References

Campbell, R. W., & Selden, S. C. (2000). Does city-county consolidation save money? *Policy Notes, 1*(2). Athens: Carl Vinson Institute of Government, University of Georgia.

Carr, J. B., & Feiock, R. C. (2002). Who becomes involved in city-county consolidations? Findings from county officials in 25 communities. *State and Local Government Review, 34*(2), 78–94.

Carr, J. B., & Feiock, R. C. (Eds.). (2004). *City-county consolidation and its alternatives: Reshaping the local government landscape.* Armonk, NY: M. E. Sharpe.

Kenefake, S. M. (2003, August). City/county consolidation: An idea whose time has come? *Kansas Government Journal,* pp. 1–8.

Savitch, H. V., & Vogel, R. K. (2004). Suburbs without a city: Power and city-county consolidation. *Urban Affairs Review, 39*(6), 758–790.

Teaford, J. C. (1979). *City and suburb: The political fragmentation of metropolitan America, 1850–1970.* Baltimore: Johns Hopkins University Press.

COOLEY, CHARLES HORTON

Charles Horton Cooley (1864-1929) is generally regarded as one of the key founders of social psychology or symbolic interactionism, the most important and lasting original American contribution to sociological theory. From his later work, Cooley's concept of the *looking-glass self* ("I am what I think you think I am") and his articulation of the social significance and aptitude of both "primary groups" and "secondary groups" have had a lasting influence on the study of social relations within and outside of sociology. The distinction between group types as well as the notion of an individual's relation to or affiliation with multiple groups has led to many important studies of urban life. It is the city where interaction between and within "secondary groups" becomes the primary mode of interaction and becomes of greater importance than traditional kinship-based ties indicative of rural or village settlements.

Cooley's earlier work, however, dealt directly with the growth and development of cities and the consequent effects on social organization and interpersonal relations. Battling both physical and mental illness, Cooley spent 7 years working toward a degree in engineering at the University of Michigan in Ann Arbor, where he was born. In 1890, Cooley returned to the University of Michigan for graduate work in political economy and sociology. His doctoral dissertation, entitled "The Theory of Transportation," completed in 1894, was a forbearer to human ecology, in general, and "central-place theory," more specifically. First published in 1894 and republished without revision in a posthumous collection of Cooley's papers in 1930, the dissertation presented Cooley's geographic and topographic theory of urban location, whereby the size and amount of population and wealth needed for a large settlement like a city to exist tend to accumulate at breaks in transportation. The first American cities that obtained populations of 100,000 or more inhabitants were located near large masses of water such as the Atlantic Ocean (e.g., New York, Boston), a river (St. Louis, Pittsburgh), or a lake (e.g., Chicago, Cleveland). Later, landlocked cities grew out of the progression of transportation from waterways to railroads.

Later in his career as a faculty member at the University of Michigan, Cooley wrote about broad subjects such as "human nature" and "social organization." He also conducted a number of ethnographic field-research projects akin to those of his intellectual brethren at the University of Chicago. Cooley's ethnographies included studies of New York's Lower East Side and Jane Addams's Hull-House in Chicago. Through such studies, he developed the method of "sympathetic introspection," a technique intended to help the researcher analyze a social actor's consciousness by putting the researcher in the place of the actor and thereby allowing the researcher to experience the actor's social reality as if he or she were a part of it.

—*Michael Ian Borer*

See also Addams, Jane; Hull-House

Further Readings and References

Cooley, C. H. (1930). *Sociological theory and social research.* New York: Henry Holt.
Coser, L. A. (1977). *Masters of sociological thought: Ideas in historical and social context.* New York: Harcourt.
Reiss, A. J., Jr. (Ed.). (1968). *Cooley and sociological analysis.* Ann Arbor: University of Michigan Press.

COUGHLIN, JOHN JOSEPH

John Joseph Coughlin (August 15, 1860–November 11, 1938), also known as "Bathhouse John," was a legendary Chicago alderman and machine politician, who with Michael "Hinky Dink" Kenna ruled the city's notorious, vice-riddled First Ward for 46 years. Coughlin's appearance and omnipresent cigar were considered the political cartoonist's ideal of a barrel-house alderman. Thick-muscled and tall, Coughlin excelled at rubbing, giving massages to men at community or "Turkish" bathhouses then in vogue in a city with little indoor plumbing. Working and eventually owning a number of his namesakes, he mingled with the city's business and political elite. He later observed that the only difference between Chicago's elite and its lower classes was that one was luckier than the other.

Coughlin became involved in Democratic ward politics beginning in the 1880s. He was considered an honest if not intelligent politician. He won election as First Ward alderman in 1892 and went on to serve a record 46 years on the city council. An informal alliance with Kenna, described as the smartest man in Chicago's saloon business, resulted in a crime syndicate unequaled for its day. Coughlin was the front man, and his outlandish dress and congenial manners made him popular with politicians as well as the public and press.

Vice operations outnumbered legal businesses in the turn-of-the-20th-century downtown First Ward. Beyond a few legitimate businesses such as department stores, the ward's only legal residents were the wealthy living in a lakefront neighborhood, who cared little for local politics, and immigrant slum dwellers who benefitted from the benevolence of their "ward heelers." Kenna and Coughlin organized the First Ward Democratic Club, the first organization of its kind, and began the practice of paying the homeless 50 cents apiece to temporarily live and vote in their ward. With other members of Chicago's so-called city council Gray Wolves, Coughlin used his resulting clout to elect politicians and peddle influence throughout local, county, and state governments.

Reform organizations chided "The Bath" repeatedly for his criminal activities. He never disputed their claims except once when reformers erroneously identified his birthplace as suburban Waukegan. Coughlin retorted that he had been born in Chicago and promised that he would die there, a prediction that proved true. From 1896 until 1909, Coughlin and Kenna hosted an annual campaign fund-raising ball in their ward. The event attracted not only public officials but prostitutes, madams, gamblers, organized-crime figures, and police. The attendees and their dress and behavior eventually led to public outcry and the ball's demise.

Beginning around 1900, Coughlin established an insurance agency. He and his operatives strong-armed the owners of the many vice businesses in his ward into purchasing insurance from his firm, along with the payment of protection money in the form of political contributions. He and Kenna controlled Levee liquor sales, dispensed patronage, and sold property tax abatements to make additional money.

Although Couglin and Kenna were eventually surpassed in influence by more organized crime figures such as "Big" Jim Colosimo and Al Capone, Coughlin was allowed to retain his aldermanic seat until his death in 1938. In his later years, he owned a private zoo in Colorado and more than 60 racing horses, but he died nearly broke. At the time of his death, newspaper accounts estimated that he and Kenna were responsible for as many as 200,000 individual acts of charity during their aldermanic years, providing clothing, money, and jobs for needy constituents. Most occurred in an era before any government welfare.

—Richard Junger

Further Readings and References

Ashbury, H. (2002). *The gangs of Chicago*. New York: Thunder's Mouth Press.
Simpson, D. (2001). *Rogues, rebels, and rubber stamps*. Boulder, CO: Westview Press.
Wendt, L. (1967). *Bosses in lusty Chicago*. Bloomington, IN: Indiana University Press.

COUNTRY CLUBS

Country clubs are private recreational and social organizations, centered around one or more golf courses and located at the fringe of urban areas. They first appeared in the 1880s, founded by upper-class elites, and brought a carefully planned landscape within reach of well-to-do suburbanites. From the outset, membership has been restricted by selective admissions procedures, large initiation fees, and high dues; thus country clubs served as important markers of status for the upper and upper-middle class. Real estate developers sometimes organized country clubs to attract buyers and integrated clubs and homes into a unified plan. Such developments were the forerunners of gated communities of the late 20th century.

Founded in 1882, the Country Club of Brookline, a Boston suburb, is considered the nation's first. Several dozen clubs immediately followed around the largest cities. Early clubs focused primarily on equestrian-related sports: coaching, racing, jumping, polo, and foxhunting. In the 1890s, however, enthusiasm for golf swept the nation and led to hundreds of new clubs. Golf's leisurely pace, association with Britain, nonviolent character, and sense of sportsmanship made it attractive to the upper class. It emphasized patience and skill rather than stamina or sheer strength, and it was much safer than polo. Further, walking the lush fairways reinforced the sense of connection with nature while testing one's skills against it. Members also found a leisurely afternoon of golf an ideal way to build social bonds with clients and customers, and corporations often supported clubs near their headquarters.

By World War I, there were more than 1,000 clubs nationwide, but the 1920s were the golden age of the country club. Estimates place the number of clubs by 1930 at more than 4,000, as they reached into smaller cities and towns and were affordable to more of the middle class.

The country club has always met the social needs of its members well beyond golf. In new suburban areas, country clubs provided a venue that nurtured community identity. Clubs adopted colors, uniforms, and seals that reinforced pride of place and created instant traditions. Further, taking their admissions policies and procedures from downtown businessmen's clubs, country club membership signified and confirmed class status. Multiple clubs appeared early around large cities, and a clear prestige hierarchy emerged. In keeping with the growing caste mentality of the upper class, clubs consistently denied admission to Jews, regardless of background or wealth. Blacks could be found only as caddies and waiters.

Clubhouses, usually converted farmhouses at first, became grand structures often designed by leading architects. The clubhouse usually sat on a hillside overlooking the vast expanse of the verdant and meticulously tended grounds. Members could sit on the veranda, be served by a retinue of uniformed and well-mannered staff, enjoy the sweeping views, and feel they had a piece of an English-landed estate.

The clubs offered recreation for the entire family in which the values and behaviors of class could be reinforced and passed on. In the 1920s, clubs supplemented simpler sports, such as archery, croquet, and ice-skating, with tennis courts and swimming pools. A year-round calendar of social events included card parties, holiday celebrations, dances, and debutante balls. Club golf tournaments for men and women integrated social life with recreation while strengthening the sense of club identification. Further, in such a setting the prospective marriage partners of young adults also could be carefully controlled.

Country clubs opened new opportunities for women while keeping them at a subsidiary status. Golf and tennis allowed women to participate in active sports and to adopt suitable attire, and women's golf tournaments date from the 1890s. Women also organized and controlled most of the clubhouse social calendar. However, clubs offered members' widows and adult single women (when they could join at all) only associate membership without voting privileges. Further, since women were considered slower golfers, they were usually banned from the course on weekends and holidays or were required to allow men to play through. It was not until after court challenges late in the 20th century that women received equal access to all facilities.

The first real estate developer to link an upper-middle-class subdivision with a country club was Edward Bouton, who was a founder of the Baltimore Country Club within his Roland Park subdivision. Bouton made sure his home buyers were the right sort for the club. J. C. Nichols of Kansas City carried the concept further and became the chief promoter and most successful developer to link country club and real estate. In 1908, he acquired 1,000 acres next to the Kansas City Country Club and called it Country Club Estates. During the next 40 years, Nichols developed an entire section of the city. With a combination of detailed restrictive covenants and homeowners' associations to enforce them, he was able to shape and control his developments for upper-middle-class buyers. He was instrumental in relocating the Kansas City Country Club and in founding three more. He sited those clubs as buffer zones to protect his subdivisions. Landscape architects in many places designed subdivisions and country clubs together. Homes were located on the edge of courses, and culs-de-sac were used to generate more house lots.

The Depression hit country clubs hard, and many that were overextended folded. Aggregate membership dropped sharply; clubs cut back on activities and some left part of their course untended. During World War II, the government terminated manufacture of golf balls, which, combined with lack of gasoline and of help, kept the clubs on a restricted schedule.

After the war the stronger clubs revived and new ones were founded, but never again would they so completely dominate golf or suburban social life. The clubs faced competition from public courses and from corporate-sponsored clubs. In 1960 there were about 3,200 clubs nationwide. By 1995 there were 4,300, but there were almost 10,000 municipal or commercial daily-fee courses. In addition, country clubs had to deal with contentious issues of discrimination in admissions and equality for female members. Second homes and long-distance travel cut into country club participation. Offsetting those developments, private clubs continue to dominate ratings of the best and most attractive courses.

In the late 20th century, as the popularity of golf increased, developers took the country club and planned subdivision a step further and created gated communities around courses and clubs. The postwar pioneer was Charles Fraser, whose Sea Pines Plantation at Hilton Head, South Carolina, was widely emulated. Not only is the gated community the successor to the country club in terms of planning, but it meets similar social needs: a sense of community combined with physical security and social superiority.

—Roger D. Simon

Further Readings and References

Mayo, J. M. (1998). *The American country club: Its origins and development.* New Brunswick, NJ: Rutgers University Press.

Moss, R. J. (2001). *Golf and the American country club.* Urbana: University of Illinois Press.

Worley, W. S. (1990). *J. C. Nichols and the shaping of Kansas City: Innovation in planned residential communities.* Columbia: University of Missouri Press.

CRIME AND CRIMINALS

Crime has been an endemic part of human societies throughout the world for millennia. As such, it's no surprise that one finds crime throughout the history of American cities. Even though longitudinal studies have demonstrated that, in the broad sweep of history, cities are safer and less violent places than the countryside, crime has been long considered a preeminent urban problem. In response to crime, Americans in the middle of the 19th century created municipal police departments; although today an array of federal, state, county, and city authorities have varying authority to arrest and prosecute offenders, the brunt of day-to-day work in the modern urban crime environment falls to the city police.

The Nature of Urban Crime

American ideas about crime were, for the most part, adapted from English models. Most states have penal codes that define what is illegal and group crimes by category. Violent crimes involve crimes against people, while property crimes include theft and arson, which, although they affect people, are literally committed against property. Urban crime also includes offenses against the public order, such as breaking traffic or parking laws and unlawful demonstrating. Crimes are grouped by their severity, with violations punished by a fine, misdemeanors by a brief period of incarceration or a fine, and felonies by longer incarcerations (and, in capital cases, death) and larger fines.

Contrary to popular belief, cities have historically been far safer places with lower crime rates than the countryside, simply because their compact nature is amenable to more intensive policing and community surveillance. Because the United States has been, comparatively speaking, a more violent and criminal place than Western Europe, its cities have also had higher crime rates. But the causes for high crime that are typically advanced, such as rapid immigration and overcrowding, economic depression, and wartime, have had demonstrably little effect on urban crime. If there is a single master cause for urban crime, historians, sociologists, psychologists, and police have yet to isolate it.

Most urban American crime falls into two broad social constructs: street or disorganized crime and organized crime, each of which has its own political, economic, and social causes and effects. Some categories of crime, such as homicide, robbery, arson, and assault, can be the work of street criminals or organized ones; others, such as sexually based offenses, are largely the work of disorganized criminals. Offenses like racketeering, loan sharking, and narcotics distribution are usually perpetrated by criminal organizations. Crimes committed by organized criminals generally differ from those committed by disorganized criminals chiefly in intent; crime syndicates may engage in murder, assault, and arson for strategic purposes that further the profit-seeking ends of the syndicate.

As the line between legal and illegal has shifted, American definitions of crime have changed as well. Earlier strictures against the profanation of the Sabbath or the distribution of alcohol are no longer law, but the possession and distribution of illegal narcotics and computer hacking now are. Therefore, any consideration of crime in the history of urban America must take into account the shifting definitions of crime and how citizens, police, and criminals socially construct criminal behavior.

Street or Disorganized Crime

Statistically, most crimes committed in major American cities are crimes of passion, convenience, or opportunity committed by individual perpetrators; these can be classed as street crime or disorganized crime. Disorganized crimes are difficult to predict and, often, difficult to solve. Because they cut across racial, class, and gender lines, disorganized crimes have fascinated historians, and there are several studies that attempt to find rational explanations for patterns in crime rates.

Organized Crime

Historian Jay Albanese noted in 1996 that organized crime is a continuing and profitable criminal enterprise profiting from illegal yet publicly popular behaviors, and it is sustained by intimidation, force, and dishonesty. Although its complete extent is unknown, organized crime is a huge business (or rather, several huge businesses) and a seemingly intractable criminal problem in American cities.

Sociologist Alan A. Block, who has studied organized crime, has concluded that it is so thoroughly interwoven into the American economy that it is impossible to draw clear lines between legitimate business interests and underworld ones. In addition to traditional criminal activities like illegal gambling, prostitution, labor racketeering, loan sharking, and narcotics dealing, organized crime has penetrated into industries as diverse as finance, waste disposal, construction, insurance, labor, restaurant/food supply, vending, and, more recently, identity theft and cybercrime.

Contrary to popular belief, organized crime in American cities is not the purview of any one ethnic or racial group, nor did it begin with Prohibition, although the criminal syndicates that flowered then were of great importance for the rest of the 20th century. The rise of organized crime in American cities, in fact, developed in reaction to the emergence of urban police forces in the mid-19th century. Before the appearance of police, pickpockets, burglars, prostitutes, and other criminals operated freely. It was only after the formation of professional police forces—and the increasing democratization of American city politics—that criminal syndicates emerged to provide protection for members and clients from the police.

The criminal gangs from which syndicates developed ran protection rackets, intimidated the police, and did other things associated with organized crime, but it was not until the 1840s, when "ward heelers" emerged as urban power brokers, that these became full-fledged syndicates. Ward bosses used gang violence to win elections and in turn allowed criminals in the gangs to have political power, immunity from the police, and police prosecution of nonsyndicate rivals. Bribery, either political or monetary, completed the alliance among criminals, politicians, and police. Organized crime, then, was the direct result of electoral democracy, not foreign criminals. Since American organized crime developed along with urban democracy and the ward system, it is a quintessentially urban phenomenon, although not limited to cities; county, state, and even national governments are just as susceptible to the collusions among police, politicians, and criminals that create organized crime.

Theorists have forwarded three models for the organization of crime. The organization model, most often used by police and prosecutors, defines organized crime as a criminal conspiracy organized into a hierarchy and masterminded by a boss who issues orders and enforces discipline through underbosses. Estes Kefauver and other anticrime crusaders, who publicized the existence of the mafia in the 1950s, hewed closely to this model. The ethnic and cultural model widens consideration of organized crime from the "families" considered by the organizational model to consider organized crime as embedded in patron-client relationships that allow patrons and clients to make reciprocal exchanges. These, rather than rigid top-down leadership, structure organized crime activities. The enterprise model, on the other hand, interprets organized crime as a series of illegal activities run on a profit basis that frequently blend into legitimate commercial activity. Historians of organized crime use varying elements of each of these models in considering the phenomenon.

Most theorists distance politically motivated crimes (unless they are specifically perpetrated by existing syndicates) and terrorism from organized crime. One might argue that terrorist organizations are continuing criminal enterprises, but they fail to meet the classically accepted criteria because they do not profit from their crimes, nor do they seek to establish monopoly control over the illicit economy. Still, criminal syndicates in the past used methods similar to those used by "terrorists" in many parts of the world. Rival Chicago-area bookmakers circa 1910, for example, were responsible for a series of bombings as each attempted to liquidate its competition.

In the cities of the United States, most organized criminal syndicates started in response to consumer demand for illegal products and services. In the late 19th century, for example, gambling syndicates emerged. These syndicates managed illegal gaming operations, ranging from policy (illegal lottery) to swank "first-class houses" (illegal casinos). They performed two functions by spreading the risk of an inherently risky business and routinizing protection arrangements with politicians and police. Crime syndicates also appeared in several immigrant communities, and they simultaneously helped new arrivals cope with city life in America by helping them secure patronage jobs and guiding them through the criminal justice system while profiting from their countrymen through illicit gambling and extortion.

With the arrival of National Prohibition in 1920, violent new syndicates moved into the manufacture, importation, and distribution of alcohol. After repeal in 1933, some bootleggers moved into legitimate business, while others specialized in gambling. Beginning in 1950 with the Kefauver Committee, a series of federal investigations raised public awareness of organized crime, particularly in regard to the control of gambling. Just as federal authorities began concerted efforts to disrupt national gambling syndicates, though, organized crime shifted into other fields, such as narcotics smuggling and labor racketeering, or diversified into legitimate fields.

Despite the success of prosecutors around the country in disrupting major organized-crime "families," organized crime continues to be a major problem in American cities. However, because organized crime is essentially consumer-driven, and those consumers show no signs of abjuring its illicit goods and services, efforts to eliminate it seem to be destined to fail, as the illicit markets are so lucrative that, as soon as one organization is dismantled, another arises to serve its erstwhile customers.

As definitions of legal and illegal have shifted and as the political structure of American cities has changed, organized crime itself has evolved. The classic early-20th-century criminal syndicate, based on the interlocking interests of ward politicians, syndicate bosses, and city police, has become a relic with demographic and political changes. Areas once dominated by syndicates, such as bootlegging, illegal gambling, and pornography, have become legal businesses (and in the latter two cases, major drivers of Internet use).

Organized criminals are constantly moving into new areas. Even cyberspace has digitally savvy criminal gangs that extort Web sites, particularly gambling ones, by threatening denial-of-service attacks. Because gaming sites are illegal in many countries, such as the United States, they cannot rely on the same police resources as other commercial sites, and because they are extremely time-sensitive (sports-betting sites make most of their profit on a few very busy days, such as Super Bowl Sunday), online gaming is particularly susceptible to this kind of shakedown. This is nothing more than the Internet equivalent of the time-honored protection racket, and it demonstrates that organized crime will continue to evolve to exploit vulnerabilities in the criminal justice system.

Policing the Cities

Because of the federal system, policing in the United States is as fractured as its political power. State statutes enumerate what is legal and illegal, but the enforcement authority devolves to the county level; criminals are typically tried in county courts and jailed in county facilities. In urban areas, city police most frequently "protect and serve" by attempting to prevent criminal acts, investigating crimes, and apprehending offenders.

This system has its origins in the middle of the 19th century, when American cities began shifting from the existing constable-and-town-watch system, in which crime control was the vague responsibility of volunteer night watchmen and fee-based constables, who made investigations or arrests only after being paid to do so by a victim. Following the example of the London Metropolitan Police, a number of American cities began fielding uniformed professional police. Because of the federal system, however, American police power remained divided among its various political units. Today, more than 17,000 different police agencies exercise power in the United States.

Originally, police were intended to deter and investigate crime and keep the public order, but as visible public servants they quickly assumed a variety of other roles, including many social welfare responsibilities, such as finding lost children and housing the homeless. By the end of the 19th century, however,

most police departments shed these social welfare roles and focused exclusively on crime.

Despite their jurisdictional autonomy, most urban police departments have similar hierarchical structures. County sheriffs, state police, and a growing number of federal agencies, including the Federal Bureau of Investigation, Drug Enforcement Agency, and Department of Homeland Security, may assist or co-opt municipal police departments' prevention and investigation of crime.

Fighting Crime

Citizens have given police the primary responsibility for deterring, detecting, and investigating crime, although private security officers have been increasingly used for deterrence purposes. In general, the police approach to disorganized crime is largely reactive; this is sensible, as most disorganized crime is, in a society that respects individual liberty, impossible to predict or prevent. Police patrols may be stepped up in areas that have seen increases in the crime rate, but besides basic actions such as this, little is done to actively fight disorganized, spontaneous crime.

Fighting organized crime, however, is a more cerebral pursuit, involving extensive visual, audio, and fiscal surveillance and the penetration of elaborate criminal enterprises. Throughout the 20th century, federal law enforcement took an increased role in combating organized crime, ostensibly because it crossed state boundaries, but often because local law enforcement, corrupted by syndicates, sandbagged investigations and prosecutions and, in some cases, actually worked in illegal syndicate businesses.

Measuring Crime

Because police power is federally fractured, there is no single source for criminal statistics in the United States. Historians of urban crime must instead look through a welter of police blotters, coroners' records, and court proceedings to conduct statistical research on crime, particularly before the 20th century.

Beginning in 1930, the Federal Bureau of Investigation began compiling the Uniform Crime Reports. These annual reports track the incidence of major crimes (murder and nonnegligent manslaughter, forcible rape, robbery, aggravated assault, burglary, larceny-theft, motor-vehicle theft, and, since 1978, arson) in cities of more than 2,500. The program, which is voluntary, covers about 95 percent of the nation and, along with the National Crime Victimization Survey, provides the first truly national, standardized gauge of crime.

In the late 1990s, following the example of New York City, several police departments across the nation began using COMSTAT (short for *computer statistics*), a system in which analysts enter data about crimes directly at the district substation level, which allows for nearly instantaneous tracking of crimes. District lieutenants are then free to change their deployments and tactics to better fight crime. In short, COMSTAT brings to fighting disorganized crime the strategic thinking that has characterized investigations of organized crime. Through the timely dissemination of crime information, urban police departments use COMSTAT to effect rapid deployment, analysis, and assessment. It will also, no doubt, provide a valuable tool for historians wishing to track criminal behavior and police responses.

—David G. Schwartz

See also Capone, Al; Criminal Justice System; Gambling; Gangs; Homicide; Nativism; Prohibition; Prostitution; Rioting

Further Readings and References

Albanese, J. (1996). *Organized crime in America* (3rd ed.). Cincinnati, OH: Anderson Publishing Company.

Albini, J. L. (1979). *The American mafia: Genesis of a legend.* New York: Irvington Publishers Inc.

Block, A. A. (1991). *The business of crime: A documentary study of organized crime in the American economy.* Boulder, CO: Westview Press.

Monkkonen, E. H. (1981). *The police in urban America, 1860–1920.* New York: Cambridge University Press.

Monkkonen, E. H. (2001). *Murder in New York City.* Los Angeles: University of California Press.

Monkkonen, E. H. (2002). *Crime, justice, history.* Columbus: Ohio State University Press.

CRIMINAL JUSTICE SYSTEM

The criminal justice system is a combination of laws regulating behavior and the institutions that enforce these laws. It incorporates police, courts, jails, prosecutors, and defense attorneys. These separate elements have existed for centuries, and each has its own history, but American criminal justice emerged as an interconnected system in the late 19th century.

In the United States, criminal justice was built around state, county, and municipal laws and enforcement mechanisms; for most of American history, it was an overwhelmingly local process. Each state has its own penal code, as do local governments. Courts have traditionally been the central instruments. In colonial America, most cases reached courts when accusers—plaintiffs—swore out complaints. Only in major cases such as murders would coroners assemble juries to formally accuse suspects. These arrangements existed because communities had no real policing mechanisms. Boston created the first police department in the United States in 1838, and few cities followed that example until the 1850s. Instead, in 19th-century Philadelphia, most cases were initiated by private prosecutions. Plaintiffs would swear a complaint before a magistrate and pay a constable to bring defendants to court. This democratic arrangement allowed everyone who could afford court fees to seek justice. State-sponsored prosecutions, however, gradually replaced private prosecutions later in the 19th century. Philadelphia established a police department in 1845 and, after much controversy, consolidated its neighborhoods under one centralized municipal government in 1854. Establishing full-time city services brought larger caseloads into courts and demanded more administrative organization.

The various elements involved in criminal justice began to operate as an integrated system by the late 19th century. Police departments acted as investigators on behalf of municipal governments. District attorneys or public prosecutors—lawyers employed by local or state government to pursue cases—became common after 1870. Defense attorneys also became players in the system, although they appeared mainly on behalf of clients who could pay them; courts hired attorneys for the poor only if they faced serious charges, and public defenders were rare. Turn-of-the-century courts in the locality that has been studied most closely—Alameda County, California—developed a pyramid structure. The courts at the base of the pyramid—variously called police courts, justice courts, or magistrate's courts—conducted initial hearings on felony charges and managed most misdemeanor cases entirely. A majority of offenses involved disorderly conduct, drunkenness, and vagrancy, and courts dispensed justice in these cases in a quick and rough fashion. Defendants might have a few minutes to explain themselves before judges issued verdicts and imposed sentences. Only at the second level of the pyramid, the superior courts that heard felonies, did prosecutors mount cases and did attorneys defend their clients. Cases at this level usually began with an information—a referral—from the lower courts. Superior courts featured juries as well as judges, but juries played only a limited role. Instead, plea-bargaining arrangements—admissions of guilt in exchange for lesser sentences—became common among prosecutors, defense attorneys, and judges. Roughly one third of Alameda County cases between 1900 and 1910 ended in a guilty plea. Only a small portion of cases reached the top of the pyramid, appeals courts, which addressed challenges to previous decisions or cases dealing with questions of law or procedure.

The criminal justice system accumulated new mechanisms at the turn of the century. Courts began to place some convicted offenders on probation, supervising them without jailing them. Courts also experimented with giving convicts indeterminate sentences—flexible terms of incarceration within a minimum and maximum range—and letting state parole boards decide the actual release date. And between 1899 and the early 1920s, almost every state established separate juvenile courts with mixed purposes of disciplining young offenders, protecting them from courts and jails, and providing treatment.

Older institutions also expanded in the early 20th century. Urban police departments grew to keep pace with the monumental population growth in industrial cities such as Detroit. Court systems became more organized as well. Chicago created the nation's first "municipal court" in 1906 to manage its legal system under a single chief justice who assigned cases to branch courts with clearly delineated jurisdictions and powers. And state prison systems added new facilities that allowed variations in functions and levels of security and came under the coordination of state-level departments of corrections.

In the 20th century, criminal justice became a national as well as local issue. This shift triggered two key changes in how justice operated. The first change was that the federal government went from playing a very small role to becoming a central figure. The Harrison Narcotics Act of 1914 made certain drugs illegal and gave enforcement responsibility to the federal government. The 18th Amendment, which prohibited the manufacture and sale of alcohol between 1920 and its 1933 repeal, and the 1932 Lindbergh Law, which made kidnapping a federal crime, after the killing of aviator Charles Lindbergh's infant son, placed more offenses under national jurisdiction. New

antidrug measures, enacted in the late 1960s and expanded during the 1980s War on Drugs, further increased federal powers. National law-enforcement agencies also proliferated. The Federal Bureau of Investigation, created in 1908, evolved into the nation's leading law-enforcement agency by the early 1930s under the leadership of J. Edgar Hoover. The second key change was that federal courts took a greater interest in local criminal justice, and their decisions generated more uniform procedures and attention to defendants' rights. This transition began with cases involving civil rights in the 1930s South; the U.S. Supreme Court found that defendants facing the death penalty were entitled to attorneys and that African Americans could not be barred from juries. In the 1960s, the Supreme Court carried out a judicial revolution in which it applied federal standards of due process to state and local courts. In a series of decisions, the Supreme Court clarified requirements that state and local law-enforcement agencies had to uphold in issues such as defendants' rights, police rules for searches and seizures, prison conditions, and the death penalty.

The expansion and standardization of criminal justice in the 20th century has done little, however, to quell concerns that the system is ineffective. A series of "crime surveys" executed in the 1920s by municipal, state, and federal governments all worried that too many criminals escaped justice. Academic criminology expressed similar concerns in the 1970s when studies of criminal justice outcomes suggested that, in the phrase of the day, "nothing works." Even the massive expansion of the United States prison population at the end of the century—the number of Americans incarcerated in prisons and jails increased from fewer than 500,000 in 1980 to just over 2.1 million in 2003—had only a loose correlation with decreases in crime rates.

—*David B. Wolcott*

See also Crime and Criminals

Further Readings and References

Friedman, L. M. (1993). *Crime & punishment in American history*. New York: Basic Books.
Friedman, L. M., & Percival, R. V. (1981). *The roots of justice: Crime and punishment in Alameda County, California, 1870–1910*. Chapel Hill: University of North Carolina Press.

Steinberg, A. (1989). *The transformation of criminal justice: Philadelphia, 1800–1880*. Chapel Hill: University of North Carolina Press.

Walker, S. (1998). *Popular justice: A history of American criminal justice* (2nd ed.). New York: Oxford University Press.

CROWDS AND RIOTS

One of the most vexing problems associated with American cities is how to maintain control when large masses of people congregate for any purpose. Given the space limitations, ethnic and racial diversity, and problems associated with the city as a whole, tensions often overflow into violence. As the mob swells, so too does the need for a response that will settle things. Historically, violence also has been a key part of public demonstrations. It has been noted that riots are not necessarily a breakdown of the democratic process, but simply conduit by other means within American society.

American history is filled with instances of people forming crowds that have then acted violently when events did not turn out as they had originally wished. Unfortunately, mob action also has fueled situations that may otherwise have ended peacefully. One of the earliest events in American history to feature a crowd turning violent was the Boston Massacre. By today's standards, the crowd was not that large (numbering perhaps 400 at most), but the event spiraled out of control as the crowd provoked the situation to the point where British soldiers shot the demonstrators.

Crowds were often fueled by alcohol or old hatreds. The infamous Aster House Riot of 1849, in New York, started because the Aster House Theatre was featuring an English actor of Shakespeare, William McCready, when the crowd was mostly of Irish origin and felt that their own Irish Shakespearian actor was far more talented. Since theaters served as gambling, drinking, and prostitution facilities as well, the mix of bravado, alcohol, and old tensions spilled over, and mayhem ensued. The police were unable to contain the violence, and eventually the state militia was called in. A squadron of infantry, armed with rifles and artillery pieces, ended the riot, in which 22 people were killed.

The same issues of ethnicity and alcohol consumption fueled the Lager Riot of 1855, in Chicago. Mayor Levi Boone, a nativist, railed against the Irish and Germans who congregated and drank beer on Sundays by raising liquor licenses by 200 percent so that drinking would be curtailed. In the end, the massive Irish and German groups swarmed into downtown, and although loss of life was minimal, the riot ended a volunteer constabulary in Chicago, as well as Boone's mayoral career. The first professional police departments were created to cope with the increasing problems associated with many people congregating in small areas.

Crowds often swarm based on information that may be erroneous or that is ethnically charged. The New York Draft Riots of 1863 centered on the facts that the rich could buy their way out of the army and that whites were fighting for blacks. While the issue of race was the main point of contention, victims came from a variety of social, economic, and racial classes. In fact, race has been a driving force in many of the crowd actions that have ended in bloodshed. Mob actions in, for instance, the Tulsa Riot of 1921, the Zoot Suit Riot of 1943 in Los Angeles, and the volatile riots of the 1960s were in some form inflamed by racial mistreatment or rumors of racial injustice (most often false allegations of wrongdoing by African American males against white women).

Often, riots in one urban locale incite demonstrations or riots elsewhere. In 1877, a rail strike in West Virginia cascaded into unrest in several cities across the United States. In a short time, unrest had spread to the urban centers of Baltimore, Pittsburgh, New York, and Chicago, to name but a few cities embroiled in violence that summer. In most cases, the police were unable to contain the protests, and the militia was summoned to deal with the problems. In Chicago, Marshall Field loaned delivery vans to the police and militia so that they could better respond to trouble spots.

In most of these riots, the police were called in, but how they handled the situation depended on their manner of leadership. In the infamous Haymarket Riot of 1886, an overzealous Chicago police commander, Lt. John "Blackjack" Bonfield, disobeyed the orders of Mayor Carter Harrison and advanced police. Whoever threw the bomb did some damage, but the majority of deaths of the Chicago police officers occurred when the police fired wildly, often hitting each other. It is hard to say what anyone would do in these cases. If a person was in a dangerous situation, perhaps he or she might react in a violent manner, such as a protester hitting others with placards, a cop wielding a baton or gun, or the National Guard soldiers who fired on students or rioters to quell the chaos in major United States cities in the late 1960s. Regardless of how the protests began, the end result of violence boded ill for everyone. In all too many cases, violence occurred despite the best efforts and organization of city police departments. The inability to quell problems was not necessarily a lack of discipline, but rather a deficiency in power to control crowds or in the tactics necessary to win.

The Haymarket Riot, the Republic steel strikes of 1937, and many of the strikes of the 1930s symbolized the struggle of labor and management. While the Haymarket Riot was a result of both a common movement (the socialist movement for an 8-hour workday) and a complaint against a specific company (in this case, the Haymarket meeting was a response to violence that had occurred the day before at the International Harvester plant), the results were the same. The struggles of the masses and the rich are the result of a capitalist society. As long as people have the right to complain about what they see as injustices within American society, there will be crowds, protests, and occasionally violence.

This violence is often associated with the summer months, and tempers may often flare because of the heat, in addition to other factors. The 1919 Chicago race riot was sparked because of the hot summer and the fact that blacks could not use the white beach. While this flashpoint incident ignited the riots, the hatred between the Irish groups who felt that African Americans were encroaching on their "territory" had been building for quite some time. As with many other riots in American urban history, order was restored only after federal troops were called in. In the Chicago example, this was because African Americans felt that they would not get equal treatment from white police officers. This was true. After the riots ended, indictments were handed down against many of the "instigators," yet none of those indicted was white.

In the case of many of the riots of the 1960s, the police felt that if force was not used, then matters could quickly spiral out of hand. Others saw the attempt to control crowds as wholly unnecessary. The best example of the overbearing use of force was during 1968 when the Chicago police earned a severe reputation of using violence to stop demonstrations. Mayor Richard J. Daley's infamous commands to shoot to wound looters and shoot to kill arsonists were seen by those outside of Chicago as far more extreme than warranted. Later that summer, as the Democratic Convention drew counterprotesters to Chicago, the police again used tactics deemed Gestapo-like by many Americans. Daley noted that the police were not there to create disorder but to preserve order. The yippies and anti-war protesters countered by saying that the whole world was watching the actions of not only the Chicago police department, but the "old guard" of urban politicians, as well.

Another reason that rioting occurs more often in cities is because of the numbers of people that can assemble in a relatively short time. In cities, ethnic, racial, and societal groups have contact of an almost immediate nature, and this allows them to mobilize quickly. The crowds of protest that emerged during the start of the second Gulf War of 2003 were notified using the latest technology; numbers of 5,000 to 10,000 would not have been achieved in a smaller venue on such short notice. This scenario of an "instant crowd" was repeated often, as technology accelerated communication between groups. Other sociologists have tried to explain the psychology of crowds by saying that they are more easily prone to outbursts or other violent acts, or that the media has propelled people to commit reckless acts for "reality entertainment." Perhaps crowds turn violent because the possibility of determining the exact perpetrators is remote at best.

Urban life has been altered by crowds that often turn ugly. This shift can occur because of a verdict in an emotionally charged case, a reaction to a lost or won sports championship, or anything else related to a city of even medium size. To prevent demonstrations from devolving into violence, many cities have specially trained police units that deal with crowd control. These police are also trained to use nonlethal means of dispersement, including tear gas, beanbag guns, and tasers. This is a far cry from police mobilization in the late 1800s, when police were issued howitzers and Gatling guns to scatter protesters. Fortunately, riots, while a factor in American urban history, are not as common as many would believe.

—Cord Scott

See also Haymarket Riot/Massacre; Race Riots; Rioting

Further Readings and References

Jacobs, J. (1963). *The death and life of American cities.* New York: Vintage Books.

Lardner, J., & Repetto, T. (2000). *NYPD: A city and its police.* New York: Owl Books.

Lindberg, R. (1991). *To serve and collect*. Carbondale, IL: Southern Illinois University Press.

Monkkonen, E. (1981). *Police in urban America 1860–1920*. London: Cambridge University Press.

Ryan, M. (1997). *Civic wars*. Berkeley, CA: University of California Press.

Wiebe, R. (1985). *The search for order 1877–1920*. New York: Hill and Wang.

Wilentz, S. (1986). *Chants democratic*. New York: Oxford University Press.

CRUMP, EDWARD H.

Edward H. Crump (1874–1954), who dominated local politics and government in Memphis, Tennessee for decades, was the South's most prominent big-city boss. Controlling the vote in Shelby County and much of western Tennessee, Crump played a leading role in Democratic politics at the state and national levels as well. Unlike many political bosses who exercised power unobtrusively and kept low profiles, Crump was an eccentric showman who eagerly sought the spotlight.

A native of Holly Springs, Mississippi, Crump came to Memphis at the age of 19, married into a wealthy and socially prominent local family, and became a millionaire insurance underwriter. He entered politics as a silk-stocking reformer and won election as mayor in 1909, 1911, and 1915. Refusing to enforce Tennessee's Prohibition laws, Crump became the target of a recall petition and resigned the mayoralty in 1916. He briefly held a minor position in county government and served two terms in the U.S. House of Representatives (1931–1935) but otherwise declined to seek elective office for the rest of his life. Instead, he placed a series of surrogate mayors into city hall and managed local affairs from his palatial residence in one of Memphis's most exclusive residential neighborhoods.

Crump closely supervised the delivery of city services, and Memphis won numerous national awards for city beautification and public safety. At the same time that the city's notorious vice trade flourished, Crump's police ignored civil liberties, actively opposed trade unions, and harassed dissenters who dared to speak out against local authorities. A white supremacist and unwavering defender of racial segregation, the boss nevertheless allowed local African Americans to vote under close supervision. At a time when very few blacks voted in the Jim Crow South, Crump used the tightly controlled black vote to augment his electoral majorities in local elections. Machine operatives paid the poll taxes for local blacks, transported them to the polls, and gave them barbecue, alcohol, and money after they had voted for Crump's candidates. Crump practiced a brand of paternalism whereby he opposed the Ku Klux Klan and distributed patronage to local black politicians who supported the Democratic Party. He brooked no insubordination, however, and chased black Republicans who dared to challenge his authority out of town. After Tennessee initiated a series of election reforms in the late 1940s, including permanent voter registration and the repeal of the poll tax, Crump's influence in state and national politics ebbed. Still, the boss ruled unilaterally in Memphis until his death in 1954.

—*Roger Biles*

Further Readings and References

Biles, R. (1986). *Memphis in the Great Depression*. Knoxville, TN: University of Tennessee Press.

Dorsett, L. W. (1977). *Franklin D. Roosevelt and the city bosses*. Port Washington, N.Y.: Kennikat.

Miller, W. D. (1964). *Mister Crump of Memphis*. Baton Rouge, LA: Louisiana State University Press.

CURLEY, JAMES MICHAEL

James Michael Curley (1874–1958) served four terms as mayor of Boston, one term as governor of Massachusetts, two terms in the U.S. House of Representatives, and two terms in jail. The controversial Curley dominated public life in Boston during the first half of the 20th century. Skilled at shaping popular perceptions, he helped define the social and political character of Boston in the 20th century.

Curley was born in the Roxbury section of Boston, the son of Irish immigrants. His father, Michael, was a laborer; his mother, Sarah, scrubbed floors. Michael Curley died when James was 10, leading the younger Curley to quit school to support the family. He took jobs as a newsboy, delivery boy, drugstore clerk, machine operator, and traveling salesman.

Politics served as Curley's way up. A gifted public speaker, he was drafted by local Democratic Party leaders to speak on street corners as a teenager. He won a seat on the Boston Common Council in 1899. By 1901 he had created his own organization, the Tammany Club, and established himself as the dominant politician in Roxbury's Ward 17. He even earned election to the Common Council in 1904 while serving a term in jail for impersonating a constituent on a civil service exam. The following year he rose to the Board of Aldermen and was elected to the U.S. House of Representatives in 1910. He was first elected to a 4-year term as mayor of Boston in 1914 and was reelected to 4-year terms in 1921, 1929, and 1945.

Curley succeeded by adapting to a changing political environment. He recognized that the power of party organizations was diminishing and appealed directly to a mass electorate. A self-styled "Mayor of the Poor," he cast himself as the tribune of the blue-collar Irish, carving shamrocks in the shutters of his home and responding fiercely and often humorously to even the mildest Brahmin slight. He also backed many social reforms, built municipal bathhouses and Boston City Hospital, and reputedly passed out thousands of dollars in cash to needy constituents. These gestures helped him deflect frequent (and often credible) charges of corruption. They also helped lift him to a 2-year term as governor of Massachusetts in 1935 and a second term in Congress in 1940.

Curley's image has overshadowed his performance. His cultivation of ethnic animosities fractured a political truce between Irish and Yankee leaders, bequeathing to 20th-century Boston a sharp sense of cultural conflict. His corruption, fiscal profligacy, and inability to work with the local business community helped undermine Boston's economy through the middle decades of the 20th century. Yet he is remembered fondly, as a benevolent boss whose generosity and humor made up for the corruption, inefficiency, and ethnic polarization that characterized his leadership. The 1956 publication of Edwin O'Connor's *The Last Hurrah*, a sentimental portrait of an aging machine politician that many readers took as a thinly disguised depiction of Curley, ensured that such a perception would remain fixed in the popular mind.

—*James J. Connolly*

See also Boston, Massachusetts

Further Readings and References

Beatty, J. (1992). *The Rascal King: The life and times of James Michael Curley, 1874–1958*. Reading, MA: Addison Wesley.

Connolly, J. J. (1998). *The triumph of ethnic Progressivism: Urban political culture in Boston, 1900–1925*. Cambridge, MA: Harvard University Press.

Traverso, S. (2003). *Welfare politics in Boston, 1910–1940*. Amherst: University of Massachusetts Press.

Trout, C. H. (1977). *Boston, the Great Depression, and the New Deal*. New York: Oxford University Press.

DALEY, RICHARD J.

Richard J. Daley (1902–1976), Chicago mayor from 1955 to 1976, had a reputation as the last of the old-time, big-city, political bosses. There were, however, many Daleys—New Deal liberal, public finance expert, urban builder and redeveloper, defender of racial segregation, and, finally, hero to those fearing disorder and change.

A lifelong resident of the working-class neighborhood of Bridgeport, Daley valued family, ethnicity, and church (he was Irish Catholic), neighborhood, work, unions, and patronage-based Democratic Party politics.

From 1923 to 1955, Daley climbed the ladder of politics through hard work (11 years of night school earned him a DePaul law degree), honesty, loyalty, knowledge of public finance (he ran the Cook County Treasurer's office), and the timely deaths of politicians just above him. Daley served as state representative (1936–1938) and senator (1938–1946), Illinois revenue director (1949–1950), and Cook County Clerk (1950–1955). Meanwhile, he rose in the Cook County Democratic Party from ward committeeman to party co-chair in 1953. In 1955, he ousted incumbent Mayor Martin Kennelly in a primary. Combining endorsements from liberals Adlai Stevenson and Paul Douglas with black and inner-city votes, Daley defeated GOP hopeful Robert E. Merriam in the general election. He was reelected five times.

As mayor, Daley won political power by remaining county party chairman, evading civil service through renewable "temporary appointments," and curbing city council authority. He built a dominant coalition of downtown business, unions, public employees, Catholic Church, organized crime, African Americans, and white working-class ethnics.

Daley used his power to keep his beloved city vibrant. First, he maintained strong basic services—refuse collection, clean and well-lit streets, and abundant parks and playgrounds. In "the city that works," public employees were well paid and did not strike. Second, he managed finances ably, adding fees and shifting costs to other governmental units. Third, he backed massive construction projects that created jobs and made Chicago modern and prosperous. These included expressways, O'Hare Airport, McCormick Place convention center, downtown office buildings like Sears Tower, the University of Illinois campus, public housing, and middle-income apartments on urban renewal sites.

In the 1960s, Daley faced forces he could not control and with whom he could not bargain. First, a growing and assertive black population revolted against overcrowded, second-rate segregated schools. Next, Martin Luther King Jr. led a campaign against the color line in housing. Though unsupported by established black leaders, King's marches threatened white homeowners, who stoned King and began voting Republican. Then, the federal government pressured Daley for violating its rules for school desegregation and the War on Poverty. Next, ghetto rioting in April 1968 provoked an angry Daley to tell police to shoot looters and arsonists. Finally, hippies, radicals, and antiwar liberals at the Democratic National Convention in August 1968 goaded Daley into a profane, bigoted outburst on TV and into unleashing his police on protestors, reporters, and bystanders.

Thereafter, Daley was increasingly on the defensive. Though still applauded by whites furious with blacks and youth rebels, he was hurt by financial scandals, court rulings against public housing segregation and against patronage, continued racial conflict, election wins by black and white anti-Daley Democrats, and the presence of Republicans Nixon and Ford in the White House. Chicagoans were shocked when he died of a heart attack December 20, 1976. Academics and liberals mocked Daley for his mangled language, patronage politics, and traditional attitudes. Most observers denounce him for rigidly opposing blacks' aspirations. But Daley's heritage is substantial. One of his sons has been Mayor of Chicago since 1989, while another was a cabinet secretary and national Democratic Party figure in the 1990s. Moreover, Chicago has fared better than other big Midwestern cities. In the present era of media politics, low political participation, and hostility to the public sector, Richard J. Daley offers much to admire.

—Michael W. Homel

Further Readings and References

Biles, R. (1995). *Richard J. Daley: Politics, race, and the governing of Chicago.* DeKalb, IL: Northern Illinois University Press.

Cohen, A., & Taylor, E. (2000). *American pharaoh mayor Richard J. Daley: His battle for Chicago and the nation.* Boston: Little, Brown.

Royko, M. (1971). *Boss: Richard J. Daley of Chicago.* New York: E.P. Dutton.

DALLAS, TEXAS

Dallas, Texas developed initially as a crossroads settlement in the 1840s and established itself successively as an agricultural service center, market town, and regional metropolis with the arrival of two major railroads in the 1870s. A commercial city of 92,104 by 1910, Dallas attracted the 11th District Federal Reserve Bank in 1914 and led the region in financial and insurance services in the decades before the Great Depression. At the same time, the city developed both a light industrial base represented by manufacturers of agricultural implements and clothing and heavier industries including cotton mills and a major Ford Motor Company assembly plant.

Between 1880 and 1920, Dallas often imitated Chicago, Kansas City, St. Louis, or its rivals of similar size and age on the developing prairies. Few residents of early Dallas or other "new" 19th-century towns preferred stasis or advocated returning to a simpler time. A broad, general consensus favored growth—virtually all of the citizens of Dallas were convinced that their city was destined for greatness. Still, competing interests articulated different visions of urban growth. The commercial-civic elite, club women, populists, socialists, trade unionists, and municipal reformers competed and compromised by forming short-lived coalitions that endured only as long as their respective ambitions overlapped. Significantly, the racism of the city's white majority curtailed efforts to unite Dallas workers.

Conflicts in the 1920s and 1930s convinced a new generation of businessmen—most of them Texas natives and less cosmopolitan than their predecessors—that divisions among the elite threatened the city's regional hegemony. Businessmen led by banker R. L. Thornton matured in the 1920s and consolidated their power with the formation of the Dallas Citizens Council in 1937. Unlike the early commercial-civic elite of Dallas, this new generation excluded all voices except its own from civic affairs, aired intraclass disputes behind closed doors, and presented the public with a single option that ostensibly benefitted the city as a whole.

Political scientist Stephen Elkin considers Dallas after World War II an extreme example of the entrepreneurial political economies characteristic of Sunbelt cities in which strong alliances developed between businessmen and public officials. What distinguished Dallas was not that business leaders dominated the city but the extent and duration of their dominance in the postwar decades.

John Neely Bryan established Dallas in 1841. Most probably, he named the town after Alexander James Dallas, a U.S. naval hero. Dallas County was named for the commodore's brother, George Mifflin Dallas, who was vice president under James K. Polk. By the time Bryan built his cabin and began enticing other settlers to Dallas, the Republic of Texas had already provided funds for a military highway from Austin to the Red River to cross the Trinity River near the convergence of its three forks.

From its origins as a strategically located river crossing, Dallas benefitted from the rapid settlement of much of its hinterland. In 1841, Texas granted William S. Peters and his associates from Louisville, Kentucky approximately 16,000 square miles in the region of the upper Trinity. From Stephen F. Austin's original contract with Mexico, empresarios were barred from luring migrants already in Texas to new settlements. As a result, Peters Colony settlers came primarily from areas to the north and east. Most grew wheat instead of cotton, and few owned slaves. Unlike most migrants to Texas who had to purchase land from speculators, many Peters Colony farmers near Dallas received 640 acres of free land and, because they possessed cash reserves, developed a lively interest in trade.

Growth in early Dallas was spurred by the infusion of almost 200 skilled Europeans when La Reunion colony, a French utopian community led by Victor Considerant, disbanded in 1857. The presence of highly educated professionals, scientists, writers, musicians, artisans, and naturalists distinguished Dallas, a town of not quite 2,000 in 1860, from other county seats in north Texas.

As was typical in commercial centers catering to vast agricultural hinterlands, merchants and landowners constituted the majority of Dallas's early leaders. The commercial-civic elite established a Board of Trade, a Commercial Club, the Chamber of Commerce, and an Open Shop Association—all designed to boost economic growth—and ran for political office as Democrats in what was essentially a one-party state. Factions favoring increased municipal spending on reforms and improvements ranging from pure water and milk campaigns to street improvements outside the business district to regulations on slaughterhouses to municipal ownership of streetcar lines formed short-lived alliances with women's clubs, socialists, populists, and trade unionists to defeat fiscal conservatives.

Between 1886 and 1917, Dallas populists and socialists maintained local chapters of national political parties. Political radicals in Dallas moderated the elite's choice of candidates, since they rarely achieved electoral victories of their own. Still, they established enduring urban institutions including a cooperative cotton exchange, a night school for adults, and an employment service. With trade unionists, populists and socialists formed Dallas's first liberal coalition. Labor's champions including painter Patrick H. Golden, butcher Max Hahn, and musician John W. (Bill) Parks won state and local elections or were appointed to important municipal offices. Key strikes included a popular win by street railway workers in 1898 and a work stoppage by electrical linemen in 1919 that led to thousands of building tradesmen walking off their jobs in a sympathy strike.

In the context of trade union militancy, a fractious commercial-civic elite, and the reemergence of the Ku Klux Klan, middle-class professionals and elite allies who challenged the prevailing view that growth depended on fiscal restraint and minimal taxation saw their attempts to institutionalize social reform stymied by businessmen who sought changes in the structure of city government as a means of thwarting the Klan's political ambitions and labor's potential challenges.

Ongoing feuds involving Dallas business leaders, organizing efforts by local garment workers and at the Ford plant, and the need to raise money to cover the city's obligations to the 1936 Texas Centennial Exposition (won by Dallas boosters despite the fact that their city did not exist when the Republic of Texas was founded in 1836) led a group of powerful bankers, merchants, and utility heads to form the Dallas Citizens Council. This group's self-discipline, ability to control local media, and repression or co-optation of challengers resulted in a widespread belief among Dallas voters after World War II that "apolitical" business leaders safeguarded the interests of the entire city. Of course, the overwhelming majority of Dallas voters were white and lived in highly segregated neighborhoods north or east of the business district. Few paid attention to conditions in South Dallas, which became largely African American as whites fled the area in the postwar decades, or in unincorporated Latino/a communities west of the city where the benefits of growth failed to trickle down.

In the decade after the assassination in Dallas of President John F. Kennedy in 1963, business leaders feared that racial violence would do irreparable harm to the city's reputation. The Citizens Council expanded its membership to include professionals, and a very few women and moderate leaders of minority groups were invited to participate in forums like Goals for Dallas. Selected African Americans were encouraged to run for the city council's at-large seats. When the federal courts mandated single-district school board elections in 1974 and council districts the next year, the Dallas Citizens Council lost its stranglehold on civic affairs. By the 1980s, African American and Latino/a candidates established political bases in particular districts that gave them independence from Dallas business leaders. Although by most demographic and economic measures Dallas was still growing, more of the city's residents questioned the uneven nature of their prosperity. The quality of urban life and the Dallas public schools as compared to services and educational opportunities provided in the city's suburbs emerged as a key issue.

At the beginning of the 21st century, Dallas is undoubtedly a more democratic place. Still, the city finds itself grappling with the uneven nature of urban growth and the troubling legacies of racism and exclusion. Characteristically, Dallas has yet to closely examine contradictions between its yearning for "world class" status and "uniqueness" and its historical tendency to re-create architectural styles, landmarks, and institutions deemed successful elsewhere.

—*Patricia Evridge Hill*

Further Readings and References

Elkin, S. L. (1987). *City and regime in the American republic.* Chicago: University of Chicago Press.

Enstam, E. Y. (1998). *Women and the creation of urban life: Dallas, Texas, 1843–1920.* College Station, TX: Texas A & M University Press.

Fairbanks, R. (1998). *For the city as a whole: Planning, politics, and the public interest in Dallas, Texas, 1900–1965.* Columbus, OH: Ohio State University Press.

Hanson, R. (2003). *Civic culture and urban change: Governing Dallas.* Detroit, MI: Wayne State University Press.

Hill, P. E. (1996). *Dallas: The making of a modern city.* Austin, TX: University of Texas Press.

Leslie, W. (1998). *Dallas public and private: Aspects of an American City.* Dallas, TX: Southern Methodist University Press. (Original work published 1964)

Phillips, M. (2006). *White metropolis: Race, ethnicity, and religion in Dallas, 1841–2001.* Austin, TX: University of Texas Press.

Dance Halls

During the late 19th and early 20th centuries, few institutions figured as prominently in the social lives of urban Americans as dance halls. Rooted in the 19th-century concert saloon, dance halls surged in popularity during the early 20th century as urban, working-class youth clamored for more exciting recreational opportunities. Through visits to dance halls, young men and women not only escaped boredom and loneliness, but also devised new courtship rituals and explored alternative cultures. Although parents and reformers often identified dance halls as a source of urban disorder, their popularity among the youth of the nation's cities seldom wavered.

The origins of the urban dance hall lay in the 19th-century concert saloon, which first appeared in American cities during the 1840s. Concentrated in the vice districts of the nation's largest port cities and railroad hubs, concert saloons drew upon a growing itinerant male labor force for customers. Respectable women rarely attended concert saloons. Instead, owners hired "waiter girls," prostitutes, and other scantily clad women to amuse their mostly male clientele. Some concert saloons were simply fronts for brothels, an association that raised doubts about the morality of dancing in public.

Beginning in the 1890s, however, the number of commercial dance halls increased rapidly as Victorian taboos against public dancing receded. Neighborhood saloonkeepers converted cellars and backrooms into simple but functional dance spaces. Amusement park owners erected large outdoor dance pavilions, and professional dance instructors opened mass-market dance academies. By the early 1910s, few urban neighborhoods lacked at least one dance hall. One estimate placed the number of halls in New York City alone at over 600.

The most common type of dance hall in American cities during this period was the saloon-connected dance hall. Launched by bar owners as a way to capitalize on the growing passion for dancing among the younger set, saloon dance halls combined drinking and dancing under one roof. Some were well maintained and smartly decorated, but most were sparsely furnished, dimly lit, poorly ventilated, and large enough to accommodate only a few dozen dancers. Access to saloon-connected dance halls was free, so long as dancers purchased drinks.

The vast majority of dance hall patrons were working-class men and women in their teens and twenties. Dance halls offered these young people an exciting alternative to traditional, supervised social gatherings known as "affairs." During their visits to dance halls, young men and women not only danced with one another but also developed a new, more expressive style of heterosexual socializing that diminished the role of parents and community traditions in the process of courting and identifying prospective marriage partners. Between dances, patrons drank, smoked, gossiped, told bawdy jokes, flirted with one another, and engaged in various forms of premarital sex play. Young women, blurring the line between themselves and prostitutes, partook in these activities as enthusiastically as men did. To adults, their behavior appeared immoral and risky. However, women quickly developed new customs, such as attending dance halls in the company of other women, to help them manage their relations with the men they met.

Dance halls also fostered greater interest in African American culture among young urbanites. Jazz, whether played by all-black or all-white bands, was the music of choice among dance hall patrons, and many of the most popular dances of the era—the shimmy, bunny hug, and turkey trot—had African American origins. Nevertheless, that was the full extent of racial integration at most dance halls. Blacks and whites were not permitted to dance together, nor were Black couples and white couples allowed to dance alongside one another. Prejudice and fear—specifically of interracial sex—made such arrangements unthinkable. Except at the notorious "black and tan" resorts of the 1920s, where blacks and whites socialized, drank, and danced together, segregation on the dance floor was the standard practice at most halls.

As their numbers and popularity increased, dance hall conditions became a topic of heated debate among middle-class reformers and elected officials. Beginning in the late 1900s, various groups of child welfare and anti-vice activists identified dance halls as a potential threat to the well-being of urban youth. Citing evidence collected through privately organized investigations, they concluded that dance halls contributed to higher rates of juvenile delinquency, encouraged premarital sex, and induced young women into prostitution or "white slavery." However, in contrast to those who for moral or religious reasons had once demanded complete bans on all public dancing, these Progressive Era reformers rarely advocated closure of all dance halls. Instead, they urged elected officials to enact laws designed to curb the worst excesses of commercial dancing establishments.

Cities responded quickly to the perceived dangers of dance halls. In 1907, Chicago's chief of police established a special dance hall bureau within the department to conduct undercover investigations of the city's dance halls. Numerous other cities passed laws by the late 1910s regulating the minimum age of dance hall patrons, closing times, physical conditions, and methods of licensing and inspection. Further fueled by the temperance movement, several cities banned the sale of liquor at dance halls. Mostly, however, municipal governments lacked sufficient resources to fully enforce these laws. There were occasional crackdowns, during which police ordered the temporary closure of a handful of halls, usually for building-code violations. Otherwise, there were simply too few inspectors and police officers to monitor hundreds of dance halls and the activities of thousands of dancers on a nightly basis. The youth of the nation's cities

continued to dance when, where, and however they pleased.

During the 1910s and 1920s, increasing demand for dance space and the suspect reputation of many saloon-connected neighborhood dance halls prompted the construction of increasingly large dancing venues. These so-called dance palaces relied on lavish architecture, musical celebrities, higher admission fees, stricter codes of patron conduct, and an emphasis on dancing—rather than drinking—to improve the image of the dance hall industry. New York City's first dance palace, the Grand Central, opened in 1911, followed by the Roseland Ballroom and four others in the next 10 years. In contrast to neighborhood-oriented saloon dance halls, these large halls attracted a heterogeneous mix of dancers from across the city. Close proximity to subway and streetcar lines was crucial to the success of these halls, most of which had capacities of between five hundred and several thousand persons.

The institution of nationwide Prohibition in 1920 deprived saloon-connected dance halls of their most important source of revenue, forcing many to close. Much of the dance business shifted to the larger dance palaces, which peaked in popularity during the big-band era of the 1930s and 1940s. Following World War II, the number of dance halls steadily declined as new music styles, including bebop and rock, and new entertainment options, such as broadcast television, gained appeal.

—*Scott A. Newman*

Further Readings and References

Erenberg, L. A. (1981). *Steppin' out: New York nightlife and the transformation of American culture, 1890–1930.* Chicago: University of Chicago Press.

McBee, R. D. (2000). *Dance hall days: Intimacy and leisure among working-class immigrants in the United States.* New York: New York University Press.

Peiss, K. (1986). *Cheap amusements: Working women and leisure in turn-of-the-century New York.* Philadelphia: Temple University Press.

DEATH AND DYING

Death has always been present in the city, whether through the sudden tragedy of a fever or the hidden deterioration of cancer. The place and process of dying and death, though, have changed over time. As the primary causes of death shifted from infectious, plague-like illnesses to chronic diseases that occur largely among the elderly, urban Americans turned over the care of the dying to medical professionals and the oversight of the dead to funeral directors and cemetery superintendents. Death was not denied; the dying and the dead were simply cared for in specialized facilities, mourned in funeral homes, and laid to rest in large cemeteries separated from people's daily routines.

Early American colonists would marvel at present-day Americans' health and longevity, but they would have been puzzled by the strong separation of the world of the living from that of the dead. The colonists knew death in a way that is unimaginable even in today's poorest neighborhoods. Death was a constant companion, with cities particularly deadly. Death rates have been estimated to be roughly twice as high in cities as they were in rural areas throughout the colonial period, although rural rates began to rise with the coming of the 19th century.

Urban colonial and early national burial places were typically connected to a church, established by the town, or set aside by the family. Even though sextons oversaw the burials in the small churchyards and graveyards, many times the family dug the grave and lowered the casket. Some carved a simple wooden or stone gravestone. Professional carvers developed distinctive styles that evolved from the "death's head" to the "urn and willow" motif, and gravestone epitaphs often included lessons for the living, such as: "Life is uncertain, death is sure."

The establishment of Mount Auburn Cemetery in Cambridge, Massachusetts, outside Boston, in 1831, was a first sign of modernizing urban rituals of death. New urban cemeteries were much larger than older burial places, so they could serve several generations. A picturesque, Romantic-style landscape served as a counterpoint to the commercial cityscape of the urban grid. American sculptors were employed to decorate lots with three-dimensional monuments that celebrated the family's and society's values. The corporation retained the land rights, with the hope that the cemetery would not be disturbed by urban commercial and residential demands, and maintained the grounds to standardized upkeep.

Prior to the emergence of the funeral director, the family prepared the body, held the wake, and greeted mourners after the burial, with a minister performing the ceremony. Gifts, such as a pair of gloves, became a popular means of thanking mourners for attending

funerals in the later colonial period. In the colonial period and through much of the 19th century—and in some immigrant communities well into the 20th century—the funeral was a family matter.

After the Civil War, city funerals increasingly moved from the family home to the funeral home, where funeral directors embalmed the corpse and oversaw the details of the service and trip to the cemetery. The funeral became a well-orchestrated affair. A death was greeted with the wearing of elaborate mourning apparel, making a keepsake of hair from the deceased, and hanging memorials in the household. Strict rules governed survivors' lives, including what they wore and how soon they could reenter society. Flowers, which had played little role in the colonial funeral, became an important means of expressing sentiments. By the beginning of the 20th century, an industry had formed to watch over the dying and service the dead as well as the survivors.

Starting in the 1880s, the city became a less deadly place. Resulting largely from new sanitary and water projects, urban mortality rates declined rapidly. For instance, Chicago's mortality rate dropped by over a half between 1850 and 1925, with the decreases particularly substantial for children under the age of 5. People experienced fewer deaths in the family, among their friends, and in their neighborhoods. The dying were no longer kept at home, but moved to the hospital for terminal care.

The suburbanesque landscape and aggressive commercialism of the memorial park was representative of a new commercialized approach to death. At Forest Lawn Memorial Park in Glendale, outside Los Angeles, managers combined a lawn landscape of individual flush-to-the-ground gravestones with replicas of famous sculptures, such as Michelangelo's David and Daniel Chester French's The Republic. In the memorial parks, mourners found a consolidating industry, with a mortuary, chapel, floral shop, monument dealer, and perpetual care for the grave in one place.

These new burial places were not open to everyone, nor desirable to all. Many early 20th-century cemeteries were segregated with deed restrictions (much like those in house deeds of the time that mandated lots be sold to only Caucasians) or by a "custom" that minorities would be interred only in the least desirable sections. Only in the 1960s would the legal restrictions disappear. At the same time, immigrant and minority communities held onto traditions such as wakes in the home, family vigils over the body, upright individual memorials, and quick burials without embalming. They maintained their own cemeteries that resembled older styles of burial and memorialization.

In recent years, a growing number of Americans have embraced the alternative of cremation. The first enclosed cremation was conducted at the sleepy town of Lancaster, Pennsylvania in 1876. Cremation associations soon were founded in large cities such as San Francisco and New York and in smaller cities, such as Troy, New York. Still, as late as 1970, fewer than 5 percent of Americans chose cremation; by 2003, the figure was almost 30 percent nationwide, and it reached over 50 percent in some states, such as Hawaii, Nevada, and Colorado.

Today, Americans are dying at the lowest rate in urban history. American rituals around death, though, remain controversial and unstable. Science has made the definition of death increasingly complex, and many mobile Americans wonder what the purpose of a memorial is. Some mourners have turned to roadside shrines and other spontaneous memorials to express memories they feel will be standardized in conventional cemeteries, while others, particularly recent immigrants and their children, embrace older traditions of funeral and memorials.

—*David Charles Sloane*

Further Readings and References

Laderman, G. (2003). *Rest in peace: A cultural history of death and the funeral home in twentieth-century America.* New York: Oxford University Press.

Meyer, R. E. (1993). *Ethnicity and the American cemetery.* Bowling Green, OH: Bowling Green University Popular Press.

Sloane, D. C. (1991). *The last great necessity: Cemeteries in American history.* Baltimore, MD: Johns Hopkins University Press.

Sloane, D. C. (2005). Roadside shrines and granite sketches: Diversifying the vernacular landscape of memory. *Perspectives in Vernacular Architecture, 12,* 64–81.

DEINDUSTRIALIZATION

Deindustrialization, which refers to the loss of manufacturing jobs and facilities and the movement of capital out of basic industrial production, has occurred several times in the history of the United States. The movement of the textile industry out of New England early in the 20th century is an early example. However, contemporary usage of the term generally refers to the loss of manufacturing plants, jobs, and capital in America starting in the 1970s. Deindustrialization often occurred in conjunction with the decentralization of manufacturing facilities and jobs out of cities during the same period. Deindustrialization occurred in the United States earlier than in other countries, but other industrial societies, including those in Europe and Asia, later experienced it. With deindustrialization, the percentage of manufacturing jobs in the nation's economy fell, while the percentage in the service sector rose.

There have been numerous debates on the causes, processes, and consequences of deindustrialization, and the topic remains controversial. Barry Bluestone and Bennett Harrison give an early, penetrating analysis of the process in *The Deindustrialization of America: Plant Closings, Community Abandonment, and the Dismantling of Basic Industry* (1982). Their book's subtitle makes their view of the dimensions of the process clear. In addition to the loss of jobs, other important effects of the process include abandoned buildings and ripple effects of deindustrialization such as disinvestment in local urban communities, impoverishment of public services, heightened social polarization and disorder, increasing unemployment, and declines in real income. In terms of the national economy, the consequences include shifts to a service economy. In addition to understanding the causes of deindustrialization at the level of the national economy and the effects of the process at the national and local levels, deindustrialization also should be viewed within the context of the global economy and changes in it brought about by globalization of production and capital.

The causes of deindustrialization have been much debated. By the late 1970s, the postwar economic boom in the United States had slowed down dramatically. The growth of the economy slowed and productivity fell. Unemployment rates climbed and imports increased. Some scholars argue that rather than investing in basic industry and modernizing aging plant facilities, corporations invested in mergers, acquisitions, and foreign investment, thus leading to declining manufacturing production in the United States. American manufacturing found it difficult to compete with other industrial countries which had more modern industrial plant facilities. These conditions, part of a worldwide process in which corporations seek to invest capital in order to bolster their profits, set the stage for widespread deindustrialization beginning in the late 1970s. Other scholars link this analysis to the globalization of markets and production and to the development of trade between the more developed and the less developed countries. Some argue that these transformations led to the relocation of basic industry to less developed countries. Other influential economists argue that deindustrialization has little to do with trade between developed and less developed areas, but is primarily a consequence of successful economic development in which higher levels of manufacturing productivity lead to less need for jobs in the manufacturing sector, as noted by Robert Rowthorn and Ramana Ramaswamy in 1997. Others, including Paul Krugman in 1994, noted that slackening demand for manufactured goods also plays a role.

Some economists dispute the occurrence or importance of deindustrialization. For example, Krugman characterized the debate over deindustrialization as peculiar because deindustrialization did not take place. He argued that while the nation's share of manufacturing in terms of value added and jobs has been dropping in recent years, this is in fact a very straightforward consequence of certain trends, such as increasing productivity and declining demand for manufactured products, and is duplicated in other advanced industrial societies. These analyses do not take into account some of the essential points that other scholars make about the causes, processes, and consequences of deindustrialization. For example, Bluestone and Harrison acknowledged that some researchers see deindustrialization as a trivial problem, and they argued that this reflects a simplified view of the process.

Arguing that deindustrialization can take several forms, Bluestone and Harrison noted that shutting down an industrial plant and moving jobs elsewhere or eliminating jobs altogether is only the most obvious manifestation of the process. More subtle aspects of deindustrialization include redirecting profits from particular industrial facilities to other facilities or uses. They termed *milking* the process by which profitable plants or subsidiaries are used as "cash cows." Another aspect of deindustrialization may occur when management reallocates capital by failing to invest in replacing worn-out or obsolete machinery, leading to declining productivity. Finally, management can move or sell equipment, thus constraining how much the particular facility can produce. All of these forms of capital movement are manifested in deindustrialization and disinvestment. The disinvested capital is invested elsewhere in forms that may be profitable for

the corporation, but that may have negative social consequences for the communities in which the disinvestment occurs.

In addition to the controversies over the causes and processes of deindustrialization, there is much debate over its consequences. Economists have tended to examine the impact of deindustrialization at the level of the national economy, with a focus on overall national level statistics. Sociologists are more inclined to focus on the social costs of the process on the urban and community levels, investigating how deindustrialization has affected specific places, such as Chicago, Detroit, and various smaller cities. Economists, including Rowthorn and Ramaswamy, argue that deindustrialization is a manifestation of increasing productivity and economic development, and they tend to stress that the long-term outlook will depend on the rise of productivity in the service sector. Sociologists often argue that access to well-paying service sectors jobs requires access to training and education that are often not available to those most affected by deindustrialization.

Many social scientists argue that the key to understanding industrialization and its consequences is to focus on regional and local levels as well as the nation as a whole. For example, the percentages of manufacturing job losses are much higher in the Midwest than they are nationally. The consequences for cities and local communities in which plants closed and jobs were lost are serious social disruptions than cannot be captured by national level statistics. Some scholars argue that that the social costs of deindustrialization, especially for cities with large numbers of African Americans and Latino/as, have been disastrous. Sociologist William Julius Wilson provided an influential analysis of the effects of deindustrialization. In his 1987 book, *The Truly Disadvantaged,* Wilson investigated factors leading to increased poverty and social polarization in inner city neighborhoods. He hypothesized that five factors led to increased neighborhood poverty. One factor was deindustrialization and another was the linked process of the decentralization of manufacturing employment. Subsequent research indicates that deindustrialization is a factor in neighborhood poverty primarily in the Northeast, but not necessarily in other regions. Other studies suggest that deindustrialization is an important factor in the decline of manufacturing employment and subsequent increases in poverty and social disorganization in Detroit. In his ethnographic studies of Philadelphia inner city neighborhoods, Elijah Anderson argued in

1999 that the development of a violent code of every-day behavior, the "code of the street," is one outcome of deindustrialization and the declining opportunities resulting from it. Recent case studies widen the discussion of deindustrialization by taking a more historical approach and examining its political aspects and cultural significance in a number of different settings. Research on the causes, processes, and consequences continues with a wide range of social scientists approaching these topics from their disciplinary perspectives.

Today reindustrialization is occurring in some industries; especially those characterized by more technologically advanced production techniques. These newer technologies have boosted productivity, but they require fewer workers. Larger questions of the long-term economic health of the American economy, including the industrial sector, and its consequences for workers remain unanswered. Some scholars and policy analysts argue that the lack of an industrial policy to deal with the long-term economic and social consequences of capital mobility is troubling, while others regard such policy as unnecessary.

—*Walter F. Carroll*

See also African Americans in Cities; Chicago, Illinois; Detroit, Michigan; Economy of Cities; Industrial City

Further Readings and References

Anderson, E. (1999). *Code of the street: Decency, violence, and the moral life of the inner city.* New York: Norton.

Bluestone, B., & Harrison, B. (1982). *The deindustrialization of America: Plant closings, community abandonment, and the dismantling of basic industry.* New York: Basic Books.

Cowie, J., & Heathcott, J. (Eds.). (2003). *Beyond the ruins: The meanings of deindustrialization.* Ithaca, NY: ILR/Cornell University Press.

Farley, R., Danziger, S., & Holzer, H. J. (2000). *Detroit divided.* New York: Russell Sage.

Krugman, P. (1994). *Peddling prosperity: Economic sense and nonsense in the age of diminished expectations.* New York: Norton.

Rowthorn, R., & Ramaswamy, R. (1997, September). *Deindustrialization—its causes and consequences.* International Monetary Fund Working Paper. Retrieved June 7, 2006, from http://www.imf.org/external/pubs/ft/wp/wp9742.pdf

Wilson, W. J. (1987). *The truly disadvantaged: The inner city, the underclass, and public policy.* Chicago: University of Chicago.

DENSITY

The term *density* indicates the degree to which people within a settled area are living close together or spread out. Since the residents of cities generally live close together, that is, at higher densities than in other types of communities, density figures can help distinguish cities from suburbs and suburbs, in turn, from rural areas where the population is most widely dispersed.

Measuring Density

Density is typically measured as the number of people residing per square mile or square kilometer. While there is no minimum density requirement for U.S. cities, the Bureau of the Census does specify that a "block group," a defined portion of census tract, have at least 1,000 residents per square mile to be included in an "urbanized area" (population 50,000 or more) or in an "urban cluster" (population 2,500 to 49,999).

Table 1 shows substantial variations in densities among the 10 largest U.S. cities. Phoenix and Houston, which have incorporated large areas relative to their populations, have much lower densities than Philadelphia, which has the relatively confined boundaries typical of older cities. Since these figures represent citywide averages, a low-density city might still encompass crowded public housing projects, condominium complexes or mobile home parks;

Table 1 Population Densities of the Ten Largest U.S. Cities

City	Population (per square mile)	Area (square miles)	Density
New York City	8,008,278	303.3	26,404
Los Angeles	3,694,820	469.1	7,876
Chicago	2,896,016	227.1	12,752
Houston	1,953,631	579.4	3,372
Philadelphia	1,517,550	135.1	11,233
Phoenix	1,321,045	474.9	2,782
San Diego	1,223,400	324.3	3,772
Dallas	1,188,589	342.5	3,470
San Antonio	1,144,646	407.6	2,808
Detroit	951,270	138.8	6,853

Source: U.S. Census Bureau; Census 2000.

conversely, a high-density city might have neighborhoods of single-family homes like those in nearby suburbs.

These figures show only where people live, not where they work. It is, however, workplace densities (derived from journey-to-work, employment, and commercial real estate data) that are critical for determining the kind of transit service appropriate for a given city. Since Manhattan's office population during working hours soars to more than 200,000 per square mile, subway and rail commuter services are a necessity. In cities where jobs are more likely to be dispersed, bus or trolley (light rail) service may be used by commuters headed downtown, but for the majority, traveling in various directions, there may be no practical alternative to the car.

The Urban Revolution

The first census—in 1790—recorded that 3.9 million Americans were so dispersed across the country, mostly in farms and villages, that only 1 in 20 could be considered a city resident. While the population of the biggest city, New York, was only 33,000, all such ports, including Philadelphia, Boston, Baltimore and Charleston, had densities considerably higher than do most American cities today; in the absence of public transit or cars, city residents lived close together and within walking distance of where they worked. The busy streets, shops, and marketplaces of these compact towns gave them the crowded feeling we often associate today with big cities.

Beginning in the 1820s and continuing almost every year for a century and a half thereafter, thousands of predominantly young men and women from outlying farms and villages and from overseas streamed into American cities seeking work in downtown shops, offices, factories, and homes. In 1820, only New York could boast of more than 100,000 residents, but by 1900, there were 38 cities of that size or greater. And by then, New York, Chicago, and Philadelphia all had populations exceeding a million. Never before in history had so many people lived at such high densities—then referred to as "congestion of population." The prospect of living in crowded cities was exhilarating because they offered excitement, jobs, and entertainment; but urban slums were associated with crime, vice, and epidemics.

When social reformers witnessed thousands of poor families crowding into small rooms in slum districts, they sought to help them find healthier and more wholesome places to live in the suburbs or the countryside. Fearing that homeless street kids in the 1850s might become "the dangerous classes of New York," the Reverend Charles Loring Brace arranged for 100,000 of them to be adopted by Midwestern farm families. A generation later, police reporter Jacob Riis, in *How the Other Half Lives,* and other Progressive reformers worked for slum clearance, model housing, and low-cost commutation via subway, elevated transit, or streetcar to reduce the severe overcrowding on the Lower East Side and other tenement house districts. In the twenties and thirties, the planner and critic Lewis Mumford advocated the orderly dispersion of factories and offices to make it convenient for working people to live in garden cities outside the crowded metropolis. It was not until the 1960s, after much of the overcrowding in slum neighborhoods had declined and the deadly epidemics associated with city living had been largely eliminated, that sociologist Herbert Gans and the civic activist and writer Jane Jacobs cautioned against automatically equating high-density neighborhoods with undesirable slum living. They pointed out that neighborhoods like Greenwich Village and Boston's North and West Ends were vital and safe places, precisely because the dense hodgepodge of their apartments, shops, and small businesses created a sense of community among "urban villagers" who looked out for one other.

Neighborhood Densities

The highest population densities in most cities are generally found in neighborhoods closest to the center (just outside the business district); they then taper off, moving outward toward the suburbs. In the 1920s, University of Chicago sociologist Ernest W. Burgess drew a diagram of concentric rings around Chicago's Loop (the central business district) showing the city's poor concentrated in crowded neighborhoods just outside the Loop, wealthier people in houses on spacious lots at the periphery, and the middle class in apartments and small houses in the area in between. Professor Burgess's diagram proved to be an oversimplification in several ways: apartments and tenements built along streetcar or bus lines generated far higher densities (and higher land values) at greater distances from downtown than the concentric ring model would have predicted. Sub-centers (mini-downtowns) with offices and shops surrounded by dense housing could also be found at substantial distances from the center. And when factories located along rail lines, workers crowded into blue-collar suburbs that were as distant from the downtown as any spacious commuter suburb. These important exceptions aside, the basic principle of the "density gradient" still applies: The greater the distance from the center, the lower the population density.

In the first decades of the 20th century, the density gradient within cities fell off sharply. For example, while Chicago's Near West Side was very crowded, the city as whole, even as late as 1928, remained 30 percent empty lots. Eventually new housing and improved transit allowed many slum dwellers to move into less crowded neighborhoods. That was certainly the case on New York's Lower East Side, which was so crowded in 1900 that if its densities had been replicated throughout the rest of the city, then the entire population of the U.S. and Canada might have been housed within the city's boundaries. In 1904 construction began on the subways, which eventually drew off 70 percent of the Lower East Side population to Brooklyn, the Bronx, and Queens and nearby suburbs. Even though slum populations declined over the course of the century, the migration to American cities remained so strong that overall densities continued to climb, reaching a peak around 1950.

Suburbia Triumphant

The majority of Americans today live in neither the city nor the country, but in that vast area in between called suburbia. Suburbanization is often thought of as the mass movement which took families from city apartments to single-family homes, and in fact that was often the case, especially for those whose immigrant parents or grandparents had settled in big cities; within a generation or two, many of those families had moved (as civic reformers had hoped) to the suburbs. What this movement does not quite explain, however, is what happened to the majority who never lived in apartments or in big cities, but who also became suburban homeowners.

When Americans left the farm (only 1 family in 100 is living on a farm today), they generally settled in towns and small- to moderate-sized cities, which, while reasonably compact, were not as densely populated as their European counterparts. That was attributable in part to an inclination to live at some distance from work and to the ability of Americans to buy or rent single-family homes. In 1930, two decades before mass suburbanization, more than 60 percent of

nonfarm families (only slightly less than the percentage today) were living in such dwellings. In moderate-sized cities such as Knoxville, San Antonio, Cedar Rapids, Peoria, and Binghamton, close to 80 percent of families also lived in single-family homes. Outside of high density New York and certain other city neighborhoods, only a small percentage of city families lived in tenements or in multifamily apartment buildings. Hence, the single-family, home-owning culture often associated with 1950s suburbanization was, in fact, established not in the suburbs, but much earlier in town and city neighborhoods.

Although most Americans did not live in the biggest cities, they often settled nearby. By the mid-19th century, the populations of the outlying metropolitan areas of New York, Philadelphia, Pittsburgh, Cleveland, and St. Louis exceeded the population of the cities themselves. Throughout the 19th and 20th centuries many of these metropolitan communities were annexed by their central cities and so disappeared as independent entities. The remaining towns came to be called "suburbs," even though only a small fraction of the suburban workforce had ever commuted downtown. Much of what is called suburbia, especially in the Northeast, was a welter of old, well-established, high-density villages, towns, and cities that served as the core from which auto-based suburbanization would spread.

Modern suburbanization, which is now associated with post–World War II development, was first recognized in the 1920s. By then, city and regional planners understood that improved streetcar and bus service, access to the automobile, new highway construction, and the extension of telephone, gas, and electrical lines beyond the city limits would make it possible for a great deal of farmland and open space within metropolitan areas to be developed. The Depression and World War II delayed new home construction, but in the late forties and fifties, following 20 years of pent-up demand, development came with a rush. What surprised the planners was not that so many people came to live in the suburbs—rapid peripheral growth was predictable enough—but rather that the population was spread so thin over such a vast area. The densities of new subdivisions seemed unbelievably low. In 1929, The Regional Plan Association, a civic agency, suggested that New York area suburbs would probably develop at *no less than 10 houses per acre,* but by 1962, the association would report that zoning ordinances were restricting new development to *one or two houses per acre.*

What planners in the twenties had failed to see was that the suburban zoning regulations, which contributed to the spectacular dispersion of population, were sustainable only because the automobile, which planners presumed would be used mainly as a weekend recreational vehicle, became the primary means for getting to work in every region of the country. Access to cars, and willingness to use them for every sort of trip, meant that families were no longer obliged to live within densely populated transit corridors but were now free to settle on undeveloped land throughout metropolitan regions. And as offices, shops, and factories also spread out, driving to work became a necessity. Traffic jams and air pollution inevitably followed. Seemingly uncontrolled development rapidly consumed valuable open space. By the 1960s, city planners and civic agencies, which for generations had sought to disperse population, began calling for development to allow people to live and work close enough together that farms and open space might be preserved, as well as to make feasible the public transit services that could reduce pollution and dependence on the automobile.

Once out of the bottle, however, the genie proved so hard to contain that both the countryside and the city began to take on suburban characteristics. Today, *rural* means something quite different than agricultural, as the workers in the countryside understand that most jobs are to be found not on the farm but in prisons, in casinos, and, most important, in the shops, offices, and factories of adjoining suburban counties. Similarly, areas designated by the U.S. Census as *urban* and *metropolitan*—terms once closely associated with *city*—now practically mean *suburban,* since the suburbs are where most of the residents of those areas, in fact the majority of the U.S. population, actually live. Even the central cities began to look like suburbs by 1980. Their densities plummeted by almost 40 percent between 1950 and 1990 in part because the Sunbelt cities annexed hundreds of acres of low-density and largely undeveloped land. New neighborhoods in Dallas, Houston, and Phoenix look just like suburbs. Meanwhile, Midwestern and Northeastern cities, competing with suburban office parks and shopping malls, razed buildings in their central business districts to accommodate the automobiles of shoppers and office workers. But all too often, the residents of these older cities found that downtown had so little to offer that they, too, were obliged to drive to the suburbs to work, shop, or go to the movies. As the city lost its historic function as

marketplace, workplace, and entertainment district, the question arose—why move there? Between 1970 and 1980, the average American city, for perhaps the first time in history, lost population.

Flying over metropolitan areas today, it is increasingly difficult to distinguish city from suburb. A 2001 study by Francesca Pozzi and Christopher Small of Columbia University's Lamont-Doherty Geological Observatory, which utilized satellite photos to show the densities, vegetation, and distribution of buildings of metropolitan areas, suggested that aside from a few densely populated places, the average American city had, by the year 2000, all but disappeared.

—*James Wunsch*

See also Population and Population Growth

Further Readings and References

Abrams, C. (1972). Density. In *The language of cities: A glossary of terms* (p. 85). New York: Avon Equinox Books.

Bliss, W. D. P., & Binder, R. (Eds.). (1970). Overcrowding. In *The new encyclopedia of social reform* (3rd ed., pp. 854–857). New York: The Arno Press.

Hoyt, H. (1970). *One hundred years of land values in Chicago: The relationship of the growth of Chicago to the rise of its land values, 1830–1933.* New York: The Arno Press. (Original work published 1933)

Kim, S. (2005). *The rise and decline of U.S. urban densities.* Retrieved July 12, 2005, from http://www.soks.wustl.edu/density.pdf

Pozzi, F., & Small, C. (2001). *Exploratory analysis of suburban land cover and population density in the USA.* Retrieved July 12, 2005, from http:// www.ciesin.columbia.edu/pdf/IEEE_PozziSmal12001.pdf

Regional Plan Association. (1979). *Regional plan news: A fiftieth year review, (106)*6.

Tarmann, A. (2003). Fifty years of demographic change in rural America. Retrieved August 3, 2005, from http://www.prb.org/rfdcenter/50yearsofchange.htm

Wunsch, J. (1995). The suburban cliché. *Journal of Social History, 28*(3), 643–658.

DENVER, COLORADO

Denver, Colorado, has a population of 554,636 for the core city and county, according to the 2000 U.S. Census. Another 1.7 million reside in the metro area's suburban counties (Adams, Arapahoe, Boulder, Broomfield, and Jefferson).

Denver was founded November 22, 1858 after a gold discovery at the confluence of Cherry Creek and the South Platte River. Founder William H. Larimer Jr. named the city for James W. Denver, governor of Kansas Territory, of which east central Colorado was then a part.

Numerous other gold discoveries sparked a mass migration of some 100,000 in 1859 to 1961, leading the federal government to establish Colorado Territory in 1861. Denver was incorporated on November 7, 1861 by a special act of the first session of the Legislative Assembly of Colorado Territory. In 1867, Denver became the capital of Colorado Territory and remained the capital after Colorado became a state on August 1, 1876. Denver has emerged as the cultural, distribution, entertainment, financial, service, and transportation hub of not only Colorado but also much of the Rocky Mountain region.

Denver became a city and county with home rule when Article XX was added to the Colorado Constitution in 1902. Under the City Charter enacted May 29, 1904, Denver has a strong mayor and city council government overseen by an independent, elected city auditor. Denver is located on at the eastern base of the Rocky Mountains in north central Colorado. With an elevation of 5,280 feet, the "Mile High City" has a cool, dry, sunny climate that makes it a magnet for health seekers and those enjoying outdoor recreation year-round.

Denver's aggressive leadership, spearheaded by William N. Byers, founding editor of the *Rocky Mountain News,* and Territorial Governor John Evans, built the Denver Pacific Railway (1870) to Cheyenne, Wyoming and the Union Pacific mainline. In the isolated, sparsely populated Rocky Mountain West, these transportation connections enabled Denver to emerge as the trading center. While Denver captured the commercial and territorial capital, its one-time rival, Boulder, settled for the state university. Another rival, Golden, received the Colorado School of Mines. Denver became the urban hub for Colorado and neighboring states by constructing a spiderweb of rail lines. The largest and longest lived of these local lines was the narrow-gauge Denver & Rio Grande.

Between 1870 and 1890, Denver grew from 4,759 to 106,713, becoming the second most populous metropolis in the West, behind only San Francisco. Mining fueled this growth; Colorado led the country in silver production during the 1880s and in gold during the 1890s. Denver's railroads carried many of the hinterland's ores to Denver's smelters, the city's single largest 19th-century industry.

The Depression of 1893 and Repeal of the Sherman Silver Purchase Act abruptly ended Denver's first boom. Civic leaders began promoting economic diversity—farming of wheat and sugar beets, ranching and the Denver Livestock Exchange, manufacturing, tourism, and service industries. Denver began growing again after 1900, but at a slower rate.

Stockyards, brickyards, canneries, flour mills, leather, and rubber goods nourished the city during the early 1900s. Of many breweries, Coors has emerged as one of the three national giants. Regional or national headquarters of many oil and gas firms in the Mile High City fueled much of Denver's post–World War I growth and an eruption of 40- and 50-story high-rises downtown.

The economic base has come to include electronics, computers, aviation, and the nation's largest telecommunications center. As the single regional center of a vast mountain and plain hinterland, Denver boasts more federal employees than any city besides Washington, D.C. Most are civilian employees, although Lowry Air Force Base and Fitzsimons Army Hospital have been mainstays of the economy in Aurora, the second largest city in the metropolis with some 225,000 residents.

Sited on high plains at the eastern base of the Rocky Mountains, Denver has a semi-arid climate averaging 13 inches of precipitation a year. A drab, brown city, it was transformed into a city of parks, parkways, street trees, and handsome public buildings during the three terms of Mayor Robert Walter Speer (1904–1908, 1908–1912, 1916–1918). Speer, like thousands of others, came to Denver seeking the sunny, dry climate as a cure for tuberculosis. Speer hired America's leading city planners to master plan a "City Beautiful." As Denver's most powerful—and ruthless—mayor, Speer implemented plans for a parklike Civic Center at the heart of the city. Parkways lead to large neighborhood parks designed as mini civic centers surrounded by schools, libraries, and other activity hubs. Creation of not only city parks but also municipal mountain parks, including the Winter Park ski area and the Red Rocks outdoor amphitheater, helped make tourism a major industry.

Since World War II, the population of city and county of Denver has been relatively static, while the surrounding suburban counties have mushroomed. Jefferson County on the western edge of Denver, with its county seat in Golden, is displacing Denver as Colorado's most populous county. Arapahoe, the third largest county, with its seat in Littleton, is the most affluent suburb, with impressive modern office parks as well as wealthy residential enclaves. Boulder County to the northwest is noted for the University of Colorado and a concentration of scientific and high-tech firms, including IBM, the National Center for Atmospheric Research, and the National Bureau of Standards. To the northeast, Adams County is both an industrial and agricultural leader for the metropolis. Suburban growth has now pushed into an outer ring of counties—Broomfield, Douglas, Clear Creek, Gilpin, Weld, and Elbert.

Denver County remains the political, financial, and cultural hub. Notable institutions include the Denver Museum of Natural History, the Western History Department of the Denver Public Library, the Colorado History Museum, the Denver Art Museum, and the Denver Center for the Performing Arts, as well as the region's only mint and major league baseball, basketball, and football teams. Denver's Auraria Higher Education Center (1977) is the state's largest campus, with more than 37,000 students attending the campus shared by the University of Colorado at Denver, Metropolitan State College, and the Denver Community College. Senior among the city's private schools are the University of Denver (1864) and Regis University (1877).

Denver, where native Arapahoe and Southern Cheyenne welcomed the first whites in the 1850s, houses the state's largest Native American population—about 5,400, primarily Lakota-Sioux, Cheyenne, Ute, and Navajo. Germans were the largest foreign-born group in Denver until World War I, followed by Irish, English, Italians, Slavs, Canadians, and Scandinavians. With the exception of an 1880 Anti-Chinese riot, Denver has had fairly smooth race relations. Since 1930, Hispanics have been the largest ethnic group, leading some to forget that Hispanic settlers had settled in southern Colorado before the 1858 to 1959 gold rush. Roughly 23 percent of the core city population is Spanish-surnamed and 13 percent is African American. Denver has elected a Hispanic mayor (Federico Pena, 1983–1991) and an African American mayor (Wellington Webb, 1991–2003) in recent years. Asians, primarily Chinese, Japanese, Korean, and Vietnamese, compose about 3 percent of Denver's population. Suburban counties have populations that are predominately white.

Because of its white-collar orientation and the stabilizing of many inner city neighborhoods with protective local historic district designations, Denver has remained more stable and prosperous than many other large United States cities. It's former skid row, the area around Union Station, was transformed during the 1990s into a thriving historic district of million-dollar lots, pricey restaurants, art galleries, pubs, and the Tattered Cover Book Store. Successful redevelopment of the former Stapeleton International Airport, Fitzsimons Army Hospital, and Lowry Air Force Base into residential neighborhoods and mixed residential and business areas also facilitated core city growth. Between 1990 and 2000, the population of the core city increased for the first time since the 1960s, climbing form 467,610 to 554,636. With the 55-square-mile Denver International Airport (1993) and a light rail system (1994), Denver continues to use transportation networks to make it the metropolis of the High Plains and the Rockies.

—Thomas J. Noel

Further Readings and References

Leonard, S. J., & Noel, T. J. (1990). *Denver: Mining camp to metropolis.* Boulder: University Press of Colorado.

DESEGREGATION OF EDUCATION

In the landmark 1954 *Brown v. Board of Education* decision, the U.S. Supreme Court unanimously outlawed racially segregated schools, thereby overturning its 1896 *Plessy v. Ferguson* ruling that allowed "separate but equal" facilities. Yet by the 50th anniversary of *Brown,* some African American activists had questioned the premise of the movement, and a more conservative Supreme Court curtailed the scope and duration of prior desegregation orders. The current status of school desegregation is tenuous, and a clearer understanding of present-day dilemmas requires a historical analysis of this civil rights struggle and how it has changed over time.

Challenges to racial separation in schools emerged in the context of the 19th-century abolitionist movement in Northern states. Legal historian Davison Douglas recounted the struggles that resulted in legislative bans against segregated schooling in Massachusetts (in 1855), Rhode Island (1866), Connecticut (1868), and so on. The last holdout was Indiana, where the state legislature abolished all officially sanctioned school segregation in 1949. Yet white school officials frequently defied these laws during periods of black migration, particularly in states on the Northern border of the Mason-Dixon Line: Illinois, Indiana, Ohio, Pennsylvania, and New Jersey. For example, Cleveland and Columbus, Ohio, which had racially integrated schools in the late 19th century, both reversed themselves in the 1910s and 1920s by intentionally assigning most black students to schools by race, gerrymandering attendance boundaries, and refusing to permit black teachers in white schools. While Thurgood Marshall of the National Association for the Advancement of Colored People (NAACP) attempted to organize a Northern school desegregation campaign in the 1940s, the results were mixed, leading him to refocus attention primarily on the Southern campaign instead.

The NAACP's intensive groundwork delivered a tremendous legal victory in the 1954 *Brown v. Board of Education* school desegregation case, which prohibited segregated schooling where it had been codified by law in Southern and border states. According to historian James Patterson, initial compliance with *Brown* was most apparent in border state urban school districts—such as Kansas City, St. Louis, and Oklahoma City—where 70 percent had biracial classrooms by the 1955–1956 school year. In Baltimore, the official desegregation of public schools led other authorities to announce similar policies for parochial schools and public housing. Yet emerging lower court decisions enabled Southern districts to slow down the pace of racial change. A 1955 federal district court ruling known as the Briggs Dictum interpreted *Brown* to mean that the Constitution did not require integration; instead, it forbade government enforcement of integration. A year later, a growing white resistance movement rallied under the banner of the Southern Manifesto against federal intervention, then gained national attention by actively defying the desegregation of Central High School in Little Rock, Arkansas in 1957. Although federal desegregation policy eventually prevailed, many Southern districts simply demonstrated "token compliance" by replacing formal segregationist barriers with gradualist student enrollment practices that virtually maintained the status quo. In 1964, a decade after *Brown*, 98 percent of Southern black students were still in segregated schools.

Outside of the Southern spotlight, the 1954 *Brown* ruling emboldened activists in the North. Many insisted that the Supreme Court's ruling that separate schools are unequal schools equally applied to Northern cities with their growing, concentrated populations of black migrants. *Brown* reignited

smoldering school desegregation protests that had been taken up in earlier years by NAACP branches in New York, Detroit, and Philadelphia. In 1957, the Chicago NAACP marked an historic shift by challenging the existence of predominantly black schools, regardless of the cause. The battle over *de jure* segregation (by legal requirement) versus *de facto* segregation (as a matter of fact; for example, by housing patterns) had begun in Northern courts, though the law would remain unclear on this distinction for years to come.

Due to meager changes in racial attendance patterns in the decade after *Brown*, school desegregation advocates lobbied for more affirmative measures to integrate classrooms during the 1960s and early 1970s. President Johnson's administration began pressuring school districts into compliance by threatening to withhold Title I compensatory funds from the Elementary and Secondary Education Act of 1965. Furthermore, the Supreme Court departed from the Briggs Dictum by ruling that previously segregated school districts now had an affirmative duty to eliminate all racial discrimination in the *Green v. New Kent County* (Virginia) decision of 1968. Three years later, the Court authorized the use of specific policy tools—including mandatory busing, redrawing attendance zones, and limited racial-balance quotas—to counter the effects of segregation in the *Swann v. Charlotte-Mecklenburg* (North Carolina) decision. By 1973, the Court's affirmative school desegregation rulings crossed into the Northern and Western regions with the *Keyes v. Denver* (Colorado) case. While historians like Diane Ravitch have criticized the legal trajectory of *Brown* as a shift from a noble goal of color-blindness to a misguided crusade for color-consciousness, historians like James Patterson have countered that the evolution of desegregation policy has been justified in light of intense white resistance to racial justice.

Yet all agree that the Supreme Court's affirmative desegregation rulings soon came to an abrupt halt at the city-suburban line. In the *Milliken v. Bradley* case of 1974, a sharply divided Court struck down a plan to merge the predominantly black Detroit city schools and surrounding white suburban schools into one metropolitan district, due to the lack of evidence that the suburban schools had intentionally segregated students. In Northern cities like Boston, white antibusing protesters violently challenged a federal court plan that mandated the integration of working-class black and white neighborhoods, while leaving upper-class whites relatively untouched. Various critics charged that court mandates threatened to drive whites away from Northern cities, but historians countered that suburbanization had long preceded these 1970s events.

Nevertheless, the past two decades have witnessed a retrenchment of affirmative desegregation policy. Certain African American civil rights activists, such as former NAACP attorneys Derrick Bell Jr. and Robert Carter, questioned whether techniques for achieving racial balance had moved away from their view of the original promise of *Brown:* improving the quality of education for black students. In addition, social scientists who comprehensively reviewed the academic literature generally agreed that the positive effects of school desegregation on black student achievement were relatively small. Most important, the rise of white conservatives during the Reagan administration dramatically altered the views of federal courts on desegregation cases. In the *Board of Education of Oklahoma City v. Dowell* decision of 1990, the Supreme Court ruled that districts could be released from desegregation orders when the vestiges of racial separation had been practically removed. Despite reports by the Civil Rights Project at Harvard University and other organizations warning of trends toward resegregation, Americans lowered their expectations that public schools should be charged with the responsibility of addressing racial segregation in the broader fabric of society.

—*Jack Dougherty*

See also Housing Segregation

Further Readings and References

Bell, D., Jr. (Ed.). (1980). *Shades of brown: New perspectives on school desegregation.* New York: Teachers College Press.

Douglas, D. (2005). *Jim Crow moves north: The battle over Northern school segregation, 1865–1954.* New York: Cambridge University Press.

Patterson, J. T. (2001). *Brown v. Board of Education: A civil rights milestone and its troubled legacy.* New York: Oxford University Press.

Ravitch, D. (1983). *The troubled crusade: American education, 1945–1980.* New York: Basic Books.

Schofield, J. W. (1996). Review of research on school desegregation's impact on elementary and secondary students. In J. A. Banks & C. A. M. G. Banks (Eds.), *Handbook of research on multicultural education.* New York: Macmillan.

DETROIT, MICHIGAN

In the early 21st century, Detroit is known throughout the world as the Motor City, and as Motown, the birthplace of a distinctive genre of urban African American music. One of America's premier industrial cities, Detroit has transformed itself several times since its founding as a fur trading outpost.

On July 24, 1701, Antoine de la Mothe Cadillac, an agent for the French government and an entrepreneur hoping to make his fortune in New France, landed on the narrows of the Detroit River—*De Troit,* or "The Strait," in French—with a small party of soldiers, farmers, fur traders, and voyagers. They built Fort Pontchartrain, and for the next 100 years, Detroit was largely French in population and culture.

Detroit's location on the Great Lakes waterway had a tremendous impact upon the city's development. It was the fur trading capital of the Great Lakes during its first hundred years, as well as a strategic military point that controlled passage on the Detroit River. During the wars for control of North America, Detroit was fought over many times by the French, English, and Americans. In 1760, during the Seven Years War, Major Robert Rogers captured Detroit for the British, who controlled the fort and village until it was ceded to the United States in 1796.

When Detroit burned to the ground in 1805, it was still a small outpost of about 1,000 people. With its prime location on the Great Lakes, the city had easy access to raw materials from Minnesota's iron mines and Michigan's Upper Peninsula. During this era, with the opening of the Erie Canal in 1825, which reduced travel time from the Eastern United States to Detroit from weeks to days, the Michigan Territory experienced a great wave of settlement, which resulted in statehood in 1837. Detroit became one of the fastest growing American cities in the 19th century. By 1900, it was one of the primary industrial cities in the United States, the world's leading producer of cast-iron stoves, and the nation's leading producer of railroad cars and ships.

Socially, Detroit has always been a point of destination for immigrants. It has been a place of opportunity for entrepreneurs and inventors, and a haven for the working class, millions of immigrants from around the world, and migrants from other parts of the United States. As a result, large populations of Germans, Hungarians, Irish, Italians, Poles, Russians, and other ethnic groups in the late 19th and early 20th century made Detroit one of the most diverse cities in America. For several decades before the American Civil War, Detroit was also a major terminus on the Underground Railroad, and thousands of fugitive slaves made their way from the South to Canada through Detroit.

Detroit's most important transformation occurred in the first decade of the 20th century, beginning with its first automobiles in 1896—the horseless carriages of Charles Brady King and Henry Ford. By 1914, when Ford installed moving assembly lines in his Highland Park assembly plant, Detroit was the leading producer of automobiles in the world and the undisputed Motor City. From this time forward, Detroit's economic well-being has been closely tied to automobile manufacturing.

As the auto industry grew in Detroit, the city experienced unprecedented growth. Its population grew from 286,000 in 1900 to 1.6 million by 1930. Indeed, for most of the 20th century, it was a place where hundreds of thousands of skilled and unskilled jobs were available in the automotive industry. Until the 1980s, Detroit was a place where people without education, skills, or familiarity with the English language could land a well-paid job making cars and trucks.

In the 1930s, Detroit earned a reputation as a stronghold for labor unions. After the Great Flint Sitdown Strike held by the United Automobile Workers (UAW) union ended in February 1937, a wave of over a hundred local sit-down strikes at bakeries, dime stores, automobile assembly plants, hotels, cigar factories, and many other places were held in the Motor City. Detroit was the nation's premier "labor town" for many years, and the home of the UAW, which at its peak had over 1.5 million members.

Detroit's manufacturing prowess was demonstrated during World War II. From 1941 to 1945, working Detroiters made a major contribution to the Allies' final victory. Many men and women, black and white, joined the armed forces, but those who worked in Detroit and Michigan factories produced about 25 percent of Allied war material—tanks, bombers, aircraft engines, artillery shells, machine guns, and many other products needed to wage war.

After the war, Detroit again underwent another transformation. In 1950, it was the premier industrial center in the world, with a peak population of 1.8 million in 1950, and 90 percent of the cars and trucks purchased in the United States were made by Detroit-based automakers. However, Detroit's slow decline as an automotive manufacturing center and the nation's fourth largest city began at this time. Two small but historic auto companies—Hudson and Packard—that had produced vehicles in Detroit since the early 1900s closed their doors, unable to compete with the Big Three automakers (GM, Ford, Chrysler) and the smaller American Motors in the postwar economy. Moreover, auto manufacturers in Germany, Japan, and other countries began to sell cars in the United States. Foreign imports continued to gain market share over the years, and by 2005, only 50 percent of vehicles purchased in the nation were made by American companies.

Along with changes in the nature of automobile manufacturing, Detroit also experienced a demographic transformation. With the advent of expressways and an ongoing replacement of aging Detroit assembly plants with new factories in the suburbs, jobs and people began to leave the city. Most of these migrants were white; thus, the reason for the term *white flight.* By 1960, almost half of the city's population was African American. The black community became the majority in the city by the early 1970s, and by 2000, over 80 percent of Detroit's population was African American.

Although blacks have lived in Detroit since the first enslaved Africans arrived around 1720, the black community remained small until the great migrations of blacks moving from the South to Northern cities during the eras of World War I and II. Largely attracted by good paying jobs in the automobile industry, Detroit was also considered a good place for African Americans to settle. In the 1960s, it was considered a "model city," a place where the white and black races lived peacefully. There was a history of racial strife, there had been race riots in the 1830s, the 1860s, and 1943, but Detroit was also a base for the Civil Rights Movement, in which many prominent black Detroiters had important roles. In 1963, for example, over 150,000 people participated in the March to Freedom in the city, where Martin Luther King Jr. debuted his famous "I Have a Dream" speech. Motown Records Company was formed in 1959 by Berry Gordy Jr. In the 1960s, it released hundreds of records featuring a distinctive African American sound and put Detroit on the world's musical map.

Race relations in Detroit reached a crisis point in 1967, however, when on July 23 a police raid on a "blind pig," or illegal drinking establishment, became the catalyst for the worst race riot in American history to that time. When U.S. Army paratroopers finally quelled the riot 3 days later, over $50 million in property damage, thousands of arrests, and 44 deaths had occurred. The white flight that began in the 1950s then peaked. Within a few years, the majority of Detroit's citizens were African Americans, and in 1974, the city elected its first black mayor, Coleman A. Young. From that time until today, Detroit has remained the largest city in the nation with a majority African American population.

In the early 21st century, Detroit is a city once again undergoing a transformation. Its metropolitan population is over 4 million, but the population of the city itself has slipped to about 900,000 citizens. With the advent of computers, robotics and increased foreign competitions, automobile manufacturing jobs have likewise been dramatically reduced.

Metropolitan Detroit is still the Motor City. While it no longer makes more cars and trucks than anyplace on earth, it is the technical and research capital of the automotive world. It is still one of the most important manufacturing centers in the United States and one of the largest metropolitan areas. Detroit's future is intimately tied to the future of the automobile industry, and in this respect, it has a wealth of technical expertise and research facilities, which will, hopefully, serve Detroiters well as the city once again remakes itself.

—*Michael O. Smith*

Further Readings and References

Boyle, K. (2004). *Arc of justice: A saga of race, civil rights, and murder in the jazz age.* New York: Henry Holt.

Farmer, S. (1890). *The history of Detroit and Wayne County and early Michigan: A chronological cyclopedia of the past and present.* Detroit, MI: Silas Farmer.

Lichtenstein, N. (1995). *Walter Reuther: The most dangerous man in Detroit.* Urbana, IL: University of Illinois Press.

Sugrue, T. (1996). *The origins of the urban crisis: Race and inequality in postwar Detroit.* Princeton, NJ: Princeton University Press.

Zunz, O. (1982). *The changing face of inequality: Urbanization, suburbanization, industrialization and immigrants in Detroit, 1880–1920.* Chicago: University of Chicago Press.

DINKINS, DAVID N.

Born in Trenton, New Jersey, David N. Dinkins (1927-) joined the U.S. Marine Corps in 1945 and graduated from Howard University in 1950. After serving in the Korean War, he graduated from Brooklyn Law School in 1956 and entered politics. Dinkins joined the Democratic machine in Harlem and was elected that district's New York State Assemblyman in 1965. He served as the head of the Board of Elections (1972–1973) and city clerk (1975–1985) before he was elected Borough President of Manhattan in 1985.

As racial tensions in New York City mounted, many Democrats viewed Dinkins as less divisive than Mayor Edward I. Koch and an alternative to Koch. Campaigning as a racial healer, Dinkins ousted Koch in the Democratic Primary in 1989. With the strong support of the city's liberals and African Americans, Dinkins went on to defeat Rudolph W. Giuliani in the general mayoral election to become the first African American mayor of New York City.

Dinkins's mayoralty was marked by his inability to quell the city's deep racial divisions. His slow response in criticizing black demonstrators picketing Korean groceries in Flatbush, Brooklyn angered many whites. In 1991, Dinkins was blamed for failing to order police to intervene in a racial disturbance in Crown Heights, Brooklyn, where black rioters attacked Hasidic residents, looted stores, and killed a rabbinical student. Dinkins was also criticized the following year for his handling of a disturbance between police and Dominicans in Washington Heights in Manhattan.

Dinkins's mayoralty was hampered by a weak economy. A strong ally of labor, fiscal constraints prevented Dinkins from increasing salaries for municipal employees and effectively attacking homelessness and other social ills. The crack-cocaine epidemic increased violent crime in the city, where 2,245 murders were committed in 1990. Dinkins and Police Commissioner Ray Kelley deserve credit for the decline of crime in New York during the 1990s. Their addition of more police and focus on the enforcement of minor crimes caused the city's crime rate to drop significantly in the last 2 years of the Dinkins administration (with the number of murders down by 14 percent). In 1993, Giuliani, running on a law-and-order platform, narrowly defeated Dinkins, limiting the city's first black mayor to one term.

After his defeat, David Dinkins became a professor at Columbia University's School of International and Public Affairs and a radio personality. In 1999, Dinkins was one of several prominent African Americans to be arrested for protesting the shooting death of Amadou Diallo, an unarmed African immigrant, by four white police officers.

—Dan Wishnoff

Further Readings and References

Freeman, J. B. (2000). *Working-class New York: Life and labor since World War II.* New York: Basic Books.
McNickle, C. (1993). *To be mayor of New York: Ethnic politics in the city.* New York: Columbia University Press.

DISNEYLAND

Disneyland is an amusement park that has entered the English lexicon and the global imagination. Walter Elias Disney (1901–1966) opened his new amusement park in 1955 in Anaheim, California, then a small community surrounded by orchards of orange trees and near the route of a new freeway. Debuting nationwide on live television, with rides and costumed characters derived from its creator's successful animated films, Disneyland proved an immense success. It became one of the most popular tourist attractions in the nation, drawing 5 million visitors a year by the 1960s, and more than 10 million by 1970.

When Disney unveiled his new park, he invited tourists to experience his films and cartoon characters in physical form. More than just replicated film images, however, visitors could enjoy several distinct and self-contained realms of leisure. These included Frontierland, encapsulating the pioneering West; the small-town nostalgia of Main Street U.S.A.: Adventureland, with its references to exotic cultures and tropical atmosphere; the fairy tale realm of Fantasyland, where every dream came true; and alluring Tomorrowland, where visitors could ride the Carousel of Progress into a "great big beautiful tomorrow."

Nostalgia for a small-town past and optimism for a technological future combined seamlessly at Disneyland, just as all the technology, infrastructure, and labor required to operate the park was concealed under a carefree surface. Such illusions fit the personality of its creator, a man nostalgic for an often unhappy childhood and a self-made media mogul who gambled it all to make his first film and gambled all again to construct his amusement park. Disney dominated American media and culture to an unrivaled degree, yet successfully projected the image of a genial grandfather figure who periodically appeared on family television screens.

The park allowed Disney to achieve total control over every aspect of his creation—the architecture, the "theming" of each area of the park, the behavior and appearance of employees, and even the types of visitors admitted. Disney's team of "Imagineers" crafted every aspect of the park in minute detail. Even the buildings lining Main Street U.S.A. were constructed at slightly less than life size, thereby not overwhelming children and reconfirming the adult notion that objects recalled from childhood are almost always smaller than we remember. The result is a perfectly controlled and choreographed visitor experience, one that many tourists have found comforting but many commentators have deemed troubling.

Disneyland had multiple origins. Some were autobiographical. Main Street U.S.A. re-created the small town of Marceline, Missouri, a place Disney remembered fondly from an otherwise unpleasant and nomadic childhood. Disney's father, Elias, had pursued several avocations, mostly without success. He did, however, work as a laborer at the site of the Columbian Exposition of 1893, helping to construct the "White City" that awed tourists. World fairs and expositions clearly served as a model for Disney's park, which always combined amusement and entertainment with a sense of moral uplift and patriotism.

Disney's desire for a park that would not only entertain but also improve tourists also convinced him to avoid creating the kind of park he did not want. Tourists in search of cinema glamour flocked to Hollywood, finding a seedy and derelict neighborhood instead. He could give them a more appealing encounter with Hollywood dreams, entirely safe for family consumption. The most abject lesson for Disney, however, was Coney Island, the venerable New York theme park. Coney Island entertained generations of visitors, but Disney found it repellant—dingy, chaotic, poorly maintained, and filled with freakish sideshows. He resolved to create a park that was the exact opposite.

A final key to Disneyland's origins was the setting for the park itself—Southern California. It is tempting to view the park as Walt Disney's critique of Southern California, particularly the sprawl and smog of Los Angeles. As the orange groves surrounding the park gave way to development, the earthen berm Disney had constructed to block out views of the outside world took on a much more defensive aspect. Yet Southern California—and the ways it had been promoted and imagined—shaped the park in important ways. In some respects, the park was explicitly Western and Californian—everything from Frontierland to Main Street U.S.A. to Autotopia—a child's fantasy of freeway driving, where traffic never snarled and everyone stayed in their proper lane. It is perhaps better to think of Disneyland as its creator's idealization of Southern California, condensed and perfected, rid of the chaotic, messy realities of actual urban life and equipped with a good mass transit system in the form of a futuristic monorail.

The encroachment of outside civilization around his magic kingdom did ultimately lead Disney to look beyond Southern California to Florida, where he purchased 43 square miles to construct a new park, the aptly named Walt Disney World. Other parks in other nations would follow, from Euro Disney outside Paris to a park in Japan. All these parks testify to the global appeal of Disney's films and their optimistic worldview.

Perhaps the most amusing evidence of this, however, occurred at the original park. In 1959, the Soviet premier Nikita Khrushchev and his wife, Nina Petrovna Khrushchev, flew to Los Angeles and were taken to a luncheon with Hollywood studio heads and film stars. During the luncheon, Mrs. Khrushchev made a request to Bob Hope. What she really wanted was a trip to Disneyland. Walt Disney, a staunch anticommunist, could not tolerate the prospect of the Soviet premier and his wife frolicking in his park, and the request was refused. The Khrushchevs may not have been able to visit Disneyland, but their desire testified to its stature as a global phenomenon.

—*Lawrence Culver*

Further Readings and References

Findlay, J. M. (1992). Disneyland: The happiest place on earth. In *Magic lands: Western cityscapes and American culture after 1940* (pp. 52–116). Berkeley, CA: University of California Press.

Marling, K. A. (Ed.). (1997). *Designing Disney's theme parks: The architecture of reassurance.* New York: Flammarion.

Schickel, R. (1997). *The Disney version: The life, times, art and commerce of Walt Disney* (3rd ed.). Chicago: Ivan R. Dee.

DOWNTOWN

Most Americans think of downtown as the heart of the metropolis. Dramatic skylines, bright lights, bustling streets and sidewalks, and dynamic civic spaces are images that spring to mind. Yet precise definitions of *downtown* are elusive. The term carries no legal or political meaning, and so its boundaries may be fluid and amorphous. At its core, however, is a city's central business district, which contains office buildings, hotels, and convention centers. Beyond that core, a downtown typically includes cultural and entertainment districts, public buildings, and commercial corridors consisting of flagship department stores as well as small retail shops. Downtown is a focal point of corporate and governmental power, but it is also a place that brings together a broad array of individuals, ranging from the most affluent business executives and professionals to the poorest of the poor who wander the streets at night looking for a place to sleep.

The fortunes of downtown have changed over time. Its glory years occurred during the early decades of the 20th century when millions converged upon downtown each day to work, shop at one of its prestigious department stores, or seek diversion at a movie palace, theater, jazz club, dance hall, or saloon. By mid-century, the decentralization of jobs and residents to suburbia and beyond had exacted an immense toll on downtown, zapping it of much of its vitality and leading many observers to speculate about its possible obsolescence. At the start of the 21st century, however, the downtown district of many cities has experienced a revival, prompting some scholars to reconsider its place in America's future.

Origins and Early Development

The historian Robert Fogelson has traced the origins of the term *downtown* to the early 1800s, when New Yorkers used it to distinguish southern Manhattan from rapidly developing areas to the north of the island. But downtown increasingly came to take on a more functional, as opposed to geographical, meaning in both New York and other United States cities. At root, downtown was a place of centralized business activity, and its physical form was shaped by a number of key trends during the 19th century. First, the flourishing industrial economy required more and more space for managerial functions. As commercial and financial offices expanded, businesses providing essential support services such as legal advice, insurance, printing, and advertising also crowded into the area. Firms competed to secure office space in prominent buildings with a prestigious address at the center of the business district.

A second factor shaping the rise of downtown involved technological innovations such as the elevator, electricity, and steel-frame construction, which allowed commercial developers to build vertically instead of horizontally. After the fire of 1871 had destroyed much of Chicago's business district, the city's leaders were eager to rebuild and willing to experiment with new construction techniques. The 10-story First Home Insurance Building was completed in 1883 and was the first building with a steel skeleton. Within a decade, several more steel-framed, high-rise structures ranging from 15 to 18 floors testified to downtown Chicago's resurgence. Before long, similar office buildings began to appear in New York, Buffalo, and Pittsburgh, thus transforming the downtown districts of those cities.

Finally, advances in transportation technology further influenced the evolution of downtown. The development of mass transit systems consisting of commuter rail lines, cable cars, electric streetcars, and subways facilitated residential dispersion by enabling middle- and upper-class households to flee the congested central city for more pastoral settings on the periphery. However, this also had the effect of concentrating business activity, since such transit systems were built in a radial configuration whose center was the downtown business district. In sum, the combination of an expanding commercial and financial economy, technological advances that permitted the construction of high-rise office buildings, and the development of mass transit systems that converged in the central city made downtown the most accessible and desirable place to do business in the metropolitan area. Indeed, the growing demand for office space put intensive upward pressure on downtown property values, thus squeezing out alternative land uses—most notably industrial and residential ones. By the end of the 19th century, the modern downtown had taken shape: It was a geographically compact center of commerce and finance whose business firms were increasingly located in high-rise office buildings towering over noisy and crowded streets pulsing with human activity.

The Golden Era

The expansion of downtown accelerated in the years immediately after 1900. As engineering technology improved, developers were able to build offices that soared ever higher. Business leaders embraced skyscrapers not just for the practical advantages they offered in terms of work environment, but because they were seen as a source of prestige and a valuable form of corporate advertising. At the turn of the 20th century, New York City's skyline boasted over a dozen buildings exceeding 250 feet, as major corporations raced to see who could erect the tallest office tower. Just a few years later, immigrants arriving in New York harbor would marvel at colossal structures in lower Manhattan such as the 600-foot Singer Building (1908), the 700-foot Metropolitan Life Building (1909), and the 792-foot Woolworth Building (1913). Nor was the skyscraper phenomenon limited to New York and Chicago; Seattle's Smith Tower, for instance, stretched to 42 stories in 1914. And yet, skyscrapers remained a uniquely American phenomenon; most European cities resisted the temptation to build to the clouds by imposing strict height limitations such as 82 feet in Vienna and a mere 43 feet in Zurich.

The first decades of the 20th century marked the zenith of downtown. The dazzling skylines of major cities announced to the world America's emergence as an economic dynamo on a par with Great Britain, France, and Germany. Downtown office towers exuding power and confidence in the future provided employment for thousands throughout the metropolitan area. Many others flocked to downtown's department stores, cultural institutions, theaters, restaurants, and pubs. On a typical day in Boston in 1927, approximately 825,000 people descended upon its downtown, a number that exceeded the entire population of the city. Downtown was where the action was. It was the vibrant center of the American metropolis.

The downtown boom did not come without cost, however. Skyscrapers turned the streets below into dark, cold, and windswept canyons and lowered the values of nearby, older buildings hovering in the shadows of the new behemoths. Streetcars and automobiles full of commuters and shoppers descended upon downtown, causing traffic to slow to a crawl during rush hour. Sidewalks in some cities were jammed with harried passersby. In short, business was thriving, but conditions resulting from the downtown's rapid growth gave city planners and business leaders reason for concern.

To minimize the adverse environmental and aesthetic impacts of skyscrapers, some cities imposed height limitations. New York adopted a comprehensive zoning ordinance in 1916, requiring setbacks of skyscrapers to preserve sufficient light and air at street level, and other cities followed New York's lead. In addition, city leaders also sought to alleviate traffic congestion by advocating the construction of elevated trains or subway systems. Some cities, such as New York, Philadelphia, Boston, and Chicago, pursued these strategies, but most balked at the high cost of building subways and the unsightliness and noise of elevated trains.

Decentralization

The combination of downtown congestion and expensive real estate motivated some businesses, including department stores, entertainment enterprises, and other retail establishments, to move beyond the central core, where they would be closer to their residential clientele. Secondary business districts began to sprout in outer urban neighborhoods and the suburbs. By the 1920s, retail business was growing at a faster rate in the periphery than in the core. On the eve of the Great Depression, the downtown business district was no longer the only significant business district in the metropolitan area. The increasingly common use of the term *central business district* underscored downtown's continuing status as the primary, but not the only, business district.

Perhaps the most important factor spurring decentralization was the breathtaking explosion in automobile use by middle-class Americans, who now possessed the means to live even farther from the central city. In 1910, there were 500,000 automobiles in the United States; by 1930, thanks to Henry Ford's mass production innovations, which sharply reduced the purchase price of an automobile, there were 23 million. As more people moved to the periphery, many still commuted to work downtown, but more and more found fewer reasons to make the trip. The onset of the Depression further exacerbated downtown's woes as office growth ground to a halt, while commercial and retail businesses continued to relocate to secondary business districts throughout the region.

In response to decentralization, downtown business leaders formed advocacy organizations to make the case that a thriving downtown was essential for the well-being of the entire metropolis. They contended that downtown generated a disproportionate share of the city's tax revenue, mainly because of extremely high assessed values on downtown property, while consuming minimal public services. Moreover, downtown businesses still supplied the lion's share of the region's employment base. The National Association of Real Estate Boards launched a campaign in 1938 to address the problems posed by decentralization. Its

newly established research affiliate, the Urban Land Institute, published a report 2 years later entitled "Decentralization: What Is It Doing to Our Cities?" Downtown leaders aggressively pursued two strategies. First, they sought to rejuvenate downtown growth by improving access to downtown through the renovation of mass transit systems, which were widely criticized as slow, uncomfortable, and unreliable, and through the construction of highways connecting downtown with the suburbs. In conjunction with the latter, cities would need to greatly increase the supply of downtown parking garages. Second, downtown advocates argued that areas surrounding the central business district had experienced decay and stood as a deterrent to new capital investment. Their proposed remedy was massive slum clearance and the large-scale development of middle- and upper-middle-class housing, which would presumably enhance downtown's investment profile.

Crucial financial support for these "urban renewal" strategies came from Washington, D.C. Under Title I of the Housing Act of 1949, the federal government subsidized up to two thirds of the cost of acquiring and clearing property designated as "blighted" by a local redevelopment authority. The property would be "taken" under the redevelopment authority's eminent domain power. After existing structures were demolished and parcels of land cleared for redevelopment, the city would lease or sell the property to private developers, often at a substantially reduced price. Although Title I had initially been intended to ameliorate the severe shortage of decent, affordable housing in United States cities, downtown business interests and their allies succeeded in persuading Congress to amend the law, turning it into a vehicle for downtown redevelopment. Cities such as Pittsburgh, Philadelphia, and New Haven took the lead in using Title I to demolish "blighted" areas in and around the downtown core and replace them with commercial office buildings, civic structures, parking garages, and upscale housing. Furthermore, under the Federal Highway Act of 1956, the federal government advanced the goal of improving accessibility to downtown by providing massive subsidies to support the construction of freeways (but not mass transit) that would connect the central city with the burgeoning suburbs. The impact of urban renewal and highway development on the downtown business district was mixed at best. Although downtown districts were spruced up, redevelopment failed to stymie the hemorrhaging of residents and jobs. Meanwhile, both programs had a devastating effect upon residents and small business owners who happened to live and work in the path of the bulldozers. Black and Latino/a neighborhoods were disproportionately targeted by redevelopment authorities, a practice that provoked charges of racism and mounting protests directed at city hall during the height of the civil rights era.

Even after urban renewal was phased out in 1974, city leaders continued to promote downtown development as the key to revitalizing cities. That policy choice seemed counterintuitive to many observers, given that the severe decline in manufacturing in Rustbelt cities had wreaked havoc upon industrial neighborhoods beyond downtown. But while such neighborhoods cried out for redevelopment assistance, public officials chose instead to channel scarce resources to the downtown business district on the assumption that a downtown-based, postindustrial economy built upon corporate services, information, and technology would generate new jobs and tax revenue and spur the revitalization of United States cities.

The downtowns of many cities benefitted from this "corporate-center strategy." Commercial office construction took off in the 1960s, increased again in the 1970s, and then accelerated to even higher levels in the 1980s. Mayors pointed with pride to their new downtown skylines and proclaimed the arrival of an urban renaissance. But by and large downtown investment did not produce substantial spillover benefits in the form of good jobs for city residents and improved public services in outlying communities. The pattern of uneven development frequently resulted in a "tale of two cities" characterized by a flourishing downtown of gleaming office towers and hotels surrounded by a sea of struggling and impoverished neighborhoods. Grassroots mobilization in support of more equitable development policies emerged in some cities and in San Francisco and Boston led to significant reforms. But all too often neighborhood-based activists were blocked by a powerful governing coalition of public officials and private groups with ample resources, superior organizing capacity, and a common agenda premised upon a thriving downtown core.

Revival

In recent years, the thrust of downtown development has shifted away from commercial office development and toward residential development and the promotion of the arts, entertainment, sports, and tourism. In some cases, the goal has been to attract visitors through the creation of safe and sanitized shopping and amusement centers that replicate suburban environments. Festival marketplaces and center-city malls have been popular in cities like Baltimore and San Diego, although scholars have criticized their exclusionary character. More broadly, others have faulted city planners for attempting to turn downtowns into "tourist bubbles" and "theme parks," a revitalization strategy that ignores the distinctive appeal of urban life while failing to address the inequities of previous urban development policies.

However, other initiatives to bring people downtown to work, live, and play offer some potential to make downtown a destination for a relatively broad cross section of the population. Cities that have promoted new developments featuring varied land uses, mixed-income housing, historic preservation, and pedestrian-friendly streetscapes have succeeded in sparking renewed interest in downtown life. Demographers have documented a significant increase in the number of downtown residents during the past decade, particularly young professionals, gay men and lesbians, and empty nesters seeking proximity to jobs and entertainment within a more diverse and urbane milieu. The notion of downtown as a place where multiple communities come together within a variety of civic spaces advances the democratic ideal that downtown is "everybody's neighborhood." In the 21st century, downtown is no longer the dominant center that it once was, but in many areas it remains the heart of the metropolis.

—*Stephen J. McGovern*

See also Financial Districts; Skyscrapers; Urban Renewal and Revitalization

Further Readings and References

Abbott, C. (1993). Five downtown strategies: Policy discourse and downtown planning since 1945. *Journal of Policy History, 5,* 5–27.

Fogelson, R. M. (2001). *Downtown: Its rise and fall, 1880–1950.* New Haven, CT: Yale University Press.

Ford, L. R. (1994). *Cities and buildings: Skyscrapers, skid rows, and suburbs.* Baltimore: Johns Hopkins University Press.

Gratz, R. B., with N. Mintz. (1998). *Cities back from the edge: New life for downtown.* New York: John Wiley.

Judd, D. R., & Fainstein, S. S. (Eds.). (1999). *The tourist city.* New Haven, CT: Yale University Press.

McGovern, S. J. (1998). *The politics of downtown development: Dynamic political cultures in San Francisco and Washington, D.C.* Lexington: University Press of Kentucky.

Robertson, K. A. (1995). Downtown redevelopment strategies in the United States: An end-of-the-century assessment. *Journal of the American Planning Association, 61,* 429–438.

Teaford, J. C. (1990). *The rough road to renaissance: Urban revitalization in America.* Baltimore: Johns Hopkins University Press.

DRINKING PLACES

Though anyplace might do for some drinkers, most people seek a drinking venue that offers an opportunity for companionship, the basic creature comforts, and a ready supply of alcohol. Bars are designed for the purpose, of course, and they come in many varieties depending on such factors as clientele, furnishings, and local licensing laws. Other institutions, such as restaurants and fraternal lodges, may function as drinking places in the course of fulfilling some other mission. Outdoor locales often provide satisfactory venues as well, ranging from public parks to tenement rooftops. And finally, be it ever so humble, there is no drinking place like home for some people, whether their own domiciles or those of relatives, neighbors, or friends.

With so many options to choose from, one might think that drinkers would spend all their time exploring and sampling every venue they could find. But such barhopping is not the norm, except perhaps in the case of younger revelers, tourists, or obnoxious folk who get thrown out of place after place. On the contrary, most seasoned drinkers choose a favorite haunt or two to which they regularly return. For them, drinking is about companionship in familiar surroundings. The appealing thing about the great variety of drinking places in big cities is that drinkers may choose the particular niche that suits them best.

"A man walks into a bar," the joke begins, and immediately everyone can picture the familiar scene: the long hardwood counter, the customers perched on bar stools, and the bartender, framed by the back-wall mirror, standing ready with bottles, glasses, and assorted tools of the trade. Add tables, a jukebox or pool table, and a restroom in the rear, and the resulting barroom constitutes the most common of all drinking places in urban America.

Yet though most urban bars exhibit the same basic layout and facilities, the proprietor and regular clientele help make each establishment a distinctive drinking space. Bars differ significantly by class. The standard bar is functional and unpretentious, designed primarily with the working person in mind. The furniture is sturdy, the glassware mass-produced, the jukebox stimulating, and the pool table a showcase for physical grace. In contrast, the cocktail lounge caters to upper- and middle-class sensibilities, with padded chairs and booths, subtle lighting, soft music, and tasteful decorations reminiscent of well-appointed living rooms. At the other end of the scale are the dives and honky-tonks, with minimal furnishings, budget liquors, raucous music, and a generally unruly atmosphere. To each class its own, and seldom do customers of different classes willingly or happily intermix.

Other factors that distinguish one drinking parlor from another include ethnicity, occupation, and special interests. Urban bars in ethnic neighborhoods from Little Italy to Chinatown accommodate their customers with cultural flourishes in drink, food, decorations, and amusements. Those catering to particular occupational groups such as musicians or sailors often display fitting mementos ranging from band instruments to fishing nets. Still other bars appeal to an amazing variety of specialized clienteles, including motorcycle enthusiasts, computer geeks, nostalgia buffs, urban cowboys, yuppie professionals, gay and lesbian activists, and sports fans of every imaginable type. The ability of urban bars to serve as customized social clubs for diverse urban subgroups helps explain their enduring popularity as drinking places.

Local laws regulating or prohibiting alcohol sales have produced some creative subterfuges. Nearly every city sports a few unlicensed bars, known as "blind pigs," "speakeasies," or "after-hours clubs." Some towns that prohibit barrooms still permit cafes and restaurants to sell "set-ups" (glasses with ice and mixers) to which customers add their own alcohol purchased elsewhere. In certain "dry" towns in the South and Midwest, private "social clubs" pretend not to be bars by requiring patrons to pay membership fees before entering. In these various ways, determined drinkers often manage to thwart the laws designed to thwart them.

Many urban entertainment centers offer drinks as a sideline. Playgoers throng to theater lobbies during intermission to stretch legs and bend elbows. Denizens of dance halls and cabarets toss back a few to loosen joints and inhibitions. Game enthusiasts at casinos, ballparks, bowling alleys, and pool halls fortify themselves for the next round of competition. At restaurants, cafes, and oyster bars, many diners fill stomachs and empty glasses at a prodigious rate. In these various venues, alcohol consumption, though not the central activity, is nonetheless integral to the social experience. Such establishments derive much of their attractiveness as well as their revenue from their secondary function as drinking places.

Some private institutions also provide drinks while pursuing other goals. Private golf and tennis clubs as well as fraternal lodges maintain clubrooms where members may informally swap rounds or stage banquets and parties. And every major city boasts a few very swanky private clubs where the rich and powerful may sip and plot in exquisite exclusivity.

Outdoor drinking places entail their own advantages and drawbacks. Parks, wharves, and beaches make attractive settings, but drinkers must often contend with changeable weather and irksome bugs and police officers. For the romantically inclined, lovers' lanes and drive-in movies involve similar pleasures and pains. Party boats offer changing scenery and water sports, though boating and drinking can be a hazardous combination. In the built environment, city dwellers may organize block parties or gather on tenement stoops, rooftops, alleyways, and vacant lots. Urban bars sometimes open onto sidewalks or courtyards, with the German-style beer garden developing this idea to the fullest. Some cities even encourage a degree of street revelry, such as the Elvis-themed Beale Street in Memphis and the legendary Bourbon Street (not to mention the citywide Mardi Gras carnival) in New Orleans.

Despite the attractions of public drinking venues, some people still opt for the comforts and security of home. The home-drinking trend was greatly accelerated during the Prohibition era of 1920 to 1933. Indeed, domestic drinking became fashionable in many middle-class households, as respectable housewives began throwing cocktail parties (attired in "cocktail dresses" designed for the "cocktail hour"). Even after Prohibition's repeal, many continued to prefer home as their primary drinking place, whether for cocktail hour, patio barbecues, wedding and baby showers, or beer bashes during televised football games.

Big cities seem to offer a drinking place for every taste, making categorization a daunting task indeed. Yet though choices abound, one general rule appears to apply: Almost anywhere can serve as a drinking place if the companionship is good enough.

—*Madelon Powers*

See also Prohibition

Further Readings and References

Duis, P. R. (1983). *The saloon: Public drinking in Chicago and Boston, 1880–1920.* Urbana, IL: University of Illinois Press.

Powers, M. (1998). *Faces along the bar: Lore and order in the workingman's saloon, 1870–1920.* Chicago: University of Chicago Press.

Rorabaugh, W. J. (1979). *The alcoholic republic: An American tradition.* New York: Oxford University Press.

Rotskoff, L. (2002). *Love on the rocks: Men, women, and alcohol in post–World War II America.* Chapel Hill, NC: University of North Carolina Press.

Salinger, S. V. (2002). *Taverns and drinking in early America.* Baltimore, MD: Johns Hopkins University Press.

DU BOIS, W. E. B.

William Edward Burghardt Du Bois (1868–1963) was one of the leading social thinkers, civil rights leaders, sociologists, and public intellectuals of the 20th century. He was a pioneering figure in the American Civil Rights Movement and in the development of Pan-Africanism. In addition to his significant contributions to the study of African American life, he carried out important work in history and was a pioneering sociologist of the early 20th century. His *Souls of Black Folk* (1903) continues to be one of the central texts of the 20th century and remains in print in many editions. His comment that color was the 20th century's biggest problem has been widely quoted and influential. For Du Bois the color line provided the impetus for his scholarly and political work and was the lens through which he analyzed the world.

Du Bois played a central role in founding the National Association for the Advancement of Colored People before shifting later in life to Pan-Africanism. He died in Ghana as a citizen of that country, after leaving the United States in 1961, embittered by the lack of progress in reducing racism and prejudice and convinced that American capitalism could not reform itself. In terms of American urban history, perhaps his greatest contribution is the classic urban sociological study *The Philadelphia Negro,* published in 1899. His early life provides the context for understanding how he approached that work.

Born in Great Barrington, Massachusetts, Du Bois had an unusual childhood that shaped his views and perspectives on the world. Raised by his mother after his father deserted them, Du Bois grew up in a mostly white milieu, and although he and his mother were not well off, wealthier town residents gave his mother work and provided additional help to them. He had a relatively sheltered childhood and, although poor, grew up playing with the children of wealthier townspeople and was generally accepted by them. His intelligence and talents were recognized early by others in the community and schools, and they provided support for him in pursuing his education. This somewhat privileged upbringing gave him a sense of himself as a member of the elite. It also contributed to a sense of reserve which characterized Du Bois throughout his life. In many ways, he was a proper Victorian gentleman.

His education at Fisk College in Tennessee was not only in the classroom. He was exposed to a wide variety of African American life both on and off campus, as well as to the racism and prejudice endemic in the South at that time. He received his bachelor's degree from Fisk; then he received a second bachelor's degree from Harvard and entered graduate school there. His graduate career took him to Germany, where he studied with Max Weber, one of the founders of sociology. In 1890, with a monumental dissertation on the "Suppression of the African Slave Trade," Du Bois received his Ph.D. from Harvard, the first African American to do so. Unable to secure a teaching position at a white college, much to his shock, Du Bois began teaching at Wilberforce College in Ohio. He taught a variety of topics, but he was not allowed to teach a course in sociology. After 2 frustrating years at Wilberforce, Du Bois was invited to come to Philadelphia to carry out a sociological study of the city's African American community.

The impetus for the study originated with Susan P. Wharton, an upper-class Quaker woman active in the College Settlement Movement (CSA), a social welfare association affiliated with the University of Pennsylvania. The sociology department of the university sponsored the study and Samuel McCune Lindsay, an assistant professor in the department, oversaw it. Du Bois received a nonfaculty appointment as an assistant in sociology. He was aware that the CSA had an agenda for the study, expecting that it would validate their view that the city's African Americans were the cause of much crime and social disorganization. CSA members felt that a study carried out by an African American would strengthen the appeal of their theory. Du Bois had his own agenda. He felt that a lack of knowledge was the reason the world did not consider race correctly, and he would provide the information to help it think right.

With the work of Jane Addams on Chicago and Charles Booth's studies of the London poor as models, but drawing on his sociological training, Du Bois combined ethnographic research, social history, and social statistics to carry out a comprehensive investigation of African Americans in Philadelphia in the 1890s, especially those in the Seventh Ward. Doing all of the research himself, Du Bois examined every aspect of African American life in Philadelphia, including the history of African Americans in the city, their class structure, education, occupations, family life, health care, voluntary associations, criminality, and interaction with whites. The work reflects Du Bois's intellectual and analytical strengths, but it is compromised by his upbringing and attitudes.

In analyzing the causes of the social problems, poverty, and criminality among Philadelphia's black community, Du Bois emphasized the impact of historical conditions, social environment, and social conditions, rather than inherited factors as many scientists of the time suggested. He focused on social structural barriers to advancement and success. At the same time, Du Bois was also highly critical in a moralistic way of the shortcomings he perceived in the African American population. This condemnation or "blaming the victim" probably reflected his own upbringing and attitudes, but it may also have been a tactic to obtain a fuller hearing for his broader structural analysis, by giving his sponsors some of what they wanted.

The Philadelphia Negro is increasingly recognized as an urban sociological classic of historically based empirical analysis. The centenary of its publication was marked by a new edition of it as well as a collection of pieces examining its legacy and contemporary relevance for understanding race and ethnicity in American cities, as noted by Michael Katz and Thomas Sugrue in 1998.

After the Philadelphia project, Du Bois moved to Atlanta University, where he taught sociology and directed and published a series of sociological studies similar to his research on Philadelphia. Leaving in 1910, he moved away from sociology and academia, and into politically oriented journalism and an active and controversial political life. He joined the Communist Party at the same time that he left the United States for Ghana in 1961.

—Walter F. Carroll

See also African Americans in Cities; Myrdal, Gunnar; National Associaiton for the Advancement of Colored People; Philadelphia, Pennsylvania; Settlement House Movement

Further Readings and References

Du Bois, W. E. B. (1996). *The Philadelphia Negro: A social study*. Philadelphia: University of Pennsylvania Press. (Original work published 1899)

Du Bois, W. E. B. (2004). *The souls of Black folk*. 100th Anniversary Edition. Boulder, CO: Paradigm. (Original work published 1903)

Green, D. S., & Driver, E. D. (Eds.). (1978). *W. E. B. Du Bois on sociology and the black community*. Heritage of Sociology Series. Chicago: University of Chicago Press.

Katz, M. B., & Sugrue, T. J. (Eds.). (1998). *W. E. B. Du Bois, race, and the city: The Philadelphia Negro and its legacy*. Philadelphia: University of Pennsylvania Press.

Lewis, D. L. (2000). *W. E. B. Du Bois: The fight for equality and the American century, 1919–1963*. New York: Henry Holt.

Dumbbell Tenement

The term *dumbbell tenement* denotes the predominant type of multiple dwelling constructed during the last two decades of the 19th century to house New York City's burgeoning immigrant, working class, and poor populations. The building type, though reviled from its inception and invariably referred to as either infamous or notorious, was actually designed to provide a solution to the increasingly worrisome problem posed by overcrowded, unsanitary, and menacing slums—often windowless, dank cellar dwellings—which had emerged by the 1840s.

In 1878, Henry C. Meyer's trade journal, the *Plumber and Sanitary Engineer,* announced a prize competition for a tenement on a 25- × 100-foot lot that would maximize both safety and comfort for the tenants and profitability for the builders. This size lot, which had become New York's standard decades earlier when single-family dwellings were being constructed, was altogether and clearly unsuited for the construction of tenements designed to house some two dozen families. Indeed, the committee of five judges stated physical and moral health requirements could simply not be satisfied by a tenement restricted to a 25- × 100-foot lot. The judges nevertheless awarded prizes, including first prize to architect James E. Ware's "dumbbell" design.

The dumbbell tenement derived its name from its shape. It was basically two tenements—front and rear—connected by a narrow hallway which contained water closets and the stairway. There were fourteen rooms to a floor, seven on each side running straight back. One family occupied the front four rooms; another family the back three on each side. The four families on each floor shared the two water closets. The front (and largest) rooms measured some $10\frac{1}{2} \times 11\frac{1}{4}$ feet, while the tiny bedrooms averaged $7 \times 8\frac{1}{2}$ feet. The typical dumbbell tenement was five or six stories in height with 20 to 24 apartments. Into each apartment were frequently crowded 20 or more assorted family members and boarders, with adults often sleeping in shifts and children squeezed four or five to a bed or mattress. From the beginning, observers recognized that the design of the dumbbell tenement served the interests of the landlords, builders, and realtors (who often took advantage of the discretionary features of the law by covering 80 to 90 percent of the lot rather than just the legally mandated maximum of 65 percent) more than it did those of the tenants.

The windows of 10 of the 14 rooms on each floor opened onto the air shaft in the center of the tenement. Formed by the indentation of the connecting hallway and running from the ground to the top of the building, the shaft was some $2\frac{1}{2}$ feet in width (or 5 feet when two dumbbell tenements abutted one another), and some 50 to 60 feet in length. Enclosed on all sides, this air shaft could provide neither fresh air nor adequate light, and it frequently became a reeking, vermin-infested garbage dump, a place to cram excess furniture, a deathtrap to children playing on the roof, and a fire hazard. Residents often kept windows opening onto the shaft closed to keep out the noxious odors and to lessen the noise—some even nailed them shut.

The New York State Tenement House Law of 1879, requiring that every tenement bedroom have a window providing either direct or indirect light and air, insured the rapid multiplication of dumbbell tenements between 1879 and 1901 in New York City (particularly on the Lower East Side) to meet the spiraling demands for low-cost housing among immigrants and the poor. By the turn of the 20th century, approximately two thirds of New York's over 3.3 million residents lived in the city's more than 80,000 tenements, some three fourths of which were of the dumbbell variety. The Lower East Side, with over half-a-million people crammed into some 450 blocks, had become the most densely crowded place on the planet, with an average density of 260,000 people per square mile, some 800 people per acre, and more than 3,000 residents on some blocks.

From its inception, critics and reformers argued that the dumbbell tenements had to be either outlawed or, at the very least, made less dangerous through enforceable restrictive legislation. While momentum for reform built during the 1880s and 1890s, a laissez-faire doctrine coupled with a widespread belief in the efficacy of the capitalist marketplace stymied governmental action, while continued fascination with and faith in model tenements diverted attention away from the drive for effective restrictive legislation.

In February 1900, Lawrence Veiller, a young professional housing reformer who served as secretary of the Tenement House Committee of New York's Charity Organization Society, organized under the society's sponsorship an influential exhibition which graphically detailed through its maps, charts, models, and more than 1,000 photographs the horrendous conditions of the tenements on the Lower East Side. The exhibition drew 10,000 visitors during only 2 weeks and stimulated a huge outcry for reform. Veiller, whose zeal for tenement house reform was matched by his expertise, condemned the exhibition.

New York Governor Theodore Roosevelt told Veiller to stipulate the details of the needed housing reform legislation and he would then work to push it through the state legislature. Within months what became the Tenement House Act of 1901 was introduced, spirited through the legislative process, and signed into law. It established new housing standards which effectively prohibited further construction of the dumbbell tenements and mandated improvements to the thousands already in existence. This landmark piece of legislation, generally regarded as the most important housing statute in American municipal history, became a model for cities across the country and, though modified and amended over the years, continues to provide the basis for the design of low-rise residential construction in New York City. Veiller declared the dumbbell tenement dead upon passage of the new law, although the thousands of dumbbell tenements already in existence by 1901 continued to house tens of thousands of poor New Yorkers throughout the 20th century. The dream of relatively affordable, safe, and comfortable low-income housing which would attract builders and investors remained as elusive at the beginning of the 21st century as it had been throughout the 19th and 20th centuries.

—Allen J. Share

See also New York, New York; Slum; Tenement

Further Readings and References

Lubove, R. (1962). *The progressives and the slums: Tenement house reform in New York City, 1890–1917.* Pittsburgh, PA: University of Pittsburgh Press.

Plunz, R. (1990). *A history of housing in New York City: Dwelling type and social change in the American metropolis.* New York: Columbia University Press.

Rischin, M. (1962). *The Promised City: New York's Jews, 1870–1914.* Cambridge, MA: Harvard University Press.

Economy of Cities

Human settlements in North America prior to the 17th century hardly could be said to have had or to have been embedded in economies. Aboriginals formed relatively permanent settlements to provide for their social and physical needs, while relations of reciprocity and redistribution enabled food and implements to be exchanged. But, exchange for gain—a defining element of market economies—was absent. Only well after the continent had been colonized did market economies appear and shape the size and form of settlements, eventually becoming a major force in the development and diversification of cities. Lost was the organic coherence of aboriginal settlements in which the "economic" was indistinguishable from the "social."

When the English and Dutch colonized North America in the early 1600s, they entered a New World already populated by settlements that ranged from a few hundred to several thousand inhabitants. Spread across the continent were a variety of tribes whose relationship to the land changed with climate and the availability of edible plants, fish, and animals. Along the northwest Pacific Coast, Chinookan tribes established villages organized around fishing. In the Eastern woodlands, hunting, gathering, and farming—corn, beans, squash—anchored Mohawk settlements, while in Alaska the survival of large and permanent Eskimo villages depended on whaling and the hunting of sea mammals. Throughout the Great Plains, settlements were rare. The Sioux and Comanche were mostly nomadic and survived on hunting bison. Trade

occurred among aboriginals, but it consisted mainly of bartering.

In stark contrast, the first English and Dutch colonies in the New World were economic enterprises explicitly designed for the exporting of furs, forest products such as potash, and rice, indigo, and tobacco. These were joint-stock companies whose sole purpose was to provide commodities for the home market. Absent this export function, they were subsistence "economies" with little potential for growth. Such settlements included the Jamestown colony established by the Virginia Company (chartered in 1606); New Amsterdam, founded by the Dutch West India Company; and the Providence Islands Company, which operated in the Carolinas.

Until the early 18th century, all colonies, whether joint-stock companies or not, relied for their needs mainly on family farms, trade with aboriginal tribes, and hunting, gathering, and fishing. A number of places had strong export activities—Newport (whaling) and Norfolk (tobacco), for example—but the small size of these towns, restrictions on manufacturing by the colonial authorities, and the lack of capital kept external trade one-sided: profits accrued to foreign investors. The sole purpose of these settlements was to serve external markets.

Throughout most of the 18th century, the economy grew at a rapid pace. Population increased five-fold to 2.5 million people, mainly through immigration and, coupled with a westward movement that created new settlements extending to the Allegheny Mountains, strengthened internal trade. Foreign commerce involving Southern farmers also expanded. Trade, in turn, bolstered the growth of commercial towns. The port cities of Charleston, Boston, Philadelphia, New York, and Baltimore were increasingly prosperous. A number of them (for example, Boston) engaged in shipbuilding, and this spawned the manufacturing of ropes, sails, and related products. The economy, at least as measured by what people did to subsist, remained agricultural, however. Moreover, it was a rudimentary economy lacking in the banks and credit systems that would enable large-scale and profitable trade and thus rapid growth. Yet, the spread of settlement westward was opening new markets and creating towns that were not so easily controlled by colonial authorities. Consequently, these places were more likely to develop manufacturing and to trade with each other.

The Revolutionary War disrupted the colonial economy. English markets were no longer as hospitable, and the war created debts that had to be repaid. Not until the 1830s did the average level of living return to what it had been before independence. During these years, the country's internal market expanded eightfold to 17 million people. Arriving immigrants along with earlier settlers moved beyond the Alleghenies and into the Mississippi Valley, in part to take advantage of state land grants being used to pay for the war. The Louisiana Purchase, in 1803, made even more land available for settlement.

With the spread of population westward, river ports began to compete for regional trade. Competition also spurred the building of turnpikes and canals. Cities such as Cincinnati and Louisville made the transition from trading posts to thriving commercial centers. With agricultural productivity increasing, more and more of a surplus was produced for trade, and interregional trade became a major component of economic activity. In addition, people were able to move out of farming into urban activities. The coastal ports also grew as internal trade increased and new export markets were opened. The number of places with more than 2,500 inhabitants went from 22 in 1790 to 119 in 1840. Cities also were becoming larger, with New York topping the list with more than 300,000 residents.

Trade was fueled by growth in small-scale manufacturing. To shipbuilding was added iron production, textiles, and foodstuffs such as flour. The introduction of railroads and steamboats further spurred manufacturing, and through to the Civil War, the economy added goods production to farming and commerce. Immigration persisted—4.5 million individuals between 1830 and 1860—and settlers continued to push westward, crossing the Mississippi River into the Plains states.

The destruction of the Civil War created a demand for building materials, and the war and its aftermath fed the expansion of manufacturing. Of particular importance were the shift from iron to steel, the rise of oil refineries, and, more generally, the relocation of goods production from workshops to factories. With the country growing once again as immigration surged and rural migrants settled in the cities, factory owners were assured of labor. The combination of industrialization and urbanization created large cities such as Philadelphia, Buffalo, St. Louis, and Detroit. These industrial cities, some dominated by a single industry, as was Pittsburgh by steel, and others having more diversified economies, as did New York, were often ringed by smaller industrial satellites: for example, Chester and Camden outside Philadelphia and West Allis outside Milwaukee. And, while agriculture remained important economically, advances in productivity reduced employment in that sector and contributed to the rural-to-urban migration that enabled industries to grow.

One of the great success stories was Chicago. Railroad lines extending hundreds and hundreds of miles south and west, coupled with access to Great Lakes shipping, made that city a center for meatpacking, grain distribution, and manufactured products made there or brought from urban centers to the east. Chicago merchants and bankers organized and financed food production and commerce throughout the greater Midwest. Growth attracted migrants and investments from the East Coast. By 1890, Chicago had become the second largest city in the country.

During the years from the Civil War to the Depression of the 1930s, businesses consolidated, the banking sector was strengthened, more and more railroads were built, and settlements pushed farther and farther westward. A national economy, extending from ocean to ocean, came into existence. And although many new cities—Kansas City, Omaha, Salt Lake City—were established west of the Mississippi River, they were relatively small compared with those in the Northeast. The exceptions were San Francisco, a regional commercial and banking center and coastal port; St. Louis; and, less so, Denver. To the extent that the South lagged behind on the path to industrialization, its cities remained relatively small and functioned as commercial centers serving mainly regional markets.

In the 1920s, a booming economy and speculation in land and the stock market brought about rapid urban growth, and by the 1930s, city economies were fully industrialized. Most large cities came to depend on manufacturing and commerce for the jobs and capital that kept them vibrant. Increasingly, cities also were centers of management, finance, and entertainment along with the kinds of services (for example, restaurants, movie theaters, department stores) associated with an expansive economy. Their large size, though, was causing businesses and households to move to the suburban periphery. Rising automobile use and the introduction of trucks for the shipping of goods further contributed to the decentralization of households and businesses.

The stock market crash in 1929 stifled rural migration and, along with stricter immigration laws, dampened urban growth. The economy shrank. Businesses closed, not nearly enough jobs were available, and poverty increased nationwide. Consequently, few new cities emerged. During the decade between 1930 and 1940, the number of cities with populations of more than 250,000 went unchanged.

With the onset of World War II, the factories that had driven urban expansion were once again busy. Guns, tanks, airplanes, uniforms, hospital supplies, and innumerable other goods were needed in the war effort. Metropolitan economies were operating at full capacity. At the same time, people were postponing marriage, birthrates were low, and immigration and rural migration were meager. Most cities, with the exception of ports (for example, Oakland) and cities with a concentration of defense industries (for example, Los Angeles), experienced only minor population increases.

Manufacturing had been moving westward, and the war provided an additional boost to this migration of capital and jobs. In order to fight the war against Japan, the government built military installations on the Pacific coast and encouraged defense plants to locate there. It also favored the decentralization of defense industries, believing that factories would be less vulnerable to enemy attack in the suburban periphery. These policies harmed the older, industrial cities of the Northeast and presaged the deindustrialization that gained momentum after World War II. At the same time, they favored urban growth in the Southwest and West. The economies of Los Angeles, San Diego, and Seattle, in particular, benefited from defense expenditures. These growing economies, in turn, attracted migrants.

At the end of the war, the economy returned to domestic production. An increasingly affluent population demanded more and more goods and services. But during the next few decades, first heavy manufacturing and then low-wage manufacturing (for example, textiles and shoe production) receded in the face of foreign competition, technological advances, and the relocation of production offshore to low-wage countries. The economy shifted into personal services and such products as televisions, home furnishings, and automobiles. Prosperity enabled many households to buy into the expanding suburbs, a response to the shortage of housing in the central cities. Suburbanization, moreover, made automobiles increasingly necessary. With manufacturing on the decline, consumer and business services became more important in the economy.

All of this had a big impact on the industrial cities. Many of the smaller manufacturing cities—places such as Akron, Camden, and East St. Louis—descended in a spiral of business closings and population loss that continued into the 21st century. A number of the large industrial cities—Detroit, Buffalo, Philadelphia, St. Louis—joined them. Their manufacturing sectors were devastated, and their ports were undermined by the rise of trucking and the loss of heavy industrial products to ship. Nevertheless, a number of these cities were able to make the transition to a service economy. Boston eventually regrouped around financial services, higher education, and hospitals. New York survived the collapse of its port and the loss of much of its textile and light manufacturing to emerge as a global financial, entertainment, and media center. The story for Chicago is similar.

The deindustrialization of the Northeast generated an out-migration of businesses and people to the South and West. The smaller cities there began to grow into major urban centers. Houston rode the wave of oil production, medicine, and aerospace. San Jose grew as the surrounding region became a center for computer technology, Orlando became a family entertainment destination, and Las Vegas built its economy on casino gambling and tourism. Recreation, corporate services, light industry, education, and medical care spurred these urban, now metropolitan, economies. Industrial cities that could not make the transition lost even more businesses and households, and the younger, once smaller cities of the South and West reaped the rewards.

By the early 21st century, most of the thriving, older cities were relying on tourism, retailing, and corporate services to anchor their economies. Light manufacturing still existed in the peripheries of these places, but their ports (with exceptions such as Oakland and Newark) had all but disappeared, and their industrial waterfronts lay empty or had been transformed by marinas, restaurants, and middle-income housing. Cities had become places of consumption, a place where most people made their living selling to and serving others.

Despite all of these changes, a number of significant continuities are woven throughout the country's post-aboriginal history. One of the most important for understanding the economy of cities is the ever-present and persistent involvement of the government. The English and Dutch governments enabled joint-stock companies, the newly formed states sold land to settlers, their successors built canals and financed railroads, and the national government bought up and took over the continent. By the late 20th century, federal, state, and local governments were providing a vast array of assistance to investors, passing business-friendly legislation, educating and training labor, and generally pursuing economic growth.

Another continuity is the way in which the urban economies of the United States have been continually open to the world. The role of the first colonies was to serve as export platforms for sending basic goods to England and Holland. Today, the country's cities exist as part of large metropolitan economies that carry on significant trade within and without the nation. A number of cities have even established a pronounced global presence. The tentacles of Miami's economy extend into the Caribbean and beyond to Central and South America. New York has business links to London, Frankfurt, and Tokyo and provides legal, financial, and media services throughout the world. Seattle is connected to the Canadian economy to the north, San Diego to the Mexican economy to the south.

Last, metropolitan economies have become even more dissimilar as they search for competitive niches in a global economy. Trade initially and then industrialization diversified city economies. The service economy continued the trend. A country as large in land area, as populous, and as affluent as the United States offers a huge internal market to business. Global links have further expanded markets and increased investment opportunities. Economic diversification is one consequence; a large and complex system of cities is another.

—*Robert A. Beauregard*

See also Boosterism; Industrial Suburbs; Urbanization

Further Readings and References

Cronon, W. (1991). *Nature's metropolis: Chicago and the Great West*. New York: W. W. Norton & Company.
Orum, A. (1995). *City-building in America*. Boulder, CO: Westview Press.

EDGE CITIES

Edge city is a term coined by journalist Joel Garreau. He defined edge cities as suburban areas that could boast of at least 5 million square feet of leasable office space, 600,000 square feet of leasable retail space, and more jobs than residents. Edge cities were the exact opposite of the traditional commuter suburb, a place where one slept but did not work. They were not somnolent retreats from the commercial activity of the central city but centers of shopping, employment, and entertainment along the metropolitan fringe. During the 1970s and 1980s, these outlying business hubs developed to the point where they rivaled all but the largest central-city downtowns.

Although the phenomenon was evident throughout the United States by the close of the 20th century, edge cities differed in their origin and configuration. Many developed around suburban shopping malls. For example, the success of regional malls spawned office, hotel, and additional retail development in Tysons Corners outside of Washington, D.C., the Galleria area on the west side of Houston, King of Prussia west of Philadelphia, and the Schaumburg area northwest of Chicago. With eight department-store anchors and approximately 300 shops, South Coast Plaza in Orange County, California, quickly became the focus of hotel, office, and apartment construction. Reflecting the significance of the mall in edge city life, Orange County built its 3,000-seat, $73-million performing arts center adjacent to South Coast Plaza. A few edge cities arose in older suburban downtowns. Within a few decades, the once-quiet core of the elite St. Louis suburb of Clayton sprouted office towers housing thousands of white-collar workers. Still other edge cities sprawled along freeways, forming corridors of commerce. In Montgomery County, Maryland, northwest of Washington, D.C., a business corridor extended for 20 miles along I-270. South of Minneapolis, businesses lined the 7-mile stretch of the I-494 beltway between suburban Bloomington and Edina.

Virtually everywhere, expressway access was vital to edge city growth, and major interchanges were magnets for massive commercial development. In the Atlanta region, the Perimeter Center edge city grew around the intersection of Georgia 400 and the I-285 beltway. To the west, the Cumberland/Galleria business district arose near the interchange of I-75 and I-285.

By the late 1980s, these freshly minted business behemoths had transformed the commercial geography of the nation. In 1988, 16 million square feet of commercial office space clustered in the Perimeter Center area as compared to only 13 million square feet in Atlanta's downtown. As early as 1986, the Costa Mesa–Irvine–Newport Beach area, with 21.1 million square feet of office space, ranked as California's third largest business district, surpassed only by the downtowns of Los Angeles and San Francisco. By the late 1980s, the edge city of Southfield, Michigan could claim 20 million square feet of office space, more than existed in downtown Detroit. A city of 78,000 residents, Southfield at the beginning of the 21st century boasted a daytime population of almost 175,000.

Moreover, the central-city downtown no longer had a monopoly on high-rise office towers. Transco Tower soared 64 floors over Houston's Galleria edge city, Perimeter Center included a 31-story high-rise, and the equally tall Oakbrook Terrace Tower was the pre-eminent landmark of the Chicago area's Oak Brook district, an edge city hub that also housed the corporate headquarters of fast-food giant McDonalds. A 32-story office building and 33-story apartment tower soared over Southfield, advertising to freeway travelers that the once-stereotypical suburb had evolved into an edge city.

Although millions of Americans shopped and worked in the edge cities of the late 20th century, not everyone applauded the advent of this new metropolitan form. Devotees of the traditional city deplored the absence of history, street life, and cultural diversity that they associated with the older urban hubs. They rejected the glittering sterility of giant malls and glass-skinned corporate towers lining thoroughfares built for automobiles rather than people. Meanwhile, suburbanites complained that edge cities produced traffic jams and congestion, thereby threatening the quiet and serenity of their sylvan communities. They viewed the high-rises as symbols of an urban way of life that they were trying to escape. To protect themselves, suburban residents rallied behind slow-growth campaigns intended to reduce the pace of development and keep traffic-generating skyscrapers out of their communities.

Garreau, however, believed that these new outlying hubs of commerce represented the wave of the future; they were the emerging progenitors of a new American civilization. Unfamiliar and at odds with traditional notions of city and suburb, Tysons Corners, King of Prussia, and Schaumburg were jarring to the sensibilities of many observers. But Garreau believed that Americans would adjust and embrace this new form of life just as they had adapted to the emergence of the industrial city in the 19th century. In any case, Americans would have to adjust because edge cities would dominate the metropolitan future.

By the beginning of the 21st century, some were questioning the future pre-eminence of the edge city. In 2003, urban expert Robert E. Lang wrote of edgeless cities and claimed that commercial growth in America was not concentrated in outlying hubs but was sprawling in an amorphous pattern across the metropolitan fringe. According to Lang, the largest share of rental office space was in neither the central-city downtown nor Garreau's edge cities. Instead, it was widely distributed across metropolitan regions or scattered along highways. Moreover, during the closing years of the 20th century, office growth was more pronounced in the edgeless cities than in edge cities. Dispersion, not concentration, was the prevailing trend. The wave of the future was not, then, a series of gleaming new suburban downtowns. It was commercial sprawl.

Whether harbingers of the future or passing phenomena of the late 20th century, edge cities remained significant features of the metropolitan landscape and monuments to the automobile-induced centrifugal migration of commerce. Both the concept of the edge city and that of the edgeless city testified to the fact that the metropolitan fringe was no longer marginal to American commercial life.

—*Jon C. Teaford*

See also Irvine, California; Multicentered Metropolis and
    Multiple-Nucleii Theory; Suburbanization; Urban Sprawl

Further Readings and References

Fishman, R. (1987). *Bourgeois utopias: The rise and fall of suburbia*. New York: Basic Books.

Garreau, J. (1991). *Edge city: Life on the new frontier*. New York: Doubleday.

Lang, R. E. (2003). *Edgeless cities: Exploring the elusive metropolis*. Washington, DC: Brookings Institution Press.

Leinberger, C. B., & Lockwood, C. (1986). How business is reshaping America. *The Atlantic, 258*, 43–52.

Muller, P. O. (1981). *Contemporary suburban America*. Englewood Cliffs, NJ: Prentice Hall.

EDUCATION IN CITIES

Education consumes a great portion of the waking hours of much of the world's urban population. Schools and universities shape the geography, economies, and social lives of cities, suburbs, and rural communities as much as any other institution. In 2001, public elementary and secondary school construction expenditures in the United States topped $44 billion, compared to a total budget of about $33 billion for the U.S. Department of Housing and Urban Development. The majority of Americans' property taxes and much of their state and local wage taxes go to funding education, making it the foremost public service. Private and religious institutions make further investments in schooling and spur debates about the role of the state in civil society. Education is a hotly contested arena of urban life, as schools embody and refract Americans' deepest social, economic, and political concerns.

Historians argue that education is far more than just schooling. Learning takes place in many settings, from households and workplaces to formal institutions such as libraries, museums, child-care centers, and summer camps. However, most histories of education focus on schools, since they constitute the most deliberate, comprehensive attempts to address educational needs. Schools themselves take diverse forms. Public, private, and religious institutions of elementary, secondary, and higher education offer day, night, and weekend classes for commuter and boarding students. Many schools cater to specific populations and types of education, from students with learning disabilities to nonnative speakers of English, from high school vocational programs to professional training in university graduate schools.

Schools' roles in urban society have varied among different communities in cities and suburbs, as well as across different eras of American history. In the colonial era, churches ran most schools, and the earliest colleges trained clergymen. The mercantile elite of Boston, New York, and other large centers founded academies and colleges in the 18th century to train their growing professional classes. Some also established charity schools to serve the poor. These schools formed part of larger complexes of educational institutions. In mid-18th-century Philadelphia, for example, Benjamin Franklin and his colleagues founded the Library Company; the American Philosophical Society, the foremost center of Enlightenment science in the Americas; the Academy, College, and Charitable Schools of Philadelphia (later University of Pennsylvania); and Pennsylvania Hospital, the first teaching hospital on the continent. These institutions played a major part in making Philadelphia the political, economic, and cultural capital of the Revolutionary era.

Although schooling would be largely the purview of individual states, education became a national priority in the formative years of the United States. In the Northwest Ordinance of 1787, the Continental Congress mandated schooling as a means of socializing a national polity, even as settlers moved into the "wilderness" of the West. In cities of the Early Republic, the decline of apprenticeship left an educational vacuum for the working classes. From Buffalo to Baltimore, local philanthropic societies organized the first large-scale schools open to the public at the dawn of the 19th century. Most of these schools employed the "monitorial" (or Lancasterian) system of British Quaker Joseph Lancaster, wherein a master teacher trained older pupils, the monitors, who in turn taught the other students.

The state-run school systems that dominate American education today grew out of the efforts of social reformers, who cast education as part of a broader solution to what they viewed as distinctly urban problems. As a complement to its temperance, anti-prostitution, and prison-reform campaigns, the Pennsylvania Society for Promotion of Public Economy advocated free education as a means to combat poverty and vice. In 1818, its leaders pushed through a state act to create the school district of Philadelphia, mandating the erection of schoolhouses, hiring of teachers, and formation of a board of controllers. Their efforts to address the social and economic instability of the industrializing city were bolstered by mechanics' institutes and libraries that gave factory workers the drawing, mathematical, and scientific preparation for skilled occupations.

Statewide public education for the masses flowered in the Northeast in the 1830s and 1840s. Horace Mann in Massachusetts and Henry Barnard in Connecticut developed systems of "common schools" to mediate the growth of industrial towns and cities. For Barnard, factories contained the seeds of society's undoing—moral corruption and political unrest. The mills and boardinghouses of towns such as Lowell, Massachusetts attracted farmers' daughters from the countryside and immigrants from Europe, creating new patterns of work and residence. Barnard and Mann cast education for the whole population as the great problem of the day, the key institutional strategy to reorganize New England's working classes as industrialization remade the economy.

In the second half of the century, leaders at the local, state, and national levels used schooling to "improve" and "civilize" the working classes from the industrial Northeast to the Western frontier. Schools for African Americans and poor whites constituted a key part of federal Reconstruction programs to rebuild the South after the Civil War. "Normal schools" in every state trained young women to be teachers, feminizing the United States' primary and secondary educational workforce. As public schools served the masses, private elite and parochial institutions effectively segregated the increasingly diverse populations of America's cities.

The late 19th century witnessed the growth and specialization of higher education. In 1862, the Union Congress passed the Morrill Land Act, providing for the sale of public lands to finance public colleges serving each state's needs. This led to the establishment of agricultural, engineering, and teachers' colleges. As the professions and academic disciplines became progressively specialized, universities founded schools of forestry, nursing, veterinary medicine, and business. The expansion of university-based laboratory science helped fuel a "second industrial revolution" of petrochemicals, electronics, and mass production. Formally schooled financiers, managers, and clerks constituted a new corporate class that occupied the growing high-rise office districts of American cities. These trends toward educational and occupational specialization were mirrored in secondary education. Urban districts started vocational schools teaching basic engineering for boys and commercial skills such as bookkeeping for girls who would join the ranks of stenographers and secretaries in the expanding white-collar workforce.

Not only did late 19th- and 20th-century universities train the professional workforces of cities, but their faculty also conducted research seeking to reform cities and urban life. Professors of architecture, city planning, and medicine used urban environments and populations as laboratories for experiments in urban design and public health. National organizations such as the American Social Science Association supported inquiry by professors of law, public administration, and social work at Harvard, Columbia, and the University of Pennsylvania. Working against their cities' corrupt political machines, Progressive academics tackled such subjects as civil service and tax reform, public utility management, and—in sociologist W. E. B. Du Bois' famous study, *The Philadelphia Negro*—the condition of African Americans in cities.

The Progressive Movement of the late 19th and early 20th centuries transformed public education across the United States. As Northern cities accommodated a flood of new immigrants and unprecedented industrialization, reformers such as John Dewey and Theodore Sizer devised institutional responses to the increasing scale and complexity of metropolitan society. Addressing psychologists' concerns about the distinct phases of youth, nursery schools and kindergartens extended schooling to younger children, while junior high schools confronted the problems of adolescence. Public-school curriculums engaged community issues identified by social scientists, including health, home economics, and—especially in immigrant neighborhoods—Americanization.

The Progressive Movement expanded school reformers' influence far beyond cities, making their crusade for professionalism and systematic administrative reorganization a national affair. In rural states, officials consolidated myriad school districts—14,000 in Iowa alone. National rates of high school attendance soared between 1900 and 1940. The mechanization of farming, coupled with school calendars that allowed students to work in the fields during summer and after school, made high school both necessary and possible for rural teenagers. While many urban teens in the manufacturing belt of the Northeast and Midwest continued to abandon school for work, the rural regions of the upper Midwest and Great Plains became a sort of American "education belt."

Education played an equally important role in shaping urban and rural society in the late-19th- and 20th-century South. Concerted public and private campaigns to limit African Americans' access to education formed a prominent means of repression as whites consolidated power in the post-Reconstruction regime of Jim Crow. This struggle over schooling would remain a crucial element of African Americans' claims to full citizenship throughout the 20th century, occupying a central place in the Civil Rights Movement along with late-century lawsuits seeking to equalize school funding between poor, largely minority, urban districts and their more affluent, white, suburban counterparts. The search for access to education would also factor into many African Americans' choices to depart the South for northern and western cities in the Great Migrations following each World War.

The hot and cold wars of the mid- and late 20th century profoundly impacted education in cities and suburbs. In primary and secondary schools, basements became fallout shelters, while air-raid drills sent students and teachers cowering under their desks. World War II ushered in an era of large-scale federal funding for universities, and the nuclear buildup of the Cold War further militarized the research of engineering, chemistry, and physics departments. The GI Bill underwrote college education for veterans. Together with the later Pell Grant and Stafford and Perkins loan programs, this federal investment afforded the middle and working classes unprecedented access to higher learning. Universities and their student populations expanded rapidly in the second half of the century. Suburban campuses such as Stanford in California became veritable "cities of knowledge," while many universities in inner cities became engines of urban renewal and gentrification.

In the post–World War II decades, public schools figured prominently in debates over the state's role in civil society. The Supreme Court's 1954 *Brown v. Board of Education* decision was a landmark in the Civil Rights Movement's fight against racial discrimination, sparking an era of deep conflicts over desegregation and community control of public education. Clashes among legislatures, mayors, courts, teachers' unions, school boards, parents, neighbors, and students sometimes shut down urban schools altogether, as in the 1968 Ocean Hill–Brownsville teachers' strike in Brooklyn. Some disputes turned violent. The National Guard was summoned to keep the peace as the first African American students arrived at Little Rock Central High School in Arkansas in 1957 and when ethnic whites in South Boston revolted against busing programs that brought black children to previously all-white schools in 1974.

Schools thus occupied a central place in the urban crises of the late 20th century. President Lyndon Johnson's War on Poverty attempted to alleviate these crises partly through investments in early-childhood and secondary education, including the Head Start and Follow Through programs. Yet just as urban renewal caused as many problems as it fixed, these educational initiatives enjoyed limited success in revitalizing the inner city. Since schools were bellwethers of social and neighborhood change, debates over school reform came to reflect society's deep divisions and ambivalence over federal policies, social welfare, race and labor relations, and the economic crises of inner cities.

While suburban schools may have been less controversial, they were equally important in shaping the geography and daily life of American metropolises. "Better schools" are often cited among families' motives for moving from city to suburb. Along with churches and shopping malls, public schools have served as the principal centers of civic life in new suburbs where other community institutions have yet to develop. Parent-teacher and home-and-school associations have provided forums through which suburbanites express their visions for society. In addition, as suburbs have encountered problems of juvenile delinquency and violence commonly associated with cities, as in the tragic 1999 shootings at Columbine High School, in Colorado, schools have come to embody the social conflicts and contradictions of suburban life.

In the late 20th century, educational leaders in cities and suburbs turned their attention to the global shift from an economy based on manufacturing to a service- and knowledge-based economy. As factories departed cities in the Northeast and Midwest, universities became more important assets. Municipal governments came to depend increasingly on institutions of higher education, especially engineering and medical schools, to generate new jobs and tax revenues. The Massachusetts Institute of Technology is commonly credited with driving greater Boston's economic resurgence as a high-tech hub, while Austin, Texas, and the "research triangle" of North Carolina have developed major technology sectors through partnerships between universities and private industry.

At the primary and secondary levels, late-20th-century school reformers called into question old curriculums and institutional systems designed for an industrial and agricultural society. Charter schools run by parents or civic leaders with state funding proliferated to serve the particular interests of diverse urban constituencies. For some places with large populations of recent immigrants, charters offered an opportunity to accommodate the multilingual and multicultural concerns of parents and students. Some parents have removed their children from schools altogether, joining the growing "homeschooling" movement. Countering this tendency toward community and family control is an increasing privatization of public education, in which the operation of individual schools or entire districts has been contracted to private companies.

The struggle for control of public education also has been waged in state capitols and between cities and state legislatures. Some states, including California and Pennsylvania, have taken over urban districts, deeming local leaders unfit to govern their own schools. "School choice" has come to dominate public debate over education reform. Elected representatives in statehouses and in Washington have promoted voucher systems that would give public money directly to families, who could choose to spend it on public, private, or parochial schooling. These measures would give most students enough capital to attend Catholic schools but not elite private schools. This has inspired debate over the relationships between church and state, public and private, perpetuating schools' position as institutions through which Americans express their social and political views.

Finally, another trend in late-20th-century school reform highlights the continued role of the judiciary in mandating changes in urban education. Poor cities with limited tax bases from which to fund local public schools have sued their state legislatures and departments of education, demanding more state money and revisions to education funding systems. In one series of decisions, the three-decade *Abbott v. Burke* case, the New Jersey Supreme Court mandated that the state fund poor urban districts at the same levels that the state's wealthiest districts fund their schools. The court ordered the legislature to pay millions of dollars toward the erection and renovation of school buildings. This and other cases have made public-school funding a vehicle for promoting social and economic equity in otherwise sharply segregated regions. And the *Abbott* and other urban school-construction campaigns have made schools a major force in neighborhood revitalization at the end of the 20th and beginning of the 21st century. Although their curriculums and institutional forms have changed, schools and education have continued to play vital roles in American cities' attempts to cope with economic restructuring while building a healthy civil society.

—*Domenic Vitiello*

See also Busing; Children in Cities and Suburbs; Desegregation of Education; Museums; Public Education

Further Readings and References

Berube, M. R. (1978). *The urban university in America.* Westport, CT: Greenwood Press.

Cremin, L. A. (1988). *American education: The metropolitan experience, 1876–1980.* New York: Harper and Row.

Formisano, R. P. (1991). *Boston against busing: Race, class, and ethnicity in the 1960s and 1970s.* Chapel Hill: University of North Carolina Press.

Kaestle, K. F. (1983). *Pillars of the republic: Common schools and American society, 1780–1860.* New York: Hill and Wang.

Katz, M. B. (1987). *Reconstructing American education.* Cambridge, MA: Harvard University Press.

Labaree, D. F. (1988). *The making of an American high school: The credentials market and the Central High School of Philadelphia, 1838–1939.* New Haven, CT: Yale University Press.

Lazerson, M. (1971). *Origins of the urban school: Public education in Massachusetts, 1870–1915.* Cambridge, MA: Harvard University Press.

O'Mara, M. P. (2004). *Cities of knowledge: Cold War science and the search for the next Silicon Valley.* Princeton, NJ: Princeton University Press.

Perlmann, J. (1988). *Ethnic differences: Schooling and social structure among the Irish, Italians, Jews, and Blacks in an American city, 1880–1935.* New York: Cambridge University Press.

Tyack, D. (1974). *The one best system: A history of American urban education.* Cambridge, MA: Harvard University Press.

ELEVATORS

The long history of elevators includes the construction of the pyramids, the experiments of Archimedes, the platforms that raised gladiators to the floor of the Roman Coliseum, and the passenger elevators of King Louis XV of France and Empress Maria Theresa of Austria. The modern history of elevators begins in 1853, when Elisha Graves Otis of Yonkers, New York, invented an elevator safety device that stopped cars whose hoisting cables had snapped from falling to the bottom of the shaft. Otis marketed his elevators and their safety breaks aggressively. P. T. Barnum gave Otis a space at the center of New York's Crystal Palace in 1854, where he demonstrated his device by slashing the rope of his demonstration elevator, falling a few inches, and calling out that all was safe.

New Yorkers and the residents of other large cities did not immediately warm to elevators. The first machine solely devoted to passenger service, installed in 1857 in the Broadway department store of merchants E. V. Haughwout and Co., soon went out of service because it made customers nervous. But in the late 19th century, elevators transformed the landscape and social life of industrial cities. They had two basic effects on society. First, elevators and the advent of structural steel allowed architects to build higher than ever before, creating denser residential neighborhoods and commercial districts and offering the necessary tools to build and run skyscrapers. Second, elevators increased the tendency toward segregation of buildings and neighborhoods by class. Before, buildings with multiple tenants could not rent upper floors at the same rate as lower ones, because the walk up made them less valuable. The new mode of conveyance ended this problem, spurring the growth of luxury apartment houses and office towers with rents uniform enough to keep out people below a certain income.

Advances in the technology of elevators generally have run to three purposes: greater speed/height, increased safety, and decreased reliance on human labor. The shift from steam power to hydraulics in the 1870s and electricity in the 1890s increased the speed of elevators and the heights of their buildings (although hydraulics dominated tall buildings until the introduction of gearless traction elevators in 1902). Following Otis's invention of 1853, his company and competitors came out with an endless stream of safety improvements—systems of multiple cables, the "air-cushion" device (which locked rapidly, compressing air under a falling elevator car until resistance slowed it to a gentle stop), interlocks to stop motion until the car doors were closed, automatic car leveling, and electric eyes to protect passengers' limbs. Other inventions, such as Muzak, calmed passengers' anxieties about vertical travel without actually increasing safety.

Clearly, some safety devices also aided the shift to full automation, but the crucial technological advance involved the slow invention of elevators smart enough to deliver many passengers to different floors. Automatic, push-button elevators dated to 1892, but early models could not handle more than one call at a time and so were limited to short, mostly residential buildings. A concerted effort to develop sophisticated automatic elevators did not begin until the mid-20th century, when operators' unions drove up the price of labor and a cultural rage for automation swept America. The "Autotronic" and "Selectomatic" systems unveiled by Otis and Westinghouse in 1948 ran unstaffed elevators electronically and shifted their traffic schedule without human supervision during the course of the day; subsequent advances include Otis's Elevonic 101 system of 1979, the first method of elevator control run completely through microprocessors, and the use of fuzzy logic to increase efficiency in Japanese elevator systems in 1992.

The social life inside elevators also has evolved over time, often in response to technological changes but also according to its own logic. Early elevators inspired a fear of technical failures and awkward social encounters that were echoed in newspaper articles and the fiction of authors such as William Dean Howells and Charles Battell Loomis. Even as technological advances made elevator travel safer, passengers continued to struggle with its cultural implications. They worked to develop etiquette appropriate to elevators that dictated which way to face, whether to tip the operator, and when to take off one's hat in the presence of other passengers. By the 1920s, building managers had begun actively to cultivate social graces in their elevator operators, training them to become a friendly, soothing presence. But these efforts could not allay all negative responses. At their worst, elevators (like railroads, streetcars, and other claustrophobic modes of transportation) evoked racist and elitist impulses. The Tulsa Race Riot of 1921, for example, began with an alleged altercation between a white female operator and a black male passenger, and the prejudice of passengers encouraged some building managers to replace black elevator operators with whites.

Through the early 20th century, operators strove to play a greater role in defining the social space of the elevator, as well as to win themselves better wages and conditions. As individuals, they developed standard cultural roles—the chatty Irish operator, the obsequious black operator—that bowed to popular stereotypes but also helped them to form personal bonds with customers. Collectively, operators formed unions and held strikes. In the biggest American cities, and in New York more than anywhere else, dependence on elevators gave operators great strategic power—they could stop transportation and bring a significant amount of economic activity to a halt. By the 1930s and 1940s, union leaders had learned to use this leverage in conjunction with the growing personal amity between operators and their passengers, and they won a string of victories in strikes and arbitration. Through the 1950s, however, building developers and managers responded by installing automated elevators; by the 1960s, many operators had been displaced, their unions had lost much power, and their potential to socialize people to elevators lay ignored and widely forgotten.

As the functional and cultural roles of operators waxed and waned, the place of elevators in the popular imagination consistently grew. First an object of curiosity in the art and fiction of the late 19th century, the elevator has multiplied in its artistic and narrative roles, particularly in film. The elevator provides dramatic entrances and a space to build tension before important encounters. It can easily signify luxury or sinister claustrophobia and symbolize ascent in a corporate hierarchy (*The Apartment,* directed by Billy Wilder, 1960) or descent into hell (*Angel Heart,* directed by Alan Parker, 1987). Romance and chance encounters bloom in fictional elevators, and they can offer hope for freedom or spiritual redemption. Although elevators will continue to inspire fear and discomfort for some, these positive connotations may flourish in generations increasingly accustomed to vertical travel.

—Dan Levinson Wilk

See also Howells, William Dean

Further Readings and References

Goetz, A. (2003). *Up down across: Elevators, escalators, and moving sidewalks.* London: Merrell Publishers.

Goodwin, J. (2001). *Giving rise to the modern city.* Chicago: Ivan R. Dee.

Palladino, G. (1987). When militancy isn't enough: The impact of automation of New York City building service workers, 1934–1970. *Labor History, 28*(2), 196–220.

Wilk, D. L. (2005). *Cliff dwellers: Modern service in New York City, 1800–1945.* Ph.D. dissertation, Duke University.

ELLIS ISLAND

Ellis Island, located in upper New York Bay, has served many purposes: property of Samuel Ellis and his heirs until 1807; location of a fort and arsenal in the mid-19th century; hospital for wounded servicemen during both World Wars; prison for aliens awaiting deportation, among them the anarchists Emma Goldman and Alexander Berkman; and presently home of the Ellis Island Immigration Museum. However, the island is most famous and significant as the site of the federal government's main immigrant screening center from 1892 to 1924, during which time 71 percent of all newcomers arrived at the port of New York and more than 12 million of them were cleared for entry through Ellis Island. Since the great majority of those individuals settled in the nation's cities, almost one-third in New York and its immediate area alone, Ellis Island became the gateway to urban America and a chief source of its inhabitants. By 1910, the foreign-born and their children constituted three-fourths of the population of such cities as New York, Chicago, Detroit, Cleveland, and Boston. Late in the 20th century, roughly 100 million Americans, 40 percent of the United States, could trace their ancestry back to a man, woman, or child who had entered the country through Ellis Island.

The first immigration station on Ellis Island opened on January 1, 1892, and operated until 1897. During that period, approximately 1.5 million persons were examined and admitted to the country, including Irving Berlin, Felix Frankfurter, and Samuel Goldwyn. On the nights of June 14 and 15, 1897, fire broke out, destroying the center's wooden buildings completely. None of the 191 people on the island at the time was hurt, but valuable immigration records going back to 1855 were lost. The Bureau of Immigration hired the architectural firm of Boring and Tilton to construct a fireproof replacement. Built in a French Renaissance style of brick and limestone, the new facility reopened on December 17, 1900. Although it was designed to accommodate a half million entrants a year, the building soon proved inadequate because the actual volume of arriving steerage-class passengers (the only ones brought to the island) often exceeded that. In 1907, the peak year, almost 900,000 persons passed through Ellis Island. To handle the flood of immigrants, the government enlarged the island with landfill from its original 3 to 27.5 acres, added new wings and a third floor to the main building, and eventually erected 33 other buildings, at least 15 of which were hospital facilities.

Ferried to the island from the Hudson River piers at which they had disembarked, the newcomers were directed into the huge registry room in the main building, where immigration officials attempted to ferret out paupers, polygamists, mental defectives, contract laborers, and criminals. Unaccompanied women and children were detained until male relatives in America could be found who would offer shelter and support. After 1917, inspectors also tested the ability of adults seeking entry to read in some language. Public Health Service doctors looked for people suffering from debilitating and/or contagious illness. Those expected to recover were sent to Ellis's hospital wards for care, but those with symptoms of the then-incurable eye disease trachoma, tuberculosis, or heart conditions were rejected. Despite the feared questioning and medical examining, 98 percent of the prospective immigrants gained entry, and 80 percent did so in less than 8 hours. Once cleared, immigrants bought train tickets for destinations throughout the country and boarded railroad barges for stations in New York and New Jersey, or they took the Ellis Island ferry to the Battery.

The 1924 National Origins Quota Act ended mass immigration and provided that those seeking admission would be examined in their countries of origin. This diminished the role of Ellis Island as a screening center, and thereafter it was used primarily to detain deportees. After the Immigration and Naturalization Service moved its operation to Manhattan in 1954, the government, declaring Ellis Island surplus property, tried to sell it. Public protest and lack of adequate bids foiled the sale.

In 1965, President Lyndon B. Johnson, recognizing Ellis's historic importance, made it a part of the Statue of Liberty National Monument and placed it in the permanent care of the National Park Service (NPS). Congress, however, did not appropriate sufficient funds to permit the NPS to repair the abandoned buildings, let alone turn the station into "a handsome shrine," as Johnson had proposed. Although the NPS opened the main building to limited public visitation in 1976, the deterioration of the historic site continued unabated. In 1982, a private association, chaired by business executive Lee A. Iacocca, whose parents had emigrated from Italy through Ellis Island, set up the Statue of Liberty–Ellis Island Foundation to collect corporate and individual donations to repair and restore the two sites. Ellis Island closed to the public in 1984, and the $156-million reconstruction project on it commenced. Restored to look as it did between 1918 and 1924, the main building, housing the Ellis Island Immigration Museum, opened on September 10, 1990. Since then, nearly 2 million people a year have visited the museum dedicated to telling the story of the immigrants who built and inhabited urban America.

—*Barbara Blumberg*

Further Readings and References

ARAMARK. (2002). *Ellis Island history*. Available from http://www.ellisisland.com

Blumberg, B. (1985). *Celebrating the immigrant: An administrative history of the Statue of Liberty National Monument, 1952–1982*. Boston: North Atlantic Regional Offices, National Park Service, U.S. Department of the Interior.

Brownstone, D. M., Franck, I. M., & Brownstone, D. (2000). *Island of hope, island of tears*. New York: Barnes & Noble Books.

Hall, A. J. (1990, September). New life for Ellis Island. *National Geographic*, 90–98.

Jonas, S. (Ed.). (1989). *Ellis Island: Echoes from a nation's past*. New York: An Aperture Book, Aperture Foundation.

Pitkin, T. M. (1975). *Keepers of the gate: A history of Ellis Island*. New York: New York University Press.

Tifft, W., & Dunne, T. (1971). *Ellis Island*. New York: W. W. Norton.

EMPIRE STATE BUILDING

Since the building opened to the public on May 1, 1931, the distinctive shape of the Empire State Building has been an unmistakable part of the New York City skyline, towering above midtown Manhattan at 1,453 feet, 8 and 9/16 inches. Located at 350 Fifth Avenue on a two-acre site stretching from West 33rd to West 34th streets, the building was perhaps most famously cemented in the American psyche as the site of the giant ape's refuge in the 1933 film *King Kong*. The 365,000-ton, art deco–style building is home to hundreds of businesses employing more than 25,000 workers; it is simultaneously a cultural icon hosting thousands of visitors each day who ascend to the 86th-floor observation deck located 1,050 feet above street level.

From the outset, the Empire State was meant to be a testament to free enterprise and American ingenuity. Tycoons John Raskob and Pierre S. du Pont and former New York mayor Alfred E. Smith planned to build the tallest and most impressive building in the world amid the bull market and real estate boom of the 1920s. Architect William F. Lamb of the firm Shreve, Lamb, and Harmon originally designed a 1,000-foot structure, but competition drove the developers to add floors and a dirigible mooring mast (never actually used) to push the building definitively above the 1,048-foot height of the nearby Chrysler Building. The structural core of the tower stands 102 stories tall, capped by a 204-foot antenna and lightning rod. Upon completion, the building was the tallest in the world for 40 years, surpassed by New York's World Trade Center in 1972. Since September 11, 2001 it is again the tallest building in New York City.

Construction began on St. Patrick's Day, March 17, 1930, scant months into the Great Depression, supplying more than 3,000 much-needed jobs for laborers, ironworkers, and carpenters. Each week, four stories were added to the massive building's shell, and final masonry was laid in place on May 1, 1931, significantly ahead of schedule. Construction required seven million hours of labor, 200,000 cubic feet of stone, 6,500 windows, 10 million bricks, and more than 700 tons of steel and aluminum. Visitors and tenants are conveyed to their destinations by 73 elevators, or brave souls can climb the 1,860 stairs to the 102nd floor.

Final cost of the building and land was approximately $40 million. Because of a 114-year low-cost lease and management contract granted in 1962 by then-owners The Prudential Company to the Helmsley-Spear management agency, the building is valued at only about the same amount today. Financiers suspect that, were it not saddled with the lease running through 2076, the Empire State would be worth at least a billion dollars to a potential buyer.

—*Donovan Finn*

See also New York, New York

Further Readings and References

Pacelle, M. (2002). *Empire: A tale of obsession, betrayal, and the battle for an American icon.* New York: John Wiley & Sons.

Taurana, J. (1997). *Empire State Building: The making of a landmark.* New York: St. Martin's Griffin.

Wagner, G. B. (2003). *Thirteen months to go: The creation of the Empire State Building.* San Diego, CA: Thunder Bay Press.

ENVIRONMENT AND ECOLOGY

Cities and their metropolitan areas have major effects on the natural environment, while the natural environment, in turn, has profoundly shaped urban configurations. While these urban impacts have occurred since cities first appeared, they have accelerated with the development of industrialism and rapid urbanization during the last two centuries. The extensive growth of world cities since the end of World War II affected the environment to an unprecedented extent. In the United States, as well, urban development accelerated, and today a majority of the population lives in sizable metropolitan areas. In these areas, suburbanization increasingly resulted in the encroachment of the built environment on the natural environment.

Americans founded cities in locations where nature offered various attractions, such as on coastlines where the land's natural contours created harbors; on rivers and lakes that could be used for transportation, water supplies, and waste disposal; and in fertile river valleys with extensive food and animal resources. Rather than being passive, the natural environment frequently played an active and even destructive role in the life of cities. Urban history is filled with stories about how city dwellers contended with the forces of nature that threatened their lives, their built environments, and their urban ecosystems. Nature not only caused many of the annoyances of daily urban life, such as bad weather and pests, but also gave rise to natural disasters and catastrophes such as floods, fires, and earthquakes. In order to protect themselves against the forces of nature, cities built many defenses, including floodwalls and dams, earthquake-resistant buildings, and storage places for food and water. At times, such protective steps sheltered urbanites against the worst natural furies, but often their own actions—building on floodplains and steep slopes, under the shadow of volcanoes, or in earthquake-prone zones—exposed them unnecessarily to danger from natural hazards.

Cities have always placed demands on their sites and their hinterlands. In order to extend their sites territorially, urban developers often reshaped natural landscapes, leveling hills, filling valleys and wetlands, and creating huge areas of made land. On this new land, they constructed a built environment of paved streets, malls, houses, factories, office buildings, and churches. In the process, they altered urban biological ecosystems for their own purposes, killing off animal populations, eliminating native species of flora and fauna, and introducing new and foreign species. Thus, urbanites constructed a built environment that replaced the natural environment, creating a local microclimate, with different temperature gradients and rainfall and wind patterns than those of the surrounding countryside.

In order to fulfill their metabolic needs, cities need food, water, fuel, and construction materials. In order to meet these needs, urbanites increasingly had to reach far beyond their boundaries. In the 19th century, for instance, the demands of city dwellers for food produced rings of garden farms around cities; eventually, improved transportation drove the transformation of distant prairies into cattle ranches and wheat farms, the products of which were directed toward urban markets. Cities also required fresh water supplies in order to exist; engineers, acting at the behest of urban elites and politicians, built waterworks, thrust water-intake pipes ever farther into neighboring lakes, dug wells deeper and deeper into the earth looking for groundwater, and dammed and diverted rivers and streams to obtain water supplies for domestic and industrial uses and for firefighting. In the process of obtaining water from water-rich but distant locales, they often transformed them, making deserts where there had been fertile agricultural areas (e.g., the Owens Valley and the Los Angeles water supply) and flooding many towns and farms (e.g., the construction of Boston's Quabbin Reservoir in 1928, which flooded four towns).

City entrepreneurs and industrialists were actively involved in the commodification of natural systems, putting them to use for purposes of urban consumption. The exploitation of waterpower from rivers and streams, for instance, provided power for manufacturing cities, but it also sharply altered river dynamics, destroying fish populations and depriving downstream users of adequate and unpolluted supplies. For materials to build and heat the city, loggers stripped the countryside of forests, quarrymen tore granite and other stone from the earth, and miners dug coal to provide fuel for commercial, industrial, and domestic uses.

Urbanites had to seek locations or "sinks" to dispose of the wastes produced by construction, manufacturing, and consumption processes. Initially, they placed them on sites within the city, polluting the air, land, and water with industrial and domestic effluents and modifying and even destroying natural biological systems. In the post–Civil War period, as cities grew larger, they disposed of their wastes by transporting them to more distant locations. Thus, cities constructed sewerage systems for domestic wastes to replace cesspools and privy vaults and to improve local health conditions. They usually discharged the sewage into neighboring waterways, often polluting the water supply of downstream cities and producing epidemics of cholera, typhoid, and other waterborne diseases. In order to prevent these, downstream cities sought new sources of supply, building protected watersheds in distant areas or using technological fixes, such as water filtration (1890s) or chlorination (1912). Industrial wastes also added to water pollution, and urban rivers often became little more than open sewers.

The air and the land also became sinks for waste disposal. In the late 19th century, bituminous (or soft) coal became the preferred fuel for industrial, transportation, and domestic use in cities such as Chicago, Pittsburgh, and St. Louis. But while providing an inexpensive and plentiful energy supply, bituminous coal was also very dirty. The cities that used it suffered from air contamination, reducing sunlight and undoubtedly causing health effects, while the cleaning tasks of householders were greatly increased. Industry also used land surfaces for disposal of domestic and industrial wastes, and open areas in and around cities were marked with heaps of garbage, horse manure, ashes, and industrial wastes such as slag from iron- and steel-making or copper smelting. Such materials often were used to fill in "swamps" (wetlands) along waterfronts.

In the late 19th and early 20th centuries, reformers began campaigning for urban environmental cleanups and public health improvements. Women's groups often took the lead in agitating for clean air, clean water, and improved urban "housekeeping," showing a greater concern than men with such quality-of-life and health-related issues. Many progressive reformers believed that the moral qualities of good citizenship were related to environmental improvements and exposure to nature. They pushed for reduction of pollution and for construction of urban parks and playgrounds as a means to acculturate immigrants and upgrade working-class citizenship. Coalitions of reformers, urban professionals such as engineers and public health officials, and enlightened businessmen spearheaded drives for improvements in water supply and sanitary services. The replacement of the horse, first by electric traction and then by the automobile and motor truck, as a prime means of power for urban transport brought about substantial improvements in street and air sanitation. Campaigns for clean air and reduction of pollution of waterways, however, were largely unsuccessful or had very limited results. On balance, urban sanitary conditions were probably somewhat better in the 1920s than in the late 19th century, but the cost of improvement was often the exploitation of urban hinterlands for water supplies, increased downstream water pollution, and growing automobile congestion and air contamination.

During the post–World War II decades, city environments suffered from heavy pollution loads as they sought to cope with increased automobile use, pollution from industrial production, new varieties of exotic chemical pesticides and herbicides such as DDT, and the wastes of an increasingly consumer-oriented economy. Cleaner fuels and smoke-control laws largely freed cities during the 1940s and 1950s of the dense smoke that they had previously suffered from. Improved urban air quality resulted largely from the substitution of natural gas and oil for coal as urban fuels and the replacement of the steam locomotive by the diesel-electric. However, great increases in automobile use in areas such as Los Angeles and Denver produced the new phenomenon of photochemical smog, and air pollution replaced smoke as a major concern. Another improvement that proved temporary involved the replacement of the open dump and the pig farm with the sanitary landfill as a disposal place for urban garbage in the 1950s, 1960s, and 1970s. By the 1970s, however, it had become clear that the sanitary landfill often had substantial polluting qualities. As cities ran out of land for landfills, they began an expensive search for nonpolluting and environmentally sound alternatives.

In these years, also, suburban out-migration, which had begun in the 19th century with commuter trains and streetcars, accelerated because of exponential automobile growth, putting major strains on the formerly rural and undeveloped metropolitan fringes. To a great extent, suburban layouts ignored environmental considerations, making little provision for open space, producing endless rows of resource-consuming and polluting lawns, contaminating groundwater with septic tanks, and consuming excessive amounts of fresh water and energy. The growth of the edge or outer city since the 1970s reflected a continued preference on the part of Americans for space-intensive single-family houses surrounded by lawns, for private automobiles over public transit, and for greenfield rather than brownfield development. Even though today's environmental regulations prevent some of the environmental abuses of the past, without greater land-use planning and environmental protection, urban America will, as it has in the past, continue to damage and stress the natural environment.

—Joel A. Tarr

Further Readings and References

Deverell, W., & Hise, G. (2005). *Land of sunshine: An environmental history of metropolitan Los Angeles.* Pittsburgh, PA: University of Pittsburgh Press.

Melosi, M. V. (2000). *The sanitary city: Urban infrastructure in America from colonial times to the present.* Baltimore: Johns Hopkins University Press.

Miller, C. (Ed.). (2001). *On the border: An environmental history of San Antonio.* Pittsburgh, PA: University of Pittsburgh Press.

Rosen, C. M., & Tarr, J. A. (Eds.). (1994, May). *The environment and the city: A special issue of the* Journal of Urban History. Vol. 20, No. 3.

Tarr, J. A. (1996). *The search for the ultimate sink: Urban pollution in historical perspective.* Series in Technology and the Environment. Akron, OH: University of Akron Press.

Tarr, J. A. (Ed.). (2003). *Devastation and renewal: An environmental history of Pittsburgh and its region.* Pittsburgh, PA: University of Pittsburgh Press.

ENVIRONMENTAL RACISM

Environmental racism refers to the disproportionate distribution of environmental risks and exclusion of people of color from environmental decision making, by both environmental organizations and regulatory agencies. The increase in environmental burdens borne by people of color can come either from regulations that result in higher risks in particular communities or from the inequitable enforcement of regulations.

The first known use of the term "environmental racism" was in 1987, when Benjamin Chavis, then executive director of the United Church of Christ's Commission on Racial Justice, announced at a press conference the release of the report *Toxic Wastes and Race in the United States.* The first national-scale study of the demographic characteristics of communities near waste sites concluded that people of color, especially in urban areas, are more likely to live near uncontrolled toxic-waste sites than are whites. The report became an authoritative voice on the issue; all subsequent research about equity in the distribution of environmental risk refined, substantiated, or rejected the UCC's methodology or conclusion. Starting in 1994, a series of studies challenged the idea that people of color were disproportionately affected by environmental risks. The methodological critiques included challenges in four areas: the definition of an affected community, measurements of race and class, criteria for comparison, and measurements of risk.

Communities of color experienced higher environmental risks prior to naming the phenomenon. Much of the discriminatory distribution of environmental risks was tied to exclusionary housing and land-use practices that forced people of color to live in locations with higher pollution levels from industrial contamination. The 1971 annual report of the Council on Environmental Quality indicated that racial discrimination in urban land use and housing practices contributed to lower environmental quality of the urban poor and people of color. Efforts to improve housing, reduce trash, and reclaim vacant lots in poor urban neighborhoods were a significant part of the overall endeavors to improve the quality of life of poor people of color. Prior to the 1980s, rarely were these activities labeled environmental action; they were more often described as community organizing or neighborhood development. Community organizing to stop environmental racism began in earnest after the UCC report.

The impetus to conduct a study of the demographic characteristics of communities near waste facilities emerged from the participation of the UCC Commission for Racial Justice in a series of protest events in 1982 against a chemical-waste landfill in Afton, Warren County, North Carolina. After an illegal dumping of liquid containing polychlorinated biphenyls (PCBs) onto state road shoulders, the state of North Carolina decided to build the landfill to hold the 40,000 cubic yards of contaminated soil. The protests were part of the growing opposition to facility sitings under the Resource Conservation and Recovery Act and the Toxic Substances Control Act, but the Warren County protests stood out among the burgeoning anti-toxic movement because several prominent civil rights leaders were among those arrested, and the protesters argued that the government chose the Afton site because of environmental racism: The majority-black population in Warren County made it a place of least resistance to the politically charged decision of siting the chemical-waste landfill. The protests underscored the conviction that social and political issues, based in particular belief systems, would influence environmental decisions. Immediately following the protests, Representative Walter Fauntroy (D-DC) arranged for the General Accounting Office (GAO) of the U.S. Congress to investigate the demographic characteristics of commercial waste sites in the South. Although a very small-scale investigation, the GAO report indicated that environmental racism could be influencing the

location of waste facilities. The UCC report was designed to follow up and expand on the initial investigation by the GAO.

The early 1990s saw a flurry of activity by activists and government. In 1990, the University of Michigan organized a conference to examine the evidence of environmental racism in a wide range of situations including waste facilities, pesticides, fishery contamination, parks and recreation, and membership in environmental organizations. A group of conference attendees wrote a letter to the Environmental Protection Agency (EPA), outlining the problems of environmental racism and demanding that the agency take action to address the issues. As a result, in 1992 the first federal government report was issued, *Environmental Equity: Reducing Risks for All Communities*. Government officials were reluctant to use the term "environmental racism," and the report equivocated the role of racism in creating inequitable distribution of risk. After the EPA report was issued, activists leaned toward using the term "environmental justice" to describe their goals. In 1990, the influential book *Dumping in Dixie: Race, Class and Environmental Quality* was published and provided evidence of environmental injustice due to racism. It argued that indigenous leaders in communities of color were needed to combat it. A year later, the First National People of Color Environmental Leadership Summit was held in Washington, D.C. As a defining moment for environmental justice, the summit championed the new environmental identity and built solidarity among the disparate groups that made up the movement. The summit issued the 17 Principles of Environmental Justice, representing the attendees' understanding of the objectives of their movement. The principles outlined the civil rights needed to attain equitable distribution of risks and access to decision making. In addition, several of the principles explicitly addressed economic restructuring and democratization of production as a means of achieving environmental justice.

At the start of the Clinton administration, two major accomplishments indicated that environmental justice had an established presence on the political stage. In September 1993, the EPA established the National Environmental Justice Advisory Council (NEJAC) "to provide independent advice and recommendations to the Administrator on areas relating to environmental justice." Activists wanted NEJAC to be a primary mechanism to include the voices of those marginalized from environmental decision making. In February 1994, Clinton signed Executive Order (EO)

12898, "Federal Actions to Address Environmental Justice in Minority Populations and Low-Income Populations." The EO established an Interagency Working Group (IWG), under EPA leadership, and required the development of specific strategies for incorporating environmental justice into each agency. It also mandated future data collection and analysis to include environmental justice considerations as well as an increase in appropriate public participation and access to information.

Several legal challenges alleged civil rights violations of implementation of environmental regulations. The first such suit was filed in Houston in 1979 against the siting of a municipal solid-waste landfill but was unsuccessful. The first major victory for environmental justice came in 1991, but it was not based on civil rights law. The plaintiffs in *El Pueblo para el Aire y Agua Limpio v. County of Kings (California)* prevailed in their claim that "meaningful participation," mandated by the National Environmental Protection Act, had not been achieved because the documents used during the permit process for a hazardous-waste incinerator were not translated into Spanish. In 1992, in response to the environmental justice executive order, the EPA established the Office of Civil Rights (OCR) to review complaints based on Title VI of the Civil Rights Act of 1964. Between September 1993 and August 1998, OCR received 58 complaints and responded to only 4. Of these 4, only 1 (Select Steel) was decided on the merits and held for the defendant. As a result of the slow administrative review of complaints, plaintiffs took their cases back to the courts. The first victorious environmental justice case was *South Camden Citizens in Action v. NJ Dept of Environmental Protection* in 2001, later overturned by the third circuit court. In 2001, in *Alexander v. Sandoval*, the U.S. Supreme Court held that private individuals may not sue to enforce disparate-impact regulations under Title VI.

In addition to challenging regulations and environmental agencies, activists working for environmental justice forced traditional environmental organizations to address the problem of environmental racism. After a group of environmental justice activists wrote a letter in 1990 to the 10 largest environmental organizations accusing them of exclusionary memberships and staff as well as agendas that ignored the issues most important to urban communities, the traditional groups were forced to change their practices. All of these organizations now boast vital environmental justice programs and more diverse memberships and staff. The organizations focused specifically on environmental justice grew significantly in the 1990s. In 1994, the *People of Color Environmental Groups Directory* listed more than 600 organizations in North America, and by 2000, there were more than 1,000 groups. Twenty years after the term "environmental racism" was first used, the environmental justice movement has deeply influenced environmentalism in all arenas, including traditional environmental organizations, emerging environmental justice groups, and governmental agencies responsible for implementing environmental legislation.

—*Eileen McGurty*

Further Readings and References

Bullard, R. D. (2004). *Dumping in Dixie: Race, class and environmental quality* (2nd ed.). Boulder, CO: Westview Press.

Liu, F. (2001). *Environmental justice analysis: Theories, methods, and practice*. Boca Raton, FL: Lewis Publishers.

McGurty, E. (2007). *Transforming environmentalism: Warren County, PCBs, and the origins of environmental justice*. New Brunswick, NJ: Rutgers University Press.

Rechtschaffen, C., & Gauna, E. (Eds.). (2003). *Environmental justice: Law, policy, and regulation*. Durham, NC: Carolina Academic Press.

ERIE CANAL

The Erie Canal is an artificial waterway that was constructed between the Hudson River and Buffalo, New York, and completed in 1825. It was the first major canal built in the United States, and it became the standard for future canals. When the Erie Canal was completed, it was 363 miles long and had an elevation change of 650 feet accomplished with the use of 83 locks. The canal was 28 feet wide at the bottom and 40 feet wide at the surface; it was a uniform 4 feet deep. The canal had towpaths for horses and humans to move the boats along the canal. Eighteen aqueducts carried the canal over rivers and large streams. Construction also included a large number of bridges for traffic to cross the canal.

In the 1790s, New York was exploring options for constructing a canal across the state. There were several proposals for how to achieve this goal; there were also several attempts at building small canals or canalizing rivers. State funding was approved, and construction began in 1817, with the canal opening for traffic between New York City and Buffalo in 1825. The Erie Canal took advantage of the Hudson River, which is the only natural breach in the Appalachian Mountain Range.

Within a year of the Erie Canal's opening, 2,000 boats plus their crews were involved in the transportation of goods on the canal. Because of the grain entering the Port of Buffalo, there was a need to build grain storage facilities in that city. In 1829, 3,640 bushels of wheat were transported from Buffalo down the canal, and by 1837, that figure grew to 500,000 bushels. By 1841, more than one million bushels were shipped on the canal. Within nine years of opening the Erie Canal, the canal toll revenue had exceeded the expenditure to build the canal.

Goods shipped from New York City would be sailed north along the Hudson River to a point just south of Albany, New York, where the boats would then head west across northern New York to Buffalo, which is on Lake Erie. From there, the goods would be transferred to ships on the lake and then delivered to Ohio. Ohio was crossed by several canals that allowed for the shipment of goods to Illinois, Indiana, Kentucky, and all the cities along the Mississippi River.

New York City and Buffalo experienced both population and economic growth with the opening of the Erie Canal. They were not the only cities to enjoy growth; cities such as Troy, Utica, Oneida, Rome, Syracuse, and Rochester all experienced benefits from the Erie. There also were other canals in New York State that connected to the Erie, including Champlain, Chenango, Black River, Oswego, Cayuga and Seneca, and Genesee Valley. These canals helped bring agricultural, construction, and other materials from the outlying portions of the state to the ports of Buffalo and New York as well as helped to increase trade within the state. Almost 80 percent of the upstate population lives less then 30 miles from the Erie Canal.

Fifteen years after the canal opened, New York City was the busiest port in America. A greater tonnage moved through New York than Boston, Baltimore, and New Orleans combined.

Because of the availability of cheap power near waterfalls, a number of grist and cloth mills as well as factories were built near the canals. These industries included water-pump makers, fire-engine manufacturers, flour mills, cloth mills, salt from mines, and other industries, which all took advantage of cheap transportation provided by the canals.

Between 1836 and 1862, the Erie Canal was under constant improvement and enlargement to allow larger boats to haul more goods to market. When this phase of enlargement was completed, boats that had the capacity to carry 250 tons of cargo replaced those that could carry only 30 tons. In 1868, the Erie Canal carried three million tons of freight.

In 1882, tolls were abolished for all of the New York State canals. As the 19th century was closing, New York reexamined all of the canals in the system and determined which canals should remain open and enlarged; this project began in 1903 and was completed in 1918. The project would allow barges to ply the canal system. The entire system was renamed the New York State Barge Canal and incorporated the Erie Canal, the Cayuga and Seneca Canal, the Oswego Canal, and the Champlain Canal. The last year for commercial traffic on the canals was 1994; now the canals are used for recreational purposes.

—*Douglas K. Bohnenblust*

Further Readings and References

Carter, G. (Ed.). (1961). *Canals and American economic development*. New York: Columbia University Press.
Cornog, E. (1998). *The birth of empire: DeWitt Clinton and the American experience, 1769–1828*. New York: Oxford University Press.
Sheriff, C. (1996). *The artificial river: The Erie Canal and the paradox of progress, 1817–1862*. New York: Hill and Wang.

ETHNIC NEIGHBORHOODS

Since colonial times, enclaves of persons sharing common ancestry, national origin, language, or race and ethnicity have been significant elements in American urban environments. Today, *ethnic neighborhood* is the term most commonly used to describe such distinctive communities. Ethnic neighborhoods represent a marked category within the domain of American communities. The identification of a particular community as *ethnic* (a term derived from the ancient Greek noun *ethnos*, "nation") requires that residents inside and outside the neighborhood share an understanding of what is *non*ethnic.

Ethnic neighborhoods do not exist in a vacuum, but in the context of the surrounding Anglo communities historically defined as nonethnic. Even in cities where white Anglo-Saxon Protestants (WASPs) never were in the majority, their access to economic and political power meant that they did not suffer the discrimination and prejudice that were the daily bread for all other ethnic and racial groups. If ethnic identity is about how a group defines itself and is defined vis-à-vis other groups, then ethnic neighborhoods represent the residential dimension of that identity within the ever-changing urban landscape.

Ethnic Homogeneity, Multi-Ethnicity, and Pan-Ethnicity

Signs in languages other than English on store windows are sure indicators of a substantial ethnic population in an urban residential or commercial district. Until recently, each ethnic neighborhood was home to people sharing a common culture and speaking the language of their ancestors. In Los Angeles, driving along Garden Grove Boulevard or Long Beach Boulevard means passing through one ethnic enclave after another, as measured by the changing languages on the signs. In recent years, many of these neighborhoods have become multicultural and multilingual. Store signs in three or more language are everywhere, public schools cope with dozens of languages and cultures among their students' families, local video stores offer movies from around the world, and churches, temples, mosques, and fellowships compete for prime real estate along the boulevards.

A more expansive form of multi-ethnicity is found among Native Americans. Members of diverse tribes have learned that forming pan-Indian organizations helps them to obtain much-needed services from the Bureau of Indian Affairs and other agencies. More than 60 urban intertribal centers, spread across 38 states, offer services to the two-thirds of Native Americans who reside in urban places.

Sometimes pan-ethnic neighborhood organizations are impossible. For example, some African-origin tribal populations are unable to be neighbors with their historical enemies. Maya migrants from Guatemala cannot forget and forgive those Guatemalans who participated in massacres of Indian populations.

History

The separation of the European colonists' settlements from those of the Indians greatly diminished the prospects for building integrated settlements such as those that developed into *mestizo* communities in Latin America. In colonial America, settlements tended to be homogeneous, usually based on residents' religious practices. Even African-origin slaves lived in or near their owners' residences or workplaces, since they lacked the freedom to re-create tribal-based enclaves. According to the first national census in 1790, New York City was the largest city, with just 33,131 inhabitants; Philadelphia followed with 28,522; Boston had 18,320, Charleston 16,359, and Baltimore 13,503. Fifty years later, New York City had 312,710 inhabitants, but the next two largest cities (Baltimore and New Orleans) had only 102,313 and 102,193, respectively. The emergence of industrial production systems, especially in Northern cities, and the expansion of American settlements across the Mississippi created pressures for bringing an end to the South's traditional slave-based plantation economy. One of the unexpected consequences of the North's victory in the Civil War was the building of "freedman's towns" by former slaves on the edges of many Southern cities.

By the last years of the 19th century, changes in technology—including the introduction of horse-drawn vehicles, electric street trolleys, and steam-driven trains—increased the separation of home and workplace for America's urban residents. At the same time, millions of immigrants and refugees were coming to the New World from Europe and Asia, while even more millions were abandoning rural America in the hope of finding their futures in the great cities. As a result, hundreds of ethnic neighborhoods appeared across the American urban landscape. Poor-quality housing units (known as tenements) were built for poor, first- and second-generation immigrants. These overcrowded neighborhoods offered wonderful opportunities for ethnic entrepreneurs, both legitimate and illegitimate. Regarding Hell's Kitchen and other infamous tenements in New York City, Jacob Riis wrote in 1890 that a map of those areas colored to indicate nationalities would appear to be zebra-striped. In his analysis of urban poverty, Riis discussed the distinctive neighborhoods of the Irish, Germans, Italians, French, African Americans, Russian and Polish Jews, Chinese, Finns, Greeks, and Swiss.

Recognizing the realities of ethnic discrimination in late-19th-century America, the framers of the "Pittsburgh Platform" of Reform Judaism (1885) declared that they were more of a religious community than a nation. Nevertheless, many of the Orthodox Jewish communities concentrated in and around New York City—home to about one-third of the nation's Jewish population—continued to self-identify (and are identified) as living in ethnic neighborhoods.

By the beginning of the 20th century, most new-comers to the cities—whether southern European peasant refugees, Chinese labor immigrants, or southern African American migrants—were defined as "inferior" and "less desirable" by entrenched power holders. Struggling working-class inhabitants felt especially vulnerable to losing their jobs to the new arrivals. While the "melting pot" ideology was being proclaimed throughout the land, many large cities began to lose residents who could afford to relocate their families to new suburban communities.

During the 20th century, the transformation of urban neighborhoods came to be known as *neighborhood succession*. In its classic form, nonethnic Anglo neighborhoods became ethnic as new waves of immigrants arrived from other countries or from the countryside. Jews, African Americans, Hispanics, Asians, and Africans all participated in this long-term process. In Chicago, the working-class Pilsen neighborhood associated with Czech and German immigrants in the late 19th century passed into the hands of Poles, Croatians, Lithuanians, and Italians as the 20th century progressed. Now, Pilsen is the heart of one of the largest Mexican-origin communities in the nation.

Ultimately, neighborhood succession may lead to gentrification, the process through which affluent Anglos return—first as pioneers and then in greater numbers—to acquire control of distressed properties in deteriorating districts. As a consequence, ethnic residents may find themselves priced out of neighborhoods where they have lived for decades. Reordering urban spaces through gentrification, while ignoring the traditions of those who used to live there, is a form of historical discrimination. The practice of segregation must be avoided in history just as in contemporary society.

Segregation at the Neighborhood Level

In earlier decades, before laws about equal housing opportunity came into being, it was virtually impossible for minority families to escape the circumstances imposed on them in inner city neighborhoods. Occasionally, the urban power elite would facilitate the creation of new ethnic neighborhoods in order to accommodate the needs of the most successful members of the ethnic community. For instance, in the 1950s, before the era of civil rights and fair housing, Anglo community leaders in Dallas permitted the building of the Hamilton Park neighborhood for African Americans on the northern edge of the city. Even now, all other African American neighborhoods are located in southern Dallas—and Dallas continues to be among the most residentially segregated cities in America.

One consequence of segregation is the differential rate of poverty and violence in ethnic versus nonethnic neighborhoods. The effects of poverty and violence have been present for many decades. In July 1919, serious riots broke out in Chicago's South Side African American neighborhood. The Los Angeles Watts Riot of 1965 and the Detroit Riot of 1967 devastated ethnic districts far more than the rest of their cities. Recently, the effects of Hurricane Katrina fell most heavily upon the African American residents of the New Orleans Lower Ninth Ward neighborhood.

Tourism and Ethnic Neighborhoods

Despite the real and perceived risks associated with developing ethnic neighborhoods, in recent decades tourism and leisure activities involving restaurants, arts and crafts galleries, and historical museums have become commonplace across the nation. Certainly, the most famous fusion of ethnic neighborhood and ethnic tourism is San Francisco's Chinatown. Other ethnic neighborhoods well known as tourist destinations include Baltimore's Little Italy; Detroit's Greektown; the Portuguese community of New Bedford, Massachusetts; the Cuban community in Ybor City (next to Tampa, Florida); and the Ukrainian Village neighborhood in Chicago.

Beyond Inner City Ethnic Neighborhoods

As metropolitan areas have expanded in this era of the Fair Housing Act, many African Americans, Asian Americans, and Hispanics have followed Anglos out of the inner city with the goal of establishing their families in the suburbs. Other middle-class members of ethnic groups are returning to central-city communities with the purpose of rebuilding historical neighborhoods. This double shuffling of ethnic and nonethnic populations will not bring about the demise of ethnic neighborhoods, but it is likely to increase their number and their distribution throughout urban regions.

—*Robert V. Kemper*

See also African Americans in Cities; Gentrification; Ghetto; Harlem, New York; Mexican Americans; Neighborhood; Polish Americans in Cities; Racial Zoning; Second Ghetto; Tenement

Further Readings and References

Fong, E., & Shibuya, K. (2005). Multiethnic cities in North America. *Annual Review of Sociology, 31*, 285–304.

Lobo, S., & Peters, K. (Eds.). (2001). *American Indians and the urban experience*. Walnut Creek, CA: AltaMira Press.

Pattillo, M. (2005). Black middle-class neighborhoods. *Annual Review of Sociology, 31*, 305–329.

Prior, M., & Kemper, R. V. (2005). From freedman's town to uptown: Community transformation and gentrification in Dallas, Texas. *Urban Anthropology, 34*(2/3), 177–216.

Ricourt, M., & Danta, R. (2003). *Hispanas de Queens: Latino panethnicity in a New York City neighborhood*. Ithaca, NY: Cornell University Press.

Riis, J. (1890). *How the other half lives: Studies among the tenements of New York*. New York: Charles Scribner's Sons.

Wirth, L. (1928). *The ghetto*. Chicago: University of Chicago Press.

FAIR HOUSING ACT OF 1968

Title VIII of the 1968 Civil Rights Act, also known as the Fair Housing Act, was passed at the height of the Civil Rights movement. At the beginning of the 20th century, most African Americans had lived in the rural South, where Jim Crow laws and local tradition enforced segregation. During World War I, and again during World War II, many African Americans moved north and found jobs in industries that were now open to them because of the demand for labor created by war. However, legal and social restrictions limited African Americans to living in traditionally African American communities, so these communities were quickly overwhelmed. African Americans seeking to live outside these neighborhoods frequently faced hostility and violence. The Fair Housing Act was a key element in the fight for civil rights, because an end to legal discrimination in housing was the first step in helping African Americans become integrated into everyday American life.

Prior to 1962, the question of open housing had been a local concern. Initially, the Civil Rights Movement had focused on African Americans gaining access to job opportunities and on reducing discrimination in public areas, such as restaurants and stores. But during the 1950s, civil rights activists began their fight to end segregation in housing and pushed to open up white neighborhoods to African Americans. Their efforts had been bolstered by the 1948 U.S. Supreme Court decision (*Shelley v. Kraemer*) that made racially exclusive deed restrictions unenforceable.

In the late 1950s, Pittsburgh and New York City were the first cities to pass significant open housing legislation. President John F. Kennedy signed Executive Order 11063 on November 20, 1962, which was the first attempt to prevent discrimination at the national level. The order only applied to federally assisted housing that came under contract after that date, so its scope was limited, but it was an important first step. Under pressure from the Civil Rights Movement (such as the 1963 march on Washington), Congress supported the fight against discrimination by passing Title VI of the Civil Rights Act of 1964. The act outlawed discrimination in employment and public accommodations, and although not a fair housing law, the act barred discrimination in all federally funded activities, including housing.

The assassination of Martin Luther King in April 1968 generated momentum in Congress to support civil rights, which helped with the passage of the 1968 Civil Rights Act. Title VIII of that act, the Fair Housing Act, prohibited discrimination in the sale or rental of all housing except for housing sold or rented without the services of a broker and that did not include four or more units. Private individuals who had suffered discrimination could sue, and the U.S. Attorney General was empowered to act if there was a pattern of discrimination.

Soon after the passage of the Fair Housing Act, the U.S. Supreme Court greatly expanded the impact of the fair housing legislation. In the case of *Jones v. Mayer*, in which the Alfred H. Mayer Company refused to sell a home in suburban St. Louis to an African American buyer who then sued to force the sale, the U.S. Supreme Court found in favor of the plaintiff based on the Civil Rights Act of 1866 rather than the traditional equal protection clause of the Fourteenth Amendment. This meant that federal legislation applied to transactions between private individuals, not just discrimination on the part of the government.

Unfortunately for fair housing advocates, to ensure passage of the bill Republican minority leader Everett Dirkson weakened the enforcement provisions of the Fair Housing Act by preventing the Department of Housing and Urban Development (HUD) from enforcing it administratively. Also, Congress also did not provide the funding HUD requested to hire investigators to enforce the act. HUD deferred to state agencies where state laws were essentially the same as the federal law, but these agencies were also underfunded and thus had backlogs of cases to investigate. The primary enforcement mechanism was the right of the individual who had suffered from discrimination to sue. But many individuals who suffered discrimination did not have the resources to bring a lawsuit, and such suits usually took so long that they were not useful as a mechanism by which to gain access to housing.

Additionally, discrimination was often not obvious, so many individuals who had suffered discrimination might not be aware of it, and if they did suspect it, it was difficult to prove. Instead of telling prospective minority renters or buyers that they were not welcome, as would have been done in the past, realtors who wanted to discriminate would simply say there were no apartments available, or only show apartments or houses in areas that were already segregated (racial steering). Fair housing advocates dealt with this issue by testing the real estate market for discrimination. Testers, one black and one white but with otherwise similar economic profiles, would attempt to rent or buy an apartment or home. The testers would then compare notes to determine if the real estate agent had discriminated. This tactic was confirmed by the Supreme Court's decision in 1982 to allow testers to have standing to sue, which enhanced the ability of fair housing organizations to enforce the law.

Although the enforcement provisions of the Fair Housing Act were cumbersome, they were not useless. The Justice Department brought 300 fair housing cases between 1969 and 1978. By the late 1970s, the Justice Department had successfully persuaded the courts that it was not necessary to prove discriminatory intent; discriminatory effect was a violation of the law. This meant that some exclusionary zoning laws were illegal even though the laws were not overtly discriminatory. During the 1970s, the courts also expanded the scope of the law to include people who had been indirectly affected by discrimination, such as white residents denied the opportunity to live in an integrated community. Although the Fair Housing Act of 1968 did not end discrimination in housing, it was an important part of creating an open society.

—*Kent James*

See also Federal Housing Administration; Federal Housing and Home Finance Agency

Further Readings and References

Citizens Commission on Civil Rights. (1986). The federal government and equal housing opportunity: A continuing failure. In R. Bratt, C. Hartman, & A. Myerson (Eds.), *Critical perspectives on housing* (pp. 296–324). Philadelphia: Temple University Press.

Graham, H. D. (1999). The surprising career of federal fair housing law. *Journal of Policy History, 12*(2), 215–232.

Meyer, S. G. (2000). *As long as they don't move next door: Segregation and racial conflict in American neighborhoods.* New York: Rowman & Littlefield.

Saltman, J. (1990). *A fragile movement: The struggle for neighborhood stabilization.* Westport, CT: Greenwood Press.

FAMILIES IN CITIES AND SUBURBS

Writing in the 1830s, the French aristocrat Alexis de Tocqueville contrasted the traditional European "aristocratic" family and the new American "democratic" family. During his travels through America, primarily in cities and towns along the East Coast, Tocqueville observed that paternal power had diminished, that women were more forthcoming with opinions, and that relations among children were no longer rigidly hierarchical. In Europe, the long-standing practice of primogeniture had made the eldest son inheritor of all family property. In America, inheritance typically was shared among all children—even females. With shared inheritance, the rationale for life-long submission to the father disappeared. Adults' independence from their aging parents was furthered by high levels of geographical mobility in America, both among immigrants from Europe who settled in East Coast cities and among the pioneers who participated in the nation's westward expansion.

From Cities to Suburbs

Family structures and family lifestyles in the 18th and 19th centuries reflected the quite different circumstances of rural and urban economies and housing markets. Until the late 19th century, large cities and small towns were distributed independently across the American landscape. Communities were marked off from their neighbors not so much by their "Welcome" signs, but by their open spaces. The signs are still there, but the open spaces largely have disappeared.

As urban development expanded beyond the central city, new suburban communities were built on the edges of cities. These suburban places were intentionally incomplete. They emphasized large agglomerations of free-standing houses, arranged in elegant geometric patterns on the landscape, but often lacked essential infrastructure (for example, museums, concert halls, sports facilities). With the advent of railroads and electric streetcar systems in the late 19th century, connecting suburban communities to inner cities and to each other was greatly facilitated. The development of a vast highway system in the 20th century enhanced community connectivity. Living and working in the same place—or even in the same state—was no longer a necessity. From Boston to New York City to Washington, D.C., travelers pass through a seemingly unending stream of communities. The same is true of the Greater Chicago region, the San Francisco Bay Area, and the Los Angeles metropolitan region. For decades, large cities throughout the nation have been annexing or absorbing formerly free-standing towns at their margins. This transformation of urban and rural landscapes has converted more than half of the nation's population into suburban residents.

Families in Cities

For more than a century, waves of immigrants and refugees have sustained pressure on urban housing markets. Small houses and even smaller apartments long have been the norm in American cities. Lacking the economic resources to afford more space, working-class families "doubled up" within their living spaces. As a result, multigenerational extended families became increasingly common. As the children of the working class grew up and married, they worked to fulfill the "American Dream" by moving out into the suburbs, where they hoped to have more space and greater opportunities for their children.

In recent decades, persons of color have become significant minorities—or even the majority—in cities across the nation (for example, Washington, D.C., Atlanta, Dallas, Oakland). The federal "War on Poverty" of the 1960s and 1970s targeted America's cities, not its suburbs. Despite the expenditure of billions of dollars, economic conditions in inner cities have not improved greatly. As a result, a substantial underclass of unemployed (and underemployed) household heads has become dependent on government support programs. Single-parent families and grandmother-headed families have become more common, especially because of the high rates of incarceration among African American and Hispanic males. Recent trends in urban redevelopment and gentrification have brought young, affluent Anglo singles and families back into the inner cities. Their presence is largely offset by a rise in the number of homeless families finding their way to inner city shelters and social service agencies.

Families in the Suburbs

As they developed during the 20th century, suburbs have been more ethnically and socioeconomically homogeneous than central cities. New suburbs primarily were places for Anglos, although suburbs now are attracting a broader mix of ethnic populations. Seeking to find better residential and educational possibilities for their children, African American, Hispanic, and Asian American parents are moving to the suburbs in great numbers. This shift is documented in the results of the 2000 United States Census. During the 1990s, the Anglo population in suburban areas increased by only 5 percent, the African American population grew by 39 percent, the Asian American population by 84 percent, and the Hispanic population by 72 percent. In addition, many new immigrants from other countries, especially members of the middle and upper classes, have moved from their homelands to American suburbs.

Families in Imagined Cities and Suburbs

Social critics from Sinclair Lewis to Norman Lear to George Will have commented on family life in inner cities and in the suburbs. Especially through television programs, movies, and other media, the portrayal of American families contrasts the idyllic existence of suburban life with the stressful, competitive world of city life. Unfortunately, such depictions historically ignored (or overplayed) the diversity of family life in cities and suburbs. For example, for decades, gays and lesbians were absent from portrayals of American family life. Now, it seems that the formula for a successful program must include gay or lesbian persons. The same can be said of interracial marriages, single-parent households, multigenerational families, adopted children, and so on.

During the so-called Golden Age of television in the 1950s and 1960s, programs like *Ozzie and Harriet, Leave It to Beaver, The Donna Reed Show,* and *Father Knows Best* presented all-white family fantasies that reflected the ethnic, gender, and class segmentation then prevalent in American society. While fathers were the titular head of their families, during the daytime they disappeared to their distant places of employment. In its 203 episodes during 1954 to 1962, *Father Knows Best* provided a look at the problems of a middle-class and middle-American family composed of Jim Anderson, manager of an insurance company; his stay-at-home wife, Margaret; and their three children, Betty, Bud, and Kathy. Such programs were intended as weekly moral lessons for parents and their children grouped around the family's black-and-white television set.

Perhaps the most influential situation comedy in television history, *All in the Family,* debuted in 1971 as a satire of contemporary stereotypes about race, politics, and family life. In its 207 episodes, the program focused on a dockworker and part-time cab driver named Archie Bunker, his ditzy wife Edith, their daughter Gloria, and her college-student husband, Michael. The conflicts in this extended family household reflected the serious generational differences in Vietnam-era America. Their neighbors included the Jeffersons, an entrepreneurial African American family whose small dry-cleaning business eventually proved so successful that they moved out—and up—to a Manhattan apartment building. As a spin-off, *The Jeffersons* became a very successful situation comedy in its own right, with 251 episodes running from 1975 to 1985. The hard-edged social commentary of *All in the Family* and *The Jeffersons* was quite different from the suburban-based family shows of an earlier television era.

In presenting such different facets of family life, the popular media attempt to capture a rapidly changing social and cultural phenomenon. Commercials also are anchored in stereotypes at the same time that they target specific demographic segments of American consumers. The development of a multi-billion-dollar restaurant industry, the proliferation of microwave ovens, and a significant increase in the number of women in the workforce have hastened the end of the traditional family mealtime for many Americans. These fundamental changes in eating patterns are symptomatic of deeper transformations in family life in American cities and suburbs.

—Robert V. Kemper

See also African Americans in Cities; African Americans in Suburbs and African American Towns; Asian Americans in the Suburbs; Children in Cities and Suburbs; Gentrification; Ghetto; Mexican Americans; Middle Class in Cities; Middle Class in the Suburbs; Polish Americans in Cities; Suburbanization; Upper Class in Cities and Suburbs; Working Class in Cities and Suburbs

Further Readings and References

Bramen, D. (2004). *Doing time on the outside: Incarceration and family life in urban America.* Ann Arbor: University of Michigan Press.

Keller, S. (2003). *Community: Pursuing the dream, living the reality.* Princeton, NJ: Princeton University Press.

Liebow, E. (1967). *Tally's corner: A study of Negro streetcorner men.* Boston: Little, Brown.

Lindstrom, M. J., & Bartling, H. (Eds.). (2003). *Suburban sprawl: Culture, theory, and politics.* Lanham, MD: Rowman & Littlefield.

Palen, J. J. (1995). *The suburbs.* New York: McGraw-Hill.

Spigel, L. (1992). *Make room for TV: Television and the family ideal in postwar America.* Chicago: University of Chicago Press.

Watanabe, Y. (2004). *The American family: Across the class divide.* Ann Arbor, MI: Pluto Press.

FAMILY PLANNING

While the term *family planning* is generally a 20th-century term, referring to a couple's use of birth control methods to choose how many children to have and when to have them, the concept dates back centuries and was present in a variety of cultures. Family planning has existed throughout America's history, demonstrating the strife inherent in any attempt to control nature, as well as the fundamental significance of birth control in the American story. Early colonial records demonstrate a fairly common knowledge among colonial women of herbal remedies known to cause miscarriage, and by the late 18th century, husbands and wives began to collaborate on family planning by practicing such birth control methods as extending nursing for their existing children and coitus interruptus.

Surgical abortion, though practiced by some doctors as early as the 18th century, did not become more than a rare solution until the early 19th century when unmarried women more regularly sought abortions to terminate unwanted pregnancies. By 1840, married, middle-class women began using this process as a form of family planning, causing some to become fearful, in the following decades, of low birthrates among the middle class. Laws prohibiting abortion and the dissemination of information regarding contraception followed, most notably the Comstock Act of 1873, which outlawed the mailing of contraceptives or information about them.

Outlawing abortion and the dissemination of contraception information was largely unsuccessful, causing both of the practices outlawed to instead merely go underground. Abortions became increasingly more dangerous and some, like birth control pioneer, Margaret Sanger, became convinced that dangerous abortions could be prevented if women had proper information about and access to contraceptives. Sanger spent a number of years publishing radical papers on the necessity of women's access to birth control (a term she coined in 1915), made many trips to Europe to research contraceptives, and, in 1916, opened a birth control clinic in Brooklyn. Her clinic's opening coincided with the apex of the grassroots birth control movement in the United States, in which socialists, working-class women, and industrial workers rallied together, demanding more information about planning and limiting family size. The grassroots activists believed that birth control would grant the working classes social equality and a higher standard of living.

Sanger's clinic and the growing ranks of women desiring information about birth control were not received well, however, and proponents of birth control knew a difficult struggle lay ahead. Sexuality, particularly female sexuality, continued to be considered taboo in American society and culture. By the 1920s, it became clear that neither radical socialists nor grassroots organizers were prepared to fight the looming battle ahead; accordingly, professionals in the fields of public health, human sexuality, and other related disciplines entered the birth control movement and worked to make a new name for the movement.

These professionals embraced Margaret Sanger, in large part because she believed doctors should be the ones to educate women on and fit them for contraceptive devices. In 1921, in conjunction with these professionals, Sanger created the American Birth Control League (ABCL), which sent out birth control information to its members and lobbied for laws favoring birth control. With the onset of the Great Depression, these lobbyists fought to tie contraception to New Deal initiatives and programs, arguing that family planning would be beneficial to the growing numbers of impoverished families. Though the U.S. government would not embrace any federal approval of contraceptives during the Depression, fears about overpopulation and its ill effects on the American economy became very real for those who had suffered through the Depression. As such, birth control began to gain respectability in many circles and started the journey toward legalization.

As the birth control movement gained power and credibility, Sanger and her ABCL came together with friends and rivals alike to form the Planned Parenthood Federation of America in 1942. Planned Parenthood redirected the focus of birth control from the individual woman or mother to the family and family planning. "Family planning" was seen as a positive connotation for birth control, replacing the former, negative connotation of pregnancy prevention. This new focus drew in many liberal allies who felt that family planning would lead to social and economic stability. And though Planned Parenthood offered their services and access to birth control to women regardless of age or social class, the Federation did indeed succeed in helping droves of working-class women make new choices about work and life.

By 1950, as Planned Parenthood gained popularity and a family-oriented image, and as World War II caused fears about national and international overpopulation to resurface, Sanger and birth control advocate Katharine McCormick set about to research and develop an oral contraceptive. The scientists and doctors they recruited soon created a pill that was able to suppress ovulation and prevent pregnancy, allowing couples to plan their family size and the time between children. After successful large-scale tests in Puerto

Rico, "the Pill," as it came to be known, made it back to the United States, where it was greeted with much enthusiasm. By the end of 1959, over 500,000 women were already using the Pill, even though FDA approval was still 6 months away, and the Pill's popularity grew in leaps and bounds after approval.

The 1960s saw a number of other occurrences that would make family planning an option for more couples. In 1965, the last laws banning contraception were struck down by the Supreme Court and, that same year, federal funds became available for birth control. The modern feminist movement gave women even more individual control over pregnancy and family size with the legalization of abortion in the landmark Supreme Court case *Roe v. Wade*. Though the debate over abortion remains heated, the concept of family planning has become completely ingrained in American society. Information, contraceptives, fertility drugs, and alternative childbearing methods have become widely available through family planning clinics, classes on health and sexuality, and other resources, allowing single women, alternative couples, and families—regardless of race, age, class, and creed—to make decisions and plans for and about their families.

—*Devon Hansen*

Further Readings and References

Dayton, C. H. (1991). Taking the trade: Abortion and gender relations in an eighteenth-century New England village. *William and Mary Quarterly* (3rd series), *48*, 19–49.

Gordon, L. (2002). *The moral property of women: A history of birth control politics in America*. Urbana, IL: University of Illinois Press.

Mohr, J. C. (1979). *Abortion in America: The origins and evolutions of national policy*. New York: Oxford University Press.

Norton, M. B. (1980). *Liberty's daughters: The revolutionary experience of American women, 1750–1800*. Ithaca, NY: Cornell University Press.

Sanger, M. (1931). *My fight for birth control*. New York: Farrar & Reinhart.

FANNIE MAE

The Federal National Mortgage Association (FNMA), now known as Fannie Mae, came into existence in 1938 as a federal government initiative to create more liquidity in the mortgage market. Prior to the establishment of Fannie Mae, prospective homeowners had to apply for a loan from savings banks, credit unions, or other lenders in the primary mortgage market if they could not afford to purchase a home outright. Creditors in the primary mortgage market could rarely afford to freeze their assets with long-term amortization agreements and therefore typically offered short-term (3- to 5-year), fixed-rate loans with low periodic payments and one lump-sum balance payment at the date of maturation. This system obviously limited the number of families that could afford to own homes, and many of those that could found they could not meet their scheduled payments during the Great Depression, resulting in a wave of foreclosures across the nation. According to the Bureau of the Census, only about 46 percent of the American population owned their own homes and only 40 percent of these did so with mortgages from 1900 to 1940.

The creation of Fannie Mae opened the door to widespread homeownership in a way that had never before been possible. The Housing Act of 1934 created the Federal Housing Administration (FHA), which in turn chartered Fannie Mae on February 10, 1938 as a subsidiary of the Reconstruction Finance Corporation. (President Herbert Hoover created the RFC in 1932 in order to provide emergency loans.) Fannie Mae purchased federally insured FHA loans from primary mortgage providers and freed up capital for more home loans, thereby allowing more widespread access to homeownership, especially after Fannie Mae expanded its purchasing abilities to include those loans ensured by the Veterans Administration in 1948. In essence, Fannie Mae was created to give primary lenders an incentive to originate FHA-insured mortgages; this new system of government-assumed risk came under heavy fire as being "socialism for the rich and private enterprise for the poor." According to critic Charles Abrams, "Social purpose, the rationale for most subsidized operations, has become the palliative for the removal of the gamble from private building speculations and mortgage investments and for passing it onto the government."

For better or for worse, Fannie Mae changed the structure of mortgage lending practices. First, it standardized mortgage instruments across state lines, creating standard contracts and underwriting procedures. Second, it opened the door for savings from the Northeast and Midwest to be channeled to new investment opportunities in the South and West. Fannie Mae set up the primitive beginnings of a secondary mortgage market, although its status as a directly government-controlled, government-backed entity would soon change.

When Dwight D. Eisenhower took office in 1953, he set up a special advisory committee headed by Albert M. Cole and requested recommendations that would maintain national home building at a rate of one million plus units per year but remove the government from the business of home financing. The committee recommended that Fannie Mae remain a federally chartered organization but that financing be shifted entirely to the private sector. After critics vociferously opposed this recommendation, arguing savings and loan institutions would raise interest rates and shorten terms if given control over the direction of the central mortgage reserve, President Eisenhower compromised. In 1954, Fannie Mae became a "mixed ownership" corporation, with its U.S. Treasury stock being gradually retired as private investments grew.

The next critical change to Fannie Mae occurred in 1968 when the organization officially became a private entity. Congress and President Lyndon B. Johnson retired the $142 million in preferred Treasury stock and common stockholders henceforth held sole equity interest, a move brought on by the expenses of the Vietnam War and strongly supported by special interests like the National Association of Real Estate Brokers. Despite the empowerment of common stockholders, however, the Housing and Urban Development (HUD) secretary and Treasury continued to wield considerable influence over the organization. President Johnson hoped these changes would help build 26 million new housing units over the following decade. Special assistance programs were relegated to the newly created Government National Mortgage Association (or "Ginnie Mae"), a fully government-owned corporation within HUD. By 1970, President Richard Nixon had expanded Fannie Mae's purchasing power to conventional mortgages and began the Federal Home Loan Mortgage Corporation (or "Freddie Mac") to purchase loans from members of the Federal Home Loan Bank. (The FHLB began in 1932 in order to provide funds for local banks and credit unions that lacked sufficient savings deposits.) By 1976, Fannie Mae was purchasing more conventional than FHA- or VA-backed loans.

In the 1980s and 1990s, Fannie Mae continued to grow and expand at an incredible rate. It added multifamily loans, adjustable rate mortgages (where interest rates are tied to changes in the index), and second mortgages to its portfolio; it also raised funds in overseas capital markets beginning in 1984. Fannie Mae has recently begun paying more attention to low- and moderate-income families' needs, developing homeownership programs such as the $10 billion "Opening Doors to Affordable Housing" (1991) and "American Dream Commitment" (2001). In 1997, Fannie Mae permanently retired the name FNMA in order to avoid confusion for investors and consumers.

Recently, Fannie Mae has struggled with the aftermath of a September 2004 report by the Office of Federal Housing Enterprise Oversight that revealed serious accounting errors and that resulted in the resignations of CEO Franklin Raines and CFO Timothy Howard. Fannie Mae continues to make profits from the difference between the borrowing cost and the price of their mortgage-backed securities, and it is the nation's second largest issuer of securitized debt. Since its conception, Fannie Mae has funded over 63 million families, with an enterprise value of over $984 billion in October 2005.

—*Nancy Kwak*

See also Federal Housing Administration; Great Depression and Cities; Urban Renewal and Revitalization

Further Readings and References

Abrams, C. (1965). *The city is the frontier.* New York: Harper & Row.

Downs, A. (1985). *The revolution in real estate finance.* Washington, DC: Brookings Institution.

Hays, R. A. (1995). *The federal government and urban housing: Ideology and change in public policy.* Albany: State University of New York Press.

Jackson, K. T. (1985). *Crabgrass frontier.* New York: Oxford University Press.

FEDERAL GOVERNMENT AND CITIES

The American federal system was established by the United States Constitution.

Article I of the Constitution, which specifies the legislative authority of Congress, does not explicitly give the national government any responsibility for urban problems or any authority over city governments. For a century and a half following the Constitution's ratification, the Congress, the president, and the Supreme Court largely adhered to the doctrine that the national government's powers are limited to those enumerated in Article I. The federal government did not have a comprehensive "urban policy," nor did it pursue individual programs that explicitly focused on cities. Thus an early, authoritative work on city government, Frank Goodnow's *City Government in the United States,* published in 1904, distilled the topic of federal-local relations as simply that a city has no relations with the national government.

It remains true down to the present day that the national government does not have any authority to give commands to city officials or to control local affairs. The United States Supreme Court, under the leadership of Chief Justice William Rehnquist, issued a number of decisions in the 1990s declaring several U.S. statutes unconstitutional for exceeding the national government's authority over matters reserved for cities and states. For example, the Court in *U.S. v. Lopez,* 514 U.S. 549 (1995), ruled that Washington could not create gun-free zones surrounding school buildings, into which it would be illegal, for anyone but a police officer, to carry a gun. The Court declared it was up to state and local governments to decide whether to arrest people for carrying a gun in or near a school. It rejected claims that the federal government's power to regulate interstate and foreign commerce authorized it to legislate on this local issue. And in 1997 in *Printz v. U.S.* (521 U.S. 898), the Court voided a United States statute, commonly known as the Brady Bill, requiring local law enforcement officials to check the criminal records of people buying handguns. The Court said that what local officers do regarding handgun sales is a question to be decided by mayors, city councils, or state legislatures, not federal officials.

Under the Constitution, there are only two ways that federal officials can influence what cities do. First, the Fourteenth Amendment authorizes federal judges to overturn policies and practices of state and local officials that, on the basis of race, deny citizens the equal protection of the laws or deprive them of life, liberty, or property without due process of law. The Supreme Court used this provision to prohibit school segregation in *Brown v. Board of Education* (347 U.S. 483).

The Supreme Court's *Brown* decision, handed down in 1954, opened up an entirely new way of conducting city politics. It is not uncommon today for the opponents of a municipal project or policy to hire an attorney to allege in federal court that some activity of the city government deprives its members of their civil rights. A line of judicial decisions and congressional civil rights statutes (for example, the Americans With Disabilities Act) authorize federal officials to involve themselves in the decisions of city governments to ensure that cities provide equal treatment to racial minorities, to women, and to the handicapped.

A second source of national influence over cities since the New Deal era has been federal grants-in-aid to state and local governments. In enacting, administering, and interpreting federal legislation providing financial assistance to cities, officials in Washington and federal judges issue rulings and decisions that local officials must follow in order to continue receiving millions of dollars in federal funds. An early New Deal agency, the Public Works Administration (PWA), sought to create jobs for the unemployed by constructing housing in cities. The PWA established the U.S. Emergency Housing Corporation (EMC) to build and manage low-income housing projects in slum neighborhoods. The EMC sought to use the power of eminent domain to acquire sites for this housing, but federal courts ruled that, since housing construction was not among the powers of the national government enumerated in Article I of the Constitution, a federal agency did not have the authority to compel the owners of the condemned land to dispose of their property for this purpose. To get around this problem, the EMC provided grants-in-aid to local public housing authorities, which were established under state legislation and were authorized by state law to condemn property for the purpose of providing housing for the poor and jobs for the unemployed—activities that state governments clearly had the constitutional authority to undertake.

The 1949 United States Housing Act authorized the urban renewal program, providing federal grants-in-aid to cities to finance urban renewal projects. Local urban renewal agencies would use federal grants to purchase slum housing and dilapidated commercial facilities located in or near the central business districts of cities. This land would be sold at less than market price to developers for the construction of office buildings, retail stores, and housing for executives, professionals, and office personnel who worked downtown. The difference between the purchase price and the sale price of renewal sites would be covered by the federal grant. This "write-down" of land costs and the very extensiveness of renewal sites would encourage development that otherwise would be unlikely to occur. In this way, the renewal site would be "upgraded"—that is, the people who lived and worked in the area, and the businesses that operated there, would be better off than the poor residents and economically marginal firms they replaced.

During the two decades following World War II, Democrats largely controlled the presidency and majorities in both houses of Congress, as well as most big-city governments. Urban renewal and kindred federal programs designed to "upgrade" downtown neighborhoods and promote economic growth helped these officials to extend and solidify their party's base. As John Mollekopf argued in 1983, federal urban redevelopment programs enabled such postwar Democratic mayors as Boston's John Collins and San Francisco's George Christopher to secure the support of reformers as well as machine politicians, business leaders as well as union officials, and political spokesmen for the disparate ethnic and racial minorities in their cities.

Federal grants-in-aid to city governments grew enormously in the 1960s and 1970s. For example, the 1965 Elementary and Secondary Education Act offered funds to local school systems to provide extra assistance to "educationally disadvantaged" students. The federal government could not require local schools to give extra help to students from families that are poor, but it could cover the expense of their doing so. In this way, interests that exercise greater influence nationally than locally secure the enactment of federal statutes that provide cities with federal funds to finance activities these interests favor. The concerns of these liberal forces, and consequently the scope of federal involvement in what historically had been regarded as local matters, are indicated by the 1994 law reauthorizing the Elementary and Secondary Education Act. As Martha Derthick noted in 2001, the 1994 legislation ran to 1,200 pages and dealt with such disparate matters as math and science equipment, school libraries, teacher training, homeschooling, racial desegregation, single-sex schools, migrant education, hate crimes, gun control, prayer, sex education, gay rights, pornography, drugs, smoking, school prayer, and gun control.

There were two interrelated reasons why the number, scope, and expense of federal grants-in-aid to cities expanded greatly in the 1960s and 1970s. The first involves a change in the structure of Congress.

From early in the 20th century until the mid-1970s, its most senior members, who chaired legislative committees in the House and Senate, dominated Congress. When the Democrats controlled Congress—as they did for all but 4 years from the 1930s through the 1970s—the most senior members of the majority party came largely from the "Solid South," where Democrats faced no meaningful electoral competition. These Southerners feared that if the national government got more involved in matters that were traditionally run by state and local governments (especially schooling), "outsiders" with national influence (particularly advocates of civil rights for African Americans) would "interfere" in the Southern system of race relations. Because it was dominated by conservative Southerners, Congress refused to enact bills that liberals proposed increasing the national government's responsibilities for many matters that at the time were largely run by state and local governments.

But the influence of Northern liberals within Congress increased greatly after the Democratic congressional landslides in 1964 and 1974—the first after Barry Goldwater was overwhelmingly defeated in the presidential election by Lyndon Johnson; the second after President Richard Nixon was compelled to resign as a result of his part in the Watergate affair. The 1964 landslide enabled liberals to secure enactment of Great Society legislation greatly increasing federal grants-in-aid to city governments. And the post-Watergate landslide enabled Northern liberals to depose three conservative Southern committee chairs who had utterly dominated their committees, warning all chairs that they must share their power with other members of their committee. The newly empowered congressional rank and file found it useful to enact legislation authorizing additional grants to local governments in their districts. By expanding these federal programs and intervening to help localities secure such grants, incumbents in Congress are able to win further support from locally influential politicians.

The elements of the liberal coalition that played the largest role in designing urban grant-in-aid programs in the 1960s and 1970s were professionals in various nonprofit institutions—universities, charitable foundations, think tanks, public interest groups, and social service agencies. These nonprofit professionals considered municipal bureaucracies and school systems stodgy institutions that were not open to "innovative" approaches to dealing with the problems that their clients faced, as well as uninterested in the latest ideas—that is, unreceptive to the ideas of liberal academics, foundation executives, and social service professionals. These elements of the liberal coalition viewed city bureaucrats—police officers, teachers, social workers—as "unresponsive" to the distinctive needs of their minority clients.

Liberal forces used the influence they enjoyed in national politics to extend their sway over city governments. Liberal federal programs for cities usually took the form of "categorical grants," that is, grants for a particular purpose or category of municipal activities. To obtain categorical grants a city would submit a proposal to the federal agency administering the grant program, indicating how it proposed to spend federal monies if it received a grant. The program's administrators in Washington would then have the discretion to provide federal monies for those proposals they judged would most effectively achieve the purposes that were outlined in the authorizing statute and specified in the rules issued by the federal agency that administered the grant program. Agency officials who reviewed local applications could reject those they deemed least likely to succeed. Categorical grant legislation gave such power to federal administrators because the elites and professionals who drafted and supported this legislation were convinced that they and their counterparts in federal agencies knew how to deal with the problems of the urban poor better than did the administrators and employees of local welfare departments, school systems, and police forces. These elites did not wish to use federal funds to finance policies and programs that in their judgment had proven to be ineffective.

To obtain federal grants, local governments and school systems had a strong incentive to hire individuals who shared the views of the federal bureaucrats who administered categorical grant programs and who knew the sort of grant proposals these bureaucrats were likely to approve. Through categorical grant programs, then, upper-middle-class professionals who enjoyed influence in Washington were able to increase the power of their local allies in cities throughout the nation.

Because categorical grants were used by liberal forces to influence city governments, Presidents Richard Nixon, Ronald Reagan, George H. W. Bush, and George W. Bush sought to cut categorical grant programs and to promote the decentralization of power to state and local governments, school systems, and welfare agencies by providing them with "block

grants." Unlike categorical grant programs that focused on the problems of troubled cities, President Nixon's Revenue Sharing program and President Reagan's New Federalism initiative provided federal funds to *all* local governments—to suburbs and rural towns, as well as to big cities. Block grant programs distributed federal funds to local governments on the basis of various objective criteria (for example, U.S. Census population data), leaving little discretion to federal administrators. And city governments could use these funds as they chose, not solely for purposes specified in federal statutes and on programs that met with the approval of federal grant administrators. Under President Reagan's New Federalism initiative, federal guidelines for urban grant programs were slashed from 318 to 11 pages.

The Clinton administration sought to restore many of the urban programs that Presidents Ronald Reagan and George H. W. Bush had cut. But when the GOP won control of Congress in 1995, Speaker Newt Gingrich and his conservative allies sought to abolish or sharply reduce spending on many urban categorical grant-in-aid programs. In addition, the Republican House leadership sought to repeal "unfunded mandates"—that is, requirements that the federal government imposes on cities (such as making facilities accessible to the handicapped) without providing the funds to meet them. These efforts provoked major battles between the GOP Congress and the Democratic president; and this budget deadlock compelled many federal agencies to suspend operations for several weeks in both 1995 and 1996. But in 1996, Congress enacted, and President Clinton signed into law, the major Republican urban initiative of the 1990s— welfare reform. The new law abolished the open-ended, New Deal entitlement program providing welfare payments to single-parent families—Aid to Families with Dependent Children (AFDC). AFDC was replaced with Temporary Assistance for Needy Families (TANF), a block grant to states and localities for providing public assistance to the poor, which a mother could receive for no more than 5 years in her lifetime. Following this change in federal welfare policy, there was a marked decline in the number of persons receiving public assistance in the nation's cities.

In sum, the federal government's relationship to cities has changed in several ways over the course of American history. Some of the most significant of these changes occurred the 1960s and 1970s— changes that altered a number of practices and views prevailing in American politics. Previously, locality had played a central role in the conduct of American democracy: Voters were mobilized by locally based party organizations; national officials had no say over legislative districting at the city, state, or national levels; and local officials controlled the public policies that most intimately reflected community norms—policing and public schooling.

Because the doctrines of "states' rights" and "local control" were deployed to defend racial segregation, and local officials in the Deep South violently resisted efforts by blacks to secure greater equality, many influential Americans came to question whether localism should remain a central principle of political organization in the United States. During the 1960s, liberals began to challenge governmental procedures, public policies, and private practices that did not confer proportional benefits on African Americans, other racial minorities, women, gays, and the physically disabled. Liberals sought to use their influence in the national government not so much to promote locally dominant interests—as had many New Deal policies—but rather to alter local social structures to benefit "protected minorities." These efforts were opposed by conservatives seeking to restrict the ability of "bureaucrats in Washington" to overturn local practices. For example, Congress enacted the 1999 Educational Flexibility Partnership Demonstration Act, waiving federal rules in states enforcing performance standards for local school districts.

During the last third of the 20th century and the early years of the 21st, American politics has been very sharply and quite evenly divided between Republicans and Democrats, conservatives and liberals. As the balance of power among these national political forces has fluctuated, so too has the relationship between the federal government and the nation's cities.

—*Martin Shefter*

Further Readings and References

Derthick, M. (2001). *Keeping the compound republic: Essays on American federalism.* Washington, DC: Brookings Institution.

Goodnow, F. (1904). *City government in the United States.* New York: The Century Company.

Mollenkopf, J. (1983). *The contested city.* Princeton, NJ: Princeton University Press.

Skrentny, J. (2002). *Minority rights revolution.* Cambridge, MA: Harvard University Press.

FEDERAL HOUSING ADMINISTRATION

The United States government created the Federal Housing Administration (FHA) in 1934 to address an economic crisis. By that year, the Great Depression had wreaked havoc on the nation's housing industries, triggering a precipitous decline in both home sales and new housing starts, as well as a spate of mortgage foreclosures, that together placed the construction, real estate, and home finance sectors on the verge of collapse. By 1934, nearly one third of the nation's unemployed were in the building trades. Earlier federal efforts to shore up these markets—through creation of the Federal Home Loan Bank system in 1932 and the Home Owners' Loan Corporation (HOLC) in 1933—had provided some relief, yet neither stopped the deepening crisis. Therefore, the Roosevelt administration responded with the FHA, a regulatory and mortgage insurance program designed not simply to revive and stabilize these industries, but to create and sustain a new *kind* of market for homes. By changing the structure of the mortgage industry and its day-to-day operations, the FHA created a more accessible, flexible, and expansive market for housing and related products. By doing so, it revolutionized the ways that most Americans lived.

Two innovations proved critical to the FHA's success. First, the program insured institutional lenders (including banks, mortgage companies, and insurance companies) who agreed to issue FHA-approved mortgage loans—for home improvement or purchase—to individual borrowers. In case of default, the government indemnified the *lenders,* making their involvement essentially risk free. Second, participating lenders were required to use a particular type of financial instrument: the long-term, low-interest, fully amortized mortgage that had been pioneered by the Savings and Loans industry but that remained largely untested by other financial institutions. Among this loan's advantages—from the FHA's perspective—was its comparatively liberal terms, which promised to draw more businesspeople and consumers into the market for housing. Traditional mortgages required large down payments (up to 50 percent of the principal) and short repayment periods (often as little as 5 years), terms that generally restricted homeownership to the affluent. By contrast, the new, FHA-approved mortgage had very low interest rates, required small down payments (as little as 10 percent), and allowed borrowers 20 (and eventually up to 35) years to pay off both the principal and interest, terms that made homeownership feasible for most middle-income Americans. Another advantage of the mortgage insurance program was that it required a minimal government expenditure. The FHA did not lend money directly, while most of its operational costs were covered by a nominal fee charged to participating lenders. The program's cost-effectiveness enabled supporters to promote it as a market-friendly alternative to "socialistic" schemes like public housing.

The FHA's promotion of the long-term, low-interest mortgage quickly made it a national standard, in both the government-insured and "conventional" (or noninsured) markets for home finance. If builders qualified for an FHA-approved loan, they were virtually ensured financing for their projects, so the agency's *Underwriting Manual,* first issued in 1936, quickly standardized appraisal practices and construction standards nationwide. And by the 1940s, FHA insurance activity had facilitated a dramatic resurgence of new construction, home improvement, and sales, while giving the "average" American, for the first time, the opportunity to purchase a home. When combined in 1944 with the Veterans Administration's mortgage "guarantee" program—which operated similarly to FHA insurance—the housing-related industries began to thrive, and homeownership rates skyrocketed throughout the postwar decades.

Equally important to the FHA's success was its role in creating a *national* market for home finance, one that obeyed standardized appraisal and lending practices, thus permitting institutional lenders to buy and sell mortgages outside of their local or regional markets. Indeed, government insurance and the standardization of mortgage lending worked together—in concert with a series of related "selective credit" programs and monetary reforms—to transform the way that housing credit was created and managed. Most important, these programs were designed to increase both the demand for mortgage debt and its supply, by making borrowing more feasible while making institutional lending both risk free and more lucrative. This attracted more investors into the mortgage market, while the new liberal terms and federal oversight, meanwhile, enabled these lenders to issue an unprecedented amount of credit. And given the considerable postwar demand for housing, the market grew exponentially. In short, by establishing and regulating

economic mechanisms that enabled more people to build, sell, repair, and buy homes, federal interventions created—and sustained—a new kind of housing market, one capable of producing an enormous amount of wealth.

In many respects, these interventions were both simple and very effective. Taken together, the FHA and VA programs helped secure debt financing for up to half of all new single-family home purchases in any single year between 1945 and 1960. By 1964, they had facilitated the purchase of over 12 million housing units. In addition, selective credit programs revolutionized the conventional (noninsured) market for mortgage credit, as well, quickly fueling that sector's rapid expansion. Put simply, federal intervention made housing and related markets central to postwar economic growth. Meanwhile the FHA's standardized building and design requirements encouraged the construction of modern, larger, well-built residences. Thanks to these programs, by 1970 most Americans lived in homes that were structurally sound, comparatively spacious, and privately owned, homes that provided millions of families with unprecedented emotional and financial security.

But the FHA has long had many critics. For one, the agency actively encouraged suburban sprawl and urban decline. Because it set the lending terms, appraisal guidelines, and even construction requirements that guided the postwar housing market, the agency's preferences had a dramatic impact on patterns of metropolitan development. And the agency's preferences mirrored those of the real estate, building, and finance industries, with which FHA officials collaborated very closely to both design and operate the national insurance system. Under considerable pressure from these groups, the FHA directed the vast majority of new credit to the construction, repair, and sale of owner-occupied, single-family homes in the suburbs. It seldom insured loans for rental properties (like apartment buildings) or for urban real estate of any kind. Always concerned with keeping FHA operations profitable (by avoiding defaults), the agency refused to insure properties deemed undesirable by the real estate industry. As a result, the postwar bonanza of residential development and sales took place almost exclusively in the nation's suburbs, a trend that further undermined struggling center cities.

This outcome is particularly controversial because, according to many critics, the FHA and related selective credit programs distorted natural market activity by giving preference to specific lenders, builders, and homeowners. Indeed, by facilitating debt financing and directing this new wealth to some economic sectors but not to others, government action now fueled—and decisively shaped—patterns of production and consumption. This fact upset many Depression-era legislators and jurists, who accused the state of interfering with the free market for property. And for decades housing economists and others have argued that government insurance and oversight have "subsidized" suburban sprawl and suburban homeownership, at the expense of central cities, renters, and those populations excluded from the benefits of metropolitan growth. Critics assert that if federal programs democratized homeownership, they did so only for some, and by means of a fundamentally undemocratic reform. There is considerable disagreement over whether or not selective credit programs constituted a "subsidy." Yet there is little disagreement that without the government's pivotal interventions and sustained involvement, the remarkable postwar expansion of suburbs and housing markets would be unimaginable.

The debate over subsidies resonates with many critics because of the FHA's most controversial legacy: its open support of racial segregation. When the agency adopted and standardized private-sector appraisal standards, it also codified two assumptions widely held by white businesspeople and economists: that racial integration would undermine white neighborhoods and that properties in nonwhite or "mixed" neighborhoods were not safe investments. Specifically, the *Underwriting Manual* prohibited realtors (and, by extension, lenders and builders) from introducing so-called incompatible racial groups into white residential enclaves. Accordingly, nonwhites were systematically denied loans for properties in white neighborhoods. Meanwhile the FHA used a system of color-coded real estate maps (inherited from the HOLC) to designate all minority or mixed-race neighborhoods as economically unstable, and used this designation to deny their residents mortgage insurance for repair, purchase, or construction.

These racial "rules" had first been outlined by housing economists and some realtors in the years before the Depression, but federal involvement quickly made this calculus a fundamental tenet of the new national market for housing. Indeed, the FHA even endorsed the use of race-restrictive covenants,

until the Supreme Court ruled such deeds unenforceable in 1948. But even then, and even after removing explicitly racial language from its underwriting procedures, the agency did little to stop the "redlining" of neighborhoods, and it continued to condone discrimination well into the 1960s. The result was that most racial minorities were systematically excluded, for decades, from the new market for homeownership—and the equity that it generated—in suburbs and cities alike. And most minorities and renters, meanwhile, were excluded from the suburban communities that were fast monopolizing the most valuable resources, public services, and even employment sectors.

The sprawl accelerated by federal programs has raised a host of other concerns. Critics argue that unregulated suburban growth damages the environment, wastes natural resources, endangers public health, and limits many people's access to public services and even public space. Meanwhile the debate continues over the government's culpability for sprawl itself. Many argue that this growth was inevitable. And to be sure, pre–World War II development patterns demonstrate long-standing popular interest in suburban living. But the evidence suggests that the particular shape and scope of postwar suburban development in the U.S.—especially the emphasis on large-lot, single-family home construction and private ownership, coupled with the systematic neglect of the central city and the exclusion of selected populations—was in no way preordained.

This leaves the FHA and related credit programs with a complicated record. Together they helped make the country's population among the best housed in the world and generated considerable wealth, both by creating home equity and by fueling the growth of numerous housing-related industries. Yet they also ensured that this new wealth would be sharply segregated, both geographically and by race. Meanwhile federal intervention ensured that both the construction and use of shelter in the U.S. fast became integral components of a postwar financial system dependent on the perpetual trade and expansion of debt. This linkage continues to shape metropolitan development patterns, architectural styles, and the availability of affordable housing, by encouraging countless Americans to view homes as equal parts shelter and investment.

—David M.P. Freund

Further Readings and References

Clawson, M. (1975). *Suburban land conversion in the United States: An economic and governmental process.* Baltimore, MD: Johns Hopkins University Press for Resources for the Future.

Freund, D. M. P. (2006). *Colored property: State policy and white racial politics in the modern American suburb.* Chicago: University of Chicago Press.

Jackson, K. T. (1985). *Crabgrass frontier: The suburbanization of the United States.* New York: Oxford University Press.

Kaminow, I., & O'Brien, J. M. (1975). *Studies in selective credit policies.* Philadelphia: Federal Reserve Bank of Philadelphia.

Oliver, M. L., & Shapiro, T. M. (1997). *Black wealth/white wealth: A new perspective on racial inequality.* New York: Routledge.

U.S. Federal Housing Administration. (1936). *Underwriting manual: Underwriting and valuation procedure under Title II of the National Housing Act.* Washington, DC: Government Printing Office.

FEDERAL HOUSING AND HOME FINANCE AGENCY

The United States Federal Housing and Home Finance Agency (HHFA) was created in 1947 to oversee all federal housing and urban development programs. President Franklin D. Roosevelt had created its predecessor, the National Housing Agency, by executive order in 1942. In 1964, the HHFA became the Department of Housing and Urban Development (HUD), and President Lyndon B. Johnson elevated the Secretary of HUD to be a member of the president's cabinet. The Federal Housing and Home Finance Agency was the agency that coordinated federal efforts in urban areas for almost two decades.

The HHFA was an attempt to coordinate growing federal housing programs. The HHFA had three major components, the FHA, public housing, and the Federal Home Loan Bank Board, all of which had different approaches to urban issues and were supported by different constituencies. As a result, these bureaucracies often saw each other as competitors for federal funds. The HHFA also oversaw the Urban Redevelopment program that was created in 1949.

The FHA was created by the National Housing Act of 1934, and it saw its primary function as jumpstarting the moribund home building industry. The FHA provided mortgage insurance to banks so that they would provide mortgages, which would increase the demand for housing and provide work for builders, developers, and the real estate industry. The FHA was essentially a conservative, business-oriented organization that took great pride in the fact that its primary programs were self-supporting.

The conventional public housing program was created by the United States Housing Act of 1937, which also created the Federal Public Housing Agency. As opposed to the business approach of the FHA, supporters of public housing were much more concerned with social welfare issues. Advocates for public housing were trying to create affordable housing for people whom the private market had failed. Pressures from the real estate industry, which was concerned about its ability to compete with subsidized public housing, forced public housing to be Spartan and concentrated it in existing low-income neighborhoods.

The Federal Home Loan Bank Board (FHLBB) was created by Congress in 1932 to charter federal savings and loans, which would accept deposits from individuals and focus their lending on residential mortgages. Savings and loans were to provide a steady source of financing to boost demand for housing ownership and help stabilize the home building industry. During the Korean War, the Eisenhower Administration used the HHFA's oversight of mortgage lending to reduce demand for housing to allow more of the economy to be devoted to the Korean War. The savings and loans pushed to have the FHLBB removed from the oversight of the HHFA and be placed under supervision of a more financially oriented department, which occurred in 1955.

Slum clearance was one of the primary goals of Urban Redevelopment, which was created by Title I of the 1949 Housing Act and was one of the major programs overseen by the HHFA during the 1950s. Urban Redevelopment, in which the federal government provided funding for land acquisition and clearance so that the land could then be utilized for development (most of which was private, profit-oriented development), was a controversial program that was generally supported by downtown property owners, who saw it as a means to save the declining values of their downtown properties by reversing the encroachment of declining neighborhoods. In 1954, under pressure from the cities, the mission and name of the program were changed from Urban Redevelopment to Urban Renewal. The new program was more sensitive to the concerns of urban residents in areas targeted for renewal. Under Urban Renewal, the HHFA attempted a more focused urban revitalization by using programs such as code enforcement to rehabilitate existing structures instead of demolishing them. Along with the highway program, the urban renewal and public housing programs cleared vast tracts of low-income housing in large urban areas and dramatically altered the face of most large cities.

The HHFA was a relatively loosely structured agency, which was largely run by its constituent parts. It was a relatively conservative organization that was generally content to allow local actors to have a large say in policy and did not advocate radical changes. The real estate industry and the home builders were powerful actors in most areas, and as such, they had a lot of influence in the HHFA. The supporters of public housing had different goals than the other bureaucracies that made up the HHFA, and by 1949 they had lost the battle over federal housing policy and thus were unable to change the private-market orientation of the HHFA.

Raymond F. Foley was appointed the first administrator of the HHFA. Foley had been an FHA director in Michigan, and he was appointed to head the National Housing Agency in 1946. Albert Cole replaced Foley after the election of President Dwight D. Eisenhower in 1952. Cole had fought the advocates of public housing during the debate over the Housing Act of 1949, and Cole had close ties to the real estate and home-building industries.

The major programs overseen by the HHFA, especially FHA mortgage insurance and public housing, reinforced local racial attitudes through regulation. The FHA underwriters manual claimed that neighborhoods that were not racially homogeneous were inherently unstable and were therefore at high risk for defaults. In addition, decisions about the placement of public housing units were left to local authorities, so public housing tended to be built only in the neighborhoods that already had low-income residents. Both of these programs reinforced existing patterns of segregation.

But the HHFA did have the Race Relations Service (RRS) provide advice on racial issues, and while their advice was frequently ignored, the HHFA was one of the few agencies that considered the impact of existing racial attitudes. In 1960, President John F. Kennedy appointed Robert Weaver, an African American, to head the HHFA. When the HHFA became HUD and was elevated to the cabinet, Weaver became the first African American cabinet member. The HHFA was a transition between the initial stirrings of federal involvement in urban issues that began with the New Deal and the more aggressive and comprehensive programs that President Lyndon Johnson created in his Great Society programs of the 1960s.

—*Kent James*

See also Federal Housing Administration; Housing Act of 1949

Further Readings and References

Hirsch, A. R. (2000). "Containment" on the home front: Race and federal housing policy from the New Deal to the Cold War. *Journal of Urban History, 26,* 158–189.

Weaver, R. C. (1963). Current trends in urban renewal. *Land Economics, 39*(4), 325–341.

FINANCIAL DISTRICTS

Financial districts are areas containing a range of financial institutions and agents and historically have been located in the central business district. The financial district is home to the institutions that control, manage, and regulate capital flows (such as banks, insurance companies, investment companies, stock exchanges, product exchanges, money dealers, and brokerage houses) and to ancillary industries that service financial firms (such as lawyers and accountants). Financial districts are nodes within cities where important financial functions are performed, most notably the issue and trading of stocks and bonds, taking of deposits and the making of loans, the maintenance of the payment system, and facilitation of international transactions.

The origins of the financial districts are to be found in the coffee shops and merchant countinghouses of the colonial city's business district. Functional separation of financial services was more by street than by district, and the colonial business district was small, unspecialized, and centered on the waterfront. From the late 18th century, however, the growing demands of a well-established commercial economy and an emerging industrial economy forced merchants and other economic elites to find new places for financial transactions to occur. Yet, even then, many merchants continued to conduct these activities in the market halls, coffee shops, and countinghouses strung along the waterfronts of America's small cities.

In the 70 years following independence, the various financial institutions combined with other businesses to form embryonic financial districts in American cities. The financial sector was transformed from a relatively unspecialized industry to a highly specialized one. In Philadelphia, for example, the London Coffee House was turned by local merchants into a financial exchange where insurance was bought and sold and information about the Atlantic shipping, business, and political worlds was exchanged in an increasing variety of centrally located venues. Similarly, specialized financial and insurance services clustered on Boston's State Street by the 1840s. Despite the growing concentration of financial and related firms into one part of the city, the financial district was not sharply etched into the urban landscape before the mid-19th century.

By 1900, the financial district had become a significant part of the central city. Wall Street, the country's first financial district, emerged in the first decades of the 19th century and became the home of a critical mass of specialized financial and ancillary activities. Greater specialization created the advantages of complementary and competitive linkages essential for the running of the city's financial industry and business community. By 1860, the major banks, the stock exchange, and other important financial institutions lined Wall Street, while other specialized financial firms spilled out into the surrounding streets. New York was not alone; embryonic financial districts also appeared in other large cities, such as Chicago, Boston, Philadelphia, and San Francisco. Economic growth in America's cities over the next 100 years fueled the growth of financial districts and ensured that large and elaborate districts grew out of the original cores. Although few districts would move dramatically over this period, they were not static. In Chicago, for example, the financial district experienced numerous moves but had stopped by 1910 when it was anchored to the Chamber of Commerce and the Chicago Stock Exchange. Despite increasing financial activity in midtown New York by the 1920s, most firms continued to be linked to the downtown financial complex.

The financial district as it developed in the 19th century fulfilled two basic functions. First, they linked urban places, connecting economic players with each other over space. They permitted American cities to operate at various spatial scales, from the regional to the national and international. Cities such as Boston, Philadelphia, New York, and Baltimore used financial district institutions to grease the movement of natural resources, manufactured goods, business information, political news, and capital across the Atlantic. The district was the nexus for trade relations between the city and its hinterland. Urban financial agents moved capital, information, and goods between America's regions. The financial districts were also centers of primitive accumulation. Merchants and other capitalists increasingly used these districts to shift capital accumulated through trade into other sectors of the economy, most notably manufacturing.

Second, they functioned as a material landscape, as a place where capital was worked upon in a variety of guises. Financial districts were bounded territories where financial and ancillary industries provided the capital, credit, and informational needs of the commercial and industrial economies. Even though a substantial share of the businesses in a financial district were directly related to the financial sector, ancillary and nonrelated businesses also were found there, such as lawyers' offices, employment agencies, accounting firms, and prestigious clubs offering the financial executive and manager the opportunity to hobnob with each other. As agents working in the financial district were not homogeneous, the districts were an internally complex landscape, elaborate and differentiated in function, form, and location. Financial districts were also a symbolic landscape, where the economic elite proclaimed their identity as power brokers orchestrating the urban, national, and international economies.

A defining feature of the financial district is its unique, built environment. It is a multistoried landscape with an array of elaborate, architecturally significant buildings. Before the 1880s, financial institutions, like other sectors of the central business district, were housed in three- to six-story buildings. The development of the skyscraper by the end of the 19th century transformed the financial district's built environment and the organizational structure of work. A revolution in building technology and techniques, most especially the steel frame and elevators, permitted buildings to exceed traditional building heights. High land values restricted lateral expansion and forced the competitors for downtown land to expand vertically. Taller buildings, which housed more companies and divisions of companies, facilitated more face-to-face contact between people and helped large financial and nonfinancial corporations to keep track of their regional and national operations. Finally, skyscrapers were symbols of corporate power and modernity. Rising above the surrounding downtown area, the skyscraper proclaimed the dominance of corporate control over most aspects of economic, political, and social life and displayed a modern, sleek, streamlined machine geared to the pulse of the industrial economy.

The centers of this revolution were Chicago and New York. Initially, Chicago's 10-story Montauk building (1882) and 16-story Monadnock building (1889) set the pace. By the 1920s, however, New York, with buildings such as the 72-story Bank of Manhattan building (1929–1930), was the leader. The ever-larger skyscrapers were built to accommodate a variety of central-city functions, not just financial ones. However, the banks, insurance companies, stock exchanges, and ancillary professional services located in the heart of the financial district by the end of the 19th century were to be found in some of the largest buildings in the city.

The scale of an individual city's financial district reflected the city's place in the urban hierarchy. New York surpassed Philadelphia as America's dominant financial center by the end of the 18th century. It became the major clearinghouse of European and domestic capital invested in opening up the western resource economy and developing the nation's new transportation (railroad), informational apparatus (telegraph), urban infrastructure (docks, public transit), and burgeoning manufacturing base. The ability of New York's financial community to gain control of the nation's financial levers and to speed up the circulation of capital was possible because it was rooted on Wall Street. By the Second World War, the financial district was one of the most visible features of the landscape in the major cities of America. Home to the offices of the major financial corporations and numerous ancillary industries, it was the nexus of power; the hub of financial, corporate, and political decision making; the coordinating focus of the industrial economy; and the symbol of a modern world.

Increasing internationalization has led to growing centralization of financial transactions and institutions in a small number of "global cities." In addition, over the past 50 years the central financial district has experienced relative decline as many financial functions have moved to the business parks and built-up fringe of the metropolitan area. Although the origins of decentralization go back more than 100 years, large-scale decentralization of many low-end segments of the financial industry to the suburbs and small towns in recent years has resulted in the declining importance of the central city agglomerations. At the same time, as the routinized parts of the industry move to back offices in the low-cost areas on the city's fringe, the core financial districts become increasingly populated by high-end functions. The need for a central location that enables people to interact face-to-face was high 200 years ago and remains high today. Financial managers continue to rely heavily on their relationships with each other and with other sectors of the urban economy.

—Robert Lewis

Further Readings and References

Bowden, M. (1975). Growth of central districts in large cities. In L. Schnore (Ed.), *The new urban history: Quantitative explorations by American historians* (pp. 75–109). Princeton, NJ: Princeton University Press.

Hoover, E., & Vernon, R. (1962). *Anatomy of a metropolis: The changing distribution of people and jobs within the New York metropolitan region.* New York: Anchor.

Ward, D. (1966). The industrial revolution and the emergence of Boston's central business district. *Economic Geography, 42,* 152–171.

Willis, C. (1995). *Form follows finance: Skyscrapers and skylines in New York and Chicago.* New York: Princeton Architectural Press.

FIRE DEPARTMENTS

Fire has historically been a serious problem for urban dwellers and a key factor hindering short-term urban development, particularly prior to the 20th century. In early America flammable materials were regularly stored near open fires necessary for the heating of homes and cooking. Catastrophic conflagrations were not uncommon. A candle in a New Orleans building set off a fire that destroyed over 800 buildings in 1788, 3 years later a Philadelphia fire spread easily through the wooden buildings on Dock Street, and an 1820 fire in Savanna, Georgia, became a conflagration after setting off a cache of gunpowder. Even after the establishment of zoning regulations, urban fires could occasionally burn out of control. Chicago's famous 1871 fire destroyed more than 17,000 structures and killed over 300 people. The great San Francisco fire that followed the 1906 earthquake killed 3,000 people and incinerated most of that city. The history of urban firefighting has been one of ongoing professionalization of firefighters, increasing expenditures by municipalities, and implementation of new technologies, all in order to control the threat of fire.

Long before the rise of the "service city" led city dwellers to expect municipalities to raise money and pass legislation in support of a wide array of urban services, governments took an activist role in protecting town and city dwellers against fire. In 1646, New Amsterdam taxed residents to pay chimney inspectors after several fires resulted from careless chimney cleaning. Officials also ordered tanned leather water buckets from Holland and introduced an official fire watch. Other 17th-century colonial cities required homeowners to keep a bucket free at all times in order to help transport water to fires. Increasing urban density as well as technological innovations led residents of the largest cities to organize volunteer fire companies in the early 18th century. Boston was the first, in 1718, and equipped its volunteers with uniforms and a small hand-operated pump fire engine. In 1736, Benjamin Franklin organized, publicized, and participated in a Philadelphia volunteer fire company, setting a standard for civic leaders also fighting fires that was followed by George Washington, Aaron Burr, and Thomas Jefferson, among others. Fire companies were patriotic hotbeds in the 1770s, as firemen in New York, Boston, and Philadelphia transformed their shared obligation to the preservation of public safety and order into active and outspoken support for the Revolution.

By the early 19th century, every American city was protected by a volunteer fire department made up of fire companies organized around hand-operated pump engines and hose trucks and voluntarily manned by the citizenry, all under the loose control of a municipal overseeing organization. Baltimore's fire department increased from three volunteer fire companies in 1790, to six in 1800, to seventeen by 1843. Because the heavy equipment required extensive manpower to transport to fires and operate, companies were large. There were close to 800 active Baltimore volunteers in the 1830s alone. Philadelphia had 17 volunteer fire companies by 1790. Volunteer fire companies were selective in their membership and combined social activities with firefighting, including visits to firemen in other cities.

One of the most notable characteristics of volunteer fire companies in the early 19th century was the occupational heterogeneity of their membership. Clerks, skilled laborers, and merchants fought fires side by side. Fire companies also provided early social services, including some of the first public lending libraries. Firehouses contained rooms for public use, and as early as 1792, fire departments set up widow and orphan funds to support dependents of injured or killed firemen. Volunteer firemen were not paid salaries, but they were absolved from jury and militia duty and received public tribute and prestige for their actions. In the decades before the Civil War, this prestige sustained firemen in their belief that their public service revealed their civic virtue. Volunteer firemen became very active in urban politics (Boss Tweed of New York started his political career in a firehouse), and although companies continued to attract diverse men to the shared masculine culture of the urban firehouse, increasingly there were fewer mature merchants and more young laborers who donned the firefighter's garb.

By the 1850s, urban volunteer fire departments had become large (often over 1,000 members), disorganized, and generally unruly. Although for the most part volunteers continued to do a good job fighting fires, firemen faced increasing criticism for their public behavior, which rarely met the standards of decorum demanded by the growing urban middle class. Drinking, competition, and occasionally elaborate public brawls drew the attention of reformers. Fire companies built houses where they pleased, which provided some parts of a city with too many companies, while generally providing inadequate protection to early suburbs. Because of fire companies' increasing involvement in both politics and violence, and because of the financial demands that these companies placed on insurance companies, citizens, and city governments, reformers began to push for the municipalization of the volunteers. Technological innovations, including the steam engine (which could be operated by just a few men and rendered the large volunteer companies somewhat obsolete) and the fire-alarm telegraph, paved the way for changes. In 1853, Cincinnati instituted a paid department manned by a small band of professional firefighters and equipped with horse-drawn steam engines. Volunteer firemen actively opposed municipalization, arguing that paid men would never fight fire as bravely as volunteers, but by the 1860s every large American city had followed Cincinnati's lead and disbanded their volunteers.

Until the late 19th century, however, most paid firemen were not full-time municipal employees. The majority worked on call, were badly paid, and were expected to leave their place of employment at the fire alarm. Although fire chiefs routinely bemoaned the poor quality of paid recruits, changes such as technological innovations, increased water supply and zoning regulations, and better organized firefighters led to ever greater efficiency and order in firefighting. As in the volunteer era, firefighters protested short-sighted funding policies that made it difficult for them to purchase equipment. In 1865, New York City introduced the first full-time, paid fire department in the country, and by the end of the century most large cities had followed their lead. Early-20th-century developments, including civil service exams and training programs for firefighters, produced firefighting forces that were well trained and highly competent.

Discriminatory hiring practices and funding issues, however, proved to be entrenched problems for 20th-century fire departments. Many firemen adamantly opposed the integration of fire companies in both Northern and Southern cities in the early and middle part of the century. While some departments admitted black members in the first decades of the 20th century, the black firemen were usually assigned to segregated houses. Most departments were forced to integrate during the Civil Rights Movement, often in the face of the open and sometimes violent opposition of white members. Los Angeles finally integrated their department in 1956, after years of turmoil following an NAACP petition for integration in 1953. Segregation in St. Louis's firehouses didn't end until 1961. African American firefighters still complain that it is more difficult for them to gain positions over equally qualified white firefighters in some American cities.

Women have faced even greater difficulty becoming firefighters, in large part because firehouses and firefighting continue to be perceived by both participants and observers as highly masculine. Women replaced missing firemen in urban departments during the world wars, but it wasn't until 1973 that the first woman served as a paid firefighter in peacetime. In the later 1970s and 1980s, women lobbied for the opportunity to join municipal departments. In a case closely followed by the media, the San Diego Fire Department became the first large department in the country ordered to hire both women and minority men in 1974. In the face of organized opposition by both firemen and their supporters, the department placed five women into recruit training and then rejected them halfway through their course (the women later received out-of-court settlements). St. Louis didn't allow women to join its fire department until 1987. While more than 15 percent of the firefighters in Minneapolis and San Francisco are female, as of 2005 there were still a number of large urban departments that had no female members at all.

As in previous times, firefighting effectiveness has been improved by technological advances, particularly self-contained breathing apparatus, radios, and larger and more powerful vehicles. Unfortunately, the challenges of urban firefighting have also increased, especially with the proliferation of high-rise buildings. On September 11, 2001, 343 New York City firefighters and paramedics were killed while trying to rescue victims after the attack on the World Trade Center. As in the past, the increasing expense of firefighter salaries (which are often not as high as those of other municipal employees) and of equipment and insurance have led to ongoing funding struggles between fire departments and cities. Nonetheless, firefighters regularly rank among the most beloved urban employees. As smaller towns grow, they continue to replace their volunteer forces with paid fire departments. Although there are still many more volunteer than paid firefighters in the United States, paid firefighters have effectively protected American cities from fire for over 150 years.

—*Amy S. Greenberg*

Further Readings and References

Carp, B. L. (2001). Fire of liberty: Firefighters, urban voluntary culture and the Revolutionary movement. *William and Mary Quarterly, 58,* 781–818.

Greenberg, A. S. (1998). *Cause for alarm: The volunteer fire department in the nineteenth-century city.* Princeton, NJ: Princeton University Press.

Hazen, M. H., & Hazen, R. M. (1992). *Keepers of the flame: The role of fire in American culture, 1775–1925.* Princeton, NJ: Princeton University Press.

Lyons, P. R. (1976). *Fire in America!* Boston: National Fire Protection Association.

Tebeau, M. (2003). *Eating smoke: Fire in urban America, 1800–1950.* Baltimore, MD: Johns Hopkins University Press.

Women in the Fire Service. (n.d.). *History of women in firefighting.* Retrieved April 22, 2005, from http://www.wfsi.org/women_and_firefighting/history.php

Women in the Fire Service. (2005). *Status report, 2005.* Retrieved April 22, 2005, from http://www.wfsi.org

FITZGERALD, F. SCOTT

Francis Scott Fitzgerald (1896–1940) was born on September 24, 1896 in St. Paul, Minnesota. Fitzgerald's Midwestern family had the traditions of the upper classes, but none of the financial security to support those traditions. At a young age, Fitzgerald was aware that he was never completely a part of aristocratic society. However, he was always motivated to succeed in life and this drive ultimately led him to produce the literature he wrote. Fitzgerald entered Princeton in 1913, and in 1917 left college for an army commission. While stationed in Alabama at Camp Sheridan, Fitzgerald met his future wife, Zelda Sayre. On April 3, 1920, Fitzgerald and Sayre married and in October 1921, Zelda gave birth to their only child, a daughter, Frances Scott Fitzgerald. Fitzgerald ultimately suffered a heart attack in November of 1940 and in December of that same year a second heart attack took his life.

Fitzgerald left behind his literary masterpieces. Some of his works are *This Side of Paradise, The Beautiful and Damned, The Great Gatsby,* and *Tender Is the Night.* In Fitzgerald's novels, the settings he chose proved important. Settings used by Fitzgerald include the home, bars, schools, and the city. The city—especially New York City—intrigued Fitzgerald, but also baffled him, because while the city embodied the accomplishment of civilization and gave people opportunities, it was also a hideous place constantly threatening people with its corrupting evils. Fitzgerald saw the city as serving the double function of a physical locale and a psychological emblem. In using the city as a physical locale, Fitzgerald described the city itself in great detail. However, when he used the city as a psychological emblem, Fitzgerald placed emphasis not on what a person saw, but rather on the way a person viewed the scene.

The most recurrent setting in Fitzgerald's fiction is New York City. Fitzgerald relied on his experience as a former resident of New York City to capture the feel of metropolitan life in his literary works. Fitzgerald viewed New York City as a paradox; New York City was a mecca for glamour, romance, and opportunity, while at the same time New York City was a place of degeneration, despair, and mystery. Fitzgerald first presented the image of New York City as a symbol of the most sophisticated and glamorous qualities of urban life in his novel *This Side of Paradise* and in his short story "May Day." However, in Fitzgerald's novel *The Beautiful and Damned,* the image of New York City was blemished, and in *The Great Gatsby,* the city appeared most desolate. Both dazzled and baffled by New York City, Fitzgerald articulated this setting in his writing and sought to discover the meaning of city life.

—*Amy Hodgin*

Further Readings and References

Eble, K. E. (1963). *F. Scott Fitzgerald.* New York: Twayne.

Gale, R. L. (1998). *An F. Scott Fitzgerald encyclopedia.* Westport, CT: Greenwood Press.

Zhang, A. (1997). *Enchanted places: The use of setting in F. Scott Fitzgerald's fiction.* Westport, CT: Greenwood Press.

FIVE POINTS

For much of the 19th century, New York's Five Points district in Lower Manhattan was characterized as the worst slum in the United States. Its name derives from the intersection, formed in 1809, of three streets: Orange (now Baxter), Cross (now Park), and Anthony (now Worth) Streets. "Five Points" probably entered local idiom almost as soon as the intersection was formed, and the name was widely known to New Yorkers in the 1820s and 1830s. During the 1840s, the name also achieved international notoriety when Charles Dickens, who visited New York early in the decade, scathingly described Five Points in *American Notes* as a New World equivalent to London's East End slums.

By the late 19th century, however, Five Points had ceased to inspire horror and the name gradually dropped out of general usage. This happened in part because other areas overshadowed Five Points as symbols of urban degradation and menace. The notoriety of Five Points also faded as the district was radically altered by urban redevelopment and eventually ceased to exist as a residential precinct. The original Five Points triangle was cleared in 1833. The extension of Worth Street in 1868 further opened out the neighborhood around the Five Points intersection, and the demolition of the nearby Mulberry Bend neighborhood and its replacement with a park in 1897 further eroded the community. Additional slum clearance work was undertaken in 1916, and the few remaining traces of the old district were swept away in 1961.

Today, Five Points is a vanished neighborhood that persists in public imagination through the words and pictures of outsiders who caricatured and denigrated it. The most enduring of these representations is in Herbert Asbury's *The Gangs of New York* (1928), which demonized a place that had already been torn down. Martin Scorsese's 2002 movie *Gangs of New York* perpetuated and further sensationalized Asbury's characterizations of Five Points. The historical realities of the place are more elusive and complex than these distorting slum myths concede.

During the first quarter of the 19th century the place that would become Five Points was transformed from a network of streams and marshes on the city's borderlands, draining into the Collect Pond, into an industrial district of slaughterhouses, tanneries, breweries, furnaces, and potteries. The contaminated marshes, regarded with fear as a source of yellow fever, were drained, and the pond itself was filled and subdivided. One of city's largest concentrations of black Americans found residence there.

During the second quarter of the century black Americans were joined by other poor newcomers, most of them Irish Catholics and German Jews. Land subdivision and tenement building produced a densely settled and unsanitary environment. Symptomatic of these changes was the conversion of the "Old Brewery" during the 1830s into a rambling multifamily dwelling place. It became the focus for sensational newspaper accounts of Old World pauperism taking insidious root in American society. Suspicion of foreigners overlapped with fear of cholera, epidemics of which terrified city dwellers during the early 1830s. Cholera was known as a "filth disease," and nowhere was filth seemingly more concentrated than in Five Points. Violence also seemed to find a home there. The 1834–1835 riots, sparked in part by rivalry between black and Irish men over laboring jobs and by election-day intimidation, triggered further denunciations of the district. Commentators described a state of simmering violence between rival street gangs. The emergence of Five Points as a hub for saloons, dance halls, and the city's prostitution trade cemented its reputation as a seedy slum.

That reputation had, by the middle of the 19th century, made Five Points the focus of a thriving tourism industry. Visitors came to Five Points looking for titillation and entertainment. Many came to experience firsthand the strange sights, sounds, and smells of a district whose population was 75 percent foreign-born. Others patronized the saloons, dance halls, brothels, and bowling alleys.

Paradoxically, during the third quarter of the century many of the slumland features which attracted tourists to Five Points were visibly eroding away. What happened to the infamous Old Brewery was symptomatic of the changes. It was torn down in 1852 and replaced by the Five Points Mission. Commentators conceded during the 1850s and 1860s that Five Points was losing its reputation for violence and immorality. True, the 1857 Five Points riot was among the worst in New York's history, but the racial violence unleashed by the New York draft riots of 1863 largely bypassed Five Points, where few black Americans still lived. By the 1870s, few of the district's street gangs remained either. Most of the brothels and dance halls had also long ago left the area, and factories took their place.

Five Points continued to alter dramatically during the last quarter of the 19th century. Economic disadvantage remained entrenched, and it was tangibly expressed in multistory "dumbbell" tenements. However, population density was not as great, nor was poverty as acute, as it had been during the 1830s and 1840s. The cultural adjustments forced upon immigrants during that earlier period continued to be played out in Five Points as waves of new immigrants flooded through the area. Their homelands, however, were different. Irish and German residents were now outnumbered by Italians, Russian and Polish Jews, and Chinese. The Southern and Eastern European majority imposed a new demographic profile upon the district, with single- and extended-family units comprising the majority of households and children forming an increasing proportion of the local population.

Given the enormity of the transformations to the built environment, the social composition, and the cultural makeup of Five Points during the 19th century, it is puzzling that the slum myth persisted. It cannot be explained simply in terms of the persistence of social disadvantage in Five Points, because this was expressed very differently over time. The explanation lies rather in the visibility of that disadvantage. Five Points was called a slum because it stood within eyesight of the seat of city government and the headquarters of the city's daily press. It was seen by middle-class New Yorkers as they traveled to and from nearby Broadway and Wall Street. It was this visibility that made the idea of Five Points so shocking—and entertaining—across the nation. That image persisted whereas the place itself was totally transformed and ultimately lost its discrete identity.

The vivid content of this enduring slum image was drawn from the urban reform movement, which used slum myths to mobilize public opinion in support of redevelopment schemes, building controls, and moral improvement campaigns. These overlapping strands of slum performance and urban reform are highlighted by Jacob Riis, whose influential 1890 reformist tract *How the Other Half Lives* contended that although the old Five Points slum had been destroyed, its offshoots, like Mulberry Bend, were continuing to grow and to fester. Riis so mobilized national opinion that Mulberry Bend—the last sizeable residential enclave of the Five Points district—was destroyed.

During the 1970s and 1980s, historians began to peel back the layers of theatrical misinformation about Five Points, in order to reveal the actualities of life within this most misunderstood of American city neighborhoods. During the 1990s, archaeologists reinforced these reinterpretations, providing material evidence of lives and lifestyles about which documentary records were reticent. These accumulating findings have complicated historical understanding of Five Points. They reveal an immigrant working-class community, rough-edged and pinched by poverty, but characterized as well by a complex mix of occupational levels and lifestyle choices. The historical significance of Five Points lies not in its shocking distance from American society, but in its closeness to working-class life and culture during a century of rapid urban change.

—*Alan Mayne*

Further Readings and References

Asbury, H. H. (1928). *The gangs of New York: An informal history of the underworld.* New York: Alfred A. Knopf.

Dickens, C. (n.d.). *The works of Charles Dickens. Volume 1: American notes.* New York: Books, Inc. (Original work published 1842)

Gilfoyle, T. (2003). Scorsese's gangs of New York: Why myth matters. *Journal of Urban History, 29*, 620–630.

Riis, J. A. (1971). *How the other half lives: Studies among the tenements of New York.* New York: Dover. (Original work published 1890)

FLATIRON BUILDING

Considered the oldest remaining skyscraper in New York City, the Flatiron Building was completed in 1903 and originally known as the Fuller Building. The 21-story commercial office tower, located just below Madison Square at the intersection of Fifth Avenue, Broadway, and 23rd Streets, was rapidly nicknamed the Flatiron Building after its unusual triangular footprint and its prismatic shape that resembled the irons of the day. Immediately it became one of the city's most recognizable and beloved architectural landmarks.

It was at the turn of the 20th century that the Chicago-based George A. Fuller's steel construction company decided to move to New York and commissioned its new office building from the renowned architect and urban planner Daniel H. Burnham. Burnham had directed the Chicago's 1893 World's Columbian Exposition and designed, with his partner John Wellborn Root, Chicago's famous Rookery, Reliance, and Monadnock buildings.

The 285-foot-high Flatiron Building was the tallest edifice north of the financial district at the time of its completion. Nevertheless, its most distinctive features are its location, characterized by the surrounding void of streets that makes it frontally visible from a distance and almost isolated as a single building in the urban fabric, and its unconventional freestanding silhouette, which resembles the prow of a slender and majestic ocean liner sailing northward. Alfred Stieglitz, who captured its dramatic appearance in photographs, compared the status of the Flatiron Building in the United States to that of the Parthenon in Greece.

Designed in the Beaux-Arts style and richly adorned with Gothic and Renaissance details of Grecian faces and terra-cotta patterns, the Flatiron Building is structured like a classical Greek column. Its rusticated limestone façade is divided into three horizontal parts: a five-story base, a twelve-story shaft, and a four-story capital topped with a heavy projecting cornice. At its narrowest end, the building is just 6 feet wide, which from certain perspectives makes the structure look like a flat wall. This apparent fragility made many people fear that the building would collapse in a strong wind.

Actually, the extremely sharp angle at the northern end and the wind loads encountered at that location created special planning and framing problems that the engineering firm of Purdy and Henderson resolved by designing behind the eclectic Beaux-Arts skin of the façade a fully load-bearing steel skeleton structure reinforced with wind bracing. Also, the geometry of the site provided some major advantages, primarily the possibility for all offices to have an outside, wide-view exposure. Consequently, the building has always benefitted from low vacancy rates in both its commercial and retail spaces.

Simultaneously, it became a tourist attraction and people enjoyed viewing the city from the observation lounge and restaurant located at the top floor of the tower. At ground level, the height and aerodynamic shape of the building led to a wind-tunnel effect that raised women's skirts and petticoats. It is said that the expression "Twenty-Three Skidoo" was born on the windy corner of 23rd Street when policemen had to tell young loitering men who came to peep at a lady's bare ankle to move away.

—*Catherine C. Galley*

See also Architecture; Skyscrapers

Further Readings and References

Douglas, G. H. (1996). *Skyscrapers: A social history of the very tall building in America.* Jefferson, NC: McFarland.

Dupré, J. (1996). *Skyscrapers.* New York: Black Dog & Leventhal.

Landau, S. B., & Condit, C. W. (1996). *Rise of the New York skyscraper, 1865–1913.* New Haven, CT: Yale University Press.

FLOPHOUSES

The term *flophouse* originally described the lowest form of temporary urban housing, wherein a tenant slept either on a cot or hammock or directly on the floor of a communal room. As the migrant workers of the 19th century gave way to the more stationary, homeless population of the nation's mid-20th-century skid rows, the term came to connote a variety of housing options. Many Americans used flophouses as housing of last resort, a final protection against sleeping directly on the city streets.

Both working- and middle-class Americans required unprecedented amounts of temporary, urban housing in the industrializing cities of the late 19th century. Many migrant workers, laboring in the lumber industry, on the railroads, or in other fields, required places to stay within the cities. Similarly, middle-class workers congregating in urban areas to fill clerical and other white-collar positions sought impermanent homes. Lodging facilities soon developed to suit the needs of both groups. Middle-class workers often stayed in boardinghouses, taking their meals with their fellow boarders. Rooming houses, too, offered small, furnished rooms to some employed in the cities.

Landlords developed larger scale establishments to house laborers from the working classes. An array of lodging houses appeared, offering short-term rentals for a variety of budgets. One form, the cage hotel, would prove ubiquitous in the 20th century. Cage hotels were created by partitioning industrial spaces or warehouses into individual cubicles, ranging from approximately 5×7 feet to 6×10 feet in size. The partitions stopped 1 to 3 feet short of the ceiling, and each cage was topped with chicken wire. This construction technique allowed the circulation of both light and air, while discouraging the efforts of potential thieves. The quality of life within the cage hotels varied according to the location, management, and clientele of the residence. Some cages lacked furnishings, but many offered a bed, chair, and dresser. Residents shared communal bathrooms, which were notoriously poorly maintained. Although minimal in material comforts, such cages proved an enduring housing form because of the relative privacy they afforded residents.

By contrast, the dormitory-style lodging of flophouses offered a less expensive housing option. For a small fee, men were granted access to bunk beds or cots arranged in rows in large, communal rooms. Seeking a share of the temporary lodging market, some bars allowed patrons to spend the night sleeping in a chair or on the floor. A few enterprising bar owners even stretched ropes across the room, charging patrons for the privilege of leaning on the ropes overnight.

Postwar deindustrialization left many jobless, homeless people in the nation's urban centers. As dormitory-style lodging was phased out, the single-room occupancy (SRO) hotels became semipermanent dwellings for the skid row population. The era saw a rise in the number of older, sometimes alcoholic homeless men, for whom the SROs functioned as low-end retirement homes. Many hotel residents found them a rare, useful site for socialization and recreation in a world that increasingly denied them public space. Some men spent more than 5 hours per day in their cages or watching television or playing cards in the hotel lobby.

Public assistance paid the lodging fees for many urban homeless in these years. Some cities operated their own municipal lodging houses, providing sleeping accommodations and meals to needy homeless applicants. Some supplemented or replaced those services by issuing relief recipients tickets valid for lodging at selected hotels, as well as coupons redeemable for meals in area restaurants. Not all hotels welcomed such referrals, though, as some preferred to restrict residence to those who could pay their own way. Significantly, some hotels also routinely refused entry to African Americans, fueling the racial segregation that characterized skid row life. Although most establishments did not permit women residents, some allowed women to stay in separate areas or on separate floors.

Throughout this period, the "mission flops" administered by religious organizations continued to provide the nation's urban homeless with another type of temporary housing. Seeking to convert as many of the poor as possible to Christianity, missions such as the Salvation Army required clients to attend a religious service before serving them food. Some missions also mandated showering and sometimes delousing before bed. Uninterested in participating in such activities, many homeless avoided the missions, when possible, preferring the relative anonymity and privacy of the hotels. Men who resented the missions' prohibitions against alcohol gravitated toward the commercial establishments.

Amidst postwar prosperity, the populations of the nation's skid rows shrank considerably. Area hotels witnessed a corresponding decline in occupancy rates. Overrun with rats and other vermin, poorly maintained, and used far beyond their intended capacity, the buildings fell into disrepair, attracting public criticism.

Many American cities tore down their flophouses along with the rest of skid row as part of federally sponsored slum clearance programs in the 1950s and 1960s. Renewal initiatives swept away the flophouses of Philadelphia, Minneapolis, Detroit, St. Louis, Boston, and Chicago. In other cities, including New York, rising property values inspired landlords to convert most of the remaining flophouses into middle- and upper-class housing.

As the flophouses were demolished, some activist groups proposed the erection of new, humane facilities to house the displaced homeless population. Few steps were taken in that direction, though, due largely to political pressures brought by city residents and business district advocates. By the mid-1970s, increasing numbers of homeless people appeared in urban centers. These "new" homeless found limited housing opportunities, in part due to the decline in the supply of the temporary housing stock for low-income city residents.

At the end of the 20th century, few flophouses remained. Even on the Bowery, the nation's most infamous skid row, the last of the historic flops, such as the Andrews, White House, and Sunshine Hotels, struggled to survive, offering overnight accommodations to the city's homeless population for $5 to $10 per night.

—*Ella Howard*

Further Readings and References

Hart, J. (2002). *Down and out: The life and death of Minneapolis's skid row.* Minneapolis: University of Minnesota Press.

Hoch, C., & Slayton, R. A. (1989). *New homeless and old: Community and the skid row hotel.* Philadelphia: Temple University Press.

Isay, D., & Abramson, S. (with photographs by H. Wang). (2001). *Flophouse: Life on the bowery.* New York: Random House.

Kusmer, K. L. (2002). *Down and out, on the road: The homeless in American history.* New York: Oxford University Press.

FOLKLORE

Broadly defined, *folklore* has traditionally referred to any group of orally transmitted narratives (legends, myths, songs, etc.) told by a particular group of people in an effort to impart a lesson. And while often based upon historic precedent and even widely accepted in their subject matter, most folktales are found to be speciously plausible at best, containing considerably more imagination than truth. As with other popular national folklores, such as the German *Märchen* (wonder) tales or the French *Pourqoui* (why?) tales, these American narratives usually manifest out of some collective group's hopes and anxieties concerning the unexplainable as they search to give a credible clarification to some mysterious and arcane subject matter. The historic endurance of these tales relies heavily upon their ability both to entertain and to stir up a primal emotional or psychological response in their immediate audience.

Historically, American folklore has given rise to a few distinct traditions, such as the tall tale. Locally bound and perpetuated by the burgeoning media outlets of the 19th century, tall tales such as those about Paul Bunyan, the lumberjack of Brobdingnagian proportions, and his equally gigantic companion Babe the Blue Ox, surfaced around lumberjack camps in 1860 and were popularized by American newsmen in 1910. Their tales told amusing anecdotes of outrageous and preposterous exaggeration. In one account, Paul and Babe actually excavated the Grand Canyon when Paul accidentally dragged his pickax behind him. Sometimes, tall tales such as this one were actually born from extrapolated accounts of real-life figures. One such tale was the account of Johnny Appleseed, whose story arose from an article in *Harper's New Monthly Magazine* in 1871, which greatly inflated the agricultural exploits of the real-life John Chapman and his travels across the United States. Tales like this were considered harmless because of their obvious absurdity, and they sought largely to entertain without the didacticism or inherent proselytism of their continental predecessors (although some accounts show that the lumber industry of the late 19th century exploited the tale of Paul Bunyan for publicity and recruitment).

Similar to the tall tale in narrative strength but perhaps far more problematic in form and content, the folk song or folk ballad indigenous to America holds a far greater historical onus due to its often racial and ethnic content. While really little more, structurally, than a lyric poem with melody, this form of folk song often became imbricated within other regional mythologies and cultural mores (such as the Deep South's interest in voodoo or hoodoo) to create a small but searing set of ethnically divisive texts aimed at the social alienation and degradation of a racial minority. Derived from innuendo, rumor, superstition, and stereotype, these tales appropriated the conventions of a particular culture (for example, black

American gospel and blues music) and subverted the form to attack the culture—often through parody. In one such example, a typical black stereotype of an easily aggravated, criminal, male street thug was invented and perpetuated through song and poetry in many early-20th-century cities. Similar stories of the denizens of Jewish, Italian, and other ghettos of any large city were perpetuated to various degrees. And while it should be acknowledged that these sorts of folktales are relatively few in number, they were popular, and more important, their cultural resonances to the contemporary urban community are felt today.

More recent, urban folklore, has a direct cultural antecedent in the rise of industry and technology unique to the 19th century as proto-modern Americans began their migration into the city. Against this early backdrop, the new folklore of the American urban landscape was constructed as different cultures and ethnicities began to delineate territorial lines within districts and neighborhoods within the larger city. With newly established boundaries within this city, the individual cultural groups became relatively isolated within their own little territory, and tales and songs of incursion by outsiders, boundary crossings by other ethnicities, and idiosyncratic anomalies within the borders of the neighborhood arose in a xenophobic manner. Thus, as unknown laborers took their place on the assembly line in the bowels of some nameless factory, industrialism transmogrified the Märchen tales of wonder and fancy into darker fantasies highlighting and exacerbating minor peripheral features of competing ethnicities into greater stereotypical fears of them.

Distinguishable, yet connected, to this type of folklore is the modern *urban legend*. A term coined by American folklore scholar Jan Harold Brunvand, this new approach to urban folklore is fascinated with tales of the supernatural subsisting on and drawing from this anxiety and xenophobia of the inhabitants of the city. More often than not, the urban legend is an account drawn from second- or thirdhand sources, otherwise attributed to "a friend of a friend," and relies upon the traditional method of oral transmission to survive and be perpetuated. Likewise, upon each retelling, substantial embellishment often occurs to the primary tale to adapt it to its geographical locale and constituency, thus allowing the tales to spread across the nation.

Many of these stories are widely known and have spread outside of their local parameters as cautionary tales: In New York City, a popular folktale surrounding infant pet alligators being flushed into the sewer systems only to reemerge more fully grown to maul their former owners exists to warn citizens against animal cruelty. Likewise, Chicago's urban myth of Resurrection Mary involves a hitchhiking girl in the 1930s who was struck by a passing car and left to die, but whose spirit has been seen walking along Archer Avenue ever since seeking to hitchhike. In the late 19th and early 20th centuries, contemporary tales of the macabre and horrific became more plausible through the media. More recently, supermarket tabloids and popular mass entertainments such as the 1998 movie *Urban Legend* and the syndicated television program *Beyond Belief: Fact or Fiction* have carried these tales. Perpetuators of the folklore, with their suspenseful plotlines and almost formulaic format, hark back to storytellers with a more simple understanding of folklore as tales of entertainment and pseudoscience but are considerably less concerned with didacticism, morality, or culture.

—*Joseph Michael Sommers*

Further Readings and References

Axelrod, A., & Oster, H. (2001). *The Penguin dictionary of American folklore.* New York: Penguin Putnam.

Brunvand, J. H. (1986). *The study of American folklore.* New York: Norton.

Brunvand, J. H. (1990). Dorson and the urban legend. *Folklore Historian, 7,* 16–22.

Dorson, R. (1983). *Handbook of American folklore.* Bloomington: Indiana University Press.

FORD, HENRY

Henry Ford (1863-1947) is one of the most paradoxical figures in American history: an innovative industrial businessman about whom much is known but who in the end still remains enigmatic. He is enigmatic partly as a personality and partly as a representative of an era. Henry Ford also is a figure recognized for his popular hero appeal to the American public. He is credited with the concept of *mass production,* a manufacturing practice that the Ford Motor Company adopted toward the end of World War I for the production of its Model T car.

Henry Ford was born on a farm near Greenfield, Michigan, in 1863 and was educated in public schools.

At the age of 16, he became a machinist's apprentice. In 1888, he married Clara Janet Bryant. In 1891, he became an engineer at the Edison Illumination Company in Detroit. Henry Ford had one son, Edsel Bryant Ford, born in 1893.

Ford made his first car, the "Quadricycle Runabout," in the summer of 1896. This car had a 4-horsepower engine and could reach speeds of 20 miles per hour. He sold the car for $200 to invest in his second car, which was completed in early 1898.

In June of 1903, Henry Ford, armed with $28,000, and 11 business associates founded what has turned into one of the world's largest automobile manufacturers: the Ford Motor Company. These pioneers turned what was a small dream into a gigantic business.

In 1907, Henry Ford announced his goal for the Ford Motor Company: to mass produce automobiles. At that time, automobiles were expensive, custom-made machines. Ford produced 1,708 cars the first year. In 1908, he rolled out the Model T. His success with the Model T has been attributed to the combination of modern features and a low price that most American families could afford.

Henry Ford has traditionally been credited with combining standardized parts with the concept of the moving assembly line to form true mass production assembly in 1913. Ford's engineers took the first step toward this goal by designing the Model T, a simple, sturdy car, offering no factory options—not even a choice of color. The focus on innovation began to shift to process innovation, including the development of mass automobile production by using the moving assembly line, which was a key to the success of the Model T.

Ford also began the practice of increasing wages to improve employee morale, thus improving overall performance. In 1914, Ford workers' wages were raised to $5 a day minimum wage—an excellent wage—and the workers soon proved their loyalty to the company by purchasing their own Model Ts. Ford was called and thought a traitor by other manufacturers and competitors. He added organizational psychology that made every employee a partner in the drive for success. When the United States entered World War I in 1917, his plants switched to war production. Efficient production line methods enabled him to cut the cost of his products while simultaneously increasing wages so that his employees were the highest paid in the industry.

Although Henry Ford was man of great innovation, he refused to recognize unions, he paid attention to all of the firm's operations, domestic and overseas, and the managers were given little latitude for initiative and innovation.

In 1925, the Ford Motor Company acquired the Lincoln Motor Company, thus branching out into luxury cars, and in the 1930s, the Mercury division was created to establish a division centered on midpriced cars. The Ford Motor Company was growing. When the United States entered World War II, Henry Ford once again converted all his plants to war production.

In 1919, Edsel Ford succeeded his father as president of Ford Motor Company. When Edsel died on May 26, 1943, at the age of 49, Henry Ford again, at the age of 80, took over the presidency of Ford Motor Company. In 1945, Henry Ford retired, with an estimated wealth of $700 million. He died 2 years later, on April 7, 1947. Ford's manufacturing principles were adopted by countless industries. Henry Ford will always be remembered for his achievements in the automobile industry.

—*Alfredo Manuel Coelho*

Further Readings and References

Bonin, H., Lang, Y., & Tolliday, S. (Eds.). (2003). *Ford, 1903–2003: The European history* (2 vols.). Paris: P.L.A.G.E.

Ford, H. (1922). *My life and work.* Garden City, NY: Garden City Publishing.

Lewchuk, W. A. (1993). Men and monotony: Fraternalism as a managerial strategy at the Ford Motor Company. *Journal of Economic History, 53*(4), 824–856.

Mira, W., & Hill, F. E. (1964). *American business abroad: Ford on six continents.* Detroit, MI: Wayne State University Press.

FORT WORTH, TEXAS

Known by locals as Cowtown, Fort Worth, situated on the Clear Fork of the Trinity River in northeastern Texas, is a city closely attached to both the history and urban development of the American West. Originally settled as an Army outpost in 1849, Fort Worth has successively been a national center for the cattle industry, meatpacking, oil extraction, and the airline industry. Today it is a vibrant and cosmopolitan city of more than 500,000 no longer overshadowed by its larger neighbor to the east, Dallas.

In January 1849, United States Army General William Jenkins Worth, a Mexican War hero, proposed a line of 10 forts to mark the western Texas frontier from Eagle Pass to the confluence of the West Fork and Clear Fork of the Trinity River. Following the death of General Worth, General William S. Harney took command and ordered Major Ripley S. Arnold to find a fort site near the West Fork and Clear Fork. On June 6, 1849, Arnold established a camp on the bank of the Trinity River, which he named Camp Worth in honor of General Worth. The United States War Department officially named the post Fort Worth on November 14, 1849. Although Indians were still a threat in the area, pioneers were already settling near the fort. In September 1853, when a new line of forts was built further west, the army evacuated Fort Worth, but a community had already grown up around the Fort forming a permanent settlement.

Fort Worth soon grew and prospered, in part because of its location. As the last major, southernmost stop on the Chisholm cattle trail, it attracted soldiers, settlers, and cattle drivers alike. Butterfield Overland Mail and the Southern Pacific Stage Line used the town as a western terminus on the way to California, and while Fort Worth suffered some adverse economic effects from the Civil War and Reconstruction, the city continued to grow, with barrooms such as Tom Prindle's Saloon and Steele's Tavern welcoming travelers from across the country. Weekly newspapers such as the Fort Worth *Chief* and the *Democrat* became prominent, and in 1884, the Fort Worth National Bank was established. The post-1865 demand for cattle resulted in much of this boom, as Fort Worth offered the cowboy respite from the cattle drives to Oklahoma and Kansas to the north. Northern cattle buyers even established headquarters in the town. The Texas and Pacific Railway designated Fort Worth as its eastern terminus for the route to San Diego, completing construction in 1876, and by 1900 railroads connected Fort Worth and cattle to cities as diverse as New Orleans, Denver, and St. Louis.

Fort Worth's residents and city government believed strongly in boosterism and in 1889 constructed the Texas Spring Palace as an agricultural exhibition hall. The palace was both a form of entertainment and an important part of the town's strategy for boosting commercial expansion. It was advertised throughout the nation, and special trains brought visitors from as far away as Boston and Chicago. By the 1890s, Fort Worth, the Queen City of the Prairie, as it was known, had become a meatpacking center. With the incentive of $100,000, combined with impressive railroad links, the national meatpacking firms Swift & Co. and Armour & Co. established branch plants in Fort Worth, joining local companies in utilizing the local stockyards to make Fort Worth the nation's second largest livestock market and packing house center. The rise of the stockyards and packing plants stimulated livestock-related businesses devoted to the care of the cattle and the people working in the plants.

During World War I, the United States Army established Camp Bowie in the Arlington Heights area of the city, which trained 100,000 men, and the United States Army Air Force converted three airfields into centers of training in the burgeoning field of aviation, beginning the connections to the military and aviation that would dominate the history of Fort Worth throughout the 20th century. With the discovery of oil in far west Texas, Fort Worth benefitted, as it had with cattle, as the last commercialized town before the vast stretches of prairie land began. The town became a center for the sale of drilling supplies and for refineries. Pipeline companies—such as Sinclair Refining, Texaco, and Humble Oil and Refining Company, which later became Exxon—converged on Fort Worth, and the town became a center for oil stock exchanges. During the Depression of the 1930s, Fort Worth secured federal money for many construction projects, including the Will Rogers Memorial Coliseum and Auditorium and the renovation and building of public schools. With the outbreak of World War II, the aviation industry arrived in Fort Worth. Air Force bomber construction became a major employer in the area, and this continued after the war as nearby Carswell Air Force Base became a station for B-36 "Peacekeeper" bombers.

By the mid-1950s, following the suburban flight and inner city decline typical of most major metropolitan areas in this period, Fort Worth's downtown area had become a neglected urban space, with few beyond those who worked there visiting the central city. In 1954, the local Texas Electric Company commissioned the architect Victor Gruen to produce a new plan for the city. This plan called for a freeway loop around the central business district, the construction of underground tunnels, and the elimination of vehicular traffic inside the loop. Although the plan was never implemented because of powerful opposition from a minority of local business leaders, it emphasized the necessity of planning for the city's future needs and became a model in urban planning schools across the country in classes on how to plan the city

of the future. The 1960s and 1970s were a period of continued economic growth in Fort Worth, with major projects including the Tarrant County Convention Center, the Dallas-Fort Worth International Airport, the Amon Carter Museum, and the nationally renowned Kimbell Art Museum. Amon Carter, Sr., publisher of the Fort Worth *Star-Telegram,* successfully worked to publicize the city and secured several government installations and projects throughout this period.

Today Fort Worth trades on its reputation as a city where the Old West once reigned. Multinational businesses, high-tech industries, and even a thriving publishing industry all contribute to the economy of the city in which the Kimbell Art Museum, Amon Carter Museum, and Fort Worth-Dallas Ballet contribute to making the city a regional center for the arts and culture, combining the charm of the mythological Old West with a forward-looking and vibrant city of the 21st century.

—*Paul S. Edwards*

See also Boosterism

Further Readings and References

Cohen, J. S. (1988). *Cowtown moderne: Art deco architecture of Fort Worth, Texas.* College Station: Texas A&M University Press.

Pate, J. L. (1988). *Livestock legacy: The Fort Worth stockyards, 1887–1987.* College Station: Texas A&M University Press.

Selcer, R. F. (2004). *Fort Worth: A Texas original!* Austin, TX: Texas State Historical Association.

FRANCHISES AND FRANCHISING

The word *franchise* comes from the old French concept meaning privilege or freedom. In the Middle Ages, a franchise was a privilege or a right where the sovereign or lord granted the right to hold markets or fairs, to operate the local ferry, or to hunt on his land. Today, a *franchise* is a licence that expresses the relationship between the franchisor and the franchisee, including the use of trademarks, fees, support, and control. Throughout history, there have been three factors that have stimulated the growth of franchising: the desire to expand, the lack of expansion capital, and the necessity to overcome distance. Over the centuries, the franchise concept has changed as the economies of the world have evolved, and this business innovation has become a remarkable success story. The increased level of convenience, service, and consistency has been provided largely by franchising.

The historical origin of franchising is uncertain. Some people have suggested that it originated in the United Kingdom in the Middle Ages, when King John of England reportedly granted franchises to tax collectors. In exchange, these powerful individuals were required to protect the territory.

The first wave of franchising, as a business concept, was known as the *tied-house system.* This practice sprang up in the 18th century among German brewers who, in exchange for financial assistance, contracted with taverns to sell their brand of beer exclusively. Later, this system was transplanted from Europe to the United States.

The second wave of franchising started in the United States in the 1860s, when the Singer Sewing Machine company utilized this practice in 1863 to sell products to its own sales force, which in turn had to find the buyers. This type of arrangement, know as *product-tradename* franchising, involves using franchisees to distribute a product under a franchisor's trademark.

General Motors in 1898 and Rexall in 1902 also used this type of franchising to increase their business. After World War I, the development of gas stations and automobile dealerships contributed to the development of modern franchising and gave birth to another franchising innovation, the restaurant drive-in. This was followed by a trickle of developments until the 1930s, when Howard Johnson started his famous restaurant chain in the United States. While franchising continued to grow up until the beginning of World War II, the truly explosive growth in franchising began at the end of the war, when many of the modern giants of the franchising community began operation.

The third wave of franchising, know as the business format or *package,* was developed in the 20th century by A&W Restaurants. The earliest fast-food franchise was A&W Root Beer, established in 1924.

This type of franchising seeks to have the franchisees replicate an entire business concept in their local community, including a product or service, a brand name, facilities design, and methods of operation that are packaged into a prototype. An example of this type of franchising is McDonald's. McDonald's restaurants provides its franchisees with a tested menu, a global trademark, a store location, operating procedures, specialized equipment, advertising, and so on. This type of franchising has accounted for most of the unit growth of franchising both in the United States and abroad since 1950. Third-generation franchises exceeded product-tradename franchises in number of units during the 1980s. The growth of franchising in America continued to expand when prospective franchisees were assured of safety using federally protected trademarks and service markers. Whereas franchising has traditionally been in the restaurant, retail, and service industries, it has also been tried in other industries, such as banking. In 1982, the Interstate Bancorp of Golden, Colorado, was recorded as the first bank to franchise.

The fast-growing franchise industry in the 1960s and the 1970s did not occur without problems. It created opportunity as well as abuses (fraudulent companies that took people's money and did not deliver; many franchisors focused more on the sales of franchises than on operating their franchise systems). The International Franchise Association, which was founded in 1960, serves as "the unified voice" of franchising, a group that represents both franchisees and franchisors. The association emerged during this period to help solve the problems faced by the industry.

The fourth wave of franchising focuses on "innovative" solutions. For example, it uses strategic alliances and other forms of cooperation based on franchising principles in order to cut costs while generating new sources of revenues. Franchising can be found at all levels of the distribution chain. These alliances are development led, purchasing led, skills based, or multifunctional. Typically, they involve franchise networks in the private sector. Public service industries in this type of franchising have been hindered by higher degrees of know-how resulting in higher costs for franchisors (it might offer a vehicle for public operators to enter new markets without the need for capital investment).

Economic and Urban Relevance

Franchising has literally reshaped the retail landscape since its early years. By most estimates, franchising now accounts for $1 trillion in annual retail sales from approximately 320,000 businesses in 75 industries and employs more than 8 million workers. It is estimated that 1 out of 16 workers is employed at a franchise. In the United States, franchising accounts for more than 40 percent of all retail sales, and 1 out of 12 retail establishments are franchised, according to 2002 International Franchise Association data. Franchising has been considered one of the fastest growing U.S. exports to the world.

Franchising has become an ever-present feature of the American landscape. Franchises are normally located in heavily populated areas and are built according to franchisors' specifications. Franchising affords an opportunity for entrepreneurs to reach the national market in a relatively short time, with little capital and few risks. Franchising outlets are ubiquitous. Consumers' preferences play a major role in the expansion of franchised outlets in strip malls, suburbs, and urban areas.

Over the last few years, many initiatives (neighborhood franchise projects) have involved placing franchises in inner cities. They are designed to selectively introduce franchised operations in these neighborhoods. These initiatives are based on the "leakage" analysis, which identifies products and services that have a strong consumer demand but are either inadequately represented or nonexistent in certain locations. This initiative allows franchisors selected to participate in providing basic services that generally are not provided by other mainstream retailers.

Modus Operandi

In a typical franchise agreement, the franchisee has the right to use the trademark and operating procedures of the company at an agreed-upon location and has various rights regarding decisions to hire personnel, advertise, and so on. The franchisor maintains the rights to monitor the franchisee for quality and has other rights related to the maintenance of the value of the trademark.

Currently, there are two basic types of franchises: product distribution and business format. *Product distribution* franchises sell the franchisor's products and involve supplier-dealer relationships. In product distribution, the franchisor licenses its trademark and logo to the franchisees but usually does not supply them with an integrated system to run their businesses. This is currently the case with soft-drink distributors, automobile dealers, and gas stations. Some well-known product distribution franchises include PepsiCo, Exxon, Texaco, and Ford Motor Company.

Franchising can be described as a pooling of resources and capabilities. On one hand, the franchisor contributes with the initial capital investment, know-how, intellectual property, and experience. On the other hand, the franchisee contributes with the additional financial resources, motivation, and operating experience in a variety of markets or countries. This is not a simple buyer-seller relationship because there exists a considerable interdependence between the franchisor and the franchisee. A modern franchise system includes a *business format,* a management system for operating the business and a shared trade identity. The franchisor does not always sell products to the franchisee (for example, catering and hotel services, employment agencies, home cleaning, education).

Franchising also can be described as a network of firms in which a manufacturer or marketer of a product or service (franchisor) grants exclusive rights to local entrepreneurs (franchisees) to conduct business in an established territory by implementing prescribed methods over a time period (this is the case with the automobile and oil industries in the United States). These networks have been established worldwide, proving the success of the system. These agreements offer numerous advantages (financial returns, market penetration, brand assets). In some industries, the industrial structure has been transformed as a result of the development of franchising networks (for example, estate agency), which suggests that economies of scale might have grown in recent years.

Franchise agreements are often combined with vertical restraints (territorial restrictions, vertical-price restrictions) and combinations of elements of selective and/or exclusive distribution. While the franchisor and the franchisee may remain legally independent, economically they function much like a single vertically integrated entity. Provisions such as vertical price restrictions are not accepted by some countries of the European Union.

International Franchising

International franchising has blossomed from a modest beginning into a major expansion strategy. As business systems are evolving, so are franchising techniques to provide solutions. Franchising has emerged, in recent years, as a highly significant strategy for business growth, job creation, and economic development. As a result, franchising is becoming one of the most popular entry mode strategies for international retail companies. Of particular interest are the permutations and combinations of established and innovative franchising techniques. Because the franchise concept is still relatively new outside the United States, it is expected that in the future franchising will grow faster in other countries. Europe, Japan, Canada, and Australia are expected to provide most of the new international franchises. The rapid expansion of the franchising phenomenon internationally has reshaped the landscape and the architecture of the major cities in other countries.

A number of favorable trends are creating an environment conducive to franchising. These trends include movement toward world economic integration, improvements in communications and transportation, rising disposable income, broader acceptance of capitalism, and the reduction of barriers to trade and investment in many countries around the world. Nonetheless, internationalization of franchising on a meaningful scale did not start until the late 1960s in the United States, when the signs of saturation in the national market became noticeable.

Over the last two decades, areas not traditionally associated with franchising have been using it to extend their catchment areas, including in developing countries. This was the case of social franchising, playing a major role in some developing countries by facilitating access to drugs and transports in urban and peri-urban areas. For example, Pakistan's *Green Star* network offers a range of reproductive health products, reaching urban and peri-urban customers. Also, peri-urban and rural customers in Kenya are offered basic drugs through Child and Family Wellness.

Franchising is a prominent part of the economy and a central phenomenon in entrepreneurship around the world. Practitioners often recommend franchising as a method that entrepreneurs can use to assemble resources to create large chains rapidly where the demand is strong, especially in urban areas. Competitive franchising in urban areas could improve considerably the living conditions in some neighborhoods. The timing for franchising has never been better.

—*Alfredo Manuel Coelho*

See also Economy of Cities

Further Readings and References

Alon, I. (2004). Global franchising and development in emerging and transitioning markets. *Journal of Macromarketing, 24*(2), 156–167.

Birkeland, P. M. (2002). *Franchising dreams: The lure of entrepreneurship in America.* Chicago: University of Chicago Press.

International Franchise Association. Available from http://www.franchise.org/

Preble, J. F., & Hoffman, C. R. (1995). Franchising systems around the globe: A status report. *Journal of Small Business Management, 33*(2), 80–88.

Stantworth, J., & Curran, J. (1999). Colas, burgers, shakes, and shirkers: Towards a sociological model of franchising in the economy. *Journal of Business Venturing, 14,* 323–344.

Weber, J., & Kwan, M. (2002). Bringing time back in: A study of the influence of travel time variations and facility opening hours on individual accessibility. *The Professional Geographer, 54*(2), 226–240.

Welch, L. S. (1989). Diffusion of franchise systems use in international operations. *International Marketing Review, 6*(5), 7–19.

FRAZIER, E. FRANKLIN

Scholar-activist Edward Franklin Frazier was born on September 24, 1894, in Baltimore, Maryland, and died on May 17, 1962, in Washington, D.C. He was a political and intellectual force in the field of sociology and a pioneer in the area of urban sociology through his work on United States and African diasporic race relations. Frazier completed undergraduate studies at Howard University in Washington, D.C., received his master's degree at Clark University in Worcester, Massachusetts, and then worked with, among others, Robert Park at the University of Chicago, where he earned his doctorate in 1931. Most widely recognized for his works *The Negro Family in America* and *Black Bourgeoisie,* Frazier was a prolific social scientific scholar who published numerous essays and manuscripts, which led to his appointment as the first African American president of the American Sociological Association in 1948.

Frazier is typically associated with his studies at the University of Chicago or his tenure on the faculty at Howard University, but he had been an accomplished scholar and activist long before he set foot on the University of Chicago's Hyde Park Campus. Frazier was a socialist and feminist member of the collegiate arm of the New Negro Movement at Howard University. He later left his position as math teacher at Tuskegee in protest against the school's focus on trade education, self-published the anti–World War I pamphlet *God and War,* and, with his master's thesis at Clark University, contested two of the leading lights in scientific racism on Clark's campus, G. Stanley Hall and Frank Hankins. Frazier then studied in

Denmark hoping to apply the Danish cooperative economic movement to black Southern communities, and he contributed to the 1925 Harlem Renaissance collection *The New Negro*. In Atlanta, Frazier taught sociology at Morehouse College and organized the Atlanta School of Social Work. In 1927, he was forced to leave Morehouse after publishing the controversial essay "The Pathology of Race," in which he argued that white people had a Negro Complex that generated their abnormal behavior of racism, which bordered on insanity.

Frazier's studies at the University of Chicago led to the publication of his doctoral thesis, *The Negro Family in Chicago* (1932), and the landmark *Negro Family in the United States* (1939). In these works, Frazier was directly critical of Robert Park's inattention to the broader socioeconomic forces of slavery and persistent discrimination in theories of urban assimilation. At the same time, Frazier maintained the white cultural norms of industriousness, male-headed homes, and class distinctions within a capitalist social order as the standards through which to measure the so-called social disorganization of the black family in ways that were later appropriated by Senator Daniel P. Moynihan. However, as a faculty member at Howard University, Frazier became one of the "Young Turks" pushing to offer a forthright Marxist critique of capitalist race relations in the 1930s. Here Frazier would develop the ideas that became his most controversial and popular work, *Black Bourgeoisie* (1957), where he charged that a black middle class obsession with upward mobility created a make-believe world driven by conspicuous consumption that alienated the black middle class from both the black masses and progressive white liberals. Later Frazier would branch out to examine the centrality of race to the global economic system in *Race and Culture Contacts in the Modern World* (1957) and by serving with the United Nations Educational, Scientific and Cultural Organization (UNESCO) from 1951 to 1953.

—Davarian L. Baldwin

Further Readings and References

Holloway, J. S. (2002). *Confronting the veil: Abram Harris Jr., E. Franklin Frazier, and Ralph Bunche, 1919–1941.* Chapel Hill, NC: University of North Carolina Press.

Platt, A. (1991). *E. Franklin Frazier reconsidered.* New Brunswick, NJ: Rutgers University Press.

Teele, J. (Ed.). (2002). *E. Franklin Frazier and black bourgeoisie.* Columbia, MO: University of Missouri Press.

FREEWAYS AND EXPRESSWAYS

After 1900, the coming of the automobile set in motion a series of events that transformed the physical structure, population distribution, and transportation patterns of the modern American city. In the early auto era, some landscape architects and city planners promoted parklike motorways, such as New York's Bronx River Parkway, completed in 1923, and the Long Island parkways built by Robert Moses in the 1920s. These winding, landscaped parkways served wealthy suburban commuters and offered pleasant auto excursions for Sunday drivers, but they did not provide a useful traffic model for modernizing cities. By 1930, more than 26 million cars and trucks crowded American streets and roads. Motorists and their political allies battled with pedestrians and streetcar companies for control of the streets. Street widenings and uniform traffic regulations did little to ease the daily crush of cars heading to central business districts. In the 1920s, political and business leaders in a few cities responded to traffic congestion by supporting construction of elevated, limited-access express highways, such as New York's West Side Elevated Highway and Chicago's Wacker Drive, while Detroit began planning 300 miles of radial "superhighways" that eliminated grade crossings.

In the 1930s, rising automobile usage, relentless urban traffic congestion, and a corresponding decline of urban transit fostered new forms of urban planning to accommodate Americans' preference for private automobile travel. In February 1930, *American City* magazine announced the arrival of "The Freeway—A New Kind of Thoroughfare," and the term *freeway* caught on. The automobile industry, eyeing the huge urban market for cars, promoted the necessity for such express highways in the 1930s and after. General Motors' Futurama exhibit at the New York World's Fair of 1939 stimulated such thinking. In his Futurama exhibit and in a subsequent book, *Magic Motorways* (1940), industrial designer Norman Bel Geddes provided a glimpse of the "cities of tomorrow," with elevated freeways speeding traffic through great skyscraper cities at speeds up to 100 miles per hour. About the same time, engineers in the Bureau of Public Roads (BPR), the federal agency that cooperated with states on road-building projects, issued its report, *Toll Roads and Free Roads* (1939). Authors of the BPR report emphasized the need for high-speed, limited-access highways linking the major cities of the nation. BPR engineers also recommended an urban component to the system: expressways that would both penetrate and encircle the central cities, along with radial links that tied the urban highway network together. Embraced by President Franklin D. Roosevelt, the BPR report provided the foundation for the present interstate highway system. The completion in 1940 of the Pennsylvania Turnpike and the first segment of the Hollywood Freeway in Los Angeles offered a peek at the nation's highway future. Both roads were substantially financed through New Deal public works programs.

Between 1942 and 1946, wartime financial restraints postponed road building. The BPR issued a second report in 1944, *Interregional Highways,* mapping a 39,000-mile interstate system, but leaving the urban freeway segments for subsequent planning. The Federal-Aid Highway Act of 1944 incorporated much of the BPR's report, but funding remained inconsequential. Meanwhile, big-city mayors, city managers, city planners, and downtown commercial, financial, and real estate interests lined up in support of a major postwar reconstruction of urban America. They all conceived of inner city expressways as essential to the rejuvenation of the central business districts already threatened by population dispersion and economic decentralization. During the decade after 1945, the federal government appropriated matching 50/50 funds to the states to support highway building, but limited funding and squabbling between rural and urban interests frustrated freeway advocates. By the early 1950s, leaders in many cities, including San Francisco, Los Angeles, Seattle, Houston, Dallas, Denver, Chicago, Detroit, Cleveland, Pittsburgh, New York, Miami, and Jacksonville, began planning and building their own freeway systems. Several states, including Florida, New York, New Jersey, Ohio, Indiana, Connecticut, and Massachusetts, began building long-distance, limited-access toll highways, such as the Florida Turnpike, the Indiana Toll Road, and the New York State Thruway.

The politics of road building changed dramatically in 1954, when President Dwight D. Eisenhower announced his support for a massive interstate highway program. After 2 years of debate and compromise, Congress passed the Federal-Aid Highway Act of 1956 creating the National System of Interstate and Defense Highways that is popularly known as the Interstate Highway System. The interstate legislation anticipated a national highway network of 41,000 miles, including some 5,000 urban freeway miles, financed through the mechanism of a Highway Trust Fund derived from excise taxes on fuel and tires. The

federal government would provide 90 percent of the cost, with the states contributing the remaining 10 percent. As in the past, the BPR would provide federal oversight and final approvals, but state highway departments would be responsible for determining actual routes and for building the roads.

Passage of the interstate act set off a frenzy of expressway building in American cities over the next 15 years—a surge of construction that ultimately brought major structural change to metropolitan America. Postwar America was already being reshaped by the massive expansion of the suburban fringe. The population of most big industrial cities peaked around 1950, but then began declining, even as metropolitan area populations grew dramatically. Sensitive to changing demographic patterns, department stores and other retailers began following their markets to the suburbs. Even before the interstates, the rise of trucking and the simultaneous decline of the railroads encouraged "runaway" factories to abandon central city locations for the urban periphery, with its lower taxes and cheaper land—an early example of deindustrialization. The new urban interstates speeded up these powerful patterns of metropolitan change. Big-city decision makers and power brokers in the 1950s and 1960s endorsed the new highways to save the central business districts. However, they seem never to have anticipated that the same expressways that brought people into the cities also enabled them to live in ever more distant suburbs, or that trucking permitted department stores and factories to seek out more advantageous locations near peripheral interstate interchanges.

Expressway construction between the mid-1950s and about 1970 was closely linked to ambitious plans for urban redevelopment. Because the big new roads penetrated the heart of the cities, their construction required the demolition of wide swaths of built-up urban territory, usually involving massive housing loss. According to the 1969 report of the National Commission on Urban Problems, at least 330,000 urban housing units were destroyed as a direct result of federal highway building between 1957 and 1969. The U.S. House Committee on Public Works reported in the late 1960s that the federal highway program was demolishing over 62,000 housing units annually—housing loss that affected as many as 200,000 people each year. Urban political leaders and private redevelopers recognized that expressway construction, along with related urban renewal programs, opened the way for the demolition of slums and low-income housing near the city centers, permitting the recapture of central city space for business uses or high-income real estate development. As early as 1941, a plan for Detroit's expressways noted that such highways would clear slum areas for more productive uses. The BPR reports of 1939 and 1944 also discussed the relationship between highway building and urban slum clearance. These ideas were widespread among postwar policymakers, who conceived of freeway construction as another urban redevelopment tool.

The rebuilding of central cities in many cases came at the expense of African American communities in the inner cities. Blacks had been migrating in large numbers to the nation's largest cities since the beginning of World War II, but highway builders who worked in conjunction with local civic elites in planning and routing the urban interstates saw their neighborhoods as expendable. In Miami, a single massive downtown interchange of Interstate 95 took up 30 square blocks of inner city space and destroyed the housing of over 10,000 African Americans, as well as the entire black business district. In Nashville, the Tennessee State Highway Department deliberately altered the original routing of Interstate 40 so that it would slice directly through the center of the city's black business district. In Montgomery, Alabama, black leaders charged that Interstate 85 had been purposefully routed through a stable black community to punish the city's civil rights activists who lived there. St. Paul, Minnesota, had few blacks, but the road builders found where they lived and routed Interstate 94 directly through their neighborhood. In Baltimore, Milwaukee, Indianapolis, Cleveland, Pittsburgh, Richmond, Charlotte, and Birmingham, expressways plowed through black communities, destroying thousands of low-income housing units. An antifreeway slogan used by blacks in Washington, D.C., suggested that expressways there were nothing more than white men's roads going through black men's homes. In several cities, including Atlanta, highway planners used the roads to contain black ghettos and halt black migration to white residential areas. The freeways that ripped through black neighborhoods across the nation suggested a powerful racial component to the urban interstates. Urban expressway construction provided a mechanism to carry out local agendas on issues of race, housing, and residential segregation.

Freeway construction also resulted in demolition of white neighborhoods, historic districts, environmentally sensitive areas, and parks, churches, and schools. The extent of such devastation eventually led

to citizen movements in many cities, challenging the highway builders and the local political and business elites who supported them. The freeway revolt began in San Francisco in 1959 when the city government withdrew support for interstate construction in the face of public outrage over the massive, double-decked Embarcadero Freeway. Built in the early 1950s, the Embarcadero ran along the city's historic waterfront, cut off the city from the harbor, and enraged aesthetic and environmental sensibilities.

The freeway revolt heated up in the mid-1960s, when the final urban segments of the interstate system were nearing completion. When the newly formed U.S. Department of Transportation (DOT) took over supervision of the interstate program in April 1967, Secretary Alan S. Boyd faced some two dozen "trouble spots" on the interstate map, mostly disputed freeway segments in the cities. State and federal highway engineers typically preferred to push ahead with freeway plans despite local opposition. By contrast, Boyd supported alternative route locations where possible and rejected the highway engineers' vision that more concrete was good for America. Mounting congressional opposition to rampant freeway construction led to new environmental and preservationist legislation, including the National Historic Preservation Act (1966) and the National Environmental Policy Act (1969).

Highway opponents used these new tools to litigate the freeway revolt. In Memphis, for instance, civic leaders and environmentalists challenged the routing of Interstate 40 through the city's Overton Park, eventually taking the case all the way to the Supreme Court, where the park advocates won a major victory over the highwaymen. In New Orleans, a planned Riverfront Expressway separating the famed French Quarter from the Mississippi River spawned a decade-long opposition movement by preservationists. The battle ended in 1969 when Boyd's successor at the DOT, John A. Volpe, cancelled the Riverfront Expressway. In Baltimore, a complex freeway system was left mostly on the drawing boards after a freeway revolt led by Movement Against Destruction, an interracial coalition of neighborhood groups working to "Stop the Road." In Washington, D.C., a number of controversial and intrusive freeways were cancelled, and Congress and city leaders decided to invest in a new subway system instead. In New York City, Robert Moses's ambitious plans to drive several expressways across Manhattan were officially shelved in 1971 by Governor Nelson Rockefeller. Already served by four major expressways, Chicago's Crosstown Expressway ran into a buzz saw of opposition from aroused white ethnic neighborhoods targeted by the highway planners. In the early 1970s, plans for Phoenix's inner-loop Papago Freeway fell victim to antihighway forces. In 1974, an already built waterfront expressway in Portland, Oregon was demolished to make way for a riverfront park. The political and legal climate of highway building had changed by the late 1960s, legitimating the freeway revolt in many cities.

By 1973, the surge of freeway building had ended (although rural interstate construction continued through the 1970s). Advocates of more balanced transportation systems eventually got the upper hand in Congress. Policy changes in the early 1970s enabled governors and mayors to cancel urban freeways and reallocate appropriated funds for alternative transportation systems. The Highway Trust Fund that financed the interstate system was gradually opened up for mass transit alternatives, although such funding remained limited until further congressional action in 1991.

The commitment to build the urban interstates reflected the power and allure of the mid-century automobile culture. The freeways served motorists well, but their construction and completion had huge social and environmental costs. They contributed to the restructuring of the central cities, but they also created major physical barriers and huge expanses of wasted urban space. They undergirded and speeded the massive spread of suburban sprawl. They triggered racial transitions in many cities, as tens of thousands of blacks in demolished neighborhoods sought new housing outside the ghetto. By the end of the 20th century, urban experts and politicians had begun rethinking the necessity of freeways. Boston, New York, Providence, Pittsburgh, Milwaukee, Phoenix, and Fort Worth demolished some central city or riverfront expressways, or relocated them underground or in alternative urban corridors. Earthquake-damaged elevated freeways in Oakland, San Francisco, and Seattle have been torn down and not replaced. In many other cities, such as Birmingham, Alabama and Phoenix, Arizona, new outer beltways are under construction as metropolitan area populations expand the urban periphery. Mass transit and light rail have garnered citizen support, but the freeway remains an icon of 20th-century highway engineering and American automobility.

—Raymond A. Mohl

Further Readings and References

Brodsly, D. (1982). *L.A. freeway: An appreciative essay.* Berkeley, CA: University of California Press.

Foster, M. S. (1981). *From streetcar to superhighway: American city planners and urban transportation, 1900–1940.* Philadelphia: Temple University Press.

Gutfreund, O. (2004). *Twentieth-century sprawl: Highways and the reshaping of the American landscape.* New York: Oxford University Press.

Lewis, T. (1997). *Divided highways: Building the interstate highways, transforming American life.* New York: Viking.

Mohl, R. A. (2004). Stop the road: Freeway revolts in postwar American cities. *Journal of Urban History, 30,* 674–706.

Odell, R. (1972). To stop highways, some citizens take to the streets. *Smithsonian, 3,* 24–29.

Rose, M. H. (1990). *Interstate: Express highway politics, 1939–1989* (Rev. ed.). Knoxville, TN: University of Tennessee Press.

FRESNO, CALIFORNIA

Fresno, California, rightly known as the raisin capital of the world, lies in the flat San Joaquin Valley, one of the richest farming areas in the United States, about 200 miles southeast of San Francisco. A city reliant on surrounding agriculture, Fresno is a melting pot of people and cultures. Known as the breadbasket of the San Joaquin Valley, the Fresno area produces grapes, raisins, cotton tree fruits and vegetables as its primary products which are traded through Fresno, the urban center able to pack and transport this produce all over the country. Fresno County is the nation's leading agricultural region, with more than 250 different commercial crops worth $3 billion annually. Given this abundance, Fresno has long been a magnet for immigrants from all over America and has a uniquely ethnically diverse population, including Basque, Indian, Armenian, Hispanic, Hmong, Chinese, Portuguese, and Japanese residents.

The Yokuts people were the sole inhabitants of the region until the mid-19th century. Because the Fresno area was hot and dry, both Spanish and Mexican settlers avoided it, and the region became legal property of the United States following the cessation of the Mexican War in 1846. The first white settlers were Forty-Niners who arrived during the California Gold Rush of the late 1840s, prospecting the foothills surrounding the San Joaquin River. In the 1860s a Dutchman named A. J. Manssen settled on the site of the present city and began to farm using the abundant water found underground. He was soon joined by other settlers. Fresno's real start came in 1872, when the Central Pacific Railroad, pushing southward through the Central Valley, reached the site. In that year, the name Fresno, meaning "ash tree" in Spanish, was first applied to the area because ash trees grew along the banks of the nearby river.

Irrigation of the region, combined with the arrival of the railroad, helped Fresno become more than just another small California town. After the introduction of irrigation in the late 1870s, which many sources attribute to the work of Moses Church's "church ditches," the region's rich agricultural potential began to be realized. Frances Eisen, leader of the wine industry in Fresno County, began the raisin industry in 1875, when he let some of his grapes dry on the vine. A. Y. Easterby and Clovis Cole, the "Wheat King of the Nation," developed extensive grain and cattle ranches. Fresno County attracted farmers, ranchers, and immigrants seeking a place to settle. Lumber mills were constructed in the late 1800s, with the rich timber resources of the nearby Sierra Mountains providing the wood to supply an up-and-coming community. The discovery of gold, petroleum, and copper, along with a rich supply of oil in the western part of the county, solidified the city of Fresno as an expanding urban center for the surrounding agriculture production and mineral extraction.

Major events in the history of Fresno are rare. In 1910, Fresno was the scene of a protracted labor dispute led by the Industrial Workers of the World (IWW), and Chester H. Rowell, editor of the Fresno *Morning Republican,* became one of the leaders of the statewide progressive reform movement. However, up until the 1970s Fresno continued a pattern of steady urban growth on the back of agriculture, reaching a population of 135,000 in 1960. The first major changes in the city since the first decades of settlement came with the industrialization of agriculture in the 1970s. This led to an increased demand for labor to support this intensive farming, primarily in food processing, alongside an expansion in the associated manufacturing economy that specialized in farm machinery, transportation equipment, and vending machines and other smaller industries associated with food production and distribution.

Such rapid growth left the city of Fresno unprepared for the population gains it was beginning to

experience. What had been a relatively sleepy city suddenly had to cope with an immense demand for urban amenities. The city originally planned to do this by refashioning downtown into a pedestrian-only superblock of 36 acres, with parking and loop roads in a similar fashion to those in Fort Worth, Texas, designed by the architect and planner Victor Gruen. However, following opposition, the plans were changed to incorporate only a 24-square-block downtown pedestrian mall, which opened in September 1964. This pedestrian mall won praise across the country for its innovative approach to redesigning the central city and was awarded a Design Excellence Merit Prize by the Department of Housing and Urban Development (HUD) in 1968. However, even this pedestrian zone and work on building a new convention center and other cultural facilities could not prevent the increasing suburbanization of Fresno, as despite the efforts of Gruen and the city's administrators, Fresno followed the pattern of mass suburbanization of the majority of American cities at this time.

Fresno today is a thriving, multicultural city of more than 450,000. While still dependent on the surrounding agricultural production—most especially through the export of 60 percent of the world's raisins—in recent years, the city's economy has expanded to include manufacturing, service, and industrial operations. Much of the growth has been fueled by the arrival of families from the more crowded Los Angeles and San Francisco metropolitan areas, who have been attracted by Fresno's affordable housing and low cost of living. The relocation of businesses from other urban areas has offered new employment opportunities for these incomers, and Fresno looks likely to continue its phenomenal economic and population growth of the past 30 years.

—Paul S. Edwards

See also Fort Worth, Texas; Pedestrian Malls; Suburbanization

Further Readings and References

Clough, C. W. (1994). *Fresno County in the 20th century: From 1900 to the 1980s.* Davis, CA: Amer West Books.
Schyler, R., & Patterson, W. K. (1988). *M. Theo Kearney: Prince of Fresno.* Fresno, CA: Fresno Historical Society.
White, R. (1996). *Journey to the center of the city: Making a difference in an urban neighborhood.* Downers Grove, IL: Inter Varsity Press.

GAMBLING

Gambling is as old as human civilization, and it is no surprise that it has played a role in the culture of American cities. For much of American history, and in most places, gambling has been illegal but extremely popular. From the middle of the 19th century on, criminal syndicates became increasingly influential in gambling. Gambling has been legalized sporadically, and usually briefly, from colonial times, but states did not begin to systematically sponsor legal gaming until the 1920s. This trend accelerated in the 1960s, and by the 1990s, several states had embraced gaming in casino resorts, originally developed near Las Vegas, Nevada, as revenue enhancers and urban redevelopers.

Illegal Urban Gambling

Gambling in America predates European colonization; Native Americans, particularly in the western half of what would become the United States, were known as avid gamblers. English colonists in all regions gambled, betting with each other on card games and horse races and participating in public lotteries. Early laws generally left the practice of gambling unmolested but attempted to mitigate problems arising from it.

Most states in the early American republic chose to make public gambling illegal while tolerating private wagering, particularly games among social equals. The rise of market economies in the 1820s and 1830s, however, brought a general turn against entrepreneurial gambling (games such as lotteries in which players bet against the house—and usually lose). Although New Orleans experimented with municipally sanctioned gambling, licensing casinos in 1823, the city abandoned the scheme in 1835, concomitant with a national antigambling backlash that saw professional gamblers move from the river towns of the South and West directly to riverboats.

After the Civil War, gambling entrepreneurs organized themselves into syndicates in order to share the risks associated with bankrolling games of chance and to systematize protection arrangements with local authorities. New York was at this time the undisputed gambling capital of the nation, with hundreds of places to gamble that ranged from low dens, where hardscrabble gamblers played cards or dice by candlelight, to "first class hells," with plush fixtures and complimentary gourmet meals.

Syndicates also sponsored other forms of gambling. By the turn of the 20th century, slot machines had become popular in most American cities. From that period through the 1930s, horse rooms or poolrooms were the most prevalent loci of gambling in most American cities. Ostensibly illegal, these rooms were usually "hidden" behind a candy or tobacco store, though many of these rooms had doormen posted outside to steer patrons inside. Once within, patrons could bet on horse races at tracks throughout the United States, thanks to telegraphed race odds and information. Illegal lotteries, also called policy and numbers games, also flourished in most American cities.

After World War II, the anticrime and antigambling movement became increasingly powerful, peaking with the Kefauver Committee's hearings on Organized Crime in Interstate Commerce in 1950 and 1951.

After this time, citizens in most cities demanded stricter enforcement of antigambling statutes. Though sports betting emerged, with the rise of televised broadcasts of professional and amateur games, as a major illegal gambling form, the horse rooms, slot machine routes, and clandestine casinos of earlier years soon disappeared.

Legal Gambling Explosion

Urban gambling suffered a steep decline in the years after World War II, and relatively affluent middle- and upper-class Americans who wished to enjoy the pleasures of gambling without bringing its negatives into their communities sought gambling establishments elsewhere. They found a haven along the Las Vegas Strip, where operators opened a series of plush, self-contained casino resorts, neat analogues to the subdivisions and shopping malls that were sprouting near freeways and arterials throughout the country. These casino resorts soon became the underpinning of the economy of Nevada, which emerged as an international center for gambling and entertainment tourism.

Beginning in the 1960s, state legislatures expanded gambling, often adding state lotteries to pari-mutuel horse race betting and charitable gaming (bingo). Lottery advertisements frequently asked players to "bet their daily numbers," and in effect sought to duplicate the success of earlier illegal numbers runners.

Beginning with New Jersey in 1976, other states sought to duplicate Nevada's use of gaming for economic development. Garden State voters decided in that year to legalize casinos in Atlantic City, a decaying resort town, to boost state revenues, provide employment, and serve as a "unique tool for urban redevelopment." In the 1990s, a series of states in the Midwest authorized riverboat casino gaming for the first two purposes, though they did not usually tie gambling to urban development as had New Jersey. In sum, casino resorts have proved remarkably effective at creating jobs and economic growth, but because of their inherently self-contained nature they have not been entirely successful at redeeming decayed cities.

By the turn of the 21st century, legalized gambling had become nearly ubiquitous. For the most part the public's appetite for gambling had been channeled into legal, regulated, and heavily taxed, state-sanctioned forms. What, a century earlier, had been nominally illegal and subject to periodic vice raids, has now become a centerpiece of state budgets and a legitimate recreation.

—*David G. Schwartz*

Further Readings and References

Asbury, H. (1938). *Sucker's progress: An informal history of gambling in America from the colonies to Canfield.* New York: Dodd, Mead.

Findlay, J. (1986). *People of chance: Gambling in American society from Jamestown to Las Vegas.* New York: Oxford University Press.

Haller, M. H. (1979). The changing structure of American gambling in the twentieth century. *Journal of Social Issues, 35*(3), 87–111.

Schwartz, D. G. (2003). *Suburban Xanadu: The casino resort on the Las Vegas strip and beyond.* New York: Routledge.

Schwartz, D. G. (2005). *Uneasy convictions: American gambling, crime, and the Wire Act, from the telegraph to the Internet.* New York: St. Martin's Press.

GANGS

Gangs in the urban United States range from youth groups to criminal corporations that work through an honor complex, use violent criminal behaviors to establish social position, and use symbols to express collective identity. Gangs in this country have traditionally arisen in areas where populations do not benefit from the institutions of U.S. society. As substitute institutions, gangs are made up of people marginalized from the dominant system who must manufacture alternative forms of identity in order to survive both literally and symbolically. Each urban area in the United States has given birth to its own forms of collective, often adolescent, gang identity. This essay describes where, after 100 years of gang development, this history has brought us.

Pre-1900 patterns of gang development were deeply intertwined with immigration to the United States from Europe. New York gangs were similar to so-called townsmen or kinship groups around the world who gave each other supportive aid in a new locale. In the slums of New York, this support was linked early on to criminal enterprise that resulted from the extreme economic exclusion and racism new immigrants faced. Gang development is still influenced by immigration patterns to varying degrees. Whether or not they are immigrants, gang members transport social identities across boundaries and blend real or imaginary ideas of historical process with group-based concerns.

Literally hundreds of academic publications treat gangs as social groups that emerge from situations of constraint. Since 1927, with the work of sociologist Frederic Thrasher, gangs have been regarded as groups whose shape is intricately woven into the urban landscape. According to Thrasher, gang membership is a form of collective behavior with distinct structures and traditions. Thrasher describes gangs as emerging from the interstices of industrial society. In Chicago, gangs have historically taken the hierarchical shape of the corporate-like Italian Mafia, if not of the industrial city itself. In Los Angeles, gangs exhibit looser leadership styles, due as much to the lack of a Mafia presence as to the multicentered nature of the city itself.

Today, gangs exist in urban and rural, industrial and postindustrial landscapes. They are common not only to first worlds but also to second, third, and fourth worlds. In the United States, gang formations have been particularly strong. Migration patterns, public policies, and mass media have contributed to the spread of gangs from urban centers like Los Angeles and Chicago to rural areas, and from the United States around the globe. In all of these locations, gangs are part of symbolic if not literal interstices. And while the larger society has the power to hold gang members accountable for their actions, the "outlaw" status of gang members denies them the ability to hold the larger society accountable for behaviors in relation to either themselves or the disenfranchised populations from which they arise.

While many of today's urban gang systems began as youth cultures based in ethnic communities, they are now multigenerational institutions whose core membership involves youth and adults, families and children. Though scholars, police officers, and gang members generally agree on very little about gang life, all agree that at their core gangs are about protection. "Respect" is the ultimate street commodity, the foundation for individual, group, and even family protection. It may seem ironic, then, that gang members are far more likely than those who are not gang members to die from lethal violence that they themselves initiate.

Gang violence can be best understood as a form of low-level warfare between roughly equivalent but antagonistic groups. While individual gang members commit violent acts, the endemic violence gangs exhibit stems structurally from two places. First, it stems from gangs themselves, from local battles over respect and resources and from the inability to control violence through strong hierarchical leadership. Second, gang violence stems from changes in state policies. Any changes the state makes with regard to its policies can destabilize communities in already impoverished areas. Such changes range from global to more local concerns, such as changes in job availability and demographic patterns. Also key are the influx of new technologies (like those used to produce new types of guns) and the availability of drugs, as well as the patterns of policing and punishment that accompany them. Deindustrialization has been a particularly powerful force in the growth of gangs around the United States because it has created a situation in which few viable employment options exist in U.S. urban areas. Beginning in the 1980s, dealing crack-cocaine provided gang members with a solvent, if lethal, safety net that countered this state of economic disenfranchisement.

Gang involvement in the drug trade varies widely across the United States. Gangs across the country share the practice of exploiting the economic potential of neighborhood space on a block-to-block basis. Gang political economies are thus wholesale organic uses of space that belie core-periphery models in which one "locates" an economic center. Instead, gangs have created a kind of scatterplot economy dependent on residential patterns and in which gang members literally develop economy where they stand. Each corner, each street, and each alleyway carries economic potential. Gang members work through the drug trade and other criminal enterprises to realize this potential and thus to gain an illicit economic foothold in society.

Despite their ties to the illegal economy, gangs are not solely economic entities. They are total social institutions with rich political, cultural, and artistic traditions. For the Navajo, gangs are part of a self-made coming-of-age mechanism traditionally missing for Navajo youth who are both disenfranchised from the larger society as Native Americans and alienated from their own communities and elders. In Chicago and New York, gangs have nurtured a complex, quasi-religious symbolic ideology. In California, the Mexican Mafia prison gang has begun a system of taxation among local Los Angeles gangs, creating groups of elites within a formerly egalitarian social structure. On the international front, Bloods and Crips battle it out on the street of Belize. Jamaican posses travel from Kingston to New York, bringing with them styles of warfare and prestige, as well as illegal drugs. In El Salvador, Los Angeles gangs like 18th Street or Mara Salvatrucha replay Los Angeles–style geographies in new cities, infusing them with their own local traditions. Today, prison is a powerful extension of street gang life. Prison gangs use the violence of state punishment as a basis for their own coercive power both in prison and in the neighborhood.

As widely varied but little-understood groups, gangs are easily exploitable by the larger society as scapegoats for societal problems. According to criminologist Malcom Klein, gangs are their own call for social intervention. Currently, the most pressing needs for gang studies are both ethnographic and historical. Very little grounded fieldwork exists of gang groups, and as gangs expand geographically and evolve socially, their trajectories must be charted by holistic and relativist research. As historical entities, gangs have perhaps more to tell us about links between the built environment, social evolution, and the power of symbols than any other existing cultural group. Gangs reflect society's global strengths and weaknesses. They represent connections based on the realities of people's lives, which often contradict stricter lines of formal political economy or immigration policy. Gangs expose in us our weaknesses: social inequality, institutionalized racism, selective opportunity. To follow gangs is to follow the most telling trend of a global social world as well as its most dire outcomes.

—*Susan A. Phillips*

See also Crime and Criminals

Further Readings and References

Hayden, T. (2004). *Street wars: Gangs and the future of violence.* New York: New Press.

Klein, M. (1995). *The American street gang.* New York: Oxford University Press.

Phillips, S. (1999). *Wallbangin: Graffiti and gangs in L.A.* Chicago: University of Chicago Press.

Thrasher, F. M. (1927). *The gang.* Chicago: University of Chicago Press.

Vigil, J. D. (2002). *A rainbow of gangs: Street cultures in the mega-city.* Austin: University of Texas Press.

GARBAGE AND GARBAGE COLLECTION

Human civilizations have always produced waste, but how we have managed that waste has changed across the ages. And over the past hundred years or so, how waste has been managed has had an impact on urban politics. During the 1880s, particularly in industrial centers like Chicago and New York City, some household garbage and other waste was simply thrown into the streets where scavengers and animals would pick through it. The streets of many urban centers in the United States were, therefore, quite filthy well into the 19th century. Industry and consumers at the time were producing an enormous volume of solid waste. Unfortunately for communities populated by the working poor, immigrants, and people of color, waste was often dumped in close proximity to their homes.

In the first decade of the 20th century, major cities like Chicago and New York experienced a garbage crisis, having few designated spaces for waste dumping. The *New York Herald*'s political cartoons featured "King Garbage" as a symbol of how trash reigned over that city. Officials in Chicago were filling in swamps and wetlands with garbage. The Citizens' Association of Chicago loudly protested these practices as unacceptable, which in part led Chicago to adopt a different technology: reduction. The Chicago Reduction Company stewed organic garbage in large vats and separated grease, oils, and fats and other materials for sale. Soon, reduction became the most common method of waste management used in large cities.

It is important to contrast solid waste management in the pre–World War II era with contemporary practices. Waste reuse and source separation, for instance, were routine components of garbage hauling in the early days. Source separation today involves separating garbage from recyclables, but as early as 1895 in New York City, residents were required to separate garbage (food, organics), rubbish (nonorganic trash), and ashes into different receptacles. Typically the rubbish and garbage would go to the incinerator while noncombustibles (ash, etc.) would go to the city dump. Suellen M. Hoy and Michael C. Robinson noted in 1979 that renowned New York City sanitation commissioner Colonel George Waring built the first rubbish sorting plant in the United States where salvageable goods were sold and the revenue went to the city. While waste reuse was common, incineration technologies were being adopted in many places as well (with the first such machine put to use in 1885). But given the unpopularity of incineration with many health-conscious citizens concerned with air pollution, new forms of waste disposal were sought out. In response to a citizen's lawsuit against its waste incinerator in 1932, the Scavengers' Protective Association in San Francisco adopted what was an innovative technology of the day: the sanitary landfill. Sanitary landfills were distinct from the more traditional, open dumps, because they were covered with soil at the end of each day to lend the appearance of cleanliness. This practice continues today.

Throughout the 1930s, new practices were emerging in garbage collection to reduce costs and improve performance. For example, the "Dempster Dumpster" was introduced in 1934. This was a large steel box designed for use by a mechanical truck. The Dempster Dumpster and the hydraulic mechanism used to empty it are said to have eased the back and arm strain many scavengers experienced regularly; but they also signaled the beginning of labor displacement by automation in garbage hauling. In the 1950s and 1960s, two other major technological changes emerged that would threaten the end of salvaging and reuse: automatic waste compactor trucks and plastic garbage bags. The compactor truck was devastating to traditional reuse businesses because it crushed not only trash, but all salvageable items as well. Petroleum-based plastic trash bags were problematic because they hid the salvageable materials that the traditional system of open garbage cans had always revealed.

In the 1960s, solid waste was dubbed "the third pollution" (after air and water pollution). The public demanded better ways of dealing with this problem. Finding suitable space to place a dump was challenging given increasing suburban sprawl and stringent zoning regulations. A popular saying in the industry at the time was, "Everybody loves the garbage man when he picks it up, but hates him when he puts it down."

Soon the ecology movement emerged and articulated a view of garbage not as waste, but as a resource for community building (and as a by-product of a materialist, consumption-oriented American culture). Organized recycling began around the first Earth Day in 1970 not so much as a business venture but as a social cause. This was a time of great excitement among environmentalists as environmental legislation was passed and institutional support became available. In 1970, the United States Environmental Protection Agency (USEPA) was established and the 1965 Solid Waste Disposal Act was amended, creating the Resource Recovery Act (RRA). The RRA required the federal government to publish waste disposal guidelines. The 1980s was a time when the environmental movement successfully used the media to frame ecological problems as national and global crises warranting immediate attention. For example, the journey of the Mobro 4000, or the "Garbage Barge," was a major "eco-event." In 1987, this barge filled with municipal waste from New York City sailed down the East Coast, through the Bahamas, to Belize and Mexico, being denied entry at each port. After 6,000 miles of sailing, the ship returned to New York City, its payload to be buried on Long Island, where it originated. The Mobro 4000 was a dramatic symbol of America's trash problem.

Conclusion

Today, many environmental activists believe we can achieve a "zero waste" society. Unfortunately, the United States appears to be heading in the opposite direction. In the U.S., from 1998 to 2001, the amount of municipal solid waste grew by 66.6 million tons, or 20 percent, to a total of 409,029,000 tons per year. Of that total, about 60 percent is landfilled, 7 percent is incinerated, and 33 percent is recycled and composted, as noted by Nora Goldstein and Celeste Madtes in 2001. Alice Horrigan and Jim Motavalli pointed out in 1997 that the U.S. has only 5 percent of the world's population but generates 19 percent of its wastes.

In 2001, after 50 years of operation, the Fresh Kills landfill in New York City closed. This is was a major event because Fresh Kills was one of the largest landfills on the planet, and because the closing was a missed opportunity for the city to take a more serious approach to recycling and composting. Instead, most of the garbage will be sent to landfills and incinerators. This event must, unfortunately, be viewed as a marker of where Americans stand on the importance of ecologically sound waste management at the dawn of the 21st century. More solid waste crises are sure to follow.

—*David N. Pellow*

Further Readings and References

Environmental News Service. (2001, March 22). *Dumping ends today at world's largest landfill.* Retrieved June 28, 2006, from http://www.ens-newswire.com/ens/archives/2001/mar2001archive.asp

Goldstein, N., & Madtes, C. (2001). The state of garbage in America. *Biocycle: Journal of Composting and Organics Recycling, 42,* 42–54.

Horrigan, A., & Motavalli, J. (1997, March/April). Talking trash. *E: The Environmental Magazine.* Retrieved June 28, 2006, from http://www.emagazine.com/march-april_1997/0397feat1.html

Hoy, S. M., & Robinson, M. C. (1979). *Recovering the past: A handbook of community recycling programs, 1890–1945.* Chicago: Public Works Historical Society.

GARDEN CITIES

The term *garden cities* refers to the concept of new town development as originally envisaged by Ebenezer Howard (1850–1928). Originally proposed in 1898 in the book *To-morrow: A Peaceful Path to Real Reform,* Howard's garden city was the most radical solution to problems evident within the towns and cities of industrial Britain during the Victorian era. Inspired by the "magnets" of town, country, and town-country (that is, suburban environments), Howard proposed a new form of urban development, known as garden cities, which he envisaged would establish a new urban system. The garden cities were formed in such a manner by Howard as to take the best aspects of both urban and rural living, and included surrounding each garden city by a greenbelt so as to limit urban sprawl. Howard's new settlements would in effect be composed of a number of self-contained satellites (the population in each being 32,000) located around a central city (with a population of 58,000), which would be linked together by a system of transportation. Thus one collective settlement (that is, central city and satellites) would have a maximum population of 250,000.

The influence of the garden city should not be underestimated. Just a year after Howard's idea was published in 1898, the Garden City Association was formed, and by 1904 the first garden city, a new town situated north of London, had been planned. Letchworth, the first garden city, although planned by Barry Parker and Raymond Unwin, contained many of the ideas put forward by Howard. While not all of the social notions embedded within Howard's original idea were used in Letchworth, cottage-style houses were arranged in low-density forms within a leafy environment, industry was separated from housing areas, and a greenbelt was formed so as to contain the sprawl of the settlement. Slow-growing Letchworth had a major influence on urban development in Britain prior to 1914 and led to the forming of garden suburbs, low-density extensions added to existing urban settlements, and the creation of the Housing, Town Planning, Etc. Act in 1909—the world's first legislation to contain the words "town planning" in the title. After the end of World War I, Howard continued to pursue garden city development, and this led to the forming of Welwyn Garden City.

Although the original garden city was heavily influenced by elements of British society at the end of the 1800s, this has not inhibited the growth of garden cities in other countries. This is in part due to the comprehensive nature of Howard's original idea and the fact that it led to the creation of environments of high quality because it encouraged human settlement with nature—and thus has resonance with modern sustainable development—and it promoted notions of community via providing housing for all social classes. Finally, the garden city highlighted the collective benefits to be derived from collective land ownership. The success of the garden city thus must be seen as the result of not only the comprehensive nature of Howard's idea but also its practical use after its inception at Letchworth. Significantly, the original idea subsequently has been taken apart and reshaped into many different forms. In America, for instance, the garden city idea was dismantled and widely applied, most evidently in 1929 in Clarence Stein and Henry Wright's new town of Radburn, New Jersey, with the garden city concept applied to address the needs of commuters. And in Britain the idea found popularity within garden suburb schemes following the creation of Letchworth. Yet, it is significant to note that during the 20th century the name *garden city* was widely used, often to imply low-density, leafy housing environments, and as a consequence a confusing use of the term—after the wide incorporation of its values—has resulted. Many "garden" enviroments bear little social resemblance to Howard's dream. Given this situation, understanding the garden city Howard envisioned requires focusing attention on the purer garden city forms, that is, the two settlements in England founded by Howard, Letchworth Garden City and Welwyn Garden City, which despite bearing the title "city" are in effect towns, as well as Hampstead garden suburb. However, to study Letchworth means to consider the ideas and work of Parker and Unwin, the town's planners, as well as those of Howard.

The general plan of Letchworth, covering originally nearly 4,000 acres, highlighted spatial and visual order through the exercise of generally formalized layouts, particularly so as to emphasize the town square, the focal and civic center. Housing layouts were a major element of Letchworth's plan and in many respects reflected the pragmatic views of Raymond Unwin, the planner of Letchworth and designer of many of the housing forms within the settlement. Unwin was noted to have said that the promoters of the garden city did not essentially want an artistic complex but one in which people reside in decent houses. The layouts of housing areas in Letchworth, such as Bird's Hill, with their low-density form, established a new paradigm for the housing of working people. Houses were arranged to form changing streetscapes as one moved through and around the streets of the town, gardens were provided, and the general aesthetic of the houses followed closely the English vernacular cottage style. Residential districts varied subtly and an agricultural belt around the town acted as a greenbelt, a major characteristic of metropolitan development and urban planning throughout the world in the 20th century. Commerce and industry, as well as housing, were notable elements of Letchworth's town plan, and space was purposefully set aside solely for industrial and commercial development. A buffer of trees was placed close to factories to cushion the sound of industrial production and to shield the onlooking eye from the often ugly form of British factories.

The underlying factor in the work of planners such as Barry Parker and Raymond Unwin at Letchworth, and later at Hampstead garden suburb in North London, was their aspiration to improve the living environments of the working classes. This aspiration was fed by a personal architectural and social ideology which sought to bring together cultural, social, and aesthetic convictions through the employment of architectural concepts such as unity and *repose,* a term relating to items being designed so to fit into their proper place. The planning employed for "garden" environments therefore was meant not just as a means to arrange the urban form but as an astute device of social reform. In addition, it was highly architectural in its principles.

The slow growth of Letchworth resulted in its being almost immediately surpassed by Henrietta Barnett's 1904 garden suburb project at Hampstead, which was more explicitly visual, social, and economic in nature and strengthened the aesthetic and environmental dimensions in garden city planning. Composed by Raymond Unwin, the garden suburb at Hampstead marked a design and planning development from Letchworth through combining formal and informal design elements. Unwin discovered Camillo Sitte's ideas about urban design after creating his initial plan for Letchworth, and he utilized them at Hampstead. Thus, space at road junctions was stressed and often enclosed by surrounding groups of houses in an intimate way to give a human scale to the community. However, buildings were sometimes composed to a bigger size for enhancing street pictures, while building lines were usually set back along the streets to establish added visual variety. The composition of street pictures, one of the main characteristics of the suburb, raised town planning to a new level. And the immediate success of Hampstead garden suburb ensured that prior to the onset of the First World War in 1914, the garden city—or more precisely, low-density residential districts filled with foliage—would dominate British urban planning and ensure that Howard's carefully created concept was lost.

Despite the onset of war in 1914 and the transition of British society by war's end in 1918, Howard still promoted it as a means to resolving urban problems. Although the Garden City Association by this time was not particularly interested in the idea of creating further new towns, by 1920 Howard nonetheless had created a second settlement based on his garden city concept, called Welwyn Garden City, which he hoped would ease the overcrowding within London. Welwyn Garden City, which was designed by Louis de Soissons and differed in many ways from Letchworth, is assured its place in the history of urban development and planning because it acted as a bridge between the 1898 garden city idea and the post-1945 New Town movement in Britain.

—*Ian Morley*

See also Howard, Ebenezer; Satellite City

Further Readings and References

Ashworth, W. (1954). *The genesis of modern British town planning.* London: Routledge & Kegan Paul.

Creese, W. L. (1966). *The search for environment.* London: Yale University Press.

Hall, P., & Ward, C. (1999). *Sociable cities: The legacy of Ebenezer Howard.* Chichester, UK: John Wiley.

Miller, M. (1992). *Raymond Unwin: Garden cities and town planning.* Leicester, UK: Leicester University Press.

Purdom, C. B. (1949). *The building of satellite towns.* London: J. M. Dent.

Unwin, R. (1990). *Town planning in practice: An introduction to the art of designing cities and suburbs.* London: T. Fisher Unwin.

GATEWAY CITIES

Gateway cities are spaces through which people, goods, and trade pass. As such, they are nodes in a larger urban network or system and function as transition points or starting points for movement (of goods and people) to other parts of a region or country, as well as the globe. Although the term *gateway cities* was originally used in the United States to refer to pioneer towns, the contemporary literature is generally divided between discussions of gateway cities as points of entry into the United States for immigrants and travelers and of gateway cities as points of entry for commercial activities. With increased speed and intensity of globalization since the 1960s, there has been an acceleration of global flows of people and goods, leading to more attention on gateway cities in the literature. In addition, increasing urban competition, urban entrepreneurialism, and place-marketing has led to many cities advertising themselves as "gateways" to economic opportunity and as serving gateway functions.

Gateway city also is a concept that should be understood in relation to central place theory in geography. Central places are settlements that provide goods and services to a surrounding area. The term *central* is important, as it references a settlement that interacts with a range of people and activities in all directions, and thus does not function as an entry into an area or primarily as a long-distance transportation link. Gateway cities, on the other hand, are located at the edges of (or hinges between) hinterlands, regions, manufacturing processes, markets, and (long-distance) transportation networks. As "gates," "doors," or "windows" to other spaces and resources, gateway cities provide access to areas that may extend for many miles in one direction or may fan out from the city like spokes on a wheel, as noted by A. F. Burghardt in 1971.

In addition to geographic differences, there are differences in the functions of central places and gateways. Central places produce goods and services that are provided to surrounding areas. Gateways, in contrast, are associated with the functions of transportation, distribution, and access to other areas and resources (for example, through personal networks and communication systems), making urban spaces like warehouse districts important parts of the cities' form, as noted by Leonard Eaton in 1989. Gateways are generally not associated with manufacturing, production, or a concentration of command centers. Terms often used to describe them are *financial gateways, transportation gateways, network gateways, trade gateways,* and *immigration gateways.* While *gateway* traditionally has described the city on the physical edge of some connection or region (for example, a rail network, waterway, or manufacturing district), the term has also been used to describe a place with connections that are not physically contingent. Such places include gateways to national economies or gateways to networks and services that access national economies, as well as producer services that offer access to international trade and global connections. Shanghai and Hong Kong are examples of cities that are "gateways" to China. New York and London are said to be "gateways" to the global economy.

Thus the gateway city literature builds on the world cities literature. Some assert that a focus on gateways shifts our attention from a few world or global cities and toward a vast array of cities and how they all are affected by globalization. Gateway cities may compete globally through their role as access points to potential hinterlands of capitalist expansion (for example, as Shanghai provides access to China), and such expansion is believed by some to be increasingly important for any region's development. By developing gateway functions in particular, these cities may attract investments and new immigrants. Those who work within the hierarchical frame of the global cities concept suggest that gateway cities are "not yet" global cities because of their "limited" functions. Similarly, gateway cities may be represented as places that are "not yet" central places and which may, over time, absorb more functions (such as production) with increased prosperity. St. Louis is a common example of a gateway city that became a central place with development.

The term *gateway* also is widely used to describe migration and travel processes. Cities such as Los Angeles, New York, Miami, Chicago, and Houston, often termed *immigration gateway cities,* may be the final destination for international travelers or immigrants, or they may literally be the "opening" or gateway for settlement in other locations. As large immigrant population centers, some suggest these cities are command centers in and of themselves, while others describe such immigrant gateway cities as hinges in longer distance flows of people and services. Common topics in studying immigrant gateway cities are assimilation, segregation, discrimination, class formation, and the building of ethnic communities and places (for example, Chinatown, Little Italy, and Little Havana).

With globalization, some large metropolitan centers (that is, gateway cities) in the United States have seen a significant increase in the number of immigrants settling in the city. These demographic shifts are also reflected in changing labor markets, work patterns, residential segregation, and development of ethnic communities. Some note that with deindustrialization immigrant gateway cities have tried to revitalize their city centers by capitalizing on the new flows of people and capital to develop new ethnic districts, leading to rich and diverse urban social worlds and economies. Overseas investments in these ethnic places may conflict with long-standing interests and residents in the communities, echoing contradictions in globalization processes elsewhere.

—*Lisa M. Hoffman*

See also Urban Immigration

Further Readings and References

Burghardt, A. F. (1971). A hypothesis about gateway cities. *Annals of the Association of American Geographers, 61*(2), 269–285.

Eaton, L. K. (1989). *Gateway cities and other essays.* Great Plains Environmental Design Series. Ames, IA: Iowa State University Press.

Sassen, S. (Ed.). (2002). *Global networks: Linked cities.* New York: Routledge.

Short, J. R., Breitback, C., Buckman, S., & Essex, J. (2000). From world cities to gateway cities: Extending the boundaries of globalization theory. *City, 4*(3), 317–340.

GAY MEN'S CULTURES IN CITIES

Although same-sex sexual desires and acts can be documented across the span of American history, only in the late 19th century did groups of men begin to form urban communities and cultures based on same-sex sexual preferences and orientations. By the early 20th century, one knowledgeable commentator was referring to Boston, Chicago, Milwaukee, New Orleans, New York, Philadelphia, St. Louis, San Francisco, and Washington, D.C., as homosexual capitals. Gay cultures have also been documented in the early 20th century in smaller cities, including Jackson, Mississippi; Long Beach, California; Newport, Rhode Island; Portland, Oregon; and Seattle, Washington. Mass mobilization during World War II contributed to the growth and development of multicultural urban gay communities, and after the war an organized homophile political movement developed in many U.S. cities, beginning with Los Angeles. But across the late 19th, 20th, and 21st centuries, urban gay men have struggled against a wide variety of antigay religious, political, scientific, and popular forces. In June 1969, a police raid on the Stonewall Inn, a gay bar in New York City, led to several nights of rioting and then to the emergence of a grassroots gay liberation movement. By the late 20th and early 21st centuries, complex gay cultures existed in small and large cities in every region of the United States, influencing and being influenced by larger urban developments.

Although gay cultures also developed in rural regions of the country in the late 19th and early 20th centuries, cities were particularly attractive for men interested in same-sex sex in this period. Urban wage labor and other economic opportunities offered men greater independence from traditional familial, religious, and communal authorities. At the same time, new relationships between the worlds of work, family, and leisure created expanded possibilities for living unconventionally in one or more of these spheres. Cities also featured boardinghouses, bachelor apartments, and other types of housing that catered to unmarried men and encouraged alternative living arrangements. Meanwhile, large urban populations created the perception of safety in numbers, and multicultural urban diversity promoted sexual heterogeneity.

As amusement, leisure, and vice districts took shape in urban environments, men who were interested in same-sex sex came together in new erotic zones. City bars, bathhouses, cafeterias, clubs, parks, streets, and restaurants that acquired reputations for catering to gays appealed to those interested in making same-sex social and sexual connections, as did urban cultural institutions such as cinemas, concert halls, opera houses, and theaters. Over time, visible gay cultures took shape in various urban neighborhoods, including Northside (Boys Town) in Chicago; West Hollywood and Silver Lake in greater Los Angeles; Greenwich Village, Chelsea, Times Square, and Harlem in New York; Center City in Philadelphia; the Barbary Coast, Castro, Mission, and North Beach in San Francisco; and Dupont Circle in Washington, D.C. Meanwhile some smaller towns and cities, including Ogunquit, Maine; Provincetown, Massachusetts; Cherry Grove and the Pines on Fire Island in New York; Atlantic City and Cape May, New Jersey; New Hope, Pennsylvania; Rehoboth Beach, Delaware; Miami Beach and Key West, Florida; and Palm Springs, California, acquired reputations as popular gay resorts.

Gay cultures in American cities since the late 19th century have struggled against an array of antigay forces. Religious, political, and scientific authorities have launched campaigns against gay practices and institutions, constituting homosexuality as sin, crime, and disease. Gay men and gay youth have encountered physical violence and verbal assaults from family members, neighbors, coworkers, and strangers on the street. Police forces have conducted raids on places where gay men congregated, arresting, imprisoning, harassing, entrapping, demanding payoffs from, and committing violence against those who were present. Organized criminals who owned, managed, or demanded kickbacks from gay commercial establishments have taken advantage of the vulnerabilities of gay men, sometimes in cahoots with the police and the courts. Meanwhile, gay men have encountered discrimination in employment, housing, and public accommodations, and they have been confronted with the inadvertent cruelty of reformers seeking to clean up vice, save sinners, rehabilitate criminals, and cure the diseased.

In the midst of these hostile forces, men interested in same-sex sex have found ways to converge and connect. Coded language and clothing have often been used to announce identities and interests to others and to determine who was gay or gay-friendly and who was not. Gay men have protected one another by sharing warnings about dangerous individuals and locations, helped one another obtain jobs and housing, and pooled resources to deal with economic difficulties. Newcomers have been introduced to local gay geographies, youth have been educated about gay mores, and networks of friends have performed many of the traditional functions of family in looking after the sick and the elderly. In countless ways, gay men have come together for culture, drink, fellowship, food, conversation, entertainment, politics, sex, and support. This is not to suggest that the gay world has been conflict free, but gay cultures have allowed gay men to overcome the obstacles of isolation, internalization, and invisibility.

In many respects, it makes more sense to refer to multiple and heterogeneous gay cultures rather than to a singular and homogeneous one. Some gay cultures have favored monogamous, domestic, and privatized relationships that have had many characteristics in common with normative straight counterparts; others have favored sex with multiple partners, public sex, and sex for pay. Some gay cultures have overlapped substantially with interracial, lesbian, sex work, straight, transsexual, and transgender cultures; others have not. In some contexts the dominant gay cultural system has promoted sex between masculine and feminine (or older and younger) males, in others the dominant system has favored partners with similar gender attributes (or similar ages). In the former, the tendency might be for the masculine or older partner to perform sexual activities that were commonly defined as active; in the latter sexual activities might be more mutual and reciprocal. The term *gay* itself has had different cultural meanings in different cultural contexts, so that only some men who engage in same-sex sex have referred to themselves as *gay*. Others have used terms such as *chicken, fairy, jocker, queen, pansy, punk, stud, wolf, queer,* or *trade,* and each of these words has distinct gendered and sexualized meanings. Moreover, many men who have had sex with men (especially if they have seen themselves as conforming to dominant masculine norms) have viewed themselves as *normal* men who, under certain circumstances, would be as ready to have sexual relations with a male partner as a female one.

Many of these differences correspond to class, race/ethnic, nativity, and generational differences. For example, the working-class fairy and "her" queer or normal partner might have found acceptance in early-20th-century working-class gay cultures but have been criticized by middle-class gay men attempting to avoid the taint of effeminacy. The African American or Latino gay man might have found ways of negotiating gay life in the ghetto or the barrio in the mid-20th century but have been excluded from gay bars and events in the predominantly white gay neighborhood. Gay urban cultures have been marked by class conflict, racial oppression, and ethnic prejudice, and the eroticization of class, race, and ethnic differences has both promoted and challenged ongoing social hierarchies. Over the course of the 20th century a white, middle-class gay culture became hegemonic and in many respects marginalized alternative same-sex sexual systems. Yet great cultural diversity continues to mark both the self-defined gay world and the larger universe of men who have sex with men.

Periodizing gay urban cultures is quite a difficult undertaking, and it can be dangerous to generalize before further research is conducted. Most scholars agree, however, that urban gay cultures first took shape in the late 19th century, though there are disagreements about how accepted and integrated these cultures were (within dominant, working-class, and minority racial/ethnic communities) and when and why crackdowns occurred in the Progressive 1910s, the Roaring 1920s, and the Great Depression of the 1930s. While some see the first third of the 20th century as a period of relative tolerance, acceptance, and visibility, others point to the dramatic growth of urban gay communities and the emergence of an organized homophile movement in the second third of the century (and especially during and after World War II). A "lavender scare" has been linked to the "red scare" of the early 1950s, but while some see this as a relatively temporary reaction of a nation that had experienced decades of economic turmoil and military conflict, others believe that the crackdown extended through the 1950s, 1960s, and perhaps beyond. For those who see the homophile movement of the 1950s and 1960s as tame and accommodationist, the Stonewall riots of the 1960s mark a turning point in gay urban politicization. Others, struck by the militancy and radicalism of the pre-Stonewall movement, see the radical gay liberation movement of the late 1960s and early 1970s as but a brief and passing phase, or point to continuities between the pre- and post-Stonewall gay worlds.

In any case, it is difficult to deny that gay urban cultures developed an unprecedented level of visibility and influence in the last third of the 20th century, even as they were devastated by the effects of the AIDS epidemic, damaged by the problems of urban decline, and distressed by the nation's conservative turn. Openly gay candidates were elected to local office, gay constituencies were courted by city politicians, gay neighborhoods were redeveloped and gentrified, and gay tourism and gay businesses became important components of urban economies. From the homophile demonstrations and sit-ins that began in the 1960s through the post-1969 gay pride parades that mark the anniversary of the Stonewall riots, gay cultures have taken to city streets to demand change and celebrate diversity. Urban spaces have witnessed major conflicts between progay and antigay forces, perhaps exemplified most dramatically in the murder of openly gay San Francisco City Supervisor Harvey Milk in the 1970s and the demonstrations of the AIDS Coalition to Unleash Power and Queer Nation in the 1980s and 1990s. In the early 21st century, as is evident in same-sex marriage controversies in Boston, New Paltz, Portland, and San Francisco, cities continue to serve as catalysts and incubators of sexual, social, cultural, and political change in the United States.

—*Marc Stein*

See also Lesbian Culture in Cities; Queer Space

Further Readings and References

Beemyn, B. (1997). *Creating a place for ourselves.* New York: Routledge.

Boag, P. (2003). *Same-sex affairs.* Berkeley: University of California Press.

Boyd, N. A. (2003). *Wide open town.* Berkeley: University of California Press.

Chauncey, G. (1994). *Gay New York.* New York: Basic Books.

D'Emilio, J. (1983). *Sexual politics, sexual communities.* Chicago: University of Chicago Press.

Howard, J. (1999). *Men like that.* Chicago: University of Chicago Press.

Maynard, S. (2004). "Without working?" Capitalism, urban culture, and gay history. *Journal of Urban History, 30,* 378–398.

Stein, M. (2000). *City of sisterly and brotherly loves.* Chicago: University of Chicago Press.

GENDER

Biology distinguishes the sex of a person, yet cultures link a wide variety of attributes—behaviors, expectations, and proscriptions—to a person's sex. In some cases, a characteristic may be so intricately tied to one's sex—woman's maternal instinct or man's competitive nature, for example—that cultures describe the characteristic as a "natural" or "essential" quality of being male or female. Similarly, expectations related to gender are so embedded within traditions and social institutions that individuals may not think to question them. The term *gender* refers to the social and cultural characteristics associated with a person's sex by people of the same culture or society.

Since the 1970s, academics from a variety of disciplines have studied the dynamics of these cultural attributions that form identity. By asking what value a culture attaches to the activities of men and women, the attributions of gender have been teased away from the biological distinctions of sex. Comparisons over time, across countries, and within cultures have established a body of evidence that documents extensive variations in gender characteristics. If these gender characteristics were linked to our chromosomal material, the variation would not be so apparent. The characteristics linked to sex would remain relatively constant.

Examination of the impact of gender upon the history of cities could begin with studies of the respective actions of women and men and their relations within each group and with each other. However, the greater significance of gender analysis, like that of critical race theory, rests in how it changes what we know about familiar United States history themes and how we understand the systems of ideas, economics, politics, and social relations that have made our American culture. Historical research has documented gender's impact in many of those arenas in the history of cities, three of which will be discussed here: the use of urban space, urban politics, and social relations, particularly sexuality.

The Gendered Use of City Space

Observing how groups of people occupy specific parts of the city reveals patterns and transitions in social relations. We may be familiar with the division of urban space into areas of wealth and areas of poverty. Similarly, we know that neighborhoods reflect ethnic and racial segregation. Yet, the use of space in cities also tells us about class, race, and gender relations. Women of the working class have occupied the streets, markets, and doorsteps of their neighborhoods for as long as cities have existed. Their lives and those of their children have been lived partly outside their tenement homes and in the neighborhood streets. Christine Stansell's *City of Women* illustrates the permeable boundaries of public and private space for

working-class families in New York City during the first half of the 19th century. The presence of members of the working class on the city streets led some among their middle-class contemporaries to view their behavior as unruly and potentially dangerous—in other words, as behavior that needed to be regulated. In Stansell's study, the behavior of the white working class raised concerns among New York City's moral reformers, but the black working class resisted regulation of every aspect of their lives. Tera Hunter's *To 'Joy My Freedom* traces the ways in which Atlanta's black domestic workers created a physical and familiar space for themselves in which to enjoy their leisure and their families in the violent years of the Jim Crow South.

Another gendered use of public space occurred in urban commercial districts at the end of the 19th century. The downtown streets and shops, once filled predominately by men, would by the 1890s be shared with women. Whether women were working in the factories, retail stores, and offices of the commercial districts or shopping or attending cultural events or club meetings, their presence downtown changed the character of the city center. In Boston, Sarah Deutsch found that women claimed particular areas of the city for their activities and by doing so transformed the negative assumptions attached to women in public places.

This late-19th-century move into public spaces by middle-class women did not take place seamlessly or with homogeneity. When Jane Addams and Ellen Gates Starr founded their settlement house, Hull-House, in the center of Chicago's working-class immigrant enclaves, the distrust of their new neighbors and the dismay of their friends indicated the strangeness of this cross-class endeavor. When professional women sought lodgings near their new jobs in cities, they were guided to working women's hotels where not only would they find room and board but also their morals would be protected. Civic women's clubs formed to provide an arena for privileged women to educate themselves on civic issues and move beyond the earlier focus on self-improvement. These single-sex clubs existed as a fact of sex segregation, yet they also provided women the opportunity to set their own course of action to change their cities. For whites, public spaces such as parks, theaters, and public transportation became sex-integrated public spaces by the 1920s. Yet during those same years, these public spaces remained racially segregated—if not by law, by practice. Public parks, transportation, and theaters became the stage upon which the civil rights confrontations took place between the 1940s and the 1970s.

Politics and Culture

Looking at the history of cities through the lens of gender informs our understanding of major institutions such as urban politics. At the end of the 19th century, the great cities of the nation, such as New York, Chicago, Boston, and San Francisco, governed with a specific structure of politics—the political machine. It relied not only on particular party interests and specific organizational structures but also on a system of male homosocial relations. The neighborhood bar served as the precinct meeting place, male workers filled the patronage jobs in the ward, and the selection of candidates came from the all-male party loyalists. Whether in working-class precincts, black wards, or Irish city machines, the homogeneous social relations maintained an exclusively male political culture.

Political historians did not examine the way in which gender structured city politics for several reasons. First, historians thought that public activities were bifurcated by sex into public and private spheres of activity, with women ascribed to the latter. Men, by law and practice, had represented the family in politics. Second, because we expected the norm in politics to be male political practice, it was assumed that women's political practices would look the same as men's. As a result, women's political actions became invisible—with the exception of suffrage campaigns. However, if urban politics are construed as a wider set of activities that shape policy, public affairs, and even legislation, that is, activities that occur outside office holding and voting, then women's entrance into urban affairs was evident at least by the mid-19th century.

Studies of organized women written over the last 25 years demonstrate that women moved into urban politics first as citizens seeking to improve the areas of life that most affected them, home and family, and then as voters. As Maureen Flanagan has argued, the urban agenda of early-20th-century white women reformers looked different from that of their male peers in Chicago, because these women wanted the public sector to address the problems that affected their lives—housing, food, health care, and education. They called their work "municipal housekeeping," referring to women's traditional work in the home and its extension into the city. Furthermore, as Kathryn Kish Sklar and Linda Gordon have shown, organized women worked to expand the duties of local governments to include vital services for youth, community health, and family welfare. The impact of organized women's political activities, then, was no less than helping to create a prototype of the modern welfare state.

Today, we understand urban politics of the early 20th century as cultural systems circumscribed by sex, class, race, and ethnicity, in which women had a well-established tradition of civic work, gender shaped the policy agendas of both men and women, and political reforms increasingly broadened citizens' rights to participate in the democracy over the course of the 20th century.

The Social Relations of Sex

A third and final area of urban history that has benefitted from gender analysis is sexuality. Cities have created opportunities for Americans to meet and mix with people entirely different from themselves. Population density, migration, and the expansion of educational, cultural, and social opportunities throughout the 20th century fostered a modern urban culture; one in which the traditional restrictions on behavior by community and family dissolved. Men and women socialized in a new context generated by commercial markets in such leisure outlets as amusement parks, public dances, movies, and nightclubs. Single working women in Chicago, described in Joanne Meyerowitz's *Women Adrift,* and working-class young adults, described in Kathy Peiss's *Cheap Amusements,* are two examples. Cities also became magnets for lesbians and gay men. Leaving the isolation of small towns, they built communities and created subcultures in the nation's major cities. George Chauncey's study of the emerging gay community in New York City and Nan Boyd's study of gay San Francisco illustrate the unprecedented opportunities and challenges for gay men and lesbians afforded by city life.

At the same time, the loosened bonds of urban life created movements to limit or regulate change in social relations. The 19th and 20th centuries are full of examples of countervailing actions to control sexuality in the city. The moral reform movements of the 1840s, the purity crusades of the 1880s, the vice squads of the 1910s to 1930s, and the anti–juvenile delinquency campaigns over the course of the 20th century are examples of the perceived crises in America's cities. Single women often felt the brunt of regulation, particularly when prostitution was involved. Although present around the country, prostitution became more visible (as did its regulation) in cities.

Many more aspects of urban history could be included here. Occupational segregation of the workplace, consumption and commercialization, popular culture and urban leisure economies are all areas in which gender has changed and expanded our idea of urban life. How and where the lives of women and men are separate and where they interact explains social relations and systems of power. How those systems intersect with class and race relations further defines those systems. In 1916, Carl Sandburg paid poetic homage to the Chicago industrial workers whose labors ran the city's economy. There is no question that the engine of industrial capitalism in the early 20th century belonged to men who made Chicago the "City of the Big Shoulders" and carved out the city's place in the nation. Sandburg focused on the laborer in juxtaposition to the capitalist whose investments funded the industries. Yet, those legendary workers had partners in city building. Examining the city through the lens of gender analysis expands and explains the dynamics of city building as a multidimensional process.

—*Joanne L. Goodwin*

See also Bosses and Machines; Masculine Domesticity; Prostitution; Settlement House Movement; Woman's City Clubs; Women and Public Space; Women in Cities

Further Readings and References

Boyd, N. (2003). *Wide-open town: A history of queer San Francisco to 1965.* Berkeley: University of California Press.

Chauncey, G. (1994). *Gay New York: Gender, urban culture, and the making of the gay male world, 1890–1940.* New York: Basic Books.

Deutsch, S. (2000). *Women and the city: Gender, space, and power in Boston, 1870–1940.* New York: Oxford University Press.

Flanagan, M. (2002). *Seeing with their hearts: Chicago women and the vision of the good city, 1871–1933.* Princeton, NJ: Princeton University Press.

Hunter, T. W. (1997). *To 'joy my freedom: Southern black women's lives and labors after the Civil War.* Cambridge, MA: Harvard University Press.

Meyerowitz, J. J. (1988). *Women adrift: Independent wage earners in Chicago, 1880–1930.* Chicago: University of Chicago Press.

Peiss, K. (1986). *Cheap amusements: Working women and leisure in turn-of-the-century New York.* Philadelphia: Temple University Press.

Stansell, C. (1986). *City of women, sex and class in New York, 1789–1860.* New York: Alfred A. Knopf.

GENTRIFICATION

Few who use the term *gentrification* agree completely on its meaning. As applied loosely in the popular press, it refers to the movement of new middle-class residents into poor and working-class inner city neighborhoods, spurring the rehabilitation of a district's previously abandoned or neglected housing stock and the revitalization of its commercial life. Even that simple definition, however, is controversial, to the extent that it neglects the broad economic repercussions and remote historical origins of a much more complex process. Most critics of gentrification, for instance, insist that it involves as well the displacement of existing residents, usually with some experience of economic hardship or disadvantage.

If we think of the process as having a historical beginning, it would be with the collapse of urban industrial economies after World War II, leading to the structural unemployment of urban working-class populations and the economic and physical decline of their residential and commercial environments. But there are even earlier precedents. The grand reconstructions of medieval European (and some Latin American) cities at the turn of the century, led by Baron George-Eugene Haussmann's "boulevardization" of Paris and Ildefons Cerda's planned rebuilding of Barcelona, created early geographical examples of what the French called *embourgeoisement,* which in the English-speaking world we would later term *revitalization* and, eventually, *gentrification.*

When British sociologist Ruth Glass coined the term in 1964, the postwar trend toward gentrification was already well under way in several major American and European cities. In the United States, downtown investment was encouraged by public redevelopment projects in the hope of reshaping the built environment to accommodate an emerging shift from the manufacturing of goods in urban factories to the production of services in offices, schools, and hospitals. In Philadelphia, which saw the departure of its textile industry begin in the 1920s, political reformers were already discussing downtown revitalization on the foundations of a new kind of urban economy before the war was over. The work of progressive planner Edmund Bacon on the systematic rebuilding of the city's transportation infrastructure and reinvestment in downtown historic districts (displayed in Bacon's famous 1947 Better Philadelphia exhibit) contributed directly to the resettling of the middle class in that city's central business district beginning in 1955. What Glass witnessed in infant stages in London had already advanced somewhat further in Philadelphia's Society Hill under the auspices of a federally subsidized public-private partnership for urban "revitalization" spearheaded by Bacon's Planning Commission, financial leaders with stakes in the downtown real estate, and the city's recently elected reform government. By the mid-1960s, the Society Hill project set a standard by which downtown revitalization in other American cities would be measured.

In the 1970s, increasingly conservative American policymakers cut public housing, welfare, and other redistributive subsidies to the inner city poor. Gentrification became one desperate hope of urban regimes eroded by collapsing tax bases and inner city impoverishment and rocked by a recent history of social and political upheaval. Advocates of gentrification viewed the trend as a process of revitalization or an "urban renaissance," a healthy middle-class movement from the suburbs "back to the city" that would solve many of the financial and social problems of urban disinvestment. Indeed, that was how downtown residential investment by the American middle class was promoted in the late 1970s and 1980s, as the sort of business revitalization and urban "pioneering" or "homesteading" that could still attract private investment and federal subsidies in the prevailing economic and political climates.

This view was provisionally supported at the time by housing statistics that showed marginal increases in the income and education levels of residents in Manhattan, as well as in parts of San Francisco, Boston, Philadelphia, and Washington, D.C. The apparent increase in middle-class desire to resettle in urban locations has been attributed to many cultural and economic factors, including the maturing of the Baby Boom generation, an increase in two-income professional families, a decline in the birth-rate, rising energy costs, increases in commuting time, and a perceived decline in the suburban quality of life. The fact that in its early stages revitalization appeared to draw middle-class residents to declining neighborhoods primarily from within the city limits (thus adding little to city tax coffers) did not deter gentrification's enthusiasts, who anticipated a growing trend that would indeed fulfill many of their expectations.

While its proponents celebrated an urban renaissance, however, critics (including the residents of threatened neighborhoods, who began in the early 1970s to join antigentrification movements) countered by pointing to gentrification's damaging effects on stable inner city communities and the living conditions and housing options of the poor. As late as 1979, when the United States Department of Housing and Urban Development published its study on the subject, relatively little was known about the displacement of working-class and poor residents from gentrifying neighborhoods. In large part resulting from the absence of reliable data on residential out-movers (who are not effectively tracked by national housing statistics), the displacement debate focused mostly on general questions about whether gentrification is socially beneficial. That debate has continued until the present moment. By the mid-1980s, it was a widely accepted view (based on small studies in selected cities) that gentrification displaced the poor and working class—through evictions, harassment, condo and coop conversions, rent increases, renovation costs, and rising tax assessments—into crowded and more expensive housing in less desirable locations. In addition, the rise in the number of urban homeless across the United States has been blamed in part on the disappearance of adequate low-income and emergency housing.

Recent studies based on analyses of national housing and census data, while less than conclusive, have nonetheless been touted in the press as definitive contrary evidence that the poor experience little hardship and possibly some benefits from gentrification. Surprisingly, there has been little advance in the tracking and surveying of displacees (the main weakness of the recent studies), who according to persistent qualitative evidence are forced into more expensive and remote housing or are doubling up with families and friends. And, as urbanist Peter Marcuse long ago pointed out, displacement has never simply been a matter of who leaves at that last minute before the gentrifiers move in. Rather, it is a long-term process of conversion that includes disinvestment, abandonment, demolition, and reconstruction and in which preferential housing and locational options are eventually shifted from the poor to the wealthy. That gentrifiers tend to be white, while the former occupants of gentrifying communities in many American cities have tended to be disproportionately people of color, has added a racial dimension to the class tensions emerging over the control of urban space.

Generally, critics contend that gentrification cannot be viewed as a process separate from the rest of the economy. In larger structural economic terms, both gentrification and the neighborhood deterioration caused by disinvestment are part of an international trend in which industrial production in developing countries is managed from "global" cities in the developed world. It is the white-collar professionals working in the high-wage producer and financial services sector in the downtowns of major cities who have increased demand for urban housing, exerting upward pressure on prices, and have supplied the consumer demand for upscale retail services and entertainment in midtown Manhattan, Boston's Back Bay, Brooklyn's Park Slope, Chicago's Near North Side, and similar gentrified neighborhoods across the nation.

As gentrification accelerated in the late 1990s (after a brief recessionary slump), advocates pointed to its visibly beneficial effects on the commercial and cultural life of previously deteriorated central business districts. Critics underscored the extent to which global "postindustrial" urban economies had become divided between salaried professionals (who are disproportionately white and male) and low-wage employees (who are disproportionately people of color and female) in the service, tourist, and retail sectors—a source of class, racial, and gender conflict aggravated by the dwindling supply of low-cost, centrally located housing. Moreover, as cities have vied to demonstrate superior positions in the "symbolic economy" of urban life with projects that added high-profile cultural and retail attractions (such as downtown malls and riverfront parks), urban political leaders have sought to cleanse streets and squares of unattractive elements, including not just crime and physical deterioration but also the evidence of racial difference, poverty, and nonnormative behavior that once was the hallmark of a diverse city space to which all citizens had rights.

—*Andrew Feffer*

See also Deindustrialization; Middle Class in Cities; Redlining

Further Readings and References

Freeman, L. (2005). Displacement or succession? Residential mobility in gentrifying neighborhoods. *Urban Affairs Review, 40,* 463–491.

Newman, K., & Wyly, E. K. (2006). The right to stay put, revisited: Gentrification and resistance to displacement in New York City. *Urban Studies, 43,* 23–57.

Rose, D. (1984). Rethinking gentrification: Beyond the uneven development of Marxist urban theory. *Environment and Planning D: Society and Space, 1,* 47–74.

Smith, N. (2002). New globalism, new urbanism: Gentrification as a global urban strategy. *Antipode, 34,* 427–450.

Smith, N., & Williams, P. (1986). *Gentrification of the city.* Boston: Allen & Unwin.

Zukin, S. (1995). *The cultures of cities.* London: Blackwell.

GHETTO

Ghetto is a culturally loaded term that, like *slum,* is applied to socially disadvantaged neighborhoods in American cities. Both words are slurs that distort rather than describe the actualities of the places that are so labeled. Ghetto implies a level of separateness from mainstream society, and of internal homogeneity, still more intense than that of a slum. The term was first applied to ethnically specific immigrant enclaves within the so-called slum districts of American inner cities during the late 19th century. By the early 20th century, with the consolidation of Asian neighborhoods within some cities, and the internal migration of black Americans to many more neighborhoods, the word began to develop racial as well as ethnic connotations. By the 1960s, the term had become synonymous with the entrenched disadvantage and accumulating anger of urban blacks. In the late 20th century, the "ghetto blaster," blaring uncompromising lyrics by rap musicians about blanket discrimination and minority self-expression, caused widespread disquiet. In the early 21st century, Ghettopoly, a Monopoly-type board game in which crack houses, peep shows, and Chinese triads replace upmarket property investments, city utilities, and railway stations, caused outrage for its stereotypical view of black people and minority cultures in America.

The word *ghetto* has an uncertain etymology. It probably derives from the Italian *getto* (or foundry), as the first ghetto was founded in Venice in 1516 on the site of a foundry. Italian ghettos were city districts to which Jewish settlement was restricted by the local authorities. The Rome ghetto, for example, was established in 1556 by Pope Paul IV. Jewish ghettos developed in other European cities. The Warsaw ghetto is probably the best known, and the London ghetto (as dramatized in Israel Zangwill's 1892 novel, *Children of the Ghetto*) is probably the best described.

It was Zangwill's sense of what a ghetto represented as a cultural milieu, rather than its precise regulatory and territorial development in Europe over the centuries, that explains the word's adoption by

American observers of mass immigrant settlement in the United States at the turn of the 20th century. It had become a truism for Americans since the middle of the 19th century that immigrants from Europe were importing Old World poverty and that the immigrant poor created slums in American cities. These immigrant slums, however, were often regarded as through houses: as the new arrivals from Britain and northwestern Europe found their feet in America, they moved out of the slums and assimilated into the receiving society. This complacent viewpoint became harder to sustain by the end of the century, as the growing wave of "new immigrants" from Southern and Eastern Europe and from Asia replaced the "old immigrants" in the slums. These latest arrivals seemed to be culturally more distinct and less adaptable than their predecessors. Americans worried that the "new immigrant" poor would remain trapped in the slums because they were culturally less equipped than their predecessors to adjust to a modern society. It was in this context that Americans began to talk about the emergence of self-contained foreign "colonies" within the slums. The Chicago reformer Robert Hunter, for example, argued in 1904 that Jewish, Italian, German, Irish, and Russian colonies often made up the main portion of the slums in American cities. It was the so-called colonies of Eastern European Jews that Americans first began to label as ghettos. In New York, for example, the journalist and urban reform advocate Jacob A. Riis described "Jewtown" as an element within the city's slums in his influential book *How the Other Half Lives* (1890), but in his sequel, *The Battle With the Slum* (1902), he redefined it as the "Ghetto." He argued that Jews had lived in ghettos since time out of mind, and had recreated a ghetto within the slums of New York. When Louis Wirth wrote his classic definition of the ghetto in 1927, it had become axiomatic that the American ghetto was a segregated district within the slums in which the poorest and most backward groups of the Jewish population had congregated.

The American ghetto of the 1930s, however, was a concept in the minds of Americans rather than a tangible feature of their cityscapes. It in no way approximated to the 1930s Warsaw Ghetto. So fluid were the meanings of the word *ghetto* that the term was often applied to the other immigrant "colonies" within the supposed slums. Wirth and other Chicago sociologists argued that although the ghetto was strictly speaking a Jewish institution, its character in American cities was equivalent to that of the Little Sicilies, Greektowns, Little Polands, Chinatowns, and Black Belts. Indeed,

so closely had these foreign colonies become identified in Americans' minds with the concept of the slum that loosely worded characterizations of *slums* and *ghettos* became interchangeable. By the 1920s and 1930s *ghetto* had not only become synonymous with *slum,* it was replacing it in American idiom.

There are three main reasons for this change in language usage. First, the exotically picturesque elements in slum sensationalism that had first enthralled American audiences were especially evident in the depictions of immigrant ghettos. The new word carried greater entertainment appeal than did the old. Second, whereas "new immigration" had tarnished the image of slums as an avenue for the assimilation of aliens into American society, in the aftermath of immigration restriction laws in the 1920s (and hence the winding back of the number of foreign arrivals), it began to seem that the foreign ghettos, no longer perpetually renewed by floods of newcomers, were reasserting that assimilation function. Hutchins Hapgood had argued against the prevailing stereotypes at the turn of the century in his affectionate study of New York's Lower East Side ghetto. During the interwar period, University of Chicago urban sociologists provided influential support for Hapgood's conclusions, arguing that the cultural community of the ghetto and its strong network of stable families provided a support base for newly arrived immigrants, who later fled the ghetto to areas of secondary settlement as they adjusted to American norms. The third reason for changing usage was more disturbing. Chicago School sociologists drew a distinction between what they called immigrant and racial colonies within the ghetto. Since the late 19th century, black migration from the rural South into the cities had been creating black enclaves, but the Chicago sociologists warned that whereas earlier waves of newcomers to the ghetto had later washed out of it, race prejudice was setting African Americans apart. Segregation was halting the path out of the black ghetto and into the American melting pot.

Whereas *slum* was entirely an imaginary construct that outsiders applied to poor neighborhoods, and whereas immigrant *ghetto* was likewise in large part a label that attached insecurely to the places it so tagged, prejudice translated the black ghetto from a stereotype into an actual feature of the social geography of American cities after World War II. Ongoing rural-to-city migration by blacks after 1945, together with across-the-board discrimination in the workplace, the housing market, and the general community, turned black enclaves into vast black urban regions. The *ghetto* tag still oversimplified and disparaged the social and cultural complexities of the districts to which it was applied, but it did signal entrenched inequalities of access in American society.

Michael Harrington dramatized this looming social crisis in his 1962 book *The Other America*. Harrington argued that the old ethnic ghettos, with their vitality, their clubs, their stable families, and their culture of aspiration to move into the American mainstream, had been replaced by a new ghetto of pessimism, social disintegration, and hopelessness. The critical difference, he contended, was color, which made the black ghetto's walls higher than ghetto walls had ever been. The whole world took note when black city districts exploded into anger during the city riots of the late 1960s. The U.S. Riot Commission concluded that the flash point for this wave of violence was the racial ghetto, and that this in turn was the outcome of systemic discrimination and segregation. Continuing black migration during the last quarter of the 20th century, combined with large-scale Puerto Rican, Hispanic, and Asian immigration and massive workplace restructuring, have complicated but not fundamentally altered this bleak conclusion. The spread of AIDS, crack-cocaine addiction, and the proliferation of handguns since the 1980s have exacerbated the social problems that President Lyndon B. Johnson's "War on Poverty" had sought to address back in 1964.

Paradoxically, although the cleavages within American society have, if anything, intensified over the last 25 years, the term *ghetto* is less often used to describe and sensationalize them. Transparently, the word now struggles to encapsulate the conditions it purports to describe. In part this is because of the clear persistence of the older ethnic ghettos that were supposedly displaced by the black ghetto (a persistence which is reflected on the one hand in tourist promotion of historic neighborhoods such as the Italian neighborhood North Beach in San Francisco and on the other hand in the wave of disgust that has swept across America after incidents such as the 1989 racially motivated slaying of black teenager Yusuf K. Hawkins when he ventured into the Italo-American enclave of Bensonhurst in New York City). The word *ghetto* has been further clouded by the out-migration of ethnic and racial groups to the suburbs and by the development there of affluent "gilded ghettos." In addition, ghetto stereotypes have lost their former potency because—as the majority of Americans of all backgrounds have retreated from the cities to their hinterlands—the perceived problems of the ghetto have been subsumed within a new master symbol of social disequilibrium and menace: the big city itself.

—*Alan Mayne*

Further Readings and References

Hapgood, H. (1902). *The spirit of the ghetto: Studies of the Jewish Quarter of New York.* New York: Funk & Wagnalls.

Harrington, M. (1971). *The other America: Poverty in the United States.* New York: Penguin. (Original work published 1962)

Hunter, R. (1904). *Poverty.* New York: Macmillan.

Riis, J. A. (1969). *The battle with the slum.* Montclair, NJ: Patterson Smith. (Original work published 1902)

Riis, J. A. (1971). *How the other half lives: Studies among the tenements of New York.* New York: Dover. (Original work published 1890)

Wirth, L. (1964). The ghetto. In A. J. Reiss Jr. (Ed.), *Louis Wirth on cities and social life: Selected papers.* Chicago: University of Chicago Press. (Original work published 1927)

Zangwill, I. (1969). Children of the ghetto: A study of a peculiar people. In *The Works of Israel Zangwill* (vol. 1). New York: AMS Press. (Original work published 1892)

Ghost Towns

Ghost towns are communities that have experienced a period of thriving, followed by a decline that leads to the community being mostly or entirely abandoned. The term generally invokes visions of deserted but still partially standing buildings, but it can also be applied to sites where no physical signs of the community remain, or even sites where a few inhabitants still live but the community's existence is tenuous and marginal when compared to its economic and social zenith. While there are towns throughout the United States that qualify as ghost towns, the term is particularly evocative of Western boom towns abandoned in the wake of an economic downturn, leaving behind the shells of buildings and the artifacts of their inhabitants' lives. These sites create a landscape invested by their visitors with images and narratives of the pioneering period of the American West—images and narratives that are widely circulated through film, television, guide-books, local histories, Internet sites, and restored or fabricated ghost towns designed for tourist consumption.

Ghost towns are created by a number of variables. Most commonly, these communities were founded and experienced their boom period based on the exploitation of a single natural resource, such as oil, phosphate, silver, gold, copper, or timber. When the resource was played out, the community had no other economic base to sustain itself, and its inhabitants moved on. Another common cause of the creation of a ghost town was a shift in access to commercial transportation. If the railroad bypassed a community, the community's loss of access to essential goods and loss of the ability to send their own goods to larger markets could cause the town to fail. This issue was especially acute in the West, where great distances between communities exacerbated the economic and social isolation of losing access to the railroad.

The term *ghost town* is of early-20th-century origin, although such communities existed in the West in the 19th century, particularly in the wake of the 1848 Gold Rush, when many mining towns were founded and as quickly died. Such "dead camps" were written of in the guidebooks and memoirs of travelers in the West. These abandoned communities appeared in the works of journalists and writers like Horace Greeley, John Muir, Bret Harte, Robert Louis Stevenson, and Samuel Clemens. Making sense of these failed communities was problematic for such writers in light of their era's boosterism and optimism regarding the vast natural resources and the unlimited potential they envisioned in the westward expansion.

In 1915, the *Saturday Evening Post* published four travel articles by Charles Van Loan on "Ghost Cities of the West." His articles described Virginia City, Bodie, Aurora, and Eureka. This appears to have been the first written use of the word *ghost* to describe the abandoned settlements of the West, and by the mid-1920s the term *ghost town* was widely used. Van Loan's articles painted the "ghost cities" as places that powerfully evoked the colorful history that had been lived in them and fed an interest in the imagined "Wild West" already shaped by 19th-century writers and further defined by popular silent film Westerns such as *The Great Train Robbery* (1903).

The first half of the 20th century saw an increase in automobile tourism and the concomitant improvement of roads, allowing access to more remote areas of the country. Ghost towns provided a destination for tourists in search of sites that evoked the pioneer heritage many white, middle-class Americans constructed from popular culture images in films and books, and from the celebratory history of westward expansion taught in schools. In addition, the 50th anniversary of many towns of the Gold Rush era fell during the early years of the 20th century, and the generation of people who had settled the region were passing away, which heightened interest in recording and preserving the history of the West, including the stories of its ghost towns.

Visiting ghost towns provided an opportunity to experience what 19th-century accounts had remarked upon: the sense of a place frozen in time. The buildings or parts of buildings that remained standing and the artifacts that the town's inhabitants left behind at mining sites or in their homes might be well preserved depending on the climate of the site. The physical remains of ghost towns were touchstones for the historical, genealogical, legendary, and fictional narratives visitors associated with the site. Even if no physical remains were left, standing on the site of the ghost town could be enough to evoke an imagined past that had been richly described and populated by the stories and images that make up the mythos of the American West. In this way, ghost towns are not only iconic symbols of that mythos, but uniquely iconic in the imagined immediacy and continuity of their connection to the past.

By the middle of the 20th century, Western states were celebrating their centennials, and another flurry of interest in state history led to recognition of a number of ghost towns as historic sites and state historic parks over the decades that followed, such as Columbia, California, in 1946; Bannack, Montana, in the 1950s; and Bodie, California, which was named a National Historic Landmark in 1961 and a state historic park in 1964. The postwar period saw the continued identification of ghost towns with the values and heritage of the "Old West," even when it was constructed from relocated or copied buildings from actual ghost towns, like the Knott's Berry Farm Ghost Town, using gunfight reenactments and stagecoach rides to provide visitors with a "frontier town" experience.

Ghost towns continue to be popular sites for people to visit, preserve, research, document in photos and artwork, and discuss on the Internet. The often simplistic, hegemonic nature of the past imagined to be associated with ghost towns is slowly being reshaped into a more nuanced and inclusive history, and just as they have in the past, ghost towns continue to play a part in re-imagining the history of the American West.

—Barbara Truesdell

See also Boom Towns; Boosterism

Further Readings and References

Coleman, J. T. (2001). The prim reaper: Muriel Sibell Wolle and the making of Western ghost towns. *The Mining History Journal, 8,* 10–17.

DeLyser, D. (2003). "Good, by God, we're going to Bodie!" Ghost towns and the American West. In G. Hausladen (Ed.), *Western places, American myths: How we think about the West* (pp. 273–295). Reno: University of Nevada Press.

Limerick, P. N., & Klett, M. (1992). Haunted by Rhyolite: Learning from the landscape of failure. *American Art, 6*(4), 18–39.

Poff, C. M. (2004). *The Western ghost town in American culture, 1869–1950.* Unpublished doctoral dissertation, University of Iowa, Iowa City.

GILMAN, CHARLOTTE PERKINS

Born Charlotte Ann Perkins on July 3, 1860, Charlotte Gilman (1860–1935) began publishing under her married name in 1892. Gilman was a prolific author, lecturer, and social commentator on women's rights at the turn of the 20th century. While she never labeled herself a feminist, Gilman believed the social roles assigned to men and women in modern society were artificial and outdated. Though she wrote numerous tracts during her lifetime, Gilman is best known for her short story "The Yellow Wallpaper" and her book *Women and Economics.*

Gilman grew up in a poor Connecticut household. Despite their familial ties to Harriet Beecher Stowe, Gilman's family had little money of their own. Gilman was a voracious reader and largely self-educated. She attended 2 years of college before dropping out to marry her first husband, Charles Welter Stetson. Gilman gave birth to her only daughter, Katherine, in 1885.

Childbirth caused Gilman to develop neurasthenia, an emotional disorder similar to postpartum depression. In 1886, Gilman's husband consulted renowned physician S. Weir Mitchell in the hope of finding a cure for her depression. Mitchell advised Gilman to live as "domestic" a life as possible in order to overcome her illness. The doctor's "Rest Cure," as he called it, was unsuccessful. However, the experience did inspire Gilman to write "The Yellow Wallpaper." The story, which was first published in 1892, focuses on a depressed woman's descent into madness as she is left alone in her sickroom. Many of Gilman's contemporaries considered the story to be a critique of marriage and the medical treatment of women in the 19th century.

Gilman's marriage to Stetson ended in a controversial divorce in 1888. She firmly believed that economic independence was crucial to feminine freedom in modern society, and as such, sought to earn her own living as a writer. She followed up on the success of "The Yellow Wallpaper" in 1898 with her book *Women and Economics.* The book attacks the division of social roles in society and was hailed as a major accomplishment for a female writer. It was republished in several languages and listed as required reading at Vassar College for a brief period of time.

Gilman continued to write throughout the duration of her second marriage, which was to her cousin, George Houghton Gilman, and took place in 1902. From 1909 to 1916 she self-published a feminist magazine called *The Forerunner,* which boasted a circulation of over a thousand copies per issue. She also gave lectures on women's issues, labor, and social reform over two decades.

Gilman was diagnosed with incurable breast cancer in 1932. Following the unexpected death of her husband in 1934, Gilman committed suicide by overdosing on chloroform. She died on August 7, 1935, stating in her suicide note that she preferred chloroform to cancer. Gilman's work experienced revitalization during the Feminist Movement of the 1960s, culminating with the posthumous publication of her novel *Herland* in 1979.

—Catherine Devon Griffis

Further Readings and References

Hill, M. A. (1980). *Charlotte Perkins Gilman: The making of a radical feminist.* Philadelphia: Temple University Press.

Kessler, C. F. (1995). *Charlotte Perkins Gilman: Her progress towards utopia with selected writings.* Syracuse, NY: Syracuse University Press.

GLADDEN, WASHINGTON

(Solomon) Washington Gladden (1836–1918), a congregational minister often called the "Father of the Social Gospel," was born in Pottsville, Pennsylvania. Gladden graduated from Williams College in 1859 and taught school for a year before deciding to enter the Congregational ministry. Ordained in 1860, he took a church in Brooklyn, New York, and then moved to a suburban church (1861–1865). Between pastorates in the two Massachusetts industrial towns of North Adams (1866–1871) and Springfield (1875–1882), Gladden served as religious editor of the weekly *Independent*. In 1883, he was called to the First Congregational Church in Columbus, Ohio, where he stayed until his retirement in 1914.

Although he had no formal seminary training, Gladden had read widely in the social sciences and liberal theology, focusing on the social teachings of Jesus. A lively style and persuasive message of brotherhood and social service earned Gladden a national reputation through his many lectures, over 35 books, and several hymns. He was a promulgator of what became known as the "Social Gospel." Like Walter Rauschenbusch, Josiah Strong, and Richard Ely, he taught that middle-class Christians must take responsibility for alleviating the material problems resulting from industrialization and urbanization. Gladden exhorted his audience to work for the salvation of society and thus achieve the Kingdom of Heaven on earth.

Placing particular emphasis on brotherhood and cooperation, Gladden worked to promote understanding between workers and employers, blacks and whites, Protestants and Catholics. In Massachusetts, he had mediated between labor and management. As labor and economics issues continued to concern him, he became increasingly supportive of unions—although never of socialism. In Columbus, whose population had nearly tripled from 1870 to 1880, Gladden became involved in urban reform. He supported municipal ownership of public services, home rule, and an end to corrupt government, which he saw as a ubiquitous urban evil. He helped found the National Municipal League in 1894 and served as an independent alderman on the Columbus City Council from 1900 to 1902.

Beginning in the 1870s, Gladden had participated in the American Missionary Association, working with freedmen in the South. His interest in racial reform intensified after he met W. E. B. Du Bois in 1903. A strong supporter of Protestant ecumenism, Gladden helped found the Federal Council of Churches in 1908, endorsing its landmark Social Creed, which codified the churches' role as agents for social change as well as spiritual comfort. Gladden's inclusiveness extended to Unitarians, Jews, and Catholics; Notre Dame University gave him an honorary degree in 1905.

The Social Gospel movement peaked in the second decade of the 20th century as its proponents joined with secular reformers to bring about social justice through legislation and social service. In 1914 Gladden was, predictably, opposed to entering World War I, but he eventually came to support the American war effort. He died before postwar disillusionment and Protestant fundamentalism began to erode the effects of the Social Gospel.

—*Janet C. Olson*

See also Social Gospel

Further Readings and References

Dorn, J. (1967). *Washington Gladden: A prophet of the social gospel.* Columbus: Ohio State University Press.
Gladden, W. (1909). *Recollections.* Boston: Houghton Mifflin.

GOLDEN GATE PARK

Golden Gate Park is a 1,017-acre urban park located on reclaimed sand dunes in the western section of San Francisco. The park consists of three major elements—an expansive forest, extensive open meadows, and a connecting system of curvilinear paths and roads. Numerous gardens, lakes, and recreational features are located throughout as well. Golden Gate Park was developed beginning in 1871 from an original plan by William Hammond Hall. It was designed as a picturesque park landscape, influenced by the work of the preeminent landscape designer of the period, Frederick Law Olmsted, Sr., with whom Hall had an active correspondence. Olmsted had originally declared the project impossible due to wind and soil conditions.

In 1870, Hall surveyed the area for the new park, which stretches 3.5 miles (by 0.5 miles wide) from the center of the city west to the Pacific Ocean, with a narrow 0.75-mile-long panhandle extension on the eastern end. The site was located in the Outside Lands, an area consisting primarily of wind-raked sand dunes that had only recently been annexed to the City of San Francisco.

Hall was appointed park engineer and superintendent in 1871. Informed by a study of Olmsted's work, as well as European beach-reclamation techniques, his plan incorporated the existing topography, featuring some low rock hills and ridges as well as slight depressions among the prevailing sand dunes. Initial plantings of lupine seed sown with fast-growing barley began to stabilize the dunes and were followed by a succession of grasses, then shrubs, and finally tree seedlings. Massive amounts of topsoil and manure were imported, a park nursery established, a large underlying aquifer tapped for irrigation, and an elaborate distribution system constructed. Eventually, two windmills, the Dutch Windmill (1902) and the Murphy Windmill (1905), located at the far western edge of the park, would pump water to a reservoir atop Strawberry Hill, the central high point, from where it was fed throughout the park. Hall's design exaggerated the natural terrain by concentrating trees on higher ground, thus sheltering and helping to define the valleys, which became open meadows. Topography also played a role in the location of the lakes, several of which were sited in low areas that were already seasonal ponds. These lakes were also components of the irrigation system. In the first few years of park development, much of the area had been reclaimed and planted with seedlings that would become its forest, primarily Monterey pine, Monterey cypress, and eucalyptus. This introduced evergreen forest contrasted with the wooded areas of major urban parks in the eastern states, which consist largely of native deciduous trees. A major reforestation effort began in 1980, as the original plantings reached advanced age.

Hall's master plan concentrated recreational facilities in the eastern portion of about 270 acres. The high Victorian-style wood and glass Conservatory of Flowers (1878) was the park's first building. In 1882, the first bandstand was constructed in Conservatory Valley, providing a site for band music concerts, a popular entertainment in the period before recorded music. In 1889, the Children's Quarter, consisting of a playground, a carousel, and the Sharon Building, a canteen for children and their mothers, was completed as the first area of a public park in the United States dedicated to children. In the 1890s, active sports facilities appeared. The Recreation Grounds (Big Rec

baseball diamonds) were added in 1893, followed by tennis courts in 1894. Bicycling was becoming popular at the time, and the park's first bicycle path, which paralleled the main carriage drive, was constructed in 1896. The Stow Lake Boathouse provided rowboats for visitors beginning in 1894. The Mid-Winter Fair of 1894, an international exposition intended to highlight San Francisco's mild climate, was held in the park. It resulted in the creation of the Music Concourse and deYoung Museum of Art, which along with the California Academy of Sciences now form the core of the park's cultural center. The Japanese Tea Garden, another legacy of the fair, is the oldest of its kind in the United States.

An extensive paved path and unpaved trail system provides circulation for bicyclists and pedestrians to almost every part of the park. Paved paths were constructed of asphalt. Many of the unpaved trails were constructed of distinctive "red rock" crushed gravel. The grade separation between roads and paths, employed by Olmsted in Central Park, was also used in Golden Gate Park, primarily in the more developed eastern end. Most of the vehicular roads were graded and completed within the park's first 20 years, and the system is largely unchanged today. They were designed as curving thoroughfares providing an ever-changing series of vistas as one moves through the park. The series of meadows created by the forest plantings provide the main open spaces and contribute to the changing vistas. The oldest part of the circulation system, now a pedestrian path, was originally known as "The Avenue" and built as a curving carriageway down the center of the eastern panhandle. Eucalyptus plantings protected early carriage travelers from the strong west winds.

Golden Gate Park was conceived as a naturalistic pleasure ground park to provide a sylvan retreat from urban pressures for citizens of all classes. The edges of the park were particularly densely planted to reinforce the bucolic illusion by blocking out views of the city. This created a landscape design that successfully imitated nature and was inward looking. The advent of the park spurred nearby development, one of the prime purposes of the city fathers for locating it in the Outside Lands, and the parkland is now surrounded on three sides by dense urban fabric.

Golden Gate Park was the first application of Olmsted's naturalistic landscape park design theories in the western United States. These principles, adapted to the unique environment of San Francisco, resulted in a park quite unlike its eastern counterparts. It was also the first park to be created on reclaimed land that was formerly barren and unwelcoming, resulting in an unprecedented landscape transformation. Golden Gate Park was important in advancing the field of park design by successfully integrating active recreation features into the Romantic landscape. The park was seen not just as an urban amenity but as a force for social improvement and a benefit to the health of citizens. It helped define what urban parks should be and, in the larger context, helped define the role of parks in urban planning.

Many amenities have been added over the years without violating Hall's original scheme. These include Kezar Sports Stadium and Gymnasium, the Strybing Arboretum, lawn bowling facilities, handball courts, a polo stadium, riding stables, an archery range, a fly-casting pool, a model boat pond, statuary, and monumental entrance gates. The park today is a mature creation that remains remarkably true to its original vision.

—Tim Kelly
—Douglas Nelson

Further Readings and References

Clary, R. H. (1984). *The making of Golden Gate Park: The early years 1865–1906.* San Francisco: Don't Call It Frisco Press.

Clary, R. H. (1987). *The making of Golden Gate Park: The growing years 1906–1950.* San Francisco: Don't Call It Frisco Press.

Doss, M. P. (1978). *Golden Gate Park at your feet.* San Rafael, CA: Presidio Press.

GREAT DEPRESSION AND CITIES

In the Great Depression, unemployment rates reached a high of 24.9 percent in 1933, accompanied by a fall in gross national product (GNP) of 29 percent from 1929 to 1933. Even after a modest economic recovery from 1935 to 1937, the economy sank again, with an unemployment rate persistently in the high teens from 1937 to the outbreak of World War II. Cities, home of American industry, were the geographic locations for much of the economic tumult of the 1930s. While the economies of a few cities weathered the economic storm, the Great Depression hit most cities—particularly the industrial cities of the Northeast and Midwest—very hard, ending the era of relative prosperity for metropolitan areas that had marked the opening decades of the 20th century.

The 1920s had been a period of growth for the cities. Migrants from rural America flocked to the great metropolises to take industrial jobs, as well as find employment in the retail and service industries as the nation's consumer markets flourished. Los Angeles, for example, powered by the glamour of the film industry and its good climate, ranked among the fastest growing metropolitan areas of the country, as did the core industrial cities of Akron, Ohio, and Detroit, Michigan, as well as resort towns like Miami, Florida. However, in the late 1920s, the national economy stuttered; the economy collapsed after the stock market crash in October 1929.

Urban governments in the 1930s were not designed to manage the vicious cycle of economic distress. In the moribund marketplace, surpluses of goods mounted. Industry responded by cutting production and firing workers or cutting shifts for hourly employees. Without cash, workers and small businessmen could not cover the mortgage or the rent. Foreclosures and evictions resulted. Municipal governments were particularly vulnerable to foreclosures since most were dependent on property taxes for revenue. Their problem was made worse by the fact that the same residents who could not pay their property taxes required food, shelter, and employment that local governments were often unable to provide. Only a handful of cities had mature government social services agencies to assist the unemployed and their families. The economic earthquake often cracked the façade of order and civility, revealing the architecture of power politics in the cities.

In most cities, the Great Depression revealed the dominance of business interests. Private, not public, power was the first to respond to the humanitarian crisis. The private sector in Philadelphia, for example, formed the Philadelphia Committee for Unemployment Relief to help needy families. In Pittsburgh, the Allegheny County Emergency Association organized big business for a works program of public improvements. Across many communities, the National Association of Community Chests and Councils coordinated a network of local affiliates in 174 cities to raise $83 million for relief. But the role of business in urban affairs was not uniformly benevolent. Bankers forced the municipal governments of

New York and Detroit to adopt austerity measures or face the risk of being locked out of the bond market. In many conservative cities, such Houston, Denver, and Cincinnati, local governments enforced austerity budgets with the approval of local businesses and homeowners.

However, for urban voters in cities with radical and progressive traditions, the Great Depression shifted political orientations to the left. With the support of minority voters, Frank Murphy won the mayoral election in Detroit, promising to spur government to take action to help the unemployed. Leftist mayors with ties to socialist and labor parties held power in Minneapolis, Milwaukee, and New York for much of the 1930s.

President Herbert Hoover, whose term spanned the early years of the Great Depression, had tried to organize private charity to help citizens ride out the depression and offered some federal aid for relief. But Hoover's conservative political commitments and philosophy would not allow for an expansive federal role in domestic politics. Hoover's successor, Franklin D. Roosevelt, although elected with a strong surge of support from the industrial cities, was not a natural advocate for urban interests. FDR romanticized the virtues of the country life, and as a former governor, believed in states' rights. President Roosevelt also promised the nation that he would set out on an economizing course of action to end the Great Depression. But the weight of pressing urban problems, and the political reality of an electoral coalition built on a foundation of urban votes, forced the president's hand.

In an attempt to pump the economy and provide jobs for the industrial unemployed, the federal government gave grants and loans to city governments for construction projects. Through some of the alphabet soup federal agencies such as the Public Works Administration, the Civil Works Administration, and the Works Progress Administration, thousands of post offices, schools, and public recreation facilities were built or refurbished. The more dramatic contributions to the urban landscape and architecture include San Francisco's Golden Gate Bridge, Los Angeles's Federal Courthouse, and Miami's Orange Bowl. More broadly, regional development carried out through electrification and irrigation projects in the West and South opened those regions of the county to rapid urbanization in the decades after World War II.

The Great Depression set the stage for the emergence of exemplary political leadership. Urban leaders in the 1930s set the bar for their successors. First among them was Fiorello La Guardia, mayor of New York from 1934 to 1945. Although nominally a Republican, La Guardia established himself as a firm supporter of New Deal economic intervention in urban economies. La Guardia shared with President Roosevelt an antipathy toward regular Democrats in New York City linked with Tammany Hall and the city's other county organizations. The La Guardia-Roosevelt alliance made New York the premier New Deal city. Public works money poured into the city, transforming the landscape with vast projects such as the Triborough Bridge and an expansive airport in Queens that would later be renamed in honor of La Guardia. Other major figures among the big-city mayors in this era include Frank Murphy of Detroit, who would go on to become U.S. Attorney General; Mayor Michael Curley, the legendary "rascal king" of Boston; Socialist Party member and Milwaukee Mayor Daniel Hoan; and Chicago Mayor Edward Kelly.

The big-city mayors established a formal presence in Washington in the 1930s with the creation of the U.S. Conference of Mayors (USCM). The USCM lobbied Congress and the executive branch to send federal aid directly to the cities. The organization also established a special relationship with Harry Hopkins, Roosevelt's close aide, who among his roles administered the Works Progress Administration (WPA) in the late 1930s, as well as works programs such as the Federal Emergency Relief Administration (FERA). Hopkins's natural sympathies were with the mayors, since big-city leaders were more liberal than the governors and state legislatures, and the mayors where more disposed to deliver federal funds into the pockets of those in need. Hopkins steered aid to support a handful of big-city mayors in critical swing states to build a more formidable New Deal coalition. One of the long-standing myths of this era is that New Deal welfare programs made big-city political machines obsolete, but this is clearly not the case. The Democratic Party machine was strengthened in cities such as Chicago, Pittsburgh, and Jersey City. While the national social welfare programs spawned in the Great Depression would eventually free urban voters from having to turn to local machine politicians for help, Democratic Party machine politics persisted—indeed flourished—in cities such as Albany, Pittsburgh, Cleveland, and Baltimore with the support of the Roosevelt administration's policies.

Federal action in the housing field in the 1930s transformed the cities. Early New Deal policy subsidized and regulated the mortgage market. This had the immediate effect of stopping widespread foreclosures of homes, which stabilized municipal budgets. But the federal government also established a uniform code of insurance risk that downgraded urban properties. This would have the long-term effect of depriving cities of construction capital and accelerating the postwar movement toward the suburbs. The federal government, with the passage of the 1937 Housing Act, also started entering into partnership with local governments to construct public housing.

The Great Depression changed American cities in new ways. In previous decades, periods of urban transitions were driven by the changes wrought by economic growth. In the 1930s, cities were clearly transformed, but by the dynamics of the public sector, not the private. The economic crisis modernized many city governments. City governments expanded their roles as they implemented social welfare and economic development policies with the federal aid they received. Many layers of single-purpose governments and special authorities were created to administer much of the new public works and services. The Great Depression was also a period of political transformation for the cities. Urban voters became the anchor of the Democratic Party's New Deal coalition, a role they would serve in future decades.

—*Richard Flanagan*

See also New Deal: Urban Policy

Further Readings and References

Adams, H. (1977). *Harry Hopkins*. New York: Putnam.

Erie, S. (1988). *Rainbow's end: Irish-Americans and the dilemmas of machine politics, 1840–1985*. Berkeley: University of California Press.

Flanagan, R. M. (1999). Roosevelt, mayors and the New Deal regime: The origins of intergovernmental lobbying and administration. *Polity, 21*(3), 415–450.

Jackson, K. (1985). *The crabgrass frontier: The suburbanization of the United States*. New York: Oxford University Press.

Kessner, T. (1989). *Fiorello H. La Guardia and the making of modern New York*. New York: McGraw-Hill.

Leuchtenburg, W. (1963). *Franklin D. Roosevelt and the New Deal*. New York: Harper & Row.

McKelvey, B. (1968). *The emergence of metropolitan America, 1915–1966*. New Brunswick, NJ: Rutgers University Press.

GREENBELT TOWNS

Begun in 1935 through the New Deal's Resettlement Administration (RA), Greenbelt towns were designed to offer alternative suburban environments for working-class families residing in America's deteriorating and congested inner cities. Headed by Undersecretary of Agriculture Rexford G. Tugwell, a Columbia professor of economics and social reformer, the RA operated the program with the goals of providing construction jobs for unemployed workers, demonstrating more appropriate design guidelines to create a better quality of life, and incorporating a social component realized in part through cooperative ventures. Design principles integrated Ebenezer Howard's model of a garden city and the vision of the Regional Planning Association of America (RPAA) as implemented in the partially completed town of Radburn, New Jersey. Still, each of the town site designs—Greenbrook, New Jersey, which was never developed; Greenbelt, Maryland; Greenhills, Ohio; and Greendale, Wisconsin—reflected the distinct signature of the team assigned to it. Detractors considered the program social engineering and maintained that the government competed unfairly with private sector developers. Thus the program only lasted 18 months before legal challenges led to the decision to terminate it. By 1954, after a series of congressional hearings, the federal government had divested itself of all greenbelt town property. While the program never resulted in the widespread town-building movement anticipated at its outset, it did attract notable planners, engineers, and architects who implemented innovations in design and community building.

Established by executive order in 1935 and funded by the Emergency Relief Appropriation Act, the Greenbelt Town Program was administered by the RA through its Suburban Resettlement Division headed by John Lansill. In addition to this new suburban town building program, the RA oversaw several existing rural programs created under the Industrial Recovery Act of 1933 to improve conditions for farmers through refinancing and rehabilitating their farmsteads or providing opportunities for resettlement to more appropriate farming sites. As originally conceived, the Greenbelt Town Program would provide work relief, offer a model of community development, and develop housing for lower income families.

In order to determine the best location for these new communities, approximately a hundred urban areas were surveyed to identify those with a combination of consistent economic and population expansion, diverse industries offering sound wages and engaging in progressive labor practices, and a critical need for housing. Within the four urban areas that were ultimately chosen, town sites were identified based on their proximity to employment centers and on natural features such as topography, soils, and characteristics that would foster the combination of development, recreational, agricultural, and open spaces envisioned for each community.

Lansill worked with five consultants, Clarence Stein, Henry Wright, Tracy Augur, Russell Van Nest Black, and Earle Draper, the first four of whom were RPAA members. They functioned as general advisers and drafted studies such as cost analyses to determine short- and long-term financial outcomes associated with development and management of the towns. Frederick Bigger, also associated with the RPAA, was retained as chief of planning for the program and oversaw the daily work of the teams. At Greenbelt, near Washington, D.C., Hale Walker served as town planner and Reginald Wadsworth and Douglas Ellington as principal architects; at Greenhills, near Cincinnati, Justin Hartzog and William Strong served as town planners and Roland Wank and G. Frank Cordner as principal architects; at Greendale, near Milwaukee, Jacob Crane and Elbert Peets served as town planners and Harry Bentley and Walter Thomas as principal architects; and finally, at Greenbrook, New Jersey, near New Brunswick, town planners Henry Wright and Allan Kamstra worked with architects Albert Mayer and Henry Churchill.

Controversy surrounded the program practically from the beginning, in part due to the high cost associated with relief workers as calculated on a per-unit basis, particularly when the original number of proposed units decreased. Federal officials acknowledged that costs were probably one third higher because workers were intentionally engaged in more intensive labor due to the program's goal to provide jobs. Other criticisms focused on more fundamental concerns about the role of government in relation to the private market. Due to a lawsuit brought by an owner of extensive property and town officials in Bound Brook, New Jersey, an injunction in 1936 terminated all work on Greenbrook. The lawsuit argued that the need for public services would result in an undue hardship on nearby communities, particularly since the greenbelt town would not contribute to the local tax base. More broadly, the prosecuting attorneys argued that the entire Greenbelt Town Program, specifically the development of model communities by the federal government, represented an unconstitutional exercise of legislative powers. The Circuit Court of the District of Columbia agreed, though the United States Attorney General determined that the court's ruling applied only to Greenbrook and that development could continue on the three remaining towns. Still, no further appropriations were provided to the program, which was transferred in 1937 to the RA's successor agency, the Farm Security Administration.

While each of the three towns that were ultimately developed had a distinct design, common principles guided their development. These included implementation of large-scale master planning; retention of the project under single ownership to ensure quality, minimize operating costs, and diminish speculation; design that was responsive to the natural environment; and establishment of a greenbelt to accommodate community gardens, recreation, open space, and existing farmsteads and to limit development, buffer the community from adjacent inappropriate uses, and protect land values. In addition to these garden city principles, a 1936 RA publication outlined several design innovations featured in the partially completed new town of Radburn that planners intended to apply in the greenbelt communities. These included the use of superblocks with clustered groups of housing oriented toward interior interconnected parks, a hierarchical street system to accommodate through and local traffic, separation of the pedestrian and the automobile, and integration of a town center with community facilities that included a school, meeting place, and shopping within walking distance of the residential areas. With their proximity to large employment centers, these towns never were truly autonomous garden cities, primarily because they failed to include significant industrial sites for employment within their borders.

Upon completion of construction, the selection criteria and large pool of applicants, particularly at Greenbelt, ensured an engaged citizenry, though the goal to emulate the sociodemographic characteristics of nearby municipalities did not extend to race. The initial working-class residents were all white. With its homes entirely rented by the fall of 1938, Greenbelt had a total of 885 units, primarily in garden apartments (306) and row houses (574) with five additional detached, single-family units. Probably the best example of coordinated community building, the town included a cooperative store and the Citizens Association, which facilitated community organizing. Incorporated in 1937, Greenbelt, like the other two towns, functioned under the manager-council form of government, using payments in lieu of taxes to fund public services including those offered by the county and state. Greenbelt also most closely adhered to the superblock form of development. At Greenhills, which was incorporated in 1938, a total of 676 units were completed, with 24 detached homes, 420 row houses, 80 duplexes, and 152 garden apartments. Also incorporated in 1938, Greendale as initially completed included the largest number of detached dwellings (274) in addition to 208 row houses and 90 duplexes. Though each community contained considerable acreage for expansion, only Greenbelt accommodated new development within the first 10 years—1,000 apartment units for defense workers, completed in 1941. Designed to continue the existing superblock plan, the housing was disconnected from the rest of Greenbelt and not of the same quality.

In 1949, Congress passed Public Law 65 outlining the federal government's intent to completely divest itself of the three towns, then being managed by the Public Housing Authority. The primary concerns of the program's supporters included maintaining the greenbelts, cooperative initiatives, and community ownership of land. While these advocates negotiated with lawmakers to include a right of first refusal to cooperative nonprofit housing groups representing current tenants or veterans, and while the federal government did sell significant sections of the greenbelt areas in each community to local park and recreation departments, the law did not require adherence to an overall master plan. Thus, consistency with existing development patterns was not ensured. By 1954, the Public Housing Authority had completed divestment with the only significant sale of units (1,635) for cooperative ownership occurring at Greenbelt. By the 1960s, major highways cut through the town sites and speculation had resulted in significant increases in property values and divergent development patterns.

—*Kristin Larsen*

See also Garden Cities; Howard, Ebenezer; New Towns; Regional Planning Association of America; Stein, Clarence S.; Tugwell, Rexford Guy; Wright, Henry

Further Readings and References

Arnold, J. L. (1971). *The New Deal in the suburbs: A history of the Greenbelt Town Program, 1935–1954.* Columbus: Ohio State University Press.

Knepper, C. D. (2001). *Greenbelt, Maryland: A living legacy of the New Deal.* Baltimore: Johns Hopkins University Press.

Mayer, A. (1968). *Greenbelt towns revisited.* Washington, DC: National Association of Housing and Redevelopment Officials.

Stein, C. (1957). *Toward new towns for America.* Cambridge, MA: MIT Press.

GREENWICH VILLAGE, NEW YORK

Originally settled in 1644 by 11 African American men, formerly indentured servants, Greenwich Village largely remained a rural area throughout the 17th and 18th centuries. As a result of a series of urban epidemics—in which thousands from elsewhere in Manhattan fled to the area—and the general expansion of New York City, the Village was incorporated into Manhattan in the course of the 19th century. With real estate prices plummeting at the turn of the 20th century, the middle and upper classes moved north of the Village, whereas many immigrant families moved into Greenwich Village. They were soon to be accompanied by individuals representing the Village's most famous and cherished image: the bohemian. From the 1900s on, the public's vision of Greenwich Village would be dominated by the area's apparent difference from mainstream U.S. American culture.

The idea of *difference* resulting from the relative isolation of the Village from the rest of New York City was always prominent in the rhetoric of outsiders as well as Villagers. However, Greenwich Village has always depended on the interaction with the larger metropolis and the nation for its construction of identity. When other parts of Manhattan were plagued by a series of epidemics in the early 19th century, it was to Greenwich Village that people fled, increasing its population fourfold between 1825 and 1840. This partly coincided with New York City's general expansion north and the imposition of a rigorous grid system on the streets of Manhattan. Greenwich Village managed to avoid this imposition of rationalization and thus remained an idiosyncratic area of irregularity and Old World charm within a modern administrative metropolis. The powerful idea of *difference* was born, but it was a concept that foreshadowed a more general all-encompassing shift: the creation of distinct residential areas. With downtown Manhattan transforming into a high-intensity commercial district, the middle and upper classes relocated to the quieter areas in the north. This reorganization of urban space not only produced the typically modern separation of work and residence; it was also bound up with the developing class system, since many of the working class remained downtown, thus spatially fixing social difference.

In the first decades of the 19th century, a thriving African American community lived in Greenwich Village: African Americans operated the Grove Theater at the corner of Bleecker and Mercer streets in the 1820s, black musicians played in theaters along Houston Street, ministers founded independent black congregations, and politically oriented newspapers such as *The Colored American, The Rights of All,* and *Freedom's Journal* were published. However, with the rising real estate prices as a result of the Village's transformation into a fashionable residential area, as well as racial conflict between working-class blacks and whites, many African Americans abandoned the area and moved to districts such as Harlem.

By the mid-19th century, Greenwich Village was firmly established as a residential area for affluent whites. Painters and other artists took residence in the University Building (1835–1894), since it was here that they could come to know possible patrons and other influential people. Others rented rooms at the Tenth Street Studios at West Tenth Street, which was the first structure in the United States specifically designed as a studio building. Important writers such as Mark Twain, Walt Whitman, Tom Paine, and Henry James also left their mark on the Village through their lives and literature. In particular, James used the Village setting in his work and was partly responsible for creating its legendary status in the first place through his 1881 novel *Washington Square.* Many of these and other artists frequented Pfaff's, a beer cellar just north of Bleecker Street. Managed by Henry Clapp, who also founded the literary journal *The Saturday Press,* the café was clearly inspired by bohemian life in Paris.

At the end of the 19th century, many of the richer inhabitants had already moved north in order to escape the further expansion of New York City. This led to a general decline in real estate values in the Village, which in turn proved attractive to many immigrants. It was this combination of low rents and dynamic ethnic life that also attracted the young people from all over the nation who became the Village's most famous export product: the bohemian. Similar to the Harlem Renaissance that peaked in the 1920s, the public emergence of the bohemian in Greenwich Village was directly related to the increasing penetration of mass culture in daily life as well as New York's central role as a publishing and entertainment center in the United States. Located in one of the major hubs of the country, many artists were able to find outlets for their work that at once spoke to citywide as well as national audiences. The public image of the bohemian, therefore, was above all the result of a dialogue between the Village artists and the local and national press and publics. On both sides, its appropriation enabled the imagination of a more human yet transgressive and exciting alternative to the constraints of the increasingly bureaucratized everyday life.

Village bohemianism in the early 20th century was characterized by a unique fusion of politics and art. The publication of *The Masses* between 1912 and 1917 was one of the clearest examples of this original fusion. Directed by a group of staff writers and the poet and philosophy instructor Max Eastman, the magazine became a forum for radical left-wing criticism. Political journalism was combined with artistic and literary experiments, thereby creating an explosive—if somewhat incoherent—mix of politics and aesthetics. These intellectual and political debates were, however, increasingly overshadowed by the entertainment factor of Greenwich Village. Certainly, most prewar intellectuals performed their bohemian role with considerable flair as well, and within the Village there had emerged a network of tearooms and restaurants dedicated to this alternative lifestyle. However, starting around the end of World War I, the celebration of this bohemian lifestyle attracted more and more outsiders and led to the transformation of Greenwich Village into a nightlife zone. There were a number of reasons for this shift. The extension of Sixth and Seventh Avenues south of the Village and the widening of these streets greatly improved the flow of transport to downtown Manhattan and, by doing so, destroyed the cherished illusion of the Village as a somewhat isolated backwater. It also increased the presence of tourists. Another reason was that quite a number of Villagers actually supported this tourist invasion. Already in 1914, for example, Guido Bruno opened his Garrett at 58 Washington

Square South, which incorporated an art gallery, lecture hall, printing house, press agency, and information office, almost purely dedicated to the tourists who arrived at Washington Square. Others specialized in guidebooks, maps, and picture postcards, sold bohemian clothing, or organized sightseeing tours. Finally, Prohibition played an important role, since it gave the Village the reputation of a place where one could still get a drink: either in the Italian restaurants with their homemade wine or in the many cabarets and speakeasies that offered the combination of exotic entertainment and alcohol.

Nevertheless, despite this increasing commercialization, the Village has usually managed to accommodate various alternative lifestyles and experimental artistic endeavors. For one thing, many lesbians and gays have made Greenwich Village their home throughout the 20th and into the 21st century. Christopher Street and the Stonewall Riots in 1969 are the most powerful landmarks in this regard, but gays and lesbians have been publicly visible in the Village since the days of the balls at Webster Hall in the 1910s and 1920s. Also, without the Provincetown Players and the Washington Square Players in this formative period, experimental theater in New York would have certainly evolved differently. The success of these groups did much to associate the Village with theater and paved the way for later experiments such as Erwin Piscator's Dramatic Workshop in the 1940s and the Living Theatre and emergence of the off-Broadway scene in the 1950s. Experimental work was also produced in other artistic fields: John Cage and the Merce Cunningham Dance Company collaborated on experimental dance pieces; jazz as well as folk music was being redeveloped at Max Gordon's Village Vanguard; and many of the abstract expressionists exhibited their works in numerous galleries. At the same time, although all of these activities took place in Greenwich Village, by the end of the 20th century it was no longer possible to speak of the Village bohemian in a communal sense. Artists no longer identified themselves as bohemians, but increasingly reacted to the opinions of their own small group of acquaintances as well as global discourses. Finally, living in this area became increasingly expensive and out of reach for the overwhelming majority of the immigrants and artists that constituted the population of the Village in the early 20th century.

—*Bas van Heur*

Further Readings and References

Banes, S. (1993). *Greenwich Village 1963: Avant-garde performance and the effervescent body.* Durham, NC: Duke University Press.

Beard, R., & Cohen Berlowitz, L. (1993). *Greenwich Village: Culture and counterculture.* New Brunswick, NJ: Rutgers University Press.

McFarland, G. W. (2001). *Inside Greenwich Village: A New York City neighborhood, 1898–1918.* Amherst: University of Massachusetts Press.

Ware, C. F. (1994). *Greenwich Village, 1920–1930: A comment on American civilization in the post-war years.* Berkeley: University of California Press.

GRID PATTERN

A settlement design widely adopted in the Americas, the grid is generally characterized by a rectilinear matrix of streets dividing the landscape into standardized blocks that are then further subdivided into individual parcels. The English word *grid* is an abbreviation of *gridiron,* which in the context of urban planning refers to an orthogonal or rectangular street pattern. Many grids are structured around two central "baselines" that can each serve as a starting point for the sequential numbering of streets and houses. Depending on the distance between streets and on the geographical context, grids have come in different shapes (for example, rectangular or square) and sizes (for example, "open" grids that may extend equally in all directions as compared to "closed" grids that are confined by some barrier, such as topography or a walled enclosure). Various open spaces for squares, plazas, parks, and public buildings have often been incorporated into the general layout of grid plans in the Americas.

Pre-Columbian Grid Designs and the Spanish Colonial Grid

Over a century before European contact, the Aztec city of Tenochtitlán was laid out in a cross-axial formation, and although there is evidence that the original city contained a central plaza, the precise geometric pattern of the pre-Hispanic street system remains a subject of debate. Some scholars believe that when the Spanish conquered the Aztec Empire in the 1520s they built Mexico City upon the ruins of

Tenochtitlán in conformity with an original grid layout, whereas others have disputed this claim.

During the mid-15th century the Incas utilized grid-like patterns to lay out settlements such as Chucuito, Hatunqolla, Paucarqolla, and Ollantaytambo. There is also evidence suggesting that the Spanish grid plan of Puebla (1533) in what is now east-central Mexico was, in part, influenced by the design of the neighboring Aztec settlement of Cholula.

Although numerous early Spanish settlements in the Americas were based on the grid pattern—such as Santo Domingo (1496) in the Caribbean and Mérida in the Yucatán (1541)—it was not until Phillip II of Spain established the "Laws of the Indies" in 1573 that the grid became codified as the standard design of Spanish colonial settlements. These royal instructions were based upon the architectural writings of Vitruvius (70–25 BCE) and incorporated a rectangular plaza as part of the grid layout. The four corners of the plaza were to be oriented toward the cardinal directions, and various other open spaces were allocated for a cathedral, palace, town hall, and custom-house.

Spanish towns, or *pueblos,* were established in what is now the United States along the Gulf of Mexico as well as in the Southwest and California. Cities such as San Antonio, Texas, and Pensacola, Florida, have their origins in Spanish colonial grid designs laid out according to the Laws of the Indies.

Gridiron Cities in a Checkerboard Landscape

When the English established colonies in North America, they were not required to follow a standardized protocol for settlement design comparable to the Laws of the Indies. Nevertheless, the grid pattern was utilized for various town plans as early as the 17th century. One of the first English colonial grid plans was that of New Haven, Connecticut (1638). Philadelphia was laid out as a grid in 1682 and later became a model for other cities. The Philadelphia plan consisted of two perpendicular axes intersecting in a central square, with streets numbered along one axis and named after different tree species along the other. Each quarter of the city was to also have a smaller square, in part to prevent the spread of fires.

During the first half of the 18th century, southern cities such as Savannah, Georgia (1733), and Charleston, South Carolina (1739), were designed according to the principles of orthogonal planning. After the Revolutionary War, the Continental Congress passed the Land Ordinance of 1785, dividing much of the country west of the Ohio River into a grid of square townships that were each 6 miles to a side and further subdivided into 36 individual sections. This "checkerboard" layout provided a standardized system of spatial organization for westward expansion and later influenced the adoption of the Dominion Land Survey (1871) in Canada as well.

Thomas Jefferson was one of the leading proponents of the Land Ordinance of 1785, and when it came to designing the national capital in Washington, D.C., he proposed a gridiron plan. Jefferson's proposal was not adopted, but the official plan designed by Pierre Charles L'Enfant in 1791 combined a grid layout with the Baroque tradition of leading diagonal avenues to monumental sites. The plan divided the city into four quadrants (NE, NW, SE, SW) by two main axes, with north-south streets numbered and east-west streets lettered consecutively. Overlaid upon the grid were numerous diagonal avenues named after the states of the Union. In fact, Washington was the first city in the United States to use the French word *avenue* as a street designation, and this practice was later adopted by other cities such as New York.

In 1785, and a decade later in 1796, the Common Lands of New York City were divided into rectangular parcels, but it was not until 1811 that the city formally adopted the grid plan as the basis of urban expansion for the entire city north of what is now approximately Houston Street (excluding Greenwich Village). Urban growth accelerated rapidly with the rise of industrialization, and many 19th-century cities and towns in the United States and Canada adopted the grid plan. The grid pattern was commonly used when laying out railroad towns, and major cities such as Chicago (1830) and San Francisco (1839) embraced the utilitarian gridiron. San Francisco's grid, in particular, stands out from the rest, because it was adapted to a site of considerable topographic variation. If the grid was often utilized as a tool for real estate speculation, it was also used to plan religious communities, with Salt Lake City (1847), designed by the Mormons, being a prime example. While not all U.S. cities are laid out as grids, the United States has acquired an international reputation as a country of gridiron cities in a checkerboard landscape.

Conflicting Interpretations of the Grid

Scholars of American urban history and geography continue to debate the merits and flaws of the grid pattern as a mode of spatial organization. Some argue that the grid symbolizes the "democratic spirit" of America, whereas others maintain that the grid was an instrument of real estate speculation and the capitalist commodification of the landscape. A number of scholars, however, contend that the grid has served *multiple* purposes and, thus, that one should beware of one-sided, reductionistic explanations. When viewed from a cross-cultural perspective, these scholars argue, it becomes evident that the grid has been appropriated by both democratic and totalitarian regimes on the one hand, as well as under capitalist and socialist economic systems on the other. In most cases, however, the grid served as a means of disciplining mobility by structuring spatial interaction according to the logic of the perpendicular. While the debate over the meanings and functions of the grid continues, the search for the "origin" of the grid plan has lost its appeal for many. The traditional view in the West has been that Hippodamus of Miletus (5th century BCE) was the "inventor" of the first true grid plan. Yet, few contemporary scholars accept that the grid has only one true origin or inventor, and it is generally recognized that the grid emerged in multiple cultural contexts across the world throughout the course of human history.

—*Reuben Skye Rose-Redwood*

Further Readings and References

Gasparini, G. (1993). The pre-Hispanic grid system: The urban shape of conquest and territorial organization. In R. Bennett (Ed.), *Settlement in the Americas: Cross-cultural perspectives* (pp. 78–109). Newark: University of Delaware Press.

Johnson, H. B. (1976). *Order upon the land: The U.S. rectangular land survey and the Upper Mississippi country.* New York: Oxford University Press.

Reps, J. (1965). *The making of urban America: A history of city planning in the United States.* Princeton, NJ: Princeton University Press.

Spann, E. (1988). The greatest grid: The New York plan of 1811. In D. Schaffer (Ed.), *Two centuries of American planning* (pp. 11–39). Baltimore: Johns Hopkins University Press.

GUN USE AND CONTROL

There has long been an urban dimension to gun use and control in the United States, especially in regard to handguns. Gun ownership, especially of rifles and shotguns, tends to be concentrated in rural areas, but handguns and assault weapons—military-appearing, semiautomatic firearms—account for much gun ownership and use in urban areas. Since the 1960s, especially, guns have proliferated in America's inner cities, leading to a rise in gun violence of which young minority males are the chief perpetrators and victims. The title of Geoffrey Canada's 1995 memoir of growing up in New York City, *Fist, Stick, Knife, Gun,* recapitulates the increasing lethality of weapons used by young men in the inner city. Gun control initiatives in urban areas have been tied to the recent upsurges in violence in America's cities and to the increasing availability of firearms. For example, in 2005, Boston developed new policing initiatives to attempt to deal with an upsurge in gun violence.

City-based efforts at gun control in the United States are not new but have been tied to concerns about urban crime dating back to the 19th century. Films and television present an image of ubiquitous guns and widespread gun use in the Old West, but laws regulating and often prohibiting the carrying of weapons were among the first passed in new western towns. In the 20th century, one of the earliest gun control laws was the Sullivan Act, passed in New York State in 1911, but clearly aimed at New York City. This law gave police chiefs discretion to issue gun permits, a discretion they usually exercised to prevent immigrants from owning firearms. The law, which strictly limits the right of anyone to carry a concealed handgun, is seen by many scholars as a xenophobic response to an influx of immigrants, especially Italians, into the city. The National Firearms Act (NFA) of 1934, the first comprehensive federal gun law, was a reaction to widespread urban mob violence and the use of machine guns in that violence. The act regulated machine guns and sawed-off shotguns.

To understand gun use and control in American urban history and in the contemporary United States requires consideration of some basic facts and the larger context of intense debates over guns, gun violence, and gun control. These facts and debates frame proposals for gun control policy, at urban and other levels, and inform evaluations of the relative success of urban efforts at gun control.

Basic facts to keep in mind are the high levels of lethal violence, especially gun violence, in the United States, coupled with the extremely high numbers of firearms; lack of comprehensive national-level gun control regulation; and a highly developed gun culture, which sees the issue of gun ownership as inextricably intertwined with that of basic rights. The U.S. is also a highly urbanized nation characterized by extremes of wealth and poverty, high levels of past and present discrimination against racially defined minority groups, and continuing high levels of residential segregation, with poor African Americans and Latino/as most likely to live in inner cities. Social and economic trends in recent years, combined with the above factors, have created urban environments characterized by numerous social problems, including poor education, lack of jobs, high levels of crime, and inadequate public safety. Add the widespread availability of firearms to this situation and the linkage of gun violence and cities is understandable.

Another important context for understanding urban gun use and control is the long-standing, intense debate between gun rights advocates and gun control advocates. Gun rights advocates argue that the Second Amendment to the Constitution gives individuals a constitutionally protected right to own and bear arms. They argue that the availability and use of guns saves lives and money and deters criminals from attacks, and that guns do not, in themselves, contribute to violence in the United States. Given these arguments, they suggest that there is a net benefit to guns and that gun control does not work, so they oppose gun control regulation. Gun rights advocates note that crime rates declined during the 1990s, and that violent crimes and homicides dropped significantly in the United States since 1993. They argue that "guns don't kill people, people do."

Gun control advocates argue that the Second Amendment protects a collective right to bear arms in a governmentally organized militia, not an individual right to personal ownership, and stress that the Second Amendment—however interpreted—does not preclude gun regulation. They suggest that the availability of guns—especially handguns—contributes to high levels of lethal violence in the United States. Arguing that gun violence is an epidemic, many view handgun control as a public health issue aimed at reducing risk,

rather than a political issue. While acknowledging the declining crime rates of the 1990s, they point out that rates of lethal violence, especially homicide, in the U.S. are still much higher than in industrialized societies which have more comprehensive firearms regulation and fewer guns. Gun control advocates note the increasing rates of gun violence in American cities in the early 21st century and suggest the need for comprehensive gun regulation. They argue that "guns don't kill people, but they make it a lot easier."

Cities have tried to cope with and control the proliferation of firearms. In addition to the earlier Sullivan Act and the NFA of 1934, both Chicago and Washington, D.C., have strict handgun laws, although Congress may reverse the District of Columbia law. Some research has suggested that those laws did reduce lethal violence, but other research suggests that they have not been effective. Pro-gun rights groups regularly criticize these laws as ineffective and suggest that they demonstrate the futility of gun regulation. Gun-control groups acknowledge the shortcomings of these laws, especially the lack of strong gun regulation in surrounding areas. Individuals can obtain guns outside of Chicago or Washington, D.C., and then bring them into those cities. Gun control advocates acknowledge that long-term policies to address discrimination, crime, and other urban social problems are necessary, but they suggest that comprehensive gun regulation can also play a role in lessening urban gun violence and use.

—*Walter F. Carroll*

See also Crime and Criminals

Further Readings and References

Anderson, E. (1999). *Code of the street: Decency, violence, and the moral life of the inner city.* New York: Norton.

Canada, G. (1995). *Fist, stick, knife, gun: A personal history of violence in America.* Boston: Beacon Press.

Cook, P. J., & Ludwig, J. (2000). *Gun violence: The real costs.* New York: Oxford University Press.

McDonnell, J. (2002). Urbanism and gun violence. In G. L. Carter (Ed.), *Guns in American society: An encyclopedia of history, culture, politics, and the law* (Vol. 2). Santa Barbara, CA: ABC-CLIO.

Zimring, F. E., & Hawkins, G. (1997). *Crime is not the problem: Lethal violence in America.* New York: Oxford University Press.

HAGUE, FRANK

Frank Hague (1876–1956) was born on January 17, 1876, in Jersey City, New Jersey, the son of poor Irish Catholic immigrants, John and Margaret (Fagen) Hague. When he left school at age 13 in the sixth grade, the tall, tough, self-confessed juvenile delinquent worked as a blacksmith's helper in the Erie Railroad yards and managed a professional boxer. He began his political career when he was elected in 1896 as a constable with the help of the Second Ward Democratic Party boss. Quickly, Hague moved up the ladder to city commissioner in 1911 and mayor from 1917 to 1929. Hague married Jennie W. Warner in 1903, and they had two children and an adopted son.

Hague dominated Jersey City and Hudson County politics and was the Democratic Party boss of New Jersey from 1917 to 1947. His power base was unrivaled on the East Coast. From 1924 to 1952, Hague was also a national Democratic Party vice chairman. Often compared to Alfred E. Smith, Hague supported Smith for president in 1924 and 1928, but in 1932, Hague transferred his support to Franklin D. Roosevelt to swing New Jersey for the New Deal coalition. With President Roosevelt's support—and by controlling city and county patronage as well as most governors between 1925 and 1940—Hague created a model political machine. When women got the right to vote in 1920, Hague was quick to see the important role they could play in his political machine. He kept the railroad, oil, and utility corporations in check and prevented labor unions from disrupting the state's fragile economy.

However, his frequent and lavish vacations in Florida and Europe, as well as his expensive apartments at the Plaza and Waldorf-Astoria hotels in New York City, aroused some criticism. In 1939, the U.S. Supreme Court ruled against his side in *Hague v. CIO* (1939), which was filed by the American Civil Liberties Union to overturn civil rights violations in a local ordinance limiting free speech and free assembly. Hague prevented Norman Thomas, the Socialist Party presidential candidate, from campaigning in Jersey City and denounced the CIO in 1937 as a communist organization. The Communist Party also investigated Hague in 1938 for political corruption as mayor.

Although uneducated and often crude and abusive to his staff and critics, Hague provided efficient public services for Jersey City voters, reorganizing the fire and police departments, building schools and a modern medical center, and creating efficient child welfare programs. He was a faithful Catholic who neither smoked nor drank, and he barred gambling, nightclubs, and prostitution from Jersey City. His dapper clothing, lavish lifestyle, and fondness for horse racing, boxing, and baseball seemed harmless to most voters. He clashed with FDR during the 1940 campaign for New Jersey governor, however, and Republican victories for governor in 1943 and 1946 marked the decline of his Democratic machine. The New Deal's social welfare programs and the rise of rival Italian and Polish candidates undercut his power base. Hague resigned as mayor in 1947 in favor of his nephew, Frank Hague Eggers, who was so inept that Republicans and younger Democrats won most postwar elections. Hague supported Harry Truman's election in 1948 with a massive political rally, but he resigned as county party leader in 1949 and as Democratic national committeeman and national vice chairman in 1952. His attempted comeback in 1953 was futile, and the death of Eggers in 1954 ended his long career. Boss Frank Hague died in his Manhattan apartment on January 1, 1956, at age 79, largely forgotten as a Democratic Party leader and master machine boss. He is buried in an impressive mausoleum at Holy Name Cemetery in Jersey City. His name remains synonymous with the 20th-century urban American political phenomenon known as bossism.

—*Peter C. Holloran*

Further Readings and References

Connors, R. J. (1971). *A cycle of power: The career of Jersey City mayor Frank Hague.* Metuchen, NJ: Scarecrow Press.

Rapport, G. (1961). *The statesman and the boss.* New York: Vantage Press.

Smith, T. F. X. (1982). *The powerticians.* Secaucus, NJ: L. Stuart.

HARLEM, NEW YORK

Harlem, New York, is probably best known for being the center of black cultural and intellectual life in the United States since the 1920s. But over the course of the last two centuries, members of numerous racial and ethnic groups have called this section of upper Manhattan home. Harlem's physical boundaries have been perpetually shifting and expanding, but Harlem has been—and continues to be—much more than a location to its inhabitants. Harlem has, at different points in its history, represented gentility, opportunity, hope, the exotic, the erotic, urban decay, and most recently, urban renewal.

The Dutch town of New Harlaem was founded in 1658. It was during the early decades of the 19th century, however, that Harlem took much of its modern shape. Today, the area north of 96th Street to 116th Street and east of Fifth Avenue is generally considered Spanish Harlem. Central Harlem, as the rest of the neighborhood is known, spreads northward from 110th Street to 155th Street west of Fifth Avenue and east from Morningside Avenue to the Harlem River.

From its creation through most of the 19th century, Harlem remained quite isolated from the rest of Manhattan. Harlem was home to Dutch, English, and French families of wealth and standing who desired that Harlem remain an exclusive community where only "the best" families lived. Alexander Hamilton, for example, built an estate in Harlem that was completed in 1802.

By the 1840s and 1850s, a large wave of immigrants, including significant numbers of Irish, moved into Harlem, either buying land at inexpensive prices or simply occupying abandoned lots and establishing the first poor immigrant communities in the affluent rural village.

After the Civil War, the Irish were joined by other European immigrants. Although Harlem is known as a predominantly black community today, this was not always the case. Between 1870 and 1920 Harlem's black residents were outnumbered by its German, Italian, and Jewish inhabitants. The Jews and Italians who came to Harlem between 1880 and 1910 moved to northern Manhattan from older downtown ethnic enclaves in search of economic opportunities. A Harlem address was a sign of social mobility for members of these groups, as it was considered one of the most attractive residential areas in Manhattan. By 1910, Harlem was home to more than 100,000 Jews.

Harlem's population growth during the late 19th century was spurred by the construction, between the 1870s and 1890s, of transportation lines—particularly elevated train lines—that spanned the length of Manhattan. After Harlem was annexed by Manhattan in 1873, the building of a transportation infrastructure continued to connect Harlem to the rest of the island. As it became easier to commute to other areas of Manhattan, Harlem became much more densely populated.

By the turn of the 20th century, those African Americans who could afford the higher costs were also trying to move out of the downtown Tenderloin district to Harlem. Although blacks who attempted to rent in Harlem faced resistance from white residents, moving to Harlem was still desirable. It was considered a sign of social mobility just as it had been for the Europeans who had come a generation earlier. The African Americans who moved to Harlem paid higher rents than elsewhere in the city, but during the early years of black migration, they also lived in better quarters than they had anywhere else. A housing slump in 1904 and 1905 caused by overbuilding in Harlem, as well as the efforts of prominent African

Americans such as Phillip Payton, who established the Afro-American Realty Company, meant many more blacks began owning and renting property in Harlem.

The composition of Harlem's population was changing rapidly by the 1910s. World War I increased the number of economic opportunities available for workers but cut off the European immigration that would have filled the labor gap. During and after World War I, thousands of southern blacks migrated to Harlem, just as physical deterioration of buildings in Harlem and the construction of better, more affordable housing elsewhere was pushing Harlem's white population into the more suburban outer boroughs. By 1914, 50,000 blacks resided in Harlem.

During the 1920s, Harlem became a predominantly African American community in terms of population and earned its designation as the mecca of black cultural and intellectual life, not only in the United States but around the world. Harlem was a magnet for peoples of African descent, including the Jamaican-born Marcus Garvey, who preached his message of black nationalism and economic self-sufficiency to tens of thousands of blacks in Harlem and elsewhere. Headquartered in Harlem, chapters of Garvey's Universal Negro Improvement Association would be established throughout the United States, the Caribbean, South America, and West Africa during the 1920s.

Besides the Garvey movement, a cultural renaissance would come to define Harlem during the 1920s. The Harlem Renaissance embraced such luminous literary figures as Langston Hughes, Zora Neale Hurston, Claude McKay, and Jean Toomer. It was also the literary expression of an even broader shift in attitudes among educated blacks, in which they once again defiantly proclaimed their racial pride and demanded equal treatment within American society.

The Harlem Renaissance, however, did not feed people, and as the 1920s ended, the economic circumstances of most Harlem blacks did not reflect the prosperity that had characterized the decade elsewhere. The Great Depression ravaged Harlem's economy and increased racial tensions in New York City. Blacks were still streaming into Harlem from the South during the late 1930s and 1940s to escape racial persecution and take advantage of job opportunities resulting from war mobilization. With few other residential areas within the city open to African Americans and with job opportunities much more scarce than newcomers had imagined, racial violence exploded in Harlem on two separate occasions during the 1930s and 1940s. In 1935 and again in 1943, riots in Harlem caused millions of dollars of physical damage; recovery took decades.

Harlem residents, like African Americans in other parts of the country, were expressing their frustrations with racial discrimination, deteriorating economic conditions, and unresponsive politicians. A modern struggle for civil rights was emerging in Harlem and in other urban centers, to which these two riots were connected.

During the Depression era, formal civil rights organizations opened headquarters in Harlem. The National Association for the Advancement of Colored People, the National Urban League, and the Brotherhood of Sleeping Car Porters all had offices there. These groups protested unequal conditions. In 1934, Harlem blacks coordinated the "Don't Buy Where You Can't Work" campaign. An attempt to secure more jobs for local blacks in white-owned businesses in Harlem, it was mostly unsuccessful, but in subsequent decades, similar tactics would be employed with more success to obtain civil rights gains for Harlem blacks.

Harlemites were very active in local civil rights campaigns during the post–World War II period. Housing, job discrimination, and public school integration were the primary causes for mobilization. The 1950s and 1960s were decades of great demographic change for all of New York City. Southern Blacks—and increasingly, Puerto Ricans—continued to migrate to New York City, particularly Harlem and the Bedford-Stuyvesant section of Brooklyn, by the tens of thousands during what is known as the Second Great Migration. At the same time, whites were leaving the city for the suburbs in similar numbers.

By the late 1960s and 1970s, what came to be called white flight, the departure of middle-class blacks from Harlem, and the economic crises of the early 1970s combined to create the scenes of urban decay that plagued other inner city black communities. Harlem came to epitomize blight; the neighborhood was characterized by dilapidated buildings, rising crime rates, drug infestation, poor educational facilities, and poverty.

Since the late 1980s, Harlem has begun to rebound. Private investment and municipal and federal funds have stimulated new residential and commercial construction in Harlem. African American professionals as well as others who seek affordable real estate have bought homes in Harlem. New businesses have come to the community along Harlem's major thoroughfares, especially 125th Street, which has long been the physical and cultural pulse of the neighborhood. The second renaissance currently under way in Harlem took hold during the 1990s and sparked renewed interest in Harlem's architectural and cultural attractions, including the Apollo Theater, the Studio Museum of Harlem, the Arthur A. Schomburg Center for Research in Black Culture, and the Aaron Davis Hall for the Performing Arts. The changes that Harlem has been undergoing have not proceeded without reservations or opposition, but Harlem is definitely now, as at many times in its history, a neighborhood in transition.

—*Kristopher Burrell*

See also Harlem Renaissance; National Association for the Advancement of Colored People; National Urban League; New York, New York; Urban Renewal and Revitalization

Further Readings and References

Boyd, H. (2003). *The Harlem reader.* New York: Three Rivers.
Capeci, D. J. (1977). *The Harlem riot of 1943.* Philadelphia: Temple.
Clarke, J. H. (1964). *Harlem: A community in transition.* New York: The Citadel.
Greenberg, C. L. (1991). *"Or does it explode?" Black Harlem in the great depression.* New York: Oxford University Press.
Gurock, J. S. (1979). *When Harlem was Jewish, 1870–1930.* New York: Columbia University Press.
Osofsky, G. (1966). *Harlem: The making of a ghetto.* Chicago: Ivan R. Dee.

HARLEM RENAISSANCE

The Harlem Renaissance was a culmination of African American cultural expression and is usually associated with the "jazz age" of the 1920s. In comparison to preceding decades, the period was characterized by an increased intensity and concentration on two levels. Demographically, Harlem had benefitted from a large number of immigrants as a result of national and international immigration, turning it into an area in which black people constituted the majority. Culturally, New York City was at its height as the publishing and entertainment center of the United States, thereby increasing the chances of finding outlets and publics for African American writers and artists.

The renaissance was the result of a complex interplay of social, economic, and intellectual forces in the preceding decades. Although migration by African Americans from the South to the North had been taking place as early as the Civil War, this stream turned into the "Great Migration" in the 1910s. Encouraged by black newspapers such as the *New York Age* and the *Chicago Defender* and by the increased demand for labor as a result of World War I, nearly half a million African Americans left rural areas of the South for the cities in the North. The black population of New York alone increased from about 100,000 in 1910 to about 210,000 in 1920. Following a collapse in real-estate speculation, Harlem landlords decided to rent apartments to blacks, which resulted in many newcomers moving straight into Harlem. Finally, at the turn of the century, African Americans who were committed to a modernist view and integrationist perspective in relation to American culture proved highly influential to most intellectuals of the Harlem Renaissance.

These intellectual influences go a long way toward explaining some of the tensions active during the era of the renaissance. Writers such as James Weldon Johnson, Alain Locke, and the older W. E. B. Du Bois were the most visible and eloquent spokesmen of the Harlem Renaissance, and as a result, many debates in the 1920s were structured by a belief in art as indicator of a flourishing civilization as well as a possible mediator between black and white Americans. In general, it was argued that African Americans could achieve full freedom only if they succeeded in developing an autonomous aesthetic that was not merely a copy of European forms. Although the popular cultural nationalism of the time clearly resonated in these statements, none of these authors was willing to contemplate the more radical view of full political independence. In contrast to Irish and Czech nationalists, for example, the aim of these spokesmen of the Harlem Renaissance was not territorial separation but instead integration into mainstream U.S. culture based on a liberal view of differential equality and full participation. George Hutchinson has shown that this position was to an important extent the result of a nationalization of social relations and institutions during the 20 or 30 years before the 1920s. The sophisticated, urban, and American image of the "new Negro" would have been vastly different without this increasing embedding of social and cultural relations in national structures of communication and transportation. This also explains why Marcus Garvey is often excluded from descriptions of the Harlem Renaissance, by both his contemporaries and later critics. Although Garvey lived in New York, was editor of the *Negro World,* and organized parades of his Universal Negro Improvement Association in Harlem, his separatist emphasis on Africa as the true home of African Americans distanced him from intellectuals like Locke, Johnson, and Du Bois, who were above all interested in being and becoming Americans.

Theirs was a vision of African Americans no longer under the burden of slavery but ready to embrace the 20th century as an age of a new and positive form of racial identity. This is what Houston Baker has characterized as "Afro-American spirit work," and the transformative potential of this strategy can hardly be underestimated. Others, however, occupied somewhat different positions in this literary field. Zora Neale Hurston, for example, was less fixed on debating the distinctiveness of African American culture and instead argued that no culture could claim pure originality because every expression is always an act of mimicry. Similarly, it is only with difficulty that one can interpret the novels *Quicksand* by Nella Larsen or *Home to Harlem* by Claude McKay as representing the "new Negro" in any straightforward fashion; both novels clearly contain more ambiguity than this utopian reading allows. Finally, many of the most vocal Harlem Renaissance intellectuals entertained a complex and often dismissive relationship with much of the popular entertainment that surrounded them in Harlem: jazz, blues, musicals, and dance clubs. Much of their discomfort was based on the fear, sometimes justified, of perpetuating traditions of primitivism in which African Americans were automatically associated with sexuality and sensation. Subsequent criticism has adopted the focus on literary writings as representing the essence of the Harlem Renaissance, but in the last decades, the academic concern with the inclusion of minority groups and discourses has led to the publication of a number of studies on popular forms of culture such as music, theater, and sports, as well as examinations of gender and interracialism.

Although most scholars will agree that the hub of this activity was in Harlem during the 1920s, there are various reasons for adopting a different geographic context or time frame. Feminist scholars, for example, have argued in favor of Locke's broader term of the "new Negro renaissance" because this would allow the inclusion not only of other important centers of African American artistic activity, such as Washington, Philadelphia, and Boston, but also of black women writers all over the country, who submitted their work to Harlem magazines such as *Crisis* and *Opportunity.* Similarly, the advent of the Depression is often seen as the final moment of the Harlem Renaissance, causing a shift from a concern with race to one with class. Sometimes, this has led authors to conclude that the Harlem Renaissance was above all a period of naïve idealism, whereas the 1930s confronted these artists with hard and objective facts and injected a dose of social realism into their works. Others, however, have emphasized the continuities and have argued that the themes of race and class were part and parcel of the concerns of African American artists in both periods. Irrespective of these diverging interpretations, however, the recurrent use of this historical era in these and other debates is testimony to the continuing importance of race in American culture and the specific shapes it ought to take.

—*Bas van Heur*

Further Readings and References

Aberjhani, & West, S. L. (2003). *Encyclopedia of the Harlem Renaissance.* New York: Facts on File.

Baker, H. A., Jr. (1988). *Afro-American poetics: Revisions of Harlem and the black aesthetic.* Madison: University of Wisconsin Press.

Balshaw, M. (2000). *Looking for Harlem: Urban aesthetics in African American literature.* Sterling, VA: Pluto Press.

Hutchinson, G. (1995). *The Harlem Renaissance in black and white.* Cambridge, MA: Harvard University Press.

Wall, C. A. (1995). *Women of the Harlem Renaissance.* Bloomington: Indiana University Press.

HATCHER, RICHARD

Mayor of Gary, Indiana, for 20 years beginning January 1, 1968, Richard Gordon Hatcher (1933-) was the first African American chief executive of an American city whose population exceeded 100,000. Hailed as a Moses to his people, Hatcher symbolized the limits of black urban political power. He swept into office as a result of an anti-machine grassroots struggle, in contrast to Carl Stokes, the choice of Cleveland's Democratic hierarchy, who was sworn in several hours later that same day. Hatcher grew up in nearby

Michigan City, Indiana and graduated from Indiana University and Valparaiso Law School. Moving to Gary in 1960, he quickly rose to the forefront of struggles involving discrimination in education, law enforcement, hiring practices, access to public parks, and housing. In 1963, the 30-year-old attorney was elected councilman-at-large with help from a community organization called Muigwithania, a Swahili word meaning, "We are together." In the 1967 Democratic primary, Hatcher defeated Mayor A. Martin Katz and maverick Bernard Konrady, who siphoned off white votes from the incumbent. Following county boss John Krupa, most white precinct committeemen supported Republican Joseph Radigan in the general election. Hatcher won by 1,865 votes out of 77,759 cast, receiving 96 percent of the black total and just 12 percent of white votes. Had a federal judge not purged "ghost voters," the city might have gone up in flames.

With a bankrupt treasury, eroding local tax base, state-imposed limitations to home rule, elevated race tensions, and a wary business community, Hatcher focused on tapping into Great Society programs. His administration won praise for its imaginative Model Cities experiments, but War on Poverty revenues declined after Richard M. Nixon succeeded Lyndon B. Johnson as president a year into the mayor's first term. Nevertheless, Model Cities provided leadership opportunities for many talented ghetto residents. In 1972, Hatcher hosted a historic National Black Political Convention at Gary West Side High School. It attracted more than 4,000 delegates, including co-chair Imamu Baraka, Angela Davis, Coretta Scott King, and Jesse Jackson. White flight and business disinvestment having decimated downtown, Hatcher launched a "genesis" strategy aimed at stimulating minority entrepreneurship. During President Jimmy Carter's presidency, federal money facilitated completion of a civic center and the transformation of the defunct Hotel Gary into Genesis Towers (providing housing for seniors), but Ronald Reagan's election led to devastating cuts in city services. Plans to expand use of the Gary airport stalled after the death of Chicago's Mayor Harold Washington, Hatcher's closest regional ally.

With little cooperation from state officials, Hatcher became convinced that only a reordering of federal priorities could rejuvenate rust belt cities such as Gary. Convening a 1982 Black Economic Summit, he called for a massive aid program comparable to the postwar Marshall Plan. Twice he was campaign director for presidential hopeful Jesse Jackson. Chairman of TransAfrica, a group that pressured Congress into slapping sanctions on South Africa, Hatcher spent a night in jail after picketing in front of the apartheid regime's embassy. Although a diminishing number of Gary residents were mill workers, a 6-month steel strike ravaged the local economy. In 1987, Hatcher faced his most formidable opponent, Township Assessor Thomas V. Barnes, whose "Clean-Up Gary" campaign emphasized the need for improved services and cooperation with neighboring communities—and lost. In 1991, Hatcher failed to unseat Barnes and polled about the same number of votes as white criminal attorney Scott King, who captured City Hall in 1995. Retiring from electoral politics, Hatcher taught at Indiana University Northwest and Valparaiso Law School and vainly tried to revive local interest in a civil rights hall of fame. Twice he visited South Africa as President Nelson Mandela's guest. This was heady stuff for the son of an illiterate Georgia tenant farmer.

—*James B. Lane*

Further Readings and References

Colburn, D. R., & Adler, J. S. (Eds.). (2001). *African-American mayors: Race, politics, and the American city.* Urbana: University of Illinois Press.

Lane, J. B. (1978). *"City of the century": A history of Gary, Indiana.* Bloomington: Indiana University Press.

Nelson, W. E., Jr., & Meranto, P. J. (1972). *Electing black mayors: Political action in the black community.* Columbus: Ohio State University Press.

HAYMARKET RIOT/MASSACRE

The first large-scale incident of domestic urban terrorism in American history was the Haymarket riot. On May 4, 1886, a dynamite bomb thrown at a labor rally in Chicago's Haymarket Square killed seven police officers, injured 60 people, and killed or injured an estimated 100 spectators. Although this occurred a decade before the yellow journalism that marked the Spanish-American War, Chicago's newspapers created an air of hysteria and helped bring about the convictions of eight political radicals for incitement to murder, even though only two were present at the time of the explosion. Four were hanged, one committed suicide in jail, and three were pardoned 7 years later.

The resulting backlash against labor stymied reforms such as the 8-hour workday for decades.

The roots of the Haymarket incident date back to Chicago's first labor protests during the 1860s. Beginning a practice of May Day marches that would become international, thousands of Chicago workers marched on May 1, 1867, to celebrate passage of an 8-hour workday law. Small groups of young workers attacked recalcitrant employers, and the city tottered on the edge of chaos for several days. The largely ignored 8-hour law was subsequently repealed, forcing workers back to 10- and 12-hour workdays.

Chicago's great 1871 fire contributed to an economic depression lasting from 1873 to 1878, and a second depression from 1882 to 1886 led to massive unemployment—as much as 40 percent of the local workforce was without jobs. A survey of some 350 post–Civil War Chicago working-class families revealed that almost half were in debt or on the verge of indebtedness, 25 percent needed the second income of a wife or child, and only 7 percent owned their own house.

Resentment boiled into anger. In July 1877, a railroad strike that started in Chicago spread nationally. As many as 50 local strikers were killed, more than 200 were wounded, and it took U.S. Army troops to quell the resulting disturbances. Instead of aiding the unemployed, the strike led Chicago's businessmen to provide police with four cannons and a Gatling machine gun.

As hopelessness increased, labor organizations, both foreign and English-speaking, grew in popularity. Some were very radical. Smaller, more selective strikes spread, and "workingman's militias" began to appear around the city, even after the state outlawed paramilitary activities in 1879. Two innocent construction workers were beaten senseless by police during a streetcar workers strike in 1885, and a group of police supported by businessmen such as Marshall Field were trained in riot control. *The Alarm,* a Chicago-based radical newspaper edited by Albert Parsons, wondered who was to be shot next.

In mid-January 1886, unexploded bombs were found at a judge's house and a railroad company. The *Chicago Daily News* published drawings of dynamite bombs and listed Haymarket Square, an outdoor business district on Randolph Street between Des Plaines and Halsted, as the next location for a bombing. A strike and lockout at the McCormick Harvester factory beginning in March resulted in the police-inflicted deaths of four workers. Another two were killed during a large May Day rally. A handbill circulated in the wake of the latter killings invited workers to protest at the Haymarket Square on the evening of May 4. A German-language radical newspaper predicted police actions would be met with what it called "red terror." It promised readers would soon know what the term meant.

The evening meeting began peaceably. Mayor Carter Harrison, Sr., had issued a permit for the gathering and prohibited police interference. About 10 p.m., a light rain began, and Harrison left the square, convinced the meeting was ending. Instead, a hidden police force of as many as 200 riot-control officers marched on the remaining crowd, and a single bomb thrown by an unknown person in the crowd exploded among the front ranks of the police, just as they were nearing the speakers' stand. Gunfire from both sides erupted. Dead and dying police were taken to a nearby police station. Injured participants and bystanders were left to fend for themselves, making accurate casualty counts impossible.

The bombing's aftermath was the first large-scale media event in Chicago history. The English-language dailies reacted hysterically, predicting a violent overthrow of civil order along with anarchy in the streets. Believing what they read in the papers, many Chicagoans demanded a forcible end to all political dissent. The police were only too happy to oblige, and hundreds of immigrants and political dissidents were arrested or illegally detained.

Authorities eventually charged eight men—Texasborn newspaperman Albert Parsons and foreign immigrants August Spies, Samuel Fielden, Louis Lingg, Adolph Fischer, George Engel, Michael Schwab, and Oscar Neebe—with incitement to murder. Only Parsons and Spies were present at the bombing, both within full view of the police. The trial judge, Joseph E. Gary, had arbitrated a labor dispute in favor of the newspapers just days before the trial's start and did little to hide his contempt for the accused. The jury was either sworn or bribed to convict, and the newspapers published jurors' names, pictures, and home addresses to ensure their complicity.

In a trial that lasted 53 days, the prosecution offered no direct evidence linking the accused to the bombing; instead, prosecutors argued that the defendants' published and spoken statements, some made years before the bombing, amounted to proof of their complicity. The lead defense attorney, Capt. William P. Black, maintained unsuccessfully that the accused could not have thrown the bomb, but incendiary statements made by the defendants during the trial did not help their case. The jury deliberated only 4 hours before convicting seven of the men of death penalty charges and sending Neebe to prison. Fielden and Schwab were persuaded to ask for commutations to life sentences the following year through the intervention of dissident Chicago newspaperman Henry Demarest Lloyd. Lingg committed suicide in his jail cell the day before the executions.

Spies, Parsons, Engel, and Fischer were hanged November 11, 1887. The three living Haymarket defendants were pardoned by Illinois Governor John Peter Altgeld on June 26, 1893, in the face of irrefutable evidence of judicial and prosecutorial misconduct. Altgeld, a rising political star at the time, saw his career vanish and died in poverty. The actual bomb thrower was never officially identified or convicted, although subsequent evidence pointed to George Meng, a hardened radical who was arrested but released by police. Meng died in an 1896 saloon fire, never publicly admitting to the bombing.

—*Richard Junger*

Further Readings and References

Avrich, P. (1984). *The Haymarket tragedy.* Princeton, NJ: Princeton University Press.

David, H. (1936). *The history of the Haymarket affair.* New York: Russell & Russell.

Digby-Junger, R. (1996). *The journalist as reformer.* Westport, CT: Greenwood.

Lindberg, R. (1991). *To serve and collect.* New York: Praeger.

Nelson, B. (1988). *Beyond the martyrs.* New Brunswick, NJ: Rutgers University Press.

HEARST, WILLIAM RANDOLPH

William Randolph Hearst (1863–1951) is best known as a publishing magnate in the early 20th century, having owned magazines and newspapers throughout the United States. Hearst was a political force in New York City, running for office at various levels and assisting Democratic candidates in his role as editor of the *New York Journal.* Hearst's personal and financial interests included film, radio, mining, and architecture. Popular culture has been imprinted with

Hearst's caricature in Orson Welles's film *Citizen Kane,* loosely based on Hearst's life.

Hearst was born on April 29, 1863, in San Francisco. His father was George Hearst, a miner turned millionaire and U.S. senator. Hearst's adult personality was forged by the cosmopolitan ways of his mother, Phoebe, and the hard work and persistence of his father. After graduation from Harvard University, Hearst went to work for his father's newspaper, the *San Francisco Examiner,* which he would take over at age 23. Using Joseph Pulitzer's *New York World* as inspiration, Hearst attempted to make the *Examiner* a similar paper by using flashier illustrations and more sensational stories than his competitors.

By age 32, Hearst had bought the *New York Daily Journal* and renamed it simply the *New York Journal.* Now in direct competition with Pulitzer, Hearst had to use techniques similar to those that had revived the San Francisco paper. the *Journal* started publication in 1895, and its circulation growth was aided by the foreign conflict in Cuba. Hearst used foreign correspondents, graphic images, and sensational accounts to create a more publication-friendly conflict. Hearst also employed prominent correspondents such as William Jennings Bryan, Benito Mussolini, and Winston Churchill to get attention for the *Journal.*

Hearst used his publishing prominence for the purpose of Democratic Party activism. Hearst was elected to Congress in 1902, fusing politics and journalism at a level never before seen in American history. Following his failed attempt to get the Democratic nomination for president in 1904, Hearst attempted to run for mayor of New York City in 1905 and for governor of New York in 1906. His disillusionment with Tammany Hall spurred his support of an Independence Party, of Herbert Hoover in 1928, and of John Nance Garner in 1932.

Hearst's downfall began largely with his criticism of Franklin Roosevelt's economic policies. Hearst newspapers started to lose popularity in an increasingly competitive media climate, and Hearst lost control of his newspapers briefly from the mid-1930s until the end of World War II. Hearst was concerned during this period with his film production interests, his art collection, and other financial interests. By the end of Hearst's life on August 16, 1951, the Hearst newspapers were worth $1.3 million. Forty years later, these newspapers were worth $450 million.

—*Nicholas Katers*

See also Ethnic Neighborhoods; Hollywood; New York,
New York; Newspapers; Politics in Cities; Pulitzer, Joseph;
San Francisco, California; Tammany Hall

Further Readings and References

Cheney, L., & Cieply, M. (1981). *The Hearsts: Family and
empire, the later years.* New York: Simon & Schuster.

Nasaw, D. (2000). *The chief: The life of William Randolph
Hearst.* Boston: Houghton Mifflin.

Procter, B. H. (1998). *William Randolph Hearst: The early
years, 1863–1910.* New York: Oxford University Press.

HENRY STREET SETTLEMENT

A community institution on Manhattan's Lower East
Side, Henry Street Settlement remains one of the few
working settlement houses in the United States, where
community members and experts come together to
contend with the issues of urban living. Founded in
1893 by Lillian D. Wald and her nursing colleague,
Mary Brewster, it was first called the Nurses'
Settlement, offering health care to the families of
immigrant industrial laborers on Manhattan's Lower
East Side. Under Wald's leadership (Brewster retired
due to ill health), the settlement increased the scope of
its programs, adding Americanization classes, club
work, a theater, and summer camps. Financier Jacob
Schiff, the first of many urban elite contributors,
purchased 265 Henry Street in 1895, and settlement
offices remain in that central building.

Allying herself with networks of elite, white,
Progressive reformers, including Jane Addams and
Florence Kelley, Wald incorporated Henry Street, as it
was known by the early 1900s, into the broader settlement movement. With ideas and strategies drawn
from the women's political culture of these reformers,
Wald used the institution as a platform for Progressive
and liberal causes. Its earliest successful local campaigns advocated for nurses in public schools, sanitary milk stations, and public playgrounds. Wald
allied the settlement with unions and workers in New
York City's garment strike of 1910 and in the textile
strike of 1912 in Lawrence, Massachusetts. Citing the
cross-class and cross-cultural cooperation at Henry
Street, Wald put Henry Street at the center of struggles
for the rights of workers, immigrants, women, and
children. Public officials were often invited to dine
with the resident nurses to discuss these issues.

By 1920, Henry Street's 260 nurses worked out of
22 nursing centers and visited almost 350,000 sick
people in their homes each year, from Manhattan to
Staten Island and beyond Yonkers into Westchester
County. The settlement was home to reform work and
community celebrations, perhaps none as large as
the one held when representatives from Russia's pro-
visional government came to visit after the March
1917 revolution.

Both the nursing and settlement components of the
institution continued to thrive. After Wald's retirement
in 1930, and with the increasing professionalization of
the fields of nursing and social work, the two areas
began to grow apart. Henry Street Settlement and the
Visiting Nurse Service of New York formally divided
in 1944, 4 years after Wald's death.

Henry Street continued to pioneer urban community projects in the following decades. Its Community
Consultation Center (CCC), founded in 1946, was one
of the first mental health clinics of its kind in the
country. The CCC's day treatment program, on-site
nursery, and AIDS clinic all marked important
innovations.

Over the next half century, Henry Street's efforts
have expanded to include the contemporary issues of
homelessness, seniors' and children's health, day care,
literacy, and worker training. Even as the ethnic base
of Henry Street has shifted dramatically since its
founding, its projects continue to reflect the diversity
of its neighborhood as well as its dynamic approach to
contending with the complexities of urban living.
Work at Henry Street continues to attract international
attention and acclaim as a model for other urban
institutions.

—*Marjorie N. Feld*

See also Settlement House Movement; Wald, Lillian D.

Further Readings and References

Hall, H. (1971). *Unfinished business in neighborhood and
nation: A firsthand account by the former director of the
Henry Street Settlement.* New York: Macmillan.

Wald, L. D. (1915). *The house on Henry Street.* New York:
Henry Holt.

Wald, L. D. (1934). *Windows on Henry Street.* Boston: Little,
Brown.

HIGHER EDUCATION

Institutions of higher education in American cities form the base of each city's pyramid of intellectual life. Most early American higher education institutions (HEIs), however, were established outside of cities because their founders believed in the agrarian myth: The countryside provides the venue for moral excellence. Although a city would grow around it, even Harvard University (1736) was originally placed in a village setting. Some exceptions include King's College of New York City (1754, now Columbia University), William and Mary (1693, in Williamsburg, VA), and the College of Philadelphia (1740, now University of Pennsylvania). Despite the pervasiveness of the agrarian myth, a few founders believed the countryside to be more depraved than the city. What follows is a chronological look at HEIs' ever-growing connection with America's cities.

In the late 1800s and early 1900s, the engagement of HEIs with cities increased rapidly. This relationship depended on the changing nature of the American city, civic leadership, and the institution's sense of service to setting. Between the Civil War and 1900, HEIs became more involved in the problems and possibilities of urban life. Although the agrarian myth drove the Morrill Acts of 1862 and 1890 and their resultant agriculture-oriented, land-grant institutions, higher education began to slowly adapt to the needs of an industrial society. The source of this response was the perceived need for an intellectual class to educate the poor, workers, and immigrants. This new class could also fill the growing ranks of civil and commercial middle managers. Institutions responded by becoming more specialized and professionalized, embracing the elective system, and creating graduate and professional programs according to German university ideals. American universities generally adopted commercial-vocational rather than religious-vocational ideals, but they also came to house and respect intellectuals.

The Progressive Era imperative to condescend, as well as to maintain civic and moral virtue, also inspired the growing ranks of higher education faculty. Important objects of their largesse were poor denizens of urban areas. For instance, in 1897, a young Columbia University faculty member, Charles Sprague Smith, professor of modern languages and foreign literature, formed the People's Institute in cooperation with New York City's Cooper Union. Smith's moral urge arose from his distress over the plight of poor immigrants living in Columbia's Morningside Heights neighborhood. Others also responded to immigrants' needs. As the number of Catholic immigrants increased, Jesuits founded HEIs in major cities, such as Boston College, St. Ignatius College in Chicago (later Loyola University), Fordham in New York City, St. Louis University, and Georgetown in Washington, D.C.

At the turn of the century, Progressive Era students and faculty of HEIs applied their virtue and intellectual capabilities to various aspects of civic life. What is known generally in education history as the Wisconsin Idea involved a move by some institutions toward becoming more a part of the cities where they were located. The settlement house, an extension of urban HEIs that provided social services in poor neighborhoods, represented the sentiment of the era. New York's College Settlement was first in the movement, formed in 1889. In Chicago, three settlement houses were formed by Northwestern University, the University of Michigan, and the University of Chicago. All were operated by students.

Progressive Era faculty members increased their public presence and advocated for social concerns. Prominent among these were Charles and Mary Beard, James Harvey Robinson, and John Dewey. Robinson and Charles Beard broke with Columbia to found the New School for Social Research in 1919. The school hoped to be a scholarly center for New York and a place concerned with the plight of labor, learning for its own sake, and research. The faculty eventually included Wesley Mitchell, Emily Putnam, and Thorstein Veblen.

The University of Chicago was founded during this era, in 1892. Dewey resided there from 1894 until 1904, and he worked in and with the city, including Jane Addams's Hull-House. This period saw his most fruitful education writings, as well as experiments with the Laboratory School. Edward Bemis, an economist at the University of Chicago, advocated for the urban working poor. He sided with Pullman workers during their 1893 strike.

Just before and after 1900, institutions expanded the kinds of populations they served, which helped to democratize education opportunities for city dwellers. By 1900, Frederick Rudolph noted in 1962, almost three quarters of HEIs were coeducational. Lawrence A. Cremin wrote in 1988 that missionary societies in the

South had created 27 colleges for former slaves by 1895, and the Morrill Act of 1890 aided in the creation of 13 other African American HEIs. Catholic women's academies formed before 1900 increasingly became accredited 4-year institutions. About 70 Catholic women's colleges were founded between 1900 and 1930, as noted by Phillip Gleason in 1995. Some resided in or served large urban areas, such as Marygrove (Detroit), Mundelein (Chicago), and the College of New Rochelle (New York City). Mundelein's "Skyscraper College" attracted Chicago's middle class and daughters of immigrants for 60 years before closing in 1991.

Just after 1900, some junior colleges began to open. The Chicago public school system, for instance, opened Crane Junior College in 1911. From the start, the college's mission was contested; the debate was between pre-baccalaureate studies and a vocation-oriented curriculum for Chicago's immigrants.

A period of massive adjustment for urban HEIs followed World War II. When soldiers returned, they used funds available via the 1944 Servicemen's Readjustment Act, commonly known as the G.I. Bill, to attend colleges and universities. As a result, by 1946, enrollment in HEIs had jumped by one third from prewar levels. While enrollment at all institutions increased, a major beneficiary of veterans' education ambitions were junior colleges, recast in the 1950s as community colleges. These urban and suburban institutions saw an expansion in terms of students and offerings. The aforementioned Crane Junior College joined with five other Chicago junior colleges created in the 1950s and early 1960s to form the massive City Colleges of Chicago in 1966.

Since the 1960s, urban HEIs have increased curriculum opportunities to make schools more inclusive. A plethora of new programs have opened up scholarship in previously unexplored areas, such as urban studies, women's studies, and black studies. The hope of these programs was to make higher education more attractive to students from diverse urban areas. Whether these programs have attracted more students is unknown, but the curriculum presently provides more opportunities to study diverse minority groups. Options for women decreased during this period through the closing of women's HEIs, particularly Catholic women's colleges. Although some of these were located in urban areas, the environmental effects of these closings are not known.

Urban HEIs have fulfilled several roles in America's history. They have helped immigrant populations adjust mentally and physically to new settings. Both faculty and students, through their research and activism, have helped in this adjustment. These institutions have also helped the general population adjust to the ravages of industrialization and war. As sites of implicit and explicit debate about the meaning of democracy in urban areas, HEIs have acted as social stabilizers. Although most American HEIs were formed on agrarian premises, they will continue to fill this role.

—*Tim Lacy*

See also Addams, Jane; Catholicism; College Towns; Desegregation of Education; Education in Cities; Pullman, Illinois; Settlement House Movement; Youth Culture

Further Readings and References

Cremin, L. A. (1988). *American education: The metropolitan experience, 1876–1980.* New York: Harper & Row.

Gleason, P. (1995). *Contending with modernity: Catholic higher education in the twentieth century.* New York: Oxford University Press.

Ravitch, D. (1983). *The troubled crusade: American education, 1945–1980.* New York: Basic Books.

Rudolph, F. (1962). *The American college and university.* New York: Random House.

HISTORIC PRESERVATION

Historic preservation is historical method and includes conserving, rehabilitating, restoring, and reconstructing the built environment as a useful primary source for the study and interpretation of history. Historians have not always recognized its value, and the historic preservation movement developed to some degree without their participation. The development of historic preservation as a method is linked both to the story of the historic preservation movement in the United States and to the development of urban America.

The historic preservation movement in the United States arose from motives of community pride and national patriotism. It influenced the practice of architecture, gradually transformed itself into a broader educational project, and eventually became an important factor in the revitalization of American cities in the fourth quarter of the 20th century.

The Patriots

One of the earliest instances of historic preservation was the conservation of Independence Hall in Philadelphia in 1813. In 1853, a group of women formed the Mount Vernon Ladies Association with the goal of conserving and restoring the home of George Washington. Ann Pamela Cunningham led the creation of this voluntary citizens' group after a petition for federal support for the preservation of Mount Vernon had failed. Similar organizations—the Thomas Jefferson Memorial Foundation and the Robert E. Lee Memorial Foundation—took on the task of conserving the homes of these historic figures. The goal of these organizations was primarily patriotic, based on the belief that preserving the homes of historic and especially of heroic figures would foster renewed patriotism. Although government—local, state, and federal—was at best indifferent to these projects in the early years, eventually the Historic Sites, Buildings, and Antiquities Act of 1935 stated that preserving significant and historic sites, buildings, and objects is national policy.

The Architects

The same act recognized the role of historic preservation in the practice of architecture, calling for the Secretary of the Interior to gather information about historic structures, including architectural drawings, plans, and photographs. The third president of the United States, Thomas Jefferson, was an early advocate and practitioner of this form of historic preservation in service to architecture. During the early 20th century, historic preservation developed from the conservation of the homes of great people to the preservation of period houses that expressed the architectural taste of an era. The preservation movement became as interested in the aesthetic benefit of historical architecture as in the patriotic well-being of the American people. The Historic American Buildings Survey (HABS) was established in 1933, primarily to give work to unemployed architects. Other New Deal agencies—the Works Progress Administration and the Civilian Conservation Corps—also contributed to the support of the developing historic preservation ethic at the local level. The 1935 Historic Sites Act formalized and gave a broader meaning to the HABS, and this research arm of the historic preservation movement would outlive the government's response to the exigencies of the Great Depression. The HABS and its counterpart, the Historic American Engineering Record (HAER), continue to provide support both for architects seeking inspiration and for preservationists seeking to conserve and restore historic structures.

The Educators

Two significant projects of the 1920s broadened the scope of the historic preservation movement. Henry Ford and John D. Rockefeller Jr., funded significant preservation efforts at the Greenfield Village Museum and at Williamsburg, respectively. Both projects brought new dimensions to historic preservation by making a whole community and not a single building the focus of their efforts. In addition, both projects developed an educational objective, beyond but including patriotic inspiration or architectural appreciation. In both sites, there is a real attempt to show life as it was once lived in the United States, replicating historic places in service to historical explanation. Historic preservation in Williamsburg, however, was achieved through substantial replication or reconstruction of historic buildings, and the Greenfield Village Museum involved even greater relocation and substantial alteration of historic structures as well. The Greenfield Village Museum also reflected the interests and tastes of its founder to the detriment, in the eyes of some, of its historical value. Following on these efforts, the historic building or district functioning as a historical museum and educational institution has become commonplace. In these projects, historic preservation has taken its place as a recognized method of history, especially social history.

The Renovators

The preservation of individual buildings and the creation of restored and replicated communities launched the basic themes of historic preservation and many of its contemporary conventions. These preservation efforts had produced historical museums, isolated from any urban context even if they were located in urban areas. Earlier preservation projects sometimes took on the aura of preserving an earlier America from the urban onslaught. The creation of urban historic districts, inhabited and currently used, changed the direction of both historic preservation and urban history.

The first such district was created in Charleston, South Carolina in 1931. Like later efforts in other areas, the historic preservation movement in

Charleston sought to preserve what residents and sympathetic outsiders viewed as the unique characteristics of both community and its built environment against the depredations of unsympathetic outsiders seeking, often, to demolish both buildings and community, usually in the name of economic progress. In the most successful cases of urban district historic preservation, history played an important role in community identity. Debates about the value of historic preservation became disputes not only about the past and its interpretation but about the economic and political future of the affected areas. Although each area had its own historical as well as architectural uniqueness, very similar efforts in New Orleans, Louisiana; San Antonio, Texas; Alexandria, Virginia; Winston-Salem, North Carolina; Monterey, California; and Georgetown in the District of Columbia met varying degrees of success between 1939 and 1950. In some of these cases, the developing phenomenon of mass tourism supported the preservation movement, bringing large numbers of visitors to these cities and providing an economic justification for preservation as opposed to demolition.

These local efforts inspired the development of historic preservation offices and boards at the level of state government during the first half of the 20th century. One significant outcome was the preservation of mining towns and other historically significant urban sites in the western United States.

The passage of the Historic Sites, Buildings, and Antiquities Act of 1935 had formalized federal government involvement in historic preservation, especially through the National Park Service. New Deal programs provided substantial support, but federal attention almost stopped during World War II. Shortly after the end of the war, a private citizen initiative established the National Council for Historic Sites and Buildings in 1947, and Congress chartered the National Trust for Historic Preservation in 1949. A private, nonprofit agency, the trust served as a channel of communication between private preservation interests throughout the nation and the renewed focus on historic preservation in the National Park Service. The trust spread the historic preservation themes: patriotism, community spirit, aesthetic appreciation of architecture, and the educational potential of historic sites.

The passage of the National Historic Preservation Act of 1966 nationalized the role of historic preservation in urban preservation and, eventually, revitalization. A 1959 urban renewal study in Providence, Rhode Island, had dealt with issues of historic preservation, but the 1966 act led to spreading the idea nationally. It created the National Register of Historic Places, and for the first time, federal recognition or listing of historic districts as well as of individual structures occurred. What had been primarily the product of local enthusiasm, the preservation of districts now became a nationally supported goal of historic preservation. Together with the removal of tax incentives for demolition and the creation of tax incentives for rehabilitation in the years following, the creation of nationally recognized historic districts paved the way for a different kind of economic development and revitalization in urban areas. The 1966 Act left the actual protection of historic places and districts to local governments, but listing in the National Register could be used by local enthusiasts to argue both for local government protection against demolition and for economic development that allowed more influence from Jane Jacobs than from Robert Moses.

One example is the recognition and subsequent development of the Miami Beach Architectural District in 1979. A 20th-century resort community that had gone through at least three development cycles before 1970, Miami Beach's South Beach neighborhood was home to the world's largest concentration of Art Deco structures. The first district on the National Register to be made up of entirely 20th-century structures, the Art Deco district has demonstrated the viability of historic preservation as a tool for economic revitalization as well as a method of public history.

Historians now recognize preservation as a legitimate historical method, but, as a movement, historic preservation has also been a significant part of American urban history.

—*James F. Donnelly*

See also Jacobs, Jane; Moses, Robert

Further Readings and References

Hosmer, C. B., Jr. (1981). *Preservation comes of age: From Williamsburg to the National Trust, 1926–1949.* Charlottesville: University of Virginia Press.

Mulloy, E. (1976). *The history of the National Trust for Historic Preservation, 1963–1973.* Washington, DC: Preservation Press.

Murtagh, W. (1997). *Keeping time: The history and theory of preservation in America* (Rev. ed.). Washington, DC: Preservation Press.

Wallace, M. (1986). Reflections on the history of historic preservation. In S. Benson, S. Brier, & R. Rosenzweig (Eds.), *Presenting the past: Essays on history and the public* (pp. 165–199). Philadelphia: Temple University Press.

HOLLYWOOD

In 1923, 50-foot letters spelling *Hollywoodland* were installed at the top of Mount Lee above Beachwood Canyon in Los Angeles, California, to advertise a new housing development. Two decades later, the Hollywood Chamber of Commerce repaired the sign, which had deteriorated, and removed the last four letters, creating a world-famous icon. Today, it signifies a district of Los Angeles that runs from Vermont Avenue near downtown on the east, to Laurel Canyon about a mile from Beverly Hills on the west, to the crest of the Santa Monica Mountains along Mulholland Drive on the north, and to the City of West Hollywood on the south. Hollywood Boulevard (originally Prospect Avenue) is the area's major arterial. However, more important than its geographic reference, the word *Hollywood* is most often used colloquially to mean the American motion picture industry. By association, the word also signifies an illusory state of mind, a glamorous and profit-driven "Tinsel Town" that helped birth the movies, leaving an incalculable effect on the growth, development, and image of Southern California.

Daeida Wilcox, wife of real estate developer Harvey Henderson Wilcox, gave the area of Los Angeles its new name. In 1886, after moving from Topeka, Kansas, to fledgling Los Angeles, Harvey Wilcox bought 160 acres of agricultural land 7 miles west of the city along the foothills. On a train trip back east, his wife heard a woman speak about her country home, called Hollywood, and liking the sound of it, Mrs. Wilcox gave the name to the couple's ranch. The name first officially appeared the following year, when Harvey Wilcox filed with the county his grid map for a new residential suburb with Prospect Avenue as its main street and began selling lots. By 1903, the municipality was incorporated with 166 adults. A new trolley car line, called "the Hollywood boulevard," linked the town with Los Angeles along Prospect Avenue. In 1910, 2 years after Angelenos approved the bond measure to create the Los Angeles aqueduct, Hollywood's 4,000 residents voted for annexation to secure an adequate water and sewer system. Ironically, about a century later, in 2002, the area's residents—then numbering about 300,000—took a vote on seceding from Los Angeles and becoming an incorporated city again, with the goal of gaining more local control over the area's social and economic challenges. The proposal failed.

In the intervening years, Hollywood became synonymous with the film and entertainment industry and the widely publicized reputations of its stars. In the early 1900s, East Coast motion picture companies, beginning in 1906 with New York-based Biograph, began moving out to Southern California and settling in Edendale, Santa Monica, and eventually Hollywood. The good weather and abundant sunlight needed for making films allowed for more shooting days on a year-round basis. The area also included a wide variety of natural scenery, from mountains to prairies to the seaside. Of equal importance, the West Coast was far from Thomas Edison, who owned most of the patents related to motion picture operations and sued frequently for infringement, setting off the violent industrial patents war. In Los Angeles, companies could work independent of Edison's control, fleeing across the Mexican border if his agents came after them. In October 1911, Englishmen David and William Horsley, leaders in the war against the Edison Trust, set up their Nestor Comedies Studios. The first in the Hollywood area, it was located in the former Blondeau Tavern—which Daeida Wilcox had shut down in her local prohibition effort—on the southeast corner of Sunset Boulevard and Gower Street. Two years later, four New York transplants, director Cecil B. DeMille and producer Jesse Lasky along with partners Samuel Goldfish (who later changed his name to *Goldwyn*) and Arthur Friend, leased a barn on the southeast corner of Selma and Vine streets and began production on *The Squaw Man* (1914). By 1916, the Sunset and Gower area, known as "Gower Gulch," had become a major film center with more than 15 independent companies housed there. Soon after, Charlie Chaplin Studios opened just south of Sunset Boulevard on La Brea and De Longpre Avenues; William Fox set up shop at Sunset and Western, where D. W. Griffith's colossal Babylon sets for *Intolerance* stood; Famous Players-Lasky, at Sunset and Vine, grew to two city blocks; Vitagraph merged with Warner Brothers. By the 1920s, the studios mushroomed in size and power. Hollywood, also known as "the industry," had become a major economic generator, putting Los Angeles at the center of the film world. Despite the optimism of the Hollywood*land* sign, the place gained a reputation for excesses, brought on by tales of the wild nightlife and scandalous behavior of the artsy movie colony and its ties to the underworld.

The old Sunset/Gower mecca soon became "Poverty Row" as the smaller companies went out of business. From 1927 to about 1948, the Hollywood studio system prevailed, as eight highly organized, multidepartment operations with conservative corporate ties to Wall Street swallowed up the small independents and took control: Columbia, Fox, Metro-Goldwyn-Mayer (MGM), Paramount, RKO, United Artists, Universal, and Warner Brothers. With the advent of the "talkies" and the continuing rise in popularity of the medium, combined with the growth of neighboring Los Angeles, movie studios were soon running out of room and affordable space. Needing more and larger facilities for sound stages and back lots, they expanded farther from the city's center. Of the eight major studios, only Paramount Pictures, built on the original 1918 rental lot, remains in the Hollywood area today. Two film companies settled on the Westside: MGM studios in Culver City and Twentieth-Century Fox in an area now known as Century City, although their back lots were eventually sold off as land values continued to rise. In 1915, Carl Laemmle took Universal Studios "over the hill" from Hollywood to the vast San Fernando Valley, where the majority of the entertainment industry's facilities— including the 108-acre Burbank Studios (a merger of Warner Brothers and Columbia Pictures) and Walt Disney studios—are located today. By mid-century and the advent of television, the industry had gobbled up land in Southern California for its filmmaking plants. It needed housing for its employees—from the star-studded enclaves of Bel Air, Beverly Hills, and Malibu to tract housing in Studio City for the "below-the-line" workers. Movie theaters studded the Southland, and the rest of the country, to distribute the industry's wares.

During Hollywood's golden era, the movies themselves served the studios' self-promotion goals while at the same time becoming an effective tool for Southern California boosters and fueling the American dream machine that sparked Los Angeles's growth. From the beginning, location shooting indirectly advertised the sunshine and natural beauty of the place that figured in the background. As early as

1908, in Vitagraph's *Making Motion Pictures: A Day in the Vitagraph Studios,* filmmakers also began to satisfy the audience's growing curiosity about the movie business and stardom. Feature-length films about Hollywood would become a genre, most notably in the two 1937 behind-the-scenes films, *The Stand-In* and *A Star Is Born* (remade in 1954), with their compelling rags-to-riches story line, in *Sullivan's Travels* (1941), and in the MGM musical, *Singin' in the Rain* (1952). From all over the country, seekers of fame and fortune poured in, hoping to become one of the industry's major players, or at least to find a job, especially during the Depression.

After World War II, with the decline of the old studio system and the rise of television, the sober side of the movie business would emerge in such films as *Sunset Boulevard* (1950), *The Bad and the Beautiful* (1952), *The Day of the Locust* (1975), and *The Player* (1992). In 1958, the Hollywood Chamber of Commerce established the two-and-one-half-mile Walk of Fame along Hollywood Boulevard. There, engraved on about 2,000 star-shaped plaques embedded in the sidewalk, are the names of America's biggest entertainers. Nonetheless, the district had seriously declined, becoming a haven for runaways, drug traffickers, and prostitutes, as shown in *Pretty Woman,* until vigorous redevelopment efforts began in the 1990s.

—*Julie A. Dercle*

Further Readings and References

Ames, C. (1997). *Movies about the movies: Hollywood reflected.* Lexington: University Press of Kentucky.

Thompson, D. (2004). *The whole equation: A history of Hollywood.* New York: Knopf.

HOME OWNERS LOAN CORPORATION

The law establishing the Home Owners Loan Corporation (HOLC) signed on June 13, 1933, was the first major piece of housing legislation passed by Franklin Roosevelt's New Deal administration. Designed to protect homeowners from foreclosure during the Great Depression, it refinanced tens of thousands of mortgages facing imminent default and granted loans at low interest rates to help homeowners to recover houses lost through foreclosure. Most significant, the HOLC revolutionized the home loan process. The agency developed a uniform national property appraisal system that ultimately both fueled suburban growth and stifled inner city communities. It established the long-term, self-amortizing mortgage with uniform payments spread over the life of the debt as standard practice for mortgage lenders. Long-term, self-amortizing mortgages, which freed borrowers from the burdens of large payments and from the whims of short-term capital markets, made home loans predictable and gave American homeowners unprecedented security.

The stock market crash of October 1929 and the resulting collapse of financial institutions left builders starved for construction capital, and homeowners who faced unemployment or lowered incomes were unable to find second mortgages to refinance their homes. In 1930, about 150,000 nonfarm households lost their property through foreclosure. That number jumped to 200,000 a year later and to 250,000 in 1932. With nearly 1,000 foreclosures each day in 1933, the nation's home financing system was near collapse. Housing prices fell—a typical $5,000 house in 1926 was worth about $3,000 in 1932—wiping out vast holdings in second and third mortgages as values fell below the primary claim. By 1932, a large portion of American households faced the loss of their most important investment, the family home.

Even before Franklin Roosevelt took office, Herbert Hoover had moved to shore up the nation's mortgage markets with the passage of the first permanent federal housing legislation, the Federal Home Loan Bank Act. Passed in the summer of 1931, the law established a system of federally supervised home loan banks. It did little, however, to stem the growing numbers of foreclosures. Replacing the ineffective Federal Home Loan Bank Act, the HOLC rescued millions of Americans from losing their homes. Between July 1933 and June 1935 alone, it supplied more than $3 billion for more than 1 million mortgages, providing loans to one tenth of all owner-occupied, nonfarm residences. Nationally, about 40 percent of eligible Americans sought HOLC assistance in the 1930s.

Until the establishment of the HOLC, borrowing money for a home purchase was a risky process. In the 19th century, working-class households usually borrowed from immigrant cooperative loan associations whereas more affluent buyers often purchased homes outright. After World War I, commercial banks began financing home purchases, leading both the middle and working classes to acquire mortgages from banks and contributing to a boom in the housing industry. The typical home mortgage spanned 5 to 10 years, with the buyer paying interest at regular intervals and portions of the primary loan on a 2-, 5-, or 10-year schedule. Home buyers, then, needed to pay substantial amounts of money every few years, and when payments were due, many sought to renew their mortgages or to acquire secondary mortgages to cover portions of the first loan's payments. When money markets were running smoothly and loans were obtainable, the strategy of renewing or acquiring multiple mortgages worked well. But if a mortgage expired when money markets contracted, then a homeowner, finding it impossible to acquire new credit, faced foreclosure. The HOLC, with its self-amortizing mortgages stretching 20 to 30 years, eliminated the risks of dealing with unpredictable money markets.

But the HOLC had another, equally significant impact on the nation's real estate markets: It systematized appraisal methods across the nation and in the process initiated the practice later called *redlining*. Because the agency was handling mortgages, it needed to be able to predict the future value of the housing it financed. The agency's appraisers drew elaborate maps outlining urban neighborhoods and developed detailed questionnaires, which considered the occupation, income, and ethnicity of the neighborhood's inhabitants as well as the age, type of construction, price range, and general maintenance of the housing stock. Rather than appraising individual buildings, the appraisers determined the value of a property based on the demographics of the community, local employment markets, and the value of surrounding properties. With the assistance of local realtors and banks, the agency assigned one of four ratings to every block in every city, then recorded the ratings on secret *residential security maps* kept in local HOLC offices.

The agency's rating system, a four-tiered scheme elaborated on color-coded maps, assumed that urban neighborhoods were dynamic and inevitably heading toward decline. The agency's appraisers placed low values on high-density, aging neighborhoods where immigrants and African Americans lived, while giving the highest value to low-density, new communities described as *homogeneous*. The highest grade, called A and coded green on a map, was assigned to communities of "American business and professional men," usually new suburban areas. The second grade, blue, went to "still desirable" areas that were expected to remain stable for many years. The third grade, yellow, marked neighborhoods described as "definitely declining," while the fourth grade, red, signaled neighborhoods already blighted. Aging housing stock was almost always designated yellow, just as neighborhoods housing low-income people or a "mixed" population, residents of several ethnic or racial groups, were marked red. The practical result was that high-density, lower income urban communities, often those housing impoverished African Americans, were circled in red and designated too risky for federally financed mortgages. The agency's appraisal methods, later taken up by the Federal Housing Administration and applied by lenders across the country through much of the 20th century, left a legacy of discriminatory loan practices and of inner city neighborhoods starved for investment capital.

During the 1930s, the HOLC rescued millions of grateful homeowners from foreclosure. In radically transforming the nation's mortgage lending practices, however, the agency had the equally significant impact of devastating inner city neighborhoods while spurring the growth of largely white suburbs.

—*Margaret Garb*

Further Readings and References

Jackson, K. (1985). *Crabgrass frontier: The suburbanization of the United States.* New York: Oxford University Press.

Radford, G. (1996). *Modern housing for America: Policy struggles in the New Deal era.* Chicago: University of Chicago Press.

Schlesinger, A. M., Jr. (1958). *The coming of the New Deal.* Boston: Houghton Mifflin.

HOME RULE

Starting with the Progressive Era municipal reform movement, the phrase *home rule* identified efforts to maintain or to secure the authority to determine urban policy, law, finance, and governmental structure at the local level. Home rule came to have both legal and ideological connotations over the course of the 20th century. In a major devolution of power, a majority of states passed general incorporation laws for municipalities and legislation allowing cities to draft and amend their own charters. The principle of home rule, based on the idea that local governments are the closest to the people and therefore the best representatives of the public interest, became a powerful political appeal; federal government funded city programs directly starting in the 1930s. Home rule was also a rallying cry in opposition to regional government, planning, and regulation that threatened the autonomy of local government. By the late 20th century, however, the principle and practice of home rule came into question in light of urban problems including social inequity, failing schools, and economic decline.

Dating back to the colonial era, American towns and cities have had significant law enforcement, regulatory, and taxation powers. However, the U.S. Constitution makes no specific mention of local government, and by the mid-19th century, there was a general legal consensus that local governments were subordinate to states. Cities and counties were created by state legislatures, had no independent sovereignty, and were legally administered as divisions of the state. State legislatures (or Congress, in the unique case of Washington, D.C.) composed local government charters, determined their laws, and authorized all forms of taxation. The most influential legal assertion of state authority over local government was by Iowa State Supreme Court Justice John F. Dillon. In a series of cases in the 1860s and 1870s, Dillon ruled that municipalities were strictly limited to the powers expressly granted by state statute. Dillon obliquely referenced contemporary scandals, which included a rash of municipal defaults and bankruptcies around the country starting in the 1830s and revelations of corruption associated with machine politics. Limitations on city authority protected citizens from usury, bureaucratic overreaching, and speculation by public officials, he argued. "Dillon's rule" was upheld by the U.S. Supreme Court in the 1903 case *Atkins v. Kansas,* which famously declared that cities are "creatures, mere political subdivisions, of the State for the purpose of exercising its powers," and again in 1923 in *City of Trenton v. New Jersey.*

For much of the nation, however, absolute dominance of states over cities was neither politic nor pragmatic. The representational structure of many state governments vastly favored rural areas, and large cities were often chronically underfunded as a result.

Business associations and civic leagues proclaimed that greater independence and fiscal flexibility for cities were required to meet the demands of growing urban populations, especially in light of the technological innovations of the late 19th century. Home rule advocates promised improved services and public utilities, including expanded water supplies, modern sanitation systems, better streets, electricity, and effective law enforcement. Calls for home rule were accompanied by support for commission or city-manager charters and nonpartisan elections. City officials began to organize behind home rule, forming the National Municipal League in 1894, which issued model city charters and home rule legislation in 1900, 1916, and 1921. Although legislatures were reluctant to cede power to local officials, they could be swayed by strong public support for home rule, and voters approved referenda granting cities significant autonomy from states in the name of efficiency, reform, and local self-determination. By 1937, 21 states had adopted constitutional home rule amendments that granted one or more cities the power to draft and amend their own charters and to appoint excise and policy boards.

The Great Depression strengthened the cause of home rule. With primary responsibility for public relief, many cities faced financial ruin. President Franklin D. Roosevelt addressed the situation by forging new links between cities and the federal government, often bypassing states entirely in funding urban relief programs and working directly with mayors. Through the 1950s and 1960s, housing, transportation, and development programs reinforced the direct relationship between cities and the federal government. President Nixon's New Federalism included block grants to be spent largely at cities' discretion. At the same time, local taxes increased steadily, and an ever greater percentage of city revenue was devoted to promoting commercial development and growth as opposed to services or social programs.

In the courts, Dillon's rule succumbed to a much more permissive interpretation of the legal status of local government, which was articulated by Dean Jefferson Fordham in 1953 at the behest of the American Municipal Association. Fordham asserted cities' rights and responsibilities based on tradition, even in the absence of explicit constitutional provisions for them. To prevent judicial interference, however, he proposed that states pass general legislation formally detailing city responsibilities and discretion. By 1990, 37 states had passed generally applicable, constitutional home rule protections for cities, and 23 states had done the same for counties.

As city government grew stronger and more independent in the decades after World War II, the luster of home rule began to tarnish. Population growth and technological change again posed major challenges to urban cities and counties; pollution, traffic congestion, and low-density development strained local regulatory and service capacities. Rather than advocating for the expansion of existing governments, however, policy analysts and business associations focused on developing new regional agencies and governments at the metropolitan level. Home rule became an effective rallying cry for cities and counties as they opposed regional government that could threaten their hard-won local autonomy. Rather than regional governments, associative councils of governments formed in metropolitan areas to address metropolitan area problems and fulfill regional planning requirements, further strengthening the direct link between the federal government and cities.

In the 1980s and 1990s, calls for home rule were no longer associated with efforts for stronger local government but rather with opposition to federal oversight and regulation. Funding for cities was reduced under the Reagan administration, even as a national wave of tax revolts undermined municipal finances. This exacerbated growing problems of inequity in cities, particularly along racial lines and in terms of employment and education. In the late 20th century, Dillon's rule made a dramatic resurgence in courts around the country as home rule statutes, city authority, and the success of local policies came into question in a new political environment. Often citing urban policy that led directly to inequity, failure to meet requirements for basic services, and the exclusion of minorities from the decision-making process, courts began to assign more responsibility to state governments for overseeing and supporting urban services including education and welfare. Nevertheless, the principle of home rule, rooted in the venerable tradition of American federalism, remained compelling, and the degree of local governmental autonomy became an important legal and political question.

—Louise Nelson Dyble

Further Readings and References

Krane, D., Rigos, P. N., & Hill, M. B., Jr. (Eds.). (2001). *Home rule in America: A fifty-state handbook.* Washington, DC: CQ Press.

Pegram, T. R. (1992). *Partisans and progressives: Private interest and public policy in Illinois, 1870–1922.* Urbana and Chicago: University of Illinois Press.

U.S. Advisory Commission on Intergovernmental Relations. (1993). *State laws governing local government structure and administration.* Washington, DC: Author.

Zimmerman, J. F. (1983). *State-local relations: A partnership approach.* New York: Praeger.

HOMELESSNESS

Homelessness has been a recurrent problem in the United States. From the colonial period to the present day, the "wandering poor" have been a disquieting feature of American cities. How homelessness has manifested itself, however, what language was used to describe it, and what the response to it has been have differed across time and space.

Following English tradition, local responsibility for destitute residents was an obligation in the early years of the American republic. Although homelessness was not a serious problem in the 18th century, many communities adopted settlement laws and made clear distinctions among the different types of poverty; those individuals who were deemed not worthy or not legally the responsibility of the town could be warned out—physically banished. Often, transients were informally passed from town to town.

By the early decades of the 19th century, cities, particularly in the North, were marked by rapid physical growth and an equally rapid and growing economic inequality. Widespread destitution of African Americans and, by the eve of the Civil War, Irish immigrants, women as well as men, created the first vagrancy problem. The almshouse, the workhouse, and temporary municipal lodging houses appeared in New York City and other urban centers. In the 1850s, police stations in many cities became the providers of primitive and temporary overnight lodging for homeless men, women, and even children, particularly adolescent boys. With no uniform social welfare policy on the national level, there was only a confusion of state and local vagrancy and poor laws.

The dislocations following the Civil War and the severe industrial depression of the 1870s created a new and different type of homeless population, the so-called floating "army of the unemployed." Taking advantage of an expanding railroad network, jobless men roamed the towns and smaller cities of the West and brought an awareness of homelessness to the forefront of public consciousness, but not an understanding of its causes. Both reformers and social scientists were slow (or unwilling) to examine the connection between economic conditions and tramping men. As this nomadic and distinctly white male subculture expanded and occasionally grew violent during the even more severe economic crisis of the 1890s, it assumed the mantle of a menace and a social problem. Communities across the country passed laws to control vagrancy and restrict tramping but had little success. As a result of dramatic changes in patterns of immigration, an increasing dependence on wages, and rapid urbanization, the homeless transient worker, the self-styled hobo or tramp, became part of a highly visible, if undisciplined, migratory labor force in the western part of the United States. Forming the backbone of seasonal wage work in agriculture, timber, construction, and mining, the unattached itinerant man represented a cross section of the white working class. Whether "riding the rails" or "hopping the freights," tramping workers, whose real lives were harsh and often dangerous, became an integral part of the American myth of rugged individualism, freedom on the frontier, and the hyper-masculine romance of the road. Such well-known writers and journalists as Carl Sandburg, Jack London, Jacob Riis, and Nels Anderson were proud of having tramped in the closing years of the 19th and early part of the 20th century. Although statistically overrepresented among the urban homeless, few women were among the tramping population. Life on the road was even more dangerous and uncertain for a female, and the sight of a "lady hobo" in a boxcar or hobo "jungle" was rare. Vulnerable to sexual assault, women commonly paired up with men or masqueraded as men for protection.

The decades prior to the turn of the 20th century mark both the heyday of the itinerant worker and the creation of urban "main stems," distinct hobo districts, in cities throughout the United States. Chicago was the unquestioned hobo capital of North America. The major east-west transportation hub in the country, a clearinghouse for employment information, and a location for institutions catering to a transient population (including a "hobo college"), the city provided anonymity along with cheap shelter options, a wide variety of commercial services, and leisure activities for changing populations of homeless men. Although the numbers are unclear, a gay subculture appears to have thrived on the main stem in Chicago and in other large cities. Gender and racial segregation were the norm. Women (other than prostitutes), African Americans, and Asians were unwelcome if not systematically barred from many of the lodging house districts. Like Chicago, New York City's Bowery and other urban skid row areas became synonymous, from the late 19th century until urban renewal of the 1970s, with a homeless male subculture of derelicts and tramps, with flophouses, brothels, saloons, and squalor.

Although the language of homelessness appeared only in the 20th century, a vast network of organized charity and philanthropy focused on the persistent problem of urban homelessness in the 19th century. Street children and women suspected of being prostitutes were particular subjects of reformers' anxieties, and evangelical groups established a network of maternity homes for women and girls. But men, too, always the largest "unhoused" population, came increasingly under the scrutiny of welfare organizations and rescue missions. Although distinctions between the worthy and unworthy poor persisted, ideas about causes and treatment of homelessness changed over the decades and came under the influence of social science studies and surveys. Both public and private charities came to view male homelessness as a problem to be managed, if not solved. Shelter, not reform, became the objective prior to the Great Depression. A mixture of accommodations ranging from Salvation Army flops, wayfarers' lodges, police stations, and cheap hotels for single men and women were among the various possibilities for the homeless. Some of the homeless (then as now) avoided all institutional settings, preferring to "sleep rough" or find their own casual lodgings, but others sought out shelter. No matter how many beds cities such as New York and Chicago provided, during periods of severe economic crisis, the demand overwhelmed available space.

The Great Depression of the 1930s marked a turning point in both public attitudes and policies. The homeless now appeared as victims of an economic catastrophe, and the extraordinary situation forced the federal government to become involved. There were two major categories of the homeless in the 1930s: rural refugees of the Dust Bowl, whose situation was seared into public imagination by Farm Security Administration photographs; and the urban homeless, represented in grainy photos of men selling apples or standing in breadlines. Rural or urban, male or female, single or in family groups, the numbers of people suddenly uprooted from their normal lives and needing shelter skyrocketed; estimates of the homeless were in the millions. The traditionally destitute together with the "new poor," "respectable" women and white-collar men, overwhelmed social services in every city. As public and private agencies scrambled for ways to feed and house those without any resources in the early years of the Depression, ad hoc responses became the norm. Thousands were left out of the equation of need and made do: Men (and some women) lived in parks and shantytowns (derisively called Hoovervilles), under bridges, and even on the street. In New York City, the homeless called the subway "the five cent flop." For the first time, large numbers of white women were among the homeless. Widowed or deserted, but overwhelmingly single and unattached, many women were stranded with the disappearance of the jobs that had drawn them to the cities in the 1920s. Destitute women had never appeared in significant numbers in any prior economic crisis and, unlike men, they were not a significant presence on breadlines or on city streets. Although they remained largely invisible to officials and the public alike, women nevertheless represented about 10 percent of the urban homeless population during this period. Some cities had no facilities for needy females. African Americans, men as well as women, who had been marginalized by deep-seated racial and sexual stereotyping in both the labor and housing markets prior to the Depression, were another group that was officially ignored during the early years of the Depression and forced to turn for help to churches and other struggling institutions in black communities. Although their numbers increased dramatically in the early 1930s, the African American homeless confronted persistent and widespread discrimination. Many private shelter options were closed to them, and only in municipal shelters could black men and women be assured of a bed. After the election of Franklin Delano Roosevelt in 1932, the federal government made a massive commitment to economic recovery and assumed partial responsibility for the unemployed, the transient, and the homeless. Viewing them as unwitting victims of an economic disaster, New Deal administrators together with the U.S. Congress created a multitude of agencies and programs to stem the free fall, among them the Federal Emergency Relief Act (FERA) of 1933. FERA, followed by the Works Progress Administration (WPA) and the Social Security Act in 1935, provided direct grants to the states to aid the transient and homeless population and to create temporary jobs for those with legal residences. For the first time, single adults with no dependents became eligible for home relief. As public aid replaced begging, soup kitchens, and al fresco encampments, the problem of homelessness in urban areas gradually lessened in the years leading up to World War II.

Following that war, as skid row replaced the main stem in American cities, hoboes became bums. Defined by the language of pathology, homeless men, many of whom were alcoholics, were predominantly middle-aged white men who, although rootless, were more sedentary than turn-of-the-century hoboes and tramps. Black men, forced by discrimination to seek refuge in urban ghettos, were the "hidden homeless" in the postwar years. White or black, this floating male urban population attracted little attention and remained only a local nuisance until the mid-1970s.

There is no single explanation for the explosion of homelessness that began in the 1970s and still constitutes a major social problem in cities throughout the United States. Federal policies and legislation that affected employment opportunities, as well as fiscal, mental health, and housing decisions, were the major culprits, but local factors, including the availability of public and low-rent housing, zoning changes, work programs, welfare benefits, drugs, and gentrification were also at play in any given situation. Coupled with changing family structures and the destruction of bounded skid row districts and single room occupancy (SRO) living units, the heretofore hidden homeless spread out across urban areas and became a highly visible population of street people and shelter residents. The numbers varied depending on the locale and the method of counting, but hundreds of thousands of people were officially homeless by the early 1980s; the largest number of these were members of racial minorities—single men, unattached women, and, for the first time, mothers with children. Emerging in a period of unequaled prosperity for many Americans, the new homeless found only sporadic public sympathy and support. A collective shift in consciousness had taken place. Although the public demanded that city officials "do something," particularly for families, much of this outcry was in fact a demand to remove the eyesore—to reclaim the parks, the streets, the train stations, and other public places. The welfare hotel, the panhandler, and the "bag lady" became enduring emblems of the crisis.

A constant stream of statistics, policy studies, monographs, and investigative reports followed the growth of the new homelessness. Organized in 1982, the National Coalition for the Homeless along with many local organizations has worked to keep the problem at the forefront of the nation's consciousness and social agenda. The goal has been to force cities to provide support and adequate services for the very poor and to consider the political issues of income maintenance, affordable housing, and race.

Homelessness is, in many respects, timeless. Visible homelessness creates a sense of urban disorder and anxiety, and with the exception of the Great Depression period, people tend to see the homeless as disruptive of social order and as possibly dangerous. Homelessness is, in fact, often the end result of problems involving the issues of gender and race that much of the housed world would prefer to ignore. There is no consensus about what is wrong and how it can be fixed.

—Elaine S. Abelson

Further Readings and References

Abelson, E. (1999). Homeless in America. *Journal of Urban History, 25(2)*, 258–270.

DePastino, T. (2003). *Citizen hobo: How a century of homelessness shaped America.* Chicago: University of Chicago Press.

Katz, M. B. (1989). *The undeserving poor: From the war on poverty to the war on welfare.* New York: Pantheon.

Kusmer, K. L. (2002). *Down and out, on the road: The homeless in American history.* New York: Oxford University Press.

HOMEOWNERSHIP

The single-family owner-occupied house was, by the mid-20th century, widely seen as a mark of middle-class status and a symbol of the American dream. Yet, the American celebration of homeownership was not inherent to an American sensibility nor an inevitable result of American political ideology. Rather, it emerged out of the changing conditions of work and housing in late-19th-century industrializing cities. It was fueled by Progressive Era reform campaigns, New Deal housing programs, and postwar federal subsidies to home buyers until by 1970, more than 60 percent of Americans owned their homes. In less than a century, the single-family, owner-occupied house— whether the Cape Cod in a New England suburb, the Chicago bungalow, or the southwestern ranch-style home—had come to epitomize the American way of life.

Thomas Jefferson's vision of an agrarian republic suggests the importance early Americans placed on property. But in Jefferson's world, homeowners used their property to produce income or necessities for their households; a house sat at the center of a farm or was attached to a craftsman's workshop. A home in an urban industrial center appeared stripped of such economic purpose. A crucial fact, often forgotten, is that urban Americans placed little emphasis on homeownership through most of the 19th century.

It was European immigrants to northern cities in the late 19th century who first linked the ownership of an urban cottage to "the American standard of life." For Europeans who arrived in American cities after the Civil War, the acquisition of landed property bore both ideological and economic weight. Buying a house meant, literally, the purchase of a new status as an American and a break with Old World land tenure systems that left landed property in the hands of rural aristocracies. Homeownership in America was secured through communal efforts of loaning money for down payments, cooperative associations providing mortgages, and the boarding of recent arrivals in the dwellings of their fellow countrymen. Conceived as conferring autonomy from employers, homeownership enabled low-wage workers to augment household income with backyard gardens, boarders, and the use of houses as collateral for loans. Homeownership did not lift wage laborers into the middle classes, but it often helped sustain families struggling to survive in low-wage industrial economies.

By the 1880s, as many as 20 to 30 percent of wage workers in northern industrial cities owned their homes. In Chicago, they bought four- and six-room frame cottages, in Pittsburgh brick row houses, and in Boston two-story frame houses. Some workers built houses

themselves whereas others paid local carpenters, who typically constructed three to six houses each year. Ownership of residential property proved to be not only a short-term strategy to generate additional income but also a long-term investment, a hedge against future uncertainties and, at best, a means for leaving something of value to the next generation.

The gradual expansion of the home construction industry spurred suburbanization and drew new buyers into homeownership. In the late 1880s, a new generation of businessmen—men who purchased land, subdivided lots, and built single-family houses— began selling houses on the edges of cities. Using standardized materials and factory-made door frames, window sashes, and molding, builders could hire larger numbers of unskilled laborers and construct many more houses than a single carpenter could build in a year. Builders used the expansion of urban rail lines, which lowered the cost and time of commuting to a city center, to attract new buyers to suburban houses. When municipalities constructed sewer and water systems, builders installed indoor plumbing, which increased the costs of housing but enabled builders to market the health benefits of homeownership. Constructing larger and more elaborate houses, often priced beyond the means of ordinary workers, builders developed advertising campaigns to draw more affluent buyers into homeownership.

By the turn of the century, social reformers were contributing to the expansion of urban housing markets. Health reformers, concerned about the threat of contagious diseases, urged residents to seek healthy environments in suburban locales. Settlement house volunteers, who surveyed living conditions in impoverished communities, argued that overcrowding proved a medical and moral danger to children. Reformers such as Jane Addams in Chicago or Lawrence Villier in New York promoted a vision of family privacy, advising families to remove both boarders and servants from their homes. The owner-occupied single-family home would secure family privacy and household health.

In northern cities in the 1910s and 1920s, African Americans arriving from the rural and small-town South struggled to find loans to purchase houses. Facing increasingly rigid racial segregation, most black migrants moved into rental dwellings in largely black neighborhoods. Some black real estate entrepreneurs, for example, Philip Payton in Harlem and Jesse Binga in Chicago, provided home loans to black home buyers, and small suburbs of predominantly African American homeowners were built in the 1920s. For black Americans, faced with racial covenants attached to property titles and regularly rejected by creditors, homeownership proved a near-impossible aspiration.

By 1920, more than 40 percent of Americans owned their homes. In 1923, Secretary of Commerce (and future president) Herbert Hoover wrote that the growing number of homeowners was the sign of a solid economic society. Believing that homeownership served both the spiritual and economic needs of the nation, Hoover launched publicity campaigns and housing conferences to promote homeownership. With his Better Homes for America campaign, thousands of volunteers distributed Commerce Department pamphlets and held yearly contests to encourage their neighbors to buy houses. The home construction industry boomed through the mid-twenties.

The Great Depression devastated both the housing industry and homeowners. Between 1928 and 1933, construction of residential property fell by 95 percent. In 1930, about 150,000 nonfarm households lost their property to foreclosure; 2 years later, that number leapt to 250,000. In response, Franklin Roosevelt's New Deal passed legislation to bolster the building industry and rescue homeowners facing imminent foreclosure. The Home Owners Loan Corporation, signed into law on June 13, 1933, refinanced tens of thousands of mortgages in danger of foreclosure and introduced the long-term, self-amortizing mortgage, replacing the typical 5- to 10-year mortgage used by most buyers in the 1920s.

With the passage of the National Housing Act on June 27, 1934, Congress established the Federal Housing Administration, the federal agency most responsible for the dramatic increase in homeownership rates in the years following World War II. The FHA, designed to stimulate building without direct government spending, insured home mortgages provided by private lenders and revolutionized the home finance industry. It reduced down payments from about 30 percent to less than 10 percent, extended the repayment period for its guaranteed mortgages to 25 to 30 years, and established minimum standards for home construction that became almost standard in the industry. The FHA was later supplemented by the Servicemen's Readjustment Act of 1944, or the GI Bill.

The calamitous underside of FHA policies was the increasing racial segregation of American cities and suburbs. The FHA, using a property appraisal system developed by the HOLC, readily insured mortgages in new white suburbs while typically rejecting loans in older urban areas. Concerned with "inharmonious racial or nationality groups," FHA appraisers contended that an area would lose value if racial segregation was not enforced. The result was that suburban developers largely refused to sell houses to black buyers, and urban black neighborhoods were left starved for investment capital.

With continued federal subsidies to builders and buyers, homeownership rates expanded dramatically in the years after World War II. Single-family housing starts jumped from 114,000 in 1944 to more than 1 million in 1948. By 1950, the national suburban growth rate was 10 times that of central cities. The emblems of the postwar suburbanization and homeownership were the Levittowns, built by William J. Levitt. With his first development in 1947, Levitt blanketed 4,000 acres of potato farms in Hempstead, Long Island with rows of identical single-family houses. Each dwelling included a 12- by 16-foot living room with fireplace, one bath, two bedrooms, and a kitchen near the front entrance. Initially priced at $7,999, the houses were affordable for working-class buyers, although Levitt, following FHA policies, refused to sell to African Americans. Although architectural critics derided the "cookie-cutter lots," Levittown was wildly popular. Levitt's scheme was copied by builders across the country.

By 1972, the FHA had insured mortgages for nearly 11 million families. Racially discriminatory lending practices were challenged in the courts, and civil rights advocates were working to make homeownership achievable for an ever larger public. In 1980, homeownership rates hit 63 percent. An ideal inspired by immigrant wage laborers struggling to survive in industrializing cities, the single-family, owner-occupied house had become the American dream.

—*Margaret Garb*

Further Readings and References

Edel, M., Sclar, E. D., & Luria, D. (1984). *Shaky palaces: Homeownership and social mobility in Boston's suburbanization.* New York: Columbia University Press.

Nicholaides, B. (2002). *My blue heaven: Life and politics in the working-class suburbs of Los Angeles, 1920–1965.* Chicago: The University of Chicago Press.

Thernstrom, S. (1970). *Poverty and progress: Social mobility in a nineteenth century city.* New York: Atheneum.

Warner, S. B. (1962). *Streetcar suburbs: The process of growth in Boston, 1870–1900.* Cambridge, MA: Harvard University Press.

Wiese, A. (2004). *Places of their own: African American suburbanization in the twentieth century.* Chicago: University of Chicago Press.

Zunz, O. (1982). *The changing face of inequality: Urbanization, industrial development, and immigration in Detroit, 1880–1920.* Chicago: University of Chicago Press.

HOMICIDE

For at least two centuries, Americans have associated cities with crime, particularly violent crime. Such fears have informed public policy, infused political debates, and infected attitudes toward working-class, foreign-born, and African American city dwellers. But for most of the nation's history, urban centers have been less violent than the supposedly harmonious, morally wholesome American countryside. The nation's most urbanized states typically have had modest rates of homicide, and even New York City, long considered a cauldron of violence, had a lower homicide rate than the United States as whole for most of the 20th century. The relationship between criminal violence and the American city, however, has not been static. Urban violence has changed dramatically over the course of American history, reflecting broader shifts in the nature of city life.

Social scientists analyzing violence chart rates of homicide, calculating the number of murders and manslaughters per hundred thousand residents. By employing a standardized measure that controls for population size, scholars can compare levels of violence over time and across space. Moreover, unlike assault and battery or other forms of criminal violence, homicide has had a relatively unambiguous and unchanging definition, and therefore, rates of homicide provide the most accurate measures of violent behavior. During the last two decades, historians have produced a sophisticated body of scholarship on this topic, making it possible to identify long-term changes in violence—and to dash the centuries-old myth that cities generate violence.

Until the middle decades of the 19th century, American cities experienced little violence. Although buffeted by the unsettling effects of rapid population growth and early industrialization, cities such as New York, Philadelphia, and Boston had low homicide rates through the presidency of Andrew Jackson. From the 1840s until the 1860s, however, levels of violent death rose sharply, doubling in some urban centers. A confluence of demographic, social, and cultural factors produced this explosion of violence. High levels of immigration and poverty, for example, worked in combination with changing class and gender ideologies to forge a raucous bachelor subculture at mid-century, in which young men established their status through drinking and brawling.

In the established urban centers of the Northeast, rates of lethal violence remained steady or fell during the final third of the 19th century, despite the sudden proliferation of inexpensive guns, rising levels of poverty, searing ethnic, racial, and class conflict, and skyrocketing population densities. Urban historians have argued that cultural and institutional forces increased public order during this period, discouraging brawling, drunkenness, and other activities that spurred "recreational" violence. Employers demanded increasing regimentation in the factory; schools inculcated self-control; and law enforcers criminalized aggressive, disorderly behavior. Turn-of-the-century New York City, for example, had a fragmented and surging population but a modest level of violent crime. The city's homicide rate during the late 1910s was about half of the national rate and one fifth of Mississippi's homicide rate. Neither population density nor heterogeneity triggered high levels of violence in the industrial city.

But urban homicide rates have varied over space as well as time. Western cities and particularly southern cities, although smaller than the great population centers of the Northeast, have experienced high rates of violence, reflecting acrimonious race relations, institutional instability, and regional cultures that celebrate aggression. The homicide rate in early-20th-century Memphis, for example, was four times that of San Francisco, six times that of Chicago, nine times that of New York City, and nearly 13 times that of Philadelphia. Charleston, Savannah, New Orleans, and Atlanta also suffered from levels of lethal violence far greater than cities outside of the South. Although the gap narrowed over the course of the 20th century, southern cities continue to be more violent than their northern or midwestern counterparts.

Urban homicide rates ebbed during the Great Depression, suggesting that poverty by itself does not spark violence, and then skyrocketed from the 1960s through the 1980s. Chicago's homicide rate, for instance, dropped by 51 percent during the 1930s, but it tripled between 1960 and 1990. Cultural pressures, racial conflict, economic dislocation, easy access to handguns, a spike in the proportion of teenagers in the population, and unstable drug markets interacted and contributed to the surge in urban violence during this period. America's great cities became more violent than the nation as a whole in this era, exaggerating political and racial tensions in the process. During the final decade of the 20th century, however, urban and national homicide rates tumbled, falling by 50 percent in New York City and other urban centers. But big-city trends have increasingly shaped national trends in lethal violence. To a considerable extent, rates of homicide in late-20th-century America fell as a consequence of changes in the nation's urban centers. In 1991, New York City alone accounted for 9 percent of the nation's homicides, and seven cities accounted for a quarter of American homicides. Thus, the drop in homicides in major urban centers largely produced the drop in national homicide rates.

Just as the United States has long suffered from significantly higher rates of violence than most other nations, American cities have been—and continue to be—more violent than their counterparts in other nations; American cities have been awash with blood. Early-20th-century Chicago typically had more homicides per year than England and Wales combined. Similarly, late-20th-century New York City had a homicide rate 11 times that of London, and late-20th-century Los Angeles was 20 times more homicidal than Sydney, Australia. As social, cultural, and racial tensions shift, levels of homicide in American cities will change as well, although by international standards, urban America, like the nation as a whole, has been and remains extraordinarily violent.

—*Jeffrey S. Adler*

See also Crime and Criminals; Criminal Justice System

Further Readings and References

Blumstein, A., & Wallman, J. (Eds.). (2000). *The crime drop in America.* New York: Cambridge University Press.

Hoffman, F. (1925). *The homicide problem.* Newark, NJ: Prudential Press.

Lane, R. (1997). *Murder in America.* Columbus: Ohio State University Press.

Monkkonen, E. (2001). *Murder in New York City.* Berkeley: University of California Press.

HOPPER, EDWARD

Edward Hopper (1882–1967) appropriated the visual iconography of the American city and made paintings out of it. Timeless, haunting images of men and women in urban settings engaged in the act of being human are his trademark. Whether depicting the recognizable but stark landscape of the filling station along a rural road or a corner diner in the midst of a city block, Hopper's canvases portray human life and suggest the psychological drama that accompanies daily existence. In his work, the city forms a backdrop and a metaphor for larger human realities and conditions.

Hopper used light like a saber, slashing through interior space, throwing light into space to make known people, isolated in private rooms, alone in their thoughts or their simple tasks, detached or absorbed in their own stories. Very much of a particular era, the Depression of the 1920s and 1930s, Hopper's work is nevertheless universal in its appeal and timeless in its effect. His simple and compelling images inspire the imagination and allow viewers to construct and interpret what they see. Most of his characters seem oblivious of their surroundings, which he constructs intentionally and simply to frame what is most important—their absorption in thought. Exposed to moments that seem at the same time intensely important yet incredibly ordinary, viewers become voyeurs or spectators taking it all in from the briefest of views. Rather than referencing specific places, these interior or exterior views capture the essence of many places or even types of places, which again makes it easy for viewers to place themselves in the narrative. These paintings rely on pictorial narrative terms to suggest rather than tell a specific story; they leave impressions or compelling images that seem to speak solemn volumes. Rather than dramas full of action, they are the intense moments before people act, when they contemplate actions, moments charged with the potential of something immense.

Hopper interprets the modern human condition through his paintings, using light, the settings of American cities, and men and women turned inward in thought.

Edward Hopper was born in Nyack, New York, in 1882 and moved to New York City in 1913, where he lived until his death in 1967. In his 20s, Hopper produced illustrations for magazines, books, and even posters, and he became well known as a painter of the American human landscape while in his early 40s, meeting with immediate and significant success and recognition after a one-man show at the Frank K. M. Rehn Gallery. Known as an acute observer of American everyday life, he was a realist at the same time that he greatly simplified and abstracted what he "saw" in the real world around him. There is often a sense in his world of exclusion or withdrawal, of human beings watching life move on around them. Much of his work seems to involve individuals dealing with the problems that resulted from the industrialization of American cities. In this, Hopper is a narrator of a particular moment in the American urban experience.

—*Martha Bradley*

See also Great Depression and Cities

Further Readings and References

Hobbs, R. (1987). *Edward Hopper.* New York: Harry N. Abrams.
Wagstaff, S. (2004). *Edward Hopper.* New York: Tate P.

HORNE, FRANK S.

Frank Smith Horne (1899–1974) was born in New York City on August 18, 1899. An uncle to entertainer Lena Horne, he graduated from the City College of New York (B.A.) in 1921 and earned a doctorate from the Northern Illinois College of Ophthalmology (where he passed for white) a scant 2 years later. Horne practiced optometry in New York and Chicago between 1923 and 1926 before turning to teaching. He completed an M.A. degree from the University of Southern California in 1933 and became a dean and the acting president of Fort Valley State College in Georgia between 1926 and 1935. More than an educator or doctor, the multitalented Horne published award-winning poetry in *Crisis* and *Opportunity* and saw his work anthologized in volumes edited by Countee Cullen, Langston Hughes, and Arna Bontemps. Probably best known for "Letters Found

Near a Suicide," his contributions to the Harlem Renaissance were noteworthy, if only a prelude to a life of public service.

Horne's career took a decisive turn when Mary McLeod Bethune recruited him to be the assistant director of the Division of Negro Affairs in the National Youth Administration (1935–1938). Horne soon left that job to work for Dr. Robert C. Weaver, who helped establish the Racial Relations Service (RRS) under the U.S. Housing Authority between 1938 and 1940. By 1940, Horne replaced Weaver as the head of the RRS, becoming after World War II an assistant to the administrator of the new (1947) Housing and Home Finance Agency (HHFA).

As that agency's chief race relations officer, Horne became nationally recognized for his housing expertise and zealousness in defense of minority interests. In the late 1930s, Horne and Weaver elevated the notion of equity into a policy that not only dispensed public housing on the basis of demographics and need, but offered minority access to construction and management jobs as well. Pushing the concept of equity as far as the changing postwar world would allow, Horne became the strongest voice within the bureaucracy to champion (unsuccessfully) a color-blind policy of nondiscrimination in all housing programs. His lengthy internal memoranda warned accurately of the inevitably disastrous results that would flow from urban redevelopment and renewal carried out on a discriminatory basis. The Eisenhower administration sought the removal of this dedicated New Dealer for political reasons in 1953, but a wave of protest extolling Horne's knowledge and competence forced the Republicans to retain him in a face-saving compromise. Within a year, however, Horne's resistance to the use of government programs to reinforce the ghetto, along with his desire to apply an expansive interpretation of the U.S. Supreme Court's ruling in *Brown v. Board of Education* to federally supported housing projects, secured his dismissal in 1955. The HHFA, heretofore somewhat restrained by bureaucratic infighting, now accelerated plans that included the massive displacement and forced relocation of minorities in the name of urban renewal.

Following his forced departure, Horne moved back to New York, where he became director of the City Commission on Intergroup Relations and later a staff member of the City Housing Redevelopment Board. He was also a founder of the National Committee Against Discrimination in Housing (NCDH) in 1950 and was its honorary chair at the time of his death on September 7, 1974.

—*Arnold R. Hirsch*

See also Federal Housing Administration; Housing Act of 1949; Housing Act of 1954; Public Housing; Urban Renewal and Revitalization; Weaver, Robert C.

Further Readings and References

Hirsch, A. R. (2000). Containment on the home front: Race and federal housing policy from the New Deal to the Cold War. *Journal of Urban History, 26,* 158–189.

Hirsch, A. R. (2000). Searching for a "sound Negro policy": A racial agenda for the housing acts of 1949 and 1954. *Housing Policy Debate, 11*(2), 393–441.

Horses in Cities

In any urban area, the need to transport both goods and people is paramount. Many people in early urban history lived within typical walking distance of work. Thus, their employment possibilities were limited by how far they were willing to commute to work. As the country expanded westward, the need for transportation became more pressing, and the use of horses became more pronounced. Horses were a common sight in most urban areas until the early part of the 20th century. Horses were used to pull freight wagons and passenger coaches, as well as various other municipal conveyances.

Municipalities were called on to account for horses in the development of urban infrastructure, with a mixed record. For example, streets were usually designed to allow two wagons to pass side by side at the same time, but no provision was made for what would happen if a horse had to go over uneven or unpaved roads. In addition, equine waste disposal was rarely optimal, and open sewers made equine health difficult at times. The cities managed as best they could, nevertheless.

When the first omnibuses were introduced in cities (basically streetcars pulled by horses rather than some other sort of propulsion system), the horses seemed to be a perfect way to operate. Unfortunately, the horses strained under the physical weight of the cars, and many hurt themselves or were maltreated by the drivers. In the summer months in places such as New York and Chicago, the stress of physical exertion was such that horses often just lay down and died. To ameliorate these problems, teamsters tried to give horses breaks if they were starting long hauls, or they had extra horses on standby to help pull heavy loads up hills.

The problem of sanitation was difficult enough for cities, but it was compounded by the fact that horses also had to pull the garbage wagons. When a horse died, it often stayed where it dropped because loading a 1,000-pound animal onto a garbage wagon was difficult under the best circumstances and pulling the resulting wagon would quite likely result in another horse's death. A rotting carcass attracted vermin, further spreading disease and creating a pungent smell.

Cities also faced challenges related to boarding the horses. An average horse produces 10 to 20 pounds of solid waste a day and consumes 16 to 20 pounds of food. In addition, horses must be housed in an area that is adequate enough for them to remain healthy. With these considerations, there was limited space for horses in any city, let alone in a city that relied heavily on their use. In 1900, New York City had about 130,000 horses, even though newly designed public transportation systems such as the elevated and subway trains were already in use. In Chicago, the number of horses was not nearly as large (about 74,000), but that was still a substantial number to accommodate. Philadelphia and St. Louis maintained at least 35,000 animals apiece.

For citizens as well as city employees, the horse was both a godsend and a nuisance. Horses could transport many times the amount of goods that a person could carry, and they could travel faster than a person could walk. On the downside, horses were often easily spooked. Police commendation reports often cited an officer's bravery in slowing down runaway horses before the animals injured people. Large portions of city budgets also went for the upkeep of horses. The Chicago Police Department in 1900 employed five staff veterinarians to provide the horses with medical attention. The veterinarians had to help keep the animals that pulled emergency response vehicles in at least passable shape. Even if the horses were well cared for, their life expectancy was only 4 to 5 years.

Sickness was not uncommon. For example, in 1872, a major fire erupted in the downtown area of Boston. While the loss of life was not as severe as in the famous Chicago conflagration, the fire was unchecked for a while because the horses that pulled fire engines were either sick or dead from the great horse epidemic (called the Great Epizootic) of that same summer. The fire department hired day laborers to haul the wagons, but it did little good for many of the buildings. In the end, 14 people died, more than 1,000 lost their jobs, and 776 buildings over 65 acres were burnt to the ground.

Horses were prohibitively expensive for all but the rich to board within a city. So while the rich were able to afford a private coach, most people could not pay even the 5-cent fare to ride the city's horse cars. The first real challenges to the dominance of the horse came with the streetcars, run by steam generators or later electricity and pulled by cable or powered by electricity and run on tracks. The railroads within a city also gave competition to horse-drawn services, but horses were still retained to go places where the railroads, trolleys, and cable cars could not go. Another major threat to the dominance of the horse came in the late 1880s when the safety bicycle was introduced. The bike was seen as a better alternative to the horse, as it was easy to store, required minimal maintenance, and did not leave health-threatening waste on the street. The advent of the auto spelled the end of horse employment. Despite predictions that the horse would remain the dominant form of transportation for the rich, the car was seen as the next step in transportation technology. It did not spook like a horse, it was easier to store, and it was at the control of the driver (so long as the driver was vigilant). The horse was proven to be inferior. By the late 1910s, the horse was removed from most urban areas. Only recently have horses returned to the urban setting, but they are used primarily by the police for crowd control and by hansom drivers for tourists who want to see a city at the speed that their great-grandparents once did.

—*Cord Scott*

Further Readings and References

Goddard, S. (1996). *Getting there: The epic struggle between road and rail in the American century.* Chicago: University of Chicago Press.

Kaszynski, W. (2000). *The American highway.* Jefferson, NC: McFarland Press.

McShane, C. (1994). *Down the asphalt path.* Chichester, NY: Columbia University Press.

Miller, D. (1996). *City of the century.* New York: Touchstone.

HOSPITALS

The first permanent American hospital, Pennsylvania Hospital, was established in Philadelphia in 1752. Other early urban hospitals included New York Hospital (1771) and Massachusetts General Hospital in Boston (1821). Each hospital was founded as a charity for the care of the indigent sick, and urban hospital care in the early 19th century continued to be overwhelmingly for the care of the poor. In most cases, it was difficult to separate the physical and economic ills of the patients; reflecting this, New York's first municipal general hospital, Bellevue, was part of the city's almshouse until 1849. (Temporary hospitals such as quarantine hospitals, military hospitals, and inoculation hospitals also date back to the colonial era.)

The number of American hospitals began to increase in the antebellum period, and after the Civil War, the numbers increased dramatically. The first survey of American hospitals in 1873 counted just 178; by 1900, American institutions caring for the sick numbered in the thousands. They included hospitals of various kinds: General hospitals treated patients of both sexes, of different ages, and suffering from a variety of illnesses, and a multitude of hospitals were dedicated to the care of specific illnesses and patients. In addition, institutions referred to as asylums or homes also delivered medical care, for example, maternity homes.

The increase in hospitals was the result of public and private initiative. Municipalities and benevolent organizations founded charity hospitals in response to the growing number of Americans, usually city dwellers, who were no longer able to rely on traditional means of care and support in times of illness or infirmity. In the early 19th century, hospital affiliation and experience was a credential of elite, usually urban physicians, but doctors were not the primary caretakers or decision makers in hospitals; hospital administrators were. Cultural and religious aspects of hospital care were central to the patient's hospital experience in the 19th century. Admission requirements often included character judgments and references, and hospital caretakers often considered patients to be ripe prospects for conversion, subjecting them to heavy doses of evangelizing along with a bed, food, and nursing care. Religious hospitals were organized to offer alternatives; however, they rarely offered a different set of therapeutics. Rather, they provided a setting where patients could speak their own language, be visited by their own clergy, and eat what they were accustomed to or required to eat by their religious beliefs. Confronted with discriminatory admission practices in other hospitals, African Americans also organized their own hospitals later in the century. Urban examples include Provident Hospital in Chicago (1891) and Douglass Hospital in Philadelphia (1895). Like religious and ethnic hospitals, African American hospitals also provided physicians with an opportunity for clinical training denied them elsewhere.

The introduction of antiseptic and aseptic techniques in the 1870s made surgery safer, and as a result, the number of hospital surgeries grew in the latter part of the 19th century. Fears about the dangers of hospitals and the social stigma of hospital care remained, however. Even as the number of hospitals grew, most Americans still received health care treatment elsewhere: in their own homes, in a physician's office, or, in the case of the urban poor, in dispensaries, which provided walk-in medical care to the poor.

As hospital growth continued in the early 20th century, the hospital and its role in American medicine changed, too. On the eve of World War I, a new kind of general hospital emerged. It eclipsed all other kinds of hospitals and came to assume a primary place in the American health care delivery system. Unlike earlier general hospitals, this new institution provided acute rather than chronic care, and increasingly, patients were from all walks of life.

The professionalization of nursing was a critical factor in the reorganization of the modern hospital. Prior to the mid-19th century, with the exception of religious women who nursed, hospital nursing was considered a disreputable job. Beginning in the Civil War, American women reformed nursing and nursing education through the introduction of hospital nurses training schools. (The first of these opened in Boston, New Haven (Connecticut), and New York in 1873.) Besides opening a new occupation for American women, the training schools provided hospitals with a skilled labor force that allowed them to attract and care for a greater number of patients. A shift in attitude about hospital care was a critical factor as well. As patient populations expanded and philanthropic sources dwindled at the end of the 19th century, hospitals founded as charities increasingly required patients to pay at least something toward their care. In addition to raising hospital revenues, this also minimized some of the social stigma attached to hospital

care. (The historical designation of hospitals as public or private is misleading. The varied origins of American hospitals created a system of public and private, often referred to as voluntary hospitals in the United States. Voluntary hospitals have often referred to themselves as public because of their admissions policy. The line between public and private is also historically blurred because private hospitals have often received public support.)

Further changes in the organization of the American hospital came about as the result of deliberate efforts. Progressive Era reformers applied their hand to hospital development and were largely successful in their efforts to standardize the organization of the new modern hospital. All areas of hospital care and management were targeted by reformers, who sought efficiency through standardization. In this same period, the Carnegie Foundation's Flexner Report of 1920 greased the wheels and hastened the movement that made hospital training a required component of medical education and made hospital affiliations necessary for medical schools.

By the 1920s, the image of the American hospital as a charity was waning. Hospitals actively sought paying patients by advertising comfort in private rooms as well as the most up-to-date medicine. Hospital treatment for numerous illnesses grew commonplace, and certain procedures—for example, appendectomies, tonsillectomies, and X-ray testing, were increasingly performed only in a hospital. Hospital stays were much shorter than in the earlier period, and the ethnic and religious aspects of hospital care were no longer emphasized. The role and importance of the doctor in hospital care and treatment had increased tremendously, and most significant, the American hospital was no longer characterized as or considered a charity institution.

Regional, ethnic, and class differences still continued to distinguish the way Americans received or sought hospital care, even as, by the mid-1930s, one third of all Americans were born and died in hospitals. Hospitals and hospital care were much more common in cities than in rural areas and in the South. Urban hospitals remained under the auspices of the groups that had founded them, but increasingly, city dwellers chose a hospital because of its location, not its religious or ethnic affiliations. The cost of hospital care continued to be a problem for both administrators and patients. Reformers suggested compulsory national health insurance, but efforts to organize voluntary group health insurance plans that covered the cost of hospital care were more successful (e.g., Blue Cross).

After World War II, the role of the American hospital continued to grow in both American medicine and American culture. The Hill Burton Act (1946) brought the federal government into hospital development, expanded the geographic scope of hospital care, and gave existing hospitals funds to improve their facilities. The promise of a new era in medicine with the introduction of new technology and therapeutics (penicillin, sulfanilamide, streptomycin) revitalized and reorganized the American hospital into a much larger physical plant with numerous specialized units. Hospital services and facilities were reorganized as specialized units—for example, coronary care and intensive care—reshaping the hospital plant and the patient's hospital experience. Hospitals founded a century earlier in one small building now sprawled out over city blocks.

These hospitals employed many workers who were excluded from the New Deal era's worker gains, and they were relatively unsuccessful in efforts to unionize until the 1950s. In 1974, prohibitions that denied hospital workers the right to strike were lifted.

Just as earlier demographic changes and economic circumstances contributed to the rise of the modern hospital in American cities, so too were demographics and finances operative in more recent hospital development. Medicare and Medicaid legislation in the 1960s reimbursed hospitals for care to the elderly and the poor, but urban hospitals felt the crunch of more and more patients who were unable to pay for their care. Health care costs forced many urban dwellers to seek hospital care for all their medical treatment, and emergency rooms became ad hoc clinics in many poor neighborhoods. Some urban hospitals closed, often with tremendous opposition from neighborhoods. Others merged, erasing historical distinctions among hospitals founded for and by specific groups. As more and more health care procedures and services were delivered to patients in places other than hospitals, for example, in nursing homes, laboratories, and rehabilitation centers, the general hospital became just one of a number of institutions where Americans received health care. By the end of the 20th century, it was clear that the development of the American hospital was far from over as the institution continued to evolve in response to economic, social, and technological developments.

—*Bernadette McCauley*

Further Readings and References

Gamble, V. N. (1995). *Making a plan for ourselves.* New York: Oxford University Press.

Opdycke, S. (1999). *No one was turned away.* New York: Oxford University Press.

Reverby, S., & Rosner, D. (Eds.). (1979). *Health care in America.* Philadelphia: Temple University Press.

Rosenberg, C. E. (1987). *The care of strangers.* New York: Basic Books.

Rosner, D. (1982). *A once charitable enterprise.* Cambridge, UK: Cambridge University Press.

Stevens, R. (1989). *In sickness and in wealth.* New York: Basic Books.

Vogel, M. J. (1980). *The invention of the modern hospital.* Chicago: University of Chicago Press.

HOTELS

Hotels are sophisticated hospitality machines. For more than two centuries, they have offered lodging, food, drink, and similar amenities to travelers. Their basic function has been to sell services and goods that are usually obtained within the household—hence the expression "home away from home." But hotels historically served many other purposes: They became community gathering places, centers of business activity, political forums, and dwellings; hotels also operated as key infrastructural elements in an expanding urban system and propagated metropolitan cultures in rural hinterlands. The hotel's tremendous usefulness and adaptability make it one of the most familiar building types in the world.

The first hotels in America, which were planned and built in Atlantic port cities in the 1790s, represented a dramatic departure from the inns and taverns that preceded them. They were distinguished by their tremendous size and ambitious architectural styling, as well as their innovative internal arrangement, which combined spacious public rooms and numerous private bedchambers. Their scale and elegance made them exceptionally expensive, with costs running as high as $500,000. These hotels were the work of an urban federalist mercantile elite that wanted to accomplish a number of goals: to establish a domestic transportation infrastructure; to blunt the political radicalism of artisans and workingmen; to erect impressive monuments symbolizing the promise of an urban, commercial future for the young republic; to increase the value of their adjacent land holdings; and to provide themselves with socially exclusive venues. Early hotels quickly became important centers of sociability, commerce, and politics. New York's City Hotel hosted club meetings and society balls, the Exchange Coffee House became the clearinghouse for Boston's brokers and insurers, and the Union Public Hotel in Washington temporarily housed the U.S. Congress after British forces severely damaged the Capitol during the War of 1812.

The intensification of urban mercantilism in the 1820s led to the rapid proliferation of hotels across the United States, and in the century that followed, an integrated hotel network developed as part of the nation's expanding and maturing urban system. The completion of the Erie Canal in 1825 set off a hotel-building craze as other cities scrambled to prevent New York from dominating inland trade. Baltimore's City Hotel (1826), Washington's National Hotel (1827), Philadelphia's United States Hotel (1828), and Boston's Tremont House (1829) were all part of larger municipal strategies for establishing transportation links to the continental interior. As cities sprang up in the Ohio and Mississippi River valleys and the Great Lakes, boosters financed hotels in each as a way of establishing or improving the city's position in the urban hierarchy. The development of the locomotive and the spectacular growth of the American railroad system after 1840 led to the construction of hundreds of hotels on an advancing line of settlement across the plains, through the western mountains, and to the Pacific. Meanwhile, because railroads moved such enormous numbers of passengers from place to place, cities in the East and Midwest saw a further multiplication of hotels, some of which surpassed the 1,000-room mark by 1900. This trend continued into the early 20th century, but the golden age of the American hotel was drawing to a close. As a transportation geography based on steam and steel gave way to the automobile and the national highway system, the capital once invested in hotels was increasingly diverted to building affordable roadside motels.

The same characteristics that made hotels useful to travelers also appealed to residents of cities in which transience was a permanent condition of everyday life. In opposition to a rising middle-class culture that made a fetish of privacy and domesticity, hotels offered thoroughly public spaces where people could choose their own company, yet still savor the possibility of unexpected encounters. Americans flocked to hotels in pursuit of new social opportunities. That

such company typically included not only politicians, debutantes, and entrepreneurs, but also gamblers, prostitutes, and thieves was an accepted and sometimes sought-after part of the scene. Hotels also fostered entirely new modes of urban living. Because of the way they subdivided and sold household services such as cooking, laundry, and tailoring, hotels attracted people who sought homes free of daily drudgery or the entanglements of family. Americans used hotels as dwellings beginning in the early 19th century, and beginning around 1850, the hotel served as the preeminent social and architectural model for a new building type, the apartment house, which by the 20th century had become a dominant urban residential form.

The influence of hotels transcended their localities because they functioned within nationwide networks of travel, trade, and communication. The everyday operation of hotels made them into frontiers between small communities and the larger world and conduits that channeled metropolitan cultures into small-town and rural America. For millions of people across the nation, the local hotel was the nearest point of reception for outsiders, and as such, it became a borderland where they might buy from traveling salesmen, encounter visiting stage performers, listen to a candidate's stump speech, or otherwise come into contact with emissaries from the urban centers of cultural production and political power. Hotels also fostered change by making travelers from the hinterland into carriers of urban novelty. Guests in big-city hotels were exposed to avant-garde aesthetic styles and innovative technologies that often made their first public appearances as money-making hotel amenities. When they returned home, travelers brought with them new expectations about urbane living in the form of consumer desire for everything from damask curtains, plush carpets, and luxuriant furniture to steam heat, electric lighting, and telephones. If the place of hotels at the cutting edge of a culture of consumption was initially frowned on, by the 1940s, American hotels overseas were actively promoted as showcases of the virtues of capitalism.

Hotels were both instruments and artifacts of urbanization. The hotel form originated as a social technology aimed at making the United States a nation of cities, and it developed into a means of extending metropolitan hinterlands and anchoring settlements on the urban frontier. Hotels also offered a series of architectural solutions to the emergent problems of city life by transcending their basic function and becoming headquarters and exemplars for other urban institutions. In the process, hotels became national and global outposts of modernity: havens for a cosmopolitan citizenry and homes to a world of strangers.

—*A. K. Sandoval-Strausz*

Further Readings and References

Boorstin, D. (1965). Palaces of the public. In *The Americans: The national experience*. New York: Random House.

Groth, P. (1994). *Living downtown: The history of residential hotels in the United States*. Berkeley: University of California Press.

Sandoval-Strausz, A. K. (2006). *Hotel: An American history*. New Haven, CT: Yale University Press.

Wharton, A. J. (2001). *Building the Cold War: Hilton international hotels and modern architecture*. Chicago: University of Chicago Press.

HOUSING, OWNER-BUILT

In urban and suburban America, it was primarily working-class and impoverished families who built homes for themselves from purchased or found materials. Self-built housing—the wooden shanties lining alleys in late-19th-century Washington, D.C., the frame hovels on rear lots on Chicago's West Side, or the "shacktown" suburbs of early-20th-century Toronto—was housing built far below the costs of commercial construction. Self-built housing was most common in rapidly growing industrial cities where immigrant laborers with little cash invested labor to produce their homes. Although often small, dark spaces lacking indoor plumbing, self-built housing proved a strategy for acquiring shelter and achieving homeownership for low-wage workers in cities where housing costs outpaced wages. A survey of American cities conducted in the late 1920s suggests that as many as one fifth of all homes were owner-built. That number fell during the 1930s and declined rapidly after World War II. Still, although not widely recognized, owner-builders played a significant role in the American real estate market in the 20th century.

Housing in cities and suburbs generally was constructed by one of three producers: custom builders, speculative builders, or owner-residents. Most expensive were custom built houses, designed by architects and constructed by contractors using skilled labor. More common and less costly were the rows of near-identical houses constructed by merchant or speculative builders. Merchant builders typically purchased large chunks of land, subdivided the land, and hired skilled and unskilled workers to build from several to several hundred houses. In some cities, speculative builders constructed shells, unfinished houses that were affordable to lower income workers and could be completed by the new owners. Fully self-built housing, typically constructed from cheaper materials and generally just one to three rooms in size, was the most inexpensive but most labor-intensive for the owner.

Self-builders in the late 19th and early 20th centuries tended to be families applying household labor to lower the costs of shelter. (Single men and women lived with their families or in boardinghouses.) Many were recent immigrants or African Americans seeking homeownership in northern cities. Families purchased or rented a lot, often for a small down payment and monthly installments. They purchased some materials and often scrounged for others, scavenging from demolition sites or local dumps. Some husbands and sons were trained carpenters, but many owner-builders were low-wage workers who had learned the rudimentary skills of house construction. Although often heralded in news accounts for their individualism and self-sufficiency, men relied on the labor of their wives, children, and often friends and neighbors to help them complete their houses.

Families engaging in self-building often purchased lots on the edges of built-up sections of cities, areas where land was cheap and municipal regulation of construction was minimal. Self-builders, needing to lower construction costs and to avoid health and housing inspectors, purchased lots where municipal services such as sewer and water lines, paved streets, and garbage collection were limited or entirely absent. Homeowners sacrificed amenities—sewer lines and indoor plumbing—that might improve the health of their households in exchange for lower housing costs and an opportunity for homeownership. Self-building—in particular the lack of indoor plumbing—determined the working conditions for wives and daughters who managed their homes. It sometimes required wage-laboring household members to commute long distances to jobs in the city. New communities of self-built homes grew slowly as houses and numbers of dwellings expanded, forming working-class suburbs on the edges of industrial cities.

Although they were the majority of self-builders, poor and working-class families were not the only urban residents who constructed their own homes. In the early 20th century, a small number of middle-class families embarked on home-building projects. Young white-collar workers, responding to a barrage of articles about the "feminization" of office workers, claimed to enjoy the physical labor of home construction. (President Theodore Roosevelt, worried that American men had lost their masculinity, encouraged vigorous activity for young men.) The fad for middle-class owner building peaked around World War I with the publication of John McMahon's two guidebooks, *The House That Junk Built,* published in 1915, and *Success in the Suburbs,* published in 1917. Both offered advice on gardening and home building.

Owner building slowed in the 1920s and declined precipitously at mid-century, a result of the growth of mass-production builders and increasing government regulation of housing construction. Even in the twenties, a small but growing number of builders could produce housing that was affordable for working-class families. Mass production boomed after the war, and low-cost housing, combined with higher wages for the growing numbers of unionized workers, meant that fewer working-class families needed to construct their homes. Perhaps of greater significance to self-builders, the New Deal's Federal Housing Authority (FHA) made home mortgages available to working-class families, and federal regulations linked mortgage insurance for builders and buyers to minimal building standards. Working-class households then could acquire a house through the formal housing market. Locally, suburban governments approved new zoning legislation, and urban and suburban officials often were less willing to neglect or overlook housing and health regulations.

Self-built housing helps to explain the apparent paradox of high homeownership rates among lower wage workers in early-20th-century cities. It was crucial to the growth of working-class suburbs and to the establishment of African American suburbs in the early decades of the 20th century, and it also contributed to the growth of working-class districts within industrial cities. Although it is often difficult to distinguish self-built homes from the housing constructed by merchant builders, there is evidence of self-built communities in or around Detroit, Cleveland, Pittsburgh, Los Angeles, Cincinnati, Rochester (New York), and Flint (Michigan) in the

United States and Hamilton (Ontario) and Toronto in Canada. Self-built housing shaped living conditions and community culture of urban neighborhoods and suburbs across the nation.

—*Margaret Garb*

See also Federal Housing Administration; Homeownership

Further Readings and References

Harris, R. (1996). *Unplanned suburbs: Toronto's American tragedy, 1900–1950.* Baltimore: Johns Hopkins University Press.
Nicholaides, B. (2002). *My blue heaven: Life and politics in the working-class suburbs of Los Angeles, 1920–1965.* Chicago: University of Chicago Press.
Weiss, M. A. (1987). *The rise of the community builders: The American real estate industry and urban land planning.* New York: Columbia University Press.
Wiese, A. (2004). *Places of their own: African American suburbanization in the twentieth century.* Chicago: University of Chicago Press.
Zunz, O. (1982). *The changing face of inequality: Urbanization, industrial development, and immigration in Detroit, 1880–1920.* Chicago: University of Chicago Press.

HOUSING ACT OF 1934

The U.S. Congress passed the National Housing Act of 1934 on June 27, 1934. The most significant piece of federal housing legislation up until that time, it established the Federal Housing Administration (FHA), introduced a system of mutual mortgage insurance, created the Federal Savings and Loan Insurance Corporation (FSLIC), and authorized formation of national mortgage associations. The provisions of this legislation continue to play a major role in the housing and finance sectors of the American economy.

Prior to the 1930s, the federal government rarely intervened in housing matters. Local institutions and conditions generally determined the supply of private dwellings, as well as the methods used to finance them. Widespread economic dislocation following the 1929 stock market crash illustrated the precariousness of these dynamics. Small savings and loan banks, which financed most of the nation's home mortgages by borrowing funds from other fiduciaries, were forced to close their doors as commercial banks collapsed in record numbers—about 9,760 between 1929 and 1933. The resulting closure of savings and loans had a predictably disastrous effect on the residential mortgage market because 89.6 percent of all savings and loan assets were held as mortgages. By 1933, mortgage foreclosures were averaging 1,000 per day.

Even before the tide of mortgage foreclosures crested, the Hoover administration attempted to ease conditions by supporting passage of the Federal Home Loan Bank bill on July 27, 1932. Although this legislation assisted savings and loans by providing them with additional credit, it did not directly benefit homeowners. The Roosevelt administration lobbied for additional measures, which included creation of the Home Owners Loan Corporation (HOLC) on June 13, 1933. The HOLC reduced foreclosure rates by purchasing and refinancing mortgages that were either in default or foreclosure, but it did little to stimulate new lending or housing construction.

The 73rd Congress, with strong support from a wide range of business and financial interests, passed the National Housing Act of 1934. The centerpiece of the new legislation was the FHA. Lawmakers hoped that the FHA would entice banks to offer additional mortgage loans by insuring such loans against default. For example, if borrowers did not meet their payments, banks could respond by exchanging these impaired mortgage loans for government bonds. Borrowers themselves paid for the insurance, which took the form of a 1 percent (subsequently reduced to $\frac{1}{4}$ to $\frac{1}{2}$ percent) premium added to their mortgage payments. The federal government underwrote much of the risk incurred by mortgage lenders through this insurance program. Benefits provided by the FHA to homeowners were less direct but nonetheless tangible. The FHA standardized lending practices by requiring its loans to be fully amortized (monthly payments reduced both interest and principle) and financed over a period of 20 years (later extended to 30 years).

The 1934 National Housing Act established other programs that also influenced mortgage financing. During the 1930s, bank failures caused by unprecedented withdrawals greatly undermined public confidence in basic financial institutions. Congress created the Federal Deposit Insurance Corporation (FDIC) to address this situation. The FDIC insured accounts in commercial banks and trust companies up to $15,000. The 1934 National Housing Act launched a companion program, the FSLIC. Capitalized at $100 million,

the FSLIC initially insured individual accounts in federal savings and loans (and most state-chartered savings and loans) to a maximum of $5,000. Savings and loans were to pay specified premiums to the FSLIC until a special reserve fund equaled 5 percent of the insured accounts and obligations of all insured institutions. Policymakers hoped that renewed confidence in savings and loans (inspired by the FSLIC) would prompt additional deposits, which, in turn, would increase the amount of money banks could loan in the form of mortgages.

The authorization of national mortgage associations contained in Title III of the 1934 legislation also had an important, although less immediate impact. The mission of these associations was to purchase and resell or reinvest FHA-insured mortgage loans from banks (thus creating a so-called secondary mortgage market). Banks could use the funds they received from these transactions to finance additional mortgage loans. By increasing the total amount of money available for mortgages, a secondary mortgage market would place downward pressure on interest rates, making homeownership affordable for more people. The Federal National Mortgage Association (FNMA), however, was the other association chartered under the 1934 act. Formed in 1938, the FNMA became more commonly known as Fannie Mae. In 1968, the FNMA was split into two separate entities: a government-owned corporation called the Government National Mortgage Association (Ginnie Mae) and a newly privatized version of the FNMA, which retained the Fannie Mae epithet.

The 1934 National Housing Act had an almost immediate effect on banking, mortgage lending, and residential development. Federal insurance programs did indeed increase the availability and utilization of mortgage funds by minimizing the potential financial liabilities among lenders and borrowers alike. By 1940, FHA insurance programs covered about 40 percent of all private housing starts. Furthermore, before and after World War II, the FHA's policies opened up homeownership to millions of Americans who could not have afforded that option prior to 1934. They also reshaped urban geography by fueling post–World War II suburbanization and by explicitly encouraging racial discrimination and segregation until 1950. Still later, Congress relied on the precedents set by the 1934 National Housing Act when it chartered the Federal Home Loan Mortgage Corporation (Freddie Mac) in 1970, which quickly became one of the largest purchasers of home mortgages in the United States.

—*A. Scott Henderson*

See also Fannie Mae; Federal Housing Administration; Home Owners Loan Corporation

Further Readings and References

Henderson, A. S. (2000). *Housing and the democratic ideal: The life and thought of Charles Abrams.* New York: Columbia University Press.

Radford, G. (1996). *Modern housing for America: Policy struggles in the New Deal era.* Chicago: University of Chicago Press.

Weiss, M. A. (1989). Marketing and financing home ownership: Mortgage lending and public policy in the United States, 1918–1989. *Business and Economic History, 18,* 109–118.

HOUSING ACT OF 1937

The U.S. Congress passed the Housing Act of 1937 on September 1, 1937. This legislation had three objectives: reduction of unemployment, slum clearance, and construction of low-income housing. Although the legislation did not significantly alter employment rates, it did influence the scope of federal involvement in, as well as the cost and design standards for, many of America's first public housing projects. In doing so, it established precedents for both the location and appearance of the nation's public housing.

The federal government's initial responses to the Great Depression did not address the shelter needs of low-income groups. The Federal Home Loan Bank System, the Home Owners Loan Corporation, and the Housing Act of 1934 primarily assisted financial institutions and current or prospective homeowners. The admittedly numerous beneficiaries of these programs rarely included those who were unable to purchase or rent dwellings outside of substandard areas.

One program that did attempt to provide low-income groups with affordable housing during the 1930s was the Housing Division of the Public Works Administration (PWA). Established in 1933 by Title II of the National Industrial Recovery Act, the PWA's Housing Division was authorized to spend up to $135 million on low-cost housing and slum clearance. Ultimately, 21,800 public housing units were constructed by the Housing Division during its 4-year existence. Despite this accomplishment, several factors contributed to the division's general lack of success. Federal and local policymakers frequently disagreed over site selection and project development; the courts refused to grant condemnation powers to the Housing Division; and PWA administrator Harold L. Ickes often distrusted municipal officials, which led to intergovernmental conflict and confusion.

Reformers, eager for effective federal housing programs, found a sympathetic ally in Senator Robert F. Wagner, a Democrat from New York. Wagner introduced national housing legislation in 1935 and 1936 but failed to get it enacted. Powerful economic interests, such as the U.S. Chamber of Commerce, the National Association of Real Estate Boards, the U.S. Savings and Loan League, and the National Association of Retail Lumber Dealers, opposed any form of public housing. Many of their concerns prompted conservative lawmakers to amend Wagner's bill when the U.S. Senate considered it again in 1937. The Senate passed this revised version in late summer of that same year. The House of Representatives approved a companion bill introduced by Henry B. Steagall, a Democrat from Alabama.

The Housing Act of 1937 created the U.S. Housing Authority (USHA), a semi-autonomous agency in the U.S. Department of the Interior. Although USHA's programs were administered from Washington, D.C., actual control over housing reform remained on the local level. Municipal housing authorities, in their quest to clear slums and build low-income dwellings, could apply to USHA for loans amounting to 90 percent of a project's construction costs. USHA loans were to be issued at no less than the government interest rate (3 to 4 percent) for a maximum of 60 years. To raise the capital for these loans, USHA was authorized to sell $500 million in bonds.

A little understood but important component of the Housing Act of 1937 was its subsidy program. Contemporaries estimated that prevailing costs translated into rents of at least $11 per room per month in most urban areas; yet low-income groups, given their limited means, were usually unable to pay more than $6 per room per month. To bridge this gap in operating costs, the Housing Act of 1937 authorized a system of annual subsidies to local housing authorities. USHA would pay up to 80 percent of this subsidy, while the remaining amount would have to come from the authority itself, usually in the form of a tax exemption.

In practice, the subsidies were often large enough (when added to rents and tax exemptions) not only to cover operating costs and repayment of the entire amount of the initial USHA loan, but also to service any loan that the local housing authority had used to finance the remaining 10 percent of a project's construction costs. It was thus possible for local public housing to be underwritten almost entirely by federal funds.

Reformers were less enthusiastic about other aspects of the 1937 legislation. Cost restrictions on individual units—$1,250 per room in cities with 500,000 or more inhabitants, with total unit costs not to exceed $5,000—meant that projects were aesthetically unappealing and prone to structural deterioration. Furthermore, the number of new dwellings created by a project had to be matched by elimination of a roughly equal amount of slum housing. This "equivalent elimination" requirement had several consequences. The net gain, if any, in the total number of an area's dwellings would be insignificant—for every unit built, another would have to be razed. By linking the two issues of clearance and low-income housing, equivalent elimination made public housing an urban, not rural or suburban phenomenon. This, in turn, limited the size and scope of projects because the expense of acquiring and developing central-city land was relatively high.

With public housing under continuing attack from conservative lawmakers, the House refused in August 1939 to consider a bill to grant additional borrowing authority to USHA, effectively stopping new construction. In February 1942, the consolidation of federal housing agencies placed USHA's low-income and defense housing projects under the jurisdiction of the National Housing Agency (NHA). Headed by John B. Blandford Jr., the NHA emphasized construction of temporary defense housing, not permanent public housing. Congress did not fund any additional low-income housing programs until passage of the Housing Act of 1949.

—*A. Scott Henderson*

See also New Deal: Urban Policy; Public Housing; United States Housing Authority

Further Readings and References

Bauman, J. F., Biles, R., & Szylvian, K. M. (Eds.). (2000). *From tenements to Taylor Homes: In search of an urban housing policy in twentieth-century America.* University Park: Pennsylvania State University Press.

Biles, R. (1990). Nathan Straus and the failure of public housing, 1937–1942. *The Historian, 53,* 33–46.

McDonnell, T. (1957). *The Wagner housing act: A case study of the legislative process.* Chicago: Loyola University Press.

HOUSING ACT OF **1949**

The Housing Act of 1949 originated amid World War II, when despite thousands of units of government-built temporary housing units, plus some Federal Housing Administration-assisted, and a few "experimental" cooperative or mutual housing projects, planners predicted an unprecedented demand for decent shelter. However, in 1943, Washington's concern for a "depression-free" postwar economy loomed even larger. That year, Guy Greer, Alvin Hansen, and Charles Ascher of the soon-to-be-dismantled National Resources Planning Board (NRPB) outlined plans for rebuilding American cities. Many wartime strategies for combating urban (central city) blight, like Hansen's and Greer's, involved mobilizing federal funds to write down inflated downtown land values. These strategies informed the 1944 urban redevelopment bill drafted by Greer and Hansen for the NRPB's Special Committee on Postwar Economic Planning and Policy. Although this bill floundered, it was in basic form the Wagner-Ellender-Taft (W-E-T) legislation introduced in Congress in 1945. That bill, which also called for the creation of a permanent National Housing Administration, provided federal grants to local redevelopment authorities to purchase and clear urban slums.

From the outset, consensus surrounded the redevelopment provisions of the proposed legislation; meanwhile, opposition swirled around the inserted housing clauses. By 1945, the predicted national housing shortage had arrived. The new president, Harry S. Truman, joined by the stalwart Ohio Republican Senator Robert Taft, championed housing legislation to ease the crisis. The battle lines quickly formed. Taft and New York Senator Robert Wagner, backed by housing professionals such as Catherine Bauer Wurster and Lee Johnson of the National Association of Housing Officials, anchored the one side, which favored the resumption of a large-scale government housing program. Staunchly opposed stood Senators Jesse Wolcott and Joseph McCarthy, together with the National Association of Real Estate Boards, the National Association of Home Builders, and the American Savings and Loan League.

Taft insisted that urban redevelopment be linked to housing. As long as American GI families doubled up with parents and friends in cramped residential quarters and families in western Pennsylvania found shelter in abandoned beehive coking ovens, urban redevelopment plans, argued Taft, should be limited to urban areas that were "predominately residential" in character. Redevelopment areas, that is, should be developed for "predominately residential purposes." On the other hand, Cincinnati planner Alfred Bettman viewed redevelopment as part of the comprehensive planning process. Slums, he contended, represented one facet of the larger problem of urban blight. Therefore, he considered it wrong to clear slums for housing only. In any case, housing stood as a central purpose of Senate Bill 1070, reported in February 1949, a bill establishing a national housing objective and providing federal aid to assist slum-clearance projects and low-rent public housing projects. For the first and only time, in Title I of the bill, Congress articulated a national housing policy. The 1949 bill's preamble declared that the nation's general welfare and security required not only a remedy for the serious housing shortage and elimination of slums and blighted areas, but "the realization as soon as feasible of the goal of a decent home and a suitable living environment for every American family."

The law's most virulent opponents targeted Title II of the law, the low-rent public housing provisions, which they labeled "un-American" and "communistic." Title II authorized the building of 810,000 dwelling units of conventional low-rent public housing, divided annually over 7 years. To assure that this housing could not compete with private housing, Wagner-Ellender-Taft dictated that a gap of at least 20 percent exist between the upper rent limits in public housing and the lowest rents available in the private housing market that were affordable for tenants earning the highest income eligible for occupancy in public housing. The act also provided for the construction, improvement, and repair of farm housing.

The redevelopment provisions of the 1949 act ultimately proved irresistible, the public housing clauses notwithstanding. As urban mayors, realtors, corporate executives, architects, planners, and other subscribers

to the postwar, pro-growth agenda had long urged, the 1949 law mobilized federal dollars to cover up to two thirds of the cost of purchasing, clearing, and discounting the resale price of slum-cleared land. It required states to create redevelopment authorities and cities to officially identify slums and formally request federal aid. Municipalities had to bear one third of the cost of redevelopment projects, but this share might be in the form of labor, equipment, or the installation of streets, sewers, water mains, or other infrastructure. Likewise, the law mandated that city councils and other governmental bodies formally approve redevelopment plans and provide a feasible method for the temporary relocation of displaced families. Entrepreneurs, nonprofit hospitals, universities, and other private land developers planned and financed the actual rebuilding of the cleared project sites.

Lofty goals aside, the Housing Act of 1949 failed either to halt spreading urban blight or to provide decent shelter for America's ill-housed, low-income families. Critics charged that the law actually destroyed many more housing units than it produced. The law shoved aside poor families, who crowded the ancient tenements and aging single-room occupancy hotels of the downtown, to accommodate glitzy apartment buildings and upscale hotels. First, the Korean War forced Truman to divert housing dollars to the military; second, the enemies of public housing warred against what they denounced as the Marxist conspiracy of public housing advocates against capitalism. Instead of the 135,000 units per year of public housing envisioned in the law, the actual number of units built annually rarely exceeded 25,000. By the time Truman left office in 1953, fewer than 156,000 units had been built. Philosophically opposed to public housing, the new president, Dwight David Eisenhower, kept the figure for public housing units under 30,000. Meanwhile, with the "predominately residential" clause of W-E-T intact, the immediate result of the law was thousands of units of housing, old warehouses, and the shambles of ice houses and coal yards demolished with only white wooden fences to mark the expanses of central city land cleared but still conspicuously vacant.

—John F. Bauman

See also Bauer, Catherine; Federal Housing Authority; Housing Act of 1934; Housing Act of 1937; Housing Act of 1954; Housing, Owner-Built; Housing Segregation

Further Readings and References

Bauman, J. F., Biles, R., & Szylvian, K. (2000). *From tenements to the Taylor Homes: In search of an urban housing policy in twentieth century America.* University Park: Pennsylvania State University Press.

Bratt, R. G., Hartman, C., & Meyerson, A. (Eds.). (1986). *Critical perspectives on housing.* Philadelphia: Temple University Press.

Hays, R. A. (1985). *The federal government and urban housing: Ideology and change in public policy.* Albany: State University of New York Press.

Vale, L. J. (2000). *From the puritans to the projects: Public housing and public neighbors.* Cambridge: Harvard University Press.

Wilson, J. Q. (Ed.). (1967). *Urban renewal: The record and the controversy.* Cambridge: MIT Press.

HOUSING ACT OF 1954

The housing and urban renewal legislation of 1954 addressed the perceived shortcomings of the 1949 Housing Act, the Wagner-Ellender-Taft housing and urban redevelopment legislation. The 1949 act had spurred massive slum clearance but only modest city rebuilding and minimal progress toward the law's stated goal of a "decent home and a suitable living environment for every American family." Meanwhile, urban blight spread ominously into the city neighborhoods bordering the central business district (CBD)—the old streetcar suburbs. Racial anxieties, incipient disinvestment, and suburbanization engendered by the Veterans Administration and the Federal Housing Administration unleashed white flight and spread blight. The 1954 Housing Act aimed to halt that invidious process.

Fearing the onset of untrammeled urban blight and dubious about the effectiveness of Washington-directed redevelopment, President Dwight David Eisenhower in 1953 convened an Advisory Committee on Government Housing Problems and Programs chaired by the father of the suburban mall, Baltimore developer James Rouse. Like Rouse, urbanist Miles Colean drew inspiration from Baltimore's Waverly neighborhood, a blighted inner city district remade using a mixture of zoning, housing code enforcement, and other "conservation" tools, rather than blanket slum clearance and public housing. In *Renewing Our Cities,* Colean—who would sit on the Rouse advisory committee—featured the Baltimore plan of code enforcement, strict occupancy controls, and

housing rehabilitation as the centerpiece of what he now called *urban renewal.* Colean's concept of renewal assigned private enterprise the central role in combating blight via rehabilitation. It urged the federal government to catalyze private residential development via FHA insurance, and it charged cities with the main responsibility for eradicating (via strict zoning and housing codes) the overall problem of blight.

Rouse's report, submitted in December 1953, reflected Colean's idea for renewing entire cities through conservation and rehabilitation as well as the developer's belief in the primacy of capitalist leadership in planning and carrying out city rebuilding. The 1954 Housing Act flowed directly from the Rouse committee's findings. First, the law altered the discourse about city rebuilding from *redevelopment* to *renewal.* Simultaneously, it broadened the venue for renewal from the historic CBD into the urban gray areas (streetcar neighborhoods) surrounding the central city. In these so-called *conservation areas,* it was hoped that private enterprise would team with city planners, public health officials, and code enforcement officials to rehabilitate neighborhoods. Therefore, the word *project* was redefined to include not only the slum acquisition and clearance actions in the CBD (as defined in the 1949 law) but also the conservation of blighted and deteriorated "gray areas" by undertaking plans for voluntary housing repairs and rehabilitation consistent with urban renewal plans. Such plans could include spot removal of dangerously dilapidated structures in the broadened blight area. Indeed, as in the 1949 law, the 1954 law made federal loans and grants available for demolition as well as for the installation of streets, utilities, and other vital infrastructure. Such grants and loans were now contingent on localities presenting to the federal Urban Renewal Administration a *workable plan.* Section 701 actually provided special matching grants for states to support the planning process. It also established a renewal service to further assist the planning process. Consistent with its capitalistic intent, the 1954 law added Section 123 and Section 221 to the 1934 National Housing Act to finance the purchase, construction, and rehabilitation of low-cost one- to four-family housing in the conservation areas. Section 220 helped families displaced by renewal action to afford to purchase housing.

Although it focused on housing, the 1954 act hardly ignored rebuilding in the historic downtown.

Since 1949, developers like Rouse had decried the "predominantly residential" clause of the redevelopment law. The 1954 Housing Act allowed a 10 percent exception from the requirement that renewal areas be predominantly residential. Hospitals, universities, and other developers, for-profit and not-for-profit, could devote more federal dollars and urban space to nonresidential projects. As for public housing, the *bête noire* of the real estate lobby, Washington stipulated that new low-rent public housing should be available only for meeting the needs of families displaced by government action. For this purpose, it authorized construction of a modest 140,000 units annually over 4 years.

Consequently, the 1954 act unveiled what some housing historians have described as a business view of urban city rebuilding, one articulated by the Rouse committee in its December 1953 report. The act vastly broadened the realm for urban renewal action and eased—without eliminating—the "predominately residential" restrictions of the 1949 act. Nevertheless, by widening the opportunity for nonresidential development, the 1954 act had a liberating effect and greatly accelerated the pace of urban slum clearance. Demolitions so transformed the urban landscape that in the early 1960s, renewal unleashed the wrath of urban critics such as Jane Jacobs and Martin Anderson, liberal and conservative. Jacobs especially assailed the loss of neighborhood vitality and the sheer banality of the architecture that arose from the rubble of slum-cleared blocks.

Likewise, the 1954 law exacerbated the problem of residential displacement and family relocation. Federal and local urban renewal agencies ignored the exhortations of Frank Horne, chief of the Housing and Home Finance Administration's Race Division, that in the face of the entrenched racial discrimination endemic in urban housing markets, mass slum clearance would result in the massive displacement of poor African American families who, unless decently rehoused, would gravitate to worse rather than better housing. In other words, the law triggered "Negro removal" and transformed public housing into a warehousing strategy that dictated the construction of such towering monoliths as Chicago's Robert Taylor Homes. Four years after passage of the 1954 Housing Act, Catherine Bauer, one of the primary authors of the 1937 public housing legislation, wrote that public housing had become a "deadlock." By the mid-1960s—amid the urban riots of that decade—Bauer's phrase summed up the whole campaign against urban blight.

—*John F. Bauman*

See also Bauer, Catherine; Horne, Frank S.; Housing Act of 1949; Rouse, James W.

Further Readings and References

Abrams, C. (1965). *The city is the frontier.* New York: Harper Colophon Books.

Bauman, J. F., Biles, R., & Szylvian, K. (2000). *From tenements to the Taylor Homes: In search of an urban housing policy in twentieth century America.* University Park: Pennsylvania State University Press.

Bloom, N. D. (2004). *Merchant of illusion: America's salesman of the businessman's utopia.* Columbus: Ohio State University Press.

Bratt, R. G., Hartman, C., & Meyerson, A. (Eds.). (1986). *Critical perspectives on housing.* Philadelphia: Temple University Press.

Hays, R. A. (1985). *The federal government and urban housing: Ideology and change in public policy.* Albany: State University of New York Press.

Henderson, A. S. (2000). *Housing and the democratic ideal: The life and thought of Charles Abrams.* New York: Columbia University Press.

Wilson, J. Q. (Ed.). (1967). *Urban renewal: The record and the controversy.* Cambridge: MIT Press.

HOUSING SEGREGATION

Since the end of the 19th century, housing in American cities has been starkly segregated by race. Although the means used to achieve housing segregation changed over these years—shifting from public policies such as racial zoning to private practices such as restrictive covenants, real estate discrimination, and orchestrated campaigns of harassment and violence—the end result remained constant. Whites and nonwhites, particularly African Americans, have lived in separate and often unequal sections of cities.

Housing segregation first became prominent in cities across the country around the beginning of the 20th century. As late as the mid-19th century, blacks and whites lived together in the cities of the North and South. In the antebellum South, the intermingling of white and black residences had been dictated by the demands of slave owners, who wanted their slaves kept close at hand and, thus, under constant watch. In the North, meanwhile, the black population of most cities represented such a small fraction of the overall population that intermingling of the races went largely unnoticed. With the demise of slavery in the South and the resulting mass migration of large numbers of African Americans to the industrial North, however, both regions embarked on a new era in which housing patterns became much more rigidly segregated.

The means used to create and then continue the practices of housing discrimination and segregation have evolved over the course of the 20th century. Initially, residential segregation was promoted as the official policy of municipal governments, which used various forms of racial zoning to separate the races. Baltimore, Maryland pioneered the institution of housing segregation legislation with a 1910 ordinance that provided for the designation of all-white and all-black city blocks. Other municipal governments followed Baltimore's example, and similar residential segregation measures soon appeared in cities to the south and west. When Louisville, Kentucky adopted such a segregation ordinance in 1914, however, the National Association for the Advancement of Colored People (NAACP) challenged the law in court. In the 1917 case of *Buchanan v. Warley,* the U.S. Supreme Court held that such racial zoning was unconstitutional. The right to sell and own private property, the Court ruled unanimously, could not be limited by government at any level.

With cities and states barred from enacting public policies of residential segregation, those who sought to prevent residential integration turned to private methods. Chief among these was the racially restrictive covenant. Originally, occupancy restrictions had been written only into the deeds for individual parcels of property, mandating that such property could not be transferred to a specific racial minority, religious group, or combination of both. With the abolition of state-sponsored residential segregation, however, white homeowners banded together, often at the urging of real estate agencies and under the leadership of a local homeowners' association, to combine individual deed restrictions in a broader covenant that covered an entire street, block, or neighborhood. The restrictive covenant represented a contractual agreement in which property owners promised that they would not allow a particular group—most commonly, African Americans—to own, occupy, or rent their property. As covenants spread across the country, the

NAACP once again went to court to challenge the foundations of housing segregation. In the 1926 case of *Corrigan v. Buckley,* the Supreme Court held that racially restrictive covenants represented private discrimination and therefore did not constitute the sort of "state action" found in earlier segregation ordinances. In the decades thereafter, covenants became the key means for ensuring residential segregation across the country. During the 1930s and 1940s, their implementation was encouraged by a mutually reinforcing set of forces—real estate agents, mortgage brokers and lending institutions, and, most important, the federal government.

Real estate agents emerged as primary actors in the preservation of residential segregation. In the 1920s, the National Association of Real Estate Boards (NAREB) adopted an article in its Code of Ethics that required its realtors to refrain from selling property in a racially homogeneous neighborhood to a member of another race. Those who violated the code could be expelled from the NAREB, a penalty of some consequence, given the centrality of that organization in the industry. External pressures also encouraged realtors to refrain from selling homes in white neighborhoods to minorities. Those who did so often became the target of economic boycotts, social ostracism, and physical violence. Although the ethics provision was repealed in 1950, for many white real estate agents, the taboo against such practices persisted.

The federal government perpetuated the patterns of residential segregation during the period between the two world wars. The Home Owners Loan Corporation (HOLC), created in 1933 to provide funds for refinancing mortgages and granting low-interest loans, institutionalized a discriminatory approach to appraisal values. HOLC practices created a national standard that considered black neighborhoods risky investments for home loans and mortgages. The Federal Housing Administration (FHA) and, after 1944, the Veterans Administration (VA) adopted HOLC standards in their own massive loan programs to home builders and buyers, leading to a systemic pattern of discriminatory funding that funneled federal money to white homeowners, especially those in the suburbs, but denied funds to blacks, especially those in the central cities. Private banks and lending agencies adopted these federal guidelines as well, making it virtually impossible for most blacks to escape the poorer neighborhoods of the central city. Furthermore, when the federal government built public housing during this era, it placed such projects in those same neighborhoods, thereby deepening the poverty of the inner city and furthering the patterns of racial segregation in housing.

After World War II, the NAACP renewed its assault on segregated housing. In an important breakthrough, the organization renewed its legal attack on restrictive covenants. This time, it targeted not the covenants themselves but their reliance on the courts to punish those who broke such covenants. In the 1948 case of *Shelley v. Kraemer*, the Supreme Court sided with the NAACP and held that judicial enforcement of racially restrictive covenants essentially constituted "state action" and was thus unconstitutional. With the threat of legal sanctions removed, racial covenants lost the power they had once had. In the wake of the ruling, most cities experienced the first tentative signs of housing desegregation. In some instances, real estate agents engaged in the controversial practice of "blockbusting," in which they slowly bought up a number of properties in a single section and then suddenly sold them, en masse, to black buyers in order to panic other whites into selling as well. But often, the process of residential "racial transition" unfolded at a more gradual pace, as individual black buyers purchased properties adjacent to existing areas of black concentration.

Regardless of the origins of racial transition, the purchase of property by black buyers generally triggered fierce resistance from whites. Although they had lost their most powerful weapon with the courts' invalidation of restrictive covenants, homeowners' associations still had a variety of tactics to challenge the entry of African American homeowners into all-white neighborhoods. Intimidation emerged as the most common tactic, with whites resorting to measures ranging from picket lines and other forms of harassment to more physical attacks, which included vandalism, shooting, dynamiting, arson, and other forms of violence. Economic pressure was also brought to bear. Real estate agents who dared to deal with black customers found themselves victims of boycotts, whereas blacks who had purchased property in white neighborhoods received offers to buy back the property, often at a loss. Finally, homeowners' associations often engaged in local politics, finding powerful allies in city and state agencies sympathetic to their point of view.

Despite the strength and successes of white resistance to residential transition, many whites ultimately decided to flee from cities rather than stand their ground against the course of residential desegregation. Across the country, white flight was the term used to describe the trend for whites to remove themselves from increasingly integrated urban environments and instead establish new, racially homogeneous communities in the world of white suburbia. In place of the old structures of segregation, suburbs often used other means, such as zoning practices that were ostensibly predicated on differences of class and not caste, to keep poor blacks (and poor whites) out of their new enclaves. Meanwhile, the mass migration of whites away from the city served only to intensify housing segregation for those left behind, as the urban ghetto increased in size and sped toward further decline. Despite the massive redistribution and relocation of both the black and white populations in the postwar era, the end result—overwhelmingly black cities surrounded by overwhelmingly white suburbs—meant a world marked by a degree of housing segregation that was as high, if not higher, than ever before.

In the end, American cities found housing segregation to be a durable and perhaps intractable problem. Etched onto the cityscape by the collective actions of individual property owners, organizations of white homeowners, banks and lending agencies, and local and federal governments, the racial divisions of residence have served as a foundation for broader patterns of discrimination and an inescapable reminder of the practical persistence of segregation itself.

—*Kevin M. Kruse*

See also Blockbusting; Ghetto; Racial Zoning; Restrictive Deed Covenants

Further Readings and References

Abrams, C. (1955). *Forbidden neighbors: A study of prejudice in housing.* New York: Harper.

Hirsch, A. R. (1983). *Making the second ghetto: Race and housing in Chicago, 1940–1960.* Chicago: University of Chicago.

Jackson, K. T. (1985). *Crabgrass frontier: The suburbanization of the United States.* New York: Oxford University Press.

Massey, D. S., & Denton, N. A. (1993). *American apartheid: Segregation and the making of the underclass.* Cambridge, MA: Harvard University Press.

Sugrue, T. J. (1996). *The origins of the urban crisis: Race and inequality in postwar Detroit.* Princeton, NJ: Princeton University Press.

Vose, C. E. (1959). *Caucasians only: The Supreme Court, the NAACP, and the restrictive covenant cases.* Berkeley: University of California Press.

HOUSTON, TEXAS

Houston entered the 21st century as the fourth largest city in the United States, covering an area of 617.34 square miles. Real estate brokers John and Augustus Allen founded the city on Buffalo Bayou in 1836, promising the "great interior commercial emporium of Texas." Indeed, it served as the first capital of the Republic of Texas and attracted 1,500 people in 1837. Gail and Thomas Borden mapped out the city on a standard grid around the bayou. The Texas legislature formally incorporated the city in June 1837, with James S. Holman as mayor. Houston modified its governing structure multiple times, from an alderman system in the 19th century, to a city manager form in 1942, and finally to a strong mayor with council system. The state capital moved back and forth from Houston to Austin until the matter was settled permanently in 1872.

Houston's early economic livelihood depended on cotton and more generally on commerce. Sitting conveniently near the Gulf Coast, Houston became a major hub for supplies and products that traveled to and from the port of Galveston via small river steamships. Major exports were cotton, corn, and hides, and imports consisted of cloth, flour, coffee, lead, sugar, books, and other goods. Northwestward construction on the Houston and Texas Central Railroad began in 1853, followed by the Houston Tap and Brazoria, which joined three other lines at Pierce Junction in 1856 and linked Houston with the Brazos Valley sugar plantations. After the Civil War, the Houston and Texas Central line reached Denison, joining Houston with the national rail network in 1873. Houston developed communication systems to complement the railroad, with mail and telegraph in 1853 and 1854 and telephone in 1878. These connections ensured Houston's position in the lumber and cotton markets for the 19th century.

Commercial volume prompted several companies to attempt to dredge a ship channel to alleviate the difficult passage through Buffalo Bayou. After the Civil War, the Houston Direct Navigation Company, the Houston Ship Channel Company, and the Buffalo Bayou Ship Channel Company played important roles, and in 1876, ship owner Charles Morgan opened a 12-foot-deep waterway to nearby Clinton. In 1881, the U.S. government took on the project and dug a ship channel through Galveston Bay and Buffalo Bayou. The Houston Ship Channel opened in 1914 to become one of the largest ports in the United States.

Roadwork was difficult in the muddy Houston terrain, but all-weather highways constituted major improvements in the 1920s. In 1952, the Gulf Freeway linked Houston and Galveston Island and later joined the interstate highway system. Houston's first airport opened in 1928, followed by the Houston International Airport (later William P. Hobby Airport) in 1954 and the Houston Intercontinental Airport (now George Bush Intercontinental Airport) in 1969.

It was the discovery of oil at Spindletop just east of Houston in 1918 that brought the greatest economic boom to Houston. Because the Houston Ship Channel was somewhat inland from the Gulf Coast, it was protected from severe coastal weather and offered prime land for refineries. Major refineries in the area included the Texas Company (later Texaco), Humble Oil and Refining (later Exxon), and the Gulf Oil Corporation (later Chevron). Between 1918, when Sinclair Oil Company built the first major refinery, and 1929, 40 oil companies had Houston offices.

World War II also brought economic opportunity to the area with demand for synthetic rubber, gasoline, explosives, and ships. By 1942, the Houston Shipbuilding Corporation employed 20,000 workers to build Liberty ships. The Brown Shipbuilding Company produced more than 300 war vessels by developing broadside launching. The petrochemical industry also sprouted in Houston during this time, thanks to nearby deposits of salt, sulfur, and natural gas and government wartime contracts. Companies including Dow, Monsanto, DuPont, Shell, and Goodyear formed the foundation for what became one of the largest concentrations of petrochemical production in the country. Houston's economic base as a petrochemical capital sustained growth until the 1980s, when the oil industry suffered a downturn. During that decade, Houston lost population for the first time in its history.

With a population of 292,000, Houston was the largest city in Texas by 1930. City planners developed the city with regular urban improvements, installing electric streetlights and streetcars beginning in 1884 and 1891, experimenting with various materials such as shell, limestone blocks, and asphalt to pave muddy streets, and regulating speed for automobiles as early as 1907. Artesian wells discovered in the late 1880s provided a new and clean source of water over the polluted bayou. The city took over water regulation in

1906. Subsidence from drilling wells eventually forced the city to look to local rivers for a new supply.

Between the many local bayous and Galveston Bay, water pollution presented a special problem in the area. During construction of the Houston Ship Channel, the Army Corps of Engineers ordered the city to build a modern sewage disposal system, which was completed in 1902. Unchecked construction also led to flooding. Responding to major floods in 1929 and 1935, the Harris County Flood District emerged to ease the problem. Nonetheless, flooding continued to plague the city as late as 2001, when Tropical Storm Allison dumped an unprecedented 2 days of heavy rains on the concrete terrain, leaving behind $5 billion in damage.

Numerous planned suburban communities added to the area of the city. The earliest developments were in Houston Heights (1892), Pasadena (1892), Deer Park (1892), Bellaire (1911), West University Place (1919), and the prestigious River Oaks (1929). Clear Lake City grew from the burgeoning space program in the 1960s. In 1961, the National Aeronautics and Space Administration established the Lyndon B. Johnson Space Center along the coast of Clear Lake. The area thrived as the home of astronauts, engineers, and their families, and it was eventually annexed by Houston. Concerned with enclosure by surrounding suburbs, Mayor Oscar Holcombe and the Houston City Council began to annex local communities in the 1950s. The annexations subsided in the late 1970s, but the city took over Kingwood, a neighborhood to its northeast, in the late 1990s.

For all of its land acquisition, Houston avoided zoning, making it the largest unzoned city in the United States. Even without the influence of zoning, Houston has built an impressive skyline. One of the most important figures in building the city was Jesse H. Jones, who constructed a number of commercial buildings in the 1920s and brought Houston the 1928 Democratic Party convention. In 1929, he unveiled one of his defining works, the 37-story Gulf Building. Jones served as Secretary of commerce under President Franklin D. Roosevelt. Later Houston architecture included the Galleria shopping mall in 1970, which included an indoor ice skating rink; Pennzoil Place, one of Houston's tallest skyscrapers, in 1976; and the "eighth wonder of the world," the Astrodome, in 1965. George Mitchell was another important developer in Houston. Mitchell made his name in the oil business and went on to build the Woodlands, a planned community just north of the city. Mitchell worked to blend his structures with the environment; between 1964 and 1983, he built luxury homes, business centers, and an outdoor concert pavilion on this model.

The Astrodome highlighted the diversity of Houston's cultural scene. The home of the Houston Astros baseball team, the dome also housed the Houston Oilers football team and the world-famous Houston Rodeo. The world champion Houston Rockets basketball team, the Comets women's basketball team, and Aeros hockey team rounded out Houston's sports attractions. After the departure of the Oilers, Houston welcomed another football franchise, the Houston Texans, which claimed the new Reliant Stadium as their home. The early 2000s also saw the construction of Minute Maid Park for the Astros and the Toyota Center for the Rockets.

Major venues for the arts complemented Houstonians' enthusiasm for sports. The theater district, with the Alley Theater (1947), Wortham Center (1987), Jones Hall (1966), and the Hobby Center (2002), hosts world-class talent in the Houston Grand Opera (1956), the Houston Symphony (1913), the Houston Ballet (1969), and the Museum of Fine Arts (1924). Educationally, Houston is also home to several universities, most notably the University of Houston, which began as a junior college in 1927 with support from oilman Hugh Roy Cullen, and Rice University, which grew from an endowment by William Marsh Rice, who made his fortune in the 19th century. The Houston Independent School District began educating local children in 1877. KUHT-TV, on the University of Houston campus, was the first educational television station in the country when it aired in 1953.

The Texas Medical Center brought Houston prominence in health care. Begun in the 1940s with money from the M. D. Anderson Foundation, by 2005 the complex of 42 not-for-profit institutions, including hospitals and medical schools, was the city's largest employer. The center is especially recognized for cancer treatment and heart surgery. One of the key hospitals in the medical center is the Hermann Hospital, which was founded with a bequest from philanthropist George Hermann in the 1920s. Hermann also donated the adjacent land for Hermann Park in 1914.

—*Kimberley Green Weathers*

Further Readings and References

McComb, D. G. (1981). *Houston: A history.* Austin: University of Texas Press.

McComb, D. G. (2005, July). *The handbook of Texas online.* Retrieved July 13, 2006, from www.tsha.utexas.edu/handbook/online/articles/HH/hdh3.html

Shelton, B. A., Feagin, J. R., Bullard, R., Rodriguez, N., & Thomas, R. D. (1989). *Houston: Growth and decline in a Sunbelt boomtown.* Philadelphia: Temple University Press.

Siegel, S. (1983). *Houston: Chronicle of the supercity on Buffalo bayou.* Woodland Hills, CA: Windsor Publications.

HOWARD, EBENEZER

Ebenezer Howard (1850–1928) played a central role in the evolution of urban planning, beginning around the turn of the 20th century. Howard's significance goes beyond bringing many contemporary reform strands together into a coherent form in the garden city idea and shaping the garden city movement; in addition, his ideas provided a vehicle for individuals who developed formative modern planning notions. Howard's influence propelled professionals such as Raymond Unwin (1863–1940) and his partner Barry Parker (1867–1947) from provincial obscurity to father figures of the town planning movement in Britain. Furthermore, Howard acquired importance from his practical successes. Within 6 years of the publication of his book, *Tomorrow: A Peaceful Path to Real Reform* (1898), a competition had been held and a plan had been selected for the first garden city at Letchworth, England, acknowledged as the first attempt to express 20th-century urban planning practices.

Born in London but educated in Suffolk, Howard had by the age of 21 emigrated from England to Nebraska to work on a family venture. Although this undertaking proved to be unsuccessful, it gave Howard a number of invaluable experiences. For example, in America, he acquired firsthand experience with rural living, and after moving from Nebraska, he lived in Chicago and was able to observe its development after the 1871 fire. Following his return to England in 1876, where he subsequently worked as a parliamentary reporter, Howard had a unique perspective on difficulties within the British political system and its lack of success in resolving urban problems (poverty, poor housing, labor problems, and so on). Such know-how was no doubt vital to his formulating the utopian garden city, a new type of settlement proposed as a means to end urban and rural problems in British society. Put into practice at Letchworth (beginning in 1904) and subsequently in numerous suburbs on the garden city model, Howard's town-country amalgam was a major success. Furthermore, the comprehensive nature of the garden city model proved to be of significance not only in Britain but also in other countries. Despite the intervention of World War I from 1914 to 1918, Howard continued to encourage the development of garden cities, and immediately after 1918, a new settlement, Welwyn Garden City, was planned. Howard is often mistakenly called an urban planner; it is more accurate to describe him as an urbanist or urban thinker, for it is widely known that during his lifetime, he never actually created a town plan as such, preferring instead to let professionals take up his ideas and put them into practice.

—*Ian Morley*

See also Garden Cities

Further Readings and References

Howard, E. (1965). *Garden cities of to-morrow.* Cambridge, MA: MIT Press.

Parsons, K. (2002). *From garden city to green city: The legacy of Ebenezer Howard.* Baltimore: Johns Hopkins University Press.

Sutcliffe, A. (1981). *British town planning: The formative years.* London: Palgrave Macmillan.

HOWE, FREDERIC C.

Frederic C. Howe (1867-1940) was a Progressive Era reformer whose varied career is recounted in his autobiography. Howe obtained a Ph.D. in 1892 from Johns Hopkins University, where his favorite professor was future President Woodrow Wilson. After a stint as a journalist in New York City, Howe turned to law and moved to Cleveland, Ohio. There, he became a player in the political reform movement marked by the mayoral tenure of Tom L. Johnson (1901–1909).

Howe was elected as a Republican to the Cleveland City Council but switched his allegiance to Johnson's Democratic Party because of Johnson's opposition to political corruption. While Howe lost his bid for reelection, he was later elected a state senator and was a steadfast ally of Johnson in the latter's battle against the economic and political dominance of Senator Mark Hanna's Republican Party. Hanna repeatedly thwarted Johnson's efforts to create a publicly owned street railway company to offset the monopolistic practices of the private companies holding municipal franchises. Among his successes, Howe considered his service on the tax commission, which led to a more equitable reassessment of the city's property taxes in 1910. Howe was also an influential figure in the effort of the Johnson administration and civic leaders to redevelop downtown Cleveland. An admirer of European cities and their planning, Howe supported the Group Plan developed by a committee led by architect Daniel Burnham, which transformed a key downtown area.

With Johnson's defeat in 1909 and death in 1911, Howe left Cleveland to return to New York City. There, he headed the People's Institute, a public civic forum housed at the Cooper Union, from 1911 to 1914. Howe next became the commissioner of immigration at Ellis Island through 1919, serving the Wilson administration. However, he became disillusioned with its repressive policies after the U.S. entry into World War I. After attending the Versailles peace conference, Howe withdrew to a largely private life. He was politically active for a while with the Conference on Progressive Political Activity organized by railroad unions in 1922, which supported the unsuccessful 1924 presidential bid of Progressive Robert M. La Follette.

With the election of Franklin Roosevelt and the implementation of his New Deal to fight the Great Depression, Howe joined the Agricultural Adjustment Administration as consumer counsel. However, the interests of farmers were favored over those of their urban consumers, and Howe left in 1937. He died in 1940, having lived through the Progressive Era, the conservative 1920s, and the liberal New Deal.

Howe is best known for his writings. His 1905 book, *The City: The Hope of Democracy,* was influenced by the ideas of land tax reformer Henry George, whose ideas also inspired Cleveland Mayor Johnson. In 1925, Howe wrote his autobiography, *The Confessions of a Reformer,* which recounted his transformation into and experiences as a Progressive reformer.

—*William Dennis Keating*

See also New Deal: Urban Policy; Progressivism

Further Readings and References

Howe, F. C. (1925). *The confessions of a reformer.* New York: Scribner.

Johnson, T. L. (1970). *My story.* Seattle: University of Washington Press. (Original work published 1911)

Richardson, J. F. (1988). *The confessions of a reformer* (Introduction). Kent, OH: Kent State University Press. (Original work published 1925)

HOWELLS, WILLIAM DEAN

William Dean Howells (1837–1920), author, editor, and critic, was one of the first American writers to depict late-19th-century urban life in a realistic literary style in his works *The Rise of Silas Lapham* (1885) and *A Hazard of New Fortunes* (1890). He also encouraged realist writing during his editorship of the *Atlantic Monthly* magazine by supporting authors such as Henry James, Stephen Crane, and Bret Harte.

Born in 1837 in Martinsville (now Martin's Ferry), Ohio, Howells grew up in a large, close-knit family, the second of eight children. His father was a printer and publisher who took his family to live in a log cabin for a year as an experiment in utopian living. Howells's formal education ended at the age of 10 when he began work in his father's printing office. A voracious reader who taught himself several European languages, Howells submitted poems and articles to local papers in the 1850s and became city editor of the *Ohio State Journal* in 1858. In 1860, he was commissioned to write a campaign biography of Abraham Lincoln, who won the 1861 presidential election; Howells was rewarded with an appointment as U.S. consul to Venice, Italy, where he moved in 1861. Howells remained in Italy for 4 years with his wife, Elinor Mead Howells (whom he married in Paris in 1862), and their first child, daughter Winifred, born in 1863. The couple also had a son, John, in 1868, and a second daughter, Mildred, in 1872.

When the family returned to the United States in 1865, Howells was made assistant editor of the Boston-based *Atlantic Monthly,* and the family settled in Cambridge, Massachusetts. In 1871, Howells became editor of the magazine, a post he held for 10 years. In 1891, Howells and his family moved to New York City, where he edited *Cosmopolitan* for 6 months and then began working for *Harper's Monthly,* for whom he wrote several columns until his death in 1920. In the 1890s, Howells grew extremely dismayed by the social inequality of the city and published the utopian romance *A Traveler From Altruria* (1894).

Throughout his lifetime and at the time of his death, Howells was widely acknowledged as the dean of American letters, and he was elected the first president of the American Academy of Arts and Letters in 1908. Although Howells published more than 100 books in a variety of genres, he remains best known for his realist fiction, including *A Modern Instance* (1881), one of the first novels to treat the social consequences of divorce; *The Rise of Silas Lapham* (1885), which treats an American businessman's upward mobility in Boston; and *A Hazard of New Fortunes* (1890), an exploration of cosmopolitan life in New York City.

—*Elif S. Armbruster*

Further Readings and References

Cady, E. H. (1956). *The road to realism: The early years, 1837–1885, of William Dean Howells.* Syracuse, NY: Syracuse University Press.

Cady, E. H. (1958). *The realist at war: The mature years, 1885–1920, of William Dean Howells.* Syracuse, NY: Syracuse University Press.

HOYT, HOMER

Homer Hoyt's research revealed how cities grow; his consulting shaped the suburbs that developed after World War II. Born in 1895 in St. Joseph, Missouri, Hoyt received his bachelor's and master's degrees in economics from the University of Kansas in 1913 and, after briefly teaching economics at Beloit College, earned a doctor of jurisprudence at the University of Chicago. For the next few years, he taught economics at various universities and had a short stint as a statistician with AT&T.

In 1925, Hoyt established himself as a consultant and real estate broker in Chicago. During this period, he conducted the research for his 1933 study, *One Hundred Years of Land Values in Chicago,* which, soon after publication, was submitted as his dissertation in land economics at the University of Chicago. Upon earning his Ph.D., Hoyt embarked on a varied career:

principal housing economist for the Federal Housing Administration (1934–1940), director of research for the Chicago Plan Commission (1941–1943), and director of economic studies for the Regional Plan Association of New York (1943–1946). During these years, he cowrote *Principles of Real Estate* (1939), one of the first textbooks in real estate analysis, with Arthur Weimer. From 1946 until 1974, Hoyt directed an economic consulting firm, Homer Hoyt Associates; later, he became a real estate investor.

One Hundred Years of Land Values in Chicago is an innovative analysis of that city's rhythms of growth from 1833 to 1930. It became the basis for Hoyt's later work, specifically the research he did while at the FHA on the difficulties of securing mortgages in inner cities and his writings on economic base analysis and the importance of export industries to local and regional economies. The former appeared as *The Structure and Growth of Residential Neighborhoods in American Cities* in 1939. In it, Hoyt challenged Ernest Burgess's concentric zone theory of urban growth. Sectoral theory arrayed the areas of the city in wedges that emanated from the core, involved descending land value gradients, and followed radial transportation corridors. Hoyt also wrote on urbanization; as he did in many of his writings, he framed his topic historically and comparatively, for example, in *World Urbanization,* published by the Urban Land Institute in 1962.

As an independent consultant after 1946, Hoyt provided research and advice to state and local governments on population growth, economic development, and land use. He also prepared numerous property appraisals and market surveys for developers and real estate investors. One of his most significant contributions was the creation of analytic techniques for determining the location and size of suburban shopping centers.

Hoyt died in 1984 after a distinguished career in which he influenced the work of urban and suburban planners, shopping center developers, real estate appraisers, and property investment firms and made significant contributions to the literatures on urban growth, neighborhood change, and suburban development.

—*Robert A. Beauregard*

See also Chicago, Illinois; Federal Housing Administration; Urbanization

Further Readings and References

Hoyt, H. (1933). *One hundred years of land values in Chicago*. Chicago: University of Chicago Press.

Hoyt, H. (1939). *The structure and growth of residential neighborhoods in American cities*. Washington, DC: Government Printing Office.

Hoyt, H. (1962). *World urbanization: Expanding population in a shrinking world*. Washington, DC: The Urban Land Institute.

Hoyt, H., & Weimer, A. (1939). *Principles of urban real estate*. New York: Roland Press.

HULL-HOUSE

Hull-House was founded in Chicago in 1886 by progressive reformers Jane Addams and Ellen Gates Starr and was one of the earliest and most influential social settlements in North America. Social settlements, like other reforms originating in the Progressive Era (1890–1929), were a response to the slum conditions created by the growing urbanization, massive immigration, and rapid industrialization of the late 19th century. The flood of immigrants and rural poor who came to cities to take up new factory jobs settled in the squalid tenement districts, causing overcrowding, straining already inadequate sanitation systems, and raising the specter of social disorder. Along with protective child labor legislation, public health programs, tenement regulation, and municipal reform, social settlements were an important part of the Progressive Era's urban reform agenda.

Social settlements in the United States were patterned after London's Toynbee Hall, established in 1884 to make education and culture available to residents of poor neighborhoods. As the concept was translated into the American context, settlement workers were inspired by the social action possibilities of living and working with poor people and, as a result, broadened the objectives of American settlements to include political activism and legislative change. Settlement workers took on the job of improving living conditions in urban slums, but they also sought to change the underlying conditions that contributed to poverty. As progressive ideas gained recognition, the notion of social settlements caught on quickly, and by 1900, there were nearly 1,000 settlement houses in cities across the country.

In contrast to earlier charity organizations, social settlements were located in poor neighborhoods; social workers lived in the settlement houses and were active in neighborhood life. In 1886, Hull-House sat at the center of an urban slum that was home to four poor immigrant communities—Italian, German, Jewish, and Bohemian. Addams described the area as plagued by poor and overcrowded housing, dirty streets, poor sanitation, inadequate schools, poor street lighting, and bad pavement. Many of the tenements had no water, aside from a backyard faucet; they were not connected to the street sewer; and they lacked fire escapes, adequate light, and ventilation. It was Addams's contention that because local residents had more thorough and intimate knowledge of the neighborhood, they were better equipped than outside charity workers to accurately assess community needs. She held the view that to understand the difficulties faced by the urban poor, settlement workers needed to experience the problems of poverty firsthand.

Hull-House quickly became an important institution in the neighborhood, and by 1888, it had more than 50 rooms and attracted 1,000 people a week to its programs and activities. By the mid-1890s, that number had grown to 2,000 people a week. The settlement was open 12 hours a day and hosted a wide variety of programs, including a day nursery, kindergarten, Boys Club, sports, sewing, music and theater, and other kinds of clubs. Although many of Hull-House's early programs were targeted to children, Addams was determined that settlement programs should address the needs of the neighborhood's adolescents and adults, as well. Day and evening classes of all sorts were established for youth and adults, along with theater, folk dancing, art classes, and forums for political discussions. Hull-House contained the only library in the neighborhood. Community residents could also find practical assistance through Hull-House, including primary health care, help in finding jobs, legal assistance, counseling, information and referral, and emergency food, fuel, clothing, and bedding.

Settlement workers were particularly concerned about working women and their families, and many Hull-House programs were designed to meet their domestic and child care needs. Early in her tenure at Hull-House, Addams learned that many women living in the neighborhood did sewing work, leaving them little time or money to prepare nutritious meals for their families. She added a community kitchen to Hull-House facilities and made nutritious meals available at low cost. The meals, prepared scientifically in the kitchen, did not include the wide variety of ethnic foods desired by immigrant families, and the kitchen was used instead to serve as a coffeehouse where people gathered to discuss social and political issues.

Because there were no facilities for the children of working women, they either accompanied their mothers to the unhealthful factories where the women worked or were left alone in unsafe and unsanitary home environments. Hull-House's first program was a reading program for young women, but the second was a kindergarten. In addition to poor living conditions, settlement workers worried that the urban environment and the lack of access to safe, outdoor play areas harmed neighborhood children, and in 1894, they acquired land and built one of the first model playgrounds in the country. The playground provided supervised play with an assortment of facilities, including a sandpile, swings, building blocks, and gymnasium equipment.

When Hull-House was founded, it occupied a rented second-story space in a rambling old residence on South Halstead Street. By 1907, as the result of an ambitious construction program begun in 1891, the settlement had grown to 13 practical red brick buildings that covered a large city block. The building expansion began when the settlement acquired an adjacent saloon and transformed it into one of the country's first gymnasiums. In 1894, another floor was added to the original residence, which housed a kindergarten, nursery, and music school, and in 1896, an art gallery was enlarged to provide space for a men's residence. In 1898, with the need for worker housing continuing to grow, an entire building was added for the Jane Club, a cooperative residence for

single working women. The Jane Club provided room and board for 30 women at a cost of $3.25 a week. In 1899, a new coffeehouse with an upstairs theater was built. Between 1902 and 1907, Hull-House expanded to include a new men's club and apartment building, a new women's club, a boys' club, and a new dining hall. The construction program ended when the Mary Crane Nursery was completed in 1907.

In addition to running the programs provided at Hull-House for the local community, settlement workers lobbied for protective labor legislation for children and working women. Through their efforts, the state legislature instituted the 8-hour workday for women and prohibited the employment of children under age 14 in factories. Women from Hull-House were responsible for getting the first juvenile court established in 1899 and for establishing the first state government employment bureau. Along with their work in the Halstead neighborhood, these accomplishments focused widespread attention on Hull-House and its staff, and scholars and social workers from around the world came to visit and to study the philosophy of the settlement movement and the type of neighborhood work practiced at Hull-House.

—*Teresa Lingafelter*

Further Readings and References

Addams, J. (c. 1910). *Twenty years at Hull-House with autobiographical notes.* New York: Macmillan.

Hayden, D. (1995). *The grand domestic revolution.* Cambridge, MA: MIT Press.

Spain, D. (2001). *How women saved the city.* Minneapolis: University of Minnesota Press.

Stivers, C. (2000). *Bureau men and settlement women: Constructing public administration in the Progressive Era.* Lawrence: University Press of Kansas.

INCORPORATION

Incorporation is a term used to indicate that a specifically defined piece of land has been granted an independent political identity. It more broadly describes the process whereby a municipality is granted powers of self-government. These powers provide the legal means for municipalities to take on debt, assess taxes, undertake public works projects, and provide fire and police protection and other public services. In the United States, municipalities are "creatures of the states," and as a result, the specific forms that incorporation takes vary from state to state. Political power emanates from the top of the federal system with the federal government, which admits and grants powers to the states. Individual states, in turn, create and recognize subsidiary political bodies to govern more locally. Entities as various as counties, parishes, boroughs, and townships represent a middle ground between the state governments and incorporated municipalities. The most local forms of government are the independent (and incorporated) municipalities that bear a wide variety of names—cities, villages, towns, and boroughs, to name a few. This pyramidal structure derives from the U.S. Constitution itself, which leaves a great deal of political control in the hands of the states.

As a result, incorporation is a process that is created and defined by state legislatures in varying ways across the country. Historical control of state legislatures by rural interests created a hodge-podge of regulations in response to then-current conditions. Growing cities began to push for more local control for their "corporations" during the so-called "home

rule" movement of the 19th century. Increased power was expected to come in the form of new and expansive city charters that would remove state control of such everyday matters as police and fire commissions. Despite the pleas of reformers, legislatures suspicious of cities were slow to grant such powers. The underlying principle of state control remained strong despite a general drift toward more local control.

The large city thus emerged as the primary location of conflict over the type and nature of power accorded to an incorporated body in the 19th century. At the same time, undercurrents in the home-rule battles were changing the motivations behind incorporation. The move for home rule and rationalization in government led in many cases to modernized and standardized incorporation statutes in states across the country. For example, in 1892 Wisconsin amended its constitution to prohibit incorporation by a special act of the legislature. A law specifying general incorporation procedures replaced special acts, thus transferring incorporation from the legislative realm to the judicial. The inevitability and timetable of such changes has not been uniform across all states. Thus Maine made the switch in 1820, whereas Florida never did adopt uniform regulations and retains incorporation by special act today.

Regardless of form, the general rationalization of incorporation law made possible a proliferation of municipalities possessed of ever-increasing legal independence throughout the country. Incorporation became attractive even to small settlements as the level of services expected by "city" dwellers grew at the turn of the 20th century—services such as electric lights on the streets, improved road conditions, running water in houses, and drainage in the event of heavy rainfall. While these services were not provided uniformly in communities across the country, their widespread adoption led to widespread incorporation, as communities took advantage of the relatively easy incorporation terms created under most general incorporation statutes. Incorporation thus became a solution to the problem of municipal service provision.

Home rule thus had one anticipated effect, increased governing autonomy for growing cities, and one unanticipated side effect: the multiplication of independently incorporated municipalities. Population, industry, and commerce streamed out of core cities throughout the 20th century, creating suburban growth at the expense of cities. Annexation and consolidation battles came to characterize city-suburb relationships, topped by the metropolitan unification movement widespread in the 1950s and 1960s. In a wide variety of cases, core cities began movements that would unify the city and suburban governments, thus avoiding duplication of services and, more important, recapturing tax revenue, jobs, and residents for the main municipality.

In this hostile atmosphere, unincorporated areas surrounding major metropolitan centers began to incorporate to avoid annexation by or consolidation with the city. Legal changes allowed these areas' fears of being merged with the city to manifest themselves politically; Wisconsin passed a 1955 state law granting unincorporated towns surrounding a "first-class city" special incorporation privileges. In 1954, Maryland actually instituted general incorporation laws and granted home rule for the first time. Thus, by the middle of the century, incorporation had moved to the center of metropolitan disputes, as it became the means by which areas outside the core city could retain their independence and foil metropolitan unification plans. Large-scale suburban incorporation generally prevented major cities from expanding. Instead of becoming a solution to the problem of service provision in large cities, widespread home-rule-based incorporation had become a thorn in the side of declining large cities.

Today, uniform incorporation statutes that grant home rule to municipalities govern nearly all states. Concern exists in some states over the power that states can wield, through budgetary pressures, on municipal policy and the creation of regional special districts. Sewer, police, fire, and school districts across municipal boundaries render home rule somewhat vulnerable on occasion, as the service provision that gave rise to many of the municipalities in the first place is increasingly shifted either to larger governments, typically counties, or to special districts created by state legislatures. The typical metropolitan area is governed and provided for by a complex tapestry of taxing bodies of varying degrees of democratic control and political power. In response, some metropolitan areas have seen consolidation efforts succeed, such as Miami-Dade County, Indianapolis-Marion County, and Louisville-Jefferson County, and some have been left with partial sharing of responsibilities, such as Minneapolis-St. Paul's Metropolitan Council, which represents a federated approach to metropolitan problems. Other cities, such as Cleveland and St. Louis, saw unsuccessful efforts toward a unified metropolitan government. The legal rights and responsibilities of incorporated municipalities have changed a great deal over the past 200 years, and the growth of nongovernmental taxing units and consolidated service provision portends continued change in the future.

—*Christopher Miller*

See also Home Rule; Metropolitan Government; Miami, Florida; Minneapolis/St. Paul, Minnesota; Municipal Government; Suburbanization

Further Readings and References

Miller, G. J. (1981). *Cities by contract: The politics of municipal incorporation.* Cambridge, MA: MIT Press.

Teaford, J. (1984). *The unheralded triumph: City government in America, 1870–1900.* Baltimore: Johns Hopkins University Press.

INDIANAPOLIS, INDIANA

Indianapolis has been the capital of the state of Indiana since 1825, as well as the center of governmental, political, economic, and cultural activity in the state.

When Indiana was admitted to the Union in 1816, Congress donated four sections of land for a state capital. Four years later the legislature approved a wilderness site near the center of the state. Surveyors platted a one-square-mile area in the middle of the congressional donation, and downtown Indianapolis is still known as the "Mile Square." One of the surveyors had assisted in laying out the nation's capital, and the Washington influence is obvious in the 1821 plat: broad streets, diagonal avenues, and a circle (the intended location of the governor's residence) at the center of the city. Centrality in the state was the town's principal advantage; the adjacent White River proved unsuitable for navigation and early land routes were poor. Well into the 1840s, the capital remained a barely accessible village.

Railroad connections secured during the late 1840s and 1850s and considerable growth during the Civil War transformed the town into Indiana's principal urban center. By 1870 the population of Indianapolis was more than double that of its closest intrastate rival, and the capital had become the state's manufacturing and commercial leader. Continued growth was spurred during the 1890s by exploiting newly discovered natural gas fields northeast of the city. The 1890s also witnessed construction of the city's signature structure, the Indiana State Soldiers and Sailors Monument, located on the (renamed) Monument Circle in the center of the Mile Square.

The city's growth was heavily affected by immigration. During the mid-19th century, Ireland and Germany supplied most of the foreign-born residents. In 1870, when 22 percent of the capital's residents were foreign-born, almost half of the immigrant population was German and almost one third was Irish. Compared to other American urban areas, however, the city was largely bypassed by the "new" immigration from Southern and Eastern Europe during the late 19th and early 20th centuries. In 1920, the Board of Trade proclaimed Indianapolis a "100 percent American town." While this assertion was exaggerated, it did reflect the reality that only 5 percent of the city's population was foreign-born in that year—one of the lowest rates among northern cities. The African American population grew steadily during the decades after the Civil War. Comprising only 6 percent of Indianapolis residents in 1870, blacks accounted for 11 percent of the population in 1920; by 2000, the figure stood at 25 percent. In the post–World War II decades, Indianapolis experienced an influx of new arrivals from Appalachia, and by 1970 16 percent of the population had been born in the South. At the beginning of the 21st century, Hispanic immigrants were the fastest growing ethnic group in central Indiana (accounting for 3.9 percent of the city's population in 2000).

The years of the late 19th and early 20th centuries are often considered the city's Golden Age. In addition to benefitting from the gas boom (which ended around 1900), Indianapolis became the hub of the nation's most extensive interurban railway network. Connections could be made for most of the state's major cities, and shoppers, businessmen, and sightseers arrived and departed daily. The capital also benefitted from the automobile industry. Of negligible importance in 1900, by 1920 the industry ranked second in the city in terms of number of persons employed and value of product. While Detroit assumed command of the mass market, Indianapolis was home to such elegant and costly makes as Marmon and Stutz. Even after automobile production ceased, fabricating auto parts continued as a mainstay of the city's economy until the 1980s. Completion in 1909 of the Indianapolis Motor Speedway as a testing facility led to the inauguration two years later of the Indianapolis 500-Mile Race, "The Greatest Spectacle in Racing." The venue has recently added the Brickyard 400 (NASCAR) and the U.S. Grand Prix (Formula One) to its list of events.

The city also attained prominence in politics and publishing. Local lawyers Thomas A. Hendricks and Charles Warren Fairbanks were elected vice president of the United States in 1884 and 1904, respectively. Another Indianapolis attorney, Benjamin Harrison, was president from 1889 to 1893. And a former mayor, Thomas Taggart, chaired the Democratic National Committee in the early 20th century. The Bobbs-Merrill publishing house won both popular and critical acclaim, and the city's literary reputation was secured by the presence of such well-known authors as James Whitcomb Riley (the "Hoosier Poet") and Booth Tarkington. Several of Tarkington's novels were set in a "Midland city" based on his hometown.

The Great Depression of the 1930s affected Indianapolis much as it did other urban areas across the country. The city's economy, increasingly reliant on the production of consumer goods, was sensitive to deferred household purchases. The closure of one interurban line after another during the 1930s further weakened the local economy. Starting in 1940, however, defense dollars and defense workers began to pour into the capital. Conversion to wartime production was accompanied by full employment and growing payrolls.

The demographic history of Indianapolis after World War II mirrored the national pattern of suburban growth and central city decline. During the 1950s, the city's population grew 12 percent, but the population of the suburban ring within Marion County jumped by 78 percent. And that trend continued into the 1980s and 1990s, with much of the metropolitan area's growth during those decades having taken place in counties adjacent to the city. Population loss has been especially severe in Center Township, the core of the city, although the construction of new downtown apartments and condominiums and the "gentrification" of some older, inner city neighborhoods in recent years has partially offset the exodus to the suburbs and exurbs.

Residential deconcentration has been facilitated by the construction of multiple interstate highways in the metropolitan area. Indianapolis, once a crossroads for the railroads and interurbans, is now a crossroads for much Midwestern automotive traffic. Its strategic location and highway connections have prompted warehouses, distribution centers, and motor and air-freight firms to locate in or near the capital. The I-465 beltway, in particular, has been a magnet for development.

The most important innovation in the city's recent history was the implementation in 1970 of a consolidated city-county government dubbed "Unigov." Republicans pushed the measure through in order to incorporate thousands of suburban, mostly Republican, voters into the city's electorate. Democrats consider the consolidation a partisan power play ("Unigrab") that has had an especially pernicious effect on the political influence of the capital's African American community. After Unigov's enactment, Republicans won every mayoral contest until 2000 and controlled the City-County Council until 2004 (when Democrats eked out a one-seat majority).

In spite of its name, Unigov was not a complete consolidation of all governmental functions in Marion County. School systems, police forces, and fire departments all remain decentralized. But a single executive and a central legislative body did bring increased coherence to the formation of countywide policies. Some observers credit the reorganization, especially the creation of a Department of Metropolitan Development, with making possible a number of downtown revitalization initiatives.

Mayors Richard G. Lugar (1968–1976) and William H. Hudnut III (1976–1992) were highly successful in energizing what they described as a "public-private partnership" on behalf of the city. Lugar generally receives substantial credit for Unigov, for strengthening ties with the business and philanthropic communities, and for aggressively seeking federal aid (which had often been shunned by earlier mayors). Hudnut and his administration get most of the plaudits for orchestrating the revitalization of downtown Indianapolis and for using amateur and professional sports to raise civic visibility and boost economic development. Hudnut's successor, Stephen Goldsmith (1992–2000), focused on "privatizing" many governmental functions. Bart Peterson, elected in 2000, has undertaken a "Cultural Development Initiative," an effort to bolster the city's arts community and promote Indianapolis as a cultural tourism destination.

The Unigov consolidation expanded the city's boundaries to the Marion County lines (an area of 402 square miles) and increased the city's population from 476,258 (in 1960) to 744,625 (1970). In 2000 the Indianapolis population was 791,926, and the metropolitan area claimed just over 1.6 million residents.

—*Robert G. Barrows*

Further Readings and References

Barrows, R. G. (1990). Indianapolis: Silver buckle on the rust belt. In R. M. Bernard (Ed.), *Snowbelt cities* (pp. 137–157). Bloomington, IN: Indiana University Press.

Bodenhamer, D. J., & Barrows, R. G. (Eds.). (1994). *The encyclopedia of Indianapolis.* Bloomington, IN: Indiana University Press.

Dunn, J. P. (1910). *Greater Indianapolis.* Chicago: Lewis.

Leary, E. A. (1971). *Indianapolis: The story of a city.* Indianapolis, IN: Bobbs-Merrill.

INDUSTRIAL CITY

Cities have been centers of production and manufacture for millennia. The city of manufacture gathered producers and material together. In crowded workshops and along docks and piers workers constructed chariots and wagons, boats and sails, tapestries and clothing, boots and soap, and, with the invention of the printing press, books, newspapers, and broadsides. A visit to a weaving shop in 14th-century Flanders, a shipyard in 17th-century Glasgow, or an 18th-century Philadelphia print shop would see industrious jours (skilled workers), harassed apprentices, and nervous masters. But the labor done would share one important feature—it would be for the most part hand-powered.

Cities of manufacture gathered people together and subjected them to the filth, smells, and disease of crowds. But there was something fundamentally different between these pre-industrial cities and their later progeny. The crowds of the pre-industrial city were more mixed and diverse. Mixing in with merchants and traders, bankers, and gentlemen farmers in the city, for shopping or business, would be haulers and builders, artisans and fabricators, sailors and ship captains. The wealthy to be sure found comfort in residential areas of their peers, but not far away were homes of the poor. Masters, jours, and apprentices lived amongst each other if not in the same homes. Shops that manufactured goods often were the shops where the goods were sold, and shops also were in the same buildings as homes and taverns. Within the shops, masters, jours, and apprentices mingled freely. Although orders were given, especially to apprentices, in general those engaging in the manufacture of goods did their own work, at accustomed speed and under their own direction, and they did varied activities. The goods they turned out were as varied as the men and women who produced them.

These urban workshops were complemented by rural home production. Entering a farm community of 200 years ago, one would confront multiple centers of production. Each home was a hive of manufacturing activity, in which spinning and weaving of various items was done for local use and sale to urban markets. In barns and work sheds, wagons, harnesses, rakes, tools, and furniture were fashioned. Enterprising manufacturers sent out into the countryside the cuttings and materials for the creation of gloves, hats, shoe-uppers, and brooms, and the finished products were gathered in the commercial centers for distribution.

To a great extent, urban workshop and home production met most of the needs of the new nation, but the model of large-scale production—of using armies of workers doing similar repetitive tasks and using animals in addition to people to supply the labor to produce standardized goods—had been developed in England and proved too hard to resist. In England, animal power had been utilized for centuries to power gristmills and fulling-mills, whereas in America, water power and wind power were tapped to grind grain, cut lumber, full wool, and hammer iron. What first Samuel Slater and later the Boston Associates did was to take control of waterpower to run multiple machines tended by operatives, and when they did so, they set in motion a revolution in production that not only created new ways to produce goods but also restructured urban life and gave rise to the industrial city. To find falling water significantly powerful

enough to run machines on a regular basis, these entrepreneurs looked upstream to where rivers fell across major fault lines, then built dams, canals, and mill ponds and constructed buildings large enough and strong enough to house hundreds of machines. The building of dams large enough to capture significant waterpower, and factories whose foundations were strong enough to hold up under the strain of the workings of multiple machines, required extensive investment.

The economics of scale called for huge factories and concentrations of machines, and because the waterpower they required lay beyond the boundaries of the traditional commercial cities (which were founded along protective harbors with easy access to the sea well below these fault lines), the investors in the new industries built their mills outside of the older commercial cities. Around the mills, tenements and boarding houses were built to house the workers that gathered together each morning at the factory gates. These were instant cities that grew from small villages to huge industrial centers with thousands of workers clustered close to the mills that lined the canals. Small villages were transformed into the dense industrial cities of Lowell, Lawrence, and Holyoke in Massachusetts, Nashua and Manchester in New Hampshire, and Paterson in New Jersey.

The image of young women working powered machines, living in supervised boarding houses, and reading poetry after work intrigued the world, but it was the wealth produced by armies of workers linked to powered machines in integrated production processes that impressed those with capital to invest. Investors throughout the North looked to subdivide production into units capable of being linked to powered machinery. American rivers flowed powerfully out of the Appalachian Mountains, and once they were dammed at major fault lines, the energy of nature was harnessed to the interests of capital. But even these powerful rivers flowed irregularly. Winter ice floes disrupted production and left machines idle. Summer droughts lowered the water level behind the dams and reduced the power available to keep the machines running at full capacity. Idle machines meant wasted money. Even with upriver dams to control the water flow, sole dependence upon waterpower meant the risk of unused or underutilized capital goods.

The steam engine that was initially developed in England to pump water out of mines, and that was adapted in this country as a source of energy for locomotion (for steamboats and railroads) provided a more dependable source of energy as a supplement to waterpower or as an independent energy source. Steam engines had the advantage that they were not tied to the faults of major waterways. By the second half of the 19th century, steam engines began to replace waterpower as the central force driving machines that directed the actions of operatives. Cheap coal from northeastern Pennsylvania, western Virginia, and southern Illinois provided the energy for these steam engines, and canals linked the coalfields to the factories of the cities.

New machines such as the sewing machine, the Fourdrinier paper-making machine, and the rotary printer were linked to steam power. And more and more standardized goods poured out of American factories that still used the old term *mill,* but used it to describe not the turning of stones to grind grain but the huge buildings housing powered machines that turned out cloth, paper, and iron. Industrial manufacturing had become so important to the American economy that as early as 1860, 30 percent of New England's population was employed in manufacturing—most of which involved a significant amount of powered machinery.

The gathering of people to work in the new leviathans also brought merchants, shopkeepers, craftspeople, and day laborers, but the significant occupations of these new industrial cities were those involved in tending machines that were powered by external forces of energy and that turned out standardized goods. The operatives in these occupations did skilled and unskilled work, but the regiment of the machine usually determined the pace of their work. The dominant structures built in these cities were the mills that rose up as big blocks several stories into the air.

The mountains of goods that poured out of these mills produced great wealth, which was then reinvested in other machines and other technologies. With the development of the sewing machine, steam-powered stitching machines took over the binding of shoes, making shoe production the third largest industry in the nation (behind textiles and lumber). Once cows and pigs were slaughtered in backyards and in local butcher shops, but increasingly these animals were driven to huge slaughterhouses where they were chained up to moving disassembly lines powered by steam and worked by hundreds of meatpackers doing but one small part of the bloody process. Once dressed, the meat was shipped to markets around the country. The growth and productivity of the American farmlands encouraged

investment in agricultural machinery, the vastness of the countryside encouraged the multiplication of railroad lines, and both encouraged investment in iron and steel production. By 1860 America had over 30,000 miles of track. Railroads joined the cities of the East with each other and with the cities of the West. These lines also linked coalfields and iron mines with urban iron and steel manufacturing centers, strands of forests with lumber mills, corn and wheat fields with grain elevators, and cattle herds with slaughterhouses. By the end of the 19th century, standard gauge railroads crisscrossed the nation and, together with rivers, connected the cities of the nation into a single continental market. Utilizing local resources and labor, manufacturers turned out an array of goods destined for national markets linked to the factories by the national rail network.

With the development of steam-powered furnaces, rolling and drawing machines, and the switch from charcoal to coked-coal fuel, iron production moved from the countryside to the city. And with the development of the Bessemer and then open-hearth furnaces, steel production became an urban industry. The iron and then steel industry concentrated mills and mill workers along rivers, canals, and railroads where cheap fuel could be shipped in and iron and steel rails, tubes, and sheets shipped out. And with the industry came pollution.

Cities were always dirty places; disease and filth typified the merchant and commercial city as well as the industrial one. Wood fireplaces and small smitheries sent ash into the air of cities long before steam engines became a part of the urban landscape. But the power machines of the industrial city demanded energy, and increasingly they found that energy stored in coal. As more coal was burnt, particularly cheap bituminous coal, industrial cities became identified with smokestacks and the soot pouring out of them.

Industrial production involved heavy capital investment. That investment paid off with increased production and economies of scale. But increased production needed workers and translated into profits only with increase in sales. Large runs of standardized products reduced per-item costs, but the standardized products had to find large markets. The use of rivers, canals, and railroads to transport raw materials and finished goods opened up a growing nationwide market for these industrial goods. Farm wives gave up home spinning and weaving for factory produced cloth, while their husbands bought tools and agricultural implements that in an earlier time may have been fashioned by their fathers in the sheds behind their barns. Urban housewives bought shoes made in standard sizes and readymade clothes and pre-dressed meat, while their husbands purchased suits off the rack and read newspapers hot off the steam-driven presses.

Successful industrial enterprises needed to be located near sources of labor, or to bring that labor to them. They had to be located near a transportation axis that could bring in raw materials and ship out finished products to markets. The 19th-century industrial city was formed around these requirements. The growth of standardized machine-produced goods not only created cities along river faults but also affected older commercial cities as well. With the ability to place steam engines where transportation, labor, sources of capital, ingenuity, and markets already existed, entrepreneurs located their mills in or near older commercial centers and in the process transformed them. Factories and mills stretched out from the city center along rivers, canals, and railroad lines, from which issued coal, iron ore, cotton, leather, steel plate, grain, cows, and pigs and onto which were loaded blankets, cloth, coats, clocks, plows, rubber raincoats, shoes, shovels, stoves, watches, white flour, stakes, and pork chops. Clustered around these factories and mills and located near the rivers, canals, and railroad lines were dense networks of worker housing. Into these tenements came immigrants from abroad and migrants from rural America, some with preexisting experience of industry and others recently out of the countryside and with no experience of industry. Migration patterns steered these immigrants into like communities that clustered around mills and factories.

Steam powered the industrial city of the second half of the 19th century, but by the 20th century that power was increasingly centralized in huge power plants that turned not machinery but turbines that produced electrical energy that flowed into factories and homes. Centralized electric generators moved city residents, lit the city night, and powered the industrial machines that incorporated into themselves more and more of the production process, simplifying work without reducing its drudgery.

The flow of goods coming out of the new industries contributed to the transformation of the city. Steel beams, reinforced concrete, and steel cable (used for steam-driven elevators) allowed not only for the building of the dramatic downtown skyline of office buildings but also for the construction of huge factory mills covering acres of land with a single structure.

The new factories gathered into their yards each day not hundreds of workers but thousands. Immigrants looked for neighbors who spoke their languages and understood their customs, and they shunned those who did not. They also tended to find work through neighborhood and ethnic ties. These two forces worked to segregate the city and concentrate people in ethnic and racial neighborhoods. However, even though the demand for work, housing, and workers was great, not all those within an ethnic community could find work in the local factories, and shortages of housing as well as the need for work often pushed immigrants into finding other neighborhoods. Thus large industrial cities might have several communities of the same ethnic group. Although the neighborhoods around the factories quickly filled with worker houses and overcrowded tenements, sometimes the demand for workers outstripped the number of workers in the working-class neighborhoods that spread out from the factories. Increasingly factories drew their labor force from the larger urban setting, and streetcar lines laid down the central transportation arteries were bringing workers to the factories from far-flung urban neighborhoods. Electric driven carriages, capable of carrying dozens of riders, rolled along steel rails, moving people across an urban landscape with a 5- to 10-mile radius.

The products of industry and the production of industry re-formed the city so that the old mix of merchants, masters, jours, haulers, day laborers, shoppers and visitors, shops, tenements, homes, and artisan shops increasingly gave way to a segregated, segmented city. With separate factory districts came separate residential neighborhoods. Even before the streetcar moved people over long distances, merchants and manufacturers moved with their families to neighborhoods away from the dirt and chaos of production and commerce as well as away from the homes of middle-class tradespeople and shopkeepers—and all these comfortable families moved away from the struggles of the working class and very poor.

The streetcar railways exacerbated this pattern. Factory owners lived miles from their factories and their workers. The downtown commercial districts housed fewer and fewer people and became specialized centers for shopping and the practice of the craft of commerce—the daytime activity of insurance, law, banking, and clerking. With the exception of a few fashionable downtown areas, for the most part these urban centers housed few residential neighborhoods.

The wealthy fled to higher ground away from the mix of poverty, filth, and pollution to suburban communities reached by streetcars and where trees and parks were more common. Around the commercial core of the city lay the neighborhoods of the middle classes: lawyers, doctors, managers, teachers, successful clerks, and skilled craftspeople. Following the railroad lines were factories and mills and the housing of the working classes. Along polluted river bottoms, among older abandoned factories, and at the cities' edge away from the fashionable suburbs in low lands were to be found the urban poor. Although the industrial city did not create urban poverty, the increased segregation of the city, the hazards of industrial work, and the vagaries and impersonality of industrial employment concentrated poverty, while America's dependence upon immigrant labor and black labor from the rural South for its growing industries gave that poverty an ethnic and racial complexion.

—John T. Cumbler

Further Readings and References

Cumbler, J. (1989). *A social history of industrial decline.* New Brunswick, NJ: Rutgers University Press.

High, S. (2003). *Industrial sunset: The making of North America's Rust-Belt, 1969–1984.* Toronto: University of Toronto Press.

Licht, W. (1995). *Industrializing America: The 19th century.* Baltimore, MD: Johns Hopkins University Press.

Mohl, R. (1985). *The new city: Urban America in the industrial age, 1860–1920.* New York: Harlem Davidson.

Nye, D. (1999). *Consuming power: A social history of American energies.* Cambridge, MA: MIT Press.

Platt, H. (1991). *The electric city: Energy and the growth of the Chicago area, 1880–1930.* Chicago: University of Chicago Press.

Sugrue, T. (1996). *The origin of the urban crisis: Race and inequality in postwar Detroit.* Princeton, NJ: Princeton University Press.

Teaford, J. (1994). *Cities of the heartland: The rise and fall of the industrial Midwest.* Bloomington, IN: Indiana University Press.

INDUSTRIAL SUBURBS

Industrial suburbs have been an important element of urban development over the last 200 years. While employment was found outside the city boundaries of the colonial and mercantile city, the increase in manufacturing employment in industrial suburbs was related to the development of 19th-century urban-industrial capitalism. Industrial suburbs are important for several reasons: They reflect the changing character of industrial capitalist society, they have been a central part of metropolitan development since the middle of the 19th century, and they bring out the importance of working-class suburbanization. From the early-19th-century textile suburbs of Philadelphia to the more recent steel, electrical equipment, and aircraft districts of Pittsburgh, Chicago, and Los Angeles, the industrial suburb has been a vital presence on the city edge.

Industrial suburbs have a long history. In the 18th century, firms forced out of the city by bylaws forbidding noxious and smelly industries, as well as firms seeking a site next to a fast-running stream, were scattered over the city's outer fringe. In the early 19th century, burgeoning industrial capitalism deposited an array of industrial mill towns, such as Lowell, Massachusetts, at a distance from Eastern seaboard cities. Large-scale industrial decentralization after the 1840s built on these earlier rounds of industrial dispersal. By 1899, almost a third of metropolitan employment was located in suburban areas. The suburban share grew over the following half century, reaching four out of every ten jobs in 1947. There was great variation however. At the end of World War II only a third of the industrial workforce of Cleveland and St. Louis worked in suburban firms, while more than three quarters of the workforce in Boston and Pittsburgh did. The move of industry to the suburbs has greatly accelerated in the postwar period; most manufacturing jobs are no longer found in the central city.

Industrial suburbs are a product of urban geographical industrialization. The introduction of the capitalist factory system led to the generalization of wage labor, the development of specialized divisions of labor, the emergence of new production and process technologies, and the rise of rapidly expanding markets. Transportation and communication changes widened the basis for interfirm interaction; integrated local, regional, and national markets; and reduced costs. These social, economic, and technological processes widened the locational options open to firms. With few exceptions, most firms were concentrated in or close to the city core before the mid-19th century. The modern industrial large-scale, vertically integrated, multi-unit firm in rapidly growing industries, however, sought out different manufacturing spaces. In Chicago, firms such as Pullman, U.S. Steel, Western Electric, and Ford moved to suburban greenfields for large and cheap sites, where they installed modern methods and large workforces in extensive and sprawling work spaces linked to regional and national markets by railroad and highways. Once in place, these firms generated suburban agglomeration economies. Some firms moved to the suburbs independent of the large corporation. Many firms of all scales and from a variety of industries, however, were attracted to the urban fringe to take advantage of established interfirm linkages, localized labor markets, extensive transportation facilities, and cooperative local governments.

A collection of local and nonlocal interests oversaw the making of industrial suburbs. Property speculators converted peripheral land into lots and surveys to be used for a multitude of purposes—industrial, residential, commercial, civic, and transportation. Speculative and custom builders and contractors constructed housing, civic institutions, and essential infrastructures, while owner-builders who built their own homes operated outside the private construction sector. Before World War II, the building and regulation of roads, trolley lines, water and sewage systems, housing, and factories were controlled by local private property, transportation, and municipal interests. In the postwar period, federal policy and funding coupled with large-scale investment by nonlocal retailing companies, developers, and engineering firms have become increasingly important in the construction of manufacturing districts outside of city boundaries. These actors, despite their internal disagreements and different goals and strategies, have formed local alliances to establish the ideological, legal, financial, and institutional basis for the development of industrial suburbs.

There were four major types of industrial suburbs before 1950. The most common was the informally created industrial suburb in which firms sought out suburban advantages such as large plots of land, excellent transportation facilities, and a specific labor pool. A second type was the company town where large vertically integrated firms such as Pullman Palace Car (Pullman), U.S. Steel (Gary), and Apollo Iron and Steel (Vandergrift) built and designed housing and a host of civic institutions. Detached from the built-up metropolitan district, the satellite city had a relatively diversified economic structure and an array of civic and social institutions that serviced the local population. The old service towns of Joliet, Elgin, and Aurora became industrial satellite cities of Chicago. Finally, the planned and highly regulated industrial

park provided firms with an array of services from credit to architectural design.

In recent years, the planned or science industrial park with its highly controlled environment and practices has become an increasingly important component of the metropolitan manufacturing landscape. Whether or not the high-tech corridors and technoburbs that are said to dominate the metropolitan fringe are anything more than a contemporary version of the older industrial suburb remains to be seen. There are, however, good reasons to believe that there are important differences between prewar and postwar industrial suburbs, the most notable being the role of state planning in the suburbs, the balance of local and nonlocal capital investment in them, and the length of their inhabitants' commute between work and home. Despite these differences, the very existence of large amounts of manufacturing capital on the edge of American metropolitan areas has been a significant feature for the past 200 years.

—*Robert Lewis*

Further Readings and References

Buder, S. (1967*). Pullman: An experiment in industrial order and community planning, 1880–1930.* New York: Oxford University Press.

Lewis, R. (1999). Running rings around the city: North American industrial suburbs, 1850–1950. In R. Harris & P. Larkham (Eds.), *Changing suburbs* (pp. 146–167). London: Spon.

Lewis, R. (Ed.). (2004). *Manufacturing suburbs: Building work and home on the metropolitan fringe.* Philadelphia: Temple University Press.

Mosher, A. (2004). *Capital's utopia: Vandergrift, Pennsylvania, 1855–1916.* Baltimore: Johns Hopkins University Press.

Scranton, P. (1983). *Proprietary capitalism: The textile manufacture at Philadelphia, 1800–1885.* Philadelphia: Temple University Press.

Taylor, G. (1915). *Satellite cities: A study of industrial suburbs.* New York: Appleton.

Influenza Epidemic of 1918 to 1919

In 1918 and 1919, a new strain of influenza virus swept the world in a pandemic that killed an estimated 21 million people, including at least 675,000

Americans. How the virus mutated is unknown, but certainly the vast movement of people set off by the First World War contributed to its spread. Normally, children and the elderly are the most vulnerable to influenza, but this virus was dramatically lethal among otherwise healthy young adults. In American cities the mortality rate varied, depending, in part, on how individual cities responded to the epidemic.

Spread in droplets of mucous expelled by sneezing, coughing, and exhaling, the influenza virus that caused the 1918 epidemic was easily spread by direct contact, particularly in close quarters. The symptoms, which began with a hacking cough, fever, body aches, and exhaustion, were brought on by the body's struggle against the virus's inroads. Within a week, many victims of the virus began to develop bacterial pneumonia. In some cases, particularly among those between 20 and 40, the virus provoked a drastic immune response that quickly filled the lungs with fluid and caused lesions. The victims' skin turned blue from lack of oxygen. In those instances, death usually followed, often within days of the onset of symptoms.

During the war years, people flooded into cities, especially in the Northeast and Midwest, seeking high-paying war-industry jobs. Thousands lived in temporary, inadequate barracks-style housing, while others poured into already crowded slums. Meanwhile, the federal government hastily threw together scores of equally overcrowded military training camps with inadequate sanitation and pressed into service thousands of doctors and nurses for the war effort.

In July 1918, doctors at the Philadelphia Navy Yard reported an outbreak of respiratory illness among sailors returning from Europe. In late August, sailors and soldiers in the Boston area complained of flu symptoms, and within days, large numbers began to die. The disease spread rapidly and steadily across the county. It was readily obvious the disease was highly contagious, although, since the entire concept of a virus was unknown at the time, no one knew how it spread or how to treat it. While little could be done for patients suffering through the agonies of acute respiratory distress, for the population as a whole, a great deal could have been accomplished by aggressive public health measures. Closing schools, canceling unnecessary public gatherings, demanding that people wear face masks in public, and enforcing no-spitting ordinances could have slowed the disease and reduced the number of fatalities. But some cities, out of ignorance, ineptitude, or civic pride, rejected effective preventative measures and suffered badly.

A comparison of five major cities reveals the stark difference that effective and good local public health measures good make. With its notoriously overcrowded tenements, New York might be expected to have the highest mortality rate. But for two decades the city had invested heavily in its public health infrastructure, and its mortality rate was far lower than that of other large cities. But in both Philadelphia and Pittsburgh local authorities were hesitant to take effective action. Philadelphia's mayor was under arrest for corruption during part of the epidemic, and the head of the city health department was a political hack. In September the city held a Liberty Loan parade that drew hundreds of thousands, despite pleading from doctors to cancel it. Within 3 days (the precise incubation period), the disease broke out all over the city. For more than 3 weeks, Philadelphia suffered hundreds of deaths daily. In a scene reminiscent of the Black Death, in the immigrant district of South Philadelphia a parish priest rode a wagon through the streets calling on families to bring out their dead. Hundreds were hastily buried in a mass grave; altogether, 14,000 died. Philadelphia had one third the population of New York, but suffered almost half as many deaths.

Pittsburgh suffered the highest death rate of any American city, with about a quarter of all its reported flu cases resulting in death. Mayor E. B. Babcock and his health department failed to cooperate with state and federal authorities even when they directly ordered him to close certain public places and enact quarantine measures. Even though they were desperately needed in the city, Babcock dispatched dozens of local nurses and doctors to eastern Pennsylvania coal towns, which were also struggling with insufficient medical staff. The virus, combined with the inept local government, resulted in at least 4,000 deaths. A similar mentality affected Atlanta, which took little effective action—there were no emergency hospitals or collections of bodies. The black community, in particular, was ignored and suffered badly.

In contrast, San Francisco took aggressive action, including quarantining all its military bases and staffing a telephone line to report new cases so nurses could be quickly dispatched. Consequently, its case rate in the fall of 1918 was remarkably low. However, in December, when the threat appeared to have passed, the city lifted its restrictions and then suffered a serious epidemic, inadvertently demonstrating the effectiveness of its initial measures.

Every possible medical remedy was tried, including onion baths, herbal amulets, and vaccines made from the secretions of influenza sufferers. Some surgeons tried open thorax surgery to relieve fluid and pressure, with limited success. While most remedies did nothing more than soothe aching muscles and make sleeping easier, clean bedding and general nursing cannot be undervalued as means that moderated the severity of the disease in many instances.

Although the flu returned for at least the next couple of years, the greatest mortality occurred in 1918–1919. On the whole, the fatality rate for most American cities fluctuated between 10 percent and 20 percent of all reported cases. The worst-hit cities had death rates that approached those of the yellow fever and cholera epidemics of the previous century. African Americans suffered in disproportionately large numbers, particularly in the South, where local authorities and hospitals overlooked them entirely. Some Native American communities lost fully 80 percent or more of their pre-epidemic populations.

It was not until the 1990s that scientists unraveled some of the mysteries of the disease, collecting samples from the organs of victims buried in permafrost. The outbreaks of Sudden Acute Respiratory Disorder (SARS) in 2002 and the appearance of incredibly lethal avian flu strains in Asia in 2004–2005 accelerated research on influenza viruses and their mutation to head off another possible pandemic.

—*Roger D. Simon*
—*James Higgins*

See also Public Health

Further Readings and References

Bary, J. (2004). *The great influenza: The epic story of the deadliest plague in history.* New York: Viking.

Crosby, A. (2003). *America's forgotten pandemic: The influenza of 1918* (2nd ed.). New York: Cambridge University Press.

Van Hartesveldt, F. R. (1992). *The 1918–19 pandemic of influenza: The urban impact in the Western world.* Lewiston, NY: Edwin Mellon Press.

INFORMAL ECONOMY

The *informal economy* entered international development discourse in the early 1970s when an International Labour Organization (ILO) mission to Kenya noted the diversity of small-scale economic activities that were not recognized by public authorities. The ILO study cited that these were profitable and efficient enterprises that existed in addition to what were considered waning traditional occupations. These activities had in common that they were unrecorded, unregulated, and largely ignored by policymakers and government. Although the ILO study noted the dynamic nature of the informal economy, this economy was originally perceived as consisting of activities that were of little relevance to the formal or "real" economy of the country. Informal occupations were considered transitory in nature and predicted to disappear as development, in the form of economic growth and industrialization, progressed. Today it is widely acknowledged that the informal economy is a fixed characteristic of most countries of the world. Although understandings of informal economic activity and employment arrangements have advanced considerably, full appreciation of this complex phenomenon is far from complete.

Contrary to predictions, informal employment is on the rise in all parts of the world. In 2002, the World Bank estimated that 40 percent of the nonagriculture GNP in low-income countries and 17 percent of the nonagriculture GNP in high-income countries were generated in the informal economy. In developing regions, informal economic activity takes the shape of both self-employment and wage employment in small-scale informal enterprises, including street vending, home-based workshops, and personal services. In advanced capitalist economies, the advance of informal employment is seen in the shift to nonstandard employment relations in the form of hourly and piece-rate employment as well as subcontracting to small informal units and industrial outworkers. And the transition economies of the former Soviet Union and Central and Eastern Europe have seen informal economic arrangements of many types proliferate as economic well-being has faltered. Informal economic activities and employment arrangements in all parts of the world generally do not subscribe to official regulations nor provide worker benefits and social protection.

Traditionally perceived as comprising survivalist activities, the informal economy acquired negative connotations. However, because the majority of informal economic activities provide goods and services whose production and distribution is legal, such activities are considered "extralegal." The informal economy is widely characterized by low entry requirements (e.g., capital and qualifications), a small scale of operations, workers whose skills were often acquired outside of formal education, labor-intensive methods of production, and adapted technology. The informal economy does not include the reproductive or care economies when they consist of unpaid domestic activities, nor does it include the criminal economy.

Due to the heterogeneous character of the informal economy, numerous definitions have been elaborated. The Swedish Agency for International Development Cooperation identifies four trends in defining the informal economy: (1) definition by economic unit and whether it complies with official regulations that apply to its trade (e.g., registration, tax payment, zoning); (2) definition by employment category, whereby all work that takes place in an income-producing enterprise that is not recognized or regulated by existing legal frameworks is considered informal; (3) definition based on location or place of work, including home-based work, street trading, itinerant or temporary jobs, and labor that takes place between home and the streets, such as sorting trash; (4) definition by income or employment-enhancing potential, ranging from modern enterprises (e.g., data processing) to survivalist tasks (e.g., shoe shining, trash sorting, domestic work). Although definition by economic unit is the conventional method to define the informal economy, most observers favor definition by employment category, whereby all nonstandard wage workers who work without minimum wage, assured work, or benefits are considered informally employed. The array of definitions should be seen not as an obstacle but as an aid to understanding the varying nature and manifestations of the informal economy.

Different causal factors, at work in different contexts, explain the persistence and/or expansion of the informal economy. According to the ILO, factors relating to (1) the pattern of economic growth experienced in many developing countries, (2) widespread economic crisis or economic restructuring throughout the developing world, and (3) the globalization of the world economy explain the persistence and expansion of the informal economy. Recent evidence suggests that the informal economy is less likely to shrink if economic growth does not entail improvements in employment levels and equitable distribution of income and assets. Evidence further suggests that people will voluntarily engage in informal economic activities because of excessive regulation from government or to supplement declining incomes in the formal economy.

Countering early perceptions of the informal economy as insignificant to the formal economies of most countries is evidence of many interdependencies between informal and formal economic activity. The economies are linked through the trade of goods, raw materials, tools, and equipment, the acquisition of skills, and subcontracting relationships. Many individuals participate in both the formal and informal economies. Within the current debate, some highlight the role of the informal economy in stimulating growth in the market economy by promoting flexible labor and/or absorbing labor displaced from the formal economy. However, most observers recognize that linkages and power relations between the informal economy, formal economy, and public sector are significant and differ by which segment of the informal sector is under consideration.

While the informal economy is a significant and growing component of urban and rural life in most developing countries, regional differences are significant. In a recent fact-finding study, the Swedish International Development Agency found that in Africa employment in the informal economy accounts for approximately 80 percent of nonagricultural jobs, 60 percent of urban employment, and 90 percent of all new jobs. In Latin America and the Caribbean, the informal economy accounts for more than 60 percent of urban employment. In Asia, it accounts for 45 to 85 percent of nonagricultural employment and 40 to 60 percent of urban employment. In contrast to the formal economy, self-employment in petty commerce and home-based production drastically exceeds wage employment in the informal economy. Major donors and multilateral agencies recognize that the informal economy holds significant potential for the creation of jobs and generation of income.

Although not all workers in the informal economy are poor, the majority of the poor are found in the informal economy. The ILO has found that the relationship between working in the informal economy and being poor appears when workers are classified by employment status, industry, or trade. Informal incomes decline worldwide as one moves across types of employment. Employers within informal enterprises fare better than owner-operators, who fare better than informal and casual wage workers; industrial outworkers fare the worst. Those who toil in the informal economy are among the most exposed and poor groups within the labor market. Most face inadequate labor legislation, labor protection, and social security. They have limited access to wage workers' organizations and limited bargaining power. Their incomes are low and irregular. Work conditions are poor; they have insecure contracts and few benefits.

The link between poverty and informal employment is strongest for women, who, according to the ILO, account for 60 to 80 percent of the informally employed worldwide. Again, place matters. In India, 96 percent of all women workers are employed in the informal economy, and most are invisible. In Mexico, 58 percent of women workers are in the informal economy, and in South Africa, it's 45 percent of women. In advanced capitalist countries, women represent the majority of part-time workers, ranging from 98 percent of part-time workers in Sweden to 68 percent in Japan and the United States. Women are underrepresented in higher income employment statuses (e.g., employer and self-employed) and overrepresented in lower income statuses (e.g., casual wage worker and industrial outworker). Children who work in the informal economy predominate in the lowest paying and most hazardous occupations, such as trash picking, domestic work, and apprenticeships where they face particular dangers and hardships.

Workers and producers in the informal economy are linked in various ways to the global economy. A large share of the workforce in global industries works in export-processing zones, sweatshops, or their own homes under informal employment arrangements. Global commodity chains link individual workers and enterprises, often operating under both formal and informal arrangements, spread across several countries to one another. Economic globalization can lead to new opportunities in the form of new jobs for wage workers and new markets for the self-employed within the informal economy. In aggregate, however, globalization tends to lead to shifts from secure to insecure forms of employment and to more precarious forms of self-employment, reinforcing the links among poverty, informal employment, and gender. Consensus exists that neoliberal economic policies that promote liberalization, privatization, industrial reorganization, and migration underlie the continued growth of the informal economy in industrialized, poor, and transition economies.

The informal economy is of increasing concern for policymakers because it is the part of the economy where the majority of populations, especially the poorest, support themselves. It accounts for a significant share of employment and output in all regions of the world, and it helps meet the needs of poor consumers by making accessible low-priced goods and services. Major donors and multilateral agencies stress the importance of addressing the informal economy. In 1999, the ILO formulated a vision of "Decent Work" for all workers. It recognized that decent work deficits are more common in the informal economy and drew attention to reducing the employment gap, improving rights at work, providing social protection, and increasing the voice of workers.

Several responses to decent work deficits have arisen from grassroots sectors. The Self-Employed Women's Association (SEWA), the oldest trade union of informal women workers in the world, was founded in 1972 in India. WIEGO (Women in Informal Employment Globalizing and Organizing), a global action-research coalition, was formed in 1997. HomeNet, an international alliance of home-based workers, and StreetNet, a similar alliance of street vendors, were formed in the 1990s. The nature of the informal economy makes the right to decent work for all workers especially elusive.

—*Maureen Hays-Mitchell*

Further Readings and References

Becker, K. F. (2004). *The informal economy: Fact finding study.* Stockholm: Swedish Agency for International Development Cooperation.

International Labour Organization. (1972). *Employment, incomes and equality: A strategy for increasing productive employment in Kenya.* Geneva: International Labour Organization.

International Labour Organization. (2002). *Globalization and the informal economy: How global trade and investment impact on the working poor.* Geneva: International Labour Organization.

International Labour Organization. (2002). *Women and men in the informal economy: A statistical picture.* Geneva: International Labour Organization.

World Bank. (2002). *World development report 2002: Building institutions for markets.* Washington, DC: Author.

INFRASTRUCTURE AND URBAN TECHNICAL NETWORKS

Urban infrastructure provides the basic technological frame for the operations of the city: its roads, bridges, and transit networks; its water and sewer lines and waste disposal facilities; and its power and communications systems. These facilities have allowed cities to function as centers of commerce, industry, entertainment, and residence. But while these infrastructure networks have stimulated urban growth and diversification, they have also altered the urban landscape, causing environmental damage, disrupting communities, and generating political corruption. Over time, service provision has shifted back and forth between private and public ownership because of dissatisfaction over costs and quality of service as well as corruption. Some special institutional arrangements combined features of public and private control, including the construction and operation of infrastructures by public-private coalitions and government construction with private operation.

Many of the infrastructure systems currently in use evolved in the 19th and 20th centuries as American cities went through different stages of development. In each of these stages urban technologies, generated by both the private and public sectors, shaped the spatial, economic, and even social character of cities and surrounding metropolitan areas.

During approximately the first half of the 19th century, most cities provided only limited infrastructure and services. As cities grew, however, citizen demands for services accelerated. In the 1840s and 1850s, the concept of municipal government acting as a service provider became increasingly common. Urban politicians began to base their careers on appeals to a recently enlarged electorate and promises to deliver public works and services to their voting constituencies or specific stakeholder groups. In addition, in response to growing urban densities, private entrepreneurs began providing improved public transportation services.

Water supplies were the earliest centralized infrastructure systems provided by cities. Up until the last decades of the 19th century, the majority of American urbanites depended on local water sources such as wells, ponds, cisterns, or vendors for supply. Commercial elites, industrialists, and sanitarians, however, concerned about the threats of fires and epidemics, as well as water needs for economic development and domestic purposes, pushed for the construction of water works. The first large city to construct a municipal water works was Philadelphia, in 1799–1801. Other cities soon built water works as well. For instance, water works were built in Cincinnati and Pittsburgh in the 1820s by drawing from local rivers, and systems using upcountry water sources were built in New York City (the Croton Aqueduct, 1841) and Boston (the Cochituate Aqueduct, 1848). Between 1860 and 1880, the number of water

works in U.S. cities increased from 136 (57 public, 79 private) to 598 (293 public and 305 private). While many cities began with privately owned and operated water supply systems, many large cities, such as New York, Chicago, and San Francisco, shifted to public ownership because private companies did not provide adequate water for civic purposes such as street flushing and fire hydrants or to service distant districts. By 1880, of the nearly 600 systems, 293 were public and 305 private, most of which were in smaller cities.

Increasingly linked to water supply systems were centralized urban sewers. These sewer systems gradually replaced on-site privy vaults, cesspools, and private sewers for human waste disposal. Because of financial restraints and underestimates by city officials regarding future water use, cities almost never constructed sewer systems at the same time that they built water works. Water use and the adoption of water-using appliances such as the flush toilet, however, resulted in contaminated water overwhelming existing disposal facilities, and the construction of sewers became a higher municipal priority. Cities such as Brooklyn, Chicago, and Jersey City built sewer systems as early as the 1850s, but the great burst of sewer construction occurred after 1890. Large cities mostly built combined sewers in order to accommodate domestic wastes and storm water in the same pipe, while smaller cities installed small pipe separate sewers for domestic wastes, usually leaving storm water to run off on the surface. Nationally, the miles of sewers increased from approximately 6,000 in 1890 to about 25,000 in 1909. For cities with populations over 30,000, about three quarters of sewers were combined sewers and the remainder were sanitary sewers.

Private infrastructure was also critical, with some of the most extensive infrastructure relating to transportation. These improvements caused alterations in patterns of work and residence and the expansion of city boundaries. Until the 1850s, in cities like Boston, New York, and Philadelphia, public transportation was limited to privately owned, horse-drawn omnibuses and commuter rail lines used primarily by the middle and upper classes. The New York and Harlem Railroad began operating a horse-drawn street railway in New York City in 1831, but it was not until the 1850s that streetcar systems began to appear in other cities. By the 1870s, most cities with a population above 10,000 possessed horse car lines used by the middle class to commute to work, by women shopping in emerging downtowns, and by citizens of all classes seeking weekend recreation in parks and other pleasure spots. Most working-class people, however, walked to work.

Horse-powered transit did have a number of limitations, though, and by the 1880s mechanical systems began to replace horsecar systems. The first changes involved the construction of elevated railways and cable-driven systems in the largest cities, followed in the 1890s by electric streetcars. A few cities, like New York and Boston, also constructed subways. Because the privately owned streetcar companies relied on public franchises for their operations, they were closely linked to urban political machines and often involved in political bribery and corruption. Frequently the chief motivation of the entrepreneurs who built the travel systems was to benefit from real estate speculation rather than to operate systems that served the public efficiently.

Other urban infrastructures constructed in the 19th century included centralized fire alarm telegraph systems and street lighting (first oil, then gas, and finally electricity), both systems intended to protect the public safety. In addition, the 1880s saw the beginning of telephone networks. By the 1890s, these technologies, combined with the growing transportation networks, were transforming the compact walking city of the earlier part of the century into the much more extensive technologically networked city. While practically trained engineers had built much of the infrastructure constructed before the Civil War, increasingly colleges provided a body of trained engineers who participated in the infrastructure boom that occurred after 1890.

The development of new methods of public finance was equally important for the construction of infrastructure systems. Since city tax revenues were usually insufficient to cover capital costs, many cities followed the practice of having abutters pay for infrastructure improvements. The result was an undersupply of infrastructures in poorer districts. Increasingly, however, in the late 19th century and early 20th century, cities financed capital-intensive infrastructures with municipal bonds and services became more equitably distributed.

During the first decades of the 20th century, the urban population expanded rapidly, as did the demand for services. Progressive reformers in a number of cities, concerned over the inefficiencies and threat to democracy of political corruption and private monopolies, sought to introduce new management approaches to infrastructure provision. These concerns were reflected by a new interest in the planning of cities and the use of efficiency experts.

Transport systems, although still largely private, proved central to the development of the modern city and the thinking of planners. Electrically powered streetcars as well as subways, elevated railways, and commuter railroads provided the essential framework for the expansion of urban areas. From 1890 to 1907, for instance, the mileage of streetcars (almost all privately supplied and powered by electricity) increased from 5,783 to 34,404 miles and annual rides per urban inhabitant jumped from 111 to 250. Vast areas surrounding the central cities were opened for residential development, with transit entrepreneurs heavily involved in suburban real estate development. Streetcar suburbs proliferated along the transit routes, while commuter rails transformed small towns into commuter suburbs. Public transit accelerated the transformation of the urban core from a mixed residential, commercial, and industrial area into a true central business district (CBD) devoted primarily to commercial and business uses.

Cities and so-called system builders expanded infrastructure networks, including the development and construction of public water filtration and sewage treatment facilities, the building of large-scale private but regulated electrical power networks, and the extension of largely private telephone services. The number of waterworks increased from 1,878 to 9,850 between 1890 and 1920, the population served by filtered water increased from 310,000 to 17,291,000 between 1890 and 1914, and the miles of sewers increased from 6,005 to 24,672, while half the urban population acquired home electric service and the number of households with telephones increased to about one third. Construction and operation of great technological systems, such as streetcars and electrical power networks, not only affected the city's physical landscape but also eventually encouraged substantial changes in social and political relationships. Because of the monopolistic nature and great power of these systems, many citizens concluded that only regulation or municipal ownership would secure the necessary control over them. Some of the resulting political action represented the efforts of an elite anxious to secure the benefits of administrative efficiency, but other stakeholders, such as suburbanites, were anxious to secure the benefits of urban technologies at a low and uniform rate.

Urban infrastructure developments after 1920 were predominantly shaped by the growth of automobile and truck use. The automobile was made widely available as a result of Henry Ford's assembly-line production techniques, and its presence on America's streets led to a host of social, spatial, and administrative developments that sharply altered technological priorities and patterns. During the period from 1910 to 1930, the nation's auto registrations rose from 458,000 to nearly 22 million, or from one car to every 20 persons to one car to every 5.3 persons. The automobile dramatically impacted the urban fabric and the city's technological systems. It facilitated movement toward the city's periphery and suburbs, permitted settlement of land between radial transit lines, greatly increased congestion in downtown areas as commuter traffic grew, and jammed existing road networks. Road building advocates proved especially effective in securing highway improvements. Automobile clubs, business organizations, and engineering associations expressed the need of automobiles, motor trucks, and buses for improved roads and highways, and this resulted in extensive construction. Between 1914 and 1929, the mileage of surfaced roads increased 157 percent and the mileage of high-grade surfaced roads increased 776 percent, reflecting the fact that motor vehicles required smooth surfaces. The Bureau of Public Roads, aided by the American Road Builders' Association, the American Society for Municipal Improvements, and the American Society of Civil Engineers, developed standards and specifications that were often used in designing new roadways and the rebuilding and resurfacing of highways and streets.

Planners and members of the new engineering discipline of traffic engineering concentrated on improving automobile circulation in the central business district. They promoted the widening and double-decking of streets, the elimination of grade crossings, and the development of a variety of traffic controls. In addition, street surfacing with smooth pavements made mostly of asphalt took place throughout urban areas. Cities and counties built hundreds of bridges and tunnels to facilitate cross-river transportation, and Chicago, New York, Pittsburgh, and Los Angeles even constructed costly limited-access roadways into their downtown areas.

The problems of financing road and street construction encouraged innovations in taxation and intergovernmental cooperation. The state gasoline tax, which was instituted in Oregon in 1919 and in all states by 1929, was the most important automobile-related funding innovation of the 1920s, providing funds for highway construction. When municipal expenditures for streets and highways rose, cities depended largely on conventional means of financing such as bonds, the property tax, or special assessments to provide improvements. In the 1920s, municipal operating and capital expenditures for streets and highways were exceeded only by spending for education. Cities, counties, and other governmental authorities cooperated to improve transportation infrastructure, such as Westchester County's Bronx Parkway, Philadelphia's Benjamin Franklin Parkway, and Pittsburgh's Liberty Tunnel and Liberty Bridge.

The Great Depression of the 1930s brought municipal infrastructure spending to a halt. Some of the deficiency, however, was absorbed by New Deal programs that attempted to use construction spending to stimulate the economy and to fill deficiencies in infrastructure networks. From 1933 to 1938, the federal government accounted for approximately 60 to 65 percent of all public construction through agencies such as the Public Works Administration. These projects included almost half of all new sewer and water supply construction, over three quarters of all new municipal sewage treatment plants (1,165 of 1,310), and numerous airports, parks, hospitals, dams, and public buildings. Such federal spending provided the infrastructure necessary to keep cities operating as well as improving many services.

Following World War II, large numbers of urbanites joined the movement to the suburbs, primarily using the automobile to connect residence with workplace. As suburbs grew, many cities experienced both residential and central business district decline. The newly proliferating suburbs needed services such as water supply and sewage disposal, and they were often provided by county governments (the Lakewood Plan) or by special-purpose metropolitan districts. Many suburbs, however, especially in the decades immediately after 1945, had limited infrastructure and services compared to the central city.

Faced with rapid suburbanization and central city decline, downtown business interests and urban politicians in cities like Pittsburgh and Atlanta joined in private-public partnerships to attempt to revitalize the central business districts. These "growth machines" aimed to revive the central business districts, stimulate the return of the middle classes, and improve the economic climate of the central city. Their programs largely involved a combination of private-sector investment in office structures and public-sector investment in supporting infrastructure.

Those seeking explanations for central city decline often blamed congestion and access problems and were therefore attracted to the promise of an Interstate Highway System. Beginning after World War II, truckers, automobile clubs, highway contractors, the automobile industry, engineering associations, and business groups lobbied Congress to provide federal funding for expanded and accelerated highway construction. At the center of their plans stood the Interstate Highway System, a network of 40,000 miles (in 2002, it totaled 47,742 miles) of limited-access roadway. The Advisory Committee on a National Highway Program recommended that both national security and the health of the economy depended on rapid construction of the highway network, and in 1956 Congress approved the bill. The final legislation provided for federal assumption of 90 percent of the costs of building the Interstate Highway System, with gasoline tax revenues placed in a Highway Trust Fund to prevent its diversion to nonhighway purposes.

The Interstate Highway System was the nation's largest and costliest public works project ever. The interstate system had been sold to Congress as a carrier of long-haul traffic and a vital component in the defense system, but municipal leaders had visualized the highways as a means to solve traffic congestion problems and to revitalize central business districts. Because highway construction through congested urban areas was exceedingly expensive, cities received a large percentage of the total allocations. The Interstate Highway System, however, failed to reverse central city decline. Its construction often destroyed established inner city neighborhoods, falling with special severity on minority communities. The Interstate carried a great deal of traffic in metropolitan areas, but seldom did suburban residents drive it for shopping and recreation located downtown. The highway system actually played a key role in continuing and even accelerating business and household out-migration to the suburbs.

Throughout the 1960s, the 1970s, and into the 1980s, other urban infrastructure networks, often environmentally related, benefited from federal programs. Under various acts, such as the Federal Water Pollution Control Act (1972), federal dollars were allocated to sewer and sewage treatment projects. Between 1967 and 1977, federal expenditures for sewerage systems increased from $150 million to $4.1 billion and by 1986, 90 percent of the wastewater treatment plants required to meet the requirements of the Clear Water

Act (1977) had been constructed. Struggling urban mass transit systems had largely been taken over by municipalities after World War II, and federal support for these programs was provided through the Urban Mass Transit Administration. Between 1973 and 1977, federal funds to localities for transit systems grew from $275 million to $1.3 billion. The increasing dependence on Washington for infrastructure dollars (for new construction, not for maintenance), however, resulted in serious problems for states and localities when federal funds were reduced or programs cancelled, as occurred in the 1980s under the administrations of Presidents Ronald Reagan and George H.W. Bush.

In the decades since completion of most of the Interstate's urban mileage, several overlapping demographic, fiscal, and social trends have shaped the design and location of costly infrastructure networks. While the inner city has often experienced dramatic population declines, most sections of the outer city are undergoing a continuing boom, forming a new urban construction called the outer or edge city. Traditional suburbia as well as exurbia has attracted a mass of urban activities that were formerly a central city monopoly. By the 1970s, a host of what had traditionally been downtown-type activities, such as hotels, conference centers, office buildings, and retail shops, as well as modern industrial parks and distribution centers, had located at Interstate interchanges, ring roads, and airport locations. In many cases, special purpose authorities provided infrastructure systems whose initial capital costs were aided by federal and state funds, leaving users to finance the costs of operation and maintenance.

These outer city areas, like inner city central business districts, are very infrastructure dependent, requiring major road systems for effective circulation and power and communications lines to meet not only residential but also commercial and industrial needs. In the outer city, however, development is also quite dispersed, raising important questions concerning the applicability of infrastructure originally developed to fit the needs of a more concentrated site as well as costs. New urban forms have evolved, but technological innovation has lagged behind—with the exception of advances in telecommunications. One major trend in the 1980s and 1990s was to privatize urban services, supposedly to cut public spending and to improve efficiency of delivery, or, if the services remained public, to impose user fees. In the future, urban technologies and networks, whether developed and implemented by public or private authorities, will continue to shape the lives of urban inhabitants and the forms of metropolitan areas.

—Joel A. Tarr

See also Interstate Highway Act of 1956; Railroad Stations; Railroad Suburbs; Railroads; Rapid Transit; Suburban Railroad Service; Suburbanization

Further Readings and References

Condit, C. W. (1973–1974). *Chicago: Building, planning, and urban technology, 1910–1970* (2 vols.). Chicago: University of Chicago Press.

Graham, S., & Marvin, S. (2001). *Splintering urbanism: Networked infrastructures, technological mobilities and the urban condition.* New York: Routledge.

Hayden, D. (2003). *Building suburbia: Green fields and urban growth, 1820–2000.* New York: Random House.

Hughes, T. S. (1989). *American genesis: A century of invention and technological enthusiasm.* New York: Viking.

McShane, C. (1994). *Down the asphalt path: The automobile and the American city.* New York: Columbia University Press.

Melosi, M. V. (2000). *The sanitary city: Urban infrastructure in America from colonial times to the present.* Baltimore, MD: Johns Hopkins University Press.

Roberts, G. K., & Steadman, P. (1999). *American cities and technology: Wilderness to wired city.* London: Routledge.

Rose, M. H. (1995). *Cities of light and heat: Domesticating gas and electricity in urban America.* University Park, PA: Pennsylvania State University Press.

Tarr, J. A., & Dupuy, G. (Eds.). (1988). *Technology and the rise of the networked city in Europe and America.* Philadelphia: Temple University Press.

INTERNET AND CITIES

The Internet is an infrastructural communications network linking computers around the world. Along with other relatively new information and communications technologies (ICTs), such as cable television and cell phones, it is part of a "digital revolution" creating a new "information society." The proliferation of these technologies coincides with the increasing urbanization of the world. This raises important questions about the reciprocal relationships between ICTs, such as the Internet, and cities. Early hyperbolic analyses speculated that the Internet and increasing

digital flows of information would eliminate the need for spatially organized urban settings and make geographical distance irrelevant, thus leading to the death of cities. Newer, more nuanced and empirically based analyses have pointed to more complex relationships between the Internet and cities, in which the growth of online networks would lead to changes in the nature of cities, but would heighten their importance in some ways. Stephen Graham, one of the leading scholars in the new subdiscipline of urban ICT studies, suggested in 2004 that the concept of *cybercities* conveys the nature of the closely entwined relationships between the Internet and urban areas.

The ubiquity of online networks makes it easy to forget their relative newness. For understanding the relationships between the Internet and cities, it is useful to understand the history of such digital networks. From its original manifestation as ARPANET in the late 1960s, when it linked four computers, the Internet has grown into a global network. In 1969, the Department of Defense tasked its Advanced Research Projects Agency (ARPA) with developing a communication network that would withstand the effects of a nuclear war. Initially, engineers and scientists were the primary users of ARPANET, which became NSFNET, and then the Internet. This online network grew exponentially in terms of the number of computers and users linked and also in terms of its popularity. The availability of the Internet as an infrastructural backbone of linked computers encouraged the development of other online facilities, such as the World Wide Web (WWW), which ride on the Internet. Tim Berners-Lee created the WWW, which has probably contributed the most to the explosive growth of the Internet and enabling people around the world to access and exchange information freely. Berners-Lee views the Web as a *social* invention, and this emphasizes the importance of understanding the relationships between ICTs and cities in a social rather than strictly technological context.

Early studies and prognostications tended to discuss the "impact" of the Internet on cities, as if this technology on its own would directly change cities and possibly lead to their disappearance. A more multidimensional view recognizes that all new technologies have had important effects on social life generally and urban life specifically. Although the Internet plays a role in shaping cities and urban life, it does so within the context of the effects of earlier technologies, including existing infrastructural networks such as highway systems and power grids, and in conjunction with other ICTs, including cell phones and cable television. The relationship between any technology, such as the Internet, and cities also reflects social, economic, and political decisions and relationships. Therefore, the ultimate consequences of the Internet will be due to its interplay with other networks, other new ICTs, and the social contexts within which all of these are deployed.

Viewed within this perspective, the Internet may play a role in changing the experience of community and the nature of space in urban areas, but it may enhance rather than diminish the importance of cities. There are two broad ways in which the Internet, and other ICTs, can affect cities. First, the Internet can affect society and social life in general, and cities, as part of the social world, will be affected. Second, the Internet can affect cities directly in terms of their characteristic attributes.

The general social relationship between the Internet, and other ICTs, and cities might include possible effects on the poverty, social polarization, and lack of services in inner city neighborhoods. These situations have been exacerbated in recent years by the processes of deindustrialization and decentralization, which have been facilitated by the development of ICTs that make it possible to move production facilities and corporate headquarters away from cities. While industrialization was a centralizing phenomenon, deindustrialization has been decentralizing. The Internet contributed to these changes, but it can also lessen poverty and the *digital divide* (that is, the gap between those with and without regular access to digital technologies). For example, the creation of low-cost, wireless network access can increase the accessibility of the Internet and the Web for all urban residents. Currently, many wireless access points are in upscale retail establishments and in airports, neither of which is helpful to the poor. However, Philadelphia plans to establish wireless access in the whole city. New Orleans, post Hurricane Katrina, also plans to provide low-cost wireless access. Such access, if coupled with greater availability of and training on computers, could enable lower income residents to access the Internet and the Web, which contain important information resources on jobs and human services. Another use of digital technology is the creation of community networks to foster community development. For example, the Dudley Street Neighborhood Initiative, a community development organization in Boston, created the Virtual Village to use computers and software for community building. It would not be possible without the Internet.

The Internet can also facilitate changes in cities as spatially organized settlements and in their functions. Graham argued in 2004 that cybercities contribute to global urbanization by using the Internet to extend their control and reach well beyond their borders. An example of this is the development of London, New York, and Tokyo as global cities. Such cities use digital networks to act as command and control centers for the global economy. In addition, the proliferation of online information flows seems to lead to increasing investment and population concentration in those cities which are central to the global economy. The Internet is leading not to the demise of cities but to changes in how cities are organized and experienced. The nature of those changes will emerge more fully in the future.

—*Walter F. Carroll*

See also Deindustrialization

Further Readings and References

Abbate, J. (1999). *Inventing the Internet.* Cambridge, MA: MIT Press.

Berners-Lee, T. (1999). *Weaving the Web: The original design and the ultimate destiny of the World Wide Web by its inventor.* New York: HarperSanFrancisco.

Graham, S. (Ed.). (2004). *The cybercities reader.* London: Routledge.

Mitchell, W. J. (1999). *E-topia: "Urban life, Jim—but not as we know it."* Cambridge, MA: MIT Press.

Norris, P. (2001). *Digital divide: Civic engagement, information poverty, and the Internet worldwide.* Cambridge, UK: Cambridge University Press.

INTERSTATE HIGHWAY ACT OF 1956

In April 1939, General Motors opened its "Futurama" exhibit at the New York World's Fair. Immediately the fair's most popular attraction, each day thousands of visitors rode in cars around a track, observing the exhibit below that showed fast-flowing traffic, farmlands described as "drenched in blinding sunlight," and cities featuring buildings characterized as "breath-taking." To residents of a nation still suffering the effects of dull Depression days, Futurama's designer, Norman Bel Geddes, emphasized the idea that fast-flowing traffic on new, limited-access highways would help restore prosperity and hope to residents of city and countryside. Also in 1939, senior engineers at the U.S. Bureau of Public Roads published a report titled *Toll Roads and Free Roads.* Similar to Bel Geddes, authors of this report contended that urban road improvements would eliminate decaying properties and make way for newer, more important ones. The unlikely convergence of a World's Fair exhibit and a government report written by little-known highway engineers set in motion planning to fund construction of the Interstate Highway System (IHS). In 1944, Congress and President Franklin D. Roosevelt approved the Federal-Aid Highway Act, including authorization to construct the IHS. During the remainder of the century, competing ideas about jobs, traffic relief, urban renewal and suburban growth, and federal management of the pace of economic activity informed highway politics. In 1944, however, Congress did not allocate funds to pay for construction of the expensive IHS.

Although engineers and ordinary Americans liked the promise of traffic and urban improvements, during the next 12 years no one wanted to finance the immense costs of building a national freeway system. Objecting to higher gasoline taxes, truck operators urged federal officials to focus limited funds on construction of the costly Interstate system. Nonetheless, rural leaders argued against any plan that limited spending on farm roads. Convinced, however, that freeway construction including inner belts around downtown would relieve traffic congestion, boost property values, eliminate nearby "slums," and lure suburban shoppers back downtown, starting in the 1940s merchants and political leaders in every city had advocated accelerated construction of the IHS. Then, in 1955, members of the U.S. House of Representatives rejected a plan to freeze funding levels on rural roads while greatly increasing spending to construct the IHS. Not even support from the popular President Dwight D. Eisenhower could rescue highway legislation.

In 1956, Senator Albert Gore, Sr., and Representatives Hale Boggs and George H. Fallon fashioned IHS legislation. First, truckers relented to a small increase in gasoline and truck taxes. In turn, Congress promised increased spending on urban and rural roads not included in the IHS. Before 1956, the U.S.

government had paid 50 percent of the cost of building roads on the federal-aid systems, but in 1956, Congress and President Eisenhower agreed to pay 90 percent of IHS construction costs, leaving only 10 percent of the expenses to state highway officials. Also in 1956, Congress and Eisenhower approved creation of the Highway Trust Fund, which would designate gasoline taxes (and excise taxes on tires and trucks) for exclusive use in financing construction of the IHS and other federal-aid roads. As part of assembling successful highway legislation, early in 1956 members of the Senate-House conference committee changed the name of the IHS to the National System of Interstate and Defense Highways (but it has always been referred to in everyday conversation as the IHS). Continuing a long-standing federal and state highway practice, in 1956 Congress and the president conferred authority on engineers in the U.S. Bureau of Public Roads and their counterparts in the state highway departments to build the 41,000-mile IHS, including approximately 5,000 urban miles. During the next decades, Congress approved additional mileage for the IHS, and by 2002, the rural and urban total stood at 47,742. True to the promise of IHS enthusiasts, by the late 1980s, the compact IHS carried more than 20 percent of the nation's automobile traffic and a whopping 49 percent of the truck-trailer combinations. By early 2004, the federal government had spent more than $59 billion to construct the urban portions of the IHS and more than $40 billion to construct the rural sections.

Protests against highway building led Congress to shift control of highway construction away from state and federal engineers. As early as 1959, residents and political leaders in San Francisco blocked construction of the Embarcadero Freeway. Starting in 1962, residents of Baltimore created cross-income and inter-racial groups to protect neighborhoods from destruction by highway engineers. During the late 1960s and early 1970s, upper income residents of northwest Washington, D.C., made use of political savvy and legal know-how to block construction of the Three Sisters Bridge. By the late 1960s, authors of books with titles such as *The Pavers and the Paved* and *Superhighway-Superhoax* attracted national attention to this "freeway revolt" taking place in Washington, D.C., Baltimore, and other cities. The U.S. government responded to and sometimes led this revolt. In 1973, Congress and President Richard M. Nixon approved the Federal-Aid Highway Act that financed local purchase of buses and fixed rail systems with money taken from the formerly inviolable trust fund. In 1991, Congress and President George H. W. Bush approved the Intermodal Surface Transportation Efficiency Act (ISTEA). This act allowed local political leaders in metropolitan planning organizations to chose whether to spend a portion of federal and state funds on highways, public transit, bike paths, or other projects. Passage of ISTEA was an important element in the transfer of federal highway funds and authority from national and state engineering experts and to local politicians.

—*Mark H. Rose*

Further Readings and References

Barrett, P., & Rose, M. H. (1999). Street smarts: The politics of transportation statistics in the American city, 1900–1990. *Journal of Urban History, 25,* 405–433.

Fishman, R. (1999). The American metropolis at century's end: Past and future influences. *Housing Facts and Findings, 1,* 1–7.

Mohl, R. A. (2004). Stop the road: Freeway revolts in American cities. *Journal of Urban History, 30,* 674–706.

Rose, M. H. (1990). *Interstate: Express highway politics, 1939–1989* (2nd ed.). Knoxville: University of Tennessee Press.

Rose, M. H. (2003). Reframing American highway politics, 1956–1995. *Journal of Planning History, 2,* 212–236.

IRVINE, CALIFORNIA

Irvine, California, conceived in 1960 as a master planned city and incorporated in 1971, instantly became a closely observed laboratory. Its centerpiece was the newly established University of California at Irvine, surrounded by a network of residential villages and substantial preserves of open space. Irvine currently encompasses 55 square miles and has a population of almost 165,000. It is situated in Orange County, 5 miles east of the Pacific coast, 35 miles southeast of Los Angeles, and 80 miles northeast of San Diego.

Irvine's design by William L. Pereira reflected a self-conscious alternative to the metropolitan colossus existing in the long shadow of Los Angeles. Almost 60 percent of the inhabitants in the nation's 11 western states resided within California by the early 1960s, one quarter of them in or near Los Angeles. Los Angeles County alone experienced a bigger population increase (of over 1,887,084 people) than *any* county nationwide during the 1950s; it also overtook Cook County in Illinois as the most populated American county. California had surpassed New York in 1962 as the nation's most populous state. In nearly the same moment, it also exceeded New Jersey as the state with the highest level of urbanization. Kevin Starr depicts the five-county metropolitan region spawned by Los Angeles—whose population in 2000 was 16.4 million—as "the continuous sub/urb."

Endowed with a rich sense of history, Pereira romanticized Irvine, for which his inspiration was the garden city ideal of Ebenezer Howard that avoided the excesses of mass urbanization. His plans also reflected Lewis Mumford's calls for diminished reliance upon automobiles. As the new community evolved, it was assayed in a report on NBC News by David Brinkley, a *Time* cover story, and features in *Business Week, Fortune,* and the *Saturday Review.* President Lyndon B. Johnson spoke at the dedication of the university's campus. In a survey conducted in 1973, Irvine's attributes, viewed through the eyes of its residents, were identified as a good place to raise children; proximity to places of work as well as the natural environment; good physical design; and high quality of residences.

Not as well known is the fact that Irvine's metamorphosis in the second half of the 20th century from ranch to master-planned community is rooted in the history of California, reaching back to statehood in 1850. The seed was the Irvine Ranch, which originally comprised 125,000 acres and was closely held by the dynastic namesake family. The Irvine Company, organized in 1894 to shield this land-based empire, maintained control until 1977. Eventually the ranch became one of California's unparalleled corporation farms.

Multiple forces shaped Irvine: a succession of ambitious entrepreneurs, each vying to control Irvine's land domain, the most recent of whom is Donald L. Bren; recurrent waves of metropolitan growth emanating from Los Angeles, first taking hold in the mid-1880s and eventually spawning the multicounty metropolis in which Orange County has played a key role since the 1920s; debates over the implementation and revision master plan; and power struggles reflecting maneuvers to control or dominate Irvine's body politic. Irvine's evolution has been compounded by the rapid growth of Orange County: It surpassed 1 million in 1970, second statewide only to Los Angeles County. Totaling 2.8 million in 2000, Orange County's population exceeds the populations of 29 states.

Irvine has been a forum for sharply contested political exchanges—involving citizens, corporations, organizations, and institutions—about growth-related policies, environmental issues, housing, and transportation. A defining struggle surrounded its incorporation in 1971. The contending parties were the adjacent city of Santa Ana (a hub for the low-income, non-white population in Orange County), the Irvine Company (exercising an almost monolithic role in the implementation of the master plan), and local residents (expressing strongly held opinions to their elected representatives in the newly organized municipal government). At stake was the issue of mixed-income housing as well as the prospect of Irvine's near-monopoly on new tax revenues. When Irvine's city council rejected—in a split vote following acrimonious debate—a plan for federally subsidized housing championed by the Irvine Company, Sam Bass Warner Jr. labeled the arrangement a sort of scandal.

Irvine's official Web site (www.irvine.ci.ca.us/about/history.asp) boastfully proclaims the community a "total destination." Key features include: its role as multidisciplinary transportation center, whose dominant feature is the extensive network of freeways that crisscross Orange County as well as link it to the five-county region; an academic research complex, whose flagship is the University of California at Irvine; a magnet for technology and science; an affluent regional entrepôt for retail commerce; and a globalized corporate center. In the mid-1980s, Mark Baldassare, an observer of Orange County for many years, characterized Irvine ironically—as a *disurb* (a "dense, industrial, self-contained urban region"). Vehicular congestion was ranked as a particularly vexing aspect of daily life. Responding to local critics of his rendering of Irvine, Baldassare told a correspondent from the *Wall Street Journal* in 1987 that the naysayers expected suburban life to be as simple and uncongested as portrayed on the 1950s television program *Ozzie and Harriet.*

Contemporary Irvine fits into a distinctive niche. Myron Orfield portrays such places as contributing to the nation's *favored quarter.* Its characteristics include: upmarket housing, high-achievement school systems; easy access to transportation; abundant and lucrative employment opportunities; and a population with high educational levels. The Brookings Institution

classified Irvine as among the nation's top cities with over 100,000 inhabitants. Irvine's population grew nearly 30 percent from 1990 to 2000 (to 143,072); Orange County's decennial increase was 18 percent, California's 14 percent, and Los Angeles County's 7 percent. While Irvine reflects Orange County's demographic heterogeneity, its particulars diverge, other than the fact that the proportion of the population that is white—61 percent for Irvine and 65 percent countywide—is comparable. Irvine's largest non-white concentration is Asian, totaling 30 percent, whereas in Orange County, Hispanics comprise 31 percent and Asians 15 percent. Other data are equally telling: 24 percent of Irvine's inhabitants in 2000 held graduate or professional degrees, as contrasted with 10 percent countywide; median household income in Irvine exceeded $72,000, the county figure being almost $59,000 and Santa Ana's $43,400; median home value for Irvine was $316,800, $270,000 countywide and $184,500 in Santa Ana; and employment in managerial or professional occupations was 58 percent in Irvine and 38 percent countywide. Irvine ranked last in the percentage of students receiving free or reduced price school meals during 2002–2003, at 7 percent, as contrasted with 39 percent for Orange County and 75 percent in Santa Ana. And students enrolled in the Irvine Unified School District ranked first with a score of 862 (on a scale of 1,000) on the Academic Performance Index in 2003; the average score was 735 countywide. The Santa Ana school district's average of 613 was the lowest in the county.

In its fourth decade, inhabitants of the master-planned city of Irvine continue to debate whether it is an interdependent part of the five-county metropolis, exemplifying regional pluralism, or a vast suburban refuge into which people furtively escape. Agreement exists, despite these differences of opinion, that people aspire to live and work in Irvine.

—*Michael H. Ebner*

Further Readings and References

Baldassare, M. (1986). *Trouble in paradise: The suburban transformation of America.* New York: Columbia University Press.

Bloom, N. D. (2001). *Suburban alchemy: 1960s new towns and the transformation of the American dream.* Columbus, OH: Ohio State University Press.

Kling, R. (Ed.). (1991). *Postsuburban California: The transformation of Orange County since World War II.* Berkeley, CA: University of California Press.

ISLAM

Islam has a long history in North America. Particularly since the last century, it has been a noticeable part of the urban landscape in the United States. A few individual Muslims are known to have been on this continent as early as the 16th century, but the appearance of Muslims in considerable numbers started with the slave trade from various areas in West Africa, especially in the 18th and 19th centuries. It is generally accepted that there were several thousand Muslims among those enslaved in Africa and brought here. However, they were not able to openly practice their own religion in this country, and therefore most of them were ultimately converted to Christianity.

Muslim immigrants started to come to America in the late 19th century. This first wave of immigration took place roughly between the last quarter of the 19th century and World War I. For these early immigrants, the primary reason for immigration was economic. They were mostly poor, unskilled, and generally illiterate men from Greater Syria, which included Syria, Jordan, Palestine, and Lebanon at that time. The majority of these men stayed in the industrial cities, primarily in the Northeast and Midwest, such as New York City, Rochester, Boston, Detroit, and Chicago. Having settled in these cities, they either became factory workers or itinerant salesmen. Some of these peddlers later became small store owners, while others continued peddling in the hinterlands of the urban areas, as a result of which the Muslim population spread across the country.

The second wave of Muslim immigration took place roughly between the two world wars. These new immigrants were mostly the relatives of Muslims who were already settled in the United States. Due to legal restrictions imposed in the 1920s, rising anti-immigrant sentiment in society, and the Great Depression, the number of Muslim immigrants decreased during this period. By that time, Muslims had already started to establish communities in the ghettos of big northern cities, such as Chicago and Detroit.

The third wave, which began at the end of World War II and lasted until the mid-1960s, brought Muslim immigrants from different parts of the world, including the Middle East, all parts of the Arab world, South Asia (especially India and Pakistan), North Africa, Eastern Europe, and the Soviet Union. Along with economic reasons for immigration, these Muslims had political reasons, such as the founding of the State of Israel or the establishment of Communist regimes in Eastern Europe. These immigrants were more open to Western culture, better educated, and more urban in background than their predecessors. Their settlement patterns, however, were similar to those of their earlier counterparts. Most of them found jobs as factory workers or more skilled professionals and settled in the metropolitan areas of the East Coast and Midwest, especially in New York City, Chicago, and Detroit. Others migrated as far as California and settled either in urban centers (especially in Los Angeles) or on farms as agricultural workers. There were also many students among these new-comers, who aimed to continue with their university education or receive advanced technical training.

During the last wave, which has continued until today, the number of immigrants sharply increased. At least 75 percent of foreign-born Muslims in America came here after 1965. The immigration act passed in 1965 repealed the quota on the number of foreign immigrants. As a result, Muslims all around the world rushed into the United States. Urban areas in the East (especially Boston, New York City, Rochester, Hartford, Newark, and Washington, D.C.), in the Midwest (especially Chicago and Detroit), and also in the South and West (especially Atlanta, San Francisco, and Los Angeles) are the places in which Muslims have chosen to study, find jobs, and settle down. These immigrants have been highly different from each other in terms of their ethnic and national origins, religious sects, educational backgrounds, and professional skills. Altogether, Muslims in the United States constitute a multicultural mosaic.

The size of the Muslim population in the United States is a controversial issue. This is partly because there is not an offical source for information on religious affiliation. Public law prohibits the U.S. Census Bureau from collecting data on religious affiliation on a mandatory basis. Moreover, when information is collected about religious practices through various surveys, the survey participants might be reluctant to declare their religion because of their minority status. Still, however, it is generally estimated that the Muslim population is between 1.5 and 2 percent of the total United States population, which is approximately 300,000,000 as of 2005. In other words, the number of Muslims in this country is estimated to be between 4,500,000 and 6,000,000.

More than 60 percent of Muslims in the United States belong to orthodox Sunni sects. Shias compose the second largest group, with approximately 20 percent. There are also members of other sectarian groups, such as Ahmadis and Sufis. The ethnic distribution of Muslims also varies greatly. South Asians (especially Pakistanis and Indians) and Arabs comprise 50 percent of all Muslims, each with an equal share. Islam has also been growing among Latino/as especially in New York City, Los Angeles, and San Francisco. The presence of a mosque (a Muslim place of worship) on a Navajo reservation in New Mexico indicates that Islam has been gaining ground among Native Americans as well. Finally, in terms of ethnic origin, African Americans comprise the largest group of Muslims in the United States: approximately 40 percent.

The immigration of Muslims to the United States and the massive migration of African Americans to the big Northern cities started almost at the same time. In the ghettos of these cities, some degree of interaction between these two groups was inevitable. Due to the considerable number of Muslims among enslaved Africans, there was already a historical situation in which Islamic and black identities overlapped. The social circumstances in the industrialized metropolitan areas of North America—racism and the severe conditions of life in the urban ghettos—contributed to Islam's growing popularity among African Americans. On these social and historical grounds emerged the black Islamic movement known as the Nation of Islam (NOI). The movement was founded in Detroit in 1930 by Wallace D. Fard. Fard's successor, Elijah Muhammad, established NOI's new headquarters in Chicago in 1932. NOI had a heterodox understanding of Islam. It was not only a religious but also a nationalist movement, which mobilized hostility in its members against whites and all institutions founded by whites. When Muhammad died, his son and successor, Warith Deen Muhammad, moved the group toward orthodox Sunni Islamic beliefs. He changed the name of the movement to the World Community of Islam in the West, and it was later renamed the American Society of Muslims. Some of Elijah Muhammad's followers who disagreed with this doctrinal shift decided to preserve his teachings and formed a splinter group in 1978 using the original name. NOI has continued since then under the leadership of Louis Farrakhan.

The places of worship are central in the daily lives of Muslim urbanites, who generally prefer to have accommodation in neighborhoods near or around a mosque. The first mosque in America was opened in 1893 in New York City and was followed over the years by the opening of other mosques, such as the well-known mosque in Cedar Rapids, Iowa, which opened in 1934. By 1952, there were approximately 20 mosques in the United States. The buildings had mostly been constructed for other purposes and were later converted to mosques. However, especially during the last wave of immigration, new mosques began to be built. Among them, the Islamic Center in Washington, D.C., opened in 1957, is probably the most famous. The Detroit Islamic Center, opened in 1968, contains also one of the largest mosques in the United States. There are currently more than 1,200 mosques in this country, most of which are located in big cities, especially in California, New York, New Jersey, Michigan, Pennsylvania, and Ohio. Muslims are distinct in certain respects—physical appearance (such as religious clothes), commercial activities (such as groceries in most large urban centers serving food for Muslim consumption), exterior decoration of their houses (such as the notice on the doors of many Muslim homes stating that guests should remove their shoes before entering), and festivals (such as the Muslim World Day Parade that has taken place one day each year since 1986 in New York City), and yet, they are integrated into the social and economic life in American cities.

In order to strengthen coordination and solidarity, Muslims in North America have founded many associations, particularly since the early 1950s, such as the Federation of Islamic Associations, Muslim Students of America, Islamic Circle of North America, Islamic Society of North America, and Shia Association of North America. Having extensively organized, especially in urban centers, Islam has become one of the fastest growing religions in the United States. It is estimated that by 2015 Muslims will comprise the largest non-Christian community in this country.

—*Özgür Avci*

Further Readings and References

Dannin, R. (2002). *Black pilgrimage to Islam.* New York: Oxford University Press.

Nimer, M. (2002). *The North American Muslim resource guide: Muslim community life in the United States and Canada.* New York: Routledge.

Schmidt, G. (2004). *Islam in urban America: Sunni Muslims in Chicago.* Philadelphia: Temple University Press.

Smith, J. I. (2000). *Islam in America.* New York: Columbia University Press.

Jackson, Maynard

As Atlanta's first African American mayor, Maynard Jackson (1938–2003) strove to incorporate blacks more fully into the political and economic life of his city. Born into a politically prominent Atlanta family and educated at Morehouse and North Carolina Central University, Jackson received his law degree from the latter in 1964. After practicing law in the private and public sector for several years, Jackson jumped into electoral politics by running a losing campaign for a U.S. Senate seat in Georgia. He ran strongly in his hometown Atlanta, however, and using this momentum, he won election as Atlanta's vice mayor in 1969. In the mayoral election of 1973, Jackson won 95 percent of the black vote, defeating incumbent mayor Sam Massell on the strength of the surging black coalition, which, by 1970, composed 51.3 percent of the total city population.

Jackson opened up the ranks of the city bureaucracy to black job seekers; as a result, the number of African Americans in municipal government rose from 38.1 percent in 1970 to 55.6 percent in 1978. He leveraged city funds held in Atlanta banks to force affirmative action policies on local financial institutions, and Jackson's Minority Business Enterprise (MBE) monitored city agencies to ensure that black-run firms won a fair share of government contracts. The mayor increased the number of city contracts awarded to minority-run firms from 1 percent in 1973 to 34 percent in 1981. These policies were particularly important in the construction industry, for the Jackson era saw the development of the city's international airport and expansion of the mass transit system. The airport (one of the nation's busiest) was completed ahead of schedule and under budget, using affirmative action programs for contracts and hires that conservatives often derided as inefficient. In 2003, the facility—Hartsfield-Jackson Atlanta International Airport—honored the late mayor by incorporating his name into the title.

Jackson also shifted attention from downtown development to the neighborhoods, targeting federal money for housing rehabilitation, quality-of-life improvements, and social service provision. In an effort to improve relations between minorities and the police, Jackson shifted power from uniformed leadership to his African American civilian public safety commissioner, who increased the number of black police officers.

Under pressure from white business leaders, Jackson moderated his black empowerment themes in his second term, adopting more mainstream, downtown-centered policies, creating, for example, the Office of Economic Development to bolster corporate Atlanta. By the time he won his third term in a landslide election in 1993, the ground had so shifted under Jackson that he ran as the centrist alternative to a more liberal, neighborhood-centered opponent. His third term was shadowed by a scandal involving his political allies and concession contracts at the airport. Out of office, Jackson was a prominent attorney active in civic affairs, and he worked with his protégé and mayoral successor, Andrew Young, to bring the Olympic Games to Atlanta in 1996.

Jackson's legacy as mayor was to incorporate black interests into the traditional business-centered practices of 20th-century Atlanta.

—Richard Flanagan

See also Atlanta, Georgia

Further Readings and References

Bayor, R. H. (2001). African-American mayors and governance in Atlanta. In D. R. Adler & J. S. Colburn (Eds.), *African-American mayors and governance in Atlanta.* Urbana: University of Illinois.

Jacobs, Jane

Jane Jacobs (1916–) was raised in the suburbs of Scranton, Pennsylvania, the daughter of a doctor and a nurse. Following high school, she moved to New York City and worked as a secretary and freelance writer, producing pieces on city life for *Vogue* and *Harper's Bazaar.* During the 1940s, she wrote for industrial trade publications and then the U.S. government's information agency; she also became an active union organizer.

Jacobs's greatest influence came with the publication in 1961 of *The Death and Life of Great American Cities,* a book that grew out of her work as an associate editor at *Architectural Forum* from 1952 to 1962. In it, she attacked the policies of urban renewal and rejected the ideas that underpinned modernist planning. Jacobs blended that critique with personal observations from her own neighborhood in the West Village of New York City, where she lived with her husband, architect Robert H. Jacobs, and their three children. She characterized desirable city life in terms of four generators, or conditions, for urban diversity: mixed uses (commercial, industrial, residential), small city blocks, buildings of various kinds and ages, and concentrated population. In Jacobs's controversial view, modernist planners and architects, along with the urban renewal administrators who empowered them, failed to recognize the gap between their idealized visions and the complex dynamics of urban life.

After leaving the *Architectural Forum* in 1962, Jacobs fought for the principles in her book as a neighborhood organizer and civic leader. Her most significant victories included defeating urban renewal plans for the West Village neighborhood (1961–1962), developing an alternative middle-income housing project designed by residents (West Village Houses, 1962–1974), and halting the implementation of a proposed Lower Manhattan expressway (1962, 1968). Amid the tumultuous political climate of the later 1960s, Jacobs was arrested twice, once for protesting the Vietnam War draft and once for disrupting a state expressway hearing. In 1968, citing U.S. imperialism and two draft-age sons, Jacobs moved her family to Canada. After immigrating to Toronto, she led a movement with Marshall McLuhan to defeat the Spadina expressway (1969–1971) and advised the reform administrations of Mayors David Crombie (1974–1978) and John Sewell (1978–1980) on the St. Lawrence Neighborhood, a mixed-income housing development.

Jacobs's writings on cities achieved international influence, and many of her practical insights, such as the idea that more "eyes on the street" make neighborhoods safer, have become standard wisdom in the very fields of urbanism that originally rejected her as an uncredentialed outsider. Jacobs subsequently completed her urban trilogy with *The Economy of Cities* (1969) and *Cities and the Wealth of Nations* (1984), books that, while less popular or controversial, continue to shape the thinking of urban economists and political scientists. Her other writings have branched into the areas of ethics, ecology, social criticism, and even children's literature.

—Christopher Klemek

Further Readings and References

Jacobs, J. (1961). *The death and life of great American cities.* New York: Random House.

Jacobs, J. (1969). *The economy of cities.* New York: Random House.

Jacobs, J. (1984). *Cities and the wealth of nations: Principles of economic life.* New York: Random House.

Jacobs, J. (2000). *The nature of economies.* New York: Random House.

Klemek, C. (2006). Jane Jacobs and the fall of the urban renewal order in New York and Toronto. *Journal of Urban History.*

JAZZ

Jazz is a distinctively American music rooted in African American culture and incorporating Euro-American, Afro-Caribbean, and Latin musical traditions into its unique sound. Jazz's evolution reflects the transition of the United States from a rural to a predominantly urban and industrial nation at the beginning of the 20th century. The music has no exact date of origin; however, the music first labeled *jazz* emerged around New Orleans before World War I and became a popular music for listening and dancing across the nation by the 1930s. Characterized by polyrhythmic, syncopated, and improvisational qualities, early jazz incorporated ragtime, stride piano, brass band marching music, and the blues. Jazz musicians rely on a call and response between instruments, including the human voice, to develop their improvisations as an ensemble. Classic jazz from the earliest era was characterized by collective or heterophonic improvisation; in later jazz styles, individual solo work became more common.

Jazz evolved through several significant styles, beginning with New Orleans classic jazz, followed by swing, bop, cool, free, fusion, and modal jazz, to name the most prominent forms of the music. Some styles are remembered in terms of the cities and musicians who generated exciting new jazz variations. Chicago Jazz, for example, is represented by performers King Oliver, Louis Armstrong, and the Austin High Gang (1920s); Kansas City Swing featured Lester Young, Count Basie, and Mary Lou Williams (1920s and 1930s); bebop was played by Dizzie Gillespie and Charlie Parker and brought fame to jazz clubs on 52nd Street in midtown Manhattan (1940s and 1950s); and West Coast jazz, focused in Los Angeles, brought together cool jazz performers like Art Pepper and Gerry Mulligan (1950s).

The entertainment cultures that sustained jazz musicians and ensured their audiences have been located primarily in urban areas. First, in multicultural New Orleans, African American, Creole, and European immigrants experimented together as they created jazz, sometimes competing in contests on the streets to advertise their bands. Subsequently, jazz musicians converged in Chicago, New York, Kansas City, St. Louis, San Francisco, and Los Angeles. In its first decades, jazz was performed in many locations, for example, street parades and funerals in New Orleans.

It was also associated with the vice districts of urban areas, where zoning regulations concentrated saloons, dance halls, nightclubs, and brothels into common neighborhoods. Jazzmen found work in these "red-light districts." Entrepreneurs with ties to organized crime controlled several of these zones, for example, Tom Anderson in New Orleans's Storyville, Al Capone and Joe Glaser in Chicago, and Tom Pendergast in Kansas City. These enterprises brought jazz into close proximity with Prohibition Era speakeasies and "gin joints." Some musicians depended on gangsters as agents; for example, Louis Armstrong worked for Joe Glaser. The qualities of the locations where jazz was played shaped the attitudes of some early white jazz audiences, who went "slumming" in jazz clubs with "exotic" or deviant names, such as the Oriental, the Bucket of Blood, or the Novelty Club.

Some vice districts—notably Storyville in New Orleans—were closed by order of the War Department in 1917. Jazz musicians, already joining African Americans in the Great Migration from the rural South to Chicago and New York, looked to the northern cities for new opportunities. After World War I, young people in particular associated jazz with a modern revolt against the staid mores of the Victorian Era. Jazz and its locations symbolized for them the emergence of sophisticated sounds and the opportunity for dancing. Hence, the 1920s are often described as a "jazz age" in reference to the celebration of hedonistic and urbane values. Musicians and their audiences came together in new jazz centers, particularly Chicago, New York, and Kansas City.

Critics of jazz in the 1920s believed it stimulated immoral behavior, an accusation often based largely on the upbeat tempos of the music as well as the earlier location of its performance near vice districts and immigrant, working-class, and African-American neighborhoods. In fact, jazz was also played in many other places and for varied purposes, for example, at private parties, at social clubs, and on college and university campuses. With the end of Prohibition (1933) and the growth of legitimate nightclubs and dance halls, jazz was associated more broadly with a range of entertainment venues and less exclusively with the "sporting life." Urban reformers continued to seek regulation of the performance venues where jazz might be heard, for example, in dance halls or interracial "black and tan" nightclubs. Jazz musicians and club owners continued to negotiate various legal and zoning restrictions on live music and dance throughout the 20th century.

Musicians toured on entertainment circuits connected to vaudeville and popular theaters in many cities and towns, traveling first by railroad and later by bus and automobile. Between the 1920s and 1940s, jazz was performed in nationally prominent night-clubs or ballrooms, for example, the Cotton Club and the Savoy in Harlem, as well as in many smaller venues. Beginning in the late 1920s, radio broadcasts of live music disseminated jazz and its urban locations to the nation at large. Big Band swing jazz swept the nation from the mid-1930s through World War II, as lively dance music dominated American youth culture. Post–World War II bebop was played in smaller clubs, such as Minton's Playhouse in New York City. By the 21st century, jazz had lost most of its association with deviant urban subcultures, and it could be found in concert halls, festivals, and many different kinds of settings in American cities.

Jazz also found enthusiastic audiences in smaller towns and cities. Those located on the Mississippi and Ohio Rivers were connected to excursion tourism via riverboats, such as those owned by the Streckfus Line. Pleasure cruises featured live music for dancing and acquainted their passengers with jazz clubs in river cities like Vicksburg, Mississippi; Memphis, Tennessee; Davenport, Iowa; and Cincinnati, Ohio. Bands established outside of major metropolitan areas became known as territory bands in midwestern and southwestern regions.

Cities concentrated the economic and cultural opportunities that supported musicians, most directly by providing the greatest opportunity to gather for live audiences. Urban locations provided the homes for economic institutions that proved important to jazz, such as music publishing companies, booking agents, unions, and radio and phonograph corporations. Publications that reviewed and promoted jazz for a national audience were published in cities like New York, for example, *Downbeat*. Musicians depended on professional associations and networks headquartered in cities to help them to earn their livings. Some cities provided opportunities beyond the nightclub or ballroom. In New York, musicians worked in musical theater, for example, and in Los Angeles, musicians found employment as studio musicians in Hollywood films.

Musicians from varied backgrounds—whites and blacks, immigrants and native-born performers—found opportunities to play together and learn from each other at jam sessions in major jazz locales. The entertainment industry offered some immigrants an opportunity for upward mobility, as was the case with Jewish American clarinetist and bandleader Benny Goodman. However, the changing dynamics of urban race and class relations also restricted jazz musicians' choices. Many African American musicians pursued their musical careers in segregated venues and southern cities, which limited their occupational choices and wages. Until the Civil Rights Movement of the 1950s and 1960s successfully challenged Jim Crow laws that segregated theaters and nightclubs, whites and blacks were generally not allowed in the same venues. When African American musicians toured in the South, performers faced restricted accommodations and possible violence on the road. Racial preferences favored white musicians, who were more likely to receive better paying gigs, recording contracts, and superior promotion.

Jazz history is also traced through the careers of major improvisers and composers, such as Louis Armstrong, Duke Ellington, Charlie Parker, Billie Holiday, Miles Davis, Charles Mingus, and Wynton Marsalis—all of whom traveled extensively between cities to earn their living. Also, some jazz greats are specifically identified with their cities of origin—Louis Armstrong and New Orleans, for example—or with the cities where they established their fame, as is the case with Charlie Parker and Kansas City. Composers and arrangers paid homage to the musical inspiration provided by cities and jazz venues. For example, several songs celebrate Manhattan: "Take the A-Train," Duke Ellington (1941); "Stompin' at the Savoy," Chick Webb and His Orchestra (1934); and "Central Park West," John Coltrane (1964).

Jazz music made strong contributions to artistic movements focused in American cities. The Harlem Renaissance (1920–1935) brought together African American intellectuals, artists, and musicians, several of whom, for instance, Claude McKay, Langston Hughes, and Zora Neale Hurston, experimented with a jazz aesthetic in their exploration of African American urban life. Beat writers Alan Ginsberg and Jack Kerouac likewise incorporated jazz rhythms into their unconventional portraits of Cold War American cities; their writing became associated with the bohemian coffeehouses and bookstores of North Beach in San Francisco (1950s to 1960s). Novelists employed jazz as an urban language in works such as Ralph Ellison's *Invisible Man* (1947) and Toni Morrison's *Jazz* (1992).

—*Kathy Ogren*

See also Blues Music; Civil Rights; Harlem Renaissance; Urban Renewal and Revitalization; World War II and the City

Further Readings and References

Douglas, A. (1995). *Terrible honesty: Mongrel Manhattan in the 1920s.* New York: Farrar, Straus & Giroux.

Kenney, W. H. (2005). *Jazz on the river.* Chicago: University of Chicago Press.

Ogren, K. J. (1989). *The jazz revolution: Twenties America and the meaning of jazz.* New York: Oxford University Press.

O'Meally, R. G. (Ed.). (2001). *Living with music: Ralph Ellison's jazz writings.* New York: Modern Library.

Paretti, B. W. (1992). *The creation of jazz: Music, race, and culture in urban America.* Urbana and Chicago: University of Illinois Press.

Russell, R. (1971). *Jazz style in Kansas City and the Southwest.* Berkeley: University of California Press.

JENNEY, WILLIAM LE BARON

William Le Baron Jenney (1832–1907) has secured a permanent place in the annals of architecture for his lasting impact on the skyline of many major American cities. His designs in architecture allowed the modern skyscraper to emerge as the answer to the limits of space in cramped urban areas.

Jenney was born in 1832 to William P. and Eliza Jenney. The senior Jenney owned a fleet of commercial whalers and occasionally took William on trips to the Pacific. In 1853, William decided to pursue a career in history and architecture in Paris. At that time, Jenney came in contact with many of the revered styles of embellished architecture that were prominent in Europe. He eventually attained a degree in engineering (1856) and returned to the United States. When the Civil War erupted in 1861, Jenney joined the Union Army and was eventually appointed to the Army of Tennessee under General Ulysses S. Grant. Jenney rose to the rank of major, a title that he retained to the end of his life. After the war, he came to settle in Chicago, where he started an architectural firm.

It has been reported that in 1881, as the construction of the Home Insurance Building began, Jenney remembered his journey to the Philippines and the construction design of the local inhabitants, whose huts consisted of a strong skeletal frame with an overlay of reeds, bamboo, and whatnot. More likely, Jenney was influenced by the balloon-frame construction of the Chicago area.

The concept of the skyscraper was simple in engineering and had to meet three criteria. First, the frame had to be steel. Over a steel I-beam skeleton, masonry and glass were used to build the walls to shelter inhabitants from the elements. The use of glass from floor to ceiling was important, as electrical light was still in its early stages, and ambient light was needed to illuminate the interiors of the buildings. Second, the building had to be at least 10 stories in height. With the steel frame anchored in the sandstone foundation, granite could be used to accent the frame and corners, thus reducing the overall weight. With less weight, especially on the upper floors, higher buildings could be constructed. Third, because of the height, an elevator had to be incorporated into the building. With these elements, a skyscraper was the new answer to space in places like Chicago.

Jenney built several skyscrapers in addition to the Home Insurance Building, which was located at the corner of LaSalle and Adams Streets in the heart of the Loop and financial district. Many considered Jenny's designs to be somewhat tepid, and given his engineering background, this is understandable. Because of his overall work, however—his designs were used at the World's Columbian Exposition of 1893, and designs by him and his colleagues culminated in the Chicago School of Architecture—it is no surprise that his vision and legacy should be remembered in grandeur.

—Cord Scott

Further Readings and References

Chicago Tribune staff. (1997). *Chicago days: 150 defining moments of Chicago's history.* Wheaton, IL: Cantigny First Division Foundation.

Hines, T. (1974). *Burnham of Chicago: Architect and planner.* Chicago: University of Chicago Press.

Miller, D. (1996). *City of the century.* New York: Simon & Schuster.

Turak, T. (1966). *William Le Baron Jenney: A pioneer of modern architecture.* Ann Arbor, MI: UMI Research Press.

JOHNSON ADMINISTRATION: URBAN POLICY

The nation's cities were the primary battleground of President Lyndon Johnson's domestic policy making. Legislation enacting Johnson's Great Society not only expanded on Fair Deal and New Frontier urban programming, but also initiated new community development approaches to city betterment. These approaches went beyond traditional bricks-and-mortar rebuilding efforts, investing in cities' human capital and social structures. The Equal Opportunity Act of 1964, implementing legislation for the War on Poverty, engaged members of underserved communities in urban policy decisions. The Housing Acts of 1964, 1965, and 1968 significantly expanded the nation's commitment to public and low-income housing and to traditional urban renewal, and it established a Cabinet-level Department of Housing and Urban Development. The Model Cities Act of 1966 attempted an ambitious integration of federal social programming efforts on behalf of cities. The complexity of these programs' design, along with the fact that the federal fiscal commitment failed to match the boldness of program goals, presented often insurmountable challenges to their implementers. Nonetheless, the impact of Johnson era urban policy making is still felt, especially in the increased participation of poor and minority communities in the political processes shaping cities.

Implementation of the Great Society urban programs was influenced by several conditioning factors, including the burden of the Vietnam War and the explosive American racial politics of the era. The war in Southeast Asia monopolized fiscal resources and helped fragment traditional Democratic Party constituencies. The treatment of black Americans was the most prominent social justice issue of the period, and social programming in the areas of poverty and the cities soon came to be viewed as special programming for the black community. At a time when the interracial Civil Rights Movement was being transformed into strident, separatist calls for "Black Power," this misperception about the aims of Great Society programming undercut its support.

The Equal Opportunity Act

As successor to the martyred President John F. Kennedy, Johnson faced the task of providing a respectful continuity for the Kennedy programs while searching for the opportune moment to begin placing his own stamp on policy. A collection of social programs dealing with poverty had been under development in Democratic Party policy shops at the time of Kennedy's death. On becoming president, Johnson immediately seized on this anti-poverty package as the sort of ambitious, broad-scope program that he wanted to characterize his presidency.

In transmitting the Equal Opportunity Act to Congress on March 16, 1964, Johnson argued that a country as prosperous as the United States in the

1960s had the resources to address poverty directly and to end it. The legislation also reflected the view that in America, poverty resulted from a community's lack of political effectiveness, which prevented it from securing its share of resources. The act attempted to address poverty by providing individuals with the training and other resources necessary to access jobs and by structuring community action programs to encourage "maximum feasible participation" in program decision making on the part of the poor who were its intended beneficiaries.

Among the programs established by the act were the Job Corps (providing work training and work experience), community action, Head Start (early childhood education), adult basic education, and Volunteers in Service to America (VISTA). The budget request for the first year was $962 million, adding $500 million in new money to fund existing programs. Johnson signed the bill into law August 24, 1964.

The community action programs and the requirement of maximum feasible participation quickly came to interfere with the successful operation of equal opportunity programming. Funding for community action sidestepped both state capitals and city halls to provide federal dollars directly to grassroots organizations, groups that often became troublesome to the local political establishment. Many outsiders viewed maximum feasible participation as unwarranted federal funding of minority radicalism, eroding broad-based support for the program. Critics on the right pronounced the program misguided in attempting to override market-based incentives with government giveaways. Leftist critics argued that the Equal Opportunity Act was short-sighted in attempting to remedy societal ills through provision of services to individuals rather than by addressing the underlying, systemic causes of poverty, and they questioned the wisdom of preparing people for jobs rather than seeking to increase the number of jobs generated by the economy.

Johnson Administration Housing Acts

Johnson housing legislation in 1964, 1965, and 1968 expanded government investment in public and low-income housing and pioneered rent supplements. Johnson era housing legislation represented compromises—a strategy familiar from the landmark Housing Act of 1949 and its successors in the 1950s—between the demands of the real estate and banking industries and the requirements of the poorly housed. Liberals criticized the urban housing policy for the displacement of poor and minority citizens caused by its urban renewal components, whereas conservatives charged that the programs were pork-barrel giveaways for favored contractors.

The Housing Act of 1964 was transitional legislation, providing a 1-year extension of existing programs, including $725 million for urban renewal and a commitment to build 37,500 public housing units for the year.

Johnson's 1965 housing legislation extended federal funding for cities and urban housing but failed in its attempt to redirect federal policy toward support for community rather than commercial development. The legislation introduced an important new rent supplement program, intended by the bill's sponsors to assist moderate-income families who were ineligible for public housing. However, real estate and banking advocates limited the availability of the subsidy to low-income households qualified for public housing. The administration also lost the battle to further limit the amount of funding that could be diverted from residential to nonresidential renewal: Opponents managed to raise the existing limit to 35 percent of funding. Nonetheless, the 1965 act provided a substantial federal investment in the cities, including an additional $2.9 million authorization for urban renewal and a commitment to build 240,000 units of public housing over the next 4 years.

The final expansion of the Johnson urban program came with the Housing Act of 1968, a big bill largely drafted by the banking industry with the objective of increasing homeownership. The act called for construction of 26 million new homes over the course of the decade, and it expanded both rent supplements and the subsidies created by the 1965 act to assist low-income homeownership.

Department of Housing and Urban Development

Johnson managed to win the decades-old battle for a Cabinet-level urban affairs department in the Housing and Urban Development Act of 1965, signed into law September 9, 1965. An urban affairs department had first been recommended in 1937 as part of the National Resources Planning Board's report, *Our Cities: Their Role in the National Economy,* and a similar proposal had been made by Kennedy in 1962. Johnson's bill was assisted by his agreement, in response to private sector demand, to leave both the

Federal Housing Authority and the Federal Home Loan Bank Board autonomous and to limit the scope of the programs folded into the new department. Passage of the 1965 act was also made easier by Johnson's delay in naming Robert Weaver as HUD secretary. Weaver was director of the Housing and Home Finance Agency, HUD's predecessor, and his appointment by Johnson made him the first black Cabinet member. Opposition to the Weaver appointment had helped to stall the Kennedy bill.

Model Cities

The centerpiece of Johnson's urban policy was the Demonstration Cities and Metropolitan Development Act of 1966, or Model Cities. The act represented an important step in the transition of federal urban policy from *urban renewal* to *community development* approaches. The program was given accelerated priority after the August 1965 riots in Los Angeles's Watts neighborhood. Working from a proposal prepared by a task force convened under HUD Assistant Secretary Robert Wood, Johnson submitted legislation to Congress in January 1966. The legislation was intended to coordinate the range of federal programs available to support cities, proposing comprehensive city demonstration programs with 80 percent of the costs to be covered by federal funds. The act also called for metropolitan area-wide planning, created home mortgage insurance for veterans, provided incentives for new town developers, and addressed historic preservation in renewal areas.

The impact of Model Cities was limited by underfunding and the program's unwieldiness. The intention of Model Cities had been to provide for an experimental program implemented in a limited number of cities, allowing for a variety of approaches to be tested and permitting some failures. With a limited program, significant resources could be invested in each participating city. However, to achieve passage of the legislation, it was necessary to raise the number of participating cities from 60 to 150; in addition, Congress provided less than half of the funding Johnson requested. It was also quickly apparent that the legislation's complex structure—calling for coordination and sharing of funds among federal agencies and between the federal government and localities—would make implementation next to impossible. Cities found the application process daunting: The first Comprehensive Development Plan, for Seattle, wasn't approved until December 1968. Nevertheless,

Model Cities succeeded in disbursing $2.3 billion to participating cities between 1967 and 1973.

—Bell Clement

Further Readings and References

Andrew, J. A., III. (1998). *Lyndon Johnson and the Great Society.* Chicago: Ivar R. Dee.

Bernstein, I. (1996). *Guns or butter: The presidency of Lyndon Johnson.* New York: Oxford University Press.

Fox, K. (1986). *Metropolitan America: Urban life and urban policy in the United States, 1940–1980.* Jackson: University of Mississippi Press.

Gelfand, M. I. (1975). *A nation of cities: The federal government and urban America, 1933–1965.* New York: Oxford University Press.

Gelfand, M. I. (1981). The War on Poverty. In R. A. Divine (Ed.), *The Johnson years: Vol. 1. Foreign policy, the Great Society and the White House* (pp. 126–154). Lawrence: University of Kansas Press.

Mollenkopf, J. H. (1983). *The contested city.* Princeton: Princeton University Press.

JOPLIN, SCOTT

Scott Joplin (1868-1917), the "king of ragtime," composed lively syncopated music at the turn of the 20th century that accompanied the rise of urban America.

As a composer of ragtime, Joplin pioneered in a popular musical style that combined the forms of European music with the rhythms and melodic motifs of African American music. Syncopation, its hallmark feature, called for physical responses—toe tapping, thigh slapping, and rollicking dance movements—that contrasted sharply with late Victorian propriety. Ragtime's popularity tapped into a deep well of resistance against both Victorian hypocrisy and industrial discipline and is thus rightly seen as an important manifestation of the turn-of-the-century impulse toward modernity. Although denounced by some critics as a low form of music, ragtime appealed to men and women of all classes.

When the second son of Jiles and Florence Givens Joplin left home as a teenager to make his way as a musician, he probably did not imagine himself as a cultural rebel. His departure was enabled by the very forces that gave rise to major urban centers in the United States—railroads and industrialization.

Although Joplin likely attended the World's Columbian Exposition in Chicago in 1893, he did not emerge as a composer until later in the 1890s in Sedalia, Missouri. There he composed the *Maple Leaf Rag* (1899), which launched his career and led to his business relationship with John Stark, a sheet music publisher who was white. Both Joplin and Stark eventually moved to St. Louis, where Stark participated in the burgeoning music industry, mass-producing sheet music and selling mass-produced pianos, and Joplin immersed himself in a lively entertainment district, home to Tom Turpin, Sam Patterson, and Louis Chauvin.

In 1907, Joplin moved to New York, where he composed and taught music for a living. Joplin's ragtime marches, waltzes, two-steps, and slow drags appeared with regularity. But Joplin had grander ambitions than writing popular dance music. In 1902, he persuaded a reluctant Stark to publish *The Ragtime Dance,* which was accompaniment to a ragtime ballet. Also while in New York, he wrote a ragtime opera, *Treemonisha.* However, like an earlier Joplin opera, *A Guest of Honor* (1903), this never made it to a full-stage production during Joplin's lifetime. One performance in 1915 at the Lincoln Theater failed to impress anyone, least of all a financial backer. Joplin's mental and physical health began to deteriorate dramatically, and on April 1, 1917, he died.

In little more than two decades, Joplin published ragtime compositions that set the standard for that musical genre. Altogether, he composed 44 original works and collaborated with Arthur Marshall, Scott Hayden, and Louis Chauvin on seven others. Since the revival of interest in Joplin and his music in the 1970s, *The Entertainer* (1902), *Pineapple Rag* (1908), *The Easy Winners* (1901), and *Solace* (1909) have enjoyed renewed popularity.

—Susan Curtis

Further Readings and References

Berlin, E. A. (1994). *The king of ragtime: Scott Joplin and his era.* New York: Oxford University Press.

Blesh, R, & Janis, H. (1950). *They all played ragtime: The true story of an American music.* New York: Knopf.

Curtis, S. (1994). *Dancing to a black man's tune: A life of Scott Joplin.* Columbia: University of Missouri Press.

Moderwell, H. K. (1915). Ragtime. *The New Republic,* pp. 284–286.

JUDAISM AND JEWISH COMMUNITIES

In colonial America and the early republic, the relatively small Jewish population was concentrated overwhelmingly in the five tidal port cities—New York, Philadelphia, Newport, Charleston, and Savannah. As the pace of Jewish immigration picked up from the 1820s, new arrivals followed American expansion westward along the canals and inland river systems. Individual Jewish shops and then small but viable communities appeared in midwestern centers such as Cincinnati and St. Louis, in San Francisco (with the Gold Rush in 1849), and in smaller market towns throughout the land. From 1880 through the imposition of quotas in 1924, a tidal wave of immigration brought some 2.5 million Jews to the United States. Again, most settled in the largest centers, above all in New York, Philadelphia, and Chicago, but also in Cleveland, Pittsburgh, Baltimore, and Boston. Community leaders sought to ease the strain on charitable resources by redirecting immigration—for example, through the port of Galveston; the Industrial Removal Office (1900–1917) aimed at spreading able-bodied workers to other centers. In recent decades, Jews have followed the general population shifts especially to Southern California and Florida, and there are Jewish communities today in every state. Even so, Jews have remained overwhelmingly concentrated in the country's largest metropolitan centers. In 1957, the only year for which public census data on religious identity was collected, 37 percent of Americans, but 87 percent of Jews, lived in urban areas with more than a quarter million inhabitants. The withering of Jewish communal life in small towns throughout the country has increased this trend.

Jewish concentration in American urban centers reflects and continues the traditional economic role of Jews in Europe as small-scale merchants and middlemen. The declining economic importance of small towns (*shtetls*) in central and eastern Europe forced many young Jewish men to seek their livelihood elsewhere. Beginning in the 1820s, some came to America, where they picked up the peddler's heavy pack, often with credit provided by a fellow Jew, and sold door-to-door or farm-to-farm until they had saved enough to open a general store in town. Others, especially in later periods, passed first through the growing cities of eastern (and western) Europe where they picked up urban skills, especially in the needle trades; as a result, they were attracted to the booming ready-to-wear industries growing in New York and elsewhere in the American Northeast. Comparatively few Jewish immigrants came to America with the skills necessary to engage in agriculture.

During the years of massive migration, the neighborhoods of first settlement tended to be poorer, crowded areas closest to the points of arrival. Examples include the Lower East Side of Manhattan, the North End of Boston, and the Maxwell Street market area in Chicago. But rapid urban relocation is a central element in Jews' American experience. The more affluent quickly abandoned the old downtown in favor of upscale neighborhoods, and the less well-off sought both better housing and greater business opportunity by opening small retail shops in new neighborhoods, even if at first they had to live above or behind the store. Especially after World War II, younger Jews flocked to the tract suburbs promoted by the Housing Act of 1949 and the Federal-Aid Highways Act of 1956. Older areas, to the extent that they survived urban renovation, became iconic sites of urban nostalgia, with restored synagogues, museums, and tourist events aimed at Jews seeking their roots. There are signs that recent successes in reviving inner city areas are also affecting Jewish residential patterns: Manhattan's Jewish community, for example, has been growing younger and wealthier since the 1990s.

Urban geography has had a complex effect on American Jewish group identity. Jews have consistently tended to live close to each other, sharing religious services and each other's company. Although residential proximity has allowed for the creation of strong institutions, it has also paradoxically weakened the need for them: Cultural networks and personal bonds exist even where many, perhaps most Jews do not formally affiliate. Centralized and unified institutions on the European model have proven unworkable in the face of the size and spread of American cities, not to mention the differences in ritual, ethnicity, and then denomination among the growing Jewish population. In denser urban neighborhoods, the result was a pattern of diverse and more intimate synagogues and other associations.

In the suburbs, or "gilded ghettos" (as Albert Gordon dubbed them), on the other hand, communities were not as intimate nor institutions as diverse. Suburbia's single-family homes on large lots dictated driving to central synagogues rather than walking to smaller local institutions. The economics of larger buildings demanded broader but ideologically blander and more homogenized content aimed at attracting a mass audience to all-purpose synagogues and Jewish centers. The high shared costs of building (and rebuilding) Jewish institutions, when added to the price each family paid for housing in desirable Jewish neighborhoods nearby, has made Jewish identity very expensive, limiting the diversity of occupation within the community and making access to services more difficult for the less affluent. Meanwhile, Jewish families have been subjected to the same pressures that affect all groups in suburbia: breakdown of the extended family network, marginalization of the elderly, domesticization of women's work, and demands for conformity to unrealistic norms of behavior and idealized consumerized versions of success. (Sub)urban geography has thus reinforced and exacerbated the loss of Jewish social and cultural capital inherent in Jews' acculturation to America.

In the older neighborhoods "Jews without money" (Michael Gold's phrase)—especially the elderly—inevitably remained behind and required special services. Moreover, tensions rose between established Jews (landlords, store owners, teachers, and social workers) in these older neighborhoods and their new clienteles. Although Jews were statistically less quick than other white ethnic groups to participate in white flight from the urban core in the 1960s, the issue of black-Jewish relations became a central concern for community leaders.

Where they survived, older Jewish neighborhoods have tended to take on a more traditionalist (Orthodox) character. Survivors of the European Holocaust formed communities around charismatic Hasidic *rebbes,* moving into the cheaper housing of earlier Jewish neighborhoods and taking over their abandoned institutions. Suburbia was not attractive to Hasidim, who favor large families, insist on living within close proximity to religious and educational facilities, and are willing to forgo many of the trappings of the American dream. Within a generation, they had built large, highly organized, and very visible communities, especially in Brooklyn (Crown Heights and Williamsburg), with current expansion into other urban neighborhoods in New York, New Jersey, and elsewhere. Religious cohesion has made these groups into effective and disciplined political blocs, and some have experimented with building and moving into their own planned suburbs. There,

residential separatism is not only more evident but can even acquire de facto legal recognition through municipal incorporation (most famously in the village of Kiryas Joel, established in 1977 in Orange County, New York, by Satmar Hasidim), a development that has raised constitutional questions in view of traditional American separation of church and state.

Real estate development, sales, and investment have been attractive fields of economic endeavor for American Jews. A field that is relatively open to competition and one where relatively small speculative investments could yield high rewards, real estate appealed to members of the Jewish "minority by choice" (Simon Kuznets's phrase). Inspired by new visions of communal vitality and social progress, Jewish entrepreneurs successfully applied efficiencies of scale and mass marketing techniques to house production (William J. Levitt in Levittowns) and developed new architectural visions of commercial organization (Victor Gruen in enclosed shopping malls) to forever reshape the American city.

City life has provided the setting and the dominant themes for American Jewish fiction. Although the sufferings of immigrant poverty and the oppression of sweatshop working conditions do appear, literature and drama have generally presented the city in a positive light as a place of economic and cultural opportunity. Personal progress and freedom are often represented spatially by movement out of the Jewish neighborhood with its restrictive old-world, religious, and patriarchal value system. On the other hand, the old neighborhood soon becomes the site of Jewish authenticity; a source of humor, piety, and wisdom; the paradoxical locale of universalist ethical and artistic values; the site of women's empowerment; and the alternative to the false assimilation of upper-middle-class suburbia. In the modernist epic *Call It Sleep,* by Henry Roth (1934), the division between Jewish and non-Jewish urban space is overcome as the city literally explodes into the soul of the immigrant child-hero, biblical revelation expressed as raw electric power rising out of the city street.

—*Bernard Dov Cooperman*

Further Readings and References

American Jewish Committee. (1999–). *American Jewish yearbook.* New York: Author.

Diner, H. (2004). *The Jews of the United States 1654–2000.* Berkeley: University of California Press.

Weissbach, L. S. (2005). *Jewish life in small-town America: A history.* New Haven, CT: Yale University Press.

Juvenile Delinquency and the Juvenile Justice System

Juvenile delinquency refers to criminal and other deviant acts committed by children and youths. It encompasses a wide range of criminal activities, from less serious crimes such as drinking and shoplifting, to more serious activities such as burglary and rape. Juvenile delinquency also includes noncriminal behaviors that only children and youth can be charged with, such as running away from home, disobeying parents, and skipping school. The concept of juvenile delinquency began to take shape in the United States during the early 19th century in response to rapid industrialization, urbanization, and breakdown of traditional community ties. Juvenile delinquency has been a focus of social control activities and state surveillance. The juvenile justice system refers to a body of courts, laws, and social institutions designed to protect and treat exclusively juvenile delinquents, separate from the adult justice system. The juvenile justice system and the concept of juvenile delinquency have affected the urban landscape in various ways. Reformers and social scientists have often found the causes of juvenile delinquency in the peculiar economic, social, and cultural conditions of cities, and they have established social policies and institutions to control behavior of youths in the cities.

The development of the notion of juvenile delinquency is strongly connected to the emergence of childhood and adolescence as distinctive life stages. Childhood as a distinct life stage did not exist in early America. Children were quickly integrated into the adult world by serving an apprenticeship or contributing to the family-based economy in colonial America. Treatment of juvenile offenders was based on English common law, which defined children under 7 years old as guiltless and those over 14 years old as adults criminally responsible. Juveniles who committed serious crimes were treated as adults. Children were deemed sinful by nature and could face punishment for offenses such as laziness, disobedience, and rebelliousness. The strong emotional attachment of parents to their children was also largely absent in early America. The 19th century witnessed dramatic changes in the perception of childhood. In accordance with rapid industrialization, apprenticeship and the family-based economy that had served to incorporate children into an adult world declined gradually. With the expansion of compulsory public education, children began to remain in their parents' home and to receive special treatment for longer periods of time. Mothers began to play a central role in socializing children, and they attached new emotional values to children. Parents now rejected the idea that children were sinful by nature and emphasized the pliability of the child's nature. Children came to be seen as a source of pleasure and playfulness.

This new belief that children were more malleable than adults generated social movements to establish special institutions for child offenders, separate from the adult criminal justice system. The practice of housing juveniles with adults in prisons became a major concern for middle-class reformers because they believed that adult prisoners would corrupt malleable youths. Beginning in the early 19th century, reformers established "houses of refuge," which institutionalized exclusively child offenders, ill-behaved children, and dependent children. The house of refuge movement rested on the English doctrine of *parens patriae* in which the state serves as a surrogate parent in the child's best interests. Once housed in the houses of refuge or state-supported reformatories, children studied academic subjects taught in public schools. Children also worked at trades to acquire skills and the discipline required in industrial work settings. The refuge system laid the foundation of a separate juvenile justice system by introducing educational and vocational training, conditional release, and growing state intervention in the welfare of children.

In addition to the changing perception of childhood, the changes in urban economic structure and the development of middle-class sensibilities also contributed to the emergence of juvenile delinquency as a distinct social phenomenon in the 19th century. As the practice of apprenticeship declined in the late 18th and early 19th centuries, urban residents began to discover a large number of idle youths roaming the streets. Before full economic industrialization, there were not many light manufacturing jobs available for youths. Thus, before the expansion of public schooling, a large number of urban youths had no place to go, either at work for wages or in school. Urban middle-class residents became increasingly concerned with the problem of idle youths in the streets. The middle class developed a distinct class identity in which children develop their moral and intellectual abilities at home and school, secluded from the evils of the outside world. Prompted by the fear of violence and crime caused by delinquent youths in the streets, middle-class reformers began to criminalize children who roamed the streets, launched campaigns for public schooling, and called for the establishment of special institutions and methods to handle children in the streets.

The early 20th century witnessed the development of a new legal system that exclusively dealt with this juvenile delinquency. The Illinois Juvenile Court Act of 1899 established the Juvenile Court of Cook County, the first court for juvenile delinquents in the United States. The juvenile justice system of Illinois served as a model for other states. Based on the principle of *parens patriae,* the juvenile court intervened in family affairs and removed delinquent and dependent children from their parents' home. The primary purpose of the juvenile court was to rehabilitate juvenile offenders and prevent them from committing more illegal behavior, rather than to determine if they were guilty or innocent. Because, unlike adult offenders, juvenile offenders did not need to protect themselves against the state, juvenile court procedures were not considered adversarial. Social workers, probation officers, and psychiatrists worked with the judge to promote the best interests of the child. However, while delinquent children were provided with special care in the juvenile court, they were deprived of the constitutional rights given to adult offenders in the criminal court, including the right to counsel, the right to confront and cross-examine witnesses, and the protection against self-incrimination.

Most juvenile courts defined the notion of delinquency in highly gendered ways. Male delinquent youths were arrested for assault and theft whereas female counterparts were generally arrested for immoral sexual behavior that deviated from marital reproductive sex. The juvenile court also punished delinquent girls and boys in different ways. Female moral reformers of the Progressive Era called on the juvenile justice system to appoint female judges, police officers, and probation officers to protect young women from sexual discrimination. Female officials exercised control over delinquent girls, most of whom were charged with illicit sexual behavior. Whereas male officials were generally lenient with delinquent boys charged with sexual offenses, female officials inflicted a far more severe punishment on girls arrested for moral offenses. The juvenile court tended to separate delinquent girls from their families and commit them to reformatory institutions. As a result, the juvenile justice system exercised a great control over working-class families through regulating sexual behavior of young women.

Beginning in the 1960s, the juvenile justice system came under severe criticism. Treatment of juvenile delinquents underwent several changes after a series of U.S. Supreme Court decisions pertaining to due process protections in the juvenile court. In the case of *In re Gault* (1967), the Supreme Court considered the question of due process rights of juvenile offenders. The Court found that Gerald Francis Gault had been unconstitutionally placed in an institution for a longer period than adult offenders who commit the same crime because he was denied due process protections. The Court negated the conventional idea that juvenile offenders were protected in juvenile courts by judges who considered the best interests of juveniles in a nonadversarial setting. Contrary to the tradition of *parens patriae,* the Supreme Court ruled that juvenile offenders have due process rights: to be advised of the specific nature of the charges brought against them, to be advised of the right to counsel, to be protected against self-incrimination, and to confront and cross-examine witnesses.

The federal government began to exercise greater control over the juvenile justice system in the 1970s. Congress passed the Juvenile Justice and Delinquency Prevention Act of 1974, which encouraged states to keep juvenile offenders separate from adult offenders and to abandon the practice of institutionalizing status offenders, for instance, those who are charged with running away from home and playing truant. Congress also provided a substantial amount of grant money to states so that they would remove status offenders and other youths charged with minor offenses from the juvenile court jurisdiction and promote community-based treatment that does not rely on incarceration. As a result, juvenile courts started to define the notion of juvenile delinquency far more narrowly than before. The juvenile justice system shifted its attention from preventing juvenile delinquency by attending to status offenders to punishing more violent juvenile offenders. In the 1980s and 1990s, juvenile court procedures became more formal and punitive under pressure from popular perceptions of an increase in violent crimes committed by juvenile offenders. Juvenile courts have established new methods to deal with juvenile offenders charged with violent crimes, such as transferring serious juvenile offenders to the adult criminal justice system and incarcerating them in adult prisons and jails.

—*Chiori Goto*

See also Criminal Justice System

Further Readings and References

Bernard, T. J. (1992). *The cycle of juvenile justice.* New York: Oxford University Press.

Binder, A., Geis, G., & Bruce, D. D. (2001). *Juvenile delinquency: Historical, cultural, and legal perspectives* (3rd ed.). Cincinnati, OH: Anderson.

Odem, M. E. (1995). *Delinquent daughters: Protecting and policing adolescent female sexuality in the United States, 1885–1920.* Berkeley: University of California Press.

Sutton, J. (1988). *Stubborn children: Controlling delinquency in the United States, 1640–1981.* Berkeley: University of California Press.

KAHN, LOUIS I.

Louis I. Kahn (1901–1974) is considered one of the great architects of the 20th century due to his influence as an educator, mentor, philosopher, and practitioner in the field of modern architecture. Although he is simultaneously associated with the Beaux-Arts movement of the early 20th century and the International Style of modernism in the mid-20th century, Kahn's importance stems from his ability to remain outside of any established school of architecture. Instead, Kahn insisted that he drew from ancient Greek and Roman architecture in order to restore a sense of civic monumentality to American architecture. At times, Kahn's work is associated with the architectural style known as Brutalism, in which buildings are formed with unadorned poured concrete and feature repetitive geometric patterns. Finally, it was the city itself, especially Philadelphia, from which Kahn drew his inspiration.

Born on the Baltic isle of Osel in Estonia in 1901, Kahn immigrated with his family to the United States in 1905. Settling in Philadelphia, Kahn attended Central High School and studied architecture at the University of Pennsylvania, where he was influenced by the teachings of Paul Cret, a noted architect of the Beaux-Arts school and one of the primary designers of Philadelphia's Benjamin Franklin Parkway. Upon graduation in 1924, Kahn was hired by the firm of John Molitor, architect for the city of Philadelphia. It was here Kahn worked on the design for the buildings of Philadelphia's 1926 Sesquicentennial Exhibition.

Throughout the late 1920s to late 1940s, Kahn worked on a variety of projects, including city planning, government buildings, synagogues, private residences, and public and group housing projects. In 1929, Kahn, working in the offices of Paul Cret, participated in the Folger Shakespeare Library project in Washington, D.C. In 1932, Kahn formed the Architectural Research Group (ARG) with Dominique Berninger in Philadelphia. While only lasting until 1934, this group of young Philadelphia architects formulated a progressive philosophy of architecture that broke with the Beaux-Arts style and looked to the new modernism of European architects. The ideas formulated by the ARG would carry over into Kahn's work with the Philadelphia City Planning Commission and for the Federal Public Housing Authority.

It was not, however, until later in life that Kahn earned his reputation as a great educator and leading architect on the international scene. In 1947, Kahn became a professor at Yale, going on to design the University's Art Gallery between 1951 and 1953. In the late 1950s, Kahn returned to his beloved Philadelphia, becoming a professor at the University of Pennsylvania. It was here that Kahn designed his first landmark building, the Alfred Newton Richards Medical Laboratories on the university's campus. It was at Penn that Kahn became known as a great educator and philosopher. His later works, from 1959 to his death in 1974, cemented his international reputation. These works include the Salk Institute for Biological Studies in La Jolla, California (1959–1966); Erdman Hall Dormitories, Bryn Mawr, Pennsylvania (1960–1965); Kimbell Art Museum, Fort Worth, Texas (1967–1972); and the Jatiyo Sangshad Bhaban (National Assembly Building), Dhaka, Bangladesh (1962–1974). In addition, Kahn's protégés include such prominent modern and postmodern architects as Robert Venturi and Moshe Safdie, extending his influence into the 21st century.

—*Robert Armstrong*

See also Architecture; Modernism and the City; Philadelphia, Pennsylvania

Further Readings and References

Brownlee, D. B. (1991). *Louis I. Kahn: In the realm of architecture.* New York: Rizzoli.

Cooperman, E. T. (2003). *Louis I. Kahn.* Retrieved May 18, 2006, from http://www.philadelphiabuildings.org

Scully, V., Jr. (1962). *Louis I. Kahn.* New York: George Braziller.

KANSAS CITY, MISSOURI

Kansas City was established as a trading post in 1821 and grew as a center of commercial activity during the middle of the century. During the Civil War, the Kansas and Missouri state line that bisects the Kansas City metropolitan area was a front of intense warfare between proslavery and antislavery groups. The proslavery forces in Missouri, called the "bushwhackers," sought to impose slavery on Kansas through coercion and ballot stuffing. On the Kansas side, freestate proponents, the "Jayhawkers," sought admission of the state to the Union, with slavery prohibited. In the century after the Civil War, the city experienced much population growth and became known as a prosperous manufacturing center within the industrial heartland. Today, Kansas City ranks as an economically declining central city surrounded by sprawling affluent suburbs.

The coming of the industrial revolution established Kansas City as an agricultural processing and transportation center during the latter half of the 19th century. Plankington & Armour opened its meatpacking plant in 1870. By the turn of the century, several large meatpacking houses had located to the city, employing 20,000 workers and directly supporting one fourth of the metropolitan population. The development of seven midwestern railroads and the opening of the Union Station railroad depot in 1914 spearheaded the development of the city as an important site of cattle shipping. Up until the Second World War, the Kansas City stockyards ranked second to Chicago as the busiest meatpacking area in the world. During the late 19th and early 20th centuries, the city experienced tremendous growth in population, from 32,260 people in 1870 to 248,381 by 1910. By 1930, the city's population was 399,746, an increase of more than 151,000 people in two decades.

The growth of the industrial economy also entailed a reorganization of city government functions and changes in class relations. Land annexations in 1873, 1885, 1897, and 1909 increased the city's size to approximately 60 square miles. A building code was enacted in 1880 to control the plethora of emerging industrial and residential land uses and building construction. The Kansas City Real Estate Board was created in 1900 and the Kansas City Stock Exchange was reorganized later that year. In 1880, almost none of Kansas City's 89 miles of roads were paved. Two decades later, in 1900, electric streetcars were the dominant mode of transportation for urban workers in Kansas City. Biracial labor organizing and major industrial strikes punctuated the city, including the construction and building trades strike in 1899; the meatpackers' strikes in 1904, 1917, and 1918; the soap manufacture and railroad strikes in 1917; and the first sit-down strike against an automaker (General Motors) in 1936.

In the decades before 1940, the Kansas City, Missouri, city government was run by the political machine of Boss Thomas J. Pendergast. Pendergast entered politics in 1915 and spent the next two decades expanding and consolidating his power over city politics. By the early 1930s, Pendergast had almost complete political control over the city and the Democratic Party in Missouri due to the large blocks of votes he could deliver at election time which could make or break candidates seeking office. Pendergast's privileged position in the party also earned him considerable respect from national party leaders, such as Franklin Delano Roosevelt, who after his inauguration in 1933 granted the machine boss complete control over all New Deal federal programs in Missouri. Generous federal grants through the New Deal programs paid the construction costs for a courthouse, a police station, a city hall, a municipal auditorium, a convention center, and a baseball stadium. By the early 1930s, Pendergast's power over local and state politics had become so influential that journalists and politicians infamously referred to Kansas City, Missouri, as "Tom's Town." Pendergast's fall from power began after it was revealed that many of the machine's votes in the 1934 local elections came from "ghosts," voters whose names appeared on cemetery headstones and vacant lots. Investigative reports in 1938 and 1939 found widespread financial mismanagement, embezzlement, and fraud. In April 1939, Pendergast's indictment for tax evasion ended his multidecade rule over local politics.

The years before and after the Second World War were ambivalent times for Kansas City, Missouri. On the one hand, World War II investment stimulated the local economy and the city acquired a national reputation as an aesthetically pleasing and well-planned community, largely through the work done by the J. C. Nichols Company, a major real estate and residential development company. On the other hand, federal urban renewal and highway building, in the 1950s and later, uprooted thousands of residents living in the downtown area, transforming their residential neighborhoods into industrial and commercial land uses. From 1947 to 1950 over 228 miles of city streets were resurfaced, and by 1957 all streetcars had been removed to make way for the dominance of automobile transportation. Despite land annexations in the 1950s and 1960s that extended the city's area to 316 square miles, by the 1960s, the city was losing population and business to the burgeoning suburbs. The city's white population dropped by more than 72,300 in the two decades after 1950, from 400,940 in 1950 to 328,550 by 1970. At the same time, the size of Kansas City, Missouri's African American population increased dramatically, from 55,682 in 1950 (12.2 percent of the city's total population) to 83,130 in 1960 (17.5 percent of the total population) and 112,120 by 1970 (22.1 percent of total population). This population increase represented a 49.3 percent increase between 1950 and 1960 and a 74.1 percent increase between 1960 and 1970. Like other cities in the Midwest and Northeast, Kansas City's neighborhoods and schools went from predominantly white to almost entirely black, a transformation that was reinforced by real estate blockbusting and school segregation.

Racial conflicts and struggles marked local politics in the 1970s and 1980s, setting the stage for a protracted and bitter controversy over the problem of school desegregation. During this time, several controversial lawsuits were initiated to compel the state of Missouri and the Kansas City, Missouri School District (KCMSD) to desegregate city schools. In 1984, the U.S. District Court found that a segregated school system still existed in Kansas City and ordered the KCMSD and the state of Missouri to pay the costs of desegregating the schools. Based on the 1984 district court decision, Kansas City's school desegregation efforts focused upon rebuilding the urban schools and developing a comprehensive magnet school plan designed to attract suburban white students to the city school district within a system of controlled choice. By February 1996, $1.7 billion had been spent by the school district and the state of Missouri to rebuild the district's crumbling schools, a process that in less than a decade brought a dramatic facelift to inner city schools surrounded by poverty and deteriorating neighborhoods. In June 1995, the U.S. Supreme Court ruled 5–4 that the district court had no authority to order expenditures for the purpose of attracting suburban whites. In November 1999, the U.S. District Court dismissed the school desegregation lawsuit. In October 2000, the state of Missouri revoked the district's accreditation and effectively ended the state's responsibility for paying the costs of desegregation, a development that is sending ripple effects throughout the nation, as other cities move to undo mandatory court-ordered school desegregation.

Since the 1980s, Kansas City has faced persistent racial segregation in schools and housing, fiscal crisis and white flight, and a decline in manufacturing jobs and a shift to a service sector economy. The city's population peaked in 1970 at 507,330 and is now at 441,545, with African Americans making up 31.2 percent of the population. While indices of racial residential segregation for the city and metropolitan area have declined in recent decades, Kansas City continues to be one of the most segregated metropolitan areas in the nation, a situation that is reinforced by continuing suburbanization and inner city disinvestment. Locked into a jurisdictionally competitive economic battle with its suburban neighbors, Kansas City, Missouri, is increasingly forced to use lucrative tax abatements to attract private investment and develop new sources of revenue. The political fragmentation of the metropolitan area militates against the formation of regional planning initiatives and coordination and portends a future of racial and class conflict for the city and region.

—*Kevin Fox Gotham*

Further Readings and References

Glaab, C. N. (1993). *Kansas City and the railroads: Community policy in the growth of a regional metropolis.* Lawrence: University Press of Kansas.

Gotham, K. F. (2002). *Race, real estate, and uneven development: The Kansas City experience, 1900–2000.* Albany, NY: State University of New York Press.

Schirmer, S. L. (2002). *A city divided: The racial landscape of Kansas City, 1900–1960.* Columbia, MO: University of Missouri Press.

Worley, W. S. (1990). *J.C. Nichols and the shaping of Kansas City: Innovation in planned residential communities.* Columbia, MO: University of Missouri Press.

KELLEY, FLORENCE

Florence Kelley (1859–1932), a major force in American social reform, spent her adult life crusading for protective labor legislation for America's women and children, fighting for maternal and child health services, and implementing industrial reform through consumer activism.

Born in Philadelphia to a long line of progressives, Florence Molthrop Kelley was the third of eight children and the daughter of United States congressman William D. Kelley. She was educated at Quaker schools in Philadelphia and at Cornell University, which began admitting women in 1874, and from which she graduated in 1882. In 1883, Kelley began graduate studies at the University of Zurich in Switzerland, at which time she became a follower of Karl Marx and Friedrich Engels and joined the Socialist Party of Zurich. In 1884, Kelley married a fellow student, the Russian socialist Lazare Wischnewetzky. Their first child, Nicholas, was born in 1885, followed by a daughter, Margaret, in 1886, and a son, John, in 1888. Kelley divorced her husband in 1891.

When Kelley and her family returned to the United States in 1886, they settled in New York City, a city in the throes of economic conflict and political upheaval. Kelley was poised to play a significant role in the radical circles of the city. Her first step was translating Engels's *The Conditions of the Working Class in England,* which was published in the United States in 1887. After 5 years in New York, throughout which Kelley continued to translate and publish socialist pamphlets and prefaces, she left her husband and moved with her children to Chicago.

When she arrived in Chicago in 1891, Kelley joined fellow reformers at the Hull-House social settlement, and she lived there until 1899. In 1893, Kelley was recruited by the governor of Illinois to be the state's first chief factory inspector. The next year she achieved her first legislative success: a state law that limited the workday of women and children to a maximum of 8 hours. The law was repealed in 1895.

In 1899, Kelley moved to New York City where she became the first director of the newly formed National Consumers' League (NCL), a radical pressure group which fought for the manufacture of quality products in healthy working conditions and to be sold at fair prices. She implemented the NCL White Label for products which met the organization's fair labor practices.

Kelley also supported women's suffrage and African American civil rights, and she helped establish the National Association for the Advancement of Colored People (NAACP) in 1909. After the turn of the century, she became a regular speaker on college campuses and published books such as *Modern Industry in Relation to the Family* (1914) and *The Supreme Court and Minimum Wage Legislation* (1925). She wrote her autobiography in 1927 and died in 1932.

—*Elif S. Armbruster*

See also Addams, Jane; Hull-House; National Association for the Advancement of Colored People

Further Readings and References

Blumberg, D. R. (1966). *Florence Kelley: The making of a social pioneer.* New York: Augustus M. Kelley.

Sklar, K. K. (1995). *Florence Kelley and the nation's work.* New Haven, CT: Yale University Press.

KENNA, MICHAEL "HINKY DINK"

For politics of the 19th century, patronage was often the rule of the day. One could influence the political landscape by knowing the right people. In Chicago, the most powerful ward was the First Ward, home to both the elite of Chicago industry along Prairie Avenue and the bordellos and gambling houses of the South Levee district. If someone needed a favor in the First Ward, then Michael "Hinky Dink" Kenna and John "Bathhouse" Coughlin were the men to see.

Michael "Hinky Dink" Kenna was born in 1857 in Chicago. He quickly developed a reputation among the Irish of Bridgeport as a pugnacious go-getter. With his small frame and dour expressions, he was the physical opposite of his political partner Coughlin, who was the more boisterous of the two. They were commonly known as the Lords of the Levee, as they controlled all aspects of vice in the First Ward. They were also known as the controllers of "boodle" in the area. Boodle was a type of political power that came from informal arrangements between various groups in Chicago. For example, Kenna and Coughlin used their influence to oppose the streetcar monopoly proposed by Charles Yerkses. In exchange for their opposition to the streetcar system, Mayor Carter Harrison II turned a blind eye to certain criminal activities in the First Ward.

Kenna and Coughlin used boodle to keep an effective hold on the First Ward. The most contentious aspect of life in Chicago dealt with political alliances. For Mayor Harrison, boodle was a necessity—it was what allowed him to win re-election. To obtain the votes needed to win, Harrison had to see Kenna and Coughlin. They took care of the locals by providing food and drinks to the masses (and even drugs and prostitutes when the need arose). In return for the political support and turnout of the voters, Harrison continued to allow the illicit activities carried out in the First Ward.

Every year, the Lords of the Levee sponsored the First Ward Ball, in which the high elements of Chicago and the crime lords openly hobnobbed. The balls were events of great fanfare and copious debauchery. Waiters paid $5 just to be hired at a ball, but they made back many times that in tips throughout the evening.

The end of Kenna's political career was gradual. The changes brought about by the onset of World War I and the temperance movement in Chicago, and later the entire United States, were accompanied by changes in those who held the power in the First Ward. Kenna felt himself slowly isolated by the new mayor, "Big Bill" Thompson, and the successor to Italian crime boss Big Jim Colosimo. The new lord of the Italian mob in the First Ward, Al Capone, politely asked Kenna to step aside, and he did. Kenna spent the remainder of his life living in the Lexington Hotel. When he died in 1946, he had amassed a fortune of over $1 million. He asked that $90,000 be used for a massive mausoleum for his interment. His family, perhaps seeking an end to his notoriety, as well as his money, buried him with a simple marker.

—Cord Scott

Further Readings and References

Lindberg, R. (1996). *Chicago by gaslight.* Chicago: Chicago Academy Press.
Lindberg, R. (1999). *Return to the scene of the crime.* Nashville, TN: Cumberland Press.
Miller, D. (1996). *City of the century.* New York: Simon & Schuster.

KENNEDY ADMINISTRATION: URBAN POLICY

In the presidential election of 1960, Democratic candidate John F. Kennedy promised New Frontier policies aimed at stirring the domestic agenda after 8 years of Republican control of the White House. Urban votes were an important part of Kennedy's razor-thin victory over Vice President and Republican nominee Richard Nixon. Liberals were anxious to enact policy ideas incubated in the Senate in the late 1950s. While urban voters were a critically important part of Kennedy's electoral coalition, urban interest groups were just one of many competing factions within his governing coalition. Important housing and public works legislation aimed at urban areas passed during Kennedy's tenure in office, but big-city mayors and urban liberals in Congress were disappointed with the Kennedy administration's efforts. Kennedy's most disappointing failure in this regard was his failure to elevate urban interests to cabinet status as he had promised in his 1960 campaign. Powerful Southern and rural factions in Congress successfully watered down the "urban only" policies that the administration had created to contend with the problems of the increasingly urbanized nation.

The Politics of Urban Policy in the Kennedy Years

President Kennedy came to power after 8 years of President Eisenhower's "Modern Republicanism," a philosophy committed to limiting the fiscal and programmatic commitments of the New Deal, as well as forging collaborative ties with business as an alternative to big government. President Eisenhower negotiated with Republicans and centrist Democrats to restrain government spending. In terms of urban policy, President Eisenhower accommodated the "bricks and mortar" interests of mayors and urban businesses with federal aid for airports and highways. Eisenhower favored urban policies that emphasized economic development over aid to the urban poor. The Housing Act of 1954 reoriented the federal role in shaping the physical city to support of the urban renewal of commercial districts at the expense of the construction of public housing.

The direction of 1950s federal urban policy was a source of great frustration to liberal members of Congress, particularly those members identified with urban constituencies. In the U.S. Senate, for example, former Philadelphia mayor Joseph Clark (D-PA), Chicagoan Paul Douglass (D-IL), former Minneapolis Mayor Hubert Humphrey (D-MN), and New Yorker Jacob Javits (R-NY), among others, were inpatient with the logrolling practices of the Senate Majority Leader, Lyndon Johnson, who made common cause with the Southerners in the Senate who were more conservative and rural in orientation than their Northern and Midwestern colleagues. The frustration of urban interests was even more pronounced in the House of Representatives. In the era before the full implementation of the Supreme Court's order to states to reapportion legislatures according to population, not counties (in *Baker v. Carr* in 1962), rural-dominated state legislatures drew congressional lines to the advantage of rural voting blocs. Southern rural interests dominated critically important chairmanships too. Urban liberals in Washington were anxious to deliver new federal programs to the cities at the opening of the Kennedy administration in 1961.

As a senator from Massachusetts and a Bostonian, Kennedy had been part of the group of Senate urban liberals, and he was interested in delivering programs for the urban bloc of voters that had delivered for him in the close election of 1960. However, while urban interests had an ally in the White House, the structural constraints they faced in Congress had not lifted. The president's plans to expand federal urban policy were frustrated by Congress throughout his nearly 3 years in office.

Housing Policy

In his first State of the Union address, Kennedy called for an omnibus housing bill that included $2.5 billion for urban renewal and authorization of 100,000 new units of public housing. While Kennedy's 1961 Housing Act passed by a narrow margin, urban renewal was allocated only $2 billion, and Congress diluted the intended impact on cities by spreading the funding to smaller communities. Conservative congressional appropriations committees further frustrated the Kennedy administration's plans by not releasing funds to local development agencies to build in a timely fashion. The rate of construction of public housing remained flat in the transition from the Eisenhower to the Kennedy years. The National Housing Conference, a liberal housing advocacy group, was moved to complain that the administration's housing programs were deficient because Kennedy was not prodding Congress or state and local governments to meet the targets of the authorizing legislation. While urban renewal projects moved forward, federally sponsored public housing projects stalled in the face of local community opposition. Only 72,000 units of low-income housing were constructed in the 3 years of the Kennedy administration (1961 to 1963), a number below congressional targets and not that much different from the Eisenhower record. Still, Kennedy's housing bill was the most ambitious effort on the part of the federal government in urban affairs since the Housing Act of 1949.

One of the more notable features of the Housing Act of 1961 was the authorization of federal financing for urban mass transit to subsidize commuter rail lines in and out of big cities. Federal funding for commuter trains had been a pet project of the U.S. Senators with constituents in the metropolitan areas of New York and Philadelphia in the wake of the collapse of privately held commuter lines operated by big railroad firms. While the small group of Democratic senators had little luck convincing Eisenhower's budget experts to support their plan, they were able to convince the Kennedy administration to accept the measure.

In 1963, housing advocacy groups led by the National Housing Conference, and joined by the U.S. Conference of Mayors and other municipal groups, grew increasingly frustrated that the administration was ignoring the urban agenda. The urban coalition lobbied the White House to hold a conference on housing and community development to direct national attention to their issues. While the White House initially approved plans for the conference, support was withdrawn after the massive civil rights march on Washington in August 1963. The Kennedy administration feared giving liberals a platform for local demonstrations.

Area Redevelopment
and Full-Employment Programs

The greatest successes for proponents of federal urban policy in the Kennedy years were "area redevelopment" initiatives, polices that were not explicitly billed as big-city programs but that enjoyed the widespread approval of big-city mayors nonetheless and were designed to be sufficiently expansive to include nonurban interests. Despite the efforts of urban liberals such as Senators Clark and Douglass to target aid to distressed workers in the 1950s, President Eisenhower dismissed proposed stimulus plans as wasted effort and vetoed several congressional bills that sought to provide aid to distressed cities and regions.

Unemployment was an important Kennedy issue in the 1960 presidential campaign, and he was eager to establish a record of accomplishment. Kennedy's public works stimulus consisted of four major legislative initiatives, namely, the Area Redevelopment Act, the Public Works Acceleration Act, the Manpower Development Training Act, and the Community Facilities Act. The Area Redevelopment Act was administered by the Area Redevelopment Administration (ARA) in the Commerce Department and was responsible for overseeing much of the new spending. It lasted 4 years—until it was scuttled amid complaints from conservatives that the aid was wasted. While the work of the ARA did not meet initial expectations, the agency did pump $843 million into the economy between 1962 and 1963 through Kennedy's accelerated public works program. The grants and loans provided to municipalities by the ARA built sewer systems, libraries, and other public facilities. But the accommodation of both rural and urban interests required by Congress stripped Kennedy's public works and stimulus programs of any programmatic direction. Logrolling between members of Congress overshadowed the ARA's attempts to provide for efficiency, direction, and prioritization of federal spending. Conservatives successfully turned off the federal spigot for targeted public works by late 1963. The Manpower Development Training program, however, persisted until the mid-1970s as the federal government's major job training program.

Precursor to the Great Society

Perhaps the Kennedy administration's most imaginative and far-reaching urban policies related to its protean efforts to contend with urban social problems. Since the New Deal, mayors, members of Congress from urban districts, and the urban intergovernmental lobby had been quite familiar with federal intervention in urban politics in the form of the "bricks and mortar" approach. Amid increasing attention focused on the plight of the urban poor and the urban young in the wake of the publication of Michael Harrington's *The Other America,* the Kennedy administration began exploring the possibilities of a federal role in provision of social services in urban areas. This work would frame President Lyndon Johnson's Great Society and War on Poverty efforts a few years later.

President Kennedy's Committee on Juvenile Delinquency, lodged in the Justice Department, was Attorney General Robert Kennedy's pet project. The committee, under the influence of leading social workers, sociologists, and reformers, introduced the concept of *community pathology* to the federal government. The causes of delinquency, many on the committee argued, were rooted in the lack of opportunities offered the young in poor, urban communities. Rejecting traditional approaches that focused on providing economic opportunity through the provision of "bricks and mortar," the committee stressed the coordination of public and private social services in urban neighborhoods. They proposed the concept of *community action* to solve the problem of urban pathology. Although the term was vaguely defined, the idea of community action was that the poor should be empowered to run the federal programs that operated in their communities. This process of constructive engagement, the committee reasoned, would end the societal alienation of the perennially poor. The idea of community action later took root in Johnson's War on Poverty in the form of Community Action Agencies throughout urban America that coordinated and dispersed federal funds (often over the objections of big-city mayors).

A Department for
Urban Interests

The biggest frustration for advocates of national urban policy during the Kennedy years came from the failure to create a cabinet-level department for urban affairs. Since the Progressive Era, the idea existed that a federal department should be created to provide a clearinghouse for municipal information. In the New Deal, public administration expert Charles Merriam proposed the creation of a Department of Urbanism. Throughout the 1950s, members in both Houses introduced legislation to create a new urban department, but the plans where never seriously engaged by Washington leaders. Urban liberals and big-city mayors hoped that Kennedy and the Democratic Congress would deliver this benefit to the cities. Most notably, Chicago Mayor Richard M. Daley lobbied to include a promise of cabinet-level status as a plank in the Democratic Party platform in 1960. Kennedy took the matter seriously enough to add this issue to the docket of his important and busy chief aide, Theodore Sorenson.

Kennedy sought to elevate the Housing and Home Finance Agency (HHFA), the entity largely responsible for federal housing policy—an issue of central concern to the cities—to cabinet status, and then shift urban programs from other departments to HHFA. President Kennedy's plan was frustrated because HHFA's constituency groups feared change. Under the HHFA umbrella rested the Federal Housing Agency (FHA) and the Federal National Mortgage Association (FNMA); these organizations operated independently of the HHFA and formed tight relationships with their constituencies. The banking and financial community was particularly fearful of a liberal turn from the new department that would disrupt their cozy relationship with FNMA. Content with the status quo, bankers and builders opposed cabinet elevation of the HHFA, fearful that a powerful secretary might be created in the process. Rural interests in Congress also opposed cabinet status of the HHFA, as did some state governors who feared the thickening of direct federal-city ties that bypassed state governments.

When a plan for cabinet status for the HHFA stalled in Congress, President Kennedy took the aggressive step of enacting an executive reorganization by presidential order. He also announced that the HHFA director, Robert Weaver, an African American, would serve as secretary of the new department. However, Congress soon moved to override the president, 264–150 in the House and 58–42 in the Senate, thus dooming fulfillment of Kennedy's major promise to the cities. By issuing an executive order, and naming an African American as a potential cabinet secretary, Kennedy expanded the scope of conflict from the relatively narrow question of urban representation to the more contentious issue of constitutional separation of powers and the explosive issue of civil rights. With the terms of the fight clearly laid out, southern Democrats and Republicans found common ground to defeat the president's plan.

Thus, the failure to create a cabinet department for urban interests spoke to the broader frustrations of urban policy in the Kennedy administration. Despite the fact that the Democratic president had party majorities in both houses of Congress, his urban agenda was blocked because of more fundamental divisions within the Congress and the nation, namely, the divide between rural and urban interests, and more profoundly, the differences between racial conservatives and liberals. Evident in the Kennedy years—particularly in the fight over the HHFA and Robert Weaver—were the first stirrings within national politics of the equivalence of racial politics with urban politics, a phenomenon absent in the New Deal era, but a move that would define urban policy in the Great Society and after.

Kennedy's efforts to shape urban policy were often frustrated by Congress. The administration was rarely willing to expend all of its political capital on behalf of urban programs. While the administration was nominally committed to ambitious urban programs, its urban agenda competed against other administration priorities. The urban programs that did pass often were stymied in the implementation stage because of the political reality that the accommodation of rural interests often prevented the administration's efforts in cities from having the impact that urban advocates hoped to achieve with federal aid.

—*Richard Flanagan*

See also Daley, Richard J.; Federal Housing and Home Finance Agency; Johnson Administration: Urban Policy

Further Readings and References

Blumenthal, R. (1969). The bureaucracy: Antipoverty and the community action programs. In A. Sindler (Ed.), *American institutions and public policy: Five contemporary studies.* Boston: Little, Brown.

Connery, R., & Leach, R. (1960). *The federal government and metropolitan areas.* Cambridge, MA: Harvard University Press.

Flanagan, R. M. (1996). *Mayors and presidents: The rise and fall of national urban policy from the New Deal to the Great Society.* Unpublished doctoral dissertation, Rutgers University.

Harrington, M. (1997). *The other America.* New York: Scribner's. (Original work published 1962)

Keith, N. S. (1973). *Politics and the housing crisis since 1930.* New York: Universe Books.

Levitan, S. (1964). *Federal aid to depressed areas: An evaluation of the Area Redevelopment Administration.* Baltimore: Johns Hopkins University Press.

KERNER COMMISSION

In 1967, President Lyndon B. Johnson impaneled the Kerner Commission to examine the causes of urban race riots that plagued the nation during the 1960s. The commission's influential report was issued in the following year. It was the nation's first comprehensive examination of race relations in post–World War II America. For the first time, an official federal government document made a finding that racism existed and that it was a problem for society. The panel concluded that the nation was rapidly moving toward two separate societies, which were based on race and inherently unequal. Their report was read so widely that in April 1968 it was number two on *The New York Times* bestseller list for nonfiction.

During the mid-1960s, summer race riots erupted in many of the nation's cities, resulting in some of the worst racial disorders in American history. Between 1964 and 1968, according to one estimate, over 300 major riots occurred in over 200 cities across the country, resulting in numerous deaths, injuries, and arrests. Frustrations among inner city blacks experiencing high unemployment and poverty triggered unrest in many of the poorest neighborhoods in urban America. Some of the most serious racial disturbances occurred in the Watts section of Los Angeles in 1965, Chicago in 1966, Newark and Detroit in 1967, and Cleveland in 1968. The Detroit riot was one of the most violent and costly, resulting in over 40 deaths and property damage estimated in the tens of millions of dollars.

After the outbreak in Detroit, President Johnson, in late July 1967, issued Executive Order 11365, which established the National Advisory Commission on Civil Disorders. He appointed a panel of 11 members to investigate the causes of the recent urban racial unrest and to recommend ways to prevent it in the future. This group of political, civil rights, and corporate leaders came to be known informally as the Kerner Commission, named for Illinois Governor Otto Kerner, who chaired the group. New York City's Republican Mayor John V. Lindsay served as the vice chair. Other Kerner Commission members included Oklahoma's Democratic Senator Fred R. Harris; Representative William M. McCulloch, Republican from Ohio; California's Democratic Representative James C. Corman; I.W. Abel, President of the United Steelworkers of America; Charles B. Thornton, Board Chairman and Chief Executive Officer of Litton Industries; Katherine Graham Peden, Commissioner of Commerce for the State of Kentucky; and Herbert Jenkins, Police Chief of Atlanta. Only two of the panel members were black: Roy Wilkins, Executive Director of the National Association for the Advancement of Colored People, and Edward W. Brooke, a Republican senator from Massachusetts. Senator Brooke was the first black senator since Reconstruction, and at the time was the nation's only black senator.

On March 1, 1968, after a 7-month investigation in which the panel heard from numerous witnesses and experts, the Kerner Commission issued its report. Its basic conclusion was that the United States was racially divergent and that civil rights were anything but equal.

The commission blamed Whites for promoting racism, the major structural cause of the urban race riots, noting that racial prejudice not only had shaped American society but was now threatening its future. According to the panel, white racism had contributed to a combustible mixture in urban America that consisted of racial discrimination and segregation in employment, education, and housing; black inmigration and white exodus; and black ghettos where segregation and poverty all but guaranteed failure.

To address the causes for the disorders, the Kerner Commission's report called for a commitment to sustained national action on various fronts, including significant antipoverty efforts in the nation's urban ghettos. To that end, the panel supported major increases in federal spending for education and housing. They also called for a greater commitment to job creation in the public and private sectors, more emphasis on job training programs, and enhanced civil rights enforcement.

The panel believed that national action was imperative, even if a remedy meant enacting new taxes. Observing that the nation was moving toward two separate Americas, the panel feared that without action, the nation's racial problems would someday be too intractable to solve. According to the Kerner Commission, in a couple of decades the divisions would be so deep and pervasive that it would be impossible to unite a white population located in the suburbs, the smaller central cities, and the periphery of large central cities with blacks who were aggregated with large central cities. Such a permanently divided society would, in their view, invite sustained violence in America's cities and would repudiate traditional national ideals of equal opportunity, self-respect, and freedom.

—Dianne T. Thompson

Further Readings and References

Bayor, R. H. (Ed.). (2004). *The Columbia documentary history of race and ethnicity in America.* New York: Columbia University Press.

Boger, J. C. (2000). The Kerner Commission report in retrospect. In S. Steinberg (Ed.), *Race and ethnicity in the United States: Issues and debates* (pp. 8–36). Malden, MA: Blackwell.

Kerner Commission. (1968). *Report of the National Advisory Commission on Civil Disorders.* New York: Bantam Books.

Kurlansky, M. (2004). *1968: The year that rocked the world.* New York: Ballantine Books.

KEROUAC, JACK

Born in a French Canadian Catholic family in Lowell, Massachusetts, on March 12, 1922, Jean-Louis Lebris de Kerouac (1922–1969) spoke French before learning English in public school. Kerouac entered Columbia University in 1940 on a football scholarship, but when he broke his leg and left college, he discovered the Greenwich Village bohemian scene in New York City. After working as a sports reporter for the *Lowell Sun,* he joined the Merchant Marines (1942) and served briefly in the U.S. Navy.

After World War II, Kerouac led the nomadic existence recorded in his autobiographical 1957 novel, *On the Road.* It was written rapidly as "spontaneous prose," like all of his books and poetry, to record his restless trips hitchhiking and driving from New York to San Francisco with his companion Neal Cassady. *Dharma Bums* (1958), a more conventional novel, describes his search for self-fulfillment through Zen Buddhism. He also wrote poetry in *Mexico City Blues* (1959) and travel pieces in *Lonesome Traveler* (1960). Among his other works are *The Subterraneans* (1958), *Book of Dreams* (1961), and *Desolation Angels* (1965).

Kerouac's work popularized the term *Beat Generation* for the disaffected young Americans who dropped out of mainstream society. Kerouac and other Beats sought their identity and truth in an alternative lifestyle centered on alcohol, drugs, sex, music, travel, and Zen Buddhism. Kerouac often associated with the poets and writers Allen Ginsburg, William Burroughs, and Lawrence Ferlinghetti, as well as with many jazz musicians. Like him, they embraced the ecstatic moments of everyday life through spontaneity and free artistic expression. Kerouac's sequel to *On the Road, Big Sur* (1962), is about the Beats' retreat on the California coast.

In New York City and San Francisco, Jack Kerouac reached celebrity status as the leading voice for the Beat Generation. *On the Road,* his testament to the unconventional Beat lifestyle, is a major contribution to modern literature. It inspired the alternative beatnik movement and the later hippie counterculture. However, Kerouac was unsuited for fame or mainstream society, and he succumbed to excessive drinking. His athlete's body and dark good looks ravaged by alcoholism, Kerouac died on October 21, 1969, in St. Petersburg, Florida. Literary fans and bohemians still visit his grave in Lowell, and various sites in the city are preserved by the National Park Service in his memory. His posthumously published words include *Selected Letters, 1940–1956* (1995), *Selected Letters, 1957– 1969* (1999), and the poetry collection *Book of Blues* (1995).

—*Peter C. Holloran*

See also Youth Culture

Further Readings and References

Brinkley, D. (Ed.). (2004). *Windblown world: The journals of Jack Kerouac, 1947–1954.* New York: Viking.

Charters, A. (1987). *Kerouac: A biography.* New York: St. Martin's Press.

Clark, T. (1984). *Jack Kerouac.* San Diego: Harcourt Brace Jovanovich.

McNally, D. (1979). *Desolate angel: Jack Kerouac, the Beat Generation, and America.* New York: Random House.

KOCH, EDWARD IRVING

A three-term mayor and a consistently popular political figure, Edward Koch (1924-) took New York City out of the fiscal crises of the 1970s and into the economically expanding but socially contentious 1980s.

Growing up in the Bronx (where he was born in 1924) and in Newark, New Jersey, Koch attended the City College of New York before the World War II draft interrupted his studies. Following his discharge, he entered New York University's School of Law, and after graduation he became a practicing attorney. By the late 1950s he was well regarded among reformers in the Democratic Party, and in 1963 he defeated former Tammany boss Carmine DeSapio for district leadership in Greenwich Village. In 1968, following a city council stint, he was elected to the U.S. Congress, where he represented the 17th and 18th districts, respectively, until the mayoral contest of 1977.

Running on a platform of fiscal conservatism and social liberalism, he defeated incumbent mayor Abe Beame in the Democratic Primary of 1977 and went on to defeat Mario Cuomo in bitterly contested runoff and general elections. He began his term by building the broad, and often disparate, coalitions that became a staple of his administration, with business leaders, government reformers, Jews, working-class Catholics, and a small number of influential members of the Latino/a and African American communities all forming his base. He imposed fiscal discipline on New York City by adopting the Generally Accepted Accounting Principles in order to balance the budget and rooted out inefficiency in city agencies by threatening to embarrass publicly the leaders of the slowest performing outfits. He earned the enmity of unions by frequently battling the United Federation of Teachers over education reform and, most notably, by invoking New York State's Taylor Law in 1980 to end a strike by the city's transport workers.

The following year he won reelection in a landslide, running as the candidate of both the Democratic and Republican parties, although a subsequent gubernatorial run early in his second term ended with a primary loss to Mario Cuomo. In an effort to root out political patronage in the Criminal and Family Courts, he established the practice of having potential justices screened by an independent commission. Although he was a longtime supporter of the gay community, issuing orders prohibiting discrimination in the city based on sexual orientation and signing a gay rights bill in 1986, he also rankled this constituency by closing gay bathhouses. His third term in office was marred by a series of problems ranging from a citywide economic downturn and racial strife in the neighborhoods of Howard Beach and Bensonhurst to the corruption scandal and suicide of political supporter Donald Manes. His attempted election to a fourth term ended with a 1989 primary loss to David N. Dinkins, who went on to defeat Rudolph W. Giuliani in the general election.

Despite building a fairly conservative base in a liberal city, Koch has enjoyed popularity among many New Yorkers. Supporters in the public and among newspaper and magazine editorial boards have enjoyed his distinctive personality, which was highlighted by his campaign catchphrase, "How'm I doing?" Critics, however, have found his candor to border on the excessive and have charged him with overlooking the concerns of racial and ethnic minorities. Since leaving office he has authored autobiographical and children's books and frequently appeared as a television commentator.

—*Nicholas Anastasakos*

See also Dinkins, David N.; New York, New York

Further Readings and References

Mollenkopf, J. (1992). *A phoenix in the ashes: The rise and fall of the Koch coalition in New York City politics.* Princeton, NJ: Princeton University Press.

KU KLUX KLAN

Though several groups have used the name Ku Klux Klan in American history, none has had the national appeal of the second Klan. Formed in the second decade of the 20th century, at a time in which a new America—defined by urbanization, industrialization, and immigration—was emerging, the hooded order's rebirth corresponded to a wave of nationalism, nativism, and religious fervor. Claiming to be the voice for all "100 percent" Americans, the Klan found that by the mid-1920s, millions of men and women had joined its ranks. And yet, by the end of the decade, the group had all but disappeared. The fall of the Klan came when its members discovered that the new America really was not as threatening as they had first believed and when corruption at the top cast doubts on the purity of the Klan's crusade.

The second Klan has been one of the most debated organizations in American history. The scholars who wrote at the time of the Klan's rebirth wanted to label it a *rural* (often a code word for unsophisticated) phenomenon that was resisting the new urban reality of American life. Studies since the 1960s, however, have tended to discredit this assertion. The second Klan was popular in both rural and urban communities of all sizes, with a membership that was largely middle class.

The Klan claimed to stand for Protestantism, Patriotism, and Prohibition, all of which were popular themes, and all of which had other defenders and proponents in the wider American society. Indeed, the Klan pioneered very little when it came to rhetoric, but largely adapted for its own purposes ideas and issues that had long been a part of the American civic discourse. Its innovation was to portray itself as an active defender of American culture. The Klan further capitalized on these ideas by creating women's chapters, and in some areas of the country, "junior Klans" for children. All told, the Klan portrayed itself not just as defending family values but also as being family-friendly.

However, the second Klan's hallmarks were racism—especially antiblack racism—and religious persecution, directed especially at Catholicism and Semites. Cross burning, lynching, and other orchestrated violence against its foes were some of the Klan's most visible tactics.

The secret to the Klan's appeal came in its packaging. While it originated in the South, where the first Klan had been formed during Reconstruction and was deeply concerned with oppressing African Americans who challenged the color line, its success nationally came by tapping into the fears, pride, and routine of white, native-born, American Protestants. The second Klan was able to portray itself as the defender of traditional values against Catholic immigrants, without threatening mainline Protestant churches. Wrapping itself in the flag—during a time of heightened patriotism, thanks to World War I—the Klan was able to claim to be pro-America without having to explain what that meant. Furthermore, the Klan positioned itself as yet another fraternal lodge or secret society during a period in which Americans were joining such organizations in droves.

The Klan spread its message by using all the tools of modern America. It made movies and made news (using newspapers it owned) to get its message across. Klan leaders had a great sense of drama and knew how to play to crowds. They especially loved to use parades and public speaking events to attract attention to both the group and its message. Such activities promoted a spirit of community at a time when many Americans worried that civic identity was being lost.

That the Klan was successful in urban areas should not be surprising. It was not, after all, just immigrants who were flocking to American cities. Native-born Americans were also seeking jobs in urban industrial areas. What they saw often shocked and concerned

them. America did seem to be changing, and not always for the better. Living conditions in urban ghettos were often bad. Working conditions in factories were sometimes little better. The unity of the American people seemed to be challenged. And here was the Klan, offering to get involved, to be the people's voice, to defend their values, and to clean up the mess of urban life.

The Klan found its greatest success in small and mid-size cities where these dangers could be dealt with most easily, and where opposition was small. In short, the Klan was strongest where there was more a perception of a threat than where the dangers (as defined by the Klan) actually were. Thus, places such as Indianapolis were more apt to have a strong Klan movement than someplace like Chicago, despite the fact that Klan membership was high in both Indiana and Illinois. In fact, the hooded order's membership was greater in the Midwest than in any other region of the country.

While the Klan adopted much of its rhetoric from mainstream groups that had been talking about reforms for decades, it also duplicated the machine politics of urban areas. In part, this had to do with the Klan, especially in the North, being a political action group. And yet, even with voter slates, candidate forums, civic pride, and peer pressure all helping insure that members of the Klan went to the polls in large numbers, Klan-backed candidates often came from the local or state dominant party (and thus were often assured of victory, with or without a Klan endorsement). It also should be noted that the Klan was largely inept at translating getting its members to the polls into getting legislation out of newly elected politicians.

But while urban realities gave the Klan ammunition for its cause, those same urban realities worked to destroy it. Immigrant groups and the Catholic Church organized to fight it. In addition, not all Protestants joined the organization, and among those who did join, there was apathy when they came to believe that the situation in America was not as bad as the Klan's rhetoric implied. Electoral victories at the local, state, and national levels only reinforced the notion that real Americans were in control. Success bred tension between the Northern and Southern wings of the Klan, and there was a good deal of corruption within the organization as well. Klan scandals occurred across the country, which caused members to quit in droves. All these factors helped destroy the 1920s Klan. And while the Klan name would be used again later in the 20th century, neither its Civil Rights Era or modern incarnations has recaptured the popularity of the second Klan. Although the rise of David Duke—elected the Klan's Grand Wizard in 1974—to the Louisiana State Legislature in 1989 reestablished the Klan's profile in the late 20th century, the Klan's membership is thought to be in the low thousands in the early 21st century.

—Jason S. Lantzer

See also Race Riots; Racial Zoning

Further Readings and References

Blee, K. M. (1991). *Women of the Klan.* Berkeley, CA: University of California Press.

Chalmers, D. M. (1987). *Hooded Americanism.* Durham, NC: Duke University Press.

Jackson, K. T. (1992). *The Ku Klux Klan in the city, 1915–1930.* Chicago: Ivan R. Dee.

Lutholtz, M. W. (1993). *Grand Dragon.* West Lafayette, IN: Purdue University.

Moore, L. J. (1991). *Citizen Klansmen.* Chapel Hill, NC: University of North Carolina Press.

La Guardia, Fiorello

Born in lower Manhattan to immigrant parents, Fiorello La Guardia (1882–1947) was raised on the open plains of the American West, becoming in 1916 the first Republican since the Civil War to represent New York's 14th congressional district. When the United States entered World War I, Congressman La Guardia enlisted in the army, ultimately earning the rank of major.

Following the war, La Guardia returned to Congress, only to suffer the tragic death of his baby daughter and then his wife from the disease of the tenements, tuberculosis. He poured his energies into a progressive urban agenda, demanding attention for the poor, the exploited, and the unemployed, lashing out at monopolies, racist immigration laws, and Prohibition while campaigning for a wide array of social assistance legislation. His program finally won wide attention with the coming of the 1930s Depression, but he was swept from office with the Roosevelt landslide in 1932. As a lame duck, he helped lay the legislative groundwork for the New Deal.

La Guardia is considered by many to be the father of modern New York City. He won the 1933 mayoral election, and when he took office on January 1, 1934, for the first of his three terms, La Guardia took over a bankrupt and corrupt city that lacked a coherent municipal vision. Before La Guardia, the metropolis was a congeries of antiquated boroughs, divided into political fiefdoms, a city haphazardly administered, with parsimonious social and health services, no public housing, decaying parks, and rusting bridges. It was a city mired in graft. La Guardia brought into office outstanding experts, appointed for their skills rather than their political affiliation, and with them built a new New York, throwing new bridges over the waters and digging tunnels under them, erecting new reservoirs, sewer systems, parks, highways, schools, hospitals, health centers, swimming pools, and air terminals.

For the first time, New York offered its poor public housing, its workers a unified transit system, and its artists and musicians special training and subsidies. Relief was placed on the stable foundation of a sales tax, and government, too, was modernized. The outdated 1898 city charter was replaced by a fresh new compact that centralized municipal powers, consolidated departments, eliminated unnecessary borough and county offices, and streamlined municipal operations.

La Guardia declared unrelenting war on gamblers, closed the burlesques, and cleared racy magazines from the newsstands (under his powers of "garbage collection"). Beginning in 1942, New Yorkers could tune in every Sunday on the radio to hear the mayor tell them what to buy, how to raise their children, what to wear, how to save money, what to do in case of a German attack, and how to resolve family disputes— all in a tone that was strikingly intimate and fatherly. In what became the best remembered act of his mayoralty, La Guardia one Sunday asked his audience to bring the kiddies around and then proceeded to give a dramatic reading of the Dick Tracy comic strip.

Fiorello La Guardia redefined the role of the modern mayoralty, extending the reach of government, infusing it with integrity, and upgrading its capacity to deliver municipal services. He worked closely with the New Deal to carve out a national urban policy. Taking full advantage of his access to President

Roosevelt and New Deal largesse, he rebuilt his aging city into a modern metropolis.

—Thomas Kessner

See also New Deal: Urban Policy; New York, New York

Further Readings and References

Bayor, R. H. (1993). *Fiorello La Guardia: Ethnicity and reform.* New York: Harlan Davidson.

Brodsky, A. (2003). *The great mayor: Fiorello La Guardia and the making of the city of New York.* New York: Truman Talley Books.

LAKEWOOD, CALIFORNIA (AND THE LAKEWOOD PLAN)

Lakewood, California, gained recognition as the largest mass-produced suburb of its time when it first opened to residents in 1950. Located just north of Long Beach and 14 miles south of downtown Los Angeles, Lakewood was dubbed "the instant city" when its developers transformed 3,500 acres of bean fields into a suburban development of 17,150 tract houses between 1950 and 1954. It surpassed even Levittown as the world's largest and fastest built postwar planned suburb.

The Lakewood Park Corporation, headed by Louis Boyar, Ben Weingart, and Mark Taper, conceived of Lakewood as a model planned community. The developers not only built housing using the mass-production techniques in vogue during this period, but they also set aside land for schools, parks, churches, and shopping centers. The homes were laid out on a grid pattern, set on 5,000-square-foot lots (the minimum size allowed in Los Angeles County), and averaged between 850 and 1,200 square feet in size. The typical home had a living room, kitchen, two or three bedrooms, and one bathroom, and buyers could choose from 13 different floor plans. Lakewood homes were valued between $9,400 and $14,000 in 1954. The developers also allocated land for schools, parks, churches, and retail centers, and highlighted these community amenities in sales pitches for the suburb. They delivered most successfully in the area of retail. Lakewood Center, a 255-acre regional shopping mall, represented the physical and economic centerpiece of the planned community. It was the world's largest shopping center in the early 1950s, with a 150-acre parking lot with spaces for 10,000 cars. Provisions for parks came much more slowly, and only after active lobbying by the community's residents.

The public responded enthusiastically to the promotions of Lakewood. During the first month that homes went on sale in April 1950, more than 200,000 people converged on the sales office and more than 1,000 families bought homes. In the first 10 months, 7,200 homes were sold. Many buyers were war veterans who took advantage of GI Bill financing to make their home purchase. Most of the suburb's breadwinners worked in blue-collar or low-level white-collar jobs, many in aircraft or defense industries. By 1960, 59 percent of male workers were employed in blue-collar jobs. Despite their occupational identity, most residents became part of an amorphous, expanding postwar middle class. The suburb itself had a leveling effect on residents, conferring a sense of equality based on their status as suburban homeowners. Most adult residents shared a similar income level, were first-time homeowners, and were young adults in their 20s and early 30s. The population remained all white through the 1950s, with no African Americans and a small percentage of Mexicans living in the community. By 1970, the Spanish-speaking population had risen to 9.4 percent.

Many Lakewood families had young children—a part of the postwar baby boom trend—and the centrality of children helped shape a local culture that emphasized recreation. Residents endeavored to create a wholesome, family-centered community that emphasized children, and this goal was expressed in youth recreation programs. When the whole family participated, it reinforced community cohesion around the shared values of family, youth, and community spirit. Lakewood's recreational life lived up to this ideal: In the postwar years, local sports teams and activities proliferated. By 1960, the town had 110 boys' baseball teams, 36 men's softball teams, 10 housewives' softball teams, 75 boys' and 30 men's basketball teams, and 77 football teams, as well as local groups devoted to bowling, roller skating, and exercise, among other activities. Lakewood's social life mirrored the national suburban pattern of active club and organizational life. Historian Allison Baker argues that recreation, more than any other community attribute, came to define the suburb's identity as well as the status of residents. Achievement in sports became the key to local success and recognition.

Politically, Lakewood was incorporated in 1954, after staving off annexation attempts by Long Beach. Lakewood developed an innovative way to deliver services to residents at minimal cost: It contracted with the county of Los Angeles for its public services (including fire, police, library, sewers, and water). Known as the Lakewood Plan, this arrangement became a model for other communities; 26 cities in Los Angeles County adopted the plan by 1960. By the 1990s, 126 California cities had adopted the plan, as did cities in Arizona, Colorado, Oregon, and Washington. Although supporters lauded the Lakewood Plan for its municipal efficiency, savings to taxpayers, and assurances of local control, critics claimed it promoted self-serving economic advantage to white middle-class suburbia. It was an escape hatch because it allowed suburbanites to get inexpensive services without contributing financially to the county overall. Moreover, the Lakewood Plan fueled white flight from Los Angeles.

Since the 1970s, Lakewood has become more socially diverse and has faced challenges in adjusting to these new social realities. By 1996, the suburb's population had grown racially heterogeneous, with Latinos making up 20 percent, Asians 12 percent, and African Americans 4 percent. There was also a rise in multigenerational families and the elderly. One way Lakewood has adjusted is by retreating internally; in 1992, a gated subdivision was built in Lakewood, surrounded by cinder-block walls and abutting a trailer park in Long Beach. Long-time residents often voiced the sentiment that community spirit has declined. In 1993, Lakewood gained national notoriety over what became known as the "Spur Posse episode." Members of a gang called the Spur Posse, composed of current and former Lakewood High athletes, were charged with rape, burglary, check forgery, and assaults on children. Gang members, many of them football players, tallied their sexual conquests on a point system. The national media seized on this incident as a vivid example of the postwar suburban good life gone wrong; in Lakewood's case, it represented the ultimate corruption of the suburban recreational ethos, where figures once heralded as community heroes were implicated in an array of crimes. Although residents have struggled to reconcile complicated social realities with powerful community ideals, Lakewood, like many suburbs nationally, has had to reshape its community identity in the context of changing demography and suburban maturation.

—Becky Nicolaides

Further Readings and References

Baker, A. (1999). *The Lakewood story: Defending the recreational good life in postwar southern California suburbia, 1950–1999*. Unpublished doctoral dissertation, University of Pennsylvania.

Miller, G. (1981). *Cities by contract: The politics of municipal incorporation*. Cambridge, MA: MIT Press.

Waldie, D. J. (1996). *Holy land: A suburban memoir*. New York: St. Martin's.

LAND DEVELOPERS AND DEVELOPMENT

It was once common to speak of land and *improvements*; *development* still implies progress to a more advanced state; *conversion* is a neutral term that refers to the way rural land is transformed to urban, nonagricultural uses through subdivision and the construction of services and buildings by land developers, builders, and municipalities. Methods of land conversion have evolved over the past century and a half, but they have always expressed an American mixture of individualism, optimism, and minimal concern for long-term environmental consequences.

The Changing Process of Land Conversion

Land at the urban fringe is usually owned in large parcels; to be made available for urban uses, it must be subdivided into smaller lots, with provision for a denser network of roads. Although *subdivision* usually refers to a tract of land that has been made available for residential use, comparable tracts (containing larger lots) are also produced for office and industrial parks. Once a subdivision has been registered, the installation of urban services (paved roads and sidewalks; streetlights; water and sewer pipes, electricity cables, and perhaps gas lines) and the construction of buildings may begin, although not necessarily in that order.

In the 19th century, the process of land conversion normally involved many different agents. Land subdividers (often syndicates) purchased tracts of fringe land, which they subdivided into building plots that were sold individually to buyers, who then speculated in land as investors now play the stock market. It was common for building parcels to change hands several times before anything was constructed on them. The typical residential subdivision was small, commonly 25 to 50 lots. Because houses were often built one at a time, it might take years for a subdivision to be completely developed. In extreme cases, waves of speculative subdivision created far-flung tracts that saw little or no development for decades. For example, a number of areas that were gridded in the 1920s did not begin to fill up with houses and other buildings until after 1945. By then, the greater affordability of automobiles and a new taste for neighborhood layouts with curvilinear streets rendered many of these areas obsolete.

Over the past century, land conversion has come under the control of developers, who are involved in several and sometimes all stages of the process. There has been a trend toward vertical integration: Today, developers not only buy and subdivide land but also build houses, although many prefer to subcontract construction to a chosen stable of builders. Developers may also provide or arrange for mortgage financing. Beginning in the early 20th century, self-styled "community builders" recognized that home buyers were willing to pay a premium for lots in subdivisions where all dwellings conformed to minimum and sometimes quite high standards. This new breed of developer created some covenants (deed restrictions) to regulate construction and others to prohibit buyers from selling to members of specified minorities. In *Shelley v. Kraemer* (1948), the U.S. Supreme Court declared that racial (ethnic) covenants were legal but unenforceable by the states. Since then, developers have imposed only building regulations. Indeed, with the growth of master-planned and gated communities in the past 30 years, the extent and range of private control of land development has grown considerably. Although the fact is not widely known, beginning with the creation of planned industrial districts in Chicago and Los Angeles a century ago, comparable long-term trends have affected the subdivision of land for industrial and office use.

The package of services that are required for urban development has grown. Piped water and sewers were regarded as essential by the third quarter of the 19th century, although houses on large suburban lots often managed with wells. By the end of that century, buyers in middle-class subdivisions expected almost everything that we take for granted today, but working-class suburbs managed without many of these services until the period between World Wars I and II.

Initially, municipalities and utility companies were responsible for installing this infrastructure, recouping the costs in property taxes and user fees. As early as the 1860s, buyers were demanding an expanding array of services, giving impetus to the formation of a variety of suburban municipalities that could provide varying levels of services. After 1945, the rapid pace of urban growth encouraged suburbs to transfer responsibility for service provision to developers, who defrayed their new capital costs by raising land and house prices. This transfer of responsibility hastened the growth of large, well-capitalized land developers.

Politics, Patterns, and Consequences

Land development has always been at the center of municipal politics. Municipal finances depend on property taxes, and to enhance revenues, politicians encourage development and then redevelopment to a higher use. Municipalities have to compete for industry and development. To this end, they have often been controlled by political alliances, or "growth machines," in which the land development industry has played a central role. Their convergence of interests with politicians has given developers a particular influence at city hall.

Land developers have shaped the modern American city. Decisions about the size and shape of building lots have an immediate effect on the character of the structures that can be built in a subdivision. Those decisions continue to exert an influence decades later when piecemeal redevelopment begins to occur. Street layouts are even more permanent: Only in the instance of publicly sponsored urban renewal have existing street patterns been redrawn. The patterns produced by land conversion, then, are among the most visible and significant examples of what economists call *path dependency:* the influence of the past on the present.

Methods of land conversion have expressed the individualism and optimism of American culture better than any other industry, with environmental consequences that we are only beginning to understand. In the United States, most land is owned freehold and unburdened by the collective or customary restraints that still affect land development and patterns of land use in European cities. The prevailing assumption has been that, as far as possible, owners have the right to develop land as they see fit and to realize the speculative gains that accrue from urban growth. It is also generally assumed that land should be developed and, when appropriate, redeveloped, to make way for its "highest and best use," defined as the use that can pay the highest rent. By comparison with their counterparts in Britain or even Canada, governments in the United States have imposed only limited regulation on the process of land conversion and redevelopment. From the early 1900s, a growing number of municipalities introduced zoning controls. Because of the federal City Planning Enabling Act of 1928, local planning agencies were encouraged to regulate the form, location, and servicing of new subdivisions. These initiatives helped to reduce the worst excesses of speculative subdivision. More recently, developers have been required to assess the environmental impacts of what they propose. But public regulators have continued to permit low-density urban development, which mandates heavy use of autos and trucks; as a result, unnecessarily large amounts of land are converted to urban use every year. The process of land conversion in the United States continues to express a faith in growth that knows no environmental limits.

—Richard Harris

See also Building Industry; Building Regulations and Building Codes; New Urbanism; Sewage and Sanitation Systems; Urban Renewal and Revitalization; Zoning

Further Readings and References

Burgess, P. (1994). *Planning for the private interest: Land use controls and residential patterns in Columbus, Ohio, 1900–1970.* Columbus: Ohio State University Press.

Clawson, M. (1971). *Suburban land conversion in the United States.* Baltimore: Resources for the Future.

Cullingworth, B. (1997). *Planning in the USA: Policies, issues, and processes.* New York: Routledge.

Keating, A. D. (1988). *Building Chicago: Suburban developers and the creation of a divided metropolis.* Columbus: Ohio State University Press.

Weiss, M. (1987). *The rise of the community builders: The American real estate industry and urban land planning.* New York: Columbia University Press.

LANDMARKS PRESERVATION

Landmarks preservation, the organized effort to save significant buildings from demolition, began at least as early as 1813 in urban America, when public outcry prevented the city of Philadelphia from destroying Independence Hall, site of adoption for both the Declaration of Independence and the Constitution. Since that time, the landmarks preservation impulse has continued to function in American cities as an important social response to impending loss, although the nature of the perceived loss has changed, along with the basis for reckoning a building's significance. Also, the methods employed have become stronger and more formalized. The actual breadth of public participation, however, has been and remains problematic.

Throughout the 19th century, the objects of preservation campaigns were most often icons of the Revolution and the early Republic, typically the family home of a key figure from that era. Washington's Mount Vernon, although not urban, is the best known example. In 1853, Ann Pamela Cunningham, a South Carolina native, began a long campaign to purchase and restore the deteriorating Virginia mansion and to establish long-term provisions for its maintenance. In an approach that would be used with scores of other historic monuments, the building was acquired and preserved by a private organization interested in promulgating the patriotic narrative associated with it. On occasion, wealthy individuals did the same on their own; for example, Paul Revere's House in Boston was purchased and preserved in 1902 by a great-grandson of the patriot. In most cases, the owners subsequently operated the buildings as museums.

Particularly in the cities, this nascent preservation movement can be seen as part of a broad desire to guard against the loss of traditional American identity, which was thought to be threatened by large-scale immigration. Preservation proponents were largely members of the white, Protestant upper middle class, as exemplified by Cunningham's Mount Vernon Ladies Association. Each preservation association was independent, and all relied on wealthy individuals or capital campaigns to purchase, rehabilitate, and operate their landmark buildings.

The first legal means for safeguarding landmark buildings without actually purchasing the property was the Charleston Historic District ordinance, enacted in 1931. This pioneering legislation authorized the city to regulate changes to historic buildings in a specified area. Its enactment indicates a shift in the object of preservation from a feared loss of cultural icons to loss of the urban fabric itself. There was no claim that the protected buildings had extraordinary value individually, and neither were they unique symbols of historic narrative. Rather, they were to be protected for themselves. In addition, for the first time, it was not necessary to acquire title to the property to assure its existence and proper maintenance. Subsequent court decisions validated this and similar laws on the grounds that they protected property values, a legitimate governmental purpose.

Although the 1931 Charleston ordinance dealt with protection for groups of buildings, its innovative legal approach and the shift in the basis for protection also signaled new ways of thinking about individual buildings. In 1933, under the Historic American Building Survey program, the federal government undertook to inventory important American buildings methodically and, it was thought, definitively. Candidates were selected for their design qualities as well as their historical significance. In 1935, the secretary of the interior started to compile a list of national historic landmarks that would eventually grow into the National Register of Historic Places. These federal programs contained no explicit protections for the buildings identified but served to formulate nationally accepted criteria for evaluation and to involve government in the identification of outstanding buildings.

Following World War II, as the historic urban fabric in American cities was sacrificed to freeway construction and clearance of older neighborhoods identified as slums, the rapid physical and social changes engendered a desire to protect against the loss of urban life itself. The National Trust for Historic Places (NTHP), chartered by Congress as a nongovernmental agency in 1949, worked to strengthen landmarks preservation efforts nationally. In 1956, the NTHP published standards for historic evaluation of buildings and proposed to recognize significance stemming from architectural qualities or from state and local, rather than only national history.

In the 1960s, the role of government in landmarks preservation expanded. The National Historic Preservation Act (NHPA) of 1966 followed the lead of the 1956 NTHP evaluation standards. For the first time, the act made protection of historically significant buildings federal policy, and it also made funding available to states to establish historic preservation programs under state historic preservation officers (SHPOs).

Public awareness of and political support for landmarks preservation increased substantially at about the same time, as financially driven development led to the destruction of prominent buildings in several cities to make room for much larger modernist structures. There were several highly publicized instances. In New York City, the 1963 demolition of the Pennsylvania Railroad Station was an important factor in creation of the Landmarks Preservation Commission in 1965, while the 1966 loss of the Fox Theater in San Francisco similarly galvanized political support to establish the Landmarks Preservation Advisory Board in 1967. These public commissions and their counterparts in other cities began the regular designation of hundreds of official landmarks. Unlike earlier recognition programs, these later projects typically gave adopted landmarks stringent protections against unapproved alterations, as well as a ban on demolition. Some localities also provide positive incentives for preserving landmark buildings, usually tax or zoning benefits. As a result, local landmark programs are now often the strongest, most available means of protecting threatened buildings.

However, a question persists regarding the relatively narrow cultural origins of landmarks preservation activists, even today. Although the purpose of preservation has shifted from the conscious projection of a particular cultural narrative, activists are still most often drawn from the white middle class. Thus, the protected buildings still tend to reflect mainstream historic narratives of political, social, and commercial dominance, an effect only enhanced by the fact that the same sources also have left the most visually impressive structures, designed by the most prominent architects. In recent years, awareness of this narrow recognition has grown, and attempts have been made to broaden the cultural base for landmarks preservation. These attempts have met with only moderate success, partially because nondominant cultural groups are unfamiliar with the process, while experienced preservationists and landmarks commissioners do not immediately see the importance of landmarks related to other social or cultural visions.

Another problem arises from a tendency to see landmarks preservation exclusively as a land use issue. Sometimes, groups seize on landmarks preservation as a tool when their actual goal is to block a proposed development project; as a result, arguments for a building's historic significance may be distorted. Landmarks preservation, now firmly established as a legitimate public interest, must resolve these concerns in order to widen its public support.

—Tim Kelly

Further Readings and References

Barthel, D. (1996). *Historic preservation: Collective memory and historical identity.* New Brunswick, NJ: Rutgers University Press.

Stipe, R. E. (Ed.). (2003). *A richer heritage: Historic preservation in the twenty-first century.* Chapel Hill: University of North Carolina Press.

Tomlan, M. A. (Ed.). (1998). *Preservation: Of what, for whom? A critical look at historical significance.* Ithaca, NY: The National Council for Preservation Education.

LAS VEGAS, NEVADA

Las Vegas, located in southern Nevada, is the seat of Clark County and the state's largest city. It celebrated its centennial on May 15, 2005, commemorating the day that 110 acres of ranch land was auctioned to form the city's original boundaries. Since then, Las Vegas has swelled from a sleepy railroad stop in a vast, forbidding desert to the world's preeminent entertainment mecca. Throughout its history, the place has lured high rollers, entrepreneurs, and gangsters, all attracted to the city's get-rich-quick *zeitgeist.* A product of a consumer-oriented, capitalist society, Las Vegas has become Sin City, a flashy, neon-lit haven for indulging in the adult pleasures of sex, alcohol, and gambling, an image promoted by boosters and reinforced through the mass media. By the mid-1950s, visitors flocked to resorts along the famous stretch of its main drag, called simply and suggestively "the Strip." The city now attracts about 36 million visitors a year. About 43 percent of its municipal revenue is from taxes on gambling, now called *gaming,* which exceeded $8 billion in gross profits in the year 2000. However, aside from its raunchy image, Las Vegas is a real city, the idiosyncratic center of the nation's fastest-growing metropolitan area and the largest city created in the 20th century. Its growth pattern parallels to some extent that of Los Angeles, with which it has always had a symbiotic relationship. A desert oasis-turned-town, invented, transformed, and reinvented by money and power, Las Vegas may be the quintessential postmodern American city.

For hundreds, perhaps thousands of years, members of the Paiute Native American tribe were the sole inhabitants of the Las Vegas region. That changed in 1829, when Antonio Armijo, a Mexican explorer and trader who was seeking a more direct route to

Los Angeles, veered from the Old Spanish Trail and discovered an oasis of abundant springwater surrounded by grasslands. The site was later named Las Vegas (*the meadow* in Spanish). By the 1850s, the route was used for mail transport, immigration by Mormon missionaries, and speedy access to the California Gold Rush. With the gold and other mineral strikes in the 1860s came the first wave of European-born prospectors from the East. By the turn of the century, railroad developers had found water-rich Las Vegas Valley the ideal place for fueling steam locomotives. In 1902, William Andrews Clark, a Montana senator with copper and real estate interests, began building the San Pedro, Los Angeles, and Salt Lake Railroad, connecting the Union Pacific with Southern California. His town site officially became the city of Las Vegas. The railroad company plotted and auctioned off in a single day 1,200 lots around Fremont Street, the main thoroughfare; most of the buyers were Los Angeles businessmen. This downtown area would become known as Glitter Gulch. In 1909, the city became the seat of the new Nevada county named after Clark, and it was incorporated in 1911.

Las Vegas grew slowly in its first two decades. While other parts of the nation were suffering from the Great Depression, government spending coupled with railroad development and real estate speculation helped create the first boom. In the early 1930s, Congress authorized millions of federal dollars to construct Hoover Dam and Lake Mead, the world's largest dam and artificial lake, on a site southeast of Las Vegas. The project provided jobs for more than 5,000 Los Angeles workers. Excellent year-round flying weather also motivated the Army Air Corps to construct nearby the $25 million Nellis Air Force Base. It opened in 1941, when Las Vegas had about 8,000 residents. Later, the U.S. Department of Energy built its Nevada test site just north of the city, providing more jobs and permanent residents. By the 1950s, the metropolitan area had grown to about 25,000, reaching more than 1 million by the end of the century.

In 1931, Las Vegas legalized gambling, which had been prohibited in the state since 1910, producing a steady revenue stream that would crack the $1 billion mark by 1977. Another attraction was the Hoover Dam; by the end of the 1930s, about a quarter million people per year were visiting it. The tourism industry grew steadily, providing inexpensive vacations mostly for Southern Californians, and this gave rise to Las Vegas's international convention trade. Widespread use of the swamp cooler, made possible by a plentiful supply of cheap electricity, helped calm the desert heat and led to construction of the first luxury hotel, the Apache, located downtown, where bars doubled as brothels. To avoid taxes and city control, entrepreneur Thomas Hull built two hotels in 1941, the 100-room, Spanish-style El Rancho Vegas and the dude ranch Last Frontier, just outside the city limits along two-lane Highway 91, launching development of the famous Las Vegas Strip. However, mobster Benjamin "Bugsy" Siegel built the Strip's first big gambling resort-casino. In December 1946, he opened his lavish Flamingo Hotel with its giant pink neon sign, combining elegant, Monte Carlo-style gambling with a Miami Beach-style vacation experience. Siegel, who had close ties with both Meyer Lansky's crime syndicate and the Hollywood community, recruited top performers, cementing Las Vegas's relationship with the entertainment capital.

To improve the status of the downtown's Glitter Gulch, the swank Golden Nugget Hotel opened in 1945. By the end of the century, to compete with the Strip, Fremont Street was converted to an enclosed, $63 million neon light and sound pedestrian "experience." However, during its two major periods, post–World War II and the 1990s, casino expansion took place primarily along the Strip, where competing developers built ever larger and more elaborate hotels that eventually mushroomed into today's themed mega-resorts. During the 1950s surge, the Riviera became the Strip's first high-rise hotel. In the 1960s, Jay Sarno built Circus-Circus as a tent-shaped casino, later adding a hotel and family-oriented midway. At the time it was built, Sarno's Roman-themed Caesar's Palace was the largest hotel in the world. In December 1993, Kirk Kerkorian, who bought MGM studios and built the original MGM Grand in 1973 (now Bally's), opened his new MGM Grand Hotel and Theme Park, built at a cost of more than $1 billion, with 5,005 guest rooms and a 171,500-square-foot casino, the largest resort hotel at the time. By the late 1990s, however, developer Steve Wynn had taken the lead. He purchased the old Golden Nugget, which he restored, and the 164-acre Dunes Hotel and Country Club, and he built the Mirage, Treasure Island, and the five-star Bellagio at a cost of $1.7 billion.

The early tourist hotels had Spanish and Western motifs, while those that followed had desert references, such as the Sands, Desert Inn, Dunes, Aladdin, and, finally, the Mirage. During the 1990s, the new generation of Las Vegas resorts was competing with other cities that had legalized gambling to attract conventioneers and tourists with families. The result was a chain of self-contained Disneylands. In these themed resort environments built using multinational corporate capital, guests would suspend disbelief to eat, sleep, play, gamble, relax, be entertained, and shop in a "land" where the buildings themselves had become both sign and spectacle. At the Egyptian-themed Luxor, for example, the hotel was conceived as a giant pyramid, its entrance a looming Sphinx. At Paris LV, the hotel's façade was crafted as a three-dimensional collage of famous Belle Époque landmarks, including an Eiffel Tower at three-quarters scale. The Strip became a simulation of the world's most popular destinations, sporting replicas of an All-American New York/New York, Venice in all its Renaissance glory, and, at Wynn's Bellagio, northern Italy's Lake Como, an 11-acre water feature with lakeside dining and spectacular dancing fountains fronting the Strip.

Like Disney, resort builders borrowed motion picture set-building techniques to thrust guests into nostalgic representations of the past (Luxor, Caesar's Palace, Excalibur) or fantasies of the future (Hilton's Star Trek Experience, the Stratosphere), while obliterating reality in a 24-hour town with no clocks and nonstop entertainment. The luxurious resort interiors of Bugsy Siegel's day were inflated into multidimensional "inside-outside" experiences. This faux phenomenon would find its ultimate expression at the Forum Shops inside Caesar's Palace, where a climate-controlled shopping mall was disguised as an "outdoors" promenade along the ancient Apian Way, a formula copied at the Venetian and the Aladdin.

An extensive program in the late 1990s included new streetscaping, pedestrian overpasses, and a monorail to link the Strip's resorts, furthering the impression of Las Vegas as a giant theme park. Nevertheless, although the resorts shielded visitors from the surrounding social context, the metropolitan area was facing many of the problems associated with rapid growth: pollution, crime, and traffic congestion. From 1990 to 2000, the city's population doubled to 480,000 residents. Henderson, a suburb of Las Vegas, became the fastest-growing place in the nation. The Nevada desert is now shrinking thanks to an explosion of vast suburban tract home developments and sprawling master-planned communities. The area's infrastructure and school system have been unable to keep pace, and its water supply from the Colorado

River and Lake Mead is insufficient to sustain future growth.

—*Julie A. Dercle*

Further Readings and References

Denton, S., & Morris, R. (2001). *The money and the power: The making of Las Vegas and its hold on America, 1947–2000.* New York: Knopf.

Gottdiener, M., Collins, C. C., & Dickens, D. R. (1999). *Las Vegas: The social production of an all-American city.* Malden, MA: Blackwell.

Rothman, H. (2002). *Neon metropolis: How Las Vegas started the twenty-first century.* New York: Routledge.

LATINOS IN CITIES AND SUBURBS

A Hispanic urban neighborhood in the United States and Latin America is called a *barrio* from the Latin *barium,* meaning part of the city. Other names for Latino neighborhoods indicate the origins of a particular group living in an area. For example, Cuban immigrants created "Little Havana" in Miami, and residents from Sonora in Mexico created "Sonoratowns" in cities of the Southwest.

The earliest barrio residents were Mexicans who had lived in the Southwest since it was controlled by Spain, beginning in 1690. Mexico ruled the region from 1810 to 1848, when the United States annexed the Southwest after the Mexican War. Under the American flag, the separate Anglo settlements sprawled out and surrounded the smaller Mexican communities, and so by the late 1800s, Mexicans lived in cities controlled by Anglos.

As the Southwest economy grew, these Mexican neighborhoods became sources of labor for the cities, railroads, farms, and mines. Like European immigrants, Mexicans and other Latinos became segregated as a result of *chain migration* along with poverty and discrimination. However, as immigration increased in the 20th century, Mexicans became dominant in border cities like Laredo, Texas, which was more than 80 percent Mexican and Mexican American by 1960.

East Coast barrios formed in a more familiar way. In the 19th century, Spanish, Cuban, and Puerto Rican immigrants carved out neighborhoods where they found work: in factories, on the docks, and in construction. After World War II, Puerto Ricans settled in New York, where they worked in factories and on the docks. Others went to the Midwest, first working as farm laborers and then migrating into the cities for factory jobs. Like Cuban Jose Martí, some Latino immigrants were refugees fleeing oppressive regimes at home, and they used the barrio as a base for political activities.

In the 20th century, farm, factory, and railroad jobs lured Latinos (mostly Mexicans) to the Midwest, and in the 1920s, barrios appeared in cities. During the Great Depression, the Latino urban population declined, but with World War II, Mexican immigrants returned seeking the same kinds of jobs.

Barrios grew across the United States during the 20th century for various reasons. Latinos moved to cities for better jobs, but discrimination and poverty restricted them to poorer neighborhoods. Mechanization of agriculture after World War II decreased agriculture jobs and propelled urban migration. In the Southwest, the burgeoning Sun Belt economy saw rapid job growth in cities like Houston, Albuquerque, Los Angeles, and San Diego.

Many Latino immigrants, like other immigrants, were conflicted about leaving their homeland for the United States. Many longed for home, but once they had American-born children or they found adequate employment, they delayed the return. As a result, barrios served as transnational conduits where they could maintain connections with the old country via railroad, highway, telephone, telegraph, airplane, theater, television, and more recently computer. In the barrios, Latinos formed hometown clubs, mutual aid societies *(mutualistas),* and labor and merchant associations that also had connections to the old country. On the East Coast, Puerto Ricans, Cubans, and Dominicans owned *bodegas* (corner grocery stores) and *botánicas* (pharmacies) that provided ethnic foods and religious and health items while serving as social and information centers. Ethnic retail stores, restaurants, and bars, Spanish-language media, and arts centers also served to maintain traditions.

The barrio was thus a place for cultural persistence and resistance to assimilation, even as economic difficulties and racism isolated barrio residents from the mainstream. Barrio residents were not just victims of discrimination but social agents active in resisting Anglo American cultural domination. However, the barrio has always been a site for cultural struggle. For example, along the Mexico-U.S. border, public school teachers, middle-class Anglo reformers, and the English media promoted Americanization, while the proximity to Mexico and its media and government representatives encouraged immigrants to remain loyal to their homeland. Within this cultural struggle, many residents took a middle road, accepting aspects of Americanization including economic assistance, job training, and language instruction, but rejecting other aspects (for example, religious conversion) and maintaining a Mexican identity.

Proximity to the Latin American homeland makes barrios especially vibrant cultural milieus, constantly infused by new arrivals from the old country. The Mexico-U.S. border residents see themselves forging a third culture that combines elements of each nation. In twin cities—Tijuana-San Diego, El Paso-Juarez, Laredo and Nuevo Laredo, Brownsville and Matamoros— businesses draw customers from *el otro lado* (the other side). This transborder market results in a distinct style of food, language, religion, music, art, city planning, and public celebrations, a style that merges the cultures of the two nations.

Holding onto language and culture was especially important for Mexicans in the Southwest, who as a conquered minority claimed their right to maintain their traditions because their ancestors resided in the region before the Anglos came. Similarly, after the United States annexed Puerto Rico following the Spanish American War in 1898, Puerto Ricans on the island resisted the imposition of the English language and American history and culture. Puerto Ricans brought that desire to preserve Puerto Rican national identity with them to the mainland.

Urban settlement in crowded neighborhoods created competition for housing and jobs. In reaction to discrimination and struggles with their parents over assimilation, Latino youth formed gangs in major cities. In Los Angeles, urban Mexican youth were called *pachucos,* and in 1943, the Zoot Suit riots occurred in which Anglo servicemen assaulted *pachucos* and *pachucas* in East Los Angeles. Mexican gangs defended their turf and fought with Anglos and later black gang members. Puerto Rican gangs formed in Chicago and New York City and fought with white and black gangs. In the 1960s, the proliferation of drugs and guns increased the level of gang violence at the same time that deindustrialization and white flight drained the tax base, and unemployment increased among Latino/a youth who dropped out of under-funded public schools.

Urban renewal and freeway construction displaced barrio dwellers in many large cities. In response,

Latinos organized social movements to counter discrimination. Influenced by the Black Power movement, the Young Lords, initially composed of Puerto Rican and black gang members, Vietnam veterans, and students, became advocates for residents in Chicago and New York barrios who suffered from poor housing, inadequate health care, and abuses in the welfare and criminal justice systems. Chicanos/as in the Southwest formed organizations that supported the United Farm Workers (UFW), protested the Vietnam War, and called for improved housing, employment, and education opportunities. Throughout the country, grassroots politics encouraged Latino/a artists to transform city walls into murals that celebrated ethnic and racial pride, local history, and social activism. Ethnic pride erupted as well in prose and poetry and open readings in the city streets.

This political activism stimulated a broader Latino identity, particularly in big cities that contained a variety of Latino nationalities. Throughout the country, Latinos identify primarily with their nation of origin, but increasingly those born in the United States— second and third generations—also embrace a Latino identity and unite in political and economic movements across national lines. Despite the existence of this Latino affiliation, barrios remain the sites for struggles between various Latino nationalities for political and economic power.

Los Suburbios

By the 1990 census, almost half the nation's Latino population lived in the suburbs. Their employment as farm workers often placed Latinos outside large cities, where they settled in rural *colonias*. In the Southwest, some of these rural settlements became incorporated into new suburbs as residential sprawl ate up farmland. The continued residential suburbanization of the United States, along with the growth of suburban employment, lured Latinos to the outskirts of cities. Latinos found jobs in suburban industries and in the service economy, especially in child care, landscaping, restaurants, and hotels. After Latino suburban pioneers forged the way, they were joined by their families and friends in the hinterland communities.

As more Latinos joined the middle class, they followed the American pattern of settling in the suburbs for better schools, larger houses, parks, and lower crime rates. The U.S.-born second and third generations are especially likely to choose to live in the suburbs, but many immigrants now bypass the cities for the suburbs. In some cases, Latinos are the first minority group in a community, thus adding a new dimension to heretofore homogeneous suburbs. With more Latinos in the suburbs, they create a market for Latino-owned restaurants and stores, and suburban churches offer Mass in Spanish. Latinos have been elected recently to prominent political offices in suburban communities throughout the Southwest. The globalization of the media means that Latinos no longer need to live near each other to maintain connection to their ethnic culture, making suburbs more attractive. However, good connections to urban barrios allow suburban Latinos access to ethnic culture in the cities.

—*Joseph A. Rodriguez*

Further Readings and References

Herzog, L. A. (1999). *From Aztec to high tech: Architecture and landscape across the Mexico-United States border.* Baltimore: Johns Hopkins University Press.

Moore, J. W. (1991). *Going down to the barrio: Homeboys and homegirls in change.* Philadelphia: Temple University Press.

Padilla, F. M. (1987). *Puerto Rican Chicago.* Notre Dame, IN: University of Notre Dame Press.

Ruiz, V. L. (1998). *From out of the shadows: Mexican women in twentieth-century America.* New York: Oxford University Press.

Sánchez, G. J. (1993). *Becoming Mexican American: Ethnicity, culture, and identity in Chicano Los Angeles, 1900–1945.* New York: Oxford University Press.

Sánchez Korrol, V. (1994). *From colonia to community: The history of Puerto Ricans in New York City.* Berkeley: University of California Press.

LAWRENCE, DAVID L.

David L. Lawrence (1889–1966) was a master politician who, as chairman of the Allegheny County Democratic Committee, revitalized the party and took control of Pittsburgh away from the Republicans in the early 1930s, after decades of GOP dominance. He became mayor of Pittsburgh in 1945, serving an unprecedented four terms (1945–1957). The son of Irish immigrant parents from Belfast, he grew up in a working-class area of Pittsburgh's Golden Triangle, where he was exposed to political dialogue from an early age.

As an urban politician, he is best known for the political leadership he displayed in helping to launch Pittsburgh's famous so-called renaissance after World War II. In accomplishing this, the mayor worked in cooperation with Republican banker Richard King Mellon and a powerful civic group, the Allegheny Conference on Community Development (ACCD), which was composed of the city's most influential corporate CEOs. This alliance provides a prime example of "regime" politics—an alliance between a Republican business community and a dominant Democratic organization to bring about urban development. Among the major accomplishments of the alliance was the rebuilding of the downtown area, made possible through the use of the power of eminent domain by the newly created Urban Redevelopment Authority. This was the nation's first use of urban renewal powers for purposes of commercial revitalization. Also critical to the city's renewal was the accomplishment of two environmental goals: improving the city's air quality by reducing its smoke burden and creating the Allegheny County Sanitary Authority to begin treating the sewage of the city and neighboring towns.

In coordination with the ACCD, Lawrence also used his political power to orchestrate construction of new highways leading to the downtown and creation of a parking authority and of the Allegheny County Port Authority, which administered and improved the city and county's transit system. In 1958, after his tenure as mayor had ended, Lawrence was elected as Pennsylvania's first Roman Catholic governor. State law limited him to one term, but he had important accomplishments—the Fair Housing Law of 1961, legislation for air pollution control, and a major increase in library services. One of his last public acts was to serve as chair of President John F. Kennedy's Committee on Equal Opportunity in Housing. He died in 1966 while still active in political life.

—*Joel A. Tarr*

See also Pittsburgh, Pennsylvania

Further Readings and References

Weber, M. P. (1988). *Don't call me boss: David L. Lawrence: Pittsburgh's renaissance mayor.* Pittsburgh, PA: University of Pittsburgh Press.

LESBIAN CULTURE IN CITIES

Urban lesbian culture was—and is—exceptionally diverse and often divided. Lesbian communities have historically been marked by class, race, and even gender divisions. As lesbian communities formed in a variety of urban centers in the 20th century, lesbians of color were excluded from white lesbian bars and house parties. Elite lesbians participated in resort communities such as Cherry Grove on Fire Island; Provincetown, Massachusetts; and Key West, Florida, whereas working-class lesbians formed their communities primarily through bars and house parties. The importance of butch-femme identity, especially in the bar culture and during midcentury, worked to define urban lesbian communities by dividing lesbians into femme—or feminine—and butch—or masculine— roles. All of these diversities continue to divide lesbians, precluding the existence of a single or unified "lesbian community"—either urban or rural. To examine lesbian culture in cities, then, is to examine a variety of cultures and communities on the urban landscape.

Many queer scholars agree that both the lesbian and gay male communities became increasingly visible and more organized at the end of the 19th and the beginning of the 20th centuries, with cities playing a major role as places where lesbians and gay men could explore their identities and meet others. There is an academic temptation to group lesbians and gay men together and to combine their histories and experiences, but lesbians and gay men have created very different queer cultural identities in response to the changing forces of gender, race, and class. By studying lesbian culture as a separate experience from gay men's culture, a more complicated and complete understanding of the urban landscape emerges, opening the door to analysis at the intersection of these two cultures.

Many different lesbian cultural communities formed with rural backdrops, but the city held a particular draw for women and lesbians at the turn of the 20th century. Lesbians were able to create some urban visibility—particularly useful for attracting other lesbians—in bar communities and house parties. The city offered new freedoms from home and parental expectations. Due to the growth of industry and the turn toward industrial labor, women could find new jobs in cities that offered economic independence from parents or from the confines of marriage.

Although these jobs were strictly defined by class, race, and gendered expectations, they could be pursued away from the watchful eye of parents and home communities. For lesbians, this often meant having the financial means to live with other single women in cities, as well as an opportunity to explore their sexuality and create communities without the fear of family disapproval or the awareness of their sexuality that living in a home community might bring.

Lesbian communities of many types were an integral part of the American city during the early 20th century. Researchers Elizabeth Lapovsky Kennedy and Madeline Davis have noted four major types of intimate woman-centered relationships in the late 19th and early 20th centuries, but they suggest that one particular group was beginning to coalesce around an identity defined by their romantic and sexual interest in one another. Kennedy and Davis cite this as the beginning of a modern lesbian identity. These social groups took significant shape against the backdrop of the urban landscape. Kennedy and Davis locate their study in Buffalo, New York, but fragmented documentation and further research have indicated that similar lesbian communities existed in other cities of comparable size. Most working-class bar communities were composed of white women while black lesbians created separate spaces for community. In particular, Harlem in the 1920s was a visible and vibrant site for black lesbian identity.

In the years following World War II, lesbians established communities in a variety of towns across the United States. Although documentation is sparse, scholars have noted significant changes brought about during World War II, which placed many women in same-sex situations—especially in the absence of large numbers of men who were serving in the military— ultimately leading to the formation of lesbian communities. Women were called to work in occupations previously reserved for men, and they were encouraged to do so by patriotic propaganda. For lesbians, this meant the opportunity to associate in more women-centered communities—at work and in the cultural life of the cities where they were employed. War production towns became havens for lesbians to create community and to define a lesbian urban space. Lesbians served in the military in great numbers during World War II, and their very existence caused concern among homophobic military leaders. Ironically, this concern prompted increased conversation about lesbians in the military and gave them an increased visibility.

In the mid-20th century, some lesbians began to organize for the purpose of creating community. The most notable lesbian organization was the Daughters of Bilitis, founded in 1955 by Phyllis Lyon and Del Martin of San Francisco. This group is representative of a homophile movement that sought to offer support and improve the daily lives of lesbians and gay men. The homophile movement also represented defiance in the face of a Cold War panic mentality that had gripped the entire country. Fear of communism and communist subversives led to an increased targeting of lesbians and gay men as perverts and threats to a "safe" nuclear heterosexual family—believed to be the backbone of capitalist stability and success. Meetings of homophile organizations were held in many urban centers, initially under extreme secrecy. As a direct result of their meetings, the Daughters of Bilitis produced *The Ladder,* a publication mailed from San Francisco to locations throughout the United States. *The Ladder* provided a cultural and urban link for many rural lesbians, who were isolated from the opportunities for lesbian community offered by the urban environment.

As the Civil Rights Movement of the 1950s and 1960s gripped the country, lesbians found new opportunities to connect with each other as many involved themselves in civil rights struggles. Civil rights inspired new fervor, most noticeable in cities, for a gay liberation movement. In 1969, when police raided New York City's Stonewall Inn—a gay bar in Greenwich Village—lesbian and gay patrons fought back and symbolically inspired a growing movement for gay liberation. In addition to civil rights and gay liberation, the movement for women's liberation was experiencing a revival in the late 1960s. Many lesbian women joined the movement for women's rights and even established separatist organizations devoted to promoting lesbian feminism—separate from a male-dominated gay rights movement and a heterosexually dominated women's rights movement. The importance of these movements for creating visibility and community—particularly in urban settings—is irrefutable.

Lesbian urban culture has continued to evolve and diversify since feminism and civil rights permanently changed the lesbian urban landscape. As the initial AIDS crisis of the 1980s devastated the gay male community, lesbians became involved in radical urban activist groups, such as ACT-UP and Queer Nation, as well as support networks for AIDS victims.

As a direct result of these involvements, lesbians began to form their own radical activist organizations, such as the Lesbian Avengers founded in New York City in 1992. The Avengers have promoted visibility and radical activism—forming chapters in urban centers such as San Francisco, Chicago, Atlanta, Minneapolis, Philadelphia, and Salt Lake City.

In addition to activism, lesbians have created an urban culture involving an increasing variety of urban lesbian spaces. Women's bookstores and coffee houses, devoted to a focus on women's issues, were increasingly visible in cities by the 1970s. These spaces were the site of meetings for domestic violence groups, book clubs, women's spiritual groups, and other women-centered organizations, including many focused on the lesbian community. Women's sports, most notably local softball leagues, have long attracted lesbians eager to create culture and community in rural and urban locations. Nationally, the formation of the Women's National Basketball Association in 1996 added to the diversity of lesbian spaces by placing women's basketball teams in cities such as Charlotte, North Carolina; Cleveland, Ohio; Houston, Texas; Phoenix, Arizona; and Detroit, Michigan. WNBA games attract a diverse group of lesbians who create social space and family space in an otherwise heterosexual environment.

Women's music, record labels, and feminist presses have affected lesbian culture by promoting women's writing and song. Women-centered music and art events such as the Michigan Womyn's Music Festival, created in 1975, and Lilith Fair, an all-women's music tour born in the late 1990s, have offered new visibility for lesbians in women-centered spaces. Lesbian travel has also contributed to an intriguing itinerant lesbian community—providing intersections of the rural and the urban for women who can afford to participate in such activities as themed cruises with lesbian performers and themed weekends such as Women's Week in Key West.

Since the beginning of the 20th century, lesbian urban cultures have moved from a largely isolated and often silenced position to a place of visibility in the urban landscape. Lesbian communities continue to thrive in both large and smaller urban sites. The history of lesbian culture in cities is undeniable and is an integral part of urban space. The future of lesbian urban cultures will continue to be shaped by the geography of lesbian spaces, racial and class divisions, and at the time of this writing, the currently developing issues of lesbian and gay marriage and queer civil rights. The results of these developments will further solidify the importance of lesbian cultures and communities in the urban future.

—La Shonda Mims

Further Readings and References

Beemyn, B. (1997). *Creating a place for ourselves.* New York: Routledge.

Howard, J. (Ed.). (1997). *Carryin' on in the lesbian and gay South.* New York: New York University Press.

Kennedy, E. L., & Davis, M. D. (1993). *Boots of leather, slippers of gold: The history of a lesbian community.* New York: Routledge.

Maynard, S. (2004). "Without working?" Capitalism, urban culture, and gay history. *Journal of Urban History, 30,* 378–398.

Stein, M. (2000). *City of sisterly and brotherly loves.* Chicago: University of Chicago Press.

LEVITT, WILLIAM

William Jaird Levitt (February 11, 1907–January 28, 1994), referred to as the father of American suburbia, is known for his development of several Levittowns. These massive housing developments in Long Island, New York; Bucks County, Pennsylvania; and Willingborough, New Jersey, were model communities that revolutionized the postwar housing industry in the United States. William's father, Abraham Levitt, was a self-made man who rose from poverty to become a successful real estate lawyer and investor in the 1920s. During the Depression, he established a real estate company called Abraham Levitt & Sons, to involve William and his younger brother, Alfred. While at college, they were asked to complete an upscale project, Rockville Center, which sparked William's interest in the building industry.

In 1942, Levitt gained more proficiency in fast and efficient construction processes when Levitt & Sons obtained a federal contract to build 2,350 homes for shipyard workers in Norfolk, Virginia. He enlisted in the U.S. Navy a year later and reached the rank of lieutenant. Levitt's experience with the Navy not only advanced his knowledge of mass production techniques but also gave him time to think about America's housing crisis and the opportunities for low-cost housing construction.

With $50 million in funding, Levitt's dream community for returning war veterans broke ground in Long Island, New York, in 1947. Levittown marked the beginning of modern suburbia, and William Levitt was recognized as the biggest home builder of that period. His ability to sell pieces of the American dream as a regular, inexpensive, and accessible commodity was his most significant contribution.

William Levitt's visible achievements often overshadowed his brother Alfred's talents. Shy and idealistic, Alfred, a self-taught architect, was the great designer of the homes the brothers built. It was William's financial ingenuity, competence in implementing mass production systems, and affable personality, however, that developed and sold these units by radically changing traditional industry practices. For example, he was able to bypass labor unions, resolve difficult regulation problems, and monopolize procurement and supplier chains by establishing lumberyards. One of the most controversial subjects surrounding this suburban icon was his discriminatory practices. In Levitt's early projects, people of color were barred from purchasing property, and he responded to accusations of racism by saying that this was a business move.

As a youth, William Levitt was known to have a strong desire for wealth. His reputation for producing housing units at an impressive rate of one house every 16 minutes and in 27 basic steps brought in a fortune that enabled him to live his high-profile dream. A celebrity at one time, he resided in a $3 million mansion, owned several yachts, collected expensive art pieces, and married three times.

After constructing more than 140,000 homes around the world, William sold Levitt & Sons to International Telephone and Telegraph in 1968. His later housing developments were not successful, and he ended up with enormous debt. He was 87 years old when he died in 1994, a man who left a legacy but lost a fortune.

—Mary Anne Albanza Akers

Further Readings and References

Blackwell, J. (2005, December). *1951: American dream houses, all in a row.* Retrieved from http://www.capitalcentury.com/1951.html

Hales, P. B. (2004, August). *Levittown: Documents of an ideal American suburb.* Retrieved from http://tigger.uic.edu/~pbhales/Levittown.html

LEVITTOWN

Levittown is located on the Hempstead Plains of Long Island, a glacial outwash some 25 miles east of Manhattan in the rural community of Island Trees. The firm of Abraham Levitt & Sons built Levittown's 17,447 four-room houses between 1947 and 1951, using cost-effective, mass-production construction techniques originally developed by the military for enlisted men's and defense workers' housing during World War II.

Levitt & Sons built three subdivisions between 1947 and 1965, each of which was called Levittown. However, the name Levittown is most often used to refer to the Long Island Levittown, which has become the archetype of postwar suburban subdivisions for the lower middle class.

Although it was by no means the first American suburb, Levittown represents a marked shift in the direction of suburban development. Whereas the 19th- and early-20th-century suburbs served as bedroom retreats from the city for the more affluent, the postwar suburban subdivisions were part of a larger movement to decentralize the industrial city in response to the threat of atomic warfare. In part, this was due to the decentralization of the military-industrial complex, which in turn arose in response to the nuclear threat to concentrated population centers. By moving both the defense plants and the worker housing to the suburban fringe, postwar policies decentralized the targets of nuclear attack.

Levittown is significant for its role in the transition of America's working population from urban tenants to suburban homeowners. It represents a major socioeconomic shift in the components of the American homeowner class. As a result of two major changes in public policy—the Federal Housing Act of 1934 and the Veterans Readjustment Act of 1943 (the GI Bill)—the working and lower-middle classes were enabled to purchase houses with long-term mortgages. Because the risks to the funding institutions were underwritten by federal insurance, the banks were able to offer lower down payments and longer terms, amortizing the debt and lowering the payments so that the risk to homeowners was also reduced. This made it possible for people of modest means to spread the cost of purchasing a home over longer periods. The housing strand of the GI Bill, in combination with the terms of the Federal Housing Act of 1934, underwrote the economic risk for the mortgages provided to returning veterans.

During its construction phase, Levittown was funded under the terms of the GI Bill, and purchases were limited to veterans. Only later, when the veterans market was satisfied, did other forms of finance permit nonveterans to purchase the houses.

Levittown has become synonymous with large-scale, affordable, postwar suburban subdivisions for the lower middle class. It has also become the target for critics citing the various ills that affected postwar American society in the second half of the 20th century. Unlike the earlier bedroom suburbs, which were linked by public transportation and economics to the urban core, these communities were more likely to be self-contained entities, with fewer ties to the city.

The houses built at Levittown are also significant because they typify a major shift in the technology of residential construction that followed World War II. The first 6,000 were rental units designed in the Cape Cod style. Using wartime construction methods, the work was rationalized and based on mass-produced materials in standard sizes. Concrete-slab foundations were used to speed construction and reduce costs, and a reverse assembly line, in which the houses stood still while the workers progressed from unit to unit, streamlined the labor process.

Although inexpensive, the Levitt houses retained the basic elements of a prewar middle-class house—a kitchen and living room, a single bath, and two bedrooms, rather than those of a tenement flat—a kitchen and two chambers. The unfinished attic could later be converted into additional rooms, and the oversized lot allowed for expansion at the ground level.

Standard equipment for each unit included basic, construction-grade kitchen appliances: enameled metal cabinets, a refrigerator, stove, and an automatic washer. Following the planned community concept, Levitt included seven "village greens" with shops and play areas, nine swimming pools, and community centers for the various neighborhoods.

When the subdivision opened in 1947, the houses rented for $52 per month with veterans as the priority clientele. When Levitt & Sons withdrew from the rental market in 1948, they sold the rental units and used the proceeds to fund the construction of houses intended only for sale. Those rental units that were not sold to their tenants were included in a package sale to a not-for-profit educational organization.

By 1948, the firm was under the direction of the older of the two Levitt sons, William J. Levitt, with his brother, Alfred, serving as architect/designer. Their father, Abraham Levitt, remained with the firm but in an advisory capacity.

In 1949, in response to concerns about the marketability of the Cape Cod model and the threat of negative sales to the entire housing program, the Federal Housing Administration (FHA) withdrew funding from the Cape Cods and called for redesigned model houses. Levitt's new model, described in sales promotions as a ranch house, retained the basic configuration of the Cape Cods—four rooms with an expansion attic and a peaked roof. However, the exterior ornamentation shifted from a colonial motif to a frontier emphasis. Both models were small in scale—750 square feet for the Cape Cods, 800 for the ranches. Although the exteriors varied slightly within each model, the floor plans were identical.

Levittown, Long Island, was followed by Levittown, Pennsylvania (1951–1955), and Levittown, New Jersey (1958–1965). The Pennsylvania subdivision had greater variety in both style and pricing of the houses. This Levittown retained many of the innovations introduced in New York—standardized components, mass-produced construction, annual models, and land reserved for schools and churches. Following the new suburban trend, the Levitts constructed a large shopping center outside the development rather than small village greens within it.

The New Jersey Levittown was designed to counter the criticism levied against the earlier Levittowns. It was aimed at a more varied and affluent market and offered three basic models and price levels with three to four bedrooms. In 1964, a five-bedroom model was added. Rather than replicating one model in an area, the New Jersey project integrated the various styles within a single neighborhood. In response to the continuing barrage of criticism that the first Levittown had incurred throughout the 1950s, the residents of the New Jersey development voted to revert to the community's former name, Willingboro, in the late 1960s. Both the New York and the Pennsylvania communities continue to answer to the original name, Levittown.

The GI Bill had shifted the critical mass of American workers from renters to homeowners. Before World War II, almost two thirds of American families lived in shared or rented housing; by 1950,

that ratio had been reversed. This shift to a lower socioeconomic suburban environment resulted in a series of attacks on Levittown and the other affordable subdivisions funded by the FHA and the GI Bill.

Many of these criticisms were rooted in 19th-century beliefs about the working class and the fear that affordable housing would result in slums. In addition, the new dissociation from the city fueled fears that the new suburbs would produce a stratified and undifferentiated society. In this view, conformity and isolation would emasculate the men and drive the women to neuroses. In addition, some feared that the lack of socioeconomic variation would have a stultifying effect on the social culture of America. Architects complained that the repetitious nature of the houses stifled individuality and reduced eye appeal and marketability. Financiers warned that economic downturns would result in wholesale foreclosures and bankruptcies.

The predictions did not materialize. Levittown and its houses have increased in both size and economic value since their original construction. The stereotype of the Levittown houses, celebrated as "rows of ticky-tack," "peas in a pod," or "cookie-cutter" models, is inaccurate. Well constructed from the start, the houses have been expanded, remodeled, and upgraded by their owners. Despite the critics, the various Levittowns have been a major factor in the expansion of the American middle class.

—*Barbara M. Kelly*

Further Readings and References

Duncan, S. K. (1999). *Levittown: The way we were.* Huntington, NY: Maple Hill Press.

Ferrer, M. L., & Navarra, T. (1997). *Levittown: The first 50 years* (Images of America Series). Dover, NH: Arcadia.

Kelly, B. M. (1988). *The politics of house and home: Implications in the built environment of Levittown.* Doctoral dissertation, State University at Stony Brook, Long Island, NY.

Kelly, B. M. (1993). *Expanding the American dream: Building and rebuilding Levittown* (SUNY Series in the New Cultural History). Albany: State University of New York Press.

Lataresse, L. (1997). *History of Levittown.* Levittown, NY: Levittown Historical Society.

Lundrigan, M., & Navarra, T. (1999). *Levittown, NY* (Images of America Series). Dover, NH: Arcadia.

LINCOLN CENTER FOR THE PERFORMING ARTS

The Lincoln Center for the Performing Arts, located in central Manhattan in New York City, is a nonprofit organization that receives support from the city of New York. It comprises many different buildings, including the Juilliard School of Music, the Vivian Beaumont Theater, the Metropolitan Opera House, Avery Fisher Hall, the New York State Theater, the Guggenheim Bandshell in Damrosch Park, several Fordham University buildings, and the Library-Museum of the Performing Arts.

Lincoln Center offers presentations by internationally acclaimed artists while supporting beginning artists. Touted as the "largest cultural center in the world," Lincoln Center presents all genres of music, drama, film, and dance and offers something for people of every age and taste. Professional performances of ballet, jazz, and the symphony occupy the same area as classes to teach beginning and aspiring performers. Construction of the Lincoln Center for the Performing Arts began in 1959, and the complex has continued to grow as dormitories, rehearsal studios, movie theaters, and other facilities have been constructed, adding to the wealth of resources available for artists.

The Juilliard School of Music offers premiere music, dance, and drama lessons to promising students from around the United States and Europe. Considered a music conservatory, Julliard teaches classical, jazz, modern, and improvisational music. Instrumental, piano, and vocal music along with other musical genres can be heard throughout its halls. Ballet and improvisational, classical, and modern dance are also offered. Drama lessons provide aspiring actors opportunities to practice their craft. Plays, musicals, and performances combine with traditional classes to complete an undergraduate education. A student can either take part-time lessons at Julliard or participate in a degree program. In 2005, Julliard celebrated its 100th anniversary.

Another well-known component of the Lincoln Center for the Performing Arts is the Metropolitan Opera House. In existence since 1883, the Metropolitan Opera House is noted for its spectacular operatic presentations, combining the best costumes, stage designs, and performers. Classic operas such as *La Traviata, Aïda,* and *La Bohème* along with more modern operas are presented. Patrons are delighted with the rich ornamentation of the Metropolitan Opera House and its often expensively dressed audience; however, programs for schoolchildren and senior citizens are also offered. Technological advances have allowed synopses of the opera stories along with photos to be placed on a Web site so that audience members who are unfamiliar with a particular opera can inform themselves before attending. Tools such as these remove some of the mystery of the opera without detracting from the splendor.

—*Janice E. Jones*

Further Readings and References

The Lincoln Center for the Performing Arts Web site, http://www.lincolncenter.org
Young, E. B. (1980). *Lincoln Center: The building of an institution.* New York: New York University Press.

LINDSAY, JOHN V.

A mayor of New York City (1966–1974) known for his innovative social reform initiatives, John V. Lindsay (1921–2000) graduated from Yale University in 1943 and, after serving in the U.S. Navy during World War II, sought a career in public service. A graduate of Yale Law School in 1948, he joined the reform wing of the Republican Party and was elected to the U.S. House of Representatives in 1958, representing Manhattan's Upper East Side. During four terms in Congress, Lindsay built a reputation as a liberal, voting for civil rights and Great Society legislation. He ran for mayor in 1965 as a Republican. With the endorsement of the Liberal Party, Lindsay defeated the Democratic nominee, Abraham D. Beame, and Conservative William F. Buckley.

Promising reform, Lindsay took initiatives that antagonized the city's middle-class whites. Hours after taking office, Lindsay faced a public transit strike that shut down the city's subways. To combat police brutality, Lindsay established a civilian complaint board, only to have it rejected by the city's white voters, many of whom viewed it as a concession to minorities. To avert race riots, Lindsay walked the streets of the city's most troubled neighborhoods. When New York emerged largely unscathed by the riots that swept the nation in 1968, President Lyndon B. Johnson appointed Lindsay to the Kerner Commission, which issued an influential report on the riots.

To increase minority control over neighborhood schools, Lindsay decentralized the city's school system and established community school districts. In 1968, the city's teachers responded to the experiment in the Ocean Hill-Brownsville section with a series of strikes that shut down the public school system. The strikes further weakened Lindsay's standing among middle-class whites. Seeking re-election in 1969, Lindsay lost the Republican nomination to John J. Marchi but received the endorsement of the Liberal Party and defeated Marchi and Democrat Mario Procaccino in the general election.

During his second term, Lindsay's scatter-site housing program—building public housing projects (with mostly minority tenants) in predominantly white neighborhoods—generated more protests from middle-class whites. Switching to the Democratic Party, Lindsay was among the candidates for the presidency in 1972. After his poor showing in the Democratic primaries, Lindsay announced that he would not seek a third mayoral term.

Credited for his innovative social programs, Lindsay paid for increased municipal expenditures with new taxes and heavy borrowing. These policies led to a big increase in the city's deficit, and Lindsay's mayoral successors blamed him for the city's fiscal crisis in 1975. After leaving office in 1974, Lindsay practiced law, appeared as a television personality, and ran unsuccessfully for the U.S. Senate in 1980. He died of complications from Parkinson's disease in 2000.

—*Dan Wishnoff*

Further Readings and References

Cannato, V. J. (2001). *The ungovernable city: John Lindsay and his struggle to save New York.* New York: Basic Books.
McNickle, C. (1993). *To be mayor of New York: Ethnic politics in the city.* New York: Columbia University Press.

Llewelyn Park, New Jersey

Llewelyn Park was an early suburban neighborhood of about 50 houses built in New Jersey between 1852 and 1869. During the mid- to late 19th century, it provided the elaborate setting for picturesque houses such as those developed by Andrew Jackson Downing and Alexander Jackson Davis. The place took its name from Llewelyn Haskell, a chemical and drug manufacturer who conceived of an ideal neighborhood complete with a picturesque landscaped garden and conveniently located in Orange, New Jersey, near the new Morris and Essex railroad line connecting New York City with the community 12 miles to the east. Before this time, it was impractical to commute a great distance to work by horse or buggy. Once the railroad connected neighborhoods on the outskirts of downtown commercial areas, this changed. Thus, Llewelyn Park was the prototype for the American suburban neighborhood, an idealized, rural world of privilege, convenience, and picturesque aesthetics. Haskell himself allegedly sketched out the plan with Davis's expert advice on the various components of an illusionary wild and natural landscape. The system of streets was established in 1852 and 1853, and construction of the neighborhood's houses continued for the next 17 years.

Landscape architects Eugene A. Baumann and Howard Daniels contributed to the design of extensions to the original property. Overall, streets conformed to the swell of the natural terrain. Lots were large by contemporary standards—from an acre to as many as 20 acres—and were left without hedges or fences to subdivide the individual properties. Homes were located variously on building sites and were framed by gardens, natural forest land, and vegetation. Davis designed all the original houses in a range of styles, as well as a rubble stone gatehouse, a charming introduction to the neighborhood beyond. A communal strip of land laced through the entire development, unifying it and pulling the disparate elements of the site together in a coherent whole. At the center of the site was a 600-foot-high rocky outcropping topped by pine trees and hemlocks, and springs filtered lazily through creek beds.

In its day, Llewelyn Park made a significant departure in urban planning through its approach to comprehensive planning, landscaping themes, and communal park spaces. Like the work of Frederick Law Olmstead, it was anti-urban, fully anchored in the agrarian social theory of Jeffersonian America. As a romantic ideal, the area gave homeowners a retreat from the chaos of the industrialized and urbanized American landscape, an escape to the garden. Because the neighborhood was free of the pollution, traffic, and noise of urban neighborhoods, it was an immediate financial success that spawned countless imitations. Moreover, Llewelyn Park challenged the notion that the rational grid would spread infinitely across the American landscape to populate the wilderness with logical street systems and towns laid out according to a predetermined plan. Although it was indeed carefully planned and manipulated, it gave the illusion that it was not. Instead, it promised a particular elite way of life, separated from the place of one's employment, and a prototype for the good life that someone with enough money could buy.

—*Martha Bradley*

See also Olmsted, Frederick Law, Sr.; Parks

Further Readings and References

Kunstler, J. H. (1993). *The geography of nowhere: The rise and decline of America's man-made landscape.* New York: Simon & Schuster.

Roth, L. M. (1979). *A concise history of American architecture.* New York: Icon Editions, Harper & Row.

Scully, V. (1969). *American architecture and urbanism.* New York: Holt, Rinehart & Winston.

LODGING, BOARDING, AND ROOMING HOUSES

Sheltering acquaintances, relatives, and strangers, often in exchange for their labor, was ordinary social practice in early America and remained so well into the 19th century. But as commercial and industrial development, rural migration, and European immigration swelled the populations of cities like New York, Philadelphia, Boston, and (eventually) Chicago and San Francisco, boarding and lodging—the provision of shelter in exchange for cash—became common, if often controversial features of urban life.

Theoretically boarding, lodging, and rooming houses provided somewhat different services. Boardinghouses provided *board*—three meals a day served at a common table—and housekeeping services; lodging and rooming houses neither fed nor cleaned up after their inhabitants. In practice, however, distinctions blurred, and 19th-century Americans frequently used these terms interchangeably. Although residences erected by employers in factory towns like Lowell, Massachusetts loom largest in the historical and popular imaginations,

the vast majority of boarding, rooming, and lodging houses—in contrast to hotels—had served previous purposes. Not until the early 20th century would purpose-built rooming houses appear in places like San Francisco's Tenderloin district. The typical boarding or lodging house was an older residence subdivided to make room for lodgers—or simply a home with extra space to let.

Walt Whitman claimed in 1856 that nearly three fourths of New York City's population lived in boardinghouses. Clearly an exaggeration, Whitman's remark nevertheless captures boardinghouses' ubiquity; social historians have estimated that between a third and a half of 19th-century urbanites took in boarders or lived as boarders themselves at some point in their lives. Precise figures are difficult if not impossible to calculate, partly because boarding took so many forms. Landladies who offered lodgings in "private families" often refused to advertise their services, failing even to list themselves as boardinghouse keepers in city directories. Distinctions between private families and boardinghouses reflected differences in scale (the former often—but not always—housed fewer boarders than did the latter) and in legal and commercial status (private families skirted local ordinances that required boardinghouse keepers to secure licenses and pay hotel taxes). Yet, whether one presided over a private family or kept a boardinghouse also had a great deal to do with defining social respectability; anxious to preserve their gentility, landladies who hailed from middle- and upper-class backgrounds described themselves as hosting visiting friends—not paying strangers—or keeping private families.

Whatever form they assumed, boardinghouses were institutions of enormous economic, cultural, and social importance. They provided thousands of women (and many men) with a livelihood, for some, a supplement to family incomes, for others, their sole means of support. By providing homes for urban migrants and European immigrants, boardinghouses and, later, rooming and lodging houses underwrote both urban growth and economic development. They helped newcomers, the vast majority of whom were young and single, adapt to urban life. Seated with their housemates at common tables, new boarders learned about employment opportunities, morals, dress, and manners. (Or, as in the case of the boardinghouse reach, they learned bad manners). Similarly, the advice that was offered varied with the character of the establishment. Landladies and fellow boarders might do their best to protect recent arrivals from the dangers of the city.

Alternatively, they might introduce them to vices like drinking, gambling, and prostitution.

Boardinghouses both reflected and shaped social identities. Most residences were segregated along class, race, and ethnic lines, but within these categories lurked a surprising heterogeneity. Some establishments, like the actors' boardinghouses concentrated in theater districts and the sailors' boardinghouses clustered along city waterfronts, served particular occupational groups. Emigrant boardinghouses sheltered—and often exploited—newly arrived immigrants. Others catered to people of various proclivities: temperance advocates, vegetarians, spiritualists, and members of particular religious denominations. To a limited degree, boardinghouses also encouraged social mixing. Clerks occasionally mingled with manual workers; native-born Protestants with Irish Catholics; and very occasionally whites with African Americans. Respectable boardinghouses often housed both men and women; boardinghouses "for the lady only" were synonymous with brothels—even if they were not brothels in fact. Beginning in the 1870s, organizations like the Young Men's Christian Association and the Young Women's Christian Association erected dozens of "boarding homes," hoping to dissuade young men and women from taking up residence in disreputable places.

The YMCA and YWCA deliberately invoked the language of home, for the expansion of urban boardinghouse life coincided with the rise of white middle-class domesticity, symbolized by the private single-family home. To many middle-class Americans, boardinghouses represented everything homes were not. Novelists, advice writers, newspaper columnists, and humorists condemned boardinghouses as dirty, disreputable, lacking in privacy, and above all, creatures of a corrupt marketplace. Housewives, as various cultural commentators saw it, labored for love; boardinghouse keepers labored for money, obsessed with economizing at their lodgers' expense. These seemingly self-evident dichotomies between home and work, public and private, masked uncomfortable truths. Middle-class homes often included paid employees—domestic servants; middle-class housewives, like their working-class counterparts, took in sewing, laundry, and boarders; housework, even if unremunerated, involved considerable labor. Indeed, for most Americans, "home" represented an unachievable ideal. Attainable or not, it exerted substantial cultural power, not the least fostering the widespread conviction that boardinghouses could never be homes.

Despite these criticisms, boardinghouses persisted well into the 20th century. Increasingly, however, they were replaced by apartments, which mostly housed middle- and upper-class residents, and rooming and lodging houses, which catered to a primarily working-class clientele. If boarding and lodging had been less than distinguishable during the first half of the 19th century, by 1900, a rooming or lodging house signified a residence that offered shelter but not food or housekeeping services—a transformation that reduced landladies' expenses and labor and offered residents greater privacy. Usually located within walking distance of their inhabitants' workplaces and dependent on the presence of nearby restaurants, saloons, and laundries, rooming house districts emerged in neighborhoods like Boston's South End, San Francisco's Western Addition, and Chicago's Near North Side.

Like the boardinghouses they slowly replaced, the quality and clientele of rooming and lodging houses varied. In some cities—Boston and San Francisco, for example—the term *lodging house* described all sorts of establishments. More often, *rooming house* or *furnished room house* connoted fairly comfortable quarters that housed skilled and clerical workers, whereas *lodging house* might mean a flophouse that charged transients a few cents a night for a tiny cubicle or a spot on the floor. But because both kinds of residences catered to young single people, both gave rise to the sorts of fears that critics had once associated with boardinghouses. If 19th-century commentators condemned boardinghouses because they were not homes, Progressive Era housing reformers sought—largely unsuccessfully—to eradicate "the lodger evil."

However, rooming and lodging houses (and occasionally even boardinghouses) remained important forms of urban housing into the 1950s and 1960s. But as the combined impact of automobiles, highway construction, suburbanization, and urban deindustrialization eroded their appeal for young workers, such residences increasingly catered to the elderly and the very poor. Urban renewal projects in the 1960s and 1970s destroyed numerous lodging house districts, substantially contributing to the problem of homelessness. The fate of boarding, lodging, and rooming houses—once integral to the urban landscape—demonstrates the power of dominant ideals, especially the enduring romance of the single-family home, to shape urban policy.

—*Wendy Gamber*

See also Apartment Buildings; Hotels

Further Readings and References

Blackmar, E. (1989). *Manhattan for rent, 1785–1850*. Ithaca, NY: Cornell University Press.

Gamber, W. (2002). Tarnished labor: The home, the market, and the boardinghouse in antebellum America. *Journal of the Early Republic, 22*, 177–204.

Gamber, W. (2005). Away from home: Middle-class boarders in the nineteenth-century city. *Journal of Urban History, 31*, 289–305.

Groth, P. (1994). *Living downtown: The history of residential hotels in the United States*. Berkeley: University of California Press.

Peel, M. (1986). On the margins: Lodgers and boarders in Boston, 1860–1900. *Journal of American History, 72*, 813–834.

LOGUE, EDWARD

Few individuals played a greater role in shaping the postwar American city than urban renewal czar Edward J. Logue (1921-2000). Born in Philadelphia, Logue studied at Yale University and served as a bombardier in the Army Air Force during World War II. The many hours he spent peering down on European cities made him highly skilled at analyzing and interpreting the urban landscape and—ironically—prepared him well for a career implementing massive redevelopment projects.

After the war, Logue returned to Yale to study law, and in 1954, he was appointed New Haven, Connecticut's development administrator by Mayor Richard C. Lee. Logue and Lee spent most of the next decade resuscitating a city crippled by a middle-class exodus to the suburbs. Urban renewal in New Haven did not come painlessly; some 25,000 people were uprooted as extensive "slums" were cleared. The Wooster Square redevelopment alone displaced 2,700 households in what had been a thriving Italian American community. But New Haven's program also set standards for a more temperate approach to renewal, soliciting community input, recycling historic structures, and providing citizens with such amenities as affordable housing, new schools, libraries, and senior centers.

Logue's next challenge was Boston. Like New Haven, Boston's economy had been gutted by the flight of jobs and population to the suburbs. Several attempts had been made to lure the middle class back to the city, including the disastrous West End urban renewal project. In 1961, Mayor John F. Collins recruited Logue to head the Boston Redevelopment Agency. Logue soon completed the transformation of honky-tonk Scollay Square into Government Center, organizing a major public competition for the design of a new city hall. He undertook renewal projects in the South End, Roxbury, Charlestown, and the Back Bay, where he helped build the Prudential Center over the old Boston and Albany rail yards. Logue also succeeded in reconnecting Boston to its waterfront, in part by turning long-neglected Faneuil Hall and Quincy Market into a hugely popular "festival marketplace." The project, a collaboration with real estate visionary James Rouse, inspired similar efforts around the country. Logue's Boston years, the most fruitful of his career, helped set the stage for the city's resurgence as part of the "Massachusetts miracle" that transformed the regional economy in the 1980s.

Logue left Boston after an unsuccessful bid for mayor in 1968 and was asked by New York governor Nelson A. Rockefeller to head his new Urban Development Corporation (UDC) Unfettered by local zoning codes and flush with federal money, Logue and the UDC built more than 30,000 units of affordable housing and three new towns before going bankrupt in 1975, when federal housing subsidies ended. The best known of Logue's UDC work is New York's Roosevelt Island, a highly successful "new town in town" that Logue considered his proudest achievement. Logue ended his career in the South Bronx, turning the devastated Charlotte Street neighborhood into a model of inner-city homeownership.

Edward Logue is often compared to that other titan of urban renewal, Robert Moses. Whereas Moses was disdainful of the urban underclass, however, and routinely ignored the needs and wishes of communities affected by his projects, Logue struggled to make urban renewal a positive force in the lives of city residents. Emphasizing the importance of "planning with people," Logue actively sought citizen input. He was also an early advocate of historic preservation and pioneered the use of architectural design review in the redevelopment process. Logue's vision of the new American city was grand but inclusive, reflecting his lifelong commitment to equity and social justice.

—*Thomas J. Campanella*

See also Moses, Robert; Urban Renewal and Revitalization

Further Readings and References

Dahl, R. A. (1961). *Who governs? Democracy and power in an American city*. New Haven, CT: Yale University Press.

O'Connor, T. H. (1993). *Building a new Boston: Politics and urban renewal, 1950–1970*. Boston: Northeastern University Press.

LOS ANGELES, CALIFORNIA

The second-largest city in the United States, with an estimated 2005 population of 3.96 million residents (and more than 16.5 million in the metropolitan area) spread over 470 square miles, Los Angeles exerts its influence as a model of American urbanism not merely through its great size but also by its novel geographical configuration. Although it emerged as a major city during an era of enthusiasm for skyscrapers and urban verticality, Los Angeles was pioneering a new horizontal form of metropolitan expansion by the end of the 1920s. De-emphasizing a centralized downtown business district, greater Los Angeles instead arrayed industry, retail, and residence across a vast geographical area. Not merely suburban, this multicentered, distributed, and integrated topography proved particularly influential in the years after World War II, when many other cities, particularly in the Sun Belt, emulated this horizontal built environment. Equally important in recent years has been Los Angeles's status as a multiethnic community, without, as of 2006, a single dominant ethnic group. In particular, the addition since World War II of substantial Asian and Native American communities to the existing base of white, Latino, and African American populations has made greater Los Angeles the most diverse large city in the country, and this has contributed to the global influence of its popular culture.

Early History

Yet, for centuries, Los Angeles was neither particularly diverse nor influential. First populated at least 1,000 years ago by the Shoshonean-speaking Tongva (Gabrieleño) people, the Los Angeles basin hosted perhaps 10,000 people in at least 40 separate settlements by the time the Spanish explorers arrived in 1769. Due to the disastrous effects of conquest and colonization, the city did not approach that population level again for more than 100 years. When Gaspar de Portolá's expedition reached the basin its members christened *Nuestra Señora la Reina de Los Angeles de Porciúncula*, they observed a "populous village" of Native Californians living in the flood plain of a small, meandering river. This prosperous community was soon brought under Spanish dominion, and many of its people were subjugated to the San Gabriel mission established nearby in 1771. Due to harsh treatment and disease, the population

of the Los Angeles basin plunged to about 1,300. During the Spanish period and continuing during the 20 years of Mexican rule, the local economy relied primarily on the raising of cattle. Indeed, the pueblo of Los Angeles would remain a cow town for almost a century after its founding.

1848–1910: Frontier Los Angeles

At the conclusion of the war with Mexico in 1848, Los Angeles passed into American sovereignty with few immediate repercussions. Yet, a survey of the city by U.S. Army Lt. E. O. C. Ord, combined with the Land Act of 1852, began a process that would eventually displace many of the Mexican American owners of large ranchos in the region—the Californios. Over the next several decades, most of the ranchos fell into Yankee hands through sale, debt default, lawyer's fees, outright fraud, and, not least, the ruling of a series of land commissions that frequently found the old Mexican property titles invalid.

Although a small vein of gold had been discovered north of the city in 1842, for the most part, the transformative events of the Gold Rush passed Los Angeles by, relegating all of Southern California to continued obscurity for almost 30 years. In contrast to the northern part of the state, Los Angeles received little immigration in these years, its population rising to little more than 11,000 as late as 1880. Moreover, a smallpox epidemic hit the town in the latter half of the 1860s, further decimating the region's population of Native Californians. In the wake of this catastrophe, combined with a prolonged drought that bankrupted many Californio ranching families in the same decade, white Americans came to outnumber Indians and Hispanics for the first time in 1870 (a demographic aberration that would persist for a little more than a century).

Los Angeles's isolation began to change in 1876, when the Southern Pacific opened the first rail connection between Los Angeles and Northern California (and, from there, the rest of the United States). The next year, Angelenos sent their first shipment of oranges to the East. The marketing of the oranges in cooperation with the railroad, which culminated 20 years later in the creation of the Sunkist cooperative, widely circulated booster images of an alluring Mediterranean climate in Southern California. For the first time, tourists began to make their way to Los Angeles in substantial numbers by the end of the 1870s. Yet, it was the coming of the rival Santa Fe railroad in 1885 that dramatically increased the influx. The rate war between the Southern Pacific and the Santa Fe railroads dropped the price of a cross-country ticket to less than a dollar, spurring a population increase to more than 50,000 by the end of the decade and a speculative boom that saw land valuations increase 30-fold by 1887. Contributing to the boom was the publication in 1884 of Helen Hunt Jackson's idealized novel, *Ramona,* which although it was intended to expose the plight of Southern California's remaining Native Americans, did more to promulgate a nostalgic mythology of romantic Californio culture, which primarily appealed to wealthy health seekers and other eastern tourists.

The final years of the 19th century brought continued growth, along with increasing economic diversification, driven by the discovery of oil near downtown by Edward Doheny in 1892 and an extended battle between local business leaders and the Southern Pacific railroad over the construction of a deep-water port. With the final defeat of the railroad's preferred Santa Monica site, federal funds were appropriated in 1899 for the new harbor in San Pedro. Thus, by the end of the century, Los Angeles was poised for substantial growth.

1910–1945: Emergence of the Horizontal Metropolis

Although agriculture, and most famously citrus, was still a major economic engine for the entire region, the economy was beginning to diversify in the first decades of the 20th century, merging the natural resources of the region with modern industrial processes. Contributing to the growth of the metropolis were new discoveries of oil in 1921 in the Signal Hill district; the growth of trade spurred by 1909's annexation of the port in San Pedro and its major expansion 5 years later in anticipation of the opening of the Panama Canal; and the emergence of novel ways to commercialize the climate through boosterism and the new technology of the motion picture.

With the success of *Birth of a Nation* in 1915, Southern California established itself as the undisputed center of film production in the country, employing more than 20,000 workers by 1920. Filmed images of scenic Southern California proved a powerful tool to the booster industry, which promised pleasant bungalows as alternatives to eastern cities' crowded and heterogeneous slums. As a result of these efforts, Los Angeles's population quadrupled between 1910 and 1930; at one point in the mid-1920s, 5 percent of the city's population (43,000 of more than 850,000 people) were employed as real estate agents. The influx of midwestern migrants, whom Nathanael West, in 1993, famously called the people who "had come to California to die" (p. 23), reinforced a carefully orchestrated reputation of Los Angeles as a "better city" due to its primarily "American" ethnic stock, as Dana Bartlett put it in 1907 (p. 20).

The growing importance of boosterism fed by Hollywood fantasy reflects the ways Los Angeles began to artificially supplement the natural advantages of its climate during the early years of the 20th century. To supply the infrastructure for continued growth, the city approved construction in 1907 of a massive aqueduct to carry water from the Owens Valley 233 miles to the northeast. The project, orchestrated by city engineer William Mulholland, reached completion in 1913, spurring the city's annexation of 168 square miles of the San Fernando Valley less than 2 years later. One final economic boon brought by the application of industrial techniques to the propitious climate was the growth after World War I of the local aircraft industry.

In terms of urban form, Los Angeles in the first decades of the 20th century was a fairly conventional city. The far-flung Pacific Electric interurban railway, consolidated by Henry Huntington into the largest of its kind by 1910, stretched for more than 1,000 miles across Southern California, spurring the development of bedroom communities far into the agricultural fields (which Huntington himself purchased and developed as lucrative subdivisions). Yet, as late as 1925, about half of all business activity in the metropolis was concentrated in the compact downtown district, which hosted all of the city's department stores and movie theaters (concentrated along Broadway), banks and other financial institutions (clustered on Spring Street), and the vast majority of its professional offices. A marked prevalence of single-family homes in the outlying residential districts reflected the effects of a temperate local climate and aggressive real estate speculation, but it did not alter the fundamental concentric structure of peripheral suburbs surrounding a densely concentrated commercial core, which was typical of American cities in this period.

Yet, as Los Angeles approached a million inhabitants during the mid-1920s, many Angelenos felt that their city was sorely in need of a program of urban modernization. In particular, mounting automotive traffic was already threatening to overwhelm the compact downtown, disrupting the Big Red Cars of the Pacific Electric (and, even more, the Yellow Cars of its sister Los Angeles Railway). Leaders of the downtown business community consequently looked to build their city into a fully modern metropolis, following the vertical model established by New York and Chicago, by introducing a sophisticated transit infrastructure to the central city.

Local city planners under the visionary Gordon Whitnall fiercely opposed these plans. Influenced by Ebenezer Howard's garden city movement, these planning professionals instead sought to de-emphasize what they referred to as "the congested district" in favor of outlying developments that would ideally combine work, recreation, and housing in autonomous communities. By encouraging outlying development through subdivision control and expanded powers of zoning, and by relying on the pervasiveness of the automobile (by 1915, the county had 55,000 cars, more than anywhere else in the country), planners sought to disperse the growing population into many far-flung regional subcenters, thus preserving the existing low-density, relatively homogeneous culture of the metropolis.

In a pivotal and racially charged 1926 city transit referendum, local planners abetted by an aggressive campaign in the *Los Angeles Times* raised the specter of the city being "darkened" by eastern-style slums brought about by rapid transit. Angelenos voted by a narrow margin to reject plans for an extensive downtown elevated railway system, effectively determining that Los Angeles would not follow the pattern established during that decade by vertical metropolises such as New York and Chicago.

Neither, however, would Los Angeles develop as a cluster of autonomous garden cities. Instead, beginning with the debut in 1929 of Bullock's flagship department store in a former bean field on Wilshire Boulevard, more than 2½ miles west of downtown, a new multicentered, deconcentrated, largely horizontal development pattern would emerge in Los Angeles in the decades to come. The result is what Robert Fogelson called a "fragmented metropolis," which neither planners nor business leaders had foreseen. Los Angeles's downtown district precipitously declined after 1926, losing over half of its business activity by 1939, but commerce relocated not to

the envisioned garden city subcenters but to newly developed strips along major roadways throughout the region. The resulting metropolitan pattern, popularly referred to as *sprawl*, eventually spread to other metropolitan areas around the United States, particularly to what Joel Garreau terms "edge cities" that emerged after World War II.

For decades, Los Angeles's leaders had assiduously constructed an image of the city as a white metropolis, relegating memory of its Native Californian and Mexican heritage to a nostalgic mission mythology. This booster image was enforced in practice by a notoriously violent police department and a rigid system of restrictive deed covenants covering as much as 95 percent of the city's residential property. The covenants limited Latino, Asian, and African American settlement to what Carey McWilliams termed an "archipelago" of small enclaves near the deteriorated downtown core. This image of ethnic homogeneity began to break down during World War II, although it persisted in some form for a half-century more. The expansion of heavy industry during the war, particularly the aviation sector, and the wholesale mobilization of the city as a critical depot for the war's Pacific theater, combined with new opportunities for minority employment in war production industries, began to alter the ethnic mix of the metropolis. Most significant, perhaps, was the growth of a lively African American community and the gradual resurgence of the city's Latino population. These changes were met with escalating racial prejudice, most notably illustrated in the wartime internment of Japanese American citizens and in 1943's Zoot Suit Riots, where servicemen rioted for 3 days against Mexican American youth. Despite Chester Himes's conclusion in 1943, in the aftermath of the sailors' riot, that "the South has won Los Angeles" (p. 225), the cultural contributions of these minority communities would transform the metropolis in the aftermath of the war.

1945–1973: Sprawl and Urban Modernity

By the end of World War II, Los Angeles's novel horizontal topography began to look like unintelligible unplanned sprawl to many urban observers. Although the city was booming when the war came and grew even more quickly in its aftermath (housing 2.5 million residents by 1960), civic leaders began to search for new ways to define the region's modernity, after having rejected the dominant vertical model a generation before. Bold experiments in contemporary architecture emerged in this era (such as the famous Case Study Houses), as well as the development of a new horizontal form to match the landscape: the extensive and iconic freeway system. Yet, during the 1950s and early 1960s, there was also a developing nostalgia for a more unitary and comprehensible urbanism reflected both in official large-scale urban renewal efforts to modernize and resuscitate the largely depreciated downtown district and in the escapist private world of nearby Anaheim's Disneyland Park, which debuted in 1955 as an explicit alternative to the sprawling megalopolis to the north.

Yet, a new, unauthorized grassroots vision of urban modernity had been developing in Los Angeles for decades, for the most part far from the gaze of city leaders. During the war, African American Central Avenue had defined a new modern jazz scene, which drew people from all over the city to its clubs. By the 1950s and 1960s, as George Lipsitz and George Sánchez each has shown, the rise of rock 'n' roll brought together many different communities of Angelenos, while ensuring the city's continued dominance of the culture industry. By the time of the Watts riots in 1965, the rigidly enforced image of Los Angeles as a white city, which had prevailed for a century, was gradually eroding.

1973–Present: Multiethnic Megalopolis

By 1973, with the election of African American Tom Bradley as mayor, the character of the metropolis began to change. Bradley promulgated a new definition of the city as a gateway to the Pacific Rim, and by the 1980s, the combined ports in Long Beach and San Pedro became the largest in the country by volume of trade. Also, greater Los Angeles became the primary entry point to the United States for immigrants from all over the world (by 2006, more than 40 percent of the city's population was foreign-born). Although the aerospace industry greatly diminished in the 1990s, Los Angeles County remained the nation's preeminent manufacturing center while becoming increasingly invested in services, technology, and media. Although many wealthy Angelenos, as Mike Davis has argued, have retreated into gated suburban communities and Los Angeles remains the archetypal horizontal metropolis, in recent years, there has also been a new focus on downtown and increasingly intensive inward development. The election of Antonio Villaraigosa in 2005 marked the ascendance not just of the Latino community (the largest single ethnic group, composing more than 46 percent of the population, according to the 2000 census) but of the grassroots multiethnic coalitions that today make up the city's contemporary politics and popular culture, reflecting the ethnic demography of a city that has become more diverse than any other in the world.

—*Jeremiah B. C. Axelrod*

Further Readings and References

Axelrod, J. B. C. (2007). *Toward autopia: Envisioning the modern metropolis in Jazz Age Southern California.* Berkeley: University of California Press.

Banham, R. (1971). *Los Angeles: The architecture of four ecologies.* London: Penguin.

Bartlett, D. (1907). *The better city: A sociological study of a modern city.* Los Angeles: Neuner Company Press.

Bottles, S. L. (1987). *Los Angeles and the automobile: The making of the modern city.* Berkeley: University of California Press.

Davis, M. (1990). *City of quartz: Excavating the future in Los Angeles.* New York: Verso.

Fogelson, R. M. (1967). *The fragmented metropolis: Los Angeles, 1850–1930.* Berkeley: University of California Press.

Garreau, J. (1991). *Edge city: Life on the new frontier.* New York: Anchor Books.

Himes, C. B. (1943). Zoot riots are race riots. *Crisis, 50*(7), 201.

Hise, G. (1997). *Magnetic Los Angeles: Planning the twentieth-century metropolis.* Baltimore: Johns Hopkins University Press.

Lipsitz, G. (1989). *Time passages: Collective memory and American popular culture.* Minneapolis: University of Minnesota Press.

Longstreth, R. (1997). *City center to regional mall: Architecture, the automobile, and retailing in Los Angeles, 1920-1950.* Cambridge, MA: MIT Press.

McWilliams, C. (1946). *Southern California: An island on the land.* New York: Duell, Sloan, and Pearce.

Pitt, L., & Pitt, D. (1997). *Los Angeles, A to Z: An encyclopedia of the city and county.* Berkeley: University of California Press.

Sanchez, G. J. (1993). *Becoming Mexican American: Ethnicity, culture, and identity in Chicano Los Angeles, 1900–1945.* New York: Oxford University Press.

Starr, K. (1973). *Americans and the California dream, 1850–1915.* New York: Oxford University Press.

West, N. (1933). *Day of the locust.* New York: New Directions.

LOWER EAST SIDE

The Lower East Side, covering some 1,400 acres in Lower Manhattan, has been the first stop for immigrants for almost two centuries. Situated just north of the original Dutch colony, the area is convenient to Wall Street, the port, and the civic center. The myriad nationalities who have called it home have disagreed over what area constitutes the Lower East Side. The most inclusive definition sets the boundaries at 14th Street on the north, the Brooklyn Bridge on the south, the East River on the east and Broadway on the west. The diversity of this densely populated area created a multiethnic laboratory, which over time transformed American culture. By the early 21st century, the Lower East Side had ceded its historic role as a first home for new Americans, yet it remains an area of cultural ferment and great vibrancy.

The Lower East Side's geography bears few traces of the early colonial settlement. The street names allude to the families that once owned the area (Rutgers, Stuyvesant, and Delancey) and its bucolic origins (Cherry, Orchard, Mulberry, and Bowery). South of East Houston Street, the small blocks are framed by irregularly named streets. North of East Houston Street, the even rectangular blocks are framed mainly by wide avenues and narrow east-west numbered streets. By 1909, three bridges (Brooklyn, Manhattan, and Williamsburg) joined the area to Brooklyn. Two elevated train lines (Third Avenue and Second Avenue lines) provided rapid transit connections by the 1890s, and the subway lines soon followed. The elevated train lines came down by the late 1950s, opening up Second and Third Avenues to more intensive development. Along the East River, the small blocks were merged into superblocks for huge public housing projects, beginning with the Vladeck Houses in 1940. These housing projects limited access to the East River, as did the FDR Drive, a controlled access road completed by Robert Moses in the 1940s.

By the mid-19th century, the relentless northward march of commerce and immigration drove the gentry out of the Lower East Side. What had been the desirable neighborhoods of the early 19th century merged into a vast slum. Single-family row houses were chopped into apartments, and where the row house supply was insufficient, owners converted commercial buildings into multiple-unit dwellings known as rookeries. New building types emerged to house the mushrooming population, such as the characteristic dumbbell-style tenements. They were meant to alleviate the deplorable conditions found in rookeries, rear-yard and railroad-flat style tenements. Tenements typically stood about six stories tall, covering most of their 25- by 100-foot lots. Tenants crowded into warrens of tiny rooms, frequently doubling up with extended family and boarders. Some blocks reached densities as high as 330,000 people per square mile in the late 19th century. These squalid conditions gave rise to the American housing movement and to the first public housing in the nation—First Houses in 1936. Still, the Lower East Side provided all the necessities of life within walking distance: factories, churches, schools, settlement houses, theaters, wedding halls, saloons, and stores. Its vitality has always depended on this fine-grained mix of land uses.

Of the many nationalities that passed through the Lower East Side, the first sizable immigrant group was the Irish. Thousands entered the Lower East Side in the 1840s, clustering around the notorious Five Points and the Bowery. They quickly found employment as dockworkers and construction workers, and they established a formidable political base in the Tammany Hall club. The Germans (both Christian and Jewish) came in great numbers beginning in the late 1840s. They settled between Division and 14th Streets, calling their neighborhood Kleindeutschland. They brought advanced skills and were well-educated, allowing them to progress quickly and move out of the neighborhood.

The Irish and Germans were soon replaced by even larger waves of immigrants from eastern and southern Europe. Tens of thousands of Italians, mainly unskilled and semiskilled peasants from the southern regions of Italy, began arriving in the 1880s. They clustered in the Little Italy neighborhood, which extended from Worth Street north to Bleecker Street in a long narrow strip to the west of the Bowery. The Italians colonized other Lower East Side streets as well. An estimated half million eastern European Jews, refugees from many nations, surged into the area between 1880 and 1924. After 1924, immigration law restricted their numbers to a trickle. These Jewish immigrants shared the Yiddish language and religious customs, and they created a vibrant new common culture. Along with the Italians, they staffed the garment industry, which was then centered in New York.

Several thousand Chinese immigrants staked out several blocks near Chatham Square by the late 19th century. The loosening of immigration quotas after 1965, along with the influx of overseas capital since the 1980s, has expanded the neighborhood considered Chinatown. Chinese garment workers and business owners replaced the Jews and Italians, who had prospered and largely moved on by the 1950s.

A small number of Puerto Rican, Cuban, and other Caribbean immigrants arrived in the early 20th century. Tens of thousands more Puerto Ricans settled in the area from the 1950s onward, fleeing island poverty. Although deindustrialization and abandonment had decimated the neighborhood by the 1970s, many Puerto Ricans remain in *Loisaida,* the area between Avenue A and Avenue D. They were joined after 1965 by Dominicans, Mexicans, and other Latinos.

Finally, three other groups arrived recently in the Lower East Side. These are the bohemians (artists, intellectuals, and social rebels), who first established outposts in the 1940s; New York University students, who have pushed eastward from their traditional territory; and native-born middle-class professionals. They are all drawn by the neighborhood's distinctive culture, its convenient location, and the availability of new or renovated apartments. These three groups have settled predominantly west of Avenue A and north of East Houston Street, in the area identified as the East Village. Most recently, they have moved into Loisaida (alternatively known as Alphabet City); some have ventured south of Houston Street into formerly Jewish and Italian neighborhoods. Many of these newcomers are the descendants of immigrants who first settled in the Lower East Side.

In 2001, the National Park Service recognized about one third of the Lower East Side as a historic district, placing it on the National Register of Historic Places. Yet, the area's renown rests neither on its layout nor its architecture but rather on its historic role as an immigrant portal and its continuing role as a laboratory for cultural, political, and economic innovation.

—*Barbara Stabin Nesmith*

See also Bowery, The; Dumbbell Tenement; Henry Street Settlement; Riis, Jacob August; Settlement House Movement; Tenements

Further Readings and References

Howe, I., & Libo, K. (1979). *How we lived: A documentary history of immigrant Jews in America 1880–1930.* New York: Richard Marek.

Maffi, M. (1994). *Gateway to the promised land: Ethnic cultures on New York's Lower East Side.* Amsterdam: Rodopi.

Index

Note: Entry titles are in bold.